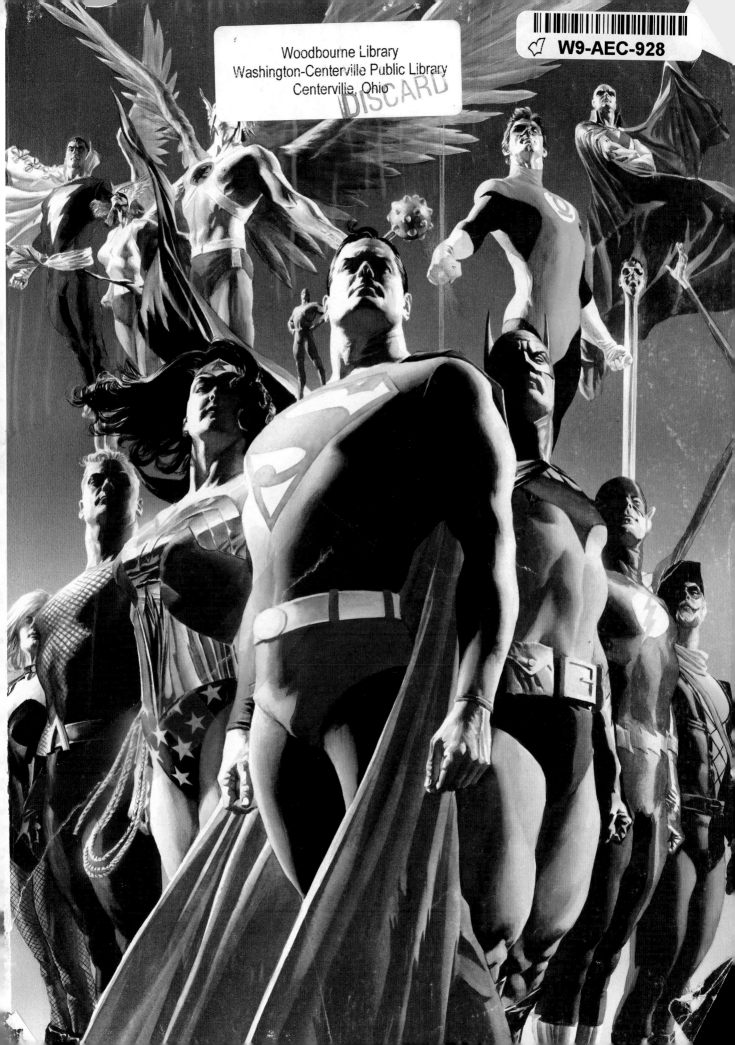

THE WORLD'S GREATEST SUPER-HEROES

stories by ALEX ROSS and PAUL DINI

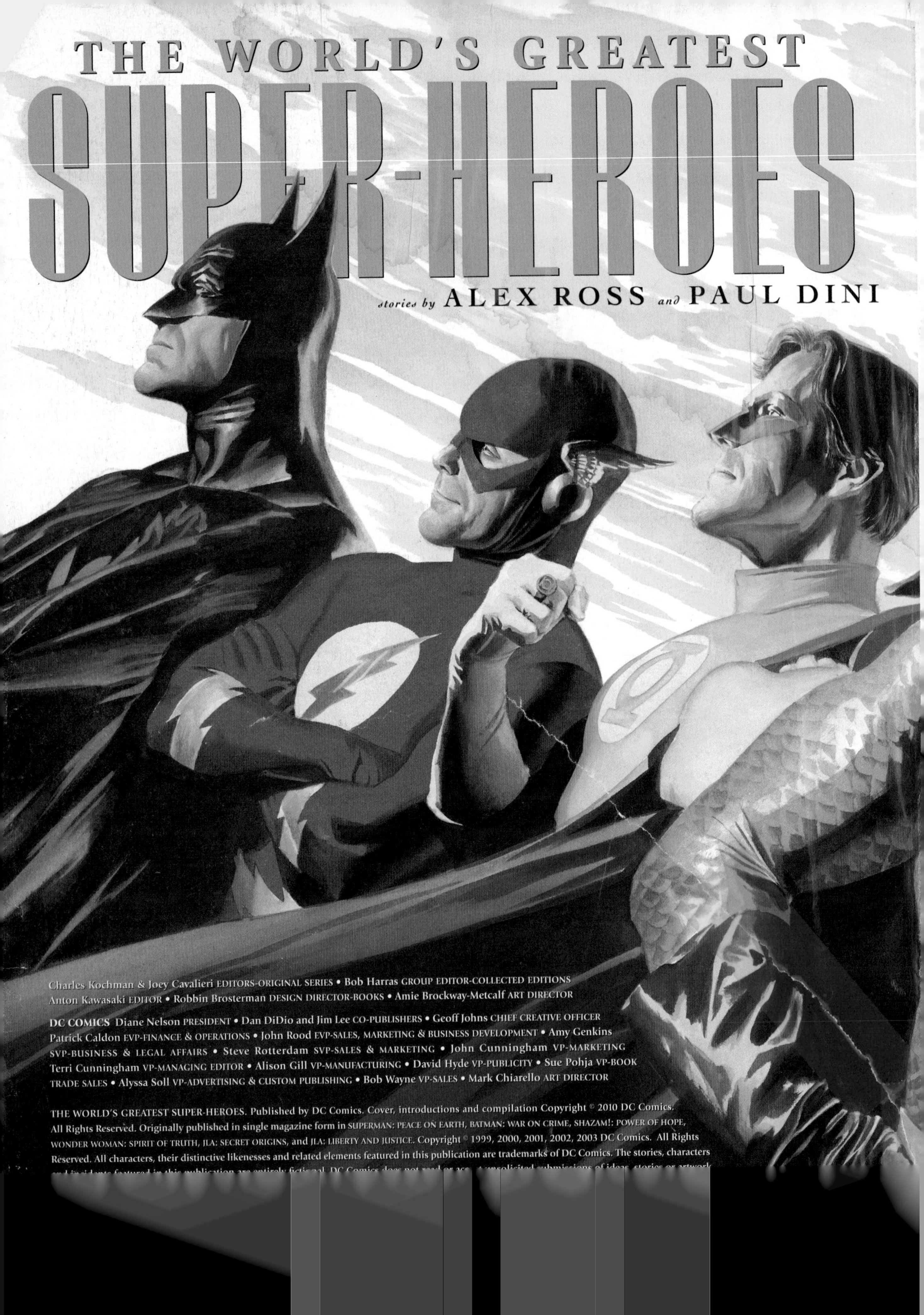

Charles Kochman & Joey Cavalieri EDITORS-ORIGINAL SERIES • Bob Harras GROUP EDITOR-COLLECTED EDITIONS
Anton Kawasaki EDITOR • Robbin Brosterman DESIGN DIRECTOR-BOOKS • Amie Brockway-Metcalf ART DIRECTOR

DC COMICS Diane Nelson PRESIDENT • Dan DiDio and Jim Lee CO-PUBLISHERS • Geoff Johns CHIEF CREATIVE OFFICER
Patrick Caldon EVP-FINANCE & OPERATIONS • John Rood EVP-SALES, MARKETING & BUSINESS DEVELOPMENT • Amy Genkins SVP-BUSINESS & LEGAL AFFAIRS • Steve Rotterdam SVP-SALES & MARKETING • John Cunningham VP-MARKETING
Terri Cunningham VP-MANAGING EDITOR • Alison Gill VP-MANUFACTURING • David Hyde VP-PUBLICITY • Sue Pohja VP-BOOK TRADE SALES • Alyssa Soll VP-ADVERTISING & CUSTOM PUBLISHING • Bob Wayne VP-SALES • Mark Chiarello ART DIRECTOR

text by **PAUL DINI**
art by **ALEX ROSS**

Lettering on JLA: LIBERTY AND JUSTICE by TODD KLEIN

Superman created by JERRY SIEGEL *&* JOE SHUSTER
Batman created by BOB KANE
Wonder Woman created by
WILLIAM MOULTON MARSTON

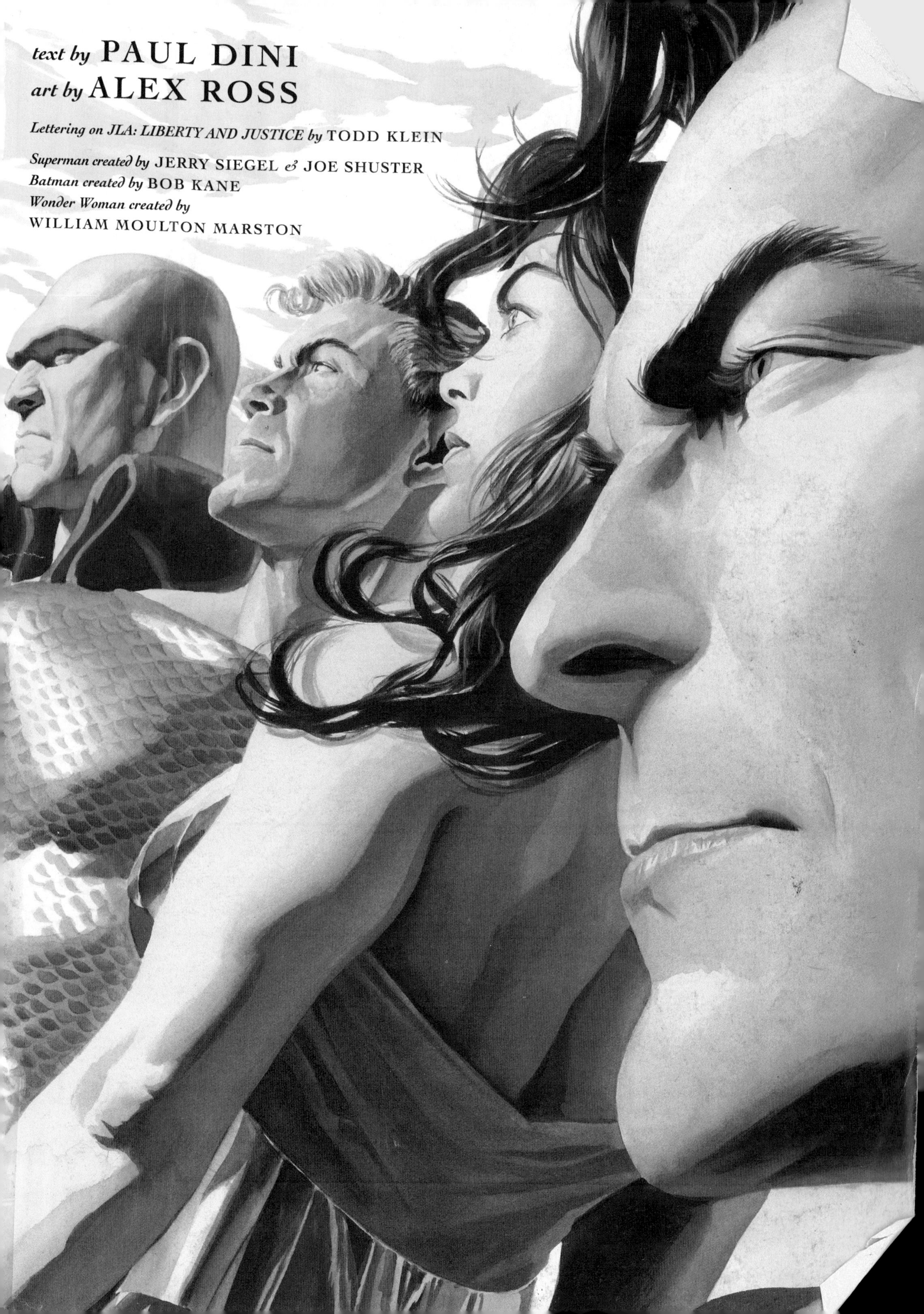

TO PROTECT AND TO SERVE...

Okay, so he makes them look real. We know that by now. And yes, it's extraordinary, and not to be taken for granted, and no, no one does it better than he does. Alex Ross is one of the most gifted draftsmen of his generation, magically conjuring super-heroes with gouache and illustration board the way Michelangelo coaxed David from a block of marble. They. Look. Real.

But what if they *acted* real? What would they do, and what would happen then? This is what intrigued Ross and writer Paul Dini when they set out to produce the series of breathtaking stories collected in this book. They are not the first comics creators to ask themselves these questions, but they are probably the first to answer them with such an astonishing effect, both visually and verbally.

For me, the greatest appeal of these characters has always been the idea that they are omnipotent, immensely powerful beings, and yet they don't want to rule the world. They want to serve it. Which is supposed to be, ahem, a Great American Ideal. Most of the members of what eventually became the Justice League were originated either during the anxieties of the Depression or on the eve of World War II by a group of young American cartoonists and writers whose first stories were often as much about fighting for social causes (workers' rights, women's empowerment) as they were about mad scientists and outlandish super-villains. Ross and Dini take the characters, now much evolved, back to these roots.

And so: Superman decides he's going to solve world hunger. Of *course* he would. The idea is so obvious you wonder why you haven't seen it before. Batman strikes at the actual core causes of crime — the unrelenting poverty and desperation that haunts the urban poor. Wonder Woman assumes the daunting task of changing what she sees as the often degrading and oppressed role of women in some cultures. Captain Marvel, that perennial man-boy, delves into the plight of disabled children. The Justice League band together to fiercely combat...a *disease*.

What gives these stories their resonant emotional power is the theme that underlies them all, one we are unused to when it comes to super-heroes: failure. Superman is blasted out of the sky while trying to deliver supplies to a war-torn third-world nation that fears and hates him. Batman grudgingly concludes that no one person, not even he, can effectively win the war on crime. Wonder Woman is branded a hussy because of her skimpy outfit and pelted with rocks by the very women she seeks to help. The Justice League does find a cure, but in the doing rouses the fear and paranoia of the rest of the world, which suspects they were responsible for the plague in the first place. The message: these problems are a LOT more complicated than they might seem and require more than short-term, quick-fix solutions, no matter how well-intended. They require thought, planning, cooperation, and care, for starters.

So while the World's Greatest Super-Heroes are left to ponder their quests, you have this book with which to ponder *them*. The illusion of reality now dazzles the heart as well as the eye. Superman and Batman may have failed, but Ross and Dini have succeeded.

CHIP KIDD
2005

INTRODUCTION

Chip Kidd is the author and designer of Mythology: The DC Comics Art of Alex Ross, Batman Animated *and* Peanuts: The Art of Charles M. Schulz. *His book jacket designs for Alfred A. Knopf (where he has worked since 1986) have helped spawn a revolution in the art of American book packaging and have won numerous awards. Chip's first novel,* The Cheese Monkeys, *was published in 2001 by Scribner and was a* New York Times *Notable Book of the Year.*

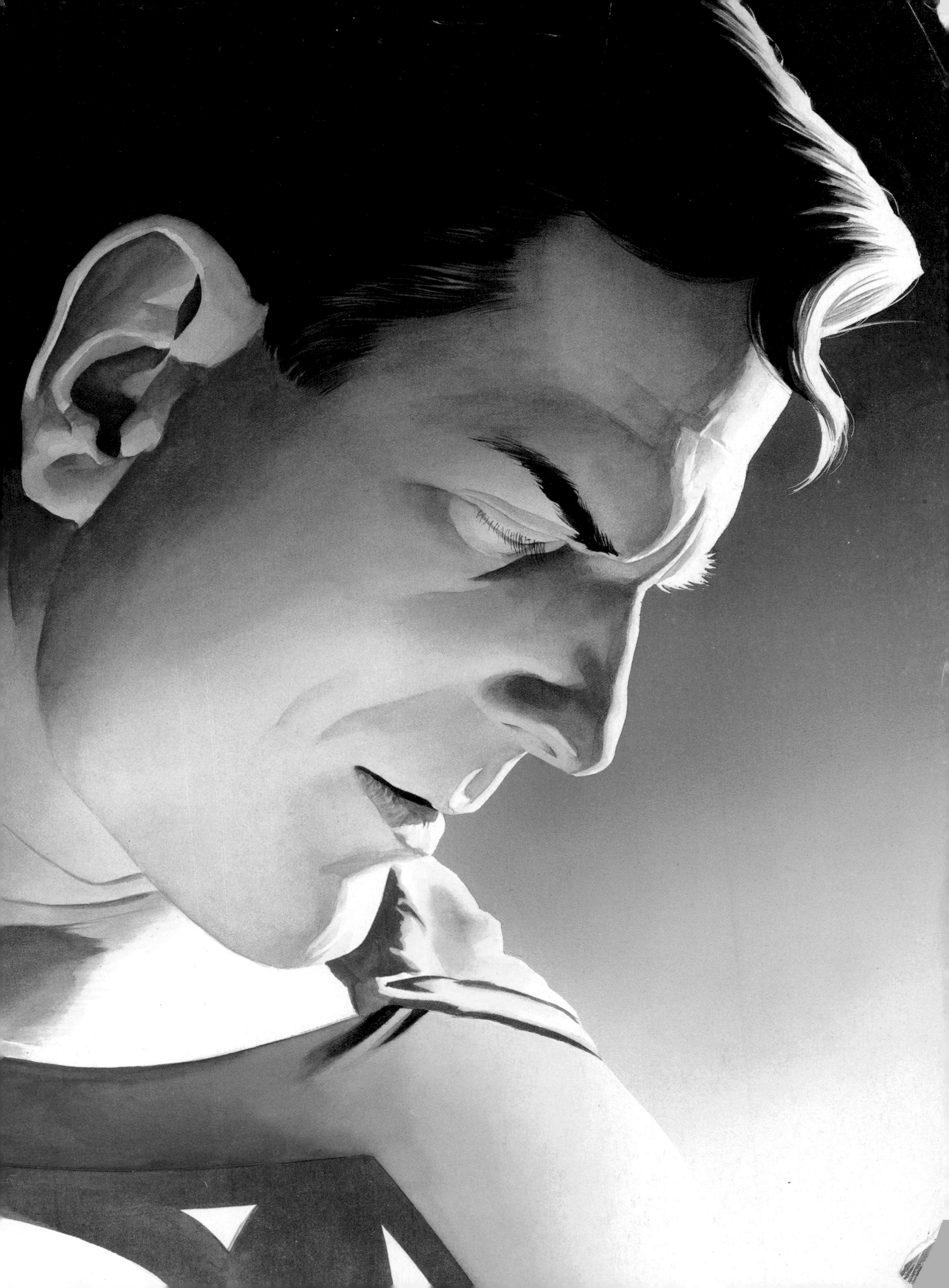

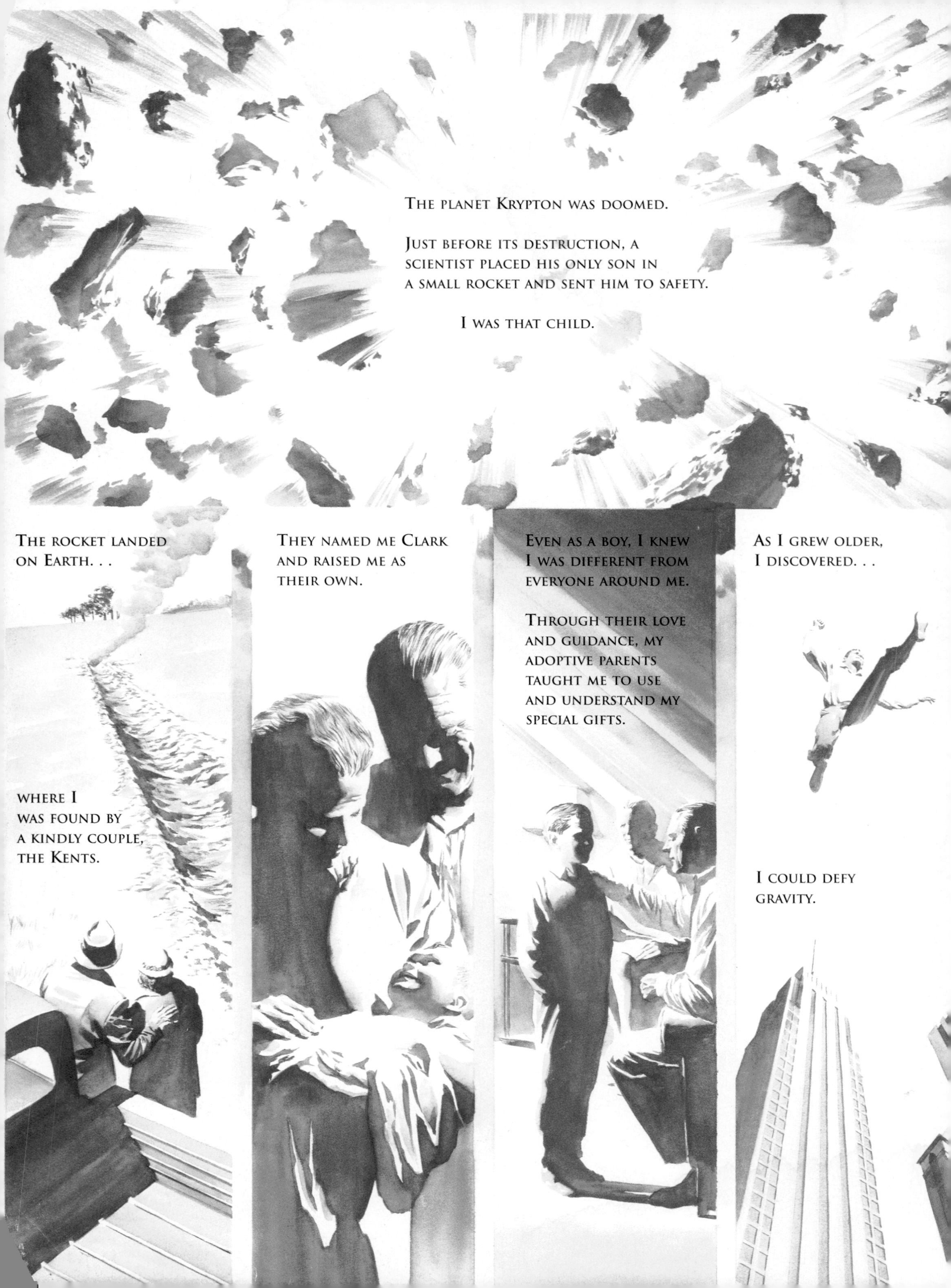
The planet Krypton was doomed.
Just before its destruction, a scientist placed his only son in a small rocket and sent him to safety.
I was that child.
The rocket landed on Earth. . .
where I was found by a kindly couple, the Kents.
They named me Clark and raised me as their own.
Even as a boy, I knew I was different from everyone around me.
Through their love and guidance, my adoptive parents taught me to use and understand my special gifts.
As I grew older, I discovered. . .
I could defy gravity.

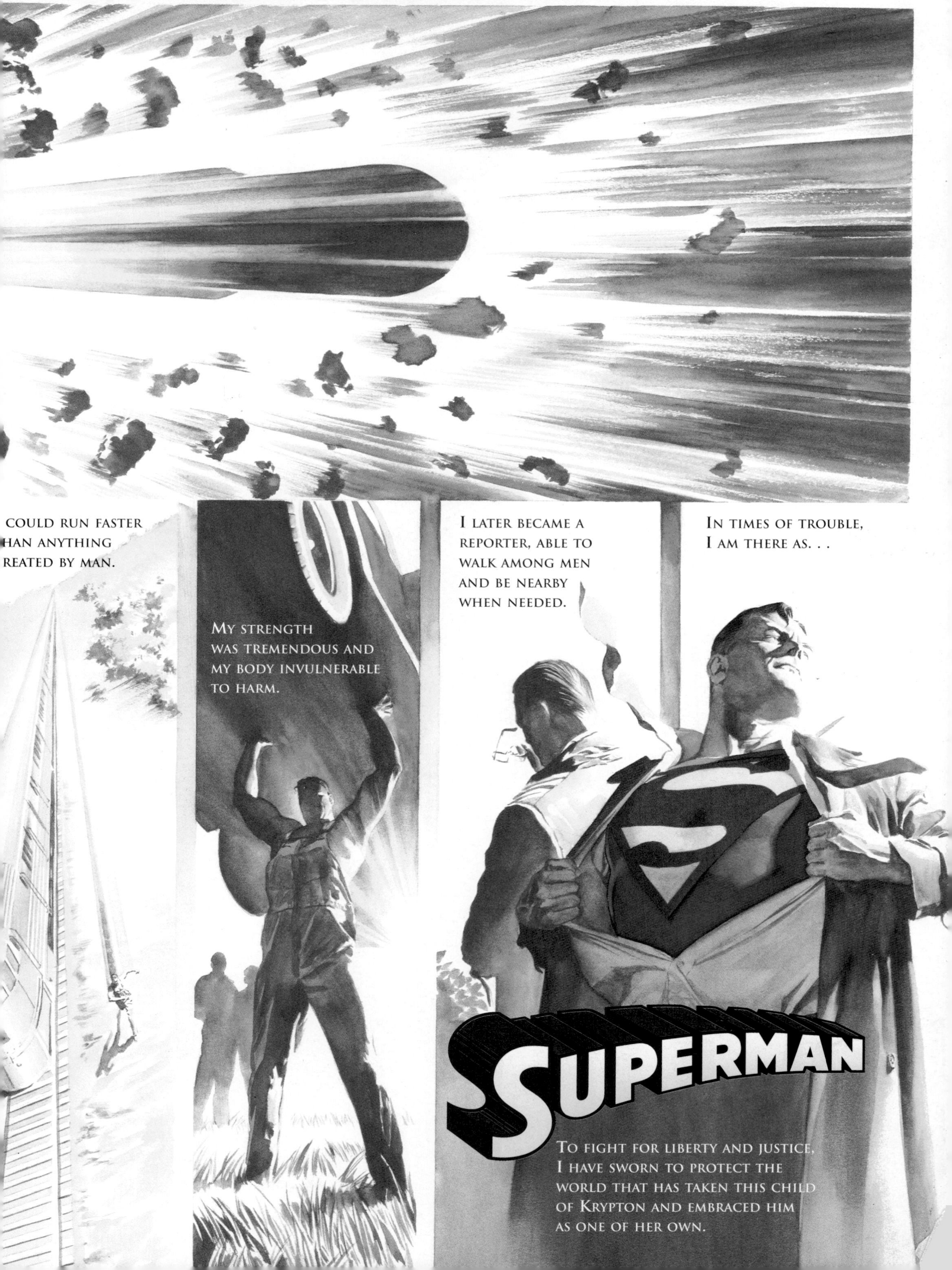
COULD RUN FASTER
HAN ANYTHING
REATED BY MAN.
MY STRENGTH
WAS TREMENDOUS AND
MY BODY INVULNERABLE
TO HARM.
I LATER BECAME A
REPORTER, ABLE TO
WALK AMONG MEN
AND BE NEARBY
WHEN NEEDED.
IN TIMES OF TROUBLE,
I AM THERE AS. . .
SUPERMAN
TO FIGHT FOR LIBERTY AND JUSTICE,
I HAVE SWORN TO PROTECT THE
WORLD THAT HAS TAKEN THIS CHILD
OF KRYPTON AND EMBRACED HIM
AS ONE OF HER OWN.

SUPERMAN
PEACE
ON EARTH

I still think back to the farm. I remember the creak of the old windmill, the smell of fresh-cut hay, and the warm spring wind in my hair.

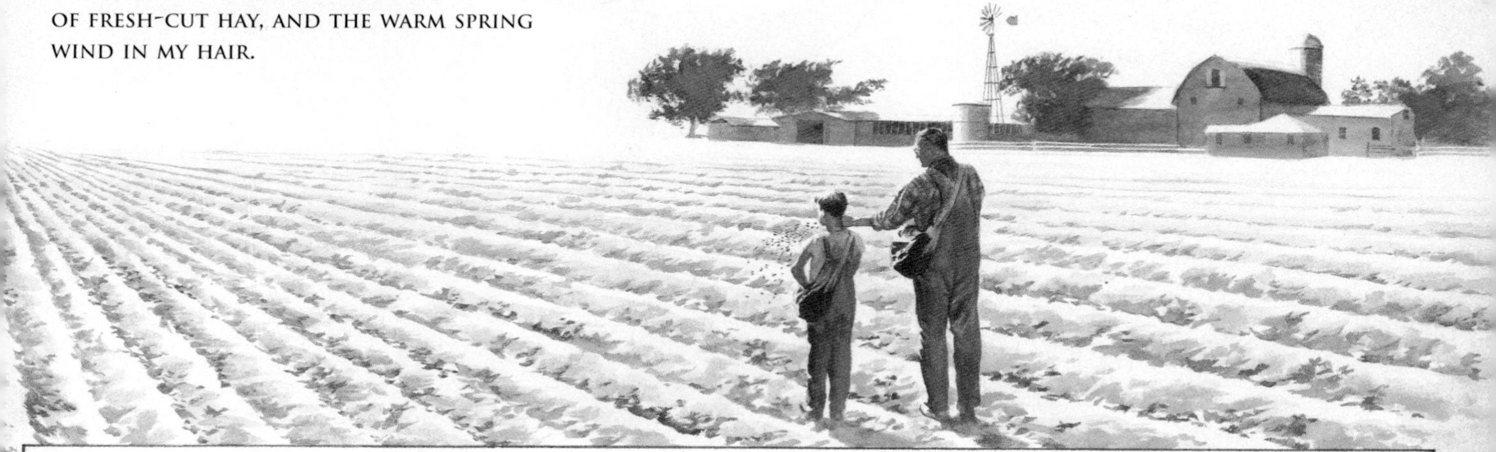

Most of all, I remember my father, patient and gentle as we worked the fields together.

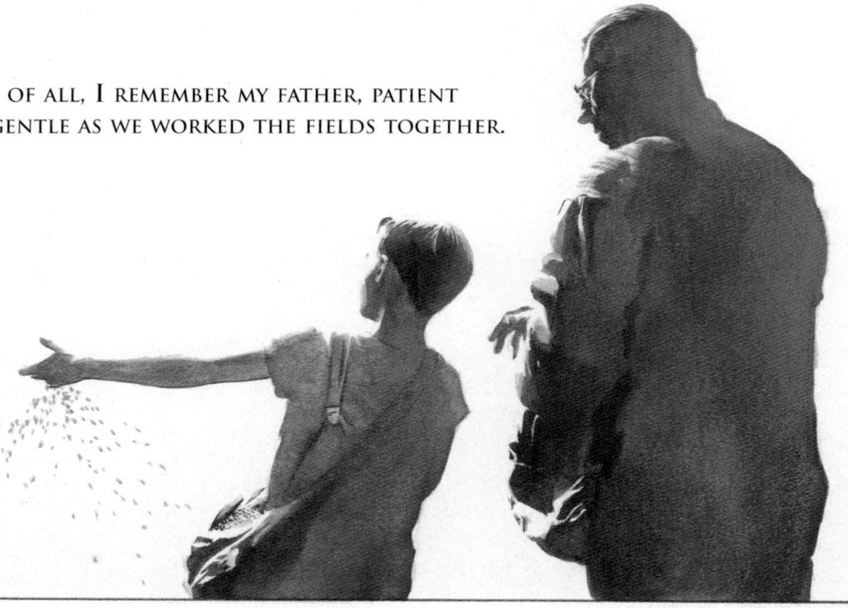

"Easy does it," he'd say. "Scatter the seeds a few at a time. Don't throw them in clumps, let them fall evenly down the rows. Give them enough space. That's the way."

He knew not every seed would make it, but Pa wanted to give each one the chance to grow.

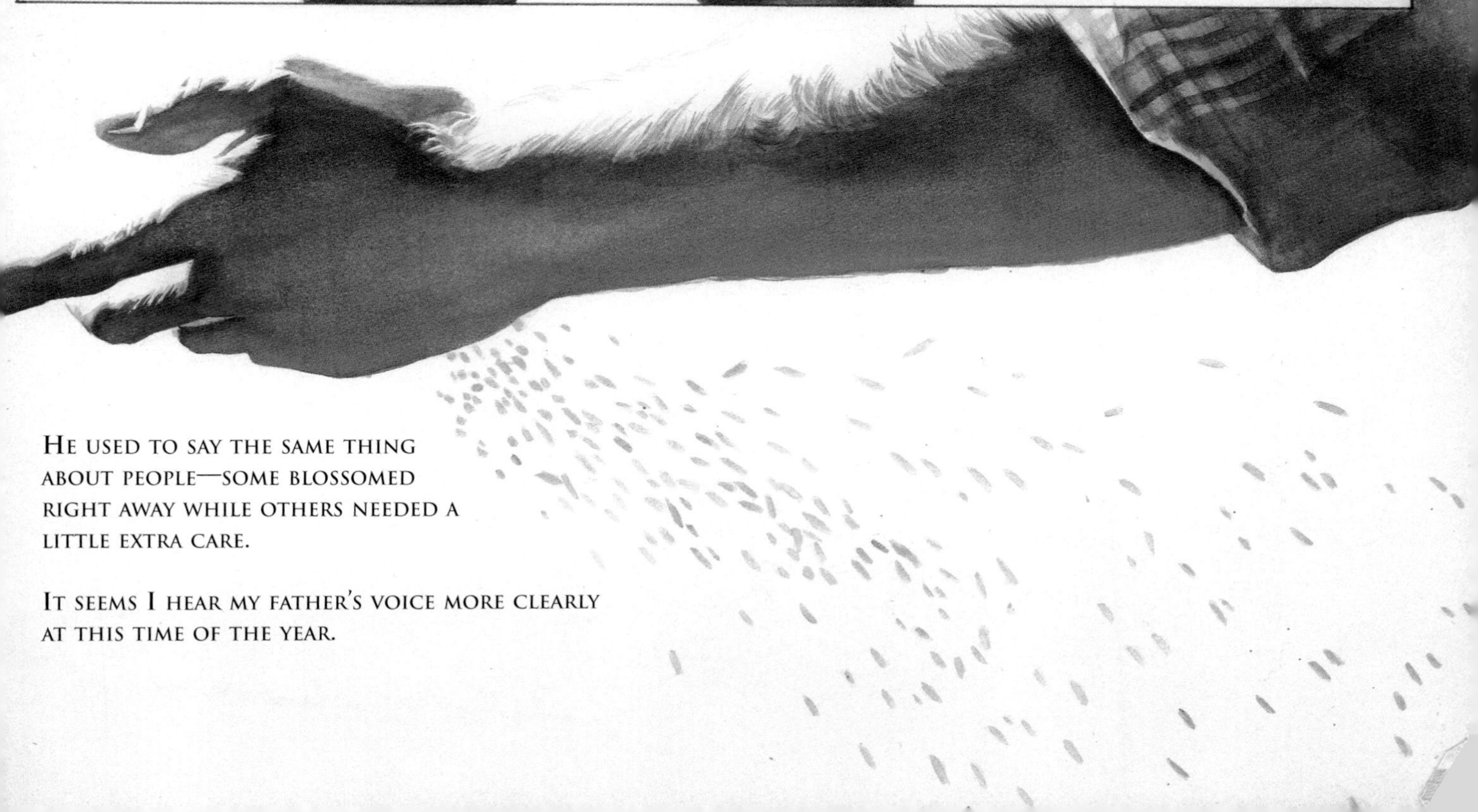

He used to say the same thing about people—some blossomed right away while others needed a little extra care.

It seems I hear my father's voice more clearly at this time of the year.

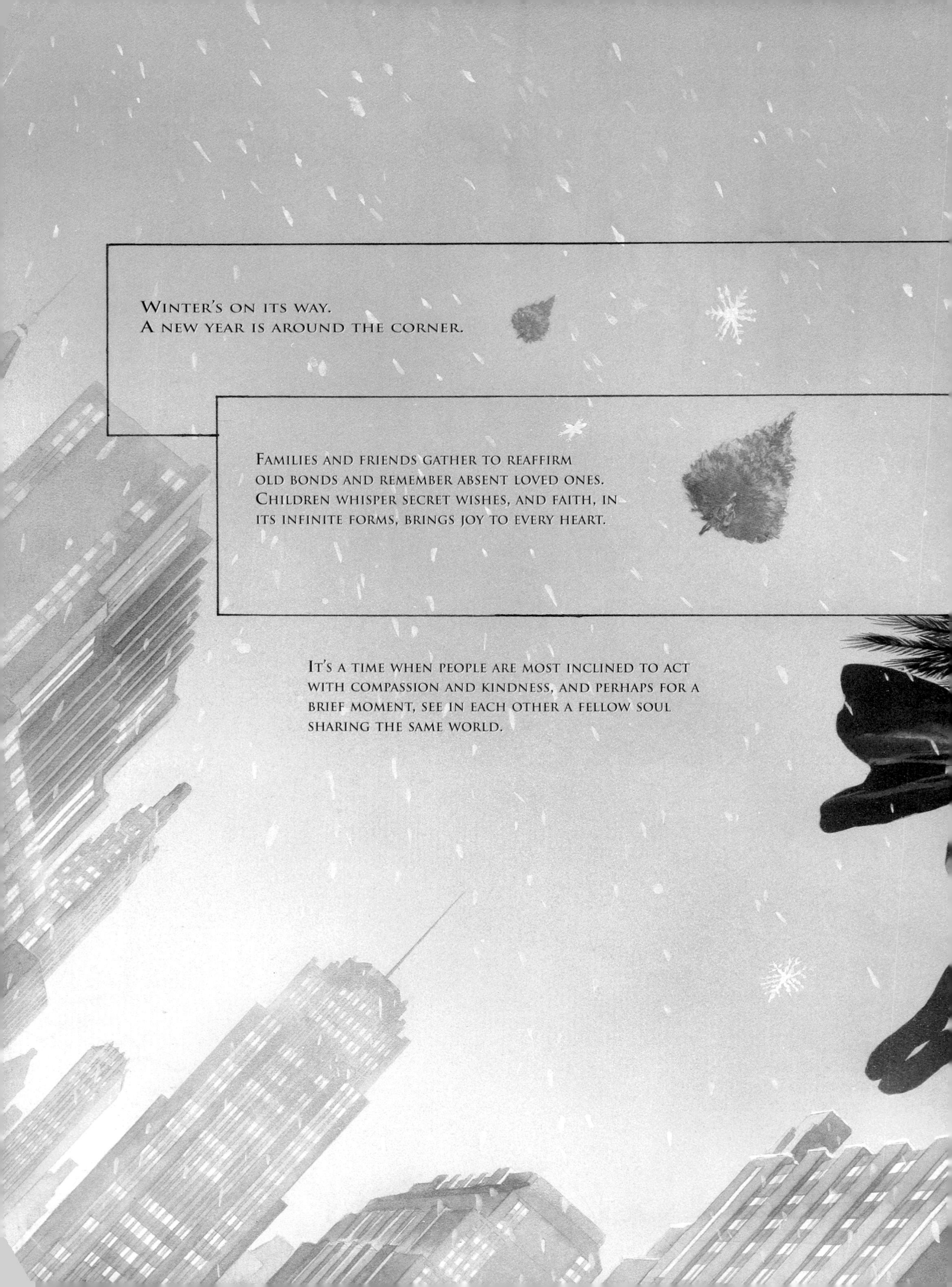
Winter's on its way.
A new year is around the corner.
Families and friends gather to reaffirm old bonds and remember absent loved ones. Children whisper secret wishes, and faith, in its infinite forms, brings joy to every heart.
It's a time when people are most inclined to act with compassion and kindness, and perhaps for a brief moment, see in each other a fellow soul sharing the same world.

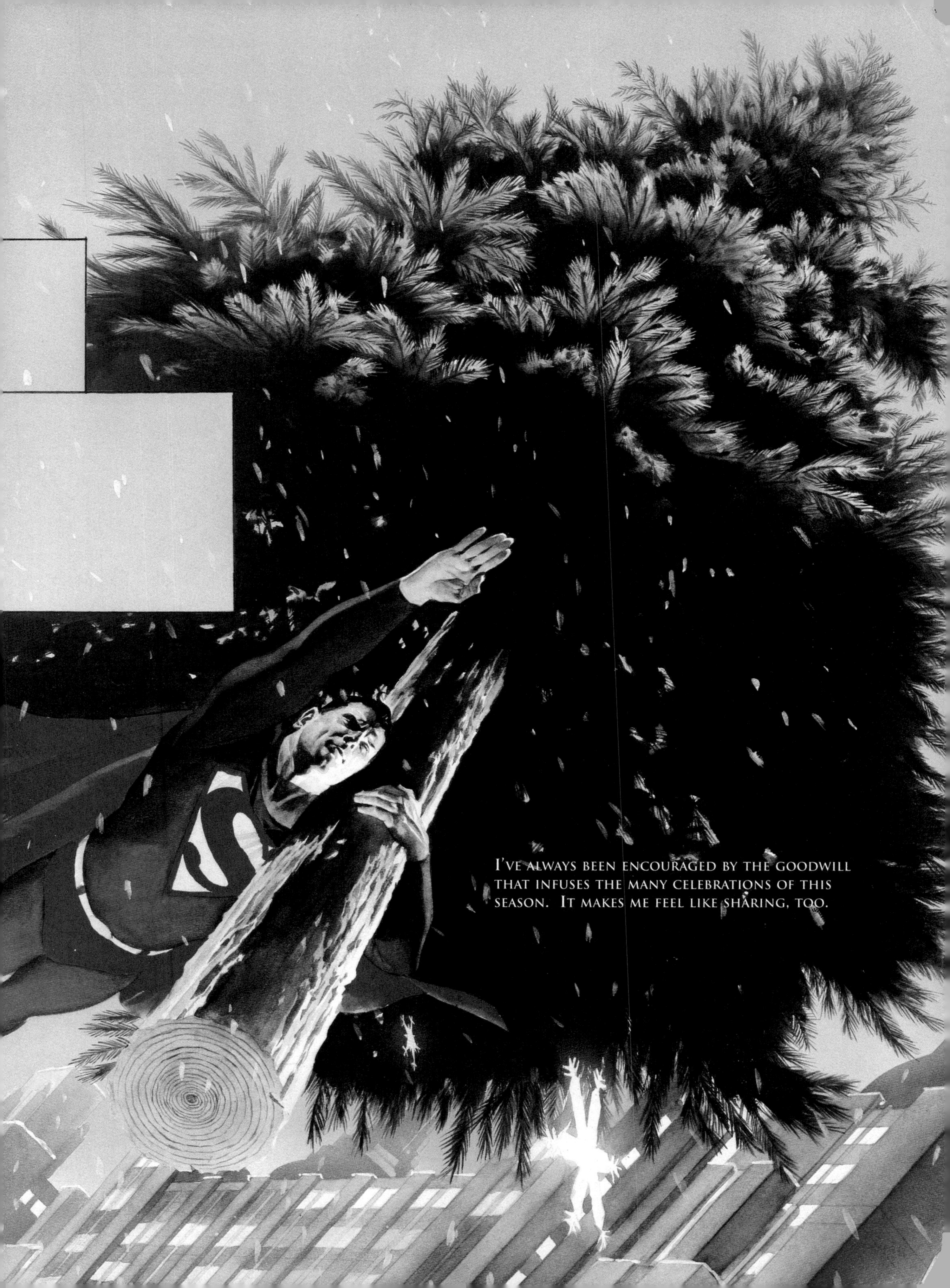
I'VE ALWAYS BEEN ENCOURAGED BY THE GOODWILL THAT INFUSES THE MANY CELEBRATIONS OF THIS SEASON. IT MAKES ME FEEL LIKE SHARING, TOO.

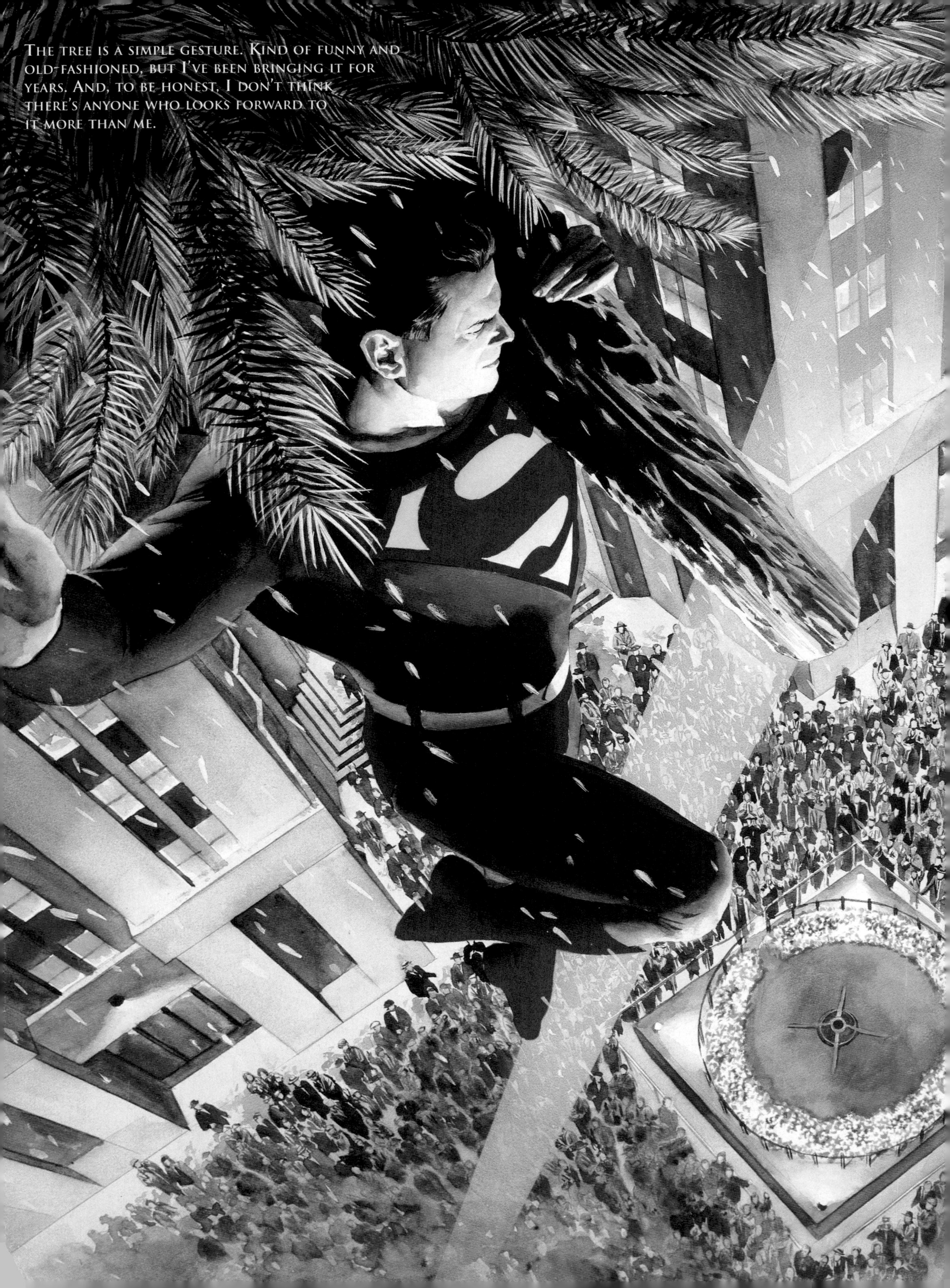
THE TREE IS A SIMPLE GESTURE. KIND OF FUNNY AND OLD-FASHIONED, BUT I'VE BEEN BRINGING IT FOR YEARS. AND, TO BE HONEST, I DON'T THINK THERE'S ANYONE WHO LOOKS FORWARD TO IT MORE THAN ME.

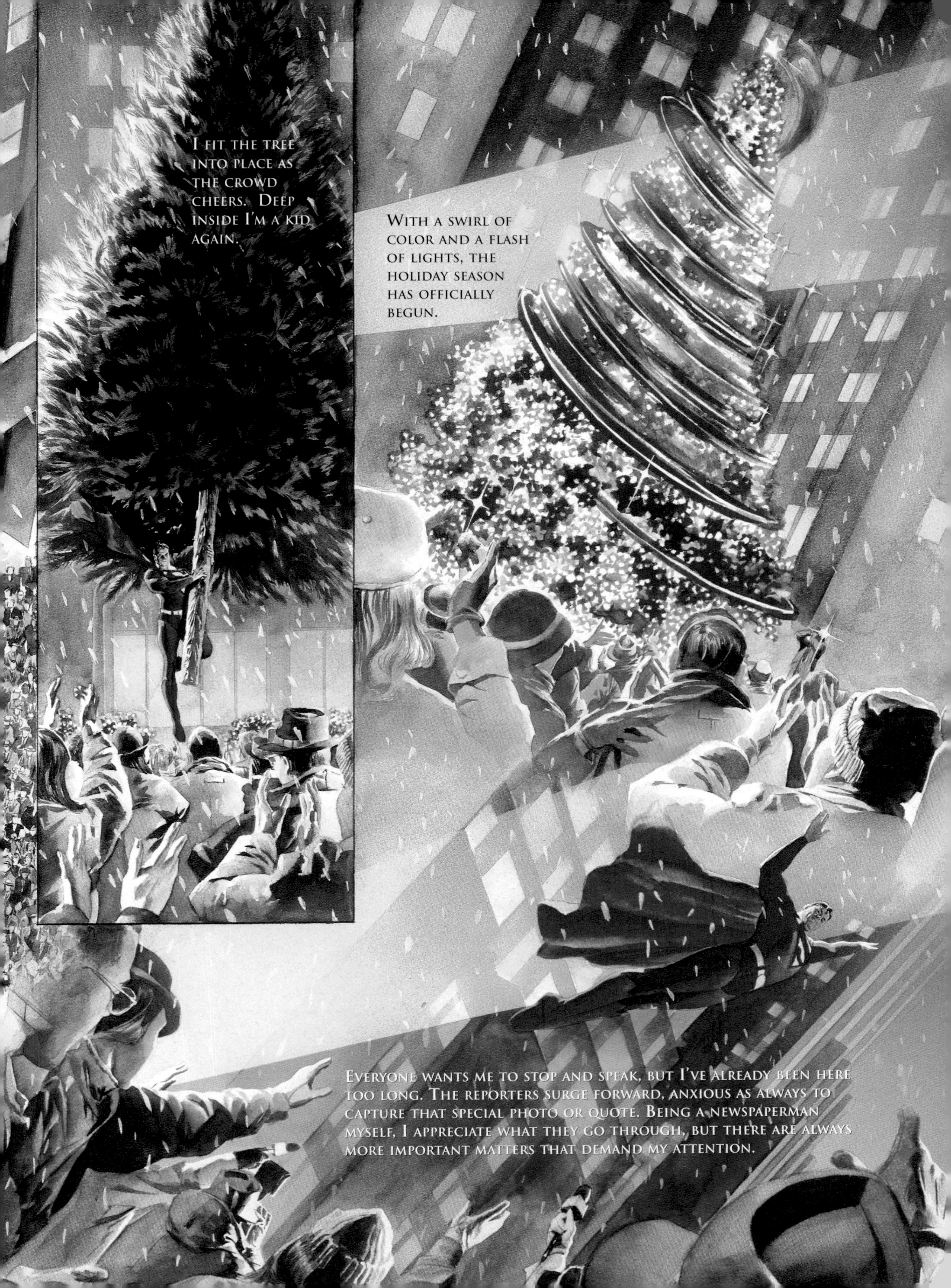
I fit the tree into place as the crowd cheers. Deep inside I'm a kid again.
With a swirl of color and a flash of lights, the holiday season has officially begun.
Everyone wants me to stop and speak, but I've already been here too long. The reporters surge forward, anxious as always to capture that special photo or quote. Being a newspaperman myself, I appreciate what they go through, but there are always more important matters that demand my attention.

THEY CALL OUT TO ME BUT I KEEP GOING.
THEN I HEAR A DIFFERENT SOUND ALMOST
HIDDEN UNDER THE ROAR OF THE CROWD.

A CRY FOR HELP.

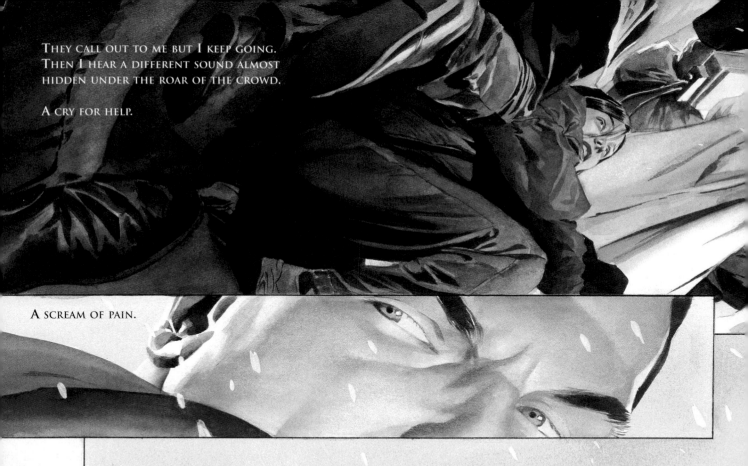

A SCREAM OF PAIN.

FASTER THAN A THOUGHT, I DIVE DOWN BETWEEN THE CROWD AND THE GIRL.
I SWEEP HER UP TO SAFETY AND SHE FAINTS.

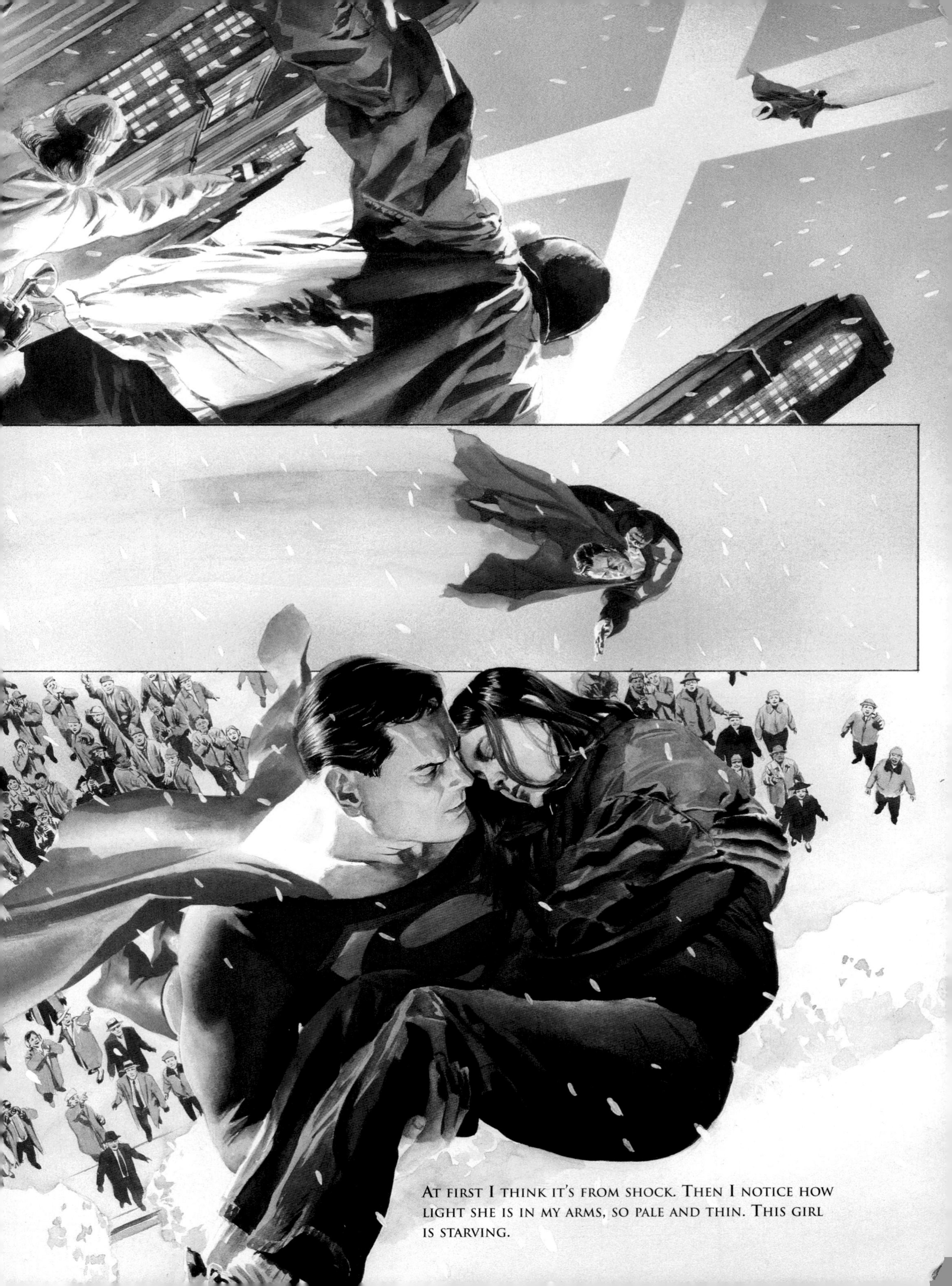
At first I think it's from shock. Then I notice how light she is in my arms, so pale and thin. This girl is starving.

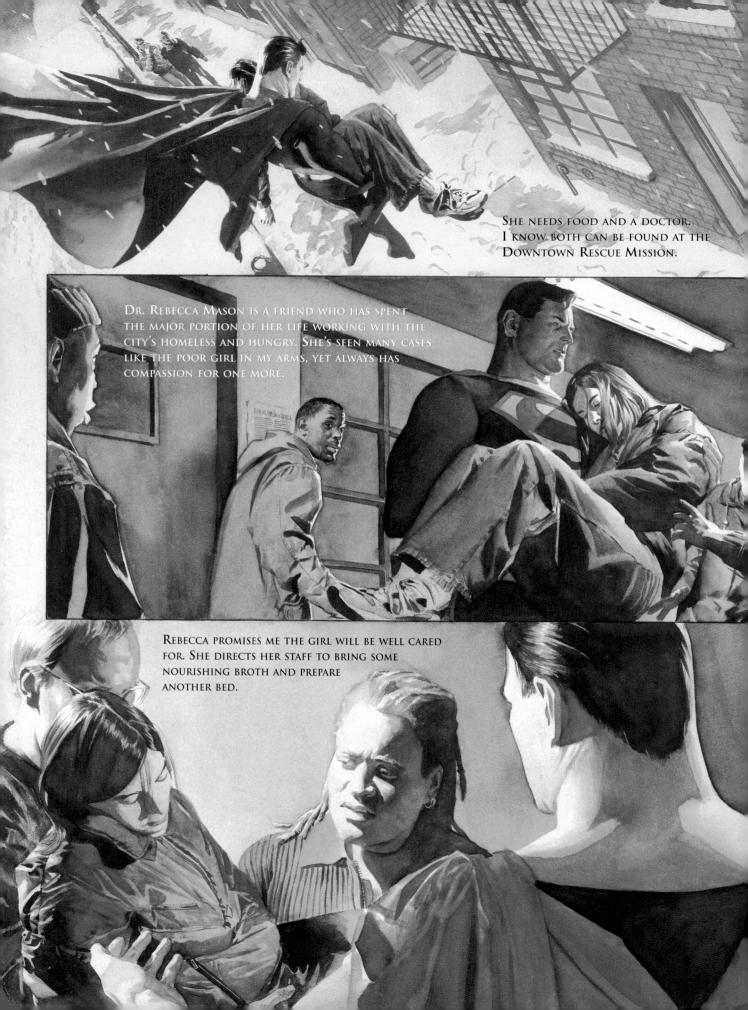

SHE NEEDS FOOD AND A DOCTOR.
I KNOW BOTH CAN BE FOUND AT THE
DOWNTOWN RESCUE MISSION.

DR. REBECCA MASON IS A FRIEND WHO HAS SPENT
THE MAJOR PORTION OF HER LIFE WORKING WITH THE
CITY'S HOMELESS AND HUNGRY. SHE'S SEEN MANY CASES
LIKE THE POOR GIRL IN MY ARMS, YET ALWAYS HAS
COMPASSION FOR ONE MORE.

REBECCA PROMISES ME THE GIRL WILL BE WELL CARED
FOR. SHE DIRECTS HER STAFF TO BRING SOME
NOURISHING BROTH AND PREPARE
ANOTHER BED.

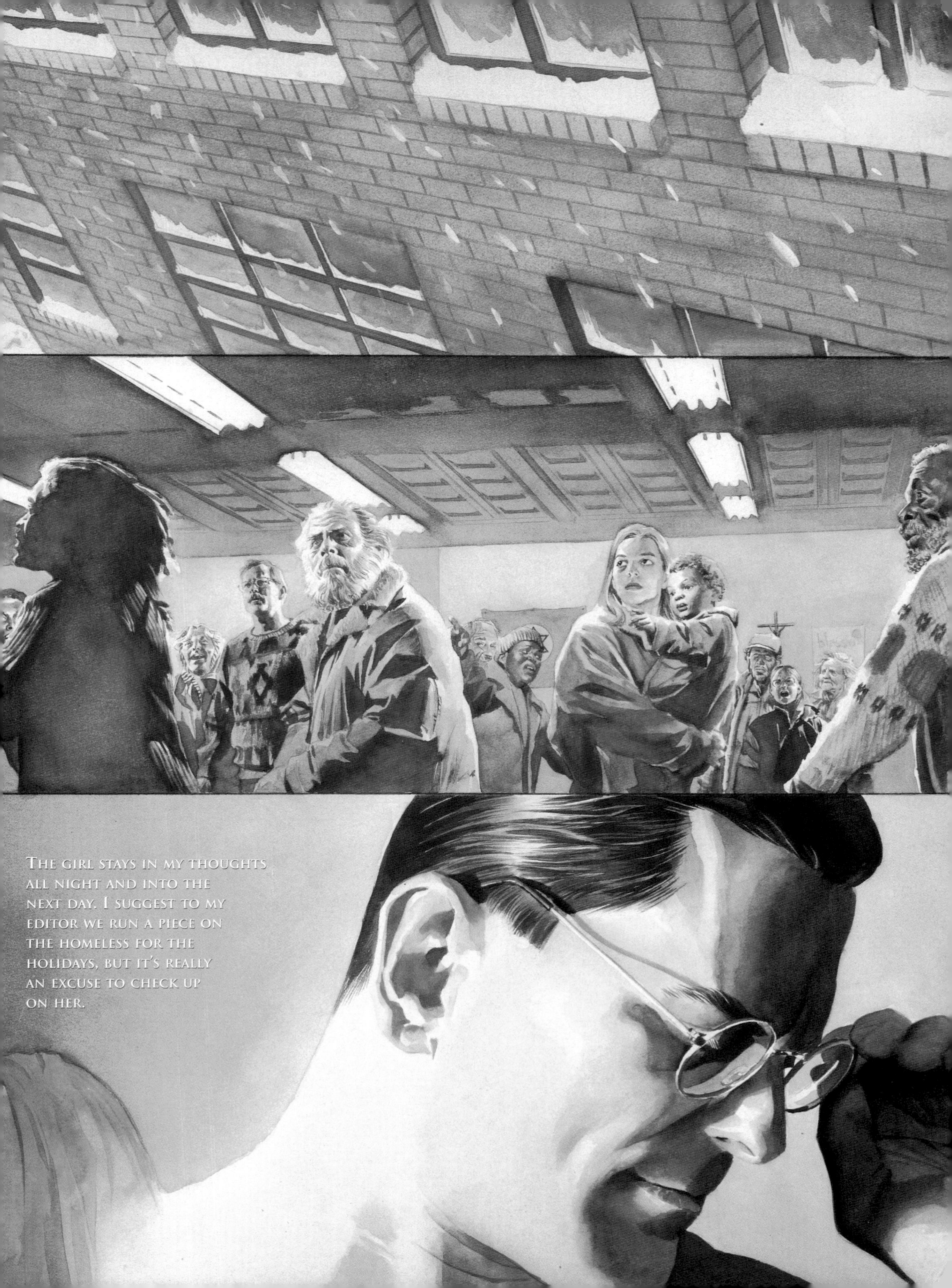
The girl stays in my thoughts all night and into the next day. I suggest to my editor we run a piece on the homeless for the holidays, but it's really an excuse to check up on her.

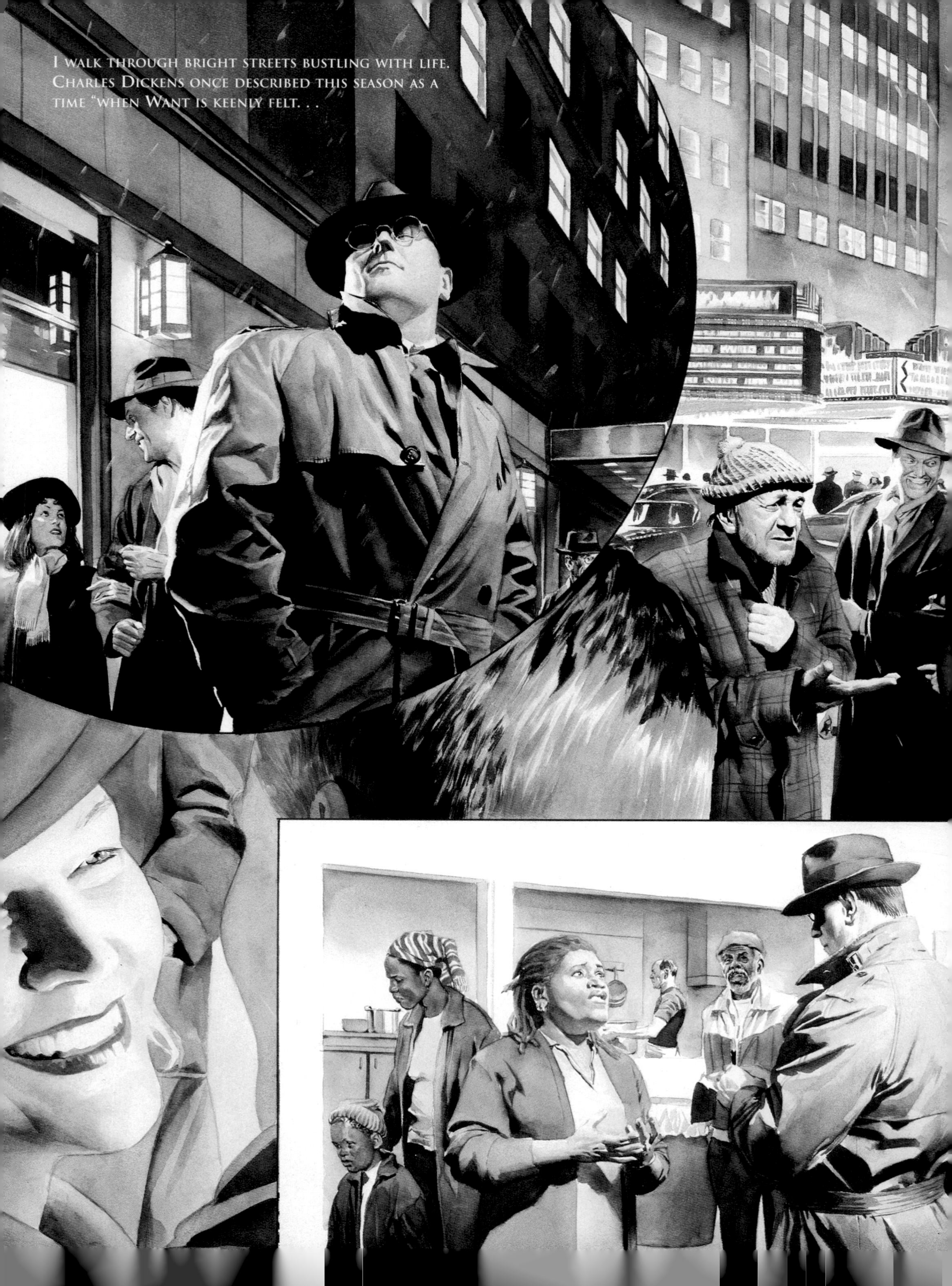
I walk through bright streets bustling with life. Charles Dickens once described this season as a time "when Want is keenly felt. . .

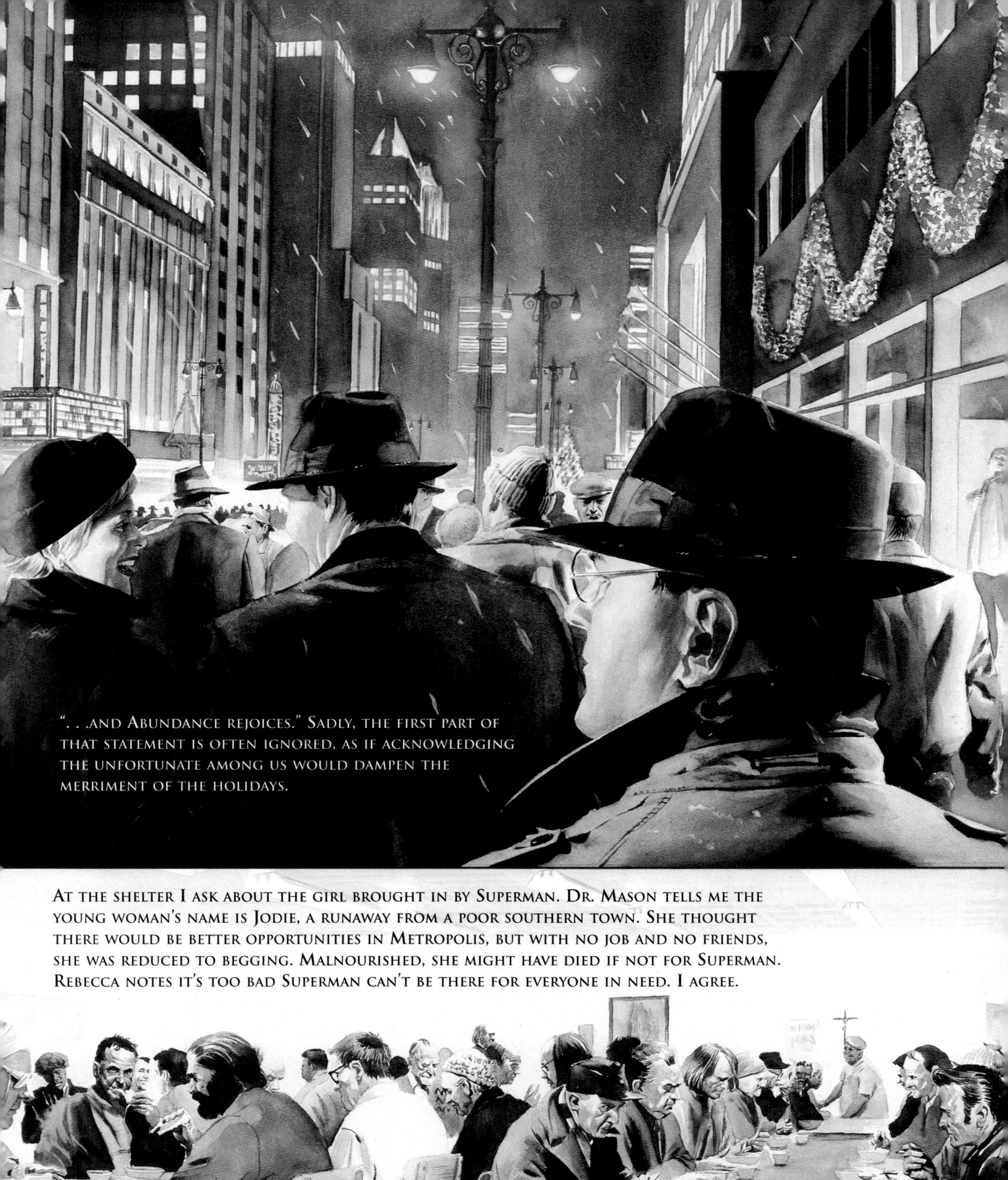
". . .AND ABUNDANCE REJOICES." SADLY, THE FIRST PART OF THAT STATEMENT IS OFTEN IGNORED, AS IF ACKNOWLEDGING THE UNFORTUNATE AMONG US WOULD DAMPEN THE MERRIMENT OF THE HOLIDAYS.

AT THE SHELTER I ASK ABOUT THE GIRL BROUGHT IN BY SUPERMAN. DR. MASON TELLS ME THE YOUNG WOMAN'S NAME IS JODIE, A RUNAWAY FROM A POOR SOUTHERN TOWN. SHE THOUGHT THERE WOULD BE BETTER OPPORTUNITIES IN METROPOLIS, BUT WITH NO JOB AND NO FRIENDS, SHE WAS REDUCED TO BEGGING. MALNOURISHED, SHE MIGHT HAVE DIED IF NOT FOR SUPERMAN. REBECCA NOTES IT'S TOO BAD SUPERMAN CAN'T BE THERE FOR EVERYONE IN NEED. I AGREE.

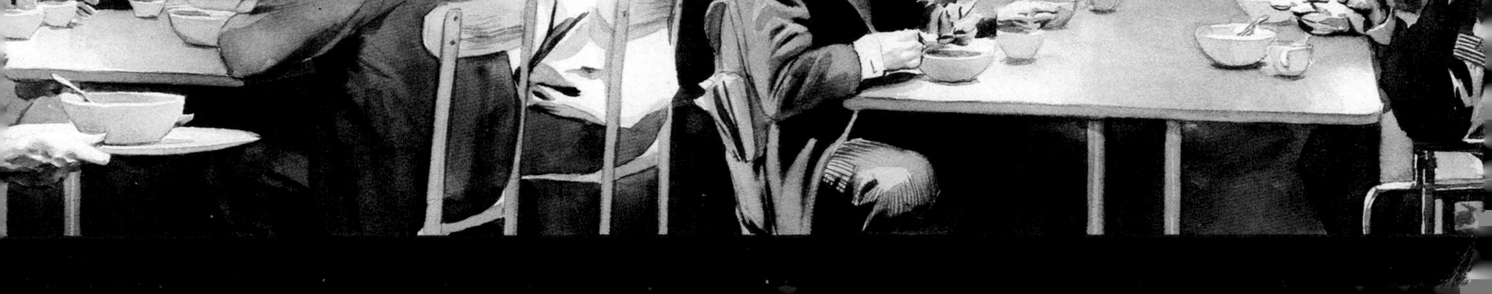

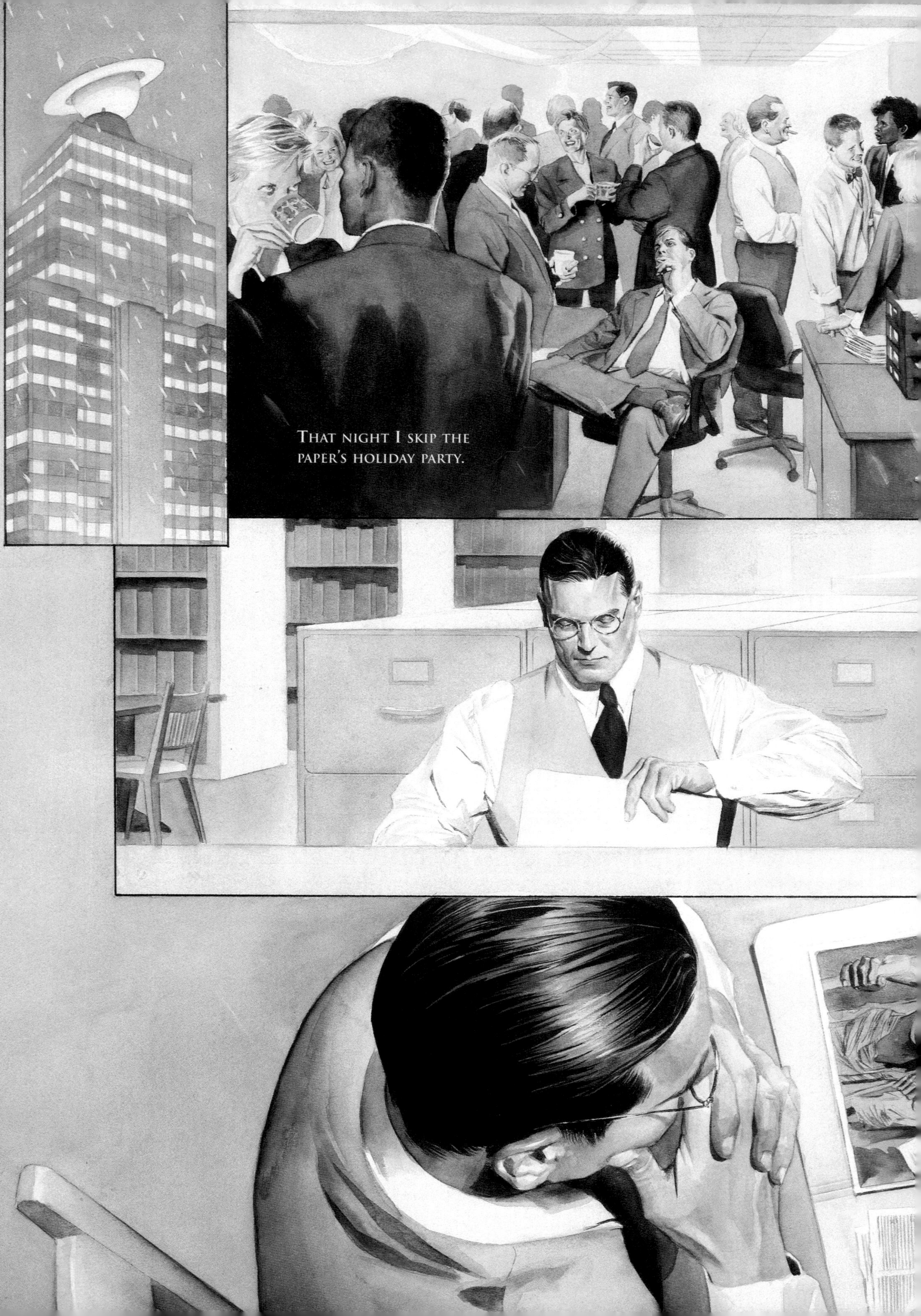
That night I skip the paper's holiday party.

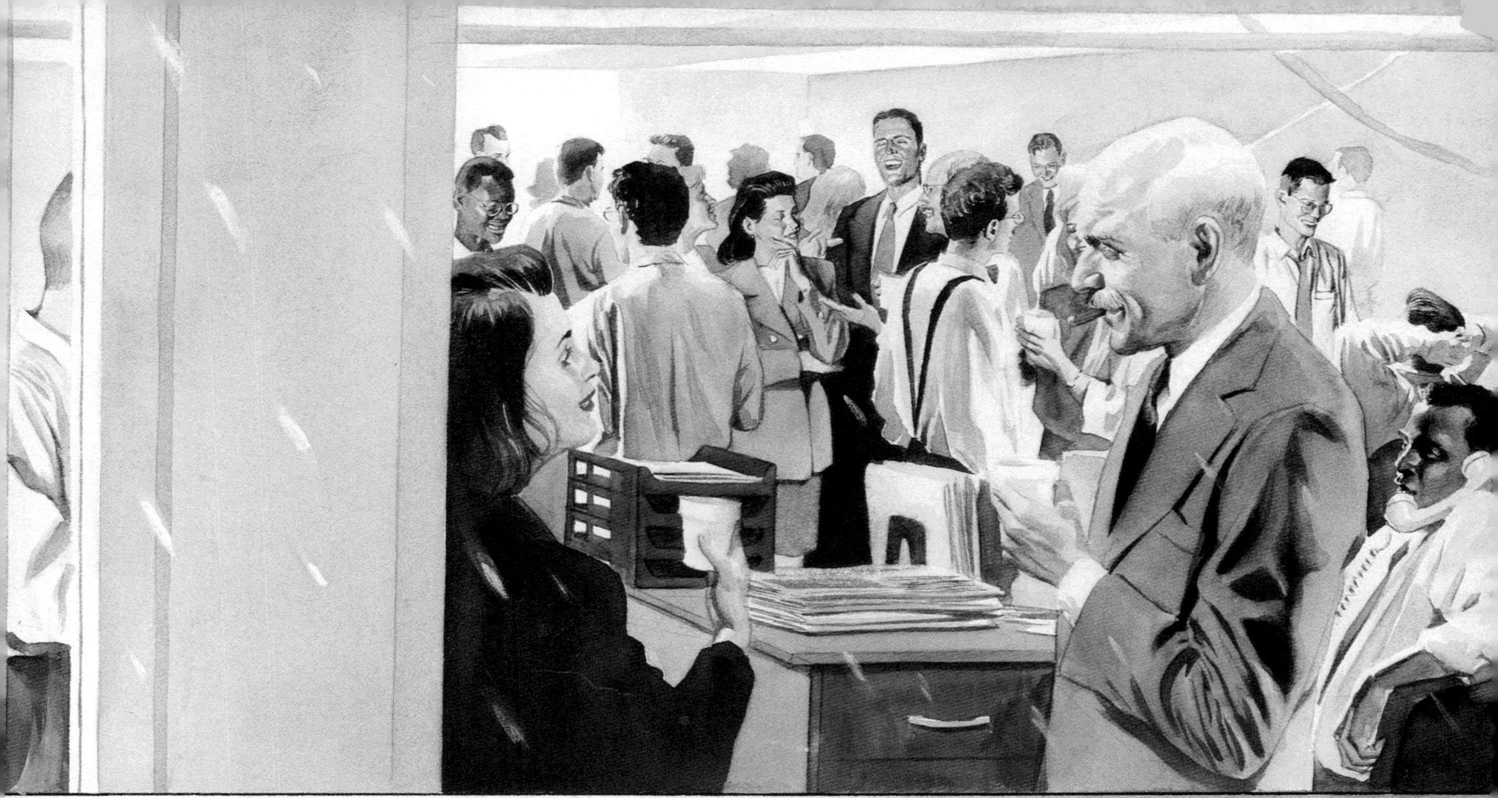

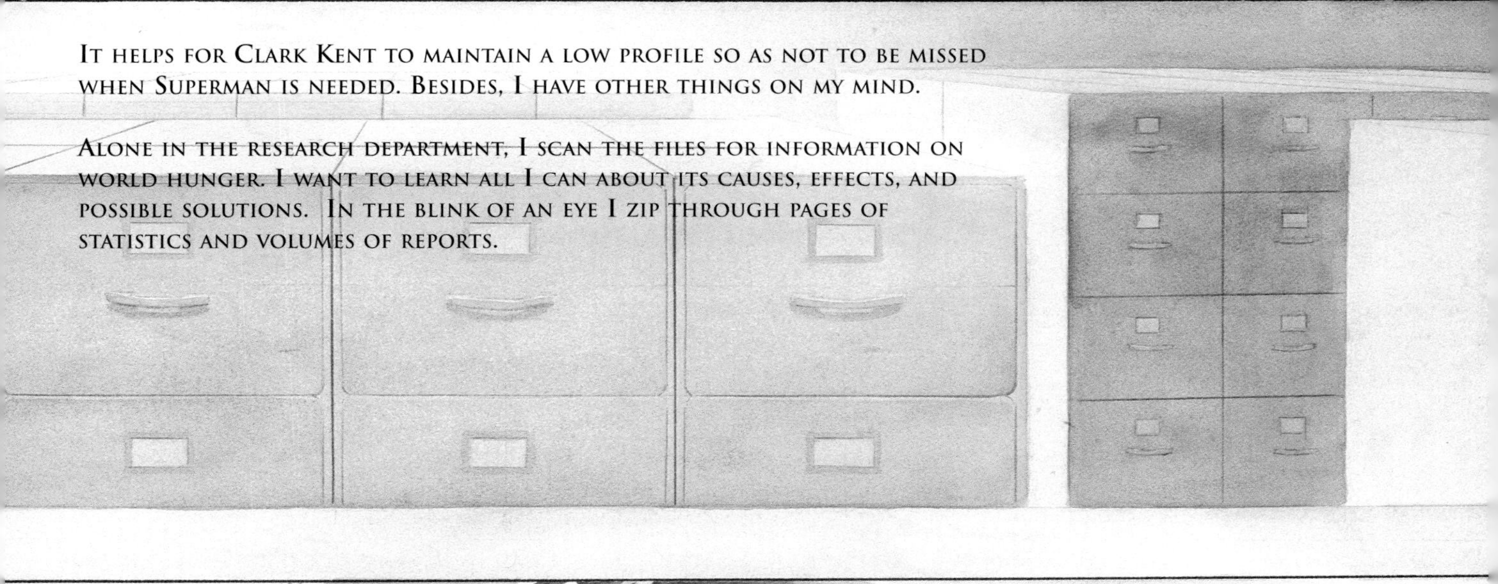

It helps for Clark Kent to maintain a low profile so as not to be missed when Superman is needed. Besides, I have other things on my mind.

Alone in the research department, I scan the files for information on world hunger. I want to learn all I can about its causes, effects, and possible solutions. In the blink of an eye I zip through pages of statistics and volumes of reports.

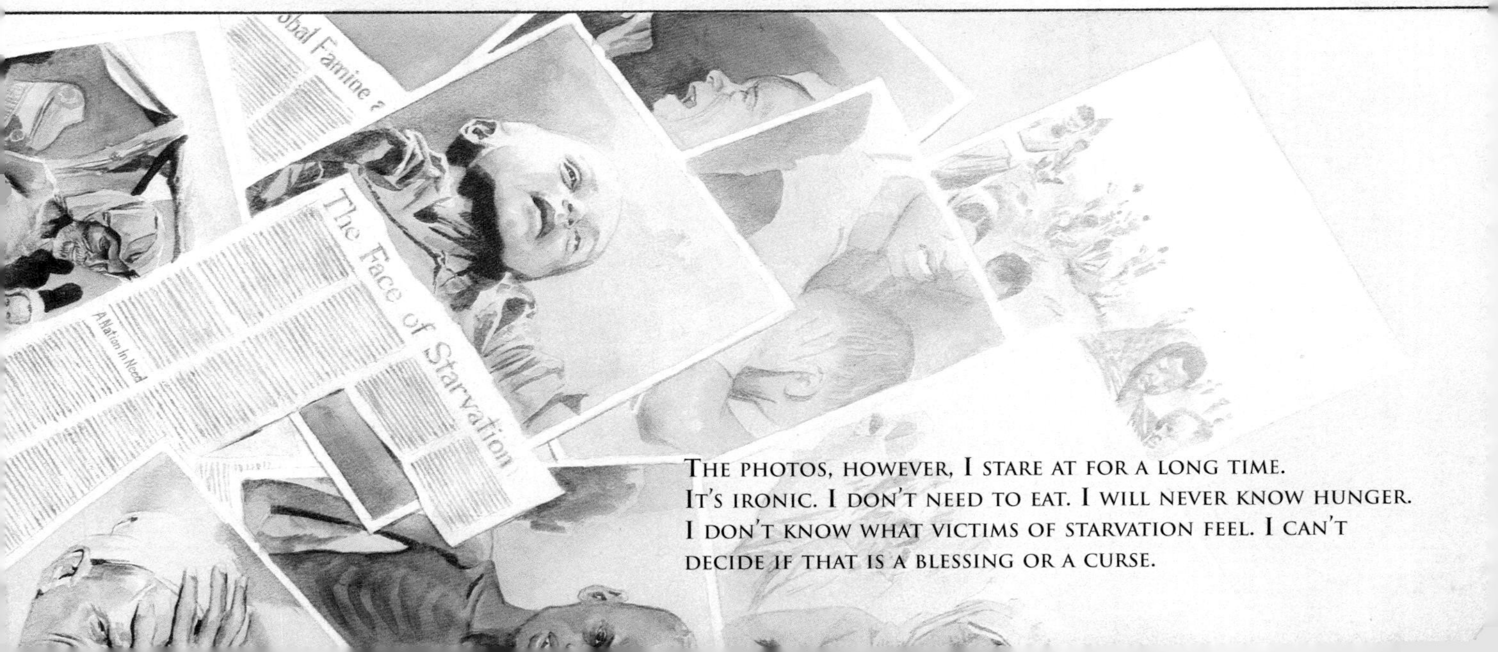
obal Famine a
The Face of Starvation
A Nation In Need

The photos, however, I stare at for a long time.
It's ironic. I don't need to eat. I will never know hunger.
I don't know what victims of starvation feel. I can't decide if that is a blessing or a curse.

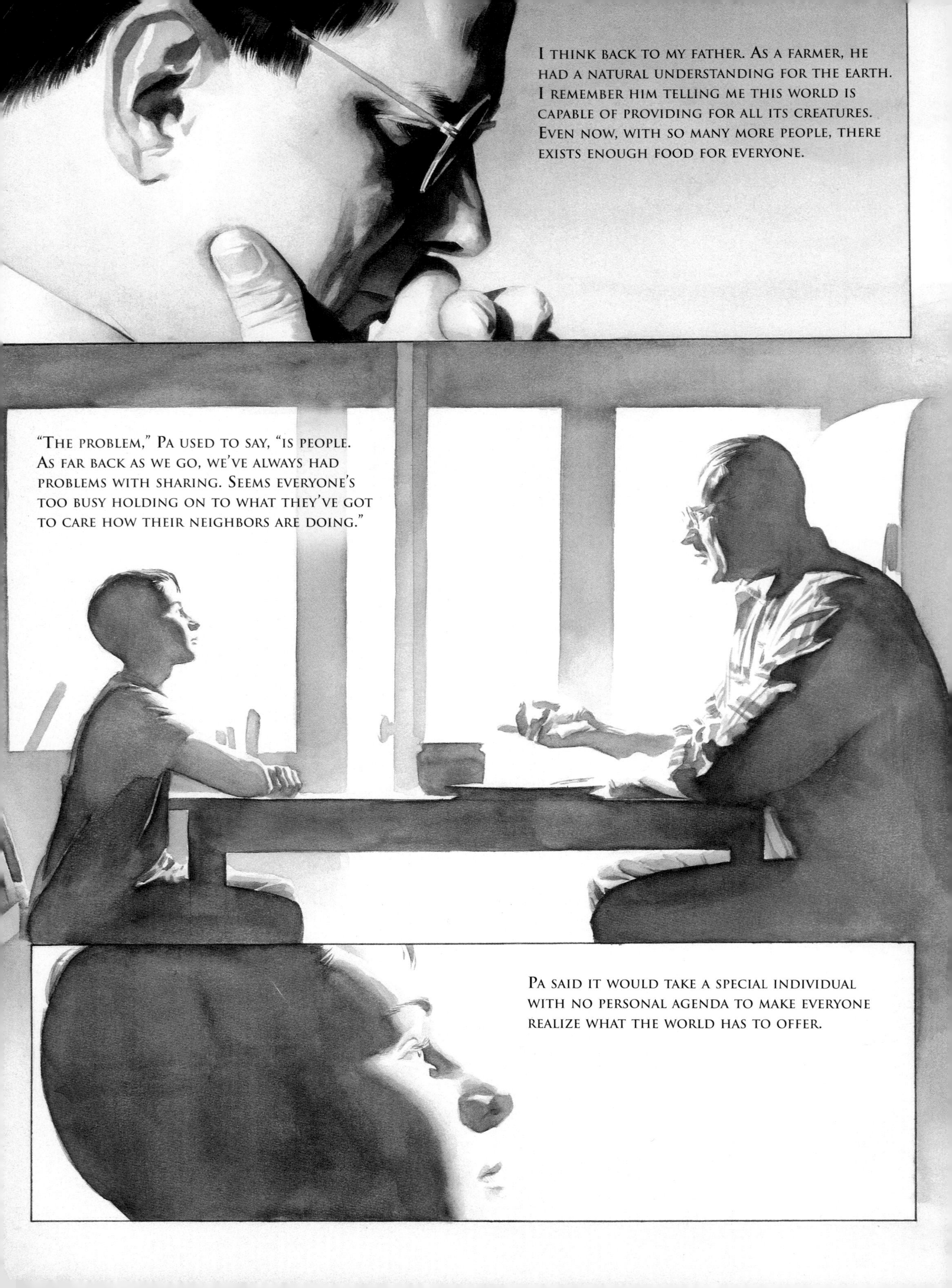
I think back to my father. As a farmer, he had a natural understanding for the earth. I remember him telling me this world is capable of providing for all its creatures. Even now, with so many more people, there exists enough food for everyone.
"The problem," Pa used to say, "is people. As far back as we go, we've always had problems with sharing. Seems everyone's too busy holding on to what they've got to care how their neighbors are doing."
Pa said it would take a special individual with no personal agenda to make everyone realize what the world has to offer.

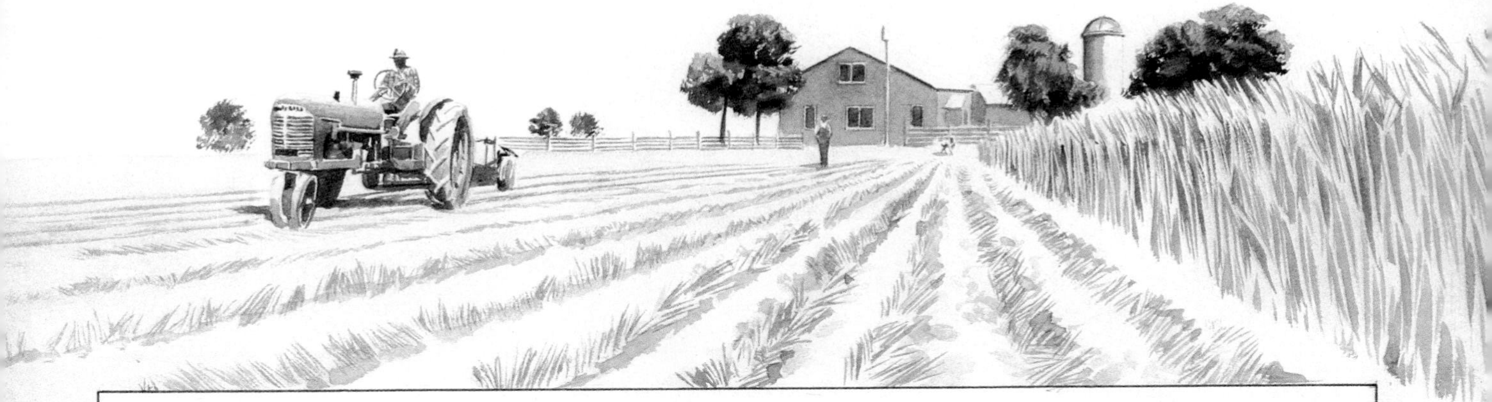

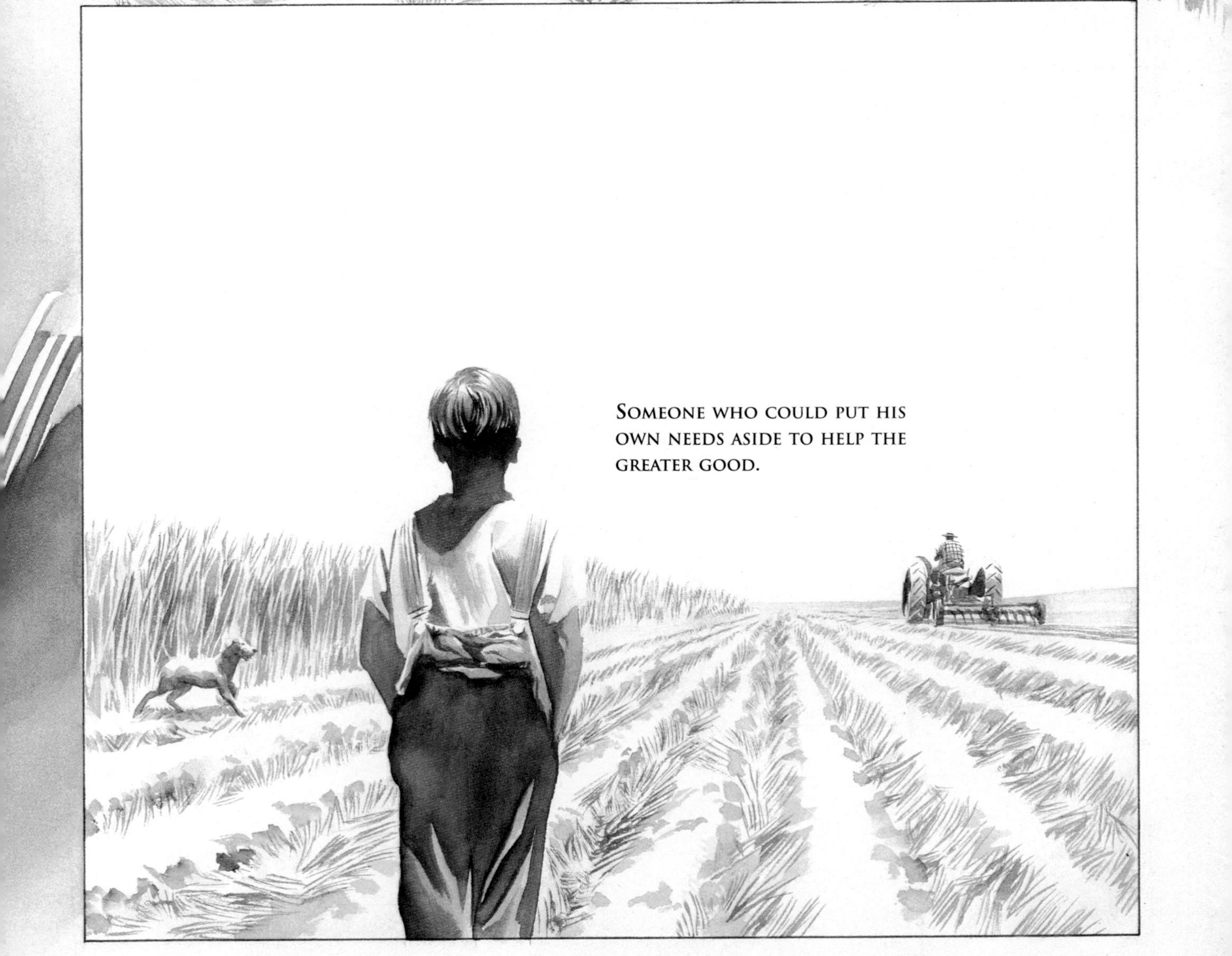

SOMEONE WHO COULD PUT HIS OWN NEEDS ASIDE TO HELP THE GREATER GOOD.

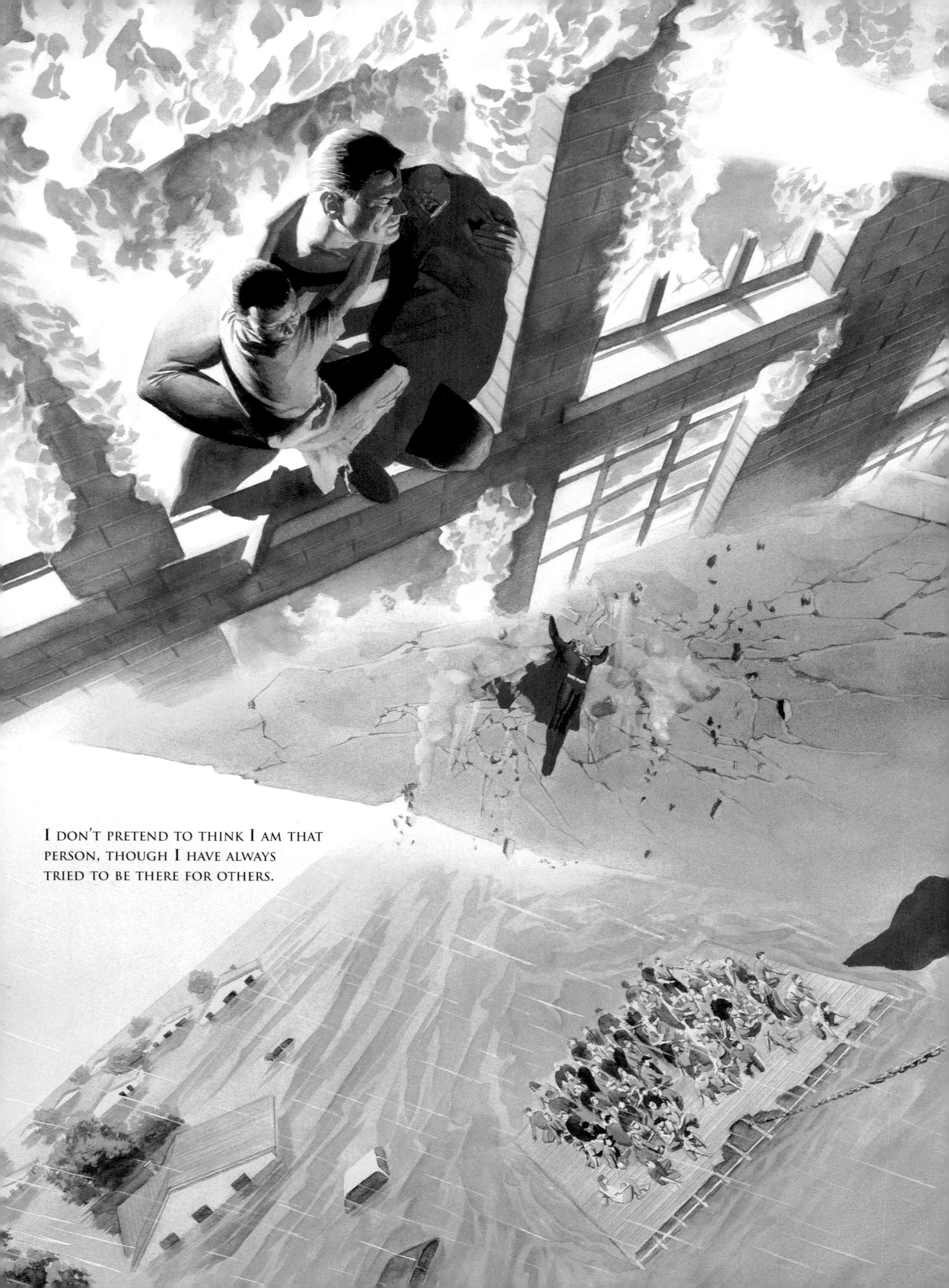

I don't pretend to think I am that person, though I have always tried to be there for others.

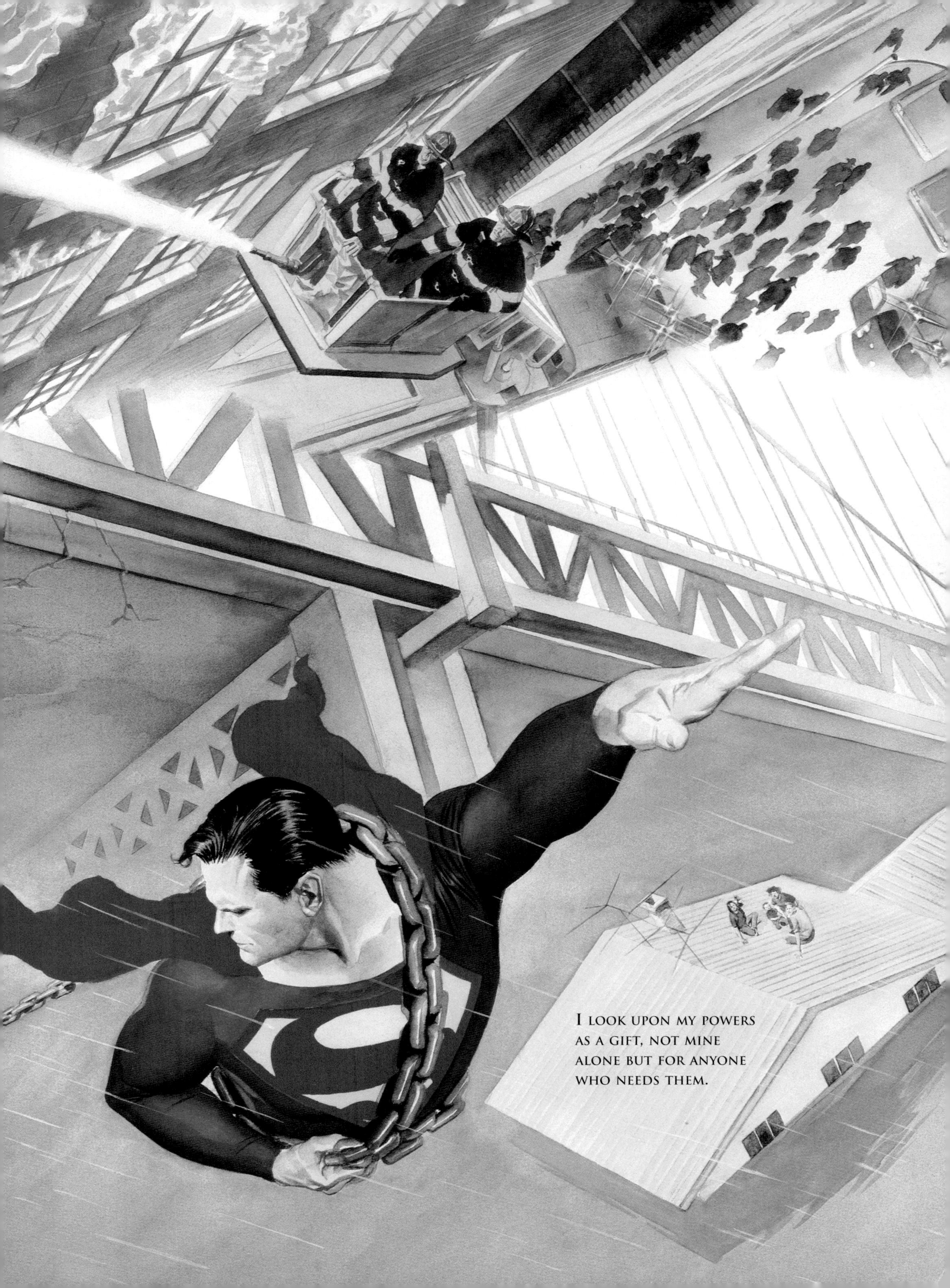
I look upon my powers as a gift, not mine alone but for anyone who needs them.

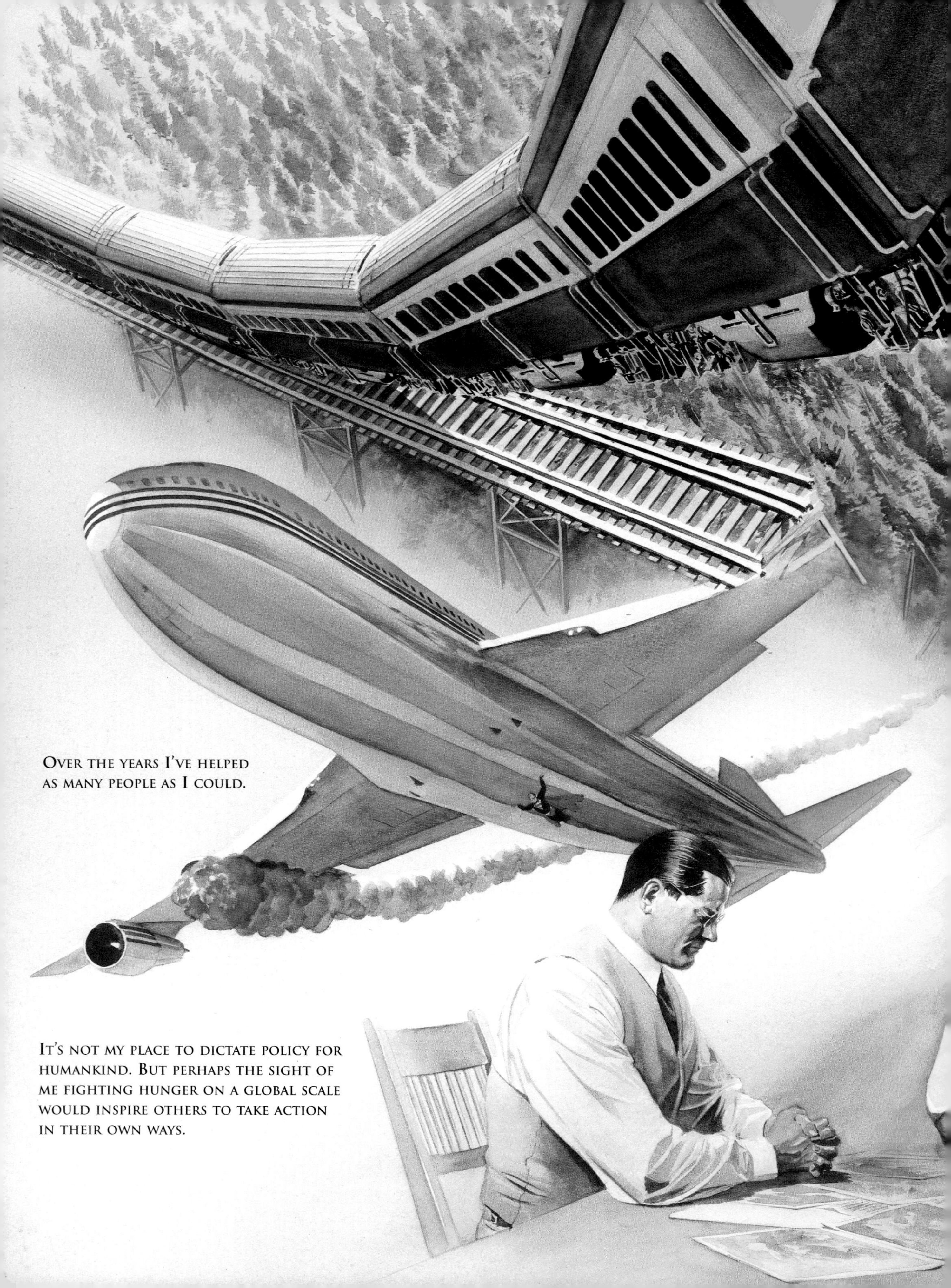
Over the years I've helped as many people as I could.
It's not my place to dictate policy for humankind. But perhaps the sight of me fighting hunger on a global scale would inspire others to take action in their own ways.

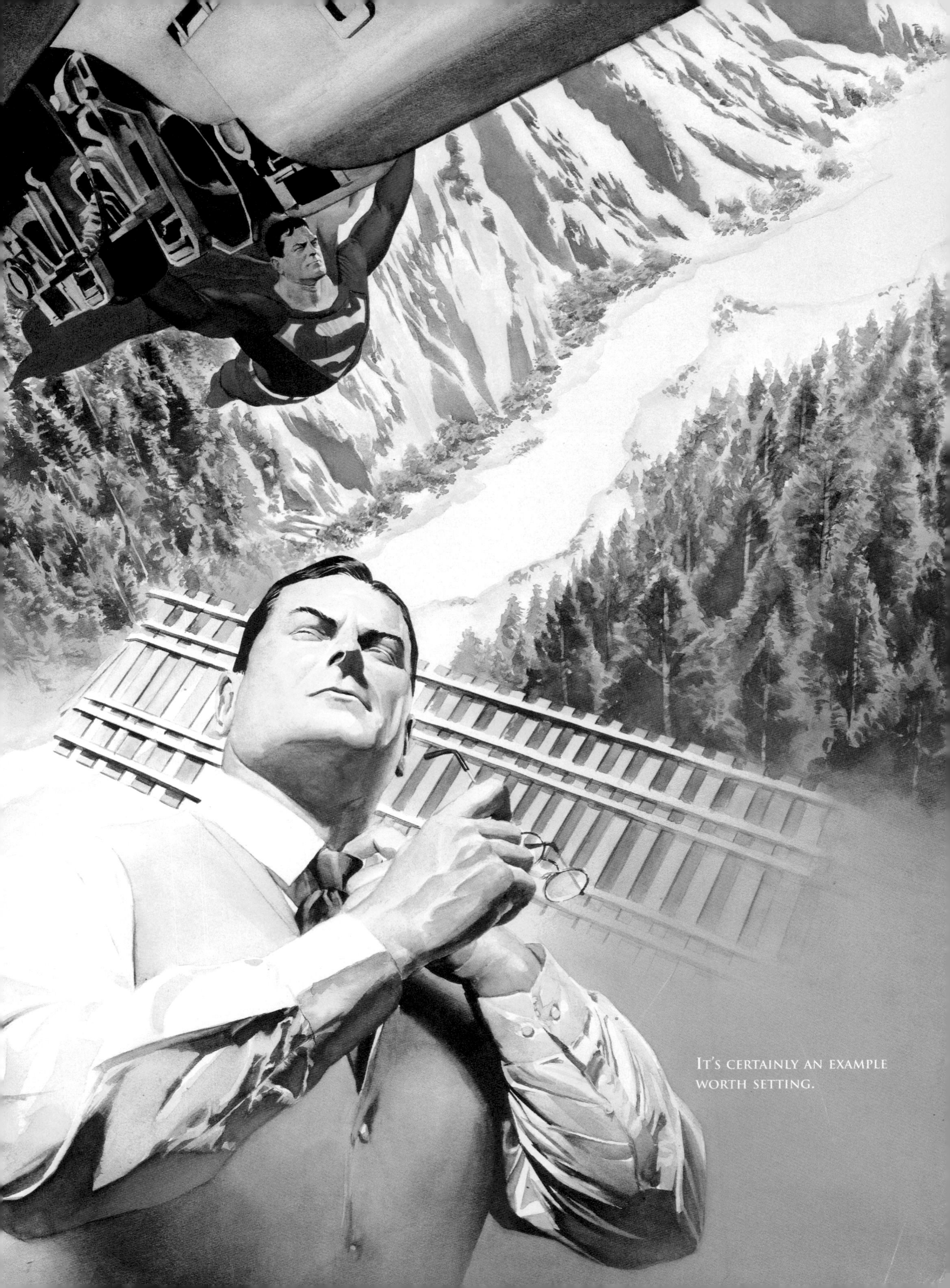
It's certainly an example worth setting.

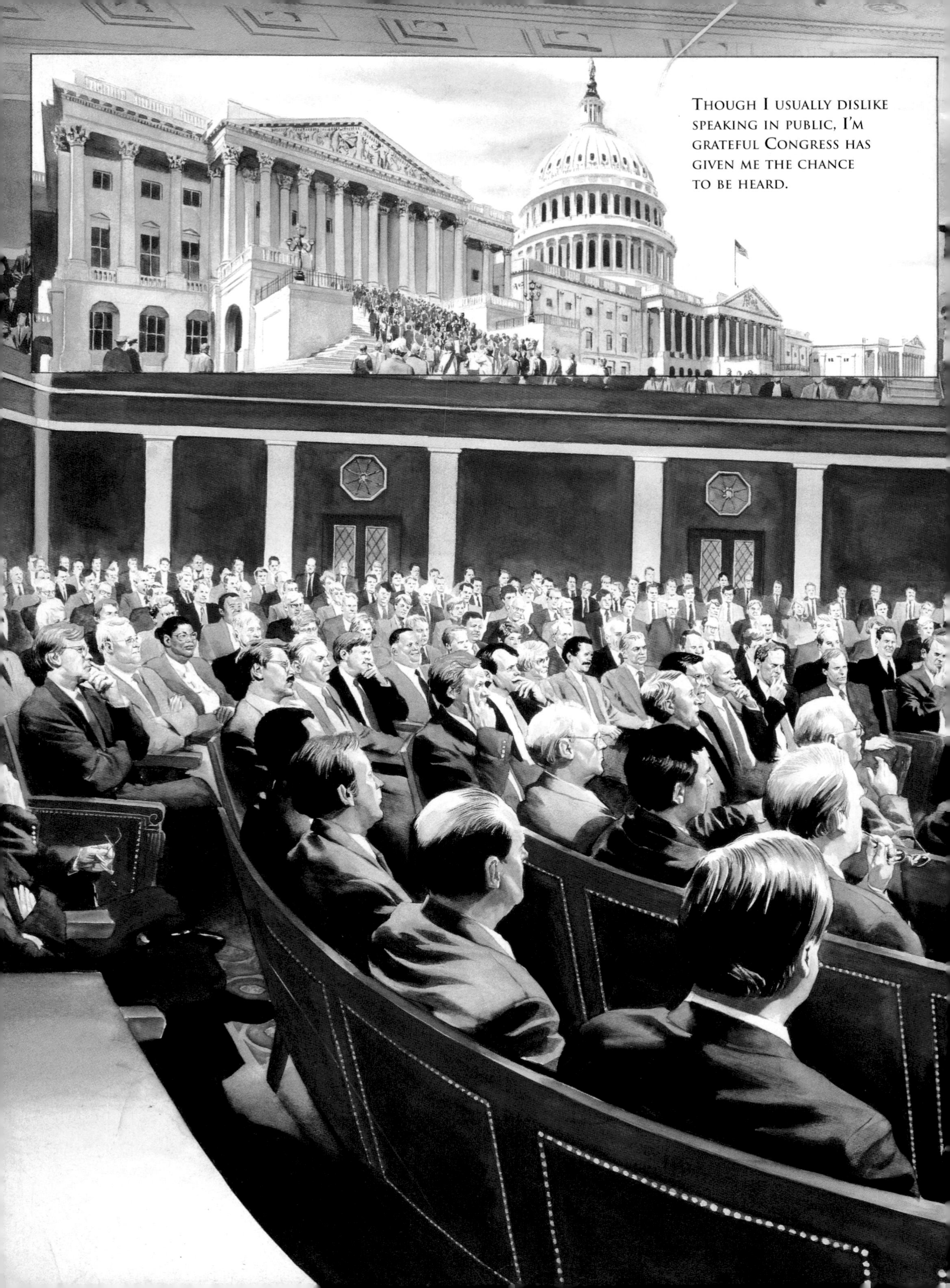
Though I usually dislike speaking in public, I'm grateful Congress has given me the chance to be heard.

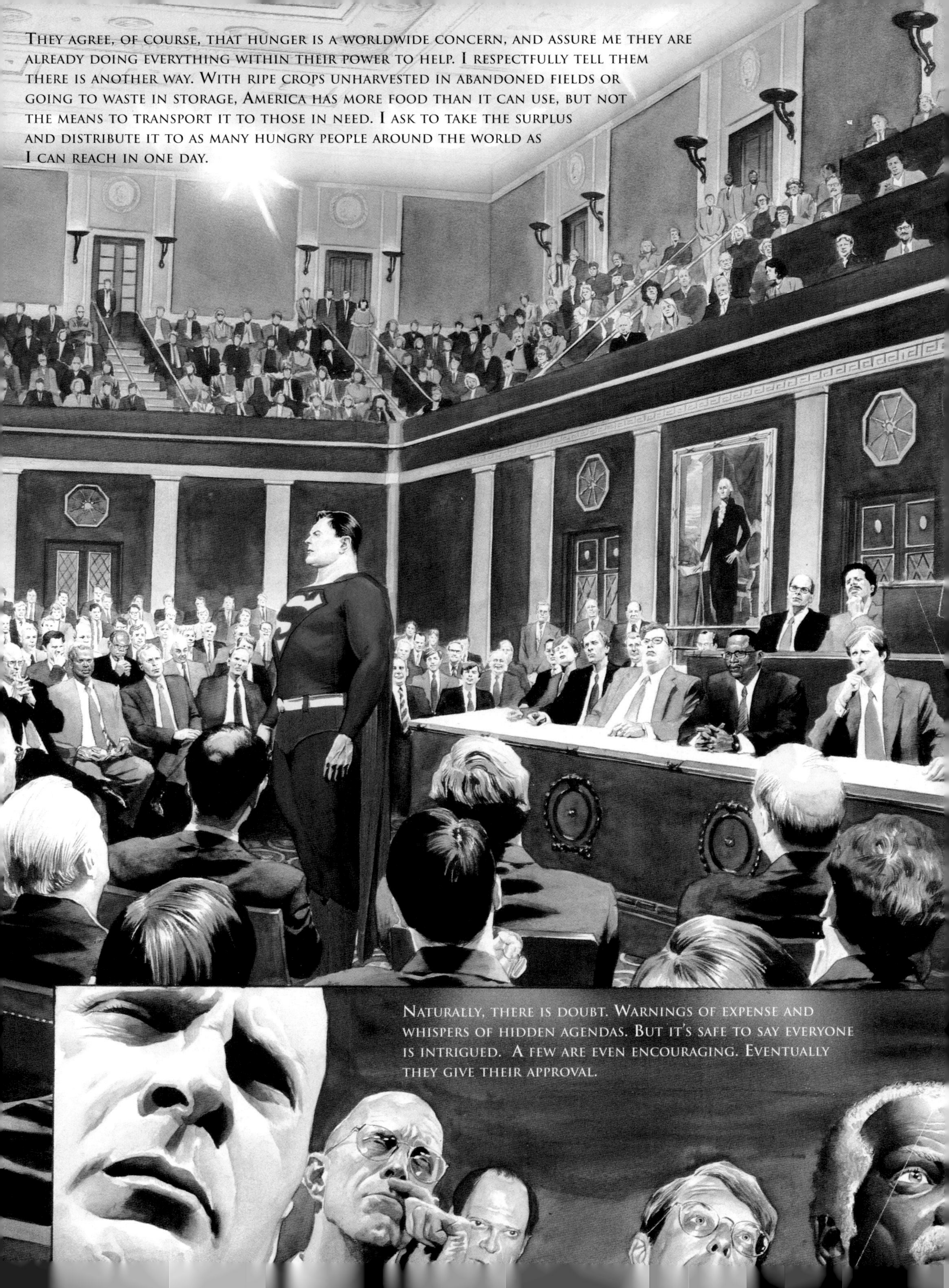
They agree, of course, that hunger is a worldwide concern, and assure me they are already doing everything within their power to help. I respectfully tell them there is another way. With ripe crops unharvested in abandoned fields or going to waste in storage, America has more food than it can use, but not the means to transport it to those in need. I ask to take the surplus and distribute it to as many hungry people around the world as I can reach in one day.
Naturally, there is doubt. Warnings of expense and whispers of hidden agendas. But it's safe to say everyone is intrigued. A few are even encouraging. Eventually they give their approval.

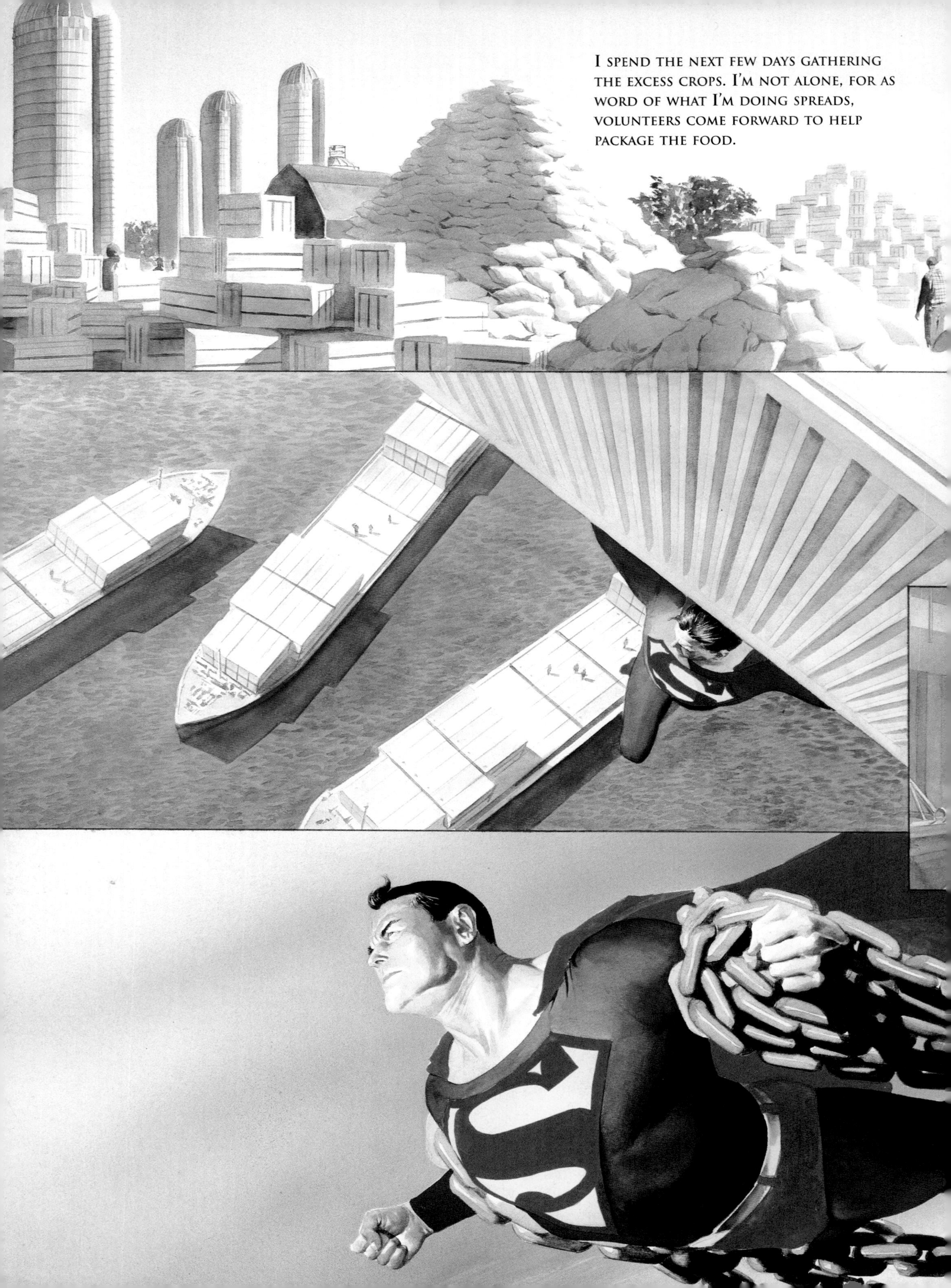
I spend the next few days gathering the excess crops. I'm not alone, for as word of what I'm doing spreads, volunteers come forward to help package the food.

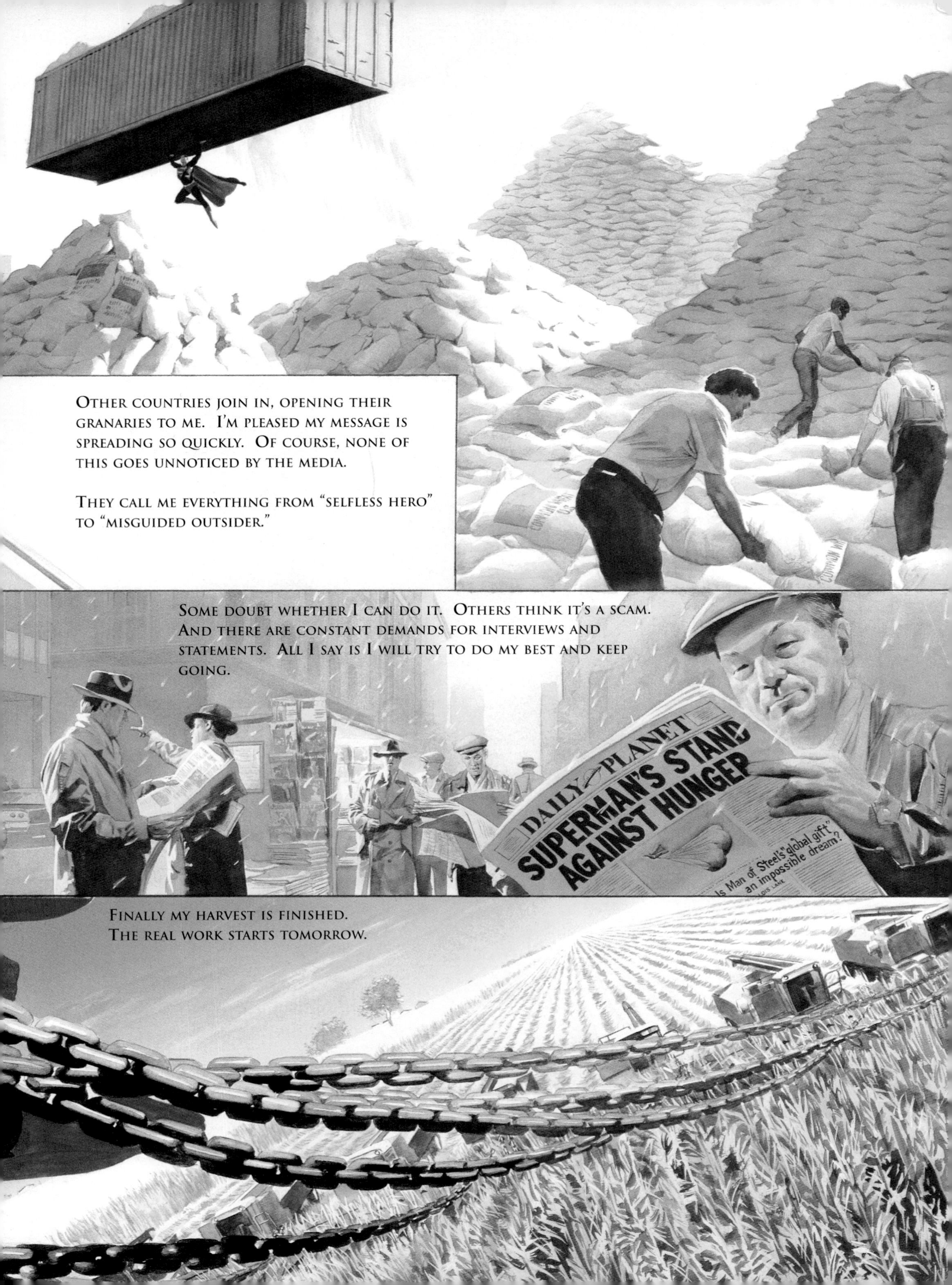

Other countries join in, opening their granaries to me. I'm pleased my message is spreading so quickly. Of course, none of this goes unnoticed by the media.
They call me everything from "selfless hero" to "misguided outsider."
Some doubt whether I can do it. Others think it's a scam. And there are constant demands for interviews and statements. All I say is I will try to do my best and keep going.
DAILY PLANET
SUPERMAN'S STAND AGAINST HUNGER
Man of Steel's global gift" an impossible dream?
Finally my harvest is finished.
The real work starts tomorrow.

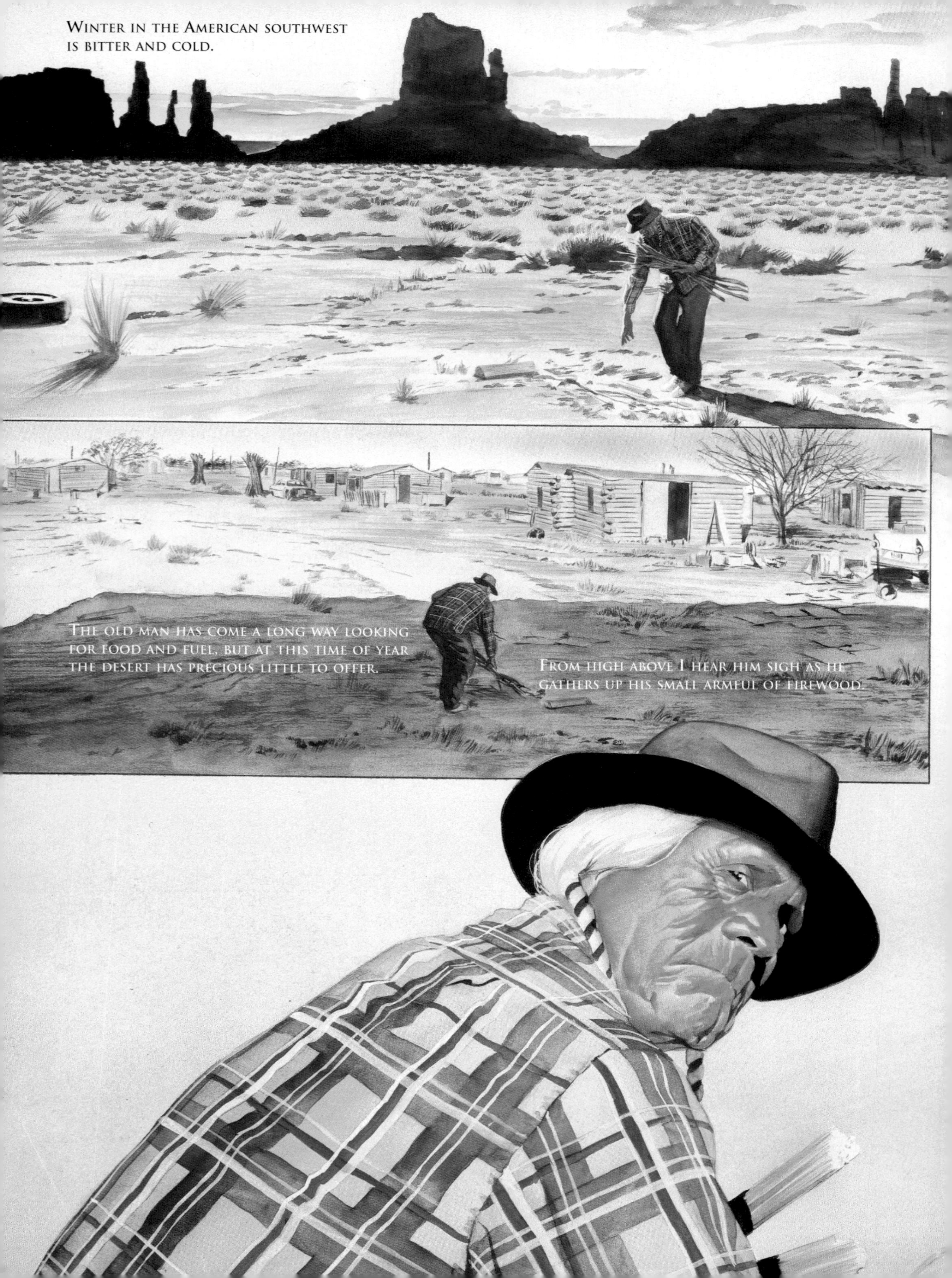
Winter in the American southwest is bitter and cold.
The old man has come a long way looking for food and fuel, but at this time of year the desert has precious little to offer.
From high above I hear him sigh as he gathers up his small armful of firewood.

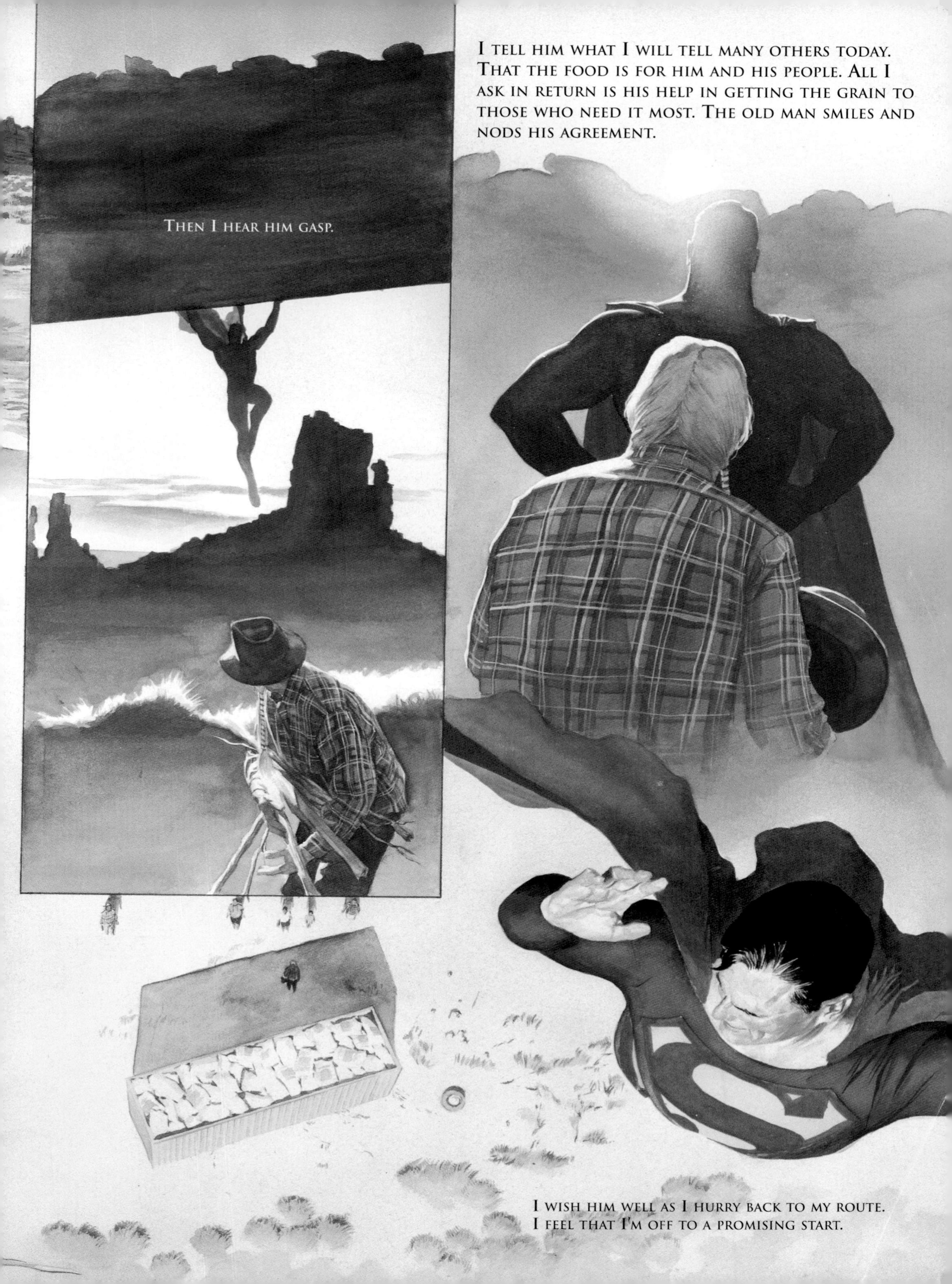
I TELL HIM WHAT I WILL TELL MANY OTHERS TODAY. THAT THE FOOD IS FOR HIM AND HIS PEOPLE. ALL I ASK IN RETURN IS HIS HELP IN GETTING THE GRAIN TO THOSE WHO NEED IT MOST. THE OLD MAN SMILES AND NODS HIS AGREEMENT.
THEN I HEAR HIM GASP.
I WISH HIM WELL AS I HURRY BACK TO MY ROUTE. I FEEL THAT I'M OFF TO A PROMISING START.

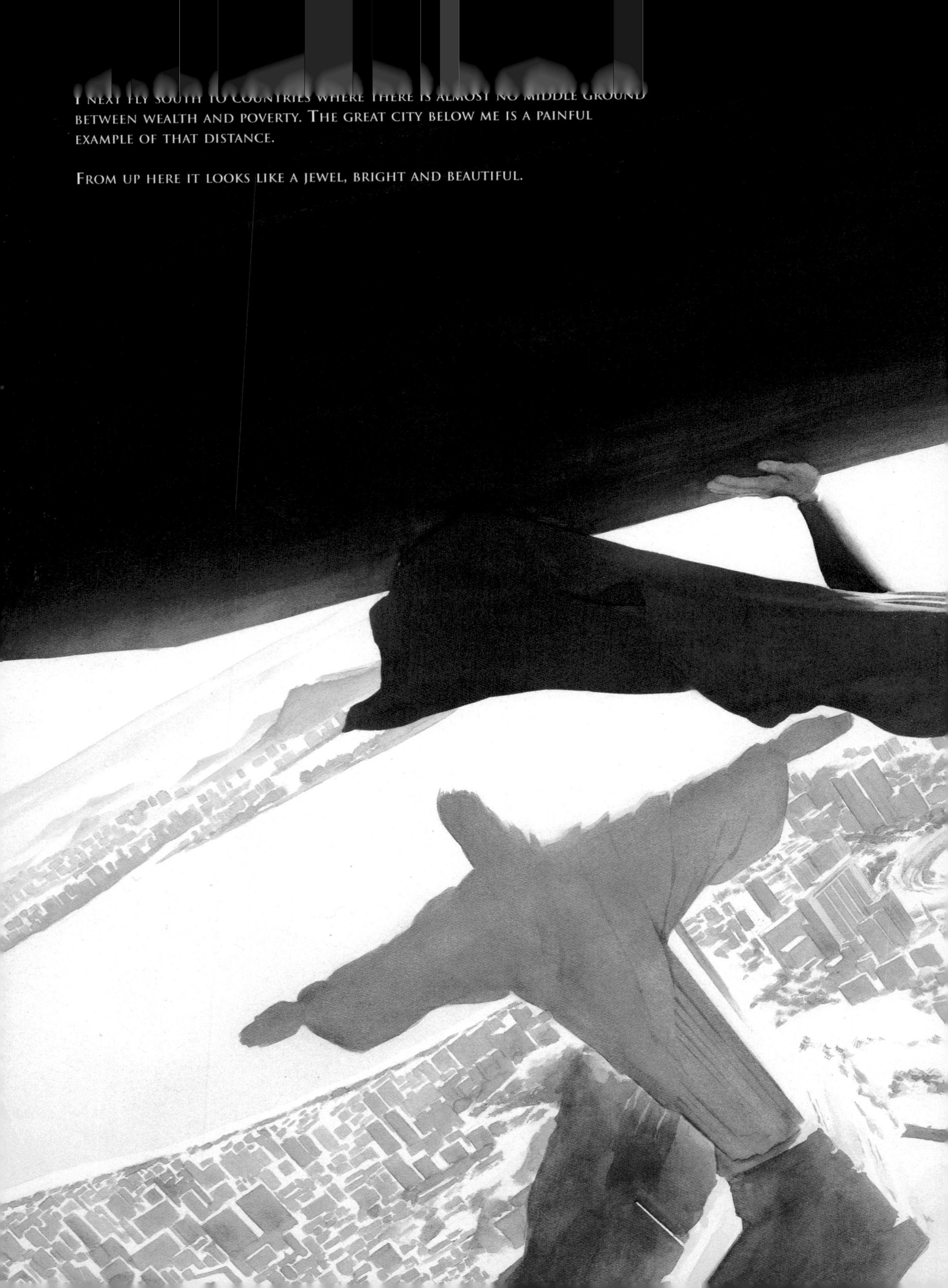
I NEXT FLY SOUTH TO COUNTRIES WHERE THERE IS ALMOST NO MIDDLE GROUND BETWEEN WEALTH AND POVERTY. THE GREAT CITY BELOW ME IS A PAINFUL EXAMPLE OF THAT DISTANCE.
FROM UP HERE IT LOOKS LIKE A JEWEL, BRIGHT AND BEAUTIFUL.

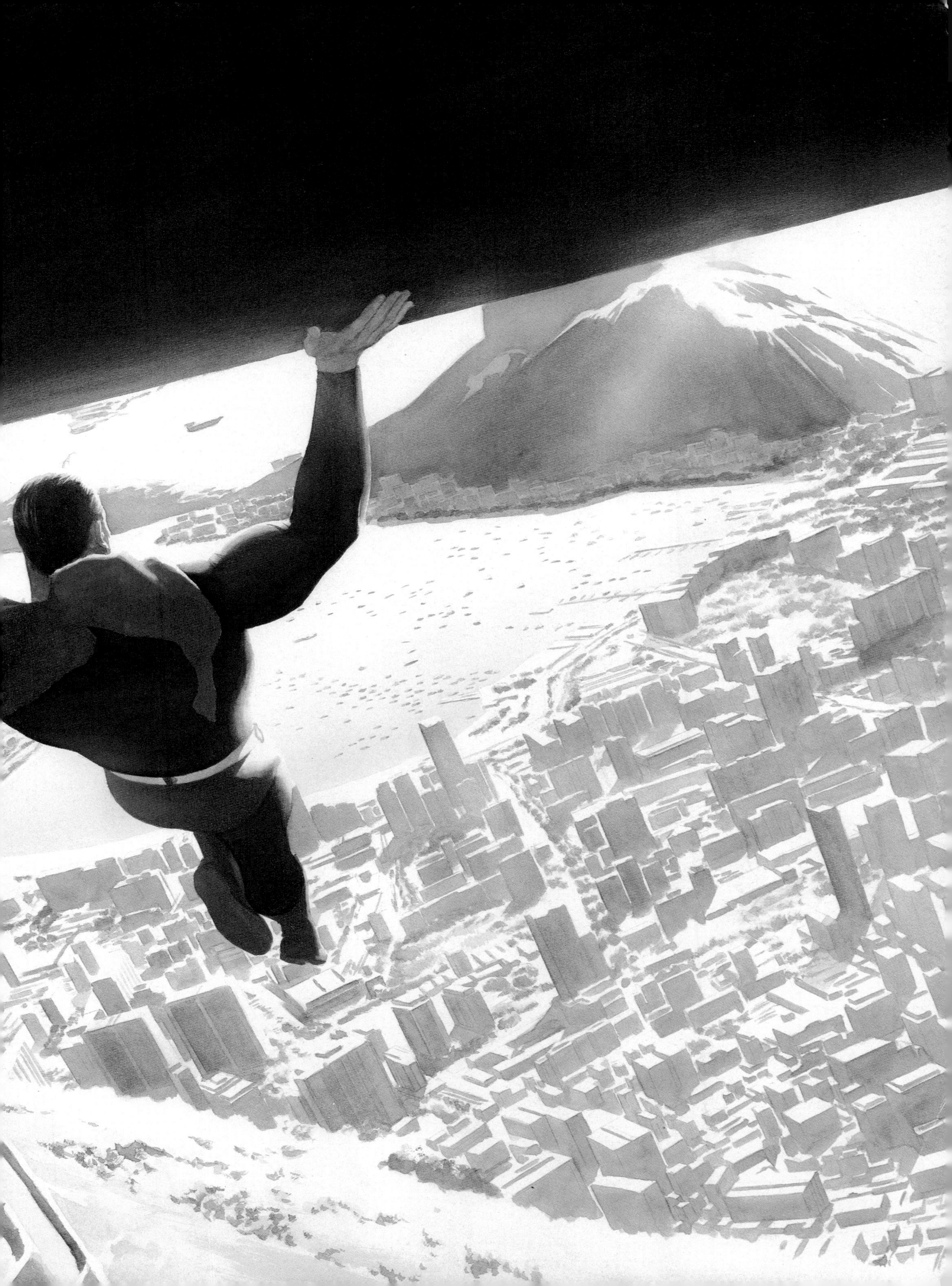

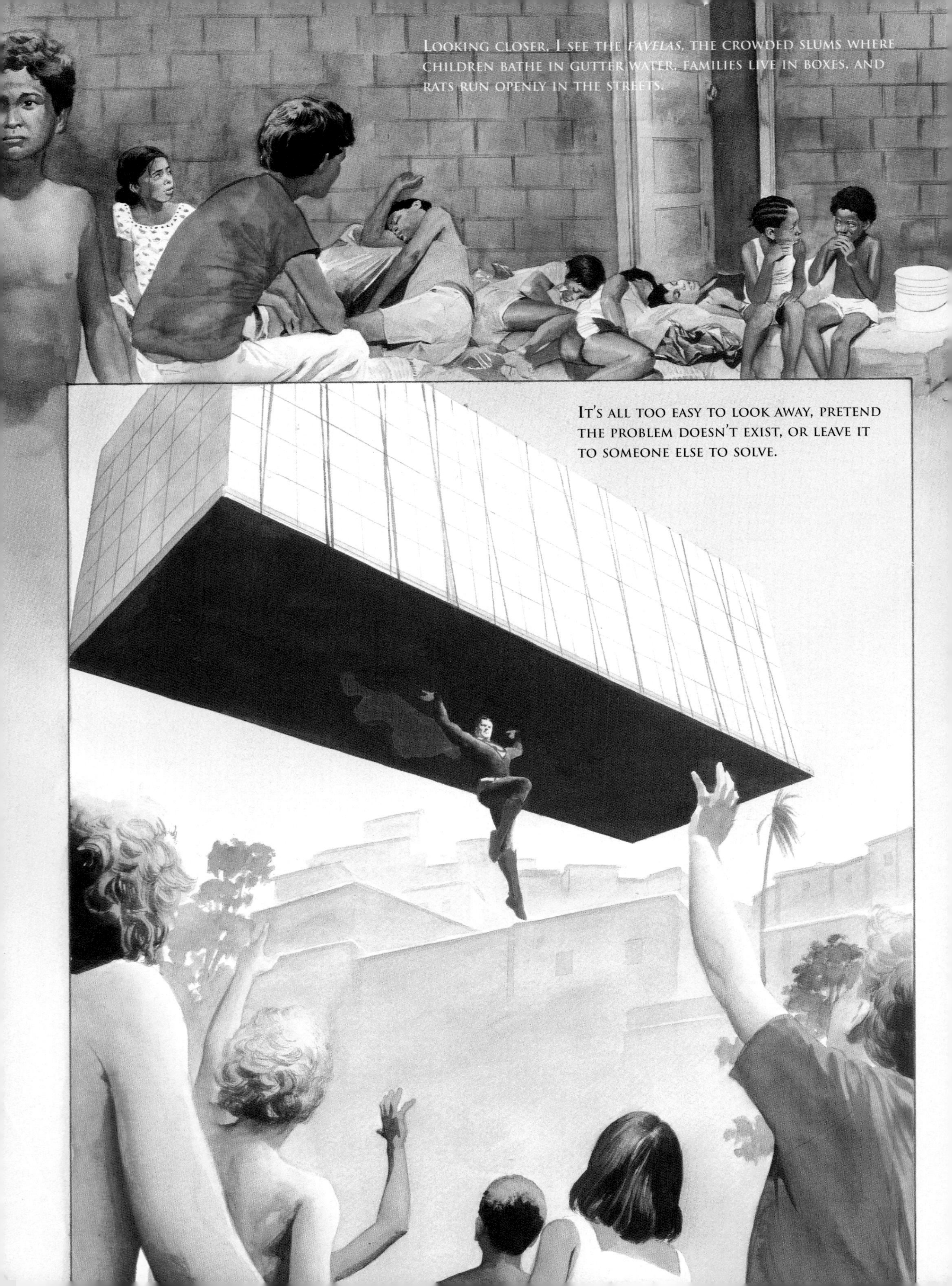
Looking closer, I see the *favelas*, the crowded slums where children bathe in gutter water, families live in boxes, and rats run openly in the streets.
It's all too easy to look away, pretend the problem doesn't exist, or leave it to someone else to solve.

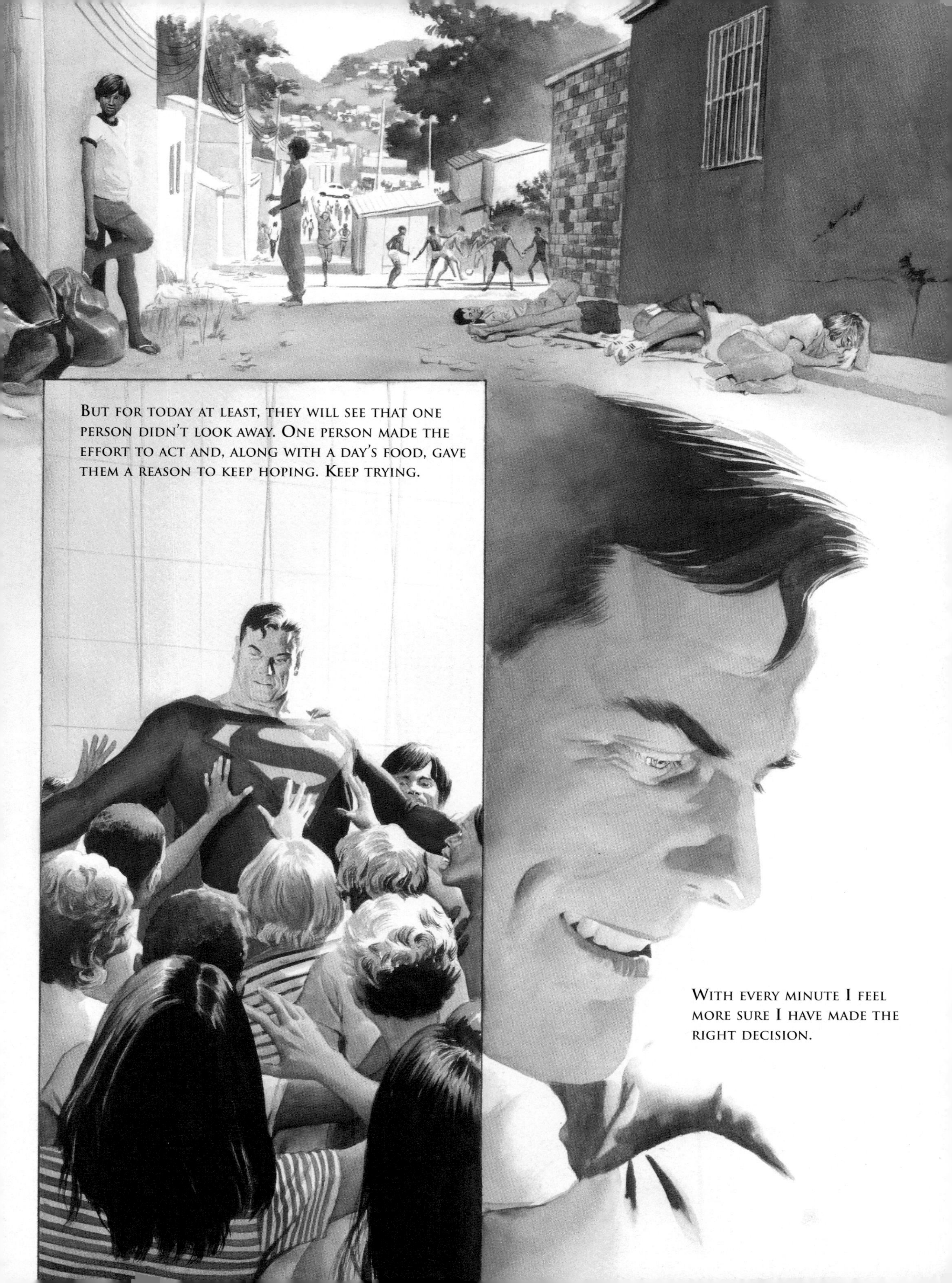
But for today at least, they will see that one person didn't look away. One person made the effort to act and, along with a day's food, gave them a reason to keep hoping. Keep trying.
With every minute I feel more sure I have made the right decision.

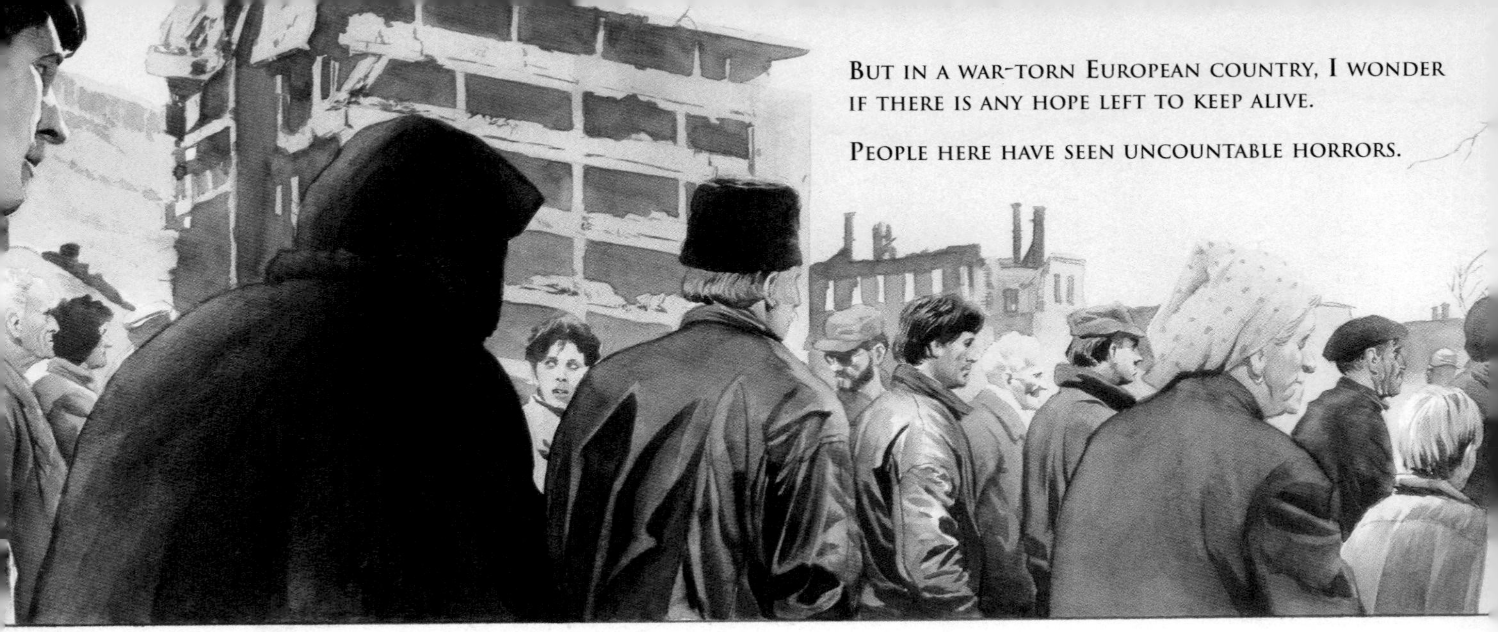
But in a war-torn European country, I wonder if there is any hope left to keep alive.
People here have seen uncountable horrors.

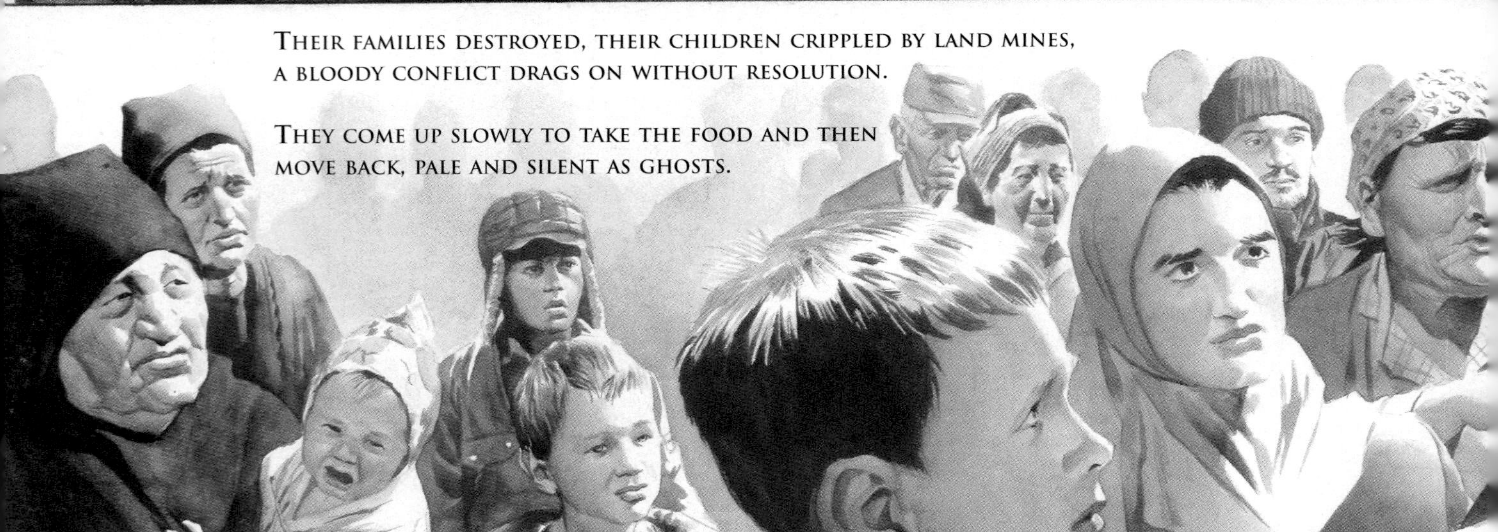
Their families destroyed, their children crippled by land mines, a bloody conflict drags on without resolution.
They come up slowly to take the food and then move back, pale and silent as ghosts.

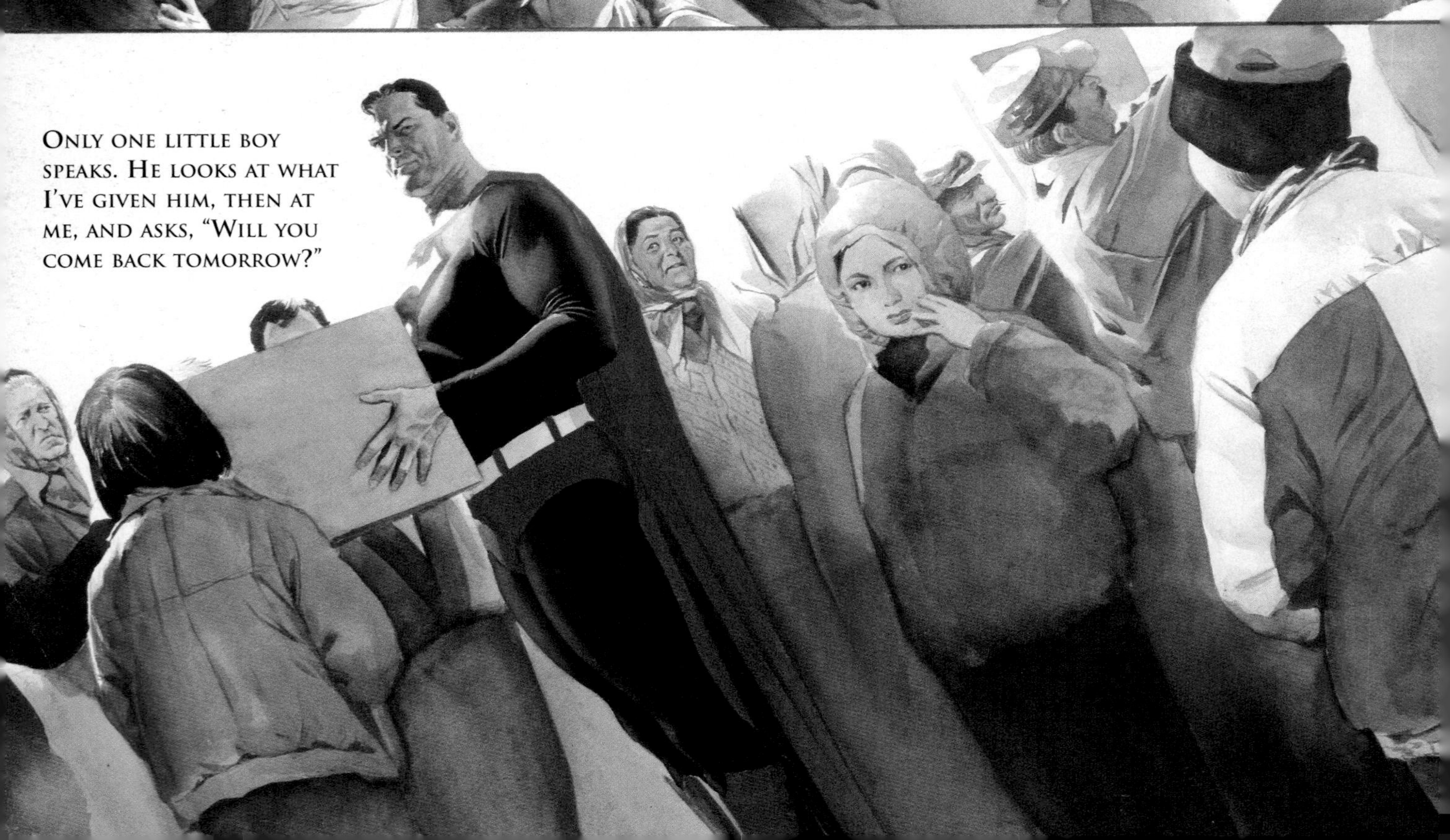
Only one little boy speaks. He looks at what I've given him, then at me, and asks, "Will you come back tomorrow?"

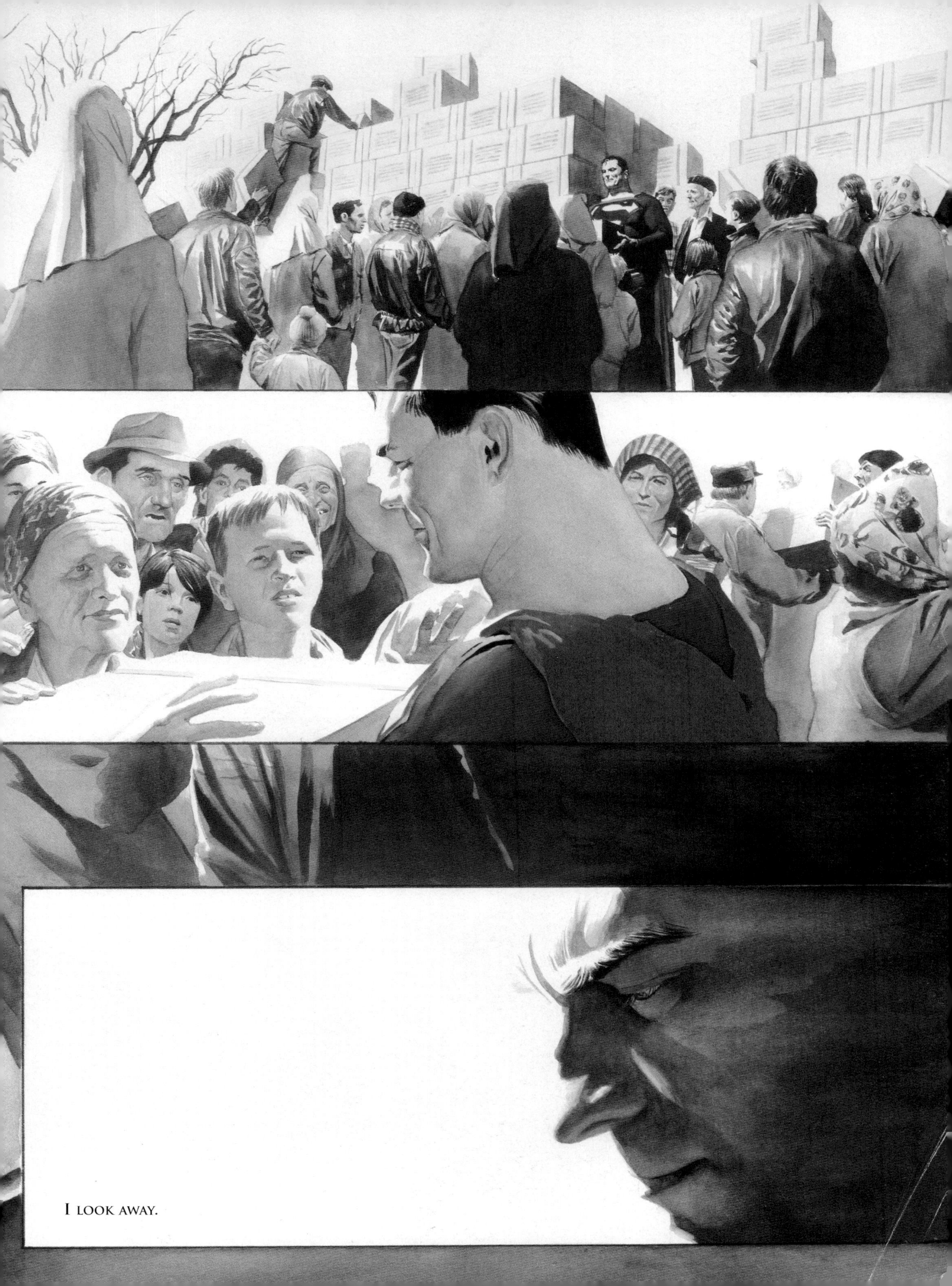
I look away.

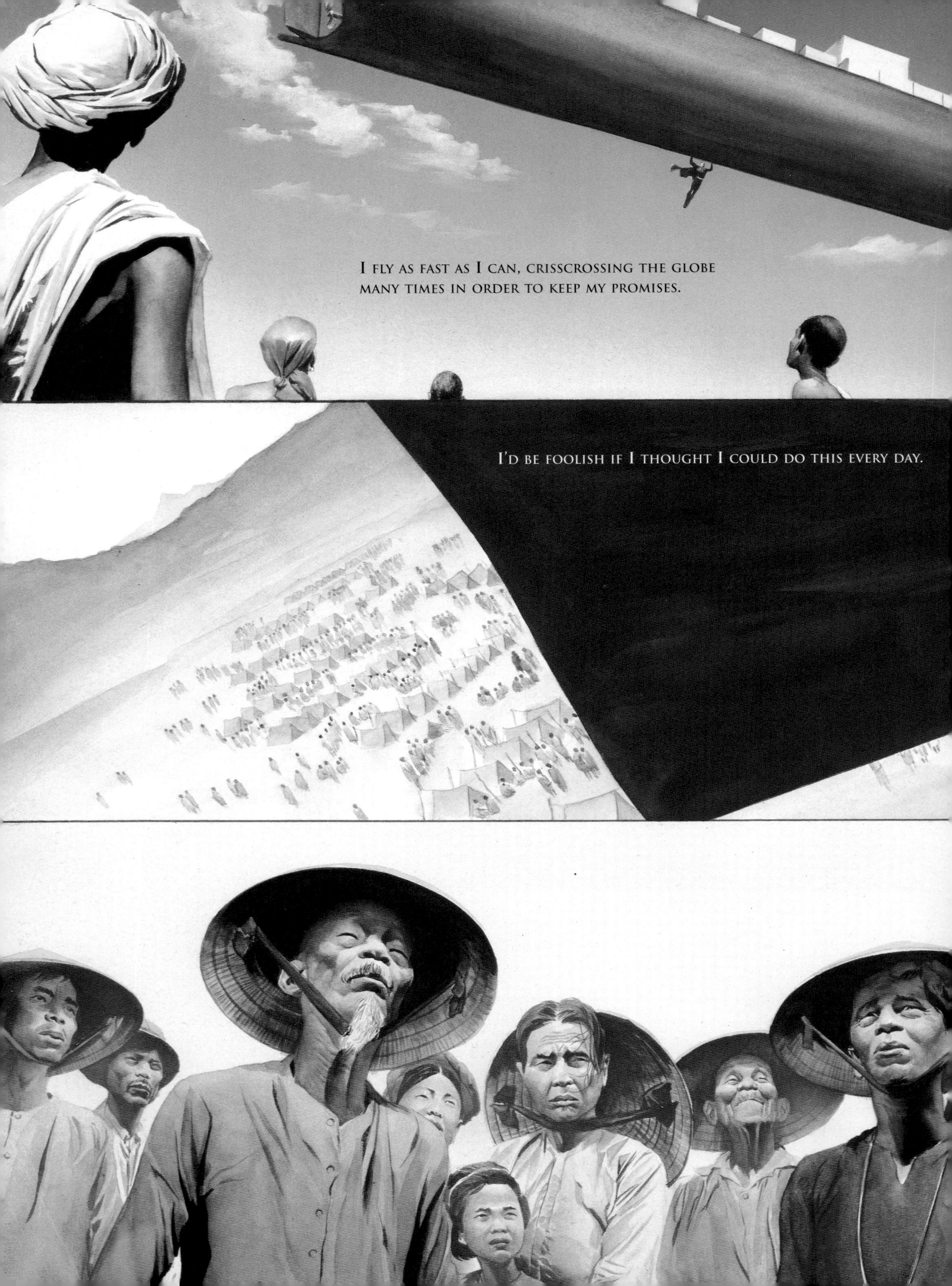
I fly as fast as I can, crisscrossing the globe many times in order to keep my promises.
I'd be foolish if I thought I could do this every day.

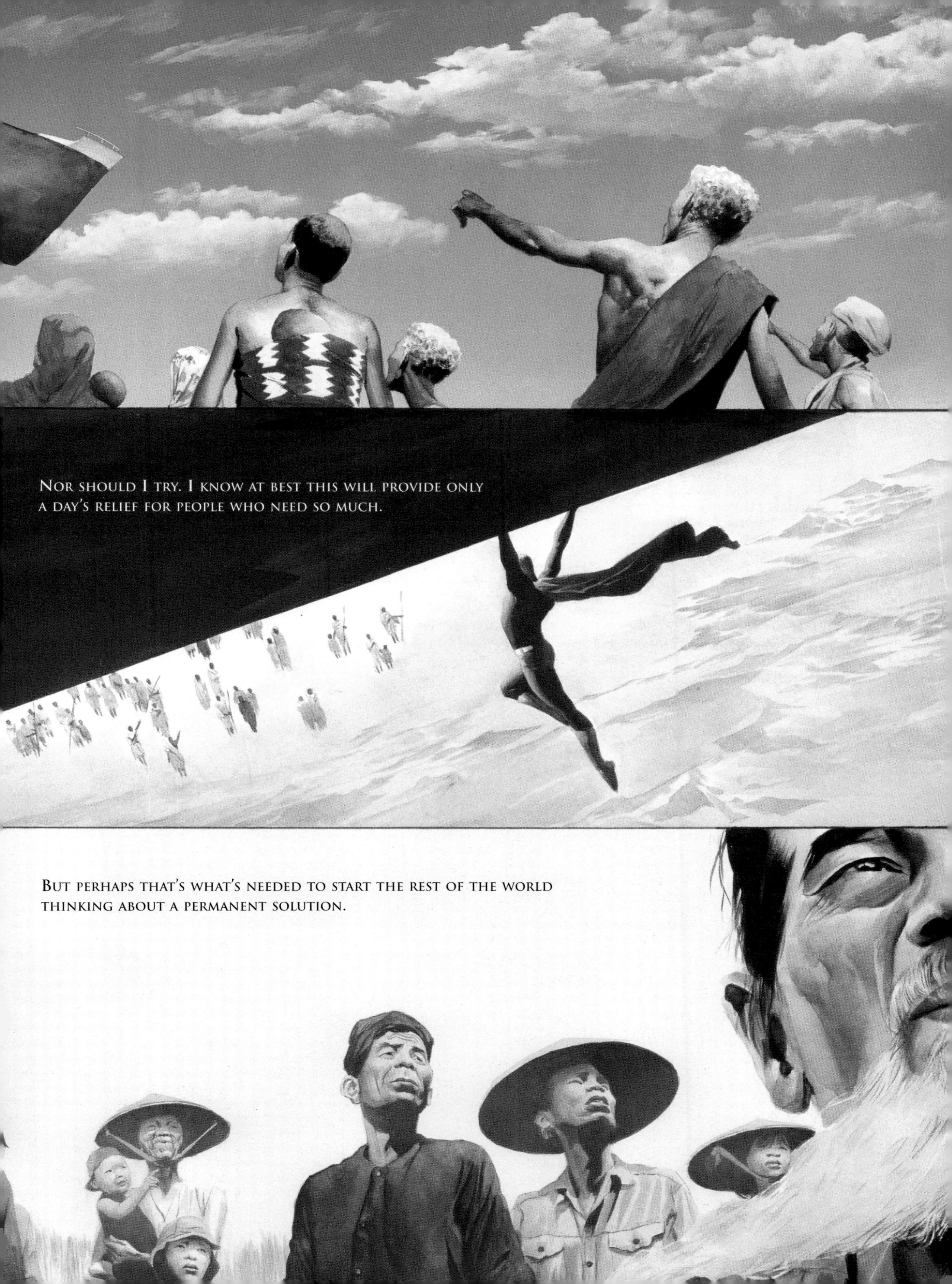
Nor should I try. I know at best this will provide only a day's relief for people who need so much.
But perhaps that's what's needed to start the rest of the world thinking about a permanent solution.

BY MIDDAY I'VE RETURNED TO AFRICA,
DETERMINED TO REACH EVERY REMOTE
VILLAGE AND SETTLEMENT.

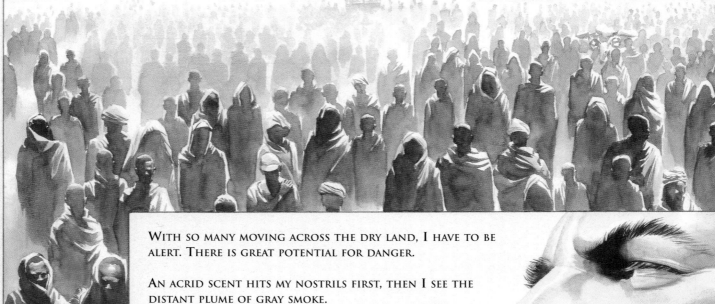

NEWS OF MY VISIT HAS SPREAD AND MANY, FEARING THEY WILL BE LEFT OUT, HAVE
ARRIVED IN DROVES. THEY SWARM INTO THE VILLAGE, SOME CROWDED INTO
RUSTING VEHICLES, OTHERS MAKING THE TRIP ON FOOT.

WITH SO MANY MOVING ACROSS THE DRY LAND, I HAVE TO BE
ALERT. THERE IS GREAT POTENTIAL FOR DANGER.

AN ACRID SCENT HITS MY NOSTRILS FIRST, THEN I SEE THE
DISTANT PLUME OF GRAY SMOKE.

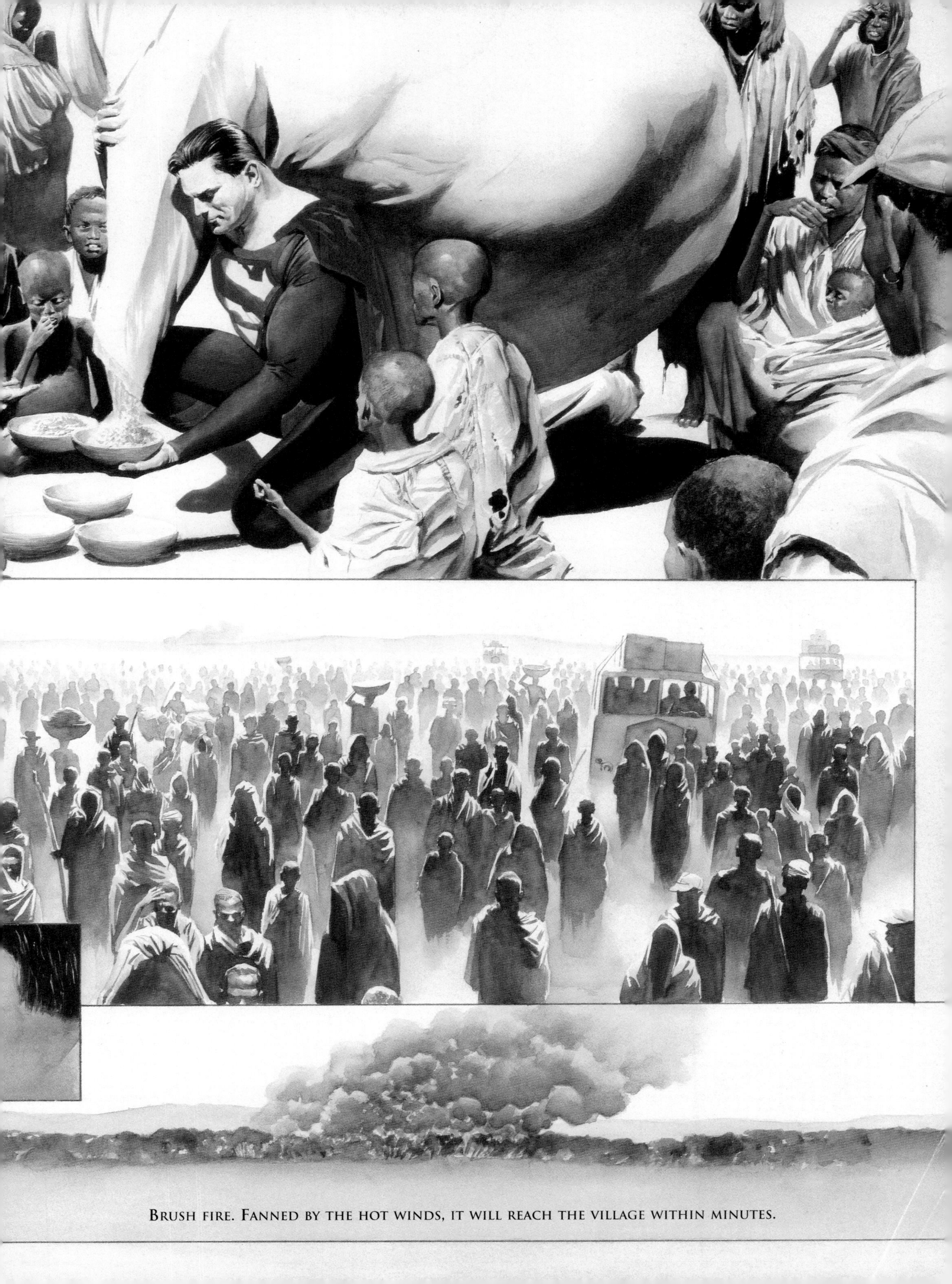
BRUSH FIRE. FANNED BY THE HOT WINDS, IT WILL REACH THE VILLAGE WITHIN MINUTES.

Wind screams in my ears as I fly toward the blaze.

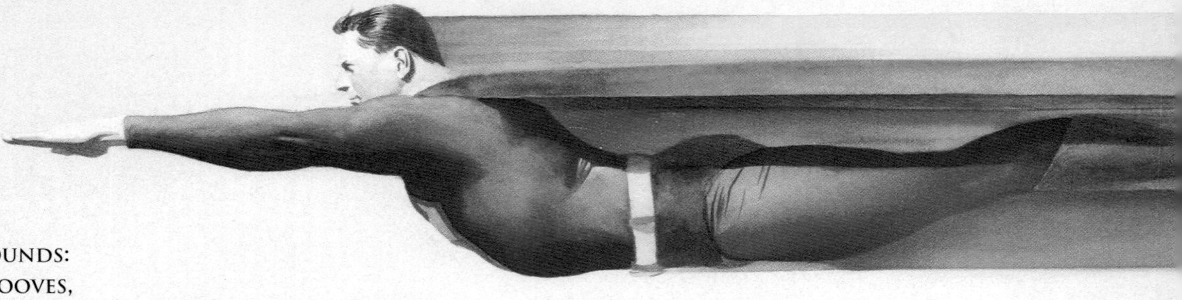

Then I hear other sounds:
thundering hooves,
fearful growls,
and thousands of hearts pounding in terror.

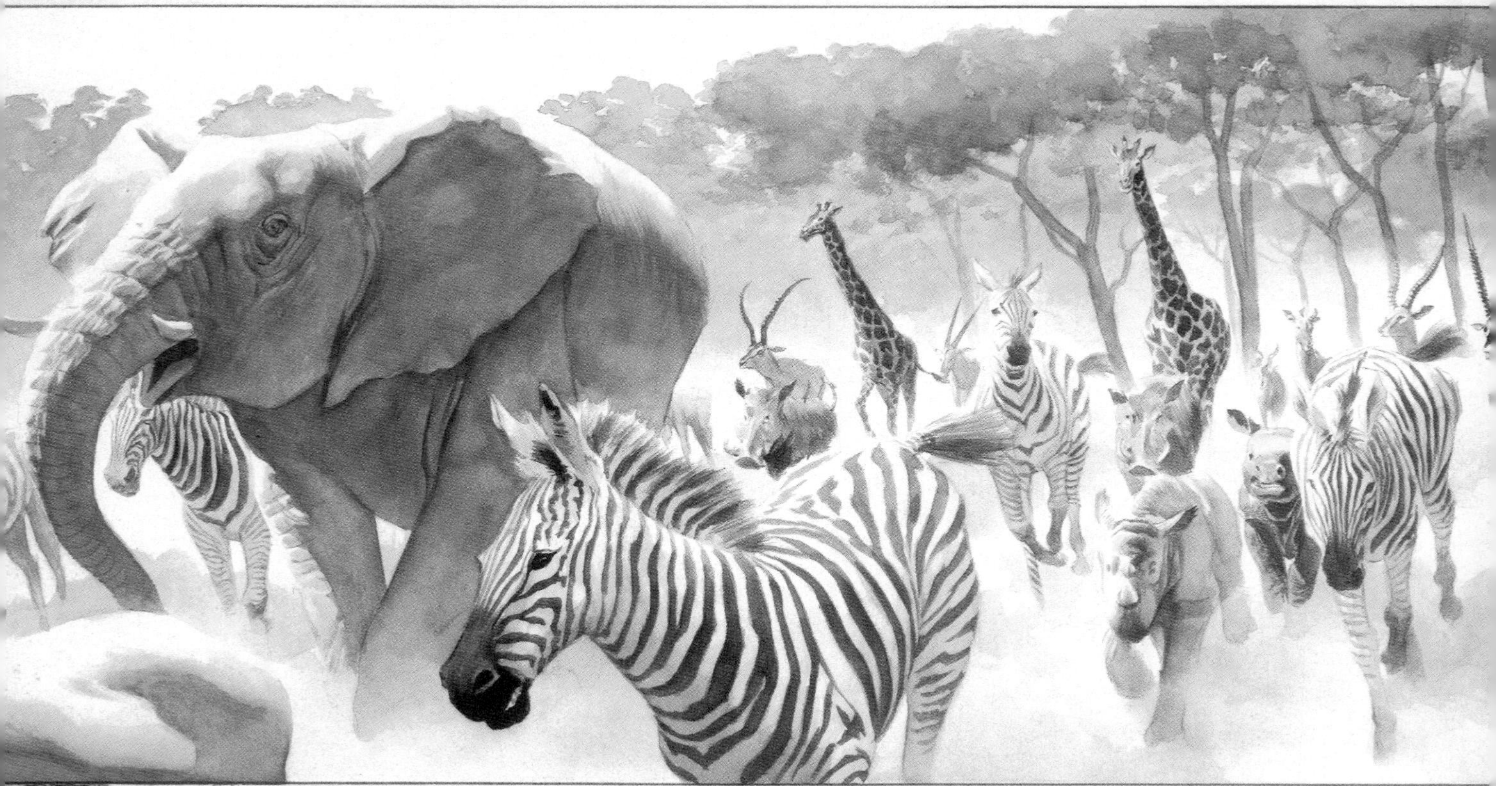

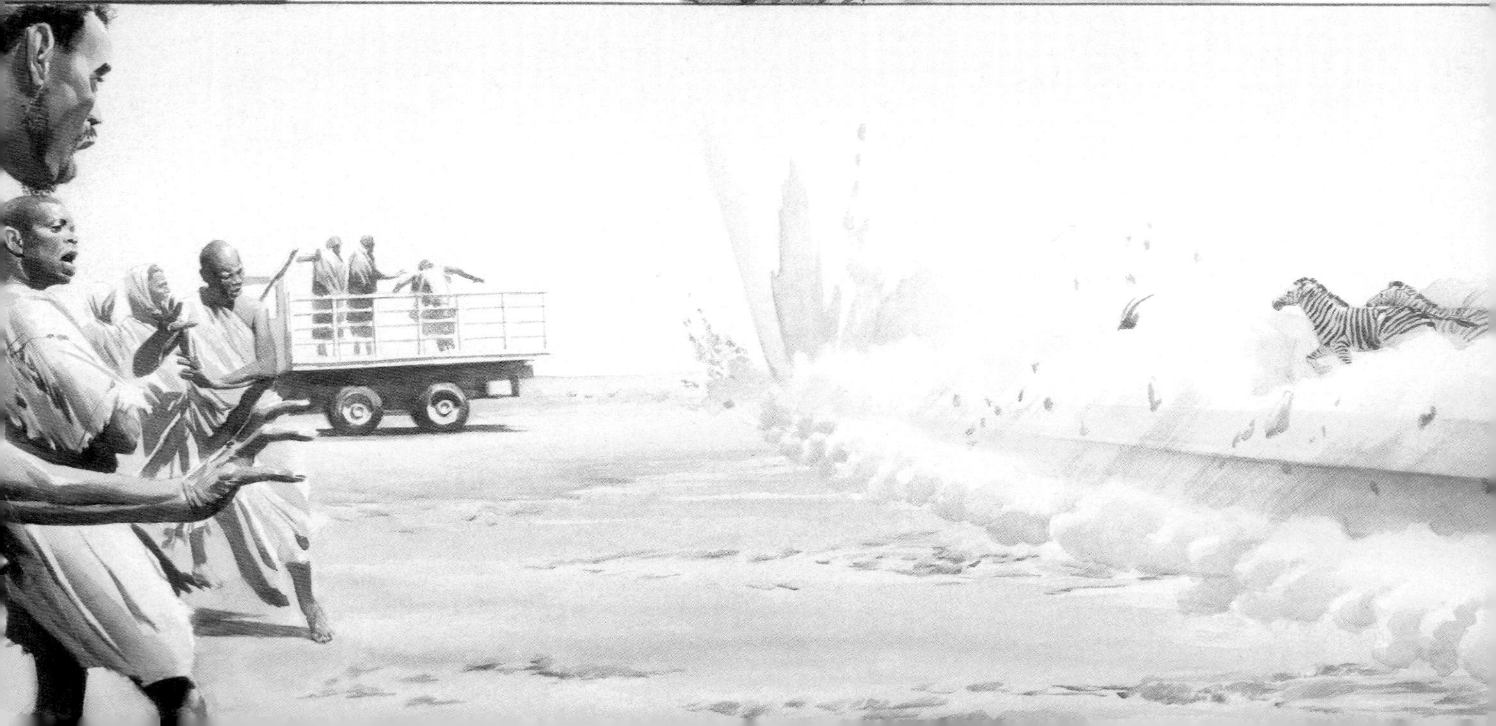

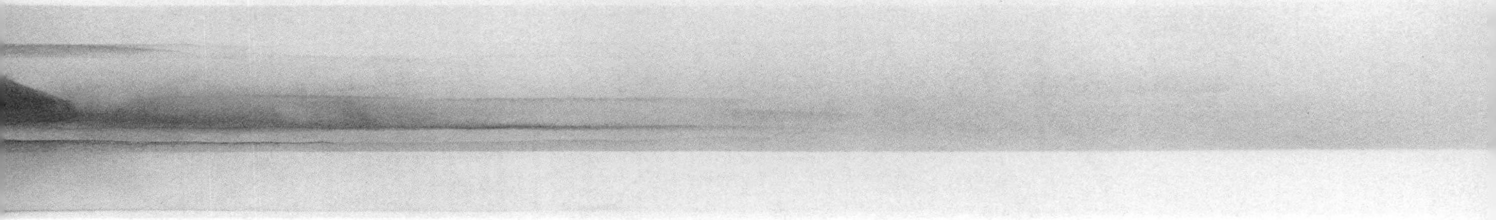

Panicked by the fire and desperate to escape, the animals will tear through the village, trampling everything in their path.

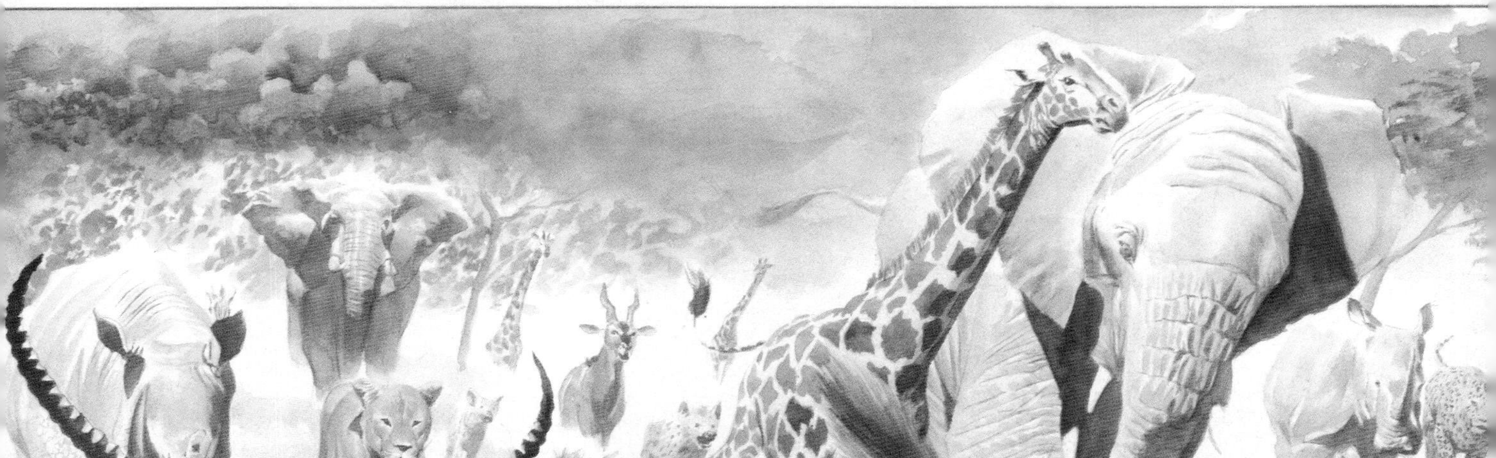

I'm not about to let that happen. The trench startles the creatures and turns many away.

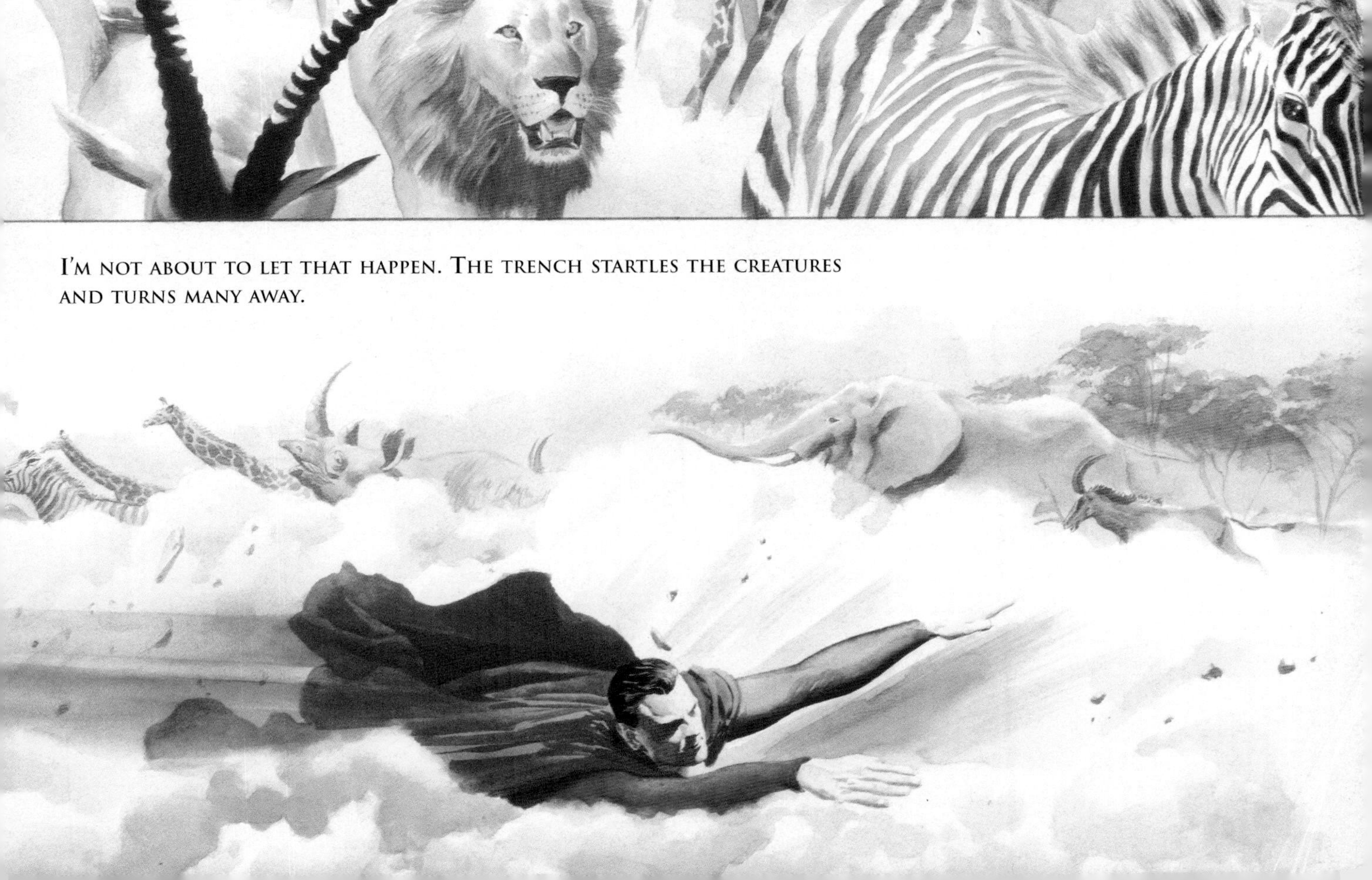

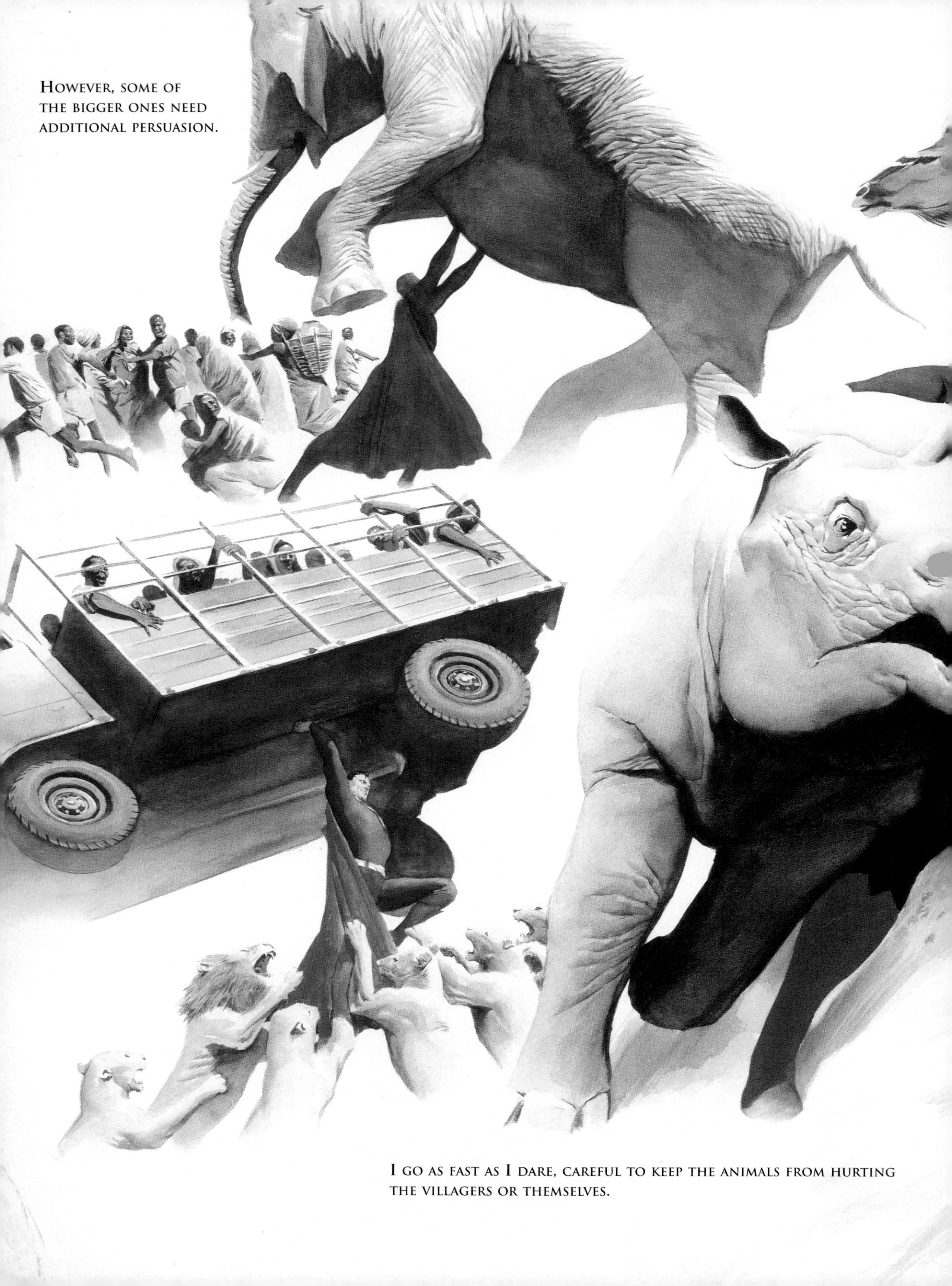
However, some of the bigger ones need additional persuasion.
I go as fast as I dare, careful to keep the animals from hurting the villagers or themselves.

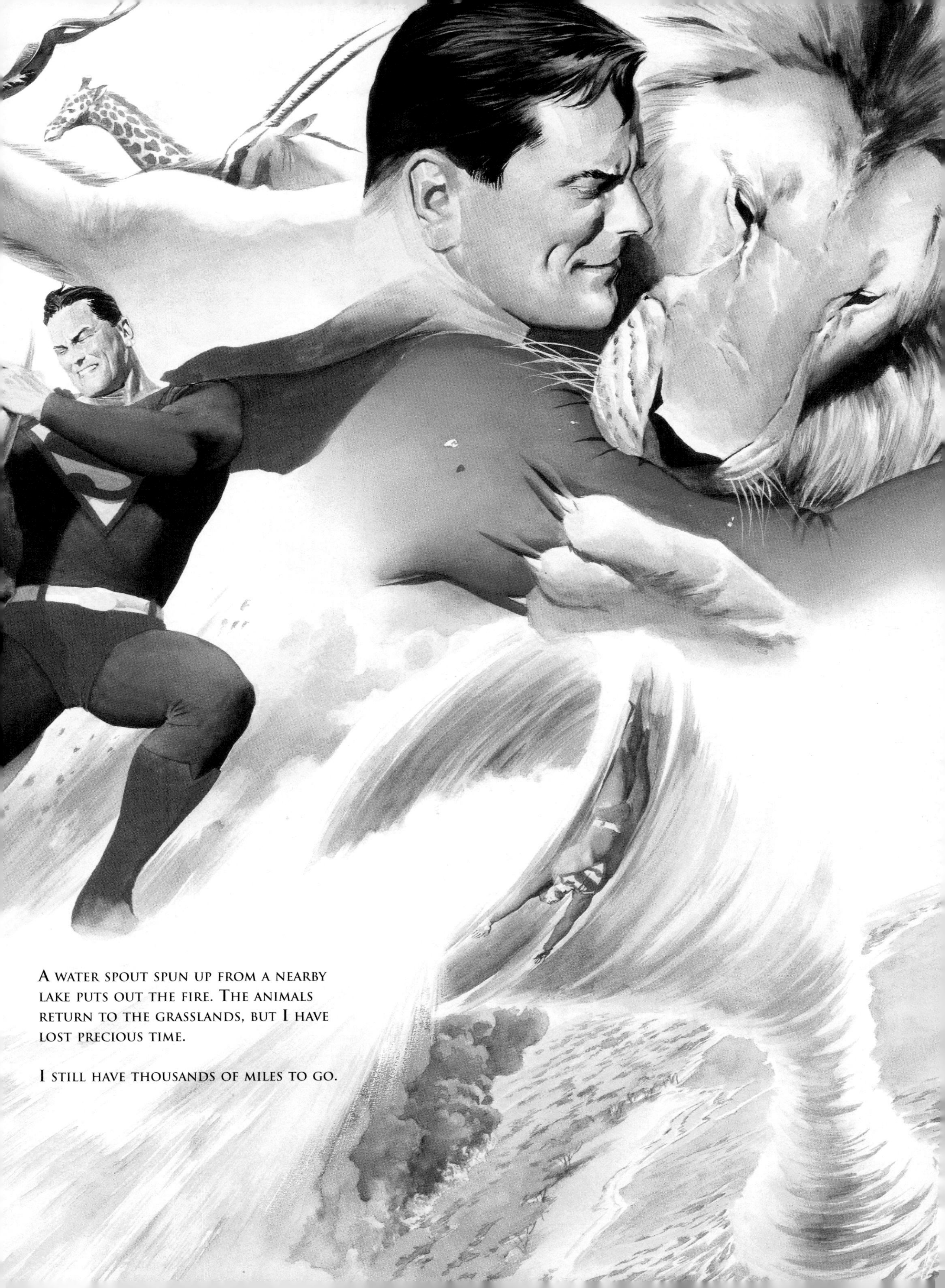
A water spout spun up from a nearby lake puts out the fire. The animals return to the grasslands, but I have lost precious time.
I still have thousands of miles to go.

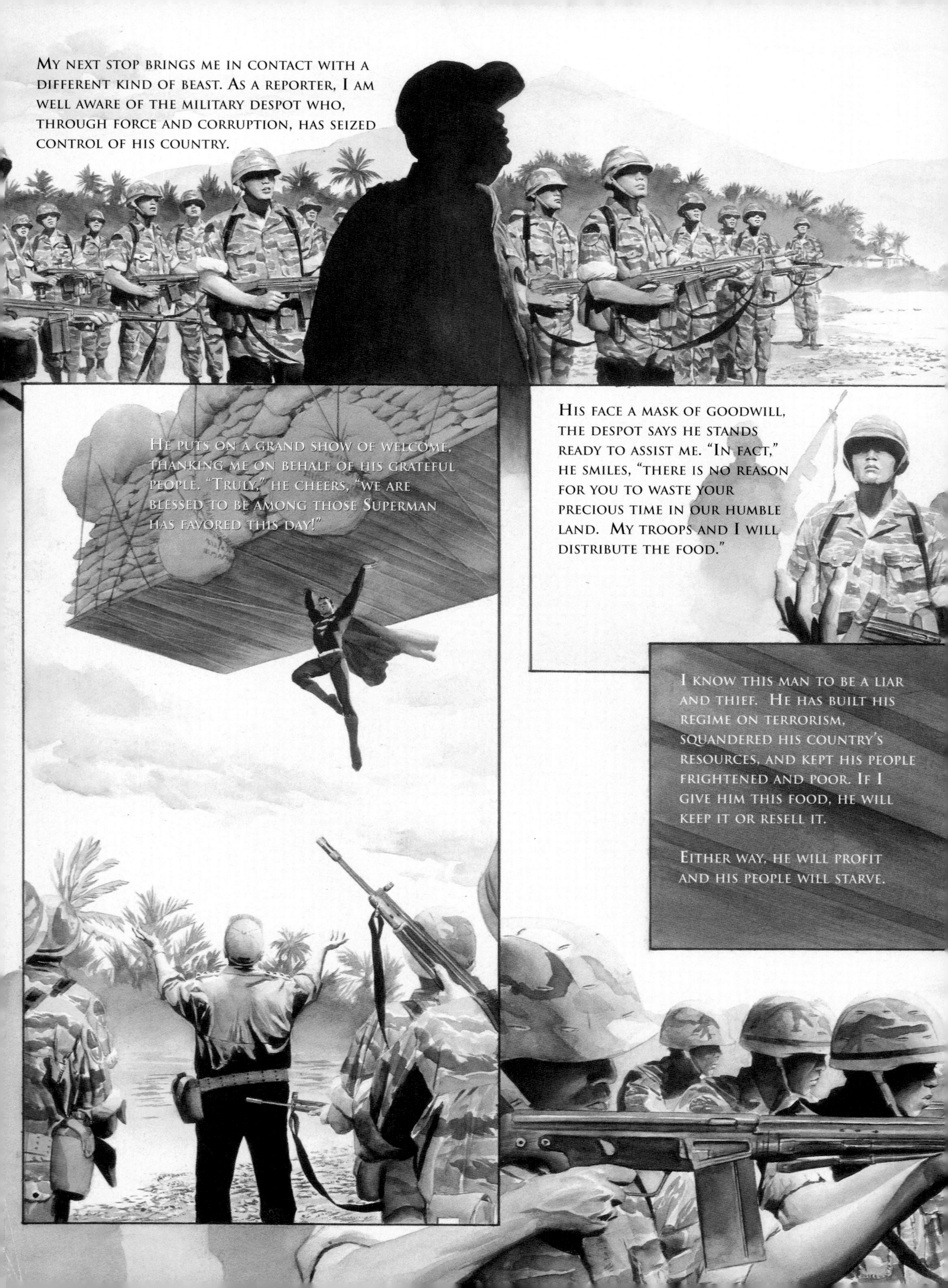
My next stop brings me in contact with a different kind of beast. As a reporter, I am well aware of the military despot who, through force and corruption, has seized control of his country.
He puts on a grand show of welcome, thanking me on behalf of his grateful people. "Truly," he cheers, "we are blessed to be among those Superman has favored this day!"
His face a mask of goodwill, the despot says he stands ready to assist me. "In fact," he smiles, "there is no reason for you to waste your precious time in our humble land. My troops and I will distribute the food."
I know this man to be a liar and thief. He has built his regime on terrorism, squandered his country's resources, and kept his people frightened and poor. If I give him this food, he will keep it or resell it.
Either way, he will profit and his people will starve.

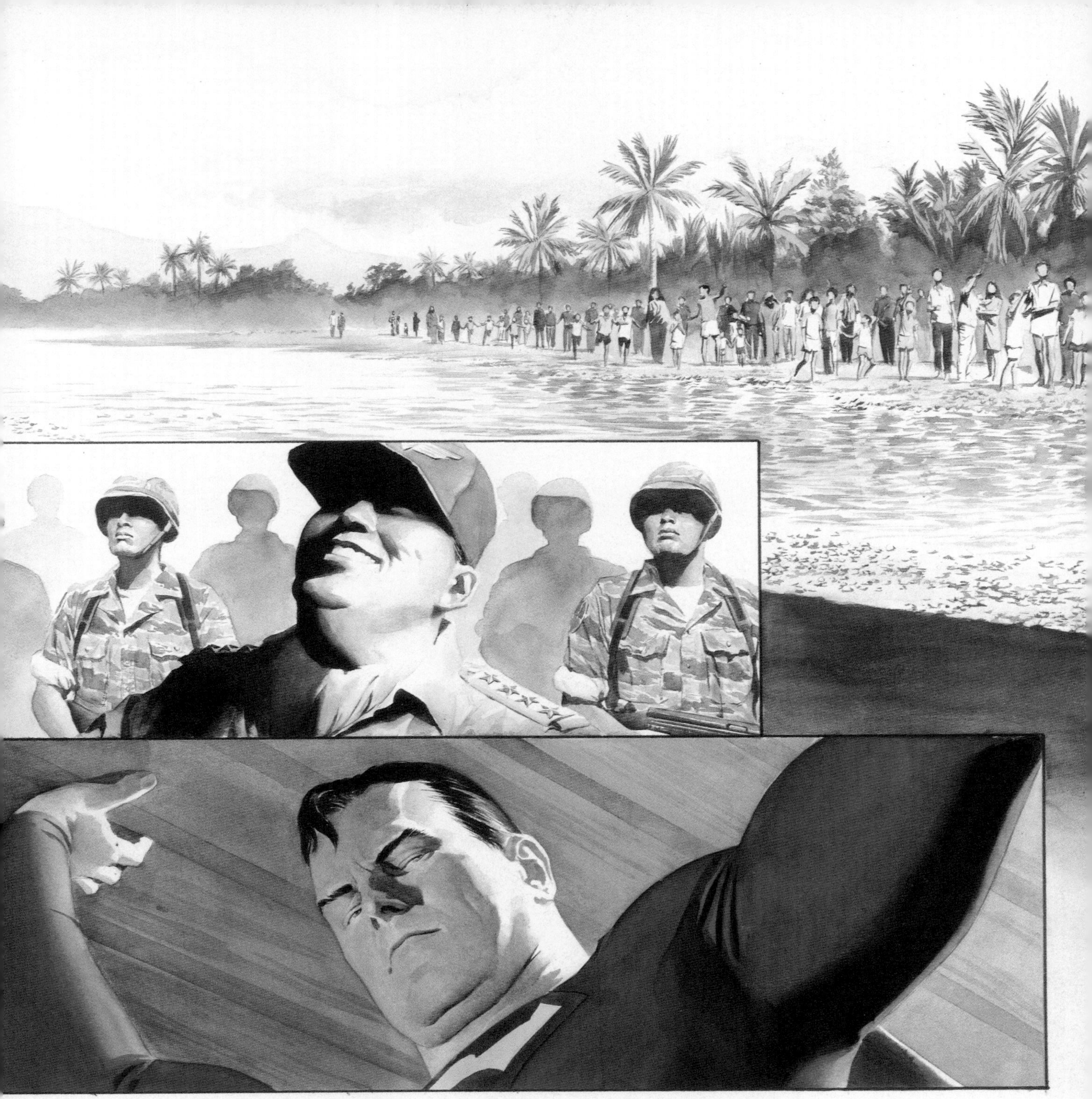

As respectfully as I can, I request permission to hand out the food myself. The despot's only answer is a grinning nod to his troops. Instantly, rifles are cocked and aimed. Not at me, but at the gaunt souls across the river.

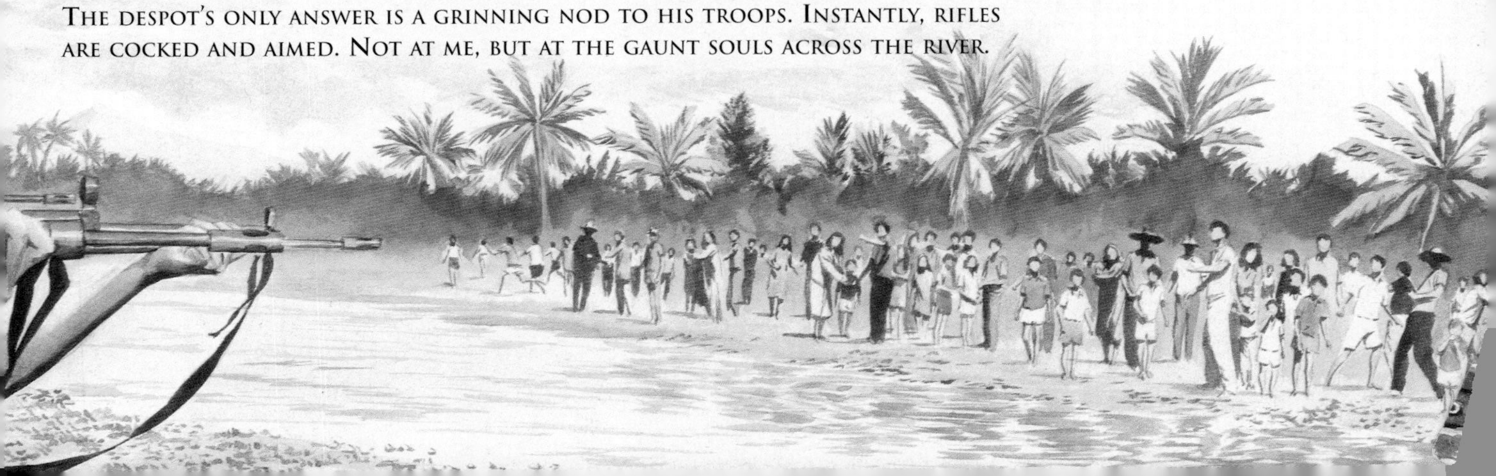

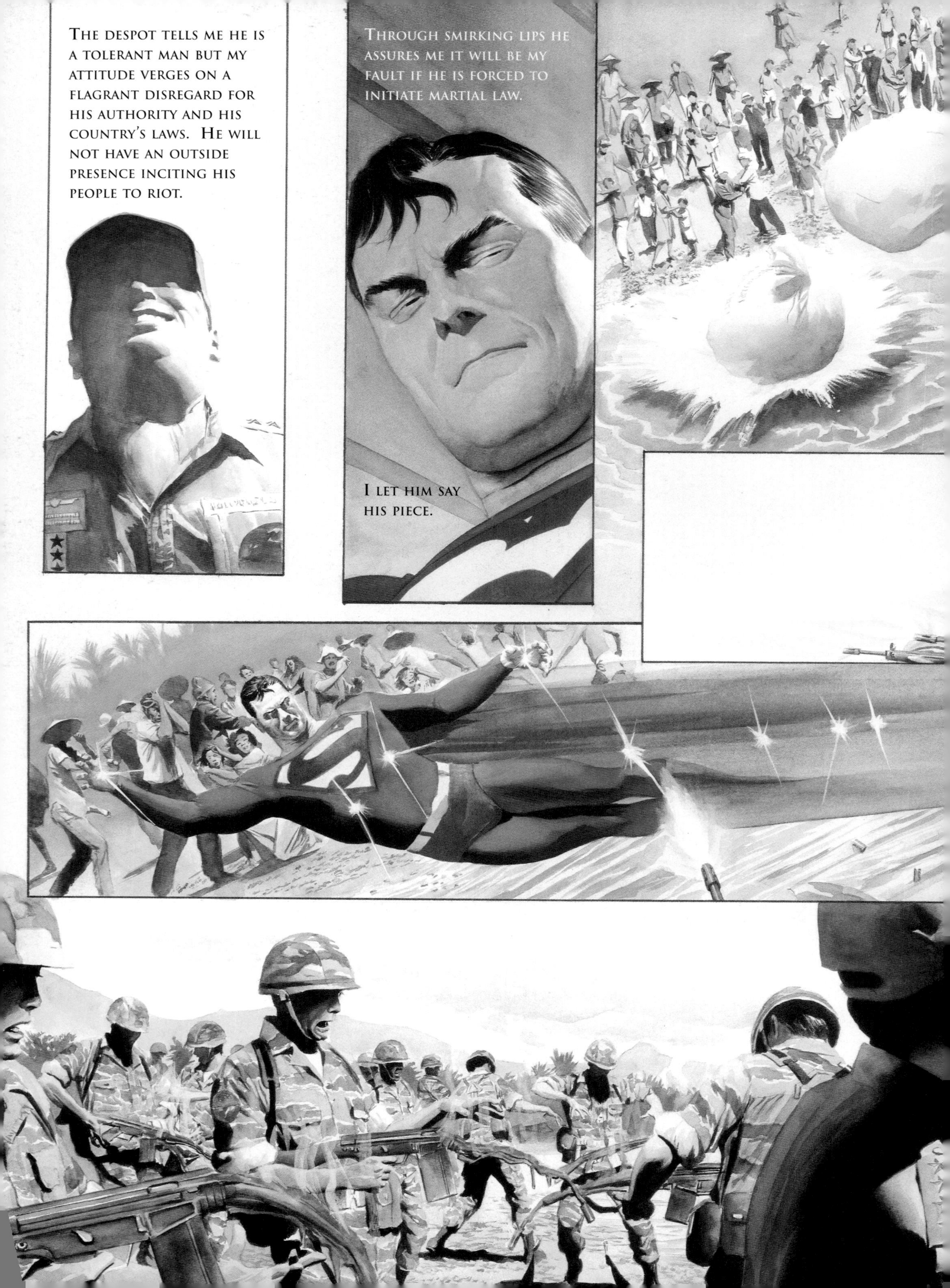
The despot tells me he is a tolerant man but my attitude verges on a flagrant disregard for his authority and his country's laws. He will not have an outside presence inciting his people to riot.
Through smirking lips he assures me it will be my fault if he is forced to initiate martial law.
I let him say his piece.

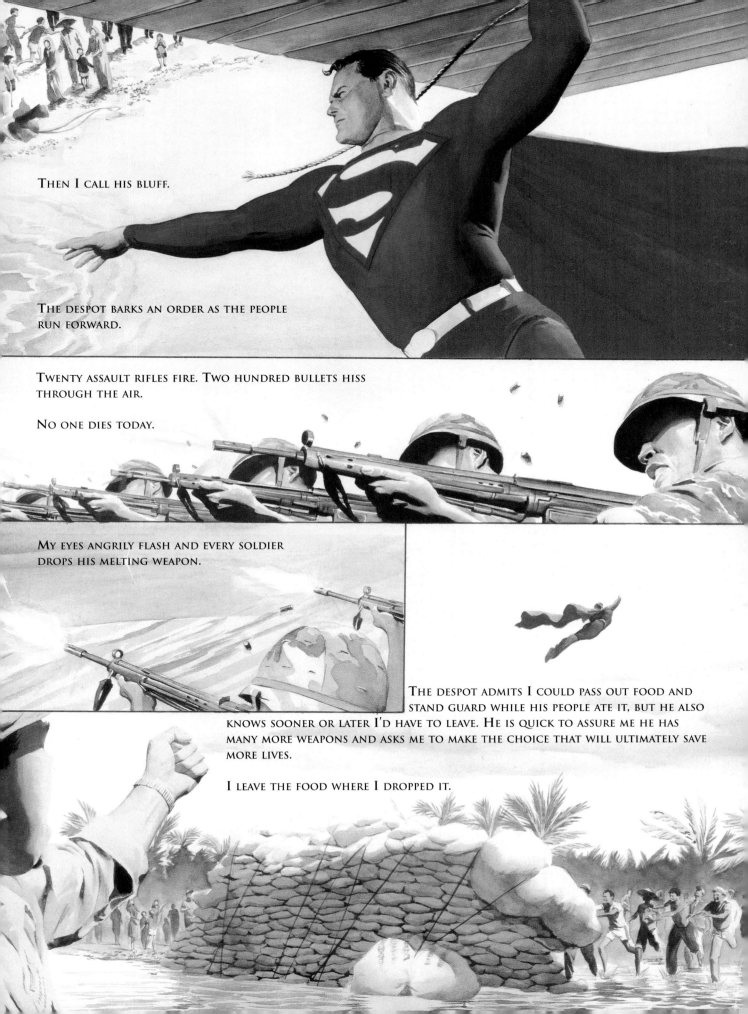

THEN I CALL HIS BLUFF.

THE DESPOT BARKS AN ORDER AS THE PEOPLE RUN FORWARD.

TWENTY ASSAULT RIFLES FIRE. TWO HUNDRED BULLETS HISS THROUGH THE AIR.

NO ONE DIES TODAY.

MY EYES ANGRILY FLASH AND EVERY SOLDIER DROPS HIS MELTING WEAPON.

THE DESPOT ADMITS I COULD PASS OUT FOOD AND STAND GUARD WHILE HIS PEOPLE ATE IT, BUT HE ALSO KNOWS SOONER OR LATER I'D HAVE TO LEAVE. HE IS QUICK TO ASSURE ME HE HAS MANY MORE WEAPONS AND ASKS ME TO MAKE THE CHOICE THAT WILL ULTIMATELY SAVE MORE LIVES.

I LEAVE THE FOOD WHERE I DROPPED IT.

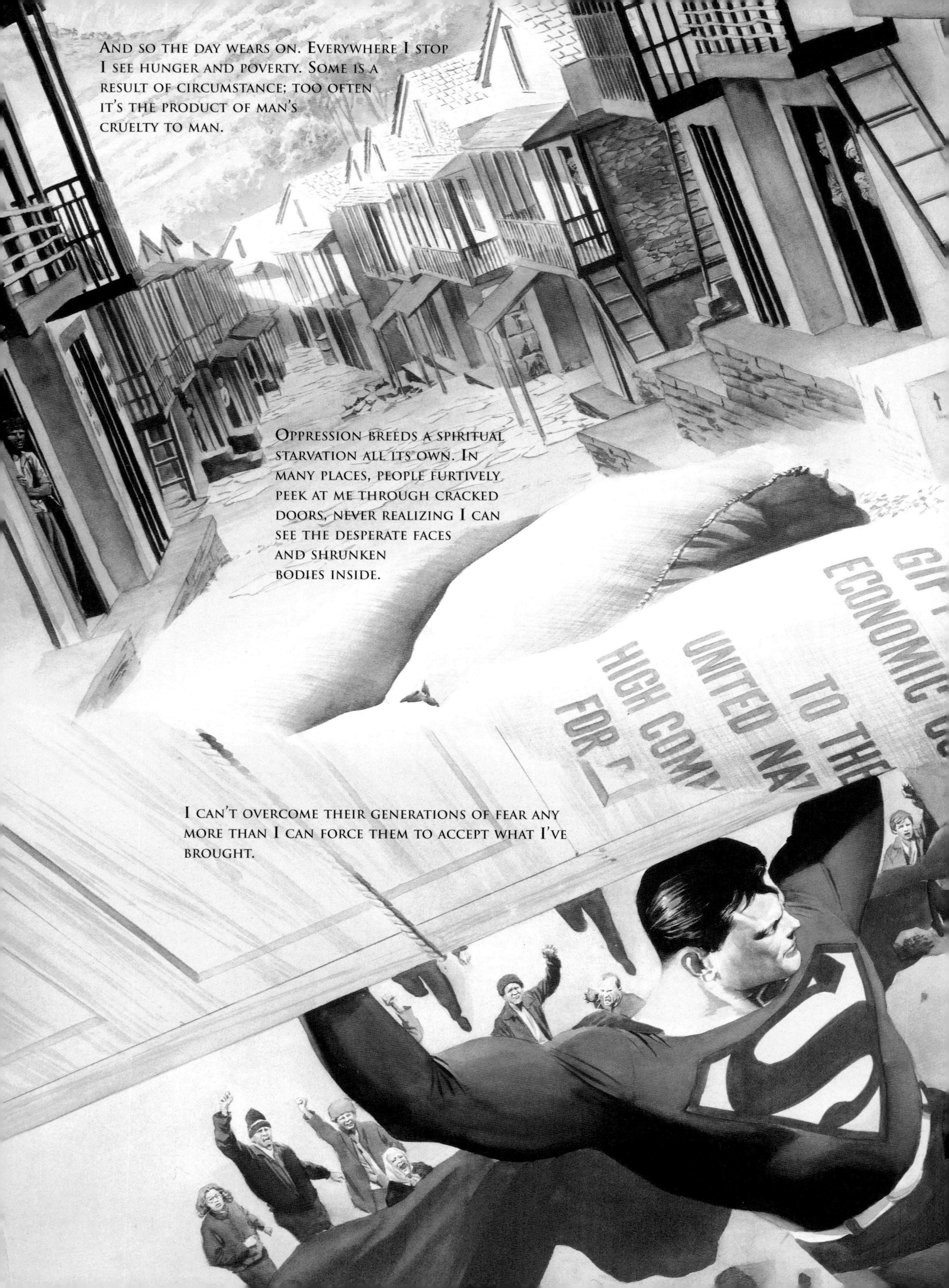
And so the day wears on. Everywhere I stop I see hunger and poverty. Some is a result of circumstance; too often it's the product of man's cruelty to man.
Oppression breeds a spiritual starvation all its own. In many places, people furtively peek at me through cracked doors, never realizing I can see the desperate faces and shrunken bodies inside.
I can't overcome their generations of fear any more than I can force them to accept what I've brought.

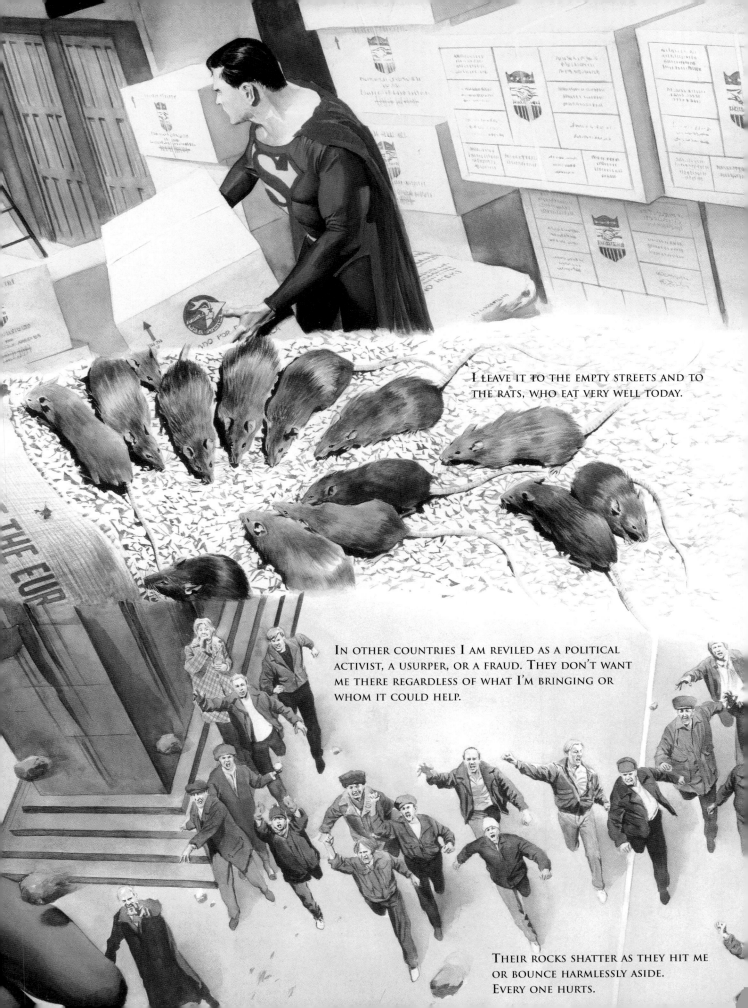

I LEAVE IT TO THE EMPTY STREETS AND TO THE RATS, WHO EAT VERY WELL TODAY.

IN OTHER COUNTRIES I AM REVILED AS A POLITICAL ACTIVIST, A USURPER, OR A FRAUD. THEY DON'T WANT ME THERE REGARDLESS OF WHAT I'M BRINGING OR WHOM IT COULD HELP.

THEIR ROCKS SHATTER AS THEY HIT ME OR BOUNCE HARMLESSLY ASIDE. EVERY ONE HURTS.

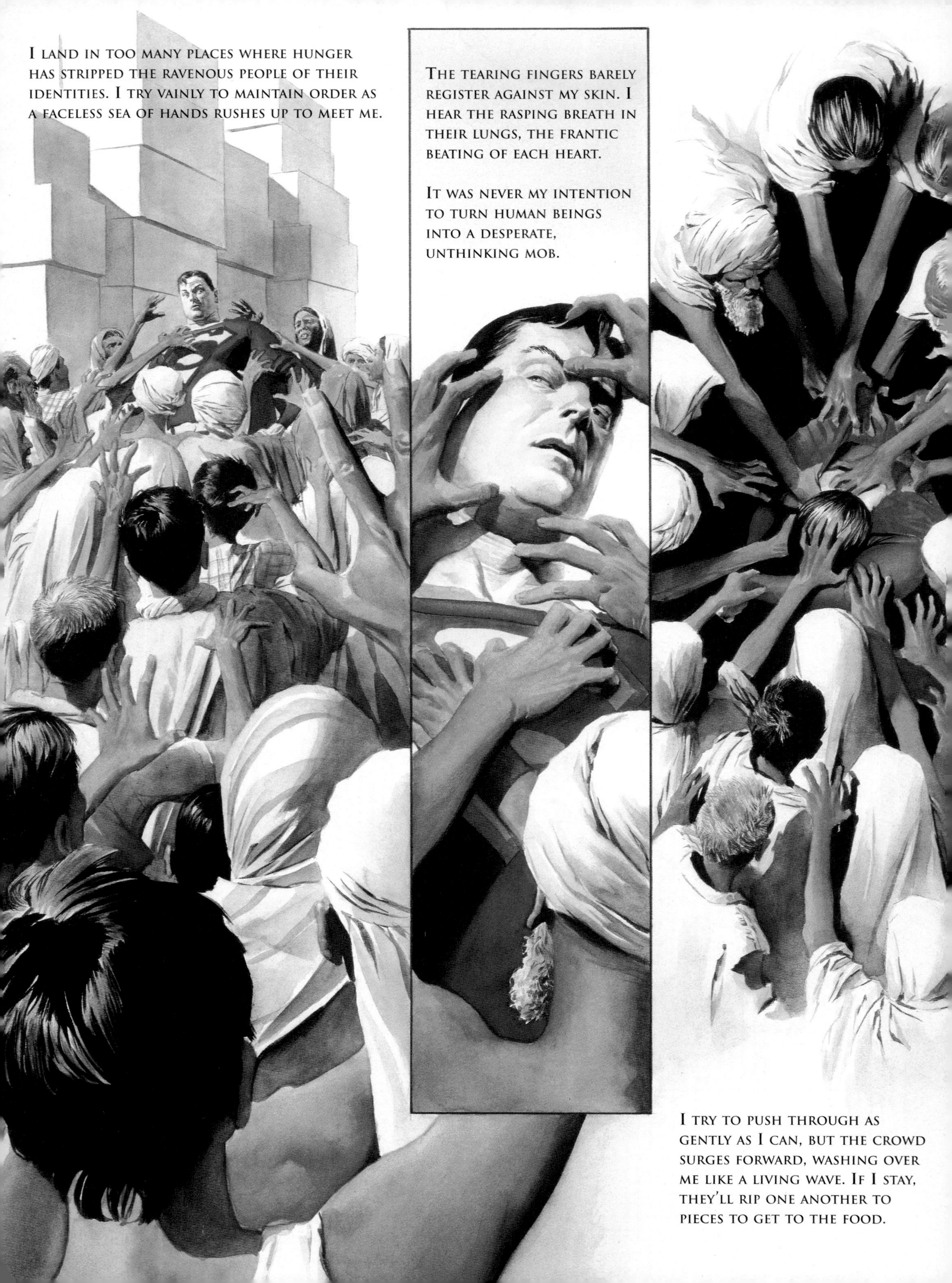
I land in too many places where hunger has stripped the ravenous people of their identities. I try vainly to maintain order as a faceless sea of hands rushes up to meet me.
The tearing fingers barely register against my skin. I hear the rasping breath in their lungs, the frantic beating of each heart.
It was never my intention to turn human beings into a desperate, unthinking mob.
I try to push through as gently as I can, but the crowd surges forward, washing over me like a living wave. If I stay, they'll rip one another to pieces to get to the food.

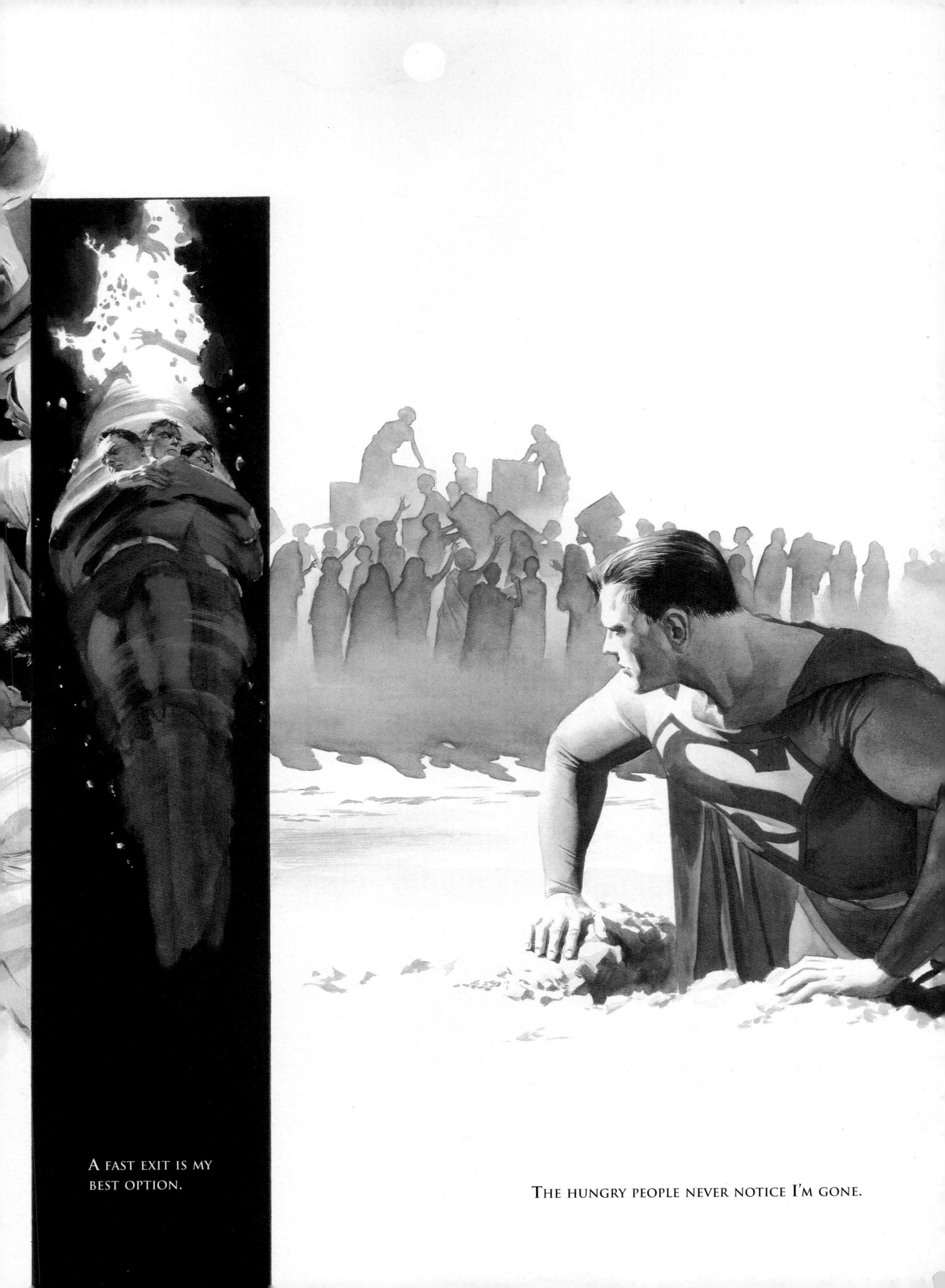
A FAST EXIT IS MY BEST OPTION.
THE HUNGRY PEOPLE NEVER NOTICE I'M GONE.

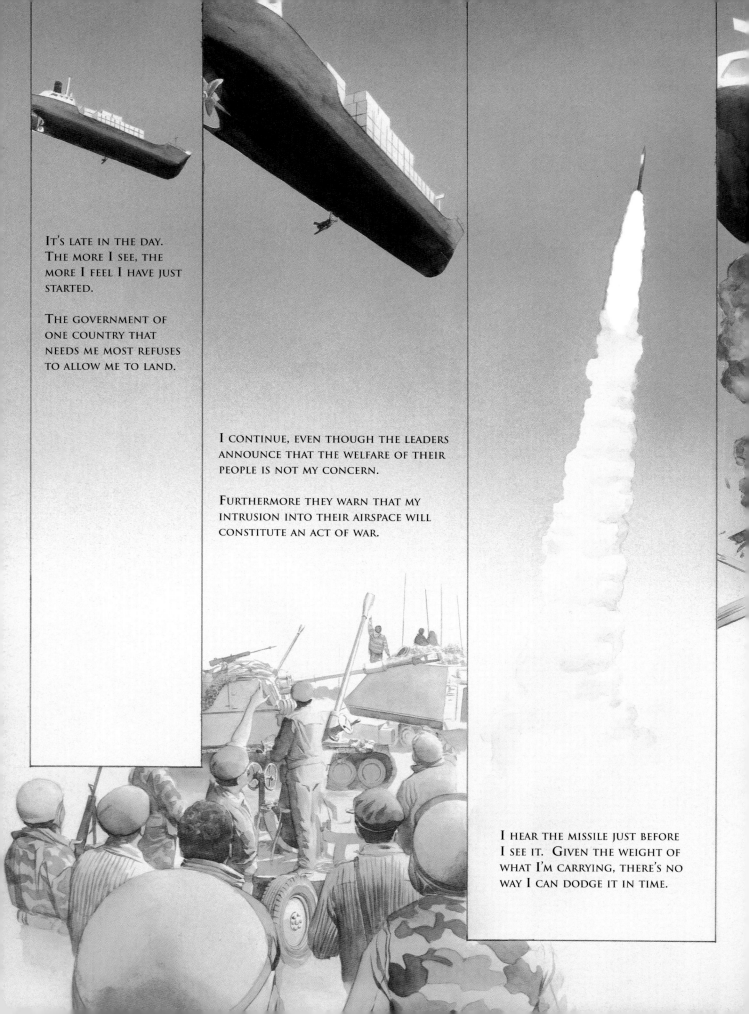

IT'S LATE IN THE DAY. THE MORE I SEE, THE MORE I FEEL I HAVE JUST STARTED.

THE GOVERNMENT OF ONE COUNTRY THAT NEEDS ME MOST REFUSES TO ALLOW ME TO LAND.

I CONTINUE, EVEN THOUGH THE LEADERS ANNOUNCE THAT THE WELFARE OF THEIR PEOPLE IS NOT MY CONCERN.

FURTHERMORE THEY WARN THAT MY INTRUSION INTO THEIR AIRSPACE WILL CONSTITUTE AN ACT OF WAR.

I HEAR THE MISSILE JUST BEFORE I SEE IT. GIVEN THE WEIGHT OF WHAT I'M CARRYING, THERE'S NO WAY I CAN DODGE IT IN TIME.

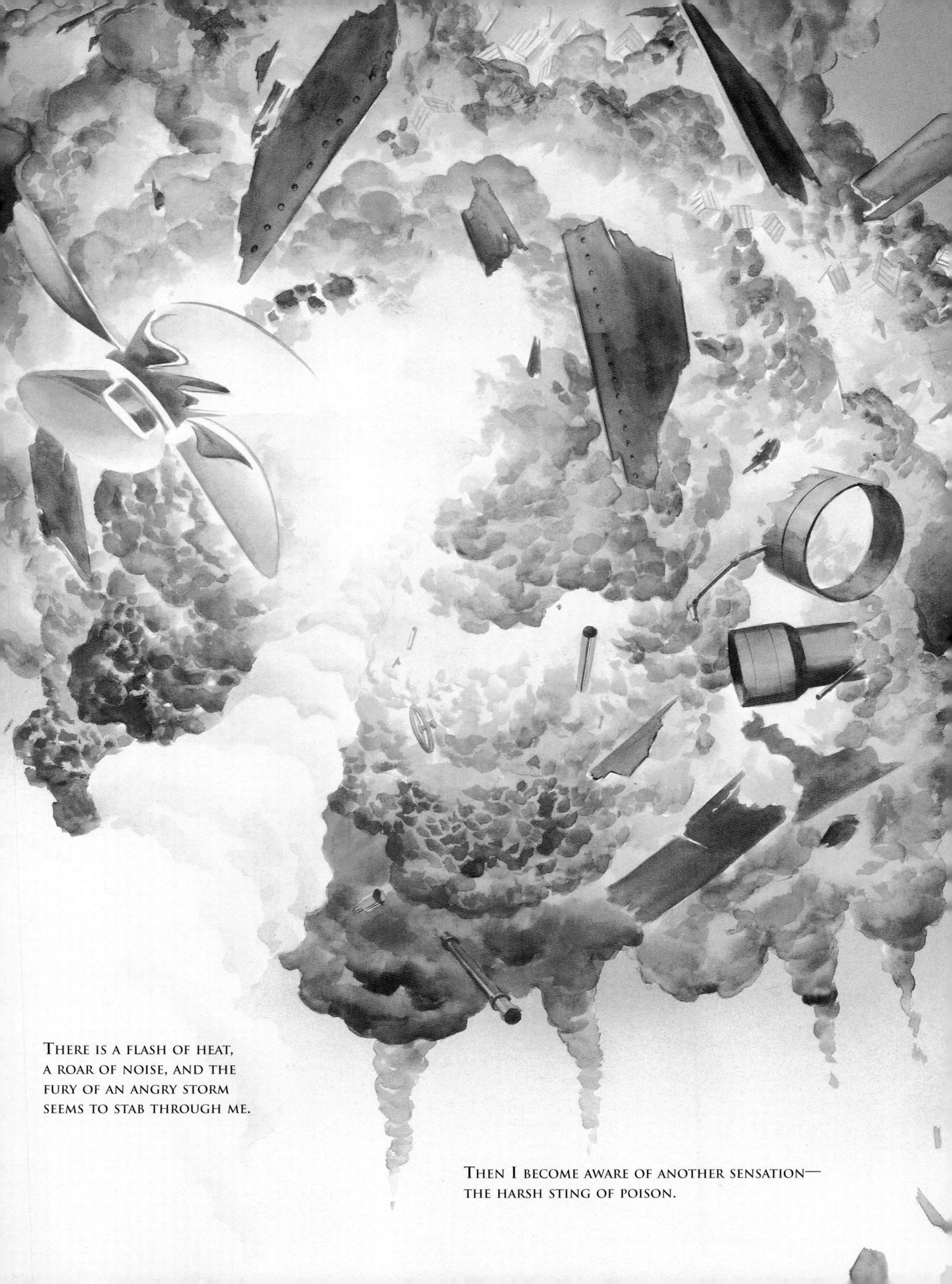

There is a flash of heat,
a roar of noise, and the
fury of an angry storm
seems to stab through me.

Then I become aware of another sensation—
the harsh sting of poison.

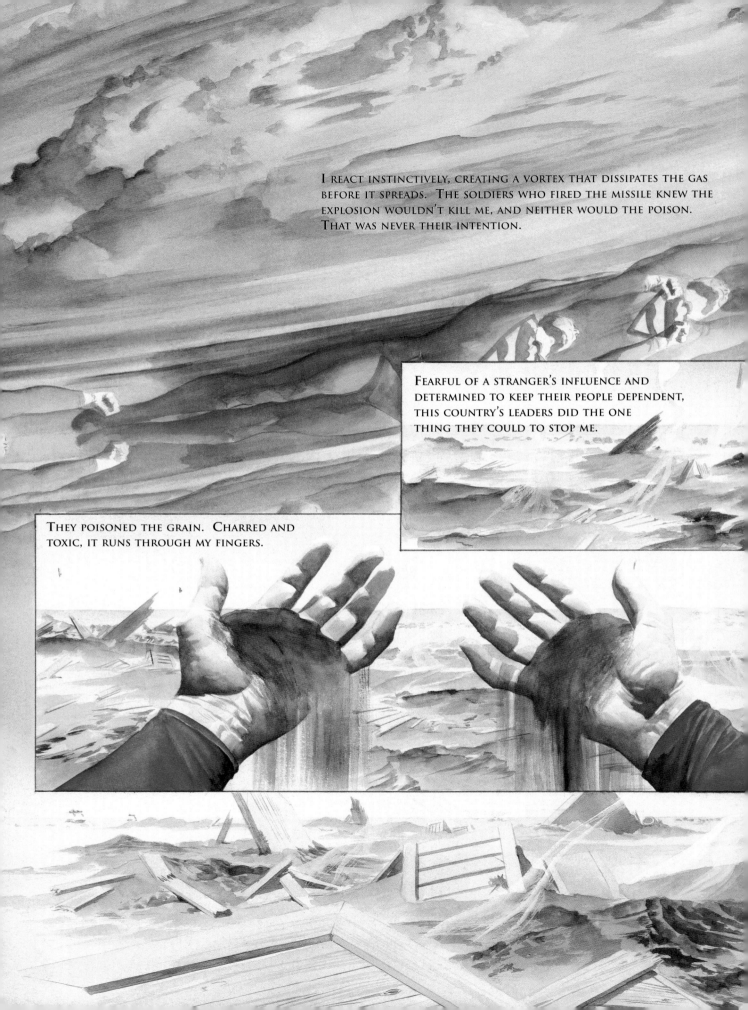

I REACT INSTINCTIVELY, CREATING A VORTEX THAT DISSIPATES THE GAS BEFORE IT SPREADS. THE SOLDIERS WHO FIRED THE MISSILE KNEW THE EXPLOSION WOULDN'T KILL ME, AND NEITHER WOULD THE POISON. THAT WAS NEVER THEIR INTENTION.

FEARFUL OF A STRANGER'S INFLUENCE AND DETERMINED TO KEEP THEIR PEOPLE DEPENDENT, THIS COUNTRY'S LEADERS DID THE ONE THING THEY COULD TO STOP ME.

THEY POISONED THE GRAIN. CHARRED AND TOXIC, IT RUNS THROUGH MY FINGERS.

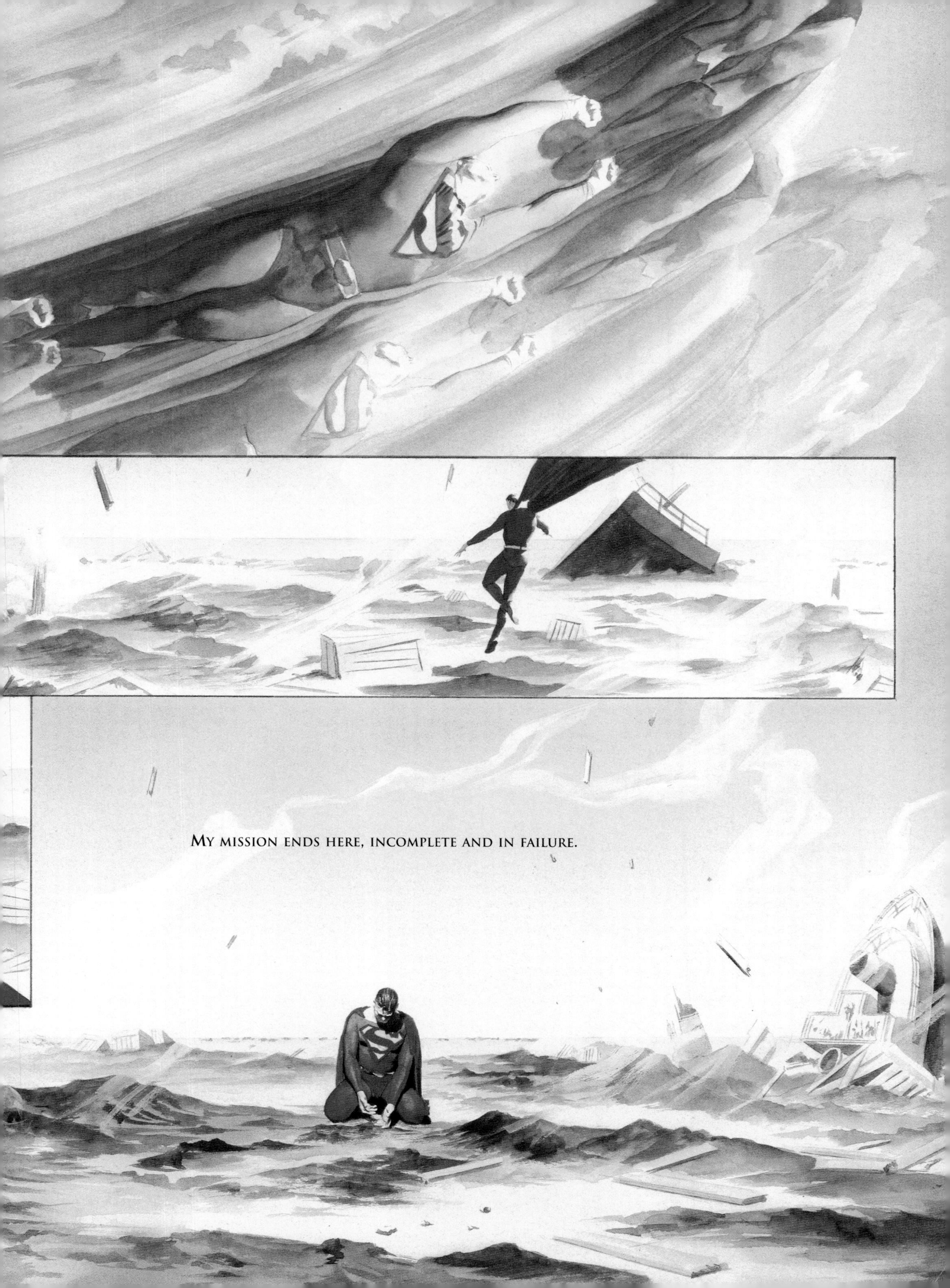
MY MISSION ENDS HERE, INCOMPLETE AND IN FAILURE.

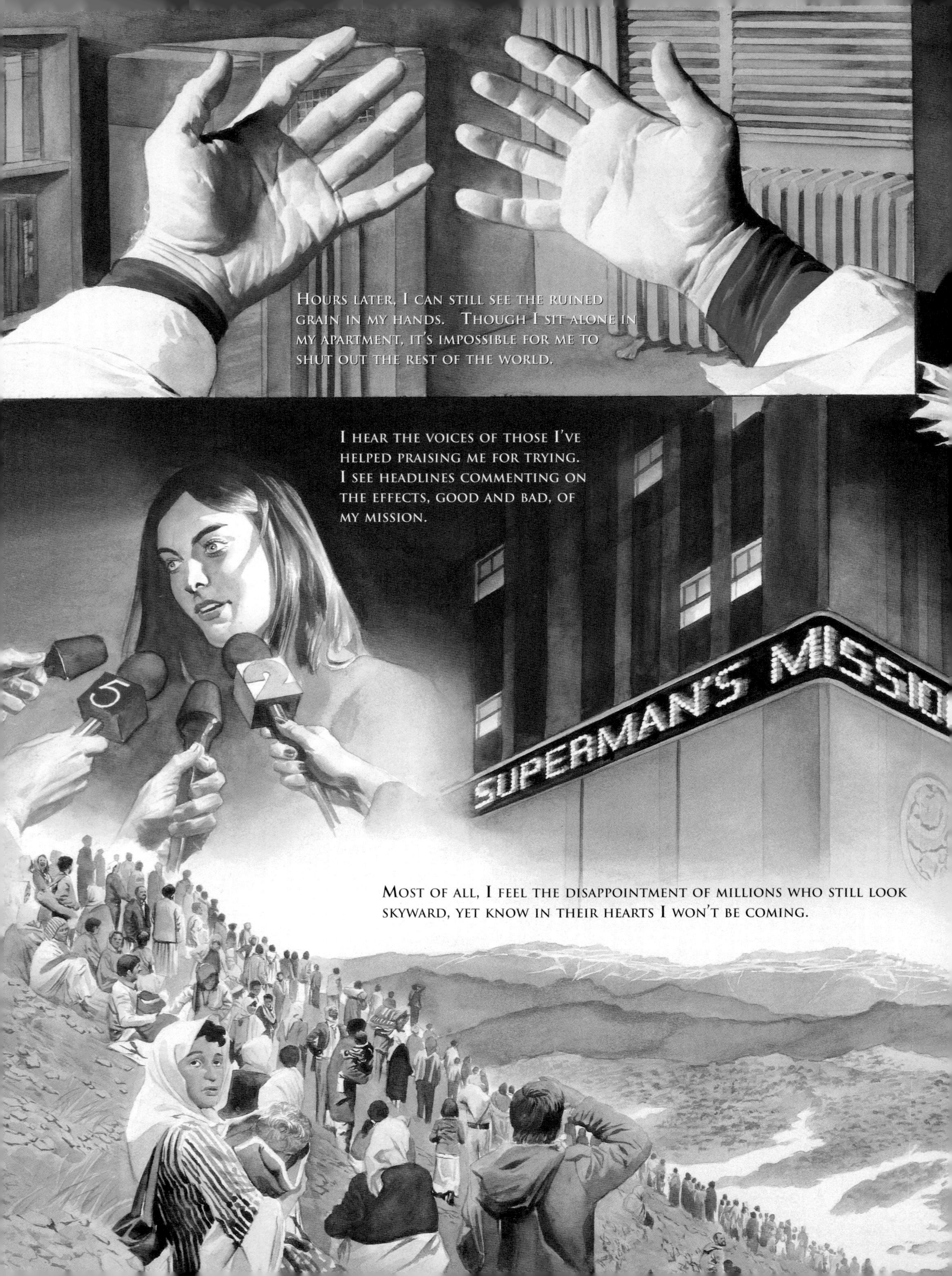
Hours later, I can still see the ruined grain in my hands. Though I sit alone in my apartment, it's impossible for me to shut out the rest of the world.
I hear the voices of those I've helped praising me for trying. I see headlines commenting on the effects, good and bad, of my mission.
5
2
SUPERMAN'S MISSIO
Most of all, I feel the disappointment of millions who still look skyward, yet know in their hearts I won't be coming.

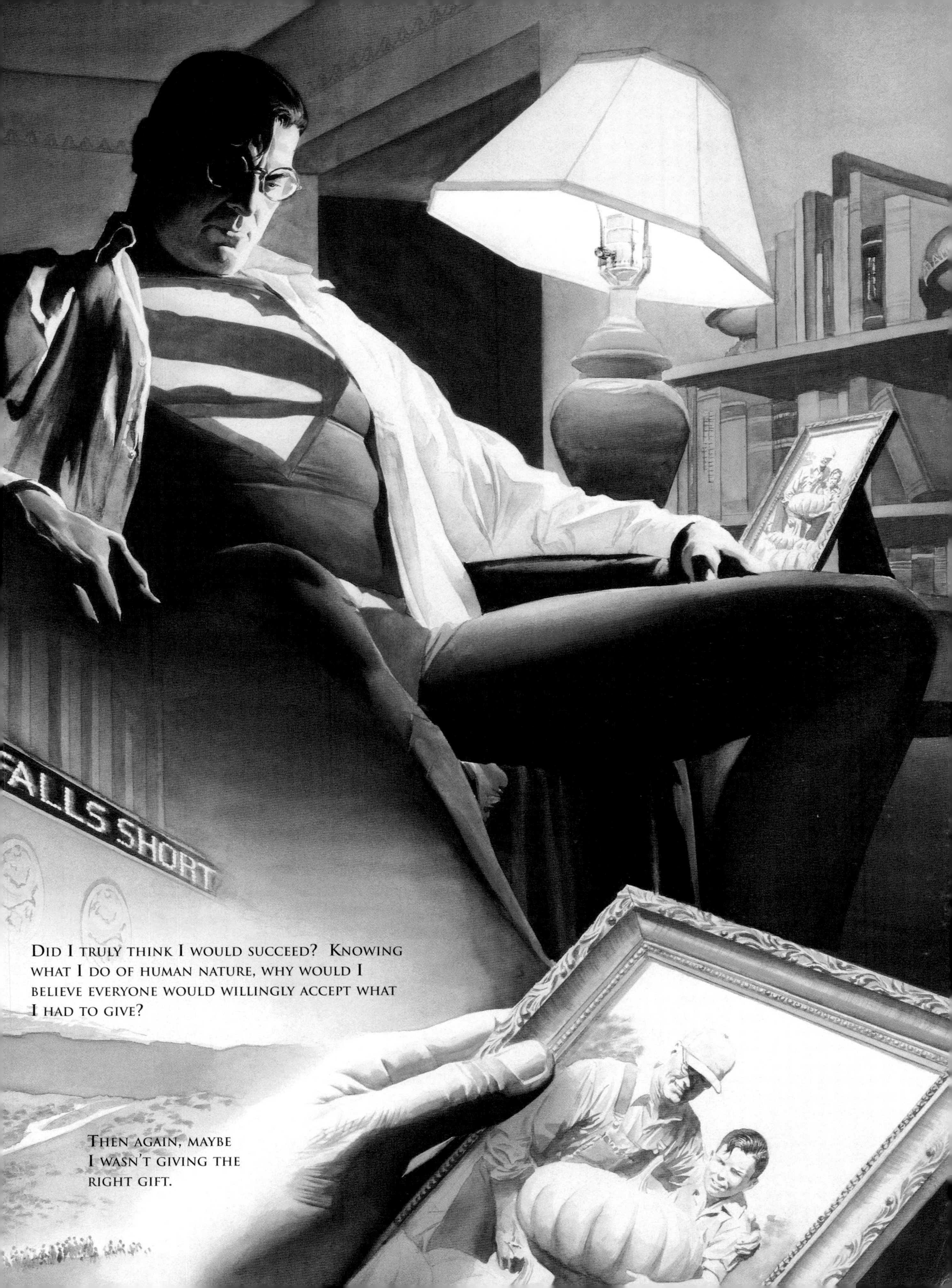
FALLS SHORT
Did I truly think I would succeed? Knowing what I do of human nature, why would I believe everyone would willingly accept what I had to give?
Then again, maybe I wasn't giving the right gift.

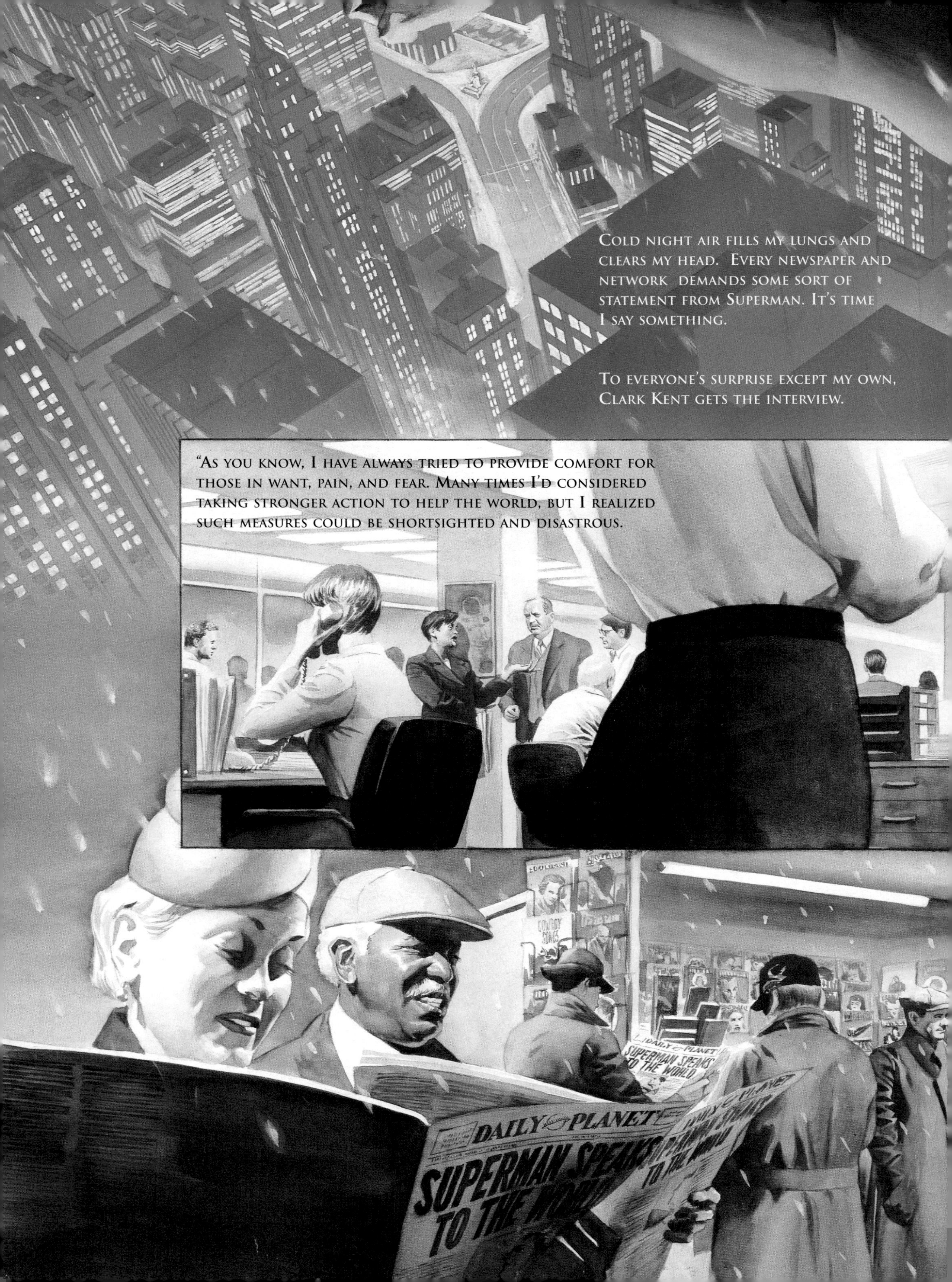
Cold night air fills my lungs and clears my head. Every newspaper and network demands some sort of statement from Superman. It's time I say something.
To everyone's surprise except my own, Clark Kent gets the interview.
"As you know, I have always tried to provide comfort for those in want, pain, and fear. Many times I'd considered taking stronger action to help the world, but I realized such measures could be shortsighted and disastrous.
Daily Planet
Superman Speaks to the World
Daily Planet
Superman Speaks to the World

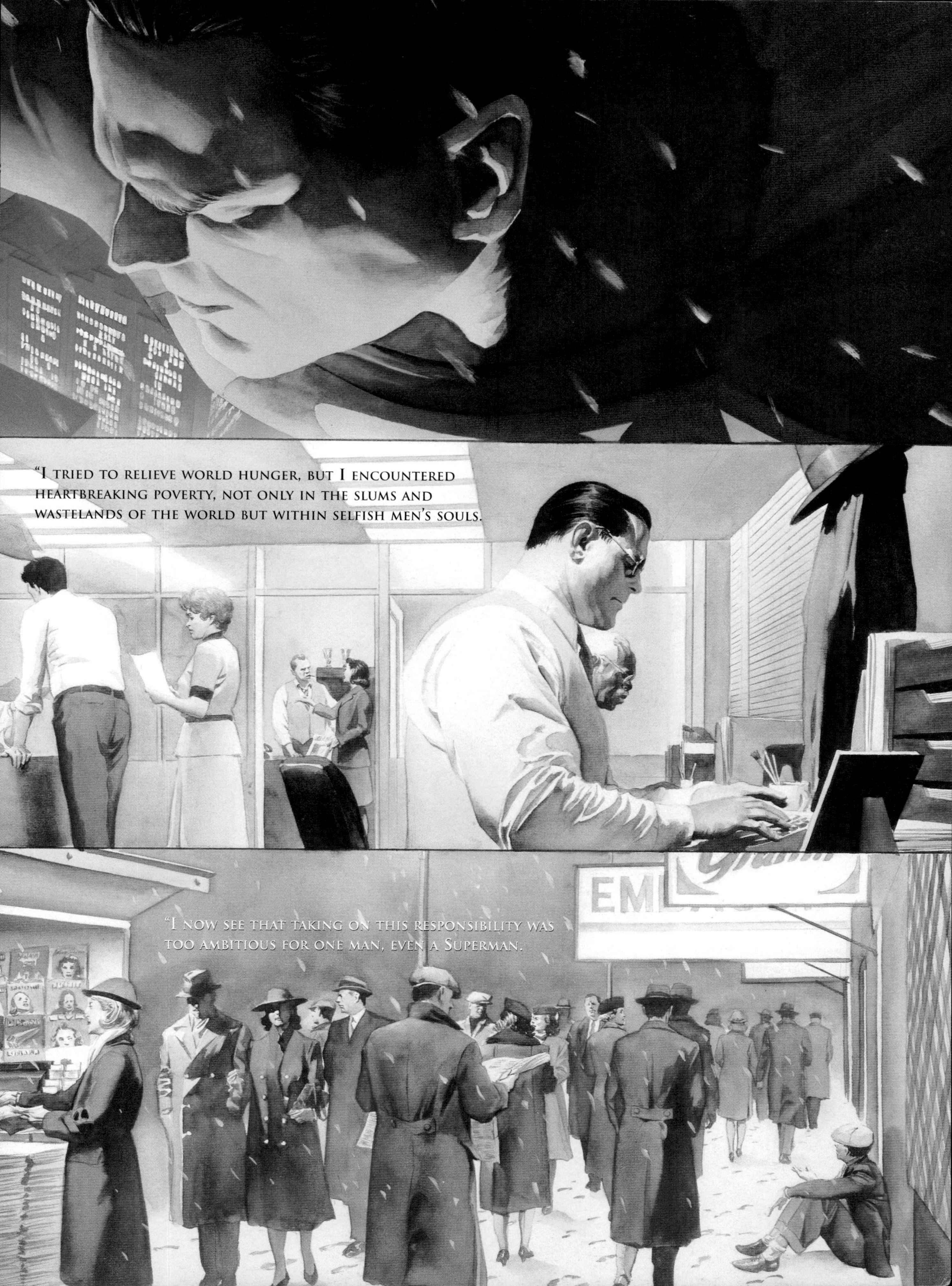
"I tried to relieve world hunger, but I encountered heartbreaking poverty, not only in the slums and wastelands of the world but within selfish men's souls.
"I now see that taking on this responsibility was too ambitious for one man, even a Superman.

"The welfare of Earth and all its people will always be my primary concern. But if there is a solution to the problem of hunger, it must be one that comes from the compassionate heart of man and extends outward toward his fellow man.

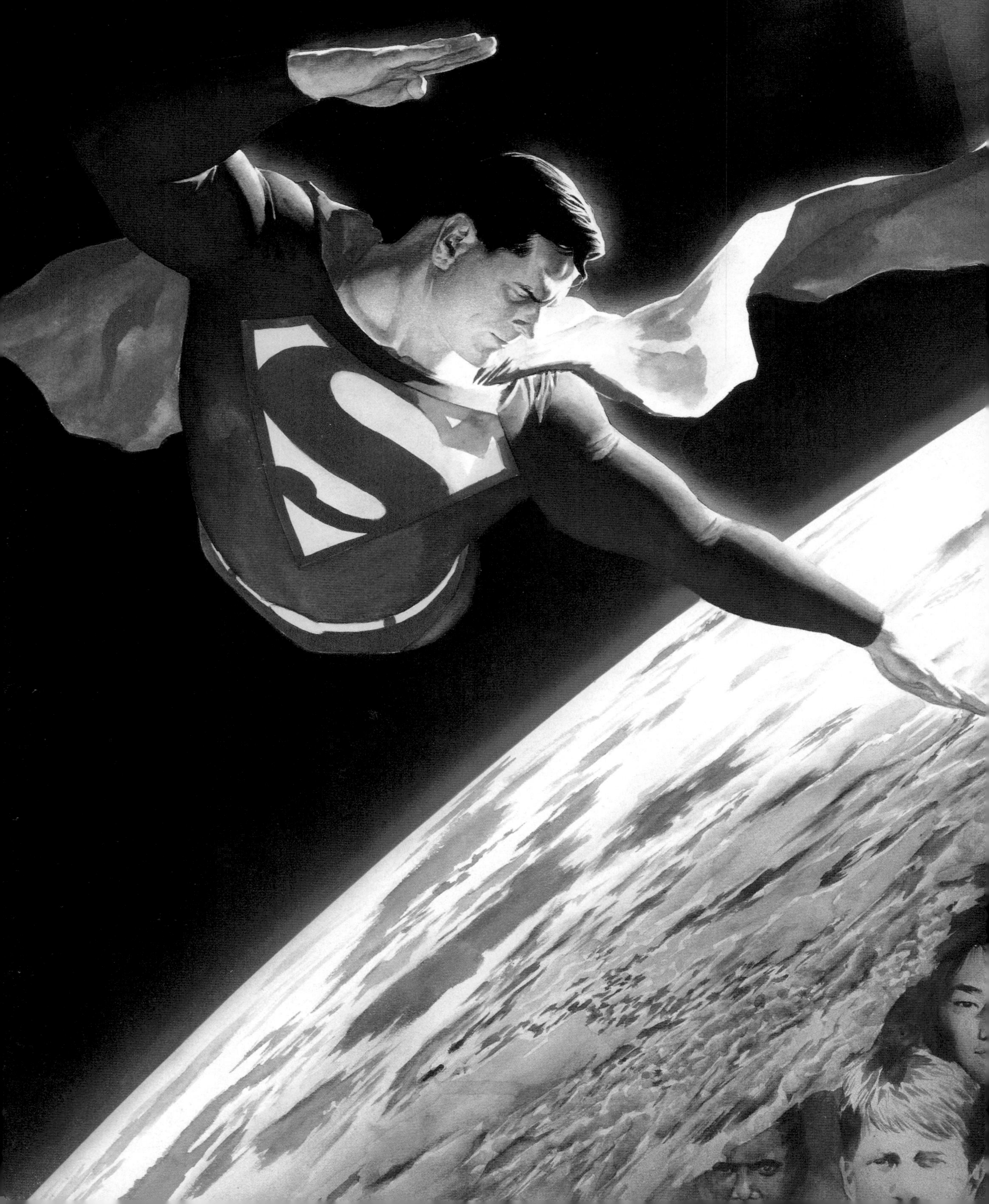

"THERE'S AN OLD SAYING: 'GIVE A MAN A FISH AND HE EATS FOR A DAY. TEACH HIM TO FISH AND HE EATS FOR A LIFETIME.' THAT SIMPLE MESSAGE ASKS HUMANKIND TO NURTURE WITH KNOWLEDGE, TO REACH OUT TO THOSE IN NEED AND INSPIRE OTHERS TO DO THE SAME. THAT IS LIFE'S GREATEST NECESSITY AND ITS MOST PRECIOUS GIFT.

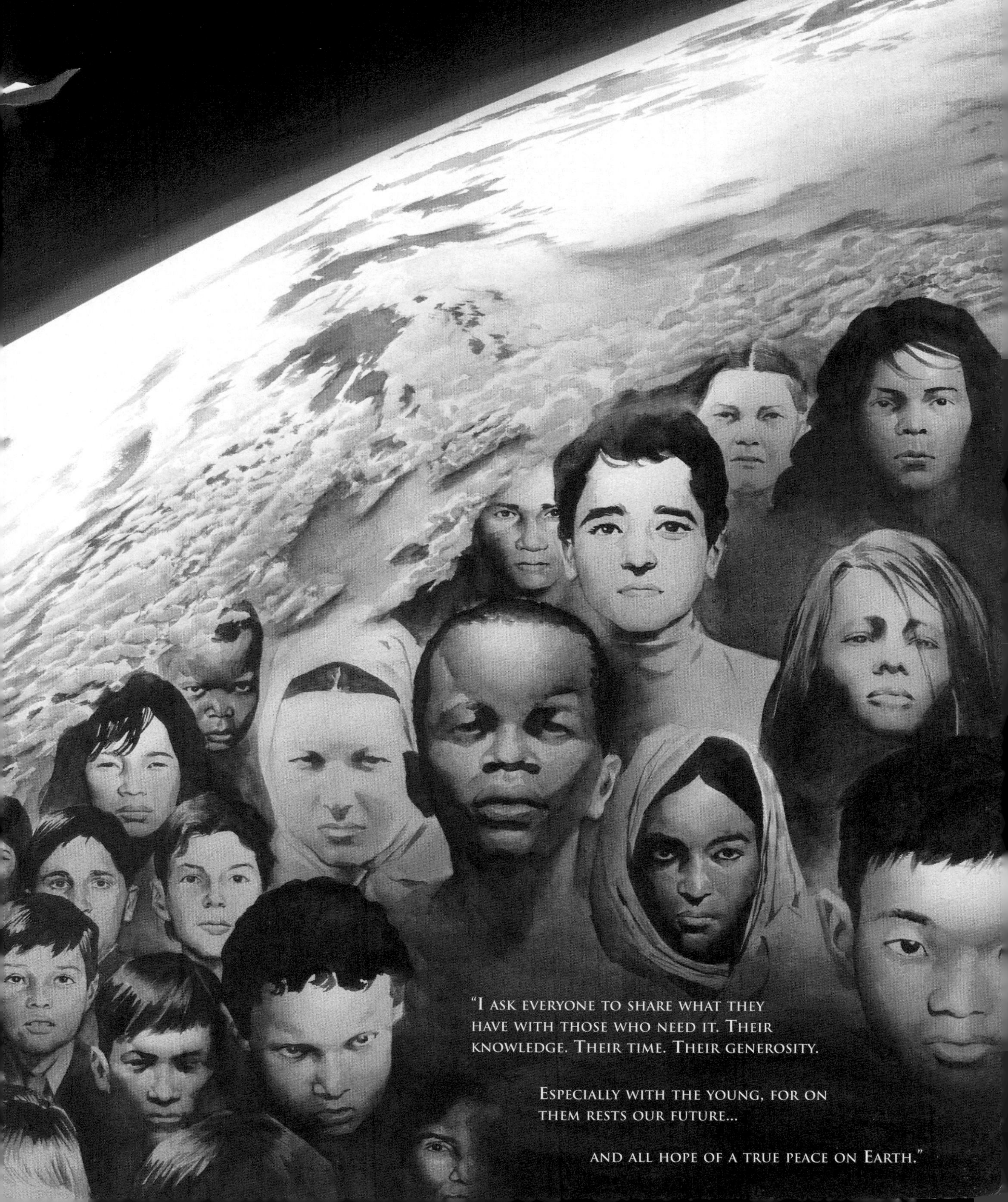

"I ASK EVERYONE TO SHARE WHAT THEY HAVE WITH THOSE WHO NEED IT. THEIR KNOWLEDGE. THEIR TIME. THEIR GENEROSITY.

ESPECIALLY WITH THE YOUNG, FOR ON THEM RESTS OUR FUTURE...

AND ALL HOPE OF A TRUE PEACE ON EARTH."

When I once again feel the warm spring wind in my hair, I make it a point to follow my own advice.

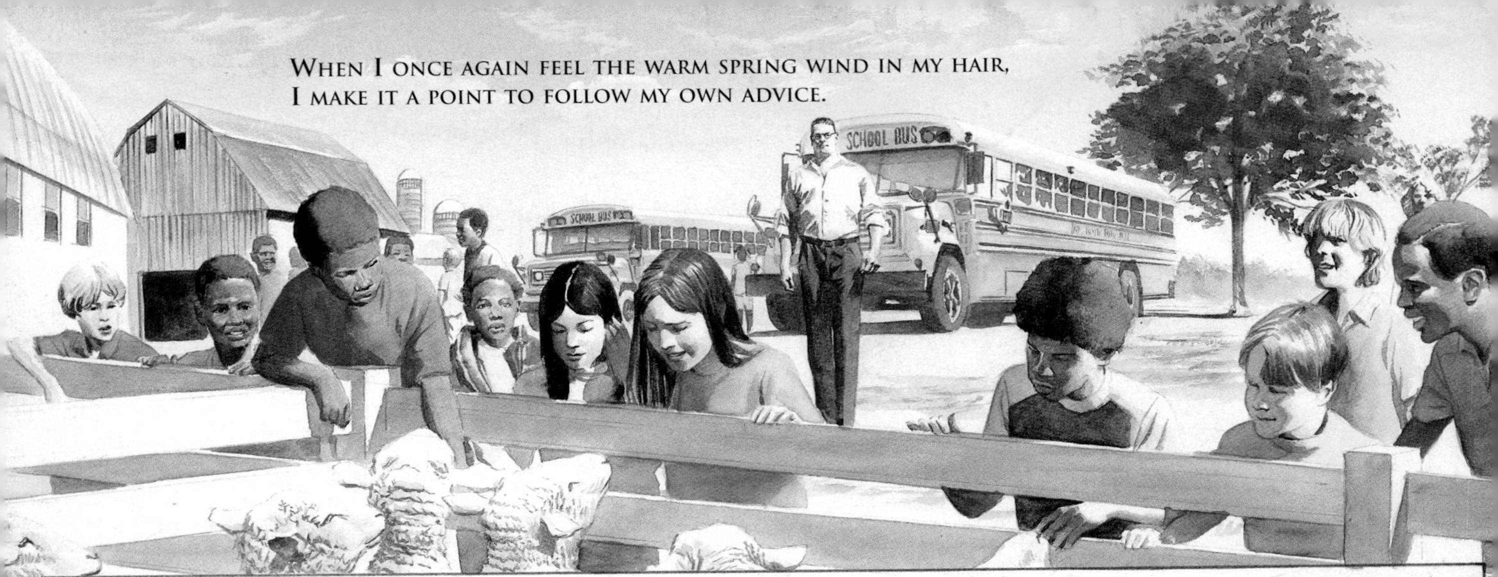
SCHOOL BUS
SCHOOL BUS

Patiently and gently, I share with others the way to scatter the seeds a few at a time, evenly between the rows so that each one will have enough space.

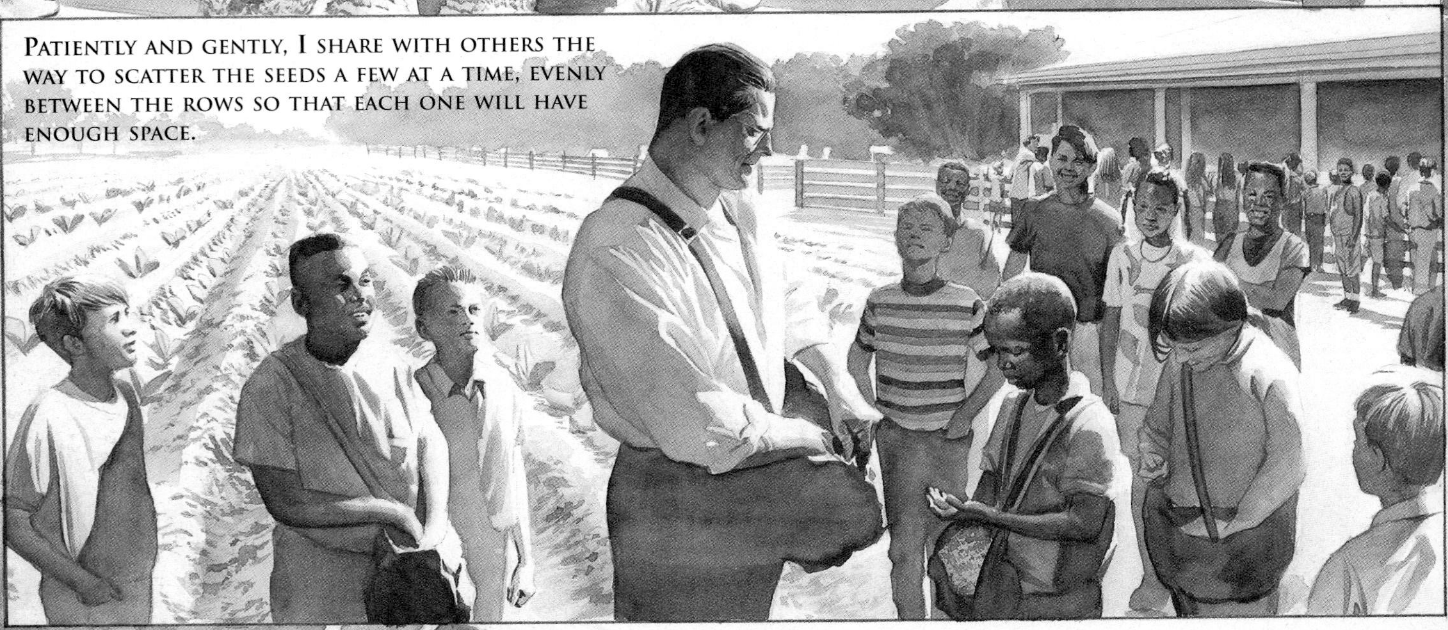

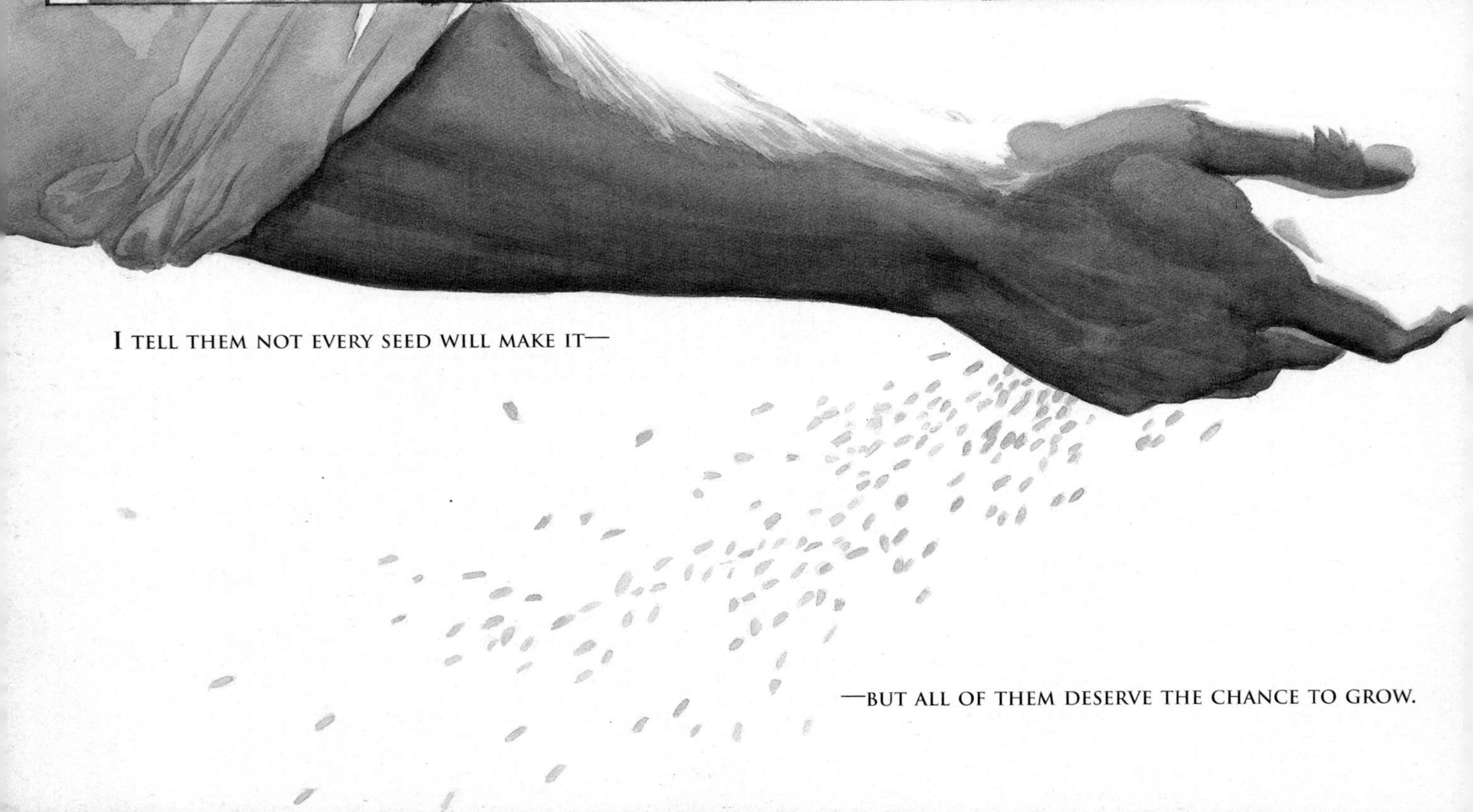

I tell them not every seed will make it—

—but all of them deserve the chance to grow.

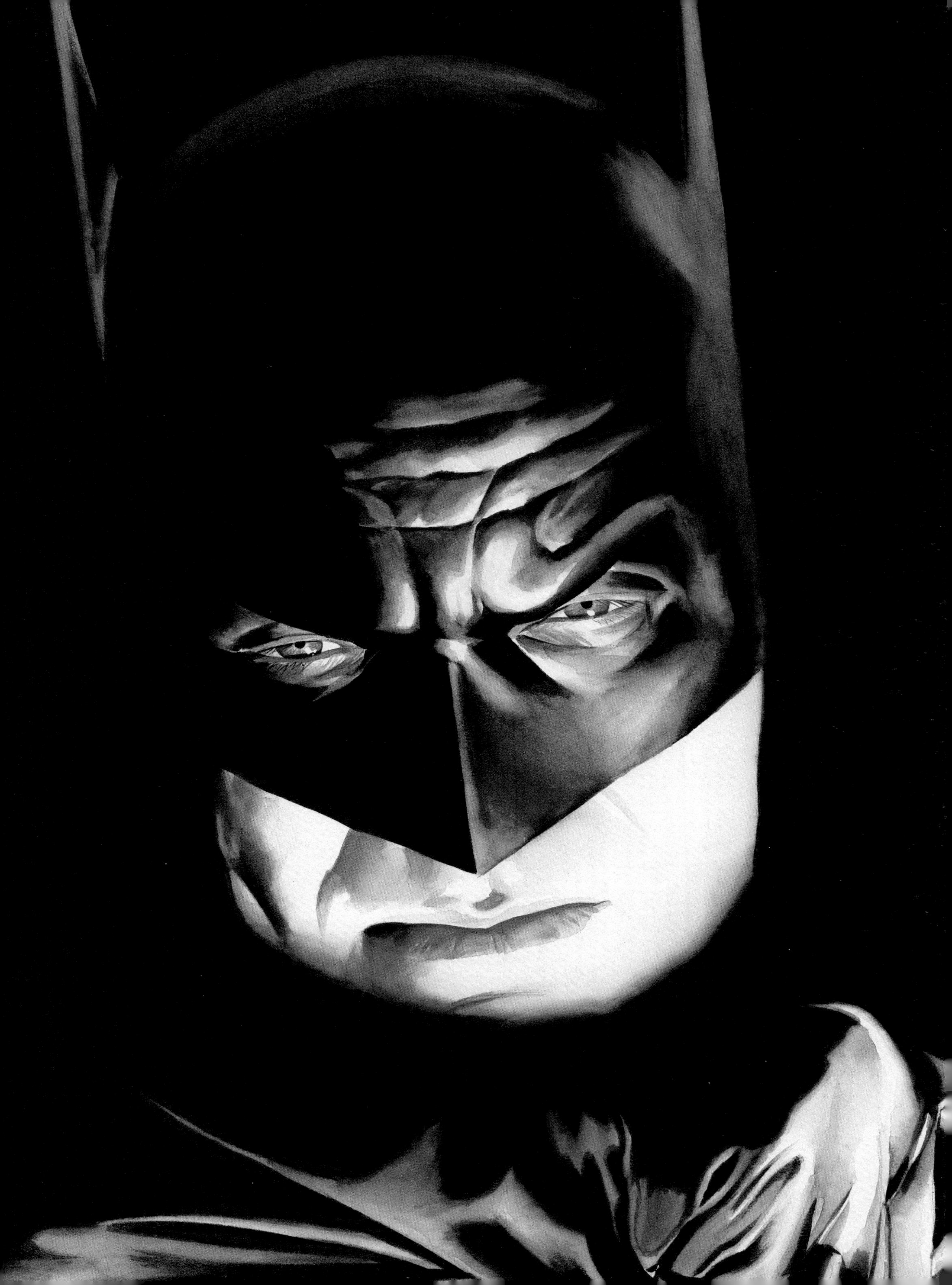

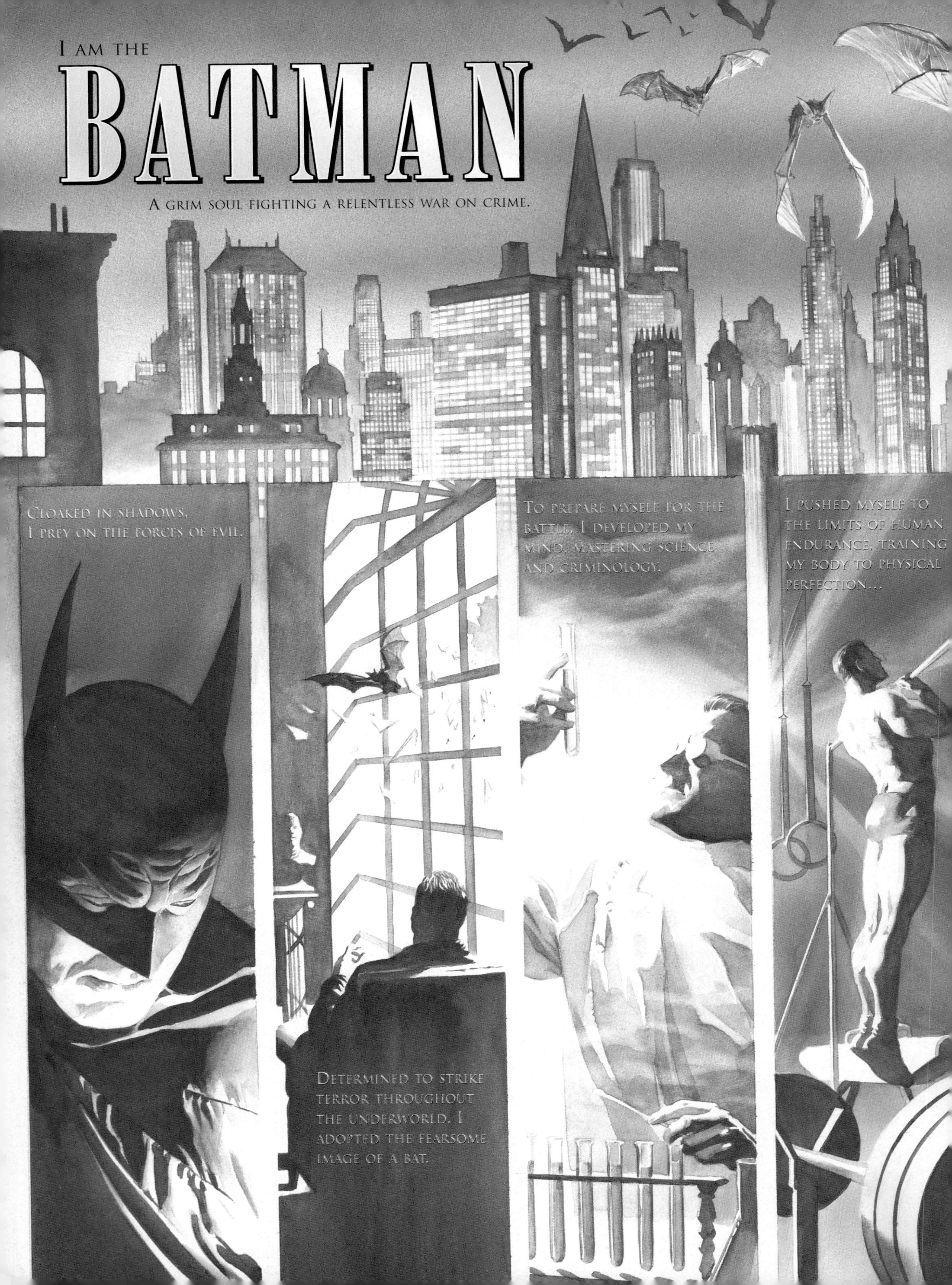
I am the
BATMAN
A grim soul fighting a relentless war on crime.
Cloaked in shadows, I prey on the forces of evil.
Determined to strike terror throughout the underworld, I adopted the fearsome image of a bat.
To prepare myself for the battle, I developed my mind, mastering science and criminology.
I pushed myself to the limits of human endurance, training my body to physical perfection...

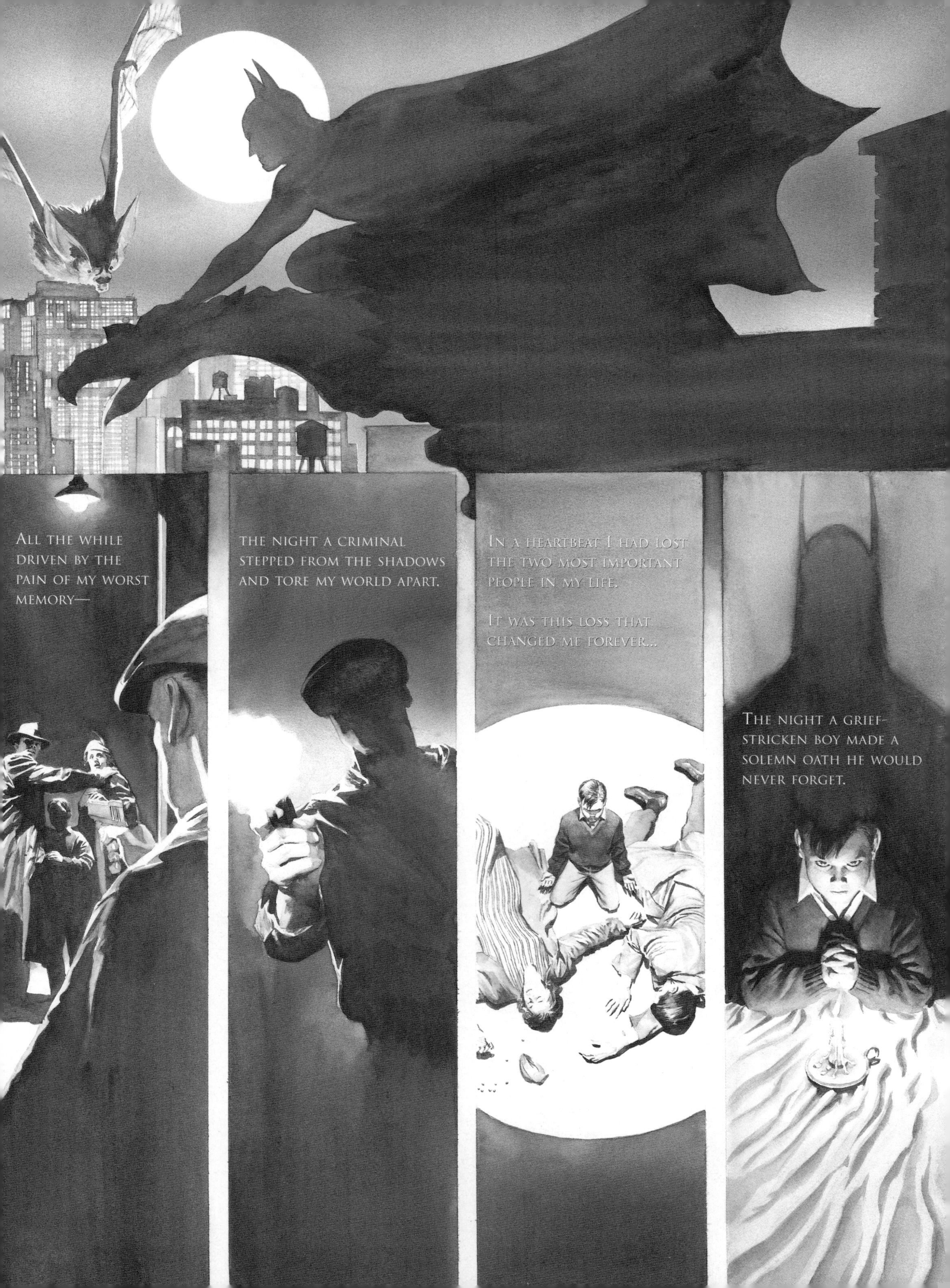
All the while driven by the pain of my worst memory—
the night a criminal stepped from the shadows and tore my world apart.
In a heartbeat I had lost the two most important people in my life.
It was this loss that changed me forever...
The night a grief-stricken boy made a solemn oath he would never forget.

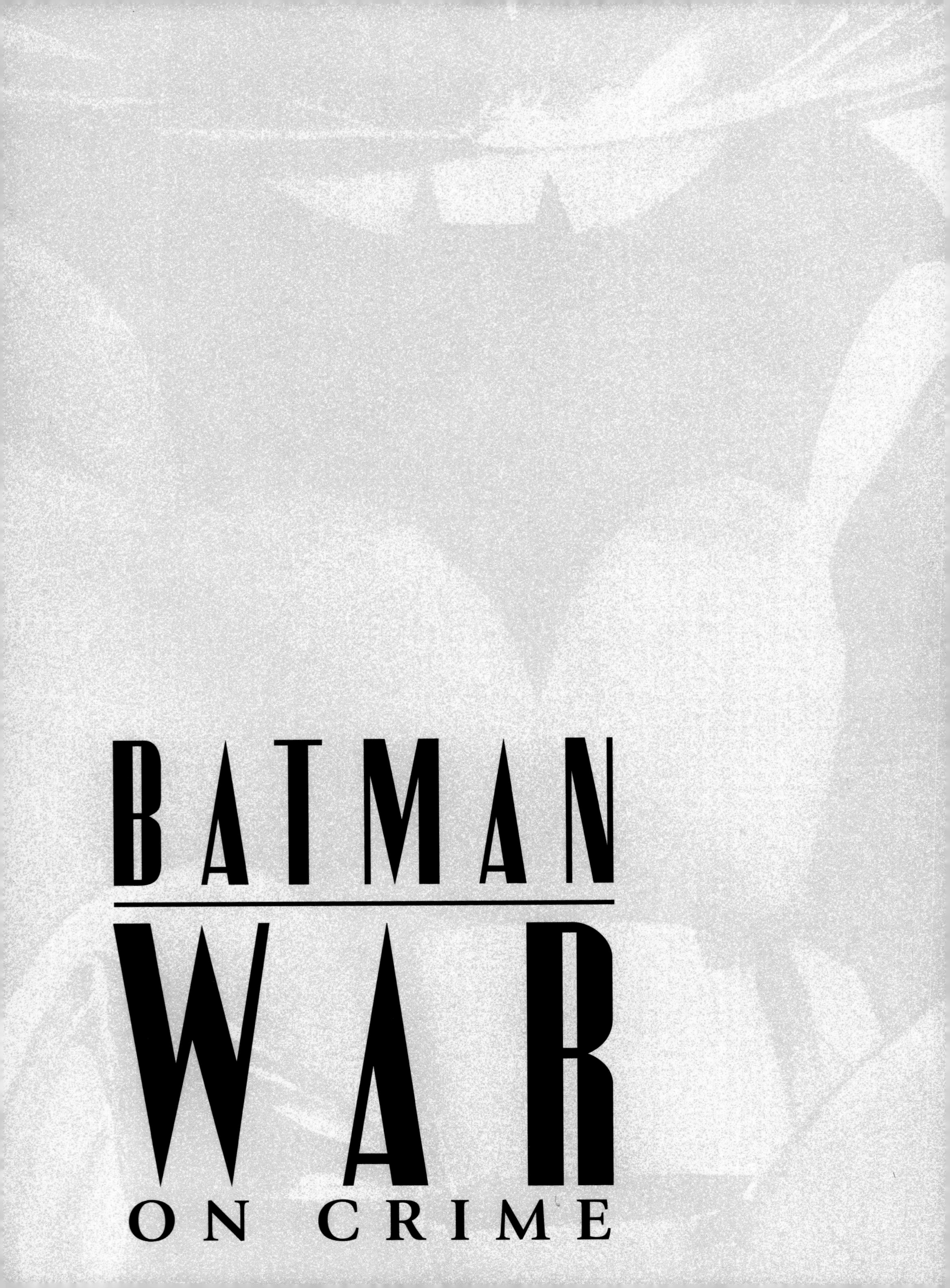

BATMAN

WAR ON CRIME

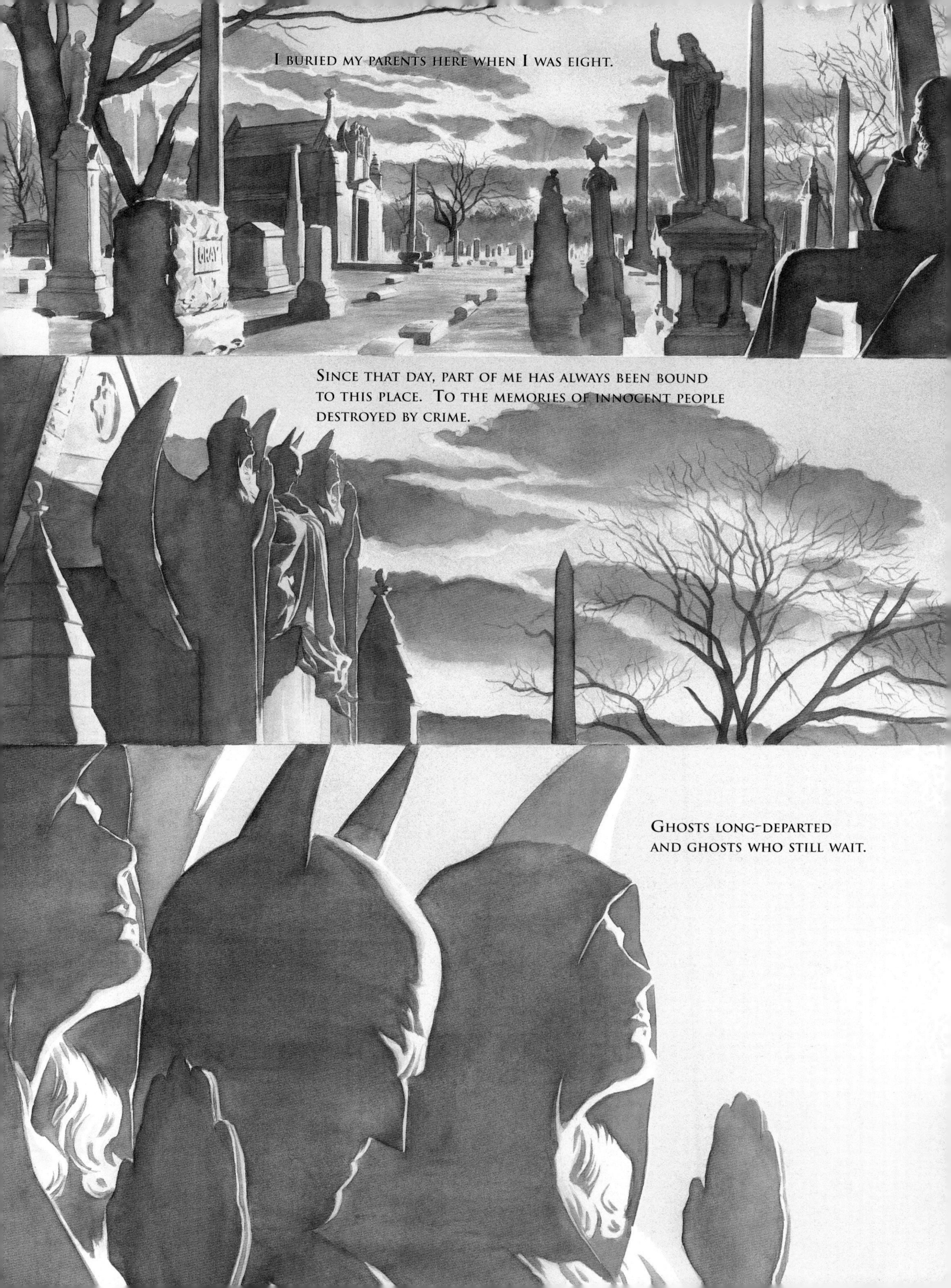
I buried my parents here when I was eight.
GRAY
Since that day, part of me has always been bound to this place. To the memories of innocent people destroyed by crime.
Ghosts long-departed and ghosts who still wait.

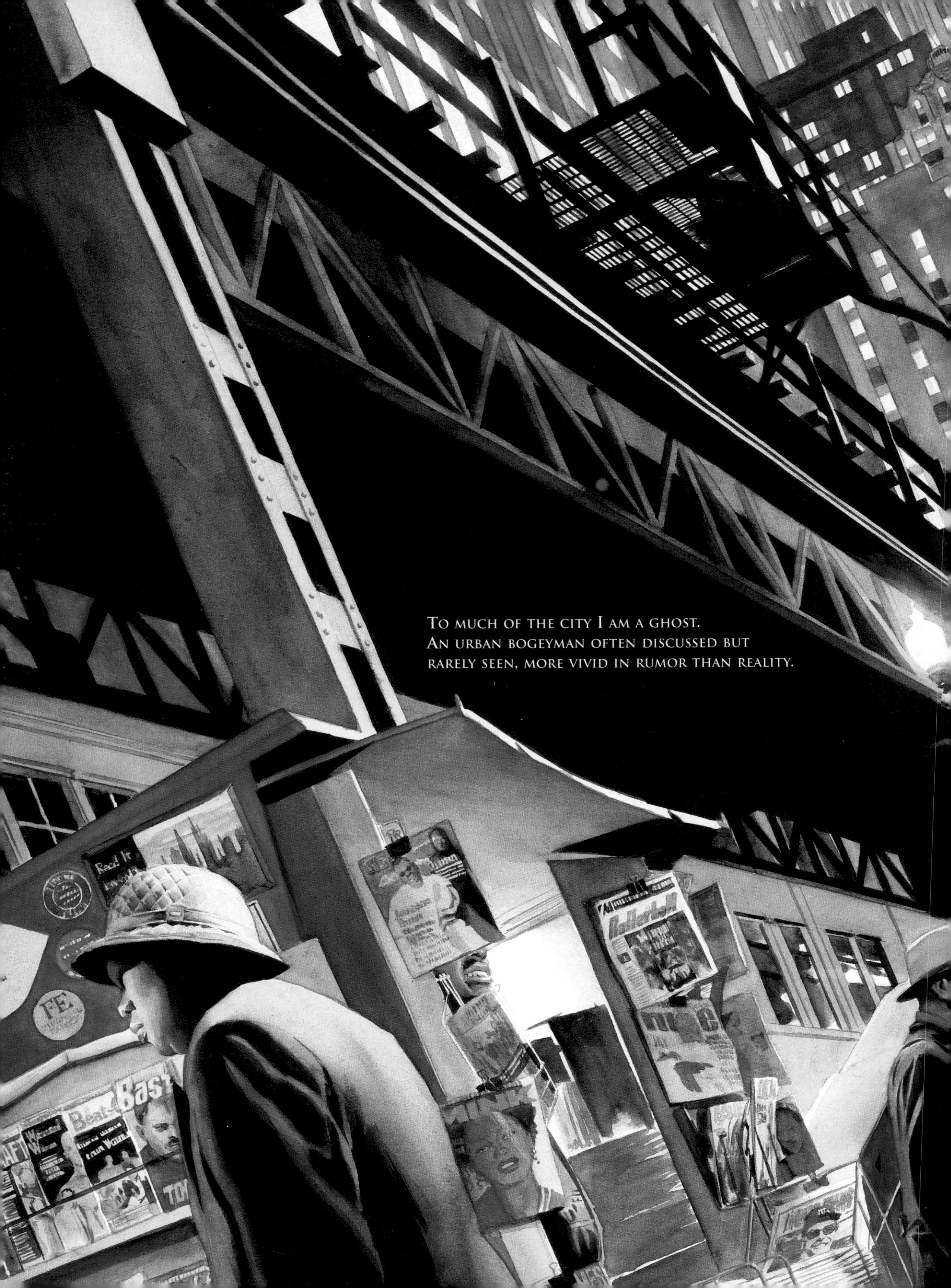
To much of the city I am a ghost.
An urban bogeyman often discussed but
rarely seen, more vivid in rumor than reality.

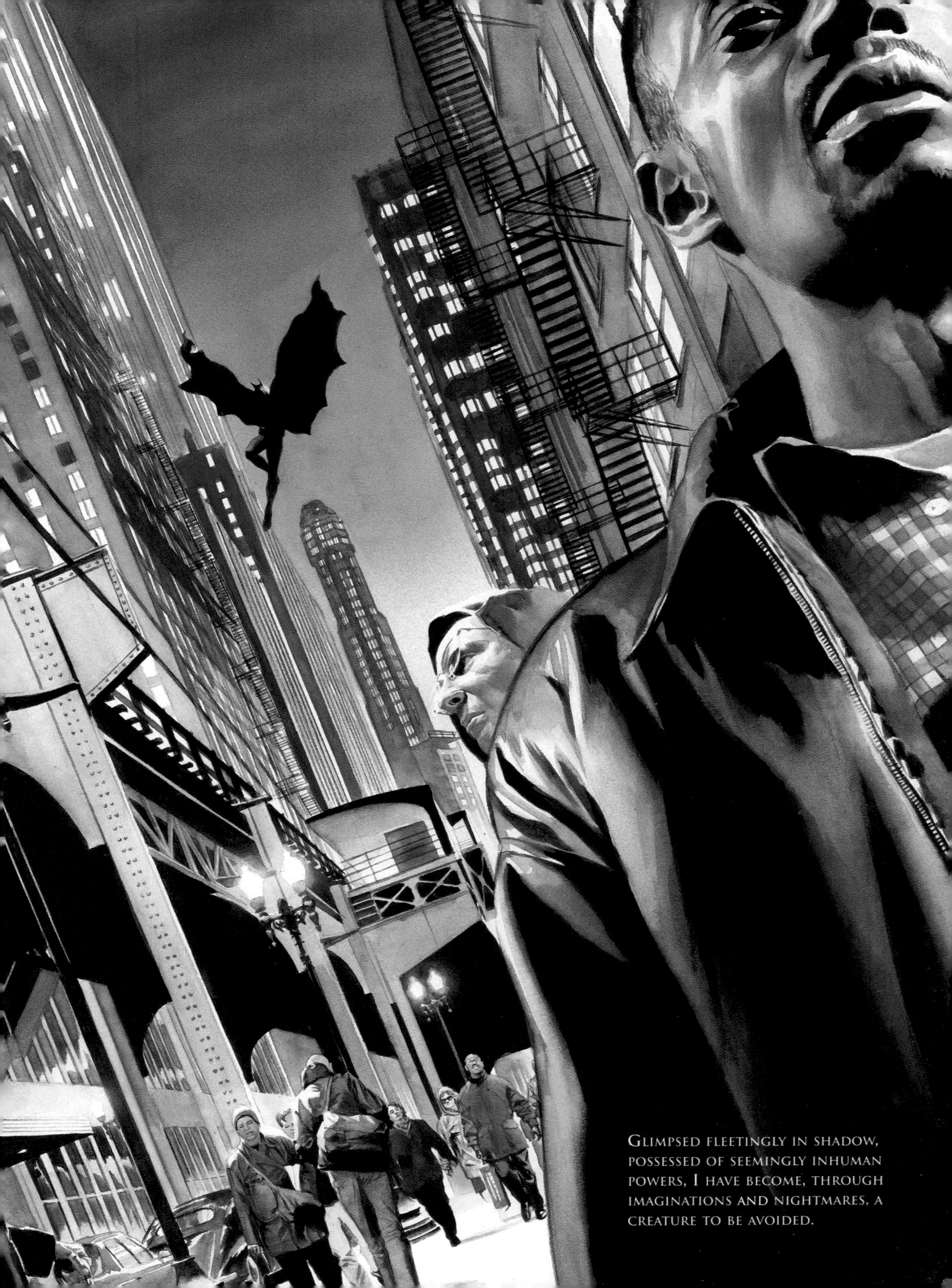
GLIMPSED FLEETINGLY IN SHADOW, POSSESSED OF SEEMINGLY INHUMAN POWERS, I HAVE BECOME, THROUGH IMAGINATIONS AND NIGHTMARES, A CREATURE TO BE AVOIDED.

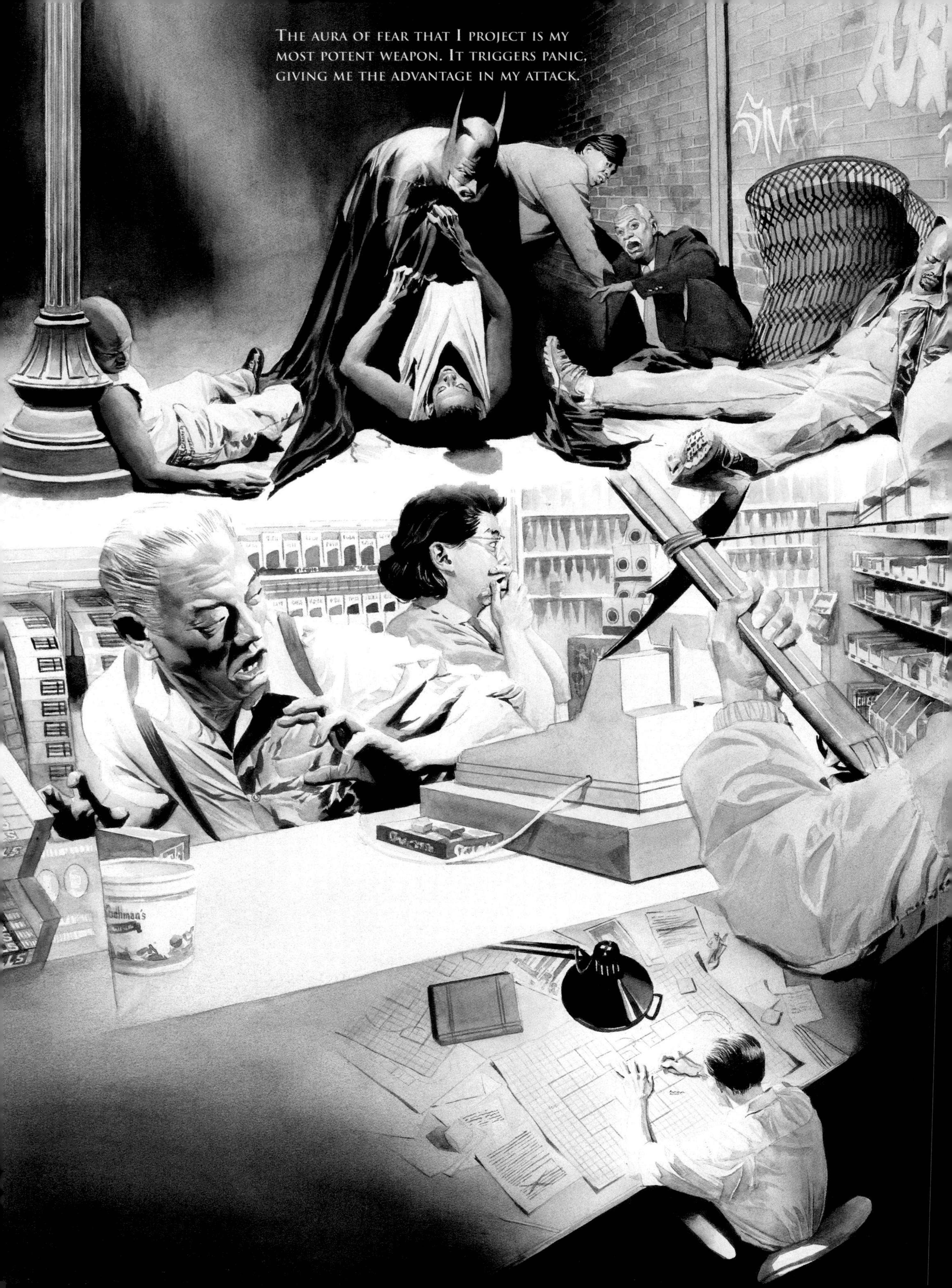
THE AURA OF FEAR THAT I PROJECT IS MY MOST POTENT WEAPON. IT TRIGGERS PANIC, GIVING ME THE ADVANTAGE IN MY ATTACK.

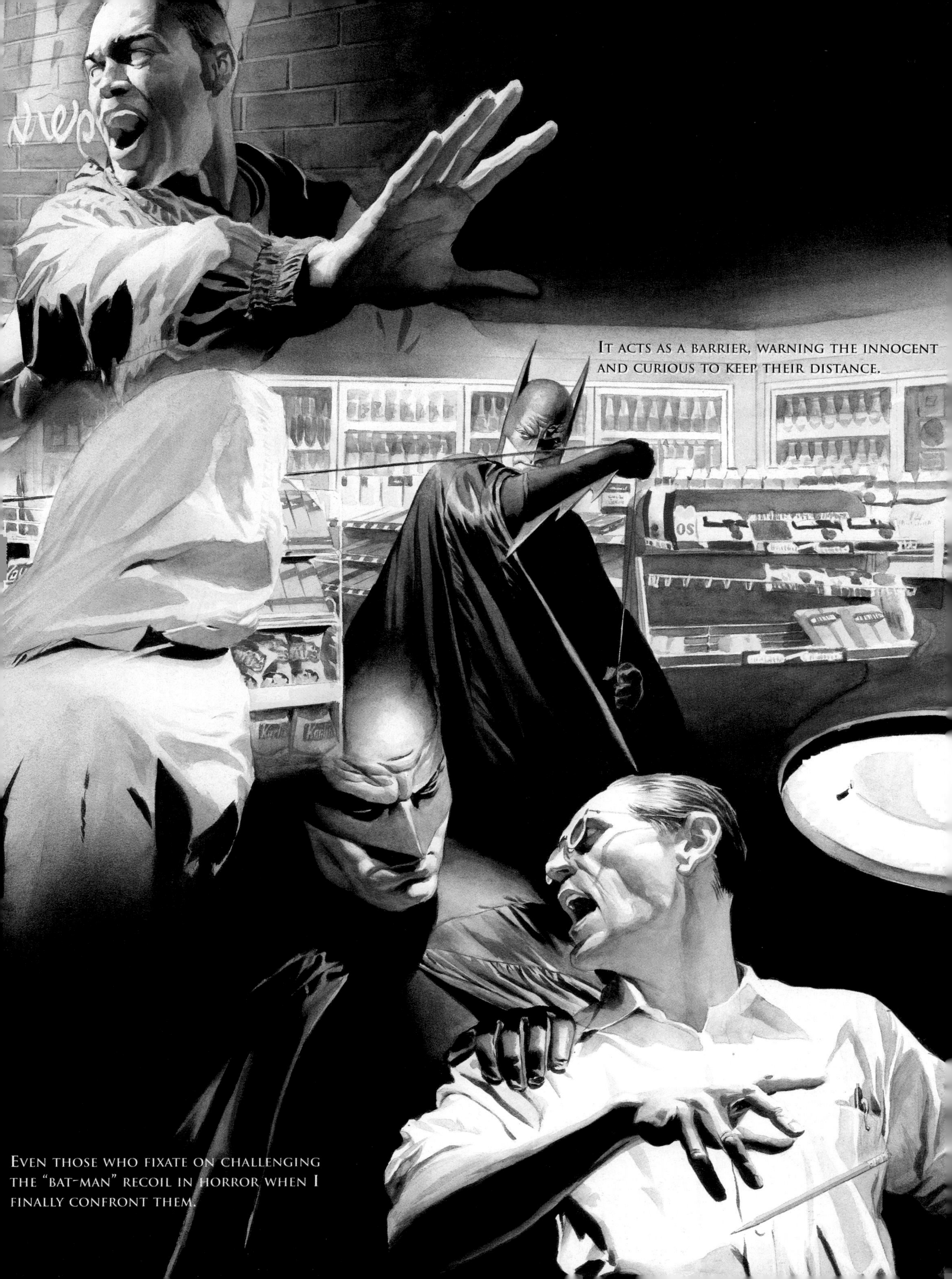
It acts as a barrier, warning the innocent and curious to keep their distance.
Even those who fixate on challenging the "bat-man" recoil in horror when I finally confront them.

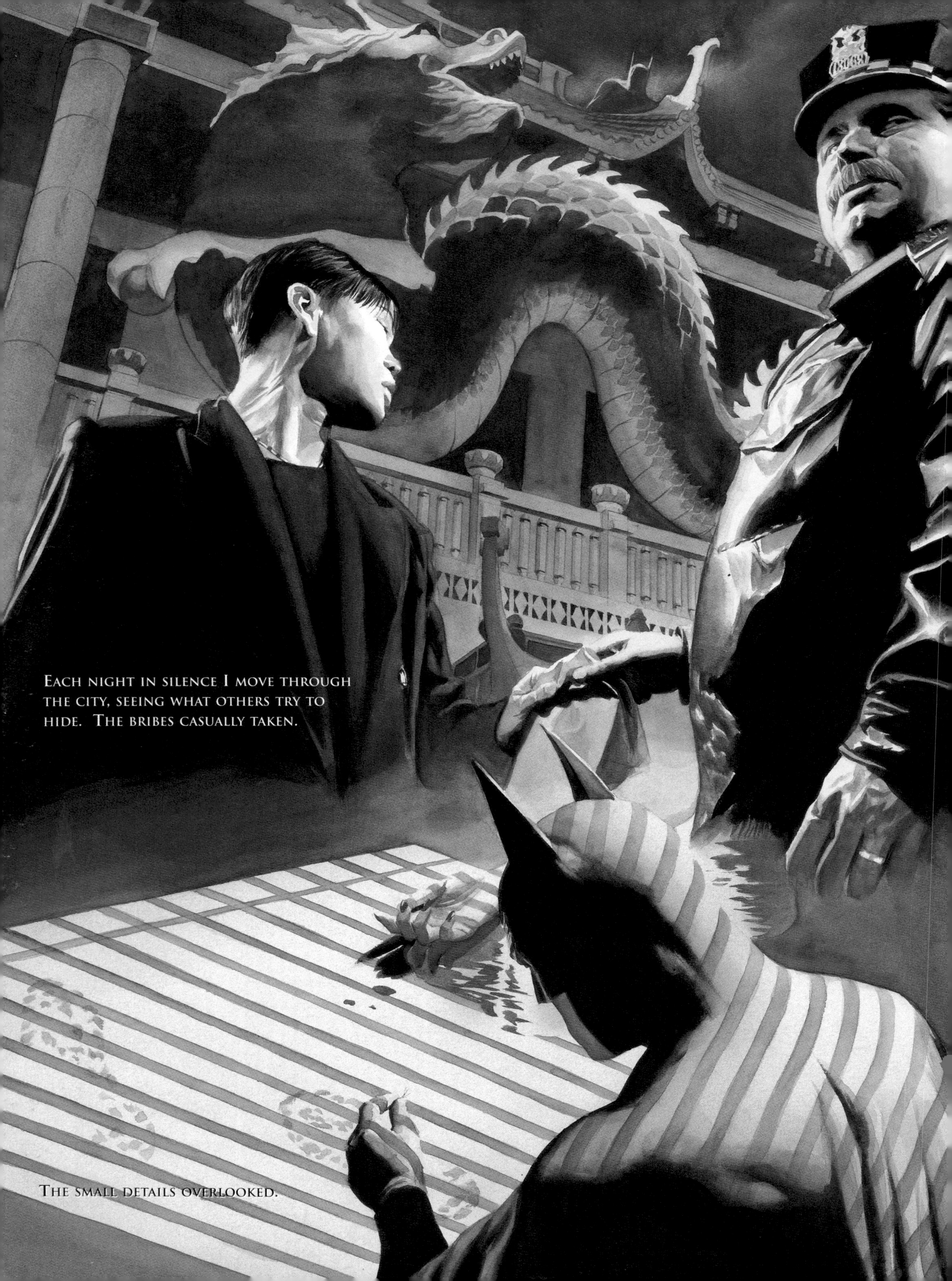
EACH NIGHT IN SILENCE I MOVE THROUGH THE CITY, SEEING WHAT OTHERS TRY TO HIDE. THE BRIBES CASUALLY TAKEN.
THE SMALL DETAILS OVERLOOKED.

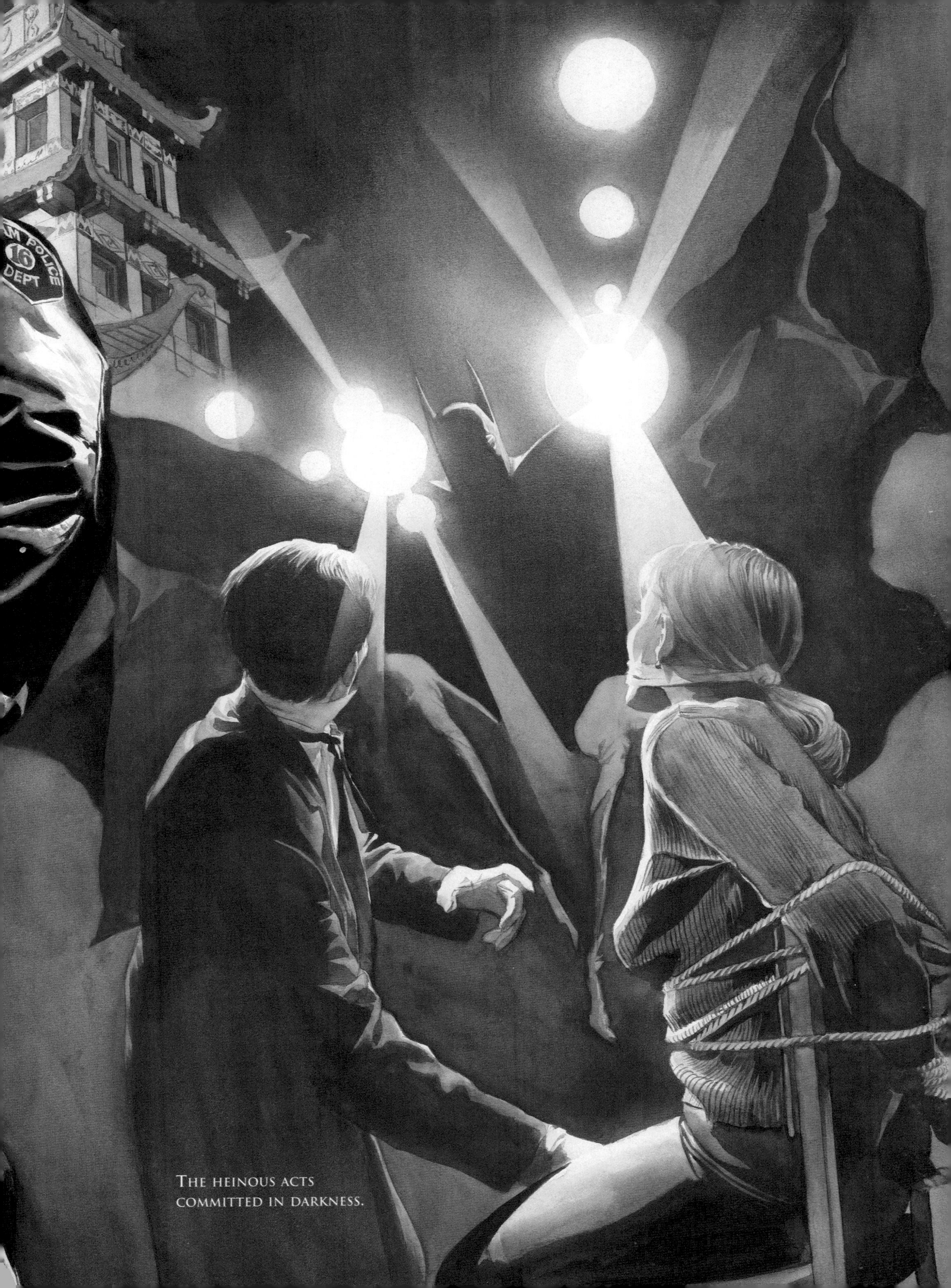
POLICE
16
DEPT
THE HEINOUS ACTS
COMMITTED IN DARKNESS.

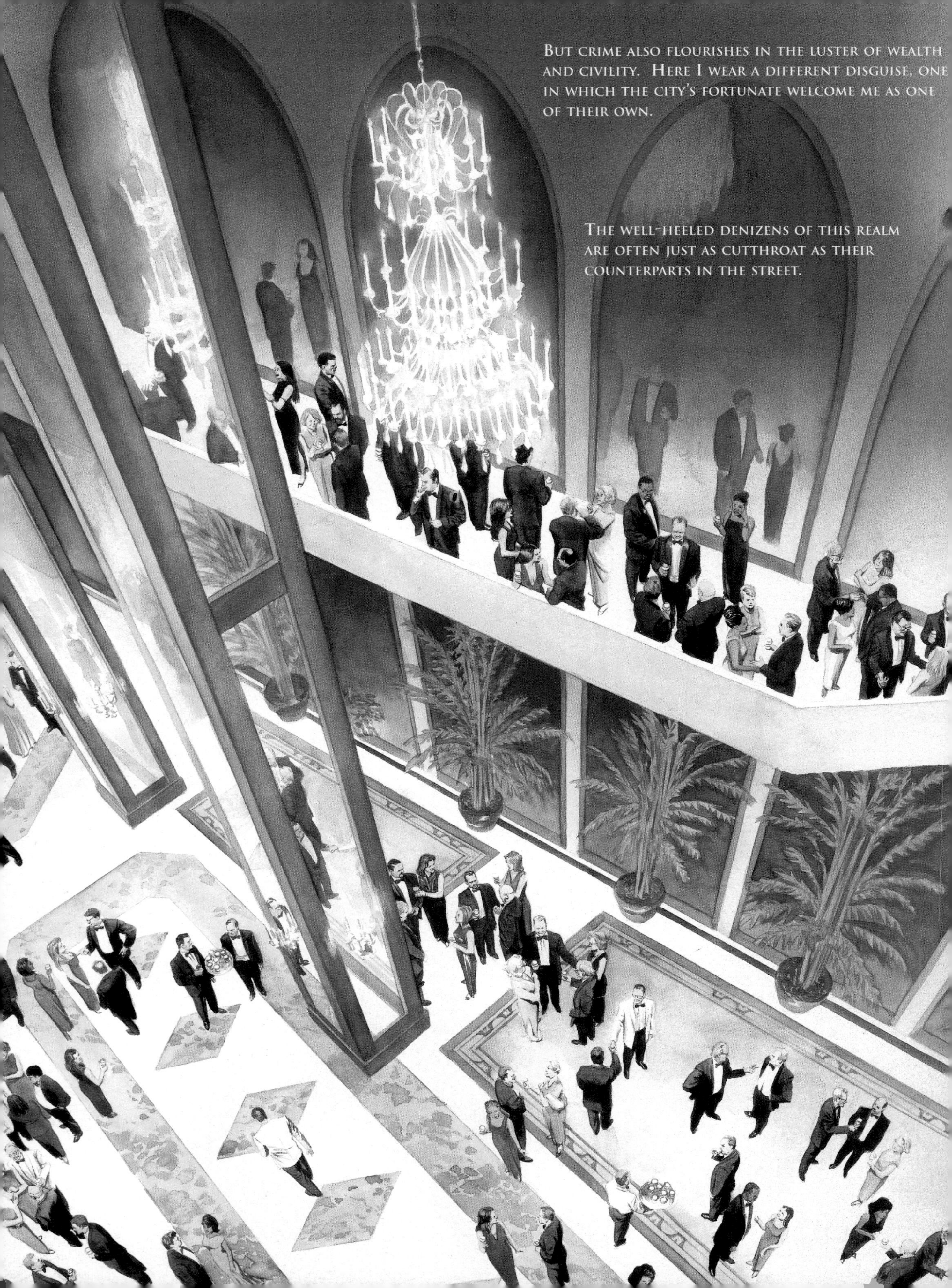
But crime also flourishes in the luster of wealth and civility. Here I wear a different disguise, one in which the city's fortunate welcome me as one of their own.
The well-heeled denizens of this realm are often just as cutthroat as their counterparts in the street.

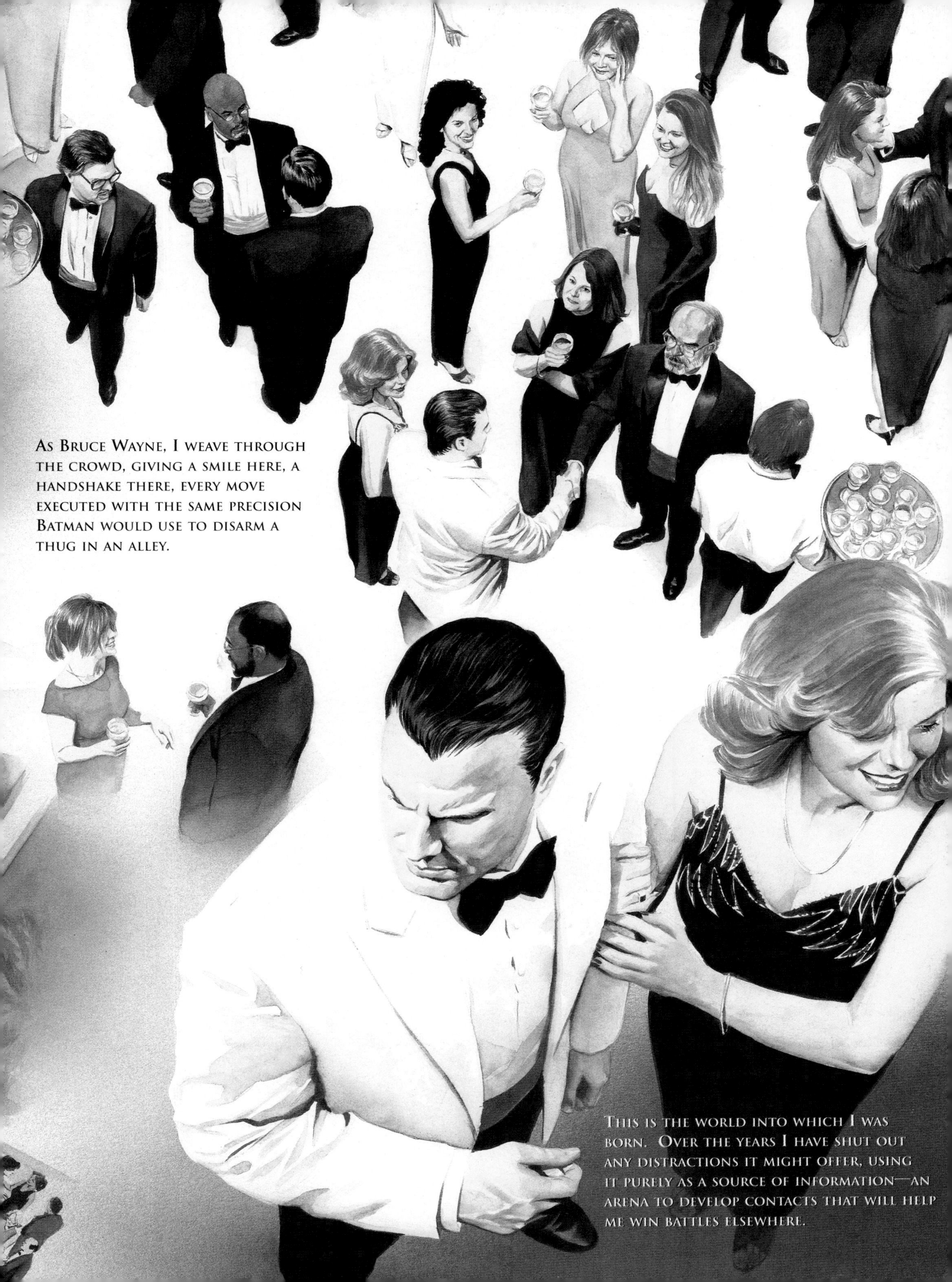
As Bruce Wayne, I weave through the crowd, giving a smile here, a handshake there, every move executed with the same precision Batman would use to disarm a thug in an alley.
This is the world into which I was born. Over the years I have shut out any distractions it might offer, using it purely as a source of information—an arena to develop contacts that will help me win battles elsewhere.

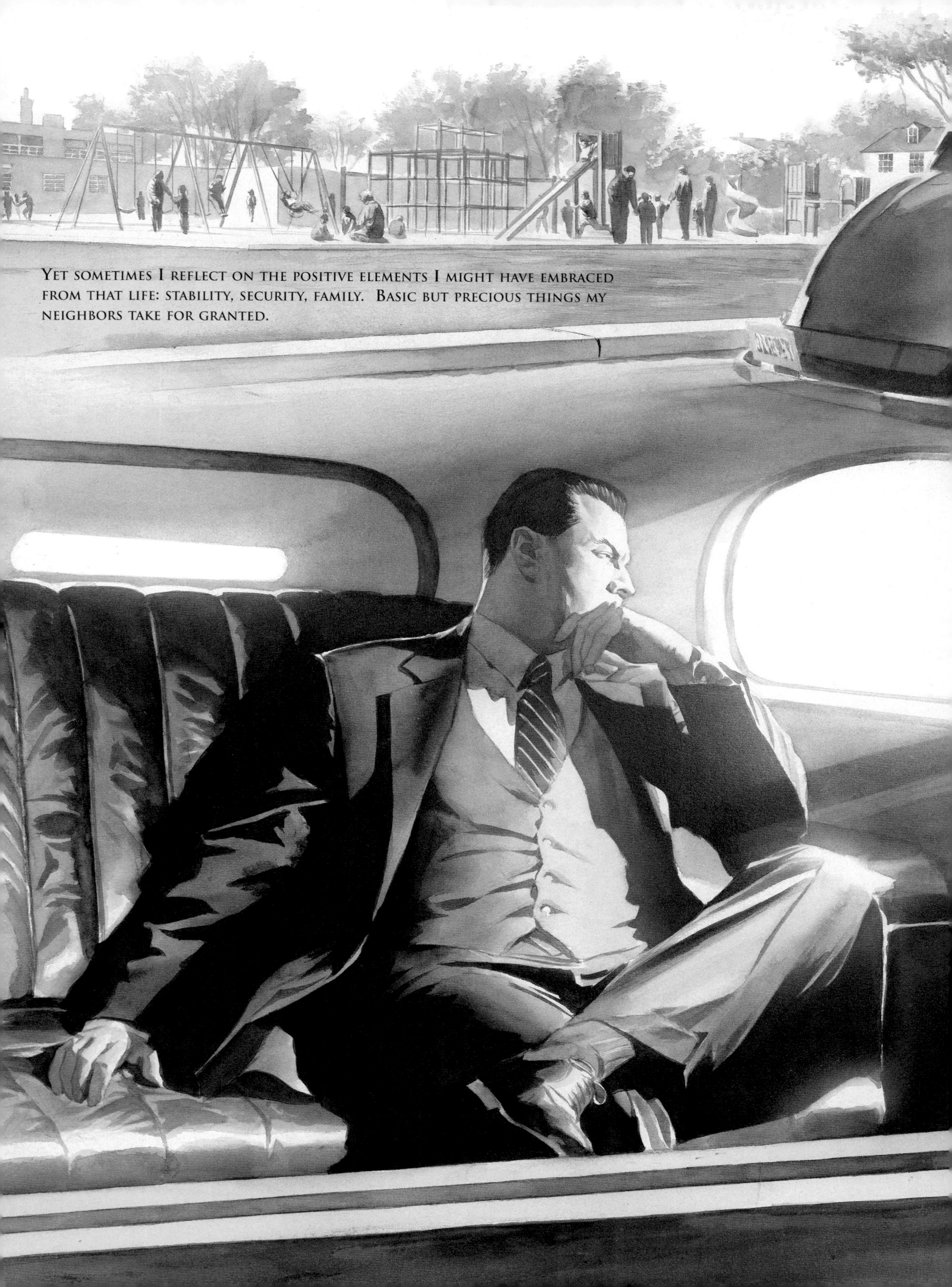
Yet sometimes I reflect on the positive elements I might have embraced from that life: stability, security, family. Basic but precious things my neighbors take for granted.

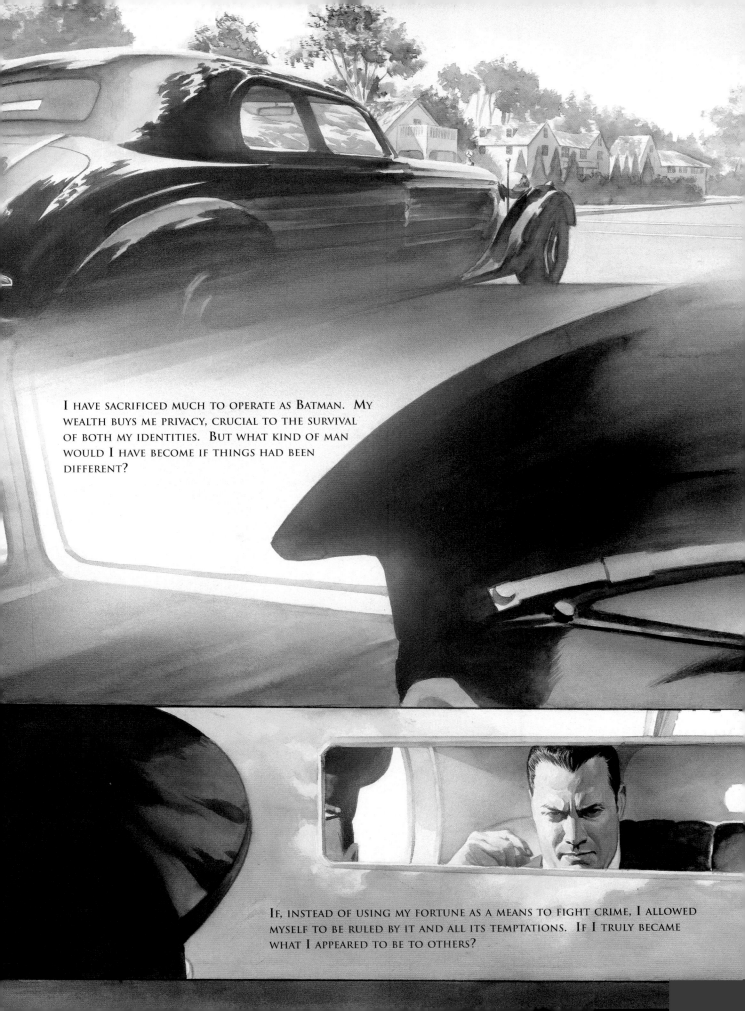

I HAVE SACRIFICED MUCH TO OPERATE AS BATMAN. MY WEALTH BUYS ME PRIVACY, CRUCIAL TO THE SURVIVAL OF BOTH MY IDENTITIES. BUT WHAT KIND OF MAN WOULD I HAVE BECOME IF THINGS HAD BEEN DIFFERENT?

IF, INSTEAD OF USING MY FORTUNE AS A MEANS TO FIGHT CRIME, I ALLOWED MYSELF TO BE RULED BY IT AND ALL ITS TEMPTATIONS. IF I TRULY BECAME WHAT I APPEARED TO BE TO OTHERS?

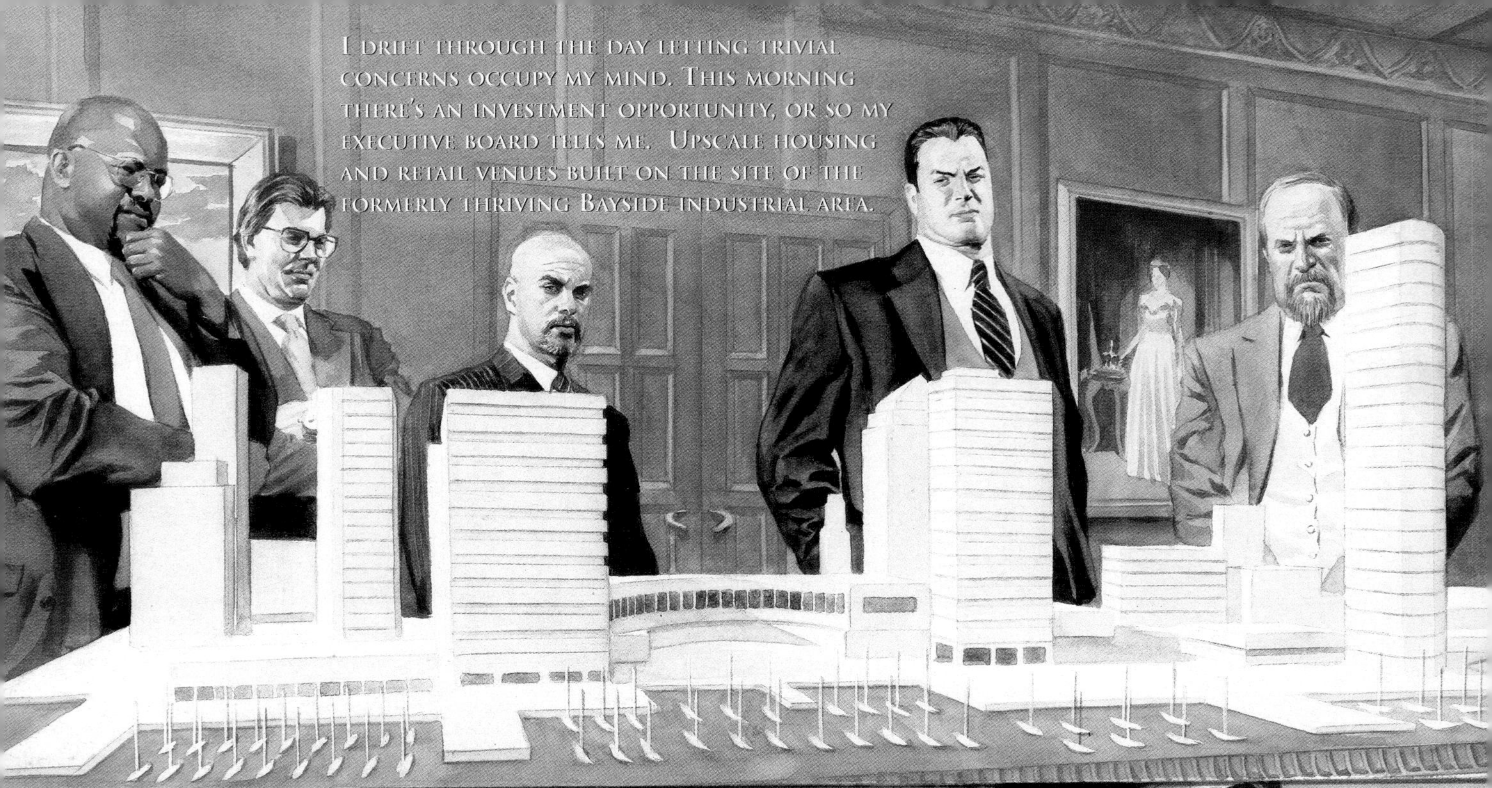
I drift through the day letting trivial concerns occupy my mind. This morning there's an investment opportunity, or so my executive board tells me. Upscale housing and retail venues built on the site of the formerly thriving Bayside industrial area.

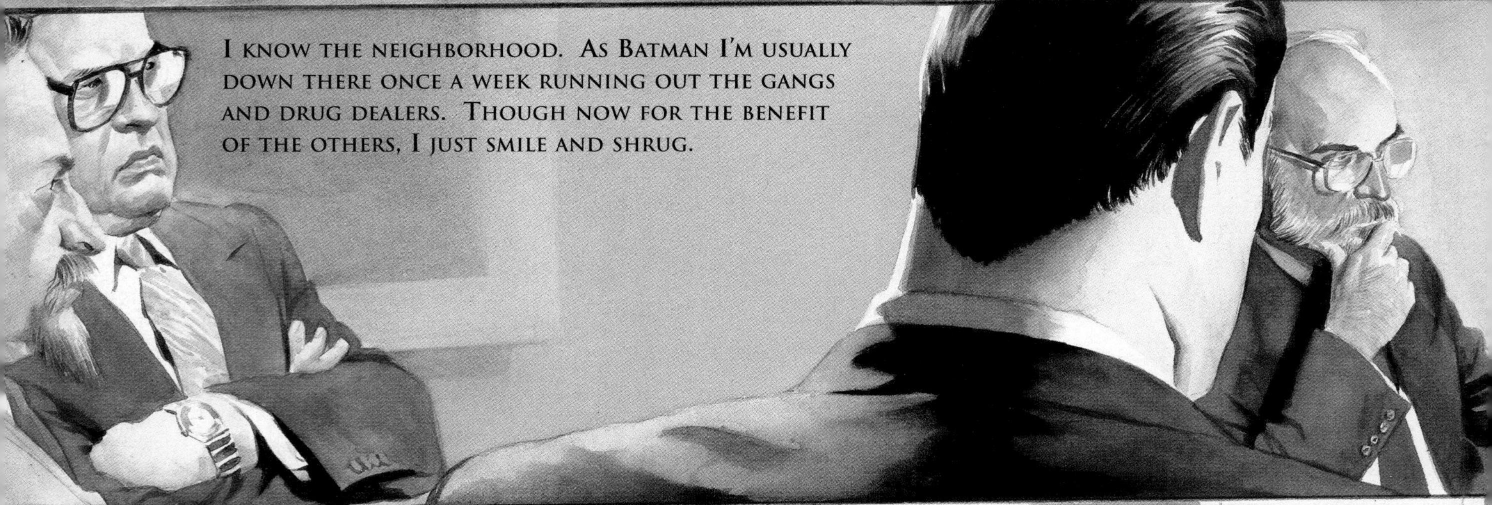
I know the neighborhood. As Batman I'm usually down there once a week running out the gangs and drug dealers. Though now for the benefit of the others, I just smile and shrug.

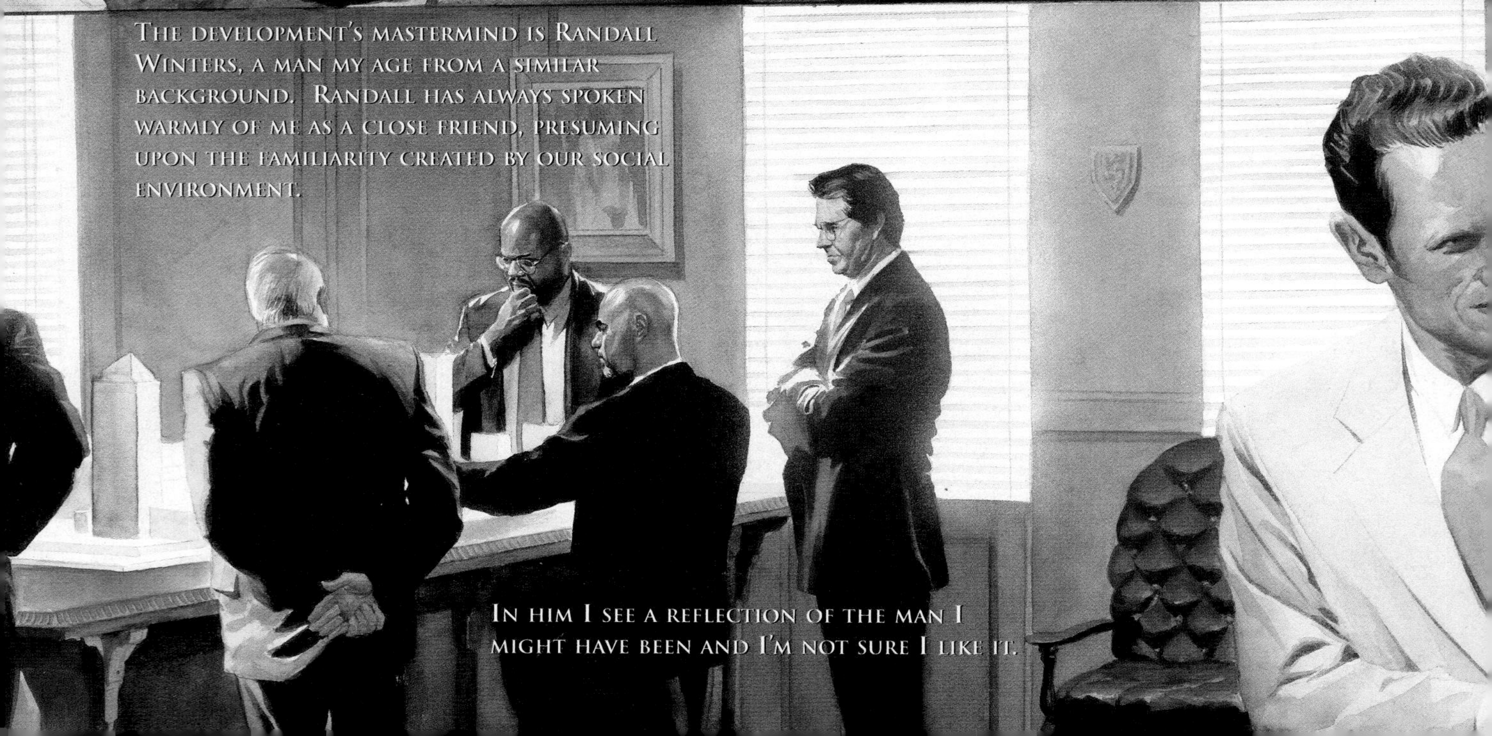
The development's mastermind is Randall Winters, a man my age from a similar background. Randall has always spoken warmly of me as a close friend, presuming upon the familiarity created by our social environment.
In him I see a reflection of the man I might have been and I'm not sure I like it.

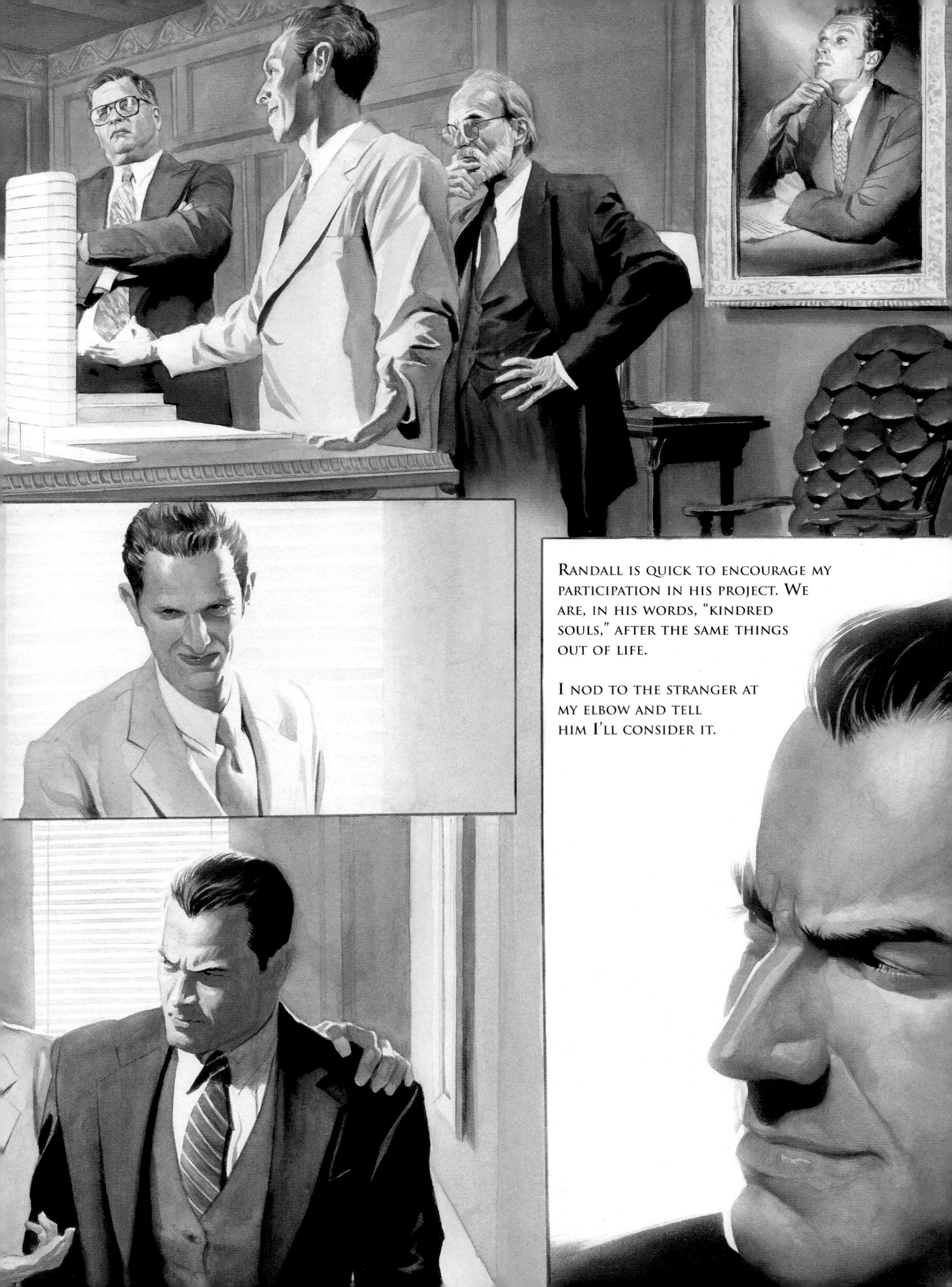
RANDALL IS QUICK TO ENCOURAGE MY PARTICIPATION IN HIS PROJECT. WE ARE, IN HIS WORDS, "KINDRED SOULS," AFTER THE SAME THINGS OUT OF LIFE.
I NOD TO THE STRANGER AT MY ELBOW AND TELL HIM I'LL CONSIDER IT.

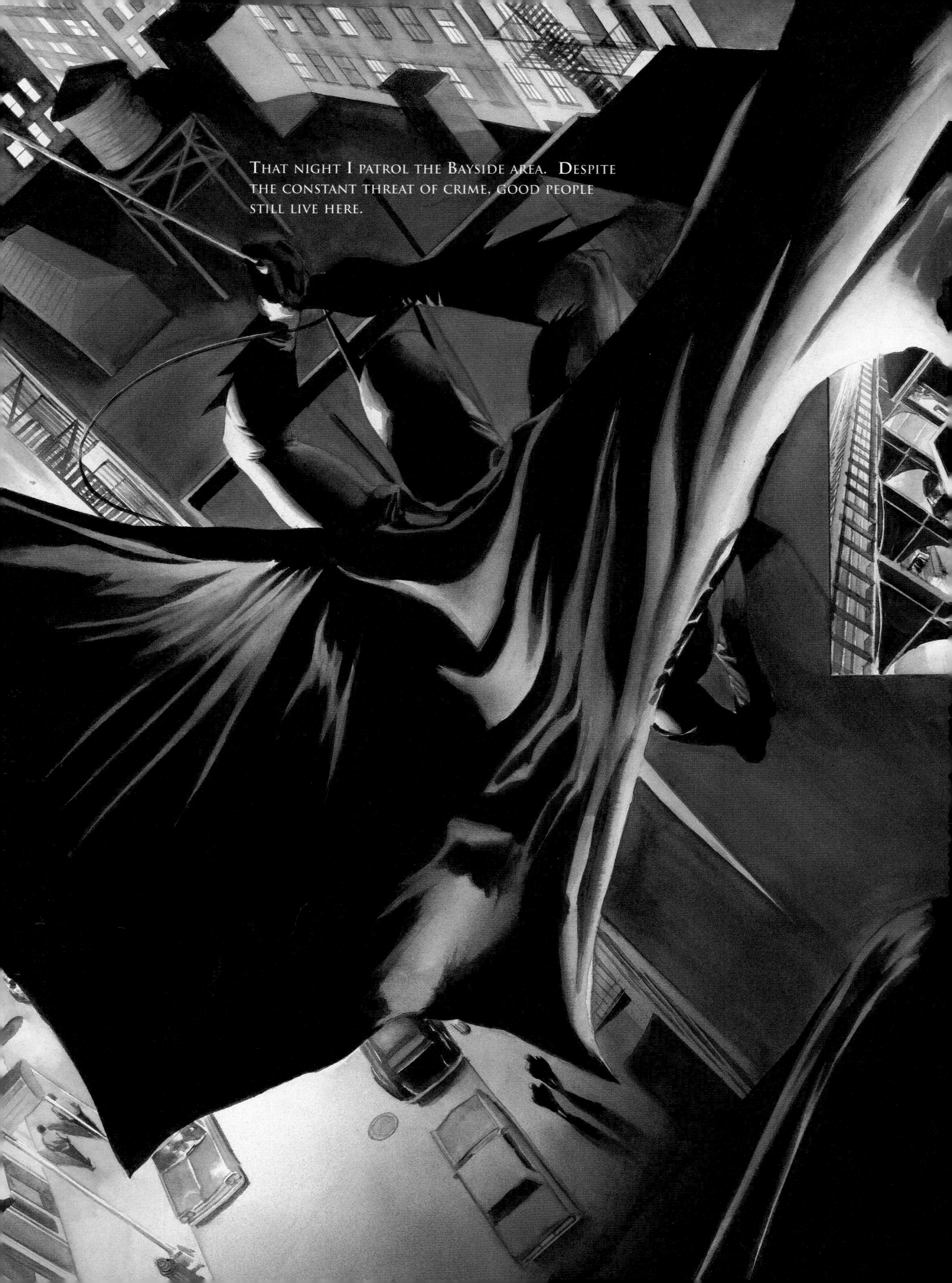
THAT NIGHT I PATROL THE BAYSIDE AREA. DESPITE THE CONSTANT THREAT OF CRIME, GOOD PEOPLE STILL LIVE HERE.

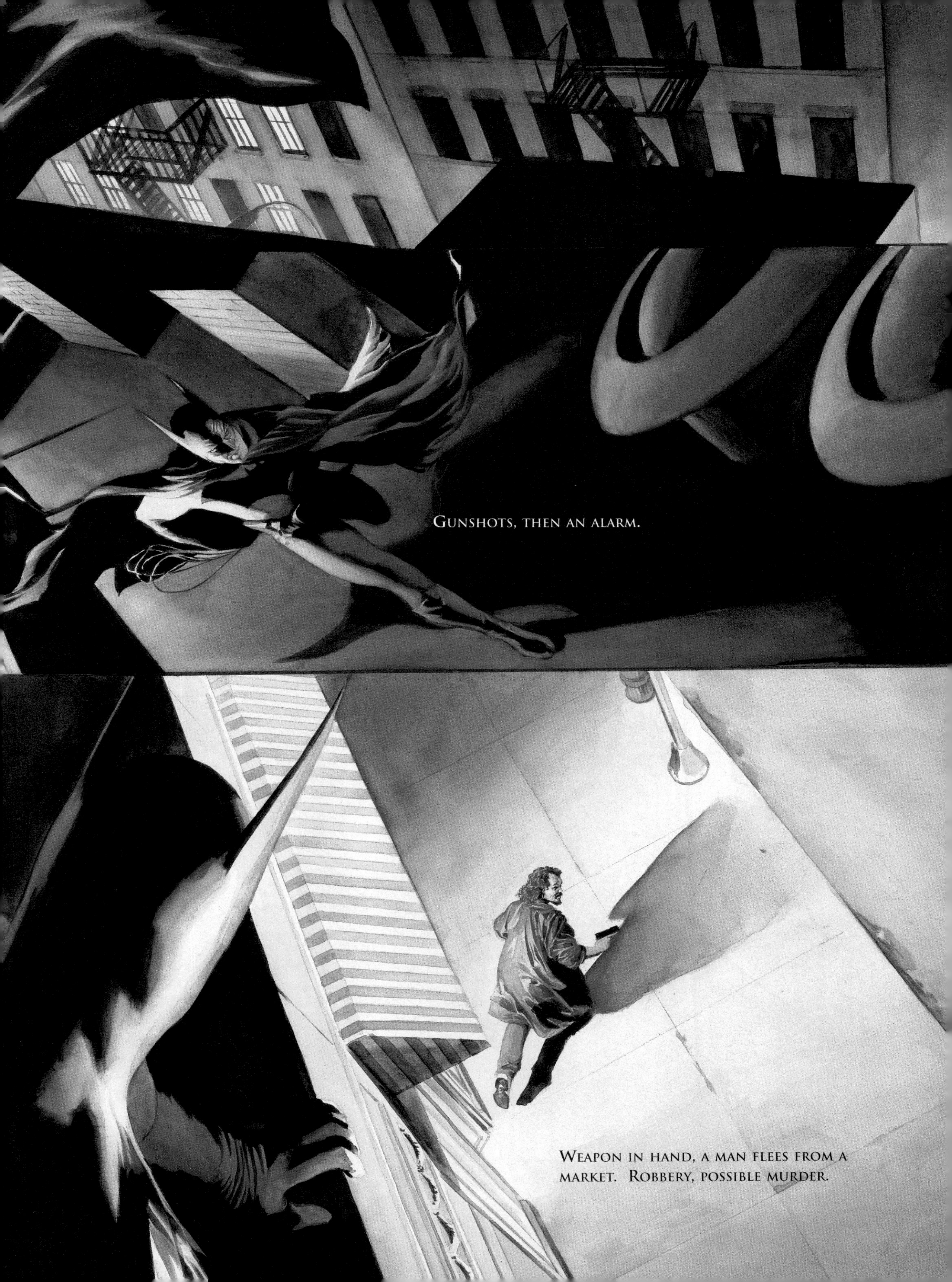
Gunshots, then an alarm.
Weapon in hand, a man flees from a market. Robbery, possible murder.

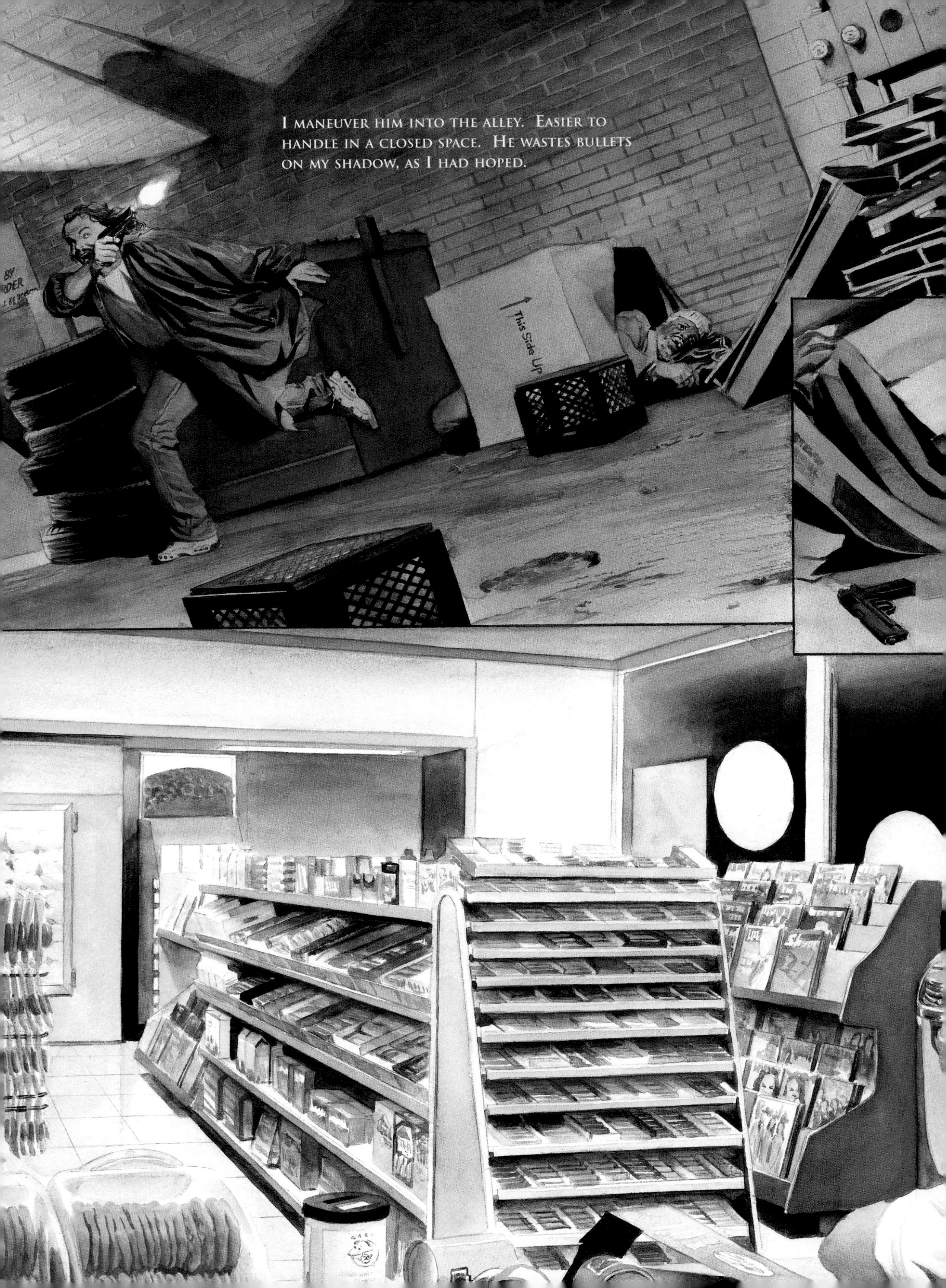
I maneuver him into the alley. Easier to handle in a closed space. He wastes bullets on my shadow, as I had hoped.
This Side Up

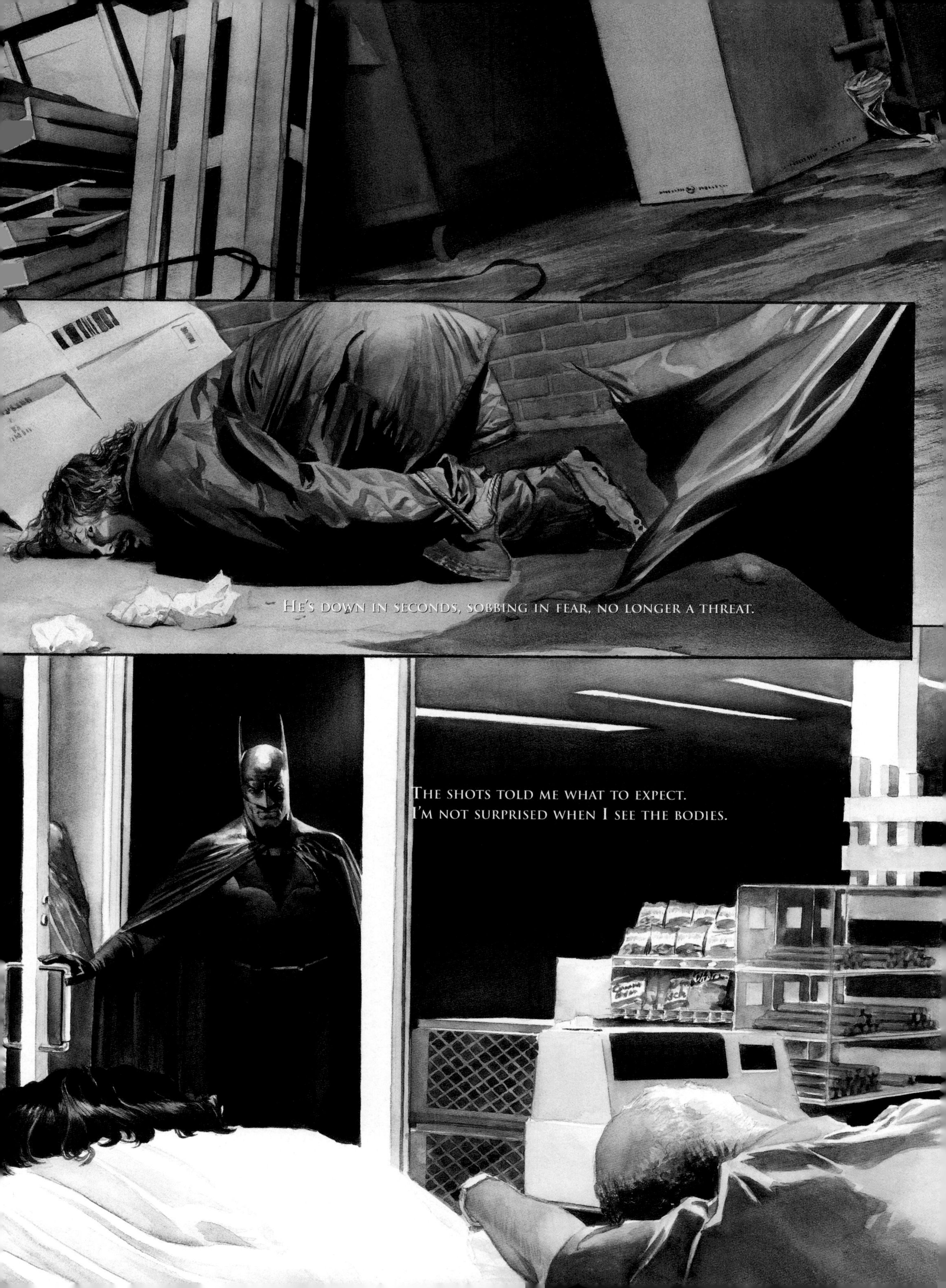
He's down in seconds, sobbing in fear, no longer a threat.
The shots told me what to expect.
I'm not surprised when I see the bodies.

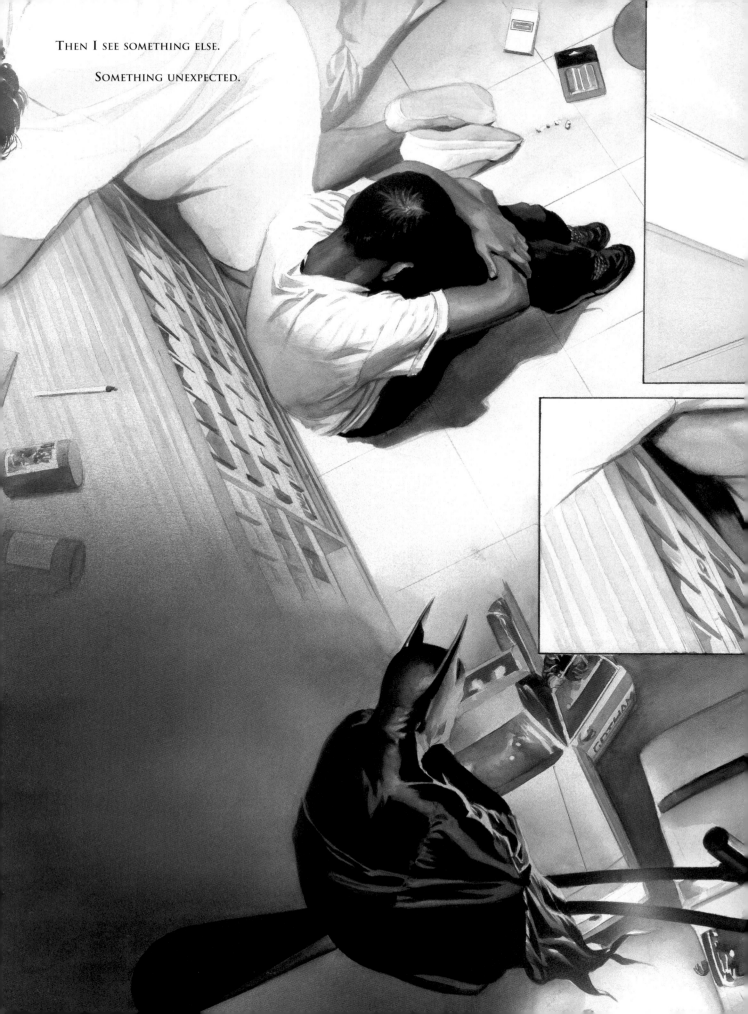

THEN I SEE SOMETHING ELSE.

SOMETHING UNEXPECTED.

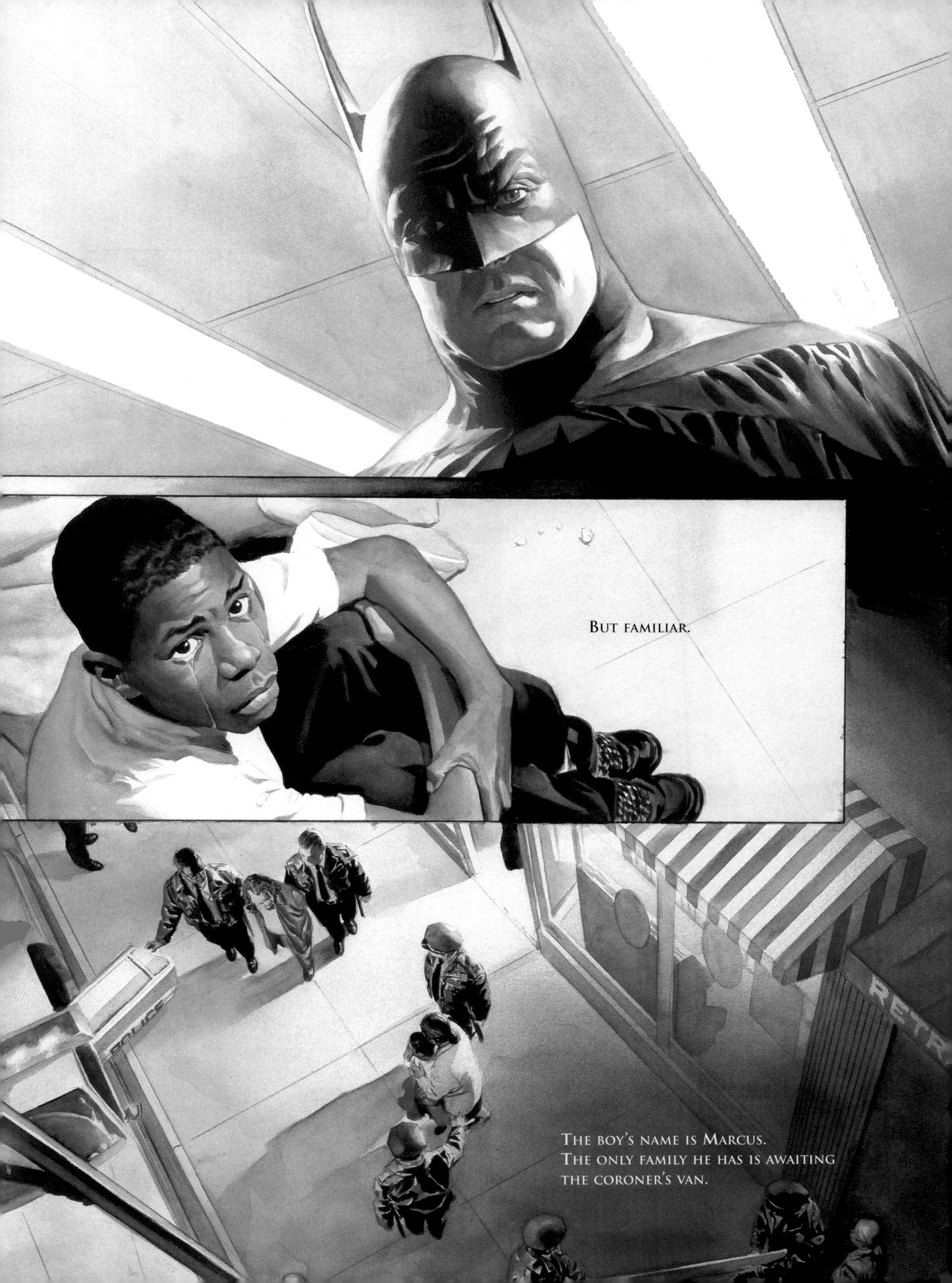
But familiar.
The boy's name is Marcus.
The only family he has is awaiting
the coroner's van.

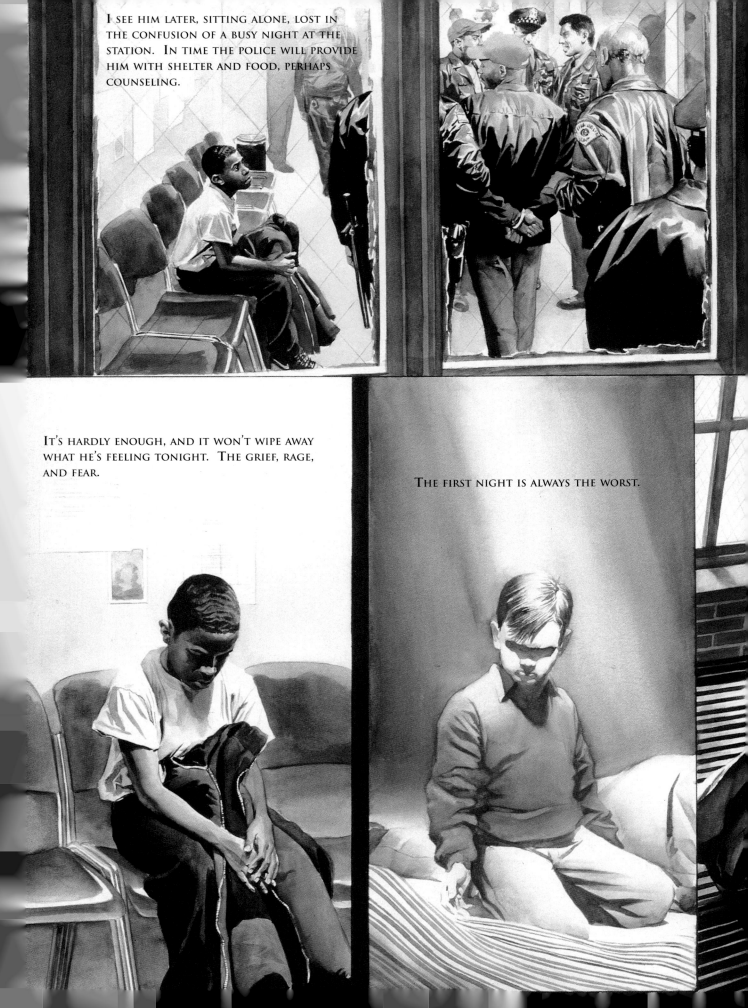

I SEE HIM LATER, SITTING ALONE, LOST IN THE CONFUSION OF A BUSY NIGHT AT THE STATION. IN TIME THE POLICE WILL PROVIDE HIM WITH SHELTER AND FOOD, PERHAPS COUNSELING.

IT'S HARDLY ENOUGH, AND IT WON'T WIPE AWAY WHAT HE'S FEELING TONIGHT. THE GRIEF, RAGE, AND FEAR.

THE FIRST NIGHT IS ALWAYS THE WORST.

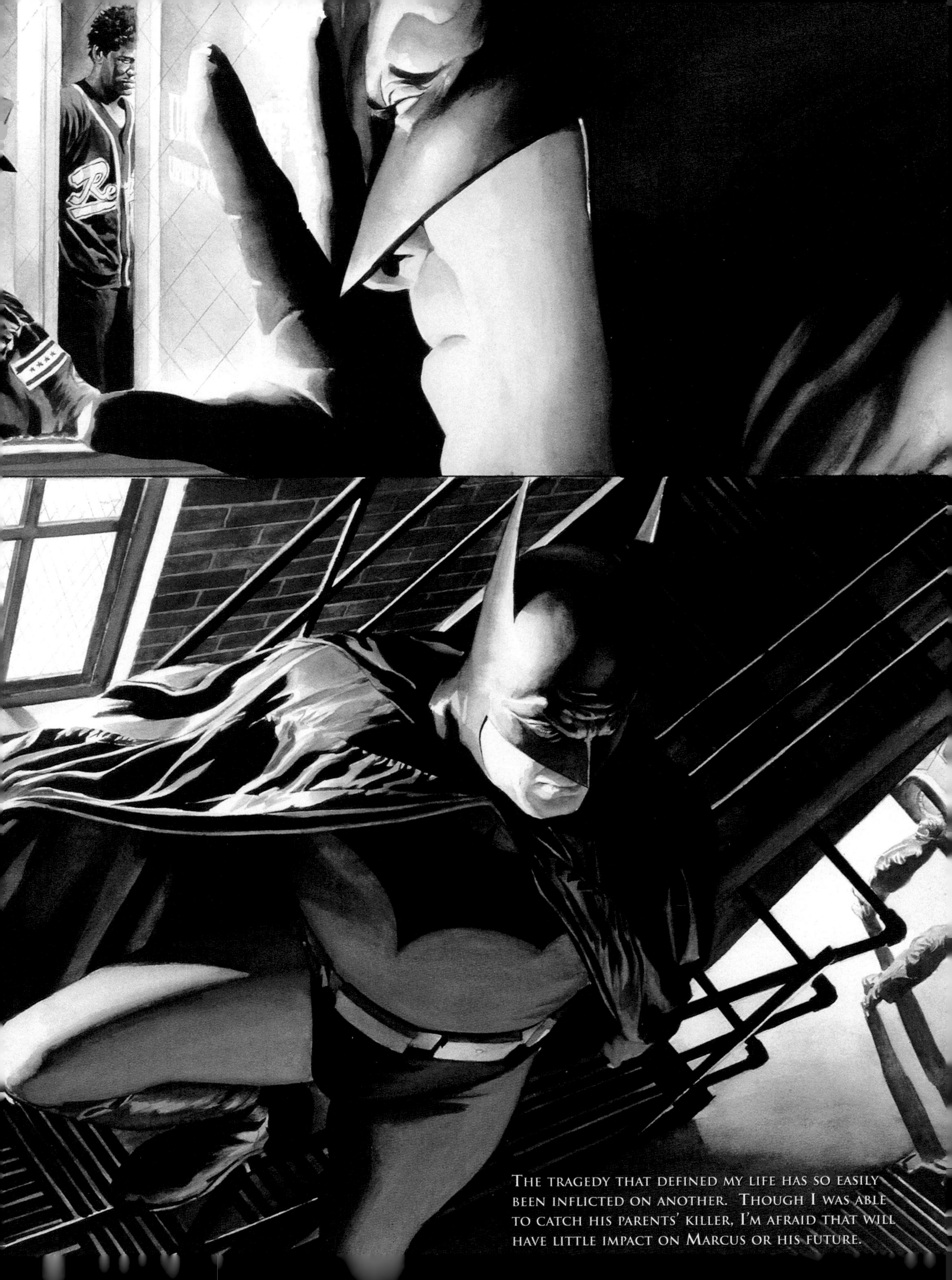
THE TRAGEDY THAT DEFINED MY LIFE HAS SO EASILY BEEN INFLICTED ON ANOTHER. THOUGH I WAS ABLE TO CATCH HIS PARENTS' KILLER, I'M AFRAID THAT WILL HAVE LITTLE IMPACT ON MARCUS OR HIS FUTURE.

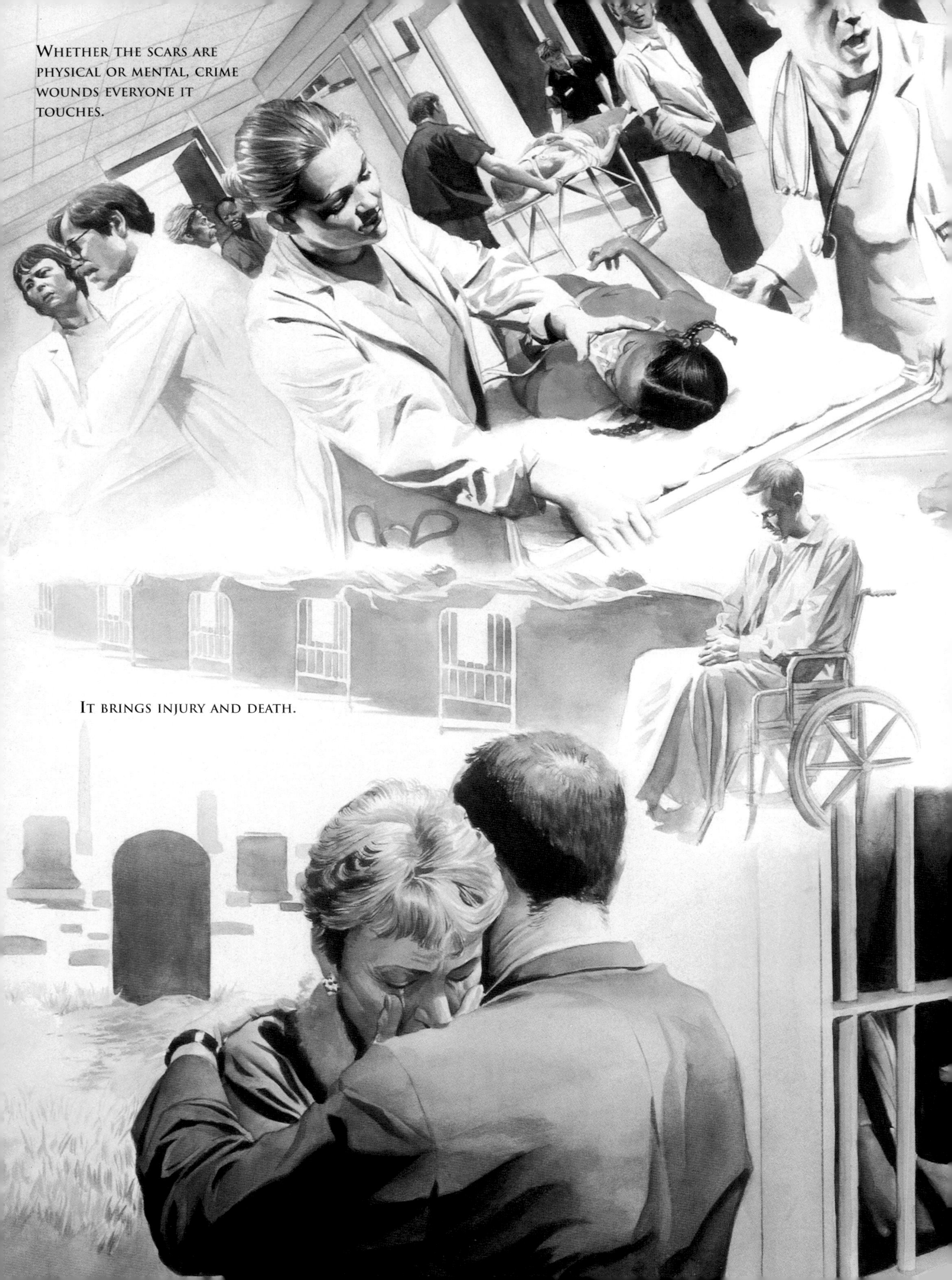
Whether the scars are physical or mental, crime wounds everyone it touches.
It brings injury and death.

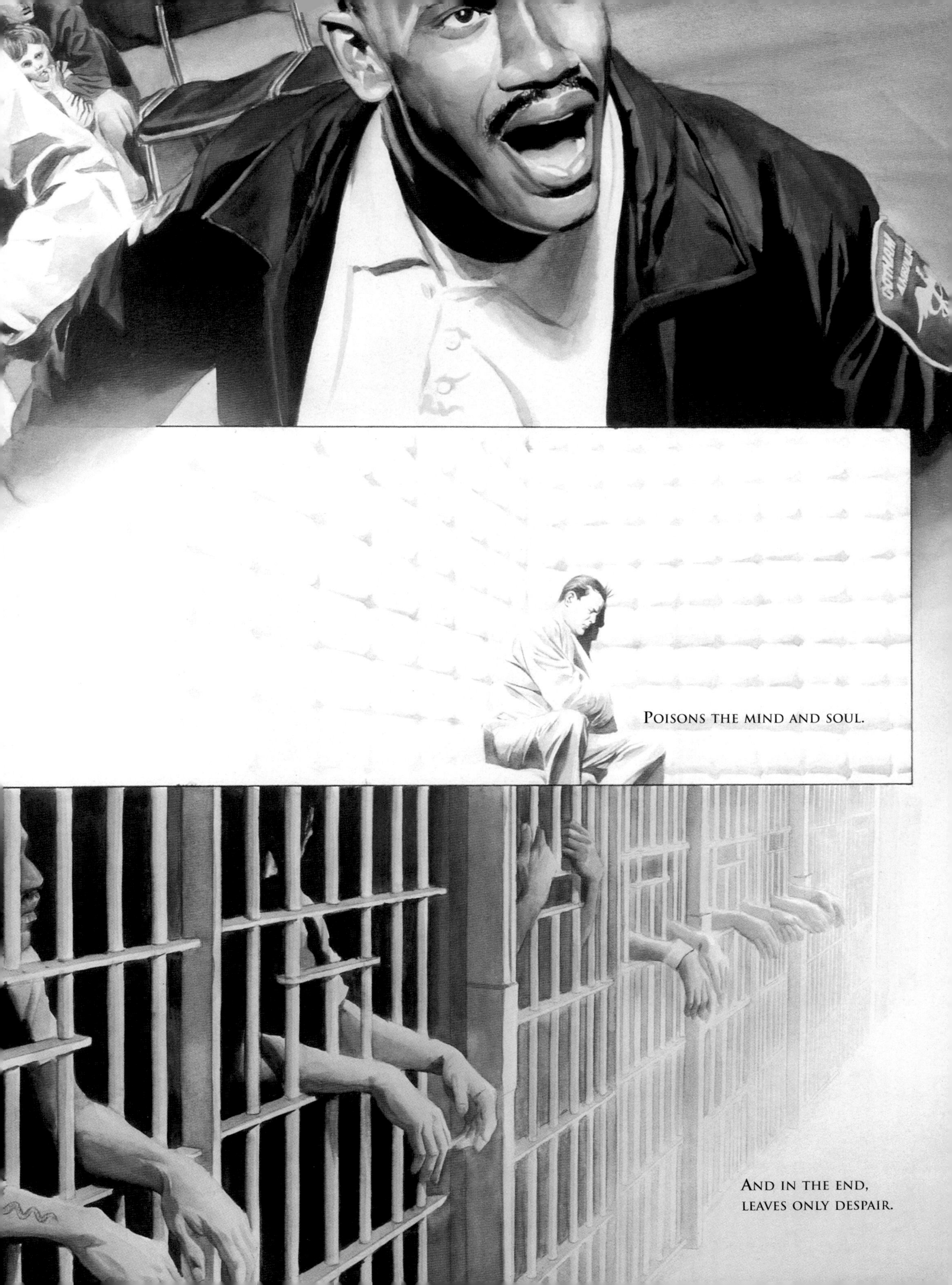
Poisons the mind and soul.
And in the end,
leaves only despair.

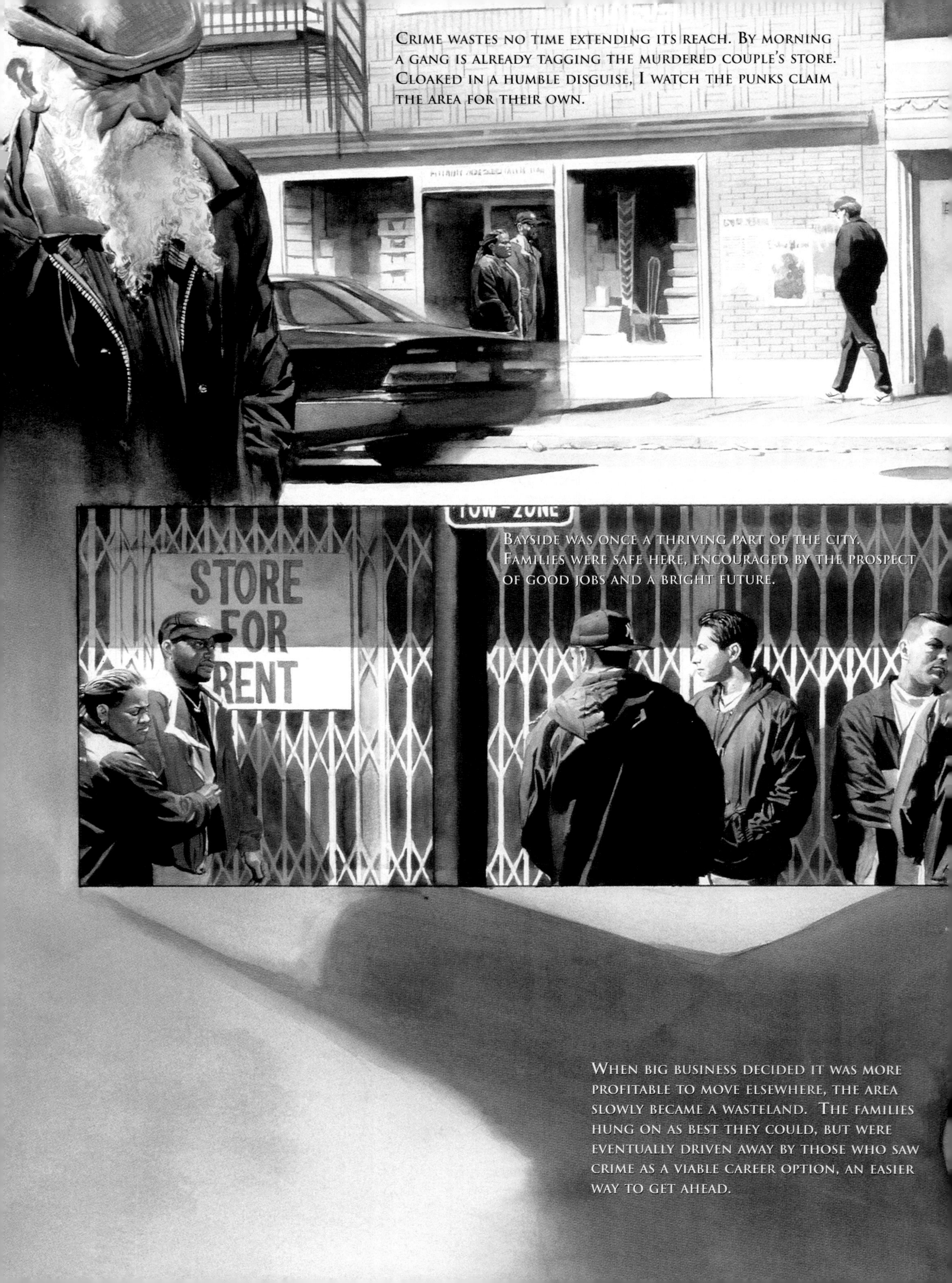

Crime wastes no time extending its reach. By morning a gang is already tagging the murdered couple's store. Cloaked in a humble disguise, I watch the punks claim the area for their own.
TOW-ZONE
STORE FOR RENT
Bayside was once a thriving part of the city. Families were safe here, encouraged by the prospect of good jobs and a bright future.
When big business decided it was more profitable to move elsewhere, the area slowly became a wasteland. The families hung on as best they could, but were eventually driven away by those who saw crime as a viable career option, an easier way to get ahead.

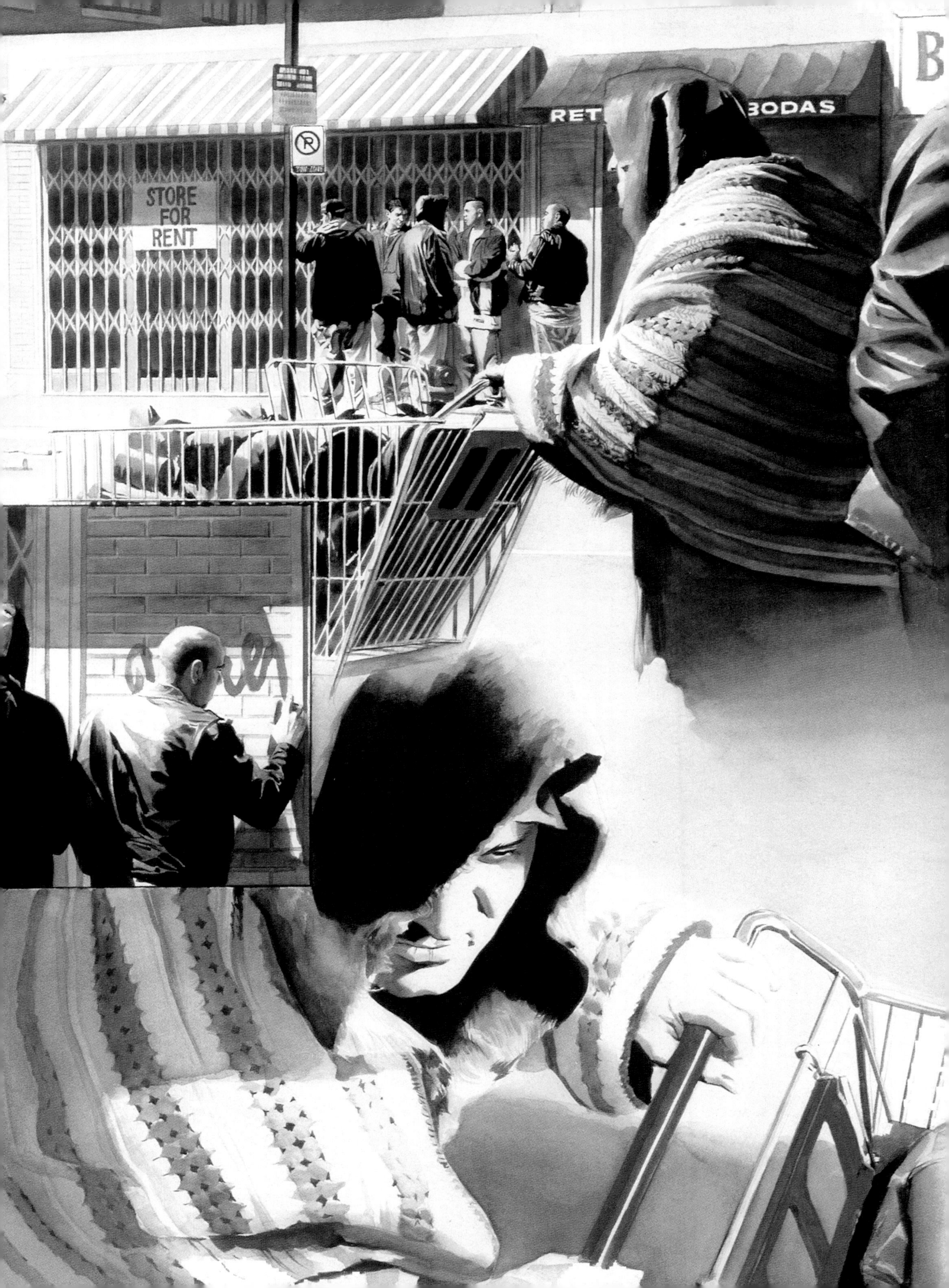

STORE FOR RENT
RET
BODAS
B

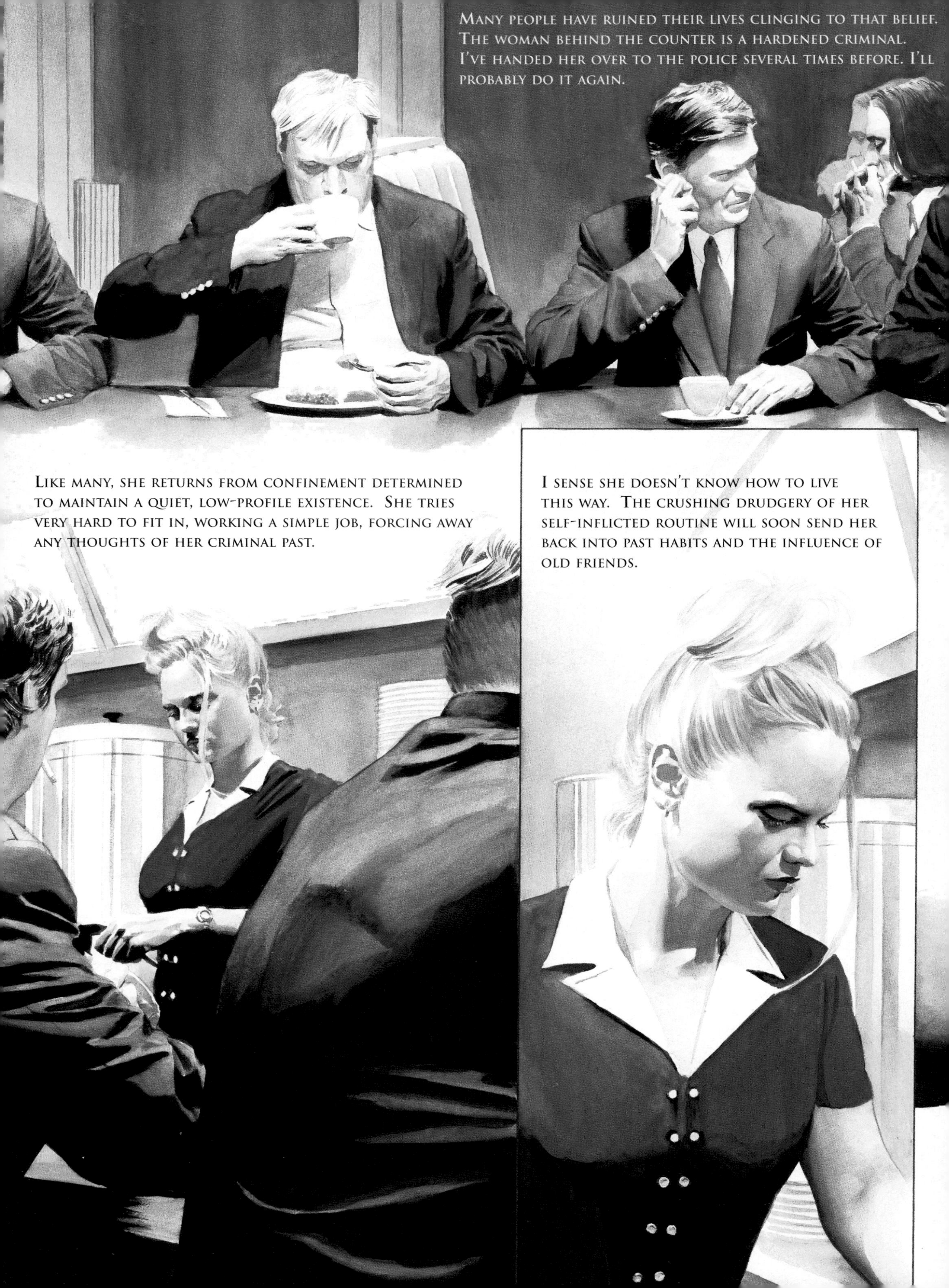
Many people have ruined their lives clinging to that belief. The woman behind the counter is a hardened criminal. I've handed her over to the police several times before. I'll probably do it again.
Like many, she returns from confinement determined to maintain a quiet, low-profile existence. She tries very hard to fit in, working a simple job, forcing away any thoughts of her criminal past.
I sense she doesn't know how to live this way. The crushing drudgery of her self-inflicted routine will soon send her back into past habits and the influence of old friends.

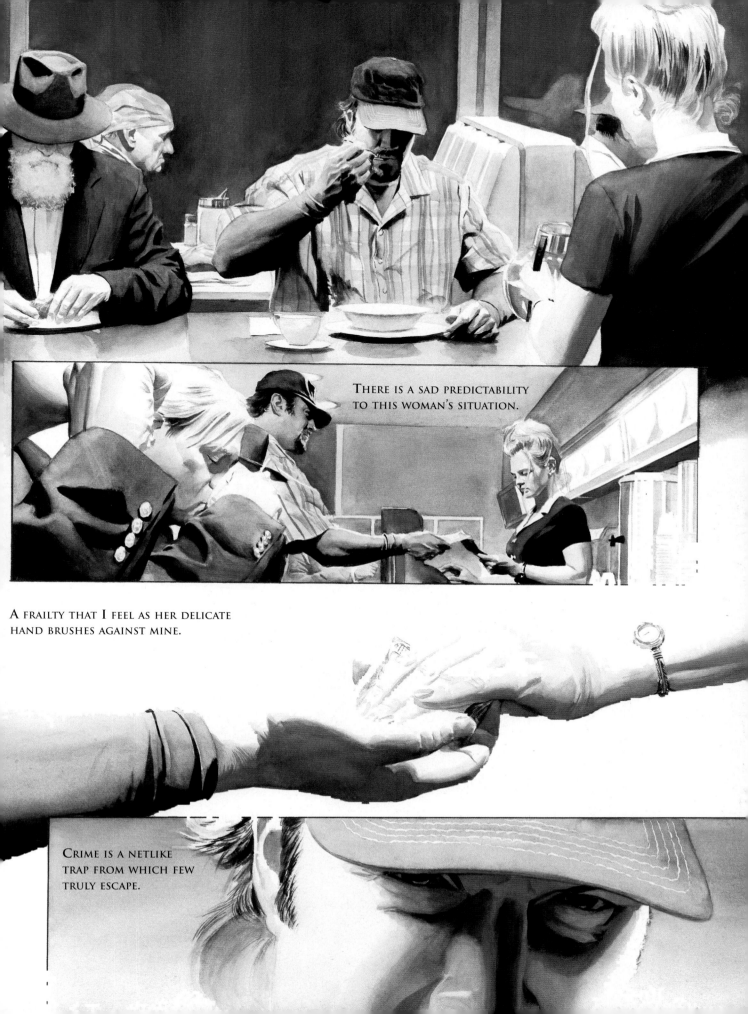

THERE IS A SAD PREDICTABILITY TO THIS WOMAN'S SITUATION.

A FRAILTY THAT I FEEL AS HER DELICATE HAND BRUSHES AGAINST MINE.

CRIME IS A NETLIKE TRAP FROM WHICH FEW TRULY ESCAPE.

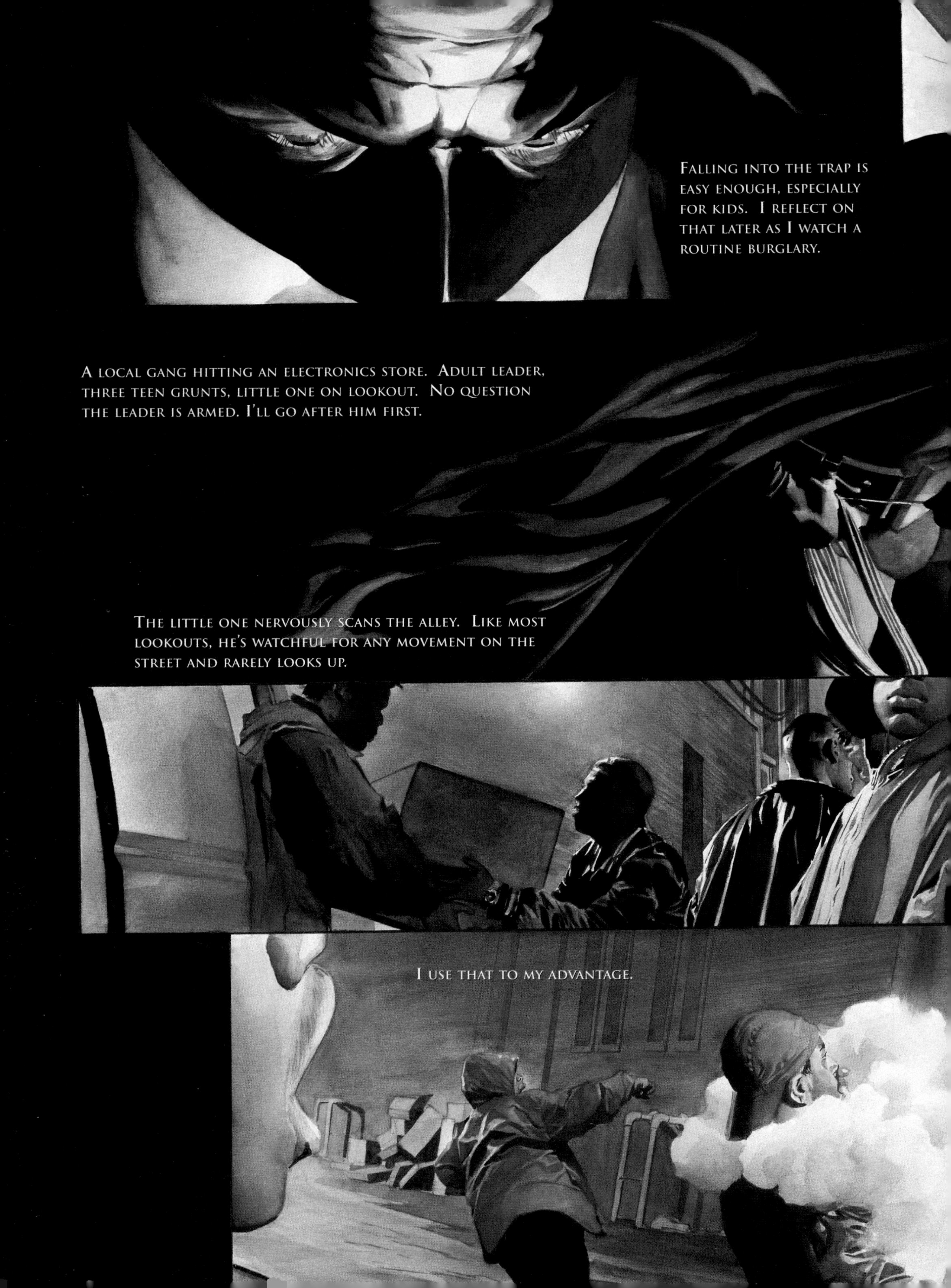
Falling into the trap is easy enough, especially for kids. I reflect on that later as I watch a routine burglary.
A local gang hitting an electronics store. Adult leader, three teen grunts, little one on lookout. No question the leader is armed. I'll go after him first.
The little one nervously scans the alley. Like most lookouts, he's watchful for any movement on the street and rarely looks up.
I use that to my advantage.

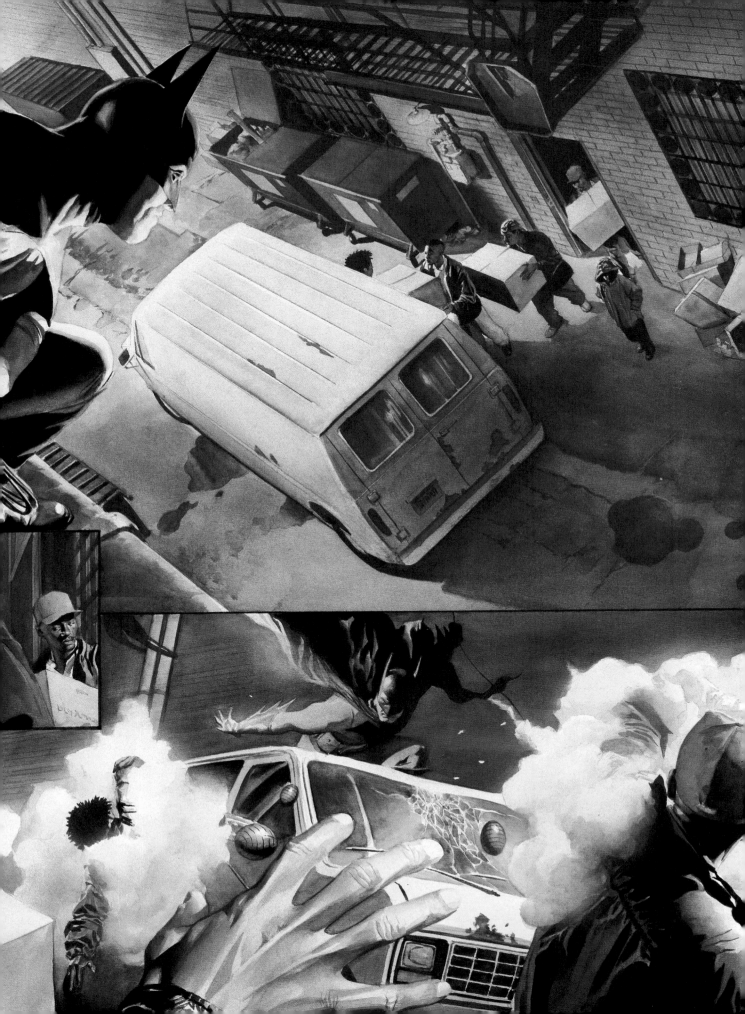

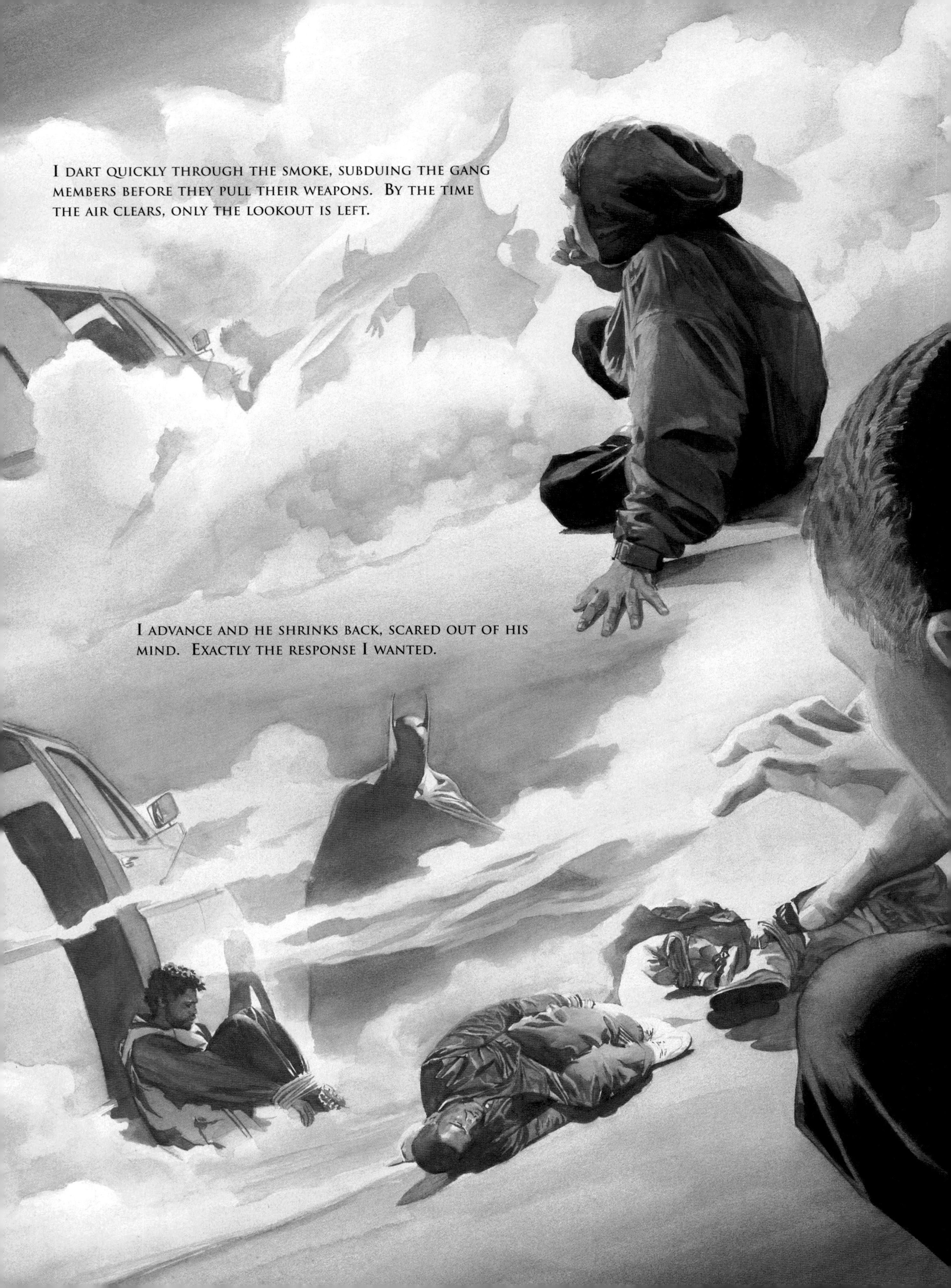
I DART QUICKLY THROUGH THE SMOKE, SUBDUING THE GANG MEMBERS BEFORE THEY PULL THEIR WEAPONS. BY THE TIME THE AIR CLEARS, ONLY THE LOOKOUT IS LEFT.
I ADVANCE AND HE SHRINKS BACK, SCARED OUT OF HIS MIND. EXACTLY THE RESPONSE I WANTED.

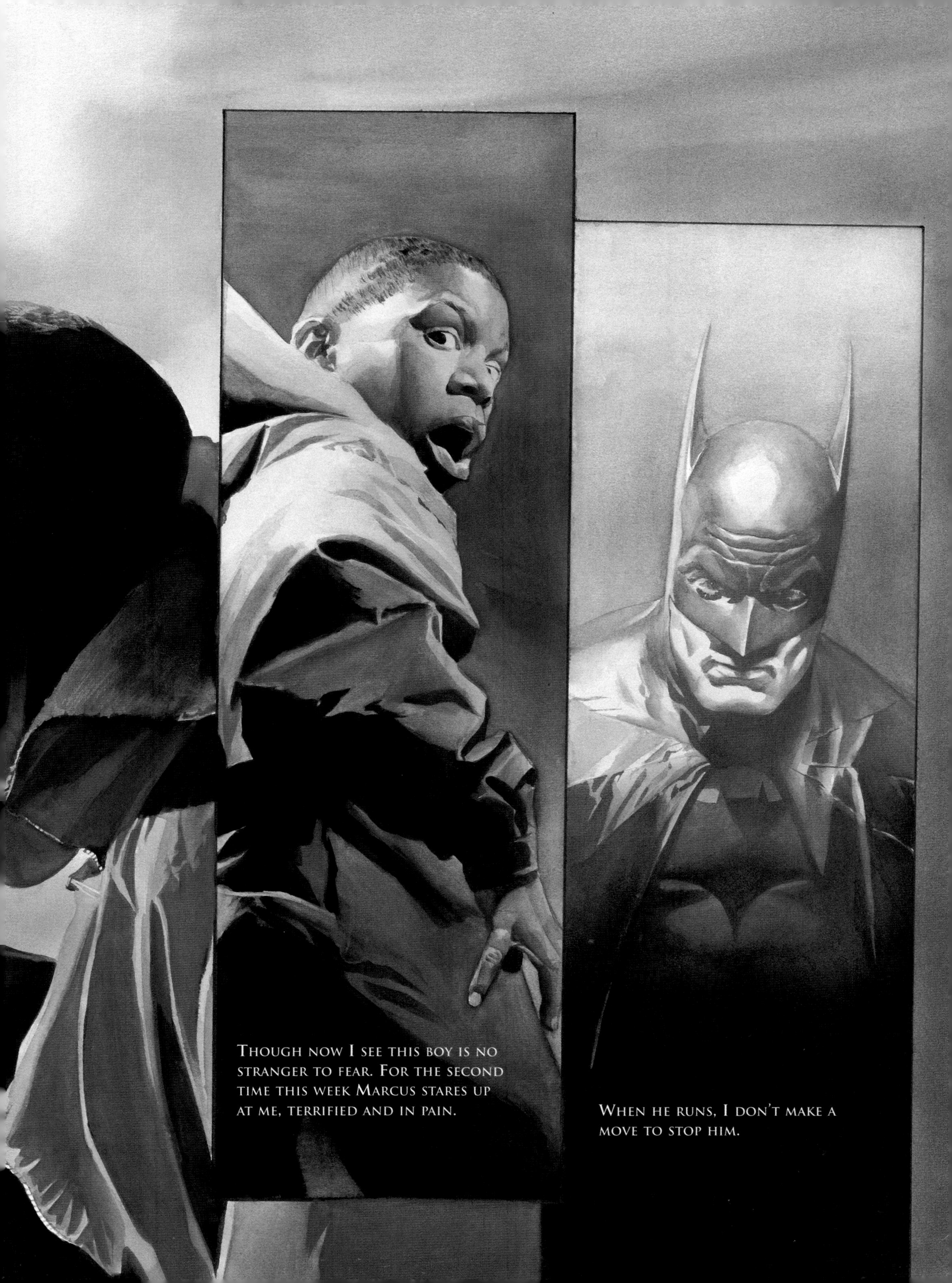
Though now I see this boy is no stranger to fear. For the second time this week Marcus stares up at me, terrified and in pain.
When he runs, I don't make a move to stop him.

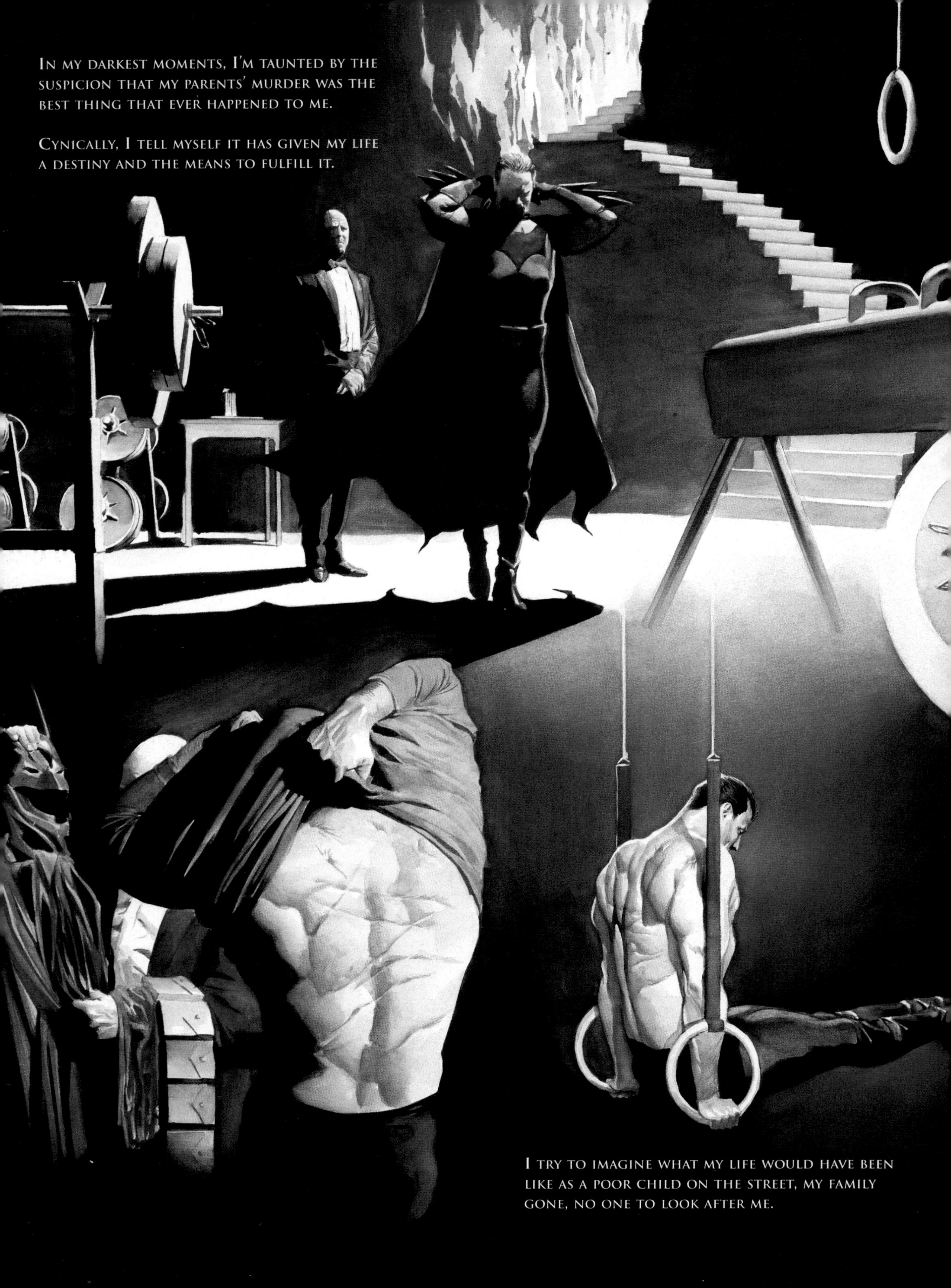
In my darkest moments, I'm taunted by the suspicion that my parents' murder was the best thing that ever happened to me.
Cynically, I tell myself it has given my life a destiny and the means to fulfill it.
I try to imagine what my life would have been like as a poor child on the street, my family gone, no one to look after me.

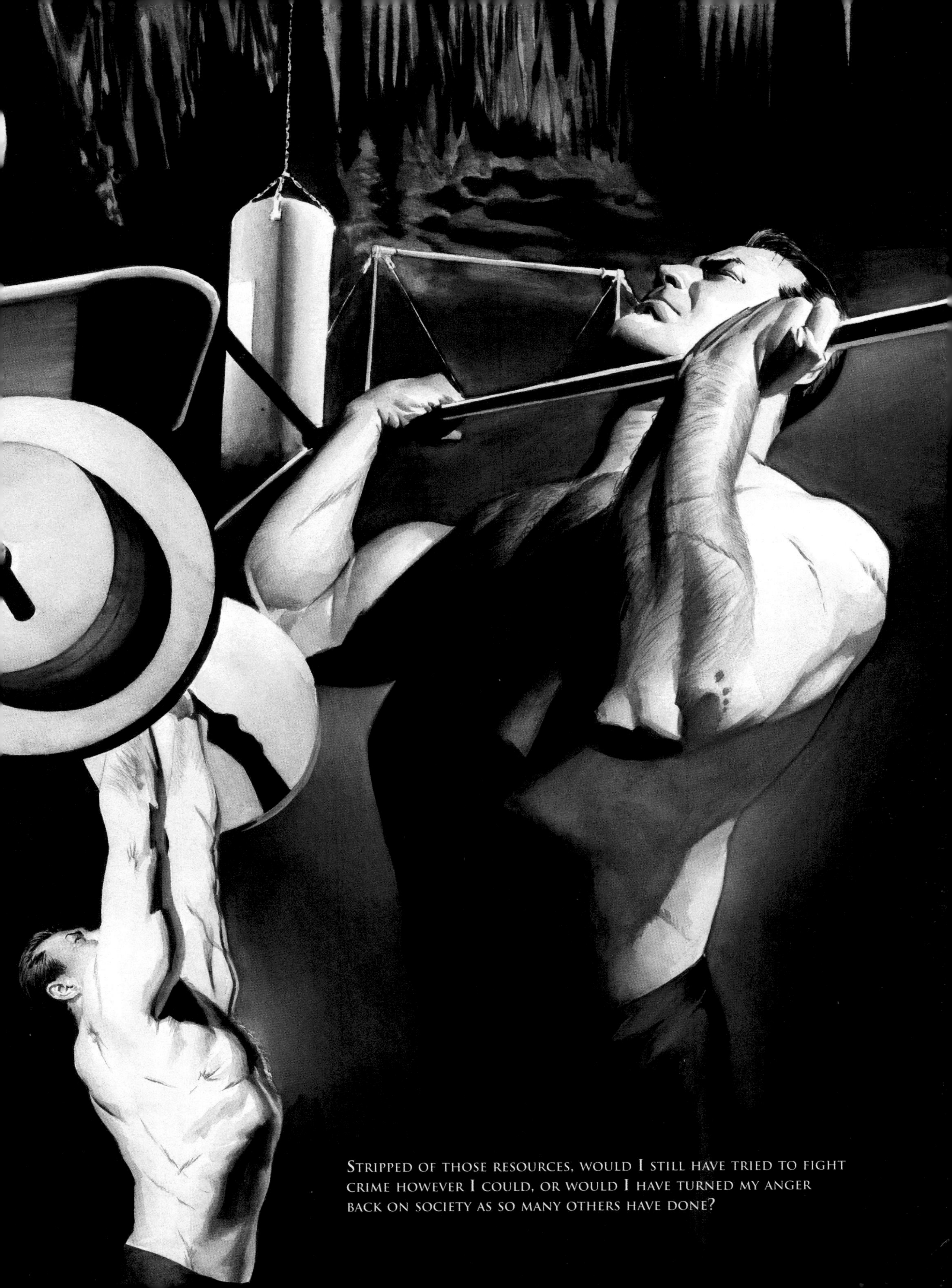
Stripped of those resources, would I still have tried to fight crime however I could, or would I have turned my anger back on society as so many others have done?

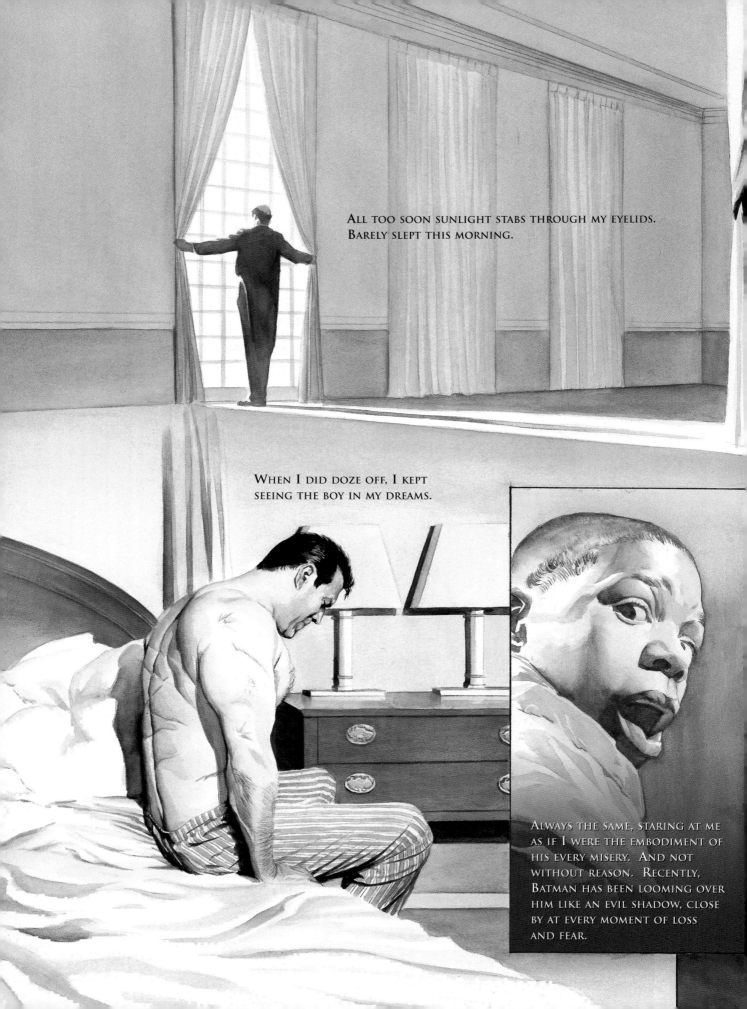

ALL TOO SOON SUNLIGHT STABS THROUGH MY EYELIDS. BARELY SLEPT THIS MORNING.

WHEN I DID DOZE OFF, I KEPT SEEING THE BOY IN MY DREAMS.

ALWAYS THE SAME, STARING AT ME AS IF I WERE THE EMBODIMENT OF HIS EVERY MISERY. AND NOT WITHOUT REASON. RECENTLY, BATMAN HAS BEEN LOOMING OVER HIM LIKE AN EVIL SHADOW, CLOSE BY AT EVERY MOMENT OF LOSS AND FEAR.

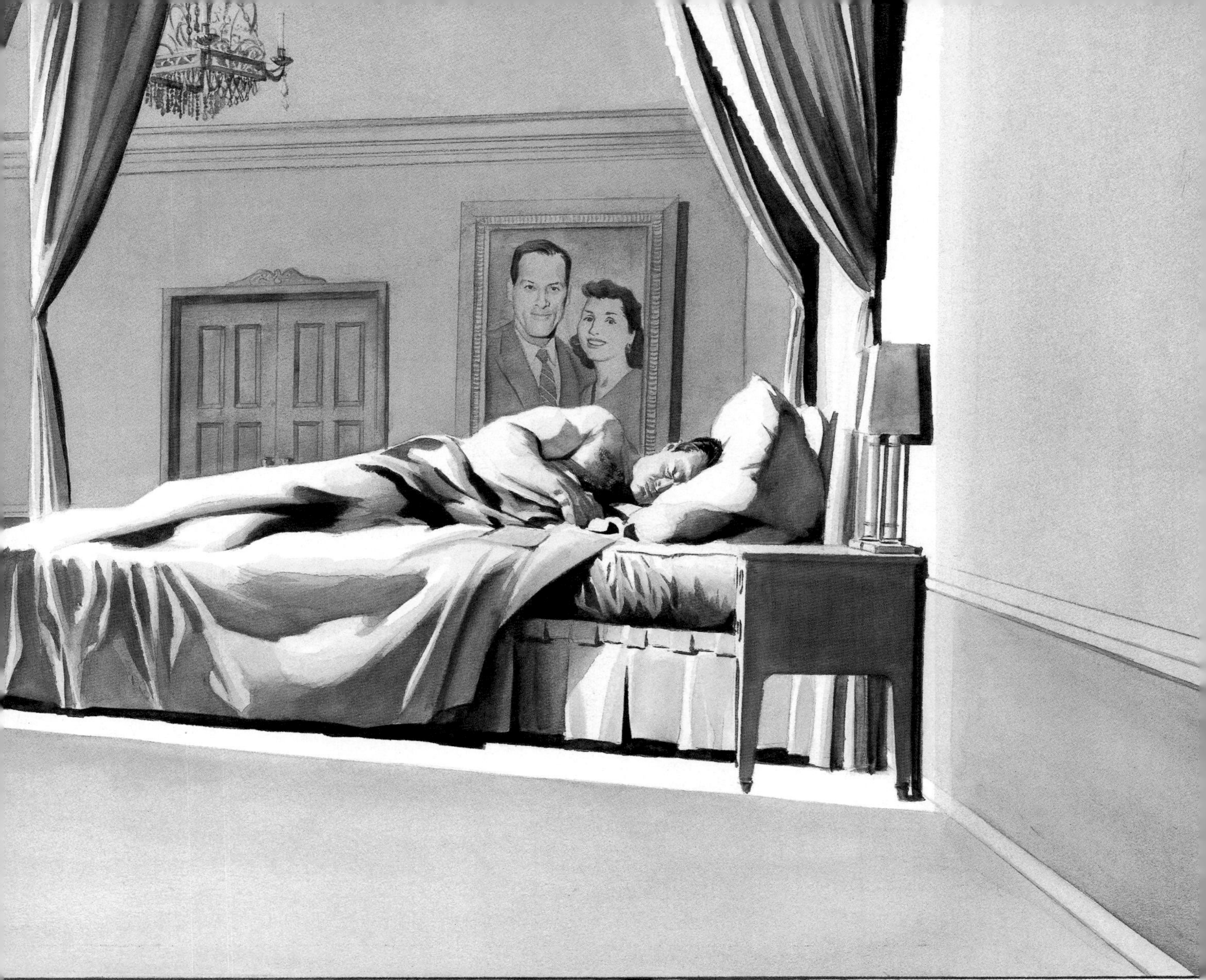

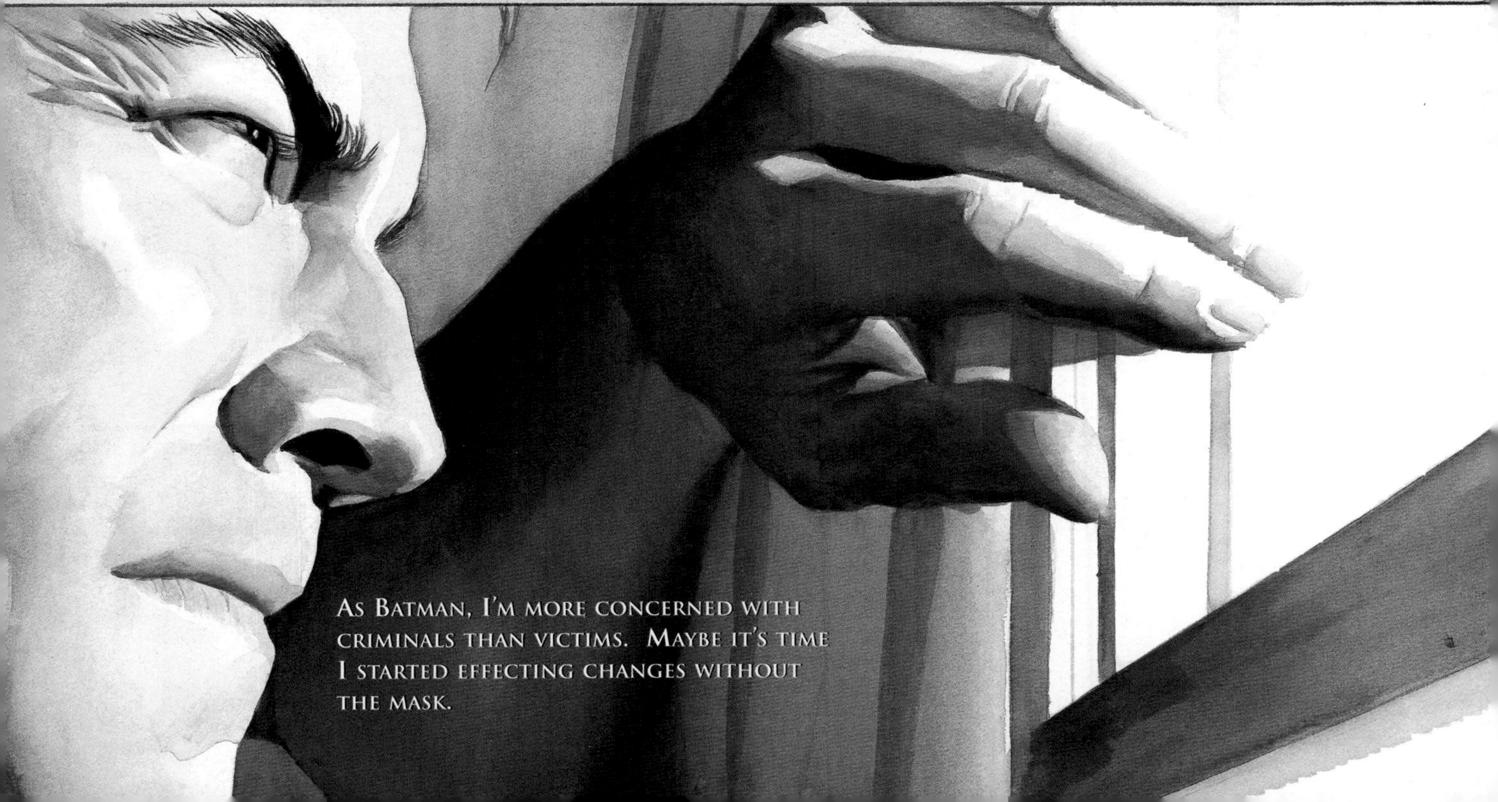
As Batman, I'm more concerned with criminals than victims. Maybe it's time I started effecting changes without the mask.

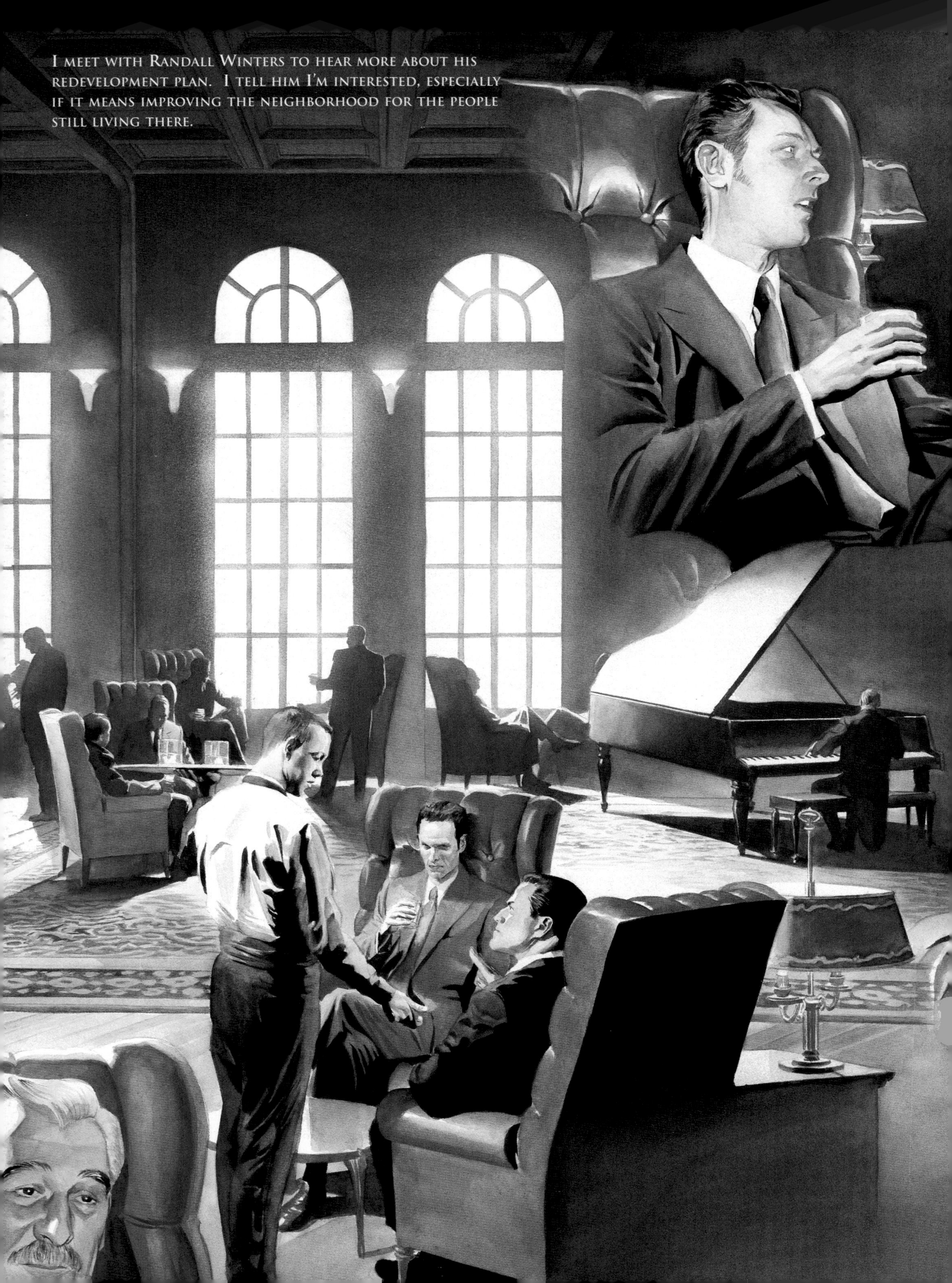
I meet with Randall Winters to hear more about his redevelopment plan. I tell him I'm interested, especially if it means improving the neighborhood for the people still living there.

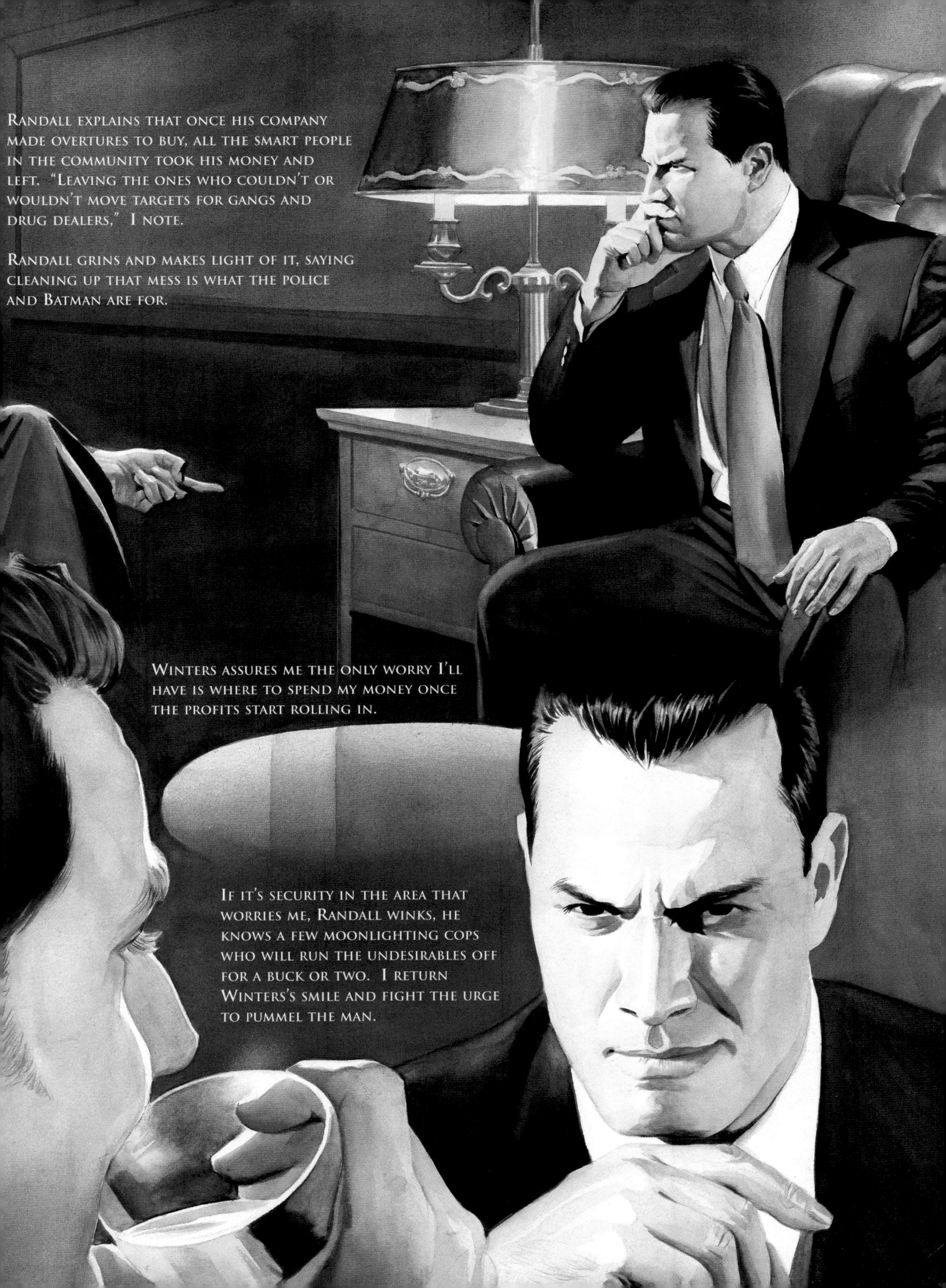
Randall explains that once his company made overtures to buy, all the smart people in the community took his money and left. "Leaving the ones who couldn't or wouldn't move targets for gangs and drug dealers," I note.
Randall grins and makes light of it, saying cleaning up that mess is what the police and Batman are for.
Winters assures me the only worry I'll have is where to spend my money once the profits start rolling in.
If it's security in the area that worries me, Randall winks, he knows a few moonlighting cops who will run the undesirables off for a buck or two. I return Winters's smile and fight the urge to pummel the man.

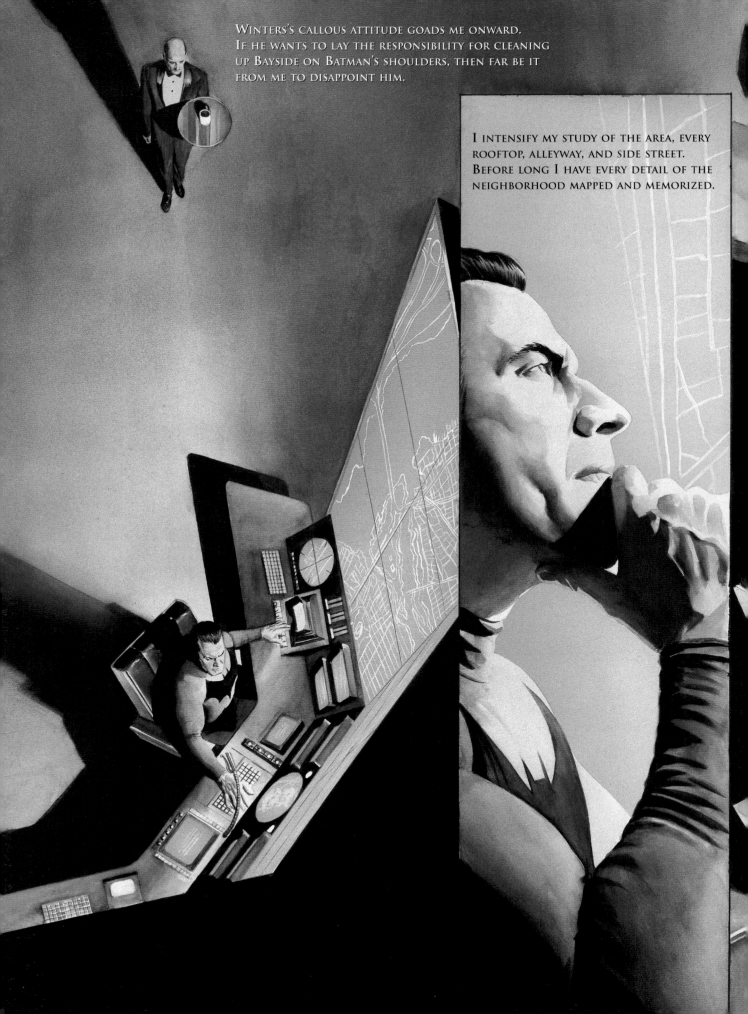

WINTERS'S CALLOUS ATTITUDE GOADS ME ONWARD. IF HE WANTS TO LAY THE RESPONSIBILITY FOR CLEANING UP BAYSIDE ON BATMAN'S SHOULDERS, THEN FAR BE IT FROM ME TO DISAPPOINT HIM.

I INTENSIFY MY STUDY OF THE AREA, EVERY ROOFTOP, ALLEYWAY, AND SIDE STREET. BEFORE LONG I HAVE EVERY DETAIL OF THE NEIGHBORHOOD MAPPED AND MEMORIZED.

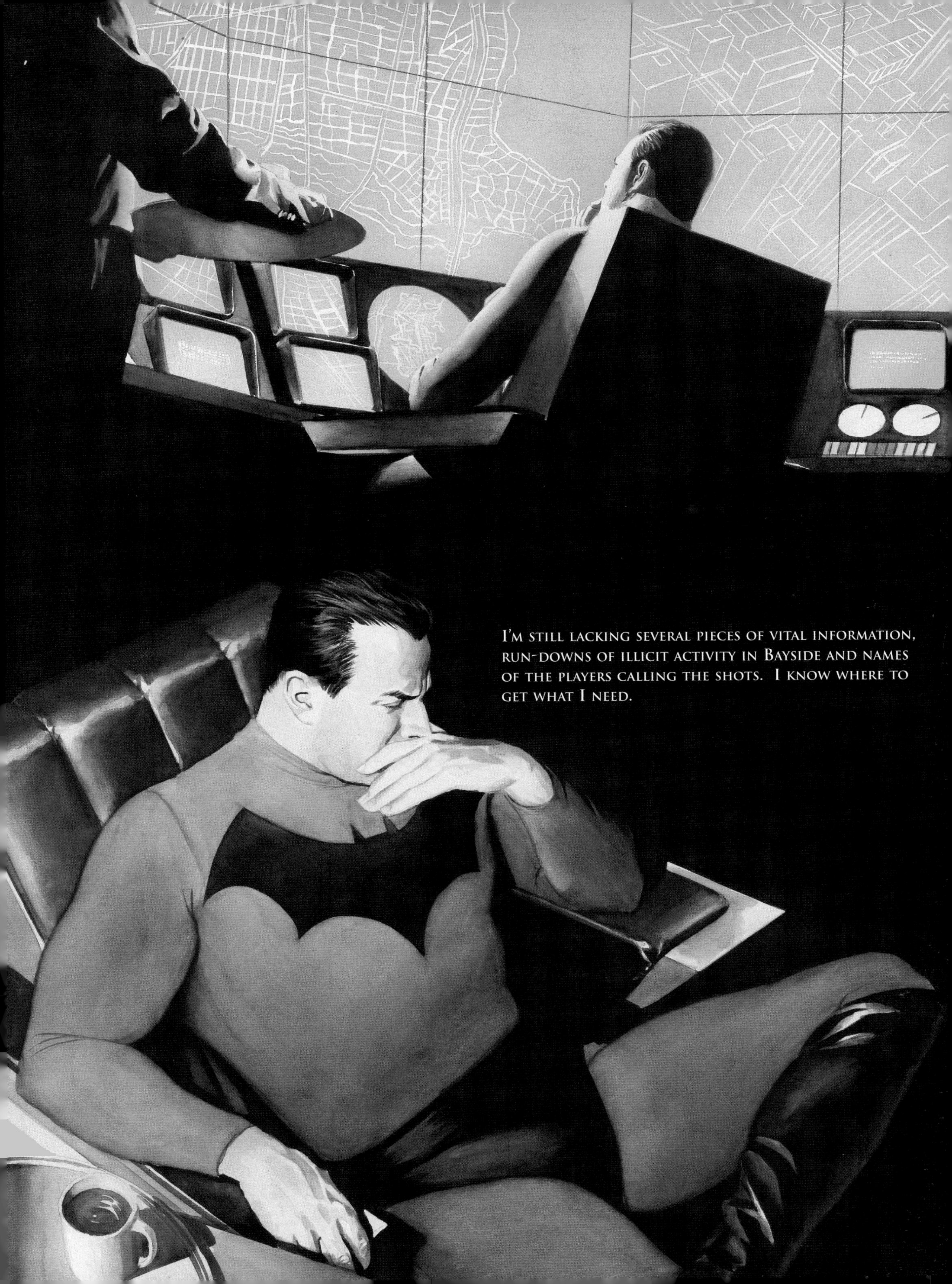
I'm still lacking several pieces of vital information, run-downs of illicit activity in Bayside and names of the players calling the shots. I know where to get what I need.

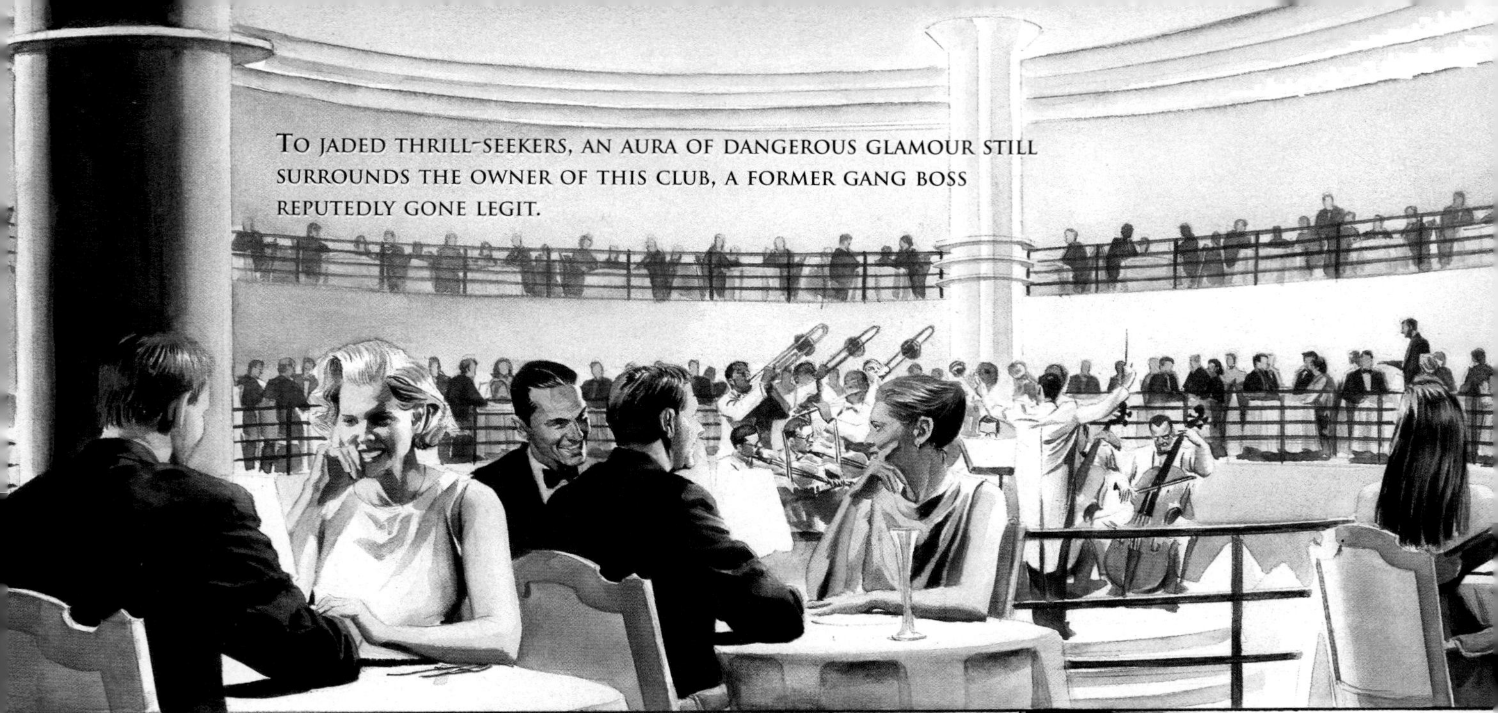
To jaded thrill-seekers, an aura of dangerous glamour still surrounds the owner of this club, a former gang boss reputedly gone legit.

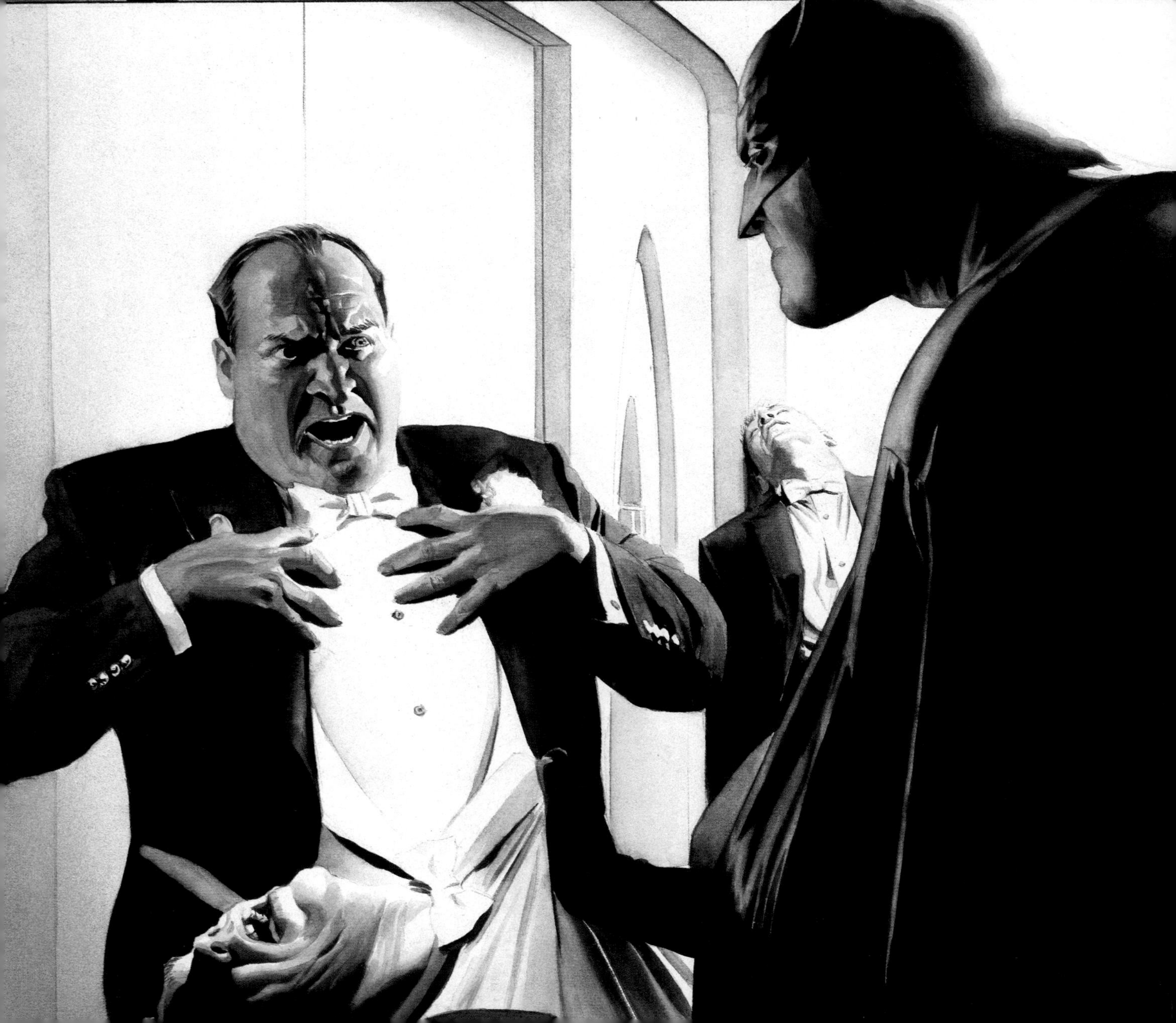

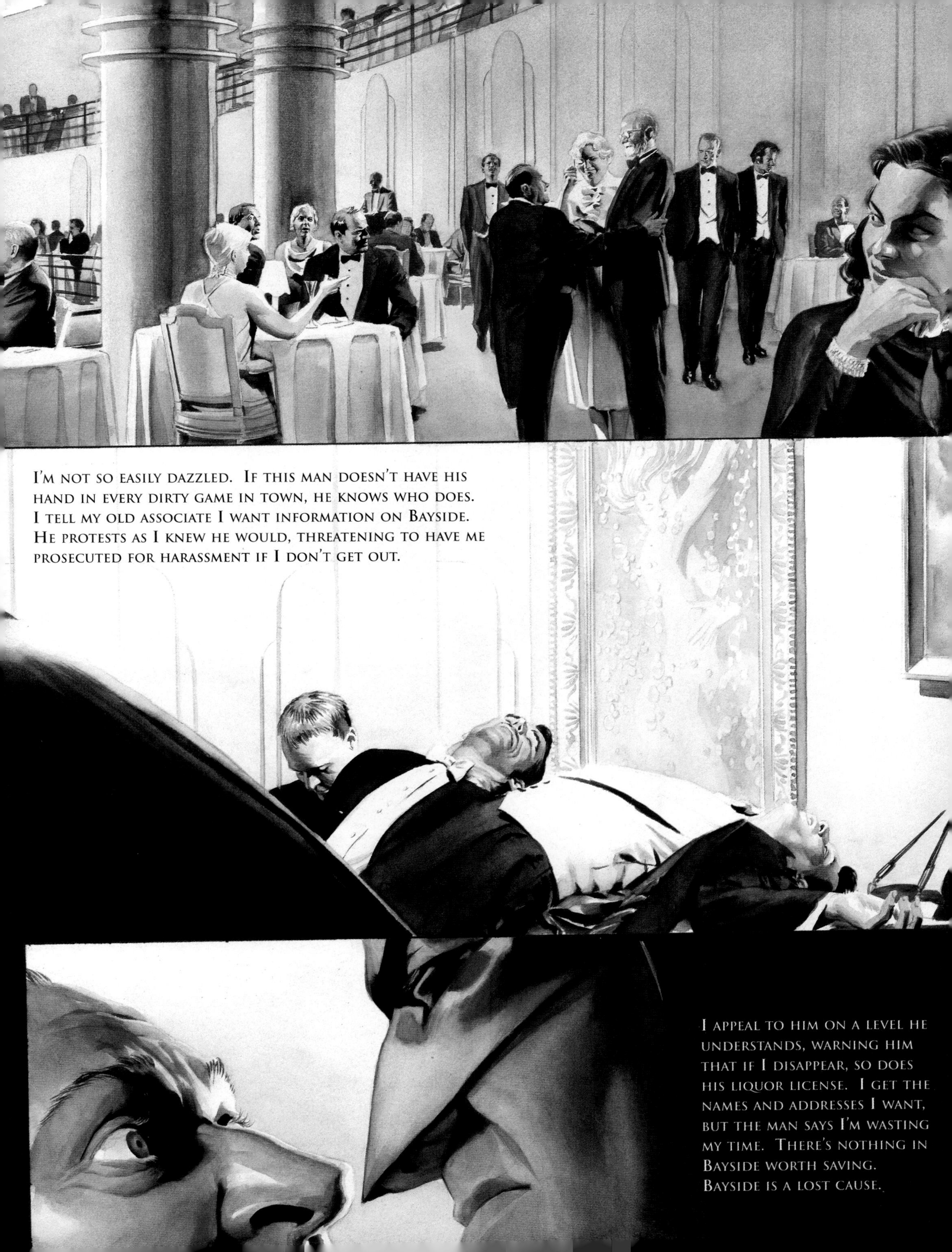
I'm not so easily dazzled. If this man doesn't have his hand in every dirty game in town, he knows who does. I tell my old associate I want information on Bayside. He protests as I knew he would, threatening to have me prosecuted for harassment if I don't get out.
I appeal to him on a level he understands, warning him that if I disappear, so does his liquor license. I get the names and addresses I want, but the man says I'm wasting my time. There's nothing in Bayside worth saving. Bayside is a lost cause.

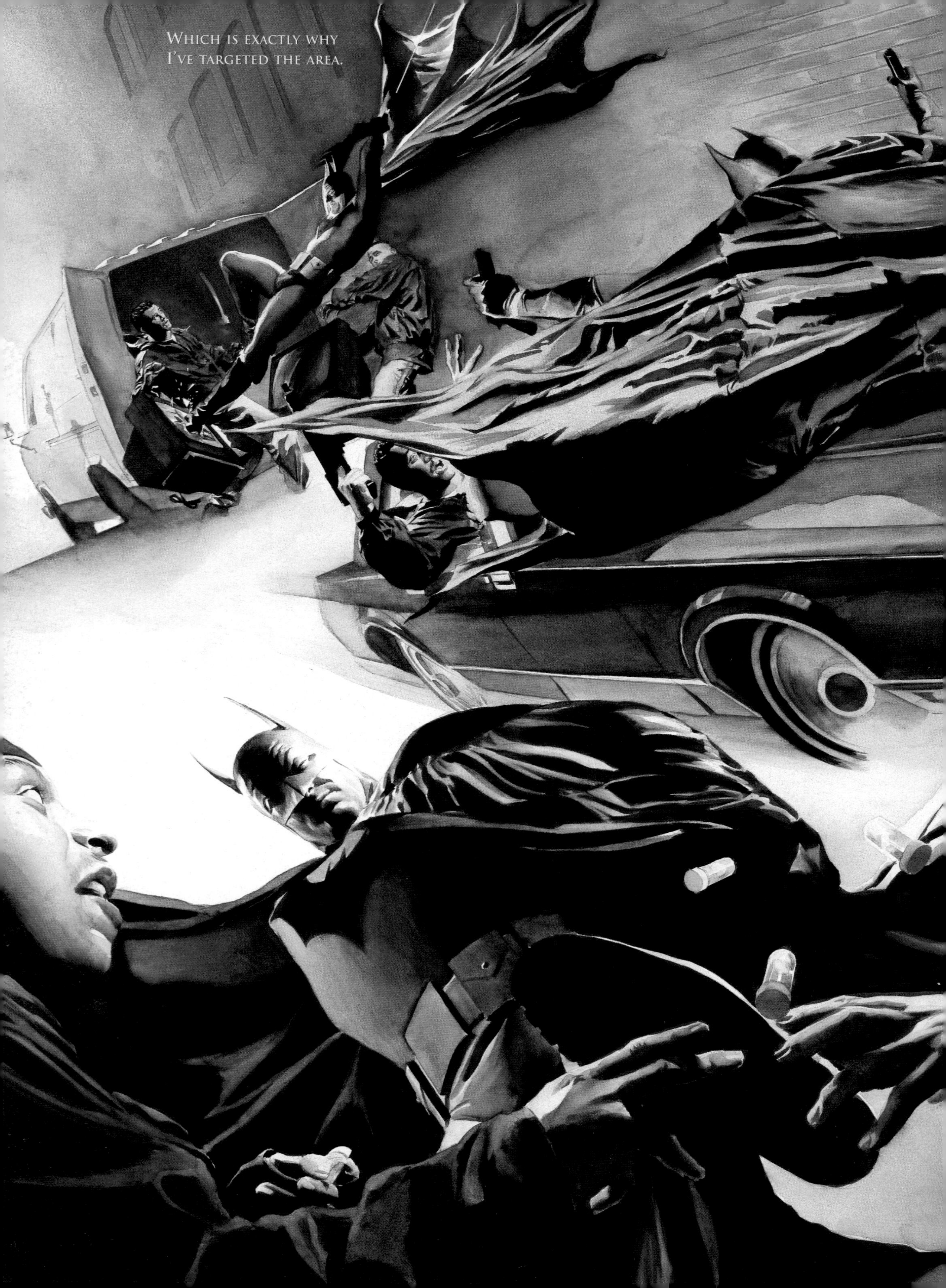
Which is exactly why I've targeted the area.

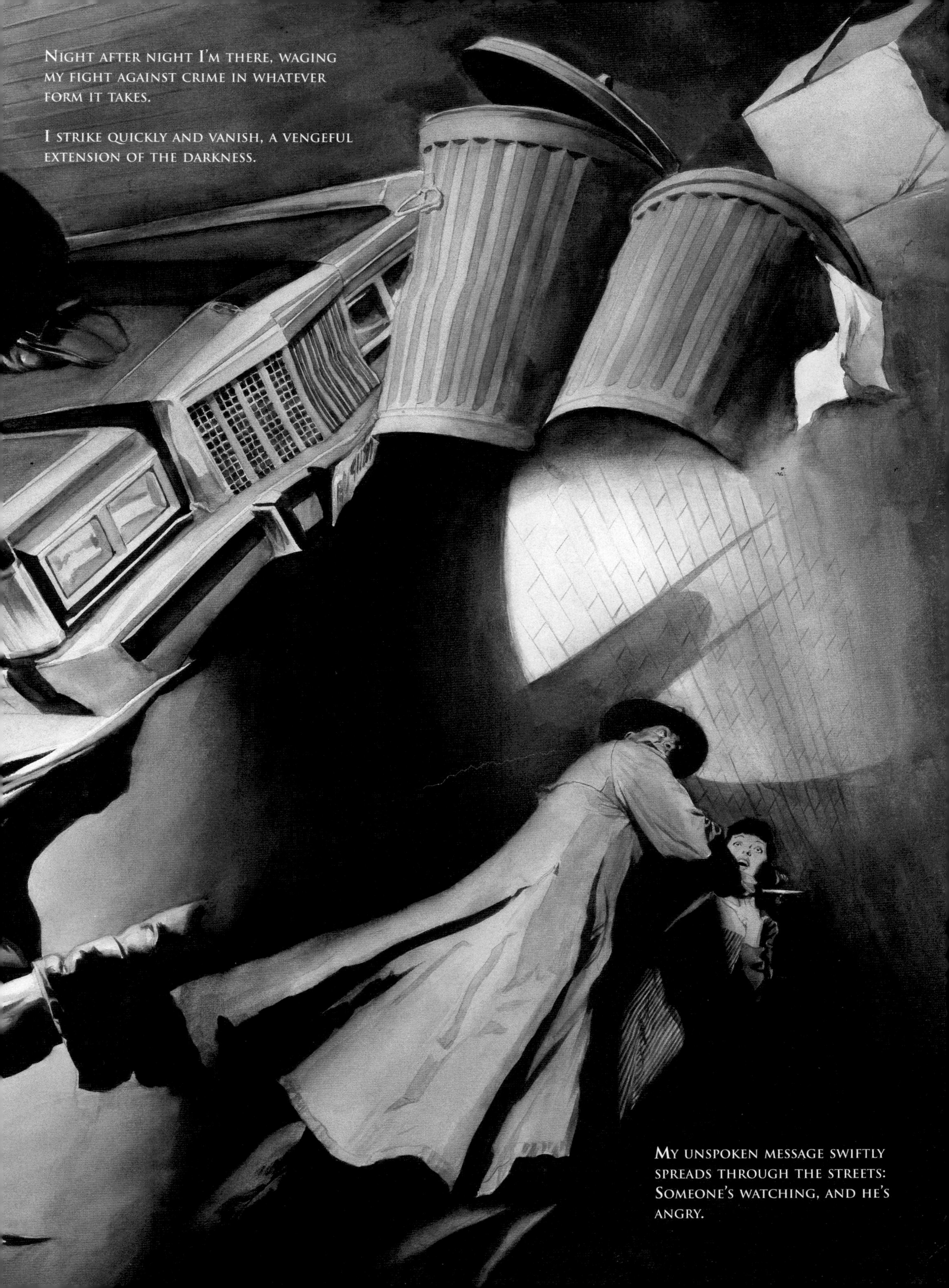
Night after night I'm there, waging my fight against crime in whatever form it takes.
I strike quickly and vanish, a vengeful extension of the darkness.
My unspoken message swiftly spreads through the streets: Someone's watching, and he's angry.

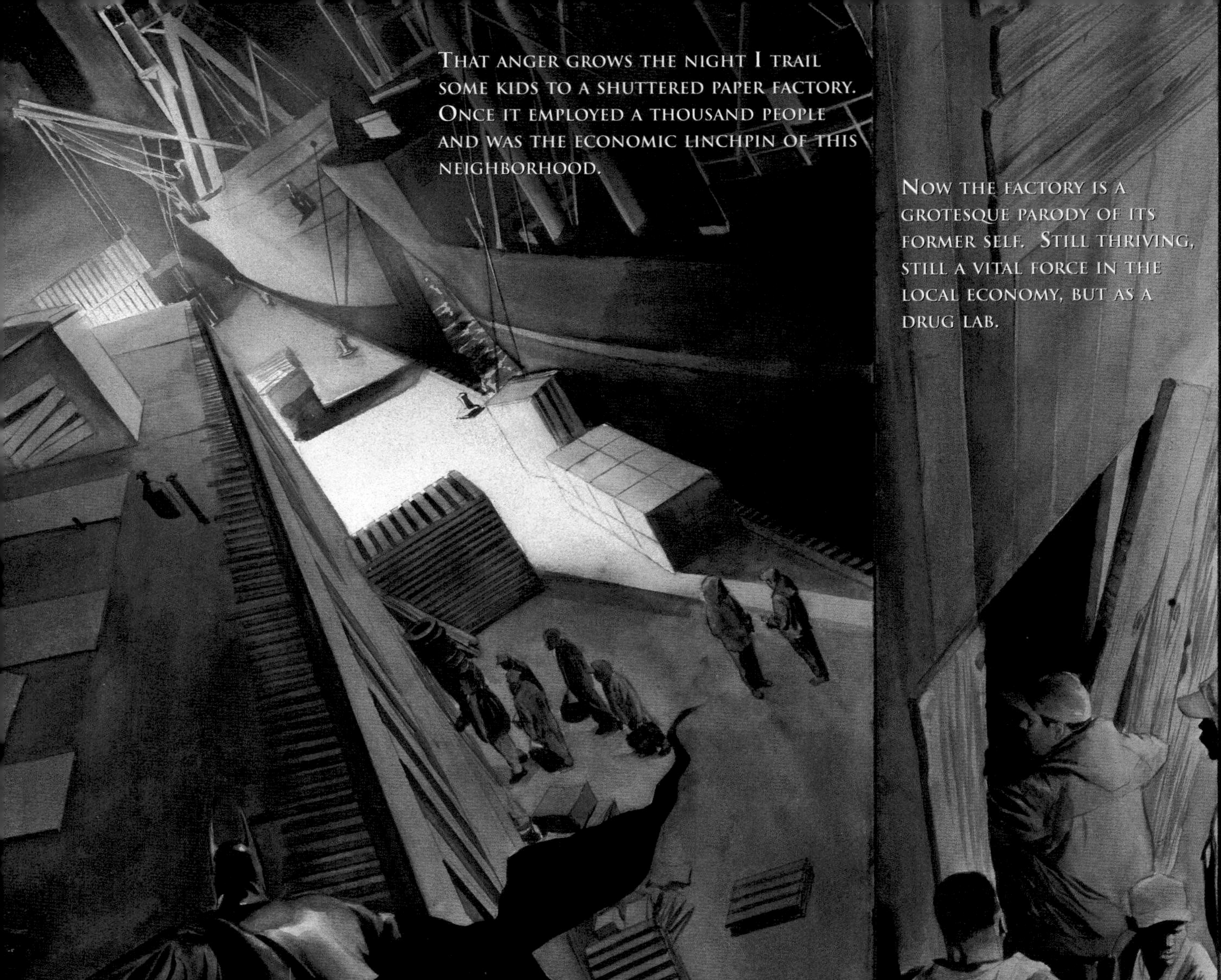
THAT ANGER GROWS THE NIGHT I TRAIL SOME KIDS TO A SHUTTERED PAPER FACTORY. ONCE IT EMPLOYED A THOUSAND PEOPLE AND WAS THE ECONOMIC LINCHPIN OF THIS NEIGHBORHOOD.
NOW THE FACTORY IS A GROTESQUE PARODY OF ITS FORMER SELF. STILL THRIVING, STILL A VITAL FORCE IN THE LOCAL ECONOMY, BUT AS A DRUG LAB.

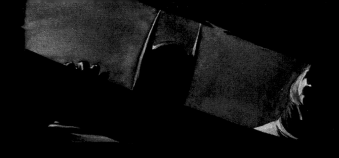

THE LOCAL GANGS HAVE PUT THE NEIGHBORHOOD BACK TO WORK. AND WHY WOULDN'T KIDS FLOCK HERE? IN THIS PART OF TOWN, IT'S THE ONLY PROMISE OF MONEY AND PROTECTION.

BUT IT'S ALL AN ILLUSION.
THERE IS NO SAFETY HERE.

LEAST OF ALL FROM ME.

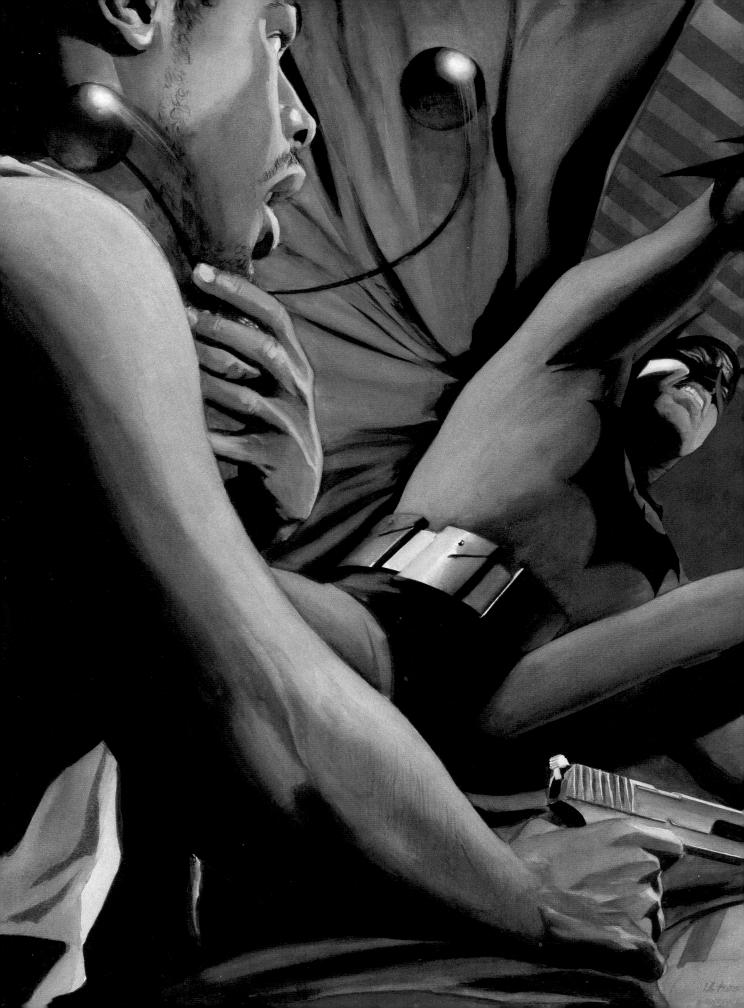

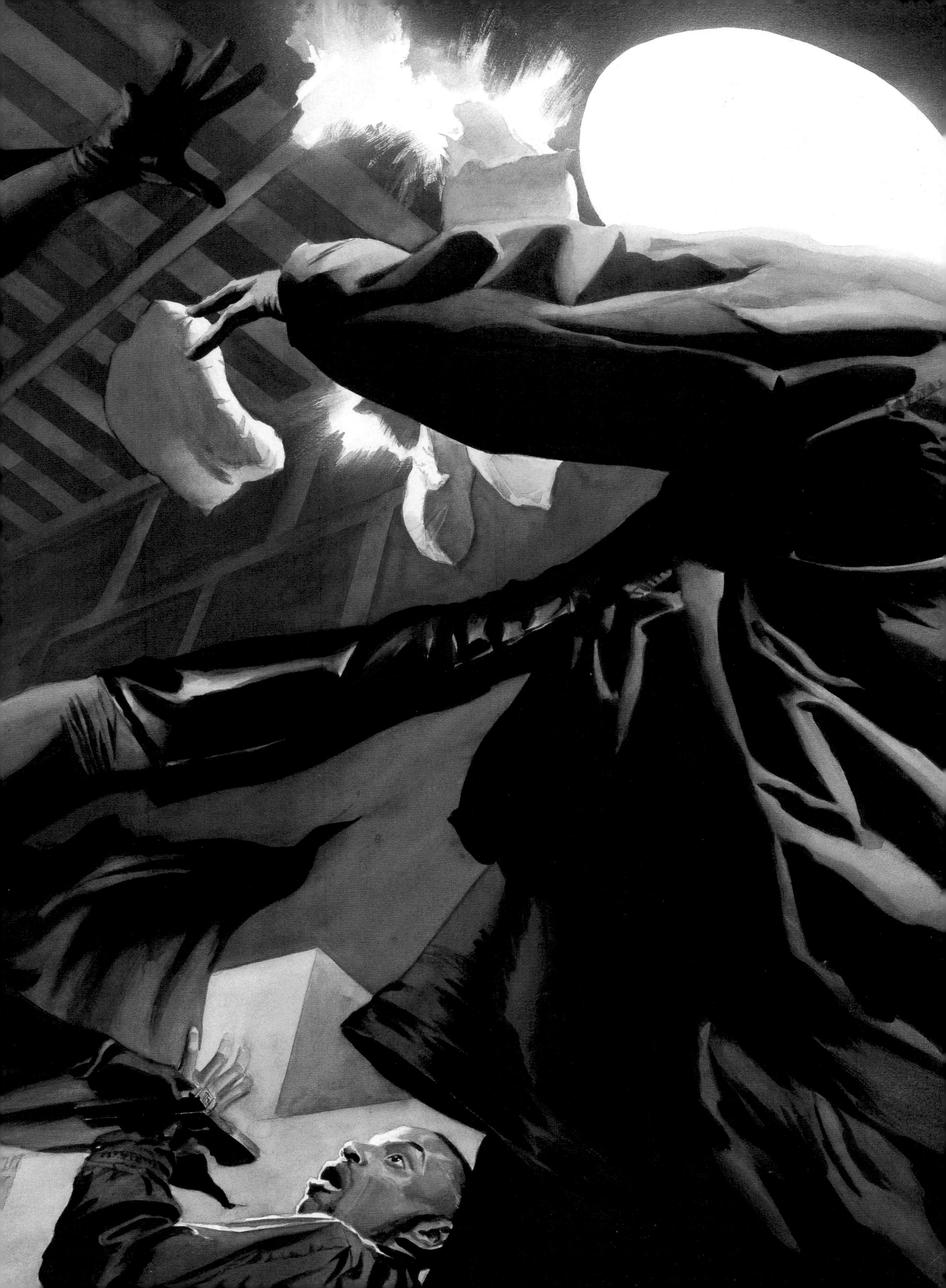

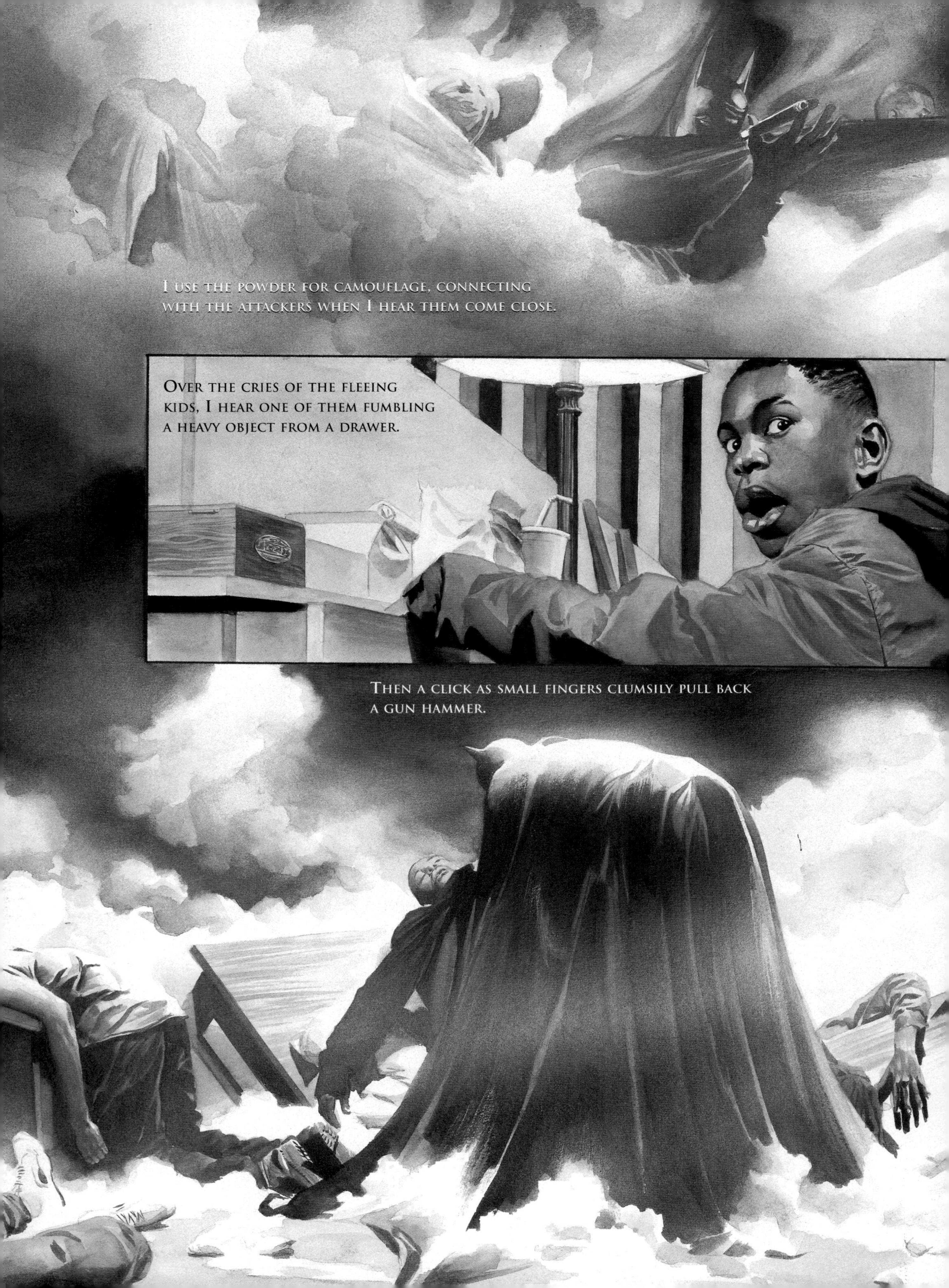
I use the powder for camouflage, connecting with the attackers when I hear them come close.
Over the cries of the fleeing kids, I hear one of them fumbling a heavy object from a drawer.
Then a click as small fingers clumsily pull back a gun hammer.

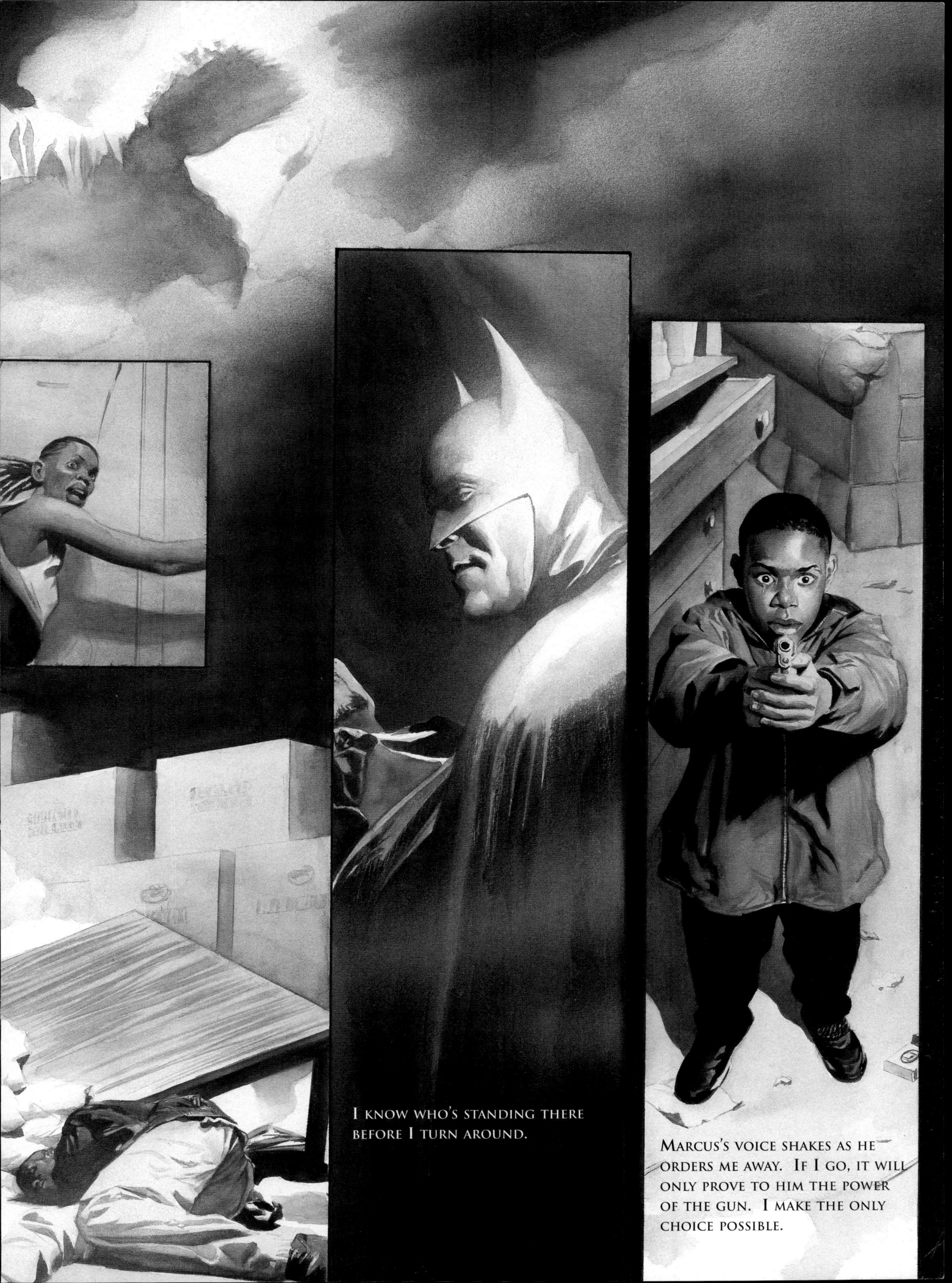
I KNOW WHO'S STANDING THERE BEFORE I TURN AROUND.
MARCUS'S VOICE SHAKES AS HE ORDERS ME AWAY. IF I GO, IT WILL ONLY PROVE TO HIM THE POWER OF THE GUN. I MAKE THE ONLY CHOICE POSSIBLE.

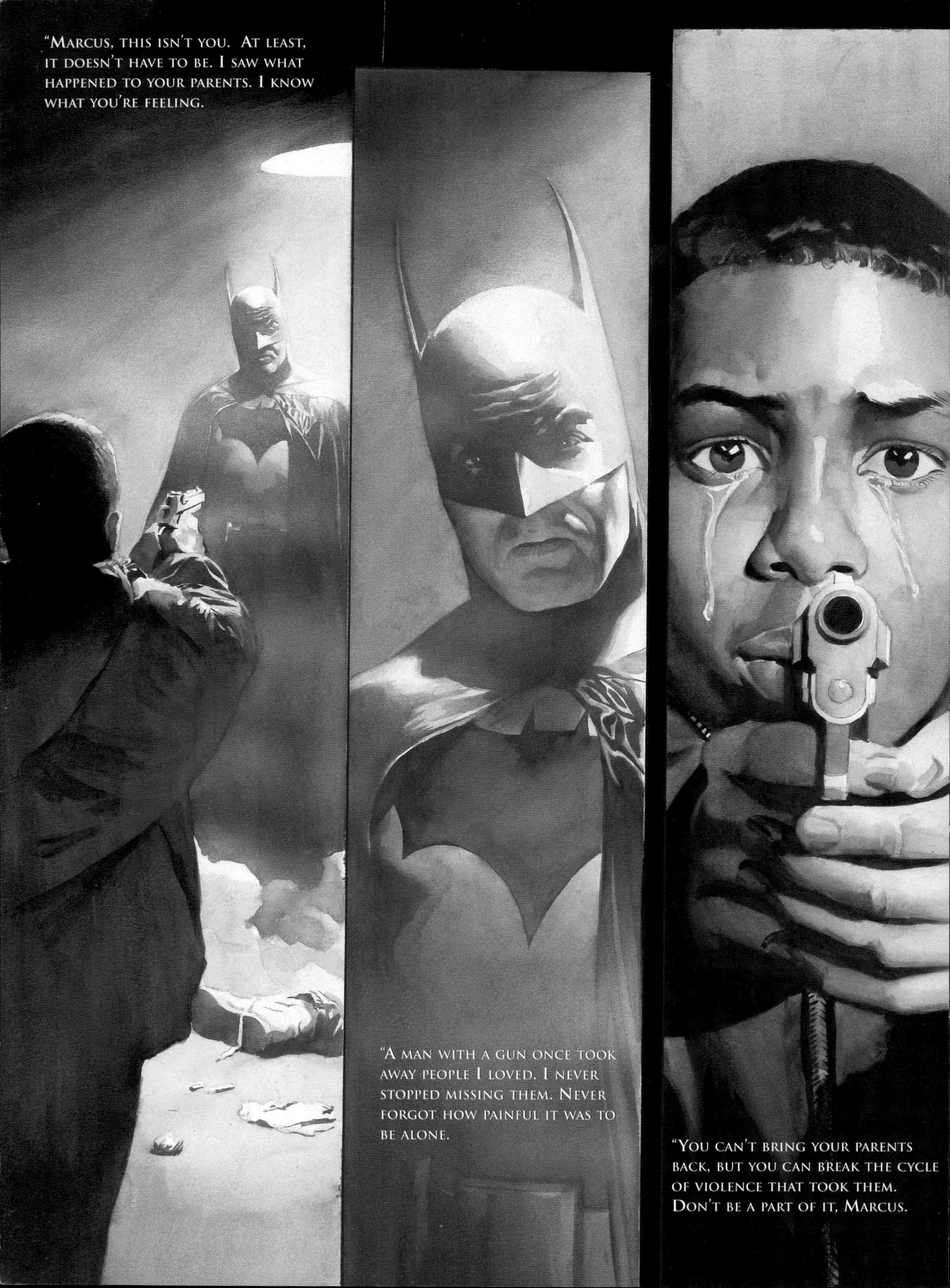
"Marcus, this isn't you. At least, it doesn't have to be. I saw what happened to your parents. I know what you're feeling.
"A man with a gun once took away people I loved. I never stopped missing them. Never forgot how painful it was to be alone.
"You can't bring your parents back, but you can break the cycle of violence that took them. Don't be a part of it, Marcus.

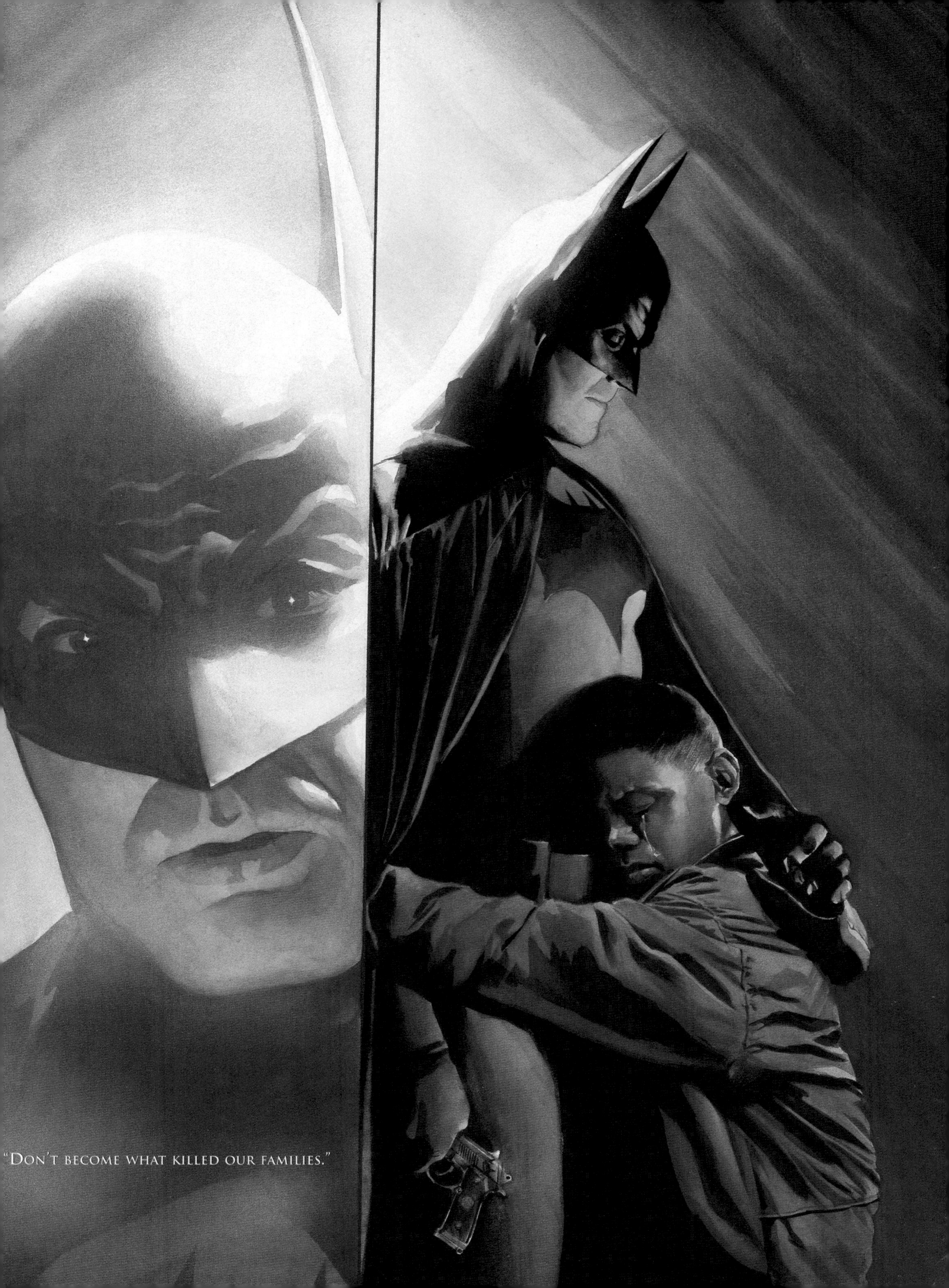
"Don't become what killed our families."

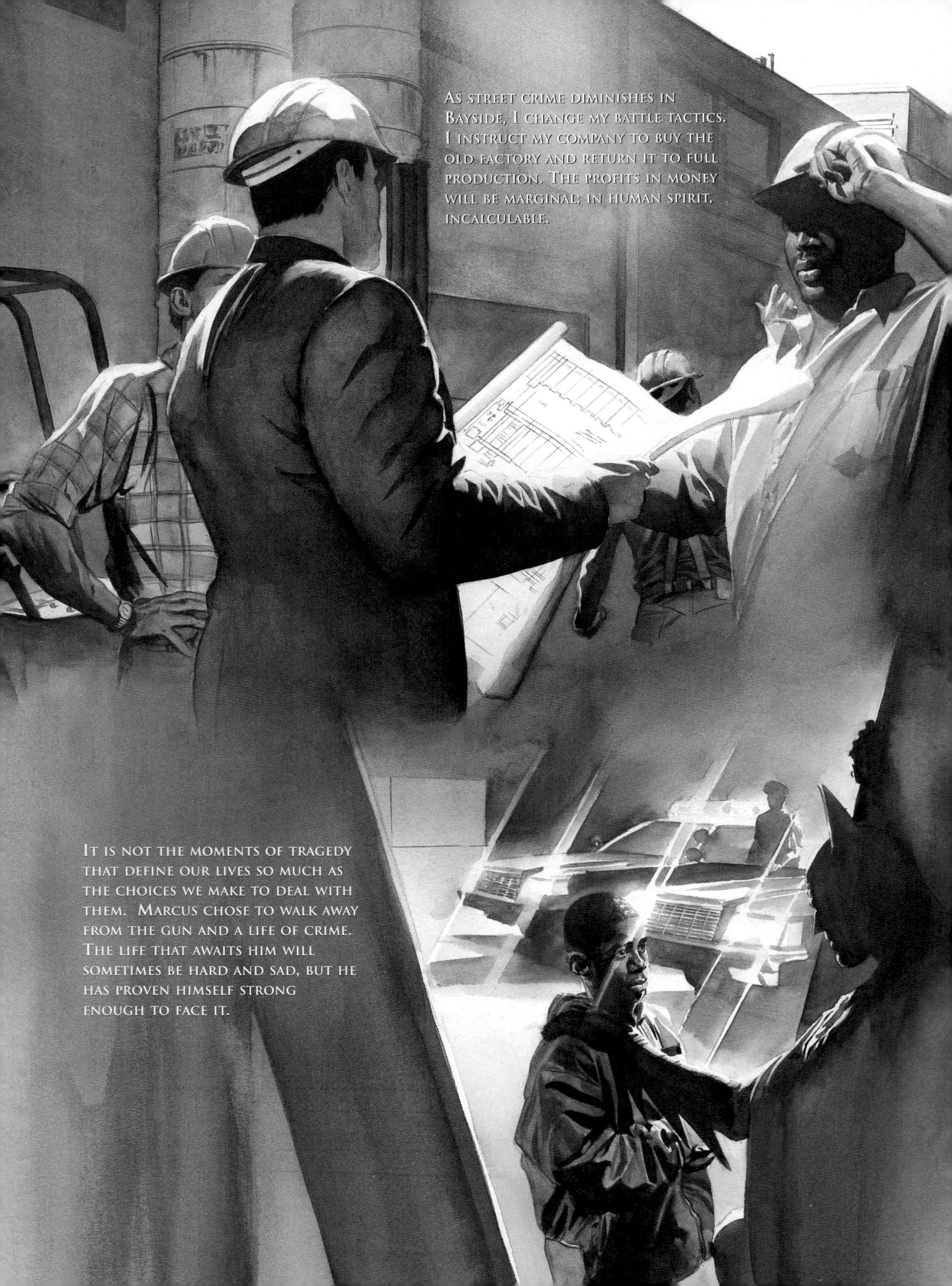
As street crime diminishes in Bayside, I change my battle tactics. I instruct my company to buy the old factory and return it to full production. The profits in money will be marginal; in human spirit, incalculable.
It is not the moments of tragedy that define our lives so much as the choices we make to deal with them. Marcus chose to walk away from the gun and a life of crime. The life that awaits him will sometimes be hard and sad, but he has proven himself strong enough to face it.

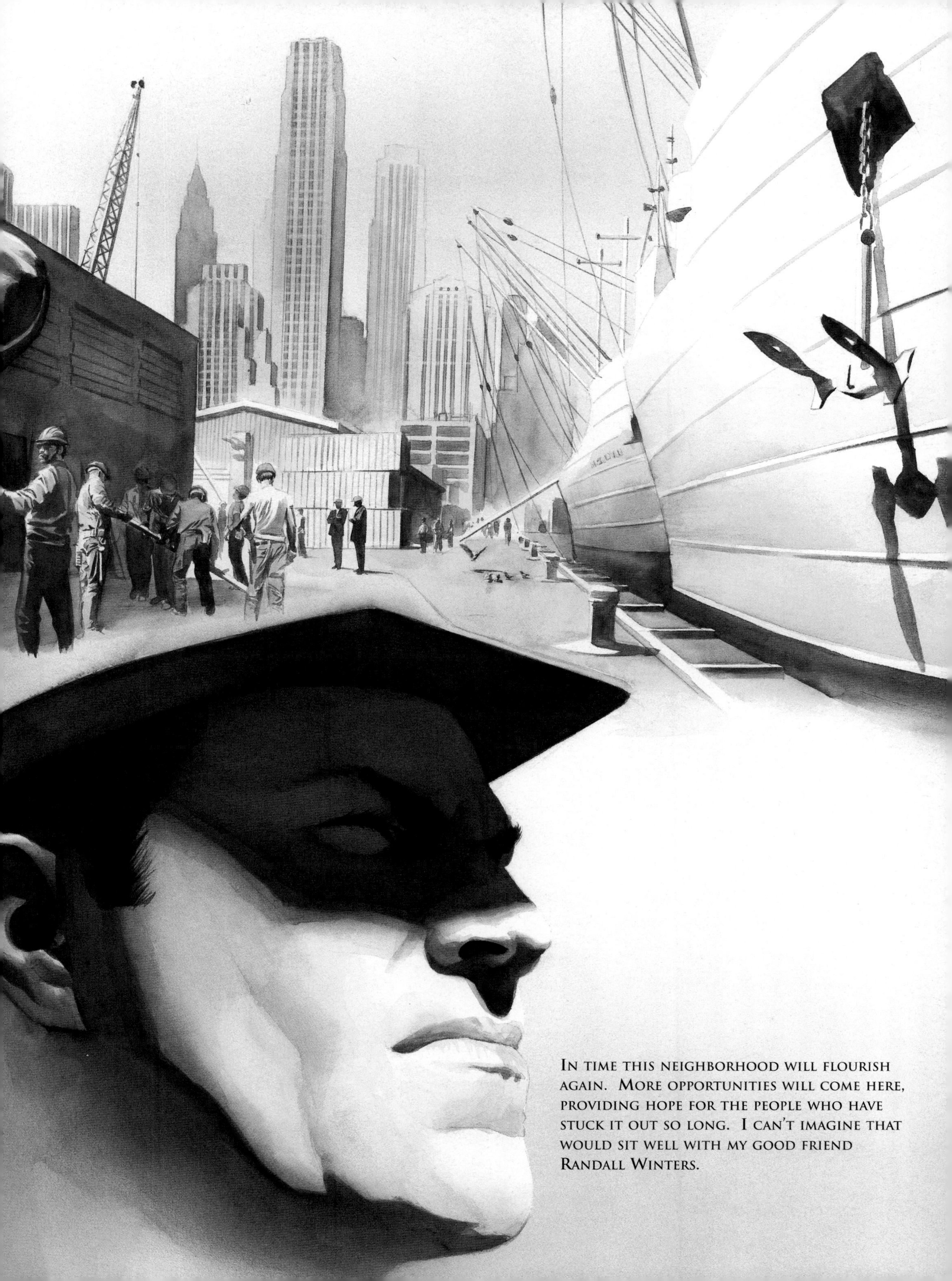
In time this neighborhood will flourish again. More opportunities will come here, providing hope for the people who have stuck it out so long. I can't imagine that would sit well with my good friend Randall Winters.

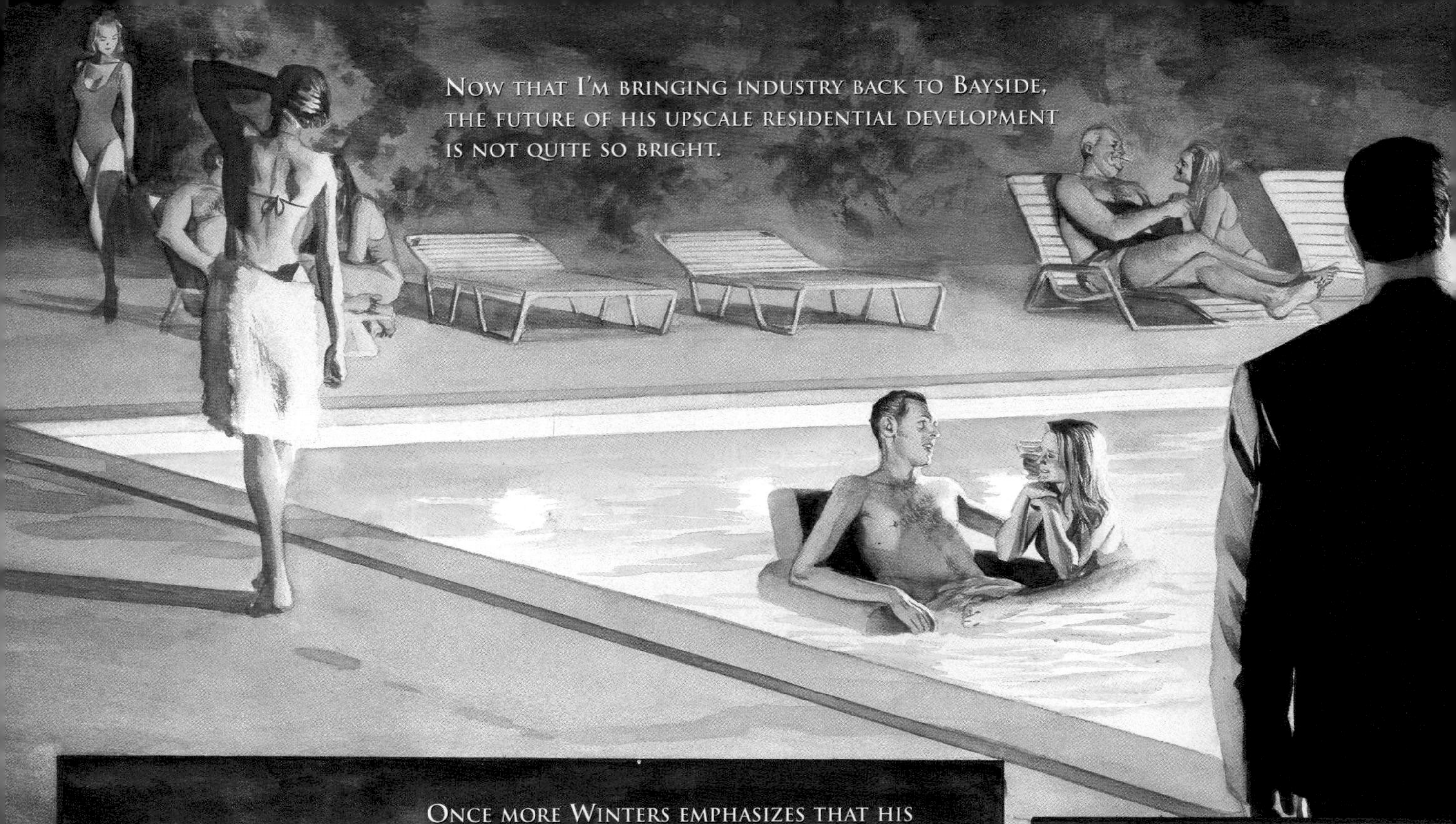
Now that I'm bringing industry back to Bayside, the future of his upscale residential development is not quite so bright.

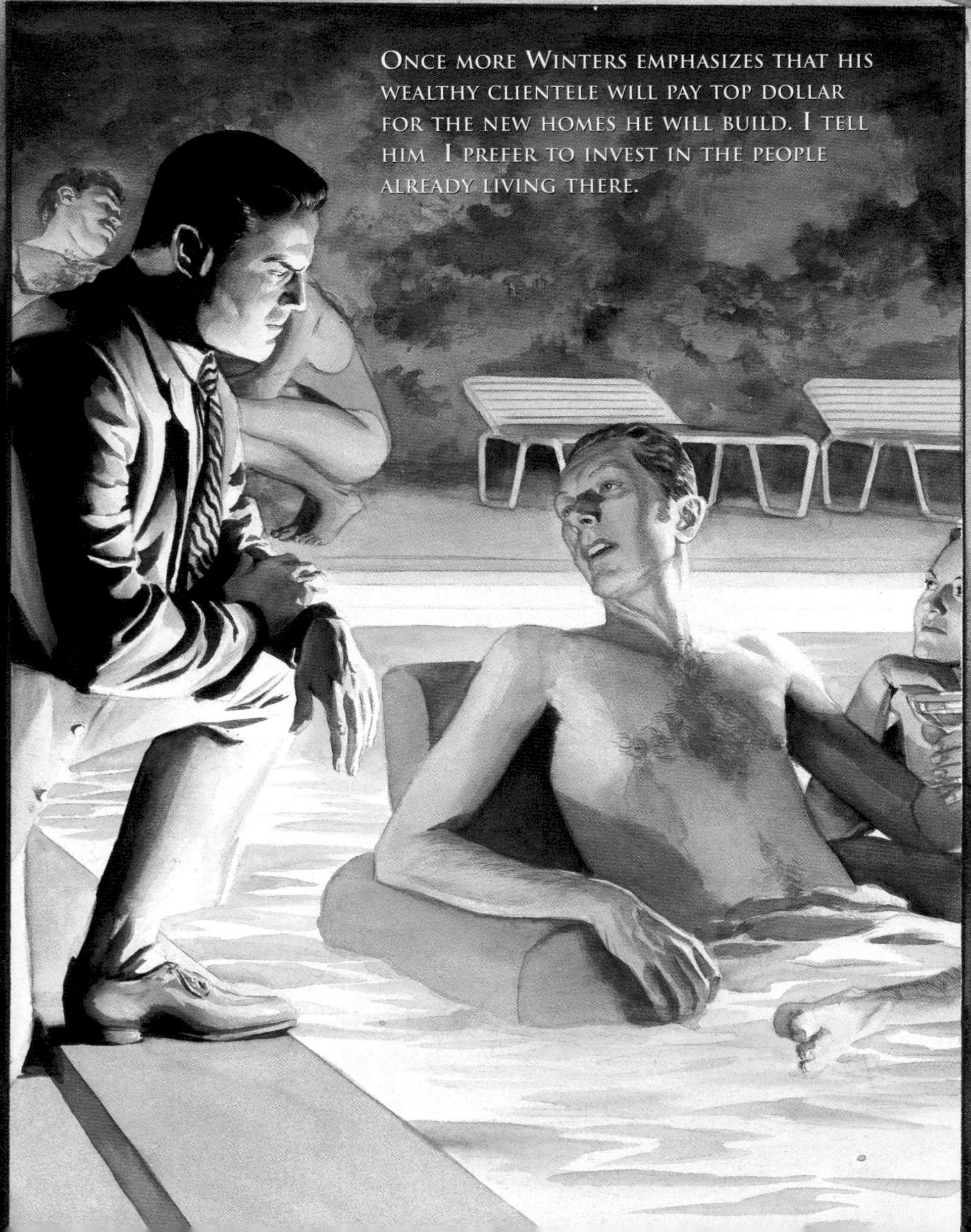
Once more Winters emphasizes that his wealthy clientele will pay top dollar for the new homes he will build. I tell him I prefer to invest in the people already living there.

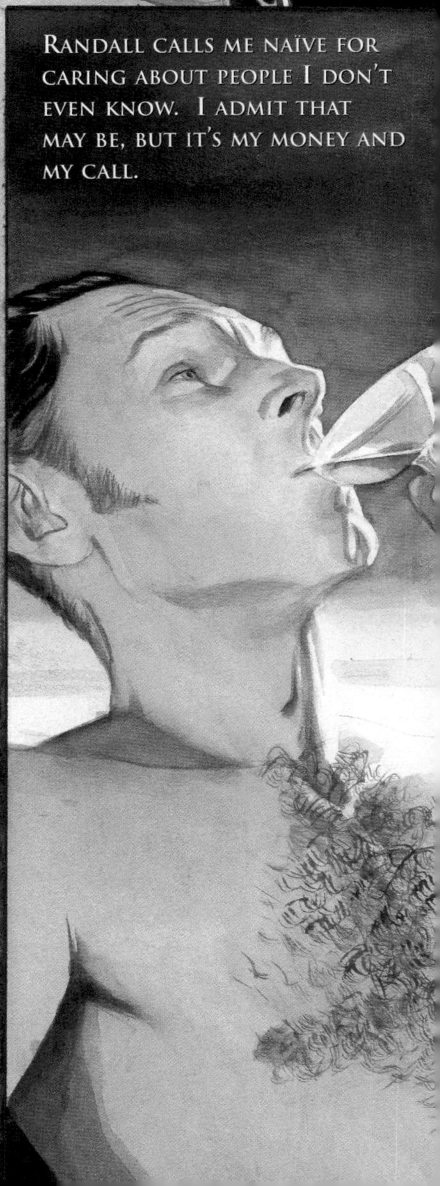
Randall calls me naïve for caring about people I don't even know. I admit that may be, but it's my money and my call.

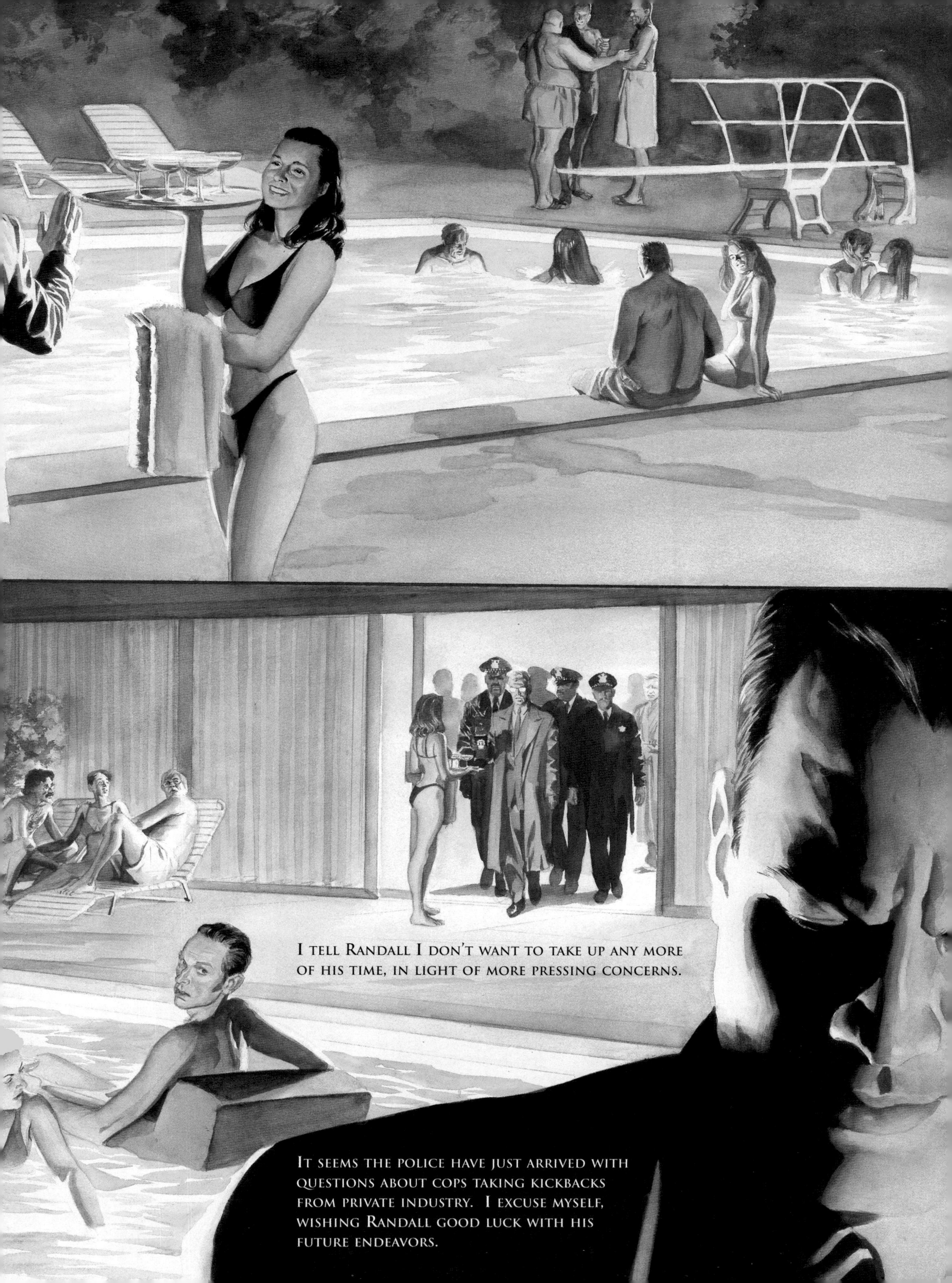
I tell Randall I don't want to take up any more of his time, in light of more pressing concerns.
It seems the police have just arrived with questions about cops taking kickbacks from private industry. I excuse myself, wishing Randall good luck with his future endeavors.

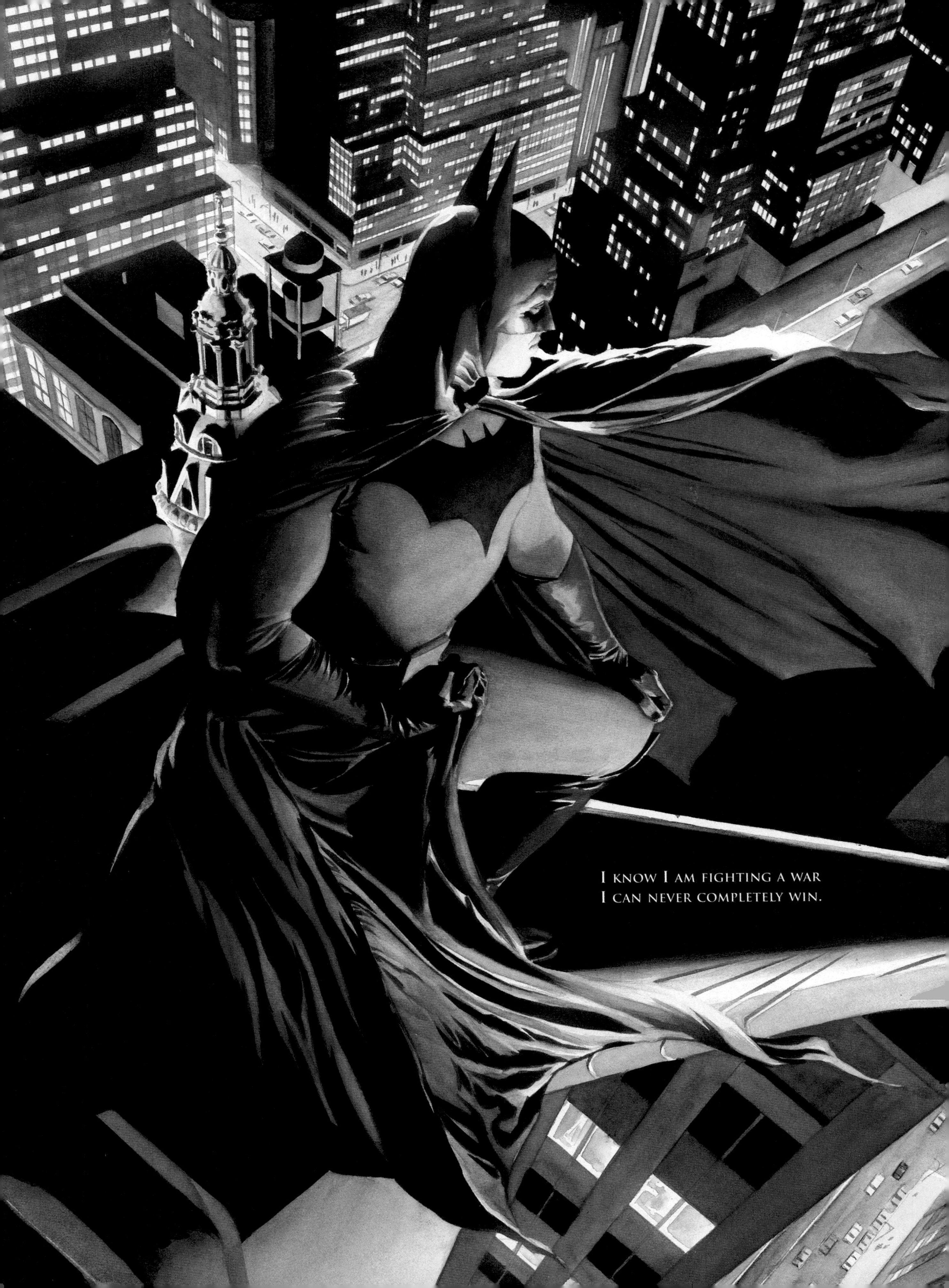
I know I am fighting a war
I can never completely win.

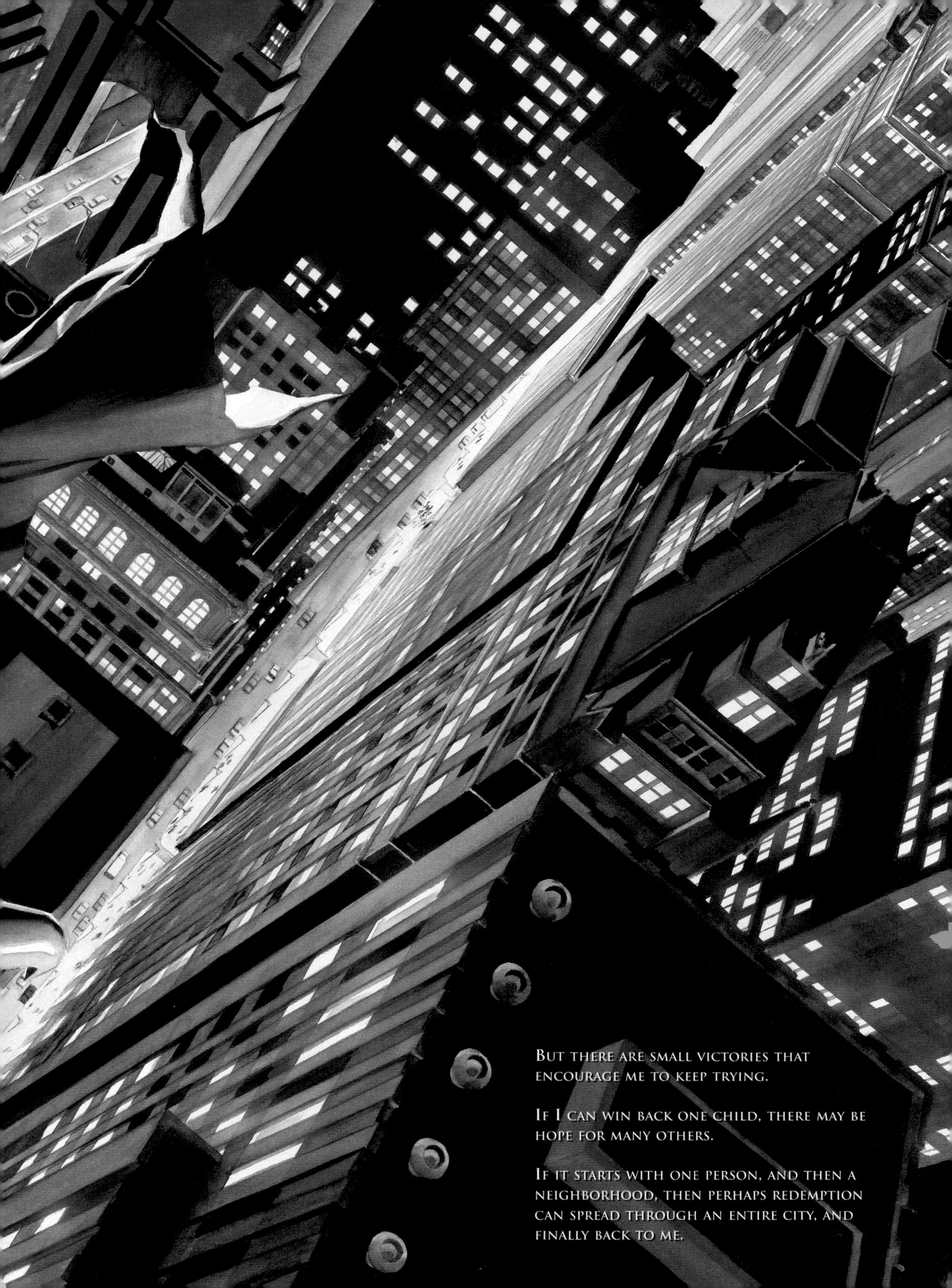
But there are small victories that encourage me to keep trying.
If I can win back one child, there may be hope for many others.
If it starts with one person, and then a neighborhood, then perhaps redemption can spread through an entire city, and finally back to me.

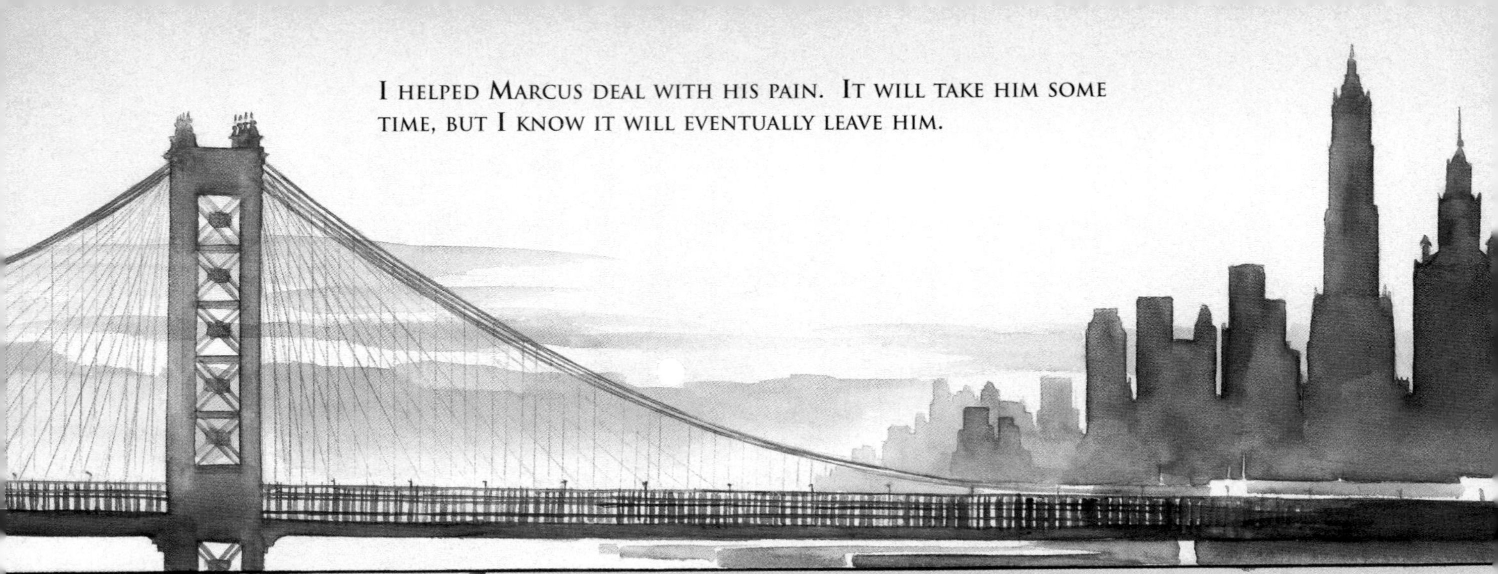
I helped Marcus deal with his pain. It will take him some time, but I know it will eventually leave him.

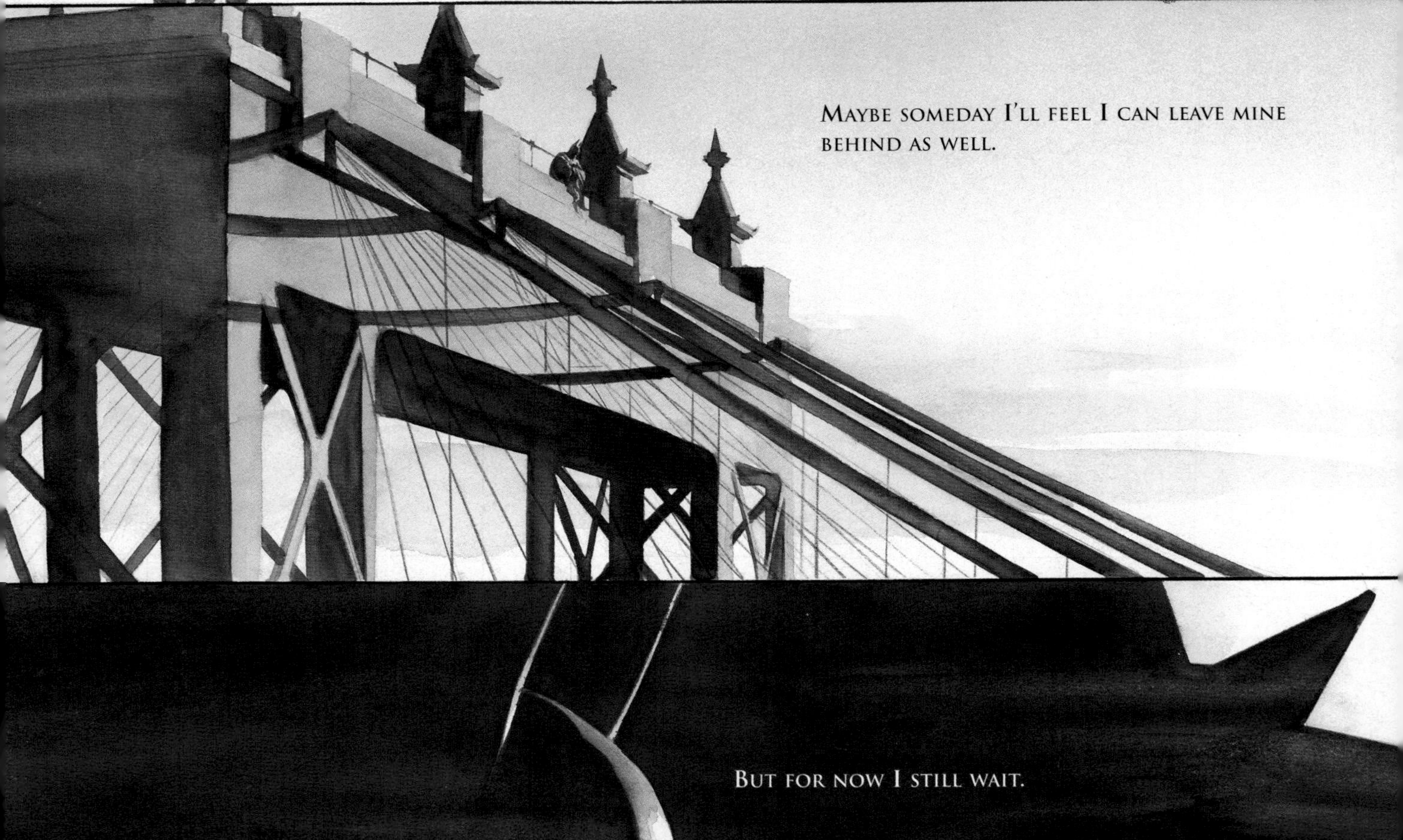
Maybe someday I'll feel I can leave mine behind as well.

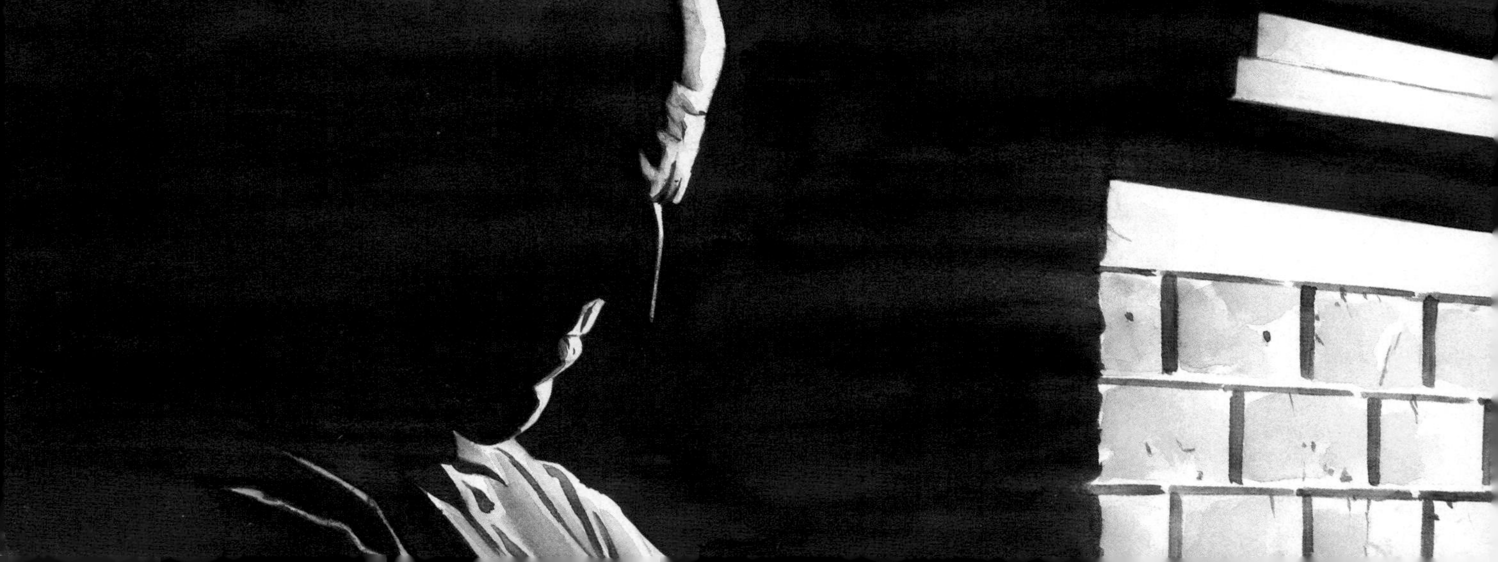
But for now I still wait.

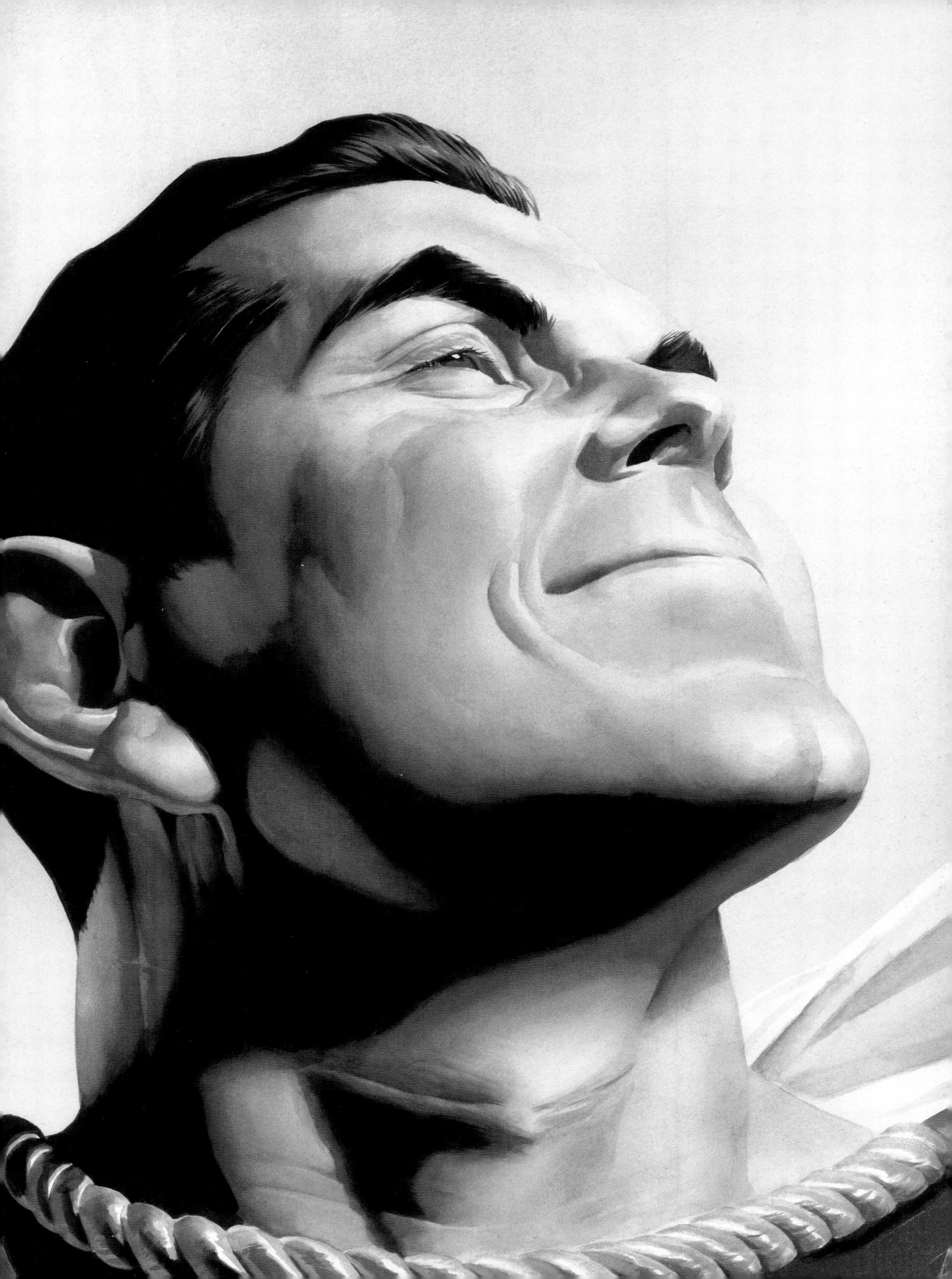

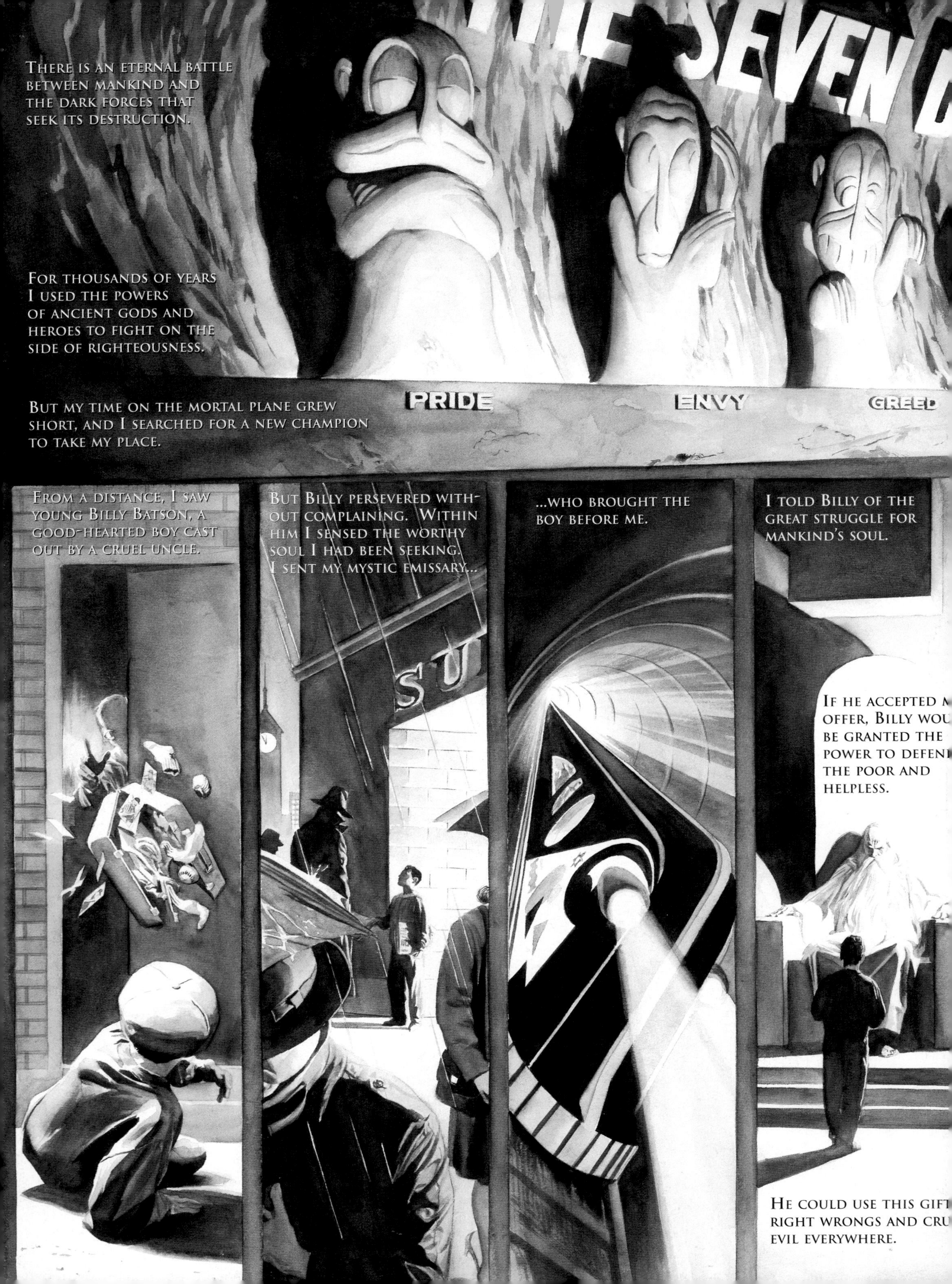
THE SEVEN
There is an eternal battle between mankind and the dark forces that seek its destruction.
For thousands of years I used the powers of ancient gods and heroes to fight on the side of righteousness.
But my time on the mortal plane grew short, and I searched for a new champion to take my place.
PRIDE
ENVY
GREED
From a distance, I saw young Billy Batson, a good-hearted boy cast out by a cruel uncle.
But Billy persevered without complaining. Within him I sensed the worthy soul I had been seeking. I sent my mystic emissary...
...who brought the boy before me.
I told Billy of the great struggle for mankind's soul.
If he accepted my offer, Billy would be granted the power to defend the poor and helpless.
He could use this gift to right wrongs and crush evil everywhere.

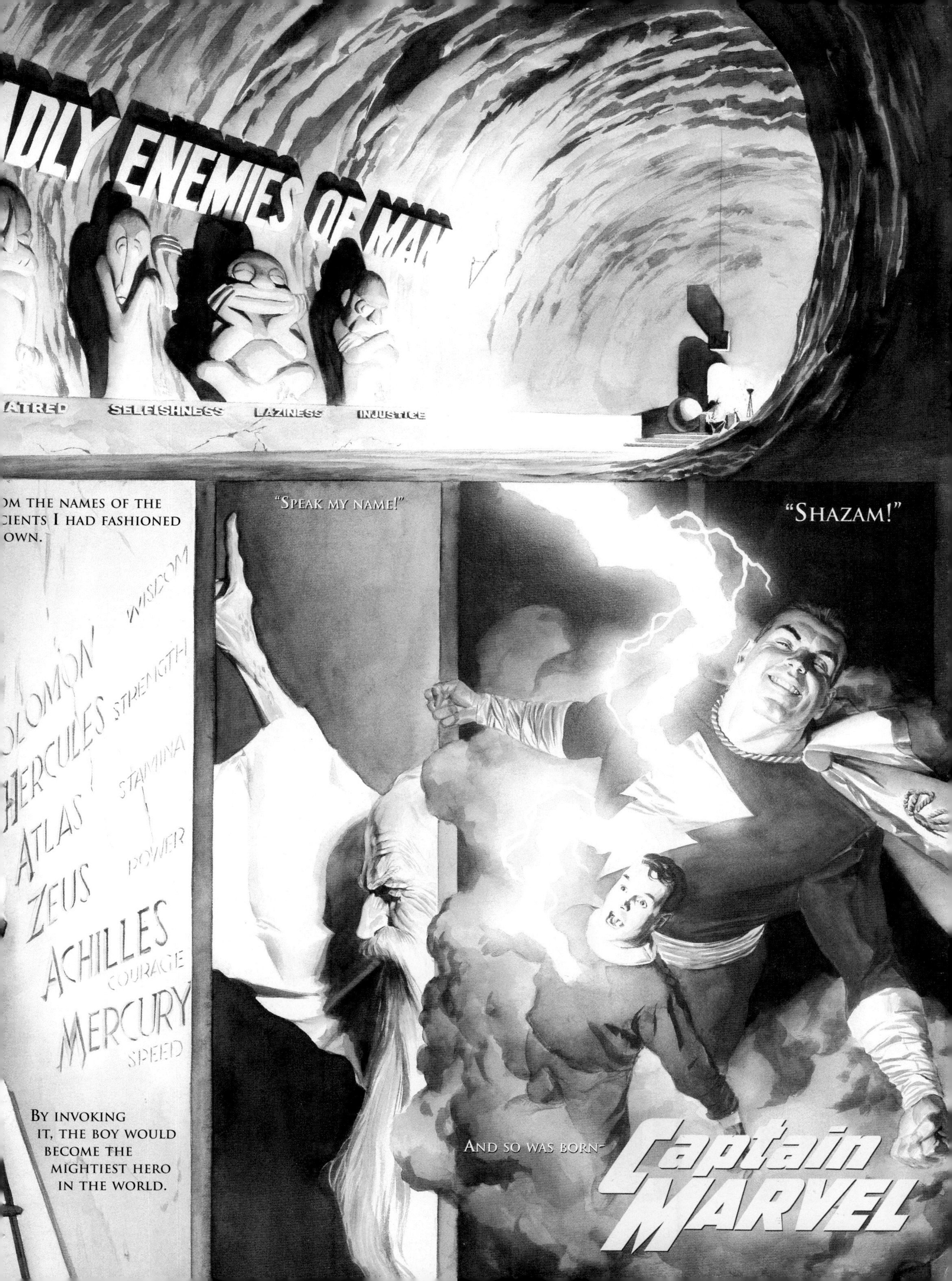

ADLY ENEMIES OF MAN
ATRED
SELFISHNESS
LAZINESS
INJUSTICE
OM THE NAMES OF THE CIENTS I HAD FASHIONED OWN.
OLOMON
WISDOM
HERCULES
STRENGTH
ATLAS
STAMINA
ZEUS
POWER
ACHILLES
COURAGE
MERCURY
SPEED
BY INVOKING IT, THE BOY WOULD BECOME THE MIGHTIEST HERO IN THE WORLD.
"SPEAK MY NAME!"
"SHAZAM!"
AND SO WAS BORN–
Captain MARVEL

SHAZAM!

POWER OF
HOPE

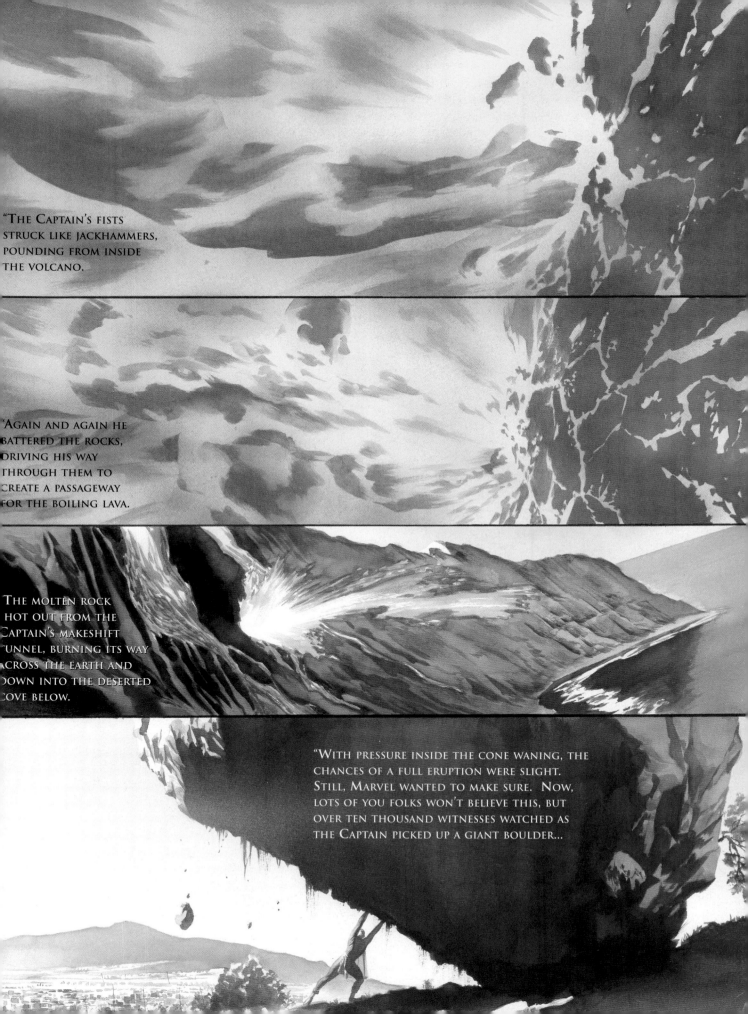

"THE CAPTAIN'S FISTS STRUCK LIKE JACKHAMMERS, POUNDING FROM INSIDE THE VOLCANO.

"AGAIN AND AGAIN HE BATTERED THE ROCKS, DRIVING HIS WAY THROUGH THEM TO CREATE A PASSAGEWAY FOR THE BOILING LAVA.

THE MOLTEN ROCK HOT OUT FROM THE CAPTAIN'S MAKESHIFT TUNNEL, BURNING ITS WAY ACROSS THE EARTH AND DOWN INTO THE DESERTED COVE BELOW.

"WITH PRESSURE INSIDE THE CONE WANING, THE CHANCES OF A FULL ERUPTION WERE SLIGHT. STILL, MARVEL WANTED TO MAKE SURE. NOW, LOTS OF YOU FOLKS WON'T BELIEVE THIS, BUT OVER TEN THOUSAND WITNESSES WATCHED AS THE CAPTAIN PICKED UP A GIANT BOULDER...

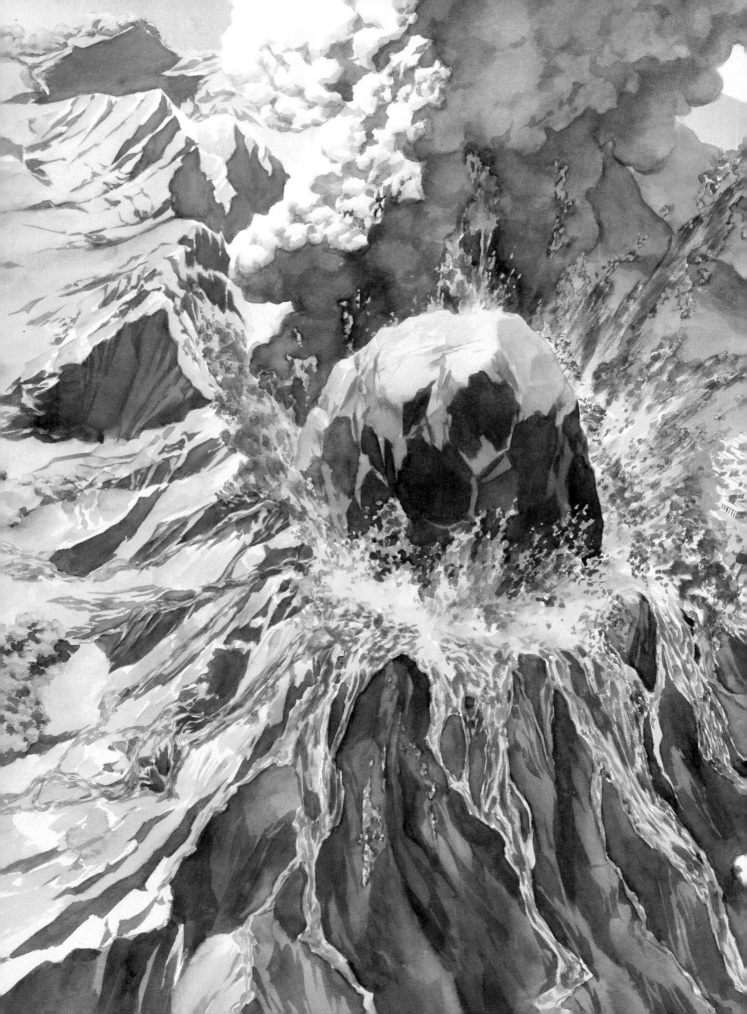

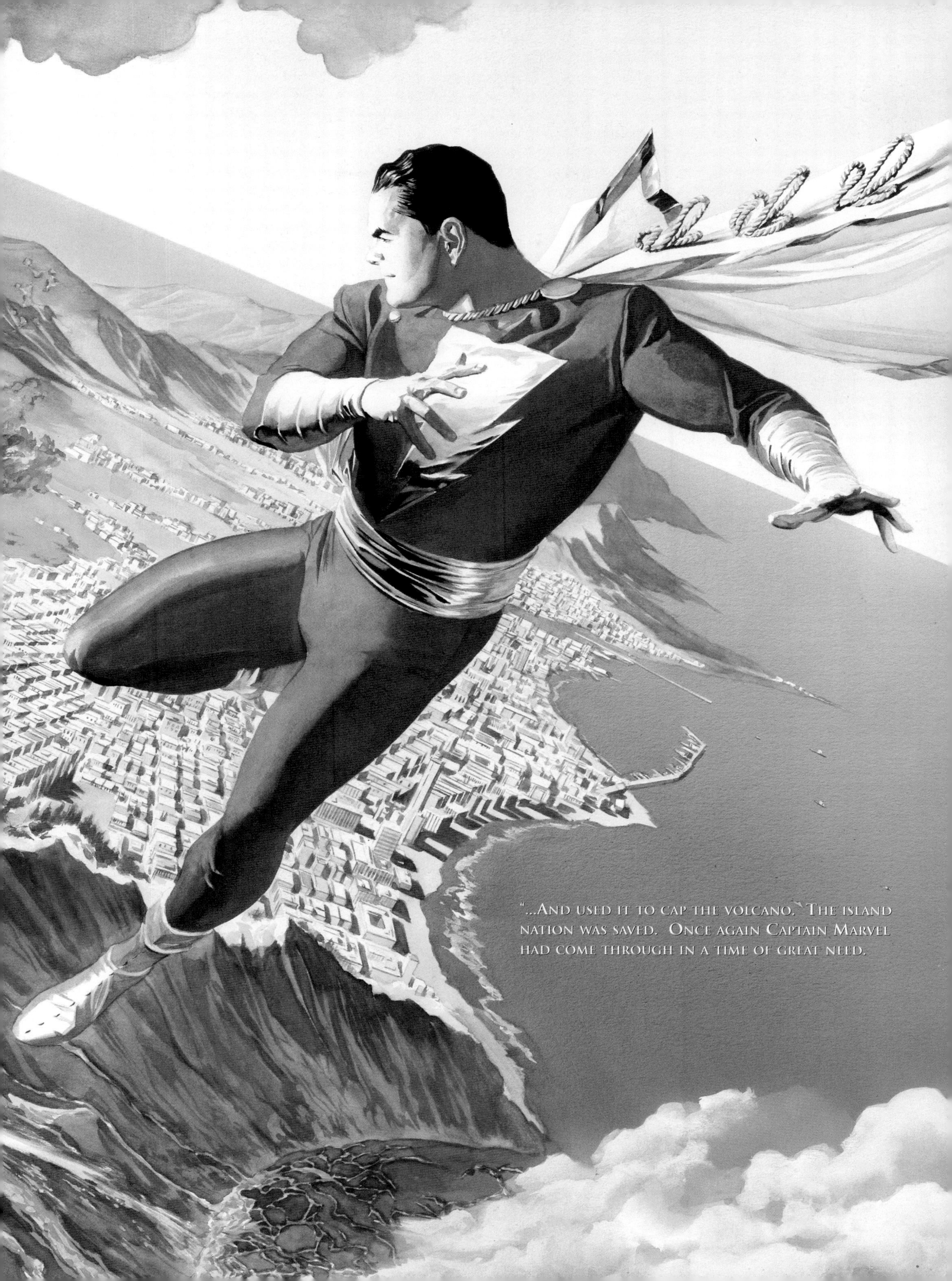

"...And used it to cap the volcano." The island nation was saved. Once again Captain Marvel had come through in a time of great need.

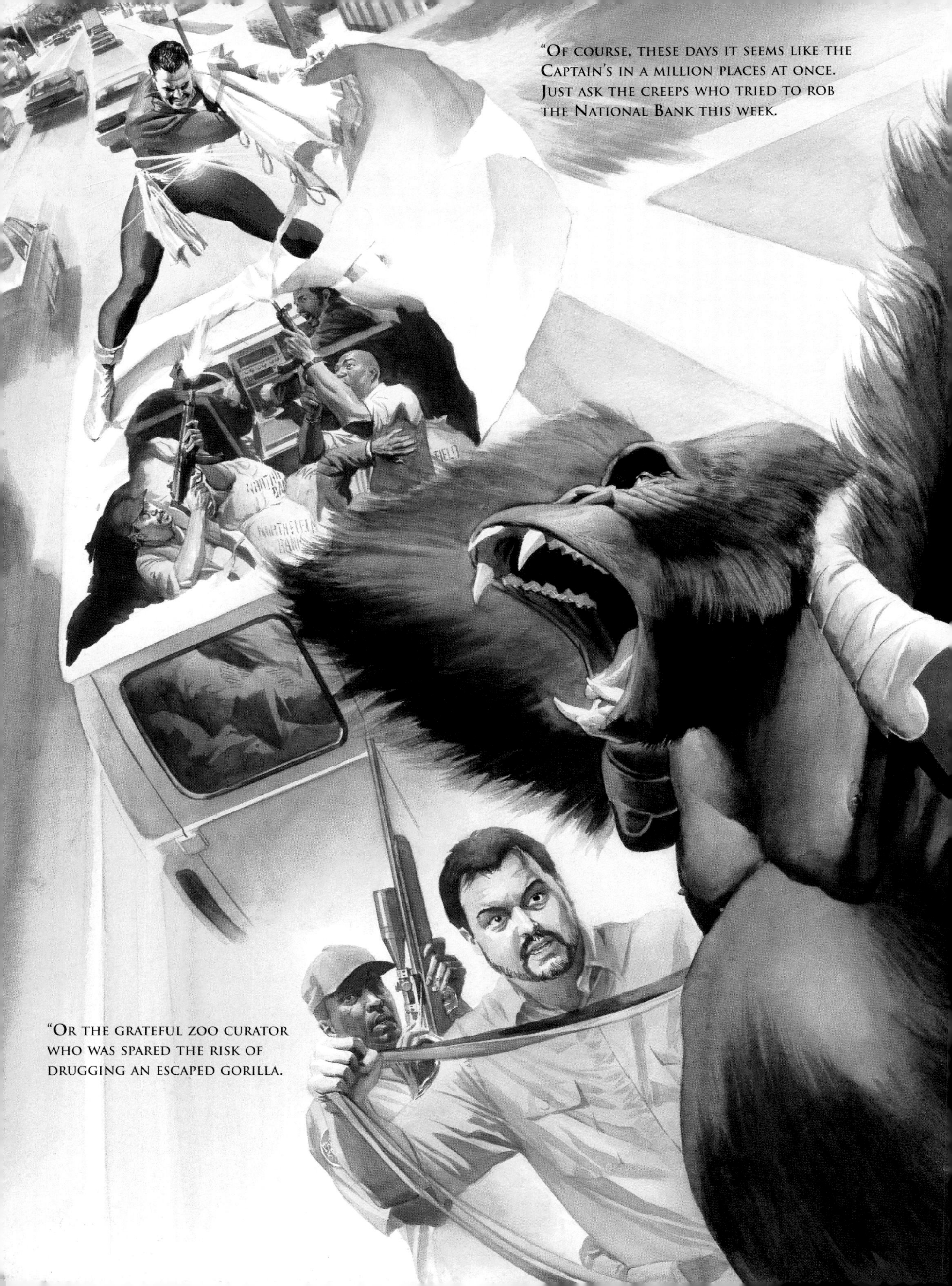
"Of course, these days it seems like the Captain's in a million places at once. Just ask the creeps who tried to rob the National Bank this week.
"Or the grateful zoo curator who was spared the risk of drugging an escaped gorilla.

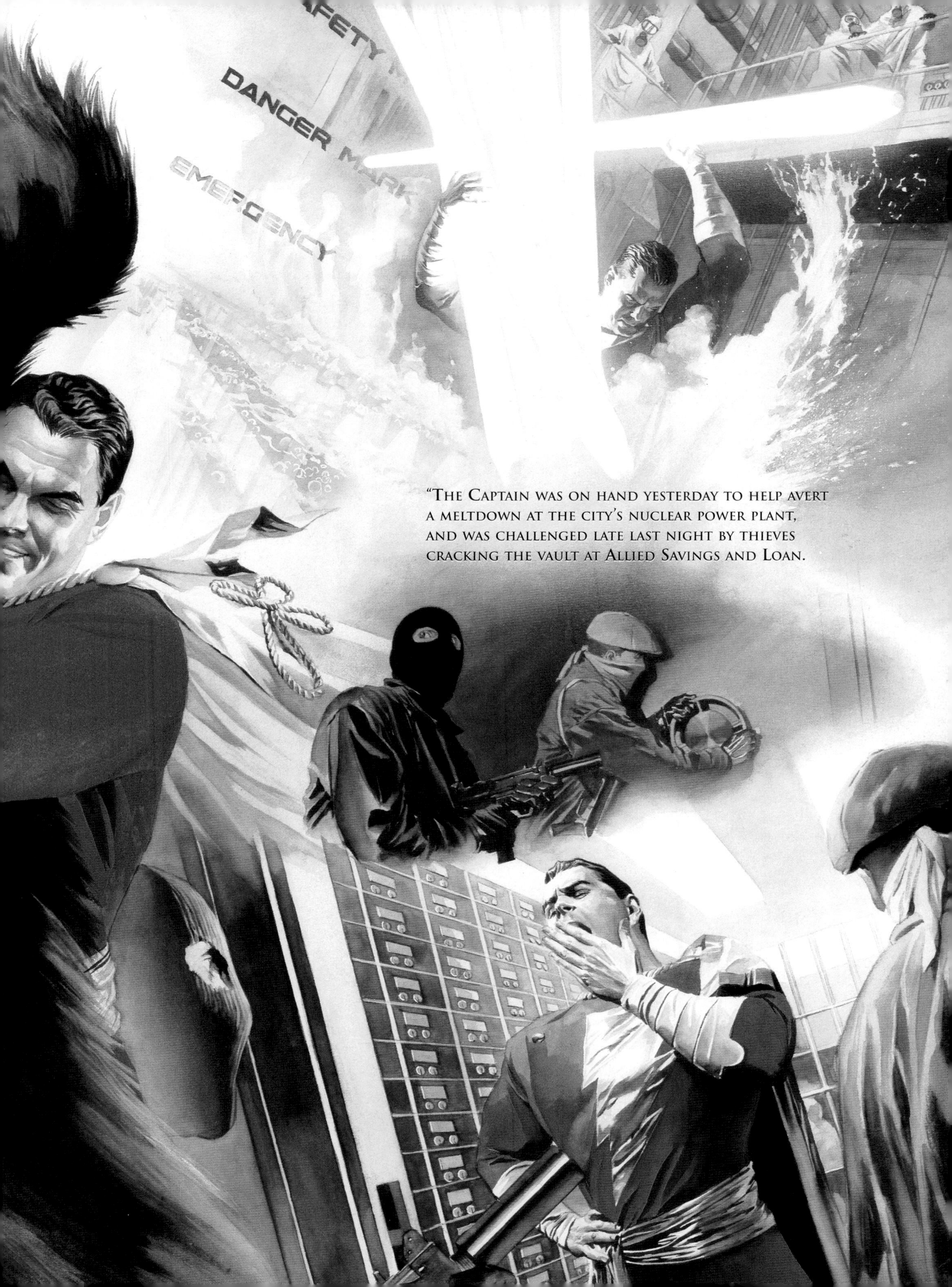
DANGER
EMERGENCY
"The Captain was on hand yesterday to help avert a meltdown at the city's nuclear power plant, and was challenged late last night by thieves cracking the vault at Allied Savings and Loan.

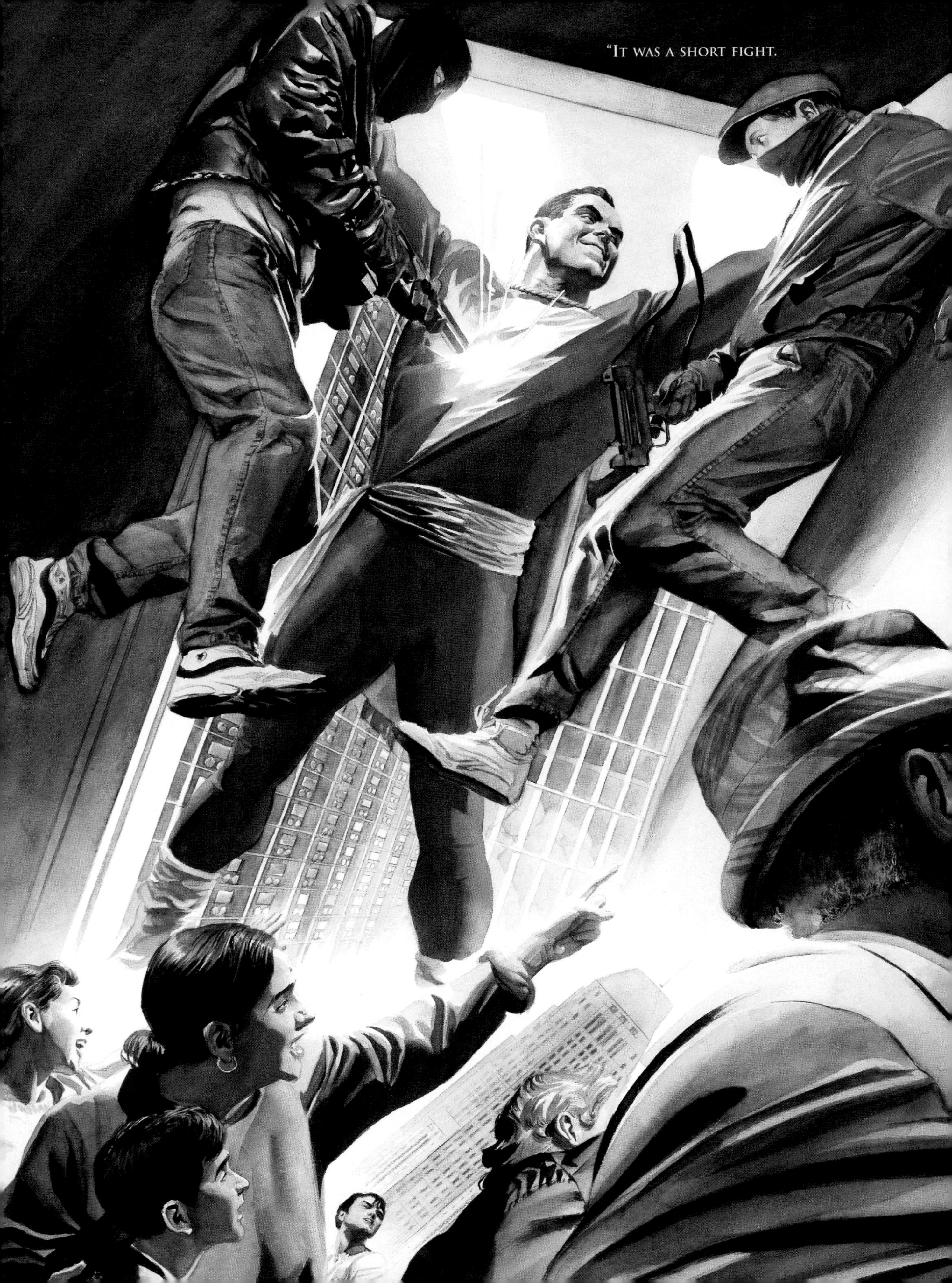
"IT WAS A SHORT FIGHT.

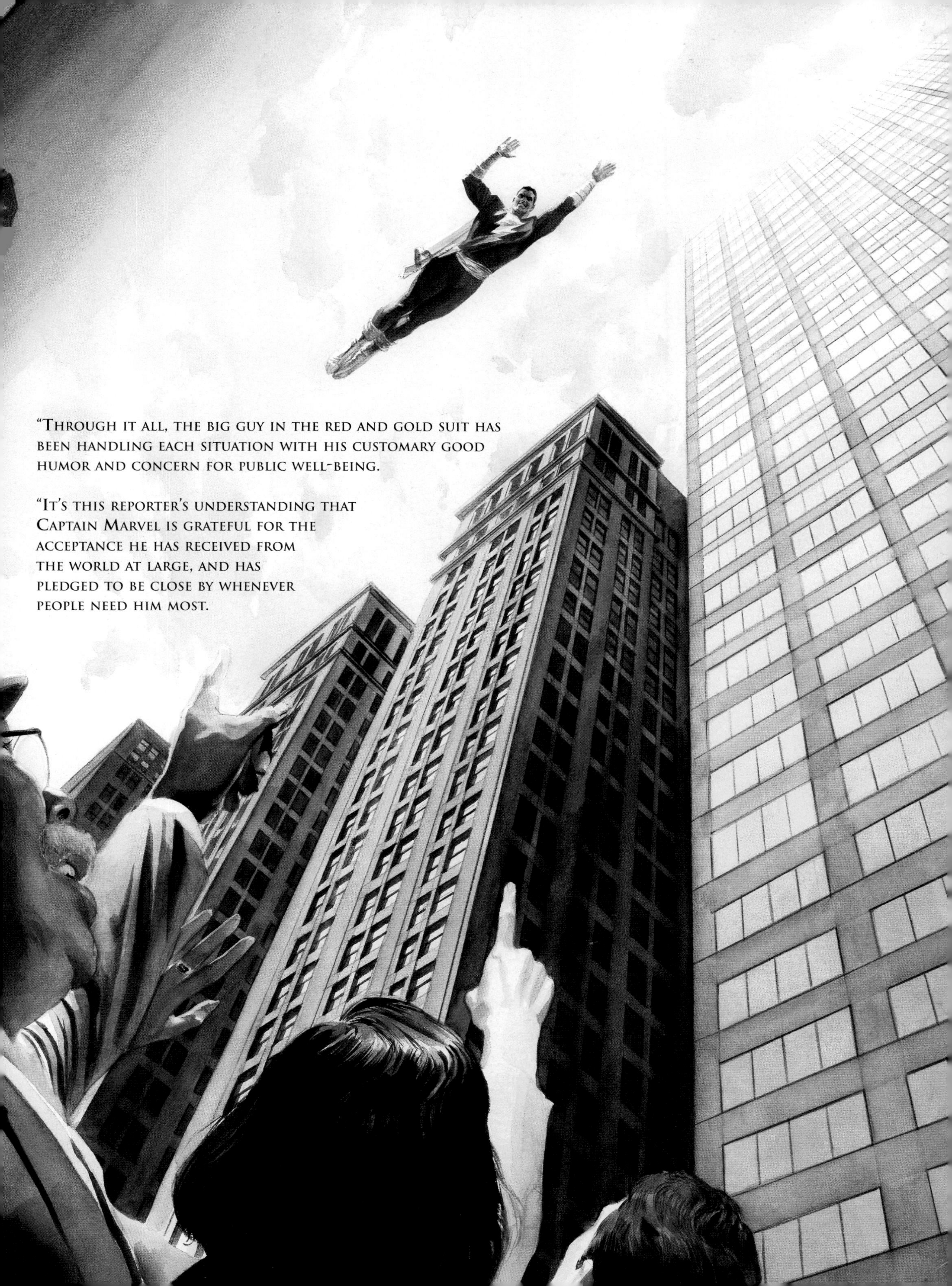
"Through it all, the big guy in the red and gold suit has been handling each situation with his customary good humor and concern for public well-being.
"It's this reporter's understanding that Captain Marvel is grateful for the acceptance he has received from the world at large, and has pledged to be close by whenever people need him most.

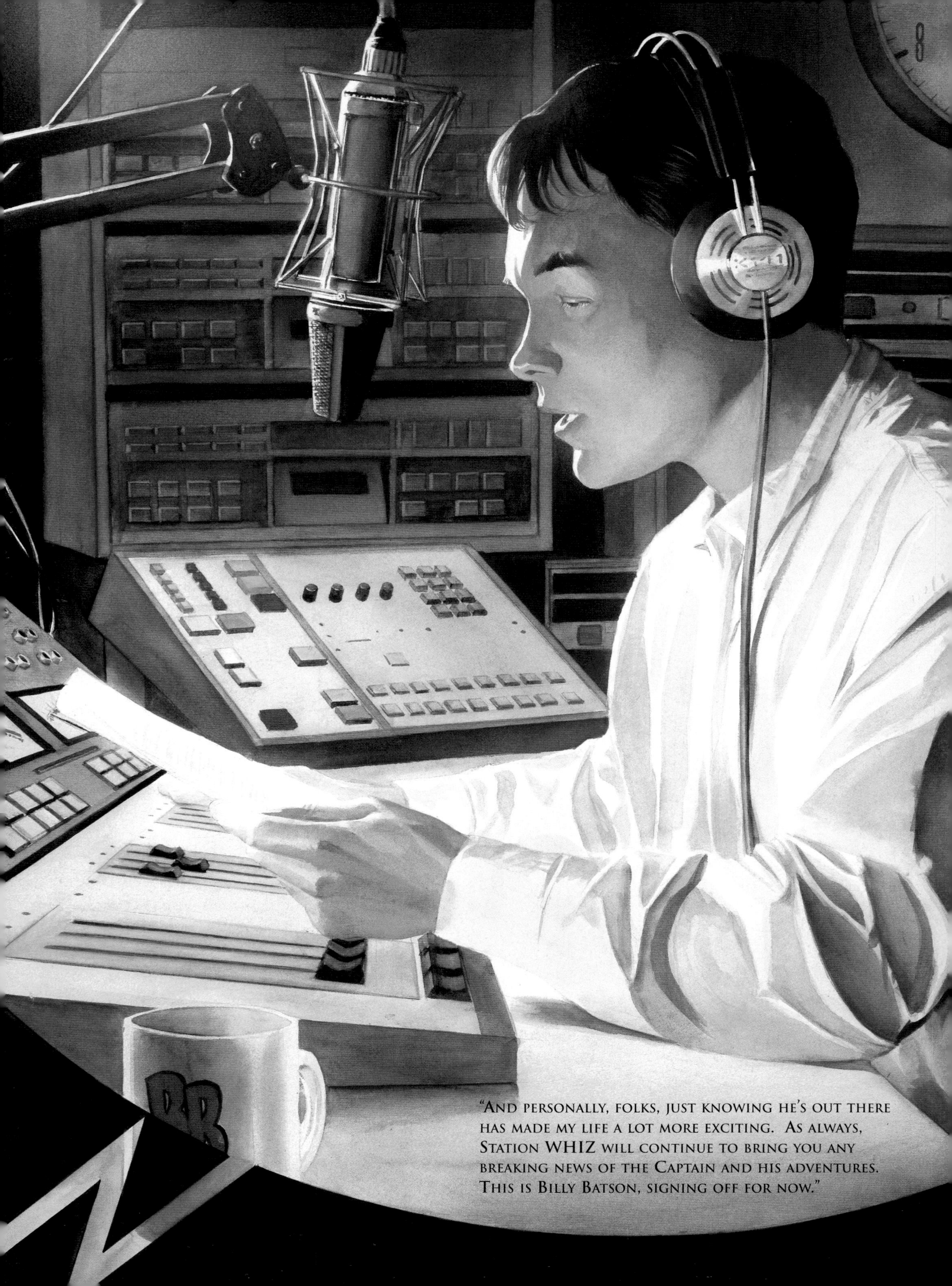
"And personally, folks, just knowing he's out there has made my life a lot more exciting. As always, Station WHIZ will continue to bring you any breaking news of the Captain and his adventures. This is Billy Batson, signing off for now."

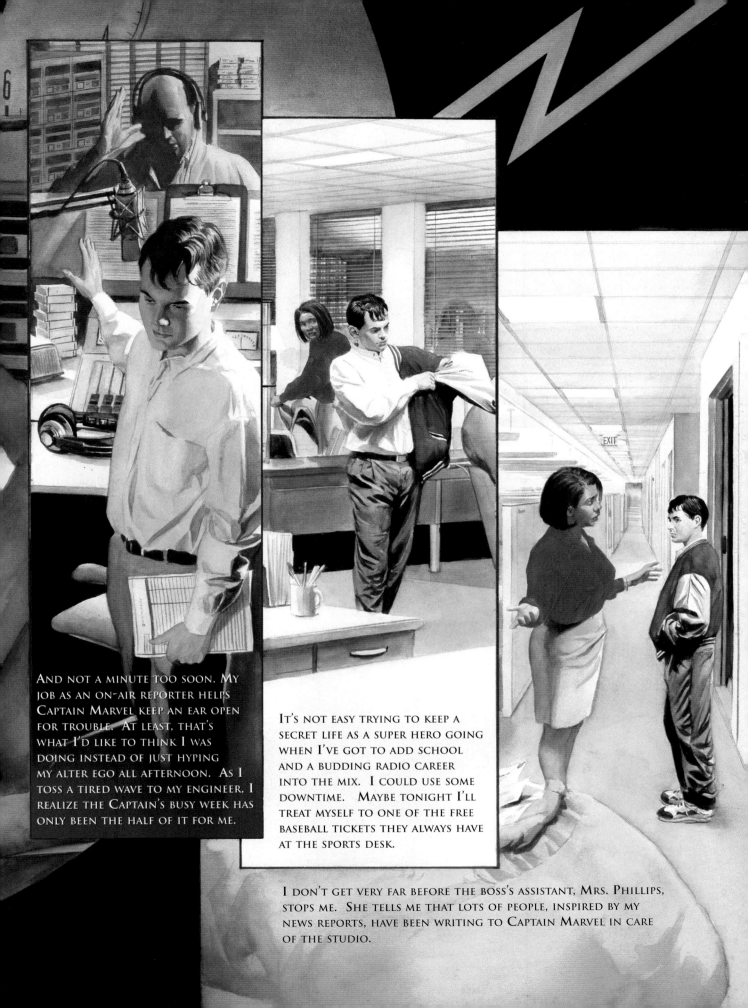

AND NOT A MINUTE TOO SOON. MY JOB AS AN ON-AIR REPORTER HELPS CAPTAIN MARVEL KEEP AN EAR OPEN FOR TROUBLE. AT LEAST, THAT'S WHAT I'D LIKE TO THINK I WAS DOING INSTEAD OF JUST HYPING MY ALTER EGO ALL AFTERNOON. AS I TOSS A TIRED WAVE TO MY ENGINEER, I REALIZE THE CAPTAIN'S BUSY WEEK HAS ONLY BEEN THE HALF OF IT FOR ME.

IT'S NOT EASY TRYING TO KEEP A SECRET LIFE AS A SUPER HERO GOING WHEN I'VE GOT TO ADD SCHOOL AND A BUDDING RADIO CAREER INTO THE MIX. I COULD USE SOME DOWNTIME. MAYBE TONIGHT I'LL TREAT MYSELF TO ONE OF THE FREE BASEBALL TICKETS THEY ALWAYS HAVE AT THE SPORTS DESK.

I DON'T GET VERY FAR BEFORE THE BOSS'S ASSISTANT, MRS. PHILLIPS, STOPS ME. SHE TELLS ME THAT LOTS OF PEOPLE, INSPIRED BY MY NEWS REPORTS, HAVE BEEN WRITING TO CAPTAIN MARVEL IN CARE OF THE STUDIO.

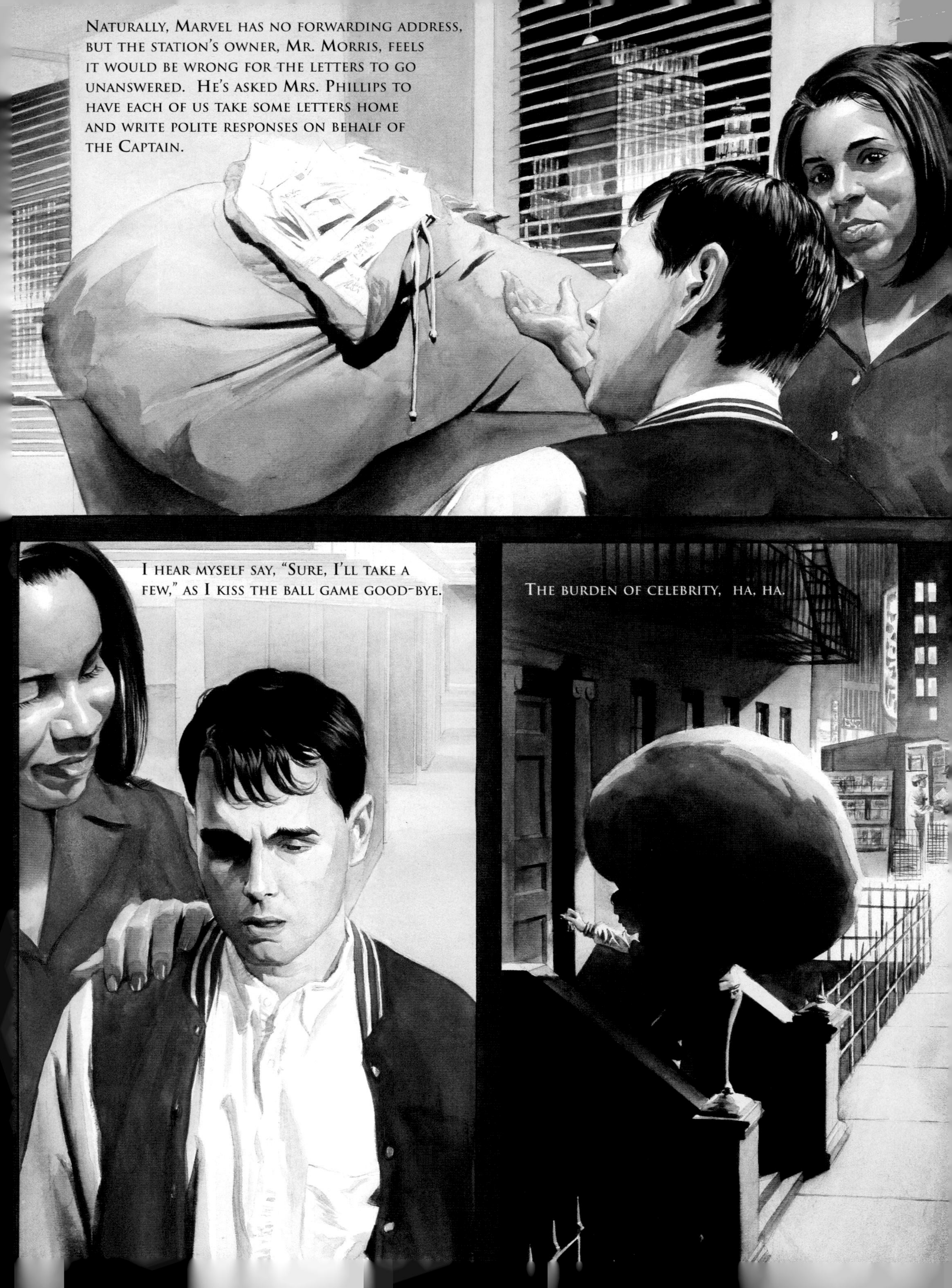
Naturally, Marvel has no forwarding address, but the station's owner, Mr. Morris, feels it would be wrong for the letters to go unanswered. He's asked Mrs. Phillips to have each of us take some letters home and write polite responses on behalf of the Captain.
I hear myself say, "Sure, I'll take a few," as I kiss the ball game good-bye.
The burden of celebrity, ha, ha.

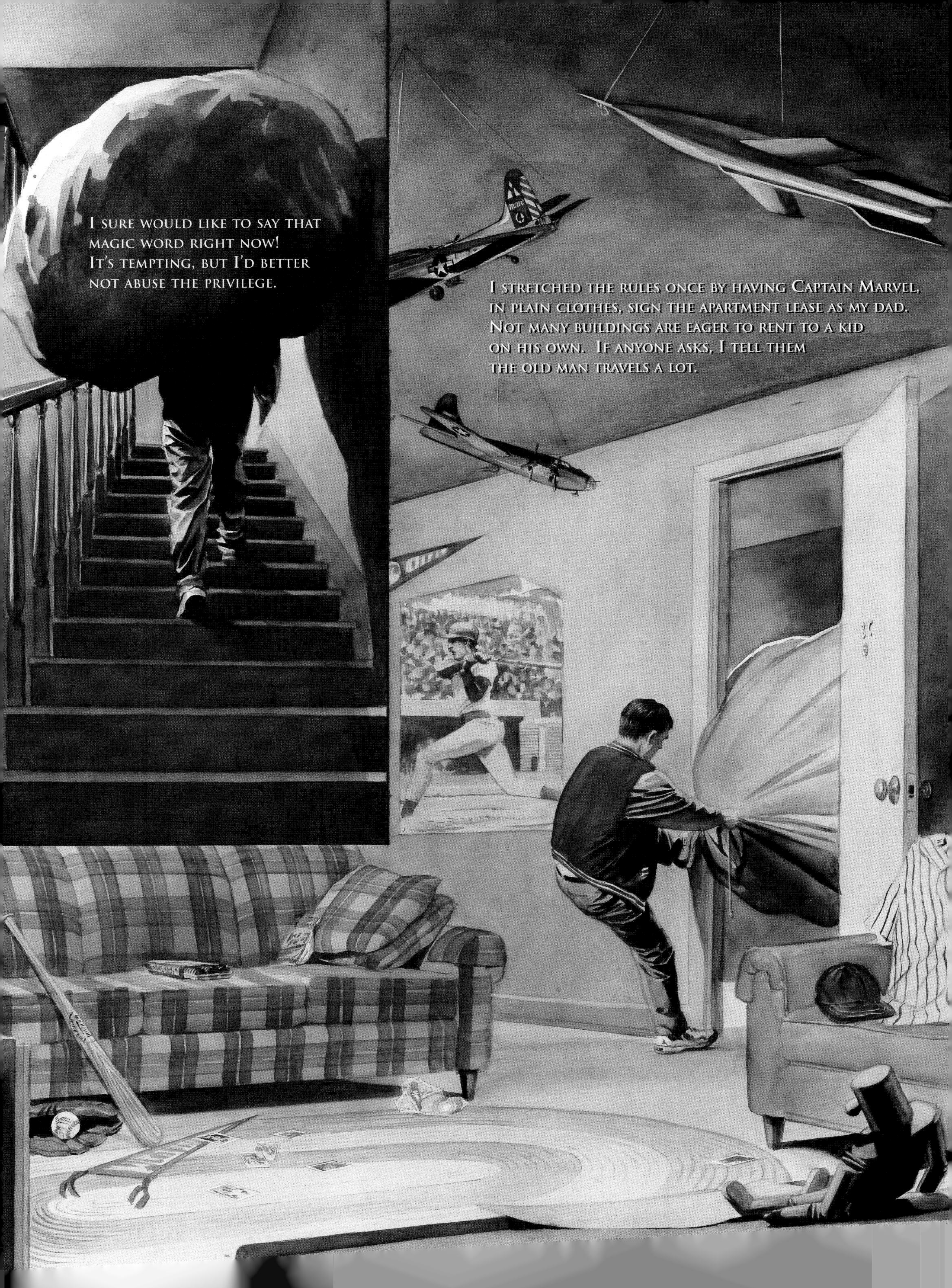
I sure would like to say that magic word right now! It's tempting, but I'd better not abuse the privilege.
I stretched the rules once by having Captain Marvel, in plain clothes, sign the apartment lease as my dad. Not many buildings are eager to rent to a kid on his own. If anyone asks, I tell them the old man travels a lot.

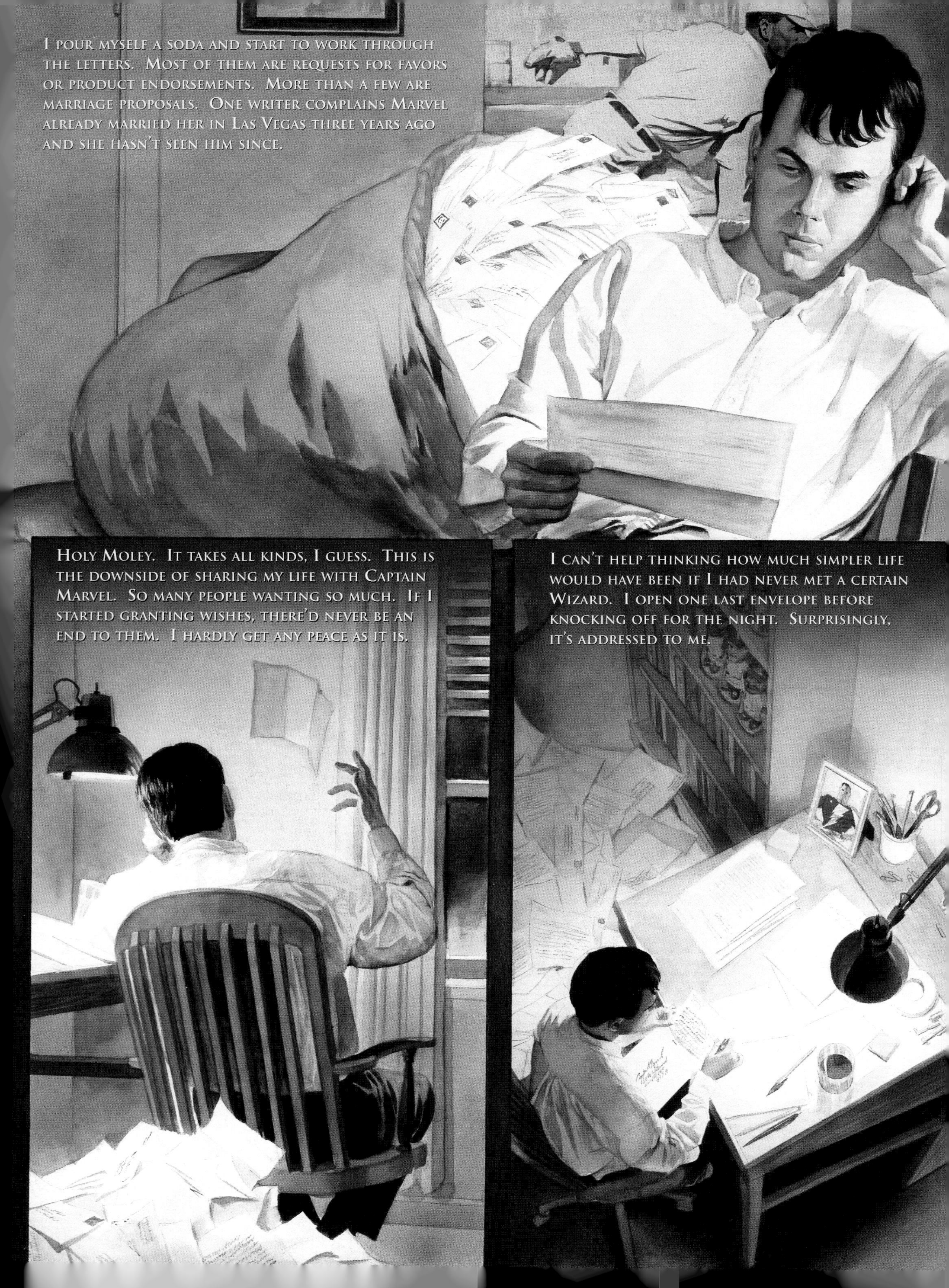
I pour myself a soda and start to work through the letters. Most of them are requests for favors or product endorsements. More than a few are marriage proposals. One writer complains Marvel already married her in Las Vegas three years ago and she hasn't seen him since.
Holy Moley. It takes all kinds, I guess. This is the downside of sharing my life with Captain Marvel. So many people wanting so much. If I started granting wishes, there'd never be an end to them. I hardly get any peace as it is.
I can't help thinking how much simpler life would have been if I had never met a certain Wizard. I open one last envelope before knocking off for the night. Surprisingly, it's addressed to me.

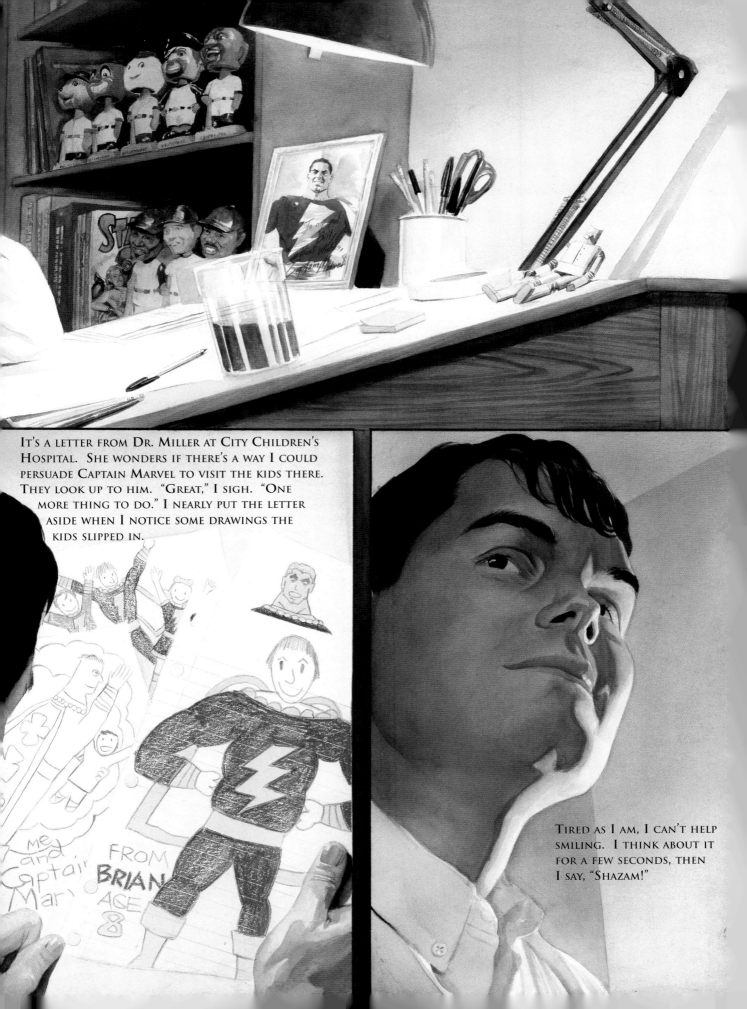

IT'S A LETTER FROM DR. MILLER AT CITY CHILDREN'S HOSPITAL. SHE WONDERS IF THERE'S A WAY I COULD PERSUADE CAPTAIN MARVEL TO VISIT THE KIDS THERE. THEY LOOK UP TO HIM. "GREAT," I SIGH. "ONE MORE THING TO DO." I NEARLY PUT THE LETTER ASIDE WHEN I NOTICE SOME DRAWINGS THE KIDS SLIPPED IN.

TIRED AS I AM, I CAN'T HELP SMILING. I THINK ABOUT IT FOR A FEW SECONDS, THEN I SAY, "SHAZAM!"

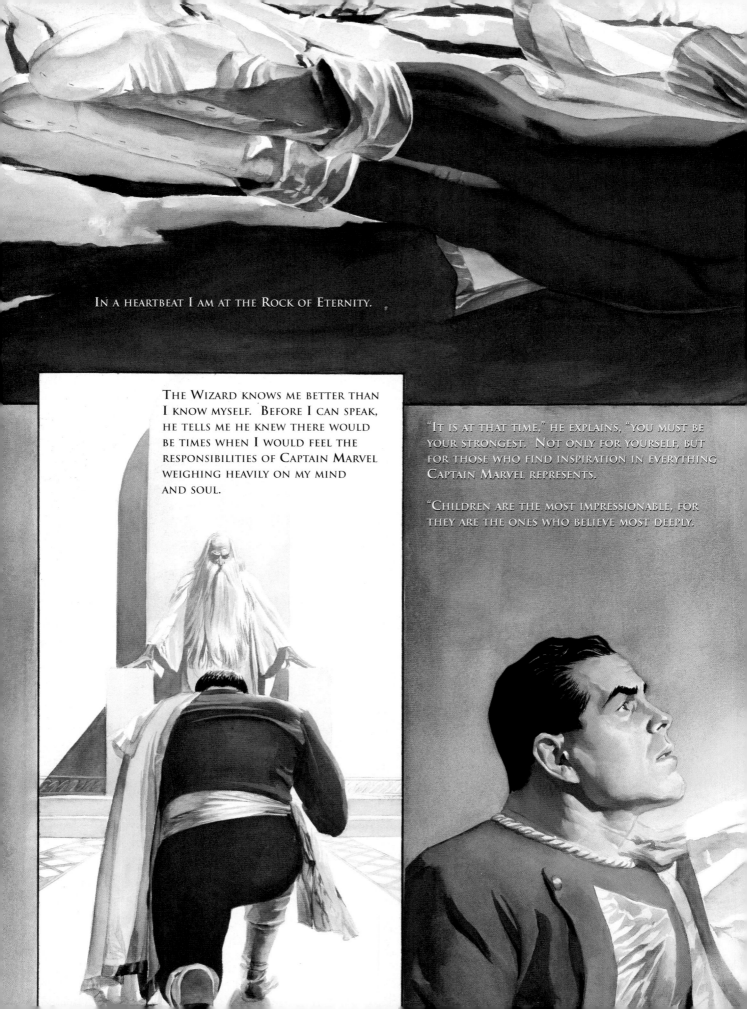

IN A HEARTBEAT I AM AT THE ROCK OF ETERNITY.

THE WIZARD KNOWS ME BETTER THAN
I KNOW MYSELF. BEFORE I CAN SPEAK,
HE TELLS ME HE KNEW THERE WOULD
BE TIMES WHEN I WOULD FEEL THE
RESPONSIBILITIES OF CAPTAIN MARVEL
WEIGHING HEAVILY ON MY MIND
AND SOUL.

"IT IS AT THAT TIME," HE EXPLAINS, "YOU MUST BE
YOUR STRONGEST. NOT ONLY FOR YOURSELF, BUT
FOR THOSE WHO FIND INSPIRATION IN EVERYTHING
CAPTAIN MARVEL REPRESENTS.

"CHILDREN ARE THE MOST IMPRESSIONABLE, FOR
THEY ARE THE ONES WHO BELIEVE MOST DEEPLY.

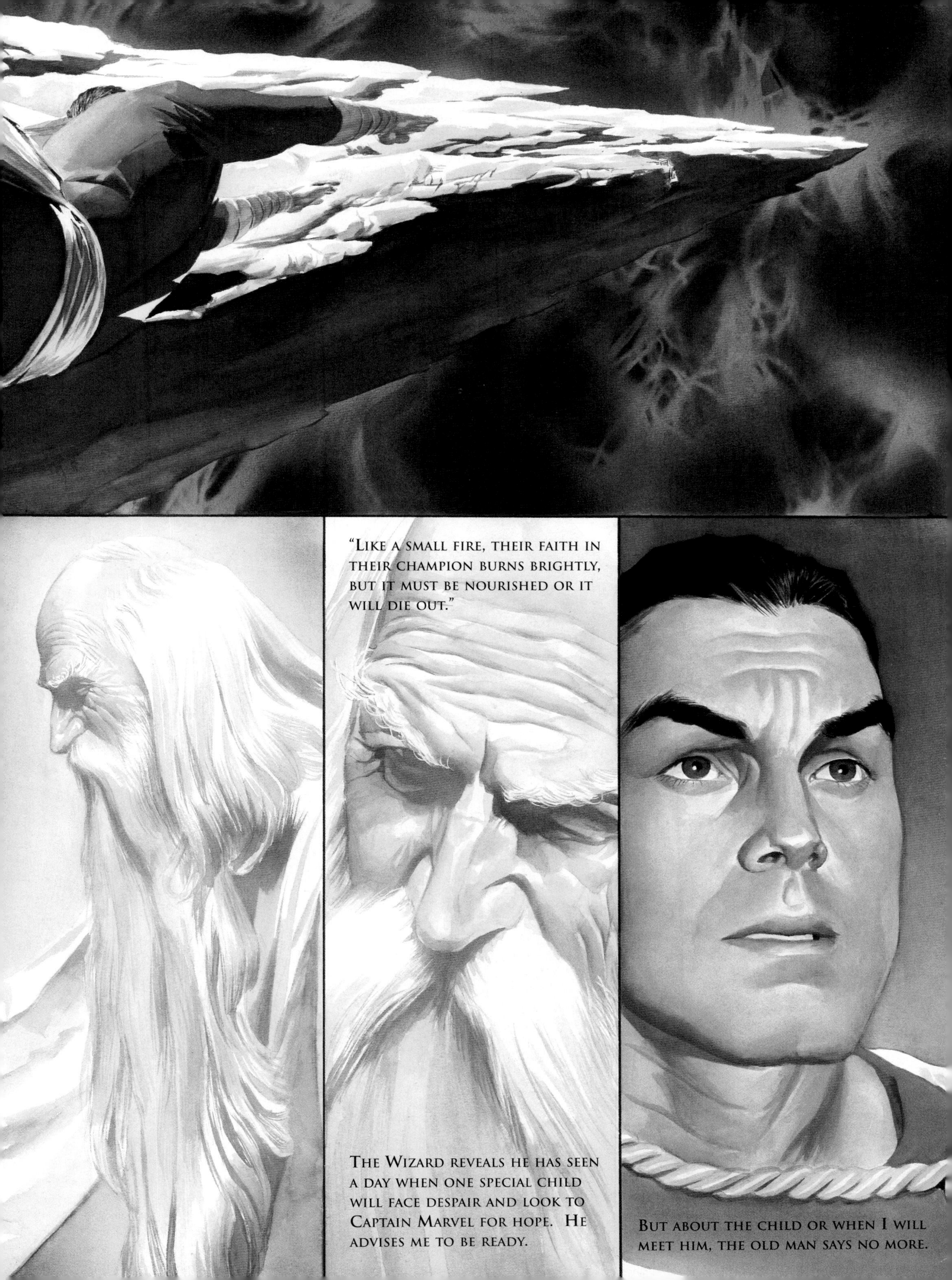

"Like a small fire, their faith in their champion burns brightly, but it must be nourished or it will die out."
The Wizard reveals he has seen a day when one special child will face despair and look to Captain Marvel for hope. He advises me to be ready.
But about the child or when I will meet him, the old man says no more.

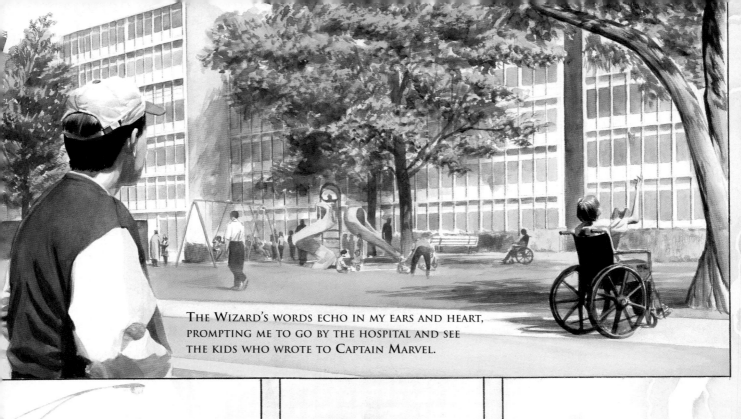

THE WIZARD'S WORDS ECHO IN MY EARS AND HEART, PROMPTING ME TO GO BY THE HOSPITAL AND SEE THE KIDS WHO WROTE TO CAPTAIN MARVEL.

ALL OF THEM ARE SICK, MANY ARE SCARED, AND MORE THAN A FEW SEEM TERRIBLY ALONE.

AND EVEN HERE, THERE IS NEED FOR THE CAPTAIN'S MORE IMMEDIATE SERVICES.

"SHAZAM!"

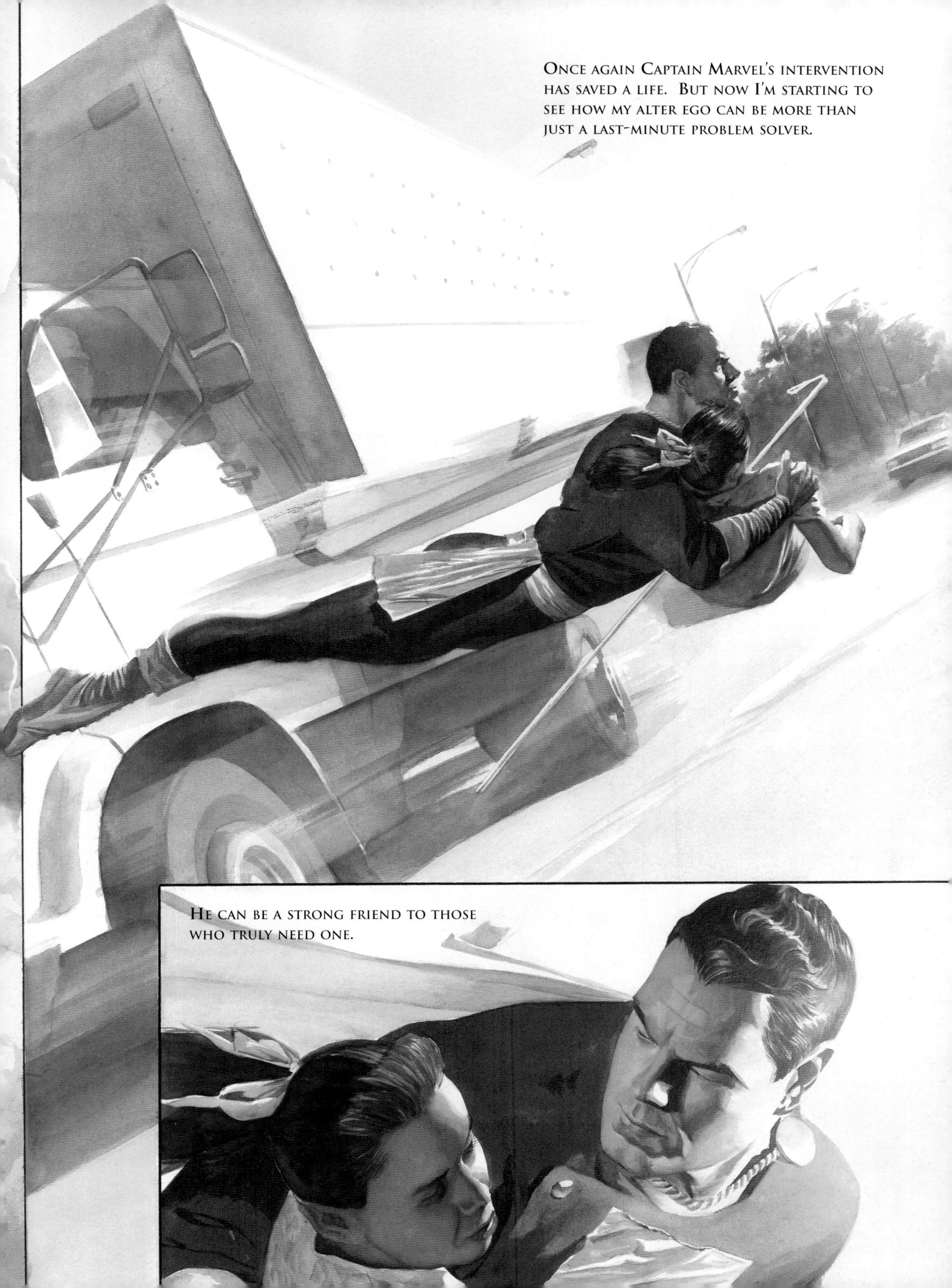
Once again Captain Marvel's intervention has saved a life. But now I'm starting to see how my alter ego can be more than just a last-minute problem solver.
He can be a strong friend to those who truly need one.

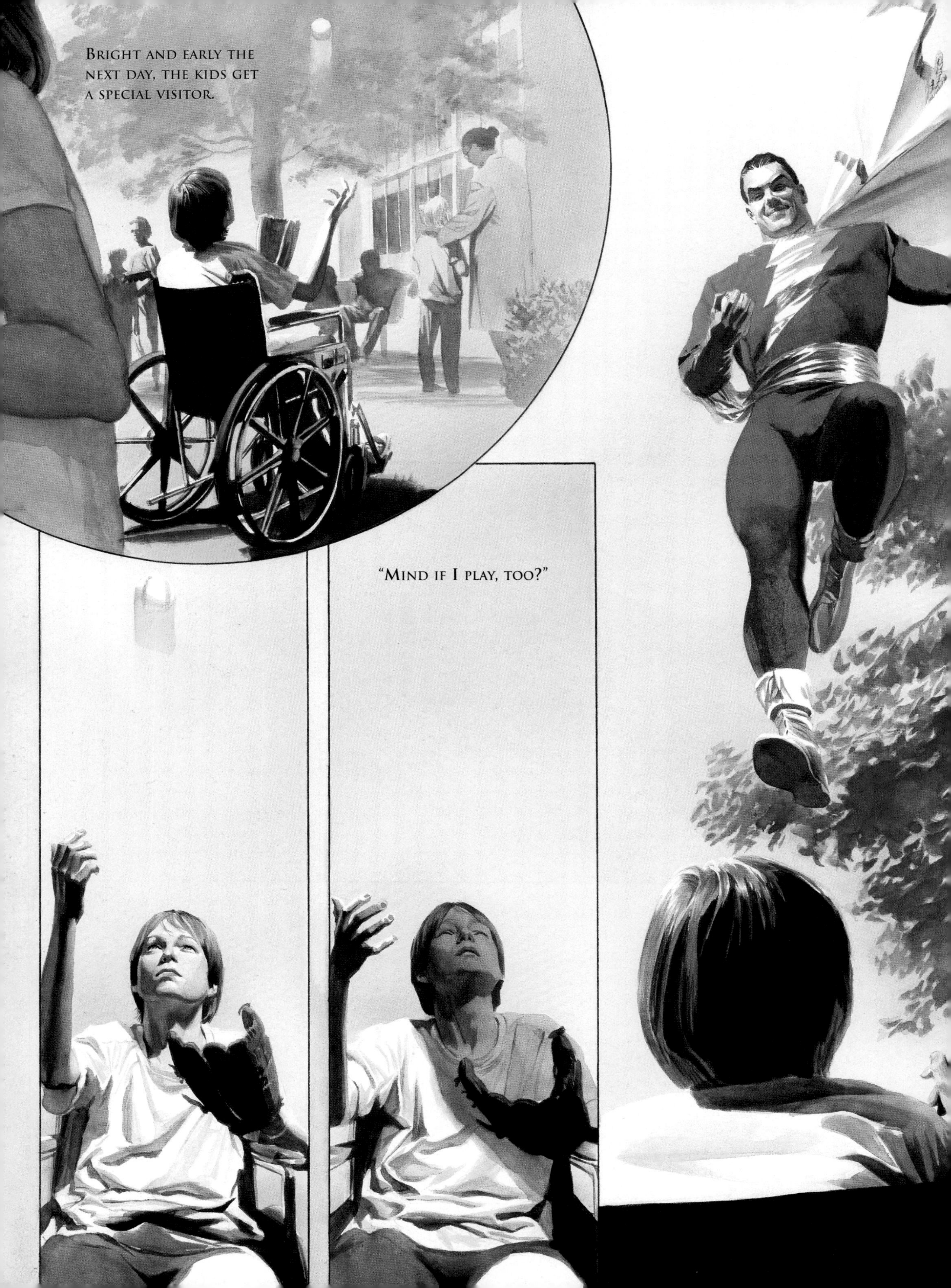
Bright and early the next day, the kids get a special visitor.
"Mind if I play, too?"

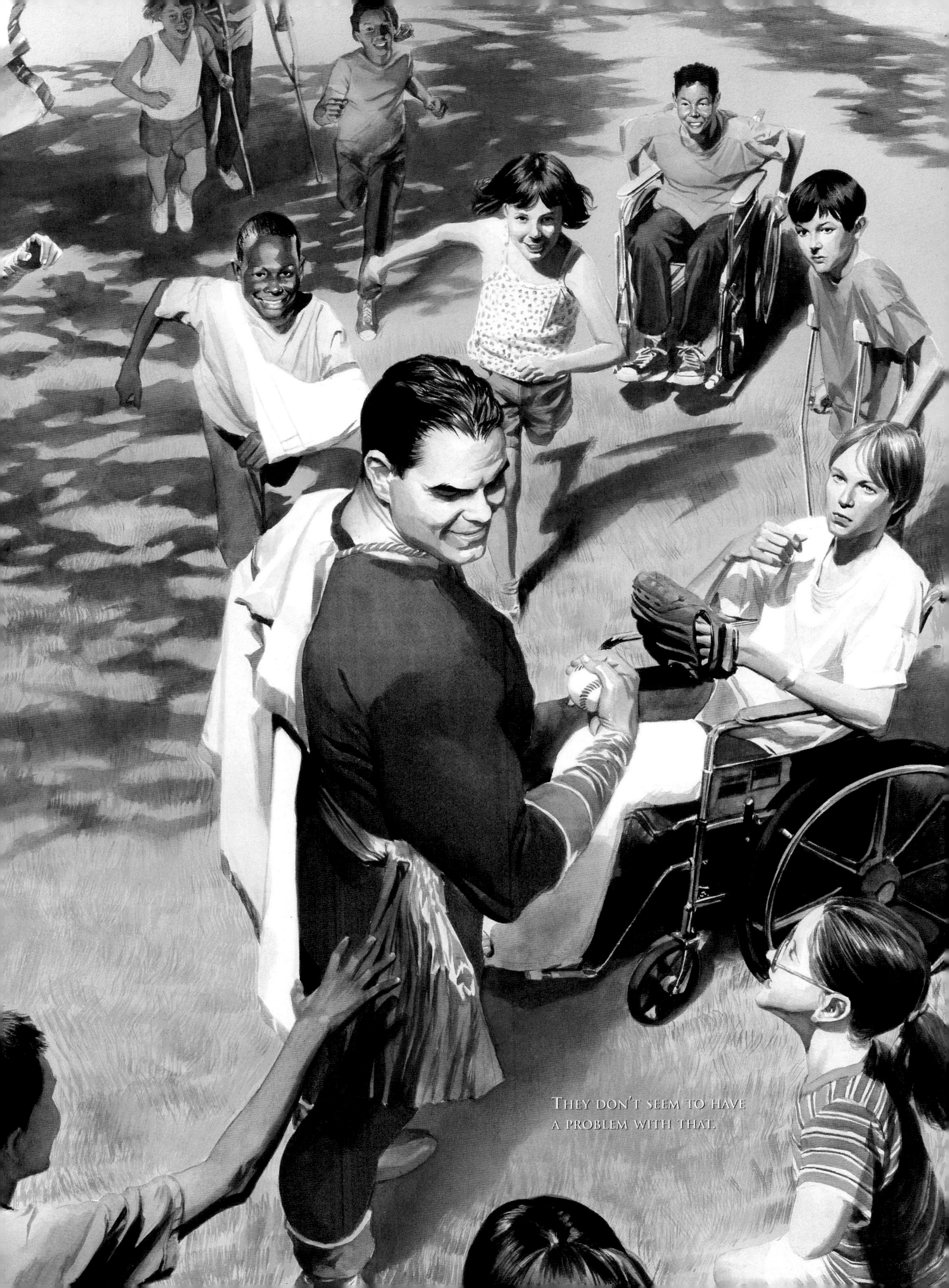
They don't seem to have a problem with that.

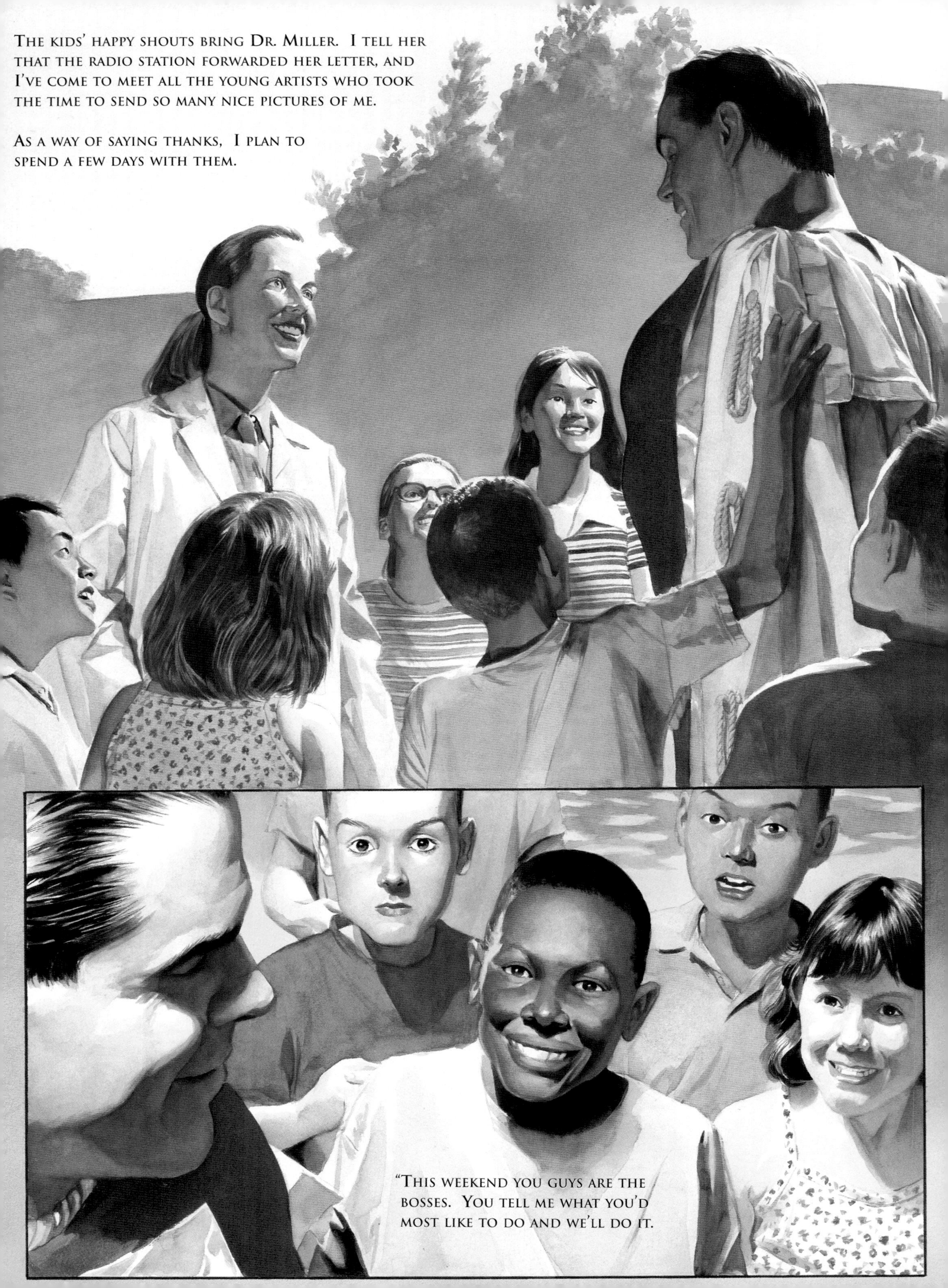
The kids' happy shouts bring Dr. Miller. I tell her that the radio station forwarded her letter, and I've come to meet all the young artists who took the time to send so many nice pictures of me.
As a way of saying thanks, I plan to spend a few days with them.
"This weekend you guys are the bosses. You tell me what you'd most like to do and we'll do it.

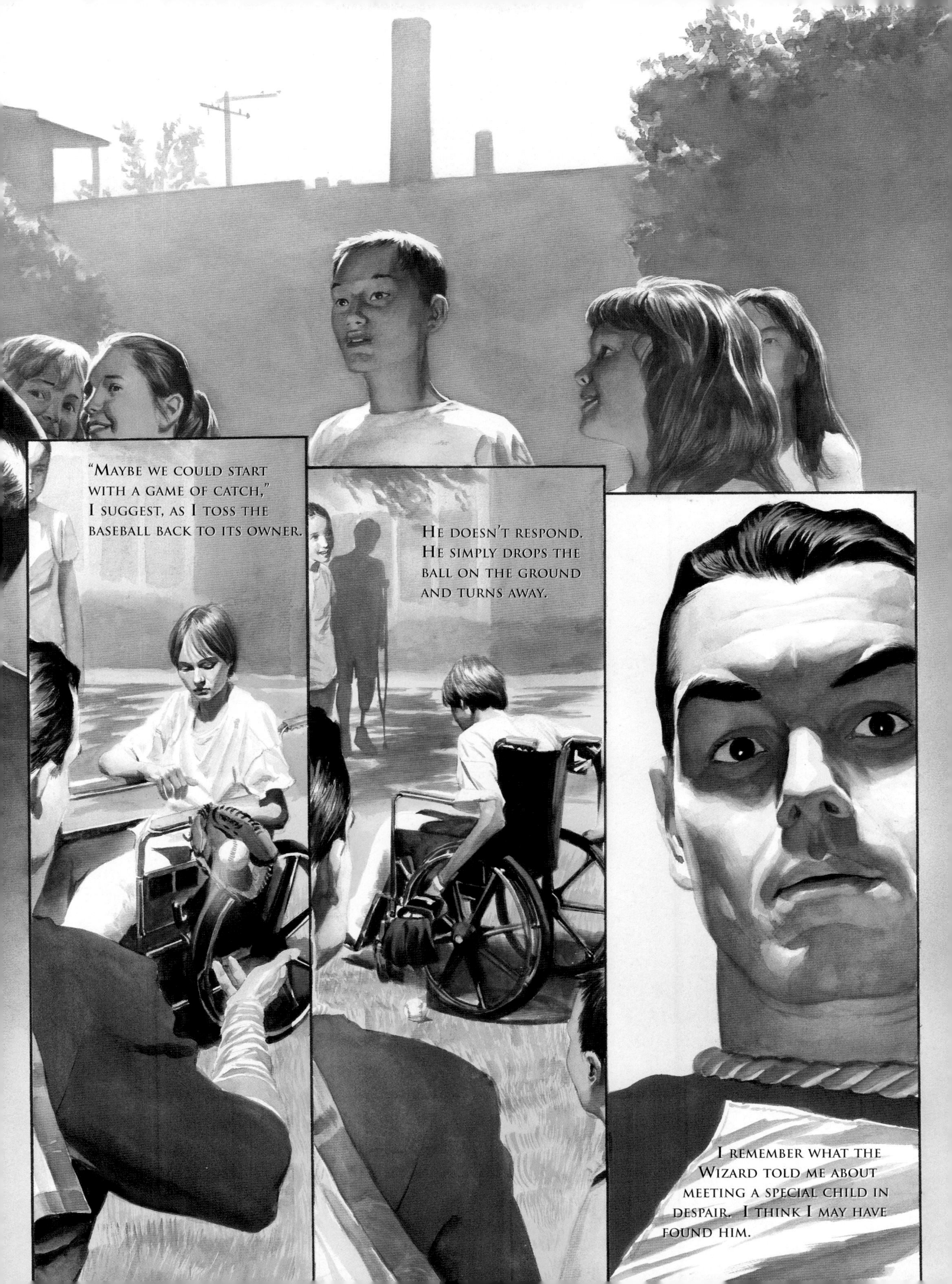
"Maybe we could start with a game of catch," I suggest, as I toss the baseball back to its owner.
He doesn't respond. He simply drops the ball on the ground and turns away.
I remember what the Wizard told me about meeting a special child in despair. I think I may have found him.

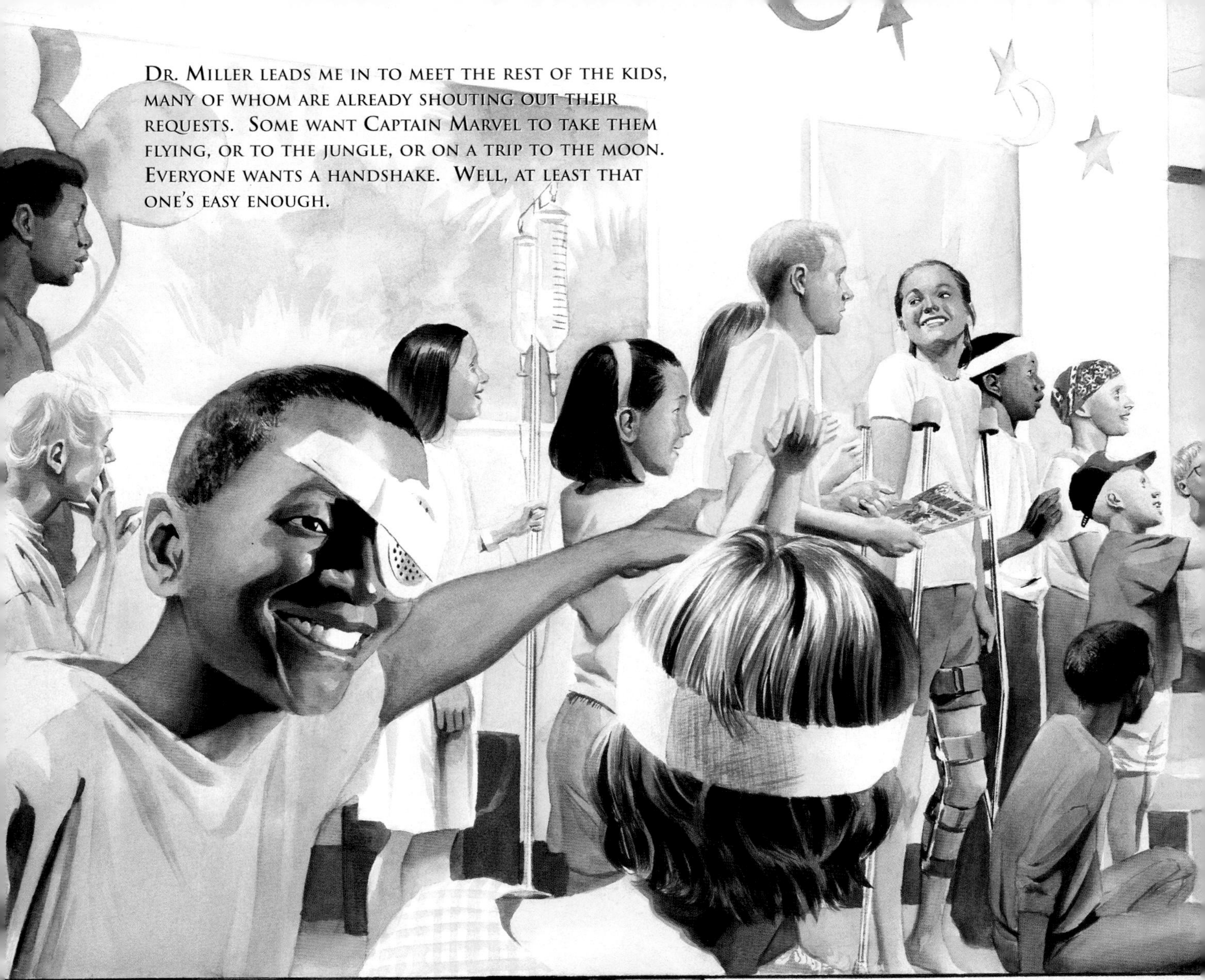
Dr. Miller leads me in to meet the rest of the kids, many of whom are already shouting out their requests. Some want Captain Marvel to take them flying, or to the jungle, or on a trip to the moon. Everyone wants a handshake. Well, at least that one's easy enough.

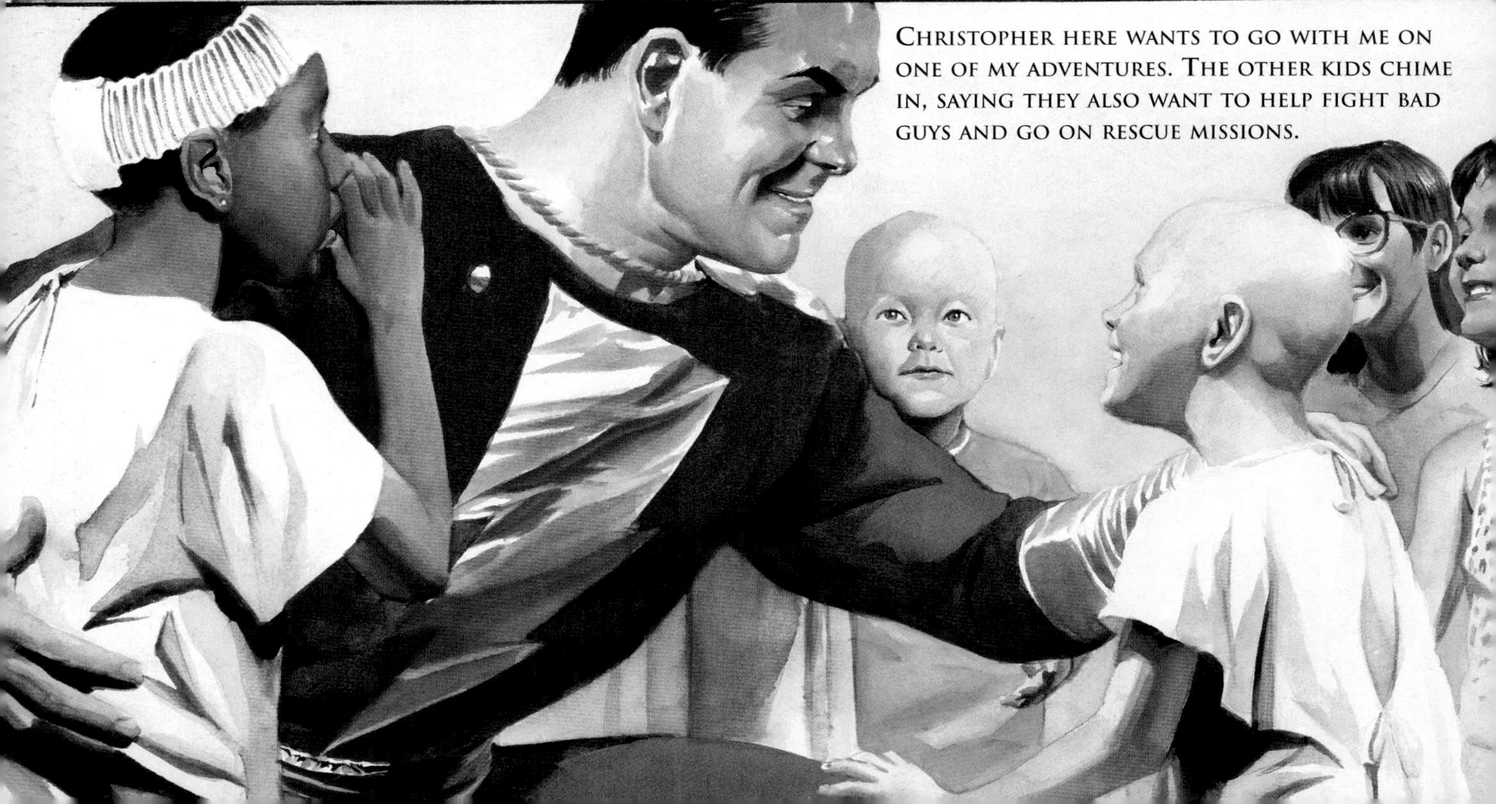
Christopher here wants to go with me on one of my adventures. The other kids chime in, saying they also want to help fight bad guys and go on rescue missions.

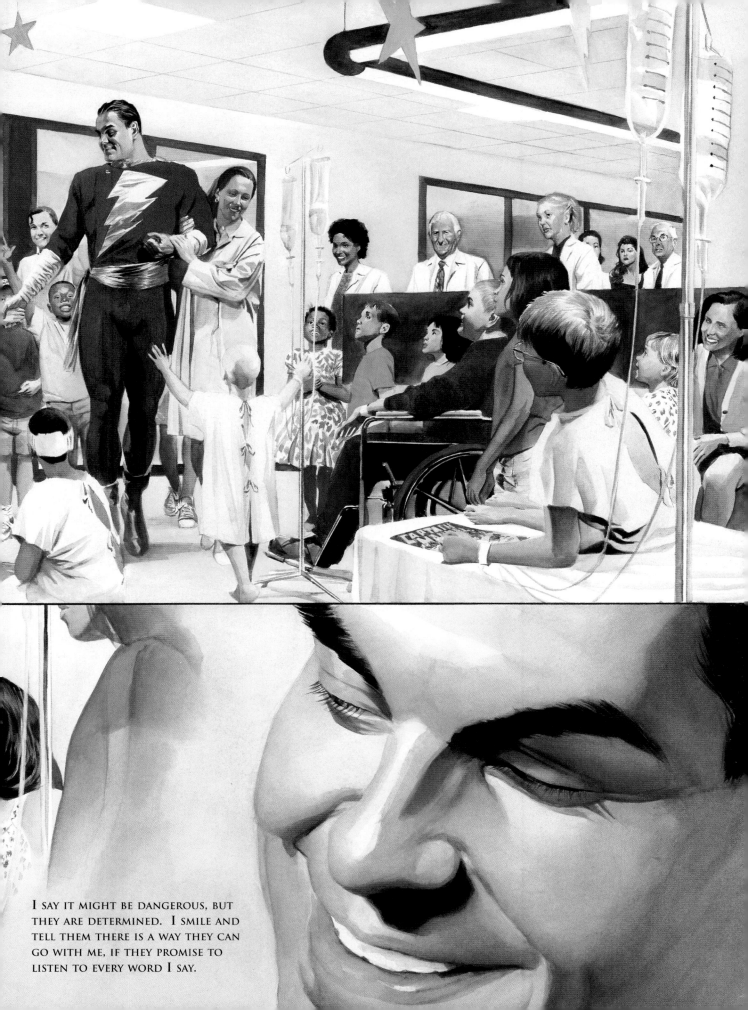

I SAY IT MIGHT BE DANGEROUS, BUT
THEY ARE DETERMINED. I SMILE AND
TELL THEM THERE IS A WAY THEY CAN
GO WITH ME, IF THEY PROMISE TO
LISTEN TO EVERY WORD I SAY.

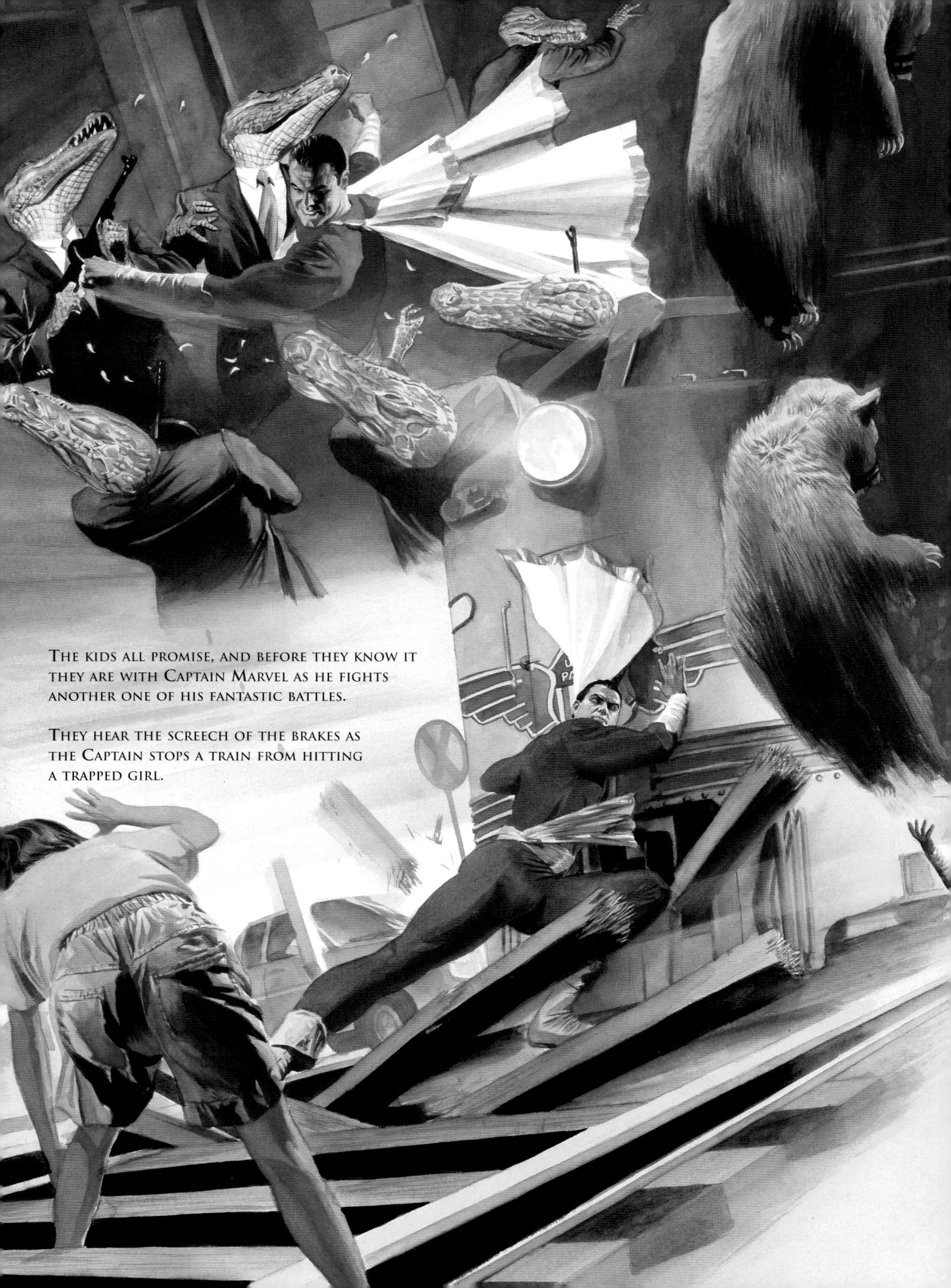

The kids all promise, and before they know it they are with Captain Marvel as he fights another one of his fantastic battles.

They hear the screech of the brakes as the Captain stops a train from hitting a trapped girl.

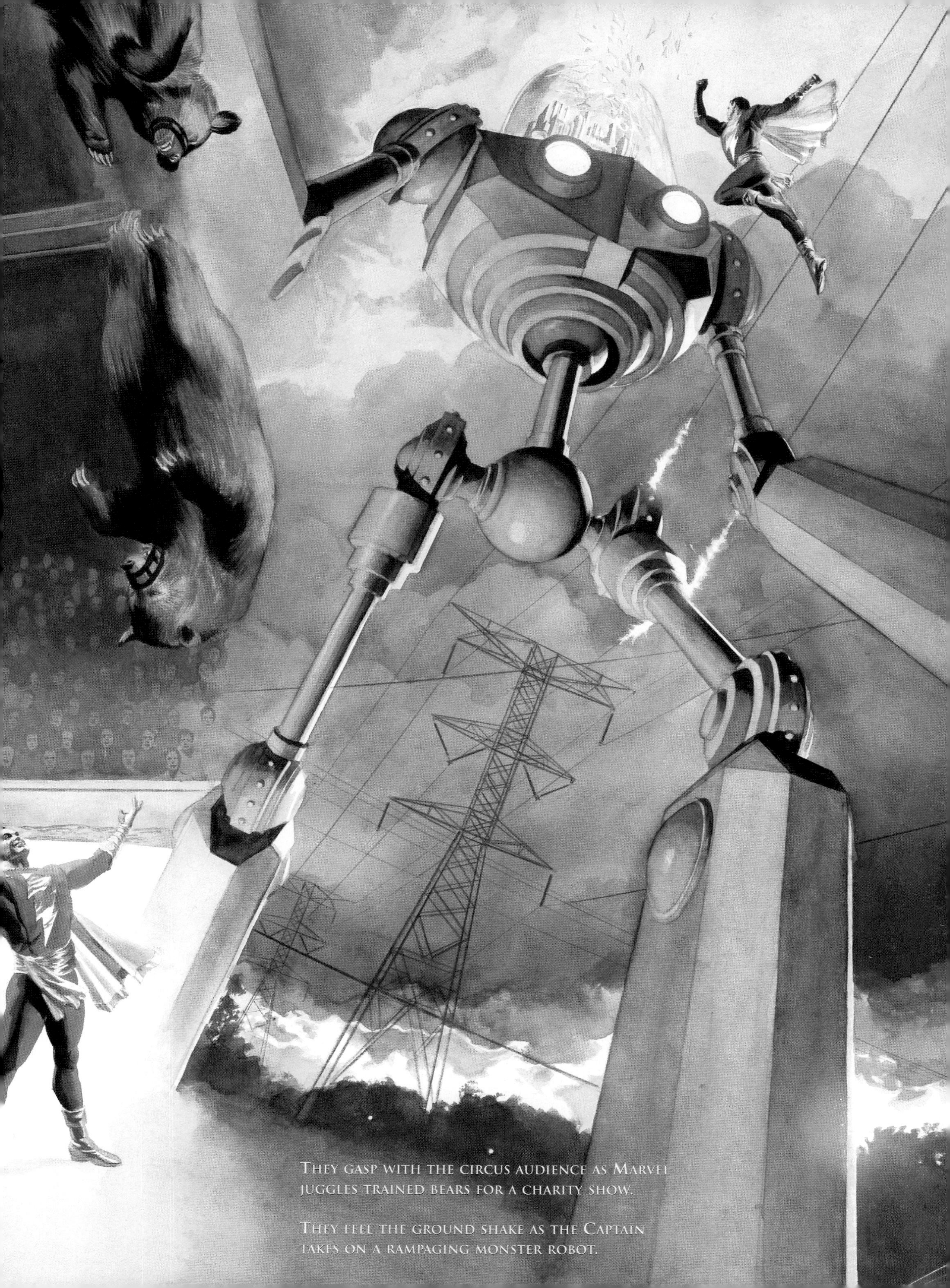
They gasp with the circus audience as Marvel juggles trained bears for a charity show.
They feel the ground shake as the Captain takes on a rampaging monster robot.

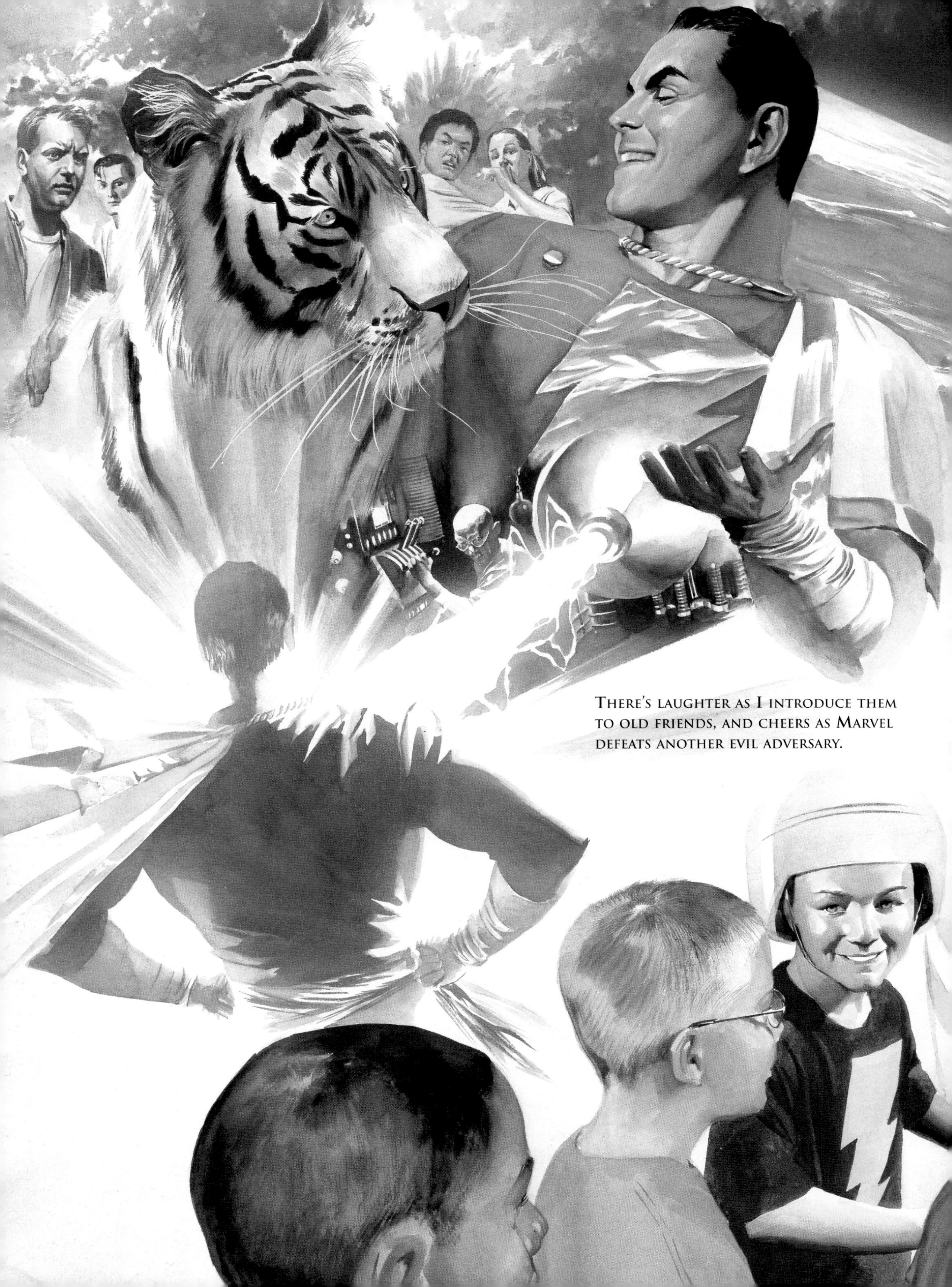
There's laughter as I introduce them to old friends, and cheers as Marvel defeats another evil adversary.

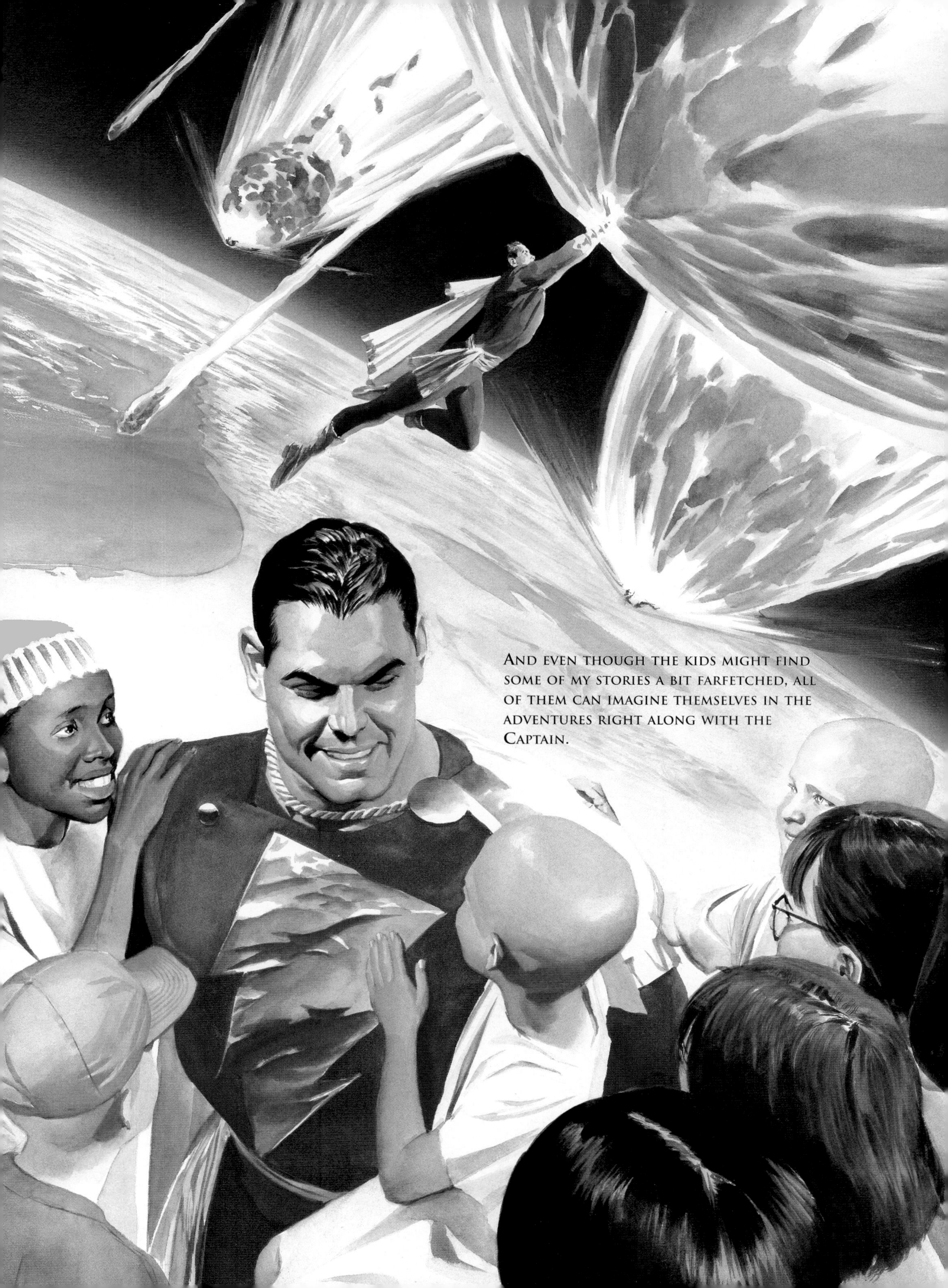
AND EVEN THOUGH THE KIDS MIGHT FIND SOME OF MY STORIES A BIT FARFETCHED, ALL OF THEM CAN IMAGINE THEMSELVES IN THE ADVENTURES RIGHT ALONG WITH THE CAPTAIN.

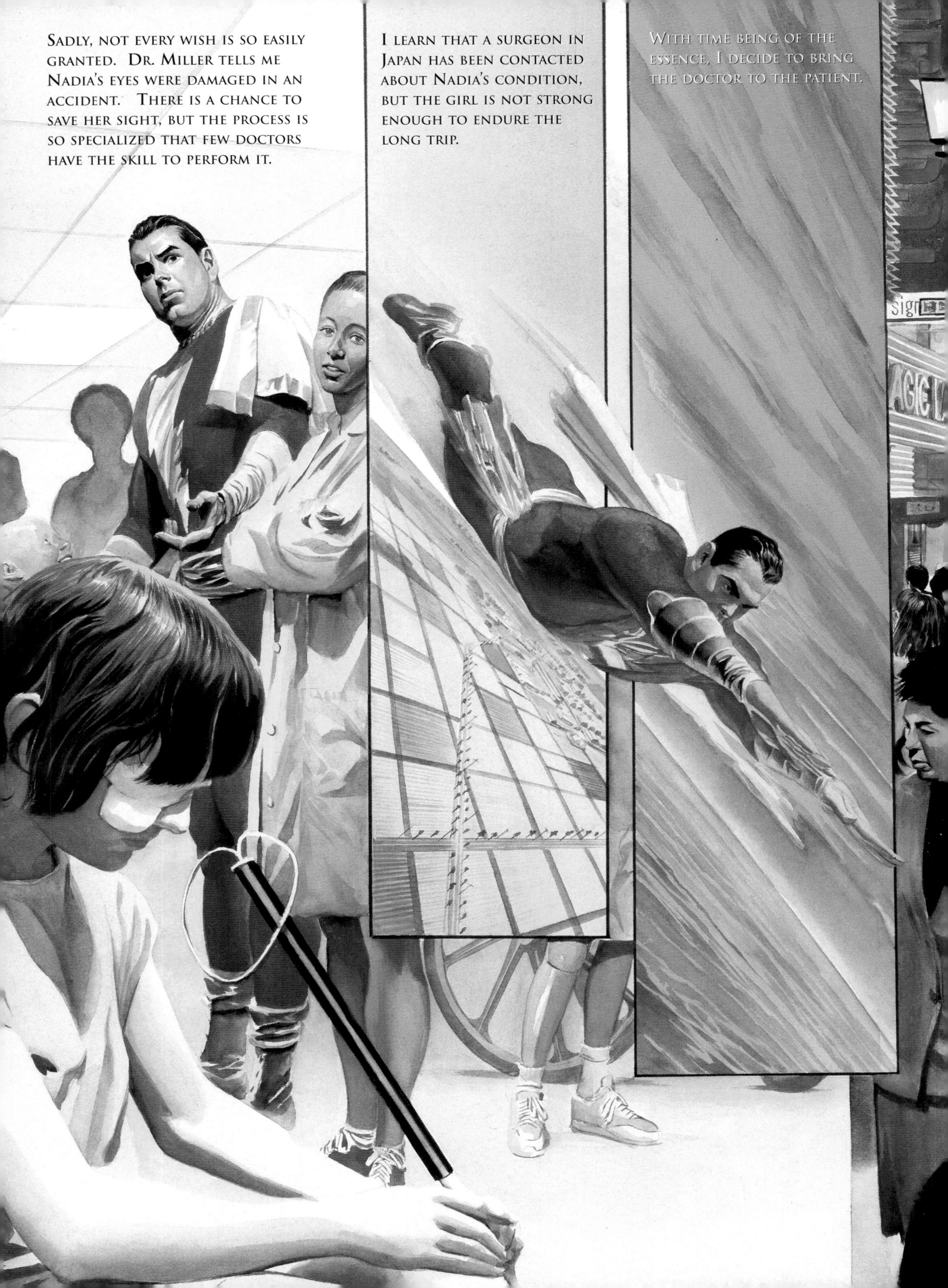
Sadly, not every wish is so easily granted. Dr. Miller tells me Nadia's eyes were damaged in an accident. There is a chance to save her sight, but the process is so specialized that few doctors have the skill to perform it.
I learn that a surgeon in Japan has been contacted about Nadia's condition, but the girl is not strong enough to endure the long trip.
With time being of the essence, I decide to bring the doctor to the patient.

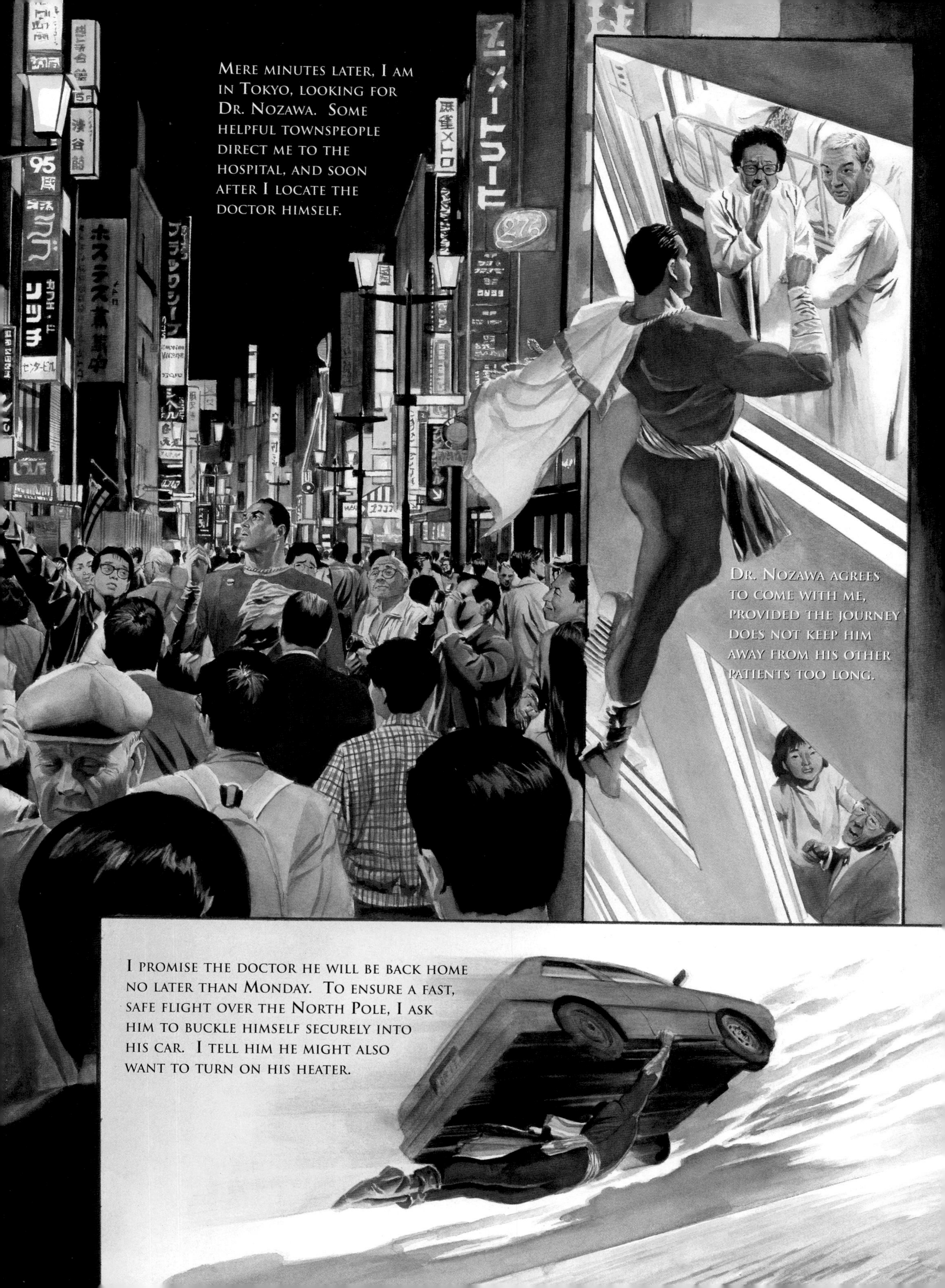
Mere minutes later, I am in Tokyo, looking for Dr. Nozawa. Some helpful townspeople direct me to the hospital, and soon after I locate the doctor himself.
Dr. Nozawa agrees to come with me, provided the journey does not keep him away from his other patients too long.
I promise the doctor he will be back home no later than Monday. To ensure a fast, safe flight over the North Pole, I ask him to buckle himself securely into his car. I tell him he might also want to turn on his heater.

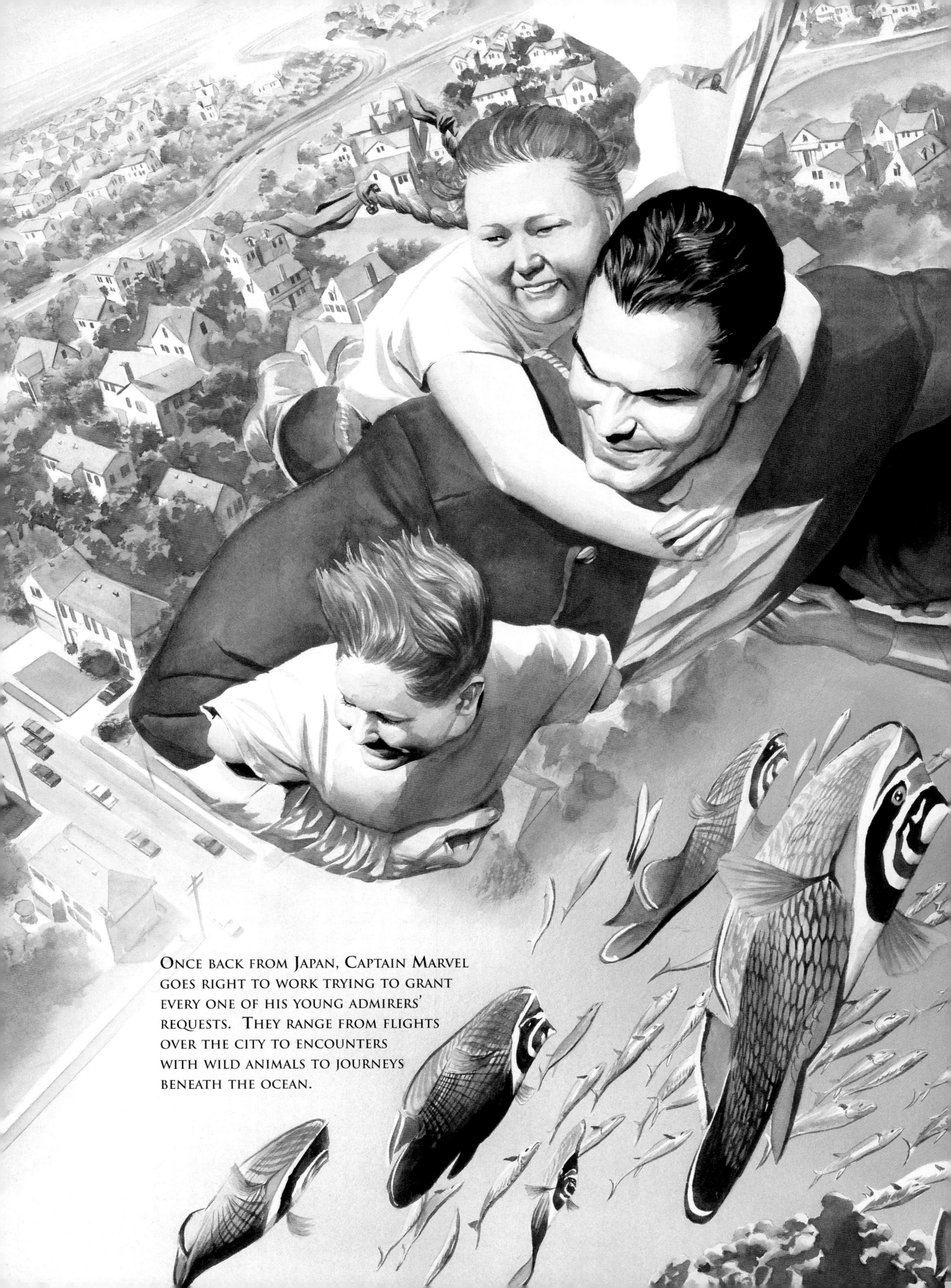

Once back from Japan, Captain Marvel goes right to work trying to grant every one of his young admirers' requests. They range from flights over the city to encounters with wild animals to journeys beneath the ocean.

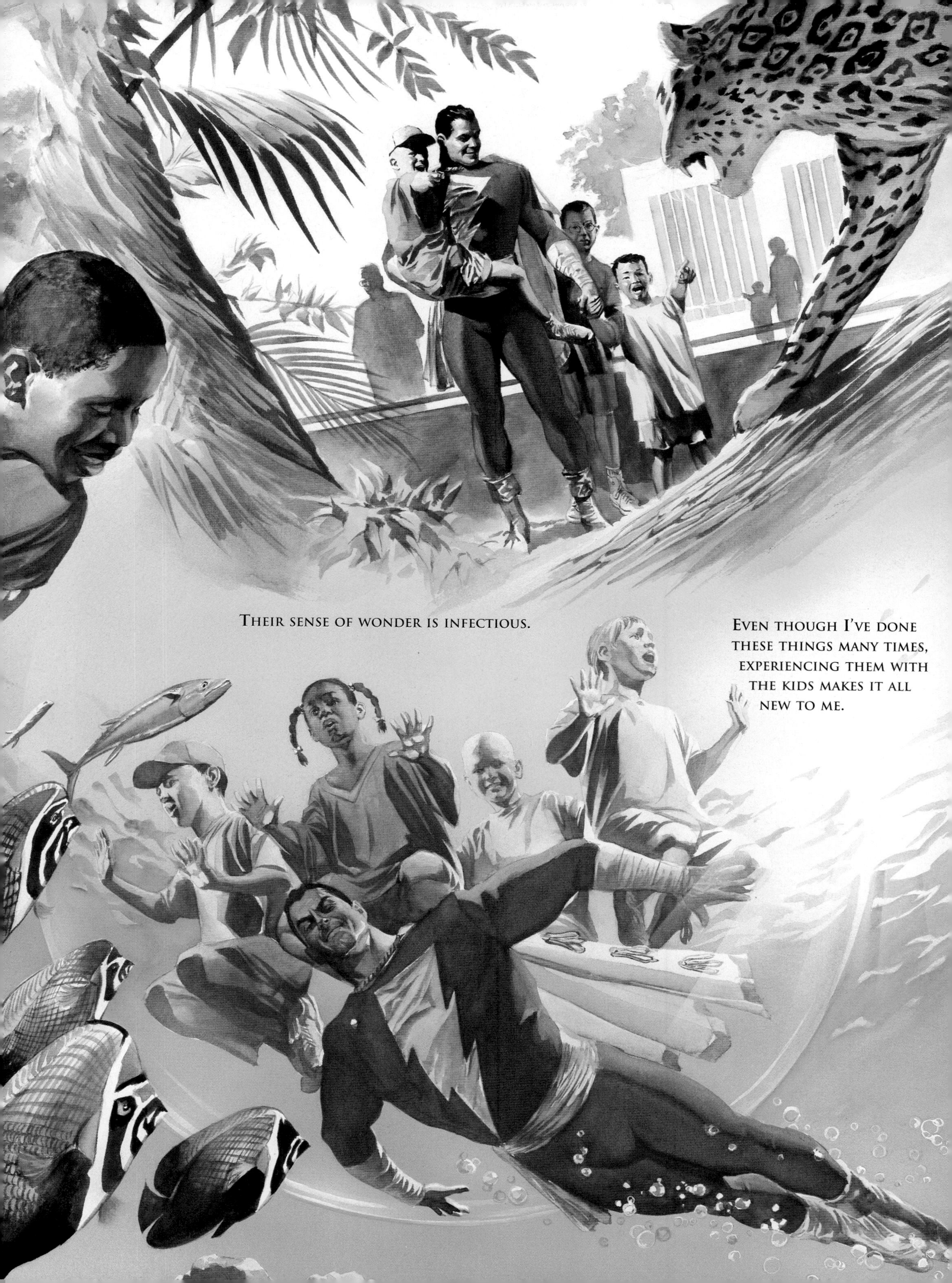
THEIR SENSE OF WONDER IS INFECTIOUS.
EVEN THOUGH I'VE DONE THESE THINGS MANY TIMES, EXPERIENCING THEM WITH THE KIDS MAKES IT ALL NEW TO ME.

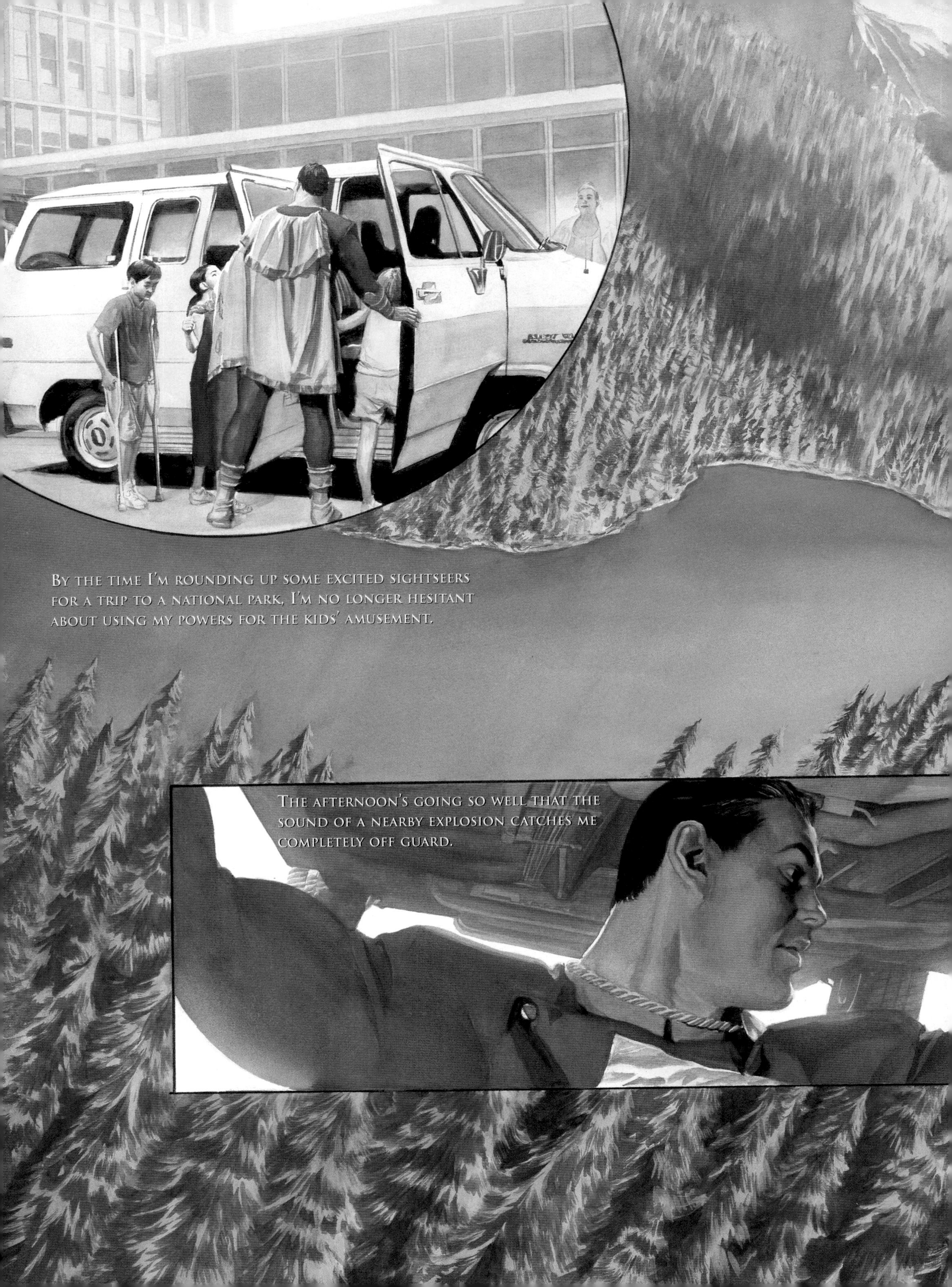
By the time I'm rounding up some excited sightseers for a trip to a national park, I'm no longer hesitant about using my powers for the kids' amusement.
The afternoon's going so well that the sound of a nearby explosion catches me completely off guard.

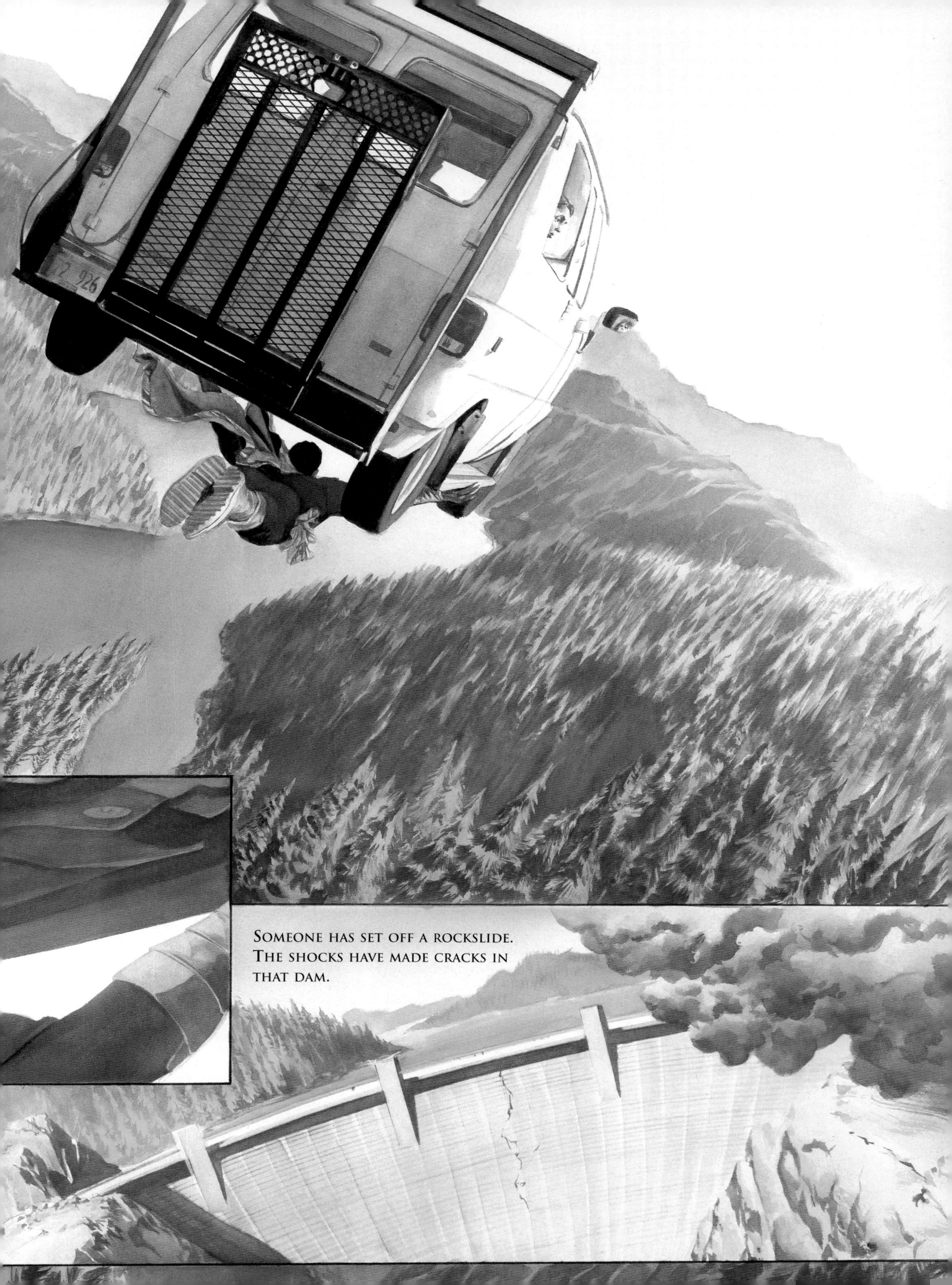

Someone has set off a rockslide. The shocks have made cracks in that dam.

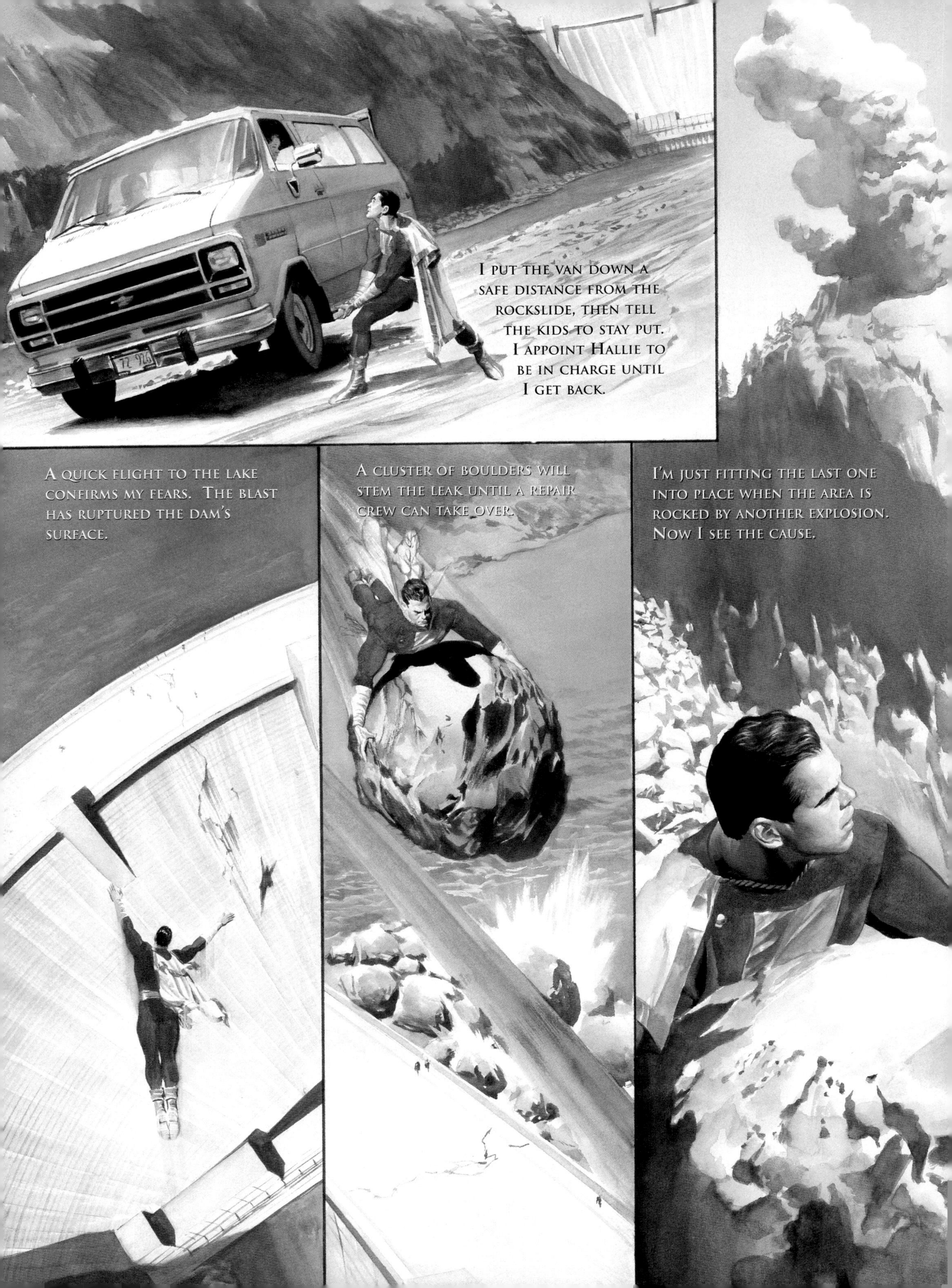
I put the van down a safe distance from the rockslide, then tell the kids to stay put. I appoint Hallie to be in charge until I get back.
A quick flight to the lake confirms my fears. The blast has ruptured the dam's surface.
A cluster of boulders will stem the leak until a repair crew can take over.
I'm just fitting the last one into place when the area is rocked by another explosion. Now I see the cause.

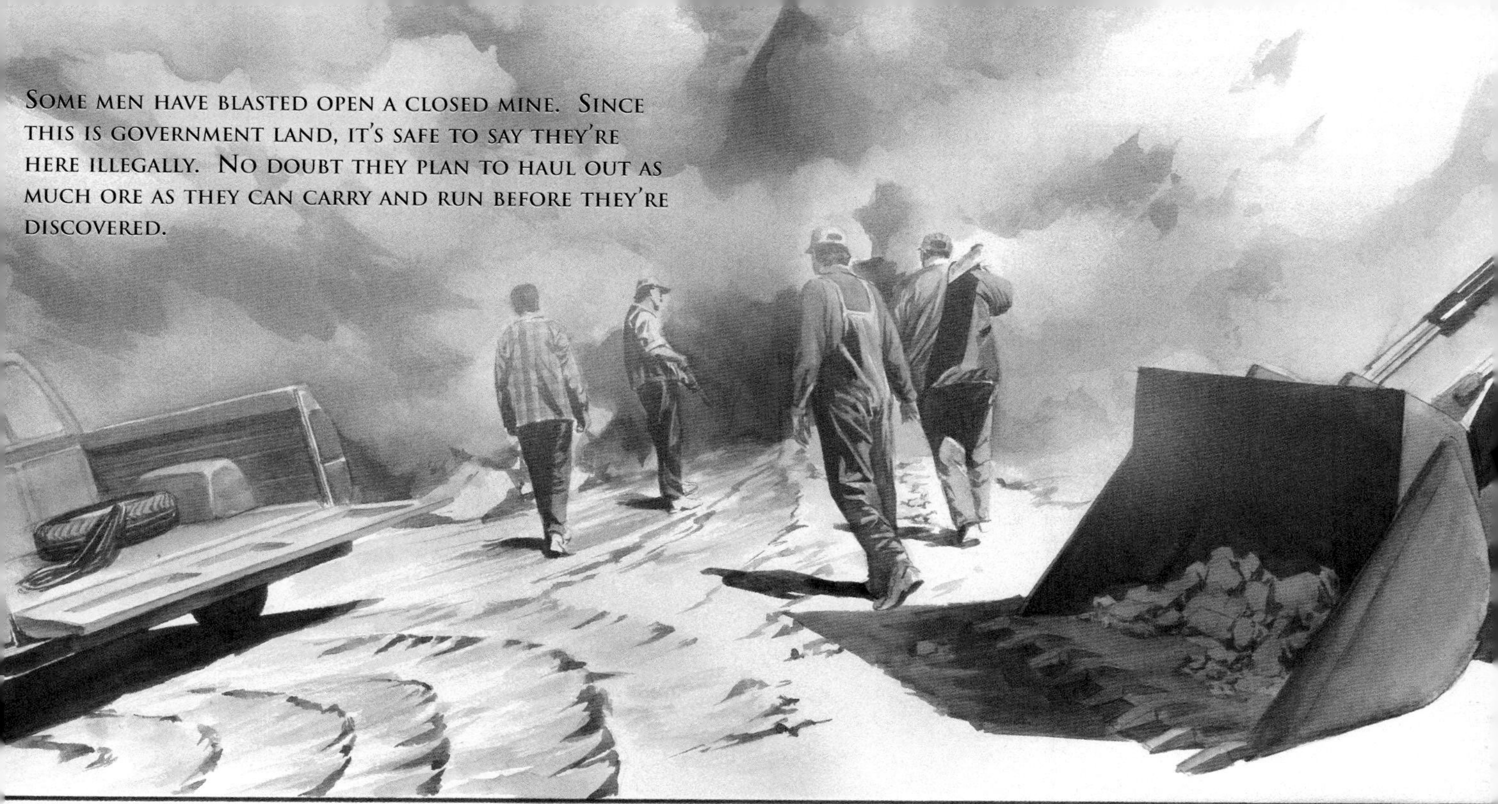
Some men have blasted open a closed mine. Since this is government land, it's safe to say they're here illegally. No doubt they plan to haul out as much ore as they can carry and run before they're discovered.

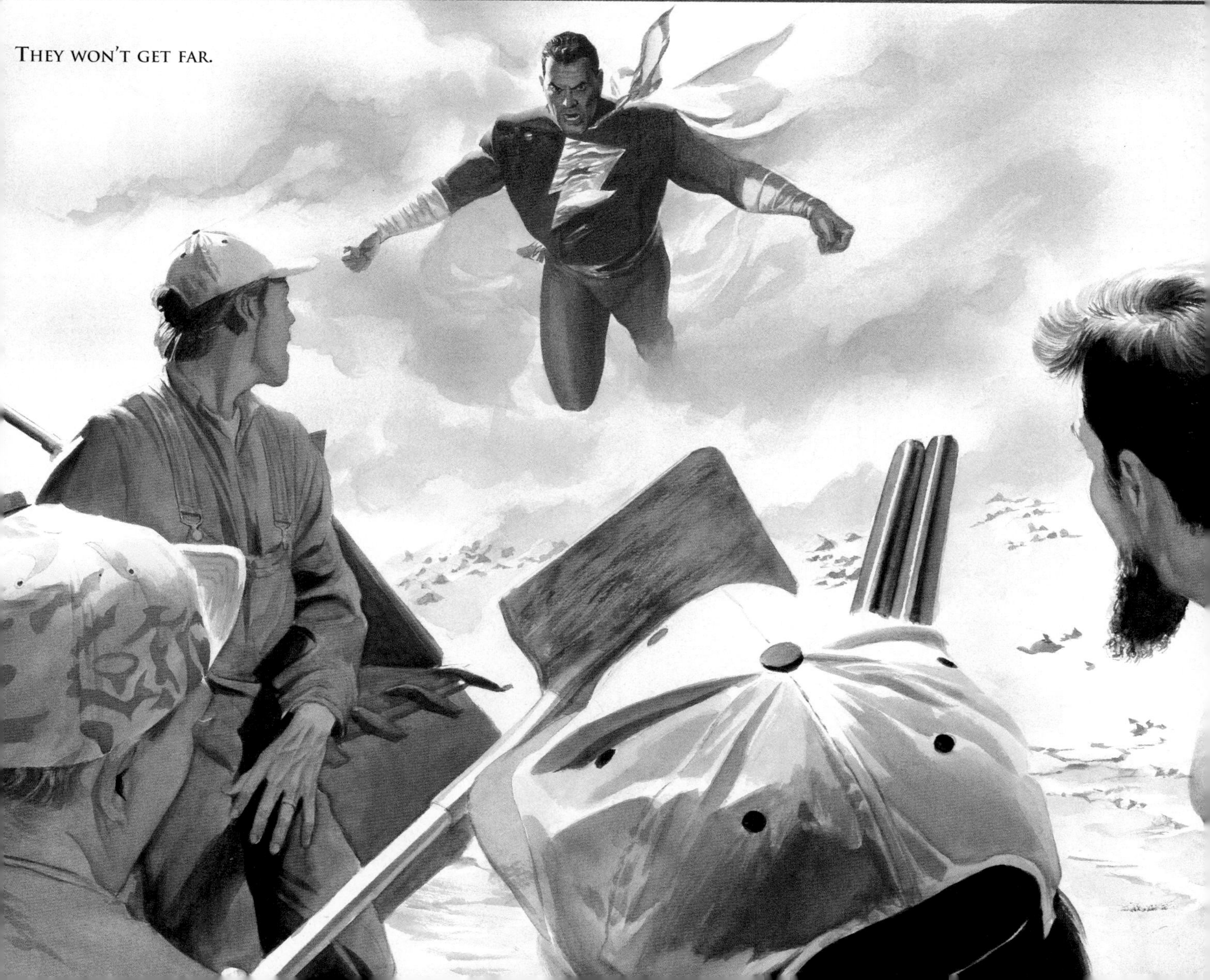
They won't get far.

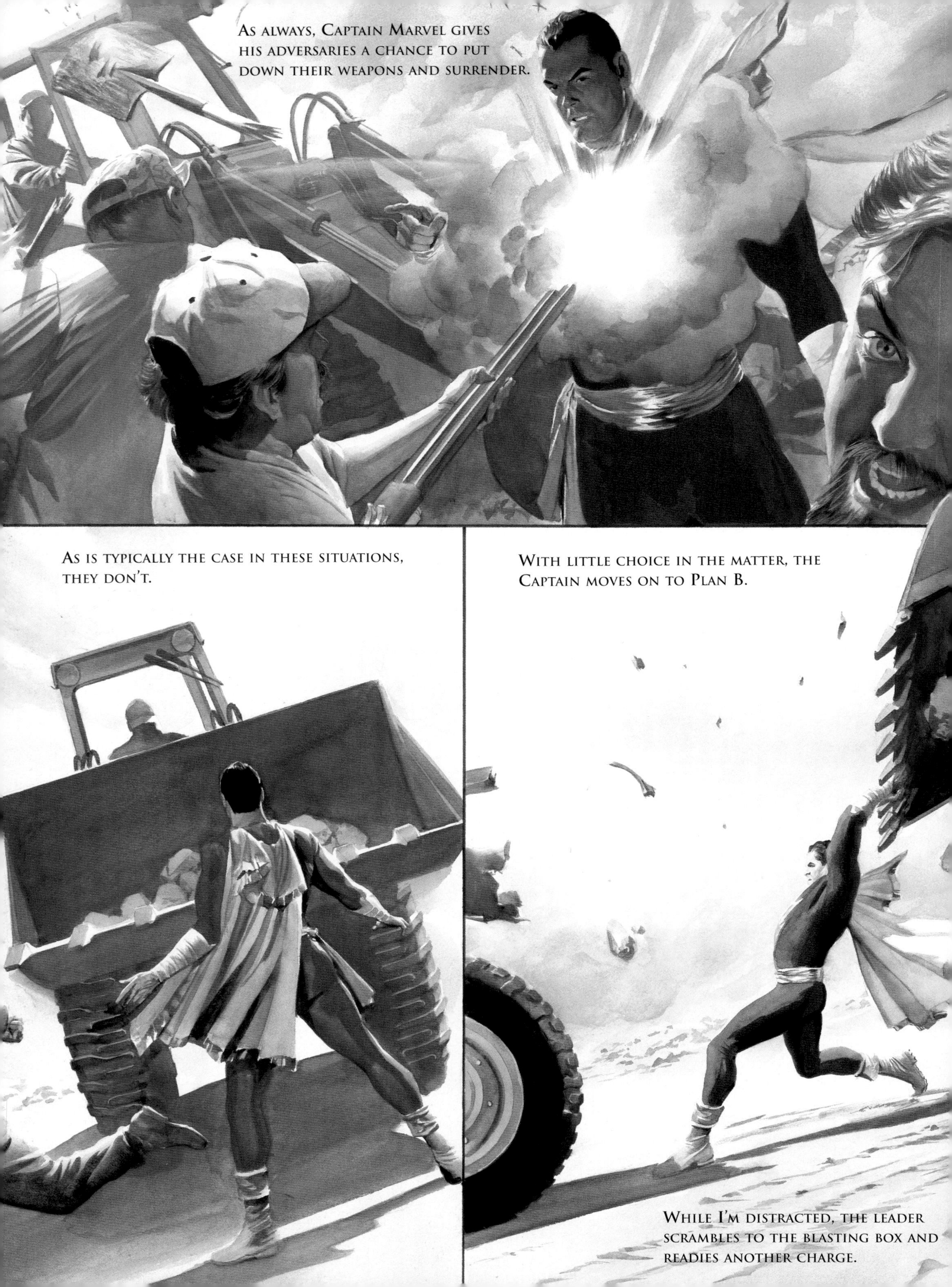
As always, Captain Marvel gives his adversaries a chance to put down their weapons and surrender.
As is typically the case in these situations, they don't.
With little choice in the matter, the Captain moves on to Plan B.
While I'm distracted, the leader scrambles to the blasting box and readies another charge.

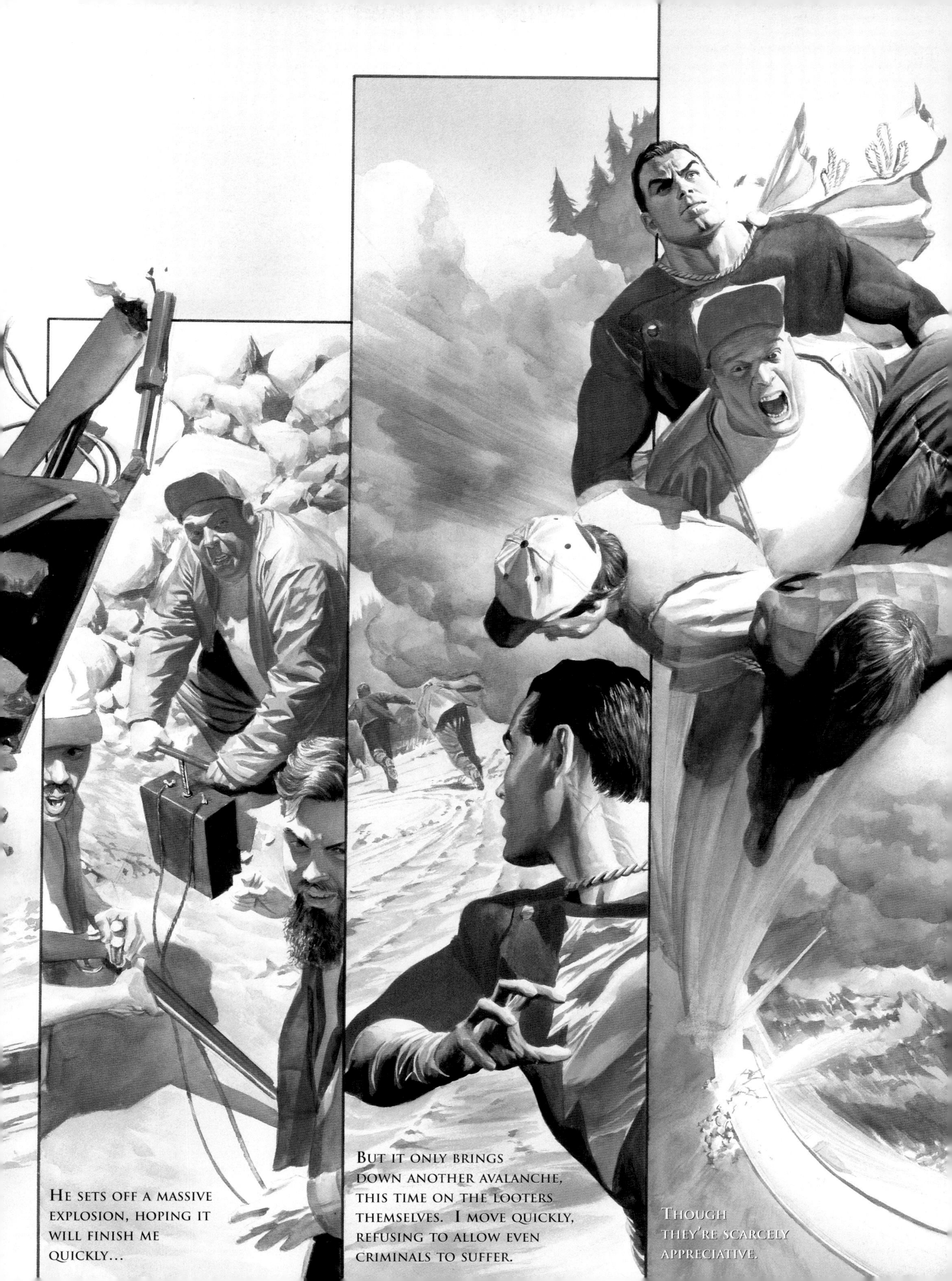
He sets off a massive explosion, hoping it will finish me quickly...
But it only brings down another avalanche, this time on the looters themselves. I move quickly, refusing to allow even criminals to suffer.
Though they're scarcely appreciative.

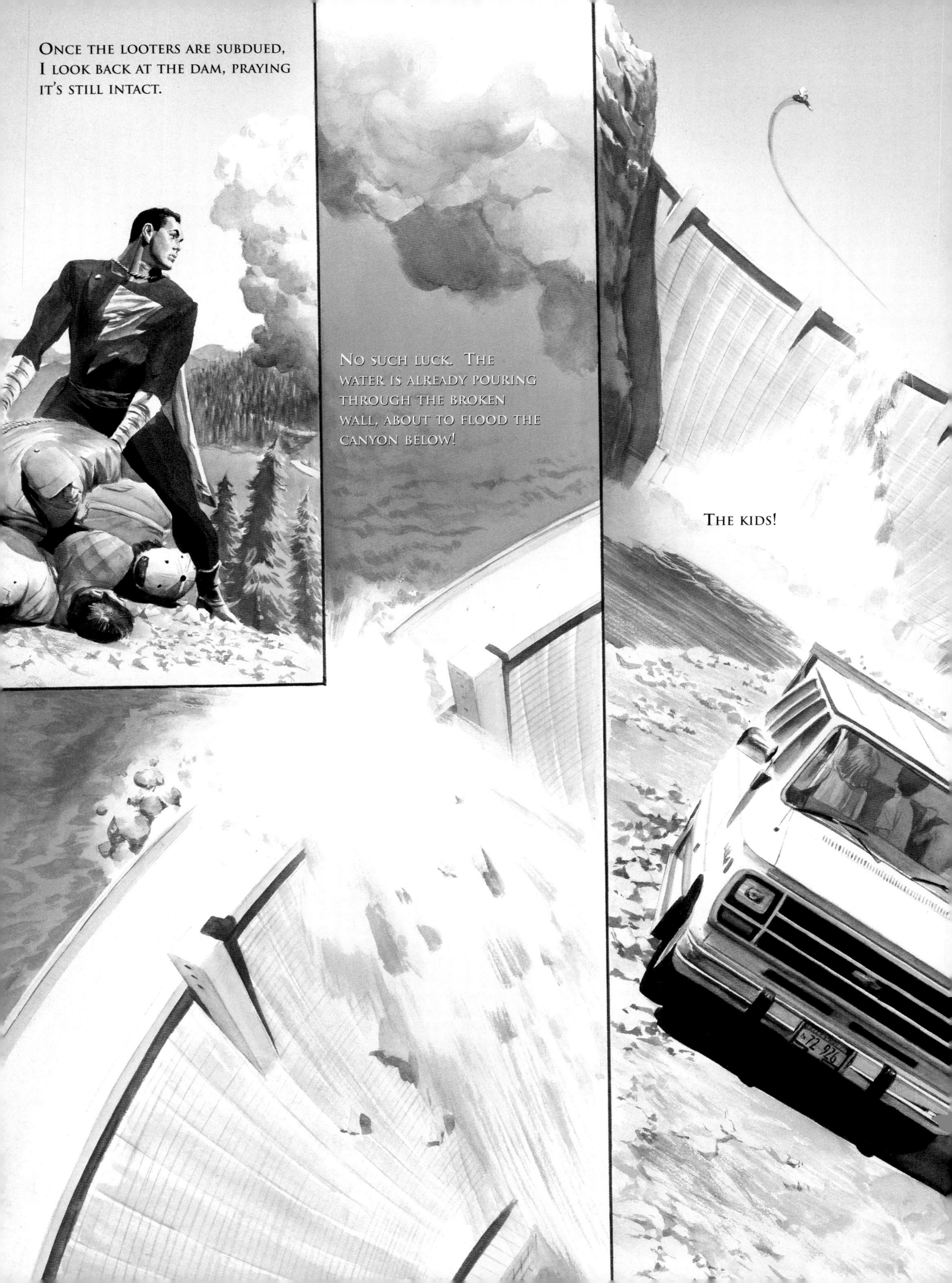

Once the looters are subdued, I look back at the dam, praying it's still intact.
No such luck. The water is already pouring through the broken wall, about to flood the canyon below!
The kids!

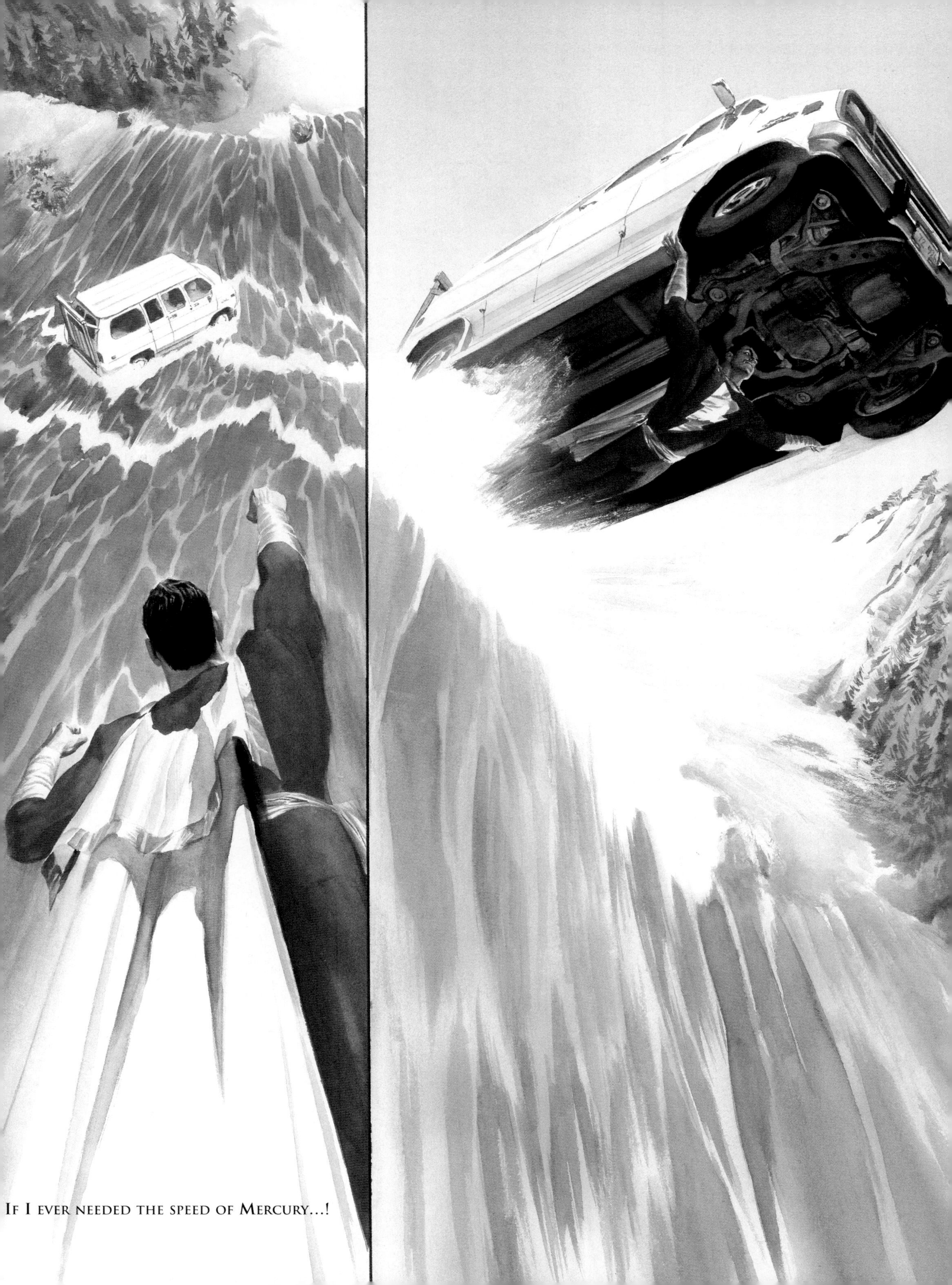
If I ever needed the speed of Mercury...!

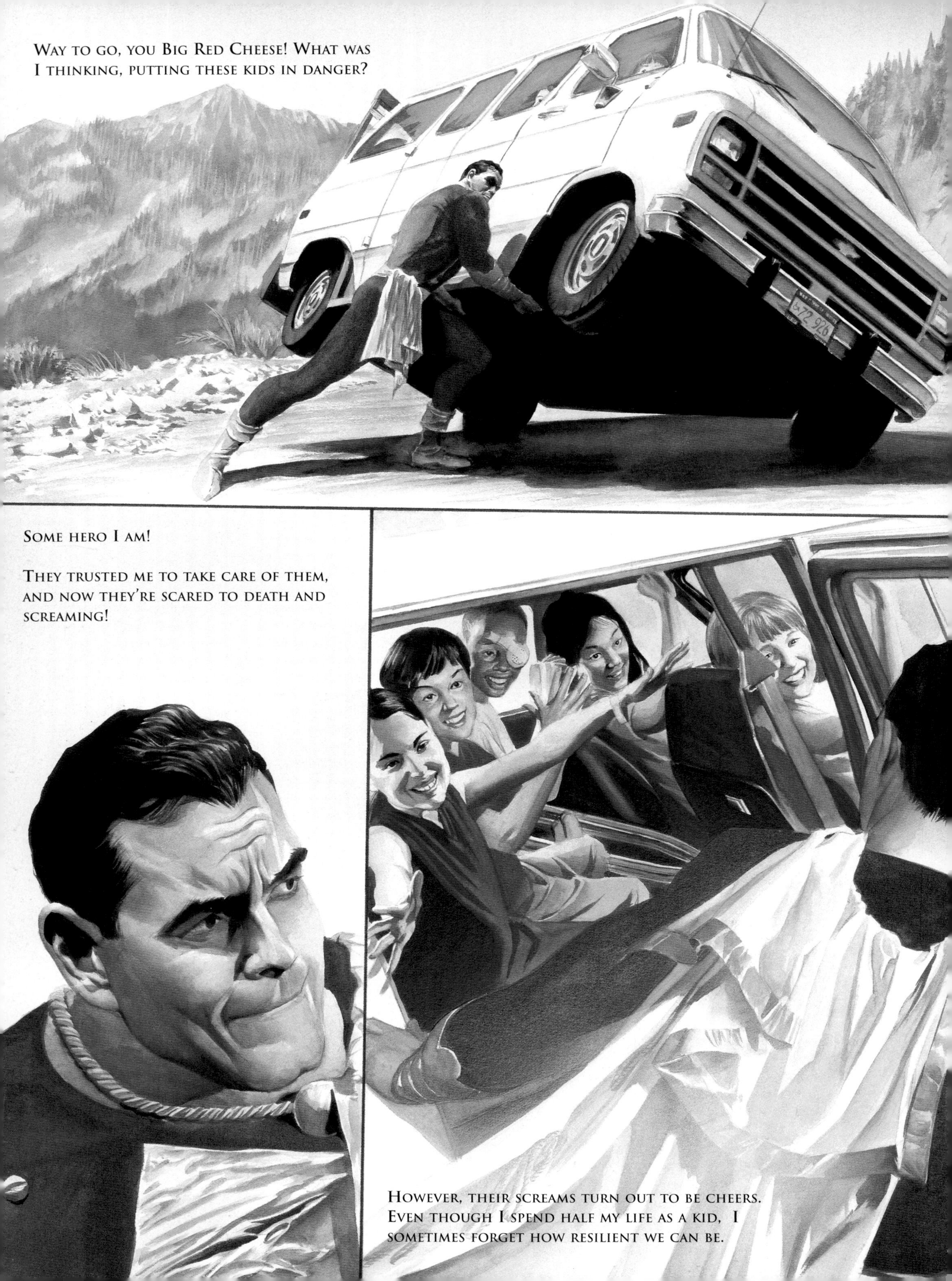
Way to go, you Big Red Cheese! What was I thinking, putting these kids in danger?
Some hero I am!
They trusted me to take care of them, and now they're scared to death and screaming!
However, their screams turn out to be cheers. Even though I spend half my life as a kid, I sometimes forget how resilient we can be.

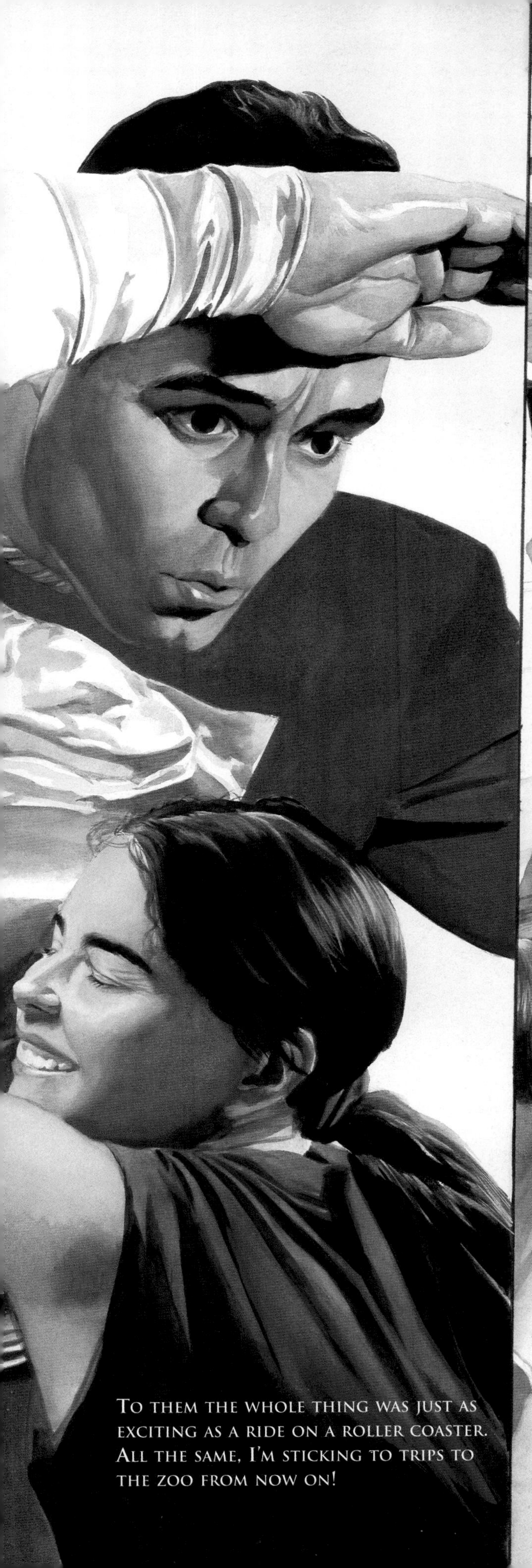
To them the whole thing was just as exciting as a ride on a roller coaster. All the same, I'm sticking to trips to the zoo from now on!

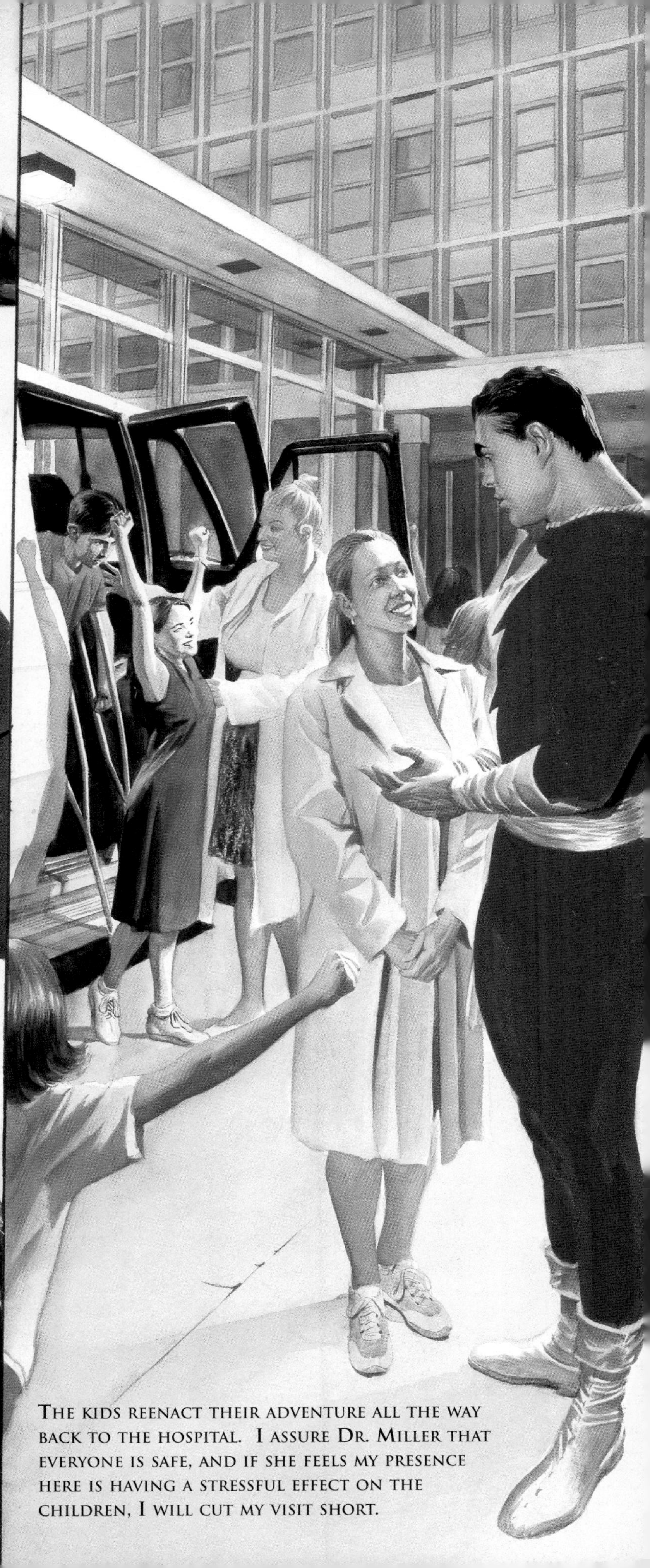
The kids reenact their adventure all the way back to the hospital. I assure Dr. Miller that everyone is safe, and if she feels my presence here is having a stressful effect on the children, I will cut my visit short.

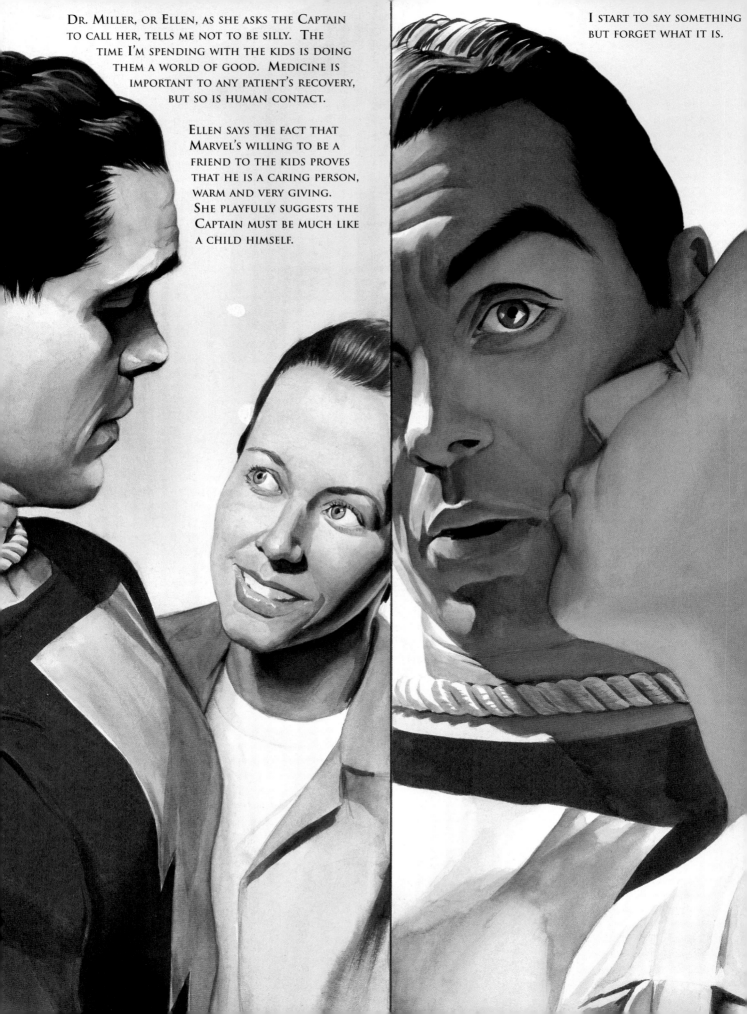

DR. MILLER, OR ELLEN, AS SHE ASKS THE CAPTAIN TO CALL HER, TELLS ME NOT TO BE SILLY. THE TIME I'M SPENDING WITH THE KIDS IS DOING THEM A WORLD OF GOOD. MEDICINE IS IMPORTANT TO ANY PATIENT'S RECOVERY, BUT SO IS HUMAN CONTACT.

ELLEN SAYS THE FACT THAT MARVEL'S WILLING TO BE A FRIEND TO THE KIDS PROVES THAT HE IS A CARING PERSON, WARM AND VERY GIVING. SHE PLAYFULLY SUGGESTS THE CAPTAIN MUST BE MUCH LIKE A CHILD HIMSELF.

I START TO SAY SOMETHING BUT FORGET WHAT IT IS.

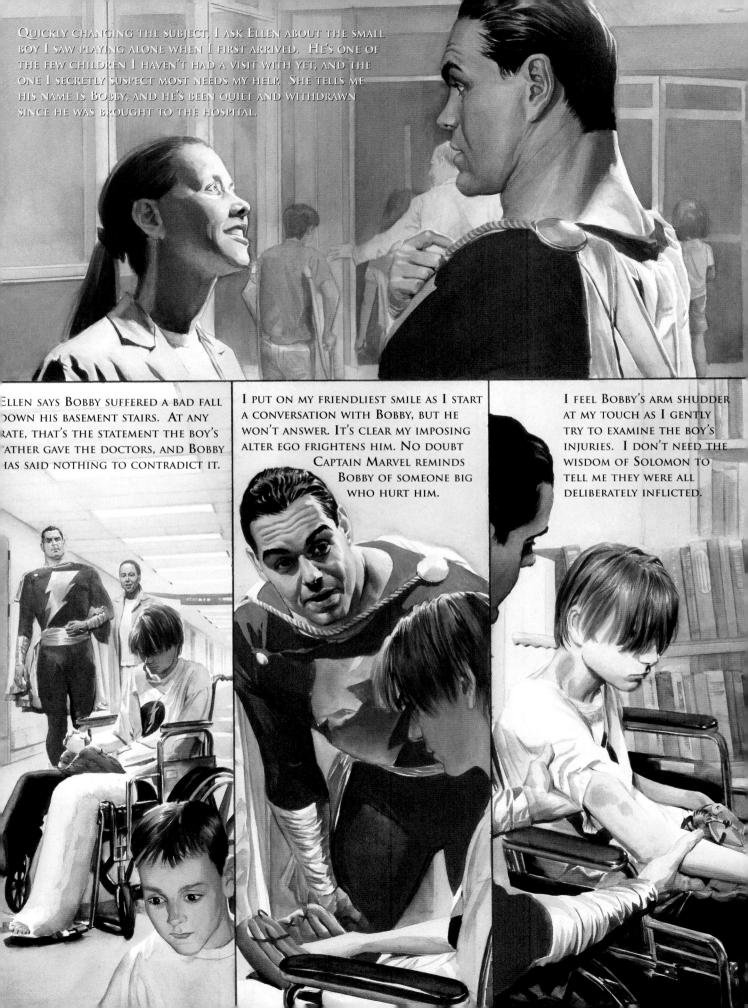

QUICKLY CHANGING THE SUBJECT, I ASK ELLEN ABOUT THE SMALL BOY I SAW PLAYING ALONE WHEN I FIRST ARRIVED. HE'S ONE OF THE FEW CHILDREN I HAVEN'T HAD A VISIT WITH YET, AND THE ONE I SECRETLY SUSPECT MOST NEEDS MY HELP. SHE TELLS ME HIS NAME IS BOBBY, AND HE'S BEEN QUIET AND WITHDRAWN SINCE HE WAS BROUGHT TO THE HOSPITAL.

ELLEN SAYS BOBBY SUFFERED A BAD FALL DOWN HIS BASEMENT STAIRS. AT ANY RATE, THAT'S THE STATEMENT THE BOY'S FATHER GAVE THE DOCTORS, AND BOBBY HAS SAID NOTHING TO CONTRADICT IT.

I PUT ON MY FRIENDLIEST SMILE AS I START A CONVERSATION WITH BOBBY, BUT HE WON'T ANSWER. IT'S CLEAR MY IMPOSING ALTER EGO FRIGHTENS HIM. NO DOUBT CAPTAIN MARVEL REMINDS BOBBY OF SOMEONE BIG WHO HURT HIM.

I FEEL BOBBY'S ARM SHUDDER AT MY TOUCH AS I GENTLY TRY TO EXAMINE THE BOY'S INJURIES. I DON'T NEED THE WISDOM OF SOLOMON TO TELL ME THEY WERE ALL DELIBERATELY INFLICTED.

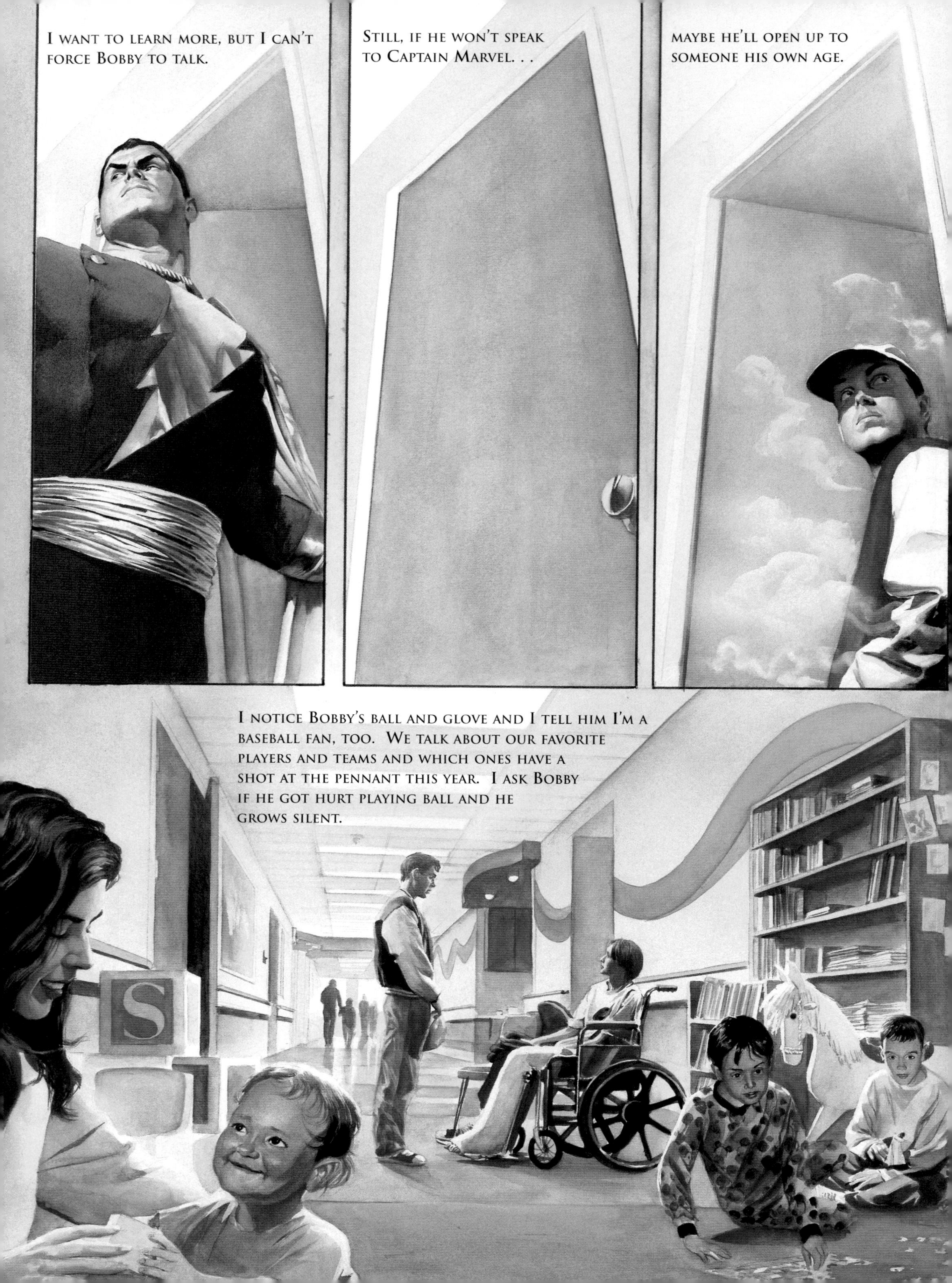
I WANT TO LEARN MORE, BUT I CAN'T FORCE BOBBY TO TALK.
STILL, IF HE WON'T SPEAK TO CAPTAIN MARVEL. . .
MAYBE HE'LL OPEN UP TO SOMEONE HIS OWN AGE.
I NOTICE BOBBY'S BALL AND GLOVE AND I TELL HIM I'M A BASEBALL FAN, TOO. WE TALK ABOUT OUR FAVORITE PLAYERS AND TEAMS AND WHICH ONES HAVE A SHOT AT THE PENNANT THIS YEAR. I ASK BOBBY IF HE GOT HURT PLAYING BALL AND HE GROWS SILENT.
S

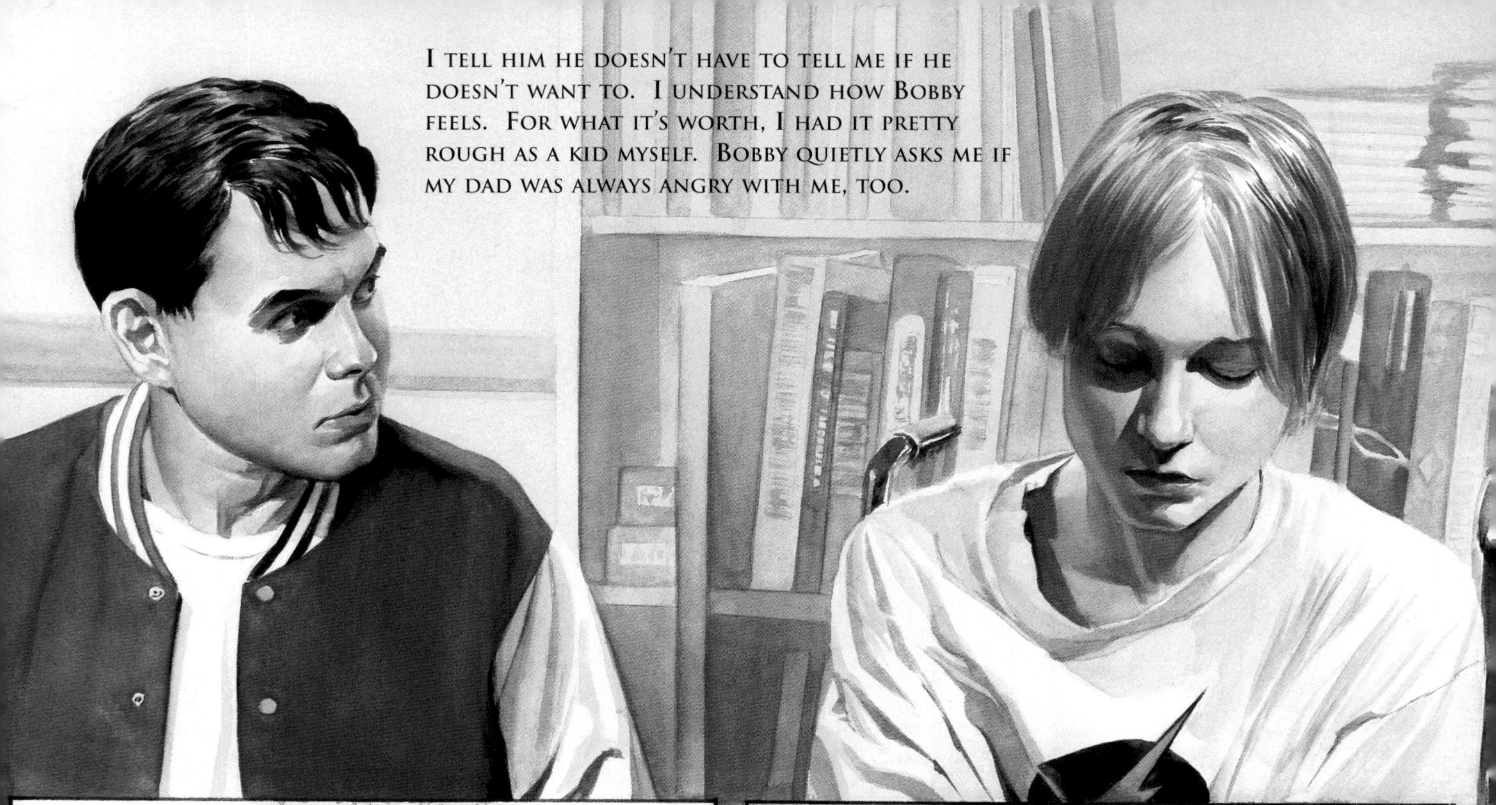
I TELL HIM HE DOESN'T HAVE TO TELL ME IF HE DOESN'T WANT TO. I UNDERSTAND HOW BOBBY FEELS. FOR WHAT IT'S WORTH, I HAD IT PRETTY ROUGH AS A KID MYSELF. BOBBY QUIETLY ASKS ME IF MY DAD WAS ALWAYS ANGRY WITH ME, TOO.

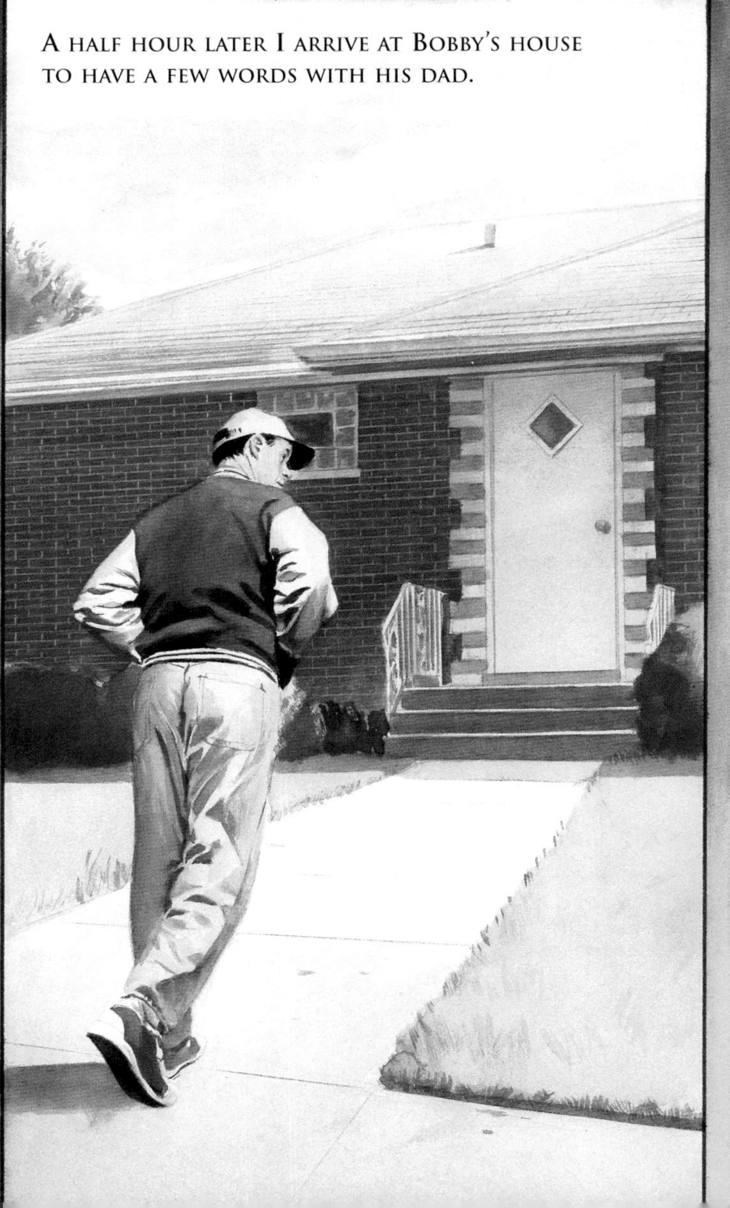
A HALF HOUR LATER I ARRIVE AT BOBBY'S HOUSE TO HAVE A FEW WORDS WITH HIS DAD.

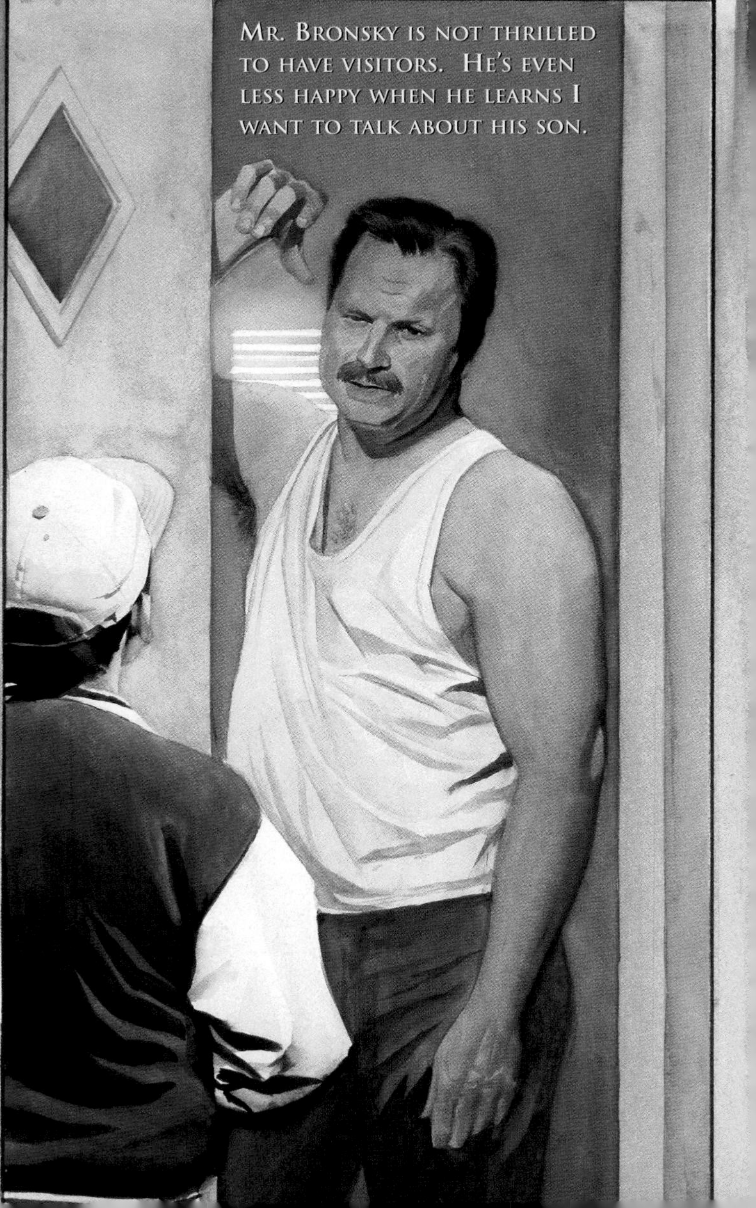
MR. BRONSKY IS NOT THRILLED TO HAVE VISITORS. HE'S EVEN LESS HAPPY WHEN HE LEARNS I WANT TO TALK ABOUT HIS SON.

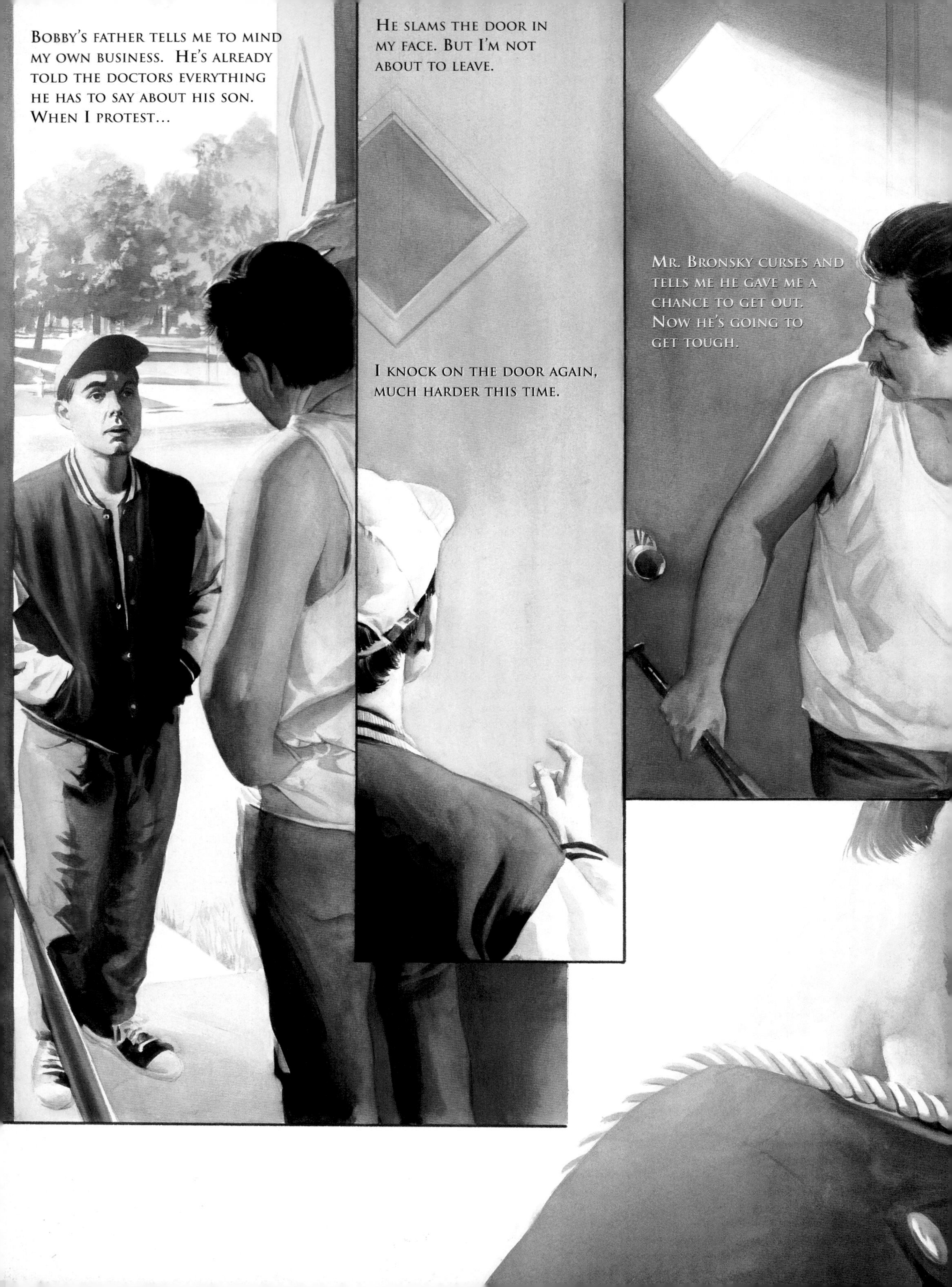
BOBBY'S FATHER TELLS ME TO MIND MY OWN BUSINESS. HE'S ALREADY TOLD THE DOCTORS EVERYTHING HE HAS TO SAY ABOUT HIS SON. WHEN I PROTEST...
HE SLAMS THE DOOR IN MY FACE. BUT I'M NOT ABOUT TO LEAVE.
I KNOCK ON THE DOOR AGAIN, MUCH HARDER THIS TIME.
MR. BRONSKY CURSES AND TELLS ME HE GAVE ME A CHANCE TO GET OUT. NOW HE'S GOING TO GET TOUGH.

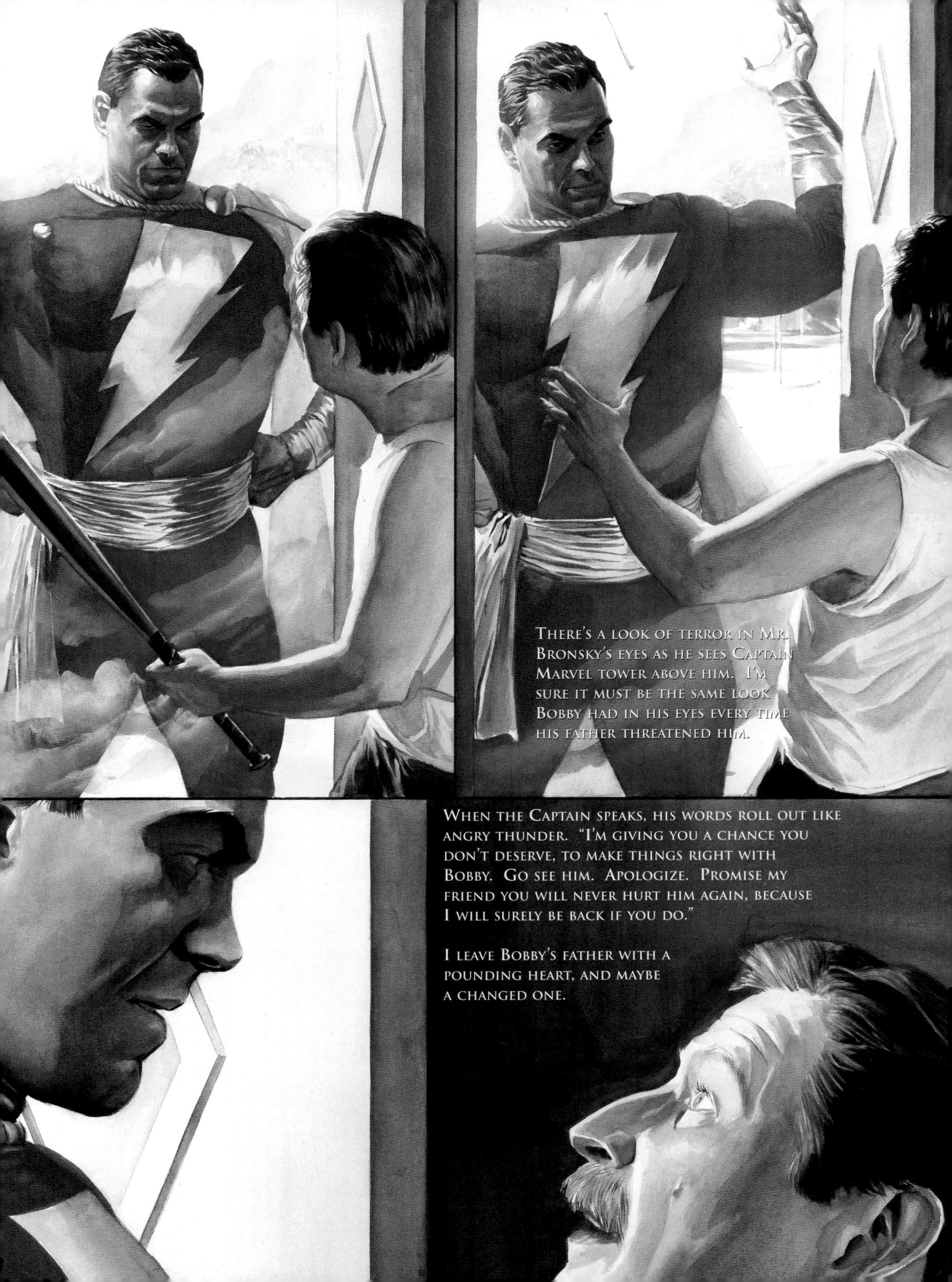
There's a look of terror in Mr. Bronsky's eyes as he sees Captain Marvel tower above him. I'm sure it must be the same look Bobby had in his eyes every time his father threatened him.
When the Captain speaks, his words roll out like angry thunder. "I'm giving you a chance you don't deserve, to make things right with Bobby. Go see him. Apologize. Promise my friend you will never hurt him again, because I will surely be back if you do."
I leave Bobby's father with a pounding heart, and maybe a changed one.

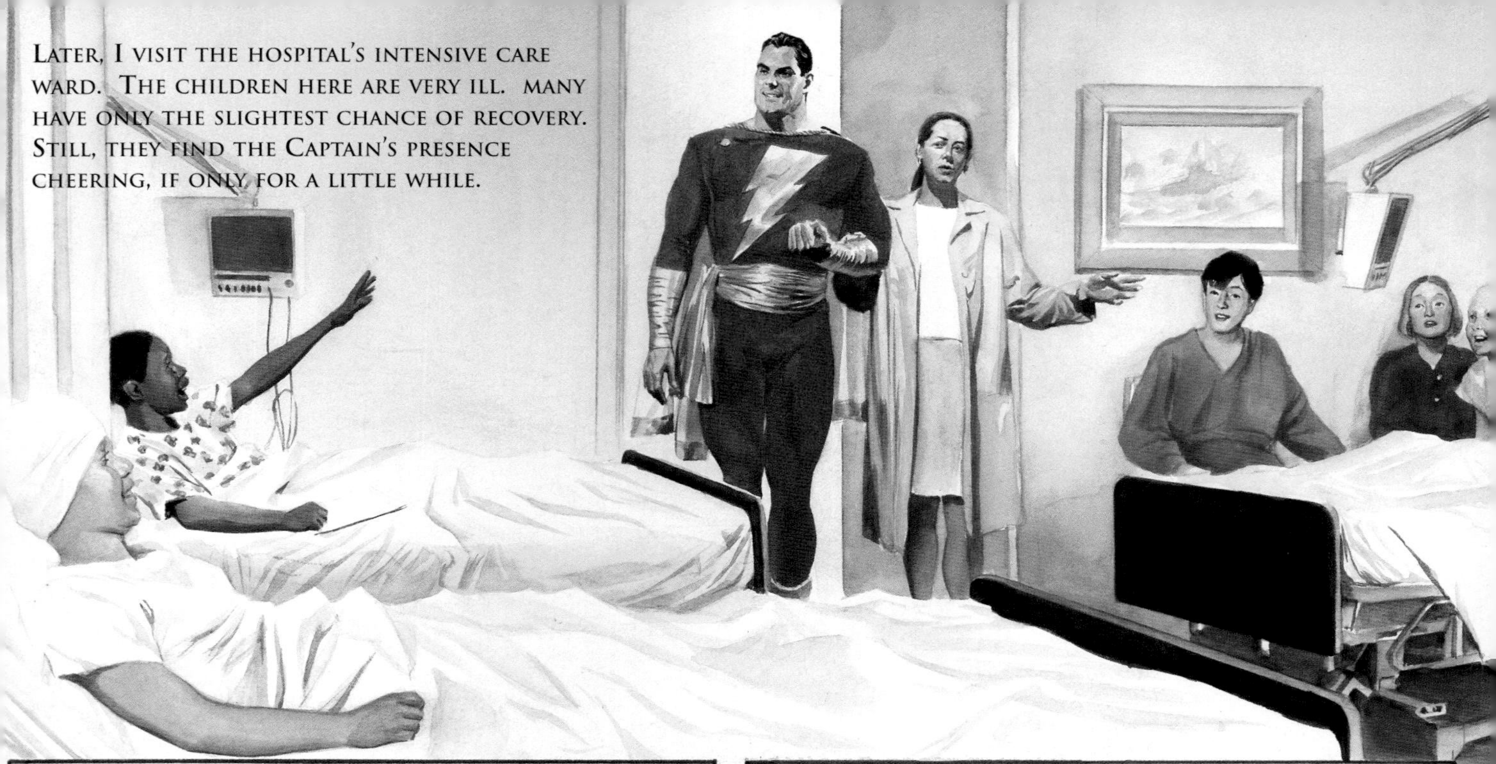
Later, I visit the hospital's intensive care ward. The children here are very ill. Many have only the slightest chance of recovery. Still, they find the Captain's presence cheering, if only for a little while.

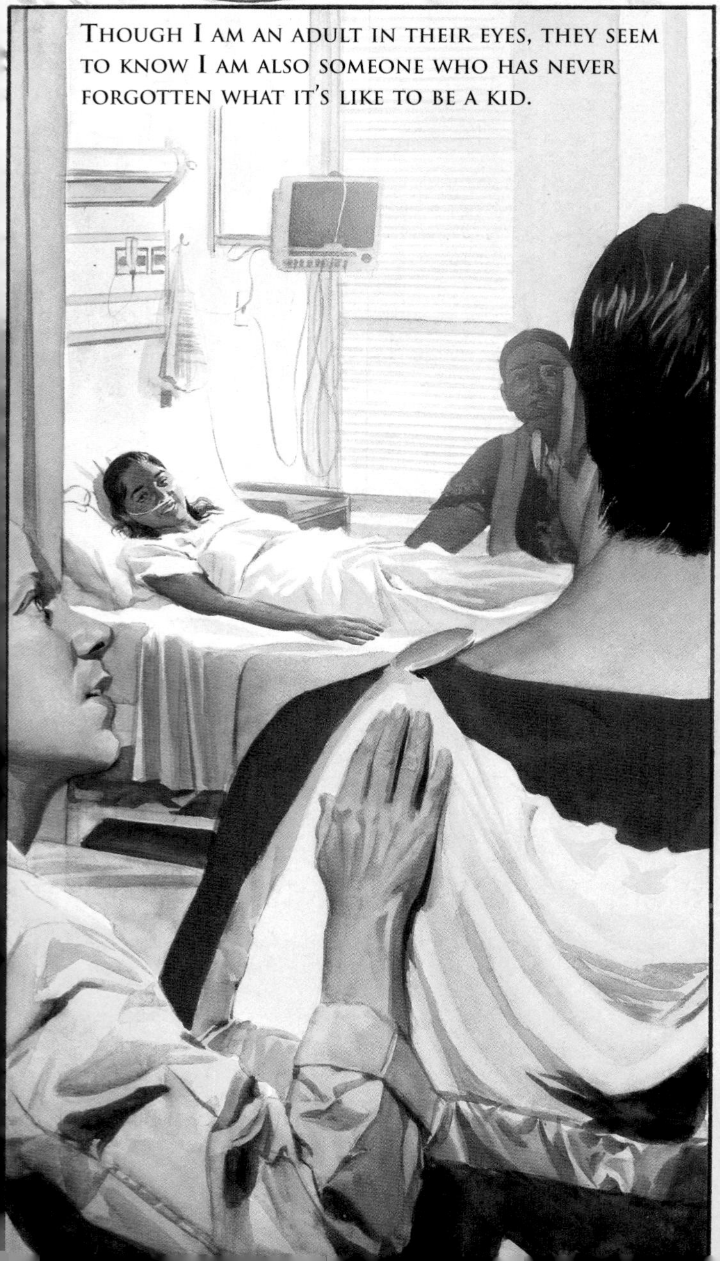
Though I am an adult in their eyes, they seem to know I am also someone who has never forgotten what it's like to be a kid.

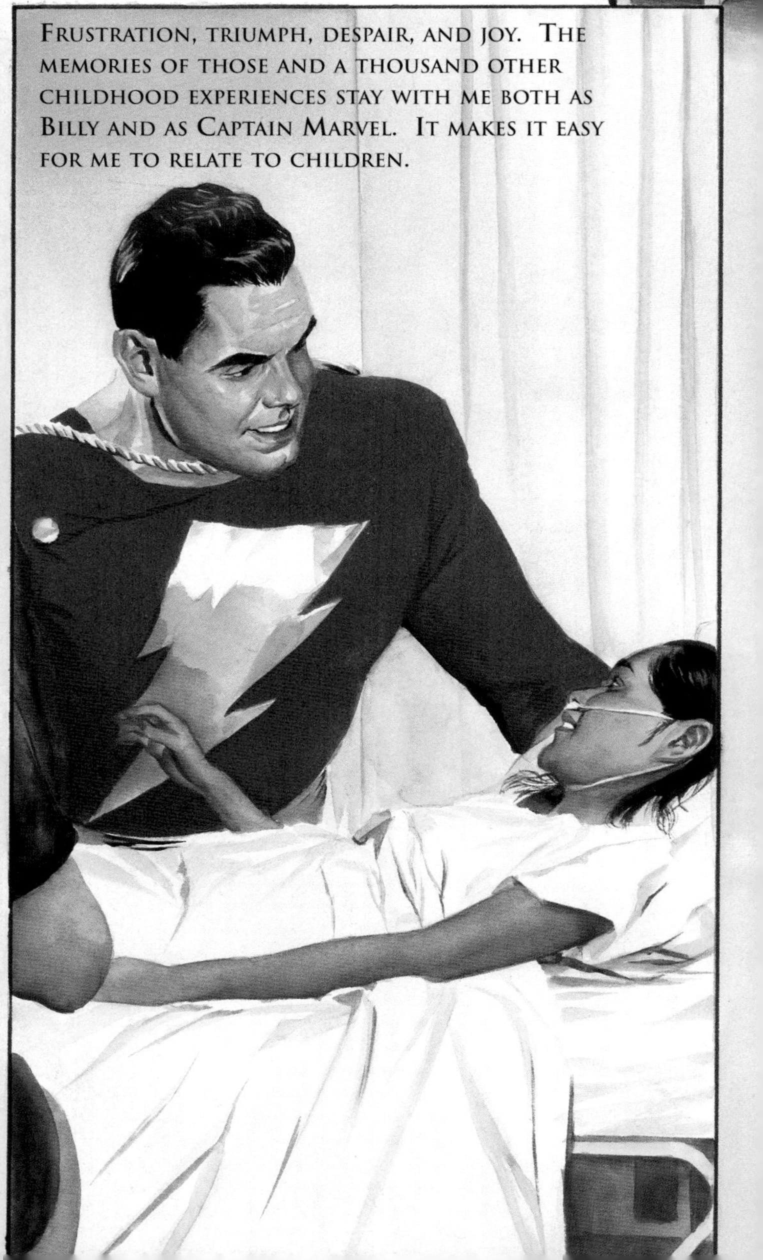
Frustration, triumph, despair, and joy. The memories of those and a thousand other childhood experiences stay with me both as Billy and as Captain Marvel. It makes it easy for me to relate to children.

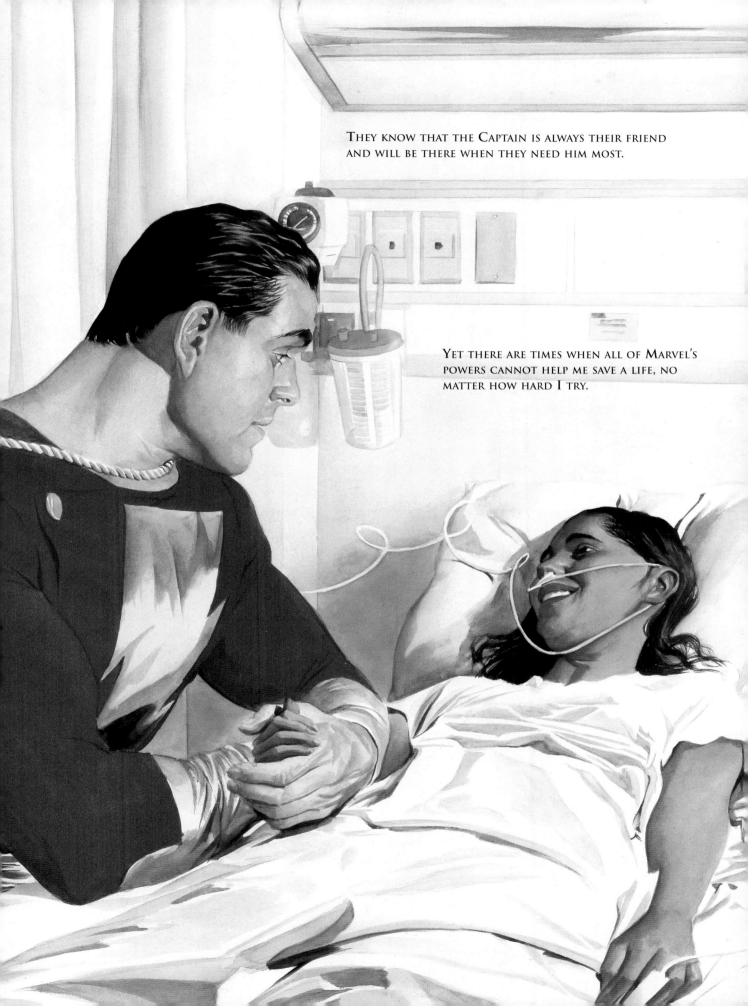

THEY KNOW THAT THE CAPTAIN IS ALWAYS THEIR FRIEND
AND WILL BE THERE WHEN THEY NEED HIM MOST.

YET THERE ARE TIMES WHEN ALL OF MARVEL'S
POWERS CANNOT HELP ME SAVE A LIFE, NO
MATTER HOW HARD I TRY.

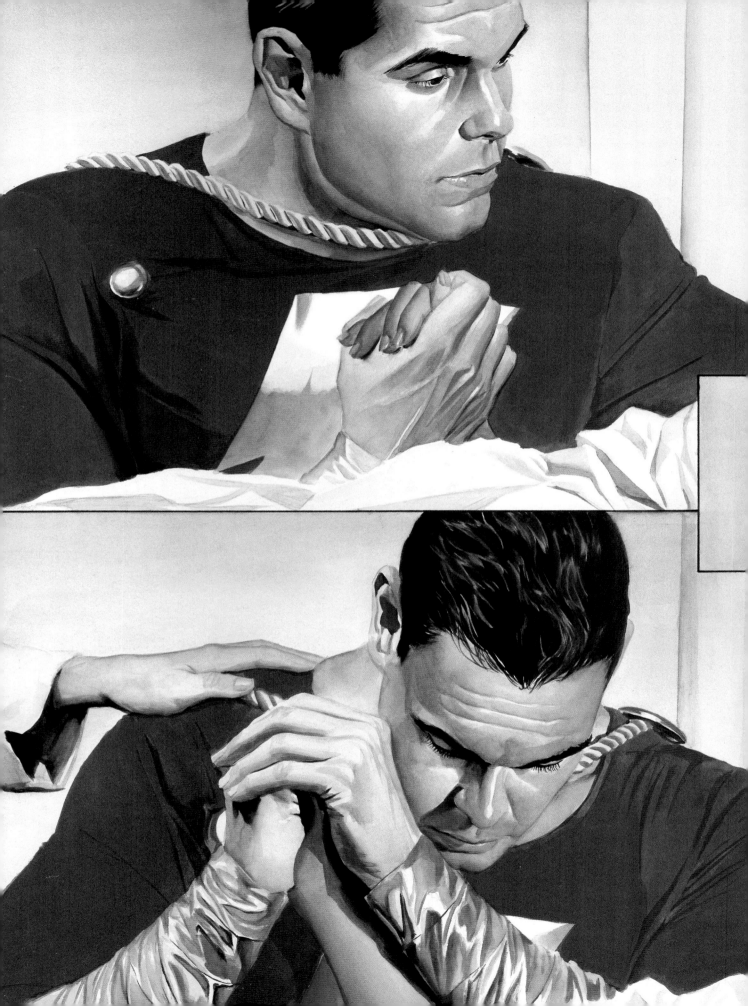

ALL I HAVE TO OFFER TANITA IS A FRIENDLY
SMILE, A GENTLE HAND, AND A FEW WORDS OF
COMFORT. IN MY MIND THAT'S NOT NEARLY
ENOUGH, BUT IT HAS MADE HER VERY HAPPY.

IT HAS GIVEN HER A REASON TO SMILE, A
MOMENT OF RELIEF FROM HER FEAR AND PAIN.

AND IN THAT MOMENT, SHE SLIPS AWAY.

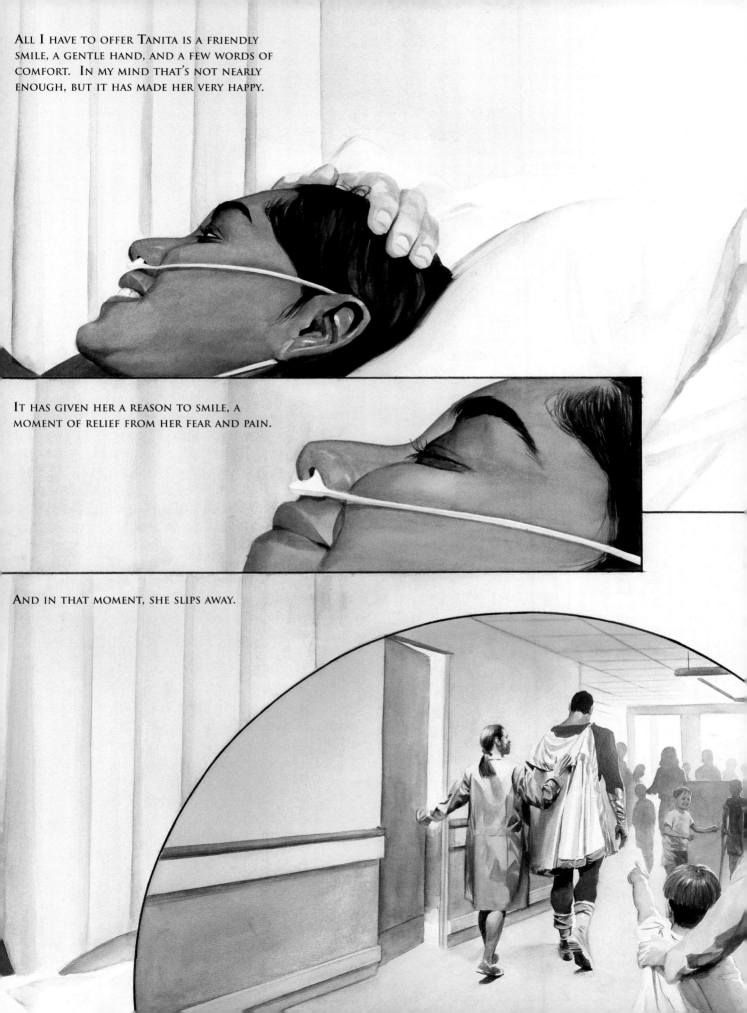

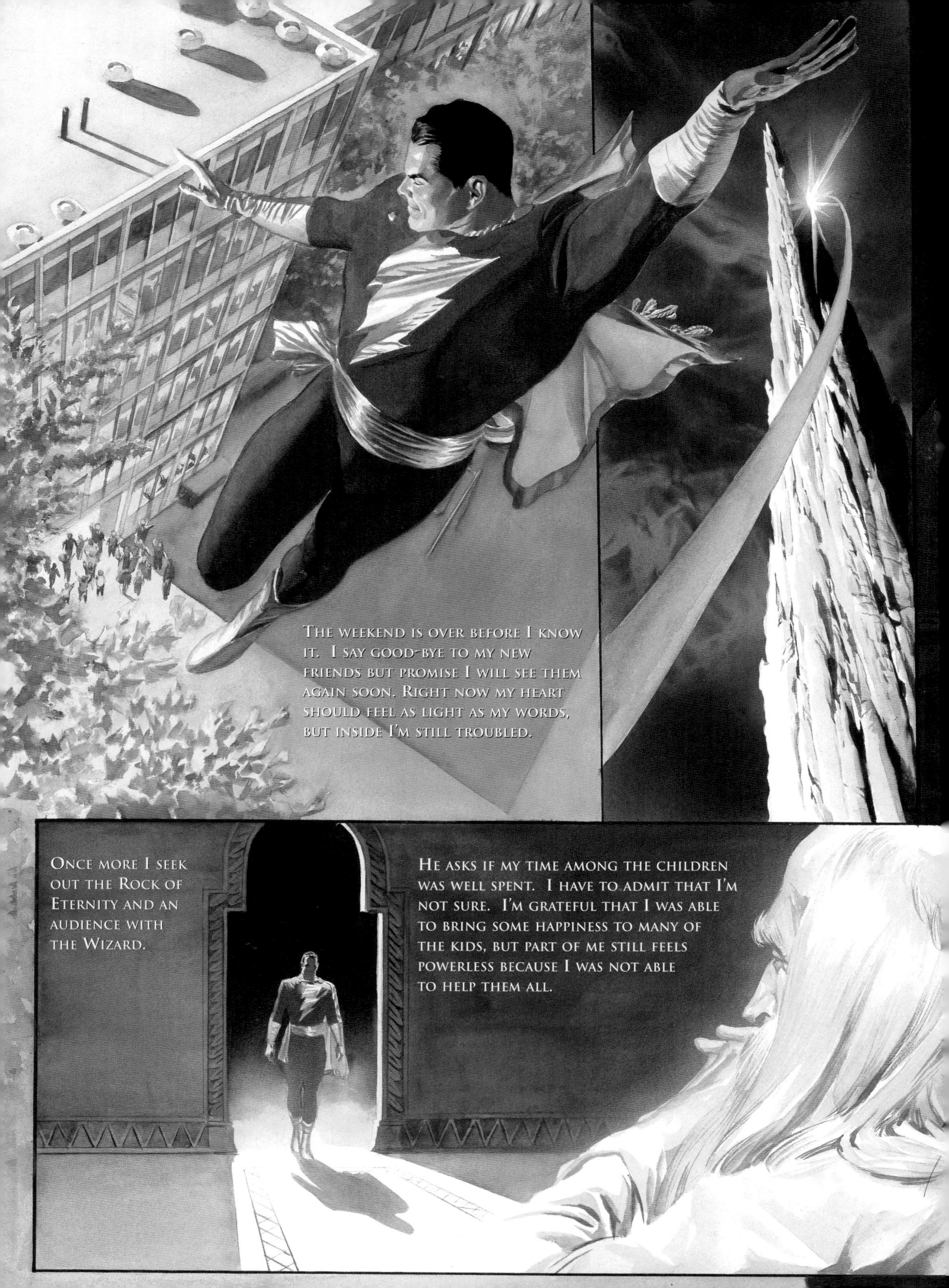
The weekend is over before I know it. I say good-bye to my new friends but promise I will see them again soon. Right now my heart should feel as light as my words, but inside I'm still troubled.
Once more I seek out the Rock of Eternity and an audience with the Wizard.
He asks if my time among the children was well spent. I have to admit that I'm not sure. I'm grateful that I was able to bring some happiness to many of the kids, but part of me still feels powerless because I was not able to help them all.

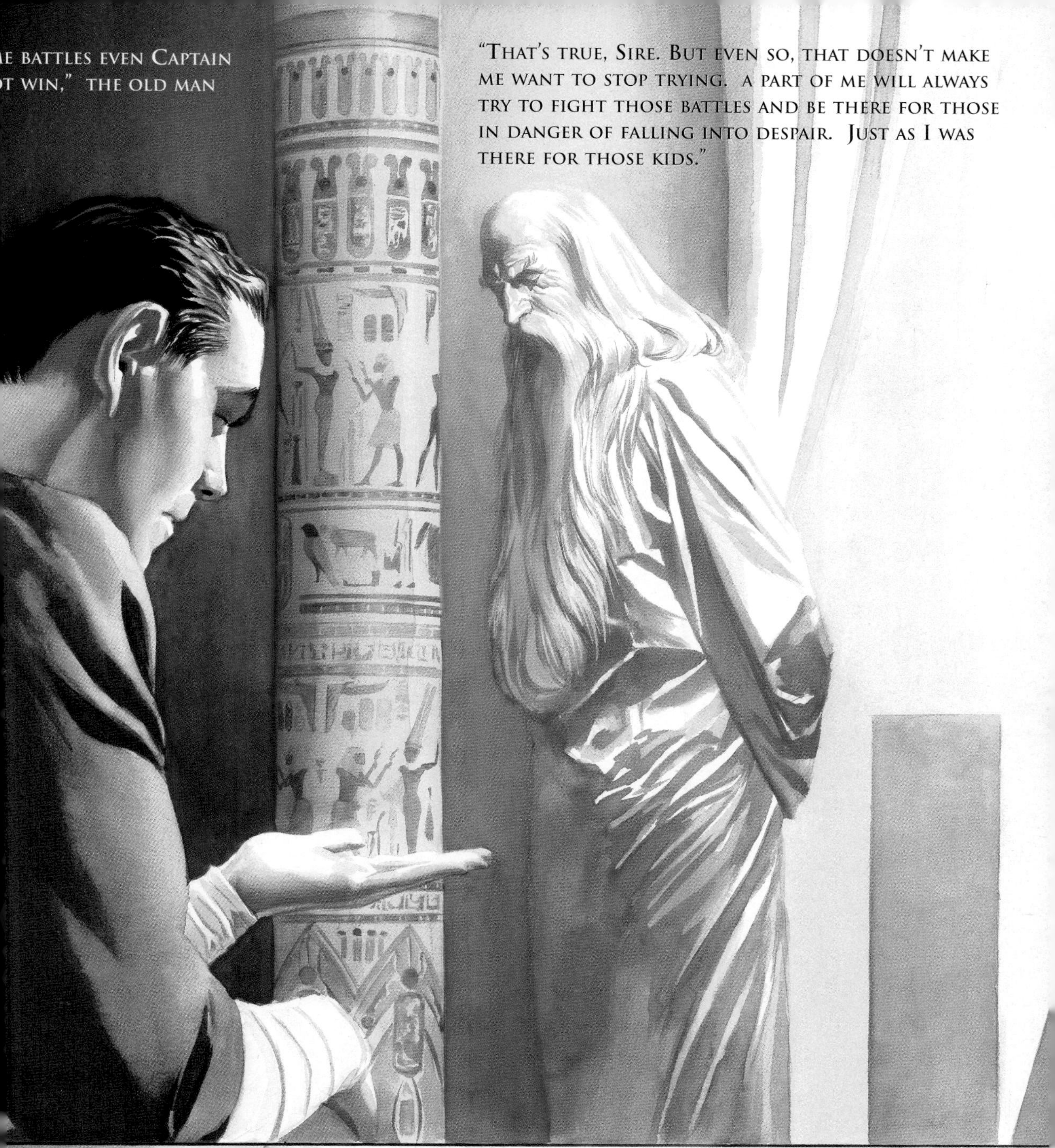
E BATTLES EVEN CAPTAIN
T WIN," THE OLD MAN
"THAT'S TRUE, SIRE. BUT EVEN SO, THAT DOESN'T MAKE ME WANT TO STOP TRYING. A PART OF ME WILL ALWAYS TRY TO FIGHT THOSE BATTLES AND BE THERE FOR THOSE IN DANGER OF FALLING INTO DESPAIR. JUST AS I WAS THERE FOR THOSE KIDS."

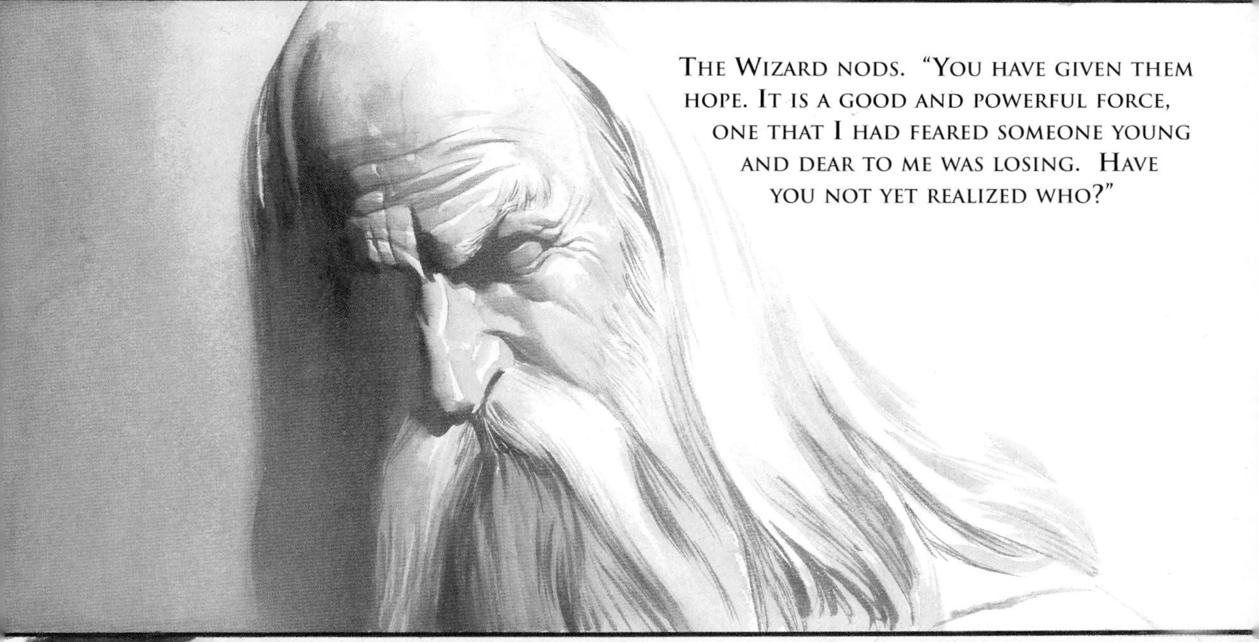
THE WIZARD NODS. "YOU HAVE GIVEN THEM HOPE. IT IS A GOOD AND POWERFUL FORCE, ONE THAT I HAD FEARED SOMEONE YOUNG AND DEAR TO ME WAS LOSING. HAVE YOU NOT YET REALIZED WHO?"

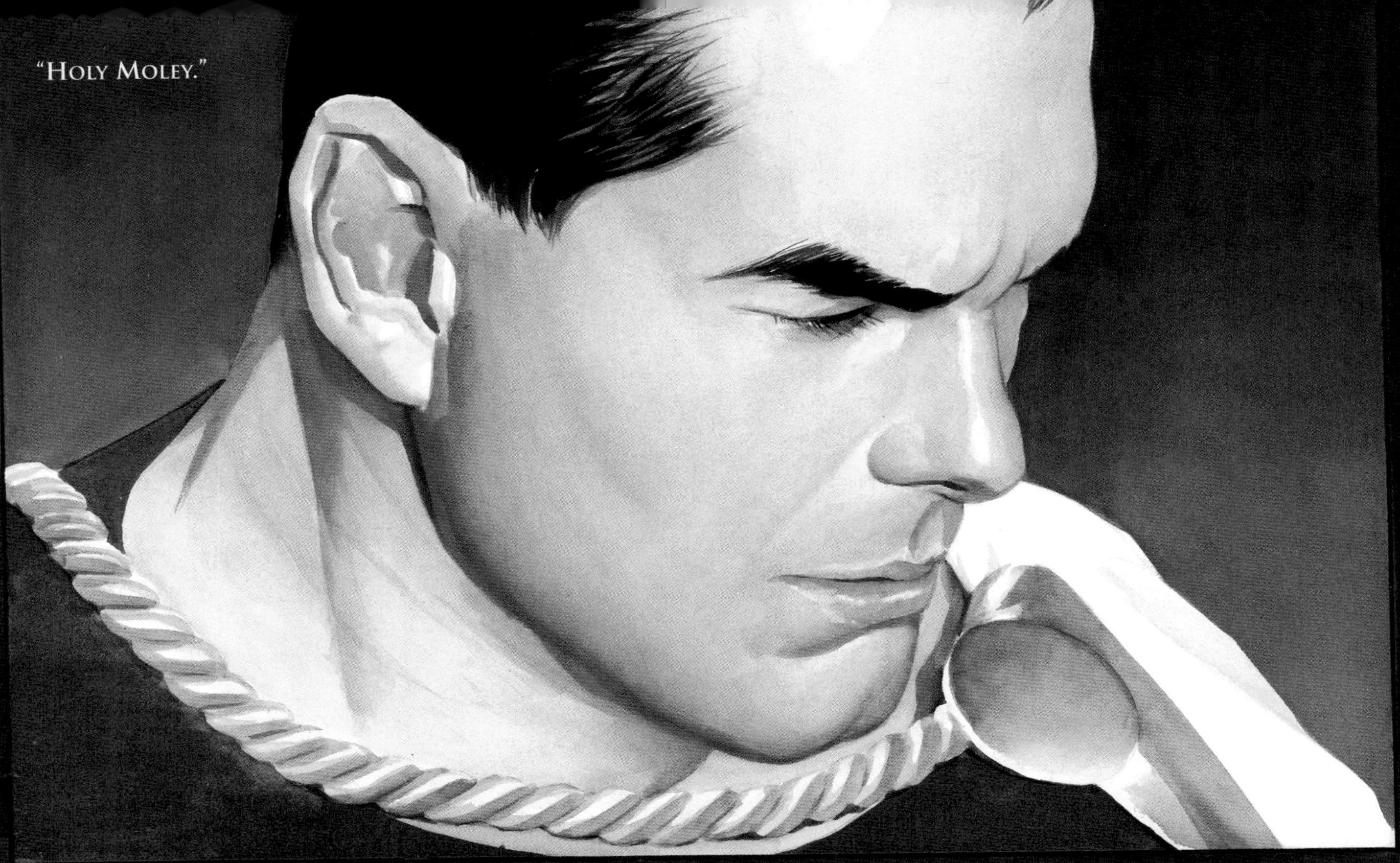
"Holy Moley."

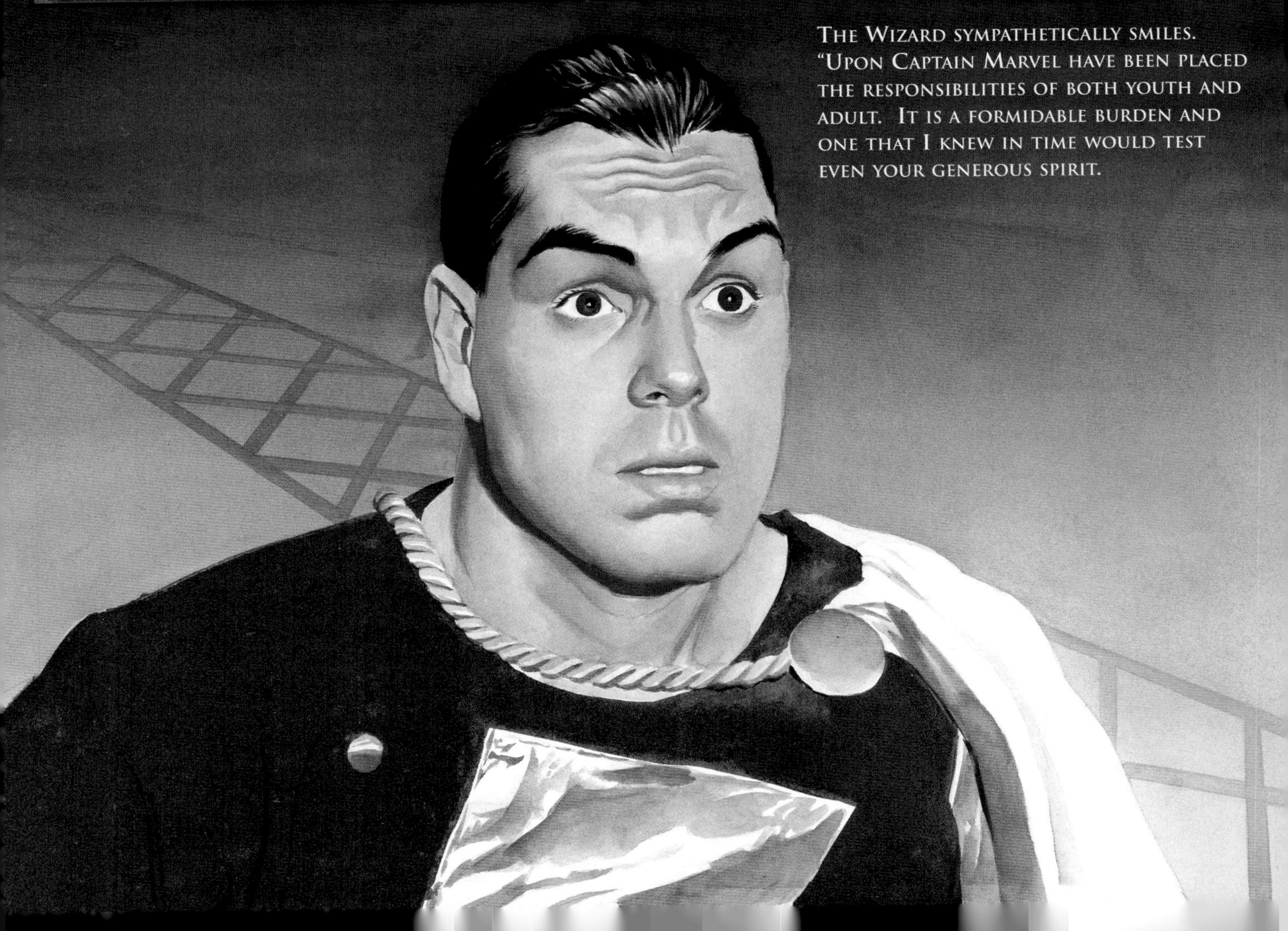
The Wizard sympathetically smiles. "Upon Captain Marvel have been placed the responsibilities of both youth and adult. It is a formidable burden and one that I knew in time would test even your generous spirit.

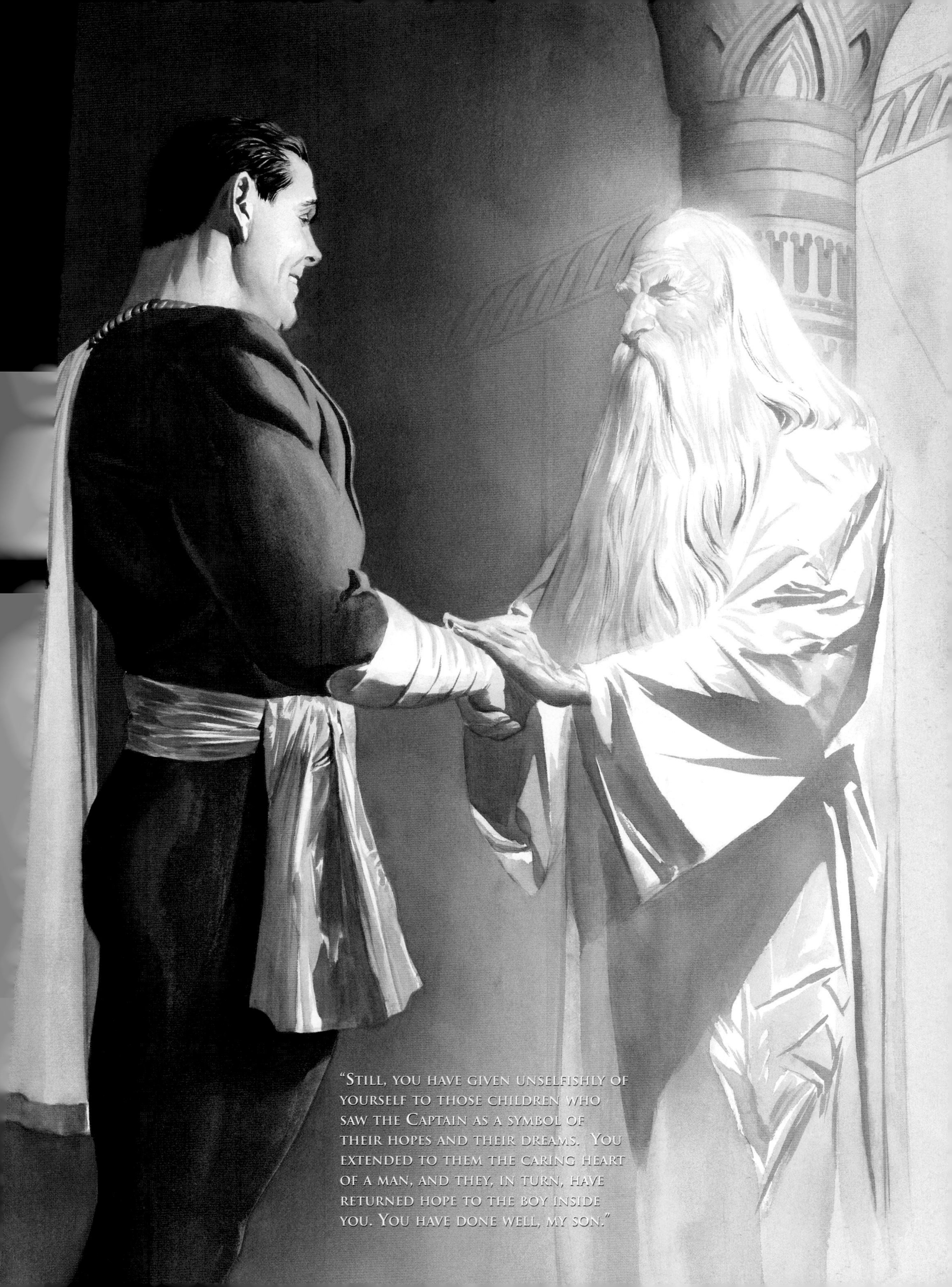
“Still, you have given unselfishly of yourself to those children who saw the Captain as a symbol of their hopes and their dreams. You extended to them the caring heart of a man, and they, in turn, have returned hope to the boy inside you. You have done well, my son.”

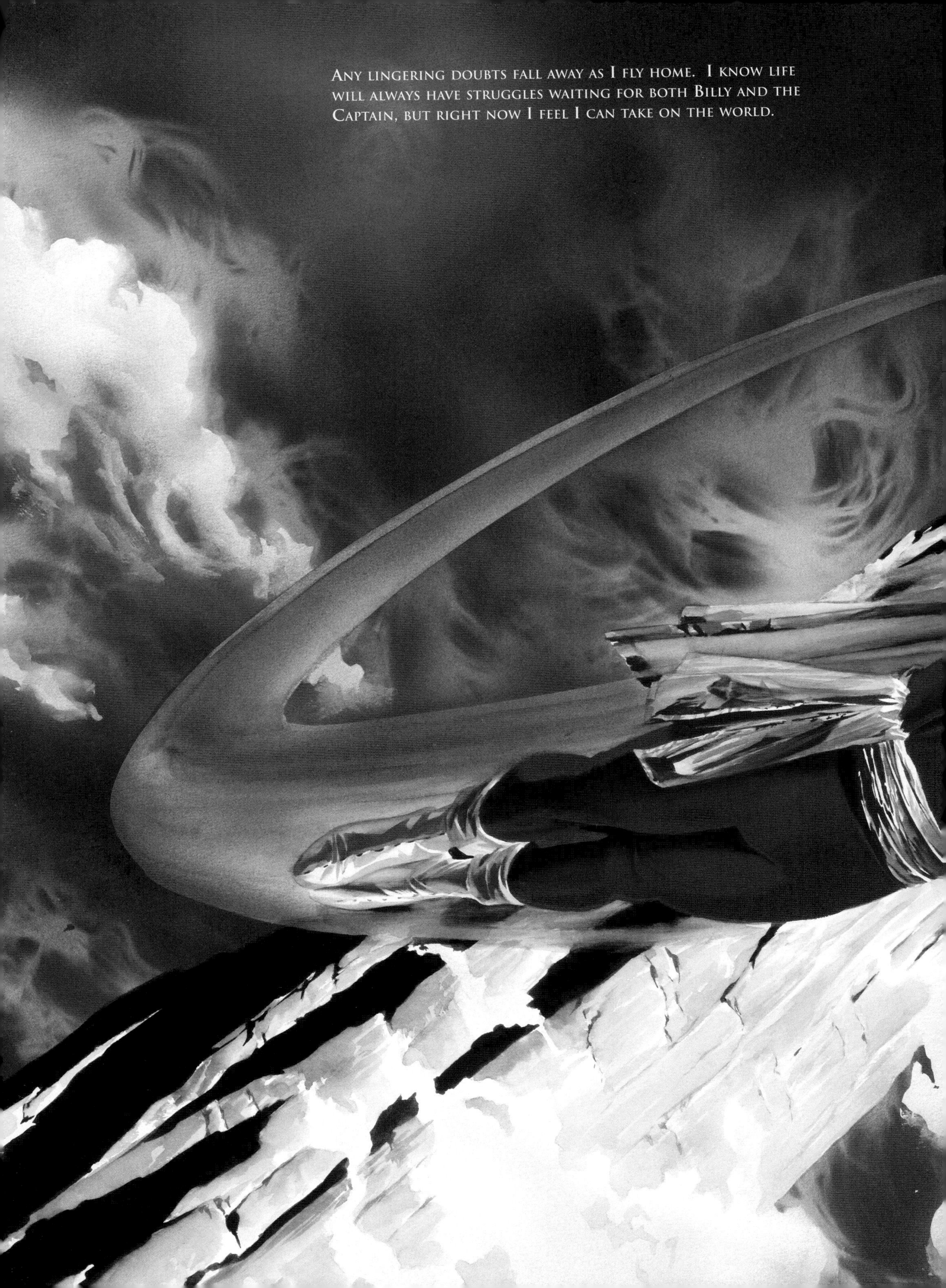
Any lingering doubts fall away as I fly home. I know life will always have struggles waiting for both Billy and the Captain, but right now I feel I can take on the world.

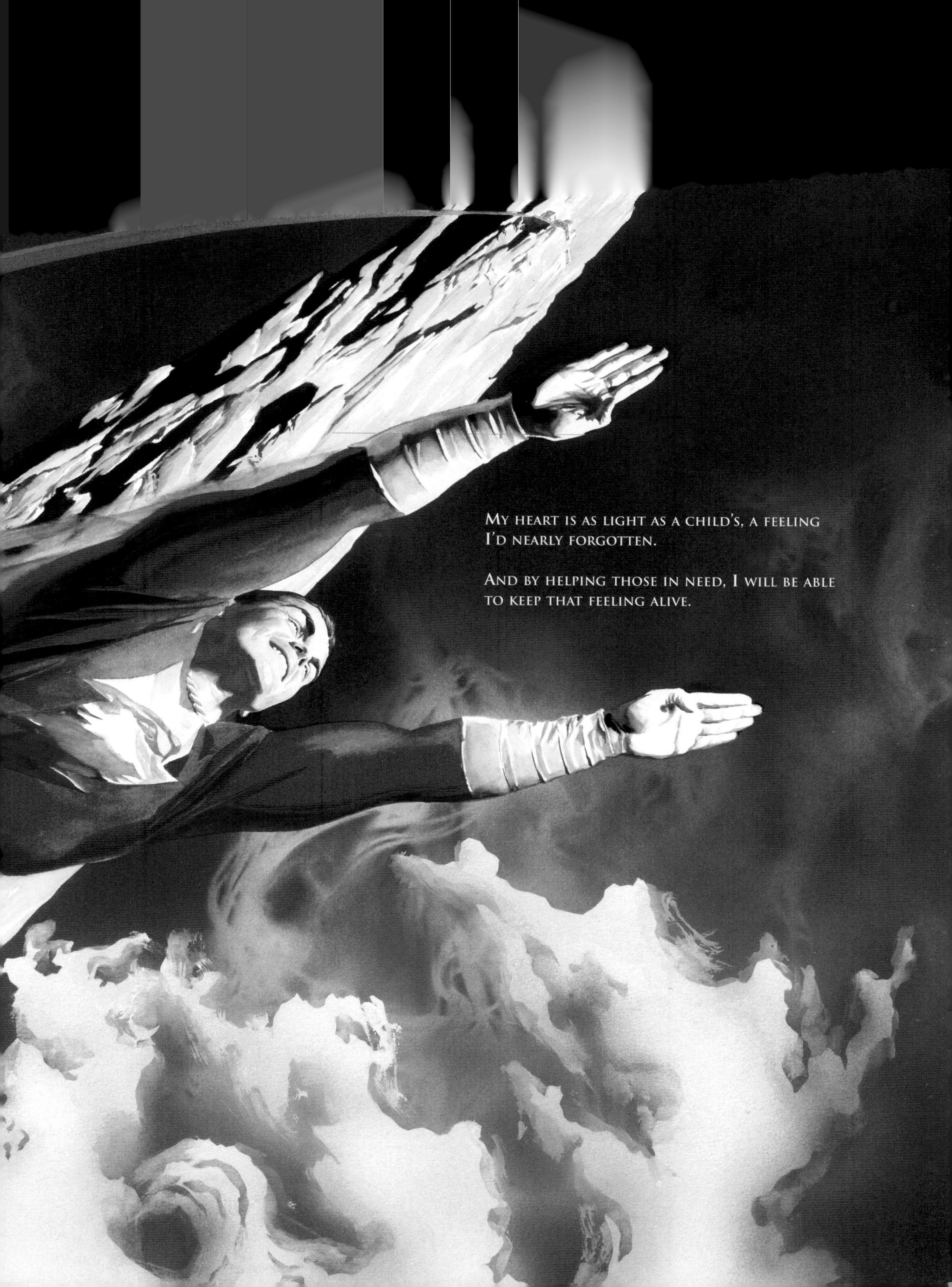
My heart is as light as a child's, a feeling I'd nearly forgotten.
And by helping those in need, I will be able to keep that feeling alive.

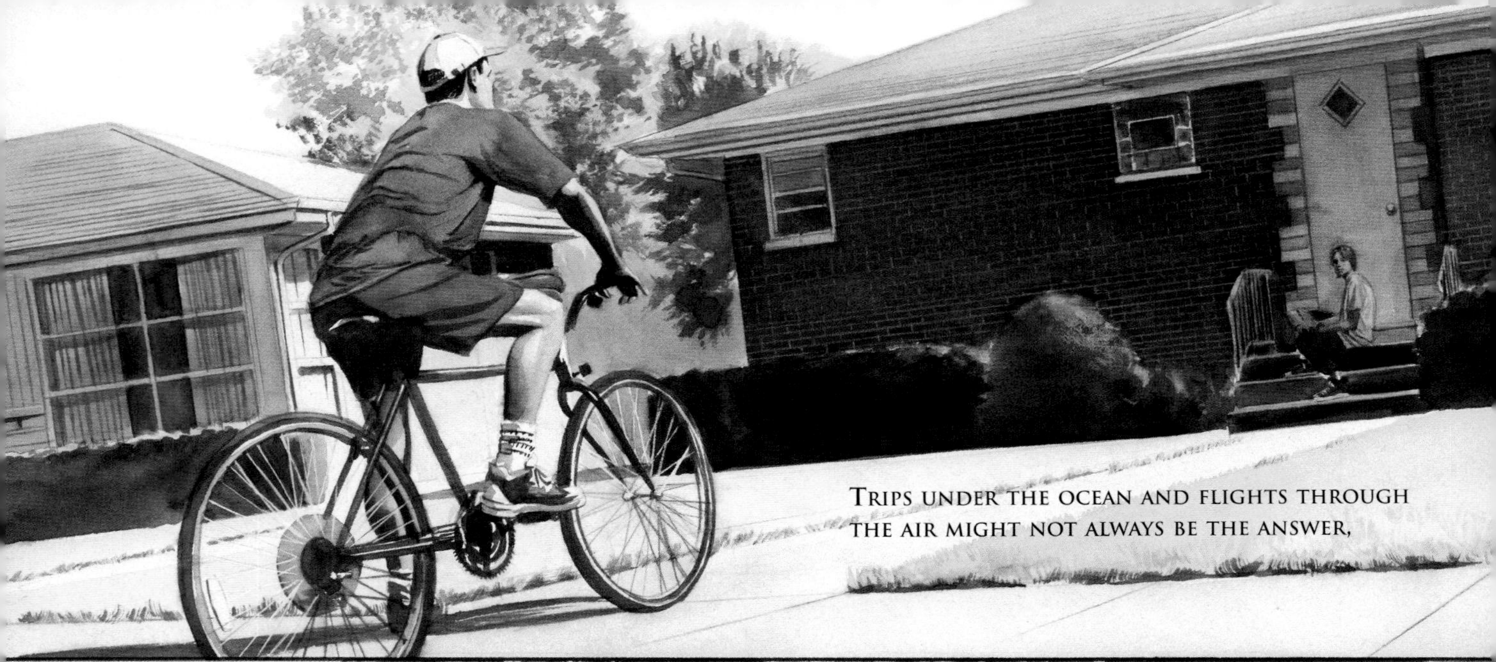
Trips under the ocean and flights through the air might not always be the answer,

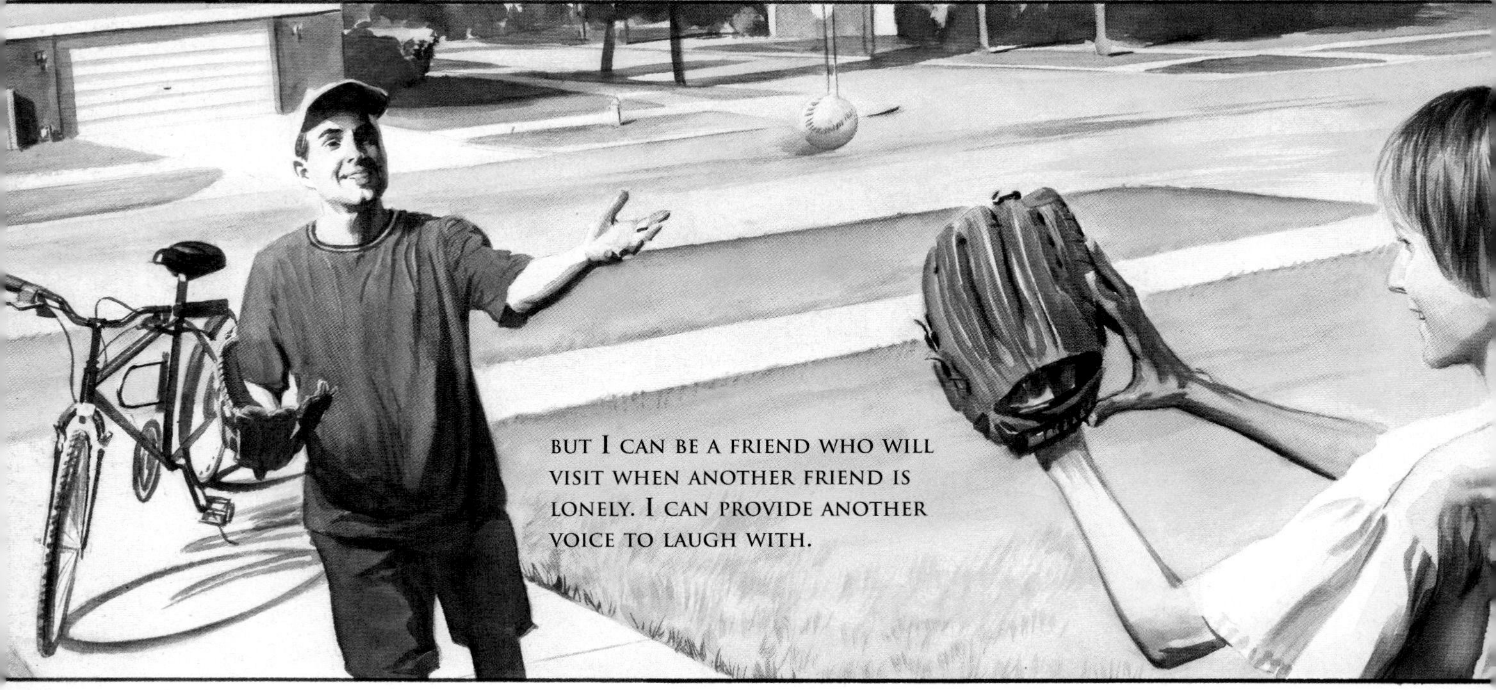
but I can be a friend who will visit when another friend is lonely. I can provide another voice to laugh with.

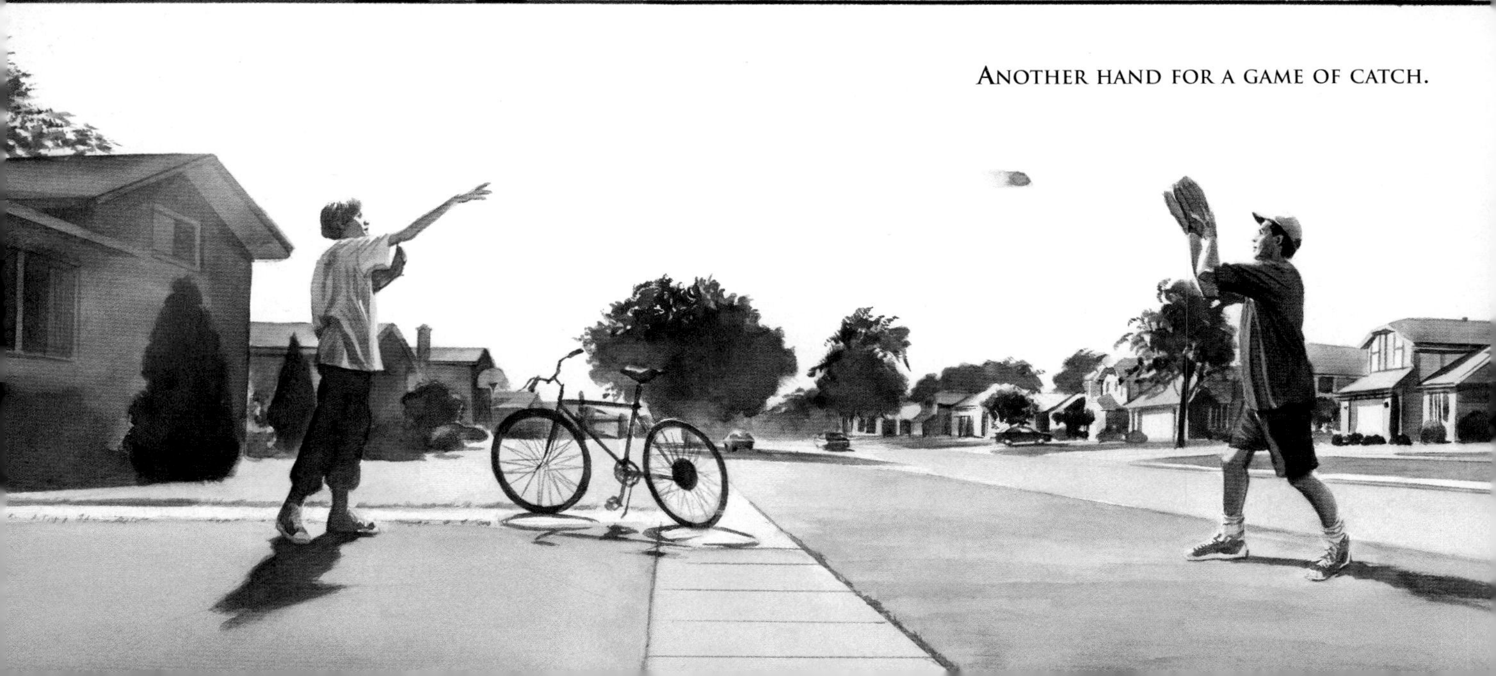
Another hand for a game of catch.

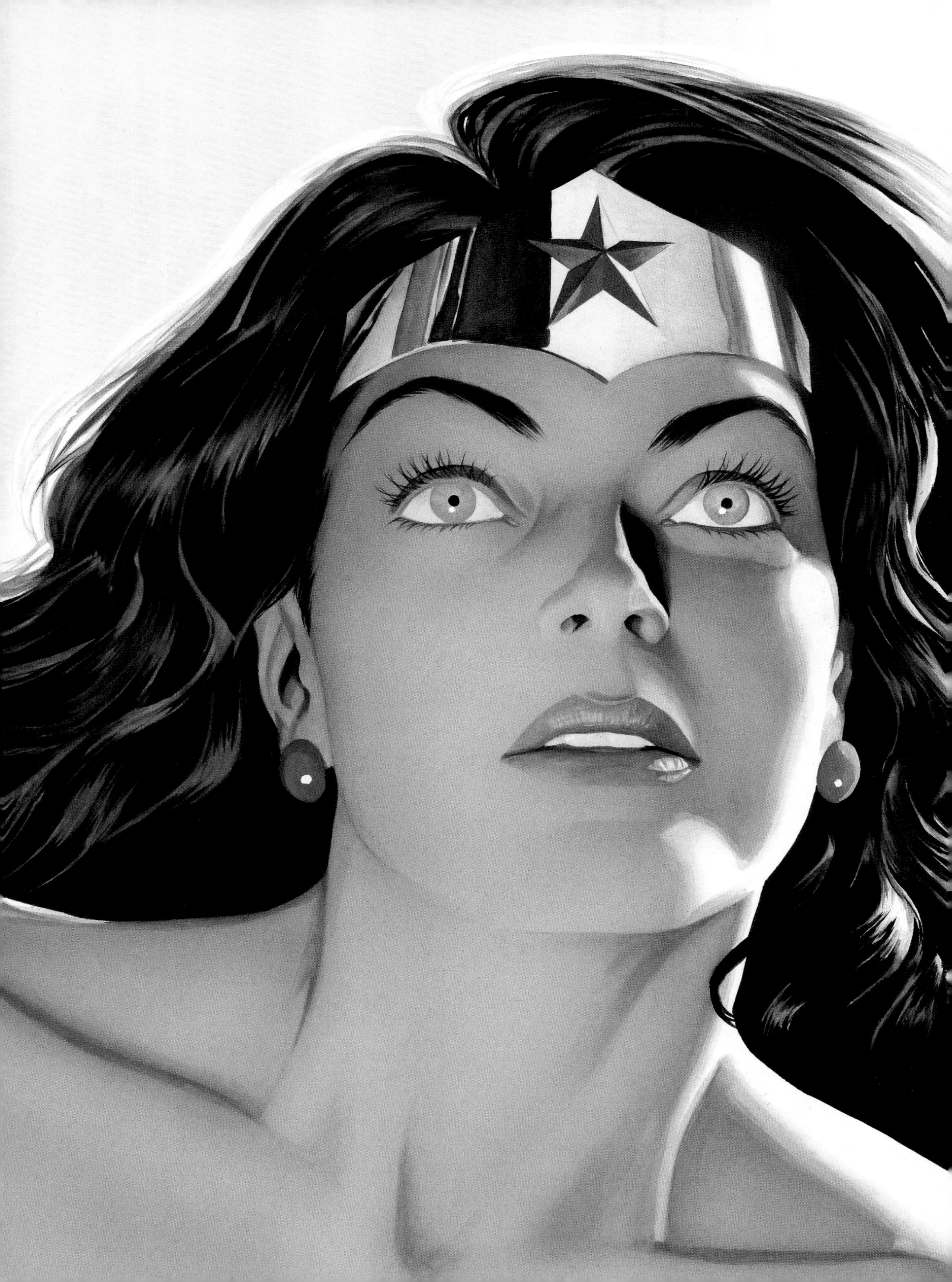

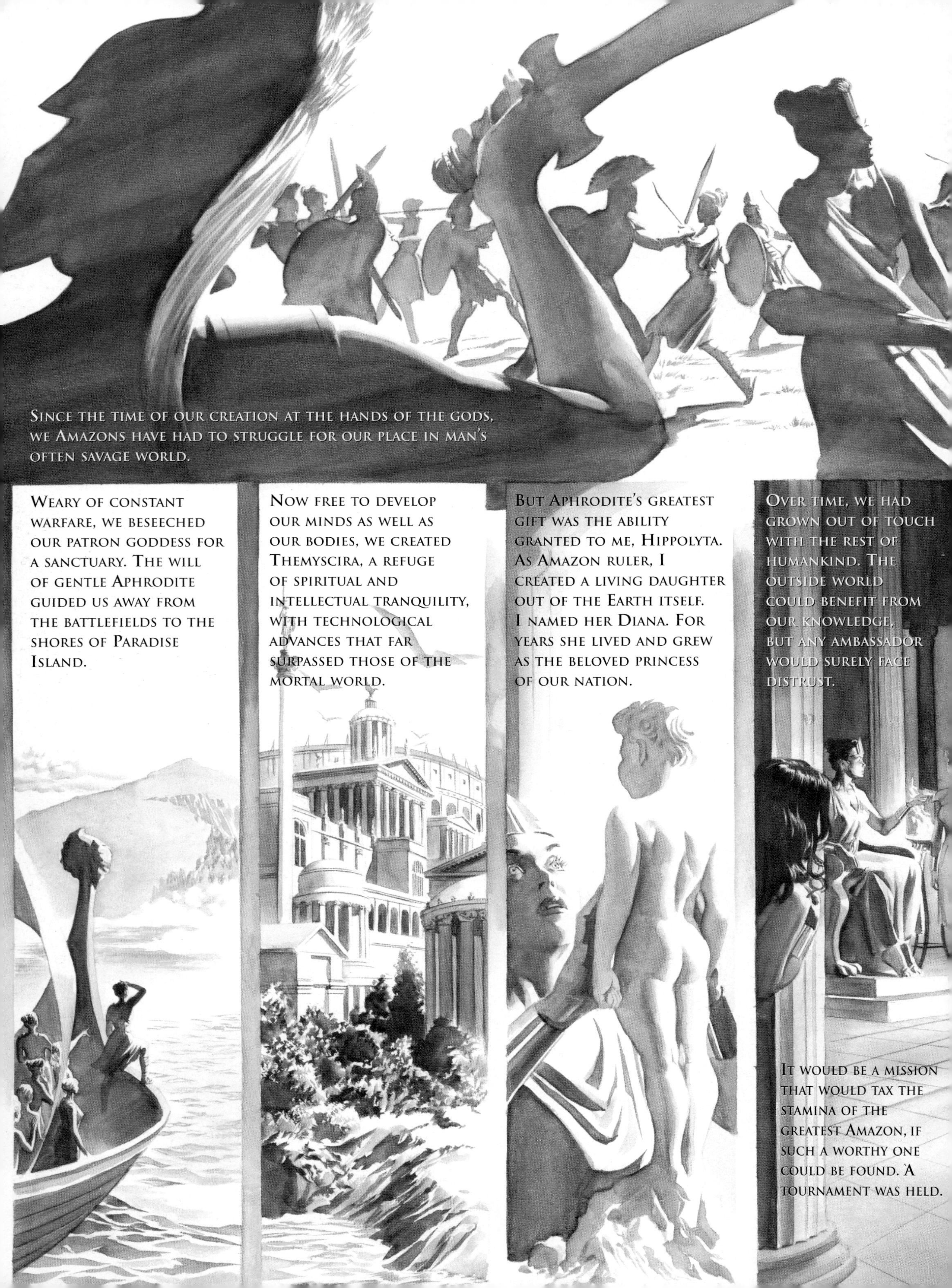
Since the time of our creation at the hands of the gods, we Amazons have had to struggle for our place in man's often savage world.
Weary of constant warfare, we beseeched our patron goddess for a sanctuary. The will of gentle Aphrodite guided us away from the battlefields to the shores of Paradise Island.
Now free to develop our minds as well as our bodies, we created Themyscira, a refuge of spiritual and intellectual tranquility, with technological advances that far surpassed those of the mortal world.
But Aphrodite's greatest gift was the ability granted to me, Hippolyta. As Amazon ruler, I created a living daughter out of the Earth itself. I named her Diana. For years she lived and grew as the beloved princess of our nation.
Over time, we had grown out of touch with the rest of humankind. The outside world could benefit from our knowledge, but any ambassador would surely face distrust.
It would be a mission that would tax the stamina of the greatest Amazon, if such a worthy one could be found. A tournament was held.

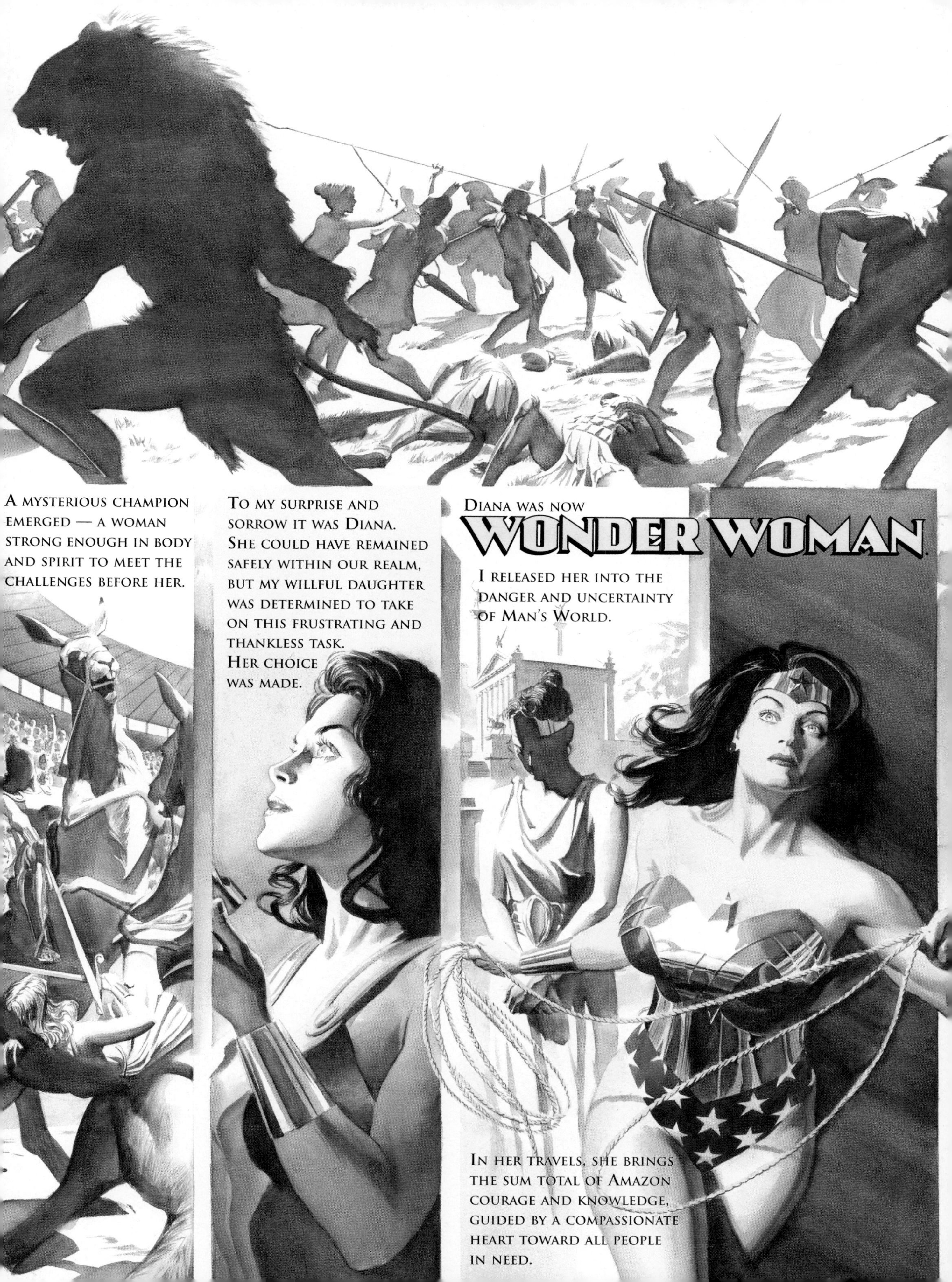
A mysterious champion emerged — a woman strong enough in body and spirit to meet the challenges before her.
To my surprise and sorrow it was Diana. She could have remained safely within our realm, but my willful daughter was determined to take on this frustrating and thankless task. Her choice was made.
Diana was now
WONDER WOMAN.
I released her into the danger and uncertainty of Man's World.
In her travels, she brings the sum total of Amazon courage and knowledge, guided by a compassionate heart toward all people in need.

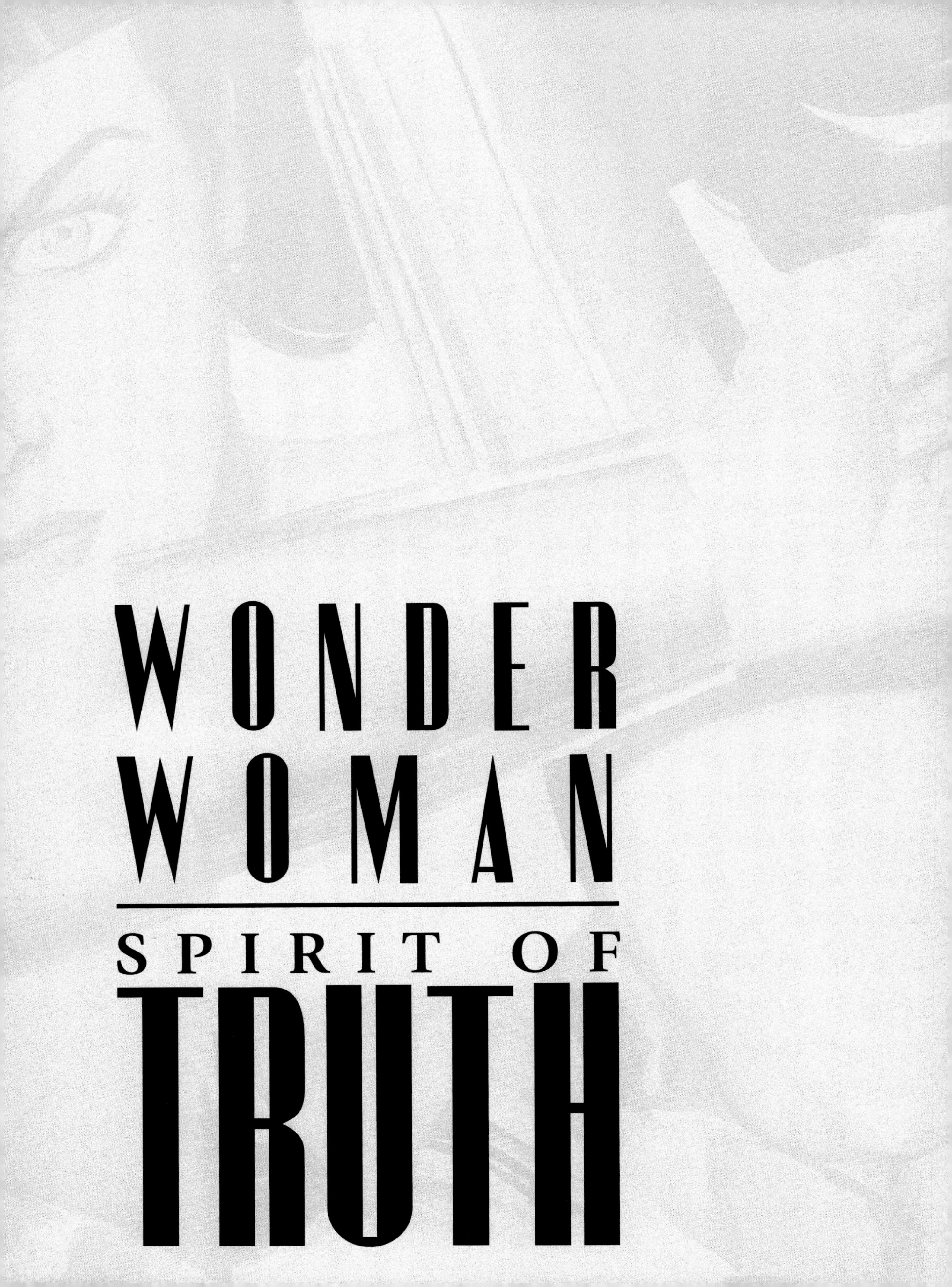

WONDER WOMAN

SPIRIT OF TRUTH

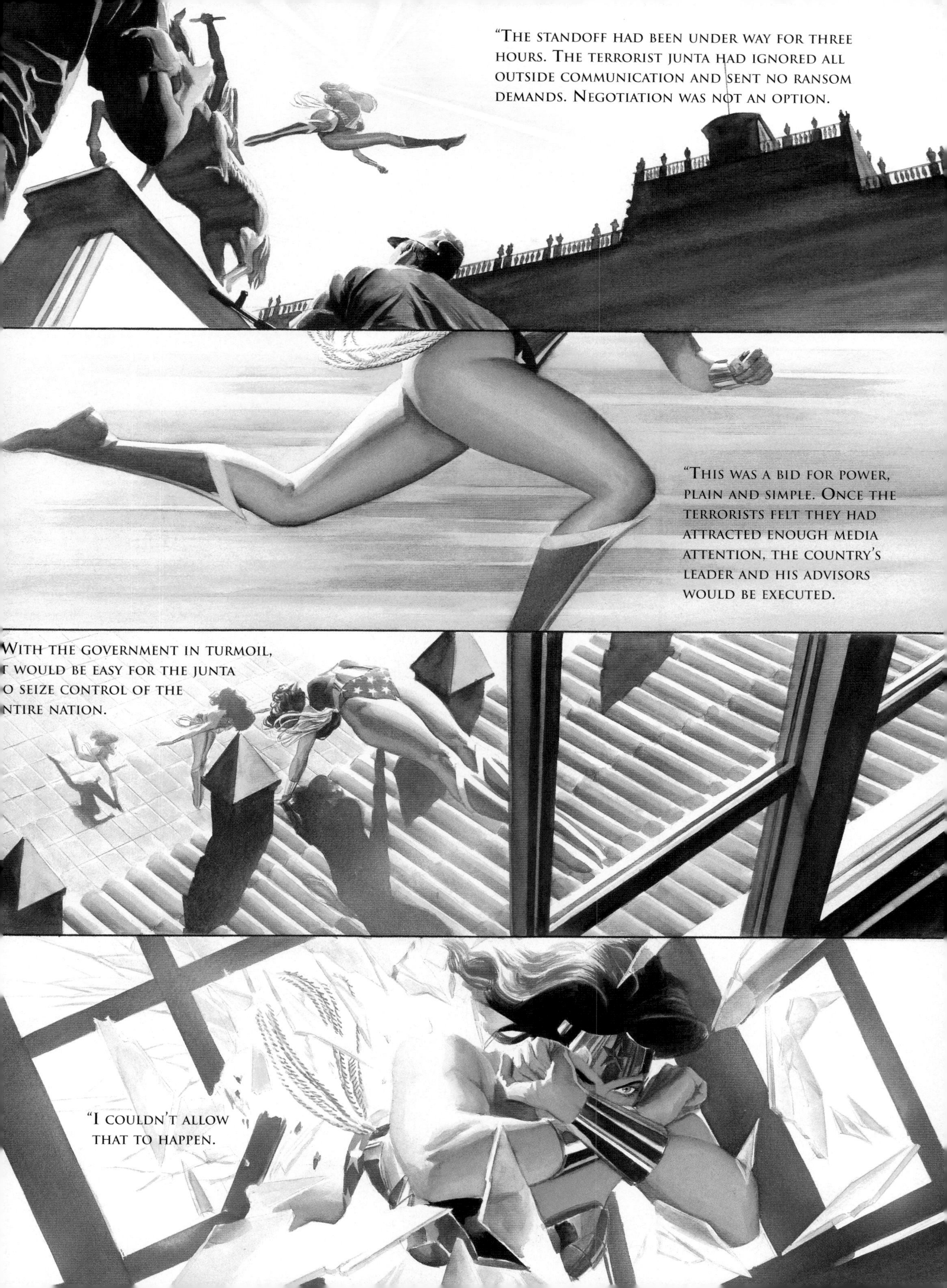
"The standoff had been under way for three hours. The terrorist junta had ignored all outside communication and sent no ransom demands. Negotiation was not an option.
"This was a bid for power, plain and simple. Once the terrorists felt they had attracted enough media attention, the country's leader and his advisors would be executed.
With the government in turmoil, t would be easy for the junta o seize control of the ntire nation.
"I couldn't allow that to happen.

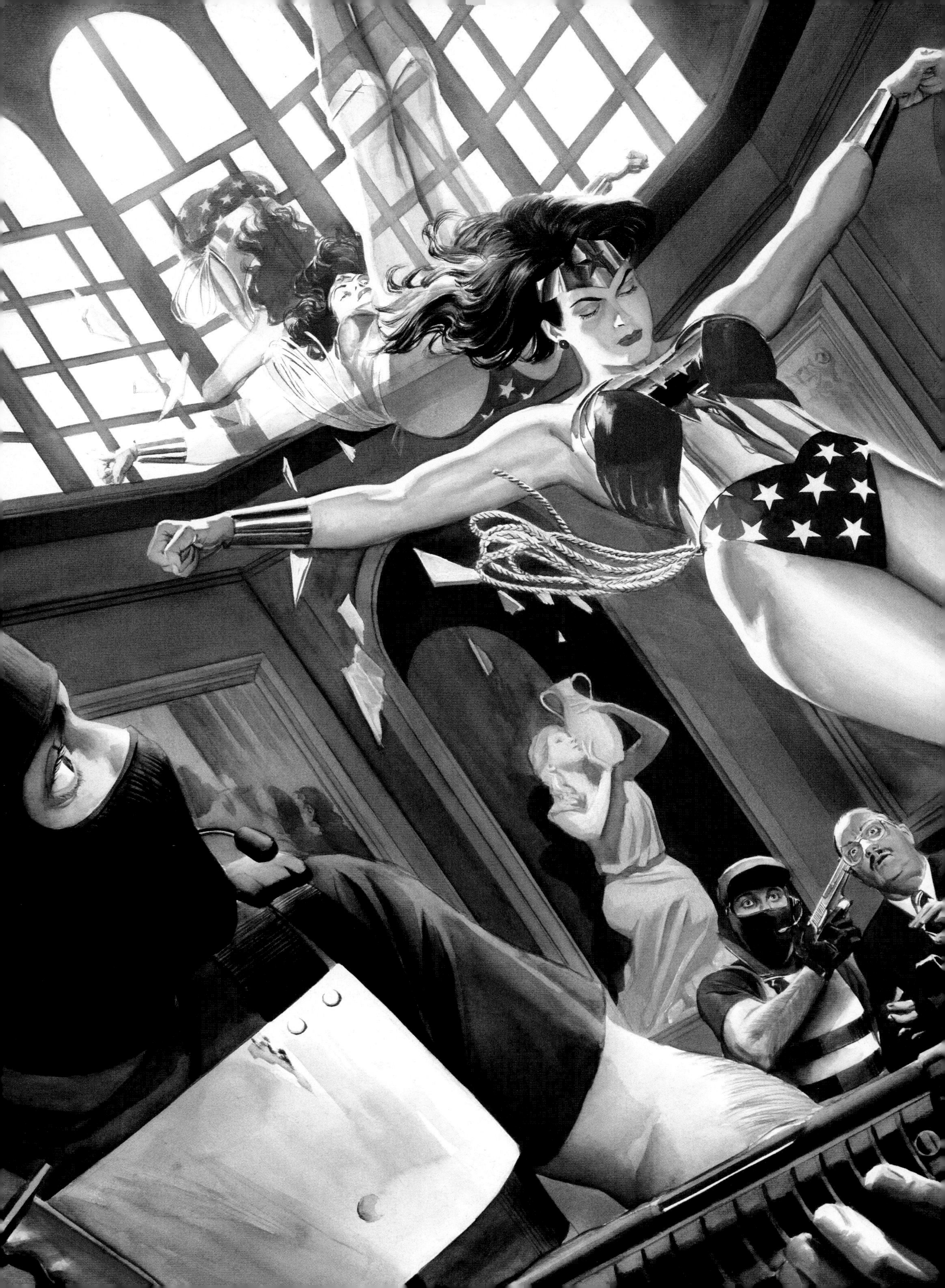

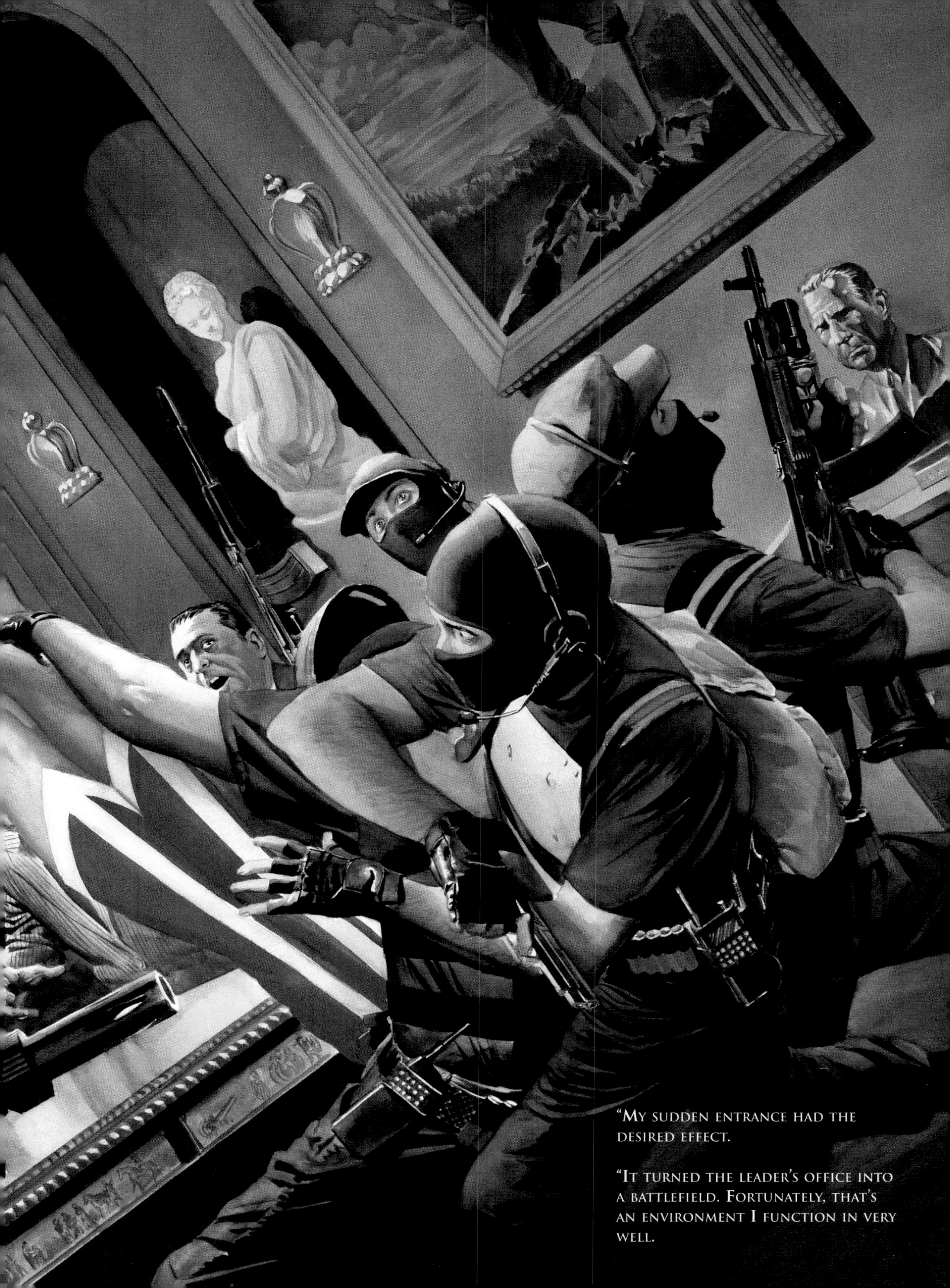
"My sudden entrance had the desired effect.
"It turned the leader's office into a battlefield. Fortunately, that's an environment I function in very well.

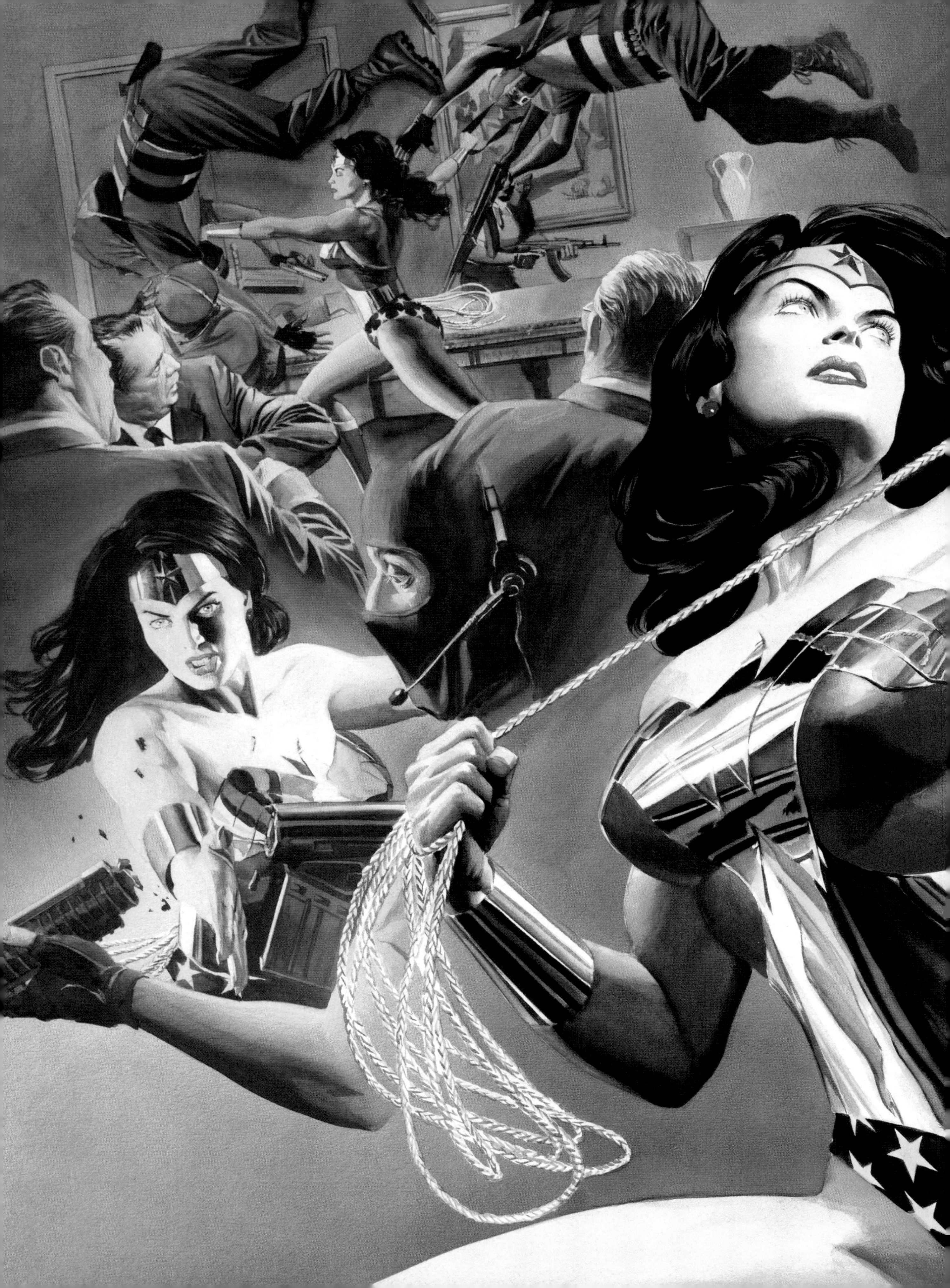

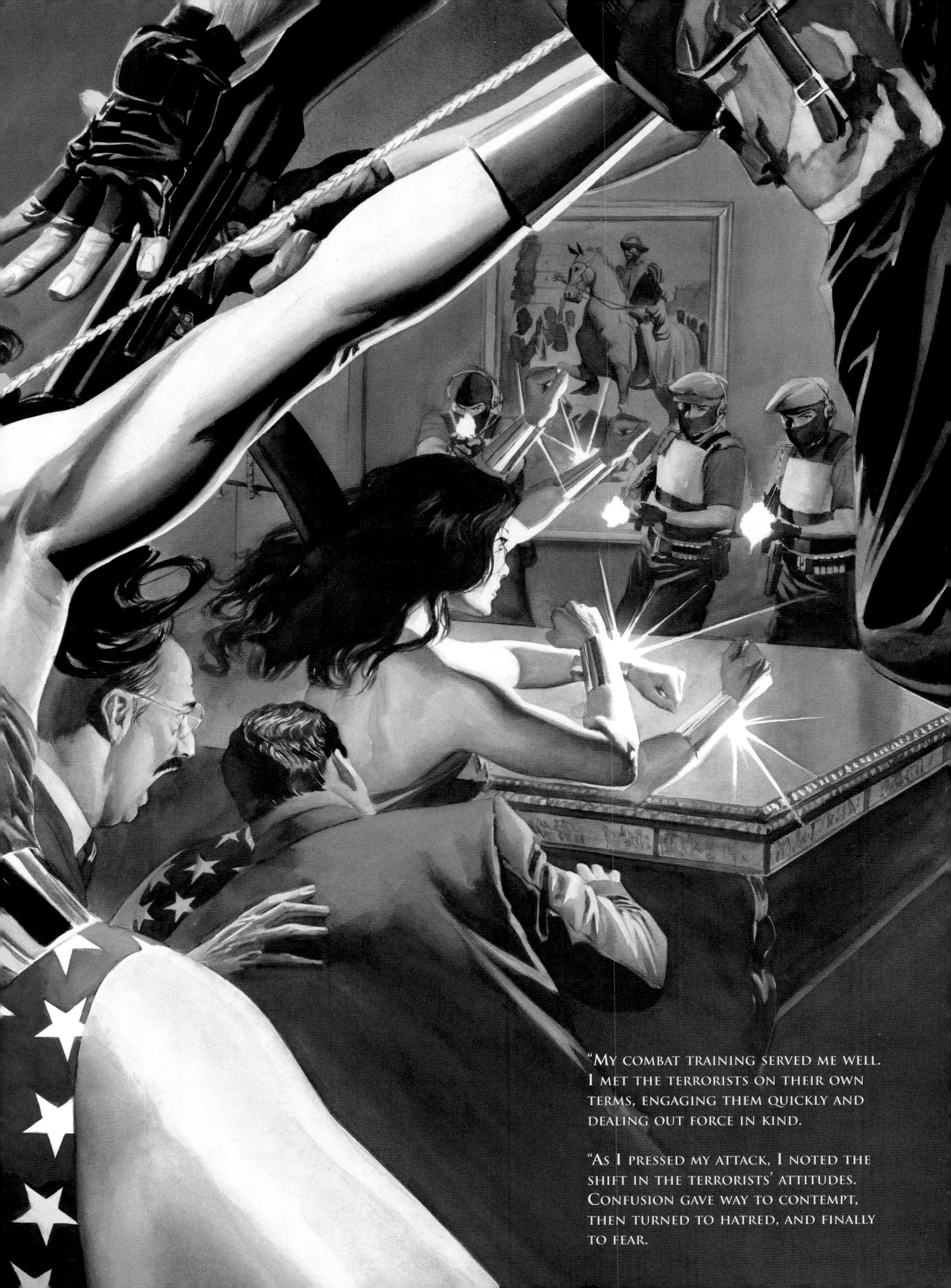
"My combat training served me well. I met the terrorists on their own terms, engaging them quickly and dealing out force in kind.
"As I pressed my attack, I noted the shift in the terrorists' attitudes. Confusion gave way to contempt, then turned to hatred, and finally to fear.

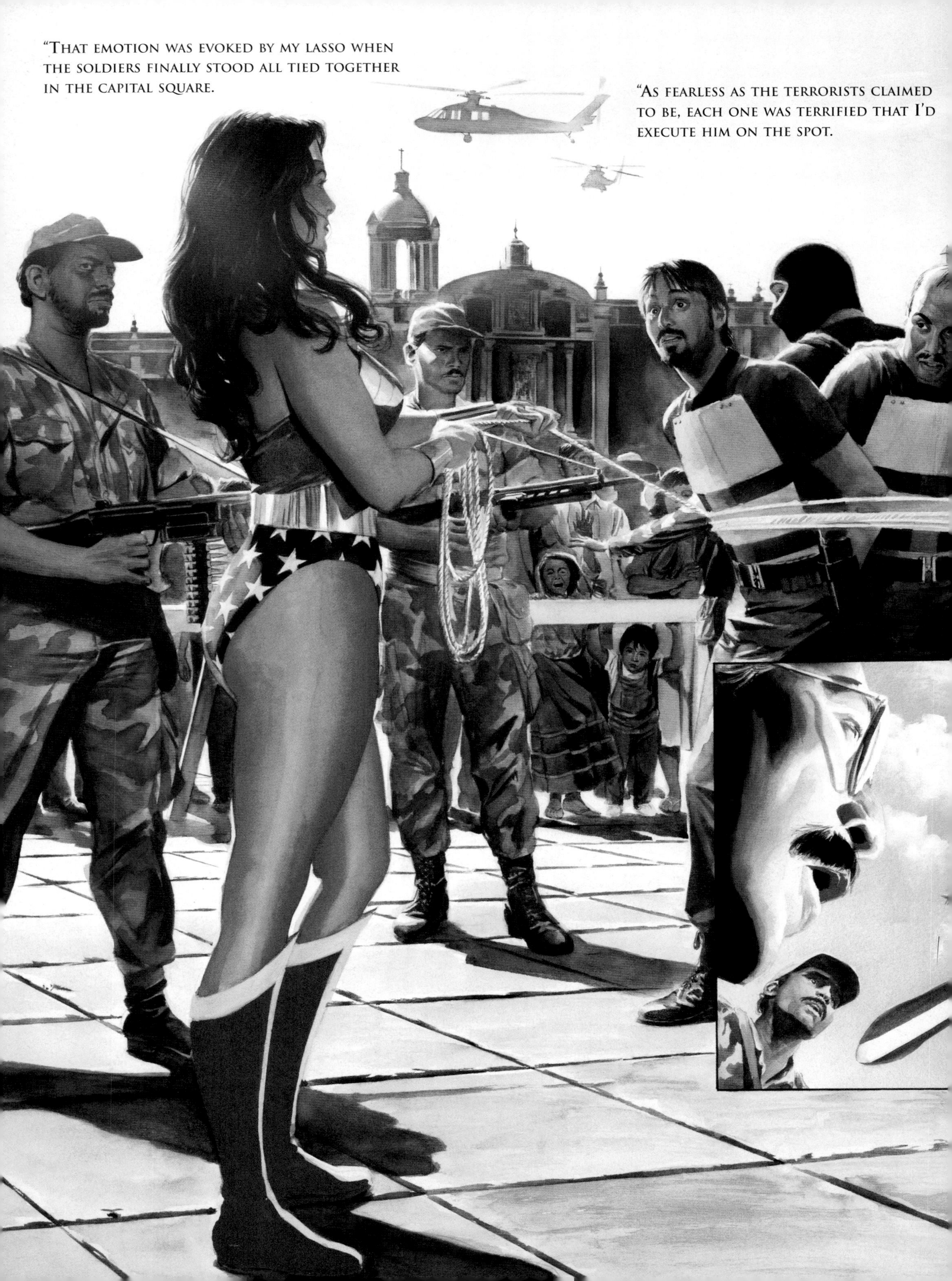
"THAT EMOTION WAS EVOKED BY MY LASSO WHEN THE SOLDIERS FINALLY STOOD ALL TIED TOGETHER IN THE CAPITAL SQUARE.
"AS FEARLESS AS THE TERRORISTS CLAIMED TO BE, EACH ONE WAS TERRIFIED THAT I'D EXECUTE HIM ON THE SPOT.

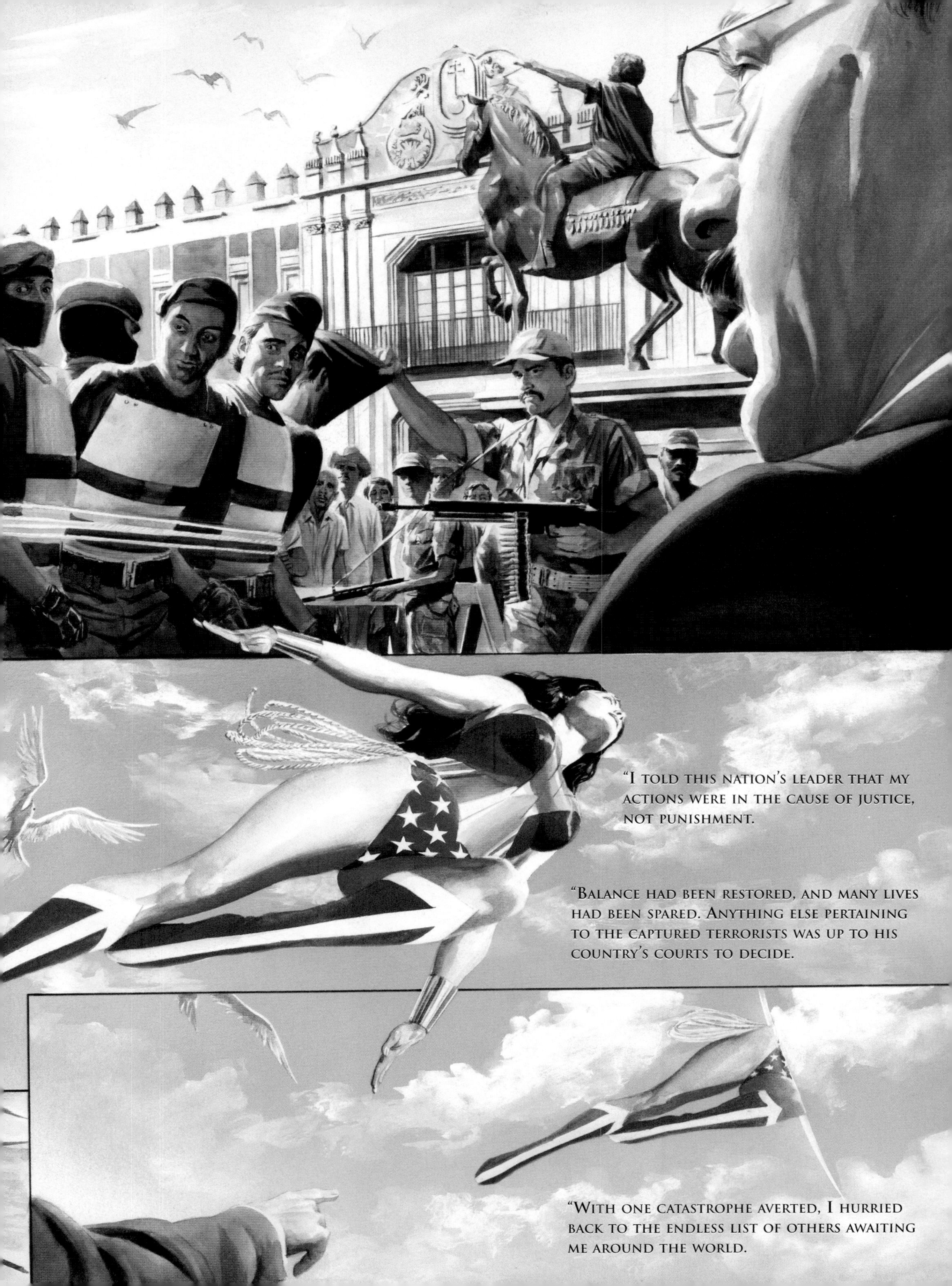
"I told this nation's leader that my actions were in the cause of justice, not punishment.
"Balance had been restored, and many lives had been spared. Anything else pertaining to the captured terrorists was up to his country's courts to decide.
"With one catastrophe averted, I hurried back to the endless list of others awaiting me around the world.

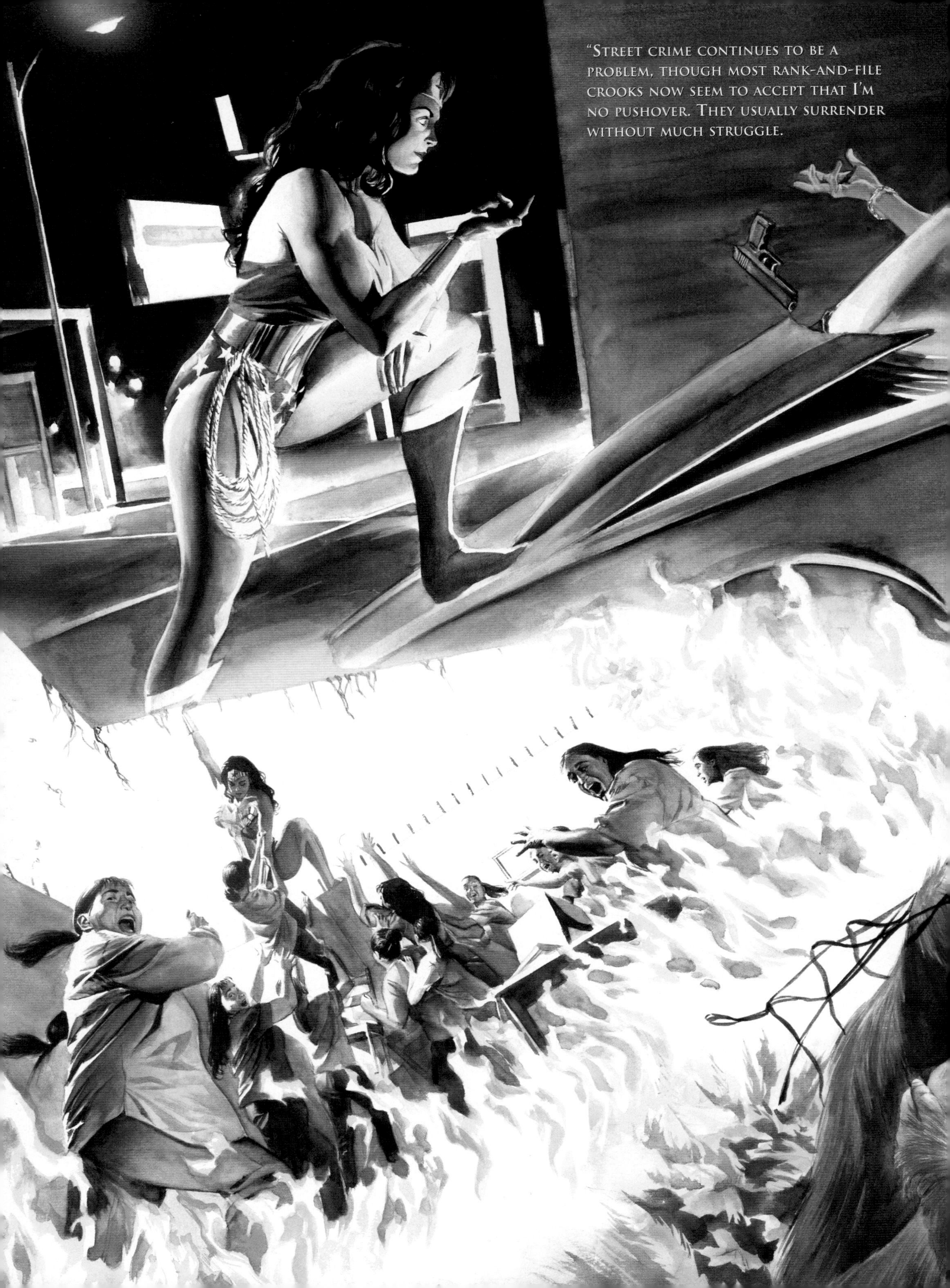
"Street crime continues to be a problem, though most rank-and-file crooks now seem to accept that I'm no pushover. They usually surrender without much struggle.

THE WORST CRIMINALS ARE STILL THE ONES WHO
OPERATE UNDER THE GUISE OF RESPECTABILITY,
SUCH AS THE SLIMY MANUFACTURER WHO PAYS OFF
A SAFETY INSPECTOR. NEVER MIND THAT ONE FIRE
COULD WIPE OUT HIS BUSINESS AND THE POOR
SOULS TOILING IN HIS SWEATSHOP.

"OR THE SOLDIERS HOPING TO MAKE BIG
MONEY BY LEADING SO-CALLED SPORTSMEN
ON AN ENDANGERED SPECIES HUNT.

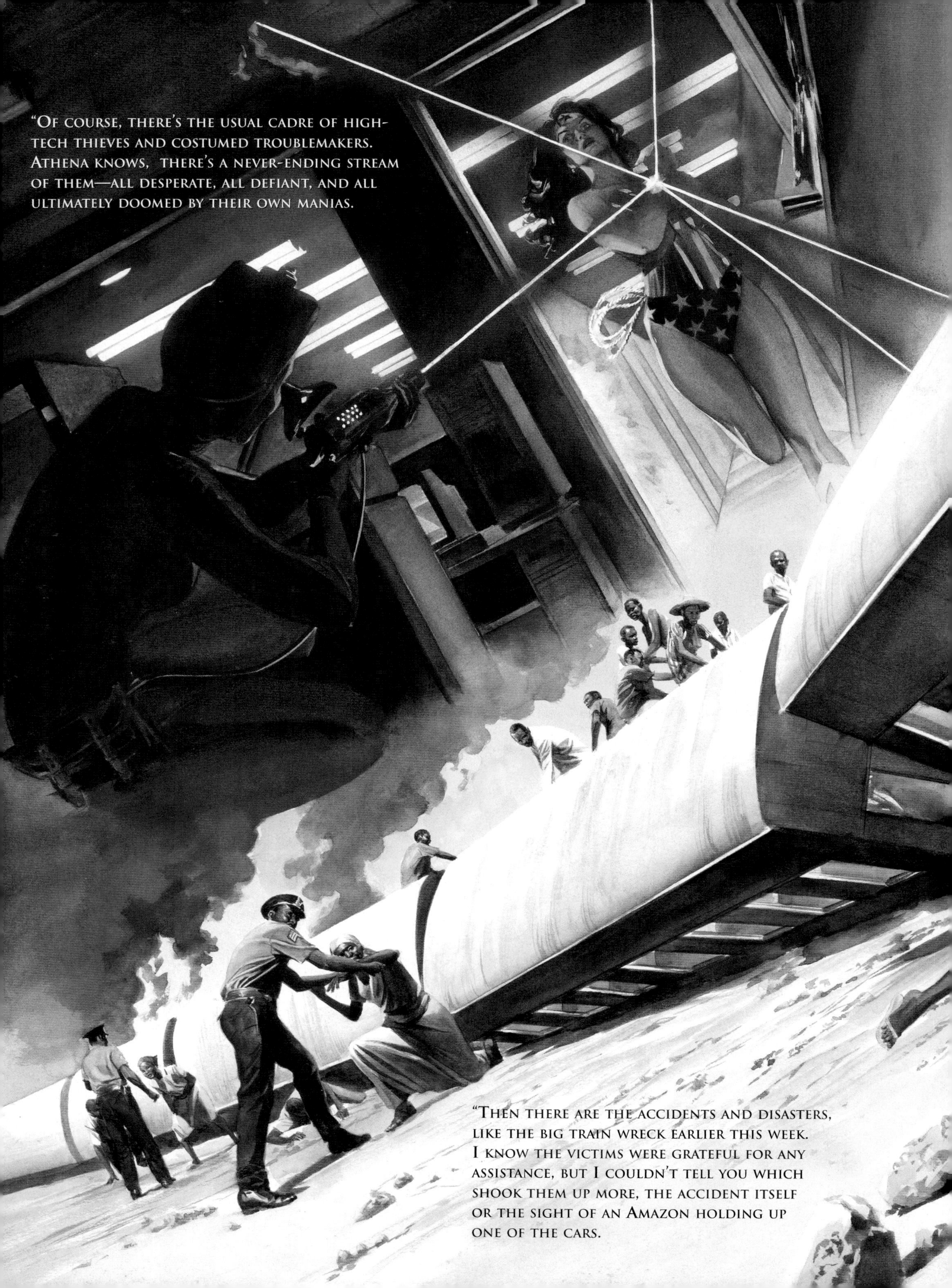
"Of course, there's the usual cadre of high-tech thieves and costumed troublemakers. Athena knows, there's a never-ending stream of them—all desperate, all defiant, and all ultimately doomed by their own manias.
"Then there are the accidents and disasters, like the big train wreck earlier this week. I know the victims were grateful for any assistance, but I couldn't tell you which shook them up more, the accident itself or the sight of an Amazon holding up one of the cars.

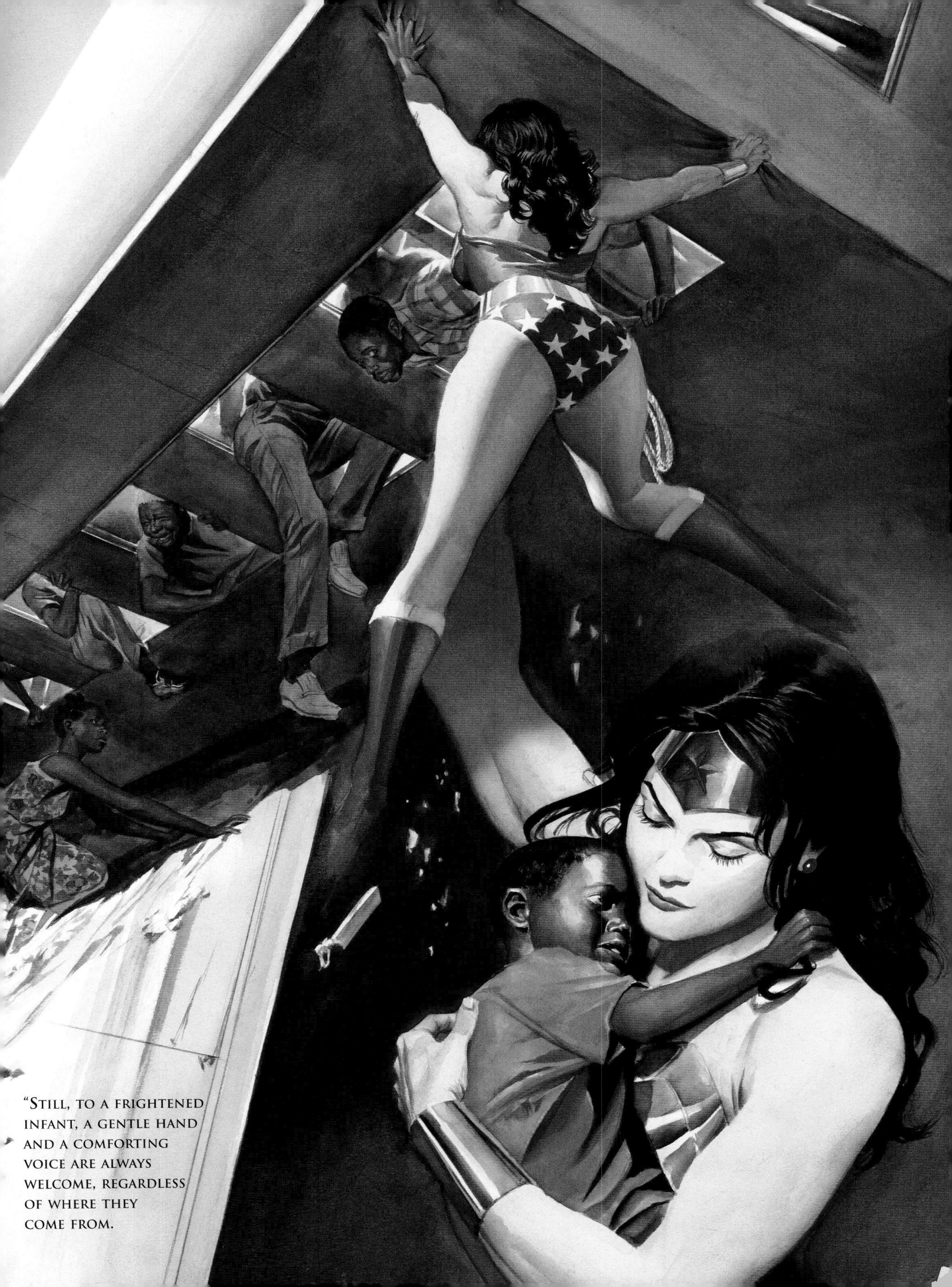
"STILL, TO A FRIGHTENED INFANT, A GENTLE HAND AND A COMFORTING VOICE ARE ALWAYS WELCOME, REGARDLESS OF WHERE THEY COME FROM.

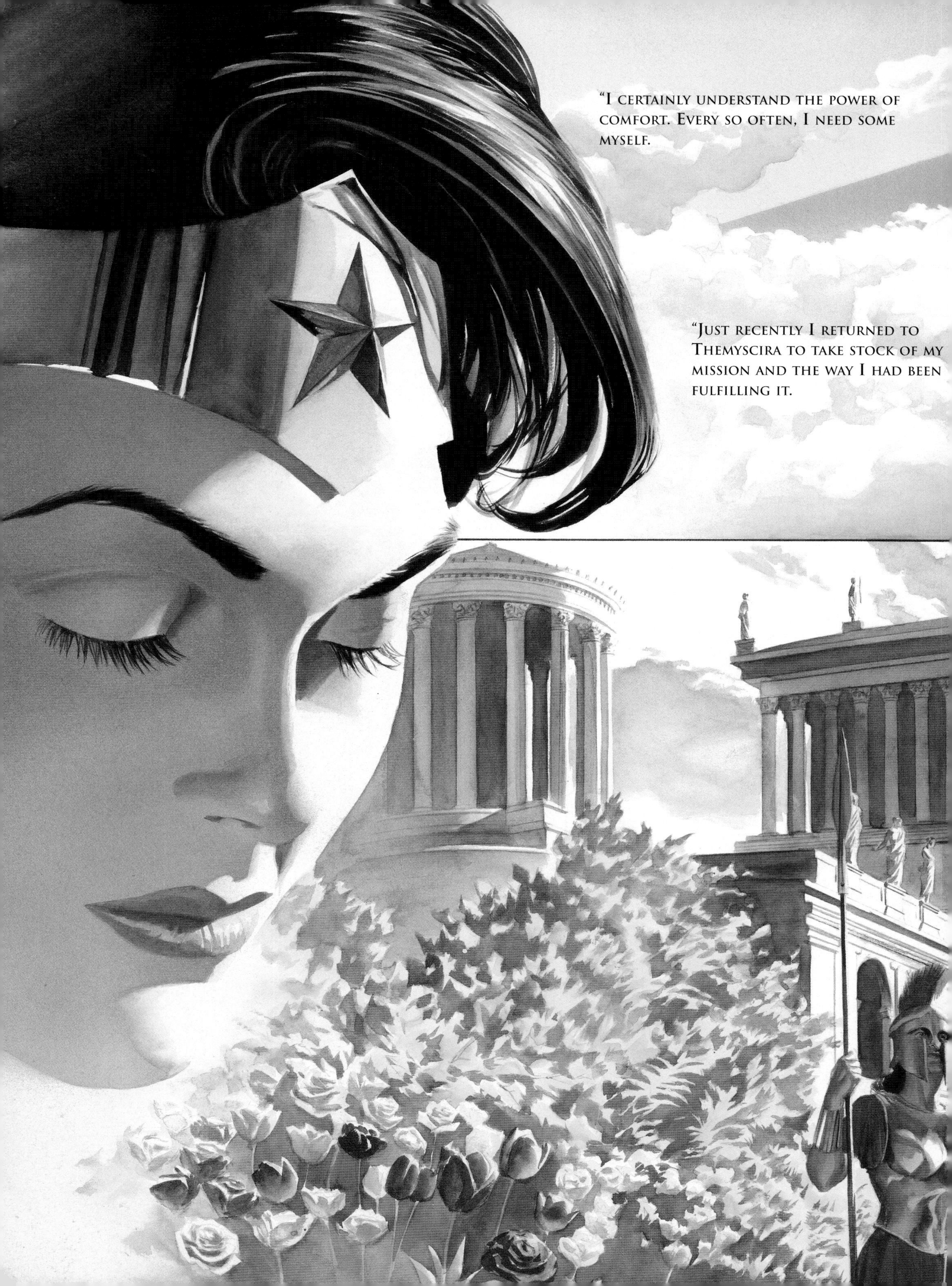
"I CERTAINLY UNDERSTAND THE POWER OF COMFORT. EVERY SO OFTEN, I NEED SOME MYSELF.
"JUST RECENTLY I RETURNED TO THEMYSCIRA TO TAKE STOCK OF MY MISSION AND THE WAY I HAD BEEN FULFILLING IT.

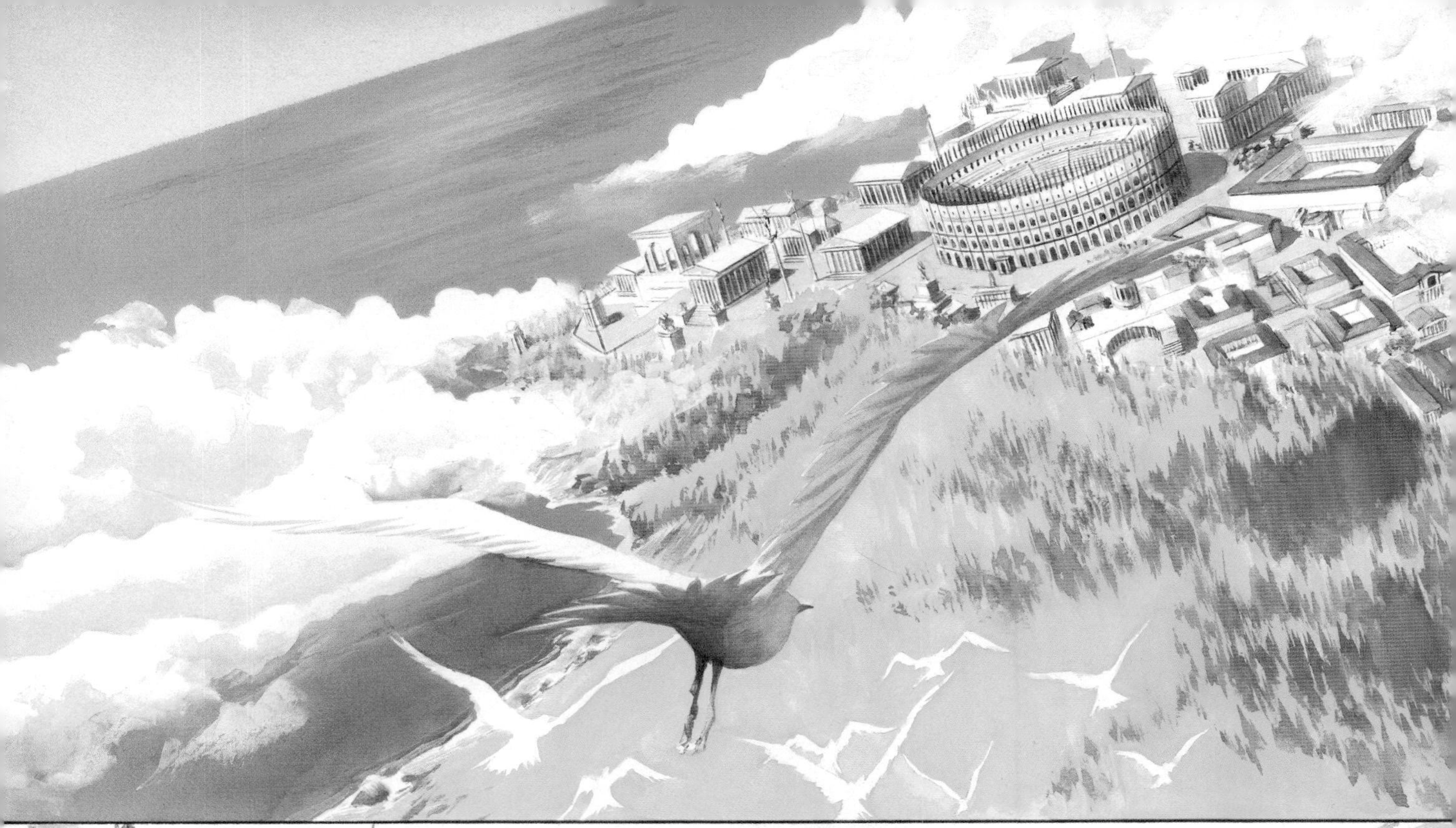

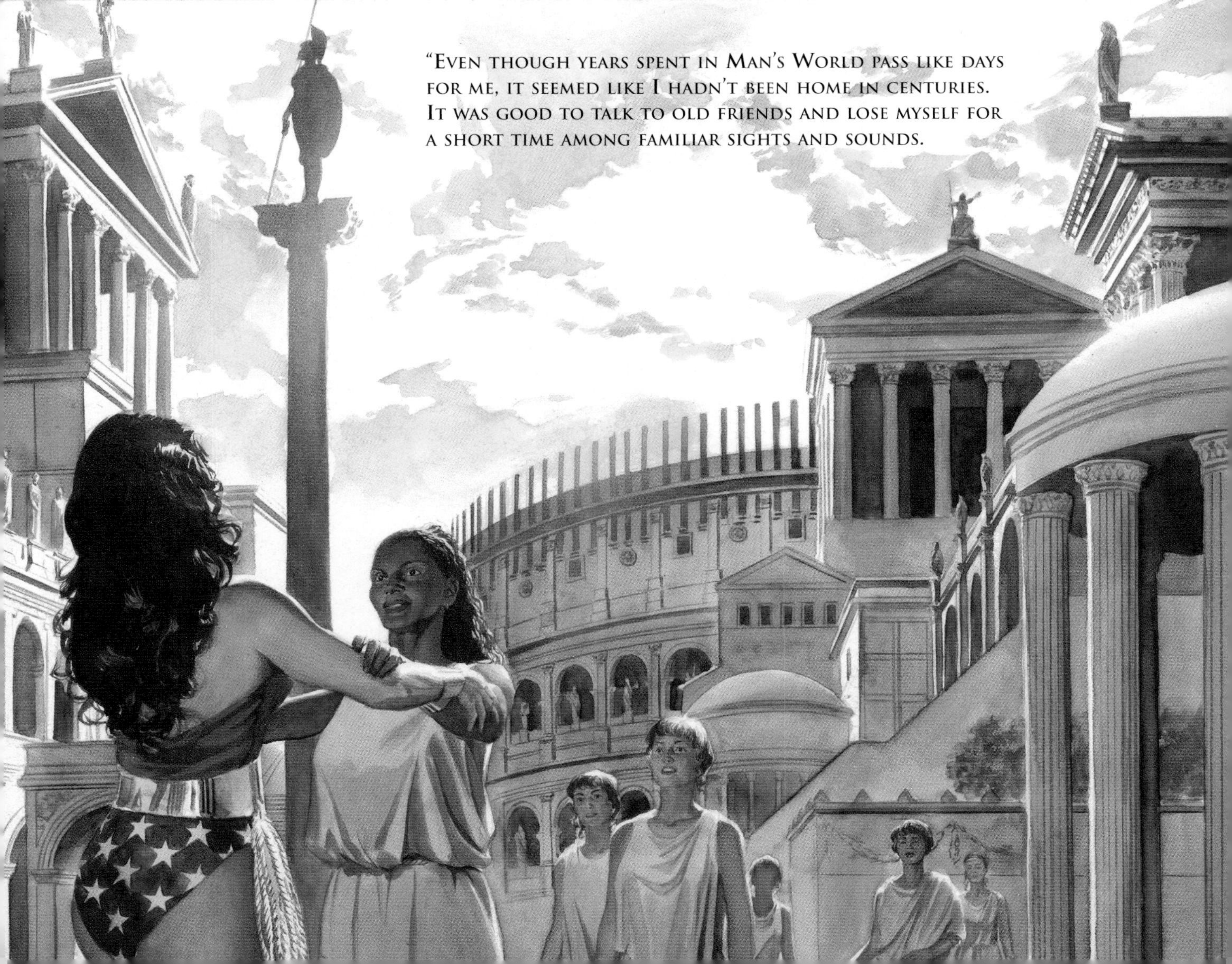
"Even though years spent in Man's World pass like days for me, it seemed like I hadn't been home in centuries. It was good to talk to old friends and lose myself for a short time among familiar sights and sounds.

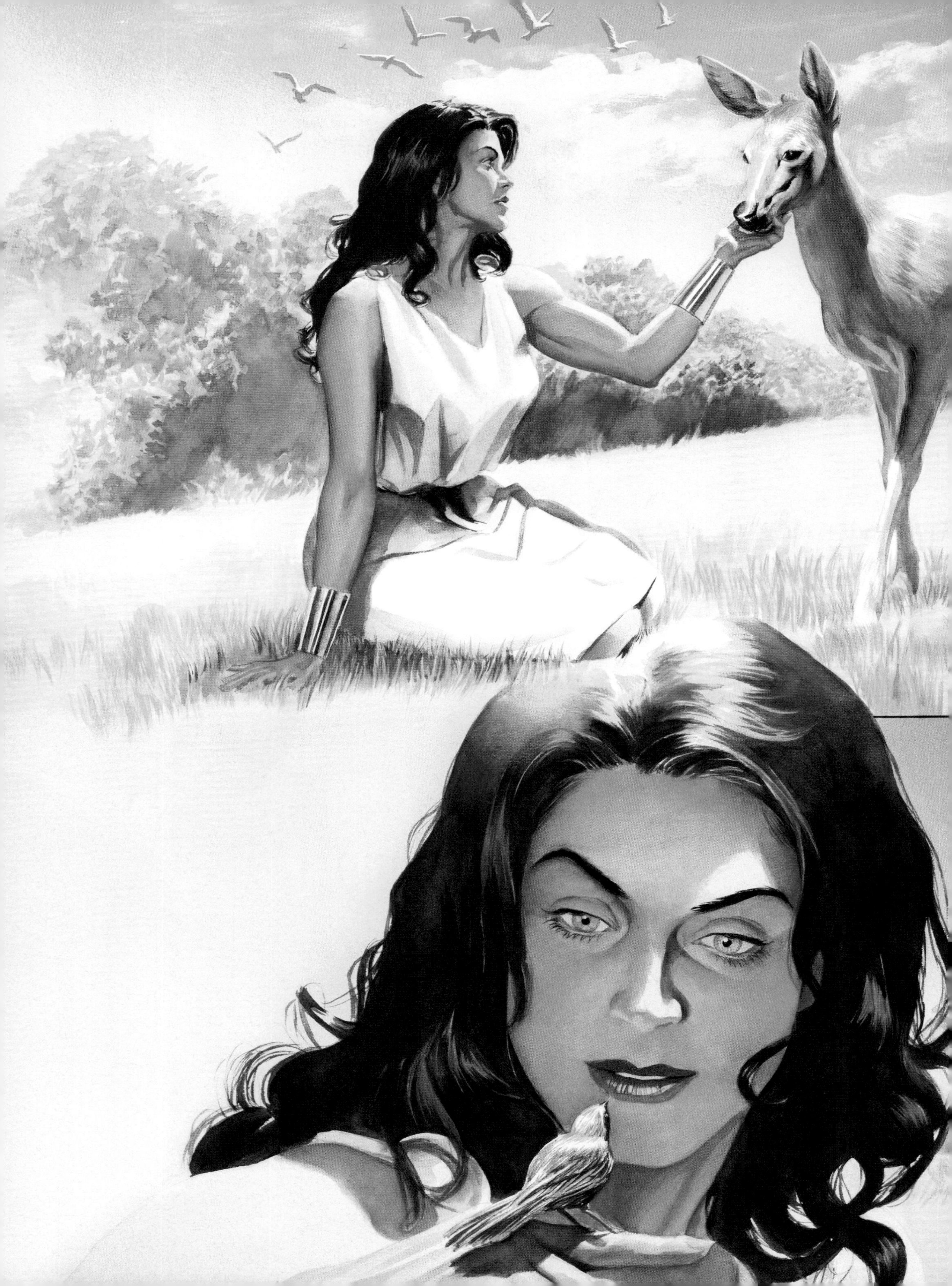

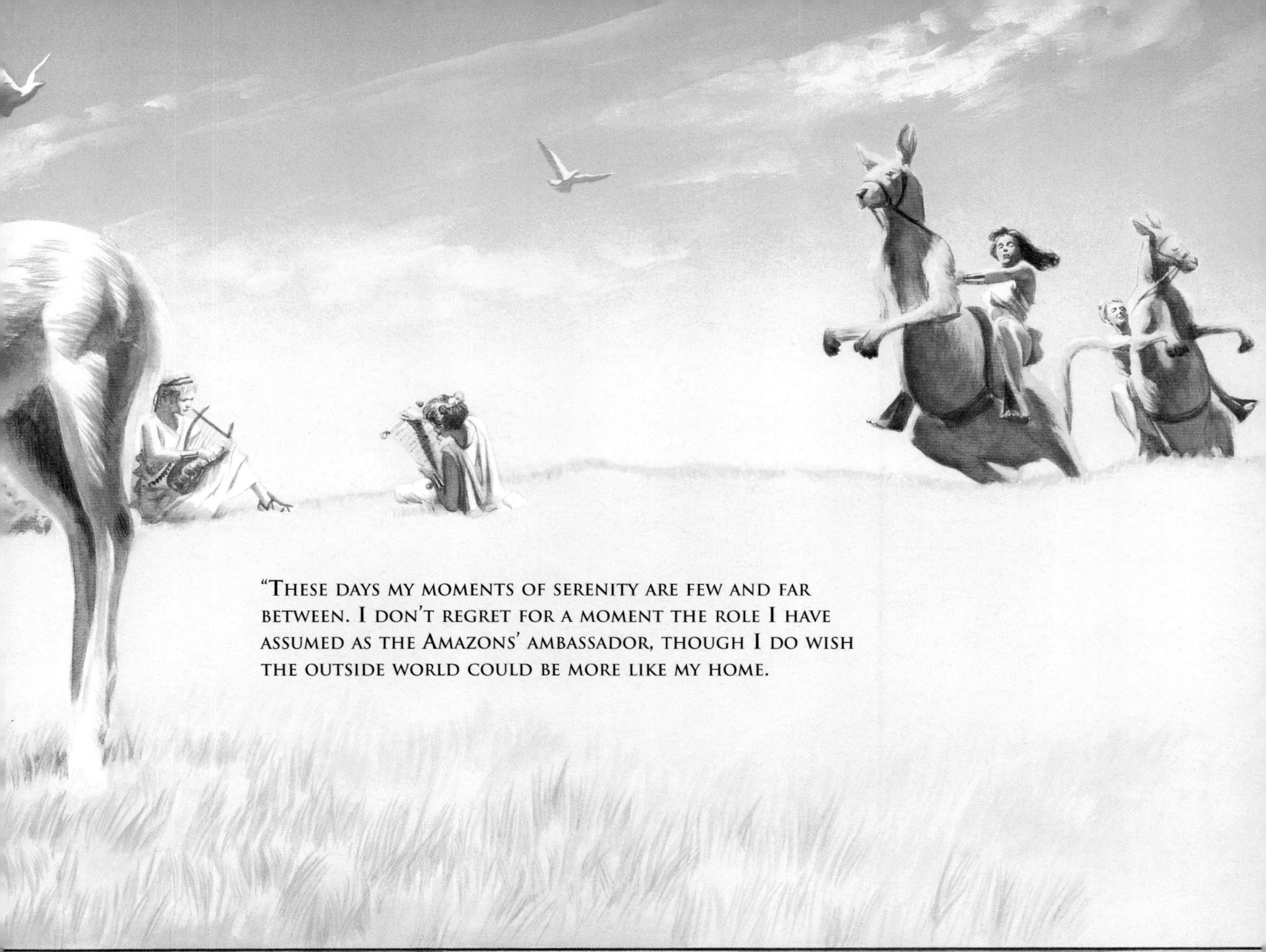

"These days my moments of serenity are few and far between. I don't regret for a moment the role I have assumed as the Amazons' ambassador, though I do wish the outside world could be more like my home.

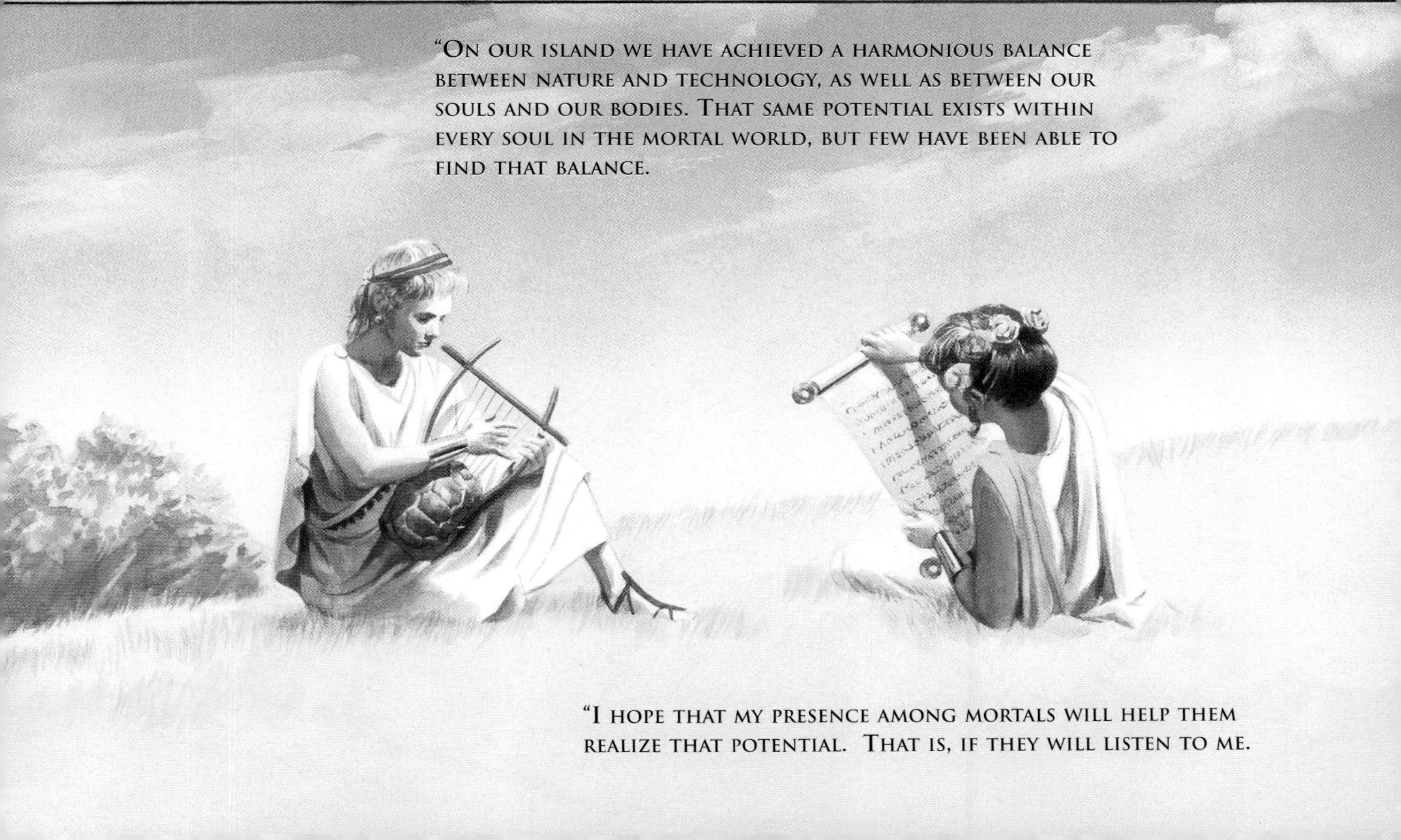

"On our island we have achieved a harmonious balance between nature and technology, as well as between our souls and our bodies. That same potential exists within every soul in the mortal world, but few have been able to find that balance.

"I hope that my presence among mortals will help them realize that potential. That is, if they will listen to me.

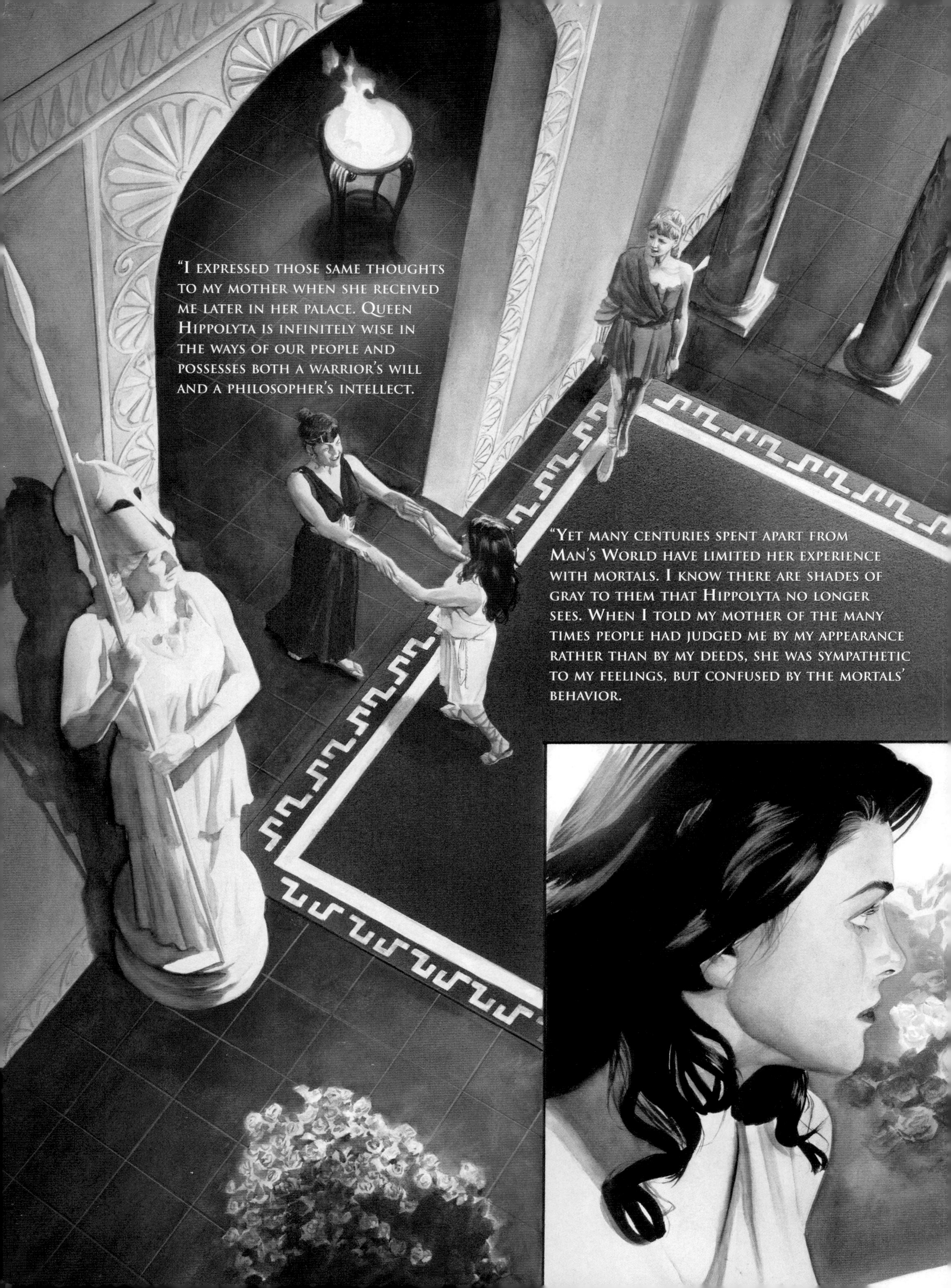
"I expressed those same thoughts to my mother when she received me later in her palace. Queen Hippolyta is infinitely wise in the ways of our people and possesses both a warrior's will and a philosopher's intellect.
"Yet many centuries spent apart from Man's World have limited her experience with mortals. I know there are shades of gray to them that Hippolyta no longer sees. When I told my mother of the many times people had judged me by my appearance rather than by my deeds, she was sympathetic to my feelings, but confused by the mortals' behavior.

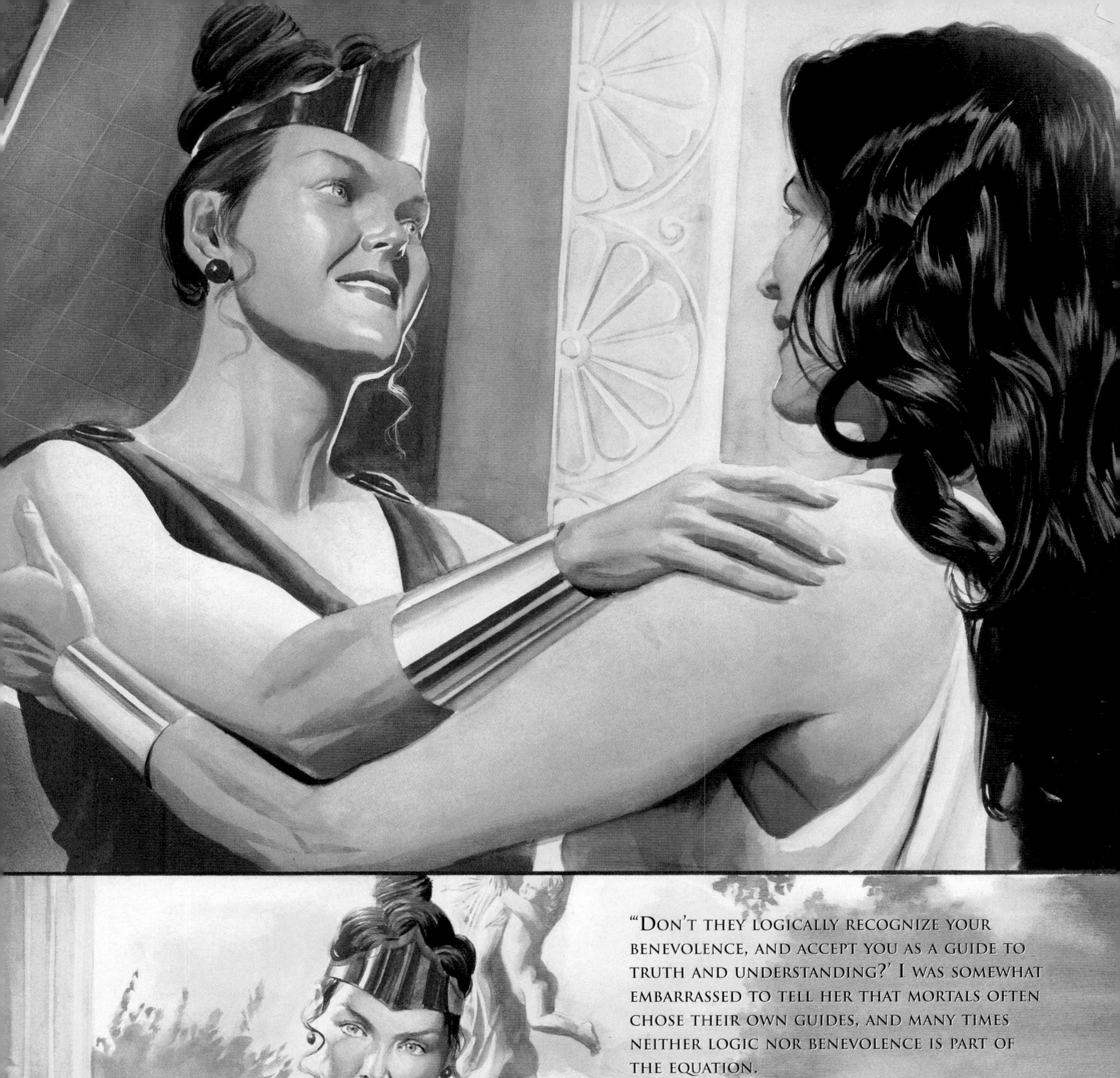

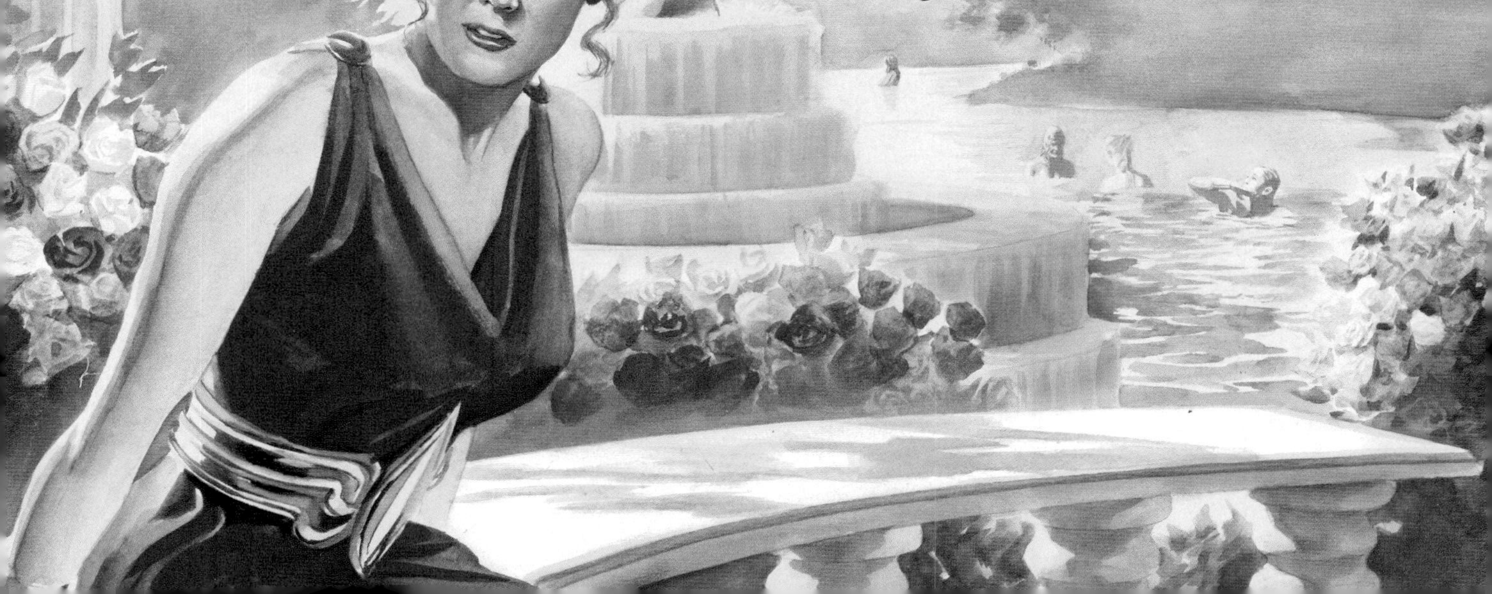
"'Don't they logically recognize your benevolence, and accept you as a guide to truth and understanding?' I was somewhat embarrassed to tell her that mortals often chose their own guides, and many times neither logic nor benevolence is part of the equation.

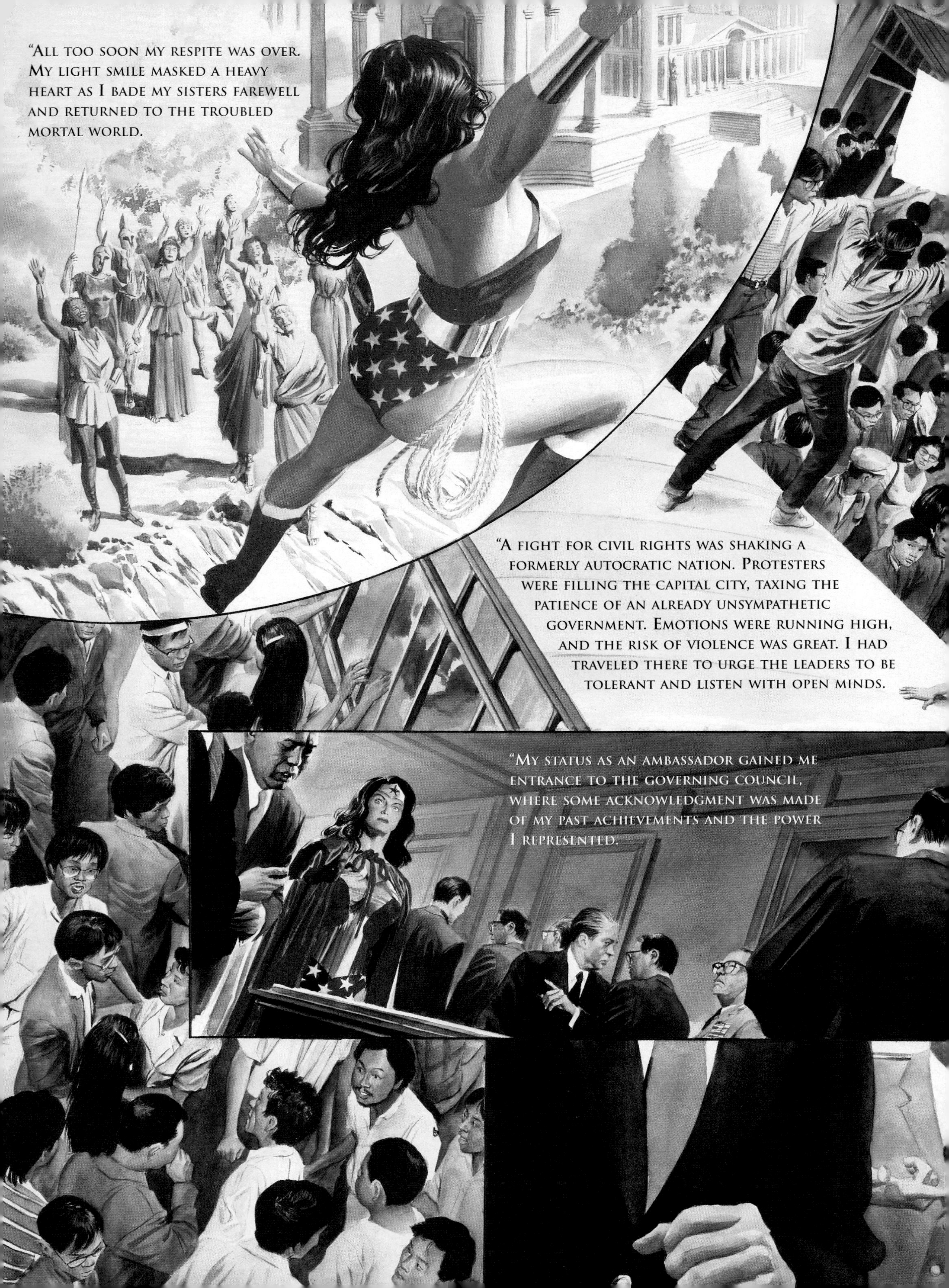
"All too soon my respite was over. My light smile masked a heavy heart as I bade my sisters farewell and returned to the troubled mortal world.
"A fight for civil rights was shaking a formerly autocratic nation. Protesters were filling the capital city, taxing the patience of an already unsympathetic government. Emotions were running high, and the risk of violence was great. I had traveled there to urge the leaders to be tolerant and listen with open minds.
"My status as an ambassador gained me entrance to the governing council, where some acknowledgment was made of my past achievements and the power I represented.

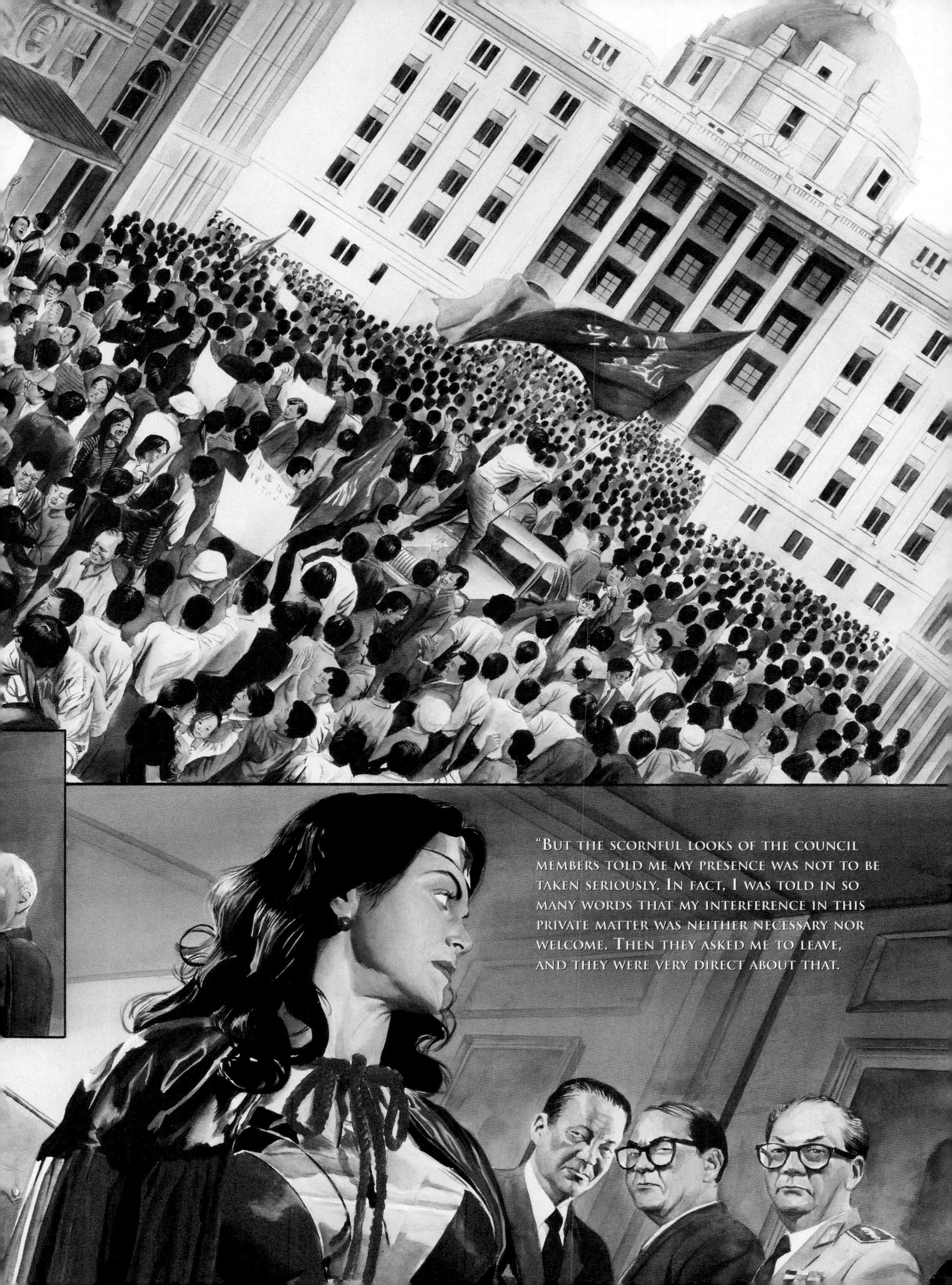
"BUT THE SCORNFUL LOOKS OF THE COUNCIL MEMBERS TOLD ME MY PRESENCE WAS NOT TO BE TAKEN SERIOUSLY. IN FACT, I WAS TOLD IN SO MANY WORDS THAT MY INTERFERENCE IN THIS PRIVATE MATTER WAS NEITHER NECESSARY NOR WELCOME. THEN THEY ASKED ME TO LEAVE, AND THEY WERE VERY DIRECT ABOUT THAT.

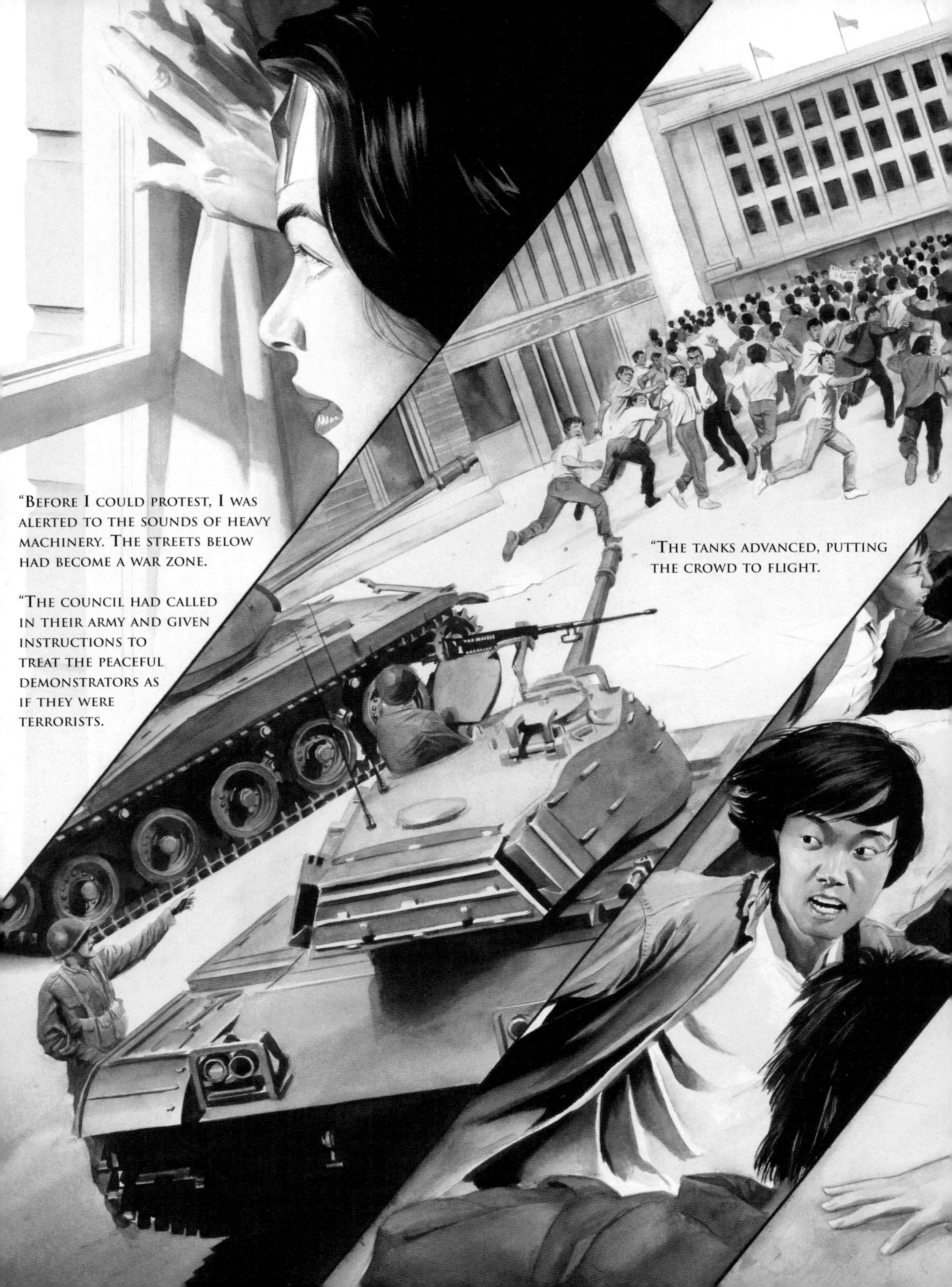
"Before I could protest, I was alerted to the sounds of heavy machinery. The streets below had become a war zone.
"The council had called in their army and given instructions to treat the peaceful demonstrators as if they were terrorists.
"The tanks advanced, putting the crowd to flight.

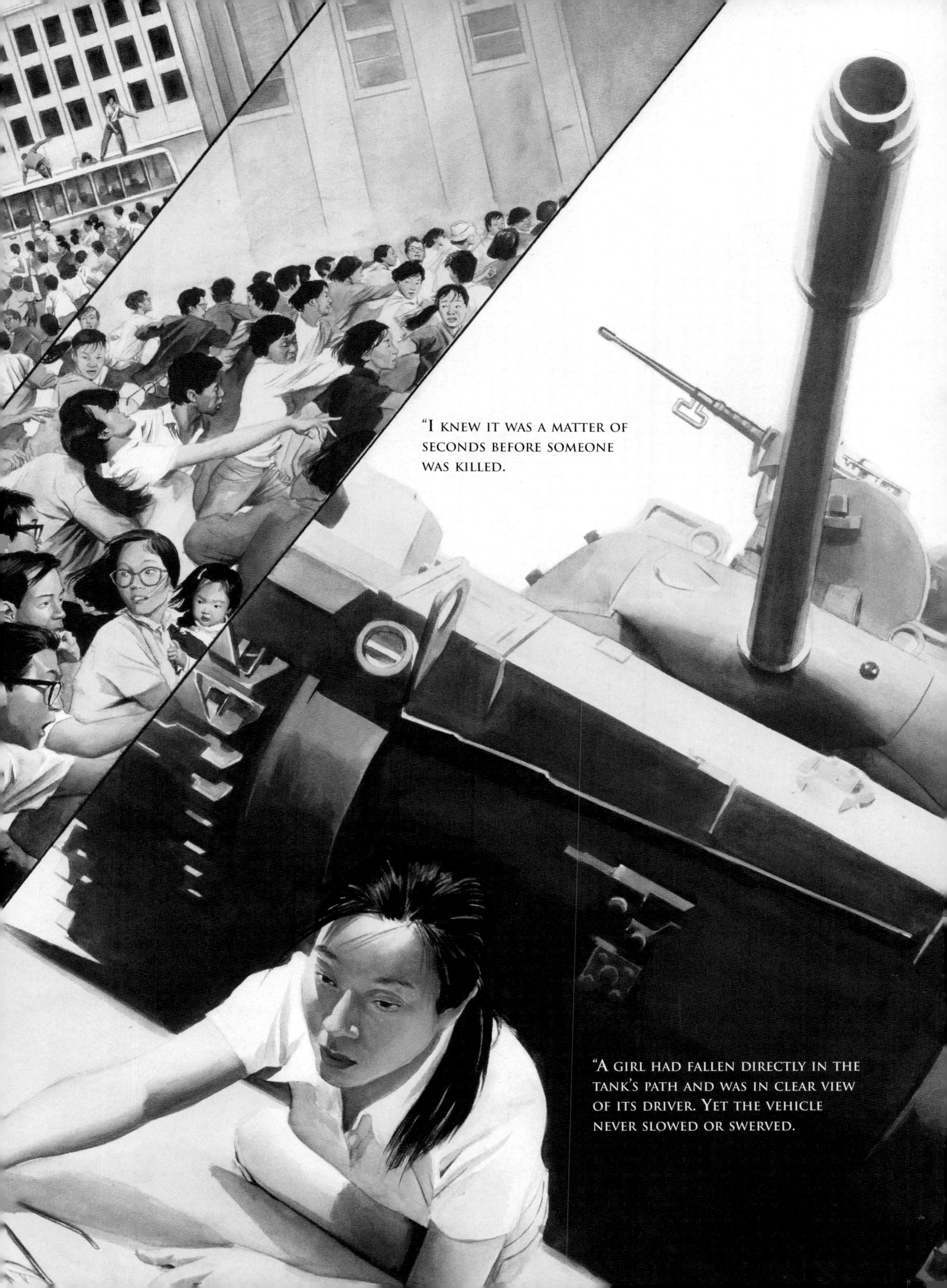
"I knew it was a matter of seconds before someone was killed.
"A girl had fallen directly in the tank's path and was in clear view of its driver. Yet the vehicle never slowed or swerved.

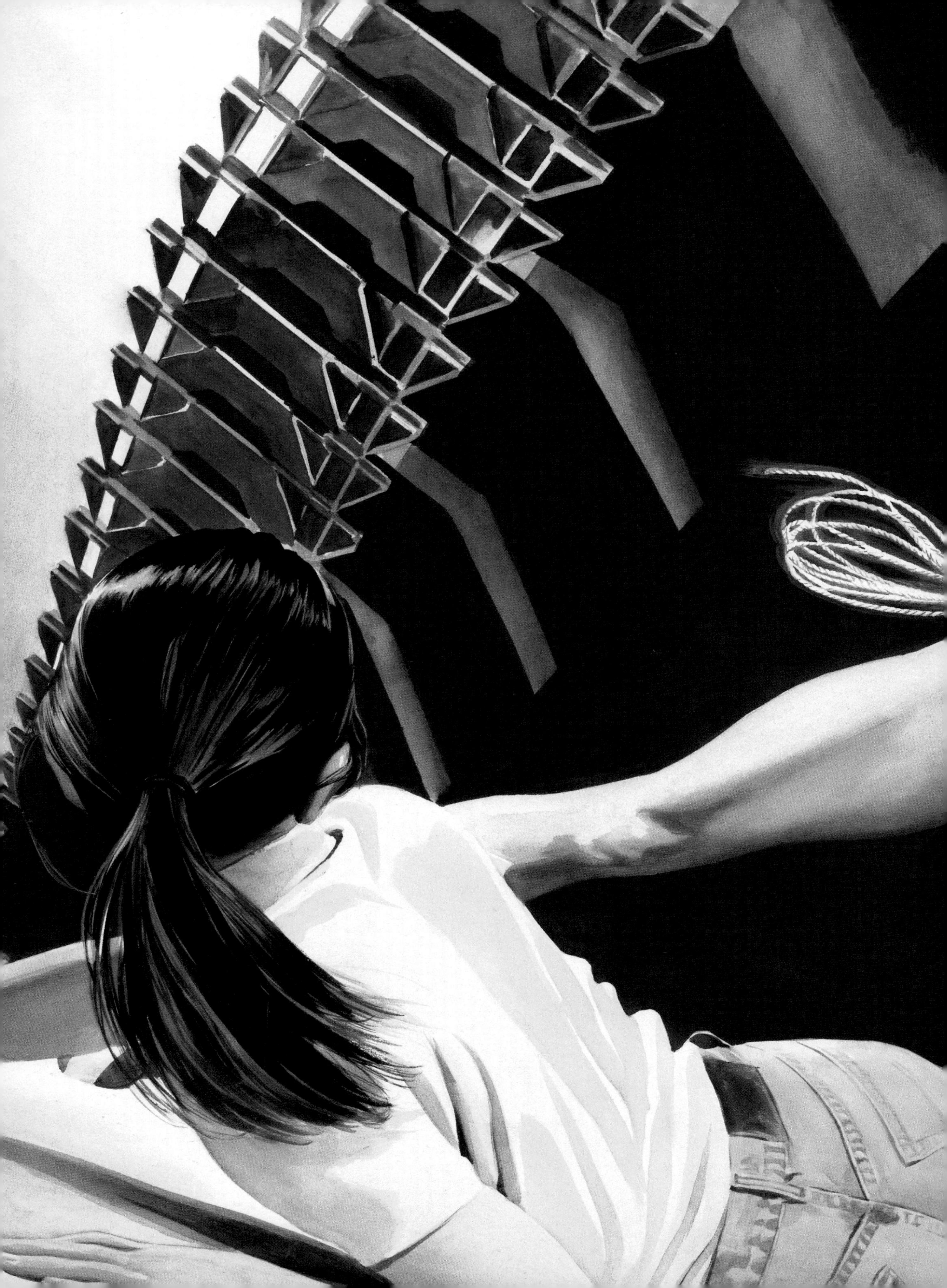

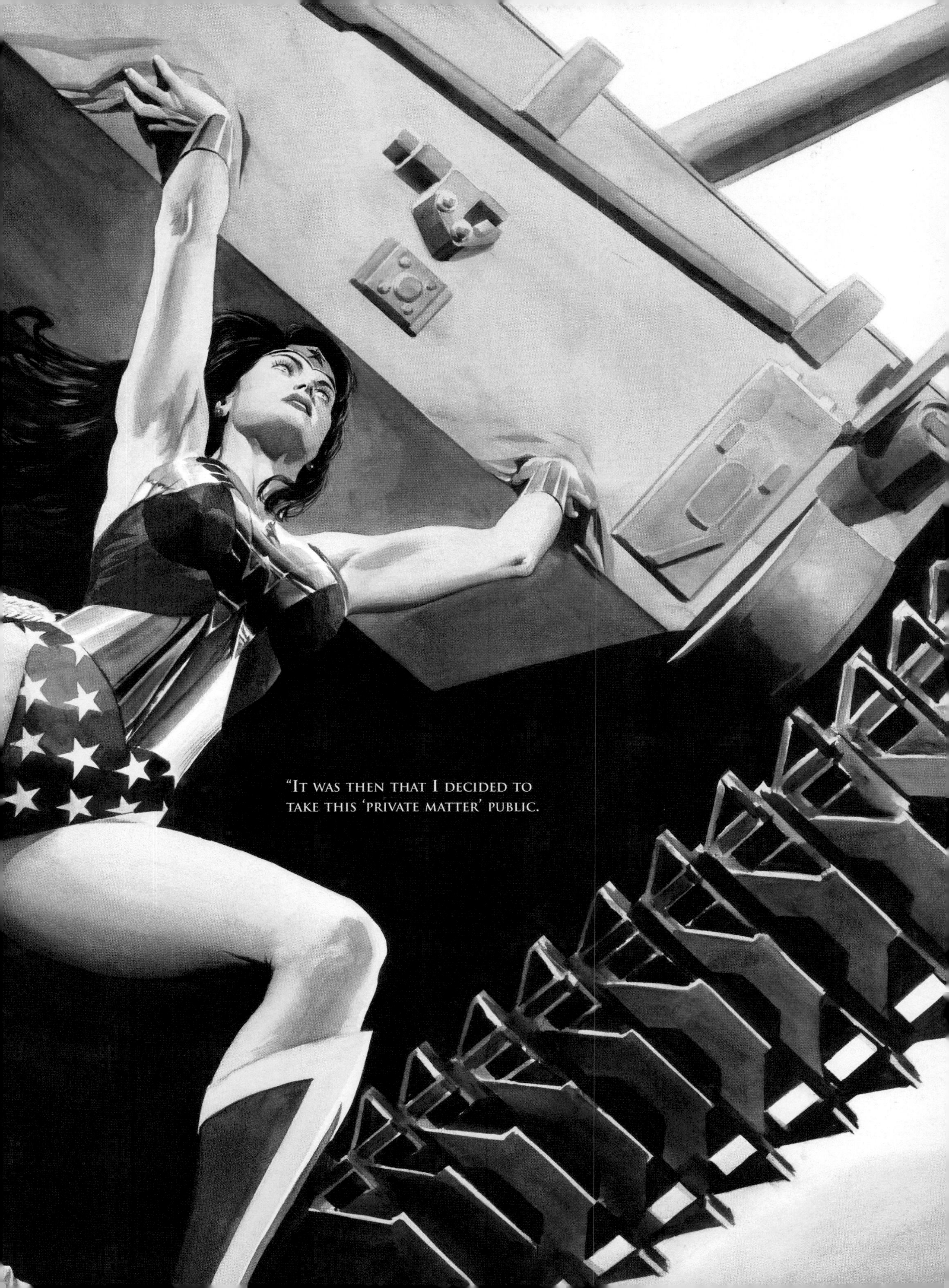
"It was then that I decided to take this 'private matter' public.

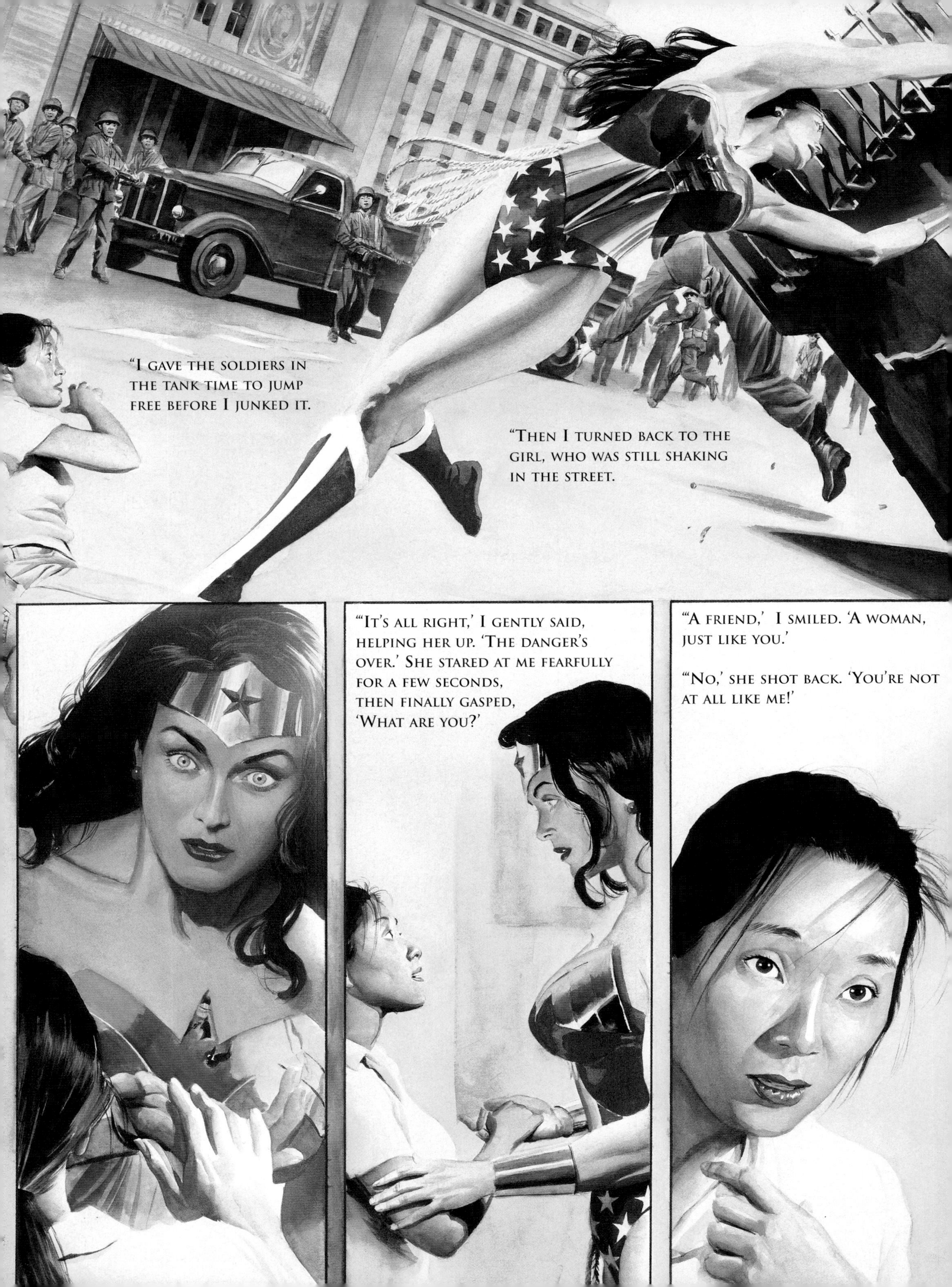
"I gave the soldiers in the tank time to jump free before I junked it.
"Then I turned back to the girl, who was still shaking in the street.
"'It's all right,' I gently said, helping her up. 'The danger's over.' She stared at me fearfully for a few seconds, then finally gasped, 'What are you?'
"'A friend,' I smiled. 'A woman, just like you.'
"'No,' she shot back. 'You're not at all like me!'

WITH THAT SHE TURNED AND RAN. THE GIRL HAD SEEN ME ONLY AS AN UNWELCOME INTRUSION INTO HER WORLD.

"A BIZARRE CREATURE EVERY BIT AS THREATENING AS THE TANK THAT NEARLY KILLED HER.

"ONCE AGAIN, I WAS MYSTIFIED AT HOW SOMEONE'S PERCEPTION OF ME COULD BE SO WRONG, AND MY KINDLY EFFORT SO COMPLETELY MISINTERPRETED.

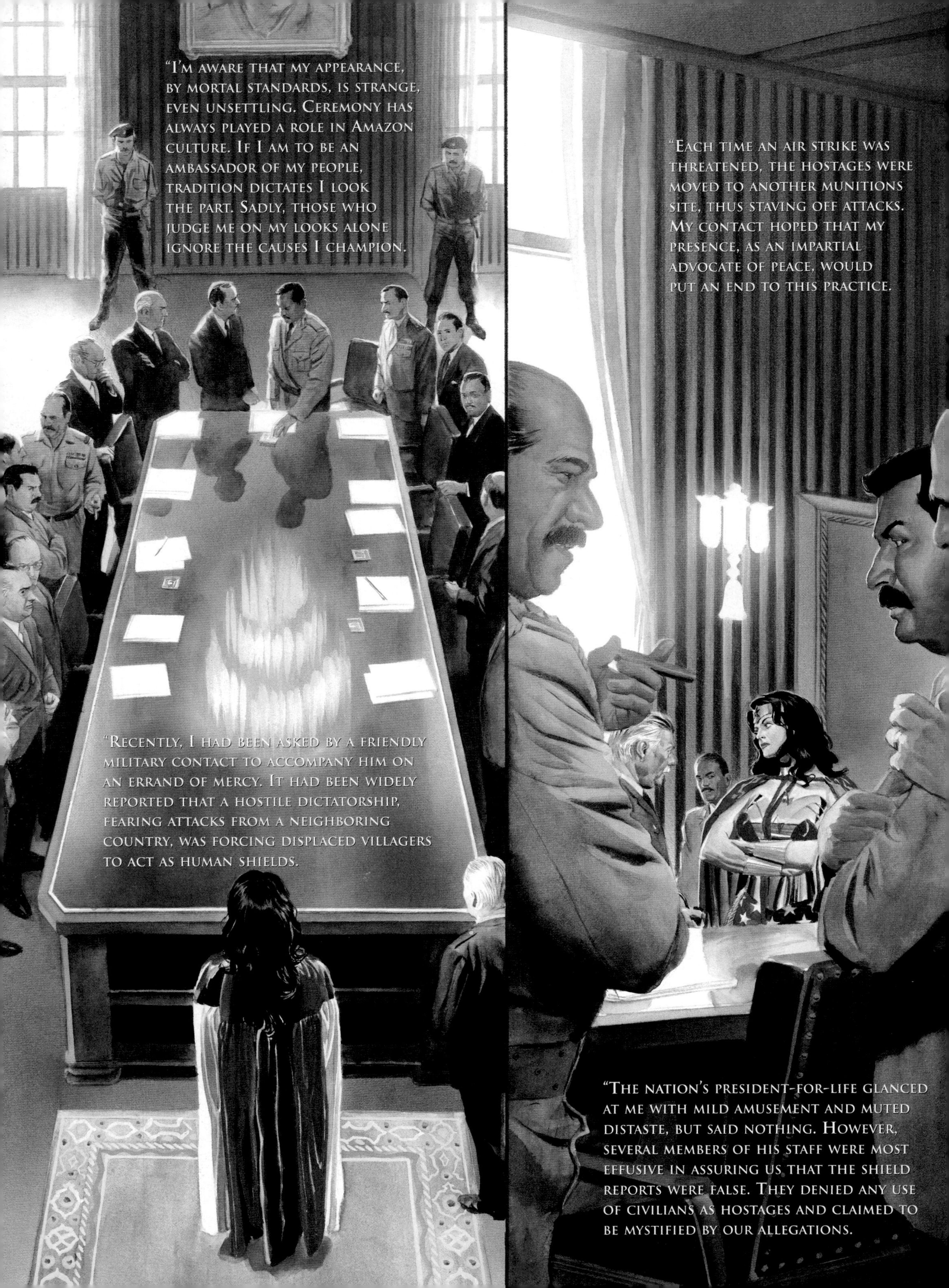
"I'm aware that my appearance, by mortal standards, is strange, even unsettling. Ceremony has always played a role in Amazon culture. If I am to be an ambassador of my people, tradition dictates I look the part. Sadly, those who judge me on my looks alone ignore the causes I champion.
"Recently, I had been asked by a friendly military contact to accompany him on an errand of mercy. It had been widely reported that a hostile dictatorship, fearing attacks from a neighboring country, was forcing displaced villagers to act as human shields.
"Each time an air strike was threatened, the hostages were moved to another munitions site, thus staving off attacks. My contact hoped that my presence, as an impartial advocate of peace, would put an end to this practice.
"The nation's president-for-life glanced at me with mild amusement and muted distaste, but said nothing. However, several members of his staff were most effusive in assuring us that the shield reports were false. They denied any use of civilians as hostages and claimed to be mystified by our allegations.

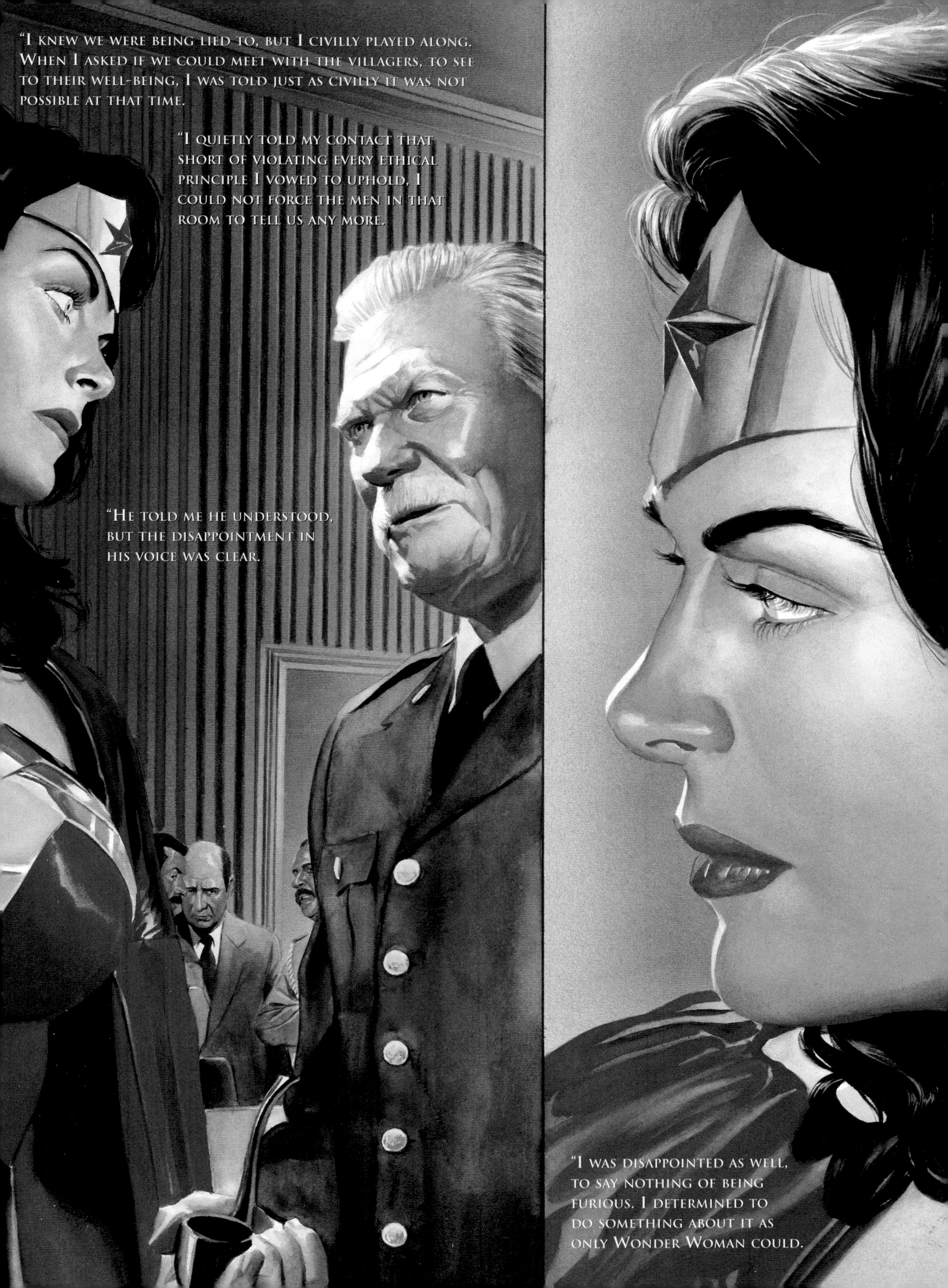
"I knew we were being lied to, but I civilly played along. When I asked if we could meet with the villagers, to see to their well-being, I was told just as civilly it was not possible at that time.
"I quietly told my contact that short of violating every ethical principle I vowed to uphold, I could not force the men in that room to tell us any more.
"He told me he understood, but the disappointment in his voice was clear.
"I was disappointed as well, to say nothing of being furious. I determined to do something about it as only Wonder Woman could.

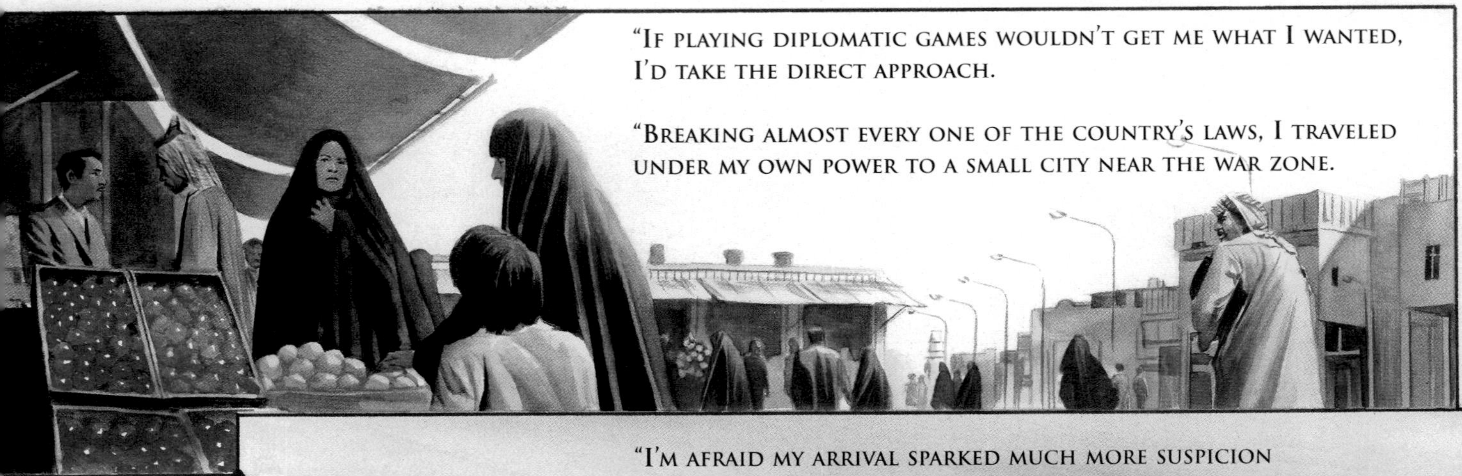
"If playing diplomatic games wouldn't get me what I wanted, I'd take the direct approach.
"Breaking almost every one of the country's laws, I traveled under my own power to a small city near the war zone.

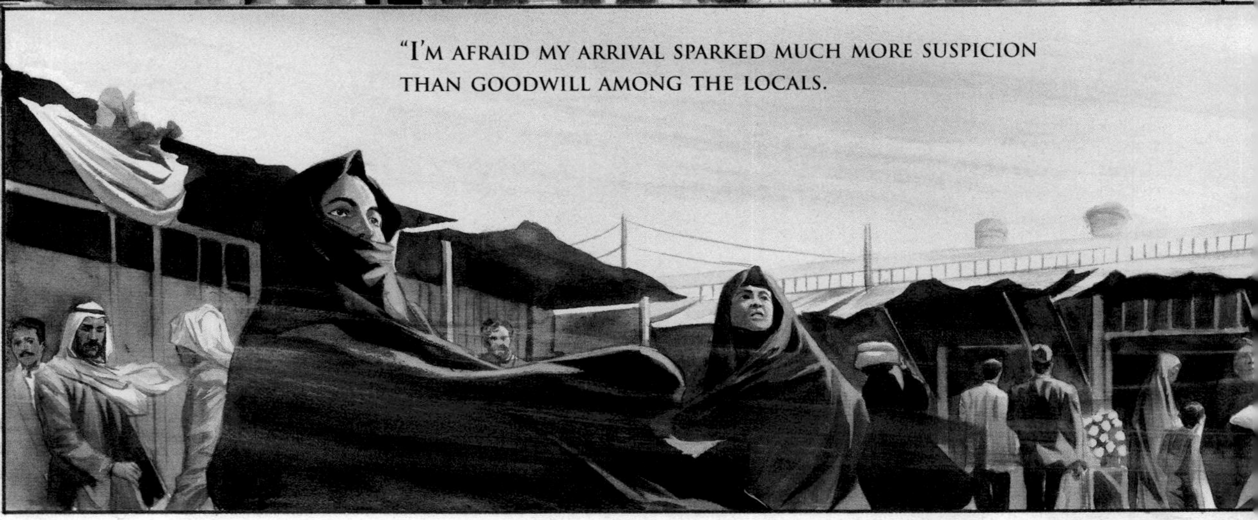
"I'm afraid my arrival sparked much more suspicion than goodwill among the locals.

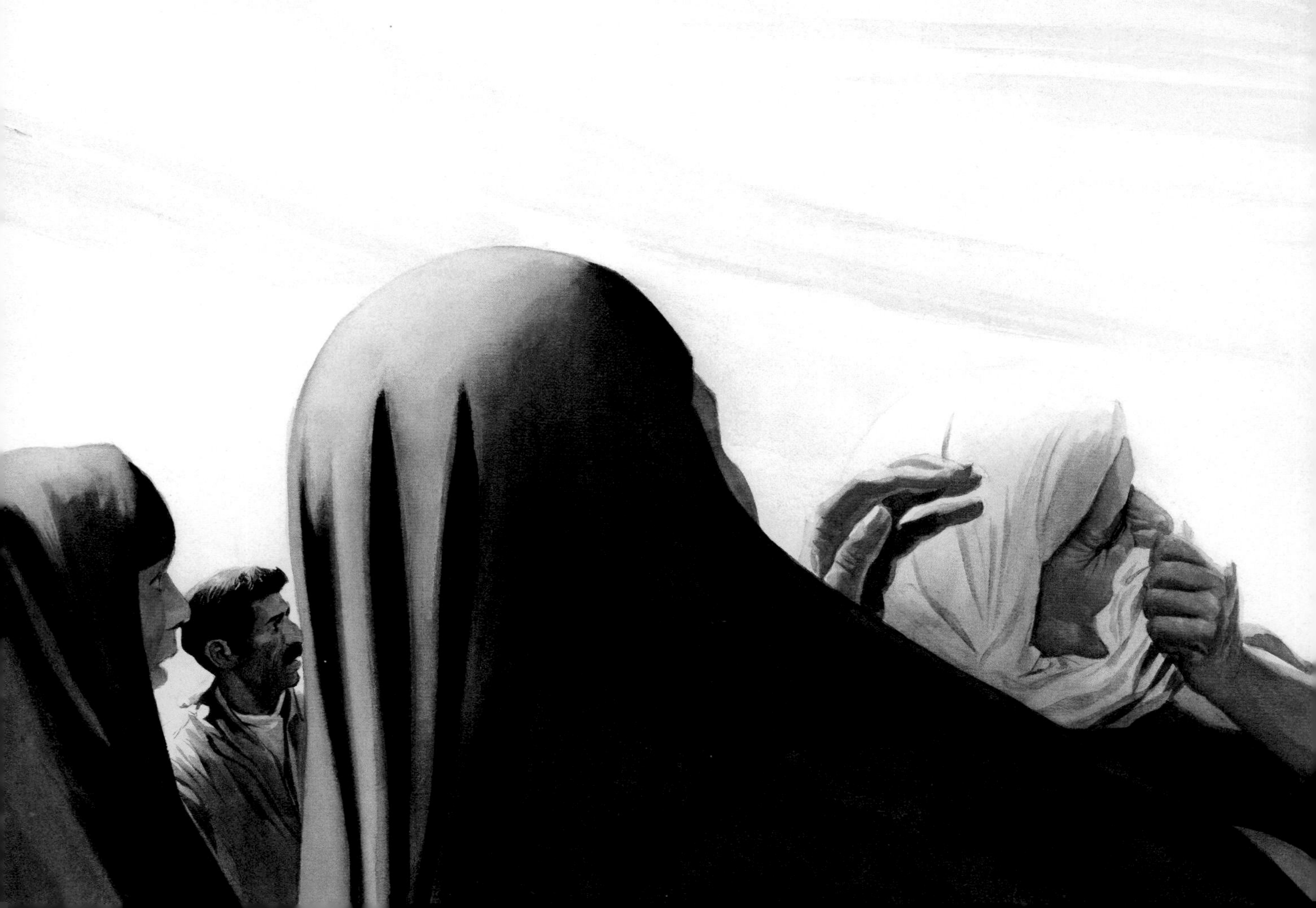

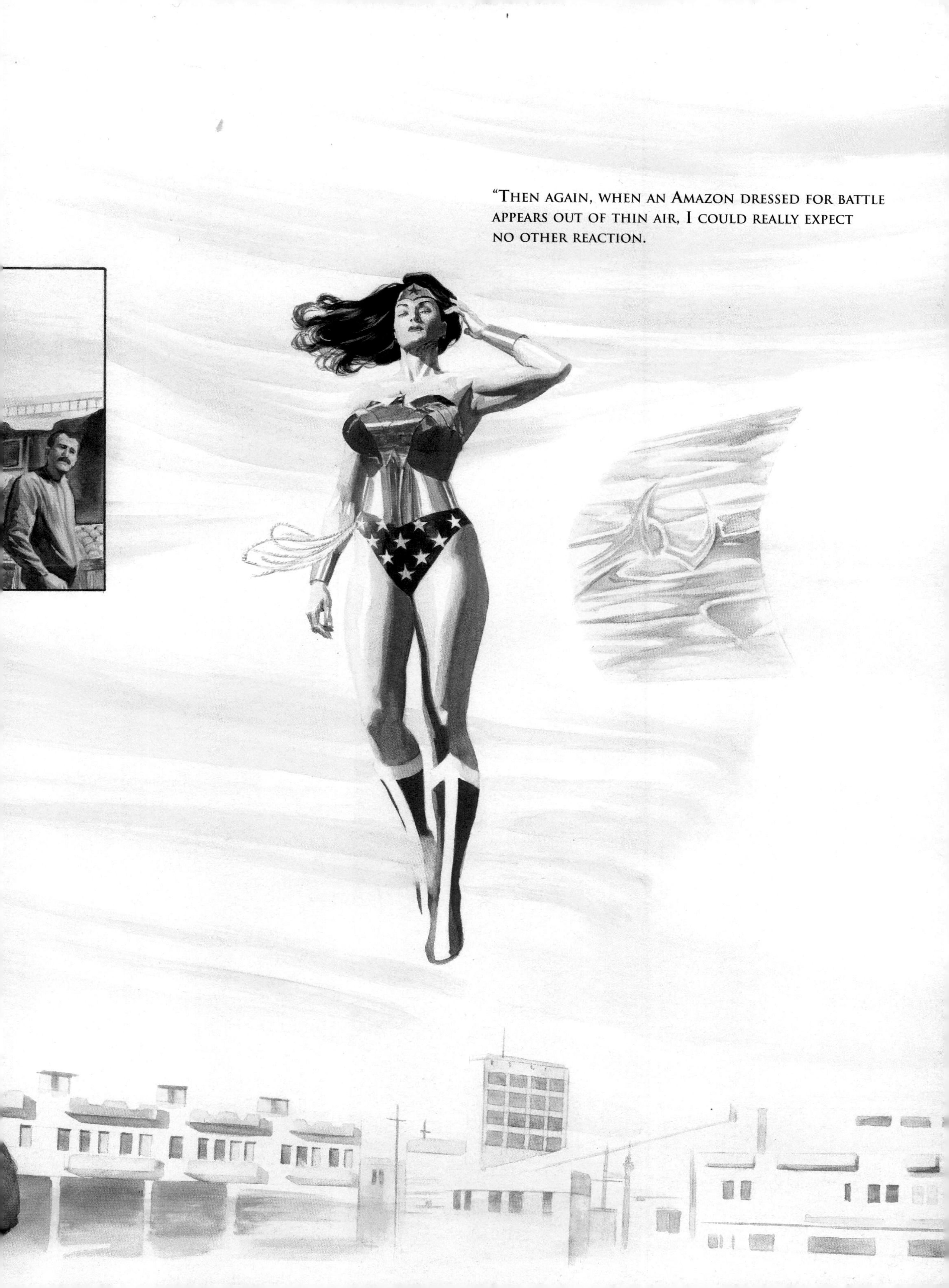
"Then again, when an Amazon dressed for battle appears out of thin air, I could really expect no other reaction.

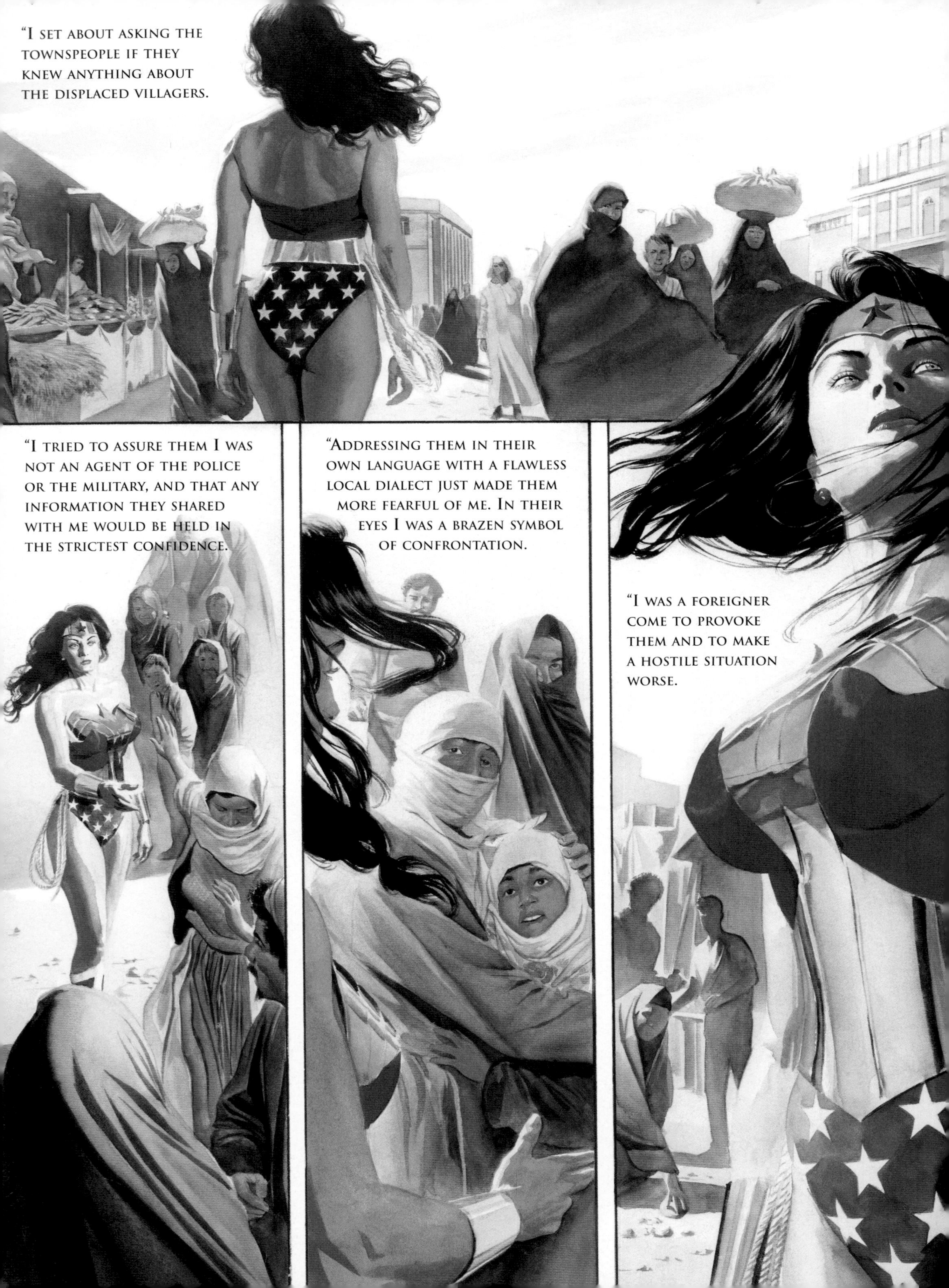
"I SET ABOUT ASKING THE TOWNSPEOPLE IF THEY KNEW ANYTHING ABOUT THE DISPLACED VILLAGERS.
"I TRIED TO ASSURE THEM I WAS NOT AN AGENT OF THE POLICE OR THE MILITARY, AND THAT ANY INFORMATION THEY SHARED WITH ME WOULD BE HELD IN THE STRICTEST CONFIDENCE.
"ADDRESSING THEM IN THEIR OWN LANGUAGE WITH A FLAWLESS LOCAL DIALECT JUST MADE THEM MORE FEARFUL OF ME. IN THEIR EYES I WAS A BRAZEN SYMBOL OF CONFRONTATION.
"I WAS A FOREIGNER COME TO PROVOKE THEM AND TO MAKE A HOSTILE SITUATION WORSE.

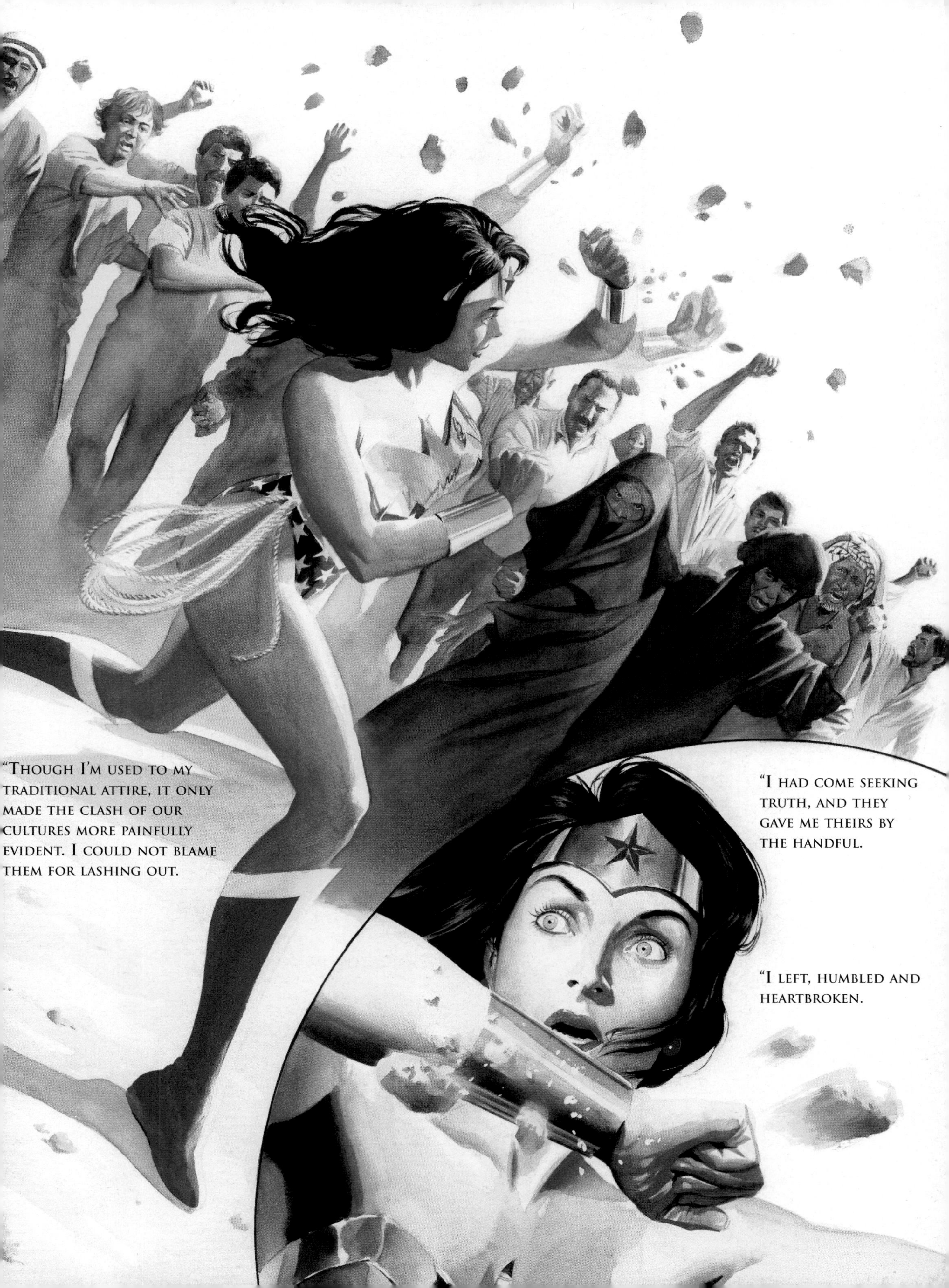
"THOUGH I'M USED TO MY TRADITIONAL ATTIRE, IT ONLY MADE THE CLASH OF OUR CULTURES MORE PAINFULLY EVIDENT. I COULD NOT BLAME THEM FOR LASHING OUT.
"I HAD COME SEEKING TRUTH, AND THEY GAVE ME THEIRS BY THE HANDFUL.
"I LEFT, HUMBLED AND HEARTBROKEN.

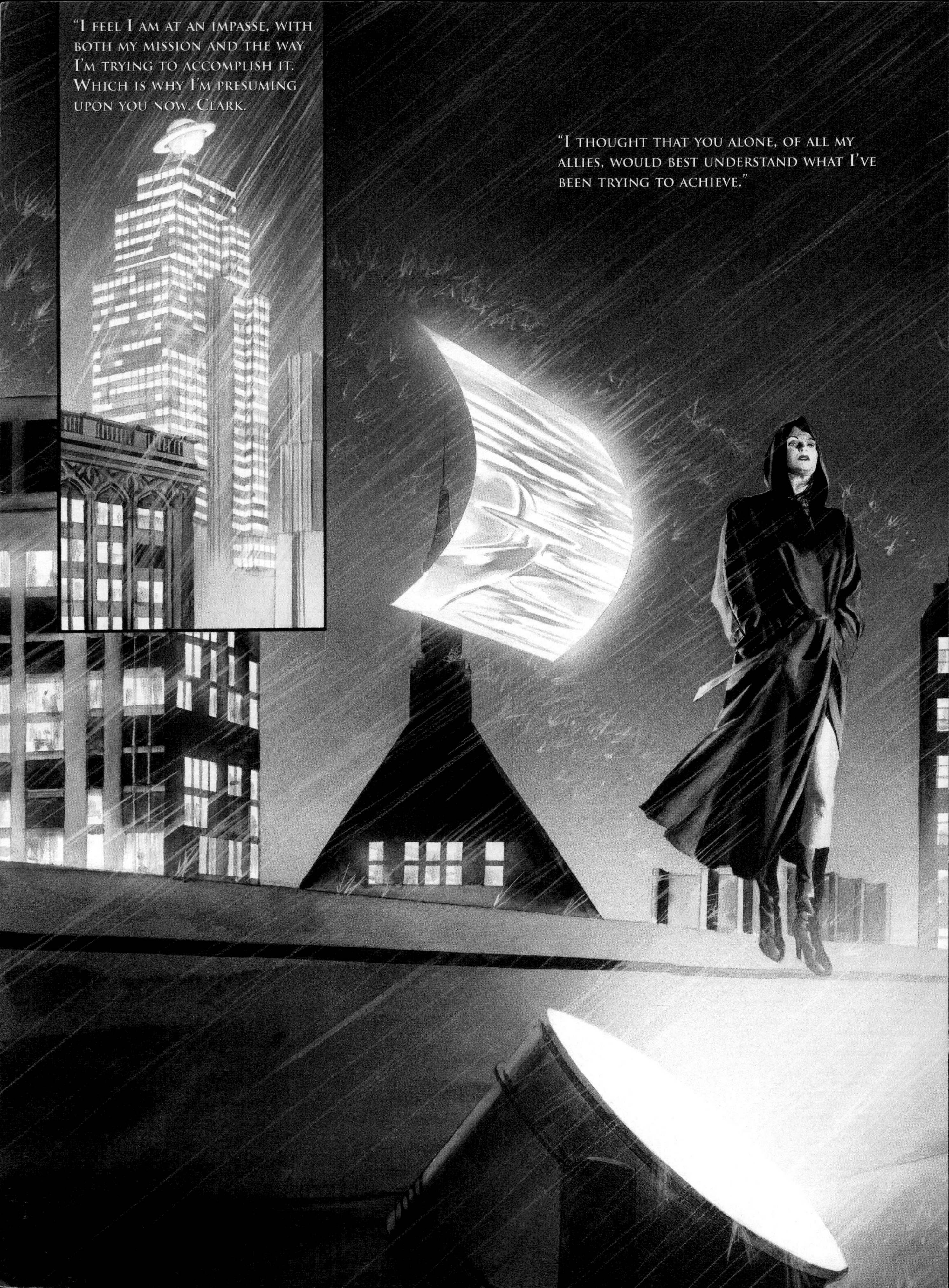
"I feel I am at an impasse, with both my mission and the way I'm trying to accomplish it. Which is why I'm presuming upon you now, Clark.
"I thought that you alone, of all my allies, would best understand what I've been trying to achieve."

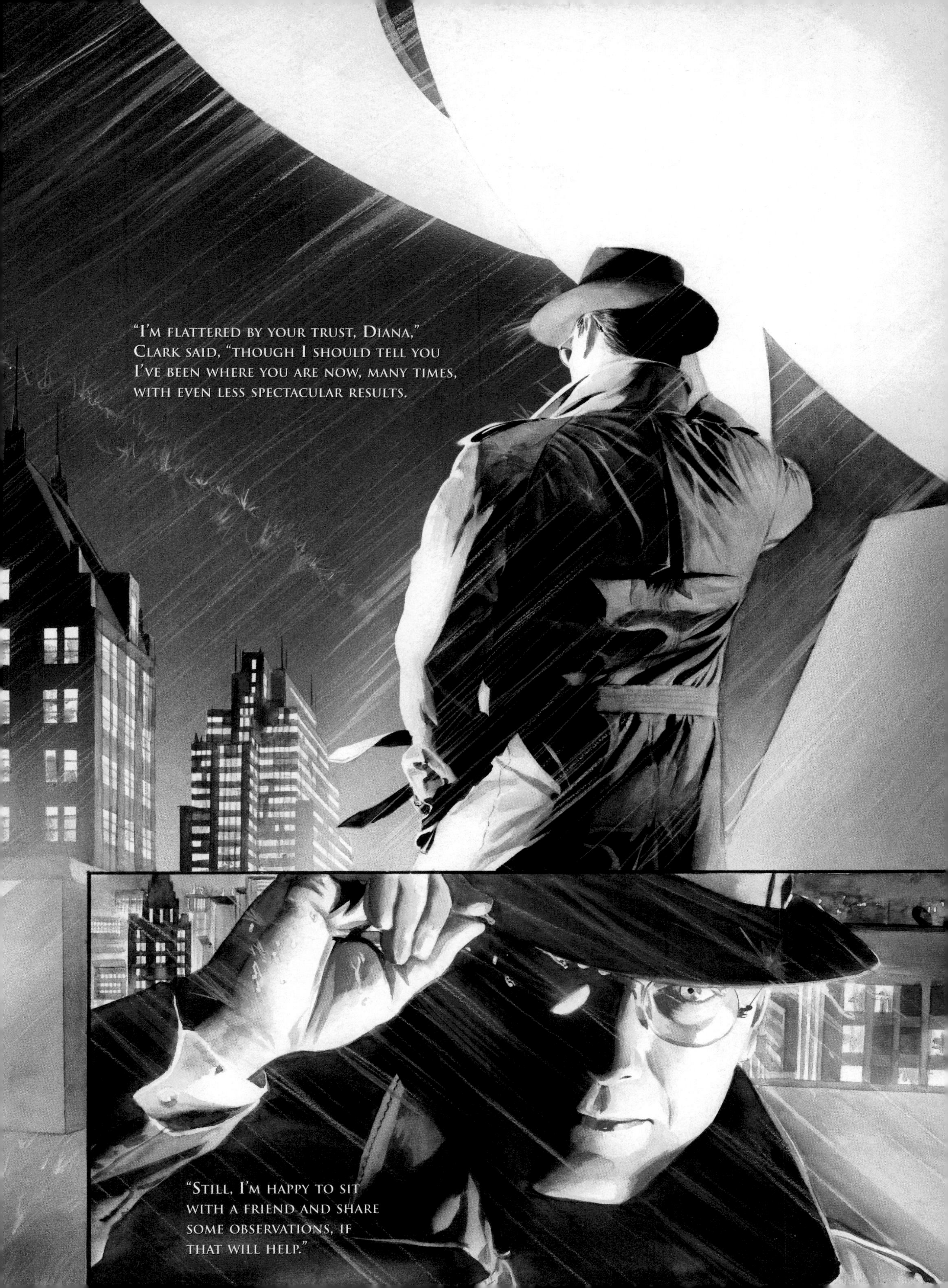
"I'm flattered by your trust, Diana," Clark said, "though I should tell you I've been where you are now, many times, with even less spectacular results.
"Still, I'm happy to sit with a friend and share some observations, if that will help."

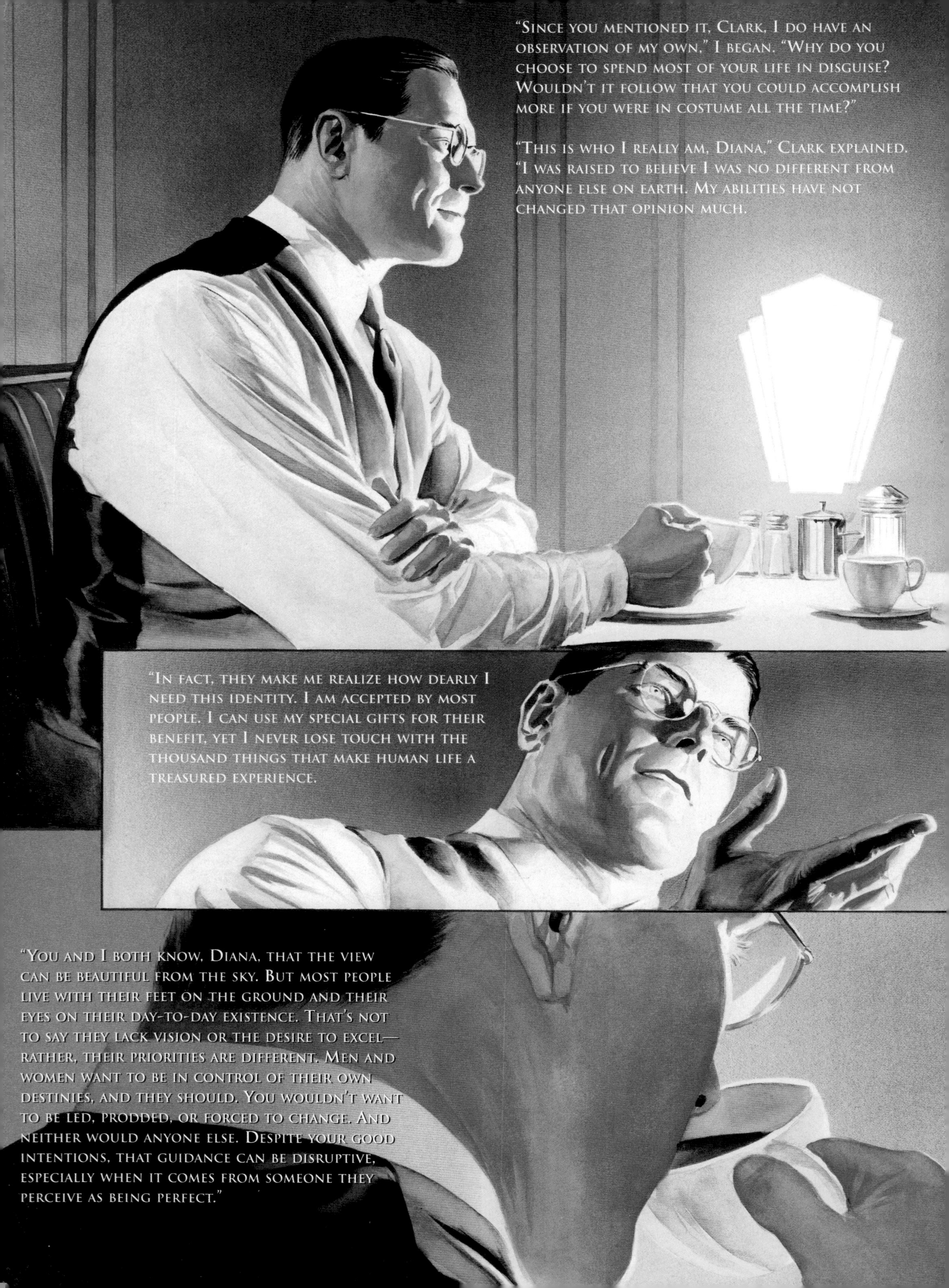

"Since you mentioned it, Clark, I do have an observation of my own," I began. "Why do you choose to spend most of your life in disguise? Wouldn't it follow that you could accomplish more if you were in costume all the time?"

"This is who I really am, Diana," Clark explained. "I was raised to believe I was no different from anyone else on Earth. My abilities have not changed that opinion much.

"In fact, they make me realize how dearly I need this identity. I am accepted by most people. I can use my special gifts for their benefit, yet I never lose touch with the thousand things that make human life a treasured experience.

"You and I both know, Diana, that the view can be beautiful from the sky. But most people live with their feet on the ground and their eyes on their day-to-day existence. That's not to say they lack vision or the desire to excel—rather, their priorities are different. Men and women want to be in control of their own destinies, and they should. You wouldn't want to be led, prodded, or forced to change. And neither would anyone else. Despite your good intentions, that guidance can be disruptive, especially when it comes from someone they perceive as being perfect."

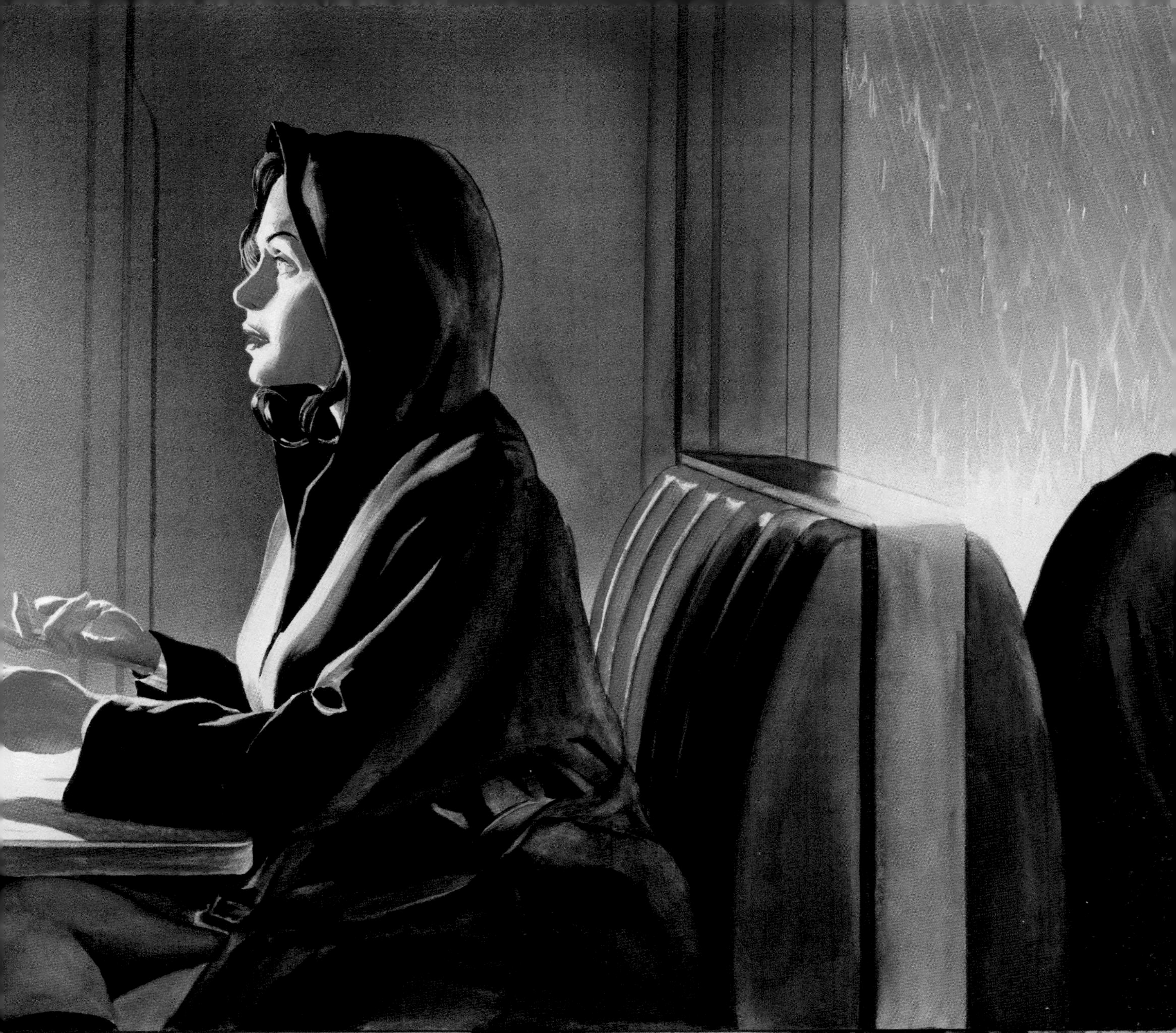

“You think I’m perfect?”

“I’m sure I’m not the first person to say this to you, but your great beauty and strength can be intimidating to most people. I can see how the rest of the world might have trouble with that. For what it’s worth, there can be a balance between the man and the superman, or woman, as the case may be. I think the best way to effect meaningful change is to work alongside people, rather than above them. At least, it’s always worked for me.”

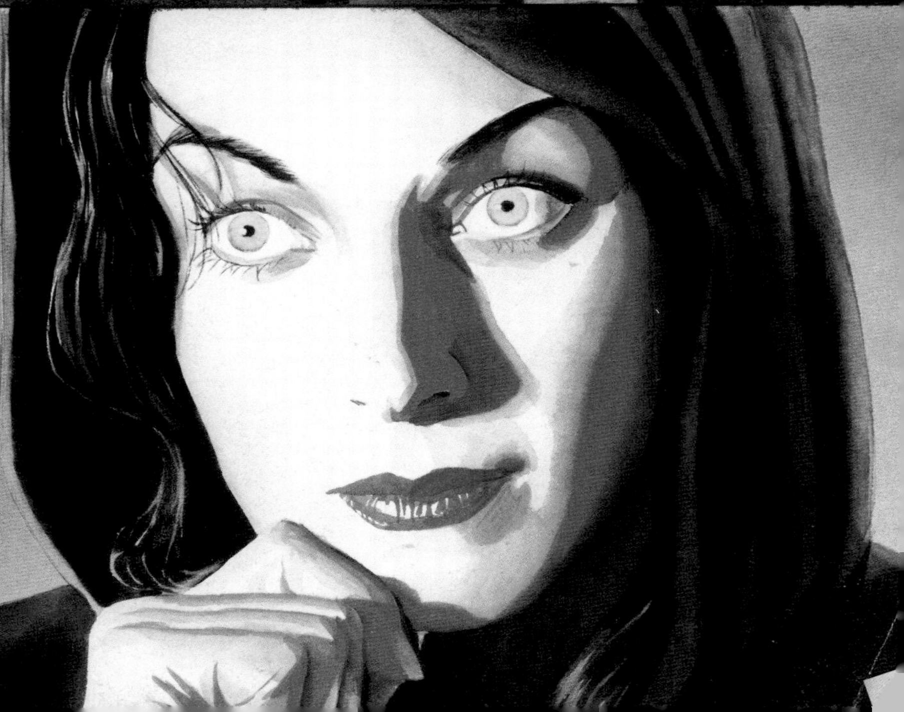

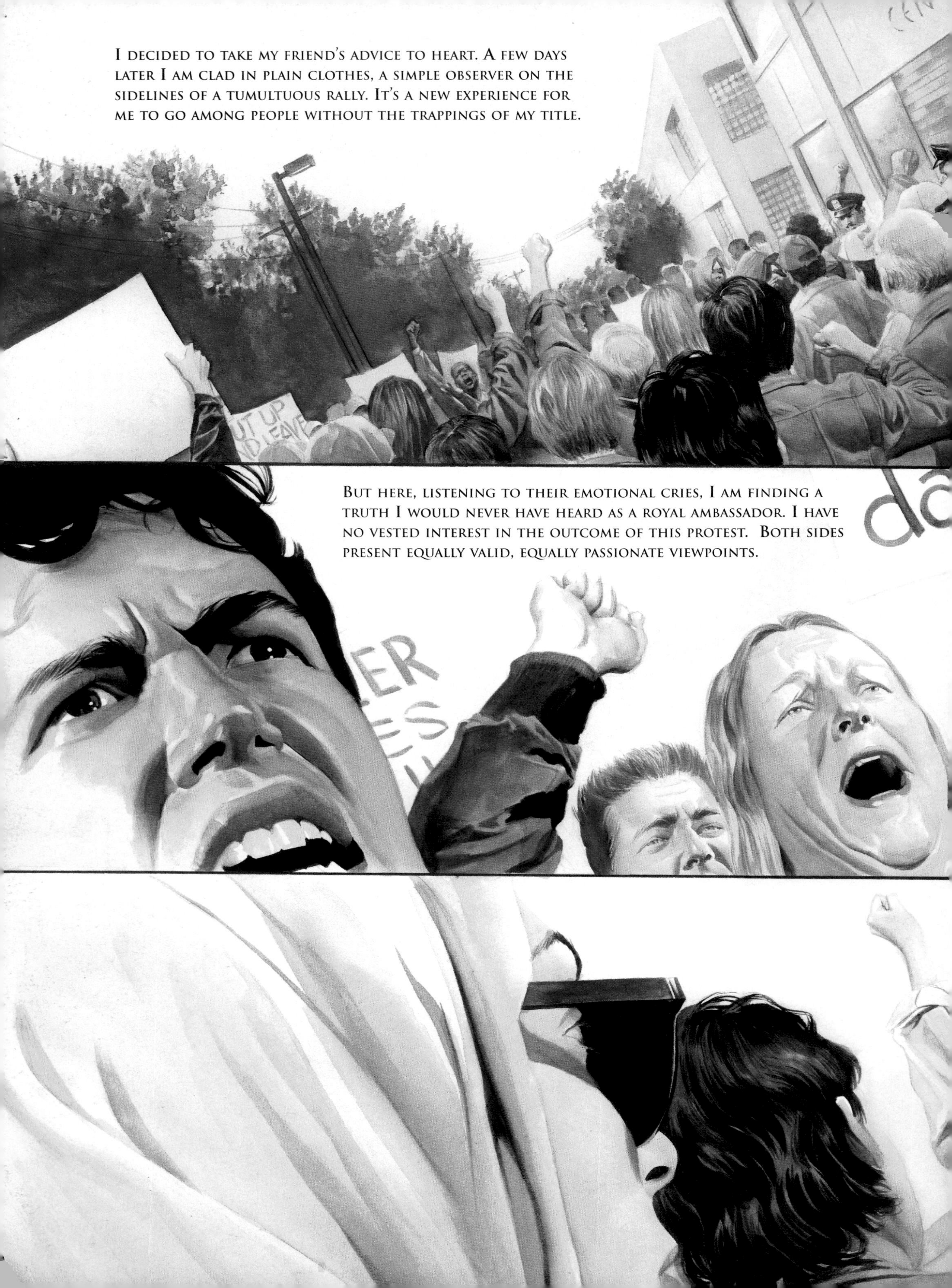
I DECIDED TO TAKE MY FRIEND'S ADVICE TO HEART. A FEW DAYS LATER I AM CLAD IN PLAIN CLOTHES, A SIMPLE OBSERVER ON THE SIDELINES OF A TUMULTUOUS RALLY. IT'S A NEW EXPERIENCE FOR ME TO GO AMONG PEOPLE WITHOUT THE TRAPPINGS OF MY TITLE.
BUT HERE, LISTENING TO THEIR EMOTIONAL CRIES, I AM FINDING A TRUTH I WOULD NEVER HAVE HEARD AS A ROYAL AMBASSADOR. I HAVE NO VESTED INTEREST IN THE OUTCOME OF THIS PROTEST. BOTH SIDES PRESENT EQUALLY VALID, EQUALLY PASSIONATE VIEWPOINTS.

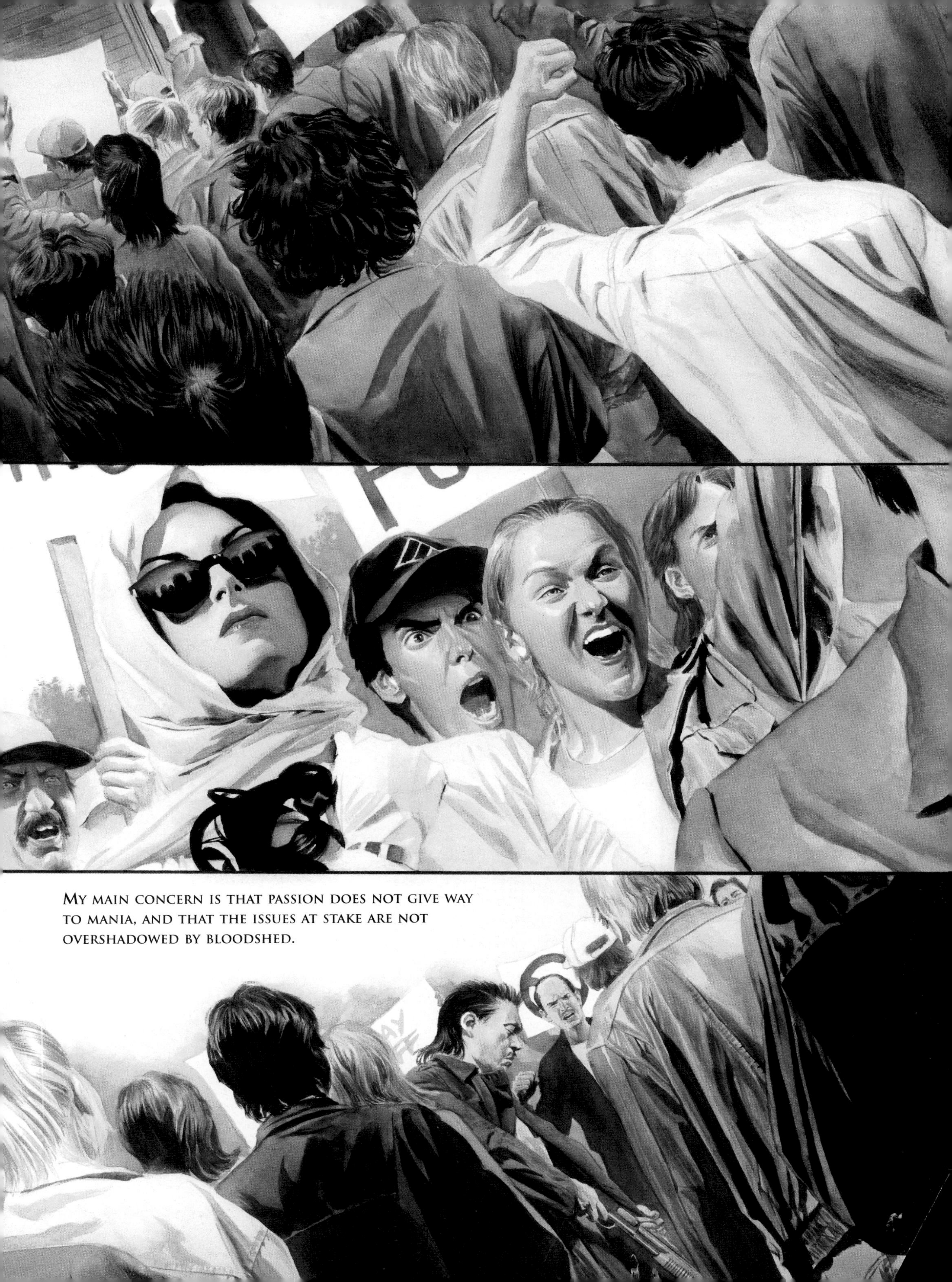
My main concern is that passion does not give way to mania, and that the issues at stake are not overshadowed by bloodshed.

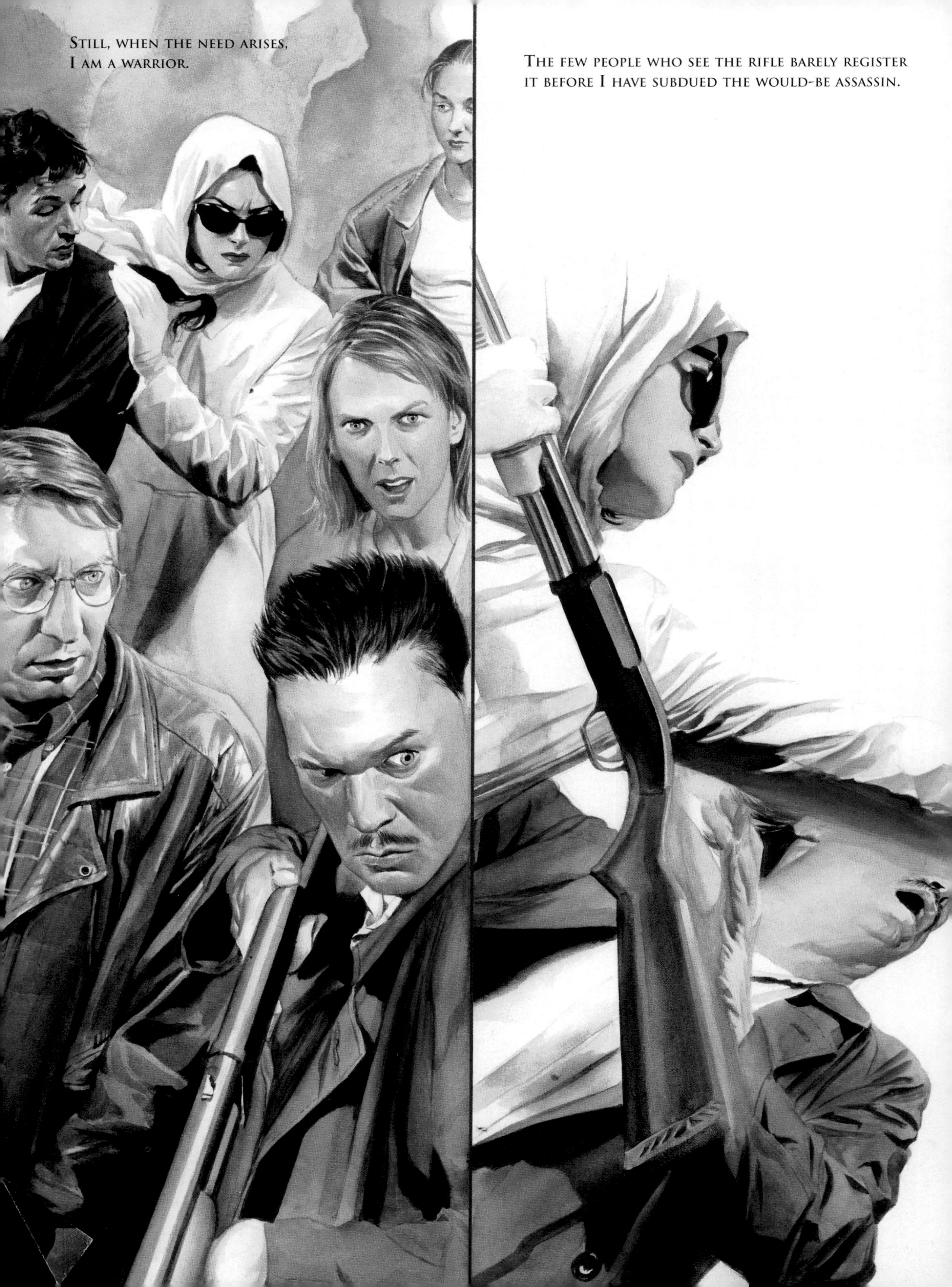
STILL, WHEN THE NEED ARISES, I AM A WARRIOR.
THE FEW PEOPLE WHO SEE THE RIFLE BARELY REGISTER IT BEFORE I HAVE SUBDUED THE WOULD-BE ASSASSIN.

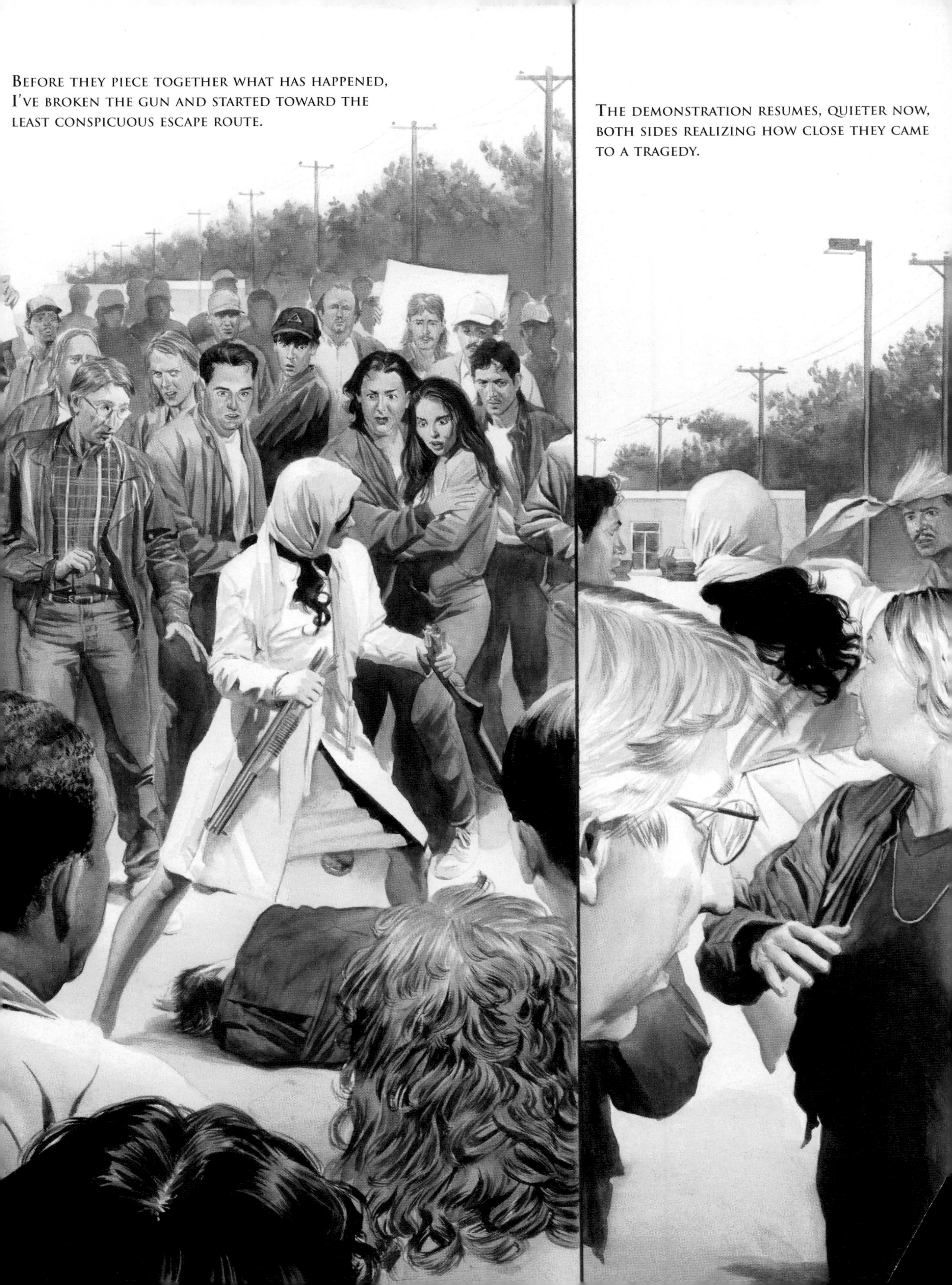
BEFORE THEY PIECE TOGETHER WHAT HAS HAPPENED, I'VE BROKEN THE GUN AND STARTED TOWARD THE LEAST CONSPICUOUS ESCAPE ROUTE.
THE DEMONSTRATION RESUMES, QUIETER NOW, BOTH SIDES REALIZING HOW CLOSE THEY CAME TO A TRAGEDY.

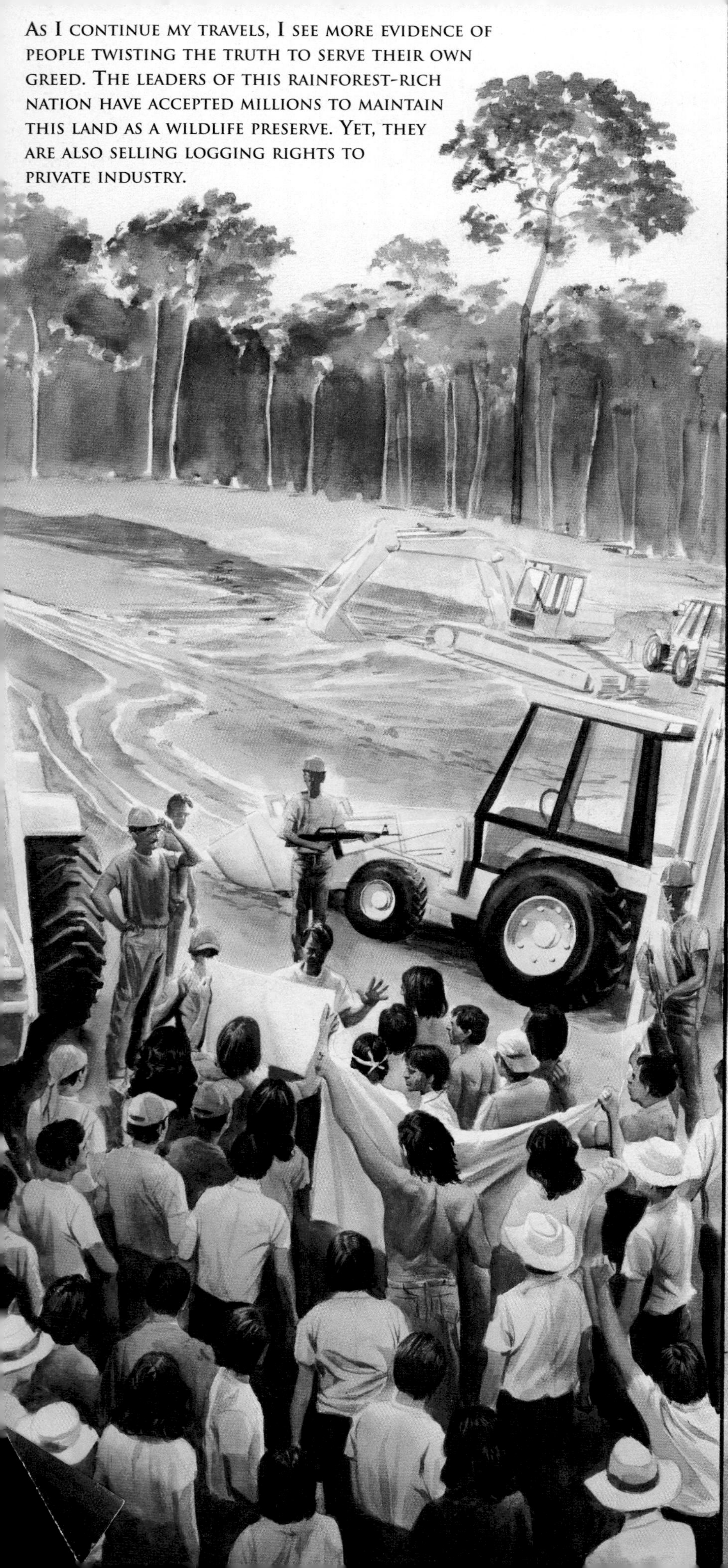
As I continue my travels, I see more evidence of people twisting the truth to serve their own greed. The leaders of this rainforest-rich nation have accepted millions to maintain this land as a wildlife preserve. Yet, they are also selling logging rights to private industry.

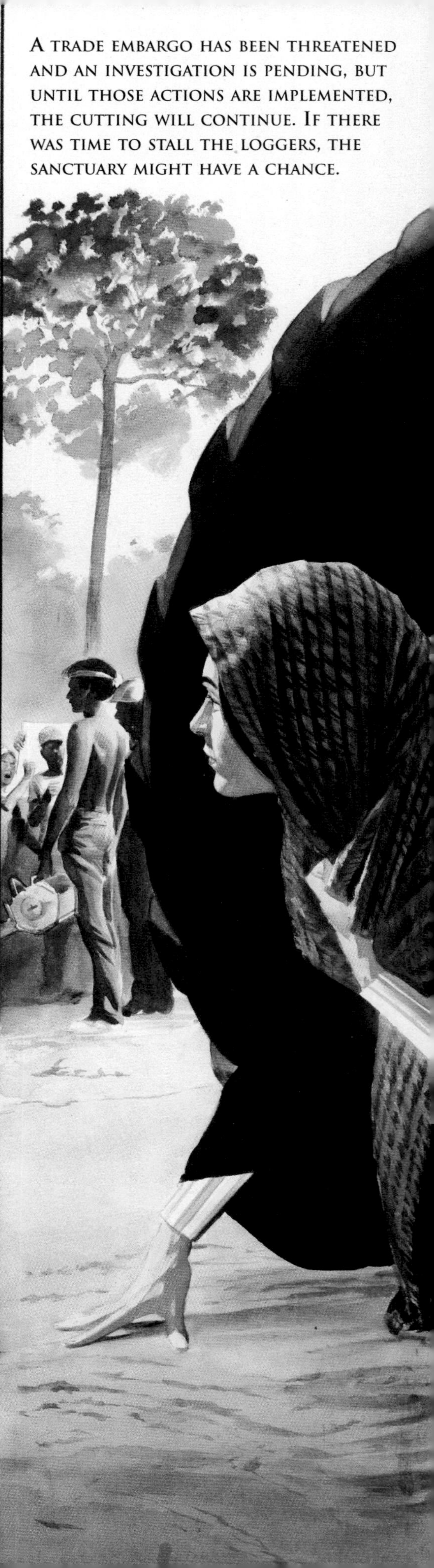
A trade embargo has been threatened and an investigation is pending, but until those actions are implemented, the cutting will continue. If there was time to stall the loggers, the sanctuary might have a chance.

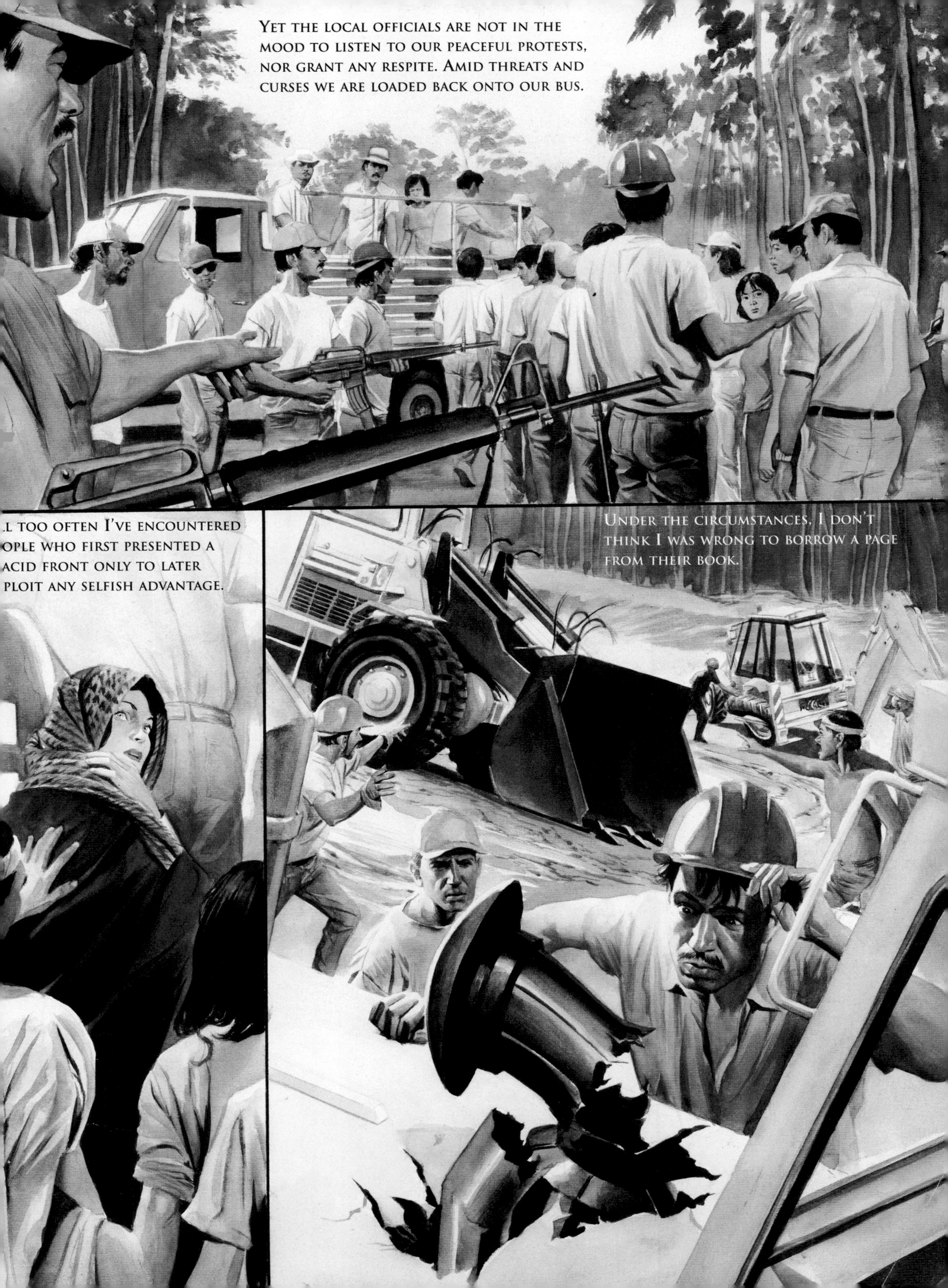
YET THE LOCAL OFFICIALS ARE NOT IN THE MOOD TO LISTEN TO OUR PEACEFUL PROTESTS, NOR GRANT ANY RESPITE. AMID THREATS AND CURSES WE ARE LOADED BACK ONTO OUR BUS.
.L TOO OFTEN I'VE ENCOUNTERED OPLE WHO FIRST PRESENTED A ACID FRONT ONLY TO LATER PLOIT ANY SELFISH ADVANTAGE.
UNDER THE CIRCUMSTANCES, I DON'T THINK I WAS WRONG TO BORROW A PAGE FROM THEIR BOOK.

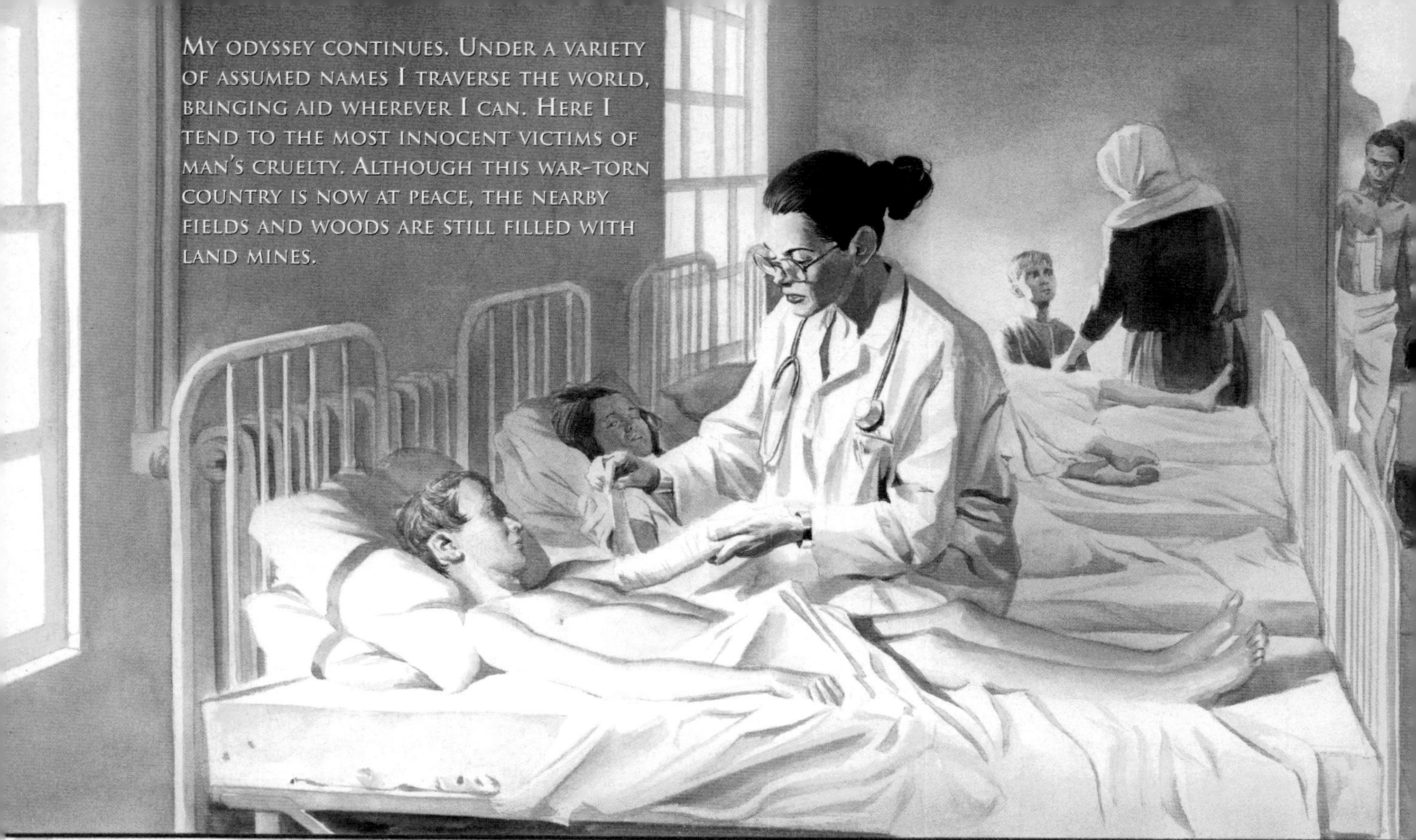
My odyssey continues. Under a variety of assumed names I traverse the world, bringing aid wherever I can. Here I tend to the most innocent victims of man's cruelty. Although this war-torn country is now at peace, the nearby fields and woods are still filled with land mines.

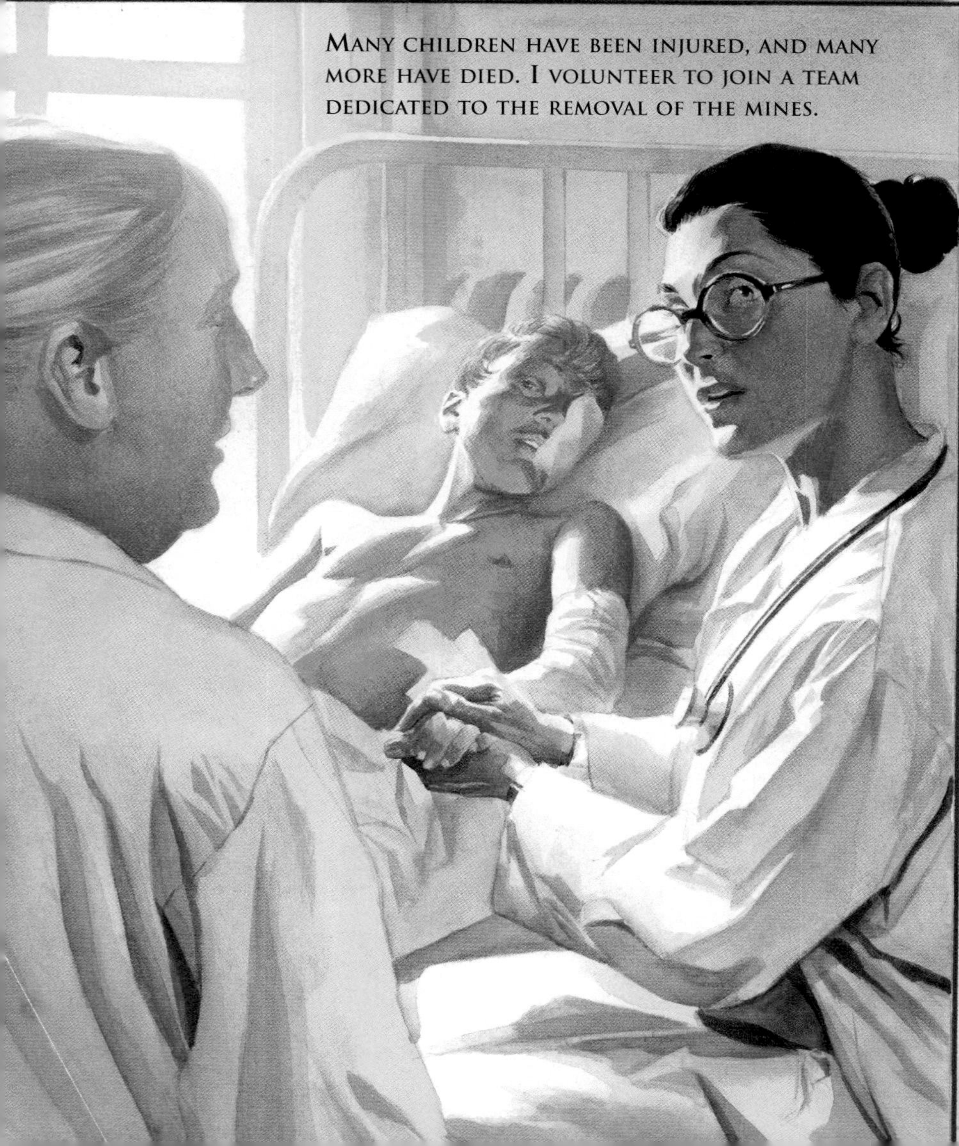
Many children have been injured, and many more have died. I volunteer to join a team dedicated to the removal of the mines.

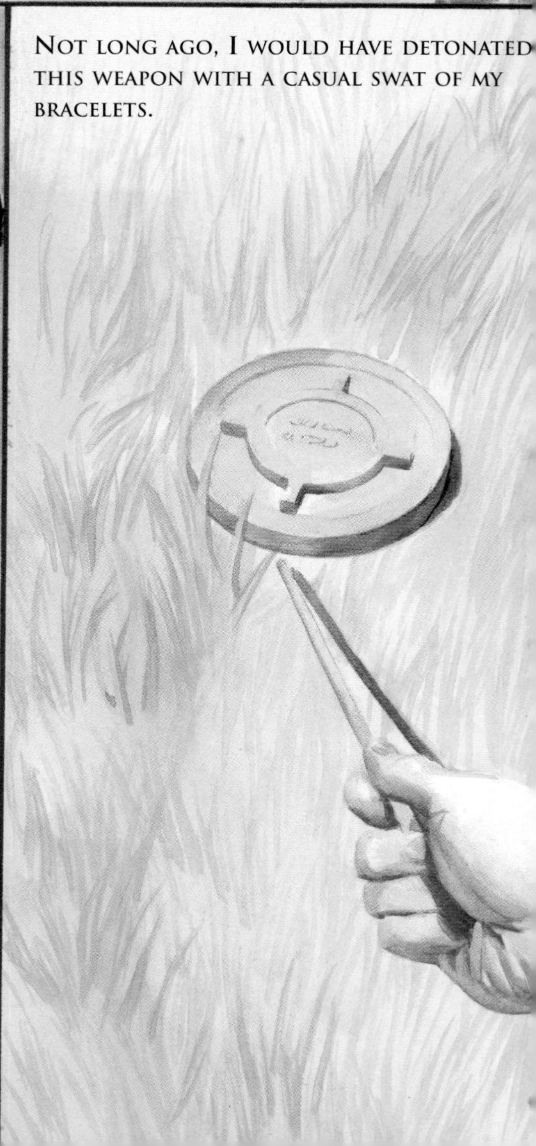
Not long ago, I would have detonated this weapon with a casual swat of my bracelets.

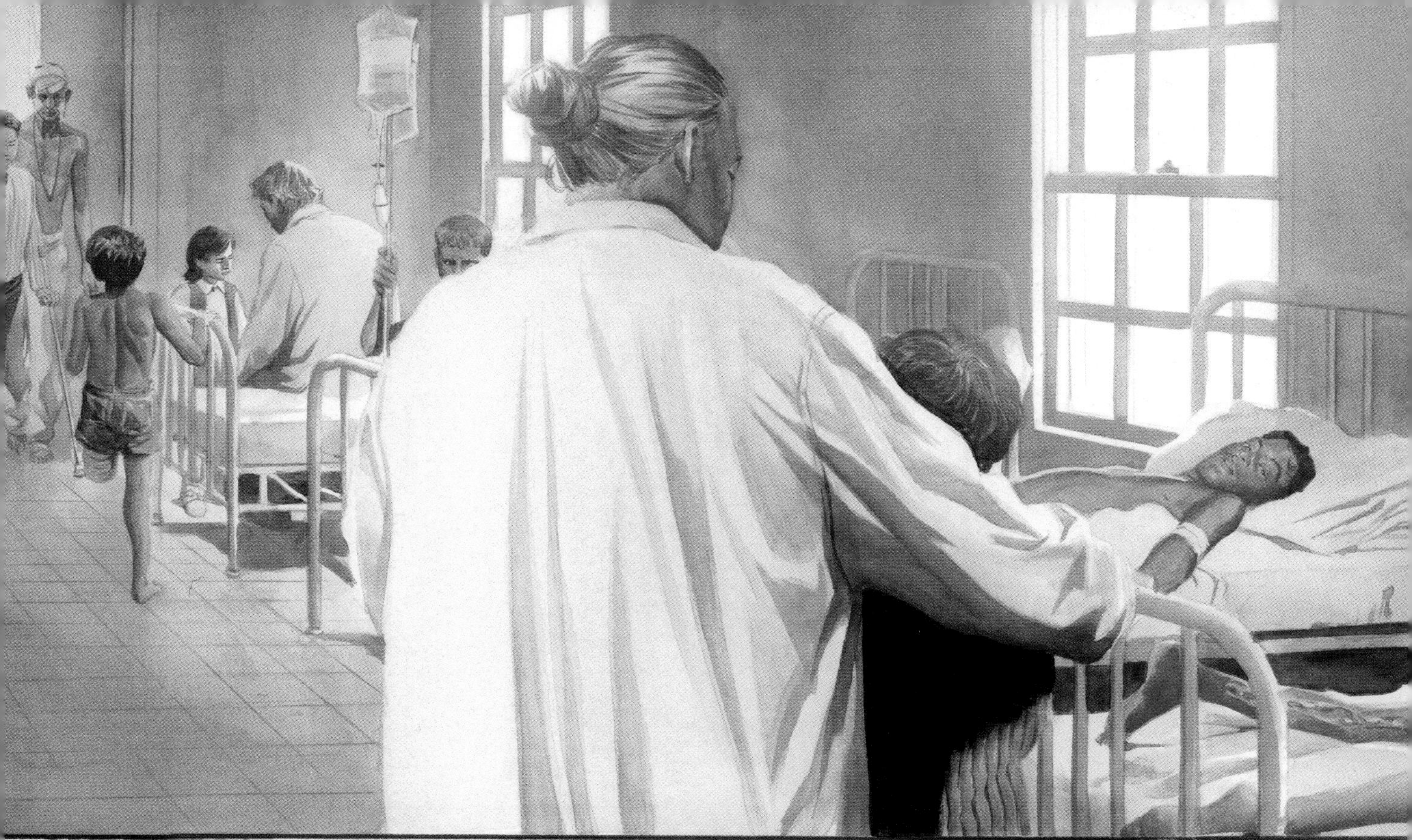

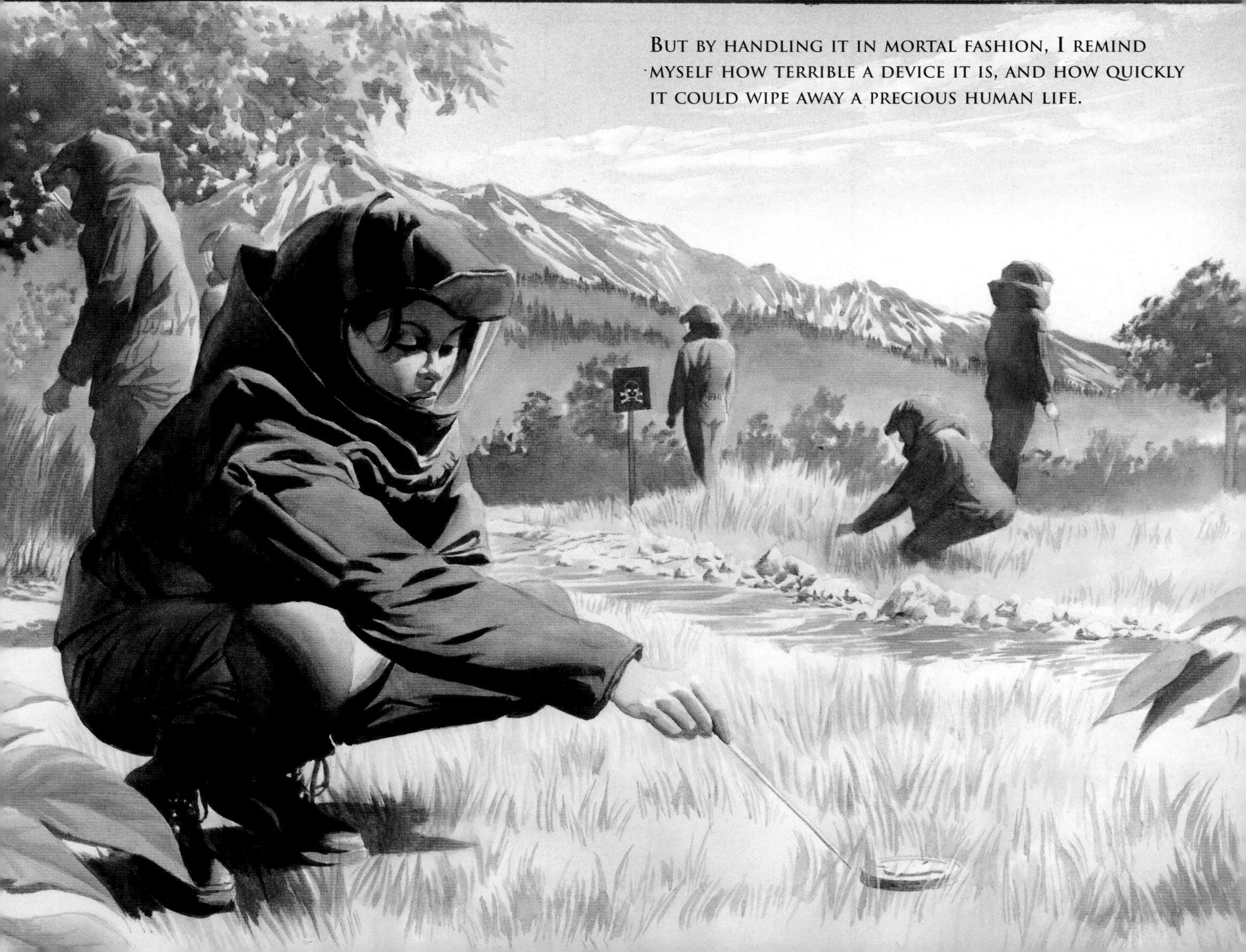
But by handling it in mortal fashion, I remind myself how terrible a device it is, and how quickly it could wipe away a precious human life.

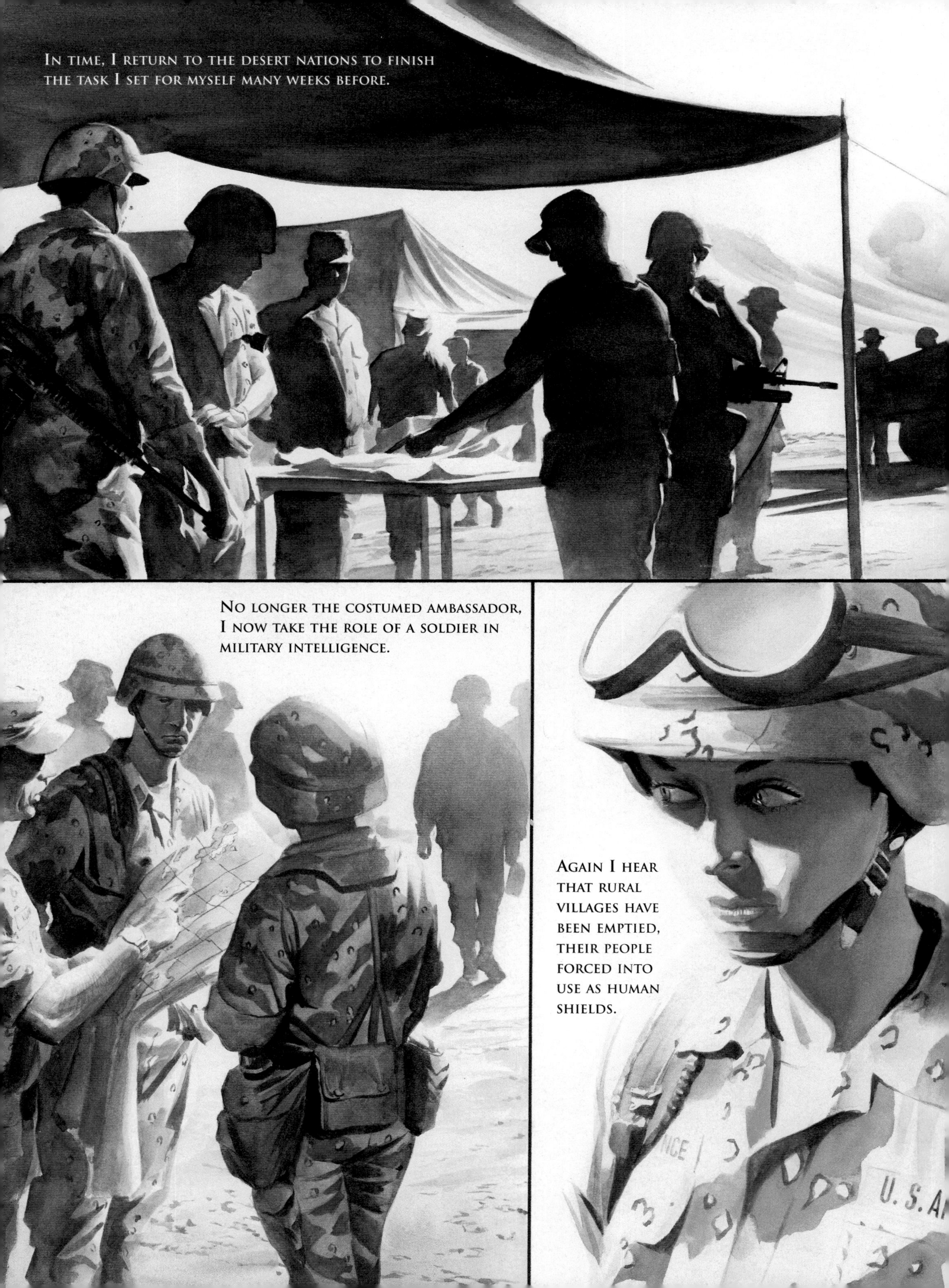
In time, I return to the desert nations to finish the task I set for myself many weeks before.
No longer the costumed ambassador, I now take the role of a soldier in military intelligence.
Again I hear that rural villages have been emptied, their people forced into use as human shields.

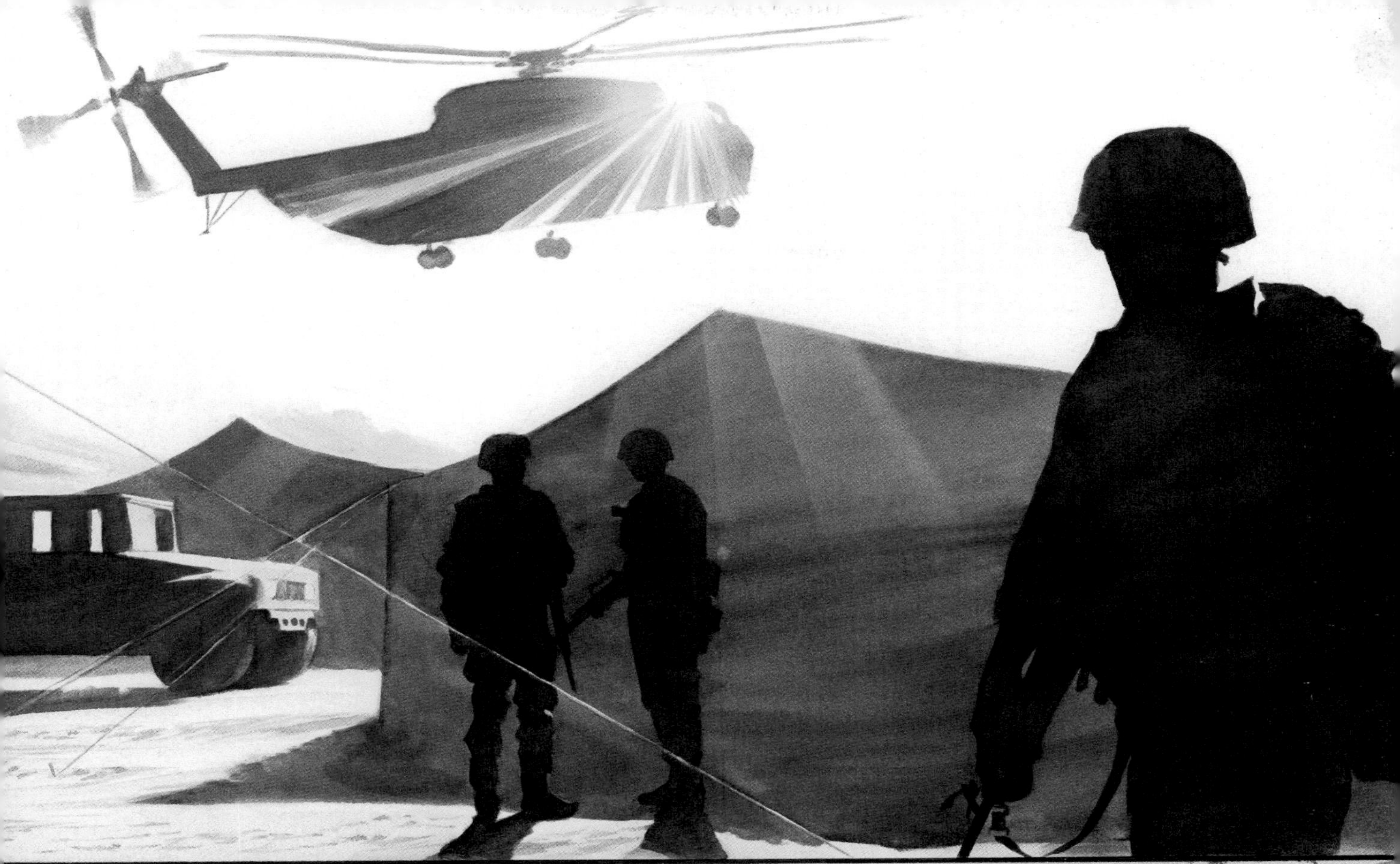

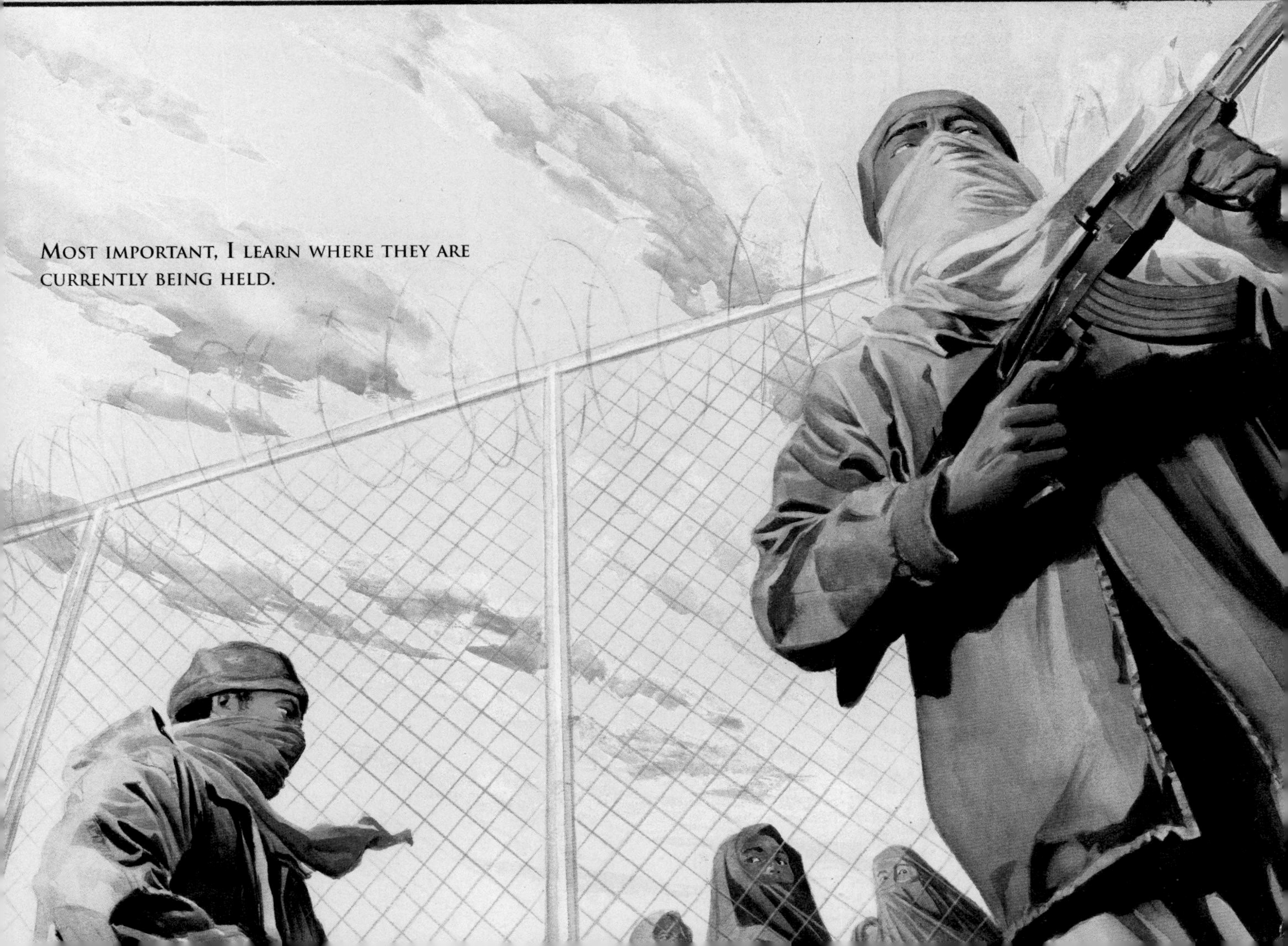
Most important, I learn where they are currently being held.

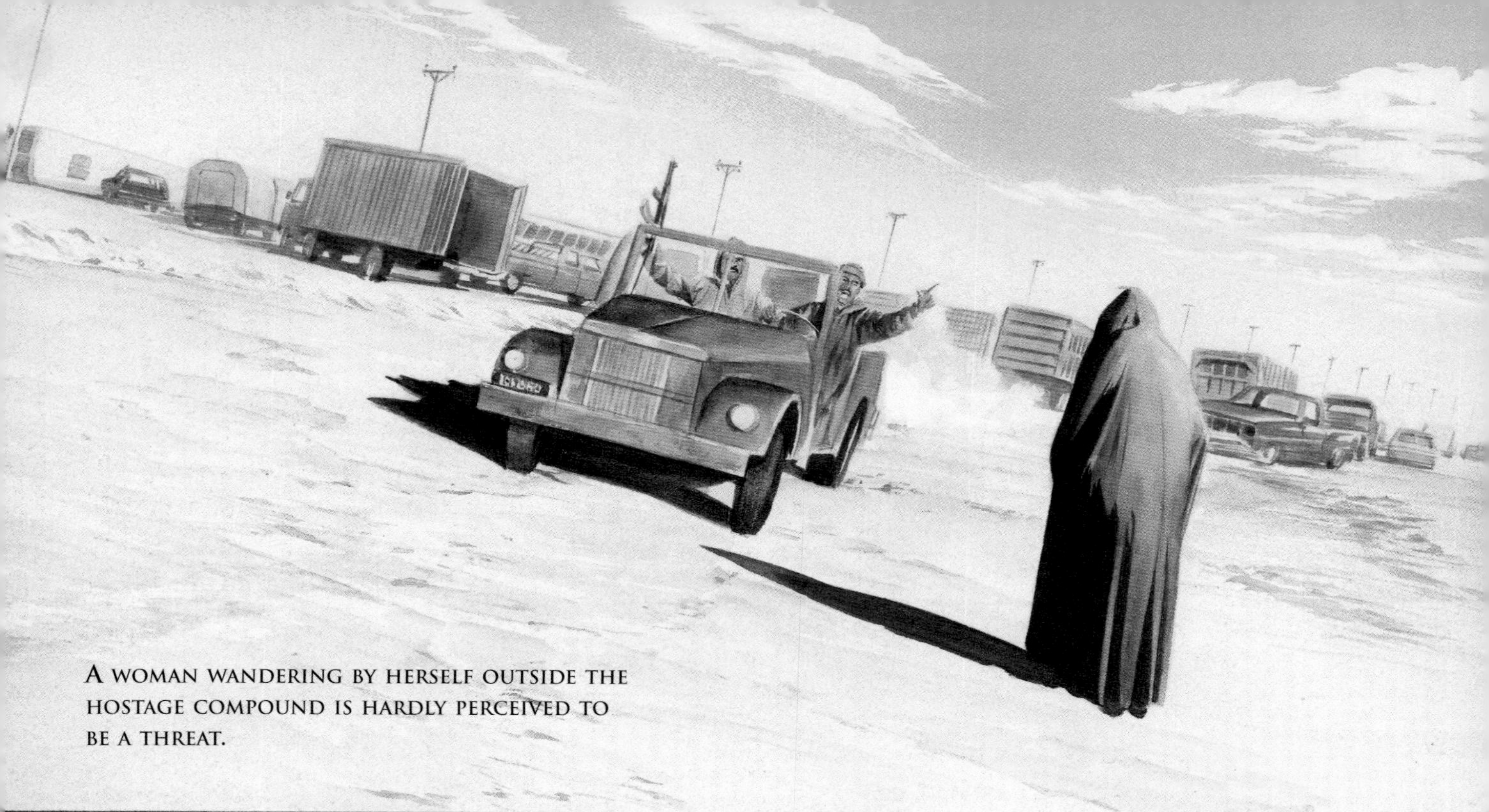
A woman wandering by herself outside the hostage compound is hardly perceived to be a threat.

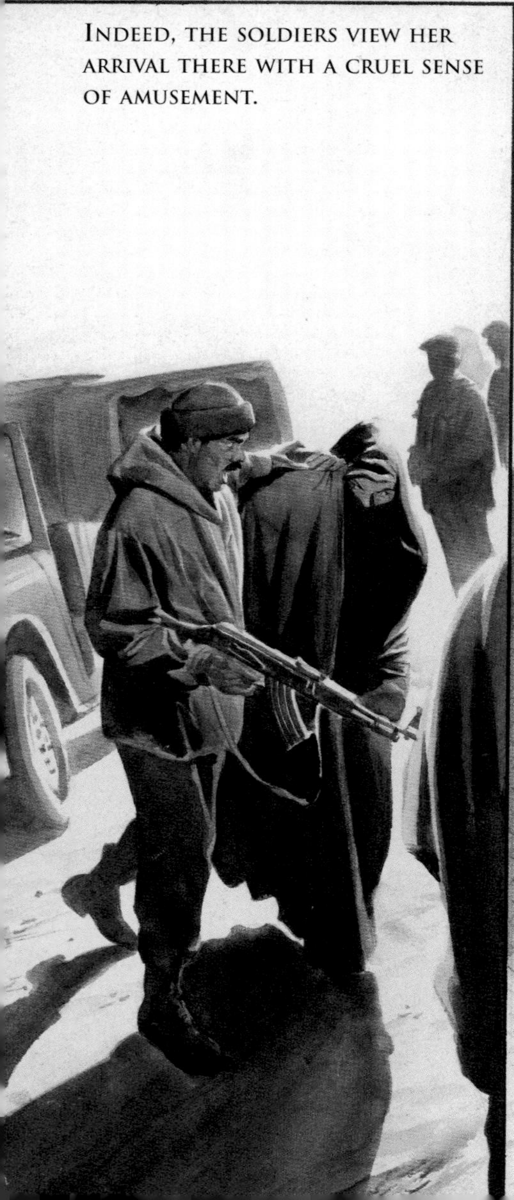
Indeed, the soldiers view her arrival there with a cruel sense of amusement.

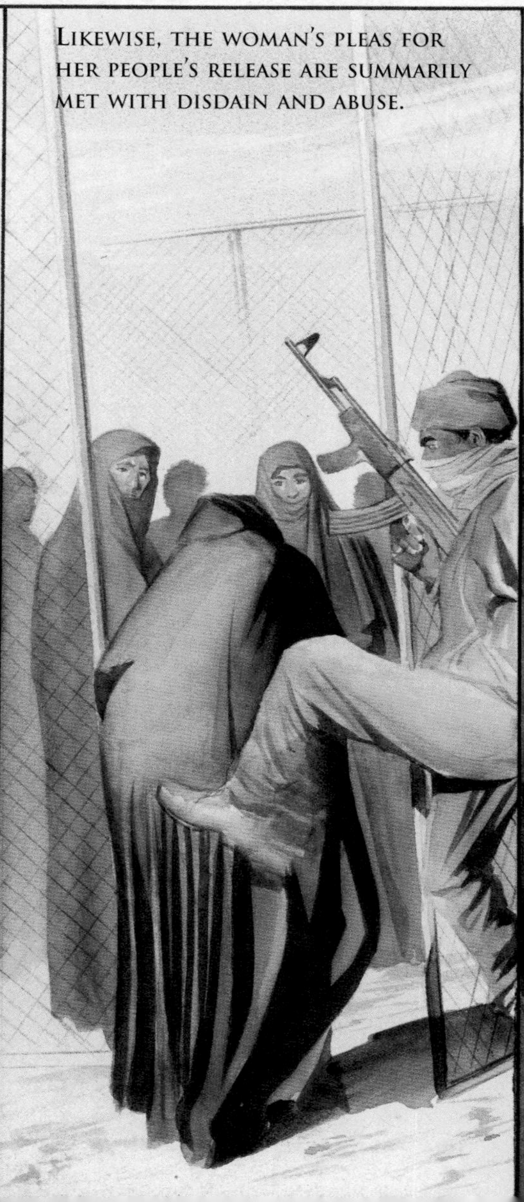
Likewise, the woman's pleas for her people's release are summarily met with disdain and abuse.

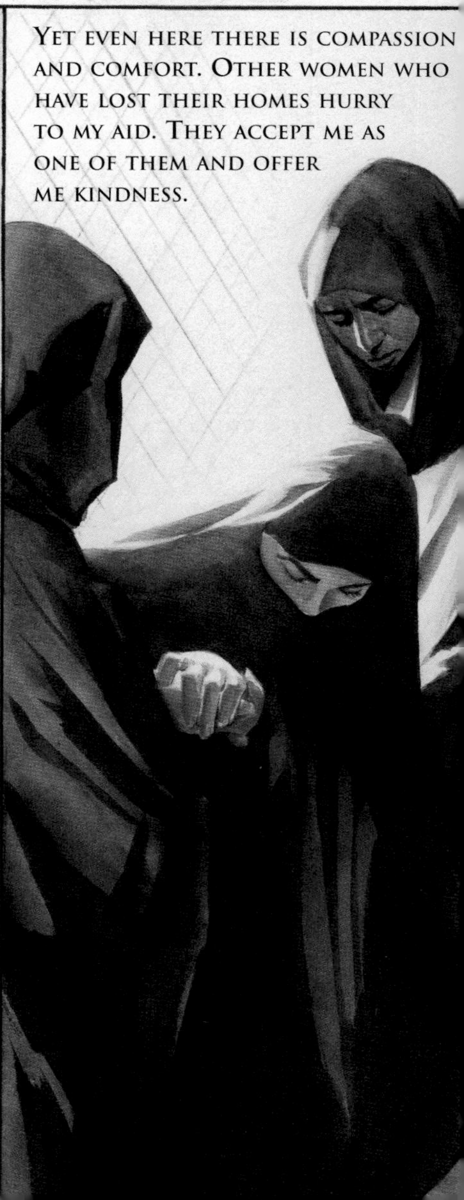
Yet even here there is compassion and comfort. Other women who have lost their homes hurry to my aid. They accept me as one of them and offer me kindness.

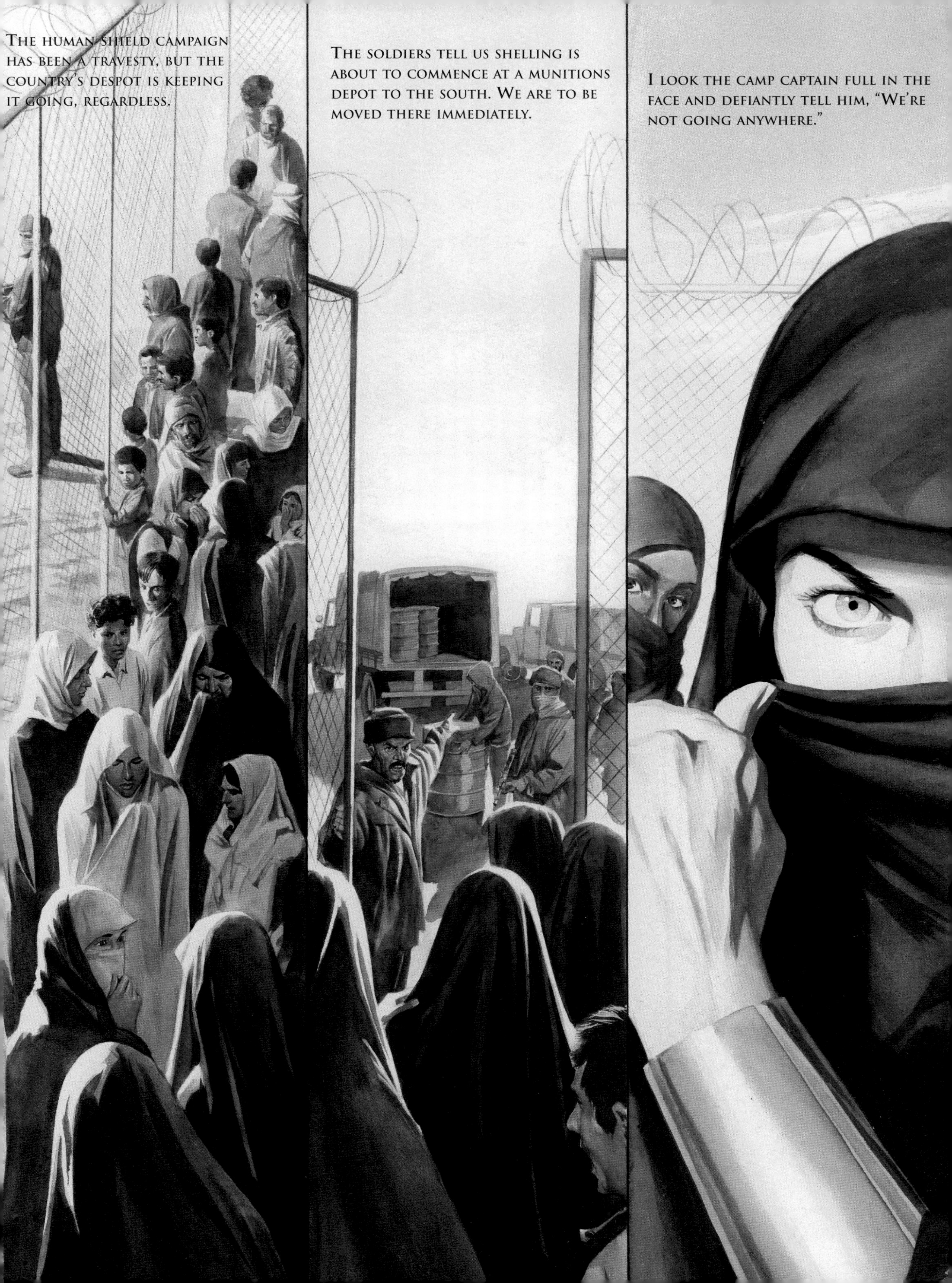
The human shield campaign has been a travesty, but the country's despot is keeping it going, regardless.
The soldiers tell us shelling is about to commence at a munitions depot to the south. We are to be moved there immediately.
I look the camp captain full in the face and defiantly tell him, "We're not going anywhere."

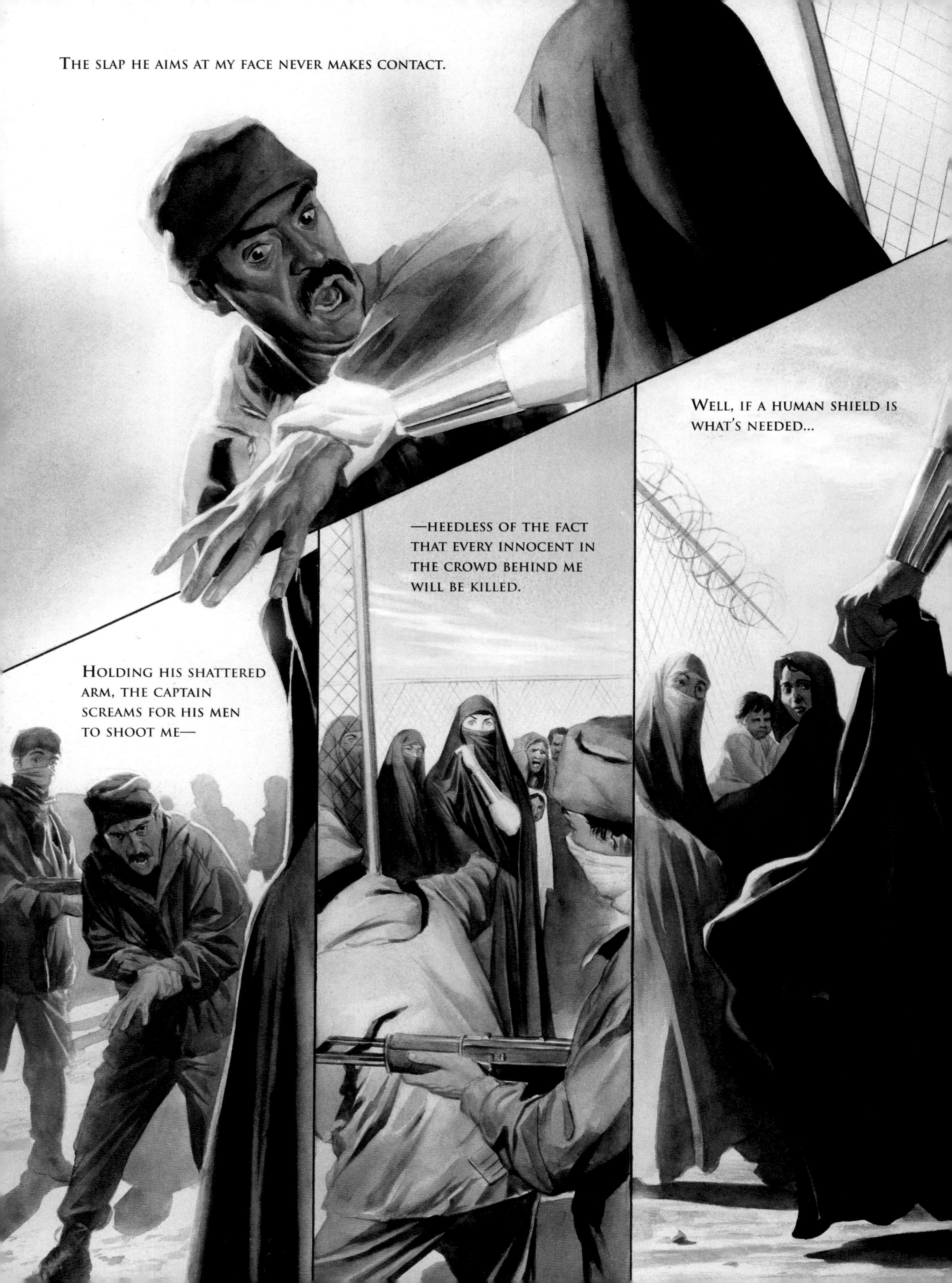
The slap he aims at my face never makes contact.
Holding his shattered arm, the captain screams for his men to shoot me—
—heedless of the fact that every innocent in the crowd behind me will be killed.
Well, if a human shield is what's needed...

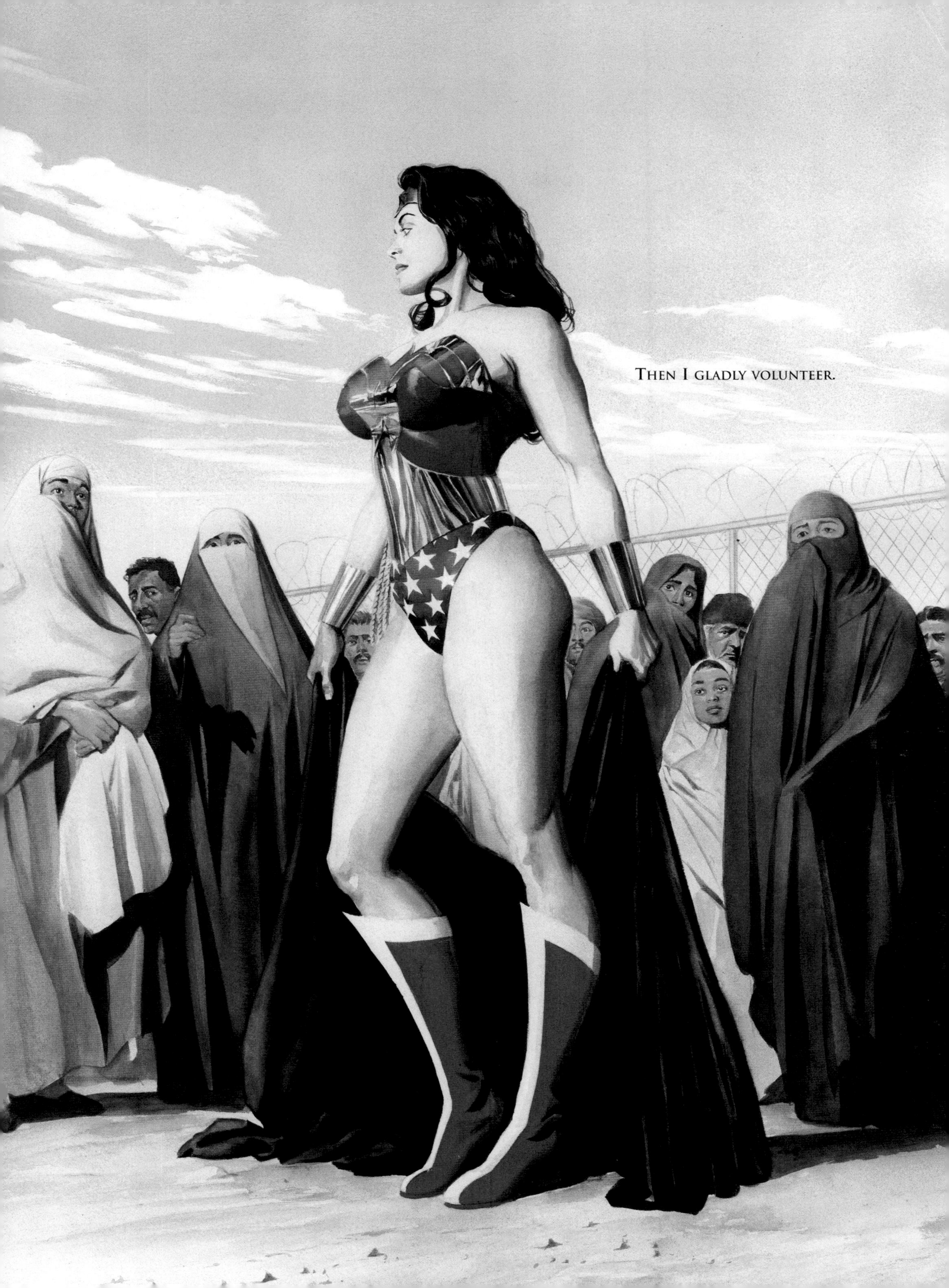
Then I gladly volunteer.

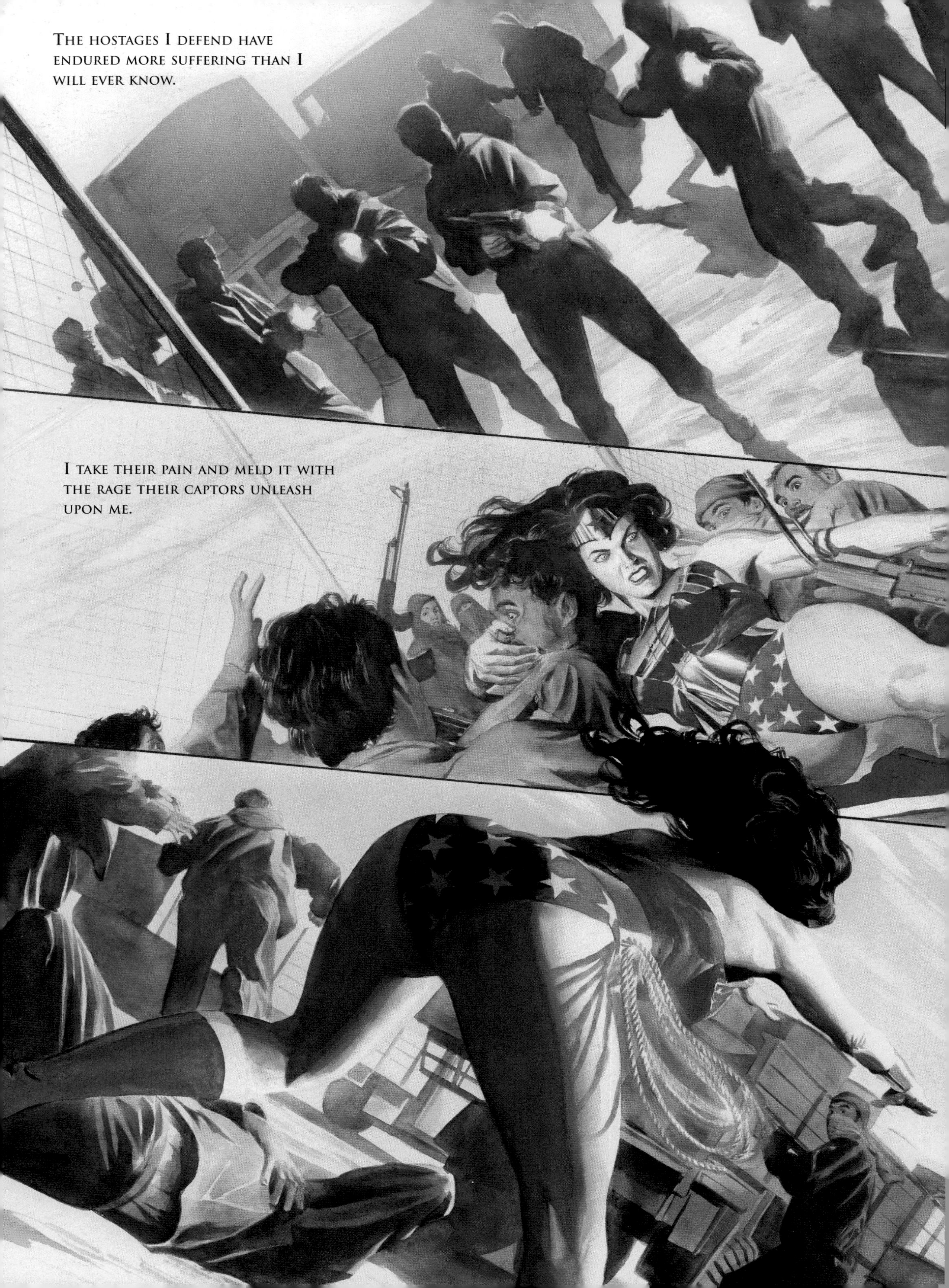
THE HOSTAGES I DEFEND HAVE ENDURED MORE SUFFERING THAN I WILL EVER KNOW.
I TAKE THEIR PAIN AND MELD IT WITH THE RAGE THEIR CAPTORS UNLEASH UPON ME.

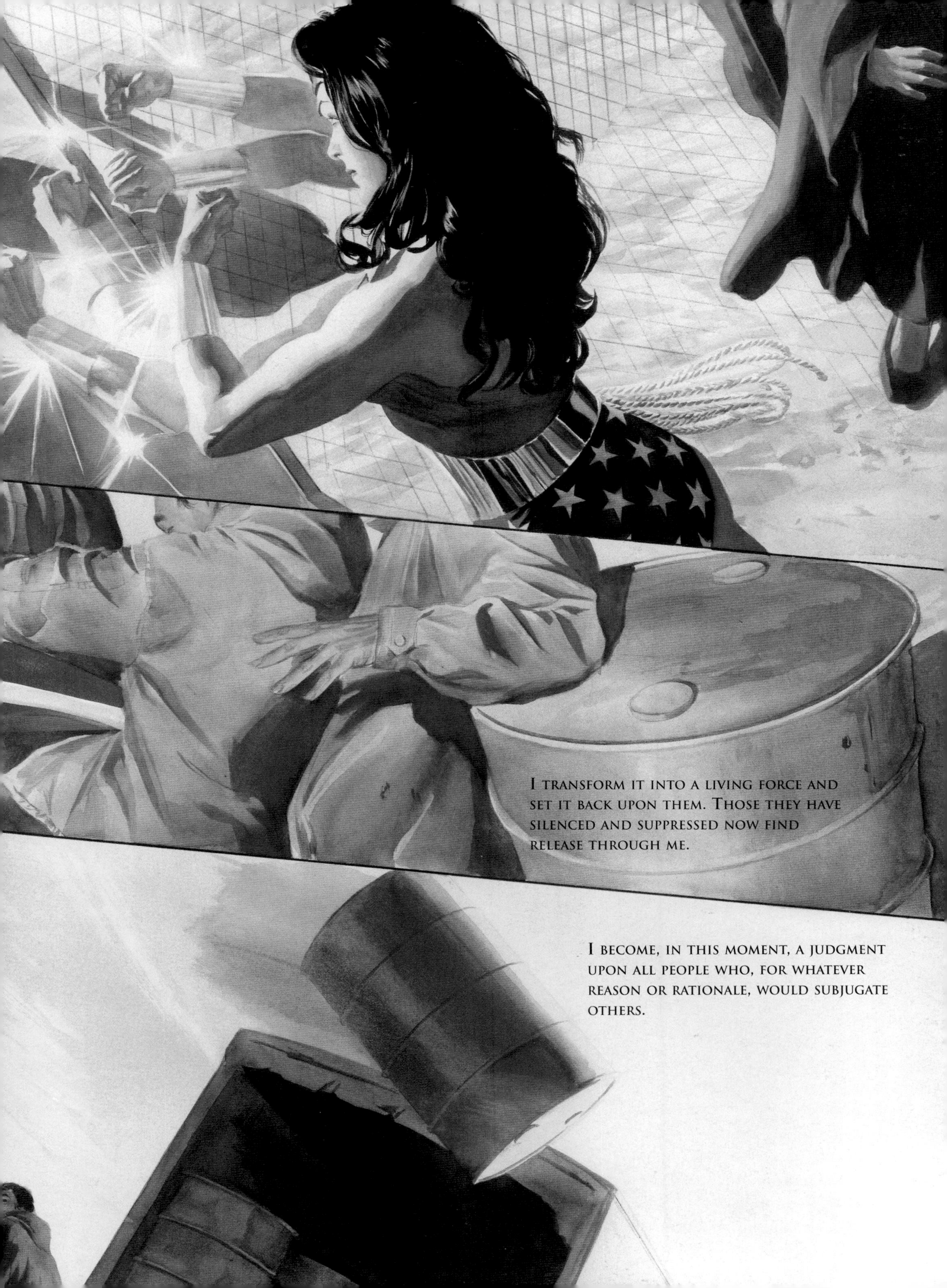
I TRANSFORM IT INTO A LIVING FORCE AND SET IT BACK UPON THEM. THOSE THEY HAVE SILENCED AND SUPPRESSED NOW FIND RELEASE THROUGH ME.
I BECOME, IN THIS MOMENT, A JUDGMENT UPON ALL PEOPLE WHO, FOR WHATEVER REASON OR RATIONALE, WOULD SUBJUGATE OTHERS.

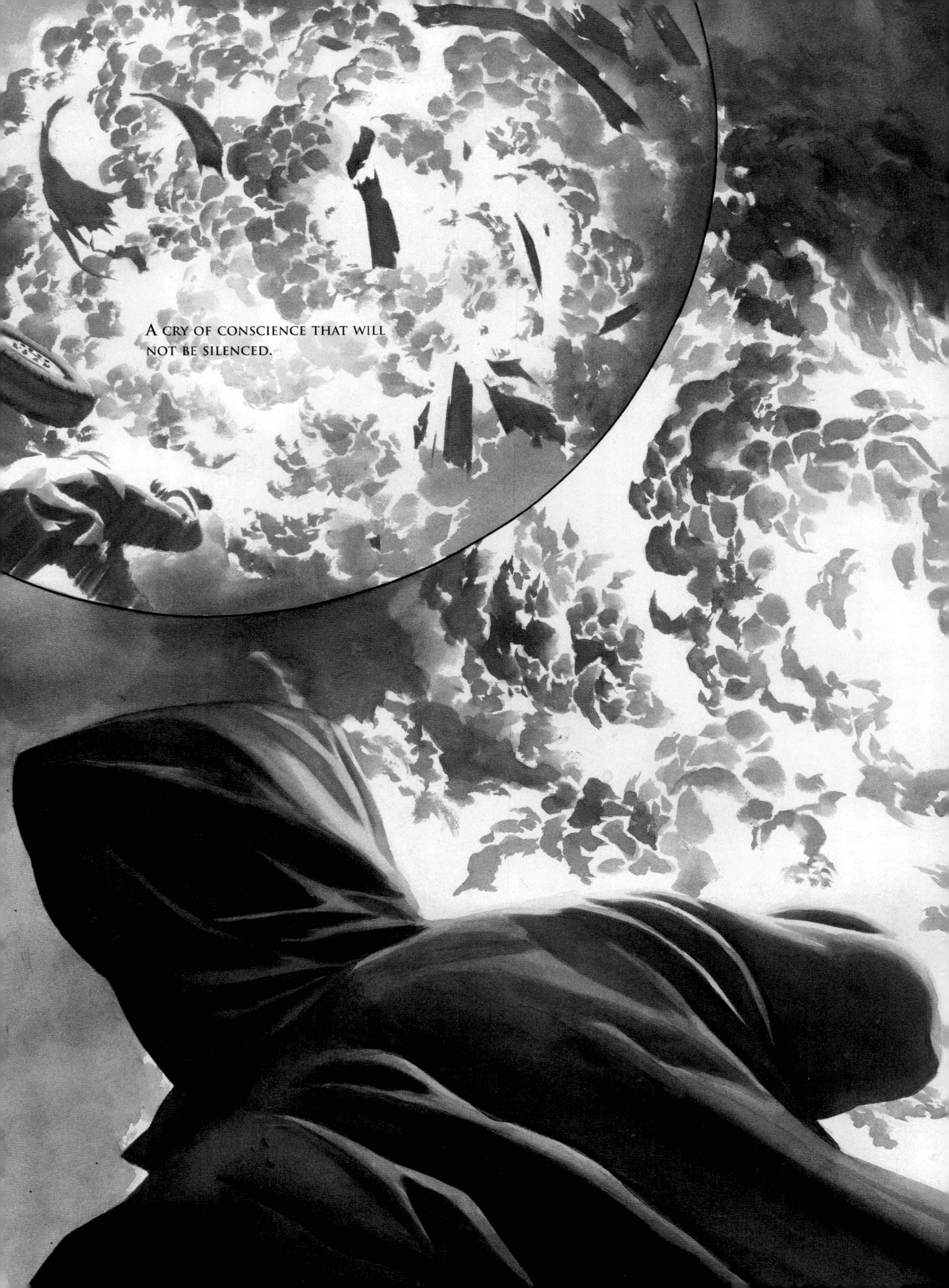
A cry of conscience that will not be silenced.

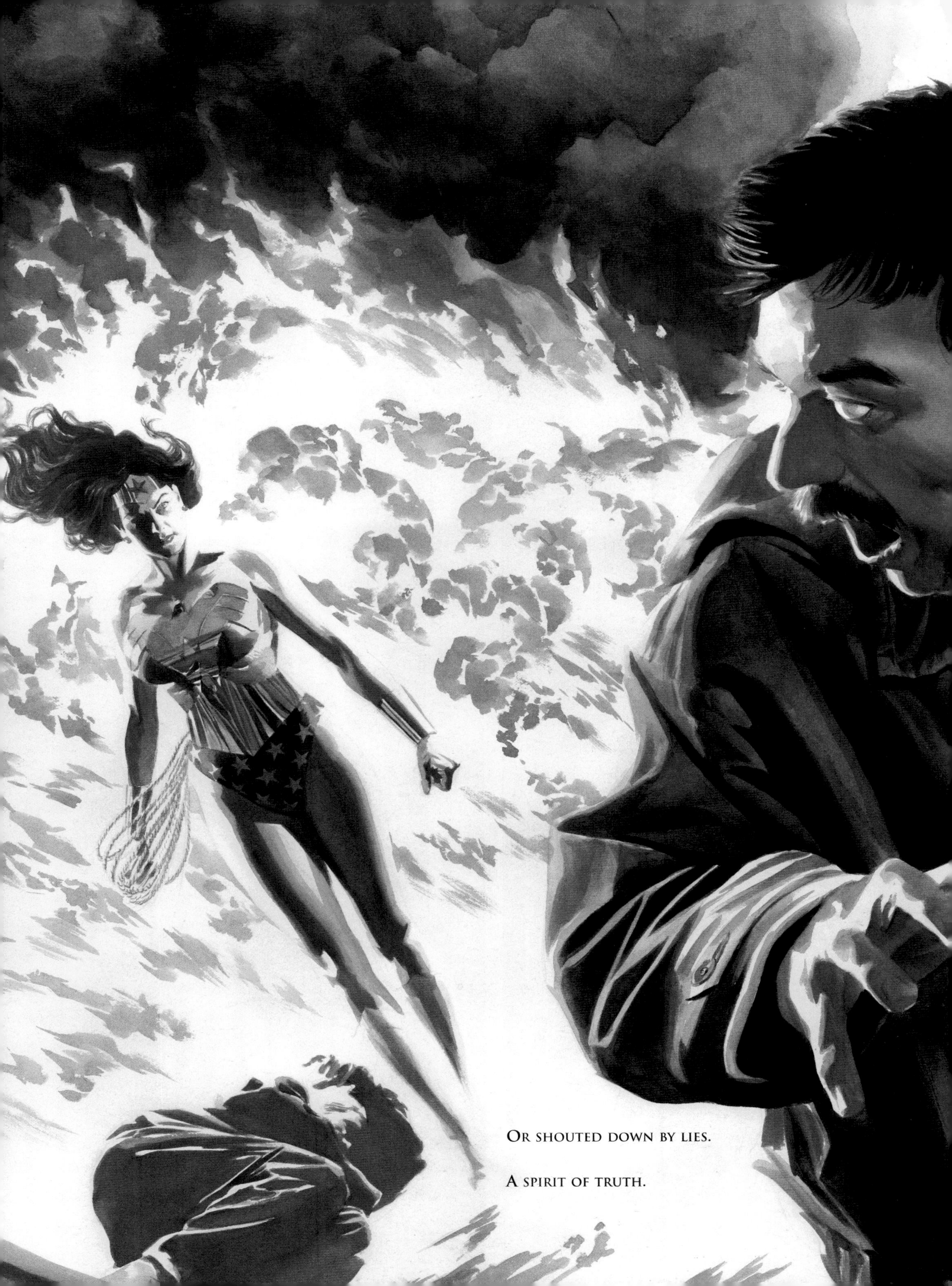
Or shouted down by lies.
A spirit of truth.

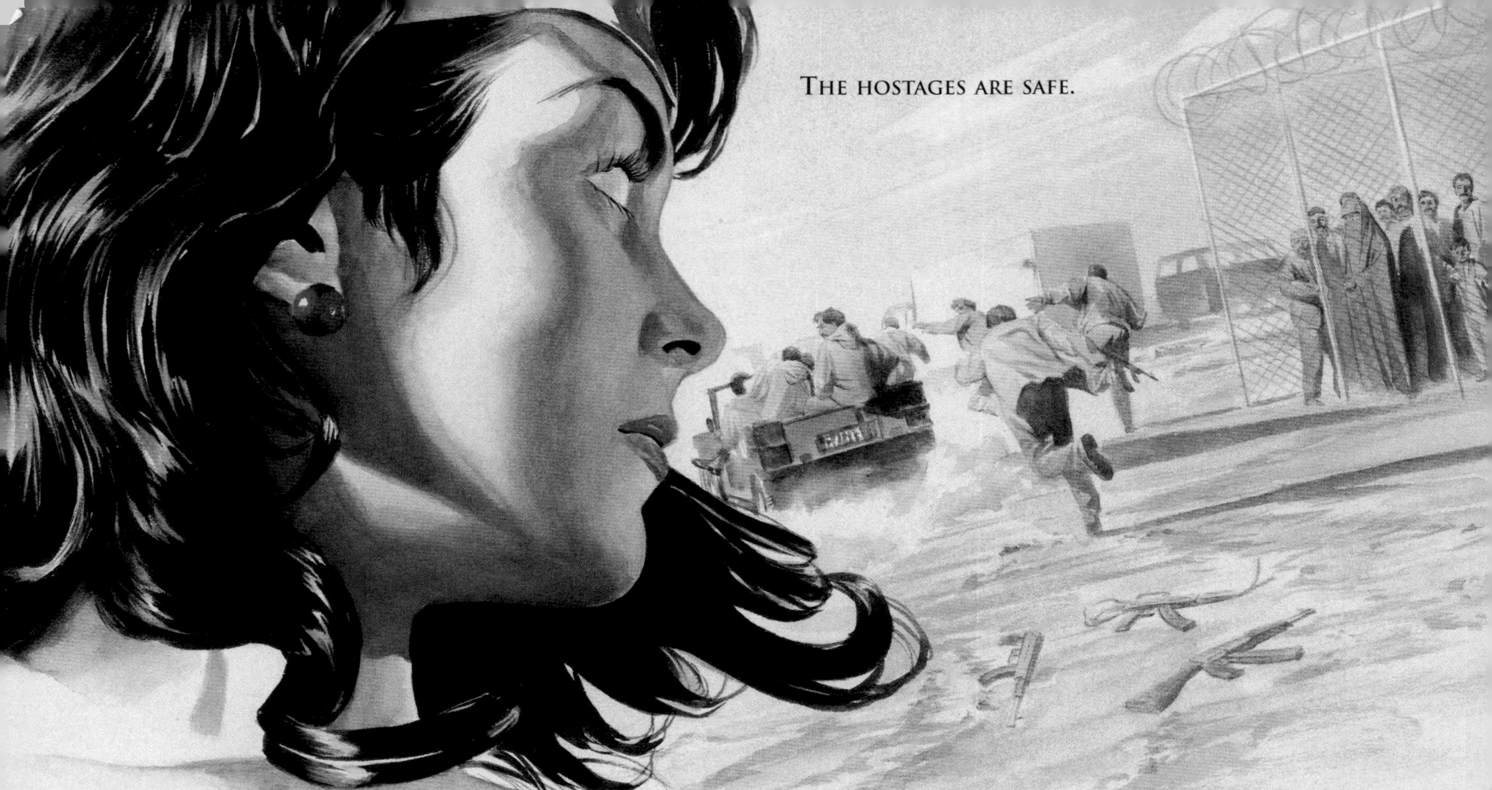
The hostages are safe.

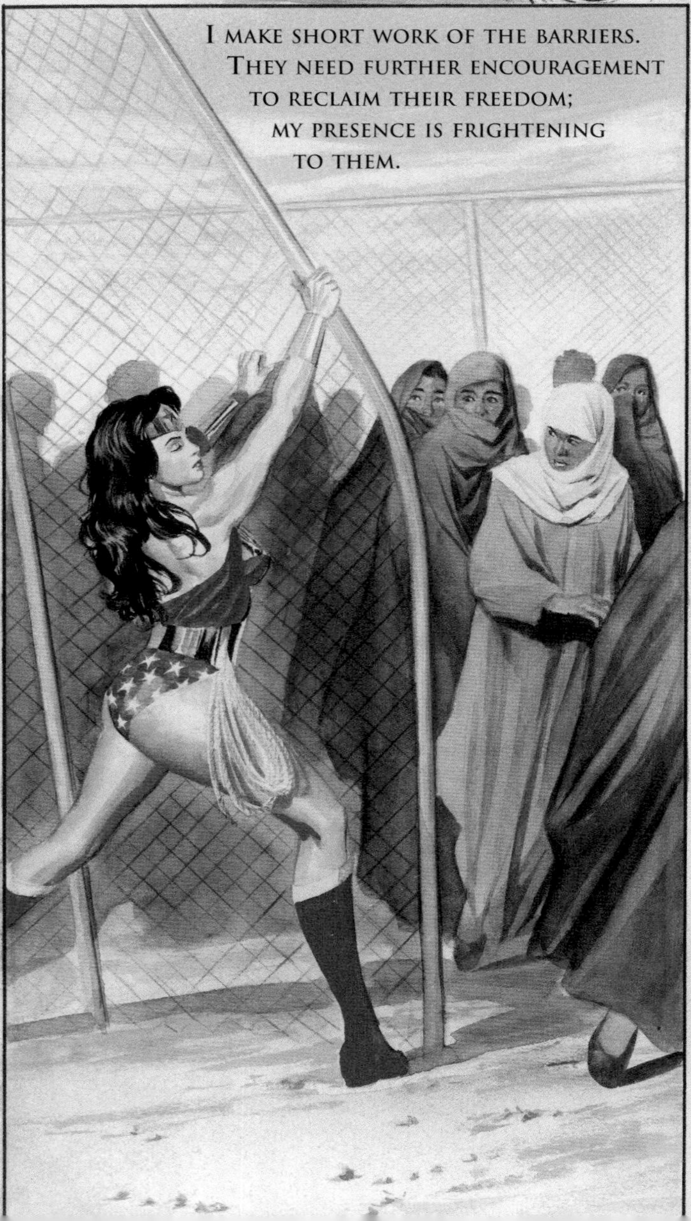
I make short work of the barriers. They need further encouragement to reclaim their freedom; my presence is frightening to them.

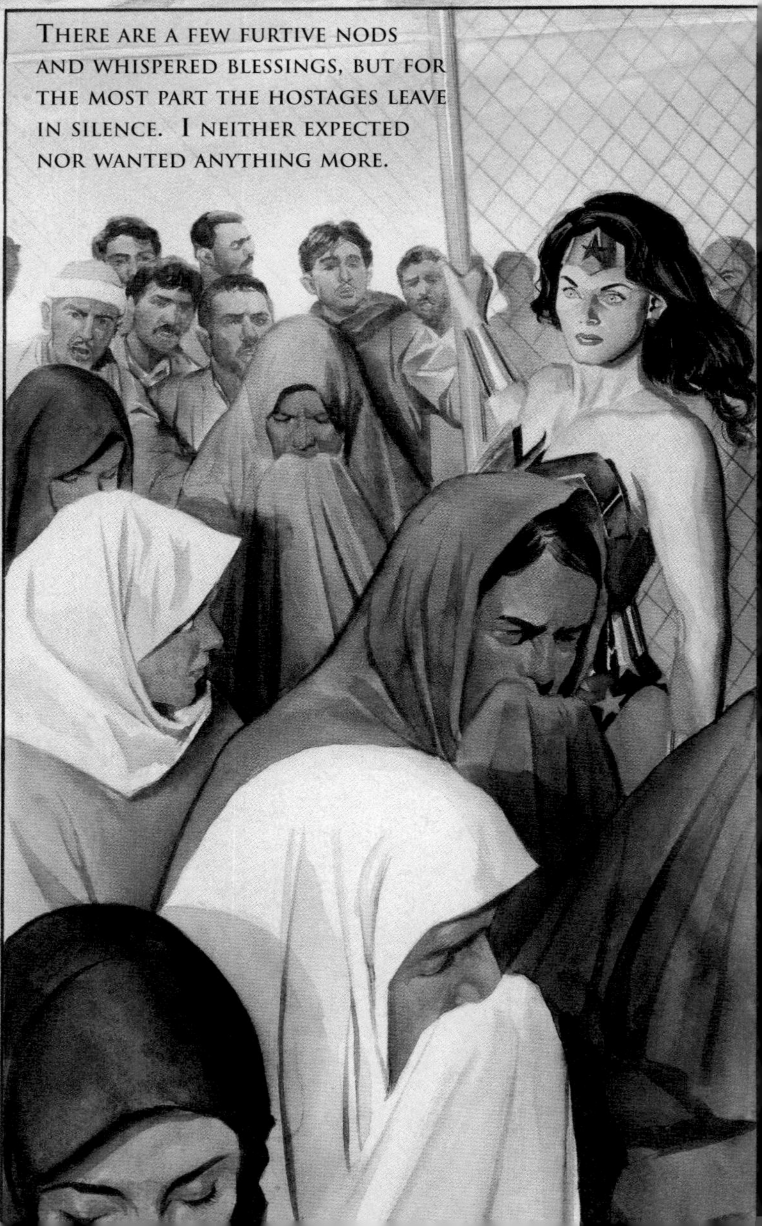
There are a few furtive nods and whispered blessings, but for the most part the hostages leave in silence. I neither expected nor wanted anything more.

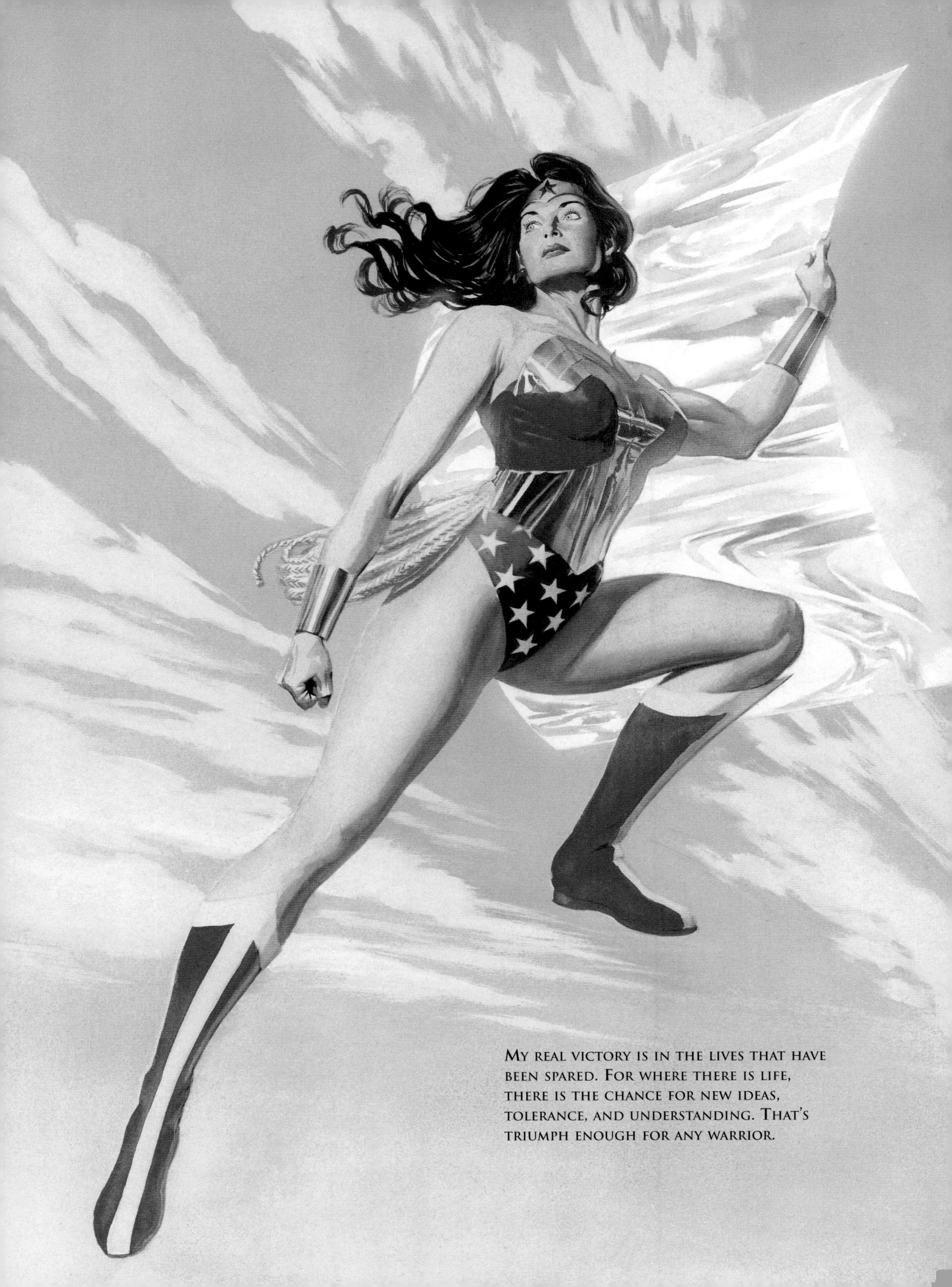
My real victory is in the lives that have been spared. For where there is life, there is the chance for new ideas, tolerance, and understanding. That's triumph enough for any warrior.

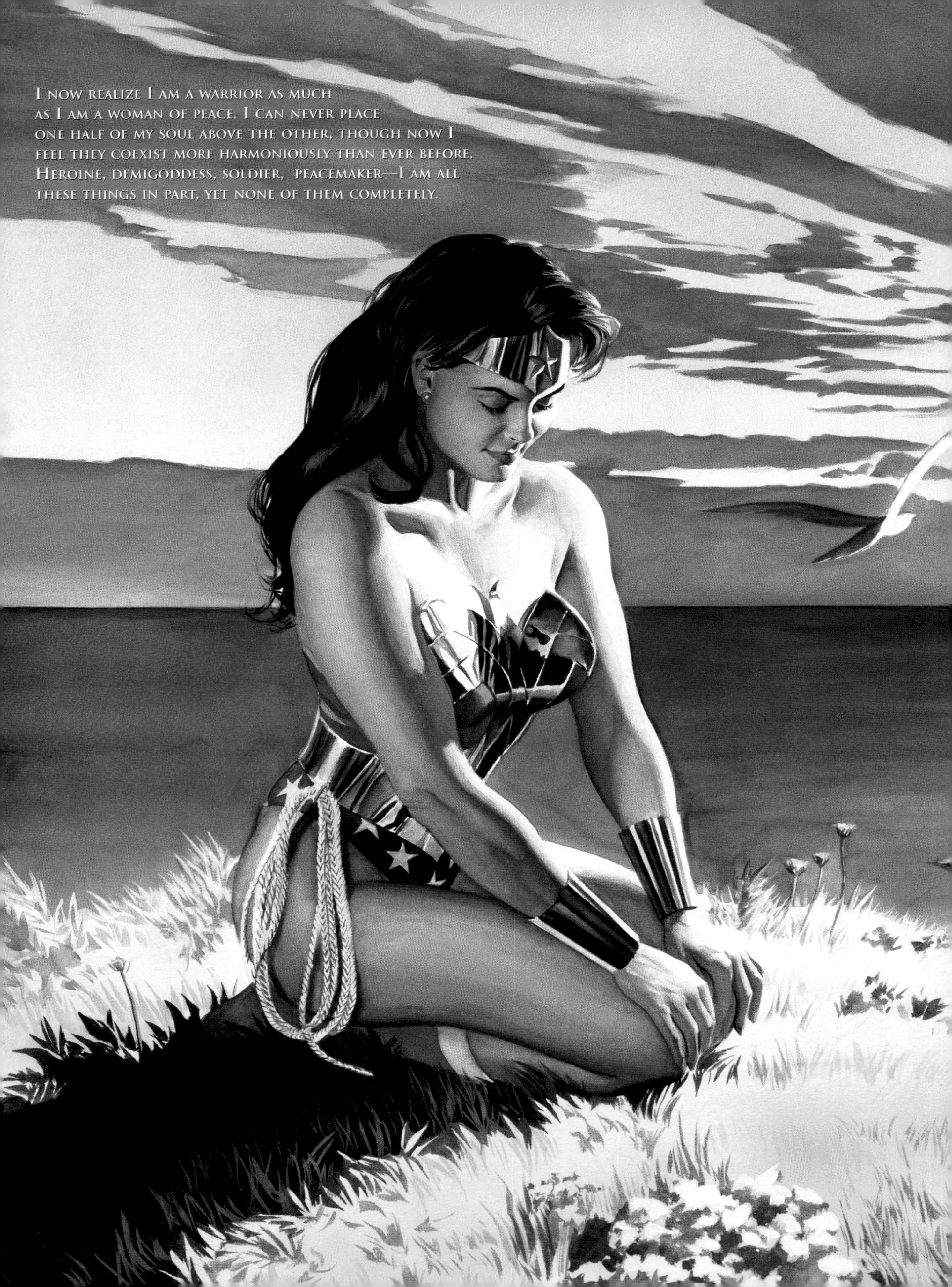
I now realize I am a warrior as much as I am a woman of peace. I can never place one half of my soul above the other, though now I feel they coexist more harmoniously than ever before. Heroine, demigoddess, soldier, peacemaker—I am all these things in part, yet none of them completely.

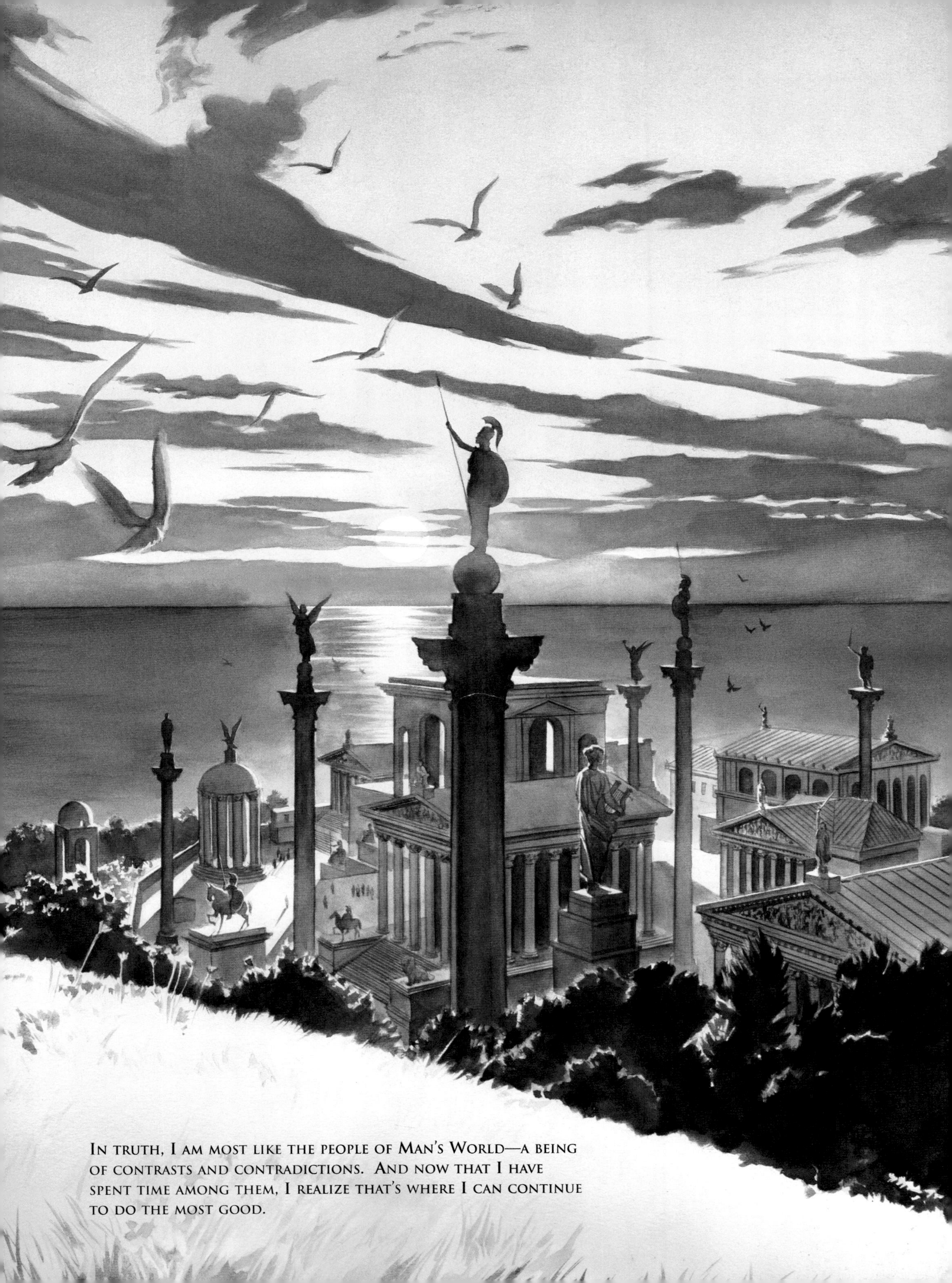
In truth, I am most like the people of Man's World—a being of contrasts and contradictions. And now that I have spent time among them, I realize that's where I can continue to do the most good.

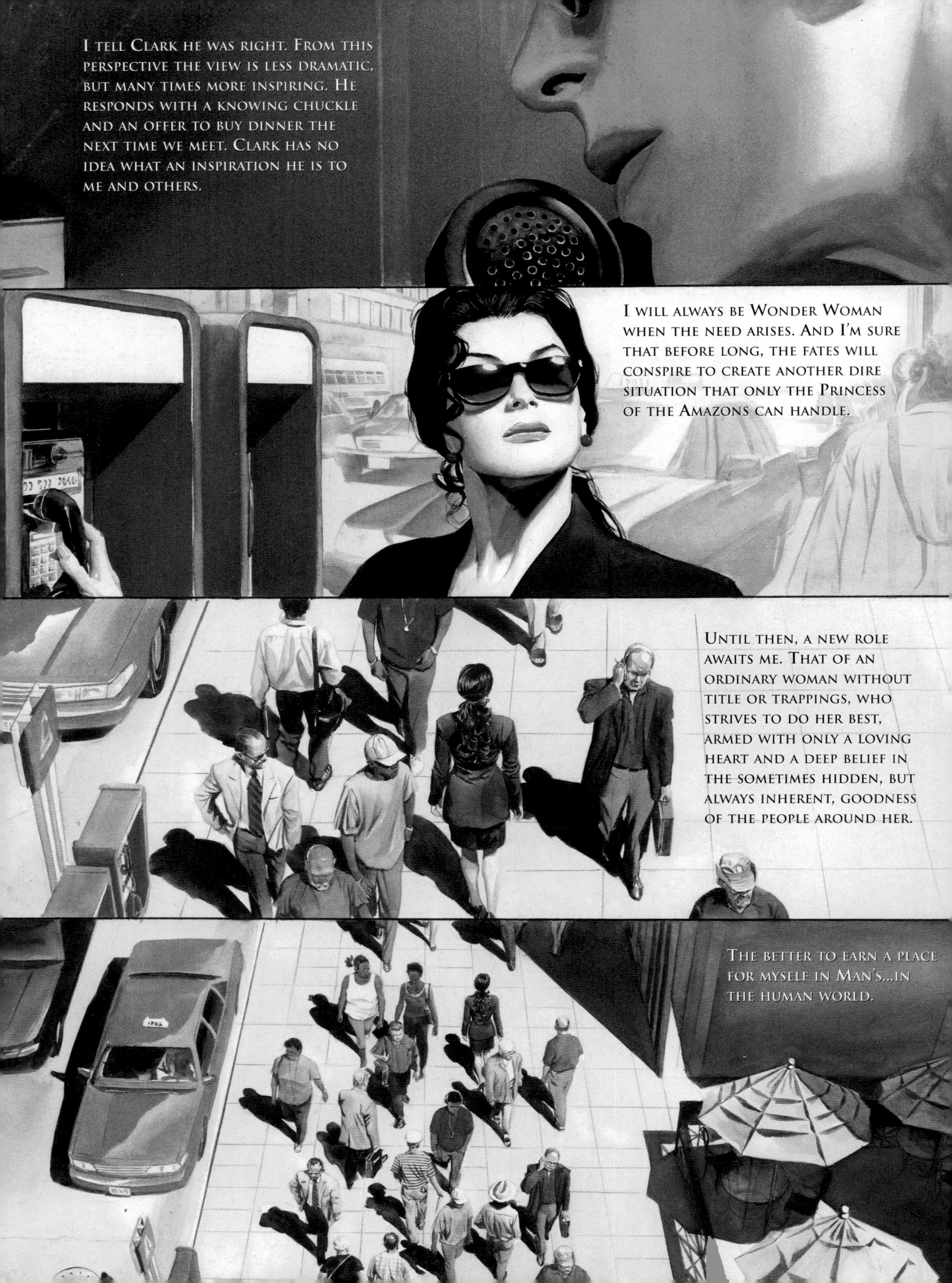
I tell Clark he was right. From this perspective the view is less dramatic, but many times more inspiring. He responds with a knowing chuckle and an offer to buy dinner the next time we meet. Clark has no idea what an inspiration he is to me and others.
I will always be Wonder Woman when the need arises. And I'm sure that before long, the fates will conspire to create another dire situation that only the Princess of the Amazons can handle.
Until then, a new role awaits me. That of an ordinary woman without title or trappings, who strives to do her best, armed with only a loving heart and a deep belief in the sometimes hidden, but always inherent, goodness of the people around her.
The better to earn a place for myself in Man's...in the human world.

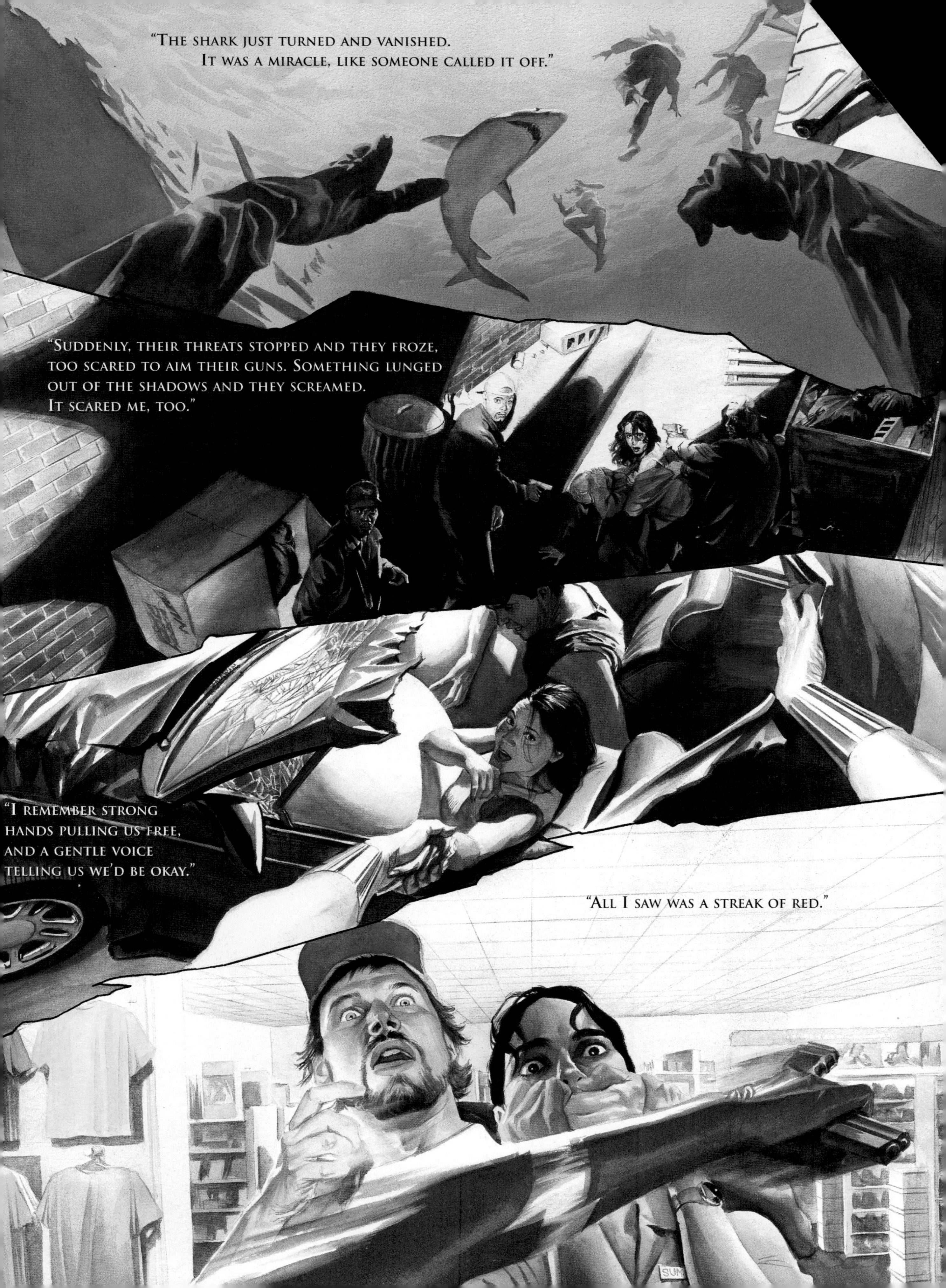
"The shark just turned and vanished. It was a miracle, like someone called it off."
"Suddenly, their threats stopped and they froze, too scared to aim their guns. Something lunged out of the shadows and they screamed. It scared me, too."
"I remember strong hands pulling us free, and a gentle voice telling us we'd be okay."
"All I saw was a streak of red."

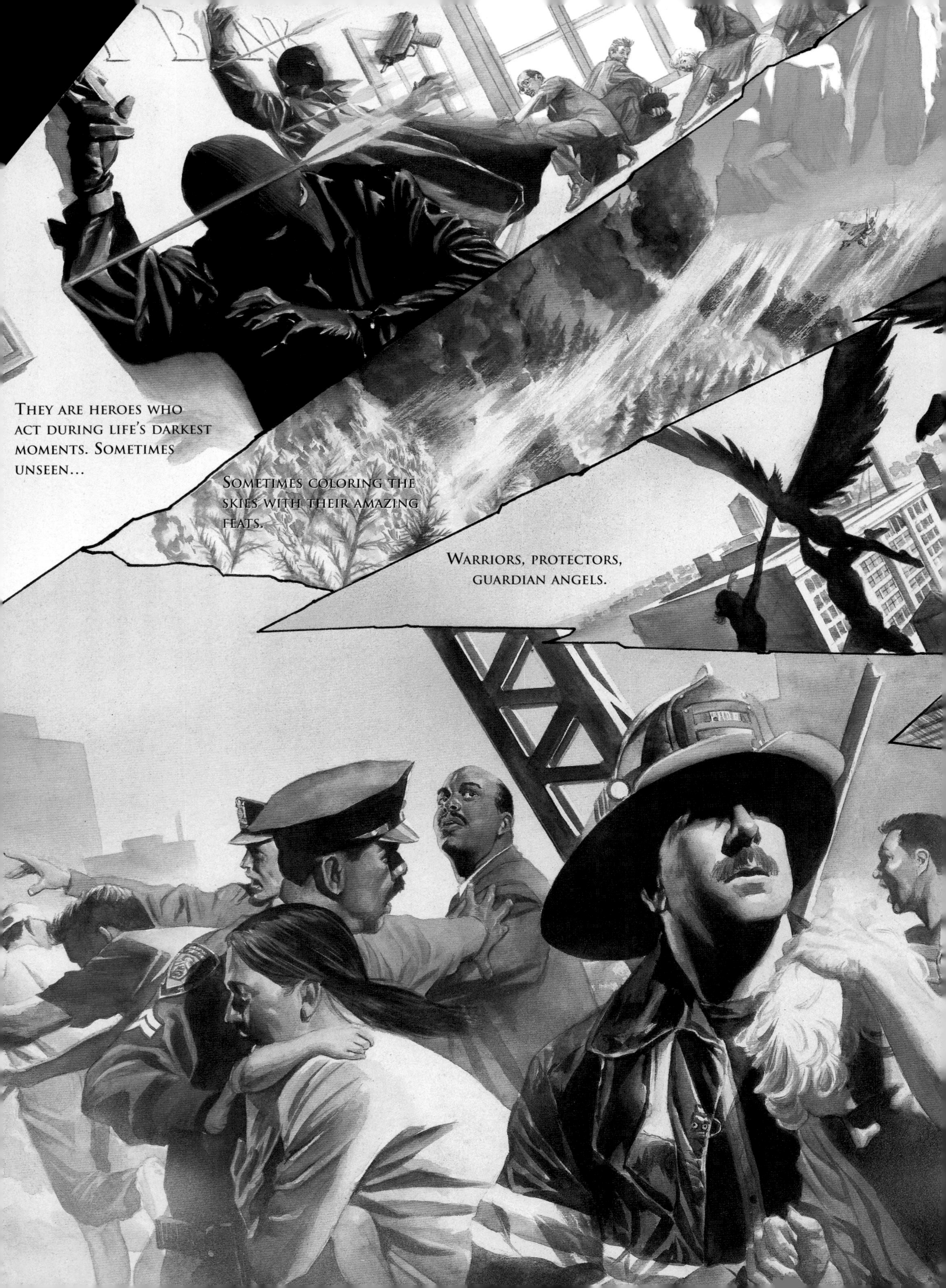
They are heroes who act during life's darkest moments. Sometimes unseen...
Sometimes coloring the skies with their amazing feats.
Warriors, protectors, guardian angels.

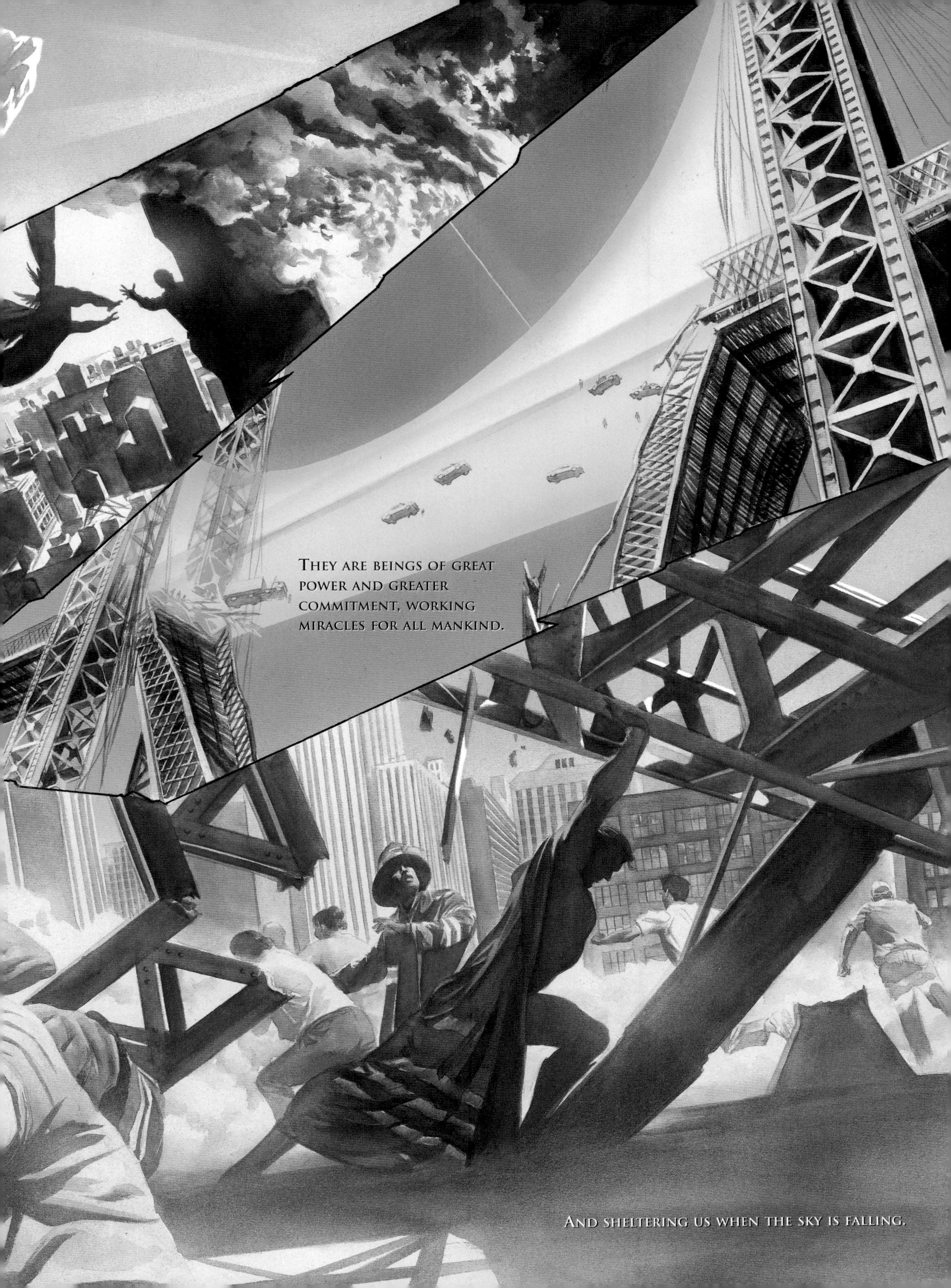
THEY ARE BEINGS OF GREAT POWER AND GREATER COMMITMENT, WORKING MIRACLES FOR ALL MANKIND.
AND SHELTERING US WHEN THE SKY IS FALLING.

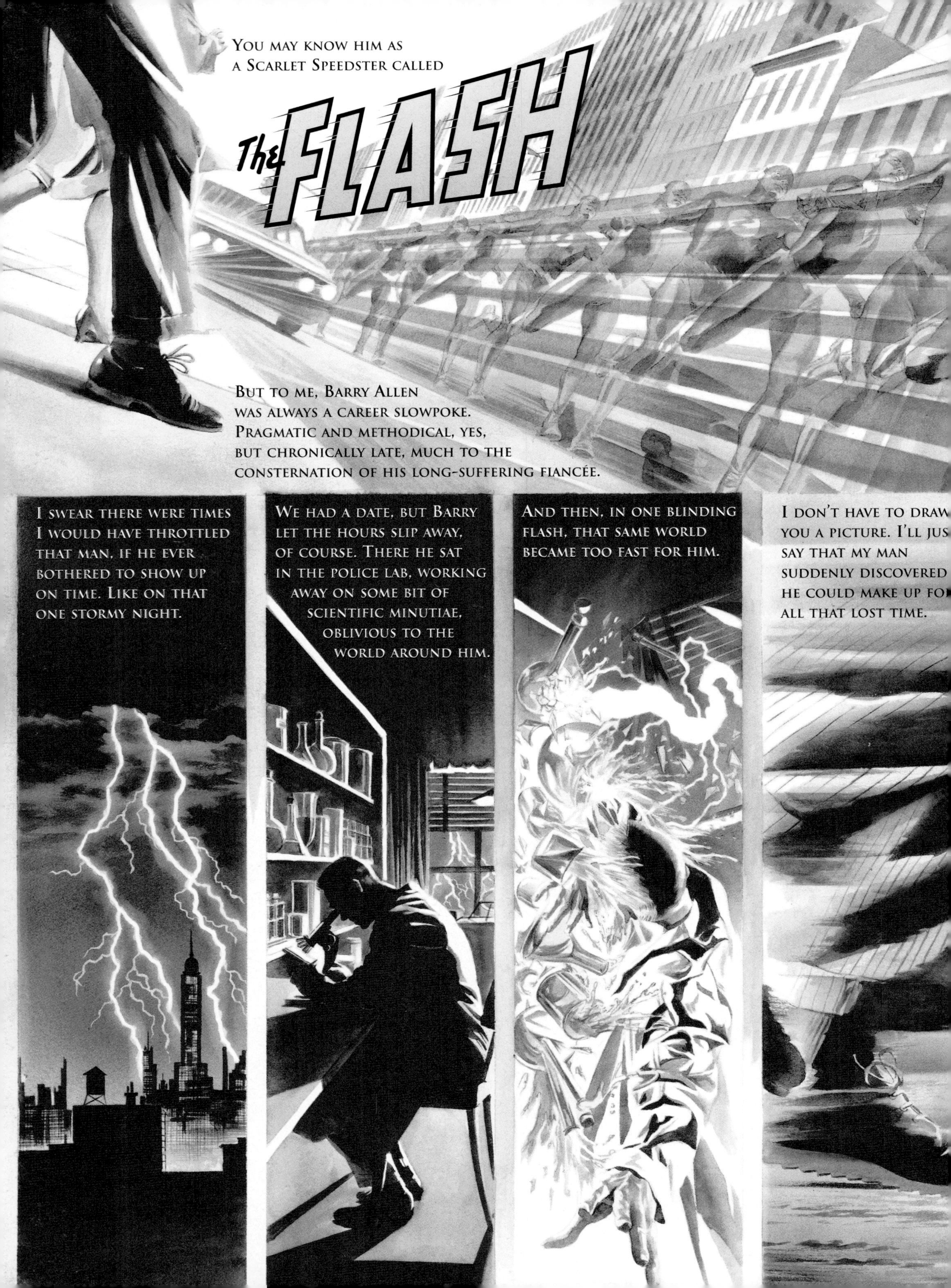
YOU MAY KNOW HIM AS A SCARLET SPEEDSTER CALLED
The FLASH
BUT TO ME, BARRY ALLEN WAS ALWAYS A CAREER SLOWPOKE. PRAGMATIC AND METHODICAL, YES, BUT CHRONICALLY LATE, MUCH TO THE CONSTERNATION OF HIS LONG-SUFFERING FIANCÉE.
I SWEAR THERE WERE TIMES I WOULD HAVE THROTTLED THAT MAN, IF HE EVER BOTHERED TO SHOW UP ON TIME. LIKE ON THAT ONE STORMY NIGHT.
WE HAD A DATE, BUT BARRY LET THE HOURS SLIP AWAY, OF COURSE. THERE HE SAT IN THE POLICE LAB, WORKING AWAY ON SOME BIT OF SCIENTIFIC MINUTIAE, OBLIVIOUS TO THE WORLD AROUND HIM.
AND THEN, IN ONE BLINDING FLASH, THAT SAME WORLD BECAME TOO FAST FOR HIM.
I DON'T HAVE TO DRAW YOU A PICTURE. I'LL JUS SAY THAT MY MAN SUDDENLY DISCOVERED HE COULD MAKE UP FO ALL THAT LOST TIME.

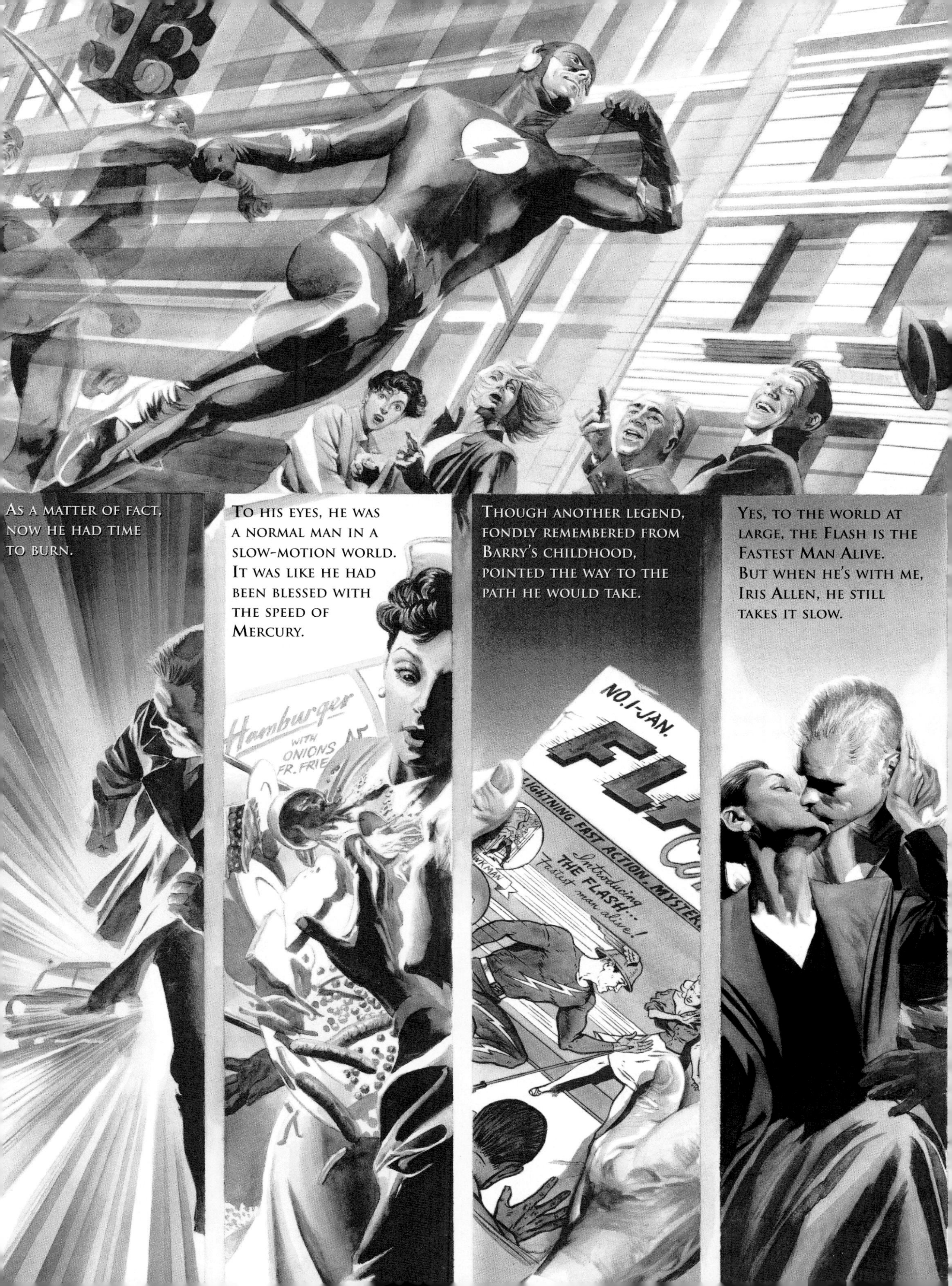

As a matter of fact, now he had time to burn.
To his eyes, he was a normal man in a slow-motion world. It was like he had been blessed with the speed of Mercury.
Hamburger
with onions
Fr. Frie
Though another legend, fondly remembered from Barry's childhood, pointed the way to the path he would take.
No. 1-Jan.
Lightning Fast Action . Myster
Introducing The Flash... Fastest man alive!
Yes, to the world at large, the Flash is the Fastest Man Alive. But when he's with me, Iris Allen, he still takes it slow.

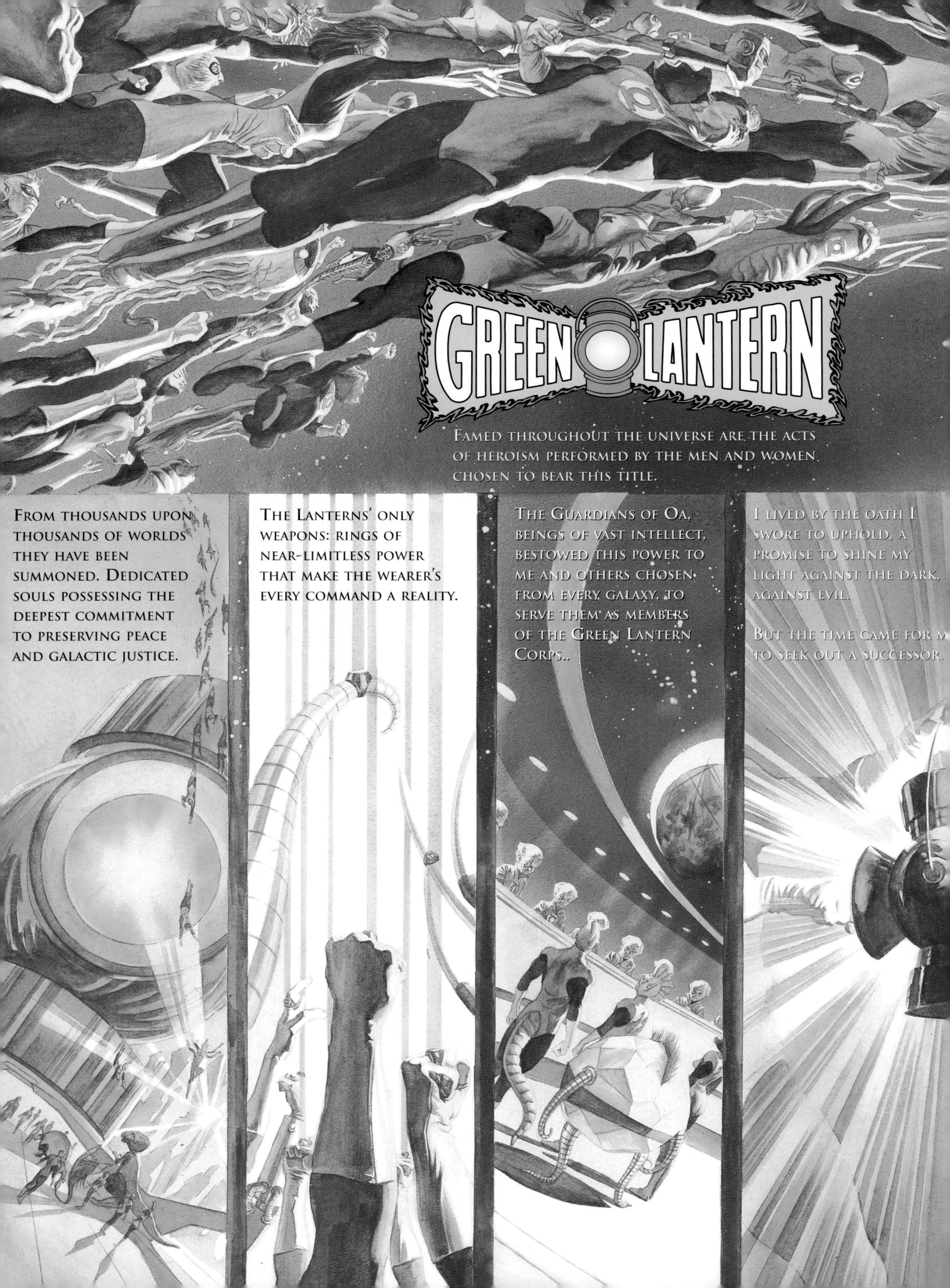
GREEN LANTERN
Famed throughout the universe are the acts of heroism performed by the men and women chosen to bear this title.
From thousands upon thousands of worlds they have been summoned. Dedicated souls possessing the deepest commitment to preserving peace and galactic justice.
The Lanterns' only weapons: rings of near-limitless power that make the wearer's every command a reality.
The Guardians of Oa, beings of vast intellect, bestowed this power to me and others chosen from every galaxy, to serve them as members of the Green Lantern Corps..
I lived by the oath I swore to uphold, a promise to shine my light against the dark, against evil.
But the time came for
to seek out a successor.

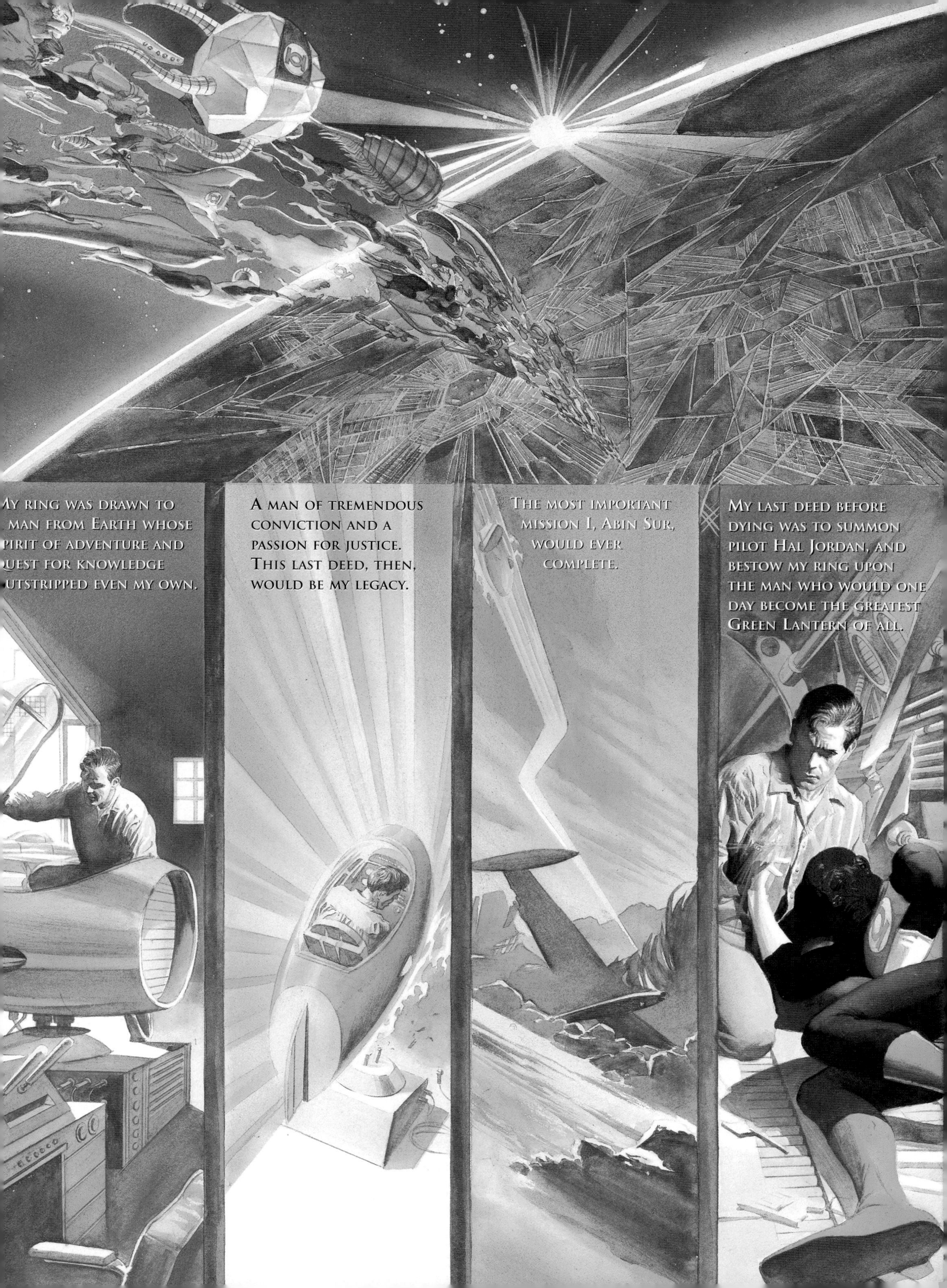
MY RING WAS DRAWN TO
MAN FROM EARTH WHOSE
PIRIT OF ADVENTURE AND
QUEST FOR KNOWLEDGE
UTSTRIPPED EVEN MY OWN.
A MAN OF TREMENDOUS CONVICTION AND A PASSION FOR JUSTICE. THIS LAST DEED, THEN, WOULD BE MY LEGACY.
THE MOST IMPORTANT MISSION I, ABIN SUR, WOULD EVER COMPLETE.
MY LAST DEED BEFORE DYING WAS TO SUMMON PILOT HAL JORDAN, AND BESTOW MY RING UPON THE MAN WHO WOULD ONE DAY BECOME THE GREATEST GREEN LANTERN OF ALL.

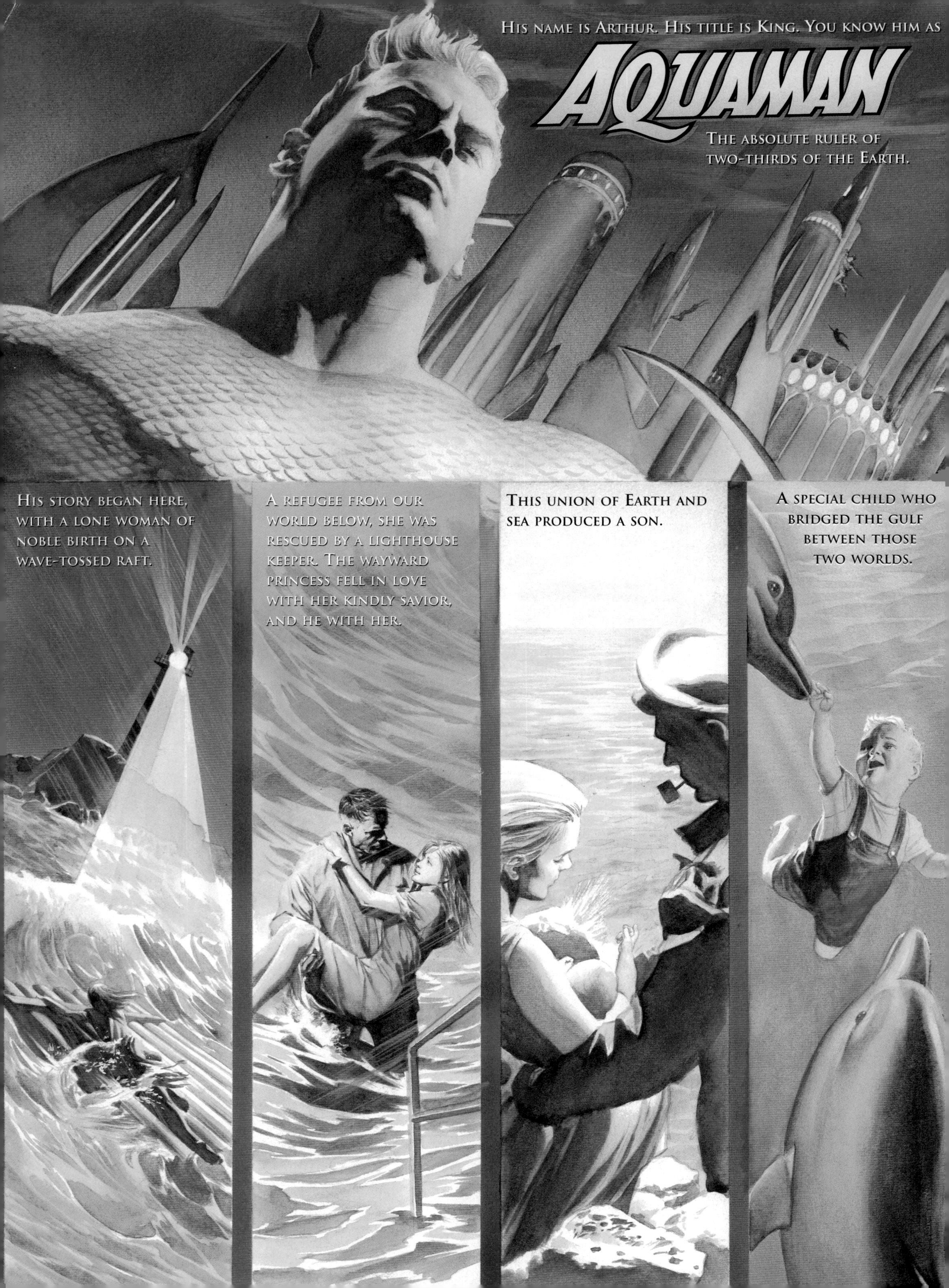
His name is Arthur. His title is King. You know him as
AQUAMAN
The absolute ruler of two-thirds of the Earth.
His story began here, with a lone woman of noble birth on a wave-tossed raft.
A refugee from our world below, she was rescued by a lighthouse keeper. The wayward princess fell in love with her kindly savior, and he with her.
This union of Earth and sea produced a son.
A special child who bridged the gulf between those two worlds.

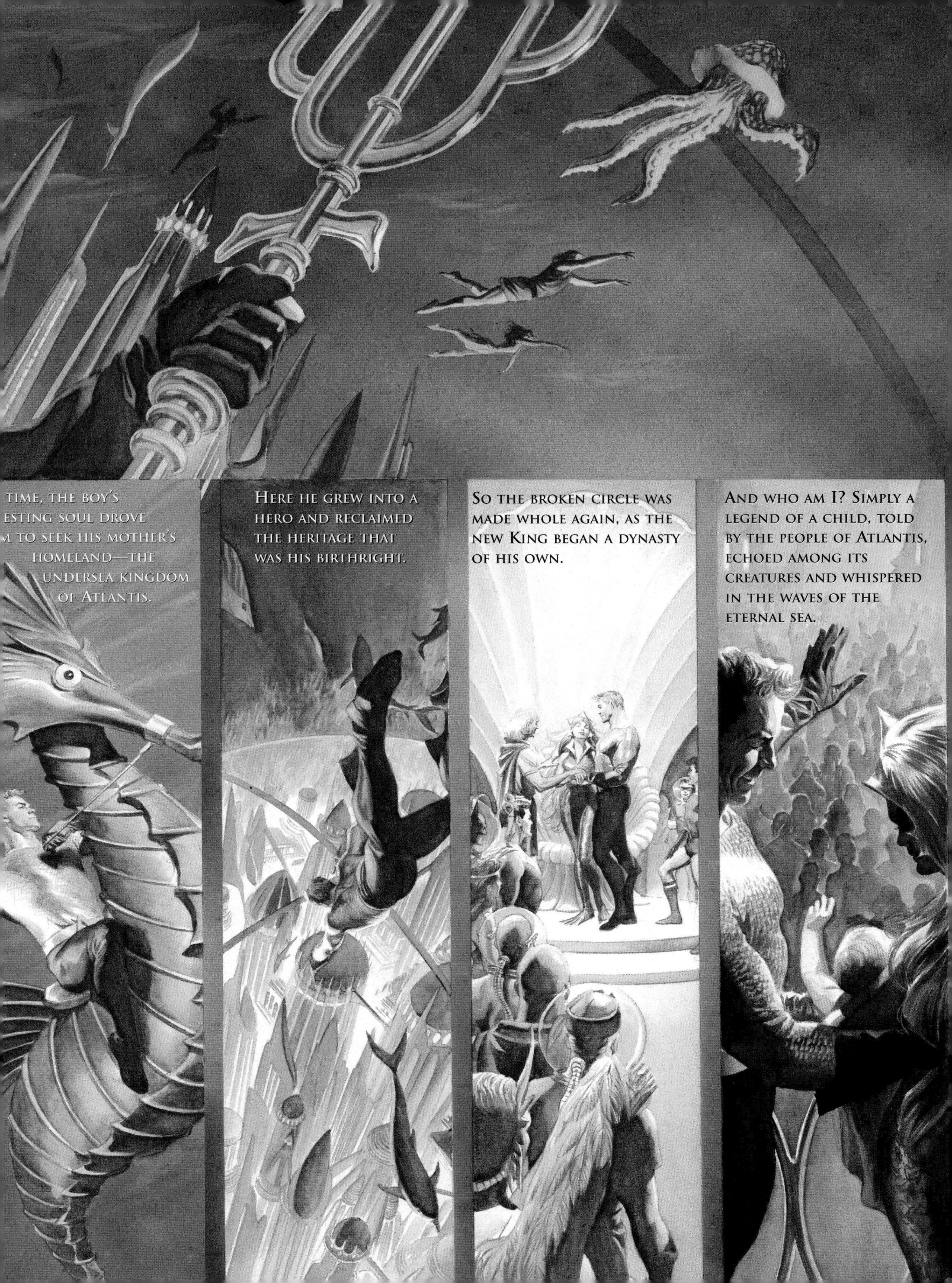
time, the boy's
esting soul drove
m to seek his mother's homeland—the undersea kingdom of Atlantis.
Here he grew into a hero and reclaimed the heritage that was his birthright.
So the broken circle was made whole again, as the new King began a dynasty of his own.
And who am I? Simply a legend of a child, told by the people of Atlantis, echoed among its creatures and whispered in the waves of the eternal sea.

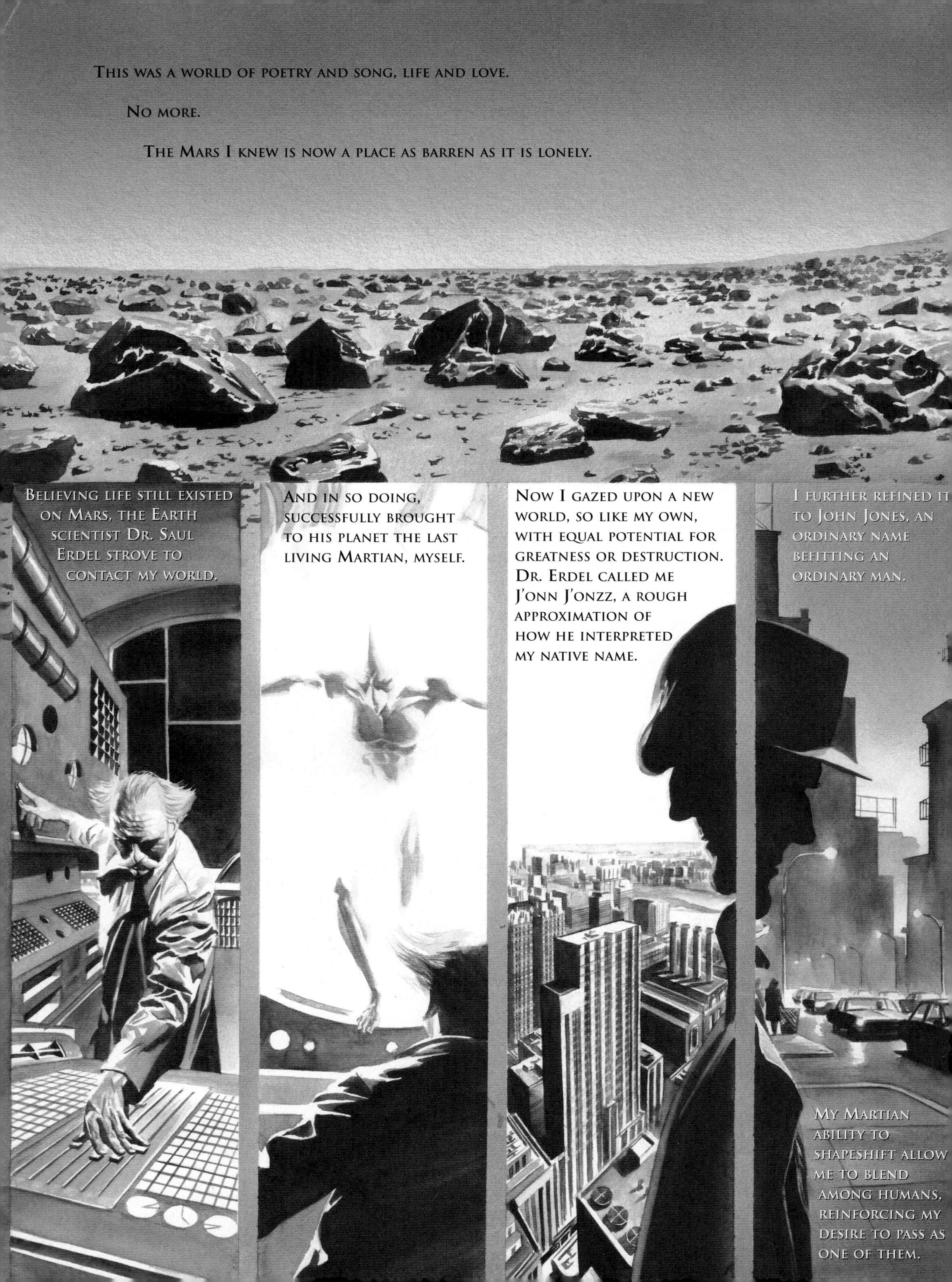

This was a world of poetry and song, life and love.
No more.
The Mars I knew is now a place as barren as it is lonely.
Believing life still existed on Mars, the Earth scientist Dr. Saul Erdel strove to contact my world.
And in so doing, successfully brought to his planet the last living Martian, myself.
Now I gazed upon a new world, so like my own, with equal potential for greatness or destruction. Dr. Erdel called me J'onn J'onzz, a rough approximation of how he interpreted my native name.
I further refined it to John Jones, an ordinary name befitting an ordinary man.
My Martian ability to shapeshift allow me to blend among humans, reinforcing my desire to pass as one of them.

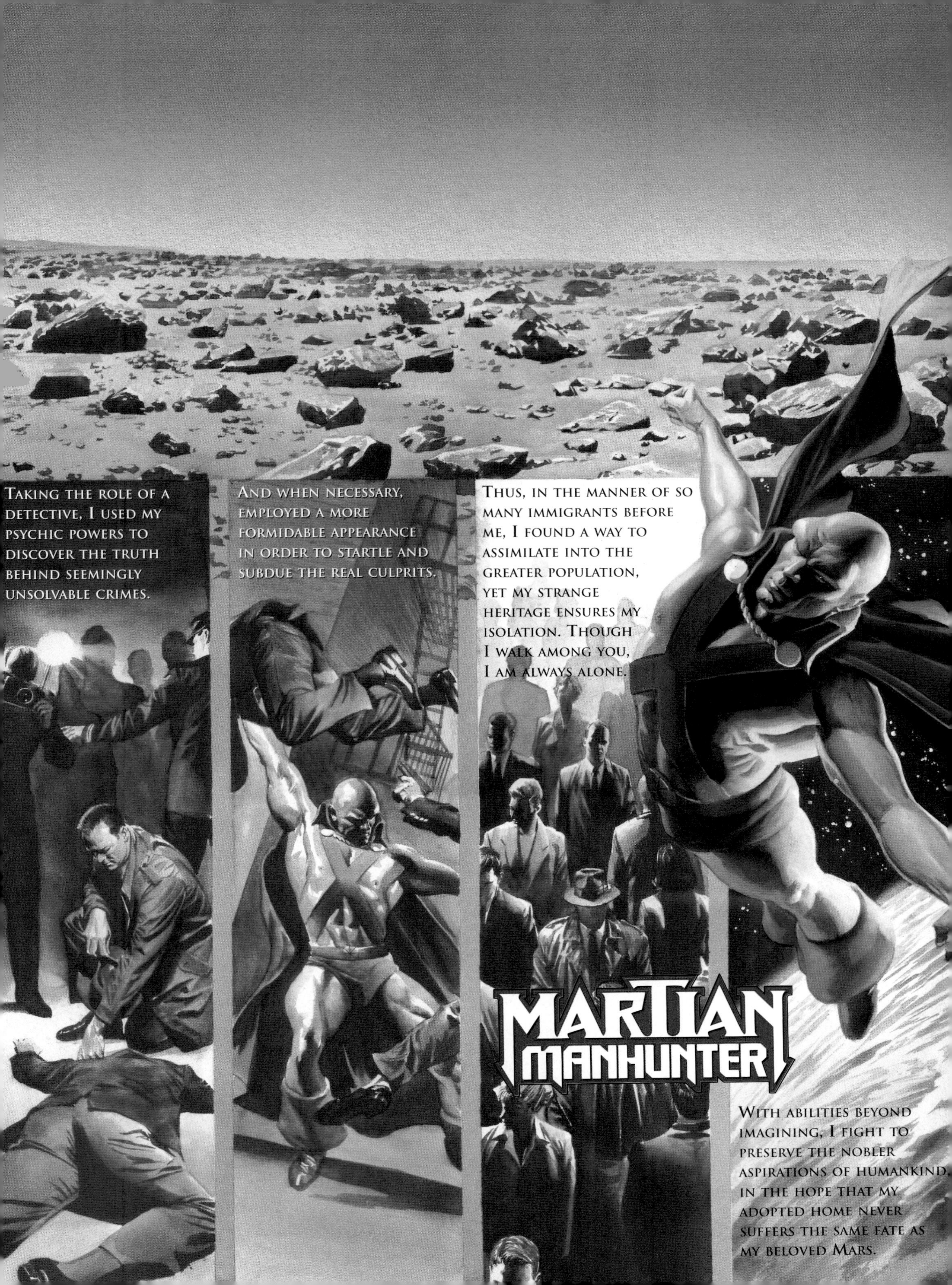

Taking the role of a detective, I used my psychic powers to discover the truth behind seemingly unsolvable crimes.
And when necessary, employed a more formidable appearance in order to startle and subdue the real culprits.
Thus, in the manner of so many immigrants before me, I found a way to assimilate into the greater population, yet my strange heritage ensures my isolation. Though I walk among you, I am always alone.
MARTIAN MANHUNTER
With abilities beyond imagining, I fight to preserve the nobler aspirations of humankind, in the hope that my adopted home never suffers the same fate as my beloved Mars.

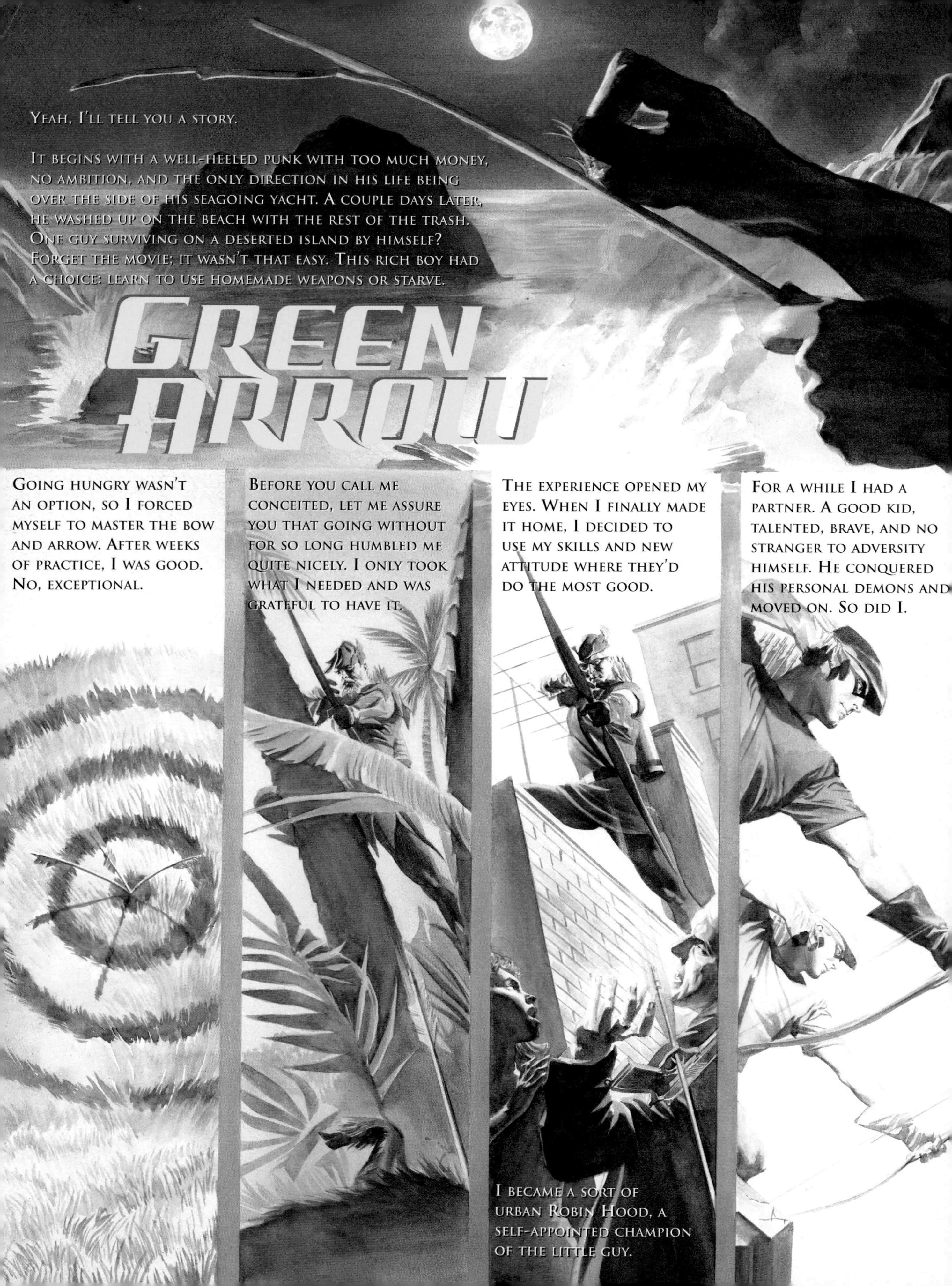
Yeah, I'll tell you a story.
It begins with a well-heeled punk with too much money, no ambition, and the only direction in his life being over the side of his seagoing yacht. A couple days later, he washed up on the beach with the rest of the trash. One guy surviving on a deserted island by himself? Forget the movie; it wasn't that easy. This rich boy had a choice: learn to use homemade weapons or starve.
Green Arrow
Going hungry wasn't an option, so I forced myself to master the bow and arrow. After weeks of practice, I was good. No, exceptional.
Before you call me conceited, let me assure you that going without for so long humbled me quite nicely. I only took what I needed and was grateful to have it.
The experience opened my eyes. When I finally made it home, I decided to use my skills and new attitude where they'd do the most good.
I became a sort of urban Robin Hood, a self-appointed champion of the little guy.
For a while I had a partner. A good kid, talented, brave, and no stranger to adversity himself. He conquered his personal demons and moved on. So did I.

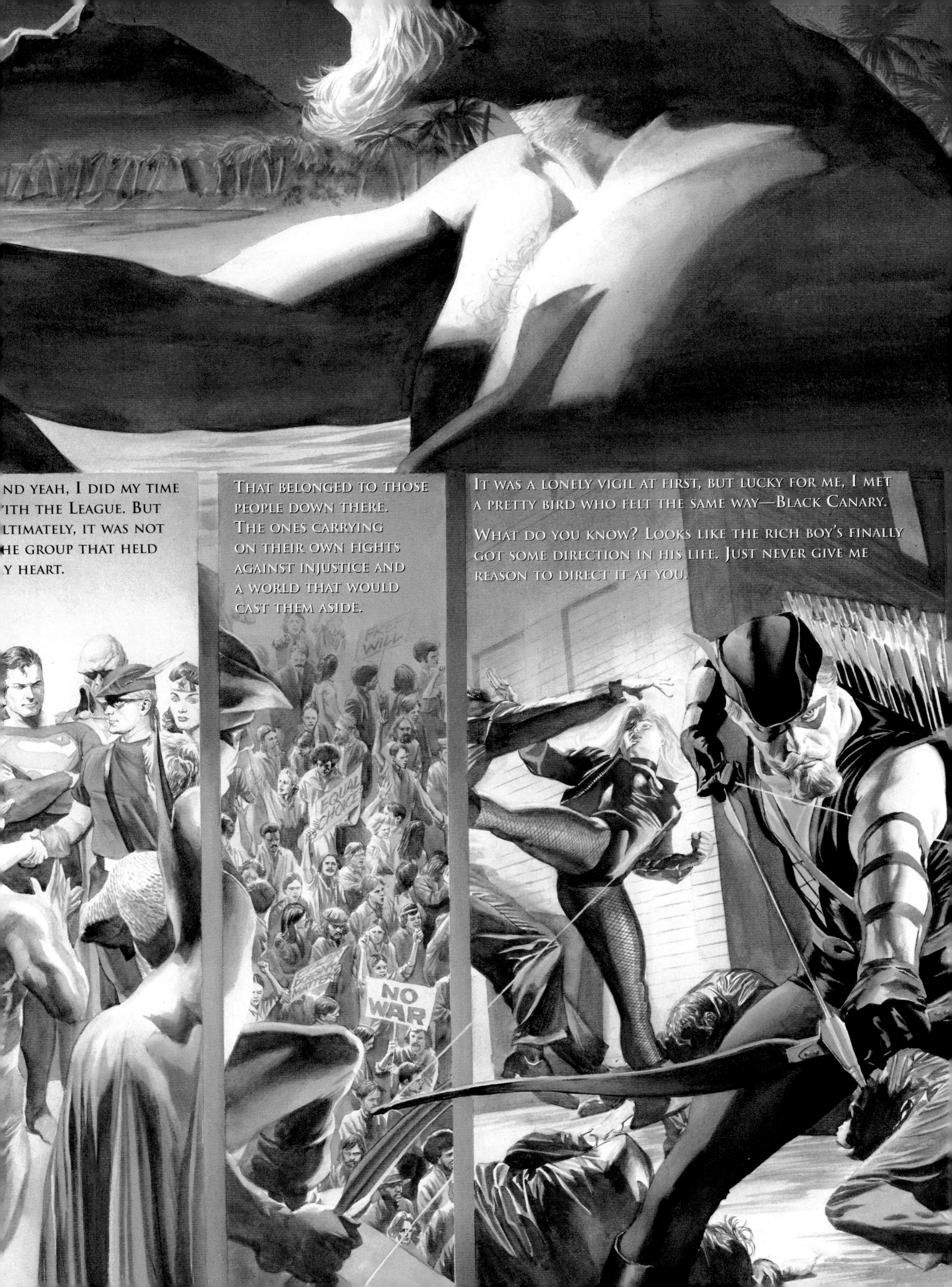

ND YEAH, I DID MY TIME 'ITH THE LEAGUE. BUT LTIMATELY, IT WAS NOT HE GROUP THAT HELD Y HEART.
THAT BELONGED TO THOSE PEOPLE DOWN THERE. THE ONES CARRYING ON THEIR OWN FIGHTS AGAINST INJUSTICE AND A WORLD THAT WOULD CAST THEM ASIDE.
FREE WILL
EQUAL CHOICE
NO WAR
IT WAS A LONELY VIGIL AT FIRST, BUT LUCKY FOR ME, I MET A PRETTY BIRD WHO FELT THE SAME WAY—BLACK CANARY.
WHAT DO YOU KNOW? LOOKS LIKE THE RICH BOY'S FINALLY GOT SOME DIRECTION IN HIS LIFE. JUST NEVER GIVE ME REASON TO DIRECT IT AT YOU.

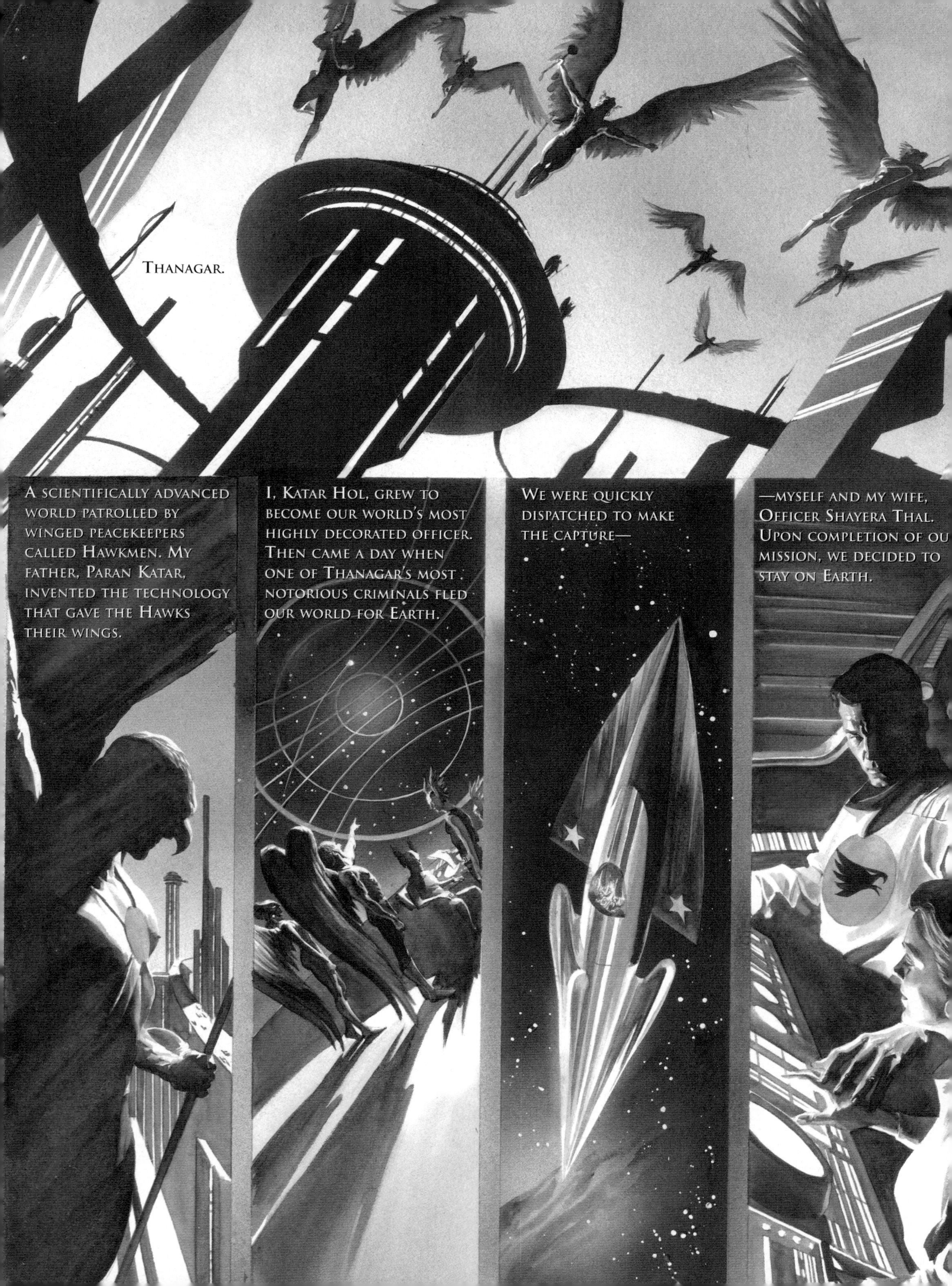
THANAGAR.
A SCIENTIFICALLY ADVANCED WORLD PATROLLED BY WINGED PEACEKEEPERS CALLED HAWKMEN. MY FATHER, PARAN KATAR, INVENTED THE TECHNOLOGY THAT GAVE THE HAWKS THEIR WINGS.
I, KATAR HOL, GREW TO BECOME OUR WORLD'S MOST HIGHLY DECORATED OFFICER. THEN CAME A DAY WHEN ONE OF THANAGAR'S MOST NOTORIOUS CRIMINALS FLED OUR WORLD FOR EARTH.
WE WERE QUICKLY DISPATCHED TO MAKE THE CAPTURE—
—MYSELF AND MY WIFE, OFFICER SHAYERA THAL. UPON COMPLETION OF OU MISSION, WE DECIDED TO STAY ON EARTH.

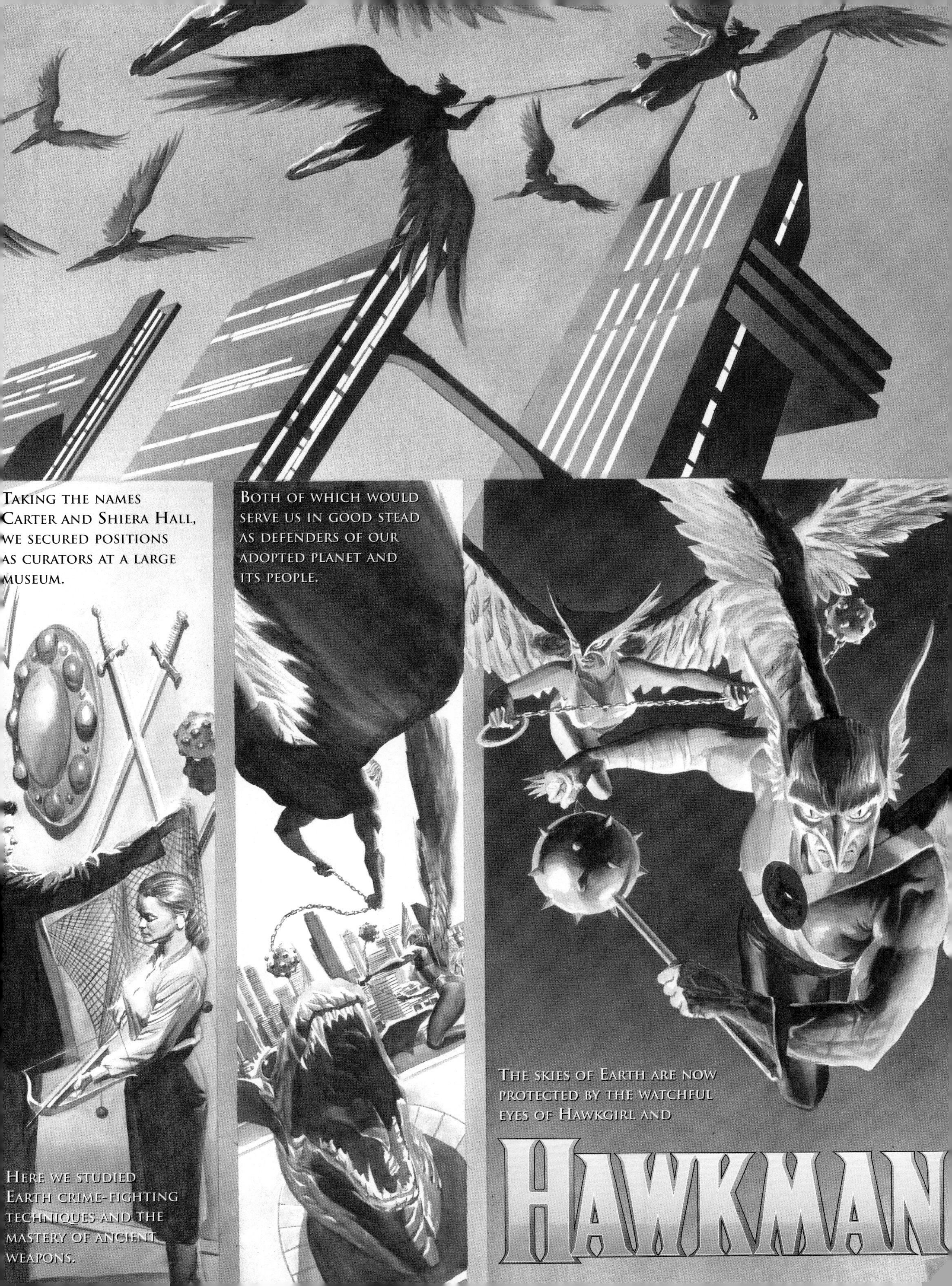
Taking the names Carter and Shiera Hall, we secured positions as curators at a large museum.
Here we studied Earth crime-fighting techniques and the mastery of ancient weapons.
Both of which would serve us in good stead as defenders of our adopted planet and its people.
The skies of Earth are now protected by the watchful eyes of Hawkgirl and
HAWKMAN

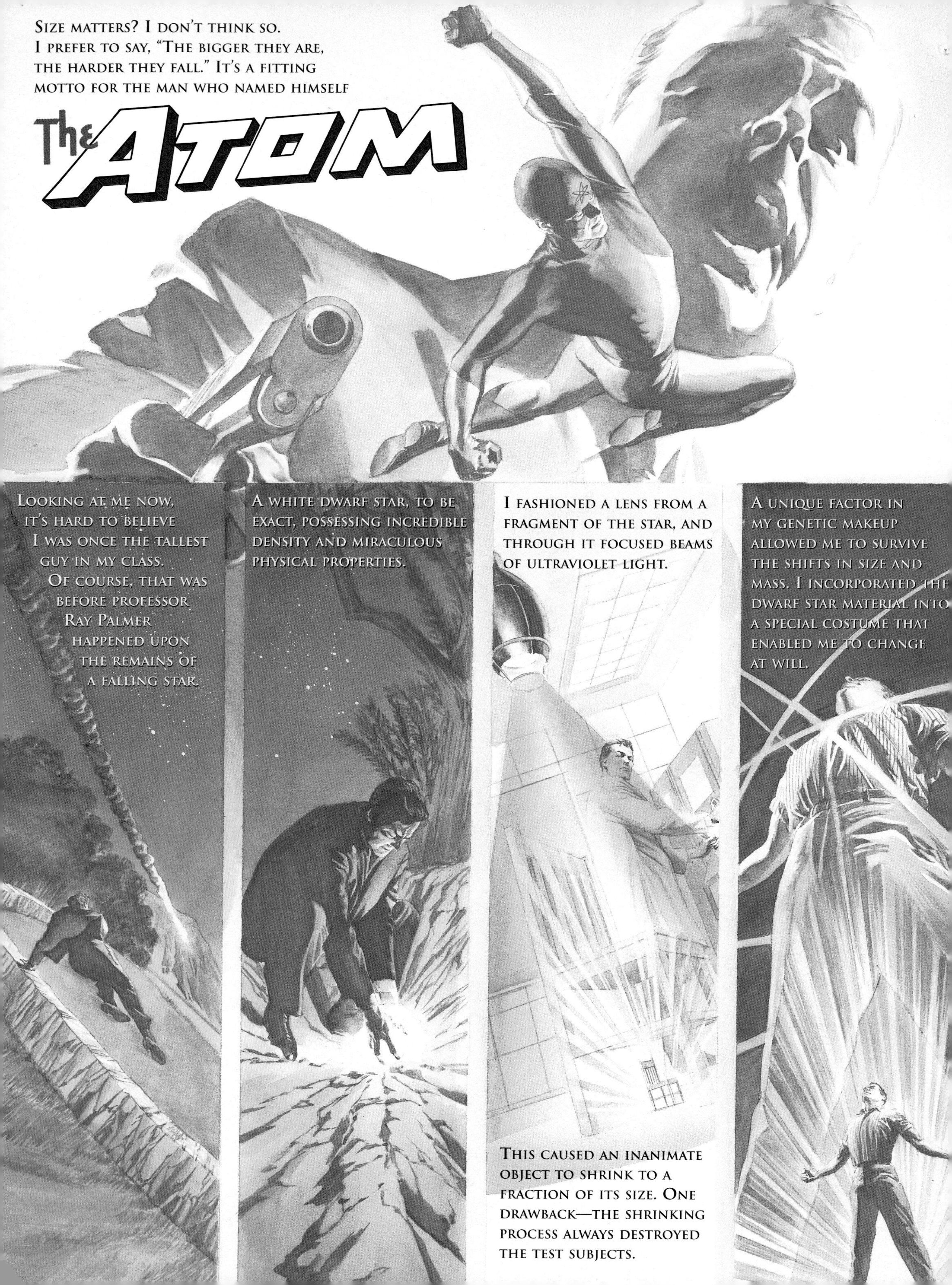
Size matters? I don't think so. I prefer to say, "The bigger they are, the harder they fall." It's a fitting motto for the man who named himself
The Atom
Looking at me now, it's hard to believe I was once the tallest guy in my class. Of course, that was before Professor Ray Palmer happened upon the remains of a falling star.
A white dwarf star, to be exact, possessing incredible density and miraculous physical properties.
I fashioned a lens from a fragment of the star, and through it focused beams of ultraviolet light.
This caused an inanimate object to shrink to a fraction of its size. One drawback—the shrinking process always destroyed the test subjects.
A unique factor in my genetic makeup allowed me to survive the shifts in size and mass. I incorporated the dwarf star material into a special costume that enabled me to change at will.

ONLY A SMALL MAN, SO TO SPEAK, WOULD HAVE KEPT THIS ABILITY TO HIMSELF. THEREFORE, I WAS DETERMINED TO USE MY SKILLS WHEREVER THEY ARE NEEDED. FOR EXAMPLE, I CAN "RIDE" ELECTRONIC IMPULSES THROUGH A PHONE WIRE INTO A CRIMINAL'S LAIR.

THANKS TO THE DWARF STAR DENSITY, I CAN COMMAND THE STRENGTH OF A MAN MANY TIMES MY NORMAL SIZE.

AND SHRINKING EVEN SMALLER, I CAN STRIDE LIKE A GIANT ACROSS INNUMERABLE SUBATOMIC GALAXIES.

BUT MY PROUDEST ACHIEVEMENTS ARE THOSE I HAVE MADE AS A MEMBER OF A TEAM OF UNIQUE MEN AND WOMEN WHO ACCEPT ME WITH EQUAL STATURE. IT JUST GOES TO SHOW YOU, NEVER UNDERESTIMATE THE LITTLE GUY.

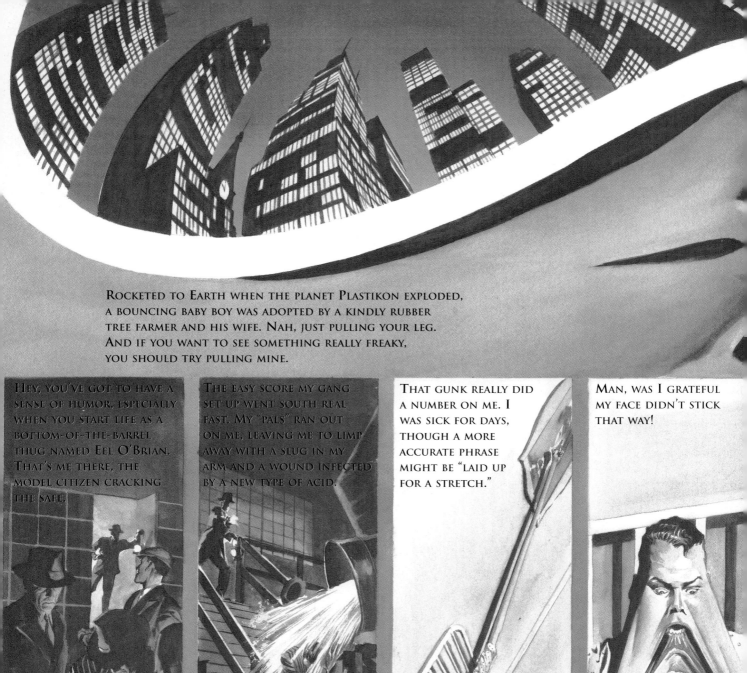

Rocketed to Earth when the planet Plastikon exploded,
a bouncing baby boy was adopted by a kindly rubber
tree farmer and his wife. Nah, just pulling your leg.
And if you want to see something really freaky,
you should try pulling mine.

Hey, you've got to have a sense of humor, especially when you start life as a bottom-of-the-barrel thug named Eel O'Brian. That's me there, the model citizen cracking the safe.

The easy score my gang set-up went south real fast. My "pals" ran out on me, leaving me to limp away with a slug in my arm and a wound infected by a new type of acid.

That gunk really did a number on me. I was sick for days, though a more accurate phrase might be "laid up for a stretch."

Man, was I grateful my face didn't stick that way!

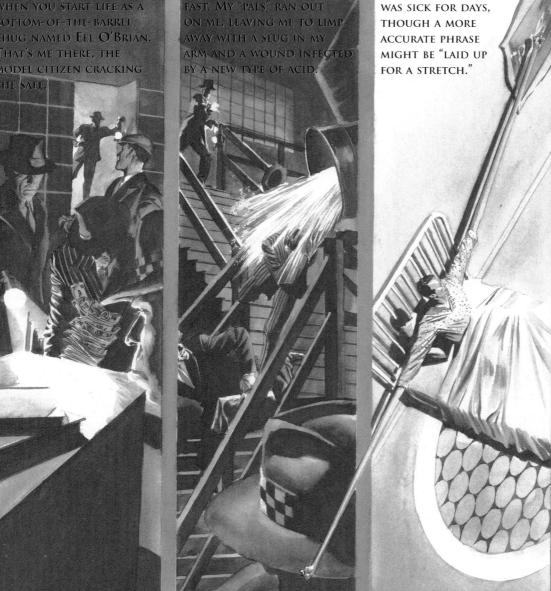

You know the rest—exposure to experimenta chemicals, radical physical changes, yadda yadda, yadda, presto! Instant mega-malleable super hero.

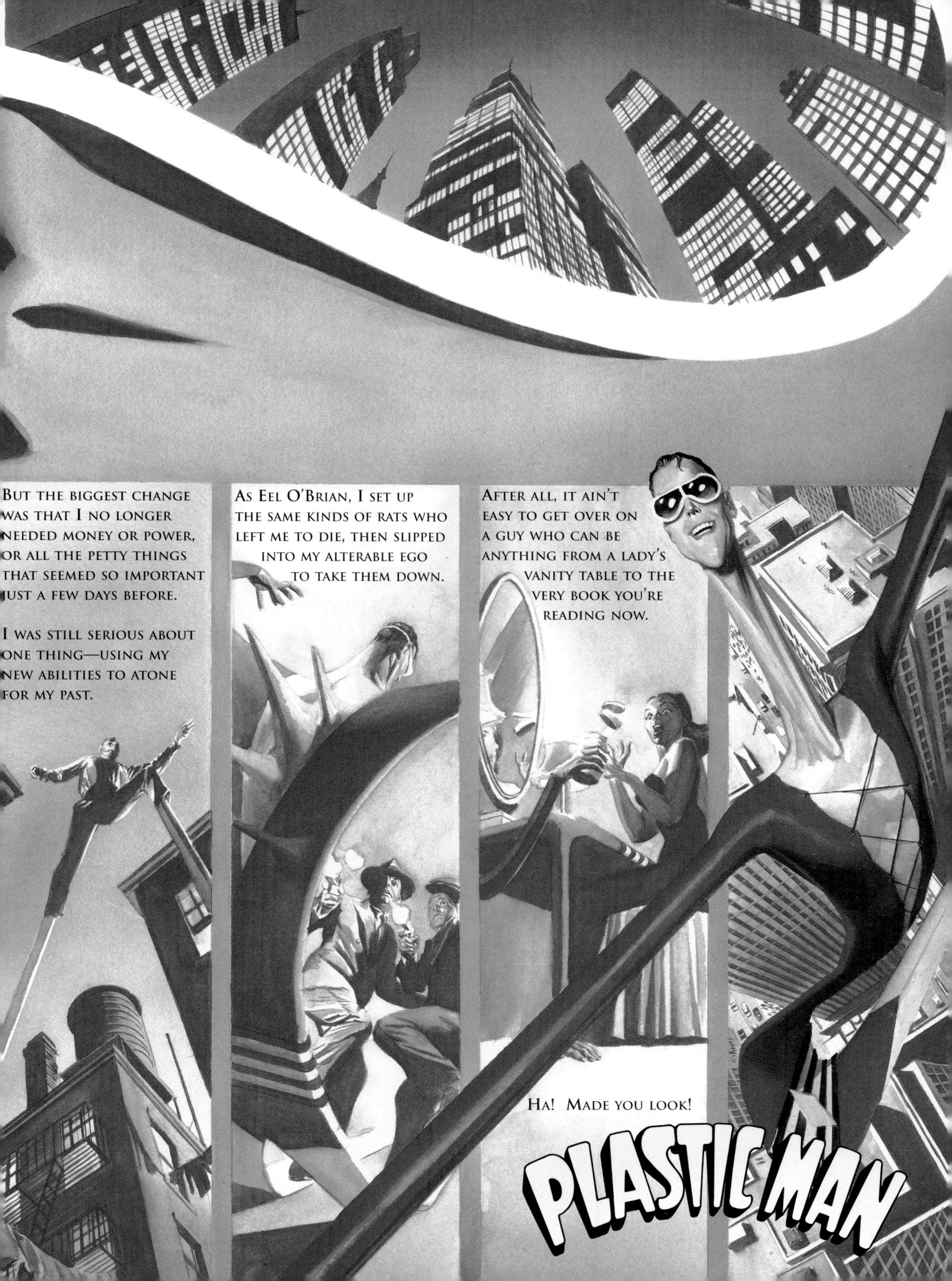
But the biggest change was that I no longer needed money or power, or all the petty things that seemed so important just a few days before.
I was still serious about one thing—using my new abilities to atone for my past.
As Eel O'Brian, I set up the same kinds of rats who left me to die, then slipped into my alterable ego to take them down.
After all, it ain't easy to get over on a guy who can be anything from a lady's vanity table to the very book you're reading now.
Ha! Made you look!
PLASTIC MAN

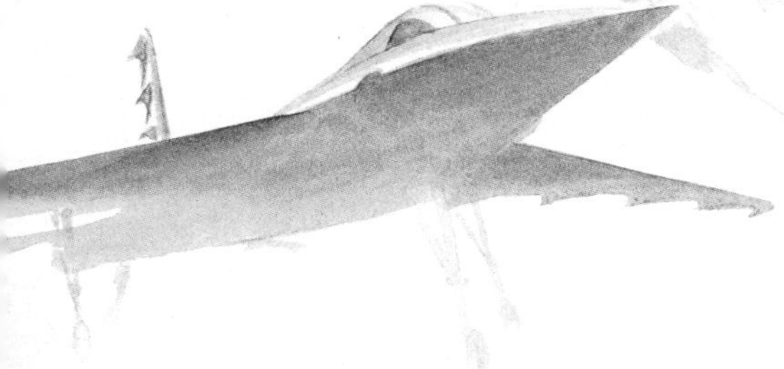

The Flash. Aquaman. Wonder Woman. Green Lantern. Martian Manhunter. Five heroes who banded together to battle a common threat from the stars.

They were soon joined by Superman and Batman, and in time, an extended team of Earth's mightiest protectors was assembled.

Each member brings to the group the deepest commitment to preserving justice and the rights and liberties of all mankind.

Over the years, many other heroes have fought alongside the League, adding their unique abilities and powers to the cause.

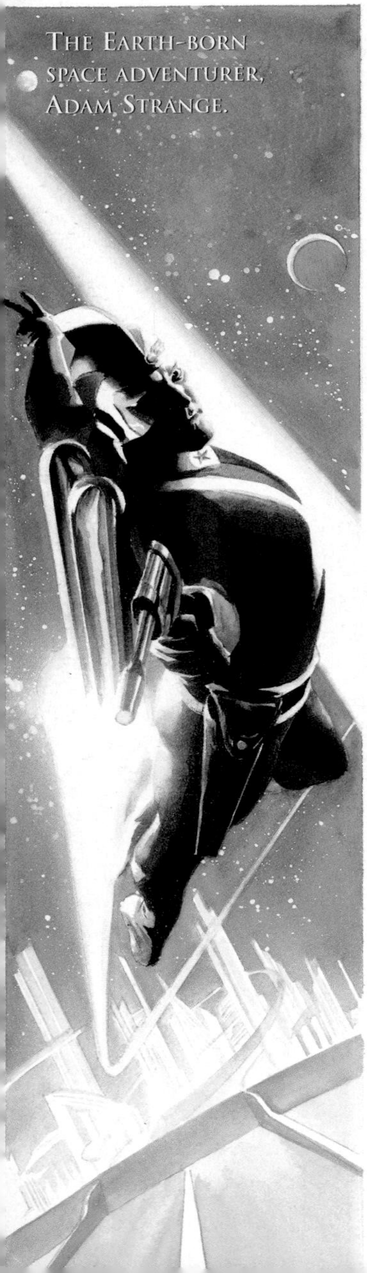

The Earth-born space adventurer, Adam Strange.

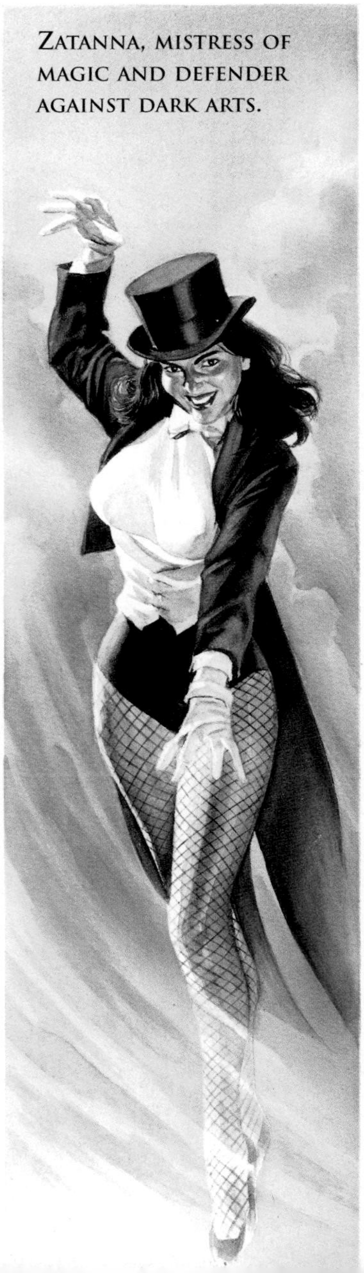

Zatanna, mistress of magic and defender against dark arts.

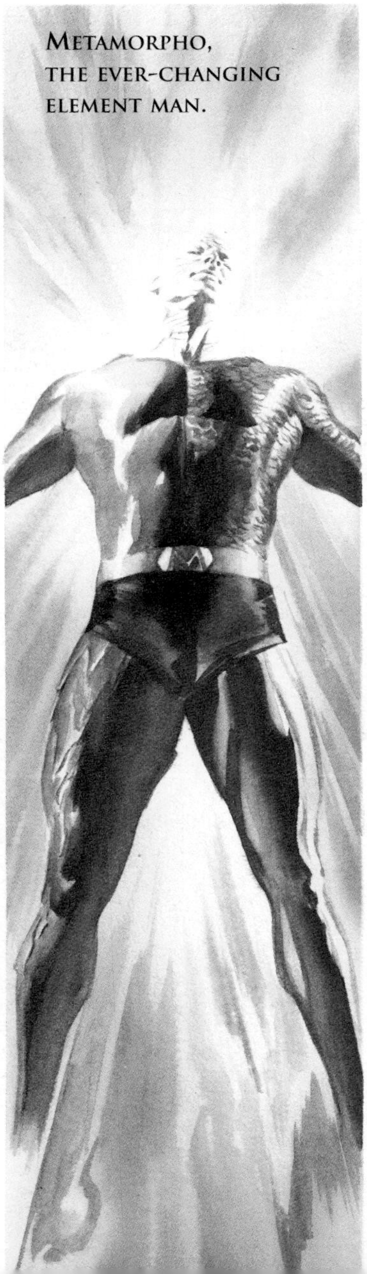

Metamorpho, the ever-changing element man.

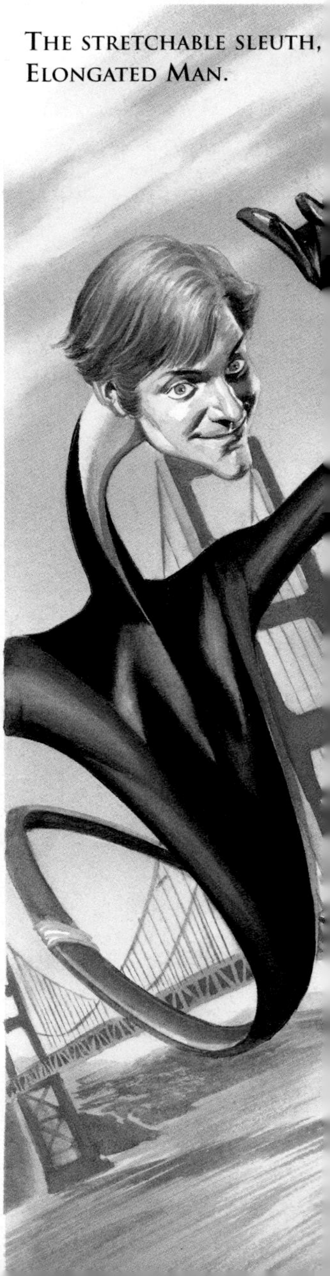

The stretchable sleuth, Elongated Man.

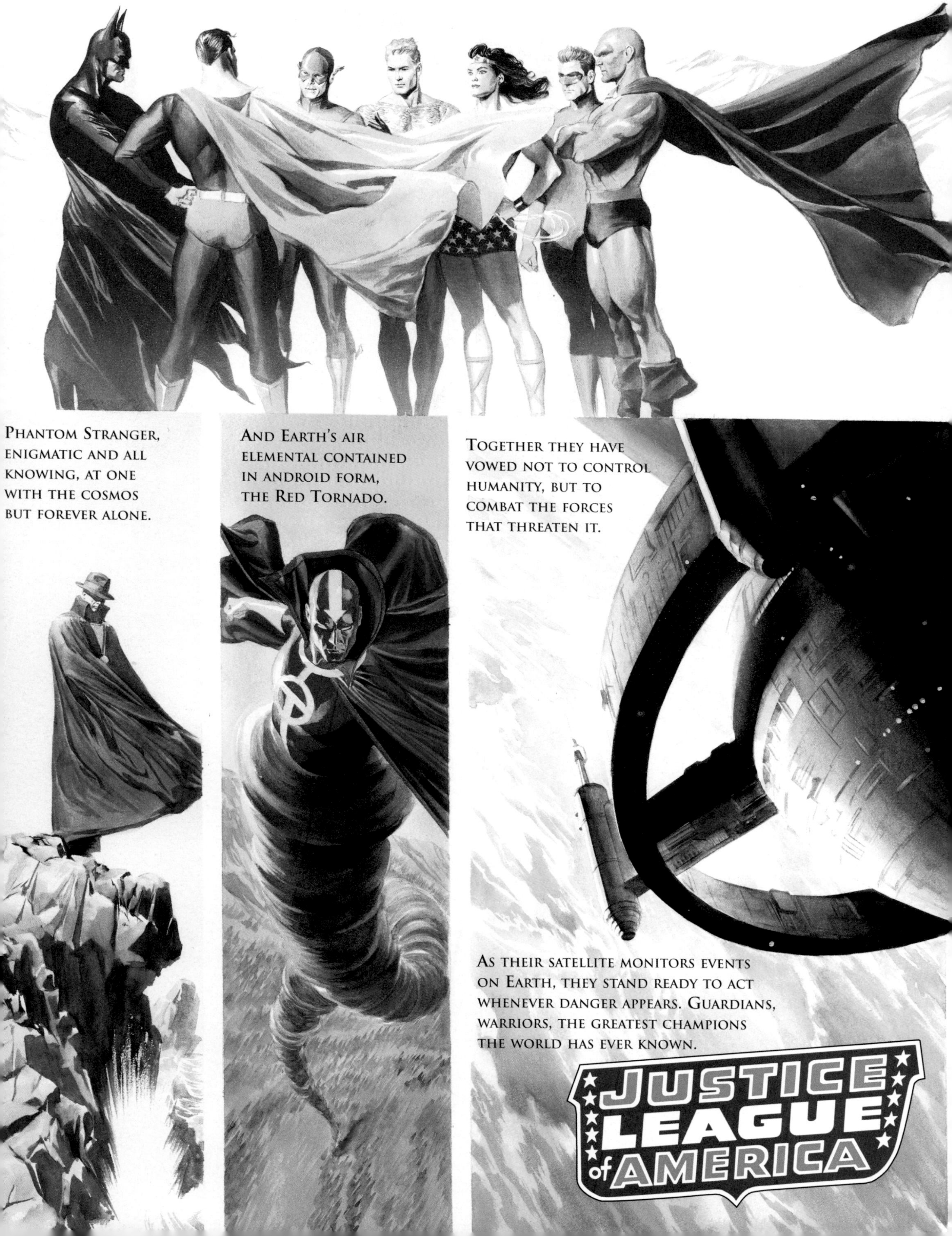
Phantom Stranger, enigmatic and all knowing, at one with the cosmos but forever alone.
And Earth's air elemental contained in android form, the Red Tornado.
Together they have vowed not to control humanity, but to combat the forces that threaten it.
As their satellite monitors events on Earth, they stand ready to act whenever danger appears. Guardians, warriors, the greatest champions the world has ever known.
Justice League of America

LIBERTY AND

J'ONN J'ONZZ
**THE MARTIAN
MANHUNTER**

CLARK KENT
SUPERMAN

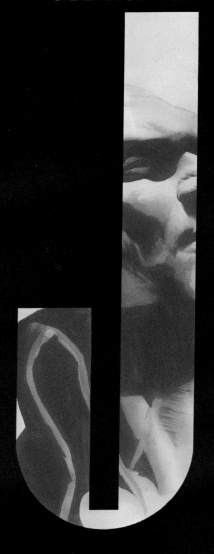

HAL JORDAN
GREEN LANTERN

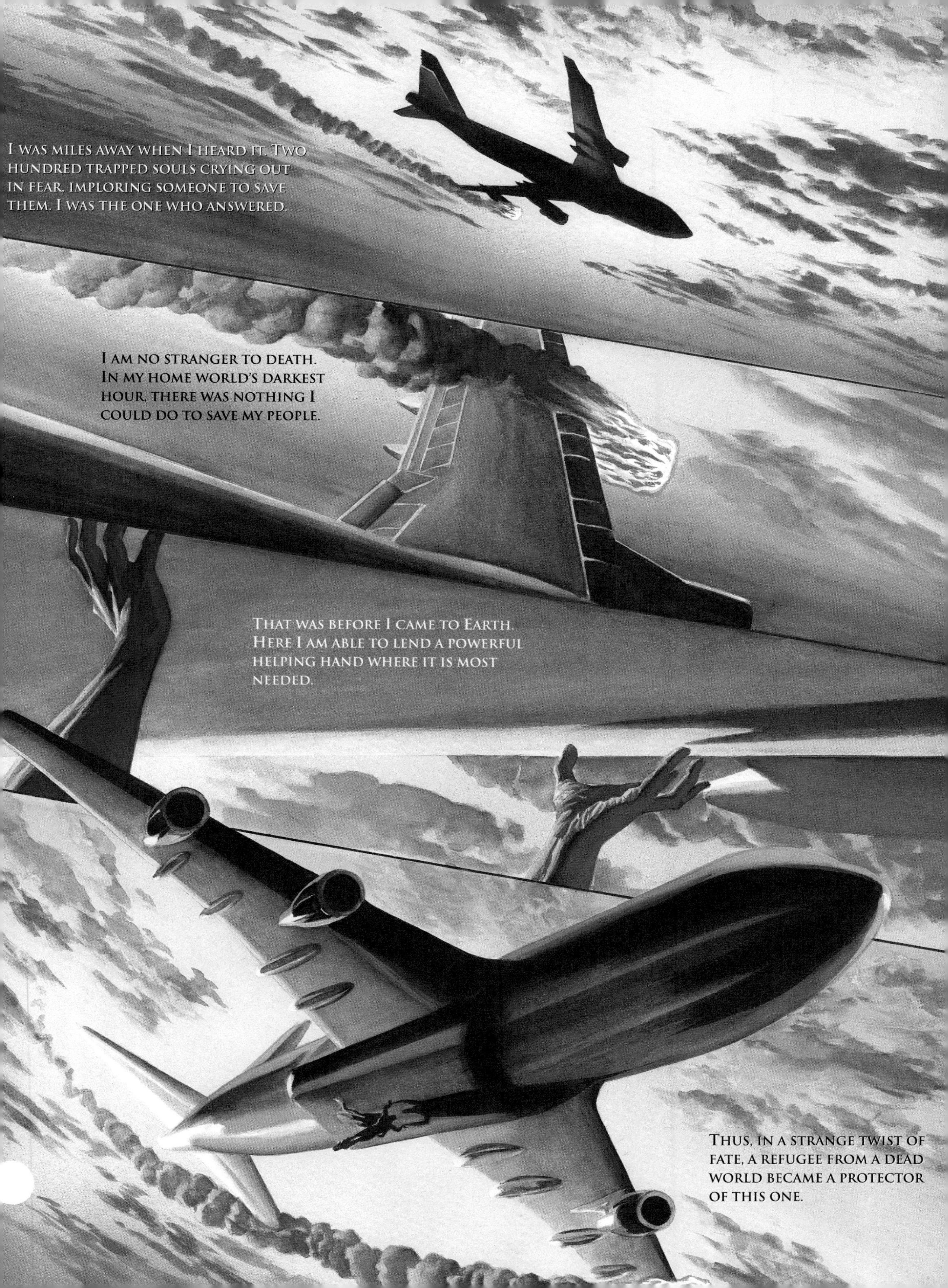
I was miles away when I heard it. Two hundred trapped souls crying out in fear, imploring someone to save them. I was the one who answered.
I am no stranger to death. In my home world's darkest hour, there was nothing I could do to save my people.
That was before I came to Earth. Here I am able to lend a powerful helping hand where it is most needed.
Thus, in a strange twist of fate, a refugee from a dead world became a protector of this one.

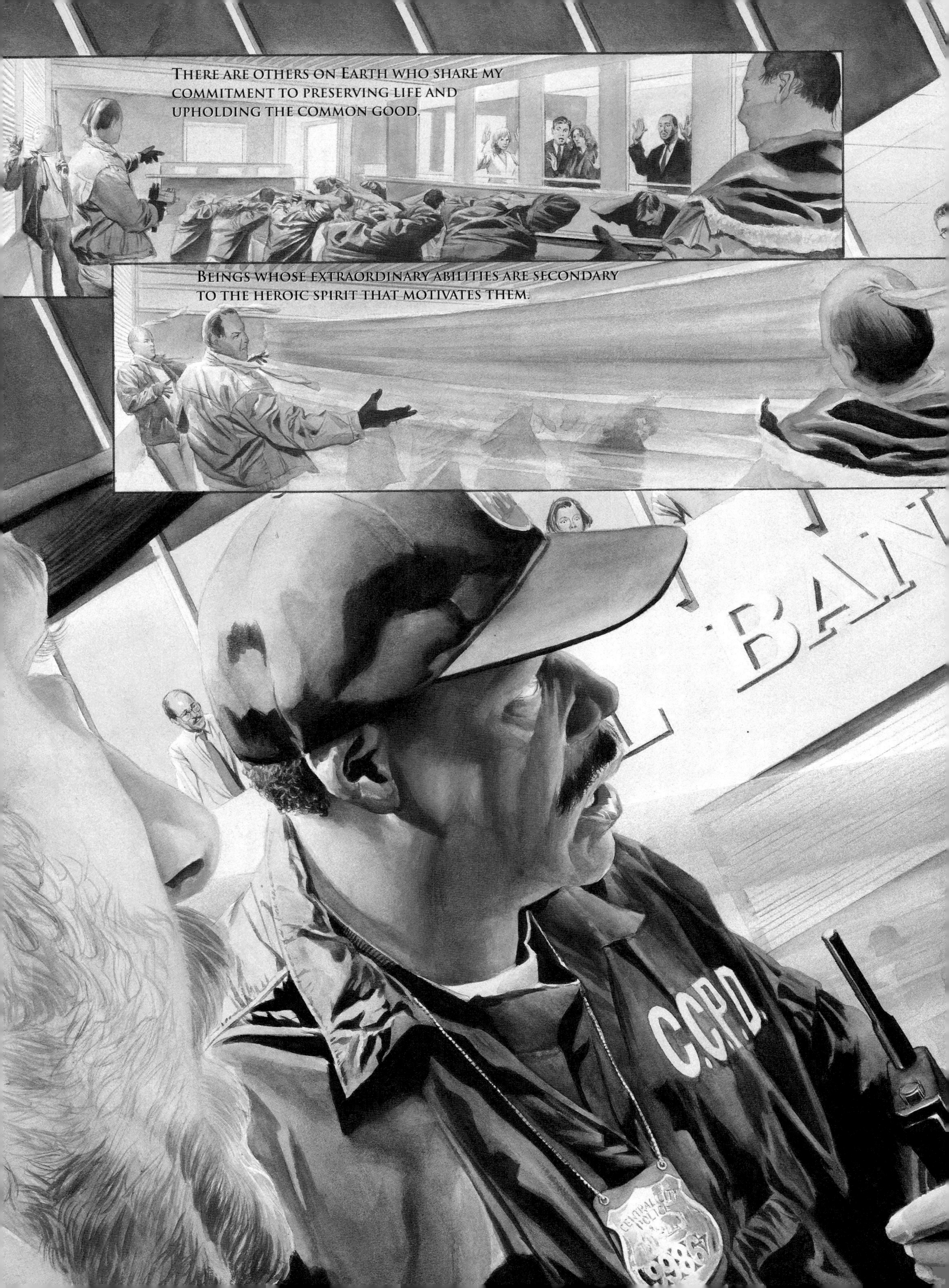
There are others on Earth who share my commitment to preserving life and upholding the common good.
Beings whose extraordinary abilities are secondary to the heroic spirit that motivates them.
C.C.P.D.

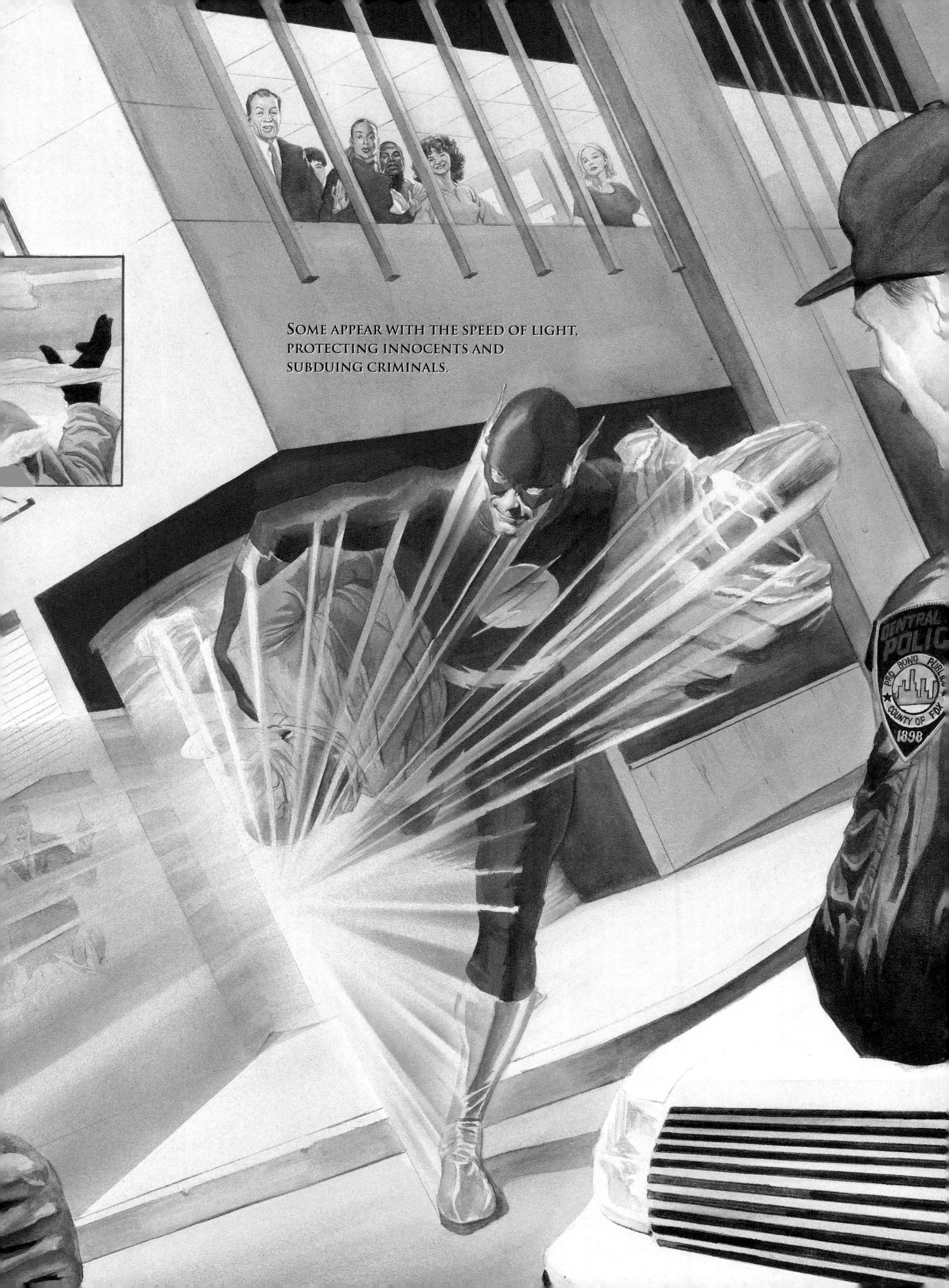
SOME APPEAR WITH THE SPEED OF LIGHT, PROTECTING INNOCENTS AND SUBDUING CRIMINALS.
PRO BONO PUBLIC
COUNTY OF FOX
1898

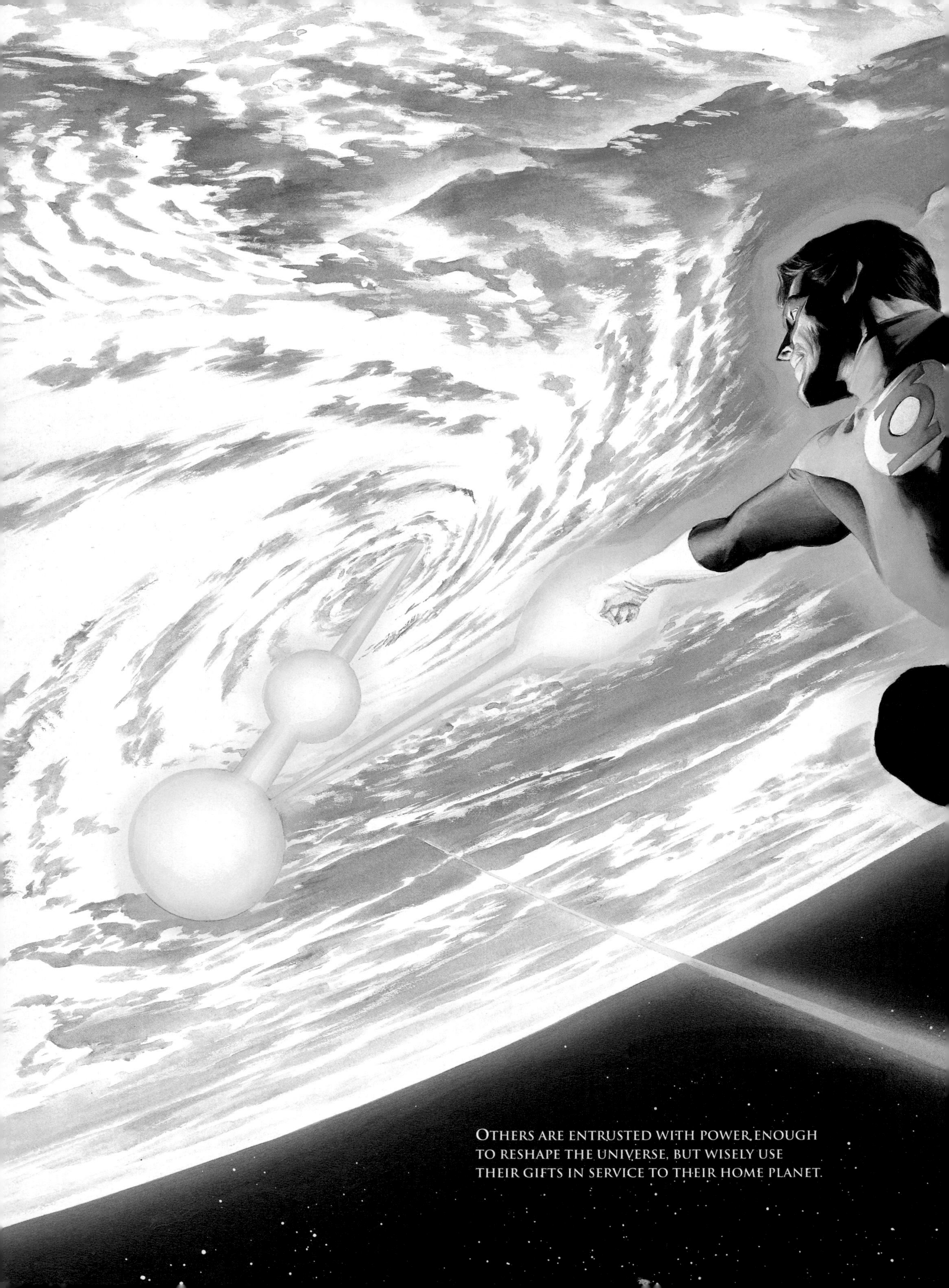
OTHERS ARE ENTRUSTED WITH POWER ENOUGH
TO RESHAPE THE UNIVERSE, BUT WISELY USE
THEIR GIFTS IN SERVICE TO THEIR HOME PLANET.

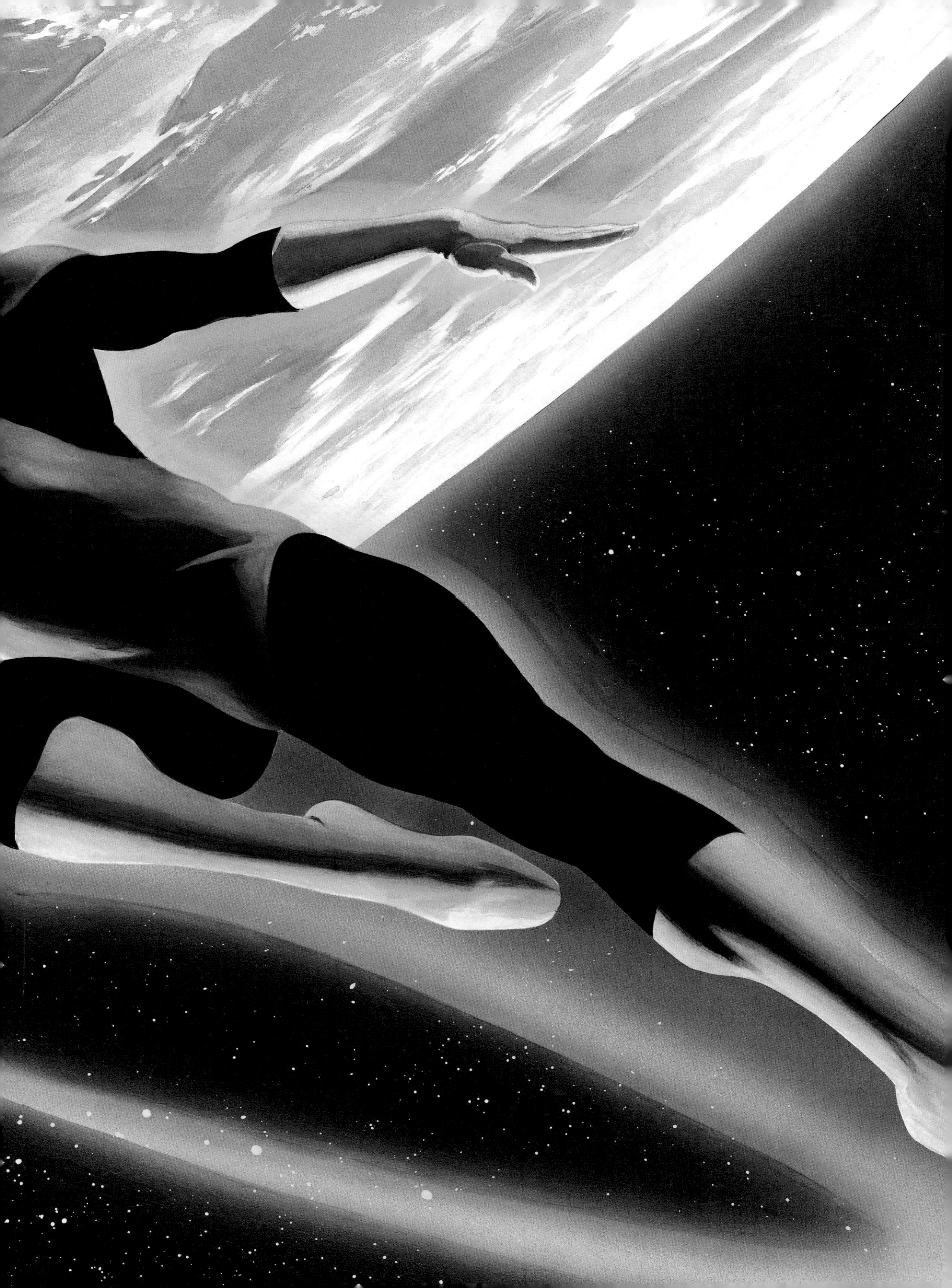

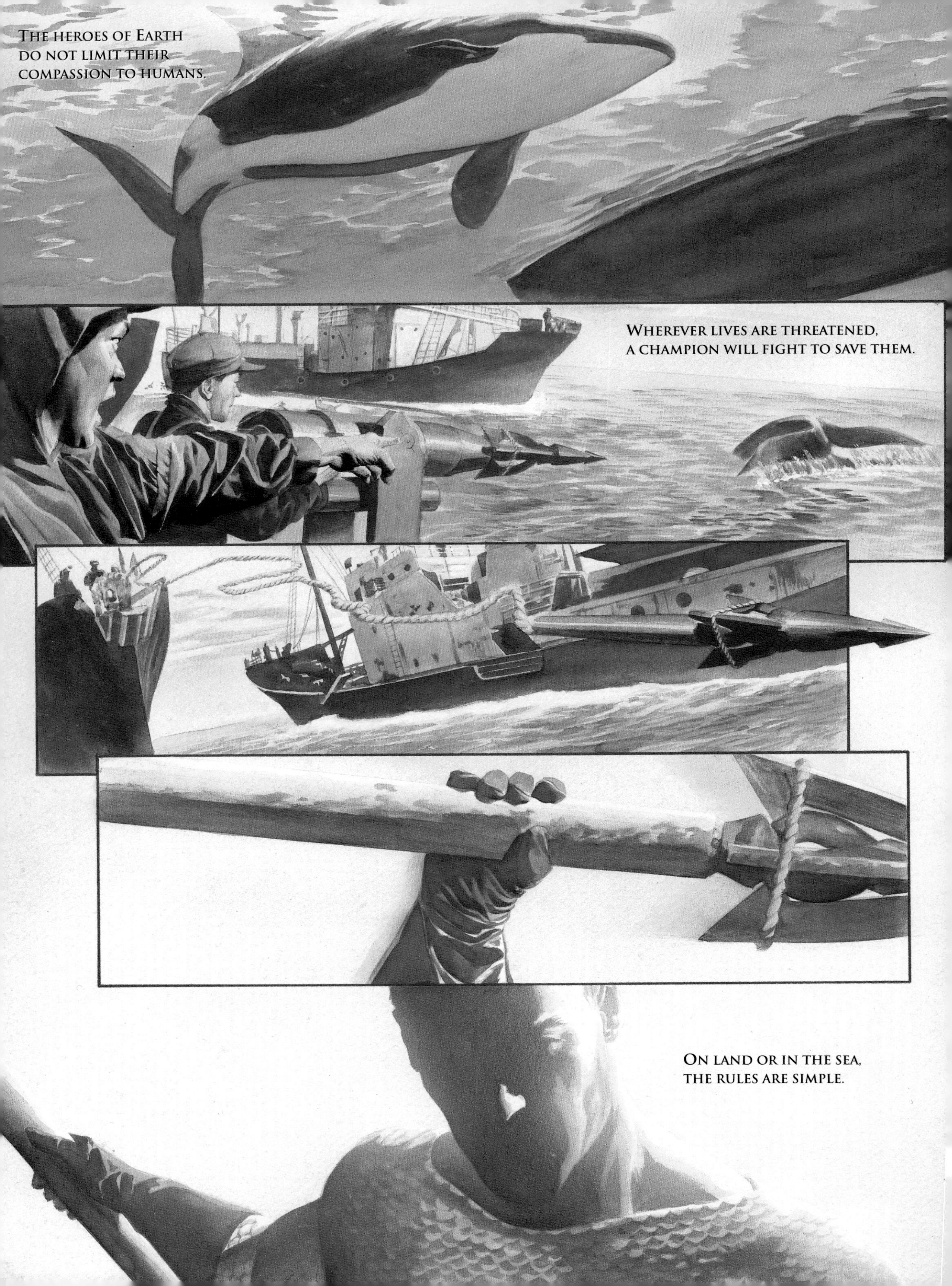
The heroes of Earth do not limit their compassion to humans.
Wherever lives are threatened, a champion will fight to save them.
On land or in the sea, the rules are simple.

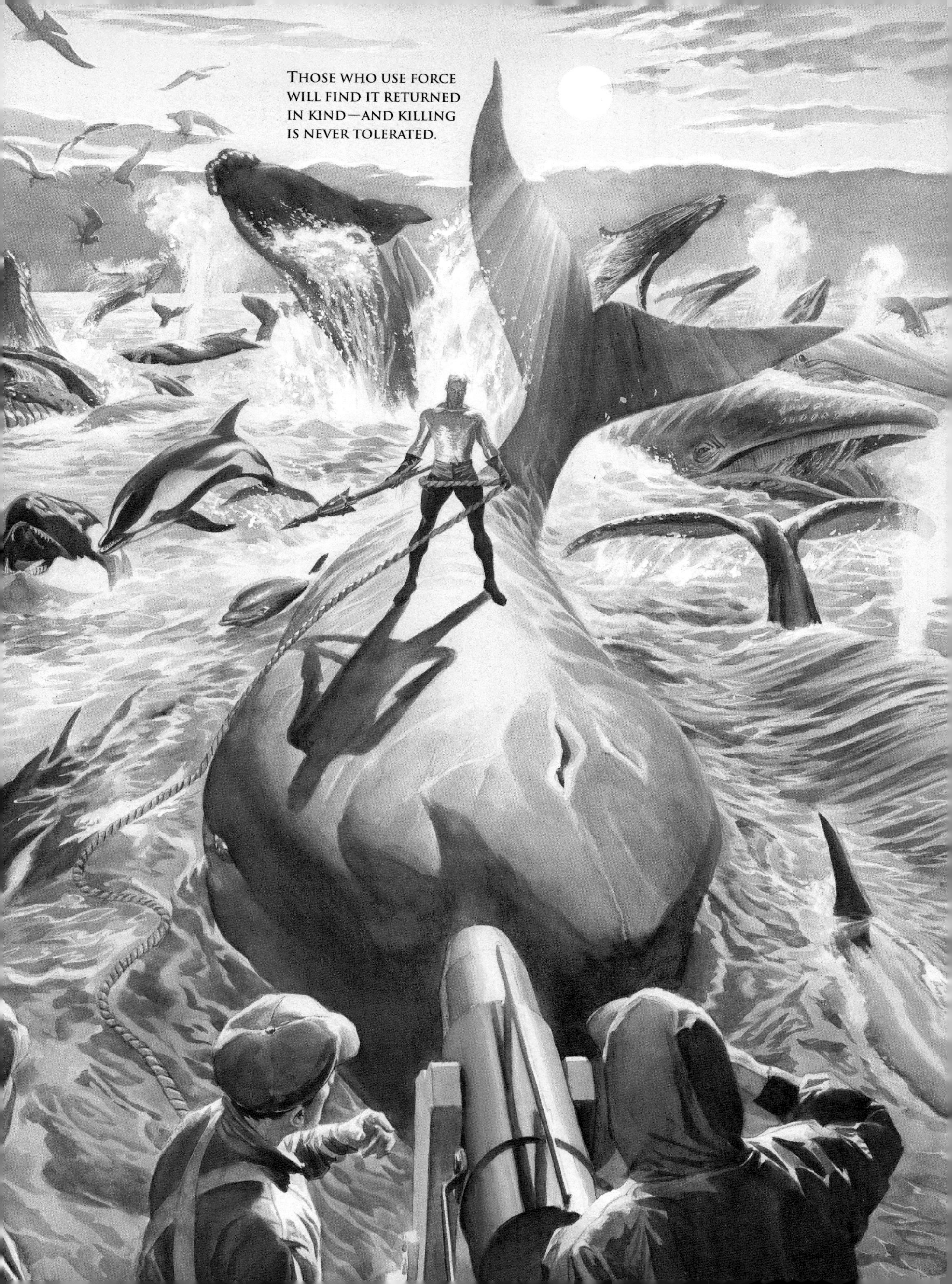
THOSE WHO USE FORCE WILL FIND IT RETURNED IN KIND—AND KILLING IS NEVER TOLERATED.

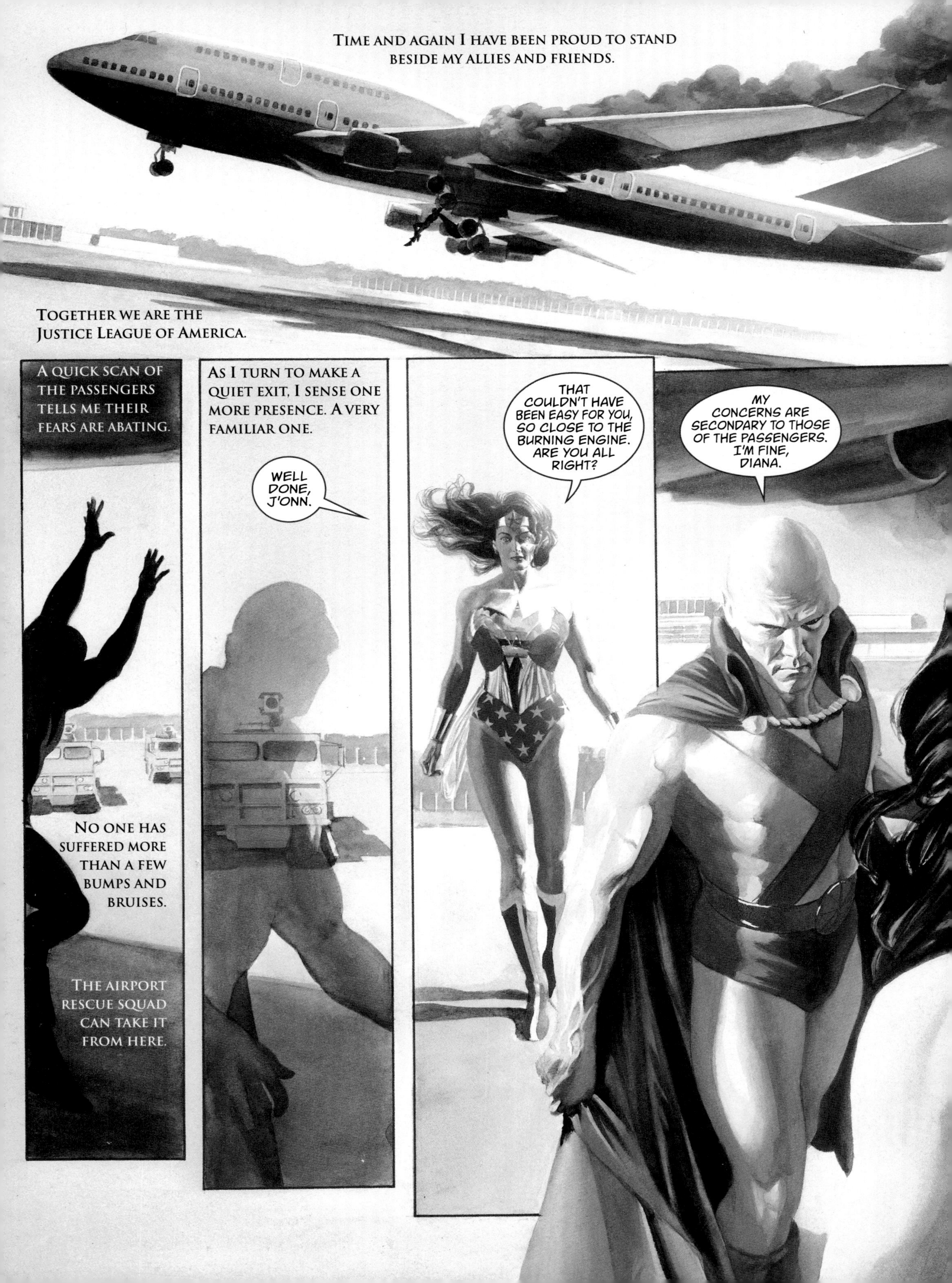

Time and again I have been proud to stand beside my allies and friends.
Together we are the Justice League of America.
A quick scan of the passengers tells me their fears are abating.
No one has suffered more than a few bumps and bruises.
The airport rescue squad can take it from here.
As I turn to make a quiet exit, I sense one more presence. A very familiar one.
WELL DONE, J'ONN.
THAT COULDN'T HAVE BEEN EASY FOR YOU, SO CLOSE TO THE BURNING ENGINE. ARE YOU ALL RIGHT?
MY CONCERNS ARE SECONDARY TO THOSE OF THE PASSENGERS. I'M FINE, DIANA.

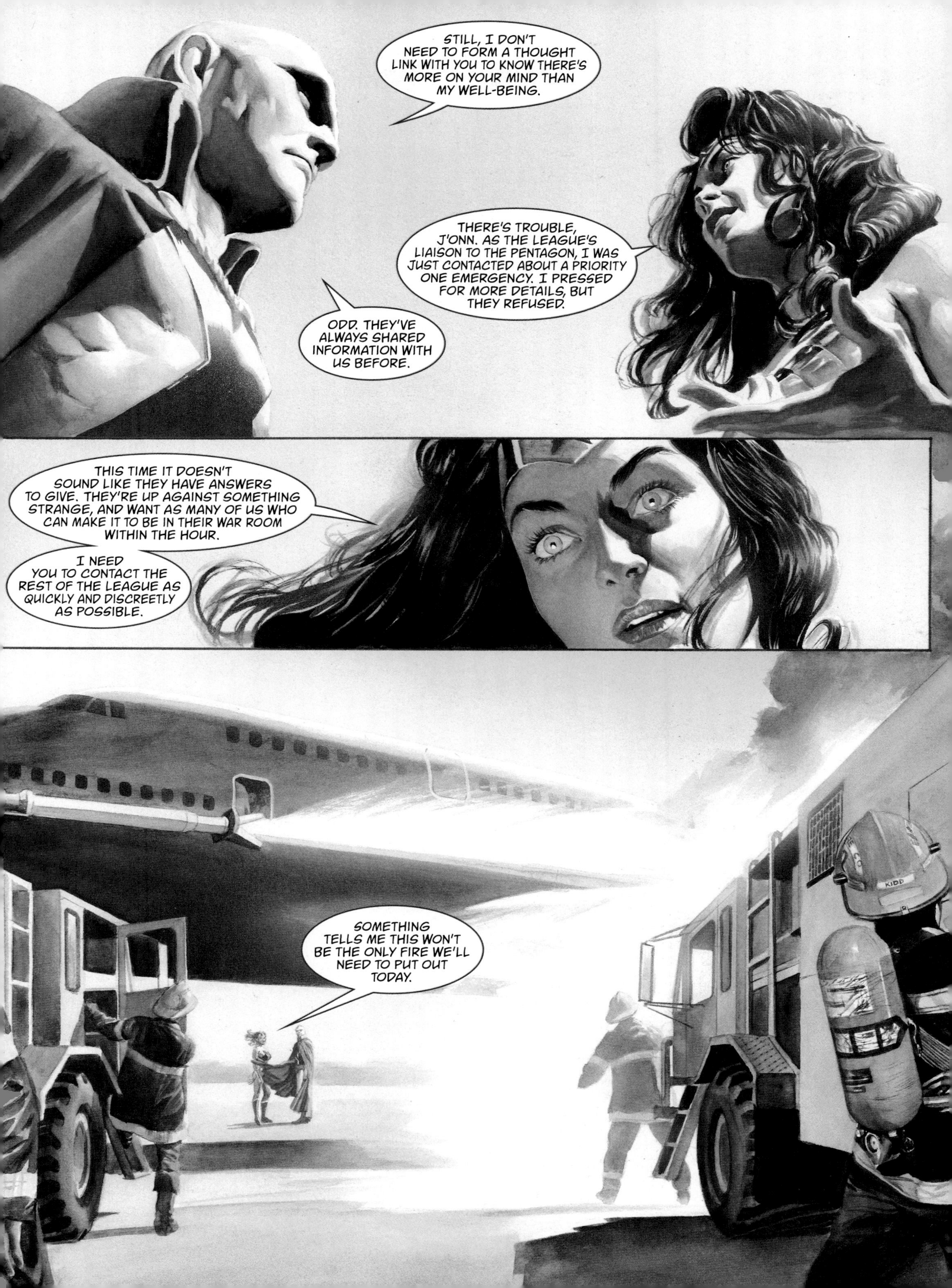
STILL, I DON'T NEED TO FORM A THOUGHT LINK WITH YOU TO KNOW THERE'S MORE ON YOUR MIND THAN MY WELL-BEING.
THERE'S TROUBLE, J'ONN. AS THE LEAGUE'S LIAISON TO THE PENTAGON, I WAS JUST CONTACTED ABOUT A PRIORITY ONE EMERGENCY. I PRESSED FOR MORE DETAILS, BUT THEY REFUSED.
ODD. THEY'VE ALWAYS SHARED INFORMATION WITH US BEFORE.
THIS TIME IT DOESN'T SOUND LIKE THEY HAVE ANSWERS TO GIVE. THEY'RE UP AGAINST SOMETHING STRANGE, AND WANT AS MANY OF US WHO CAN MAKE IT TO BE IN THEIR WAR ROOM WITHIN THE HOUR.
I NEED YOU TO CONTACT THE REST OF THE LEAGUE AS QUICKLY AND DISCREETLY AS POSSIBLE.
SOMETHING TELLS ME THIS WON'T BE THE ONLY FIRE WE'LL NEED TO PUT OUT TODAY.
KIDD

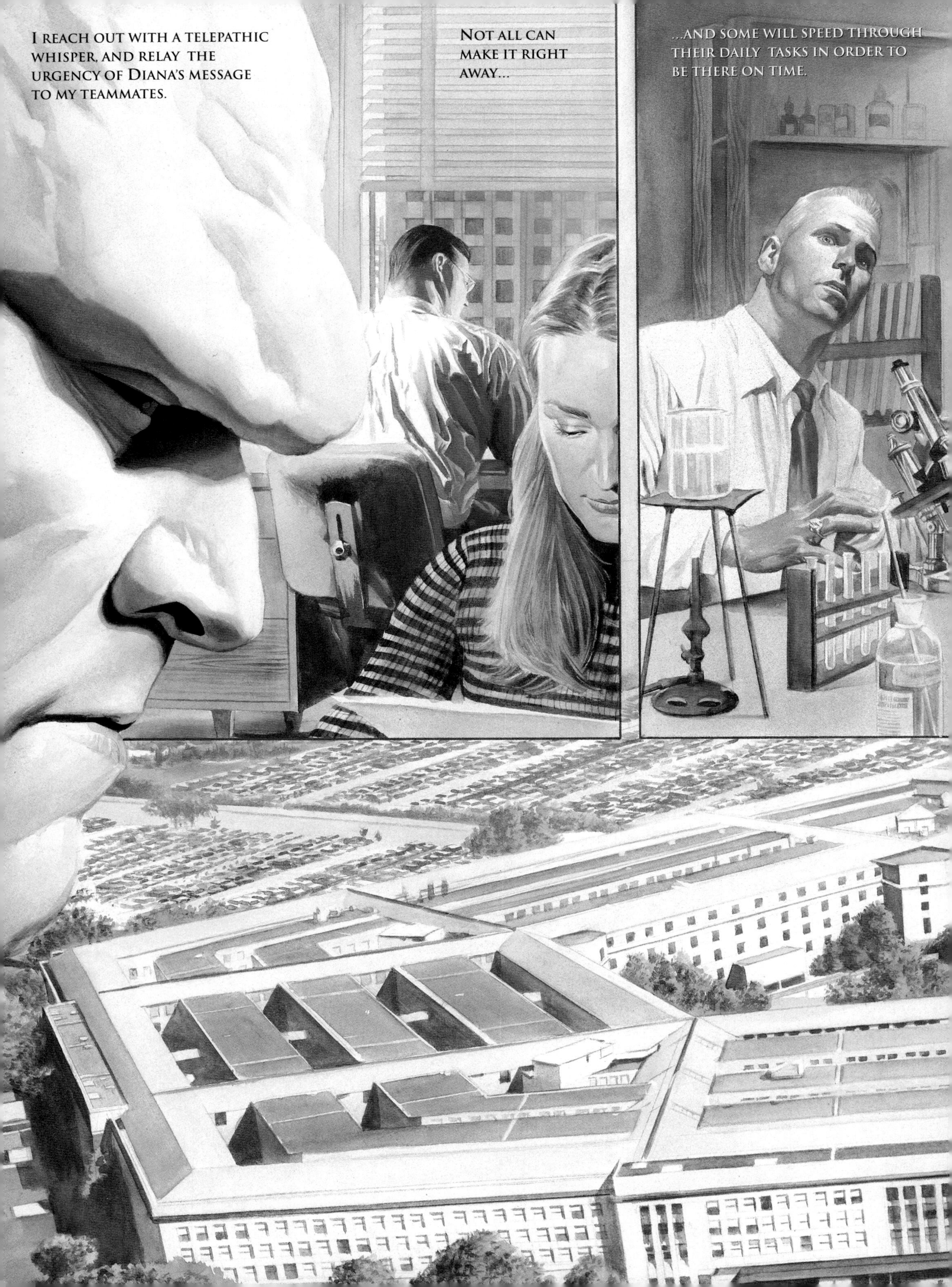
I REACH OUT WITH A TELEPATHIC WHISPER, AND RELAY THE URGENCY OF DIANA'S MESSAGE TO MY TEAMMATES.
NOT ALL CAN MAKE IT RIGHT AWAY...
...AND SOME WILL SPEED THROUGH THEIR DAILY TASKS IN ORDER TO BE THERE ON TIME.

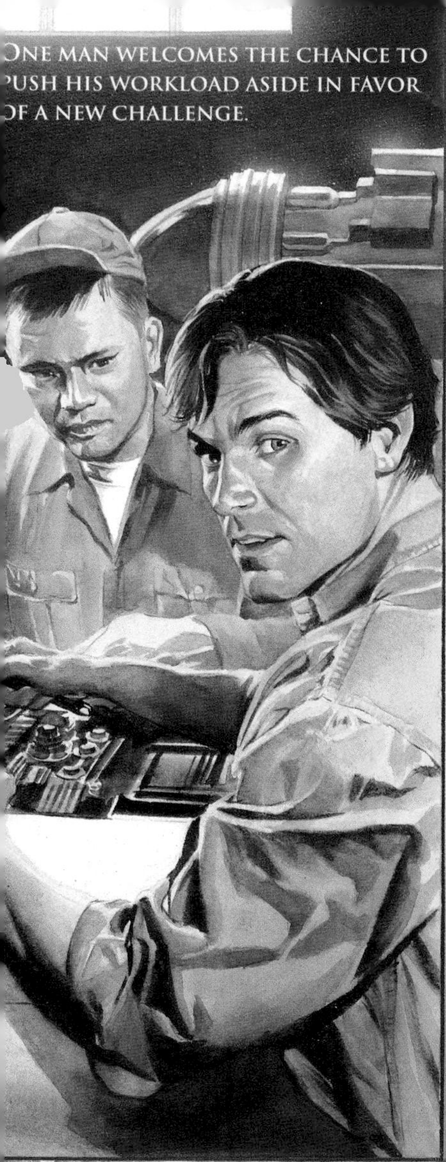
ONE MAN WELCOMES THE CHANCE TO PUSH HIS WORKLOAD ASIDE IN FAVOR OF A NEW CHALLENGE.

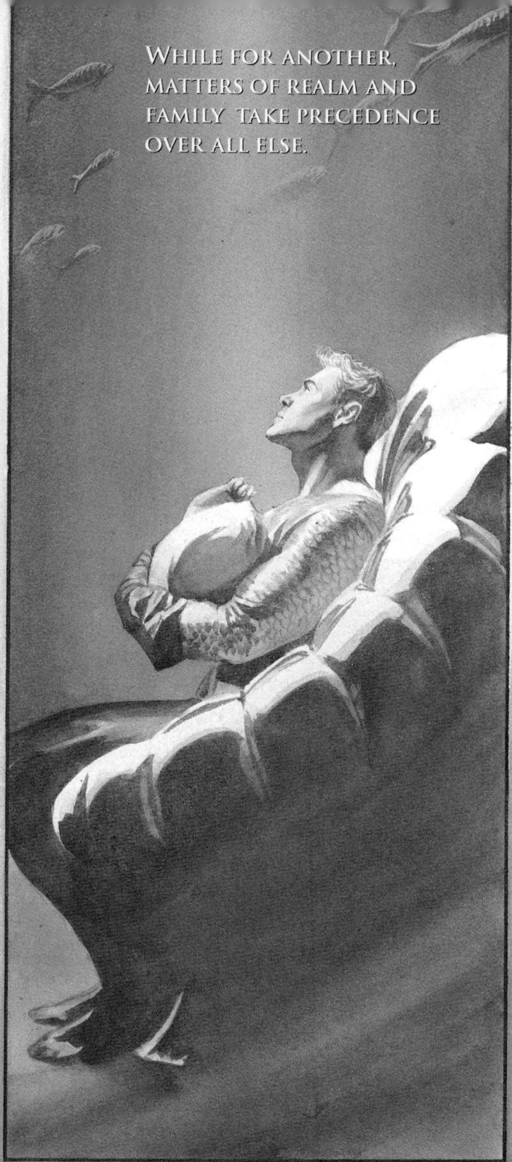
WHILE FOR ANOTHER, MATTERS OF REALM AND FAMILY TAKE PRECEDENCE OVER ALL ELSE.

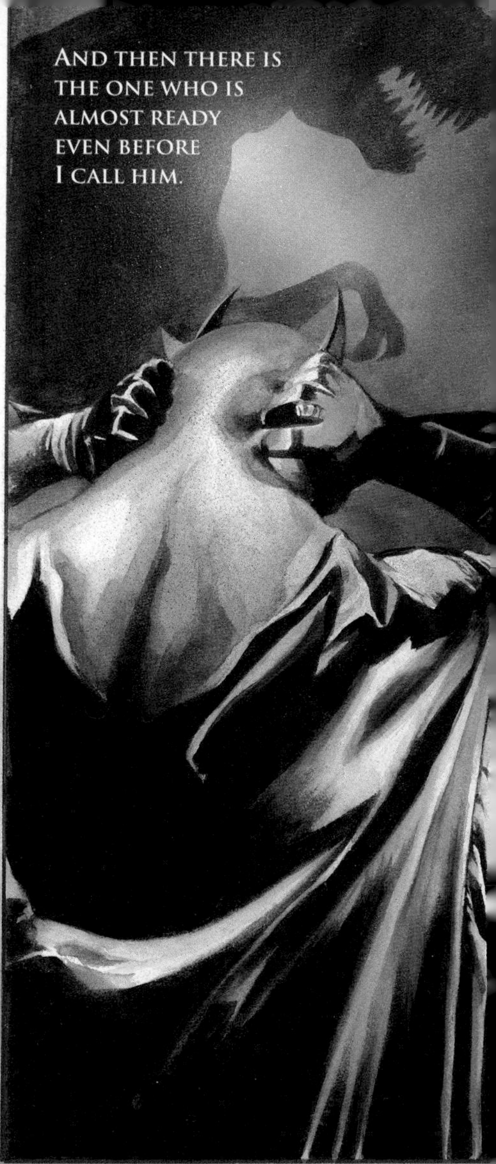
AND THEN THERE IS THE ONE WHO IS ALMOST READY EVEN BEFORE I CALL HIM.

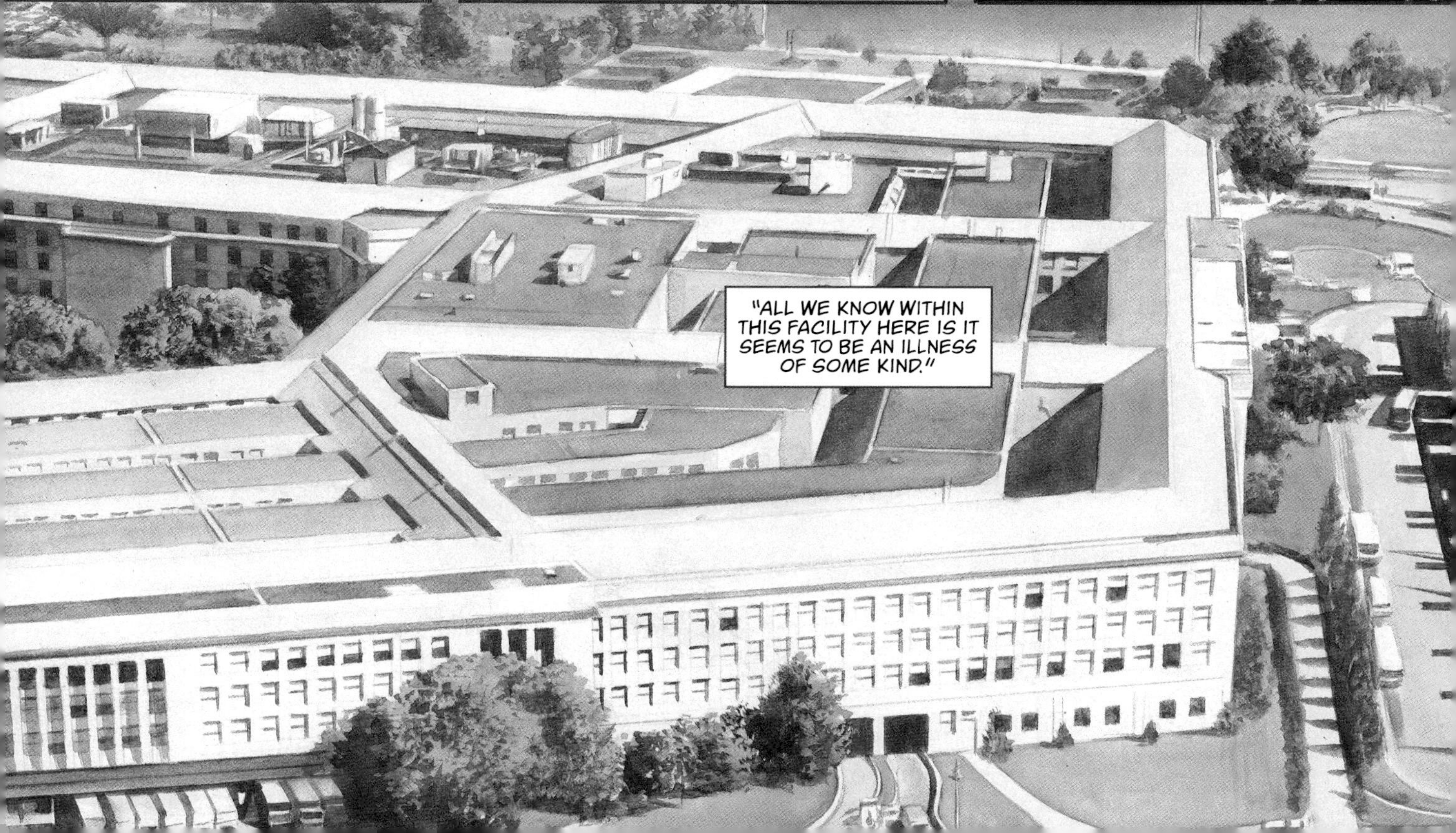
"ALL WE KNOW WITHIN THIS FACILITY HERE IS IT SEEMS TO BE AN ILLNESS OF SOME KIND."

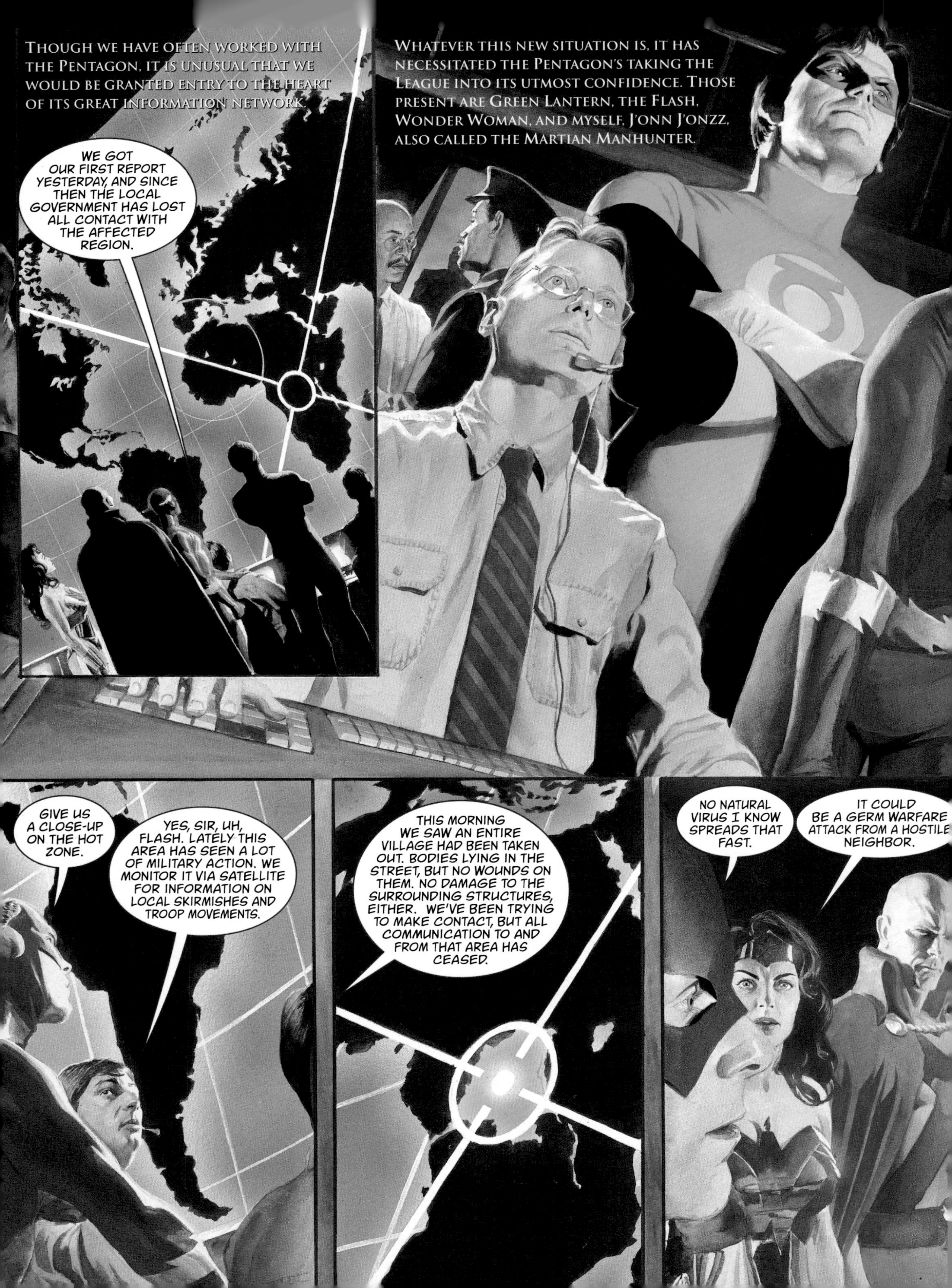
Though we have often worked with the Pentagon, it is unusual that we would be granted entry to the heart of its great information network.
WE GOT OUR FIRST REPORT YESTERDAY, AND SINCE THEN THE LOCAL GOVERNMENT HAS LOST ALL CONTACT WITH THE AFFECTED REGION.
Whatever this new situation is, it has necessitated the Pentagon's taking the League into its utmost confidence. Those present are Green Lantern, the Flash, Wonder Woman, and myself, J'onn J'onzz, also called the Martian Manhunter.
GIVE US A CLOSE-UP ON THE HOT ZONE.
YES, SIR, UH, FLASH. LATELY THIS AREA HAS SEEN A LOT OF MILITARY ACTION. WE MONITOR IT VIA SATELLITE FOR INFORMATION ON LOCAL SKIRMISHES AND TROOP MOVEMENTS.
THIS MORNING WE SAW AN ENTIRE VILLAGE HAD BEEN TAKEN OUT. BODIES LYING IN THE STREET, BUT NO WOUNDS ON THEM. NO DAMAGE TO THE SURROUNDING STRUCTURES, EITHER. WE'VE BEEN TRYING TO MAKE CONTACT, BUT ALL COMMUNICATION TO AND FROM THAT AREA HAS CEASED.
NO NATURAL VIRUS I KNOW SPREADS THAT FAST.
IT COULD BE A GERM WARFARE ATTACK FROM A HOSTILE NEIGHBOR.

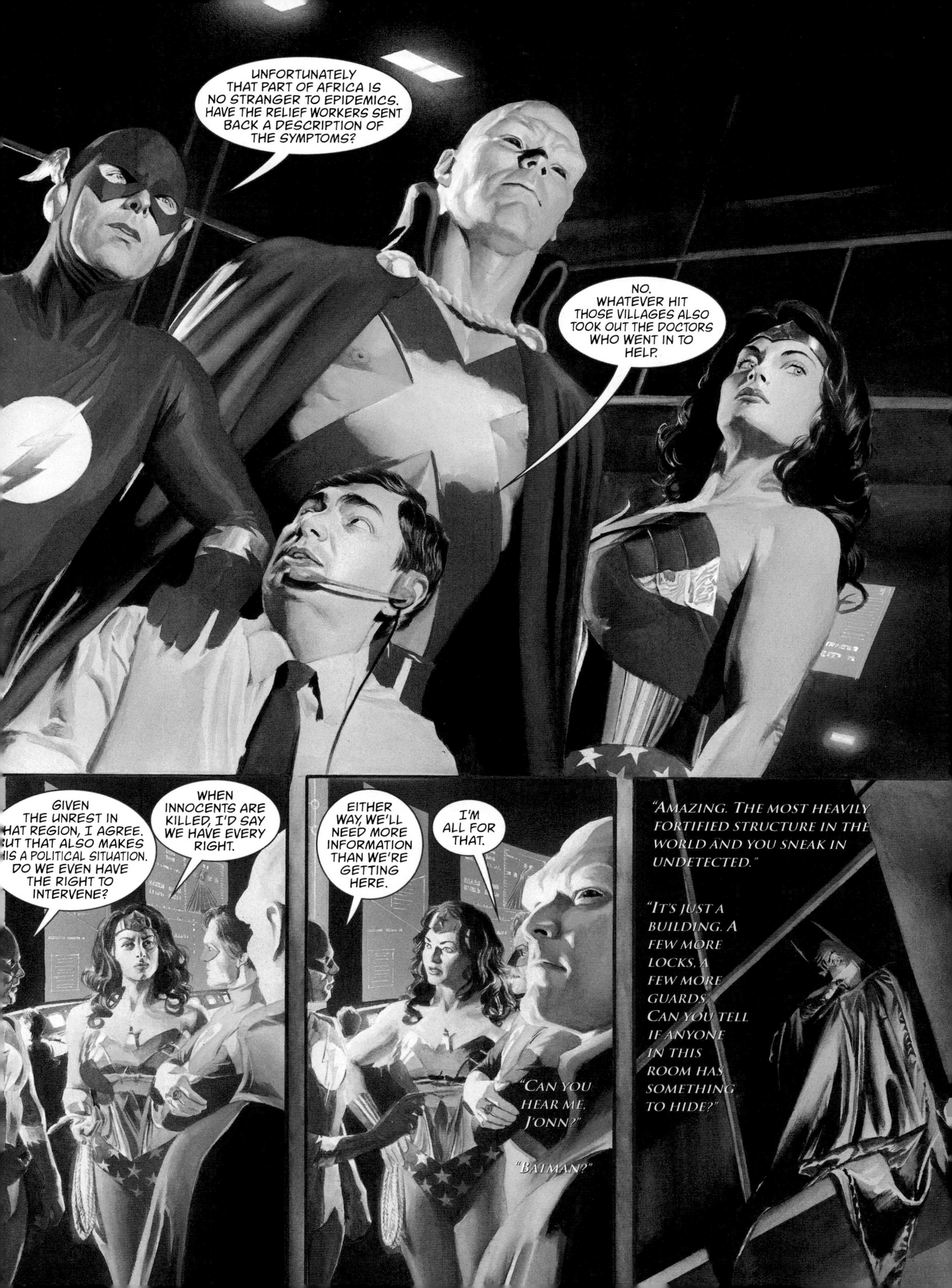
UNFORTUNATELY THAT PART OF AFRICA IS NO STRANGER TO EPIDEMICS. HAVE THE RELIEF WORKERS SENT BACK A DESCRIPTION OF THE SYMPTOMS?
NO. WHATEVER HIT THOSE VILLAGES ALSO TOOK OUT THE DOCTORS WHO WENT IN TO HELP.
GIVEN THE UNREST IN HAT REGION, I AGREE. UT THAT ALSO MAKES IS A POLITICAL SITUATION. DO WE EVEN HAVE THE RIGHT TO INTERVENE?
WHEN INNOCENTS ARE KILLED, I'D SAY WE HAVE EVERY RIGHT.
EITHER WAY, WE'LL NEED MORE INFORMATION THAN WE'RE GETTING HERE.
I'M ALL FOR THAT.
"CAN YOU HEAR ME, J'ONN?"
"BATMAN?"
"AMAZING. THE MOST HEAVILY FORTIFIED STRUCTURE IN THE WORLD AND YOU SNEAK IN UNDETECTED."
"IT'S JUST A BUILDING. A FEW MORE LOCKS, A FEW MORE GUARDS. CAN YOU TELL IF ANYONE IN THIS ROOM HAS SOMETHING TO HIDE?"

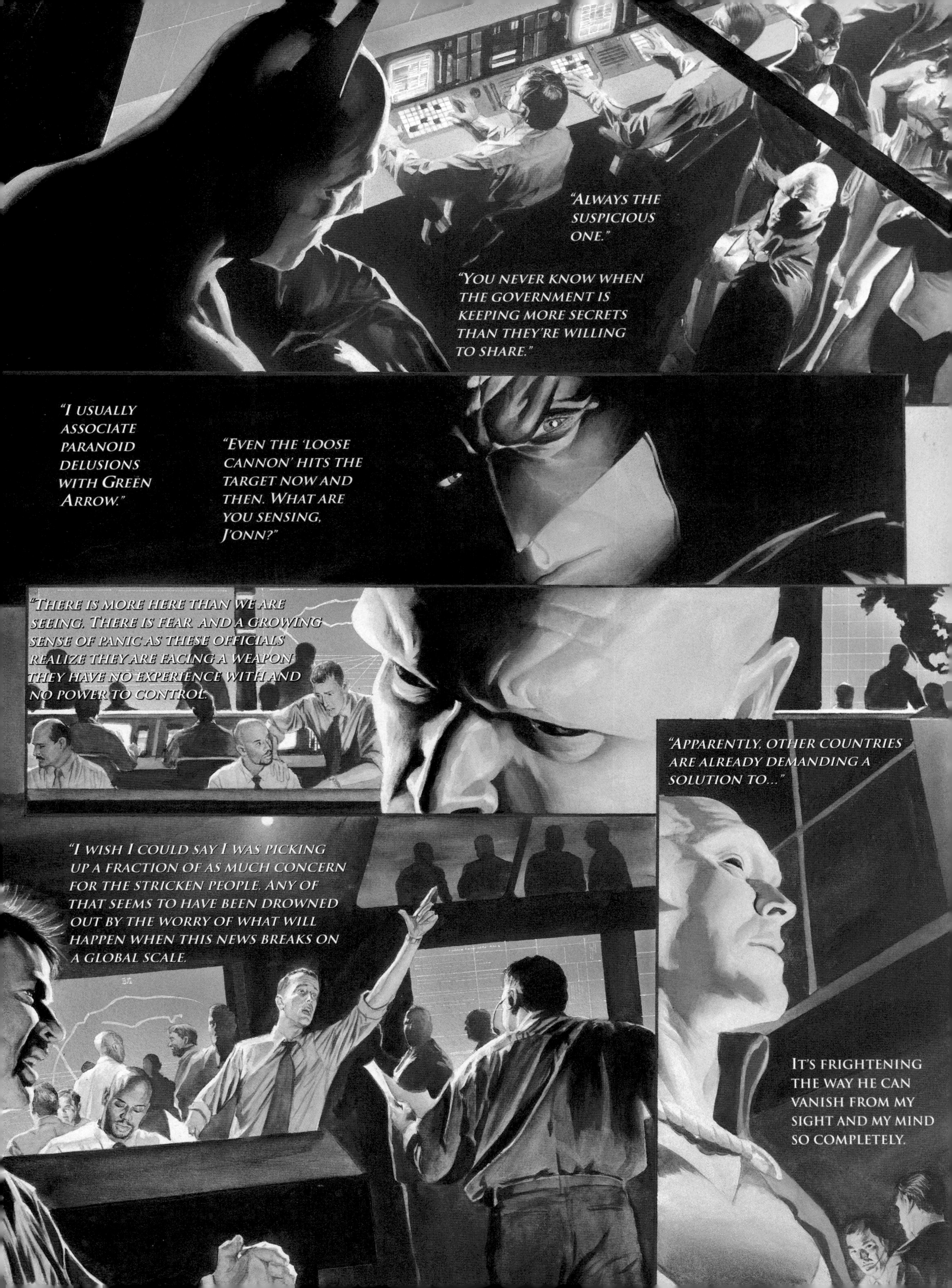
"Always the suspicious one."
"You never know when the government is keeping more secrets than they're willing to share."
"I usually associate paranoid delusions with Green Arrow."
"Even the 'loose cannon' hits the target now and then. What are you sensing, J'onn?"
"There is more here than we are seeing. There is fear and a growing sense of panic as these officials realize they are facing a weapon they have no experience with and no power to control.
"Apparently, other countries are already demanding a solution to..."
"I wish I could say I was picking up a fraction of as much concern for the stricken people. Any of that seems to have been drowned out by the worry of what will happen when this news breaks on a global scale.
It's frightening the way he can vanish from my sight and my mind so completely.

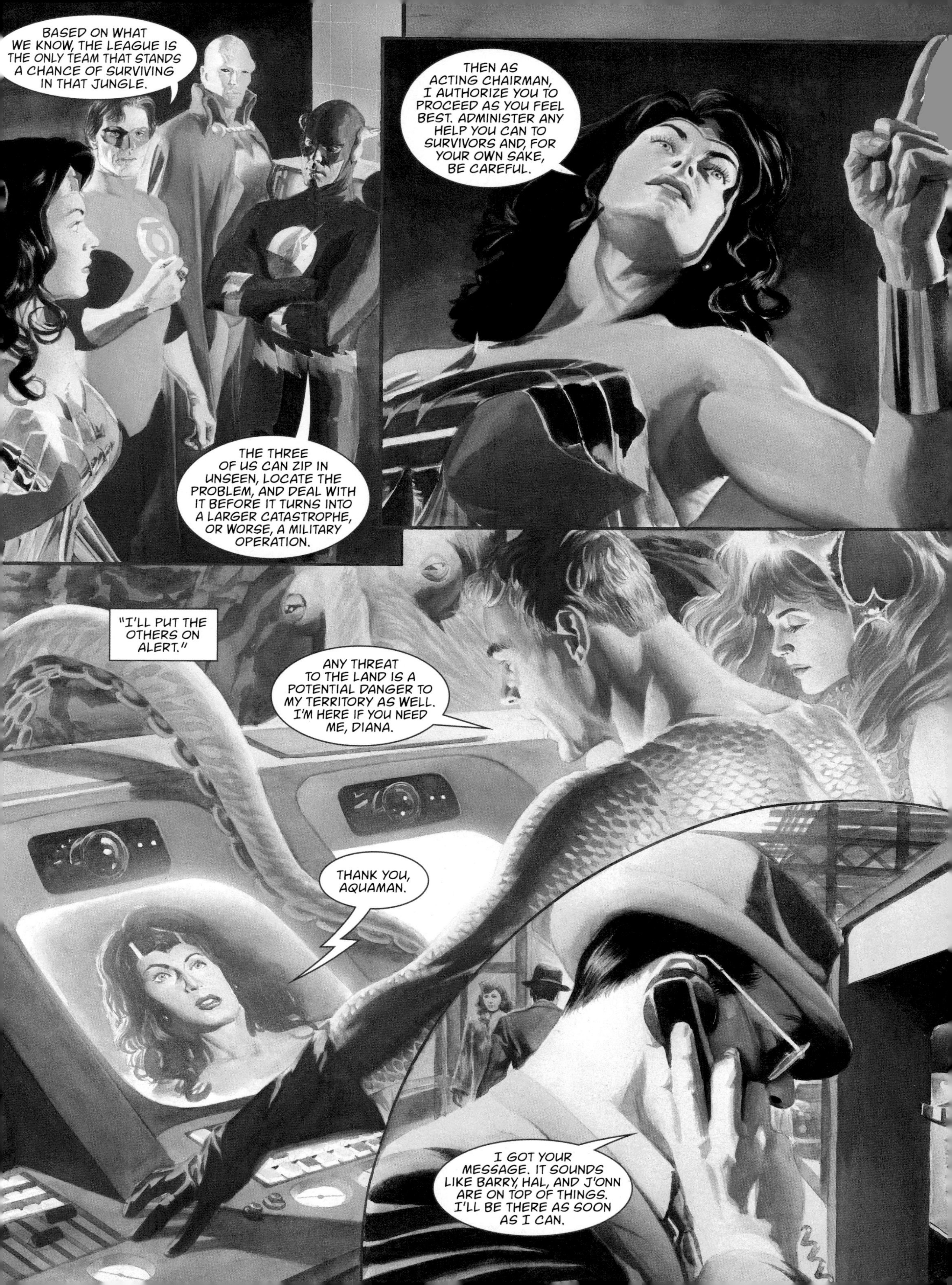
BASED ON WHAT WE KNOW, THE LEAGUE IS THE ONLY TEAM THAT STANDS A CHANCE OF SURVIVING IN THAT JUNGLE.
THE THREE OF US CAN ZIP IN UNSEEN, LOCATE THE PROBLEM, AND DEAL WITH IT BEFORE IT TURNS INTO A LARGER CATASTROPHE, OR WORSE, A MILITARY OPERATION.
THEN AS ACTING CHAIRMAN, I AUTHORIZE YOU TO PROCEED AS YOU FEEL BEST. ADMINISTER ANY HELP YOU CAN TO SURVIVORS AND, FOR YOUR OWN SAKE, BE CAREFUL.
"I'LL PUT THE OTHERS ON ALERT."
ANY THREAT TO THE LAND IS A POTENTIAL DANGER TO MY TERRITORY AS WELL. I'M HERE IF YOU NEED ME, DIANA.
THANK YOU, AQUAMAN.
I GOT YOUR MESSAGE. IT SOUNDS LIKE BARRY, HAL, AND J'ONN ARE ON TOP OF THINGS. I'LL BE THERE AS SOON AS I CAN.

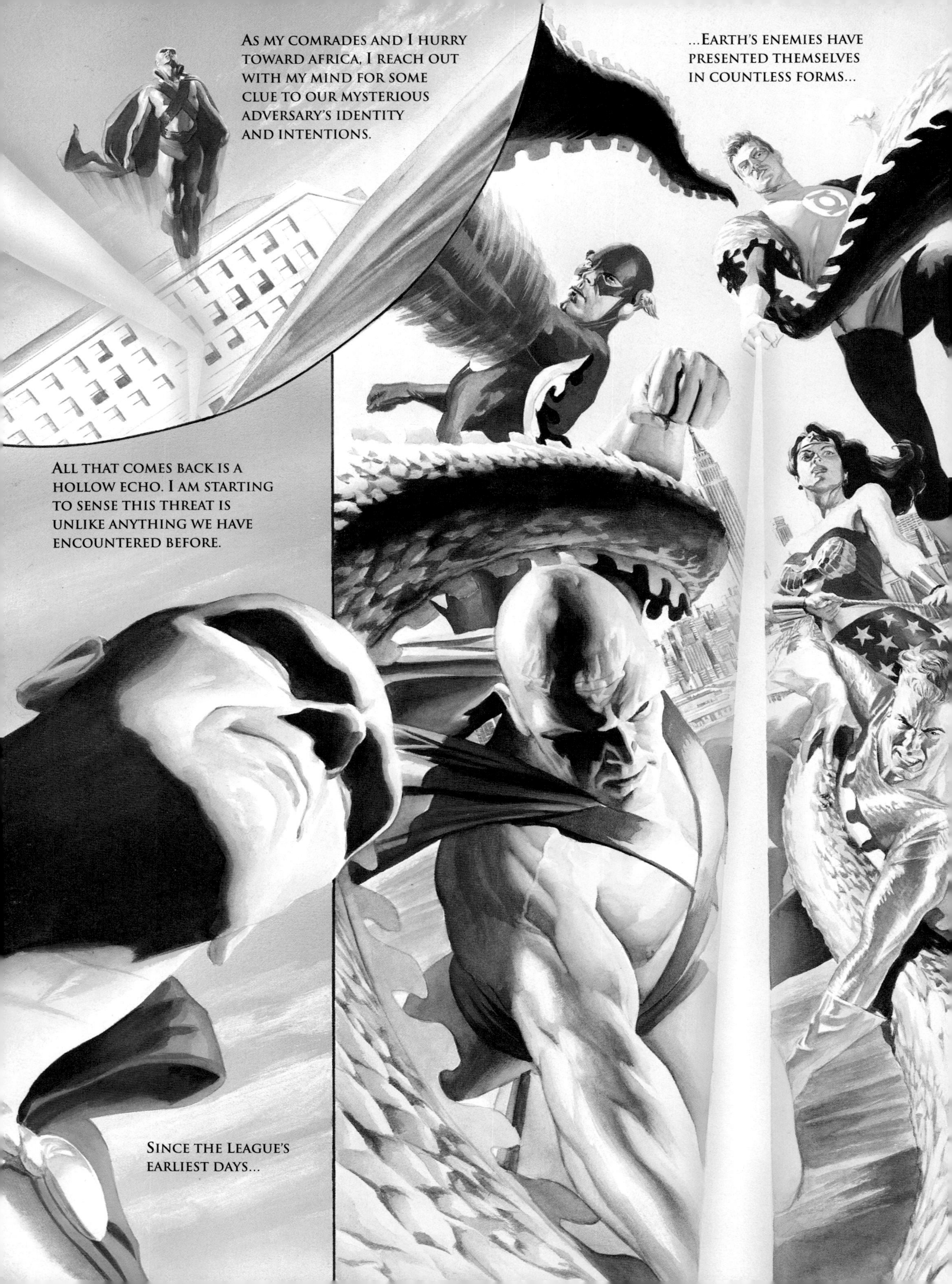
As my comrades and I hurry toward Africa, I reach out with my mind for some clue to our mysterious adversary's identity and intentions.
All that comes back is a hollow echo. I am starting to sense this threat is unlike anything we have encountered before.
Since the League's earliest days...
...Earth's enemies have presented themselves in countless forms...

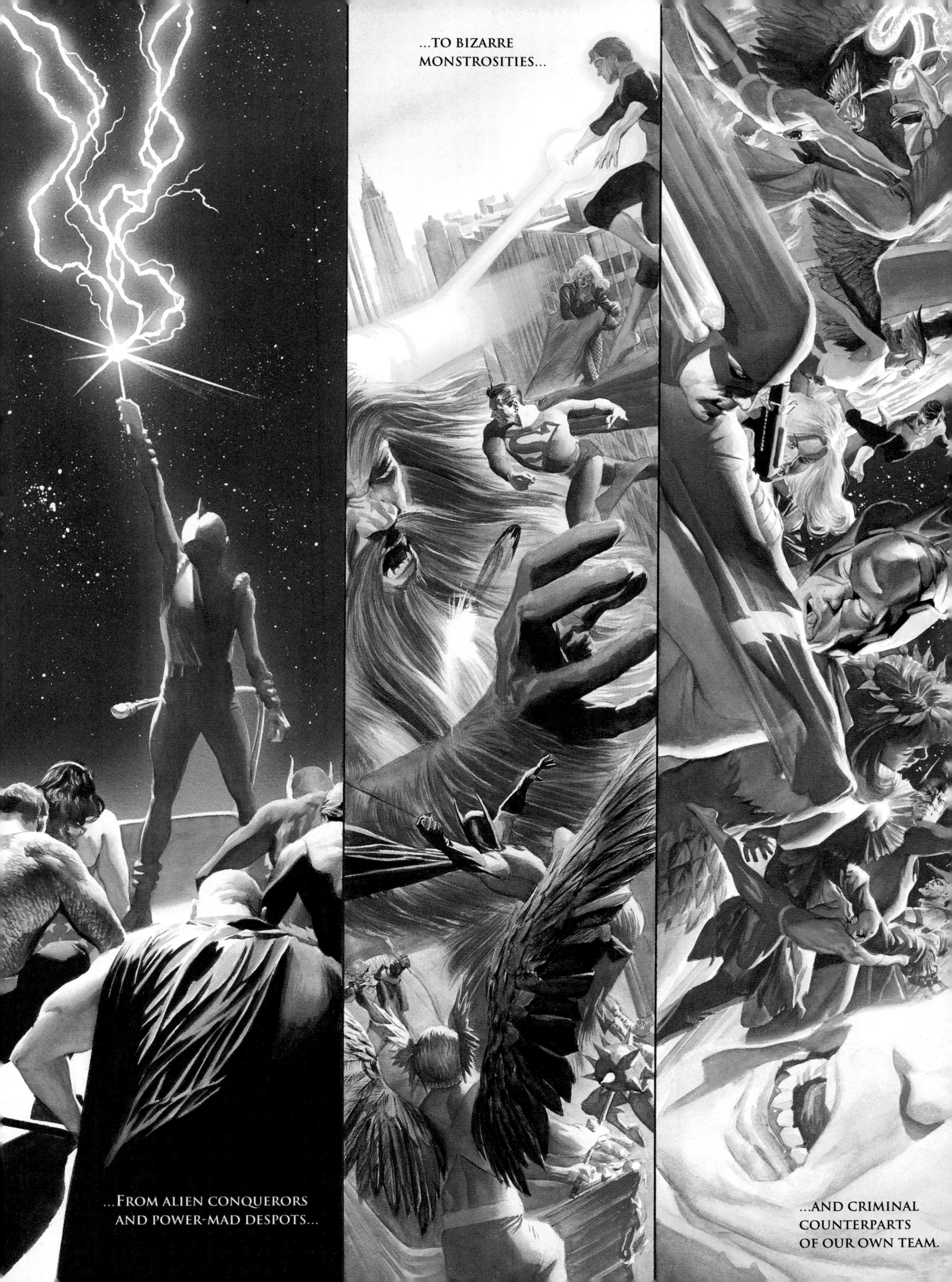
...FROM ALIEN CONQUERORS AND POWER-MAD DESPOTS...
...TO BIZARRE MONSTROSITIES...
...AND CRIMINAL COUNTERPARTS OF OUR OWN TEAM.

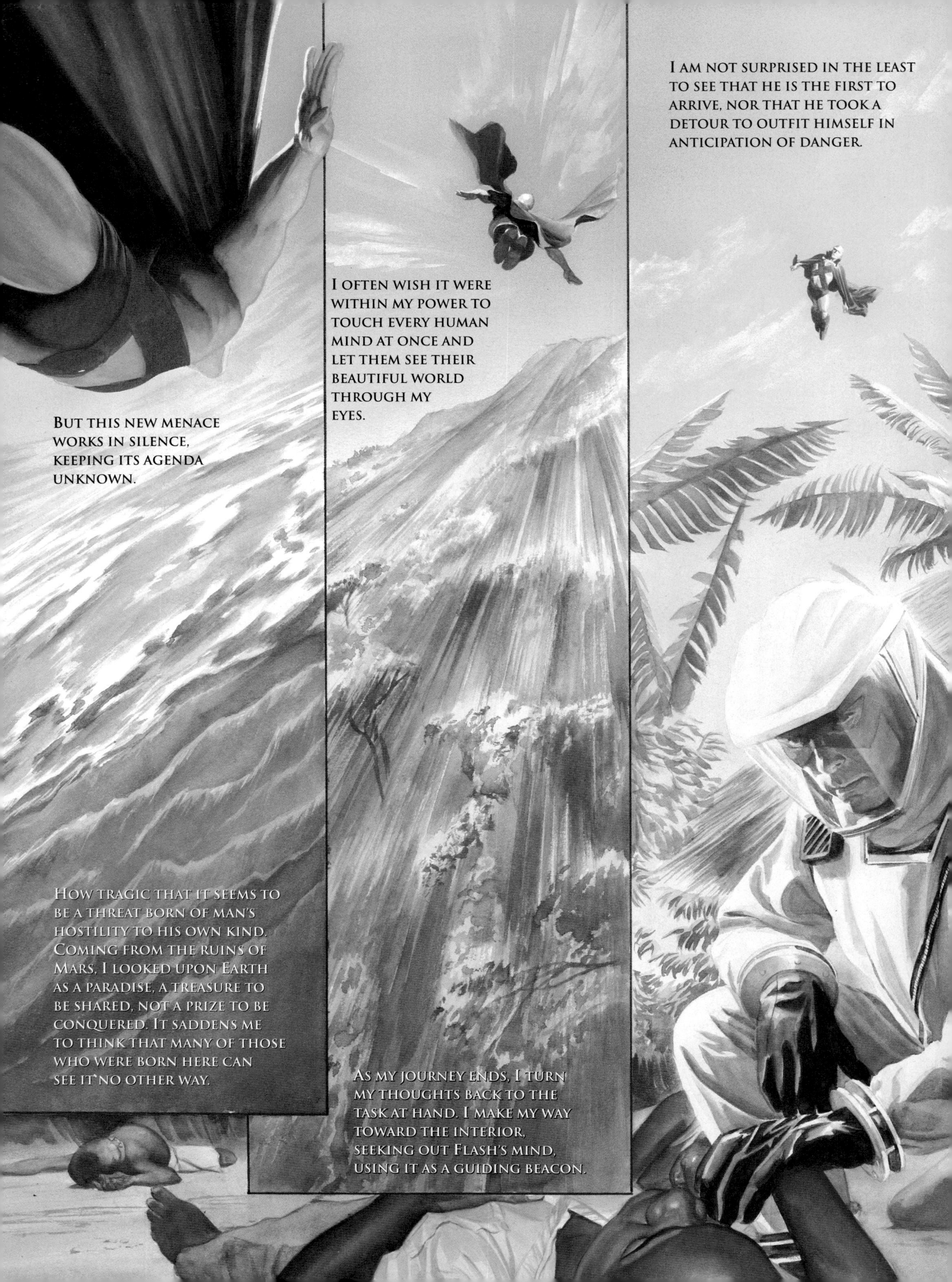
But this new menace works in silence, keeping its agenda unknown.
How tragic that it seems to be a threat born of man's hostility to his own kind. Coming from the ruins of Mars, I looked upon Earth as a paradise, a treasure to be shared, not a prize to be conquered. It saddens me to think that many of those who were born here can see it no other way.
I often wish it were within my power to touch every human mind at once and let them see their beautiful world through my eyes.
As my journey ends, I turn my thoughts back to the task at hand. I make my way toward the interior, seeking out Flash's mind, using it as a guiding beacon.
I am not surprised in the least to see that he is the first to arrive, nor that he took a detour to outfit himself in anticipation of danger.

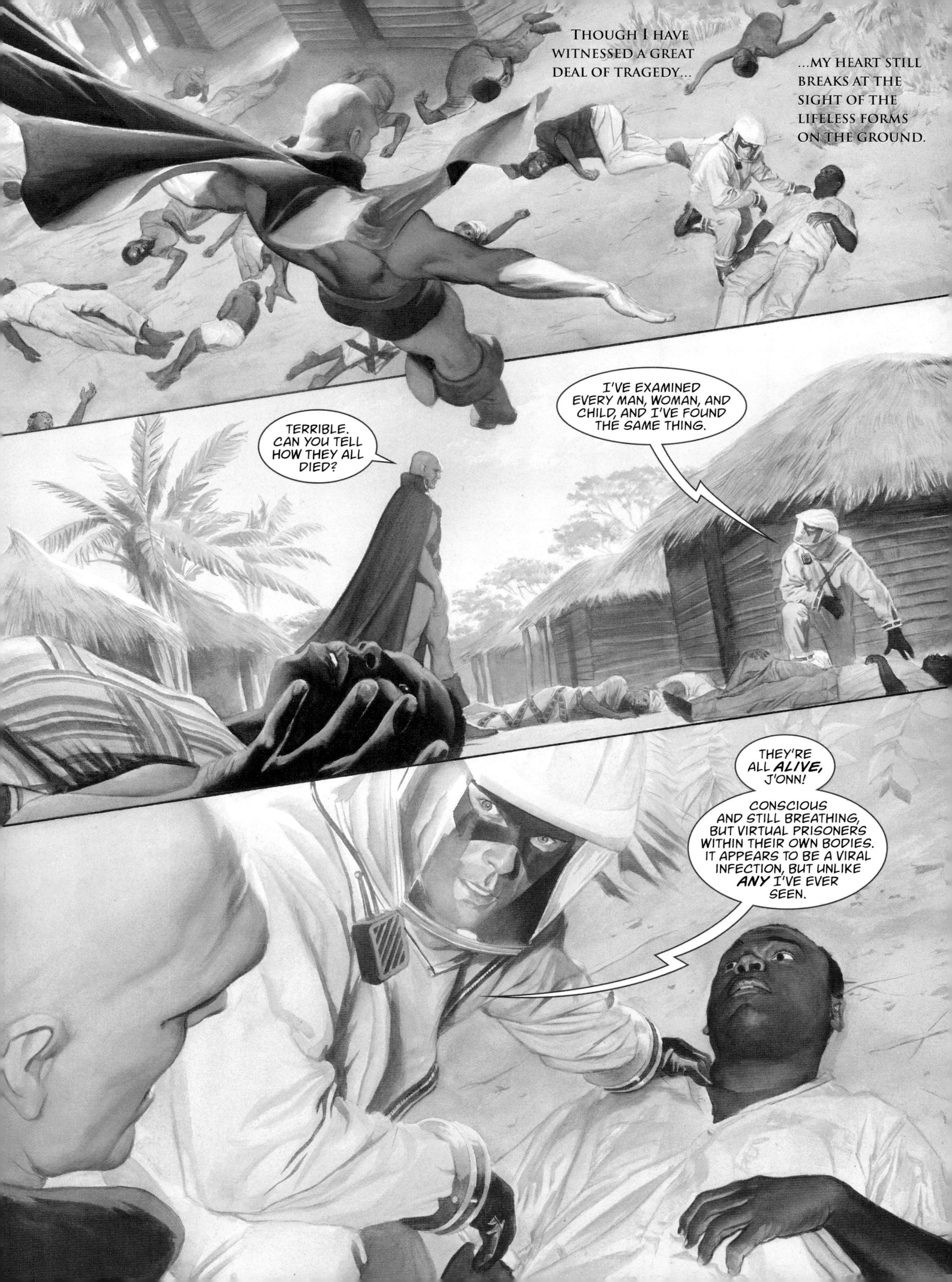
Though I have witnessed a great deal of tragedy...
...my heart still breaks at the sight of the lifeless forms on the ground.
Terrible. Can you tell how they all died?
I've examined every man, woman, and child, and I've found the same thing.
They're all ALIVE, J'onn!
Conscious and still breathing, but virtual prisoners within their own bodies. It appears to be a viral infection, but unlike ANY I've ever seen.

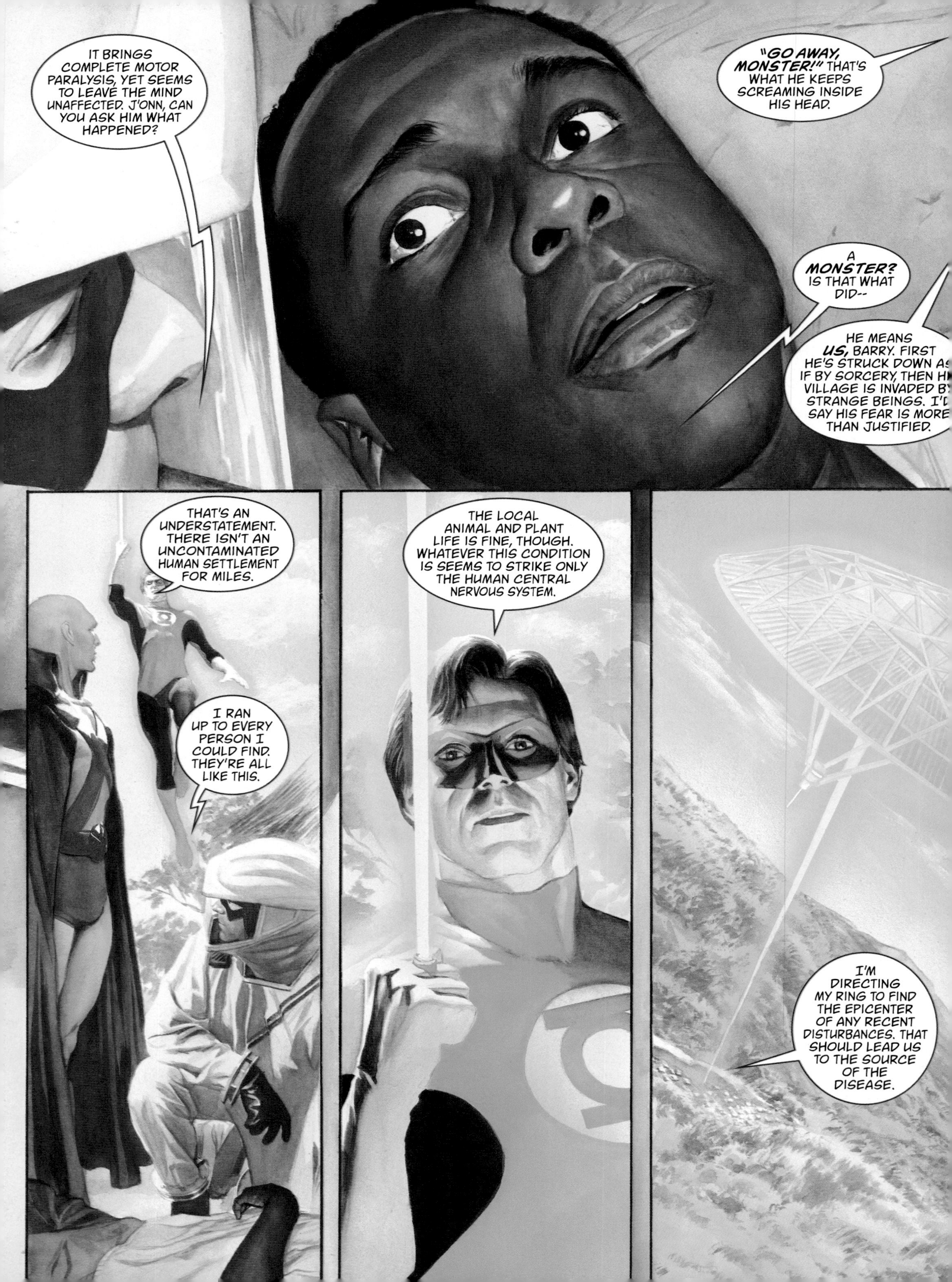
IT BRINGS COMPLETE MOTOR PARALYSIS, YET SEEMS TO LEAVE THE MIND UNAFFECTED. J'ONN, CAN YOU ASK HIM WHAT HAPPENED?
"GO AWAY, MONSTER!" THAT'S WHAT HE KEEPS SCREAMING INSIDE HIS HEAD.
A MONSTER? IS THAT WHAT DID--
HE MEANS US, BARRY. FIRST HE'S STRUCK DOWN AS IF BY SORCERY, THEN HIS VILLAGE IS INVADED BY STRANGE BEINGS. I'D SAY HIS FEAR IS MORE THAN JUSTIFIED.
THAT'S AN UNDERSTATEMENT. THERE ISN'T AN UNCONTAMINATED HUMAN SETTLEMENT FOR MILES.
I RAN UP TO EVERY PERSON I COULD FIND. THEY'RE ALL LIKE THIS.
THE LOCAL ANIMAL AND PLANT LIFE IS FINE, THOUGH. WHATEVER THIS CONDITION IS SEEMS TO STRIKE ONLY THE HUMAN CENTRAL NERVOUS SYSTEM.
I'M DIRECTING MY RING TO FIND THE EPICENTER OF ANY RECENT DISTURBANCES. THAT SHOULD LEAD US TO THE SOURCE OF THE DISEASE.

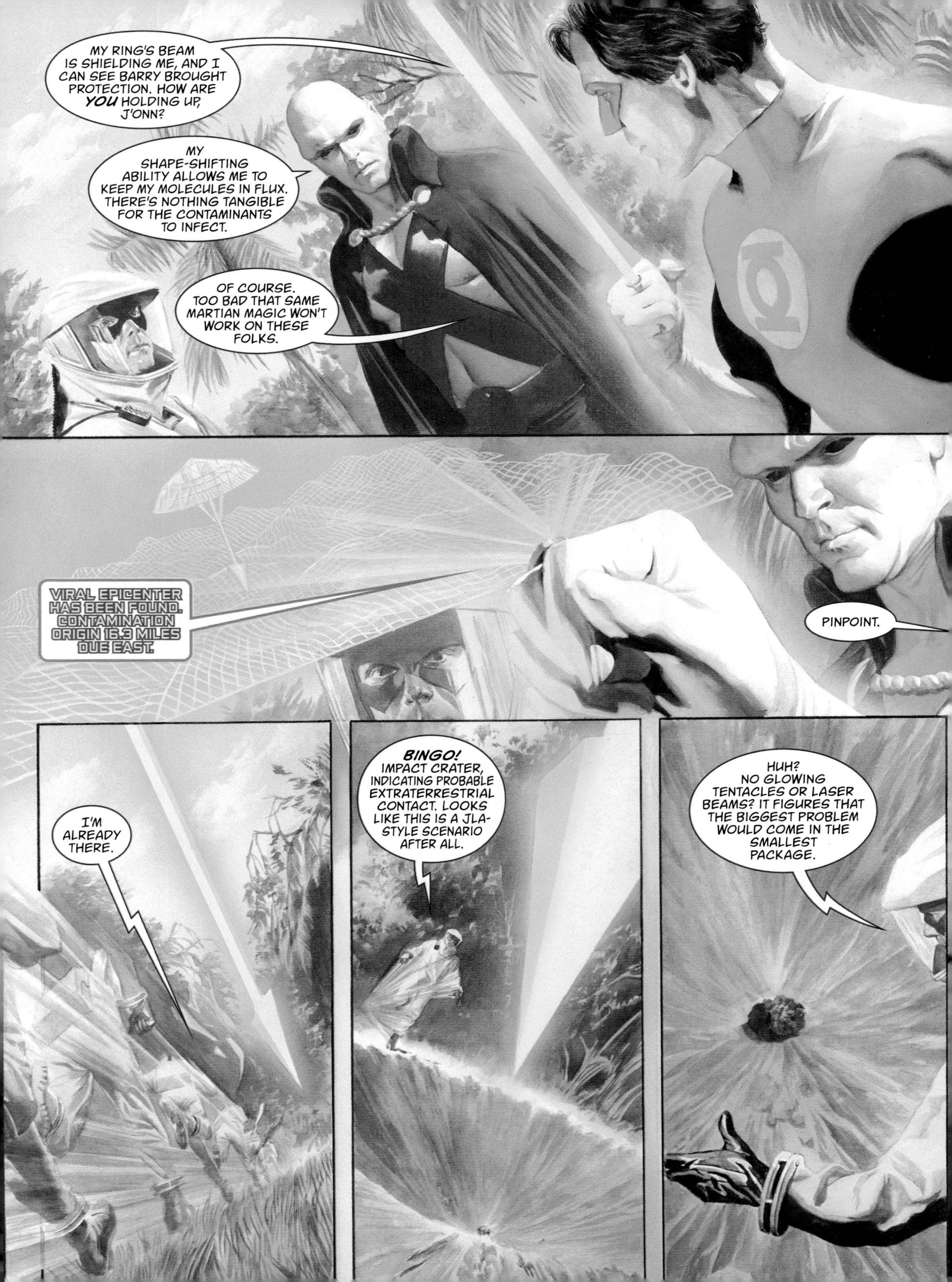
MY RING'S BEAM IS SHIELDING ME, AND I CAN SEE BARRY BROUGHT PROTECTION. HOW ARE *YOU* HOLDING UP, J'ONN?
MY SHAPE-SHIFTING ABILITY ALLOWS ME TO KEEP MY MOLECULES IN FLUX. THERE'S NOTHING TANGIBLE FOR THE CONTAMINANTS TO INFECT.
OF COURSE. TOO BAD THAT SAME MARTIAN MAGIC WON'T WORK ON THESE FOLKS.
VIRAL EPICENTER HAS BEEN FOUND. CONTAMINATION ORIGIN 16.3 MILES DUE EAST.
PINPOINT.
I'M ALREADY THERE.
BINGO! IMPACT CRATER, INDICATING PROBABLE EXTRATERRESTRIAL CONTACT. LOOKS LIKE THIS IS A JLA-STYLE SCENARIO AFTER ALL.
HUH? NO GLOWING TENTACLES OR LASER BEAMS? IT FIGURES THAT THE BIGGEST PROBLEM WOULD COME IN THE SMALLEST PACKAGE.

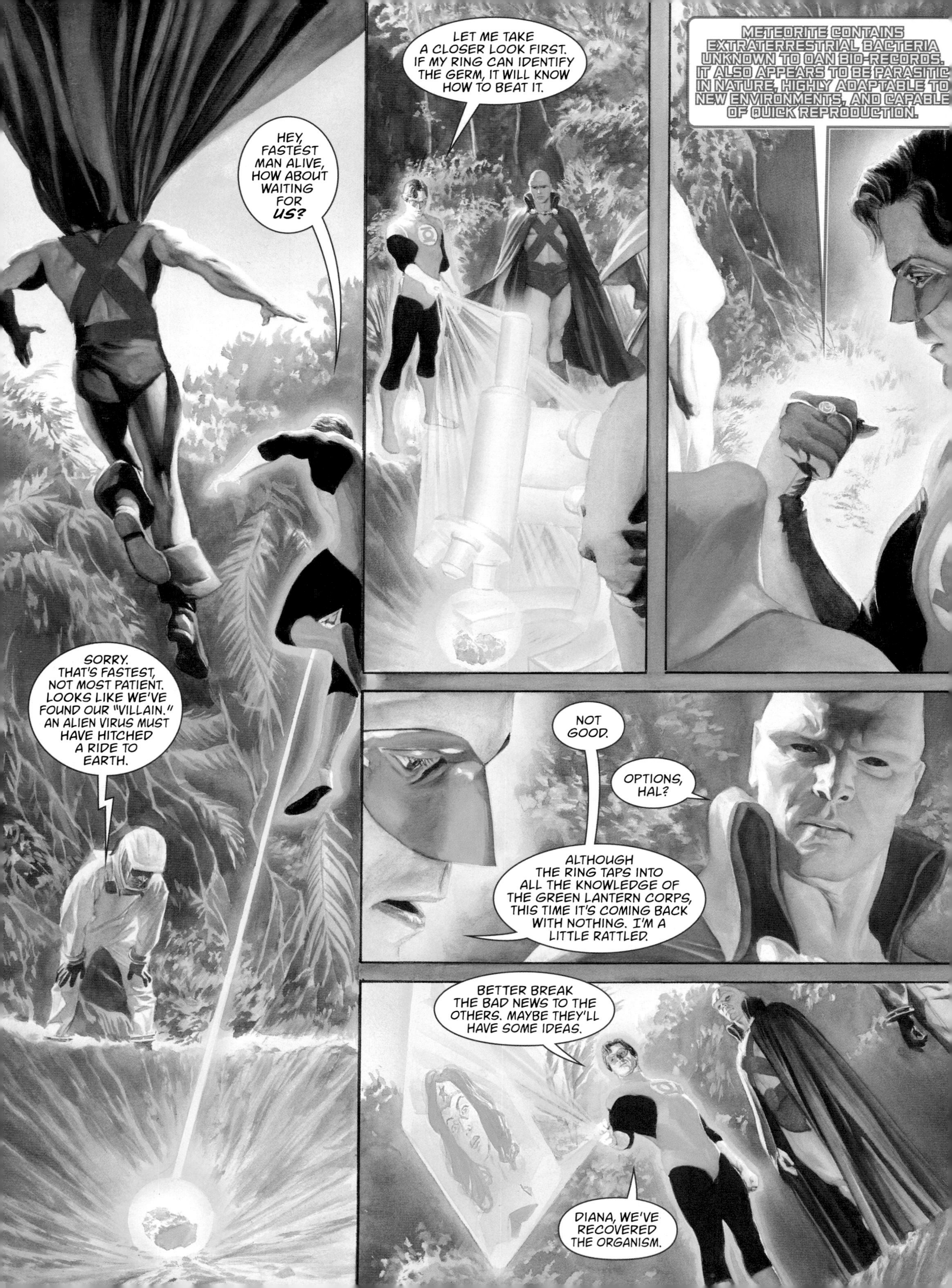
HEY, FASTEST MAN ALIVE, HOW ABOUT WAITING FOR US?
SORRY. THAT'S FASTEST, NOT MOST PATIENT. LOOKS LIKE WE'VE FOUND OUR "VILLAIN." AN ALIEN VIRUS MUST HAVE HITCHED A RIDE TO EARTH.
LET ME TAKE A CLOSER LOOK FIRST. IF MY RING CAN IDENTIFY THE GERM, IT WILL KNOW HOW TO BEAT IT.
METEORITE CONTAINS EXTRATERRESTRIAL BACTERIA UNKNOWN TO OAN BIO-RECORDS. IT ALSO APPEARS TO BE PARASITIC IN NATURE, HIGHLY ADAPTABLE TO NEW ENVIRONMENTS, AND CAPABLE OF QUICK REPRODUCTION.
NOT GOOD.
OPTIONS, HAL?
ALTHOUGH THE RING TAPS INTO ALL THE KNOWLEDGE OF THE GREEN LANTERN CORPS, THIS TIME IT'S COMING BACK WITH NOTHING. I'M A LITTLE RATTLED.
BETTER BREAK THE BAD NEWS TO THE OTHERS. MAYBE THEY'LL HAVE SOME IDEAS.
DIANA, WE'VE RECOVERED THE ORGANISM.

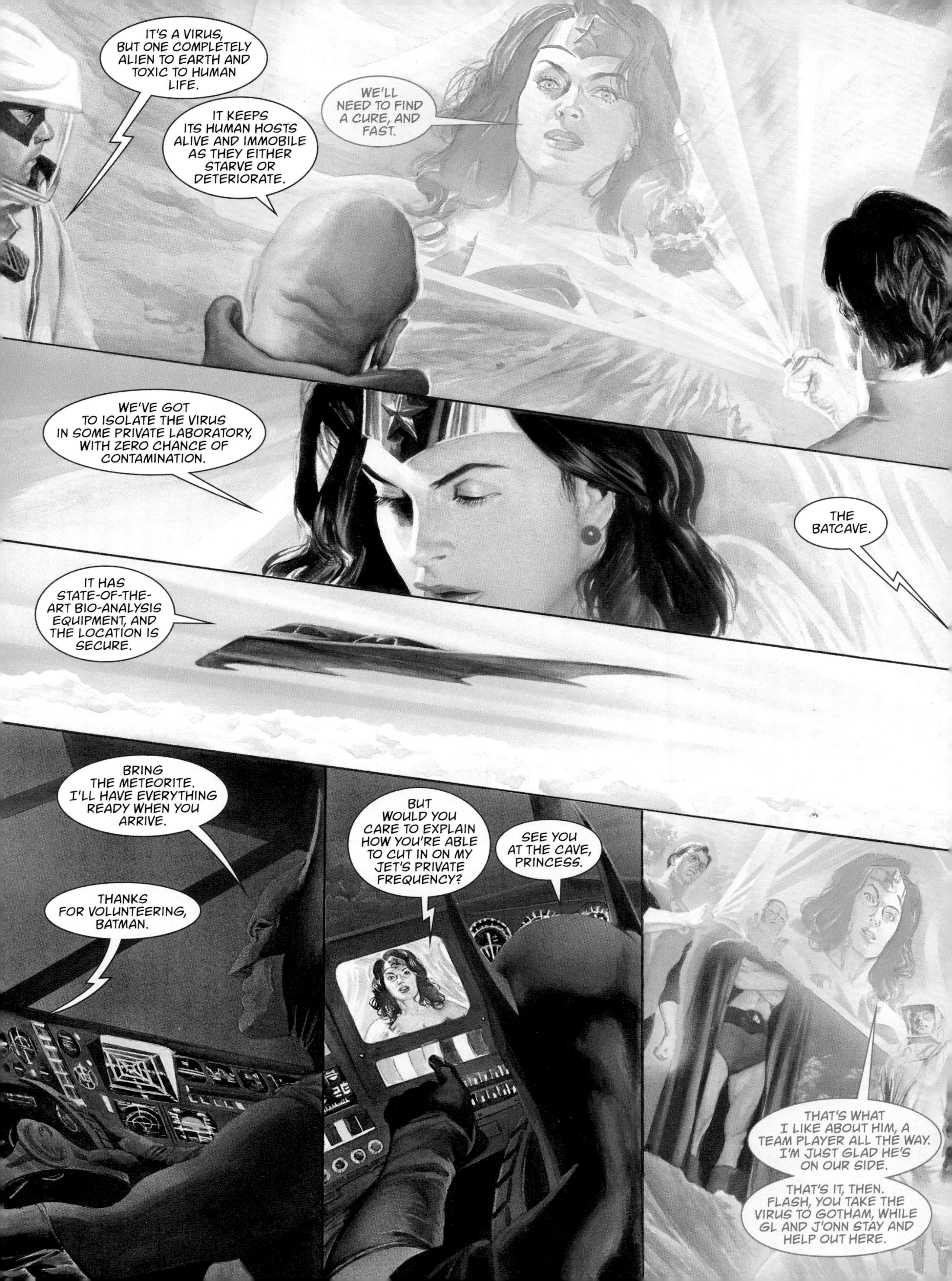
IT'S A VIRUS, BUT ONE COMPLETELY ALIEN TO EARTH AND TOXIC TO HUMAN LIFE.
IT KEEPS ITS HUMAN HOSTS ALIVE AND IMMOBILE AS THEY EITHER STARVE OR DETERIORATE.
WE'LL NEED TO FIND A CURE, AND FAST.
WE'VE GOT TO ISOLATE THE VIRUS IN SOME PRIVATE LABORATORY, WITH ZERO CHANCE OF CONTAMINATION.
THE BATCAVE.
IT HAS STATE-OF-THE-ART BIO-ANALYSIS EQUIPMENT, AND THE LOCATION IS SECURE.
BRING THE METEORITE. I'LL HAVE EVERYTHING READY WHEN YOU ARRIVE.
THANKS FOR VOLUNTEERING, BATMAN.
BUT WOULD YOU CARE TO EXPLAIN HOW YOU'RE ABLE TO CUT IN ON MY JET'S PRIVATE FREQUENCY?
SEE YOU AT THE CAVE, PRINCESS.
THAT'S WHAT I LIKE ABOUT HIM, A TEAM PLAYER ALL THE WAY. I'M JUST GLAD HE'S ON OUR SIDE.
THAT'S IT, THEN. FLASH, YOU TAKE THE VIRUS TO GOTHAM, WHILE GL AND J'ONN STAY AND HELP OUT HERE.

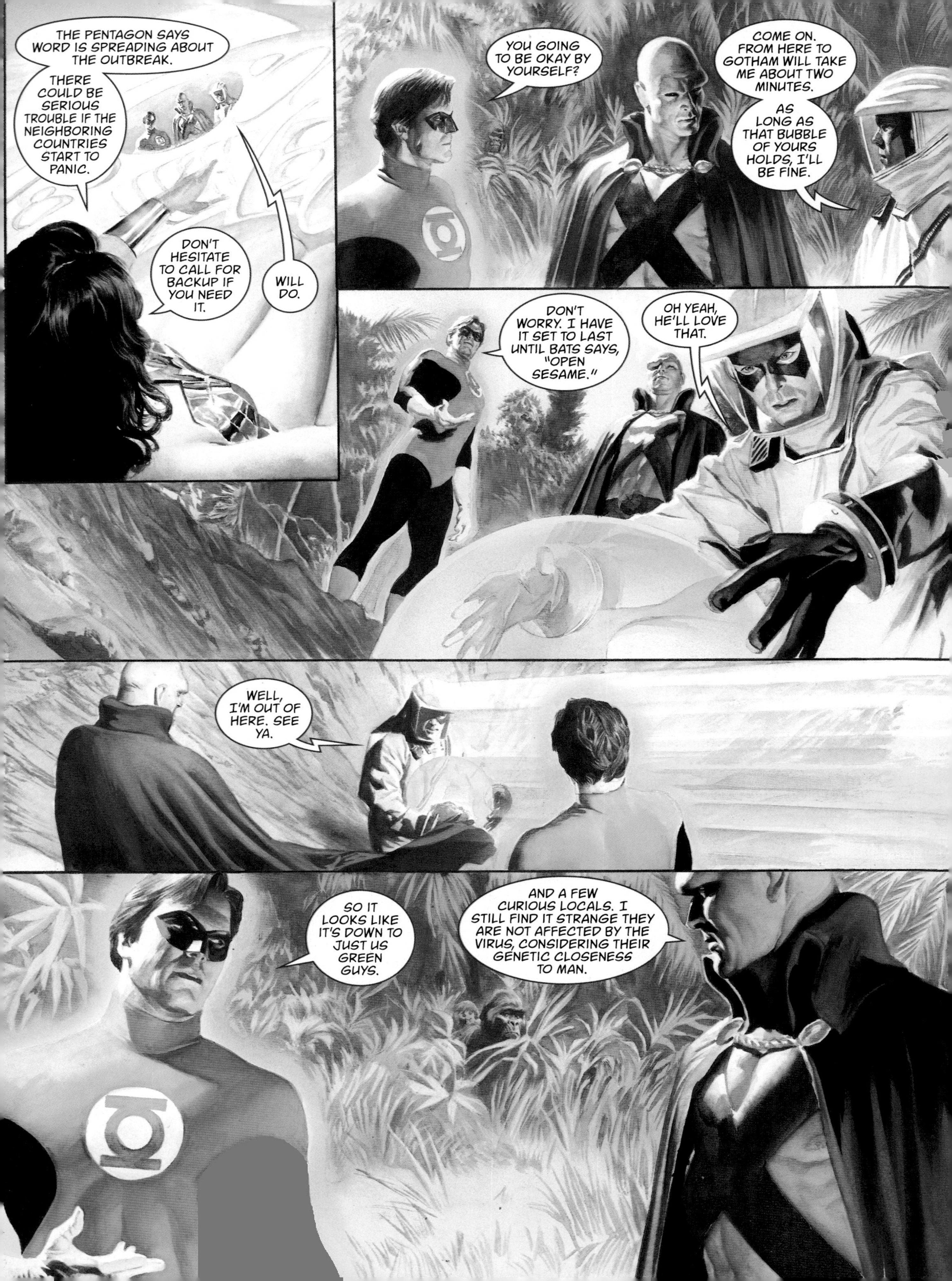
THE PENTAGON SAYS WORD IS SPREADING ABOUT THE OUTBREAK.
THERE COULD BE SERIOUS TROUBLE IF THE NEIGHBORING COUNTRIES START TO PANIC.
DON'T HESITATE TO CALL FOR BACKUP IF YOU NEED IT.
WILL DO.
YOU GOING TO BE OKAY BY YOURSELF?
COME ON. FROM HERE TO GOTHAM WILL TAKE ME ABOUT TWO MINUTES.
AS LONG AS THAT BUBBLE OF YOURS HOLDS, I'LL BE FINE.
DON'T WORRY. I HAVE IT SET TO LAST UNTIL BATS SAYS, "OPEN SESAME."
OH YEAH, HE'LL LOVE THAT.
WELL, I'M OUT OF HERE. SEE YA.
SO IT LOOKS LIKE IT'S DOWN TO JUST US GREEN GUYS.
AND A FEW CURIOUS LOCALS. I STILL FIND IT STRANGE THEY ARE NOT AFFECTED BY THE VIRUS, CONSIDERING THEIR GENETIC CLOSENESS TO MAN.

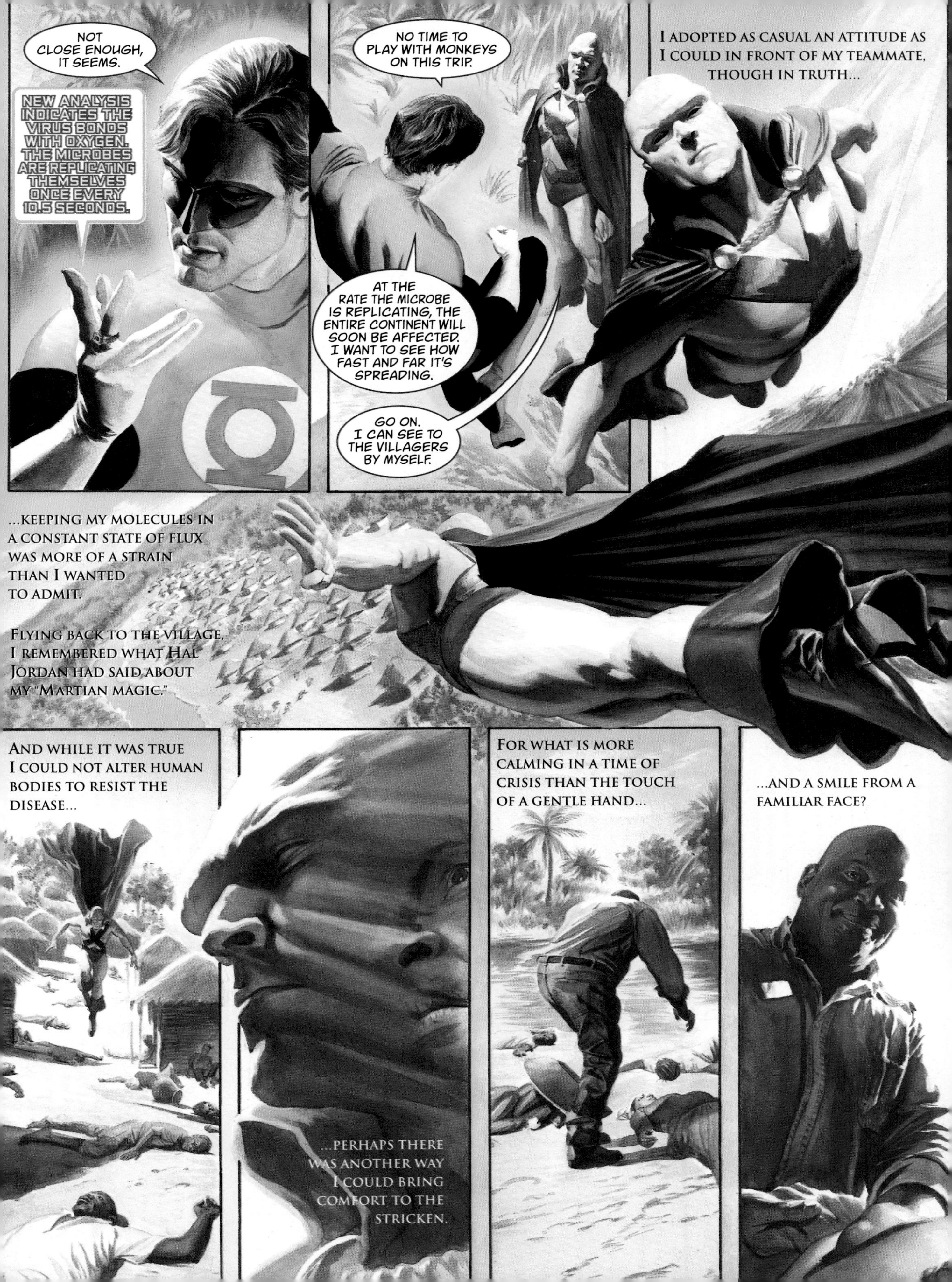
NOT CLOSE ENOUGH, IT SEEMS.
NEW ANALYSIS INDICATES THE VIRUS BONDS WITH OXYGEN. THE MICROBES ARE REPLICATING THEMSELVES ONCE EVERY 10.5 SECONDS.
NO TIME TO PLAY WITH MONKEYS ON THIS TRIP.
AT THE RATE THE MICROBE IS REPLICATING, THE ENTIRE CONTINENT WILL SOON BE AFFECTED. I WANT TO SEE HOW FAST AND FAR IT'S SPREADING.
GO ON. I CAN SEE TO THE VILLAGERS BY MYSELF.
I ADOPTED AS CASUAL AN ATTITUDE AS I COULD IN FRONT OF MY TEAMMATE, THOUGH IN TRUTH...
...KEEPING MY MOLECULES IN A CONSTANT STATE OF FLUX WAS MORE OF A STRAIN THAN I WANTED TO ADMIT.
FLYING BACK TO THE VILLAGE, I REMEMBERED WHAT HAL JORDAN HAD SAID ABOUT MY "MARTIAN MAGIC."
AND WHILE IT WAS TRUE I COULD NOT ALTER HUMAN BODIES TO RESIST THE DISEASE...
...PERHAPS THERE WAS ANOTHER WAY I COULD BRING COMFORT TO THE STRICKEN.
FOR WHAT IS MORE CALMING IN A TIME OF CRISIS THAN THE TOUCH OF A GENTLE HAND...
...AND A SMILE FROM A FAMILIAR FACE?

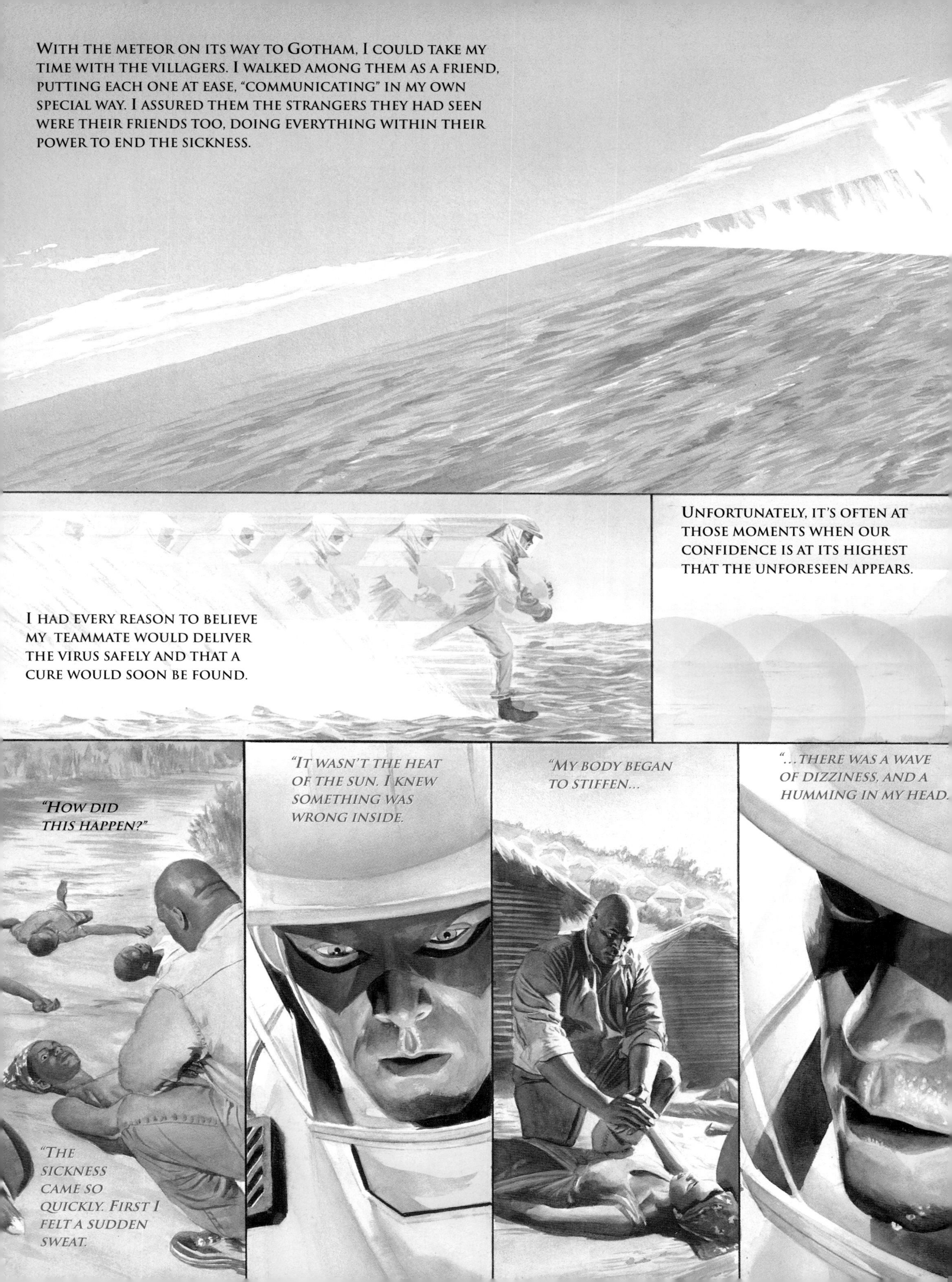
WITH THE METEOR ON ITS WAY TO GOTHAM, I COULD TAKE MY TIME WITH THE VILLAGERS. I WALKED AMONG THEM AS A FRIEND, PUTTING EACH ONE AT EASE, "COMMUNICATING" IN MY OWN SPECIAL WAY. I ASSURED THEM THE STRANGERS THEY HAD SEEN WERE THEIR FRIENDS TOO, DOING EVERYTHING WITHIN THEIR POWER TO END THE SICKNESS.
I HAD EVERY REASON TO BELIEVE MY TEAMMATE WOULD DELIVER THE VIRUS SAFELY AND THAT A CURE WOULD SOON BE FOUND.
UNFORTUNATELY, IT'S OFTEN AT THOSE MOMENTS WHEN OUR CONFIDENCE IS AT ITS HIGHEST THAT THE UNFORESEEN APPEARS.
"HOW DID THIS HAPPEN?"
"THE SICKNESS CAME SO QUICKLY. FIRST I FELT A SUDDEN SWEAT.
"IT WASN'T THE HEAT OF THE SUN. I KNEW SOMETHING WAS WRONG INSIDE.
"MY BODY BEGAN TO STIFFEN...
"...THERE WAS A WAVE OF DIZZINESS, AND A HUMMING IN MY HEAD.

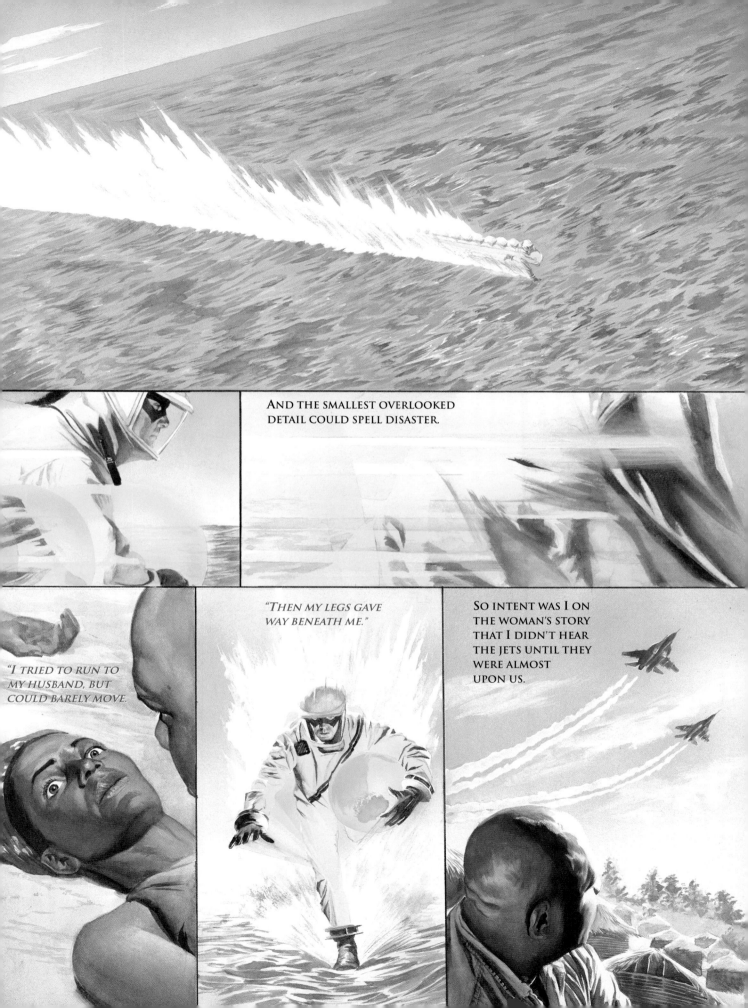

AND THE SMALLEST OVERLOOKED DETAIL COULD SPELL DISASTER.

"THEN MY LEGS GAVE WAY BENEATH ME."

"I TRIED TO RUN TO MY HUSBAND, BUT COULD BARELY MOVE.

SO INTENT WAS I ON THE WOMAN'S STORY THAT I DIDN'T HEAR THE JETS UNTIL THEY WERE ALMOST UPON US.

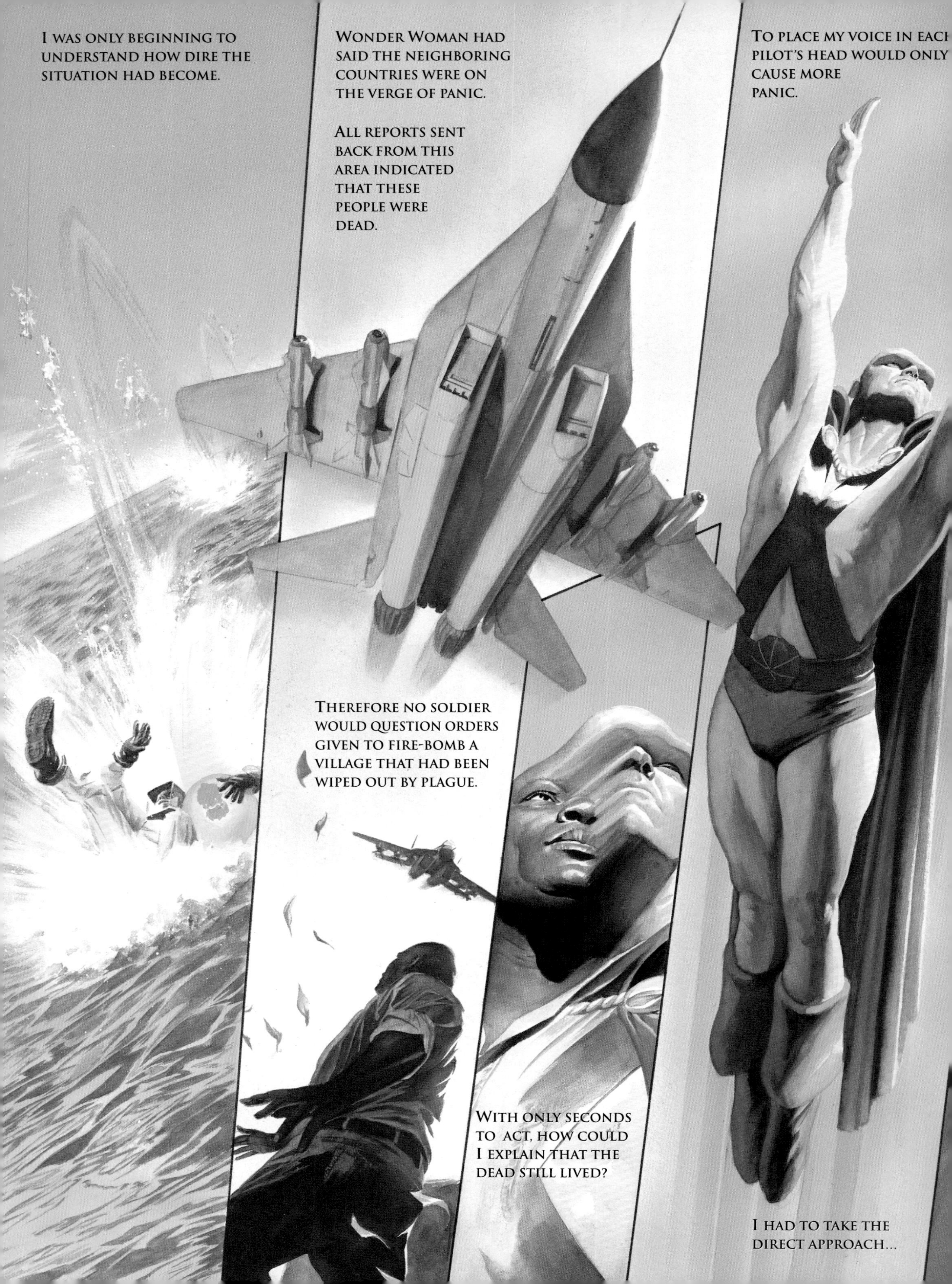

I WAS ONLY BEGINNING TO UNDERSTAND HOW DIRE THE SITUATION HAD BECOME.
WONDER WOMAN HAD SAID THE NEIGHBORING COUNTRIES WERE ON THE VERGE OF PANIC.
ALL REPORTS SENT BACK FROM THIS AREA INDICATED THAT THESE PEOPLE WERE DEAD.
THEREFORE NO SOLDIER WOULD QUESTION ORDERS GIVEN TO FIRE-BOMB A VILLAGE THAT HAD BEEN WIPED OUT BY PLAGUE.
WITH ONLY SECONDS TO ACT, HOW COULD I EXPLAIN THAT THE DEAD STILL LIVED?
TO PLACE MY VOICE IN EACH PILOT'S HEAD WOULD ONLY CAUSE MORE PANIC.
I HAD TO TAKE THE DIRECT APPROACH...

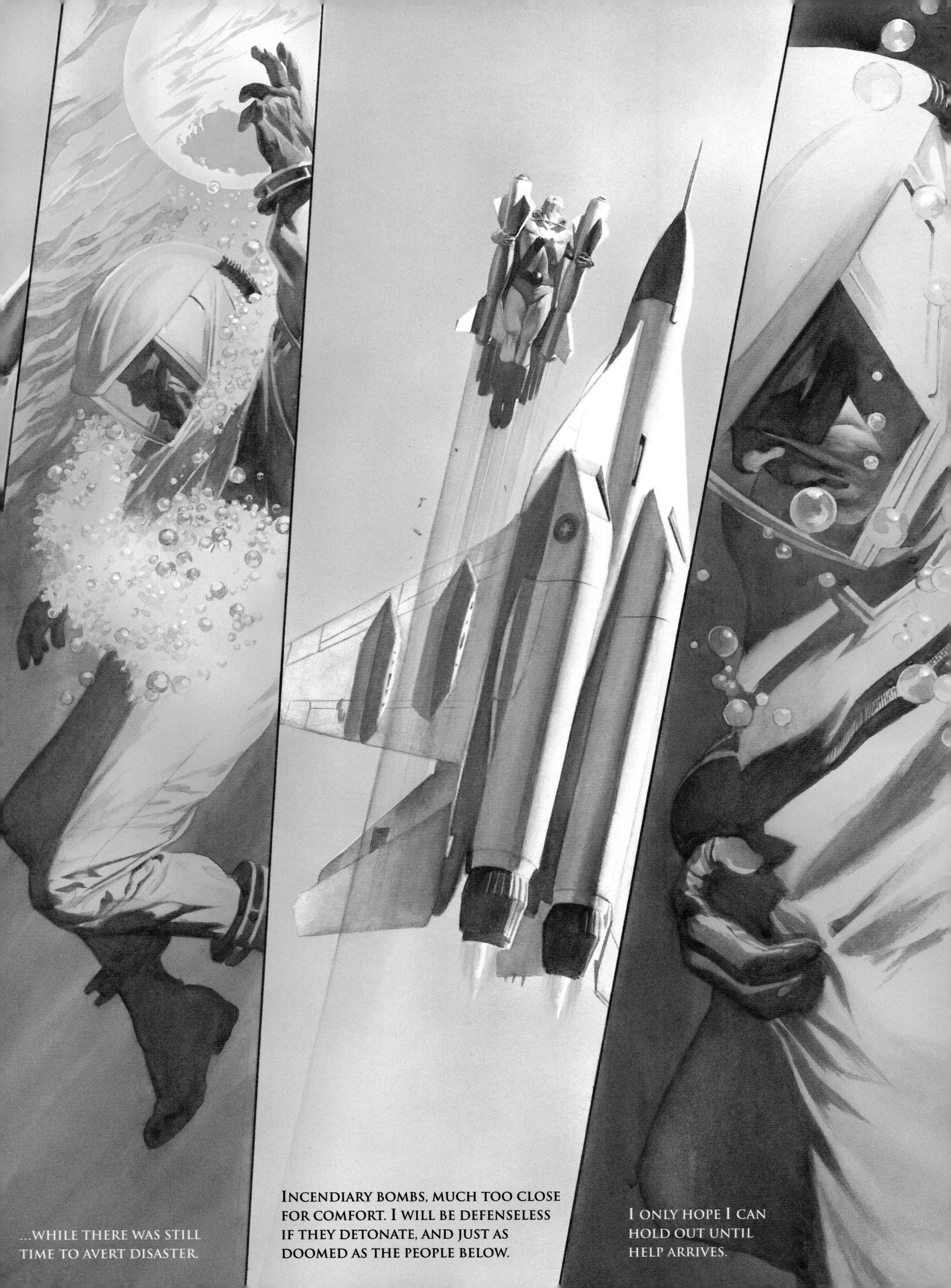
...WHILE THERE WAS STILL TIME TO AVERT DISASTER.
INCENDIARY BOMBS, MUCH TOO CLOSE FOR COMFORT. I WILL BE DEFENSELESS IF THEY DETONATE, AND JUST AS DOOMED AS THE PEOPLE BELOW.
I ONLY HOPE I CAN HOLD OUT UNTIL HELP ARRIVES.

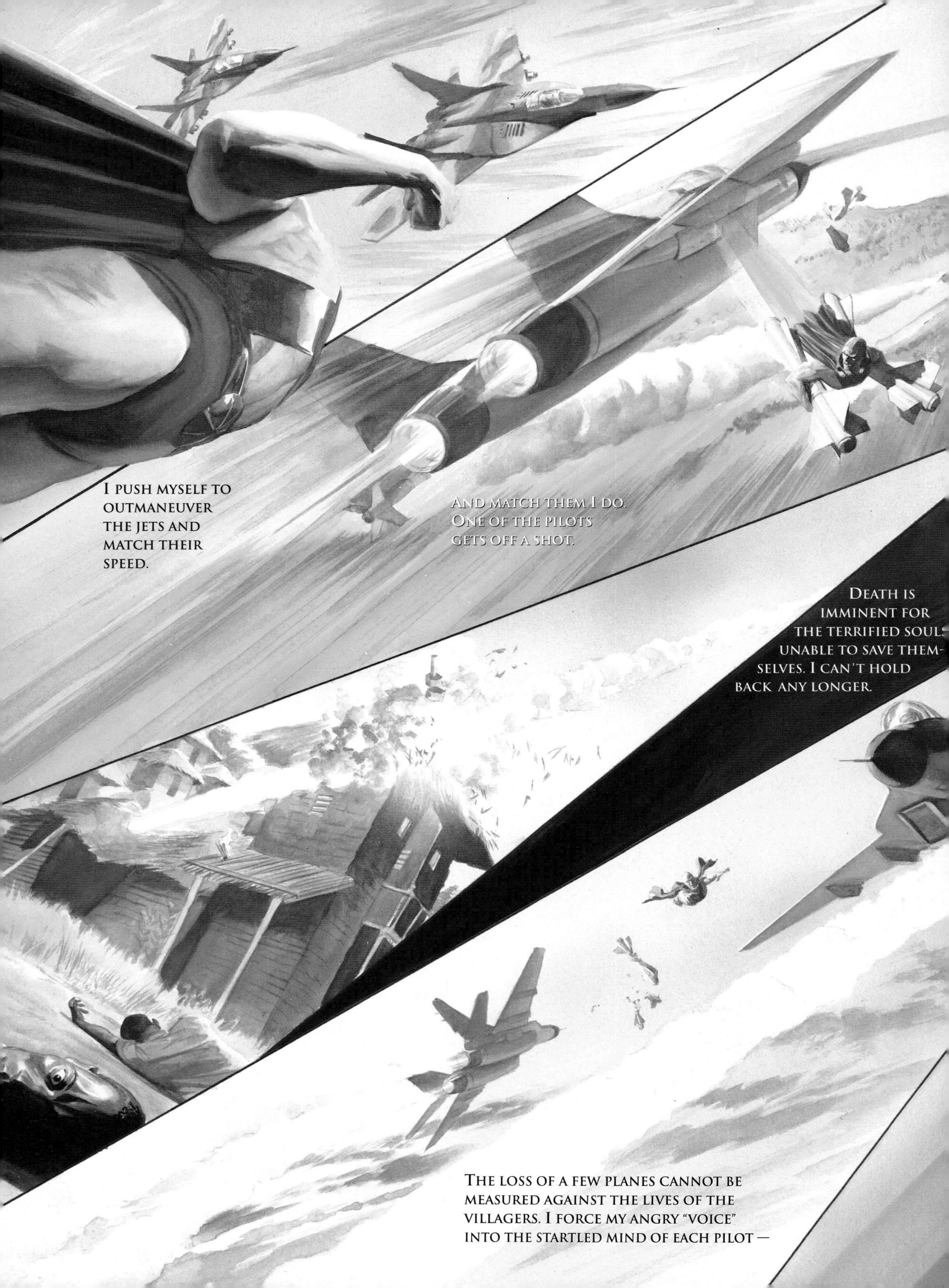
I push myself to outmaneuver the jets and match their speed.
And match them I do. One of the pilots gets off a shot.
Death is imminent for the terrified souls unable to save themselves. I can't hold back any longer.
The loss of a few planes cannot be measured against the lives of the villagers. I force my angry "voice" into the startled mind of each pilot —

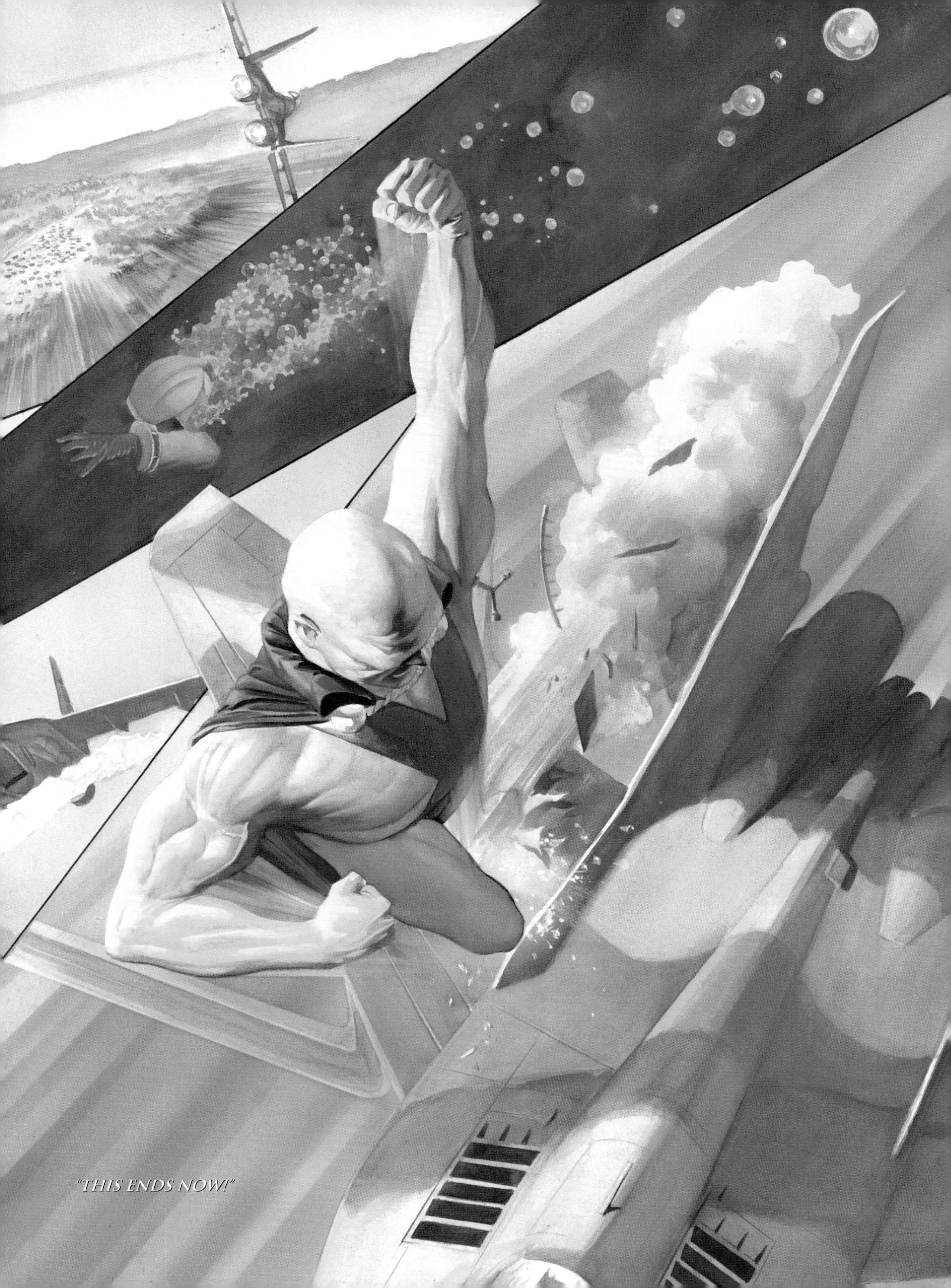
"THIS ENDS NOW!"

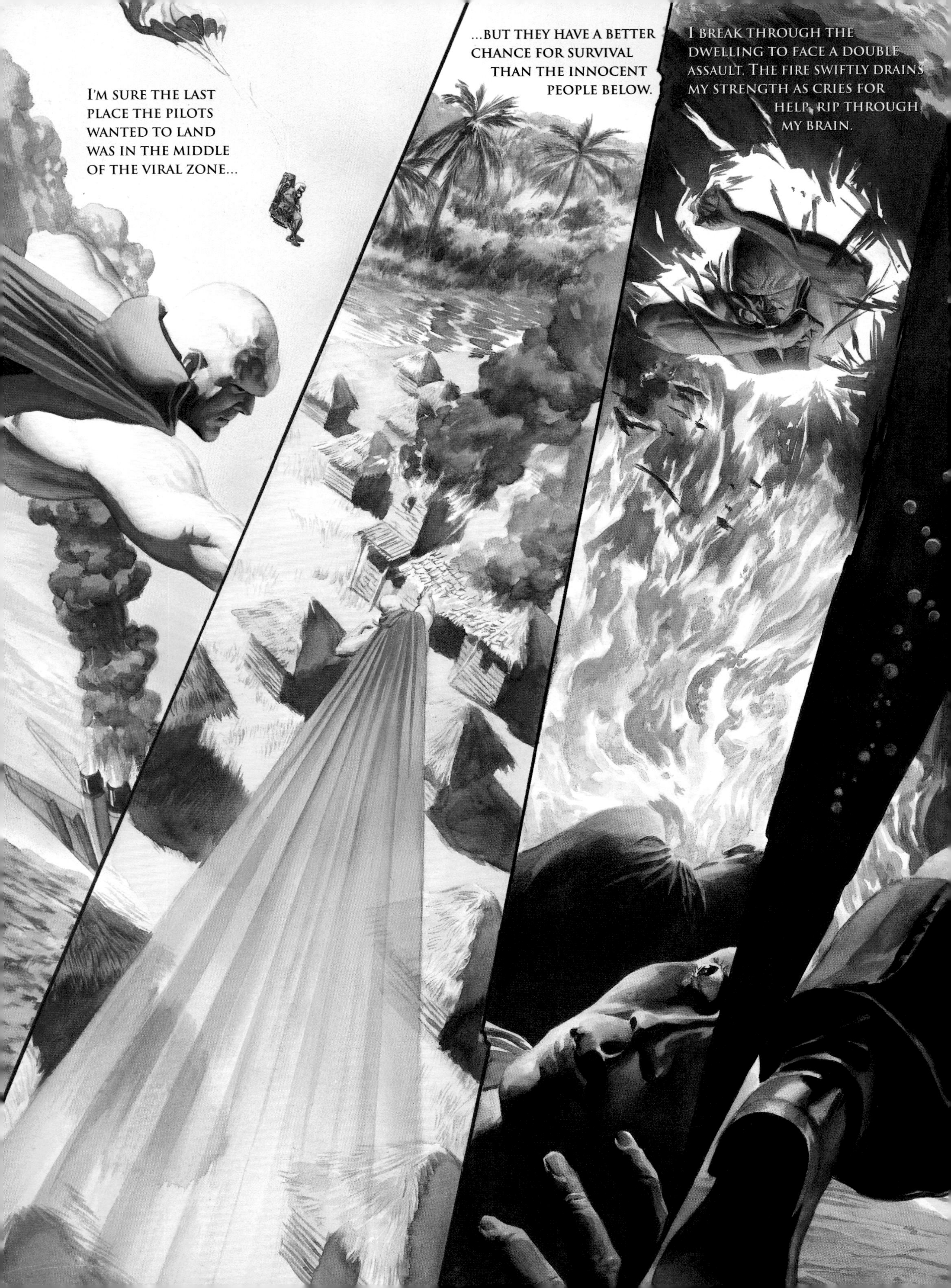
I'M SURE THE LAST PLACE THE PILOTS WANTED TO LAND WAS IN THE MIDDLE OF THE VIRAL ZONE...
...BUT THEY HAVE A BETTER CHANCE FOR SURVIVAL THAN THE INNOCENT PEOPLE BELOW.
I BREAK THROUGH THE DWELLING TO FACE A DOUBLE ASSAULT. THE FIRE SWIFTLY DRAINS MY STRENGTH AS CRIES FOR HELP RIP THROUGH MY BRAIN.

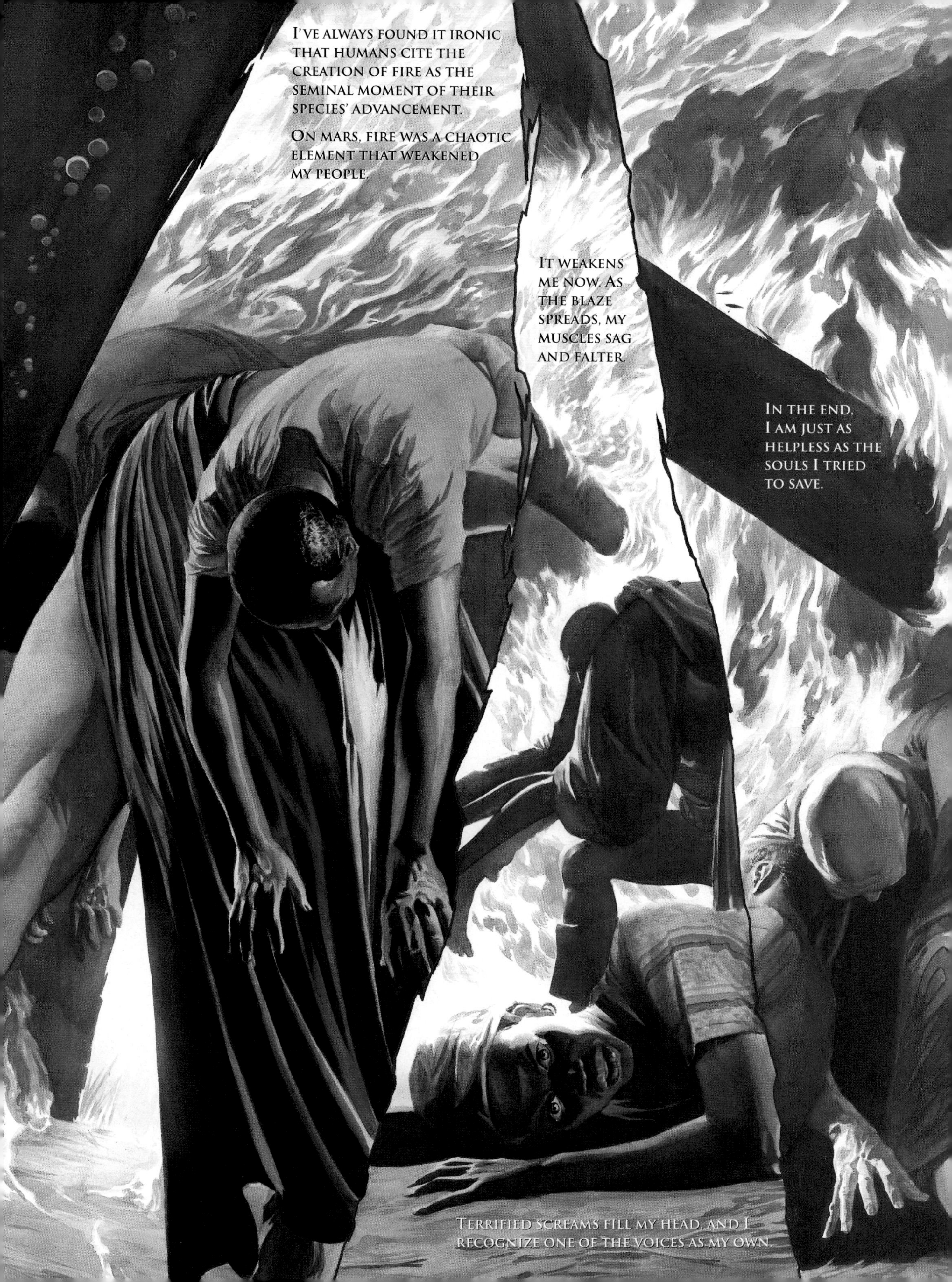
I'VE ALWAYS FOUND IT IRONIC THAT HUMANS CITE THE CREATION OF FIRE AS THE SEMINAL MOMENT OF THEIR SPECIES' ADVANCEMENT.
ON MARS, FIRE WAS A CHAOTIC ELEMENT THAT WEAKENED MY PEOPLE.
IT WEAKENS ME NOW. AS THE BLAZE SPREADS, MY MUSCLES SAG AND FALTER.
IN THE END, I AM JUST AS HELPLESS AS THE SOULS I TRIED TO SAVE.
TERRIFIED SCREAMS FILL MY HEAD, AND I RECOGNIZE ONE OF THE VOICES AS MY OWN.

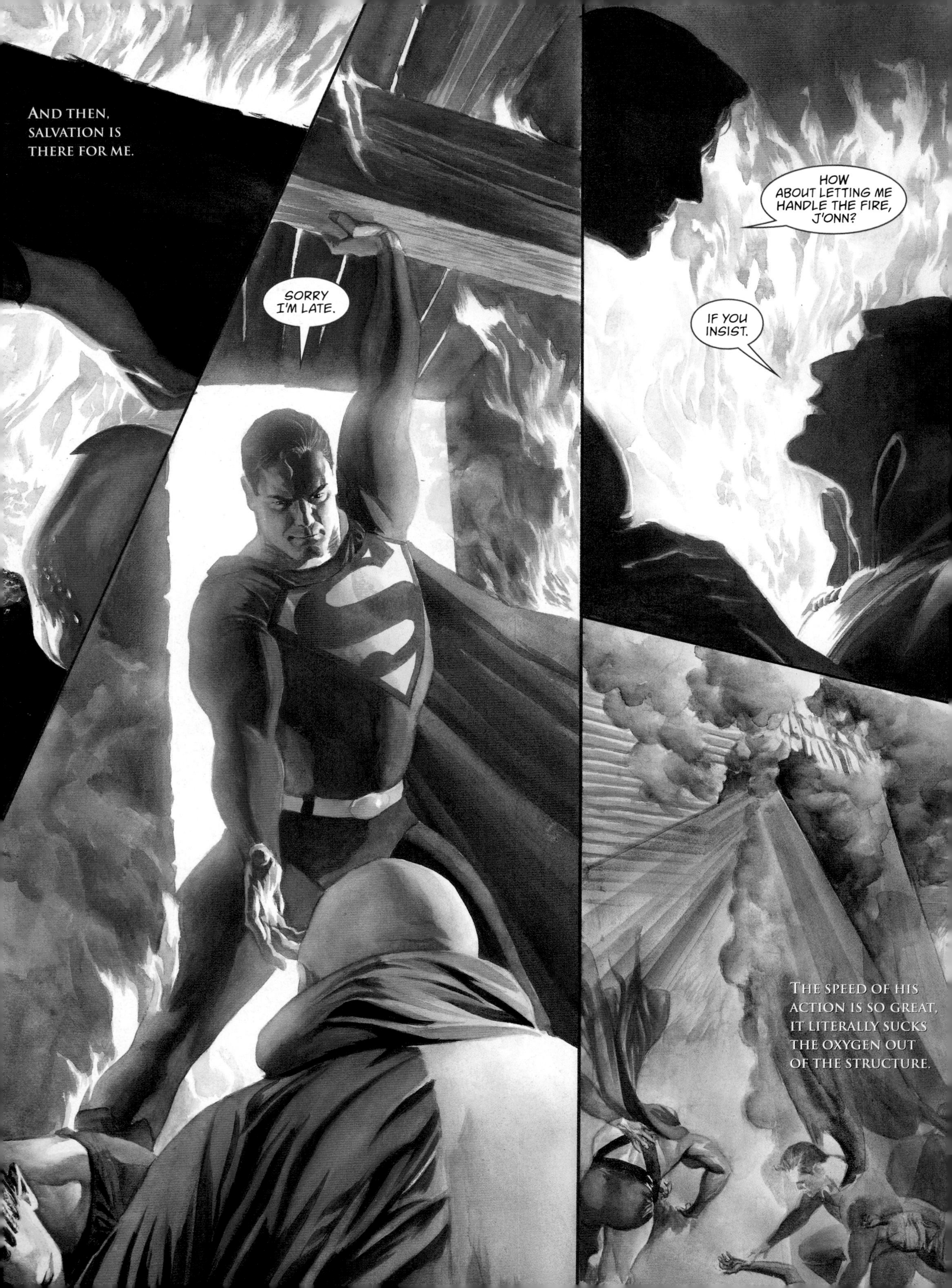
AND THEN, SALVATION IS THERE FOR ME.
SORRY I'M LATE.
HOW ABOUT LETTING ME HANDLE THE FIRE, J'ONN?
IF YOU INSIST.
THE SPEED OF HIS ACTION IS SO GREAT, IT LITERALLY SUCKS THE OXYGEN OUT OF THE STRUCTURE.

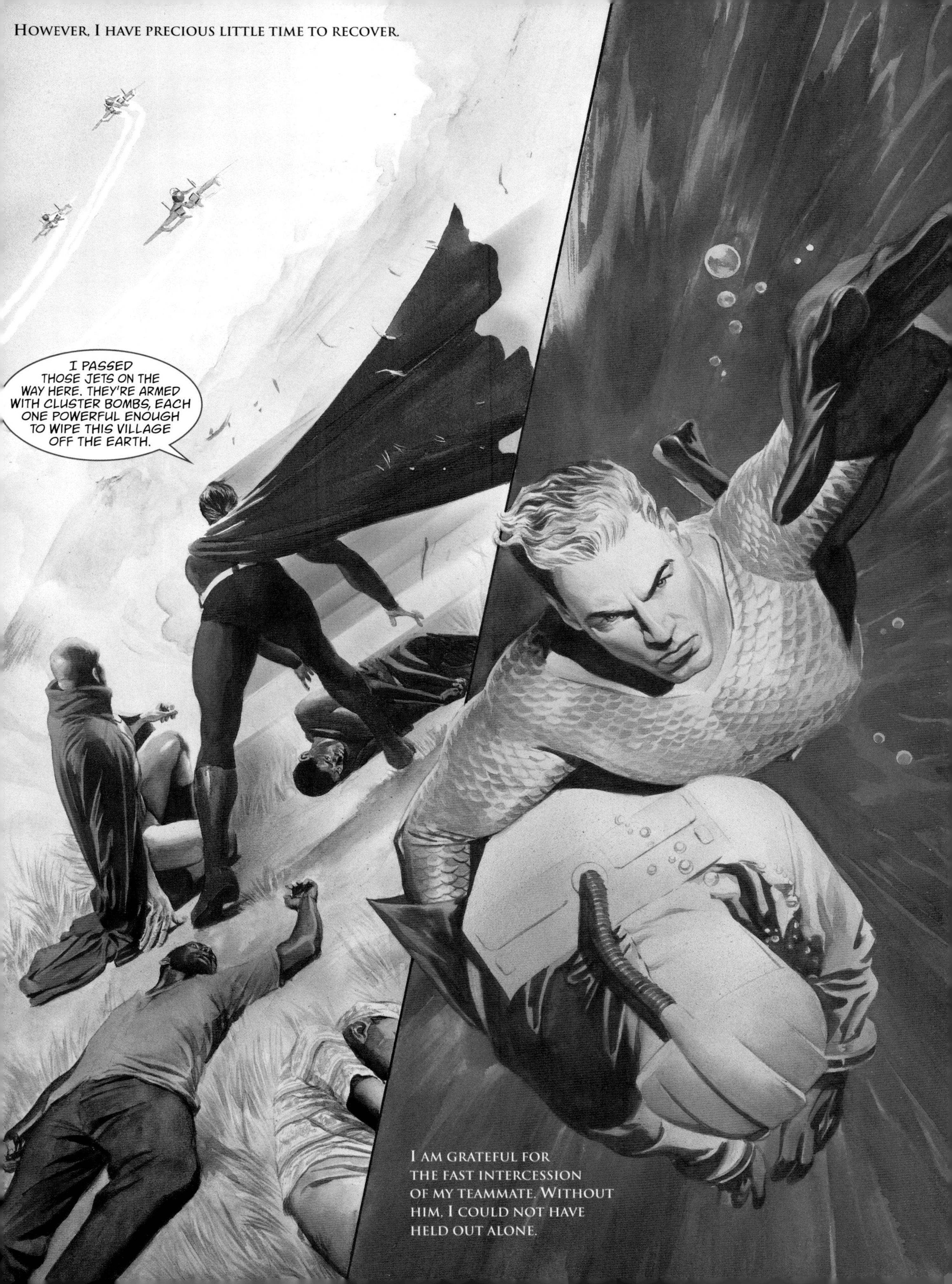
However, I have precious little time to recover.
I passed those jets on the way here. They're armed with cluster bombs, each one powerful enough to wipe this village off the earth.
I am grateful for the fast intercession of my teammate. Without him, I could not have held out alone.

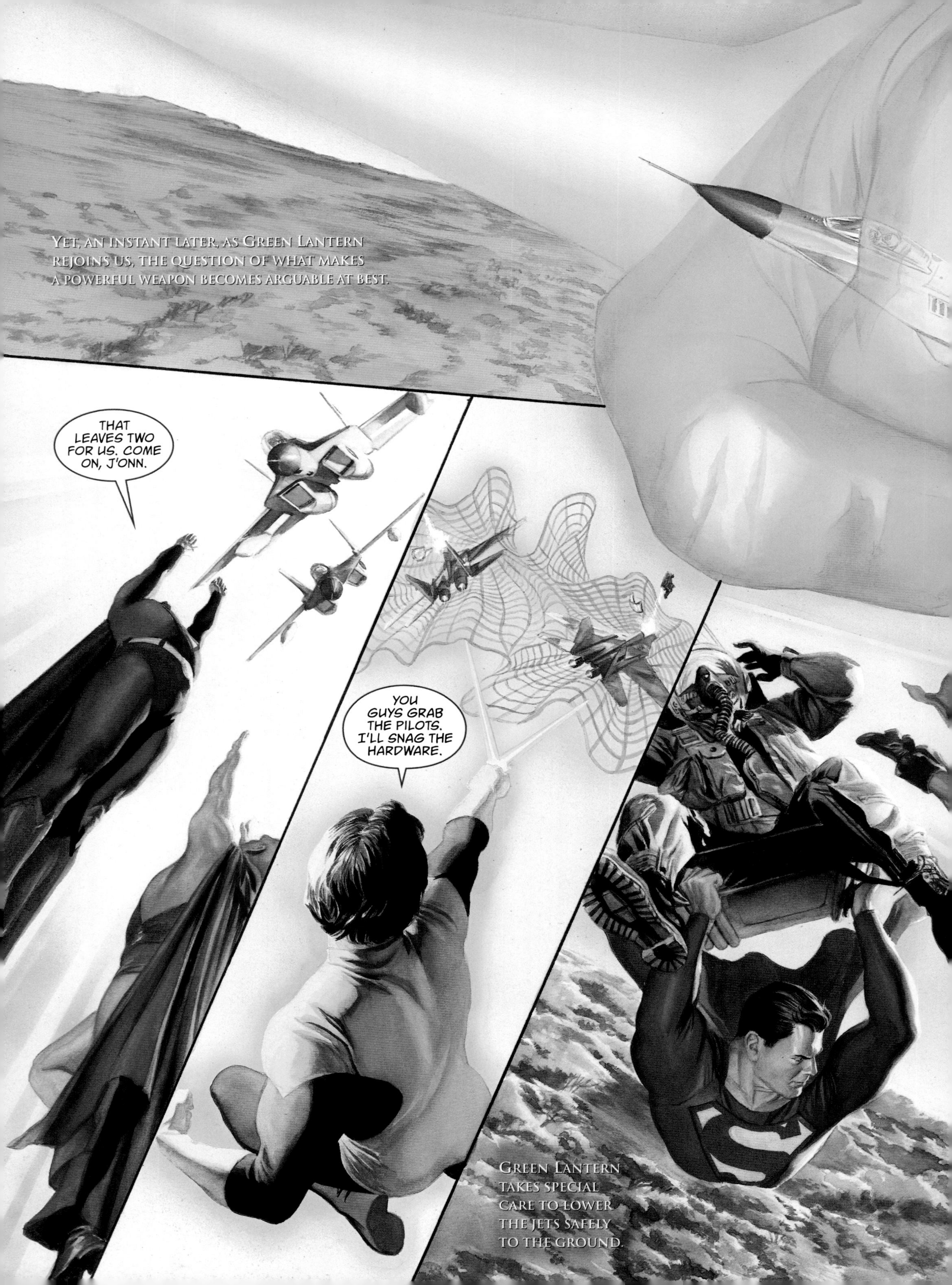
Yet, an instant later, as Green Lantern rejoins us, the question of what makes a powerful weapon becomes arguable at best.
THAT LEAVES TWO FOR US. COME ON, J'ONN.
YOU GUYS GRAB THE PILOTS. I'LL SNAG THE HARDWARE.
Green Lantern takes special care to lower the jets safely to the ground.

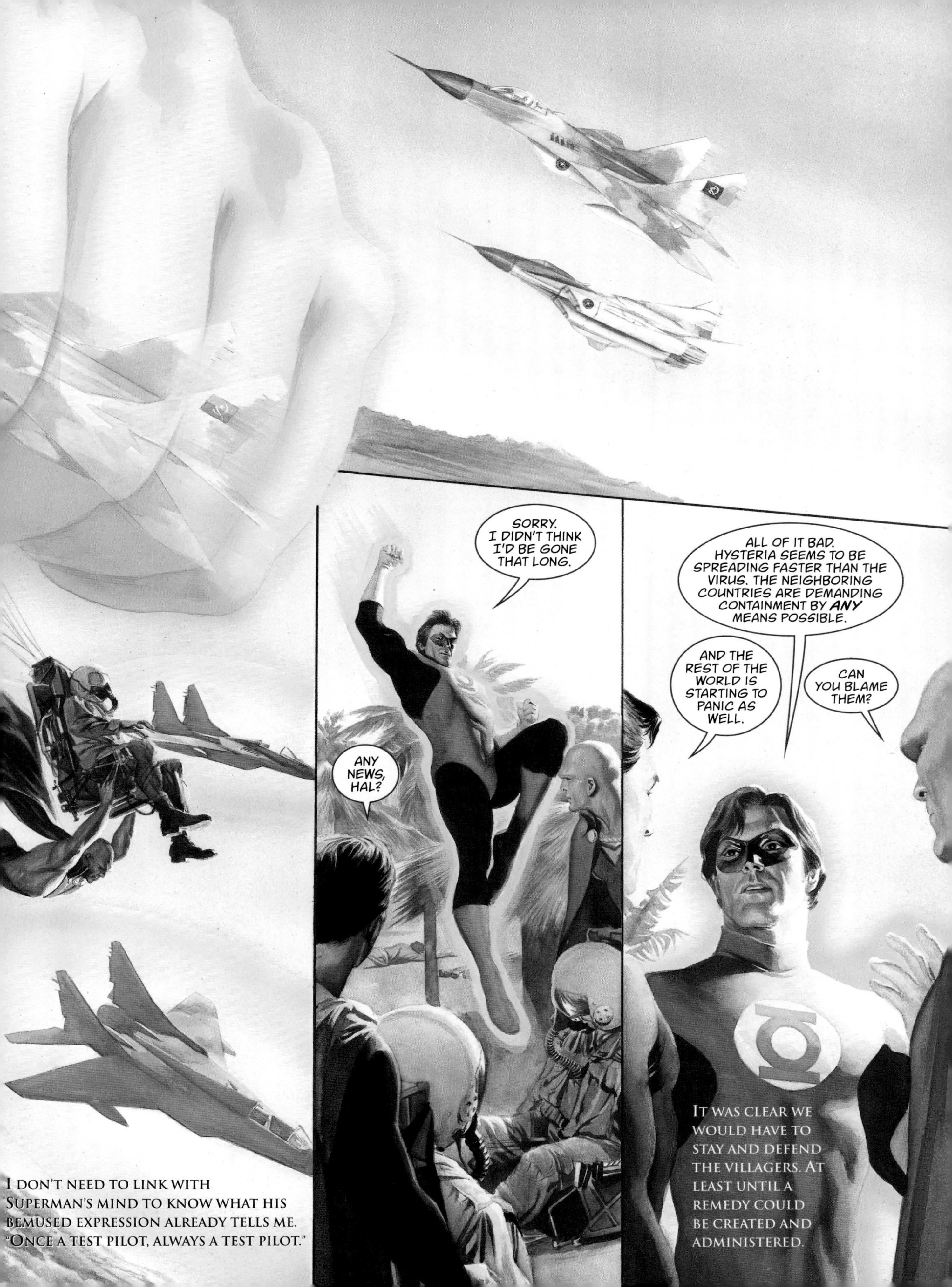
I DON'T NEED TO LINK WITH SUPERMAN'S MIND TO KNOW WHAT HIS BEMUSED EXPRESSION ALREADY TELLS ME. "ONCE A TEST PILOT, ALWAYS A TEST PILOT."
SORRY. I DIDN'T THINK I'D BE GONE THAT LONG.
ANY NEWS, HAL?
ALL OF IT BAD. HYSTERIA SEEMS TO BE SPREADING FASTER THAN THE VIRUS. THE NEIGHBORING COUNTRIES ARE DEMANDING CONTAINMENT BY ANY MEANS POSSIBLE.
AND THE REST OF THE WORLD IS STARTING TO PANIC AS WELL.
CAN YOU BLAME THEM?
IT WAS CLEAR WE WOULD HAVE TO STAY AND DEFEND THE VILLAGERS. AT LEAST UNTIL A REMEDY COULD BE CREATED AND ADMINISTERED.

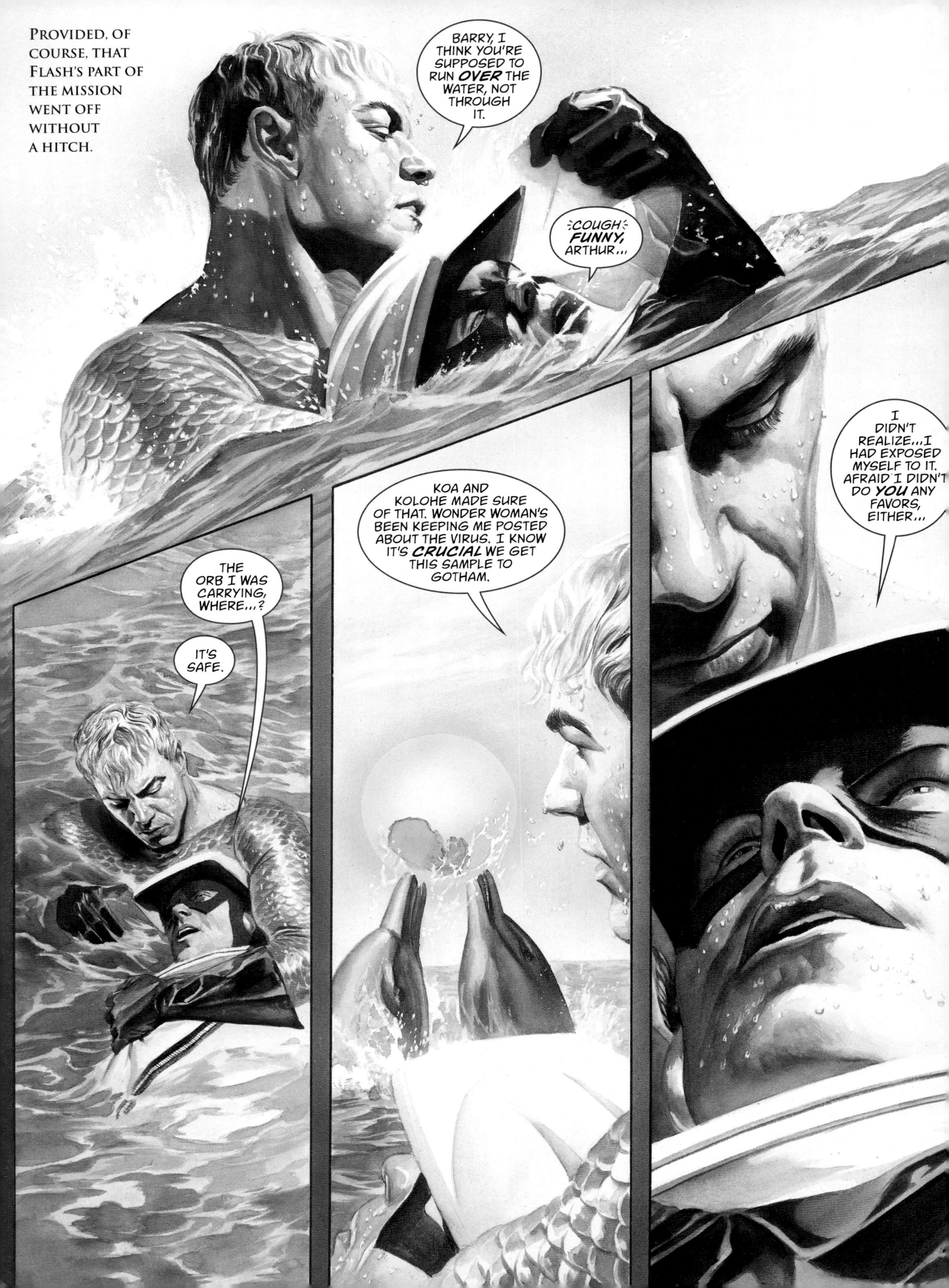
PROVIDED, OF COURSE, THAT FLASH'S PART OF THE MISSION WENT OFF WITHOUT A HITCH.
BARRY, I THINK YOU'RE SUPPOSED TO RUN OVER THE WATER, NOT THROUGH IT.
COUGH FUNNY, ARTHUR...
THE ORB I WAS CARRYING, WHERE...?
IT'S SAFE.
KOA AND KOLOHE MADE SURE OF THAT. WONDER WOMAN'S BEEN KEEPING ME POSTED ABOUT THE VIRUS. I KNOW IT'S CRUCIAL WE GET THIS SAMPLE TO GOTHAM.
I DIDN'T REALIZE...I HAD EXPOSED MYSELF TO IT. AFRAID I DIDN'T DO YOU ANY FAVORS, EITHER...

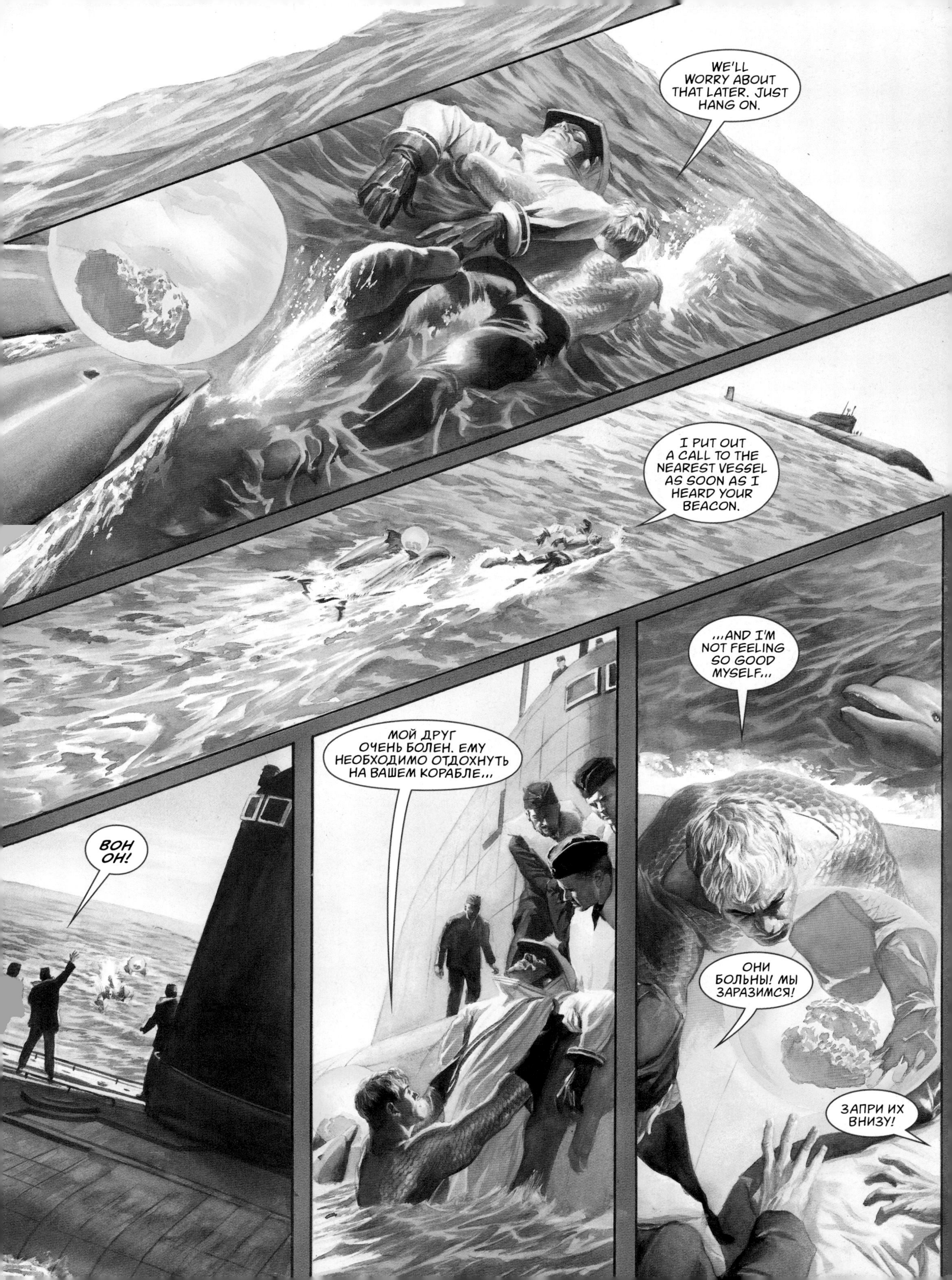
WE'LL WORRY ABOUT THAT LATER. JUST HANG ON.
I PUT OUT A CALL TO THE NEAREST VESSEL AS SOON AS I HEARD YOUR BEACON.
ВОН ОН!
МОЙ ДРУГ ОЧЕНЬ БОЛЕН. ЕМУ НЕОБХОДИМО ОТДОХНУТЬ НА ВАШЕМ КОРАБЛЕ...
...AND I'M NOT FEELING SO GOOD MYSELF...
ОНИ БОЛЬНЫ! МЫ ЗАРАЗИМСЯ!
ЗАПРИ ИХ ВНИЗУ!

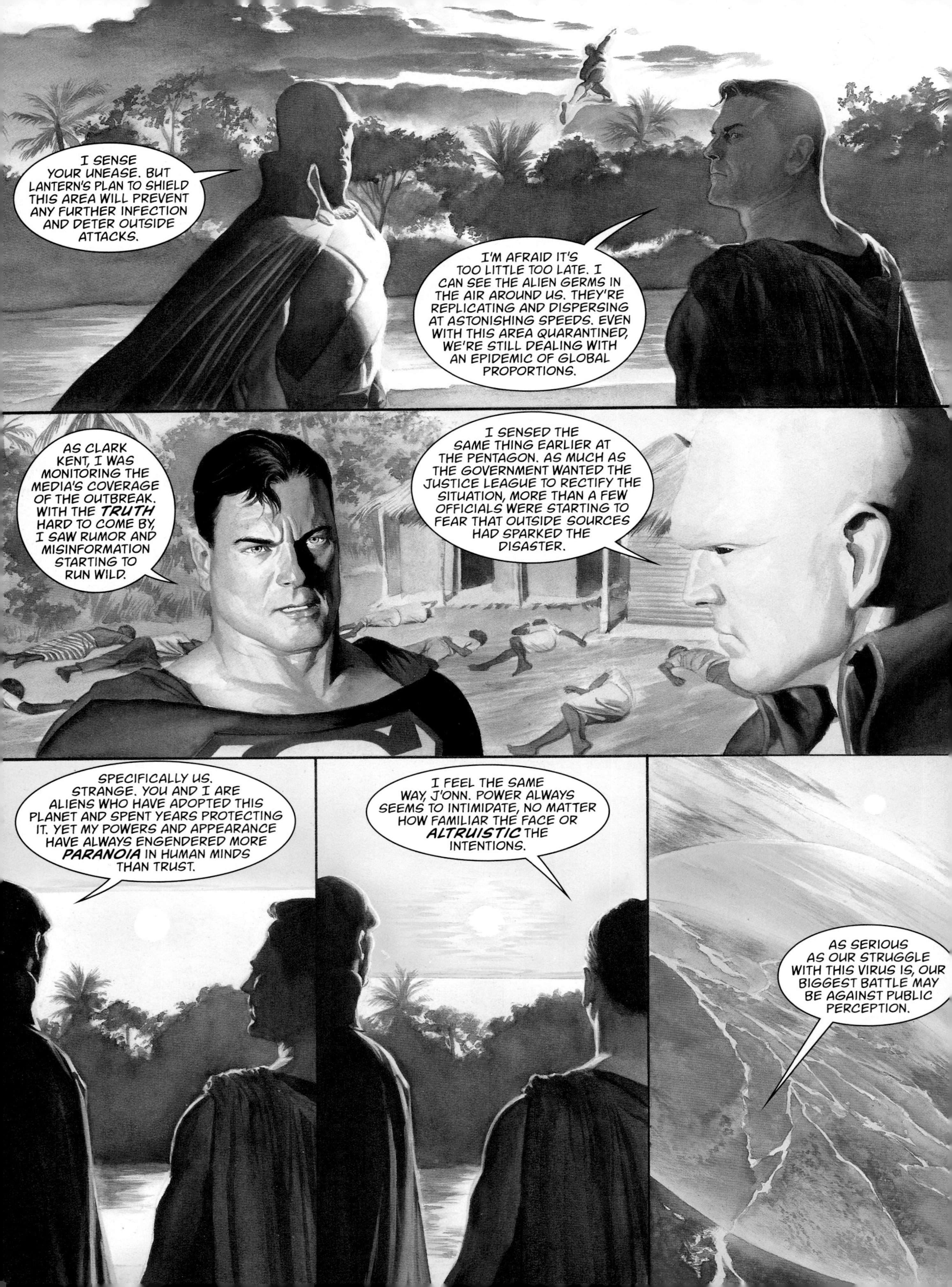
I SENSE YOUR UNEASE. BUT LANTERN'S PLAN TO SHIELD THIS AREA WILL PREVENT ANY FURTHER INFECTION AND DETER OUTSIDE ATTACKS.
I'M AFRAID IT'S TOO LITTLE TOO LATE. I CAN SEE THE ALIEN GERMS IN THE AIR AROUND US. THEY'RE REPLICATING AND DISPERSING AT ASTONISHING SPEEDS. EVEN WITH THIS AREA QUARANTINED, WE'RE STILL DEALING WITH AN EPIDEMIC OF GLOBAL PROPORTIONS.
AS CLARK KENT, I WAS MONITORING THE MEDIA'S COVERAGE OF THE OUTBREAK. WITH THE *TRUTH* HARD TO COME BY, I SAW RUMOR AND MISINFORMATION STARTING TO RUN WILD.
I SENSED THE SAME THING EARLIER AT THE PENTAGON. AS MUCH AS THE GOVERNMENT WANTED THE JUSTICE LEAGUE TO RECTIFY THE SITUATION, MORE THAN A FEW OFFICIALS WERE STARTING TO FEAR THAT OUTSIDE SOURCES HAD SPARKED THE DISASTER.
SPECIFICALLY US. STRANGE. YOU AND I ARE ALIENS WHO HAVE ADOPTED THIS PLANET AND SPENT YEARS PROTECTING IT. YET MY POWERS AND APPEARANCE HAVE ALWAYS ENGENDERED MORE *PARANOIA* IN HUMAN MINDS THAN TRUST.
I FEEL THE SAME WAY, J'ONN. POWER ALWAYS SEEMS TO INTIMIDATE, NO MATTER HOW FAMILIAR THE FACE OR *ALTRUISTIC* THE INTENTIONS.
AS SERIOUS AS OUR STRUGGLE WITH THIS VIRUS IS, OUR BIGGEST BATTLE MAY BE AGAINST PUBLIC PERCEPTION.

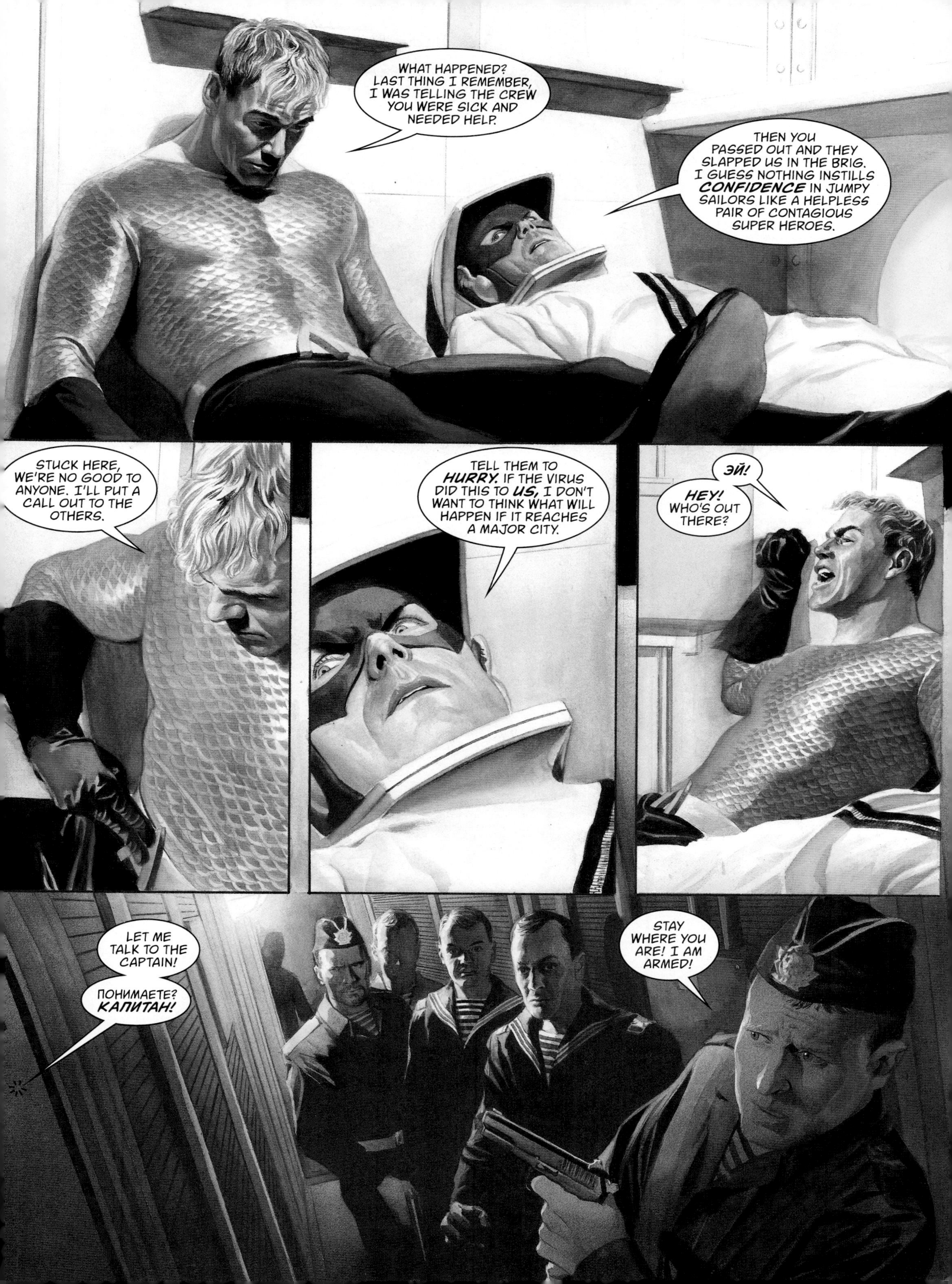
WHAT HAPPENED? LAST THING I REMEMBER, I WAS TELLING THE CREW YOU WERE SICK AND NEEDED HELP.
THEN YOU PASSED OUT AND THEY SLAPPED US IN THE BRIG. I GUESS NOTHING INSTILLS ***CONFIDENCE*** IN JUMPY SAILORS LIKE A HELPLESS PAIR OF CONTAGIOUS SUPER HEROES.
STUCK HERE, WE'RE NO GOOD TO ANYONE. I'LL PUT A CALL OUT TO THE OTHERS.
TELL THEM TO ***HURRY.*** IF THE VIRUS DID THIS TO ***US,*** I DON'T WANT TO THINK WHAT WILL HAPPEN IF IT REACHES A MAJOR CITY.
ЭЙ!
HEY! WHO'S OUT THERE?
LET ME TALK TO THE CAPTAIN!
ПОНИМАЕТЕ? ***КАПИТАН!***
STAY WHERE YOU ARE! I AM ARMED!

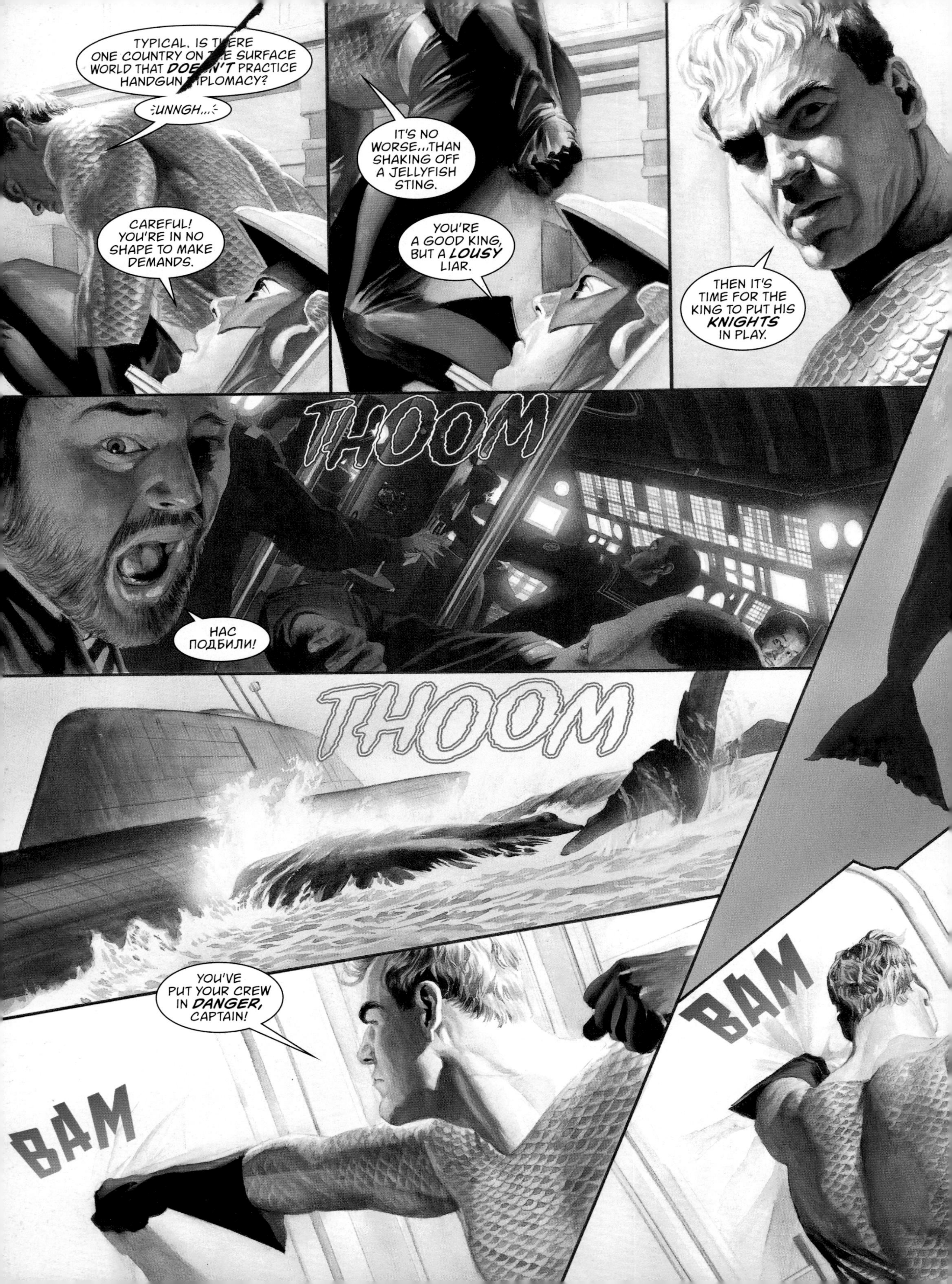
TYPICAL. IS THERE ONE COUNTRY ON THE SURFACE WORLD THAT DOESN'T PRACTICE HANDGUN DIPLOMACY?
UNNGH...
CAREFUL! YOU'RE IN NO SHAPE TO MAKE DEMANDS.
IT'S NO WORSE...THAN SHAKING OFF A JELLYFISH STING.
YOU'RE A GOOD KING, BUT A LOUSY LIAR.
THEN IT'S TIME FOR THE KING TO PUT HIS KNIGHTS IN PLAY.
THOOM
НАС ПОДБИЛИ!
THOOM
YOU'VE PUT YOUR CREW IN DANGER, CAPTAIN!
BAM
BAM

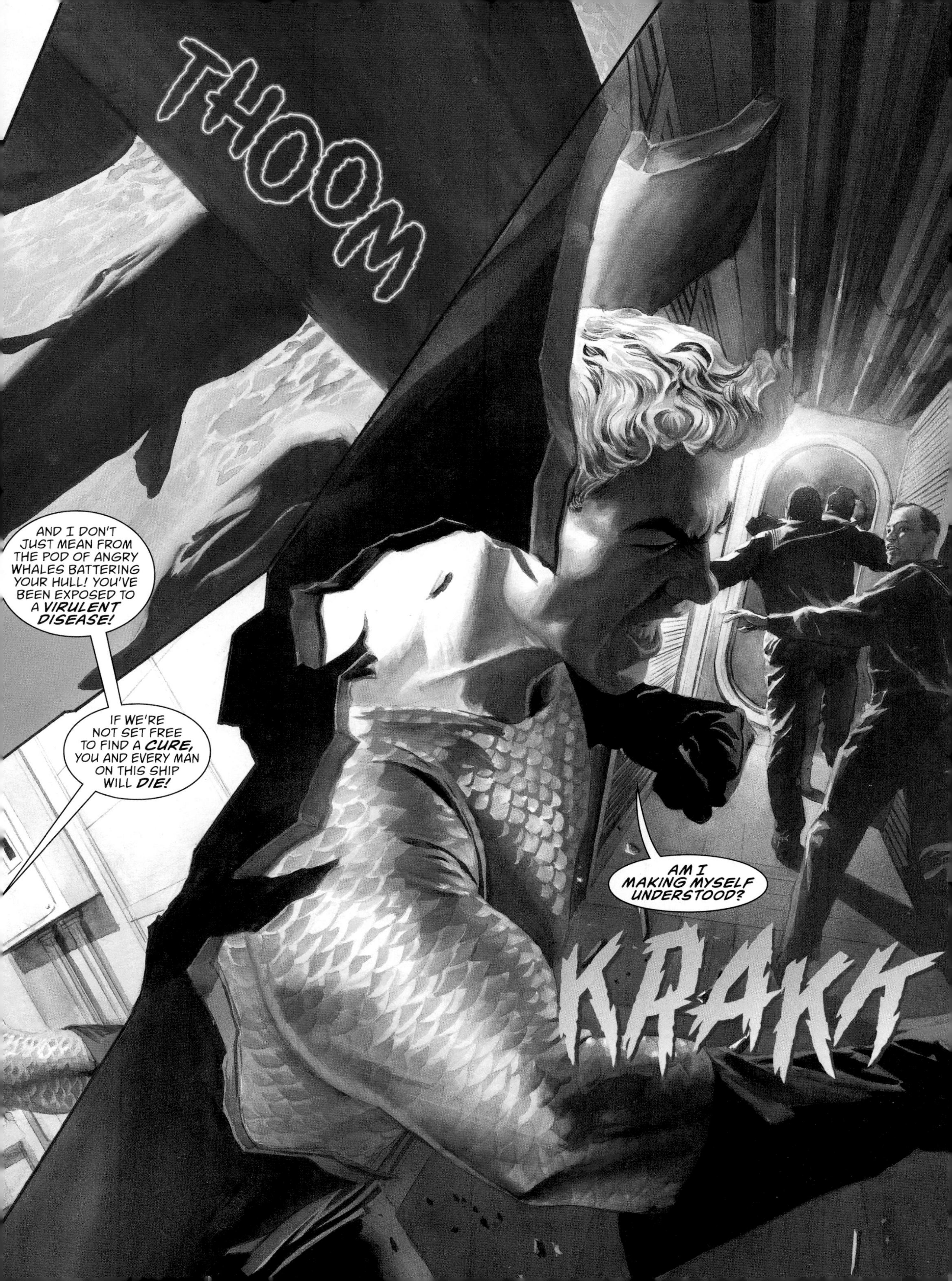
THOOM
AND I DON'T JUST MEAN FROM THE POD OF ANGRY WHALES BATTERING YOUR HULL! YOU'VE BEEN EXPOSED TO A VIRULENT DISEASE!
IF WE'RE NOT SET FREE TO FIND A CURE, YOU AND EVERY MAN ON THIS SHIP WILL DIE!
AM I MAKING MYSELF UNDERSTOOD?
KRAKK

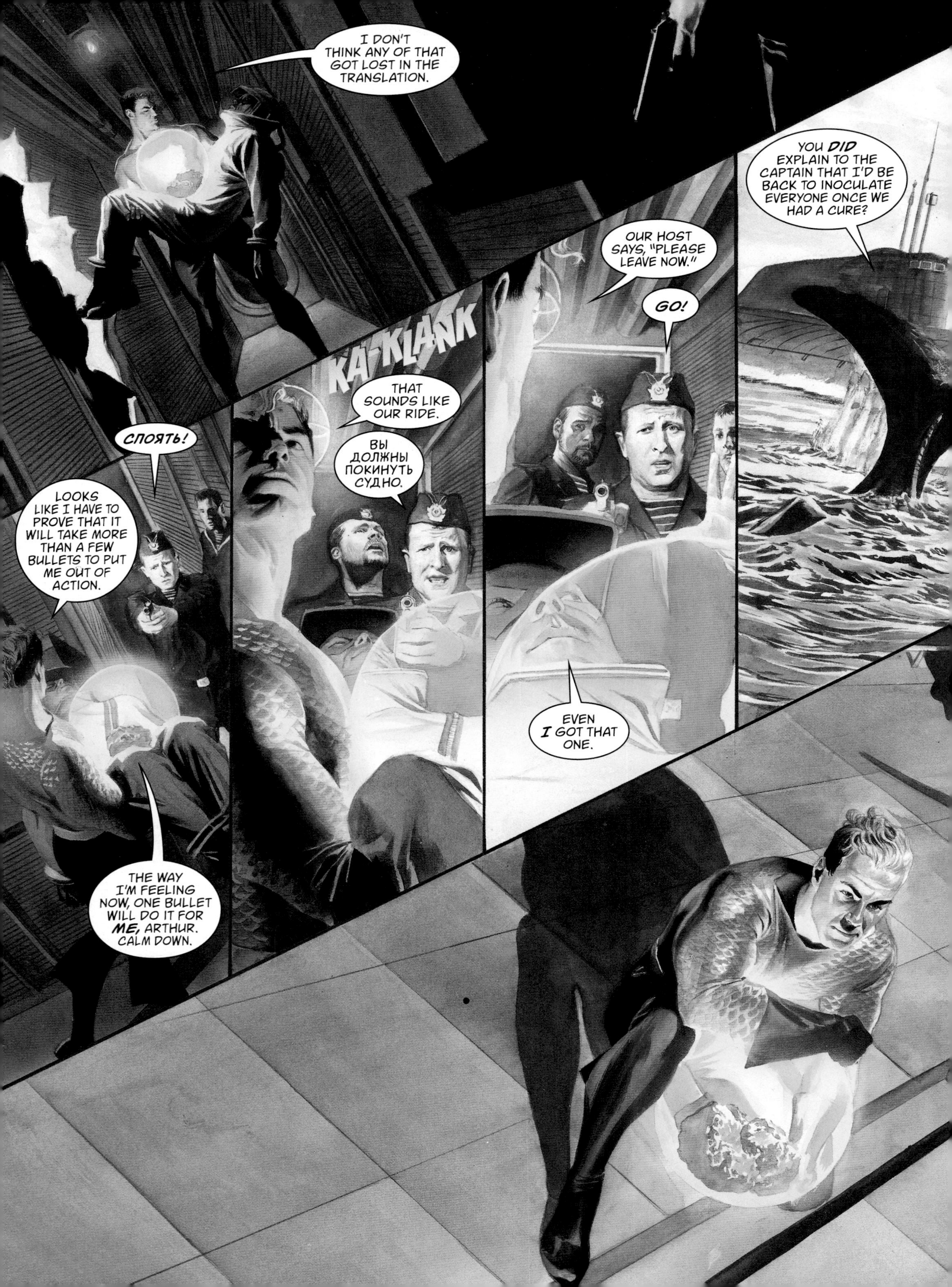
I DON'T THINK ANY OF THAT GOT LOST IN THE TRANSLATION.
СПОЯТЬ!
LOOKS LIKE I HAVE TO PROVE THAT IT WILL TAKE MORE THAN A FEW BULLETS TO PUT ME OUT OF ACTION.
THE WAY I'M FEELING NOW, ONE BULLET WILL DO IT FOR **ME,** ARTHUR. CALM DOWN.
KA-KLANK
THAT SOUNDS LIKE OUR RIDE.
ВЫ ДОЛЖНЫ ПОКИНУТЬ СУДНО.
OUR HOST SAYS, "PLEASE LEAVE NOW."
GO!
EVEN ***I*** GOT THAT ONE.
YOU ***DID*** EXPLAIN TO THE CAPTAIN THAT I'D BE BACK TO INOCULATE EVERYONE ONCE WE HAD A CURE?

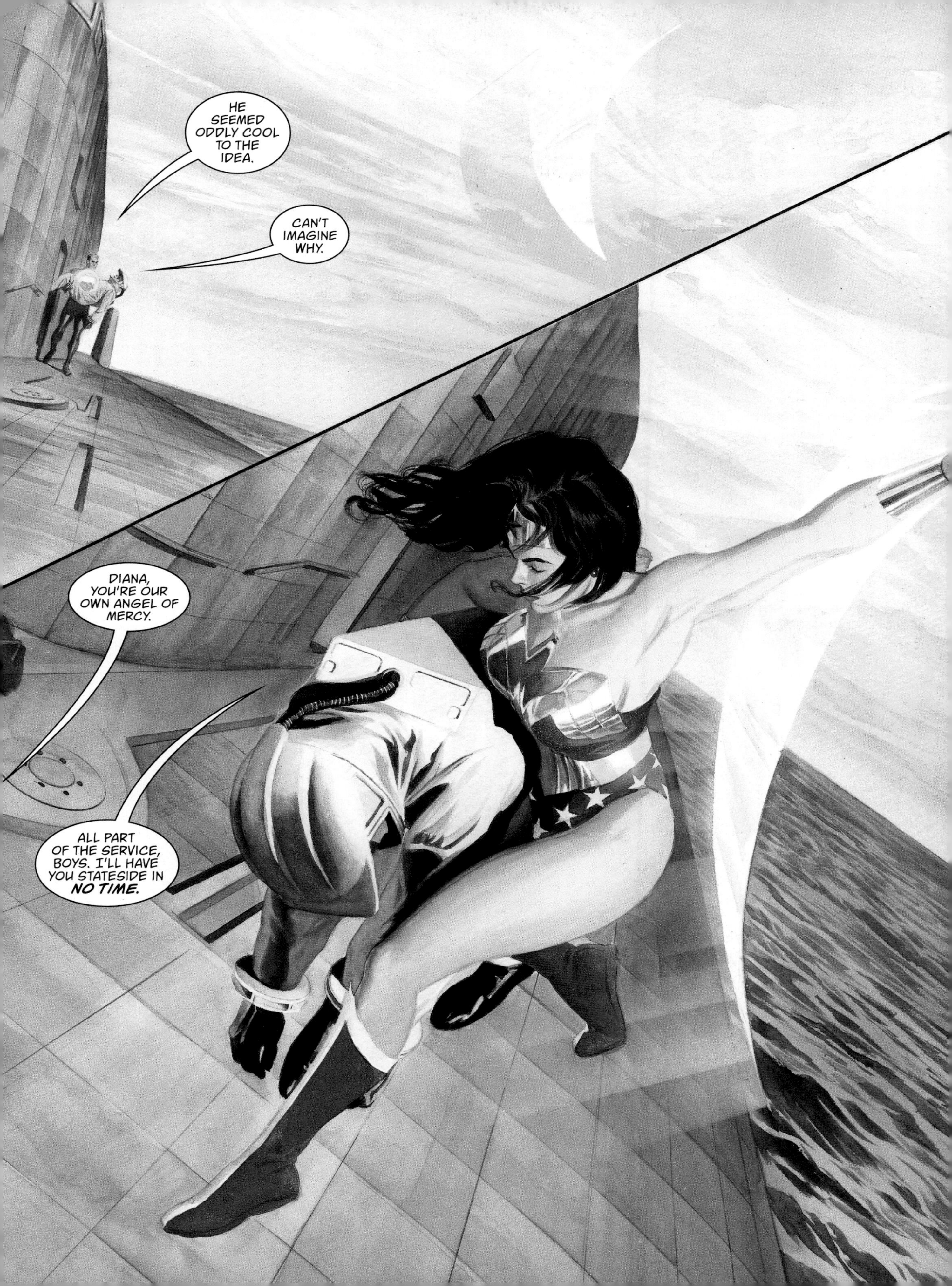
HE SEEMED ODDLY COOL TO THE IDEA.
CAN'T IMAGINE WHY.
DIANA, YOU'RE OUR OWN ANGEL OF MERCY.
ALL PART OF THE SERVICE, BOYS. I'LL HAVE YOU STATESIDE IN *NO TIME.*

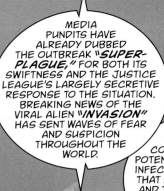

MEDIA PUNDITS HAVE ALREADY DUBBED THE OUTBREAK *"SUPER-PLAGUE,"* FOR BOTH ITS SWIFTNESS AND THE JUSTICE LEAGUE'S LARGELY SECRETIVE RESPONSE TO THE SITUATION. BREAKING NEWS OF THE VIRAL ALIEN *"INVASION"* HAS SENT WAVES OF FEAR AND SUSPICION THROUGHOUT THE WORLD.

IT'S TRUE WE ARE BEING CONFRONTED WITH A POTENTIALLY DEVASTATING INFECTION. BUT HOW DOES THAT MITIGATE SUPERMAN AND THE OTHERS ACTING WITHOUT THE APPROVAL OF THE *U.N.* OR ANY *AFRICAN* GOVERNMENT?

THIS IS A HUMAN PROBLEM, AND IN THIS REPORTER'S OPINION, FEW OF THE LEAGUE'S MEMBERS QUALIFY.

IT'S AN *ALIEN* DISEASE, AND SUPERMAN AND THREE OTHER LEAGUE MEMBERS ARE KNOWN EXTRATERRESTRIALS. *HELLO?* AM I THE ONLY ONE MAKING THE *LEAP* HERE?

IN THE PAST THESE MEN AND WOMEN HAVE GIVEN *TIRELESSLY* OF THEIR ABILITIES, AND ALWAYS FOR THE COMMON GOOD. THEY'VE *EARNED* OUR TRUST AS WELL AS OUR GRATITUDE AND PRAYERS.

THEY'VE TAKEN IT UPON THEMSELVES TO *DESTROY* SCOUT PLANES AND PUT AN IMPENETRABLE SHIELD OVER THE HOT ZONE. WHAT ARE THEY TRYING TO *HIDE?*

SEQUESTERED IN EMERGENCY MEETINGS WITH PENTAGON OFFICIALS SINCE EARLY THIS MORNING, THE PRESIDENT HAS REMAINED *UNAVAILABLE* FOR COMMENT...

SPECULATION AND PANIC OVER THE PLAGUE WAS RISING, BUT THE LEAGUE WAS TOO BUSY TRYING TO FIGHT THE BATTLES CLOSER AT HAND. SUPERMAN CAST HIMSELF IN THE ROLE OF DIPLOMAT, MEETING WITH AFRICAN LEADERS AND URGING THEM TO BE PATIENT BEFORE TAKING FURTHER MILITARY ACTION.

IRON LUNGS CREATED BY GREEN LANTERN'S RING KEPT EVER-WEAKENING BODIES FROM FAILING. TRANSFORMING MY MIND INTO A TELEPATHIC CONDUIT, I ENCOURAGED THE VILLAGERS TO SEND THOUGHTS OF COMFORT TO ONE ANOTHER. FOR THE FIRST TIME I COULD SENSE THEIR PANIC ABATING AND THE STIRRINGS OF RELIEF.

YET THE STORM CLOUDS MASSING OVERHEAD REFLECTED THE ANXIETY I COULD SENSE BUILDING AROUND THE WORLD. THE RIPPLES OF FEAR THAT BEGAN IN AFRICA WERE HEADED TOWARD NORTH AMERICA...

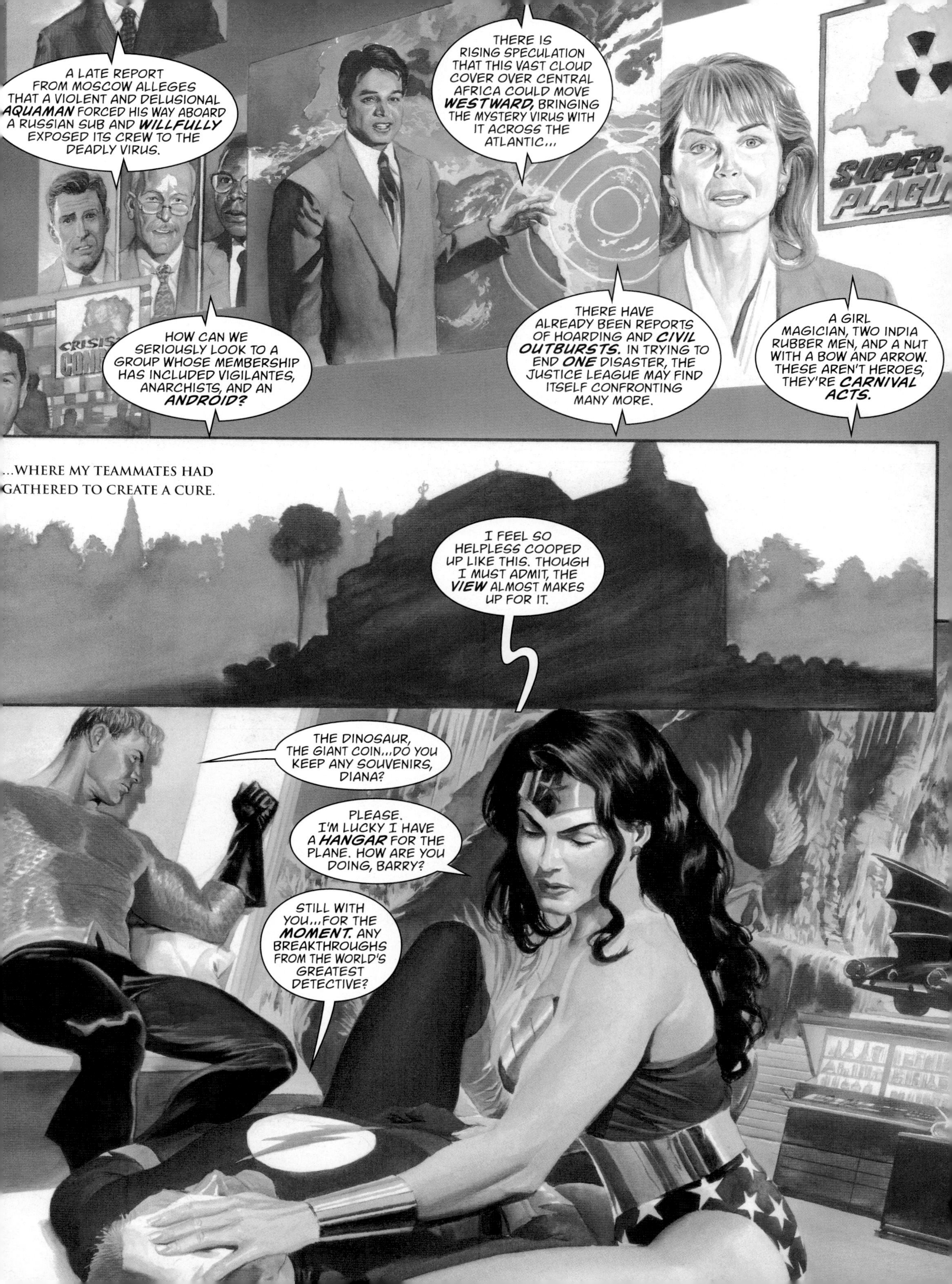
A LATE REPORT FROM MOSCOW ALLEGES THAT A VIOLENT AND DELUSIONAL AQUAMAN FORCED HIS WAY ABOARD A RUSSIAN SUB AND WILLFULLY EXPOSED ITS CREW TO THE DEADLY VIRUS.
THERE IS RISING SPECULATION THAT THIS VAST CLOUD COVER OVER CENTRAL AFRICA COULD MOVE WESTWARD, BRINGING THE MYSTERY VIRUS WITH IT ACROSS THE ATLANTIC...
SUPER-PLAGU
HOW CAN WE SERIOUSLY LOOK TO A GROUP WHOSE MEMBERSHIP HAS INCLUDED VIGILANTES, ANARCHISTS, AND AN ANDROID?
THERE HAVE ALREADY BEEN REPORTS OF HOARDING AND CIVIL OUTBURSTS. IN TRYING TO END ONE DISASTER, THE JUSTICE LEAGUE MAY FIND ITSELF CONFRONTING MANY MORE.
A GIRL MAGICIAN, TWO INDIA RUBBER MEN, AND A NUT WITH A BOW AND ARROW. THESE AREN'T HEROES, THEY'RE CARNIVAL ACTS.
...WHERE MY TEAMMATES HAD GATHERED TO CREATE A CURE.
I FEEL SO HELPLESS COOPED UP LIKE THIS. THOUGH I MUST ADMIT, THE VIEW ALMOST MAKES UP FOR IT.
THE DINOSAUR, THE GIANT COIN...DO YOU KEEP ANY SOUVENIRS, DIANA?
PLEASE. I'M LUCKY I HAVE A HANGAR FOR THE PLANE. HOW ARE YOU DOING, BARRY?
STILL WITH YOU...FOR THE MOMENT. ANY BREAKTHROUGHS FROM THE WORLD'S GREATEST DETECTIVE?

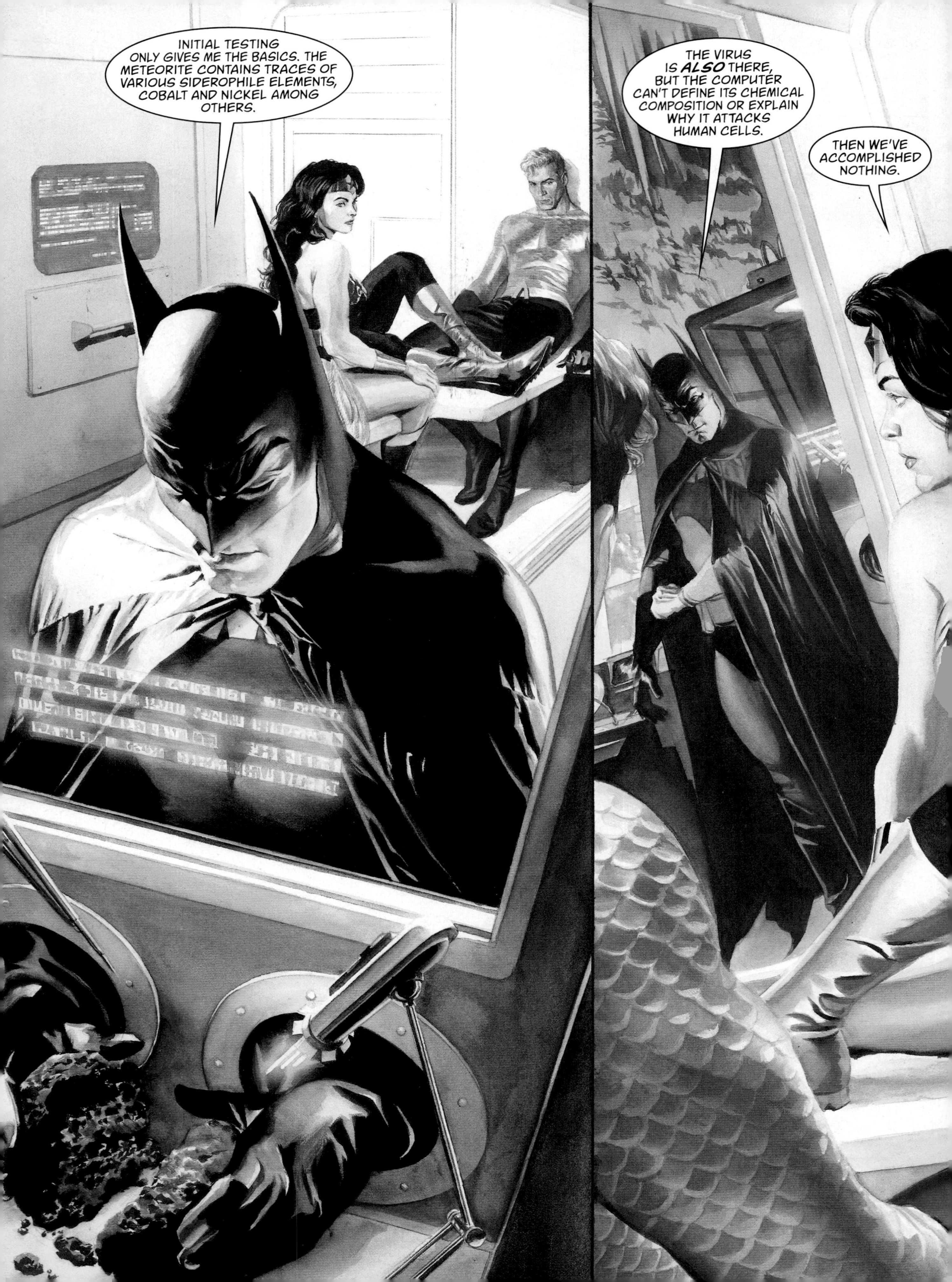
INITIAL TESTING ONLY GIVES ME THE BASICS. THE METEORITE CONTAINS TRACES OF VARIOUS SIDEROPHILE ELEMENTS, COBALT AND NICKEL AMONG OTHERS.
THE VIRUS IS *ALSO* THERE, BUT THE COMPUTER CAN'T DEFINE ITS CHEMICAL COMPOSITION OR EXPLAIN WHY IT ATTACKS HUMAN CELLS.
THEN WE'VE ACCOMPLISHED NOTHING.

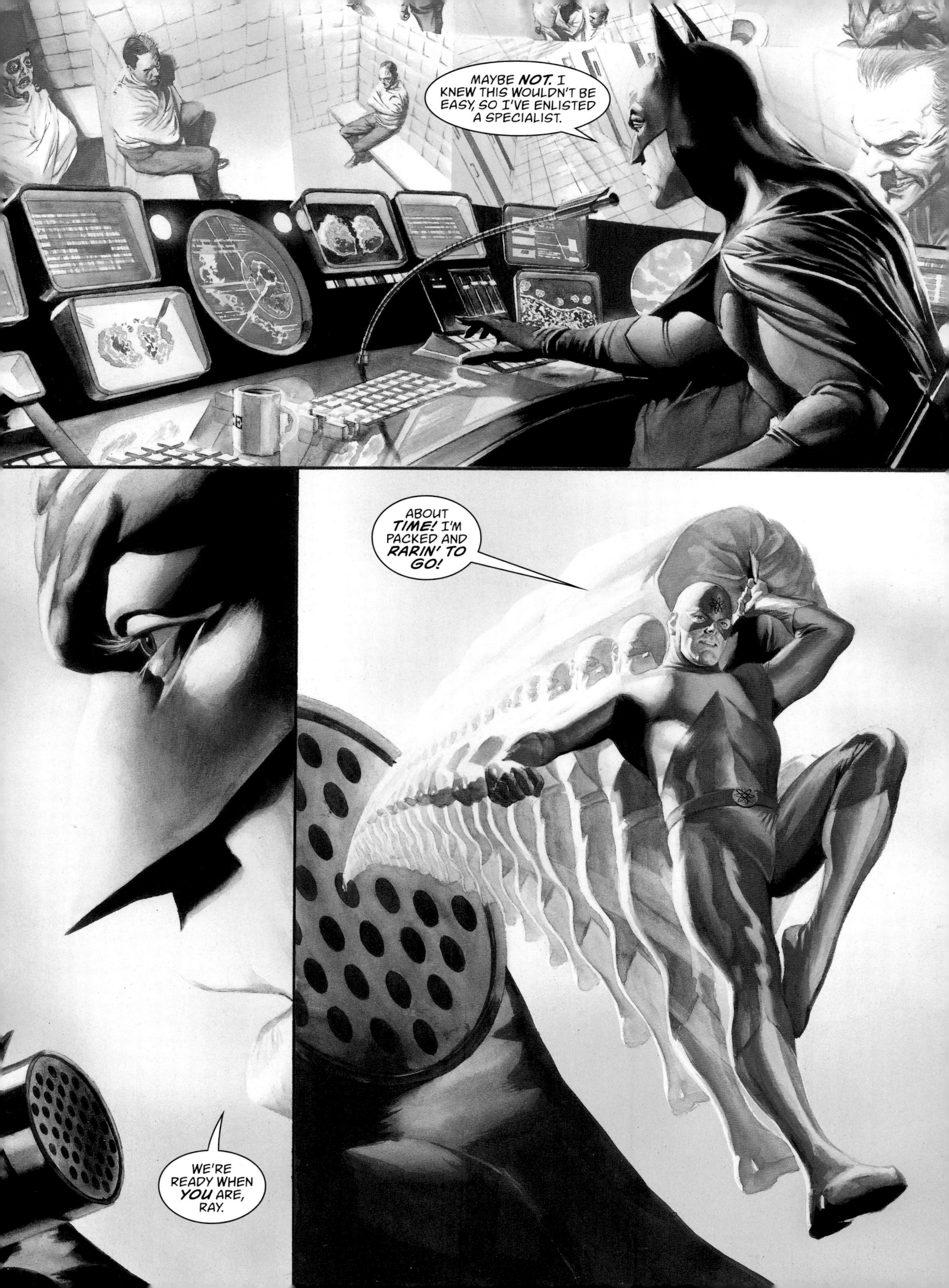
MAYBE NOT. I KNEW THIS WOULDN'T BE EASY, SO I'VE ENLISTED A SPECIALIST.
WE'RE READY WHEN YOU ARE, RAY.
ABOUT TIME! I'M PACKED AND RARIN' TO GO!

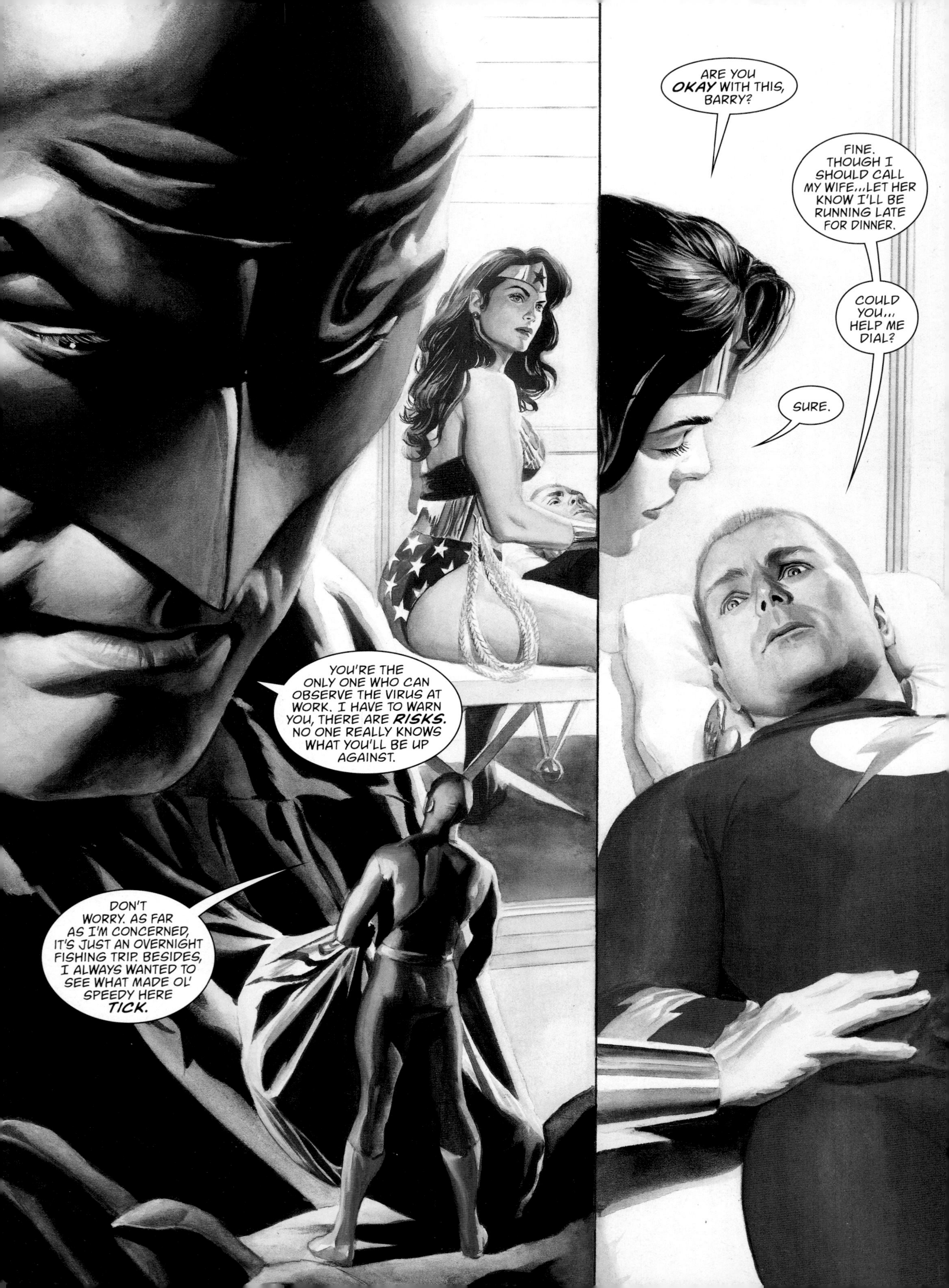
YOU'RE THE ONLY ONE WHO CAN OBSERVE THE VIRUS AT WORK. I HAVE TO WARN YOU, THERE ARE RISKS. NO ONE REALLY KNOWS WHAT YOU'LL BE UP AGAINST.
DON'T WORRY. AS FAR AS I'M CONCERNED, IT'S JUST AN OVERNIGHT FISHING TRIP. BESIDES, I ALWAYS WANTED TO SEE WHAT MADE OL' SPEEDY HERE TICK.
ARE YOU OKAY WITH THIS, BARRY?
FINE. THOUGH I SHOULD CALL MY WIFE...LET HER KNOW I'LL BE RUNNING LATE FOR DINNER.
COULD YOU... HELP ME DIAL?
SURE.

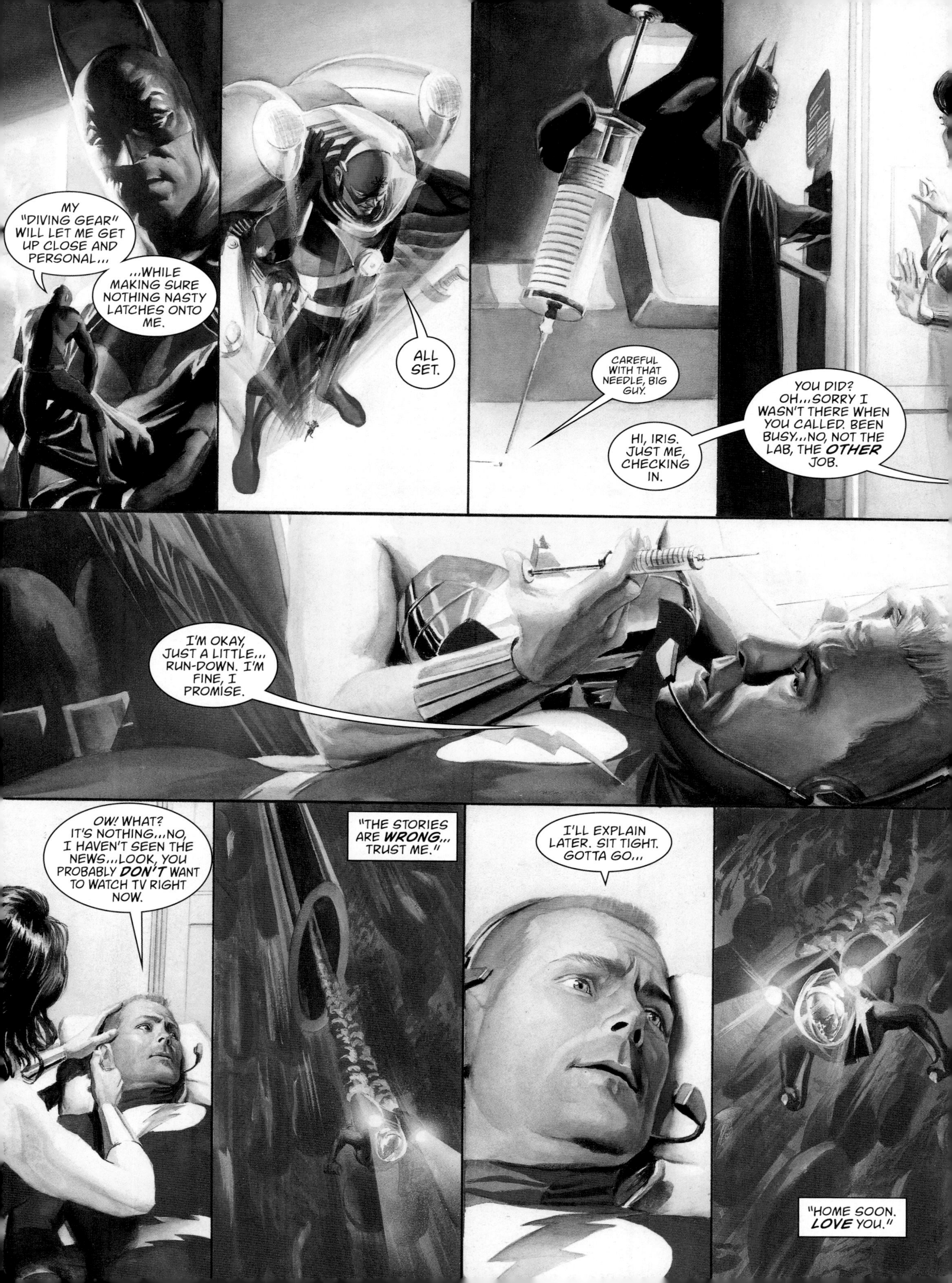
MY "DIVING GEAR" WILL LET ME GET UP CLOSE AND PERSONAL...
...WHILE MAKING SURE NOTHING NASTY LATCHES ONTO ME.
ALL SET.
CAREFUL WITH THAT NEEDLE, BIG GUY.
HI, IRIS. JUST ME, CHECKING IN.
YOU DID? OH...SORRY I WASN'T THERE WHEN YOU CALLED. BEEN BUSY...NO, NOT THE LAB, THE **OTHER** JOB.
I'M OKAY, JUST A LITTLE... RUN-DOWN. I'M FINE, I PROMISE.
OW! WHAT? IT'S NOTHING...NO, I HAVEN'T SEEN THE NEWS...LOOK, YOU PROBABLY **DON'T** WANT TO WATCH TV RIGHT NOW.
"THE STORIES ARE **WRONG**... TRUST ME."
I'LL EXPLAIN LATER. SIT TIGHT. GOTTA GO...
"HOME SOON. **LOVE** YOU."

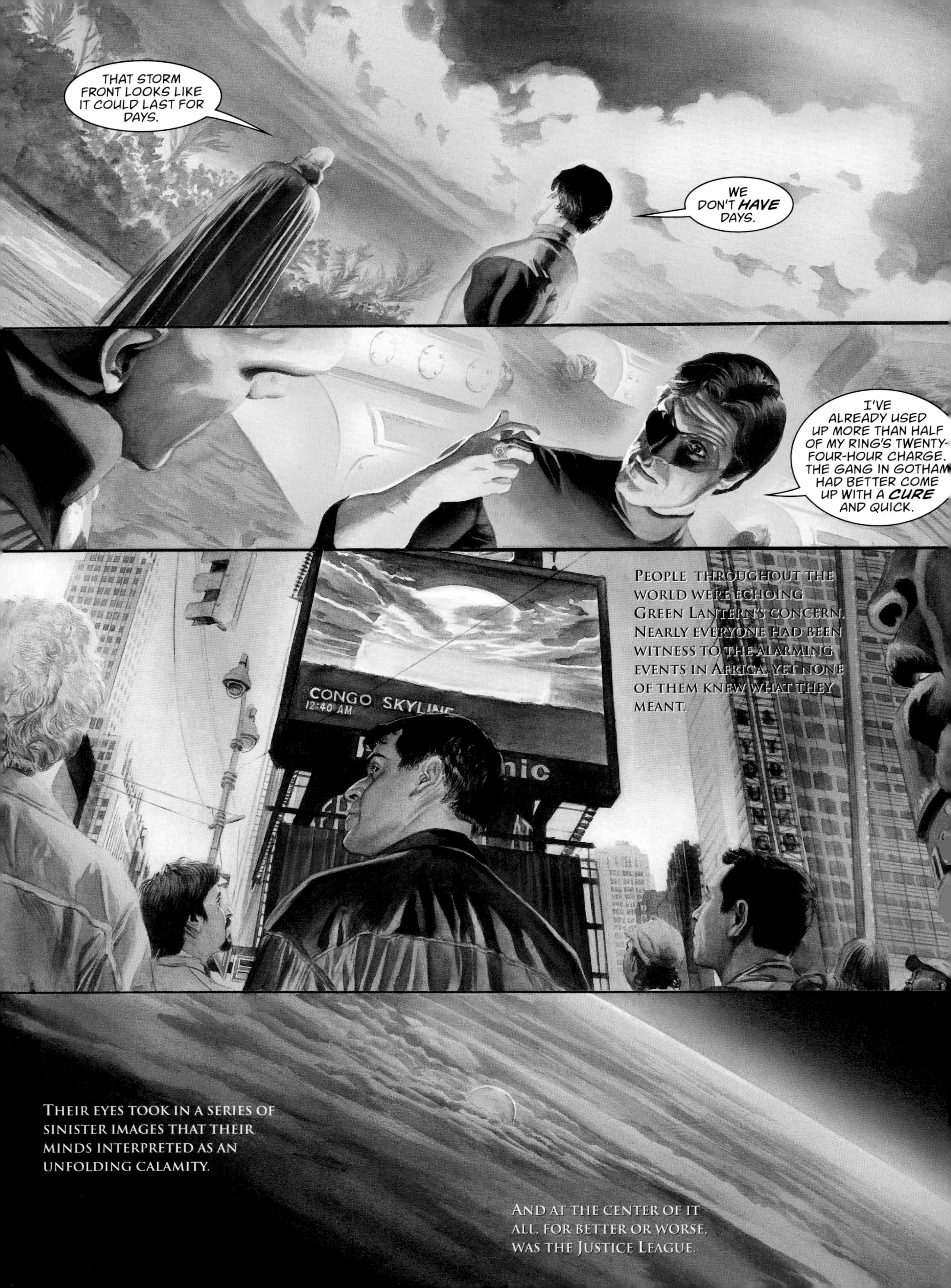
THAT STORM FRONT LOOKS LIKE IT COULD LAST FOR DAYS.
WE DON'T HAVE DAYS.
I'VE ALREADY USED UP MORE THAN HALF OF MY RING'S TWENTY-FOUR-HOUR CHARGE. THE GANG IN GOTHAM HAD BETTER COME UP WITH A CURE AND QUICK.
PEOPLE THROUGHOUT THE WORLD WERE ECHOING GREEN LANTERN'S CONCERN. NEARLY EVERYONE HAD BEEN WITNESS TO THE ALARMING EVENTS IN AFRICA, YET NONE OF THEM KNEW WHAT THEY MEANT.
CONGO SKYLINE
12:40 AM
THEIR EYES TOOK IN A SERIES OF SINISTER IMAGES THAT THEIR MINDS INTERPRETED AS AN UNFOLDING CALAMITY.
AND AT THE CENTER OF IT ALL, FOR BETTER OR WORSE, WAS THE JUSTICE LEAGUE.

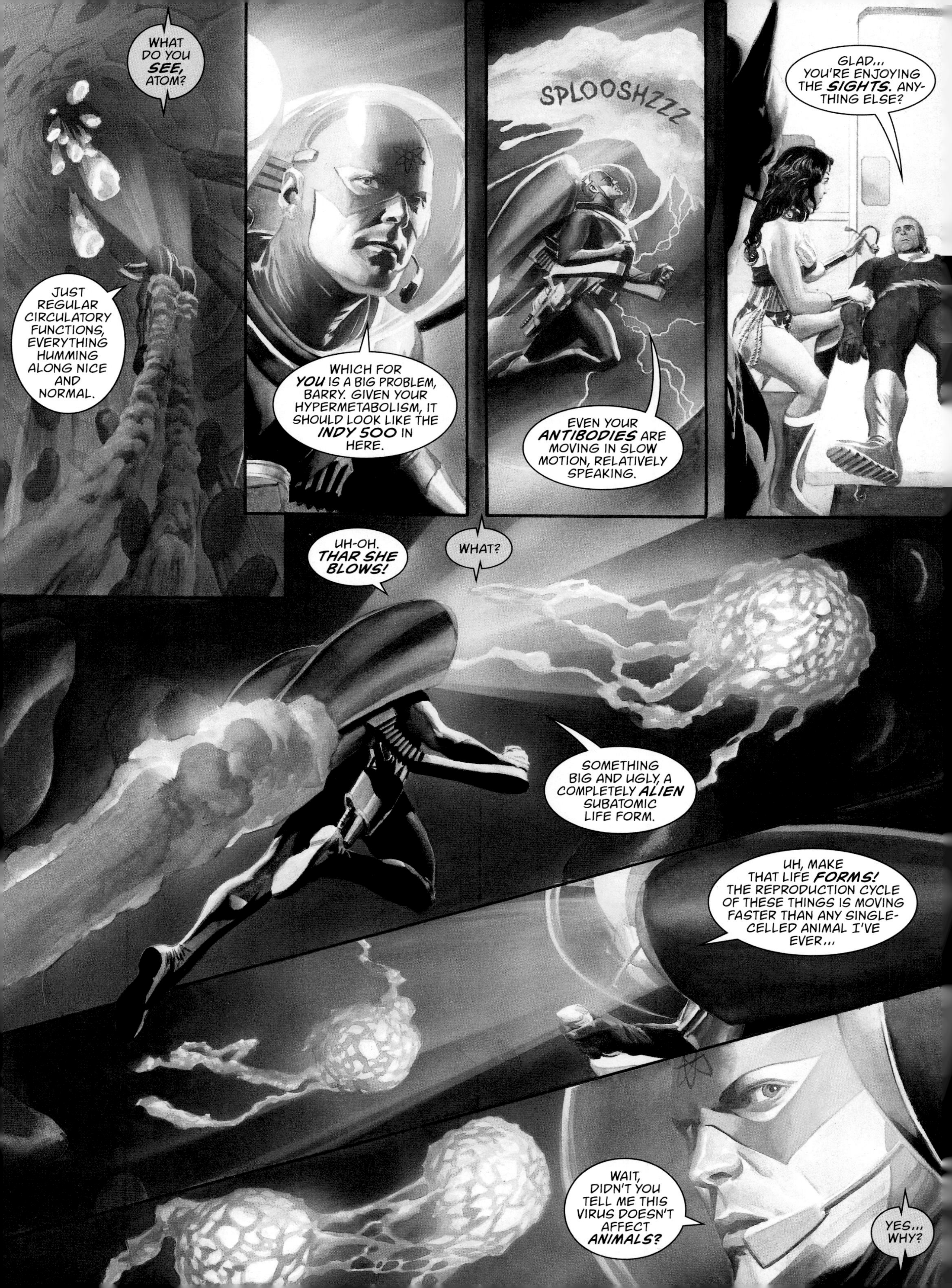
WHAT DO YOU SEE, ATOM?
JUST REGULAR CIRCULATORY FUNCTIONS, EVERYTHING HUMMING ALONG NICE AND NORMAL.
WHICH FOR YOU IS A BIG PROBLEM, BARRY. GIVEN YOUR HYPERMETABOLISM, IT SHOULD LOOK LIKE THE INDY 500 IN HERE.
SPLOOSHZZZ
EVEN YOUR ANTIBODIES ARE MOVING IN SLOW MOTION, RELATIVELY SPEAKING.
GLAD... YOU'RE ENJOYING THE SIGHTS. ANYTHING ELSE?
UH-OH. THAR SHE BLOWS!
WHAT?
SOMETHING BIG AND UGLY, A COMPLETELY ALIEN SUBATOMIC LIFE FORM.
UH, MAKE THAT LIFE FORMS! THE REPRODUCTION CYCLE OF THESE THINGS IS MOVING FASTER THAN ANY SINGLE-CELLED ANIMAL I'VE EVER...
WAIT, DIDN'T YOU TELL ME THIS VIRUS DOESN'T AFFECT ANIMALS?
YES... WHY?

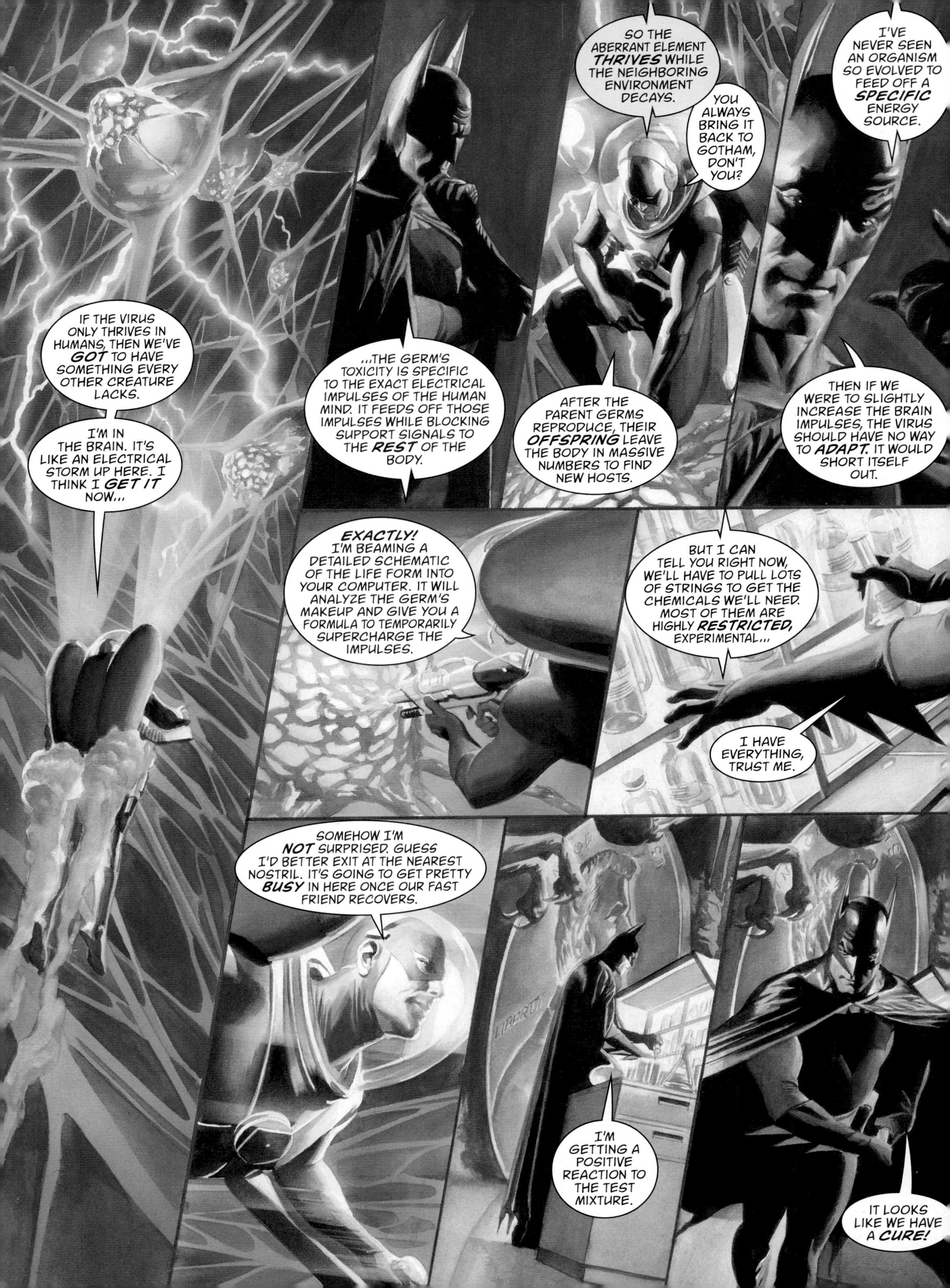

IF THE VIRUS ONLY THRIVES IN HUMANS, THEN WE'VE **GOT** TO HAVE SOMETHING EVERY OTHER CREATURE LACKS.
I'M IN THE BRAIN. IT'S LIKE AN ELECTRICAL STORM UP HERE. I THINK I **GET IT** NOW...
...THE GERM'S TOXICITY IS SPECIFIC TO THE EXACT ELECTRICAL IMPULSES OF THE HUMAN MIND. IT FEEDS OFF THOSE IMPULSES WHILE BLOCKING SUPPORT SIGNALS TO THE **REST** OF THE BODY.
SO THE ABERRANT ELEMENT **THRIVES** WHILE THE NEIGHBORING ENVIRONMENT DECAYS.
YOU ALWAYS BRING IT BACK TO GOTHAM, DON'T YOU?
AFTER THE PARENT GERMS REPRODUCE, THEIR **OFFSPRING** LEAVE THE BODY IN MASSIVE NUMBERS TO FIND NEW HOSTS.
I'VE NEVER SEEN AN ORGANISM SO EVOLVED TO FEED OFF A **SPECIFIC** ENERGY SOURCE.
THEN IF WE WERE TO SLIGHTLY INCREASE THE BRAIN IMPULSES, THE VIRUS SHOULD HAVE NO WAY TO **ADAPT.** IT WOULD SHORT ITSELF OUT.
EXACTLY! I'M BEAMING A DETAILED SCHEMATIC OF THE LIFE FORM INTO YOUR COMPUTER. IT WILL ANALYZE THE GERM'S MAKEUP AND GIVE YOU A FORMULA TO TEMPORARILY SUPERCHARGE THE IMPULSES.
BUT I CAN TELL YOU RIGHT NOW, WE'LL HAVE TO PULL LOTS OF STRINGS TO GET THE CHEMICALS WE'LL NEED. MOST OF THEM ARE HIGHLY **RESTRICTED,** EXPERIMENTAL...
I HAVE EVERYTHING, TRUST ME.
SOMEHOW I'M **NOT** SURPRISED. GUESS I'D BETTER EXIT AT THE NEAREST NOSTRIL. IT'S GOING TO GET PRETTY **BUSY** IN HERE ONCE OUR FAST FRIEND RECOVERS.
LIBERTY
I'M GETTING A POSITIVE REACTION TO THE TEST MIXTURE.
IT LOOKS LIKE WE HAVE A **CURE!**

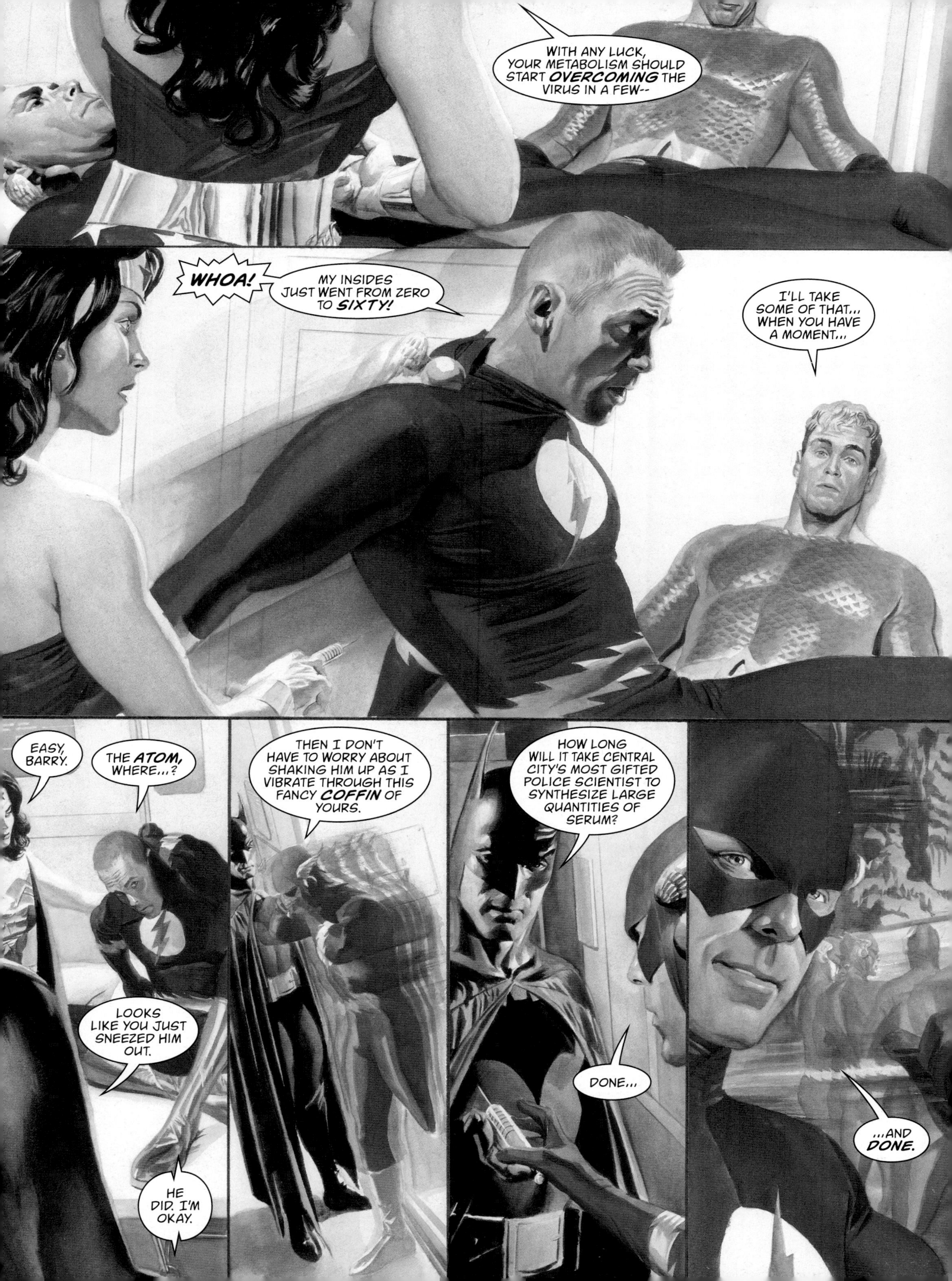

WITH ANY LUCK, YOUR METABOLISM SHOULD START OVERCOMING THE VIRUS IN A FEW--
WHOA!
MY INSIDES JUST WENT FROM ZERO TO SIXTY!
I'LL TAKE SOME OF THAT... WHEN YOU HAVE A MOMENT...
EASY, BARRY.
THE ATOM, WHERE...?
LOOKS LIKE YOU JUST SNEEZED HIM OUT.
HE DID. I'M OKAY.
THEN I DON'T HAVE TO WORRY ABOUT SHAKING HIM UP AS I VIBRATE THROUGH THIS FANCY COFFIN OF YOURS.
HOW LONG WILL IT TAKE CENTRAL CITY'S MOST GIFTED POLICE SCIENTIST TO SYNTHESIZE LARGE QUANTITIES OF SERUM?
DONE...
...AND DONE.

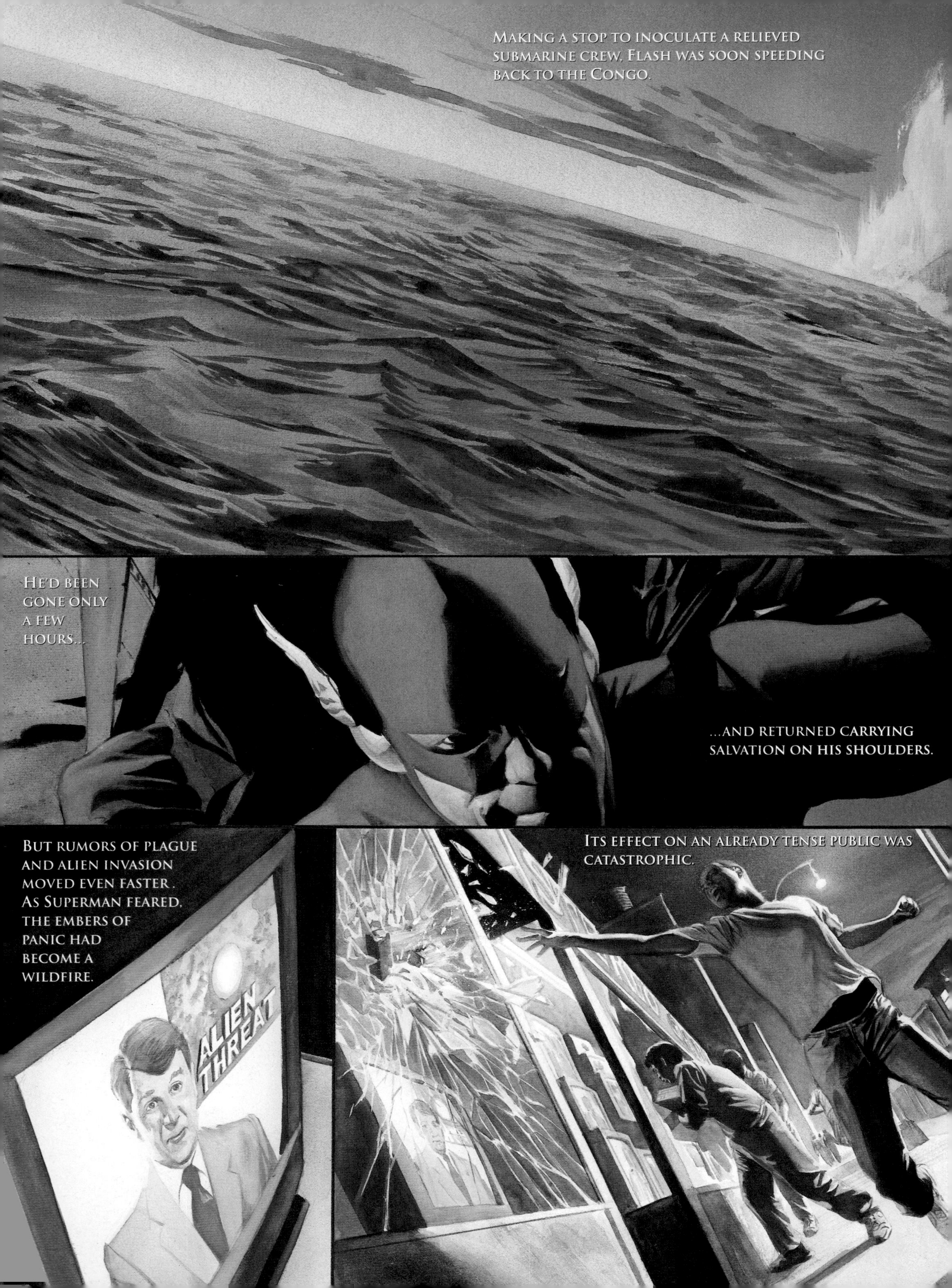
Making a stop to inoculate a relieved submarine crew, Flash was soon speeding back to the Congo.
He'd been gone only a few hours...
...and returned carrying salvation on his shoulders.
But rumors of plague and alien invasion moved even faster. As Superman feared, the embers of panic had become a wildfire.
ALIEN THREAT
Its effect on an already tense public was catastrophic.

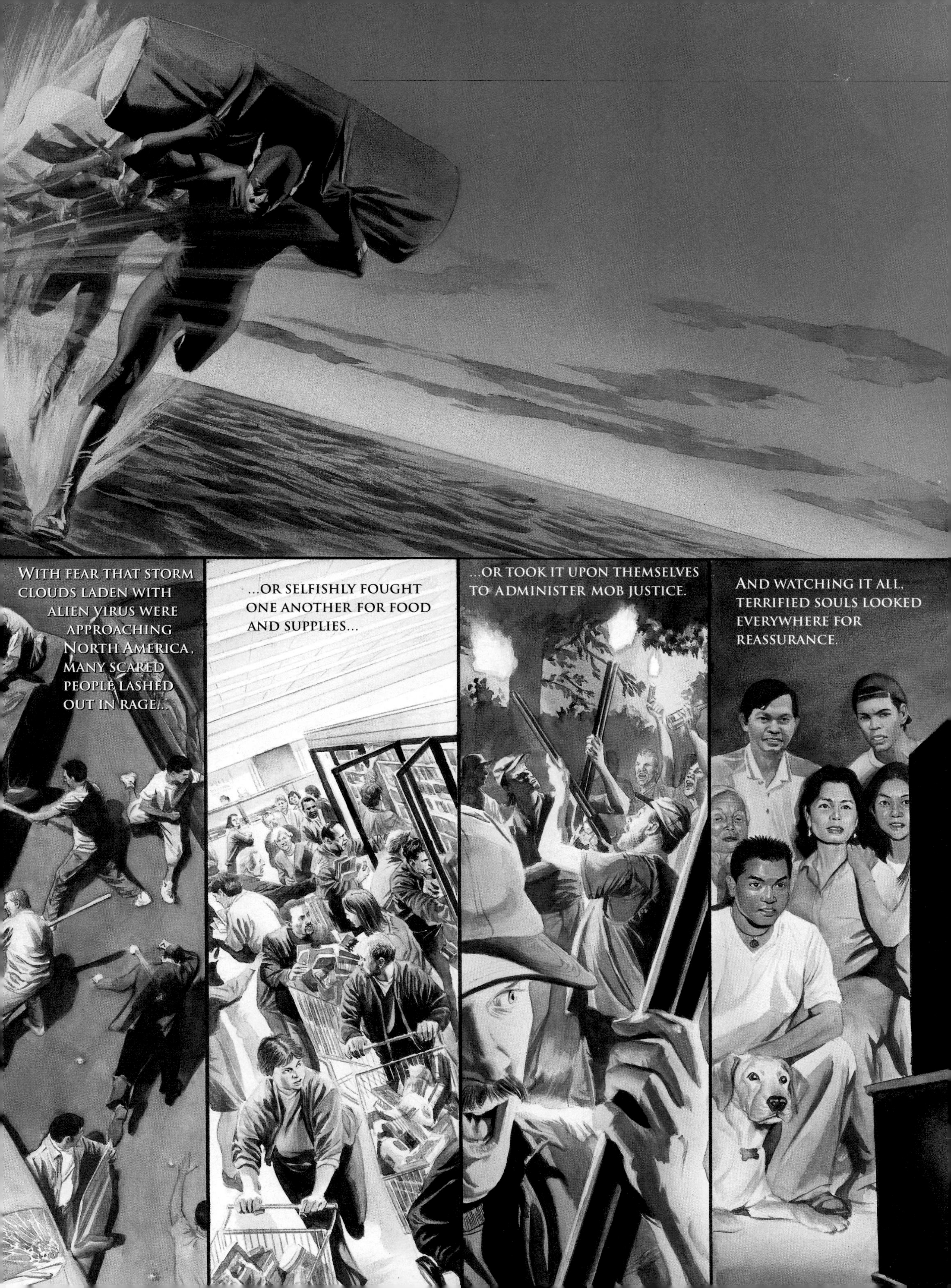
With fear that storm clouds laden with alien virus were approaching North America, many scared people lashed out in rage...
...or selfishly fought one another for food and supplies...
...or took it upon themselves to administer mob justice.
And watching it all, terrified souls looked everywhere for reassurance.

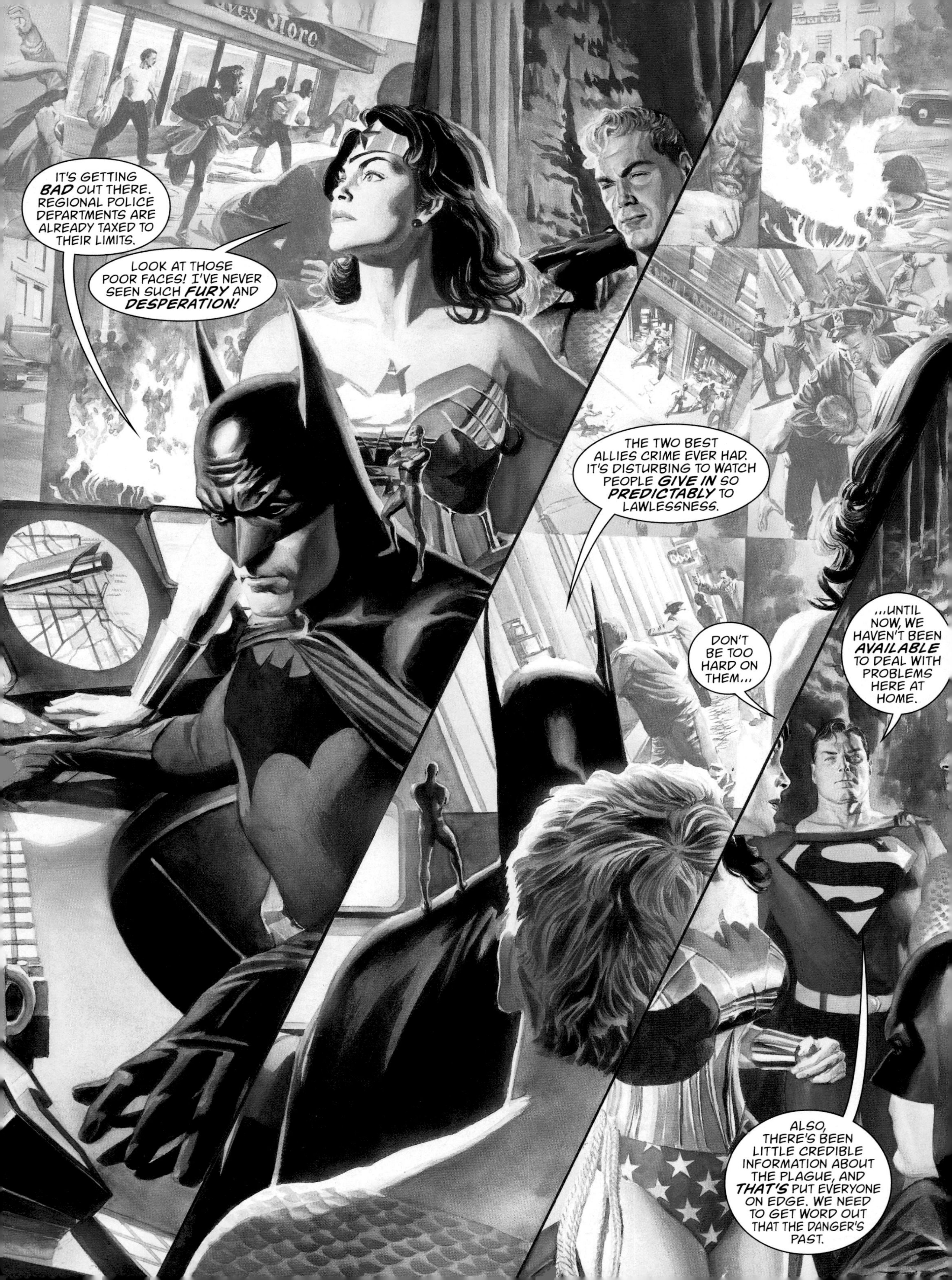
IT'S GETTING **BAD** OUT THERE. REGIONAL POLICE DEPARTMENTS ARE ALREADY TAXED TO THEIR LIMITS.
LOOK AT THOSE POOR FACES! I'VE NEVER SEEN SUCH **FURY** AND **DESPERATION!**
THE TWO BEST ALLIES CRIME EVER HAD. IT'S DISTURBING TO WATCH PEOPLE **GIVE IN** SO **PREDICTABLY** TO LAWLESSNESS.
DON'T BE TOO HARD ON THEM...
...UNTIL NOW, WE HAVEN'T BEEN **AVAILABLE** TO DEAL WITH PROBLEMS HERE AT HOME.
ALSO, THERE'S BEEN LITTLE CREDIBLE INFORMATION ABOUT THE PLAGUE, AND **THAT'S** PUT EVERYONE ON EDGE. WE NEED TO GET WORD OUT THAT THE DANGER'S PAST.

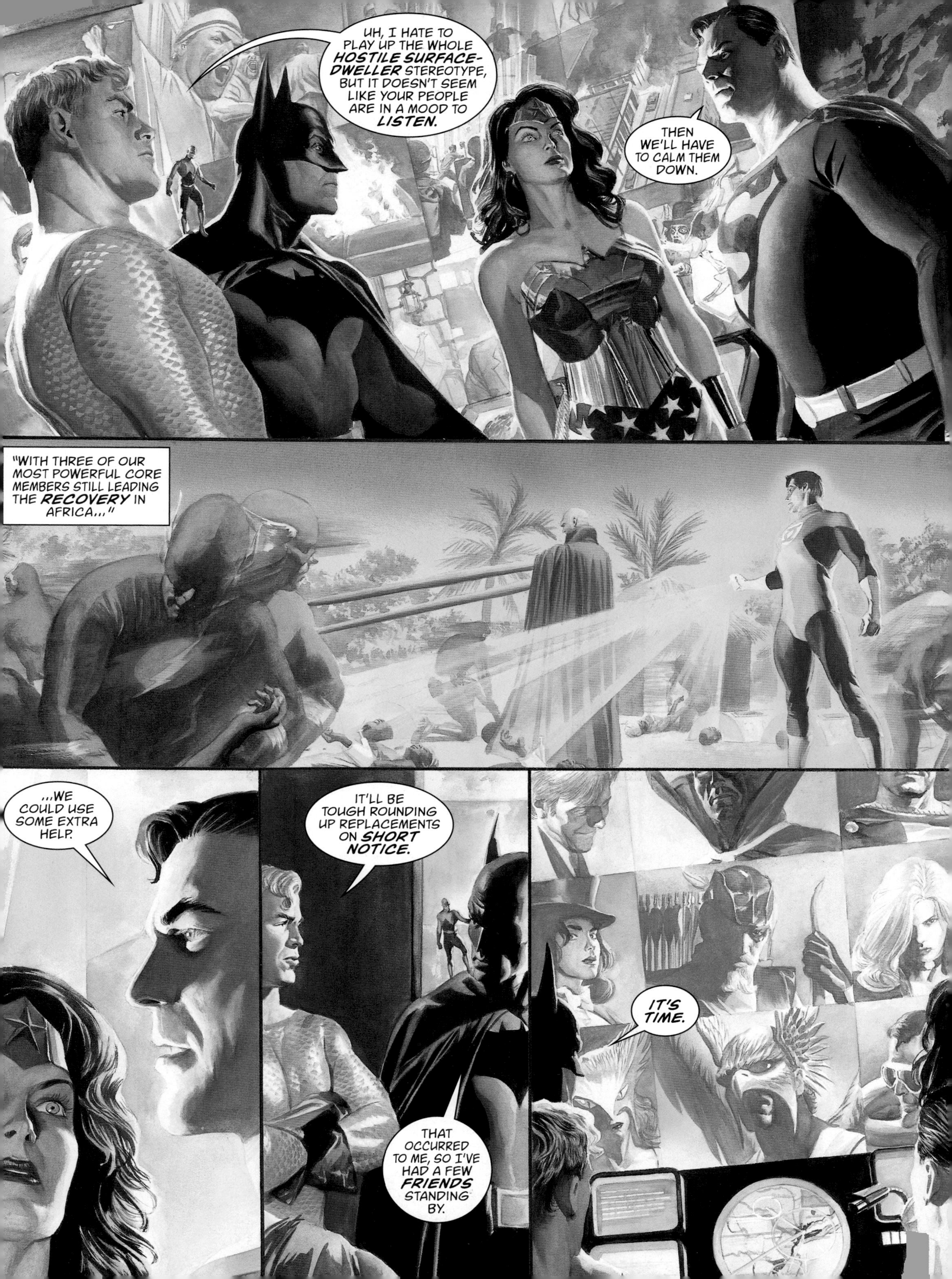

UH, I HATE TO PLAY UP THE WHOLE HOSTILE SURFACE-DWELLER STEREOTYPE, BUT IT DOESN'T SEEM LIKE YOUR PEOPLE ARE IN A MOOD TO LISTEN.
THEN WE'LL HAVE TO CALM THEM DOWN.
"WITH THREE OF OUR MOST POWERFUL CORE MEMBERS STILL LEADING THE RECOVERY IN AFRICA..."
...WE COULD USE SOME EXTRA HELP.
IT'LL BE TOUGH ROUNDING UP REPLACEMENTS ON SHORT NOTICE.
THAT OCCURRED TO ME, SO I'VE HAD A FEW FRIENDS STANDING BY.
IT'S TIME.

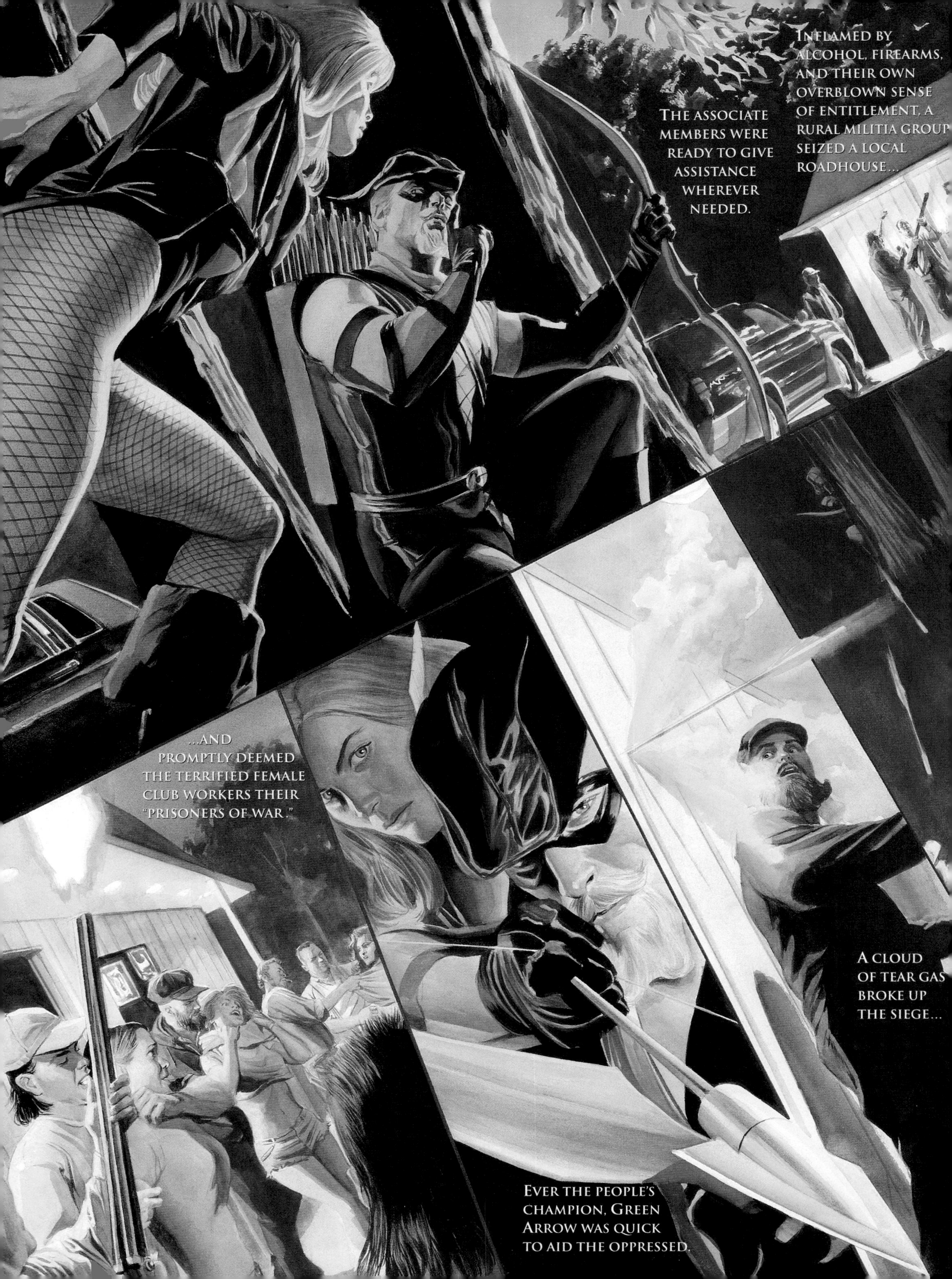
The associate members were ready to give assistance wherever needed.
Inflamed by alcohol, firearms, and their own overblown sense of entitlement, a rural militia group seized a local roadhouse...
...and promptly deemed the terrified female club workers their "prisoners of war."
Ever the people's champion, Green Arrow was quick to aid the oppressed.
A cloud of tear gas broke up the siege...

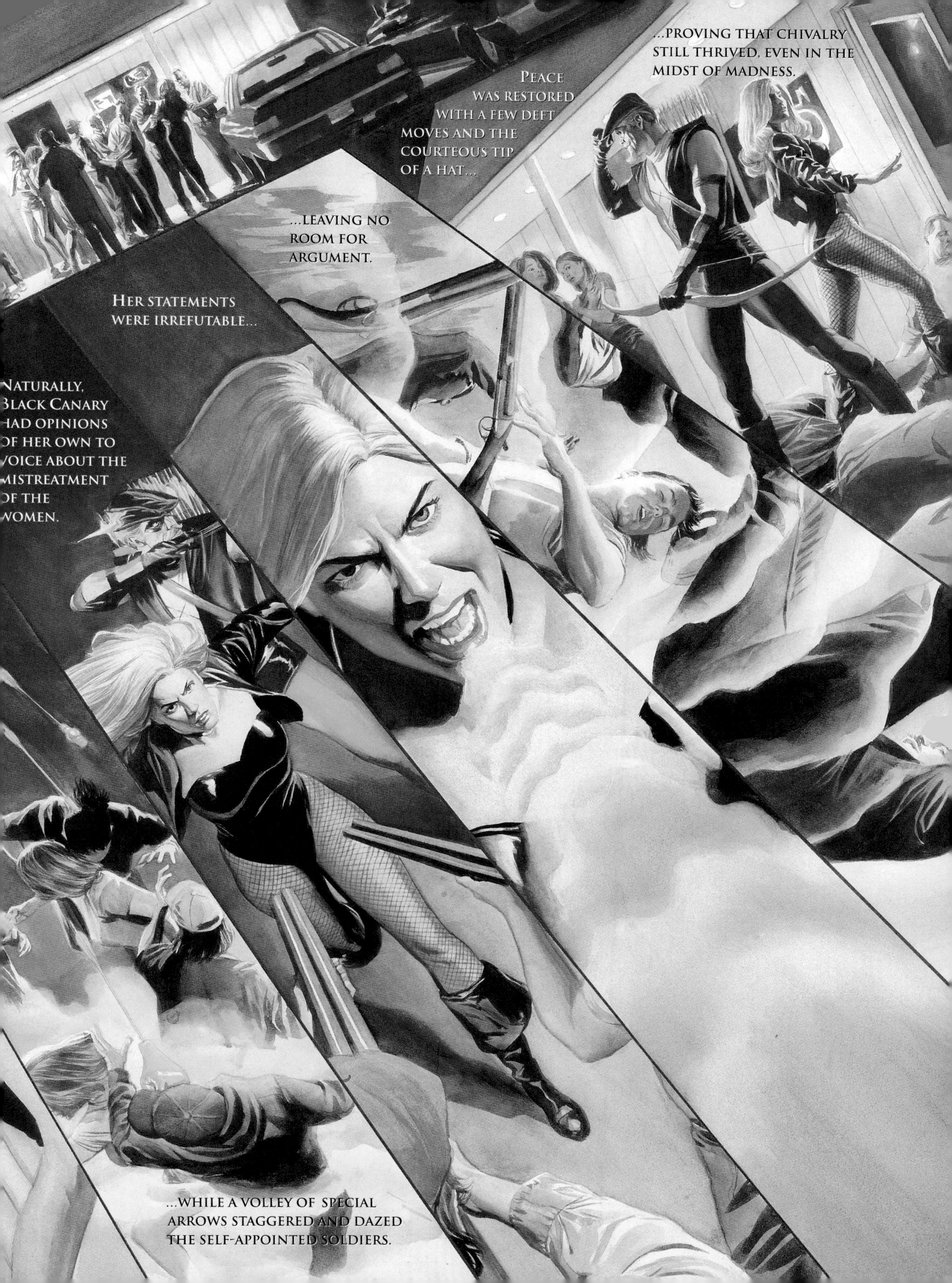
NATURALLY, BLACK CANARY HAD OPINIONS OF HER OWN TO VOICE ABOUT THE MISTREATMENT OF THE WOMEN.
HER STATEMENTS WERE IRREFUTABLE...
...LEAVING NO ROOM FOR ARGUMENT.
PEACE WAS RESTORED WITH A FEW DEFT MOVES AND THE COURTEOUS TIP OF A HAT...
...PROVING THAT CHIVALRY STILL THRIVED, EVEN IN THE MIDST OF MADNESS.
...WHILE A VOLLEY OF SPECIAL ARROWS STAGGERED AND DAZED THE SELF-APPOINTED SOLDIERS.

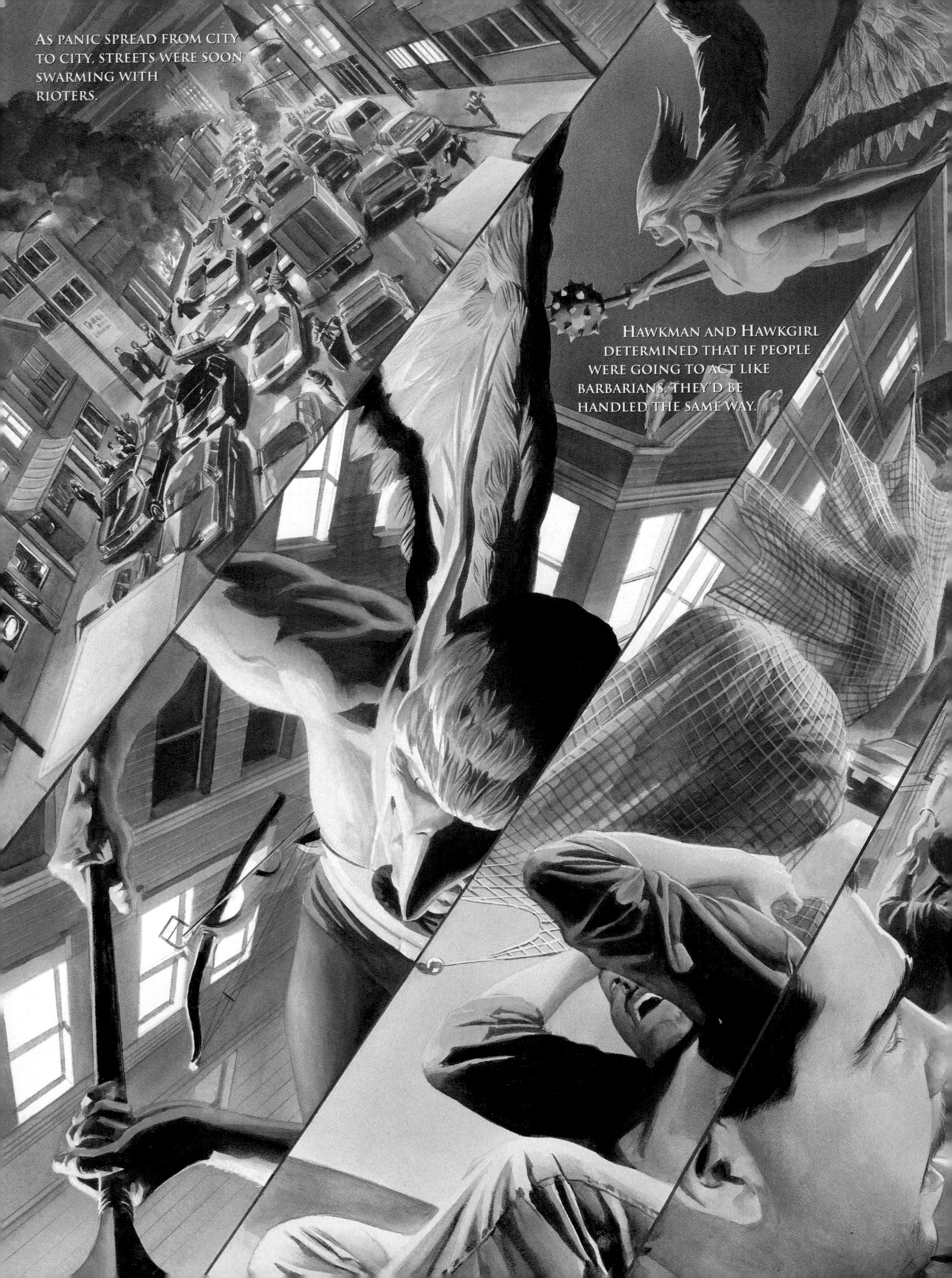
As panic spread from city to city, streets were soon swarming with rioters.
Hawkman and Hawkgirl determined that if people were going to act like barbarians, they'd be handled the same way.

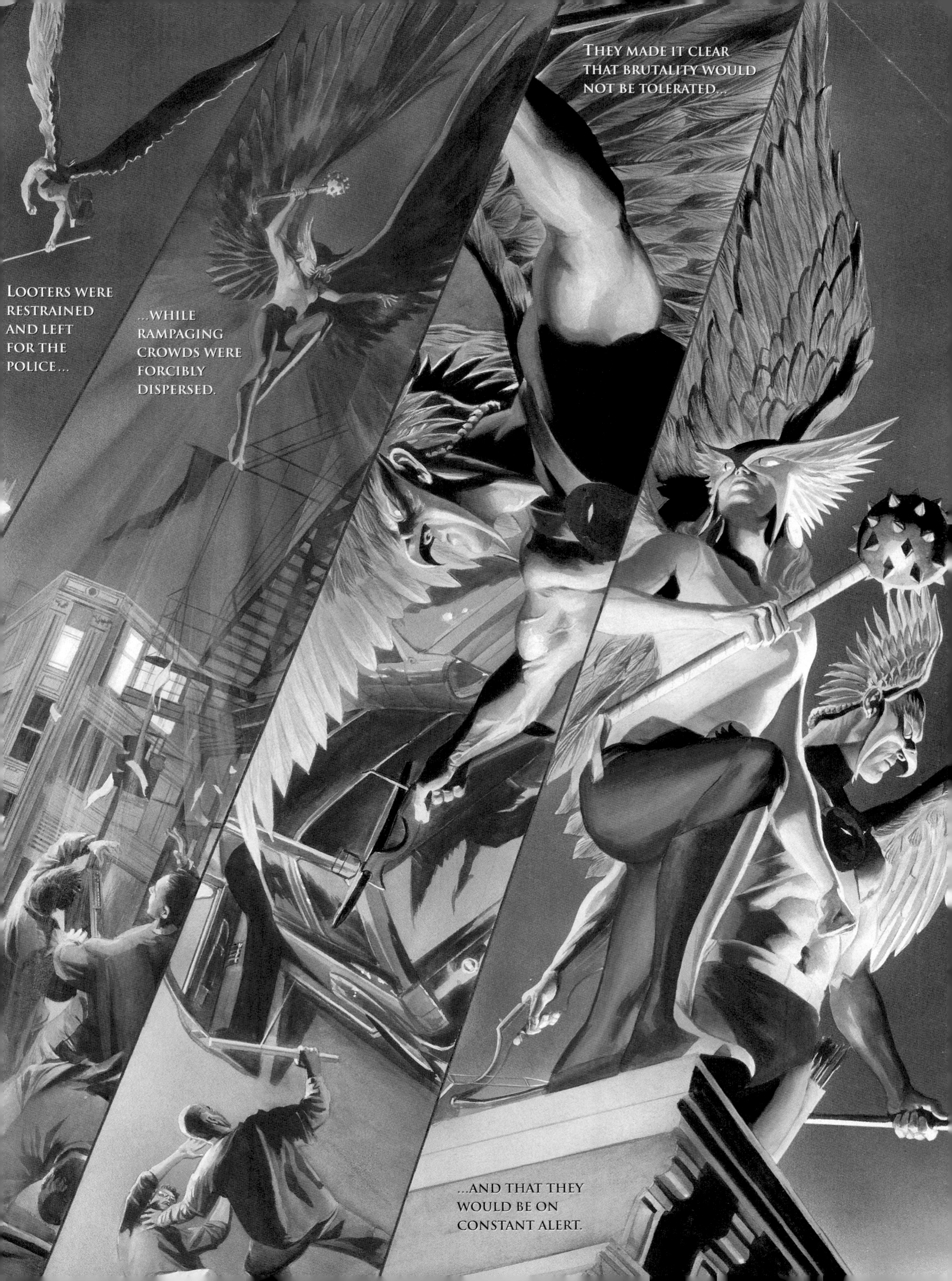
Looters were restrained and left for the police...
...while rampaging crowds were forcibly dispersed.
They made it clear that brutality would not be tolerated...
...and that they would be on constant alert.

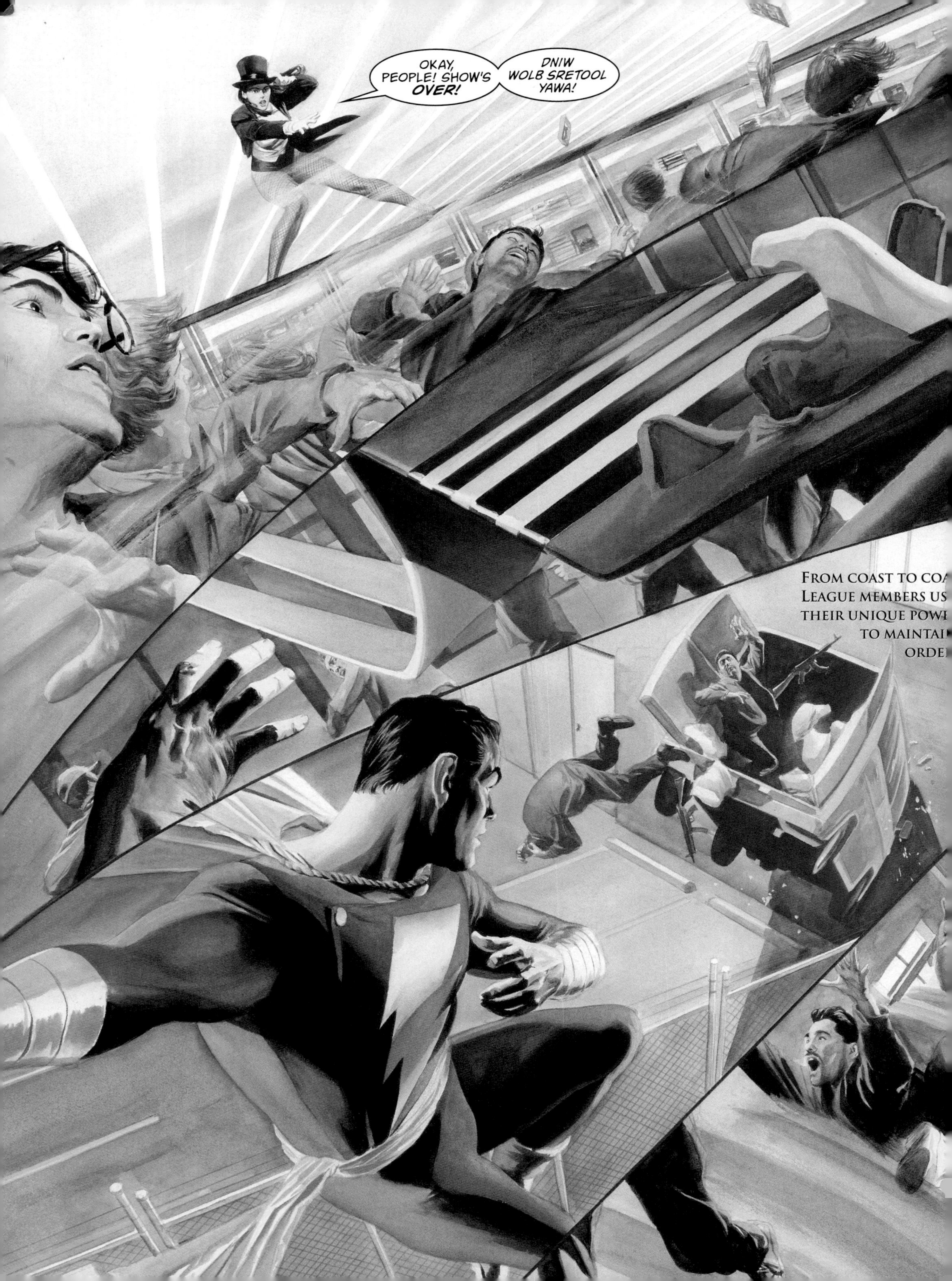
OKAY, PEOPLE! SHOW'S OVER!
DNIW WOLB SRETOOL YAWA!
FROM COAST TO CO
LEAGUE MEMBERS US
THEIR UNIQUE POW
TO MAINTAI
ORDE

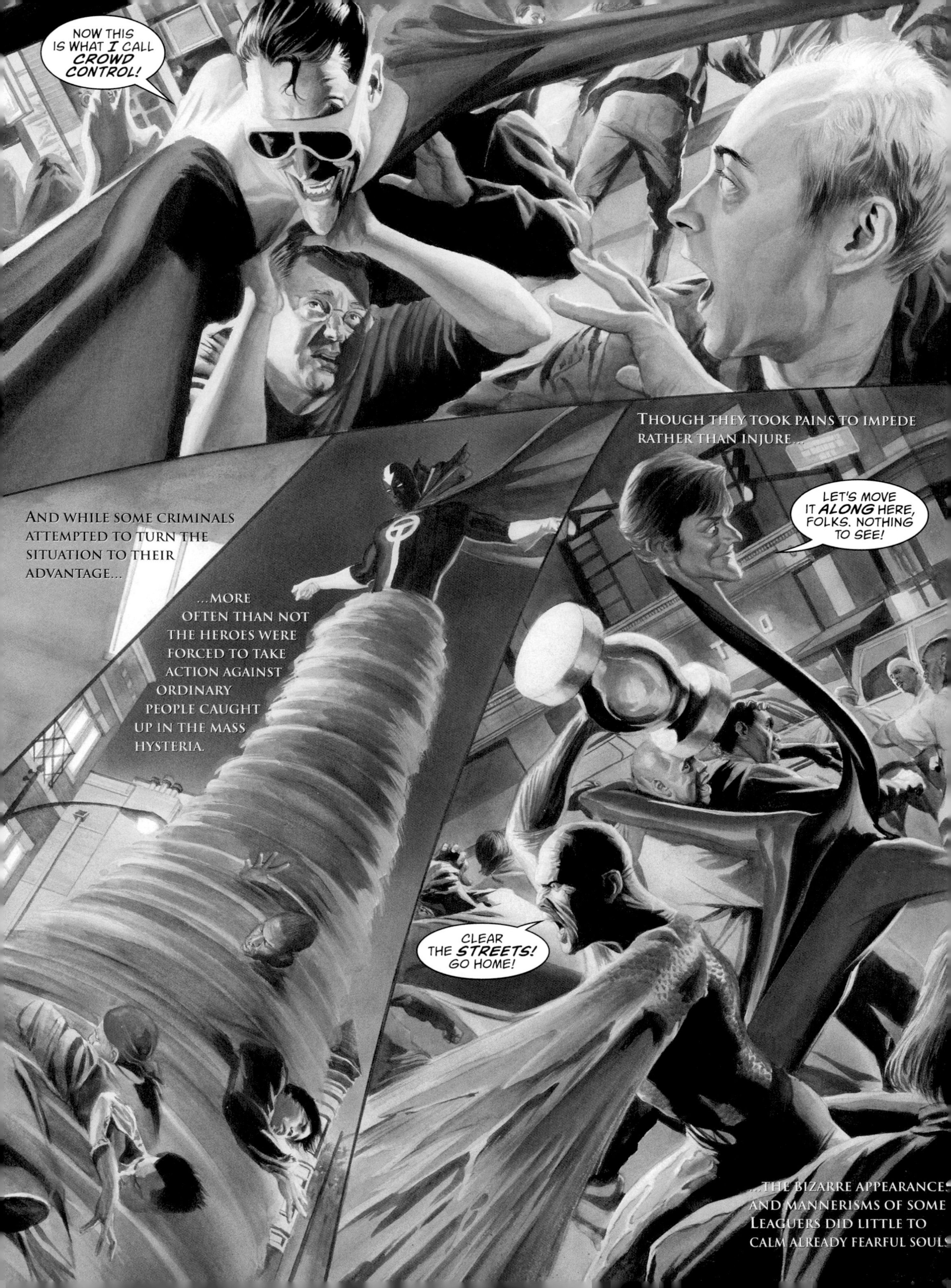

NOW THIS IS WHAT I CALL CROWD CONTROL!
AND WHILE SOME CRIMINALS ATTEMPTED TO TURN THE SITUATION TO THEIR ADVANTAGE...
...MORE OFTEN THAN NOT THE HEROES WERE FORCED TO TAKE ACTION AGAINST ORDINARY PEOPLE CAUGHT UP IN THE MASS HYSTERIA.
THOUGH THEY TOOK PAINS TO IMPEDE RATHER THAN INJURE...
LET'S MOVE IT ALONG HERE, FOLKS. NOTHING TO SEE!
CLEAR THE STREETS! GO HOME!
...THE BIZARRE APPEARANCES AND MANNERISMS OF SOME LEAGUERS DID LITTLE TO CALM ALREADY FEARFUL SOULS

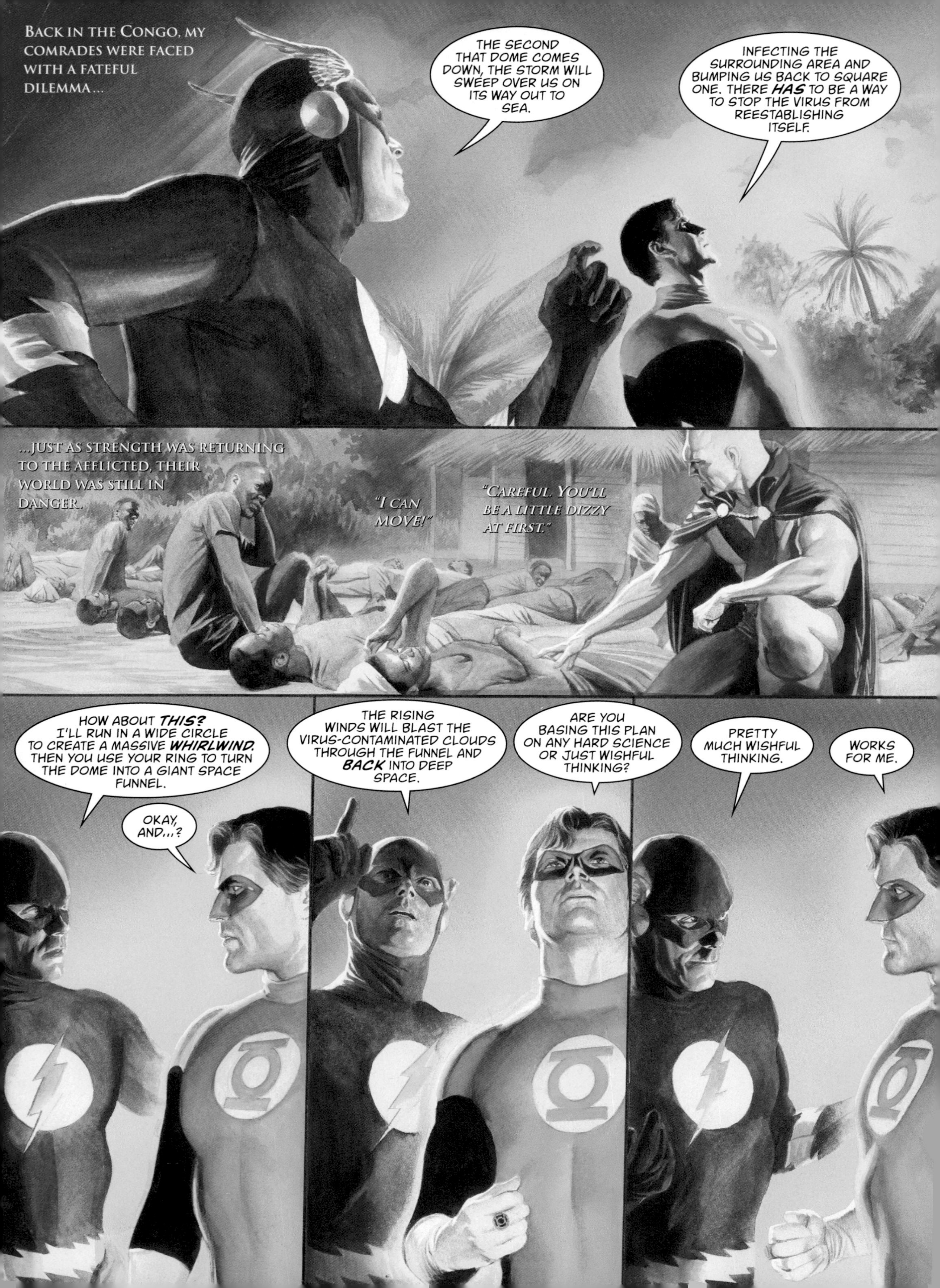
Back in the Congo, my comrades were faced with a fateful dilemma...
THE SECOND THAT DOME COMES DOWN, THE STORM WILL SWEEP OVER US ON ITS WAY OUT TO SEA.
INFECTING THE SURROUNDING AREA AND BUMPING US BACK TO SQUARE ONE. THERE HAS TO BE A WAY TO STOP THE VIRUS FROM REESTABLISHING ITSELF.
...just as strength was returning to the afflicted, their world was still in danger.
"I can move!"
"Careful. You'll be a little dizzy at first."
HOW ABOUT THIS? I'LL RUN IN A WIDE CIRCLE TO CREATE A MASSIVE WHIRLWIND. THEN YOU USE YOUR RING TO TURN THE DOME INTO A GIANT SPACE FUNNEL.
OKAY, AND...?
THE RISING WINDS WILL BLAST THE VIRUS-CONTAMINATED CLOUDS THROUGH THE FUNNEL AND BACK INTO DEEP SPACE.
ARE YOU BASING THIS PLAN ON ANY HARD SCIENCE OR JUST WISHFUL THINKING?
PRETTY MUCH WISHFUL THINKING.
WORKS FOR ME.

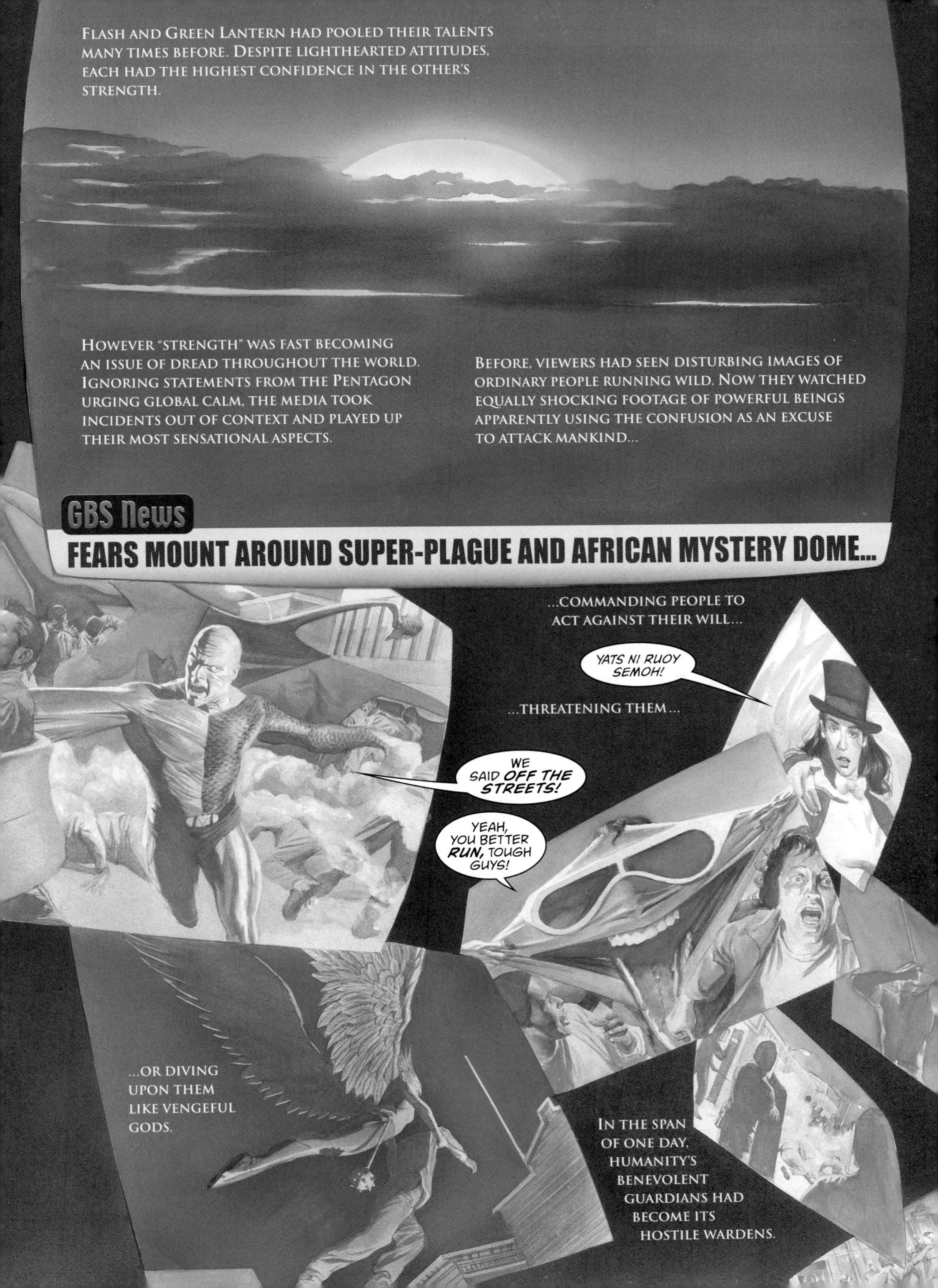

Flash and Green Lantern had pooled their talents many times before. Despite lighthearted attitudes, each had the highest confidence in the other's strength.
However "strength" was fast becoming an issue of dread throughout the world. Ignoring statements from the Pentagon urging global calm, the media took incidents out of context and played up their most sensational aspects.
Before, viewers had seen disturbing images of ordinary people running wild. Now they watched equally shocking footage of powerful beings apparently using the confusion as an excuse to attack mankind...
GBS News
FEARS MOUNT AROUND SUPER-PLAGUE AND AFRICAN MYSTERY DOME...
...commanding people to act against their will...
YATS NI RUOY SEMOH!
...threatening them...
WE SAID OFF THE STREETS!
YEAH, YOU BETTER RUN, TOUGH GUYS!
...or diving upon them like vengeful gods.
In the span of one day, humanity's benevolent guardians had become its hostile wardens.

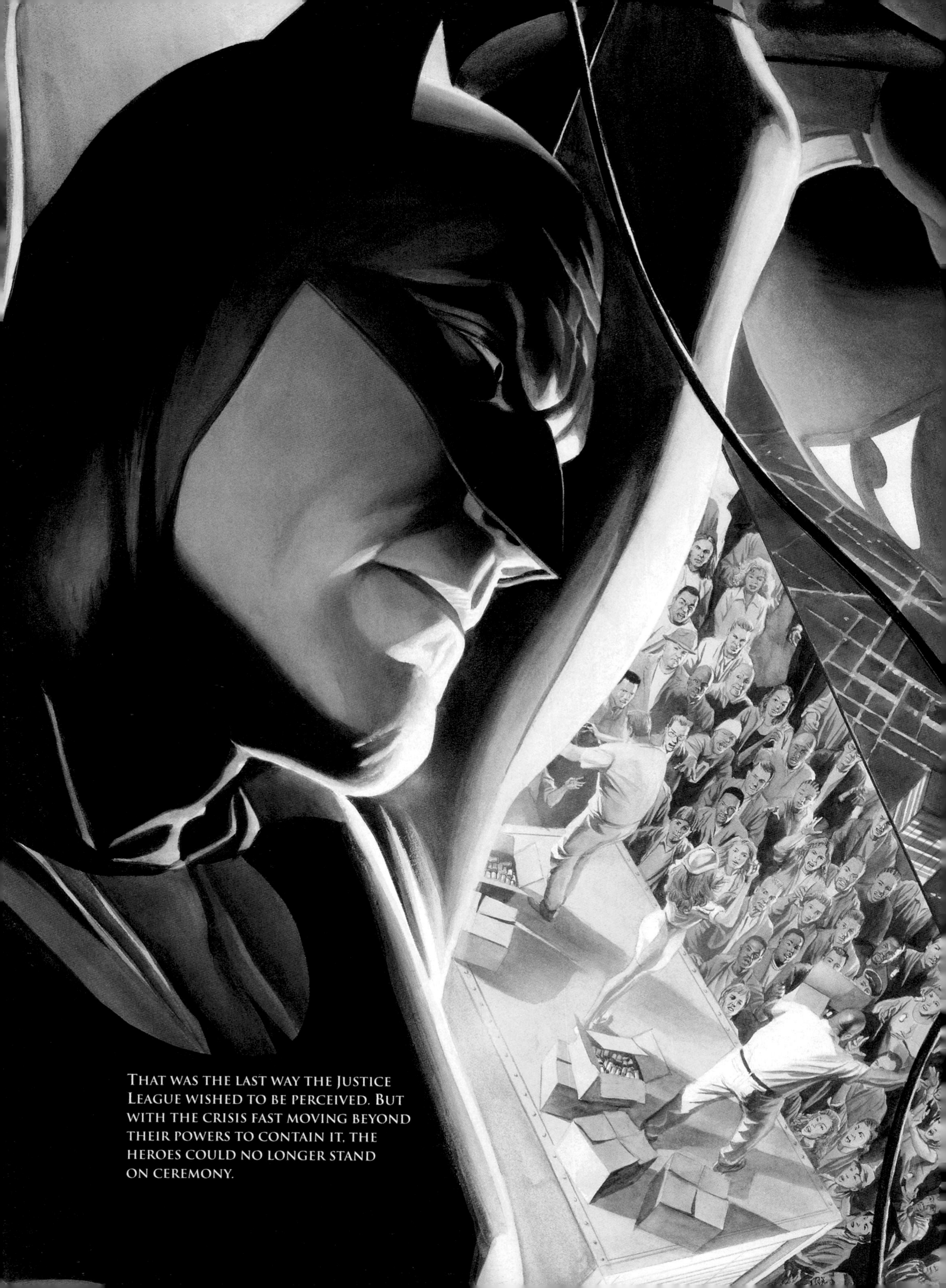

That was the last way the Justice League wished to be perceived. But with the crisis fast moving beyond their powers to contain it, the heroes could no longer stand on ceremony.

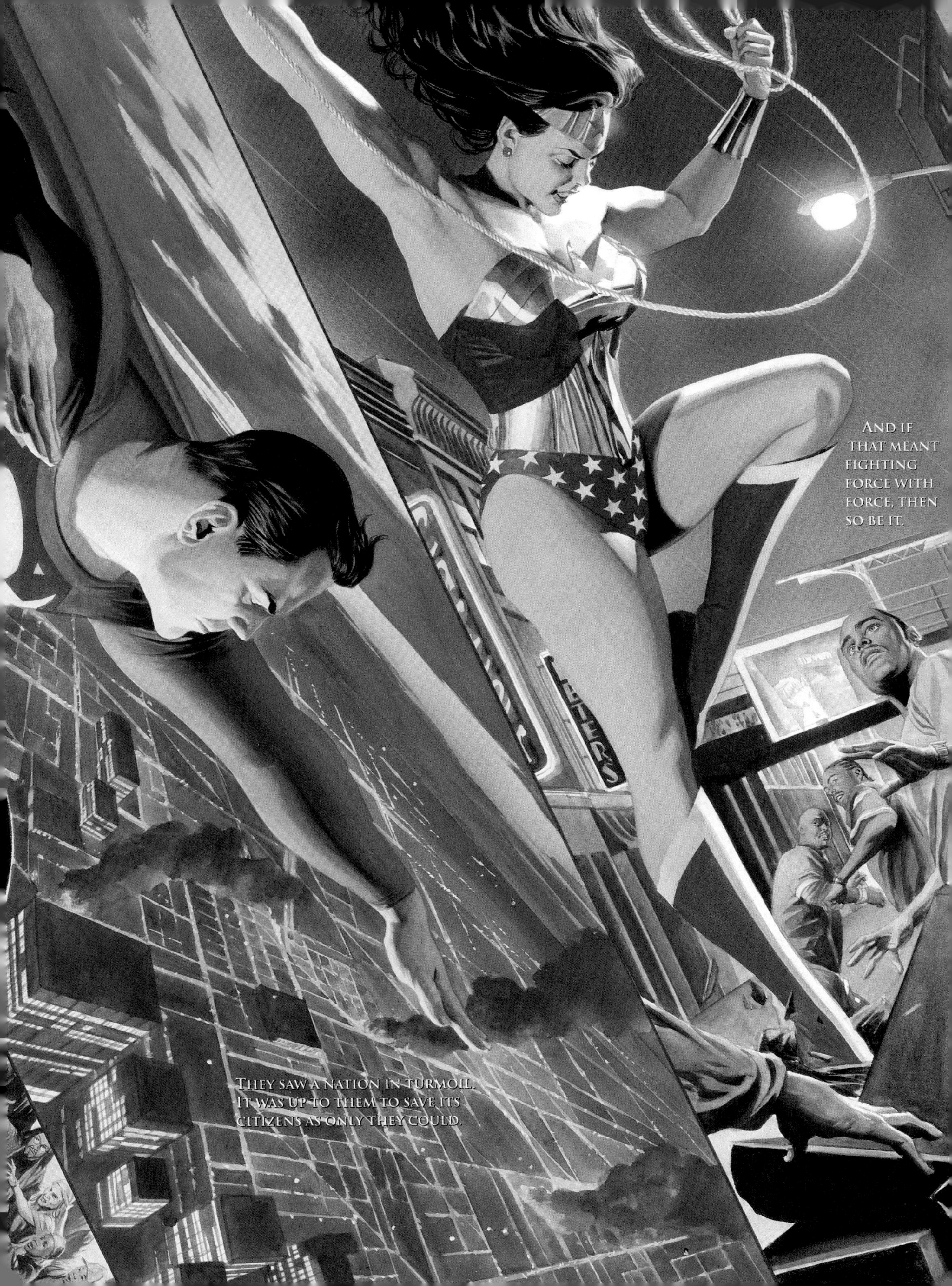
They saw a nation in turmoil. It was up to them to save its citizens as only they could.
And if that meant fighting force with force, then so be it.
ETER'S

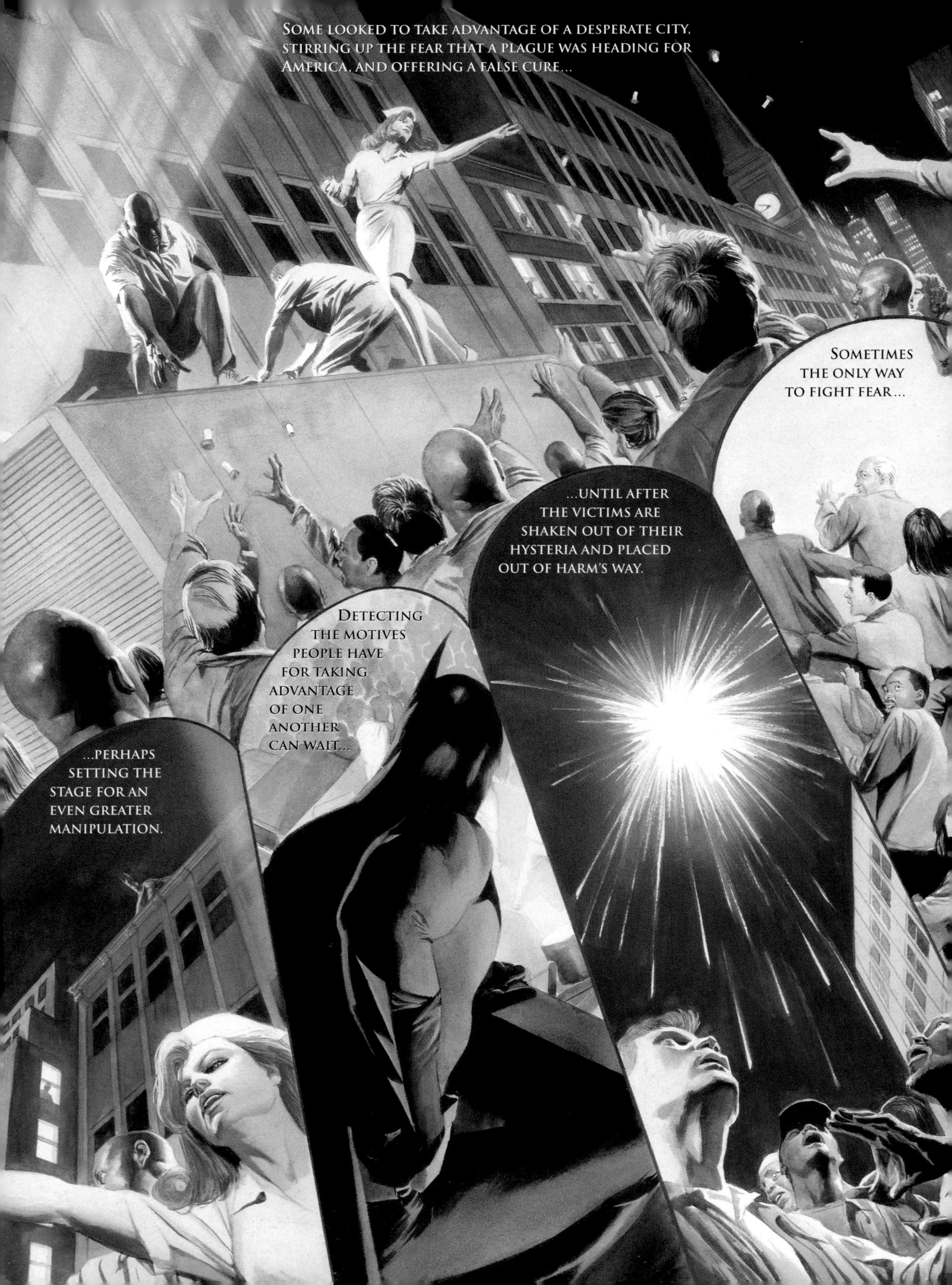
Some looked to take advantage of a desperate city, stirring up the fear that a plague was heading for America, and offering a false cure...
Sometimes the only way to fight fear...
...until after the victims are shaken out of their hysteria and placed out of harm's way.
Detecting the motives people have for taking advantage of one another can wait...
...perhaps setting the stage for an even greater manipulation.

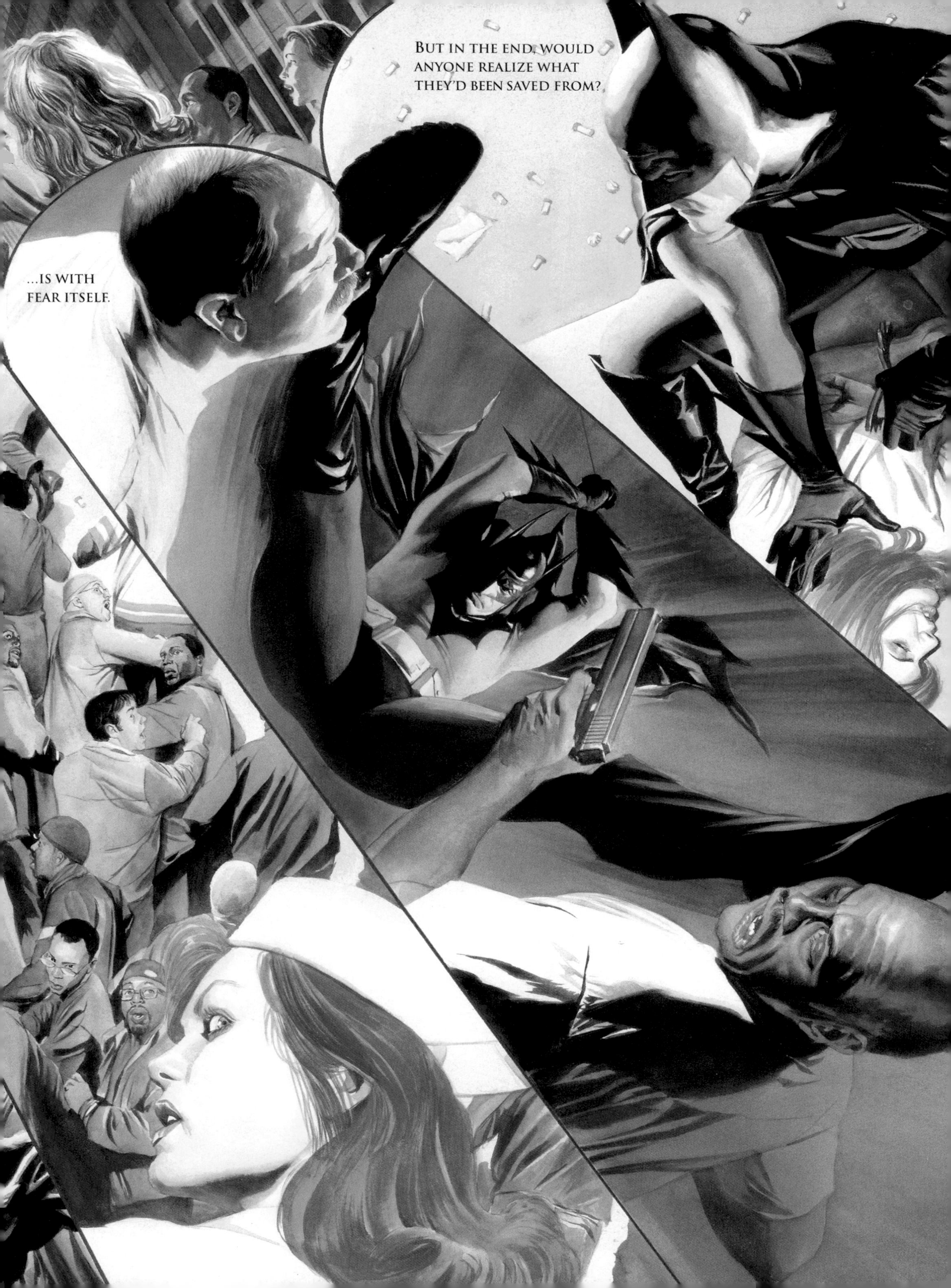
...IS WITH FEAR ITSELF.
BUT IN THE END, WOULD ANYONE REALIZE WHAT THEY'D BEEN SAVED FROM?

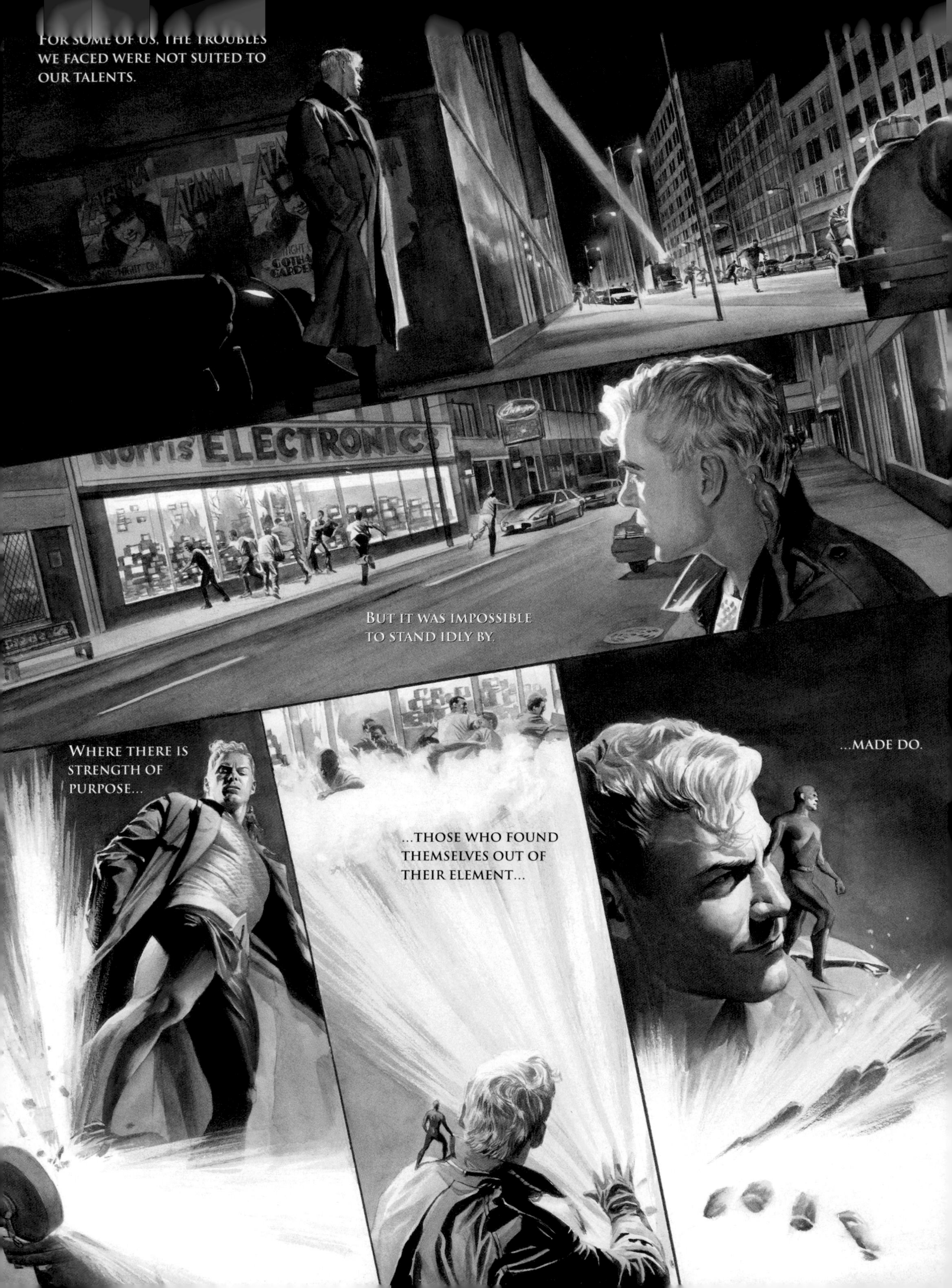
FOR SOME OF US, THE TROUBLES
WE FACED WERE NOT SUITED TO
OUR TALENTS.
ZATANNA
ELECTRONICS
BUT IT WAS IMPOSSIBLE
TO STAND IDLY BY.
WHERE THERE IS
STRENGTH OF
PURPOSE...
...THOSE WHO FOUND
THEMSELVES OUT OF
THEIR ELEMENT...
...MADE DO.

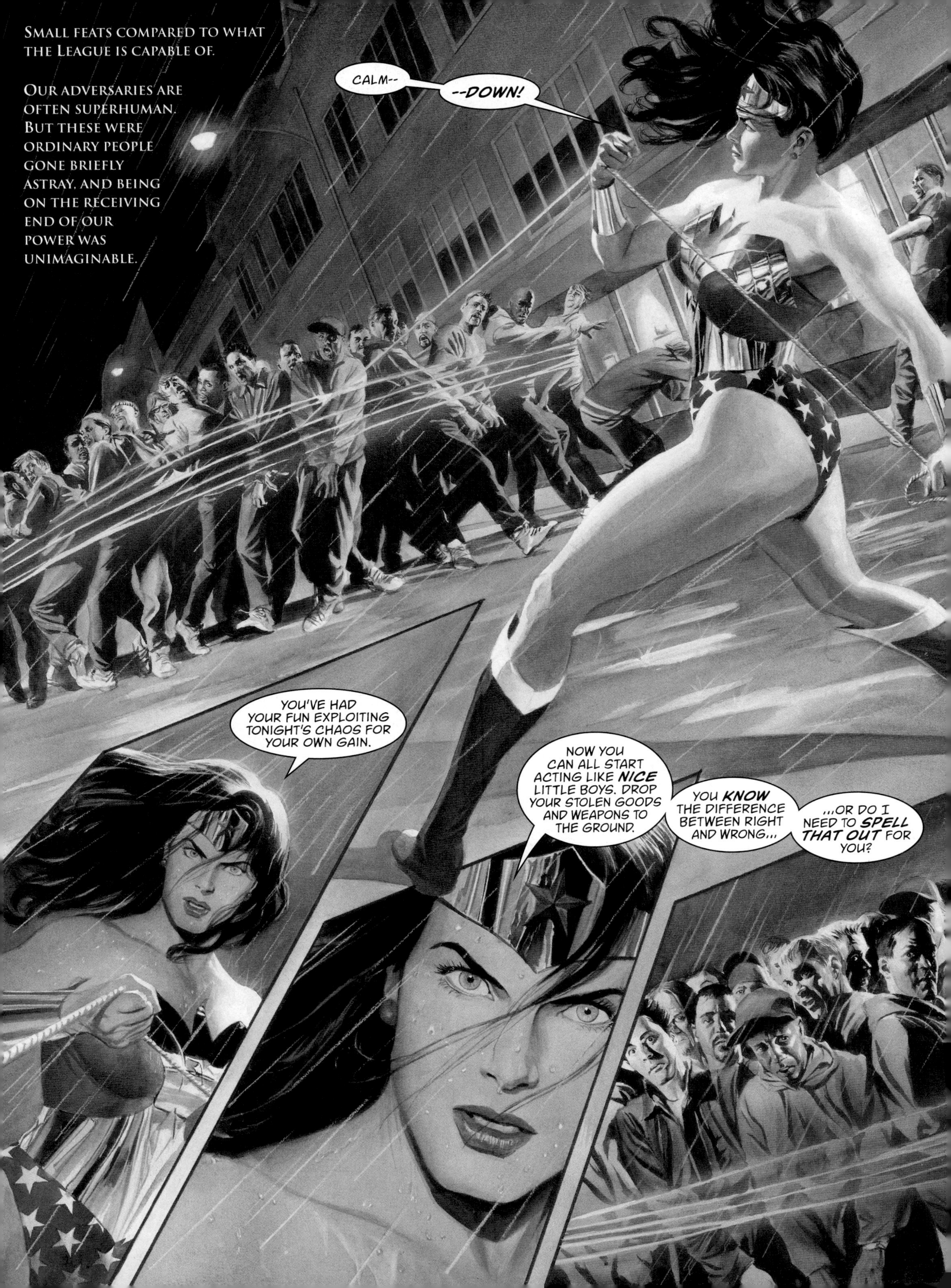
SMALL FEATS COMPARED TO WHAT THE LEAGUE IS CAPABLE OF.
OUR ADVERSARIES ARE OFTEN SUPERHUMAN. BUT THESE WERE ORDINARY PEOPLE GONE BRIEFLY ASTRAY, AND BEING ON THE RECEIVING END OF OUR POWER WAS UNIMAGINABLE.
CALM--
--DOWN!
YOU'VE HAD YOUR FUN EXPLOITING TONIGHT'S CHAOS FOR YOUR OWN GAIN.
NOW YOU CAN ALL START ACTING LIKE NICE LITTLE BOYS. DROP YOUR STOLEN GOODS AND WEAPONS TO THE GROUND.
YOU KNOW THE DIFFERENCE BETWEEN RIGHT AND WRONG...
...OR DO I NEED TO SPELL THAT OUT FOR YOU?

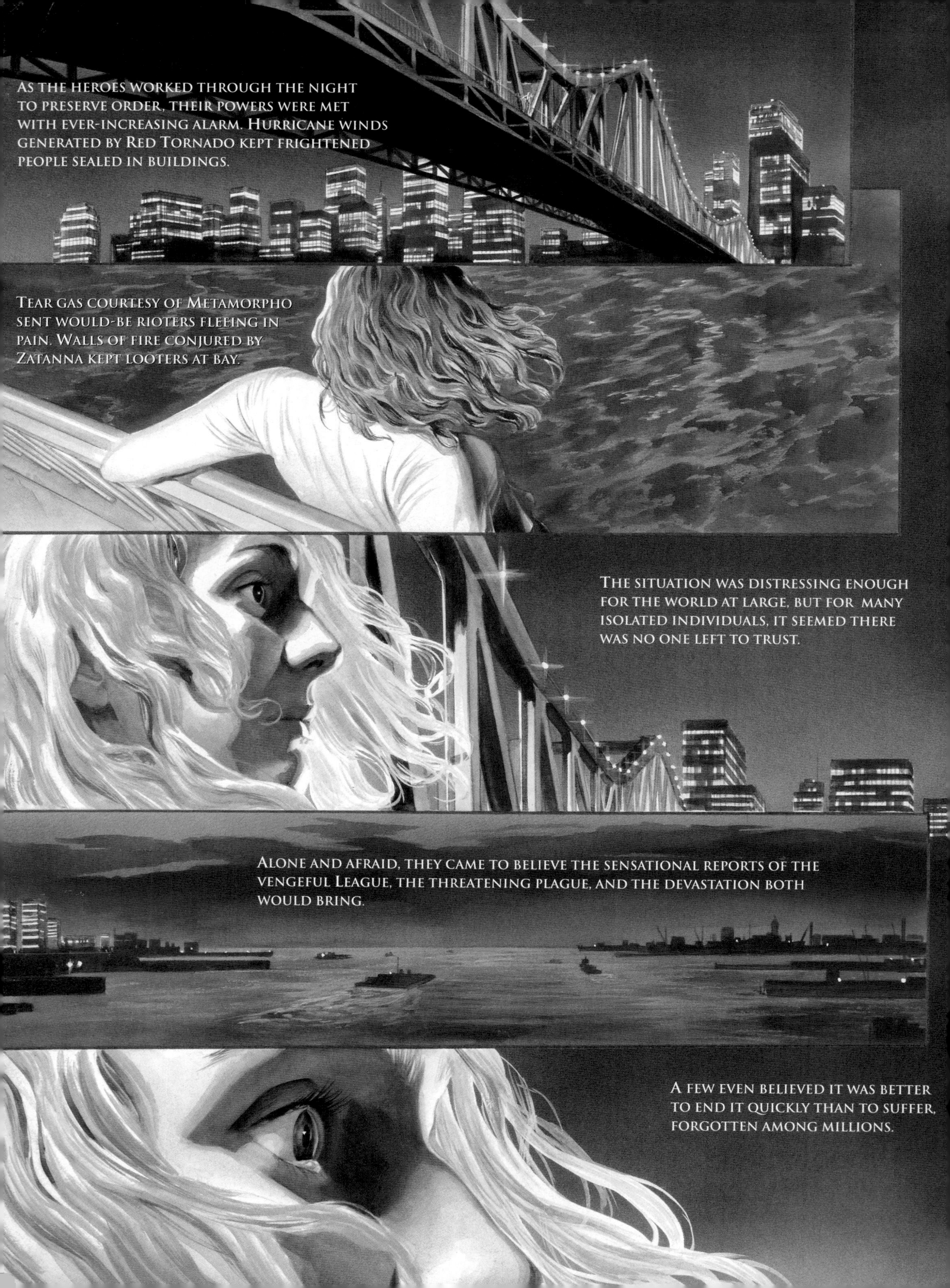
As the heroes worked through the night to preserve order, their powers were met with ever-increasing alarm. Hurricane winds generated by Red Tornado kept frightened people sealed in buildings.
Tear gas courtesy of Metamorpho sent would-be rioters fleeing in pain. Walls of fire conjured by Zatanna kept looters at bay.
The situation was distressing enough for the world at large, but for many isolated individuals, it seemed there was no one left to trust.
Alone and afraid, they came to believe the sensational reports of the vengeful League, the threatening plague, and the devastation both would bring.
A few even believed it was better to end it quickly than to suffer, forgotten among millions.

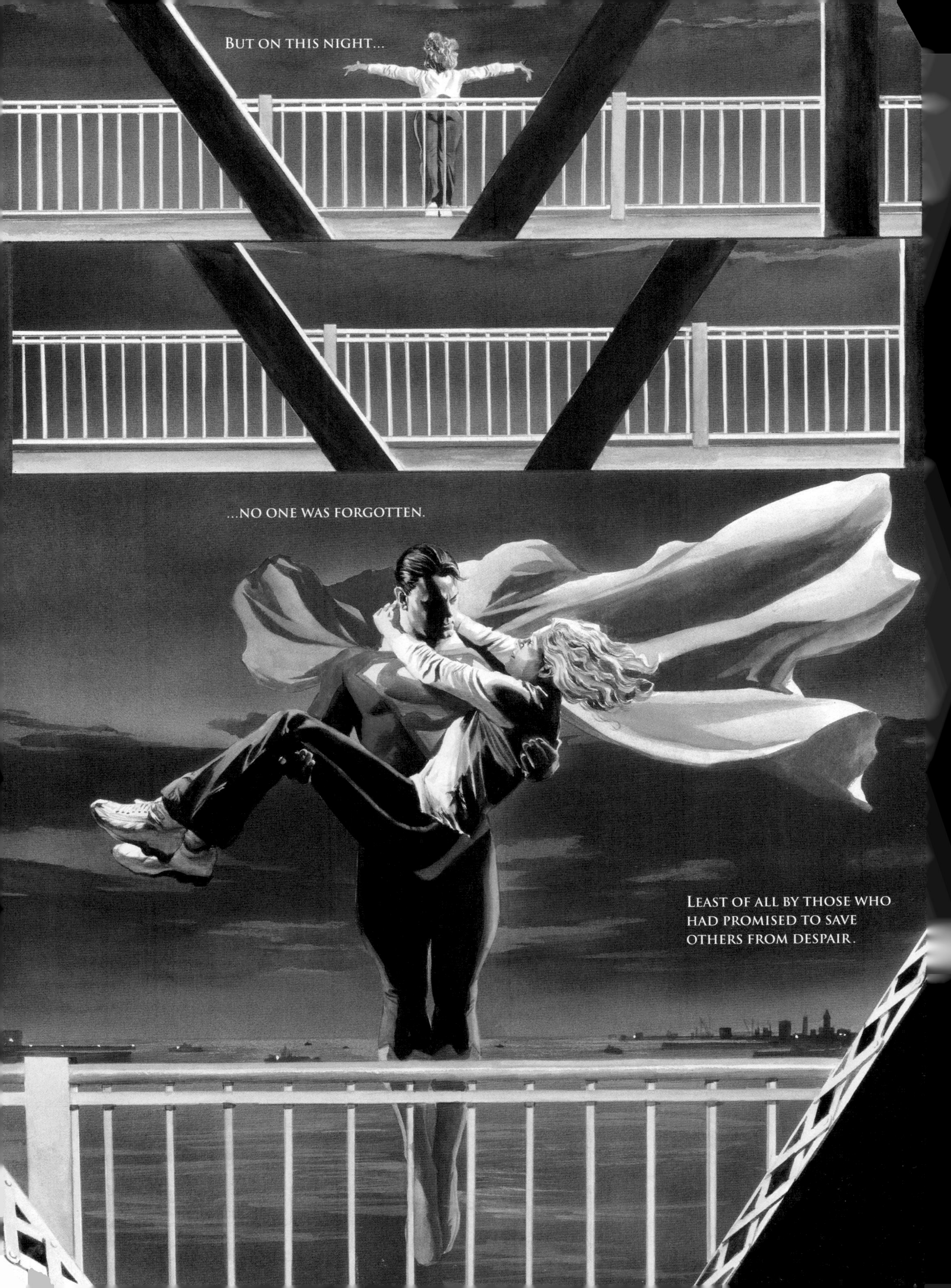
BUT ON THIS NIGHT...
...NO ONE WAS FORGOTTEN.
LEAST OF ALL BY THOSE WHO HAD PROMISED TO SAVE OTHERS FROM DESPAIR.

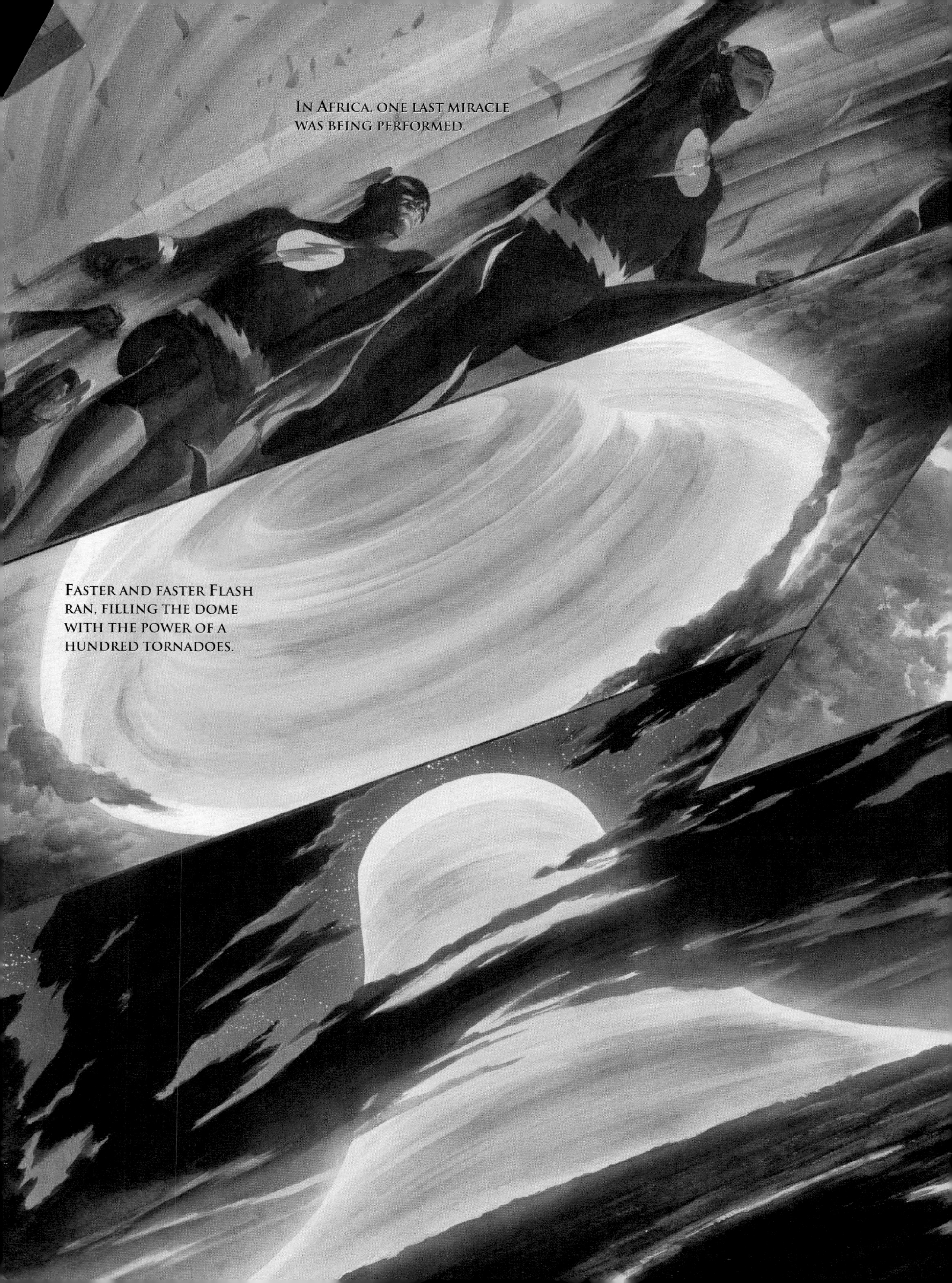
In Africa, one last miracle was being performed.
Faster and faster Flash ran, filling the dome with the power of a hundred tornadoes.

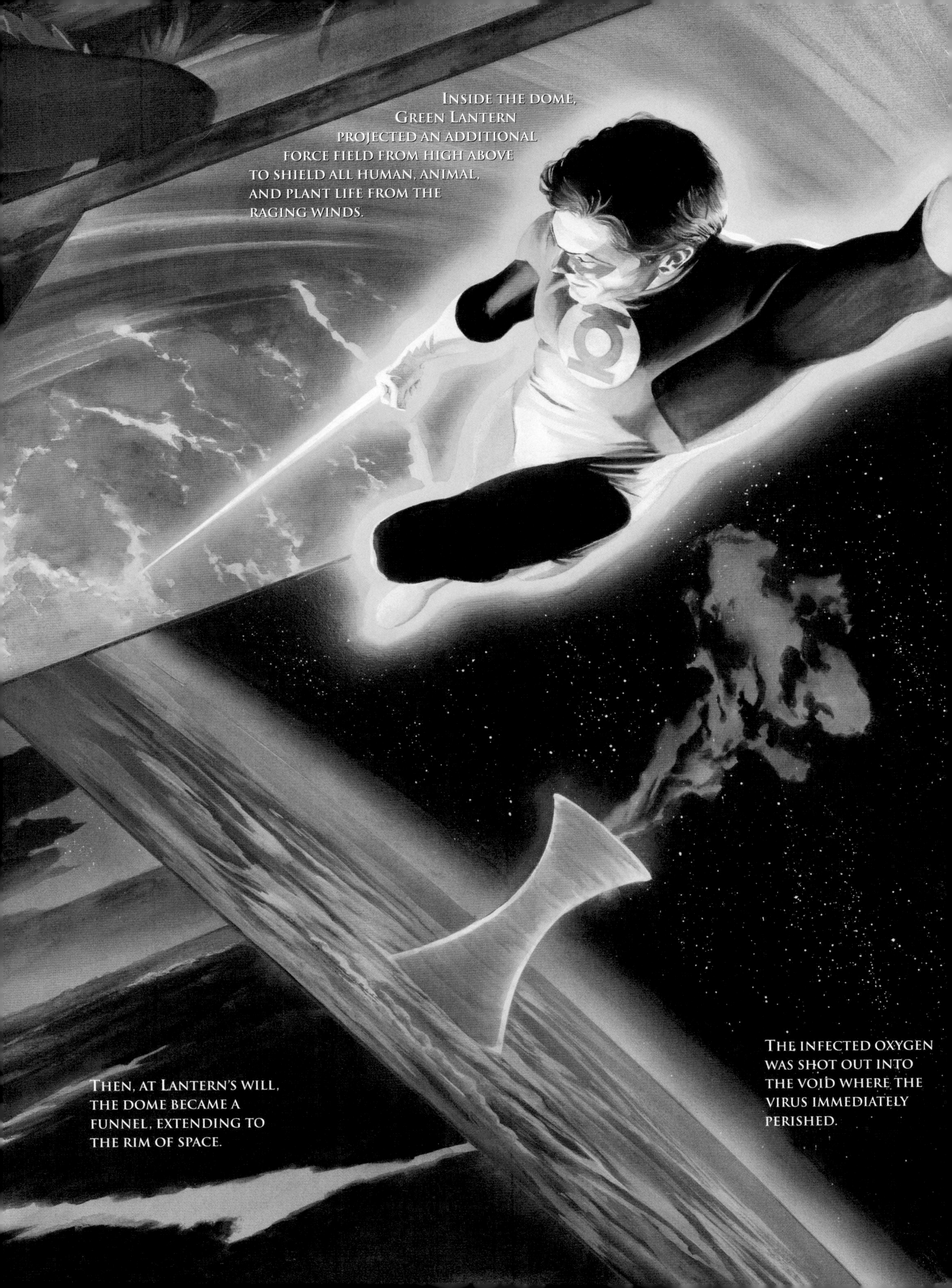
Inside the dome, Green Lantern projected an additional force field from high above to shield all human, animal, and plant life from the raging winds.
Then, at Lantern's will, the dome became a funnel, extending to the rim of space.
The infected oxygen was shot out into the void where the virus immediately perished.

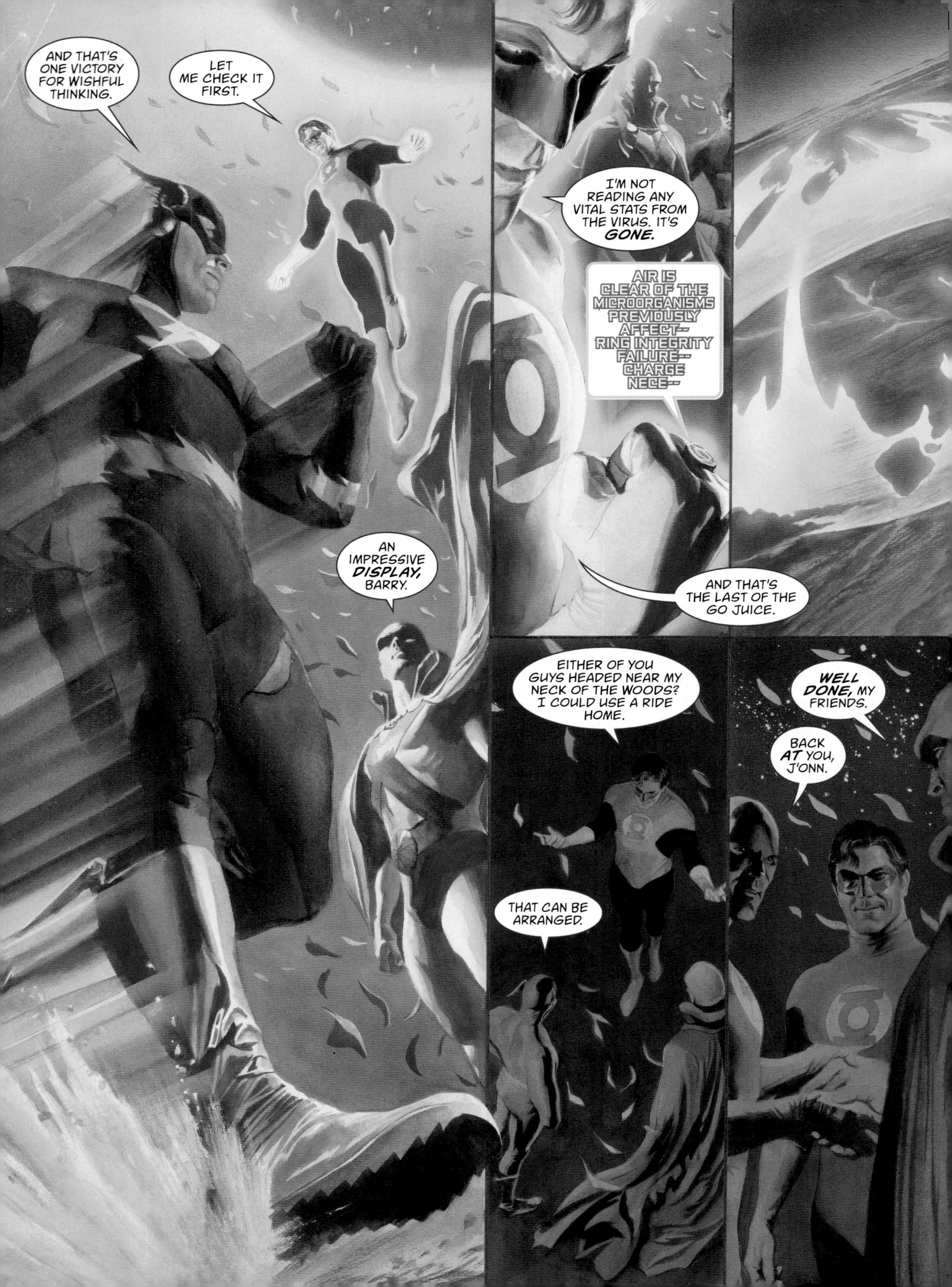
AND THAT'S ONE VICTORY FOR WISHFUL THINKING.
LET ME CHECK IT FIRST.
I'M NOT READING ANY VITAL STATS FROM THE VIRUS. IT'S GONE.
AIR IS CLEAR OF THE MICROORGANISMS PREVIOUSLY AFFECT-- RING INTEGRITY FAILURE-- CHARGE NECE--
AN IMPRESSIVE DISPLAY, BARRY.
AND THAT'S THE LAST OF THE GO JUICE.
EITHER OF YOU GUYS HEADED NEAR MY NECK OF THE WOODS? I COULD USE A RIDE HOME.
THAT CAN BE ARRANGED.
WELL DONE, MY FRIENDS.
BACK AT YOU, J'ONN.

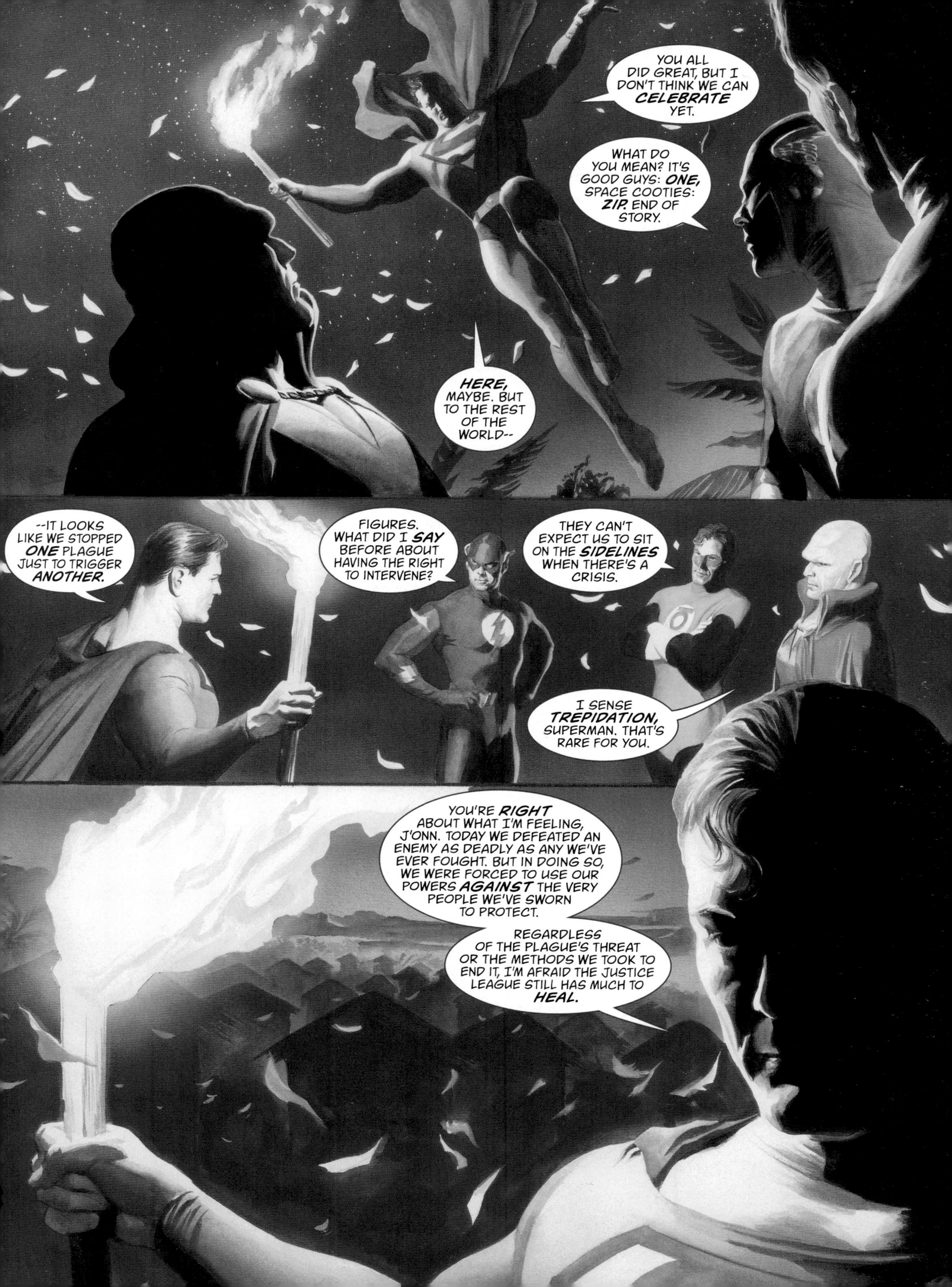
YOU ALL DID GREAT, BUT I DON'T THINK WE CAN CELEBRATE YET.
WHAT DO YOU MEAN? IT'S GOOD GUYS: ONE, SPACE COOTIES: ZIP. END OF STORY.
HERE, MAYBE. BUT TO THE REST OF THE WORLD--
--IT LOOKS LIKE WE STOPPED ONE PLAGUE JUST TO TRIGGER ANOTHER.
FIGURES. WHAT DID I SAY BEFORE ABOUT HAVING THE RIGHT TO INTERVENE?
THEY CAN'T EXPECT US TO SIT ON THE SIDELINES WHEN THERE'S A CRISIS.
I SENSE TREPIDATION, SUPERMAN. THAT'S RARE FOR YOU.
YOU'RE RIGHT ABOUT WHAT I'M FEELING, J'ONN. TODAY WE DEFEATED AN ENEMY AS DEADLY AS ANY WE'VE EVER FOUGHT. BUT IN DOING SO, WE WERE FORCED TO USE OUR POWERS AGAINST THE VERY PEOPLE WE'VE SWORN TO PROTECT.
REGARDLESS OF THE PLAGUE'S THREAT OR THE METHODS WE TOOK TO END IT, I'M AFRAID THE JUSTICE LEAGUE STILL HAS MUCH TO HEAL.

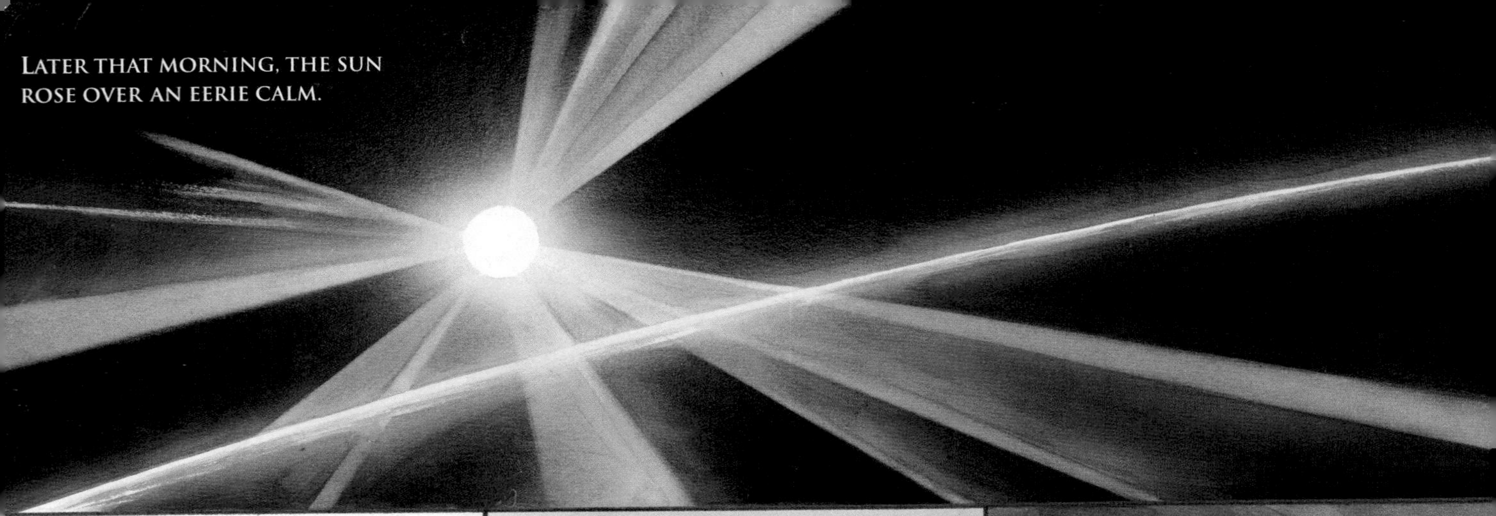
LATER THAT MORNING, THE SUN ROSE OVER AN EERIE CALM.
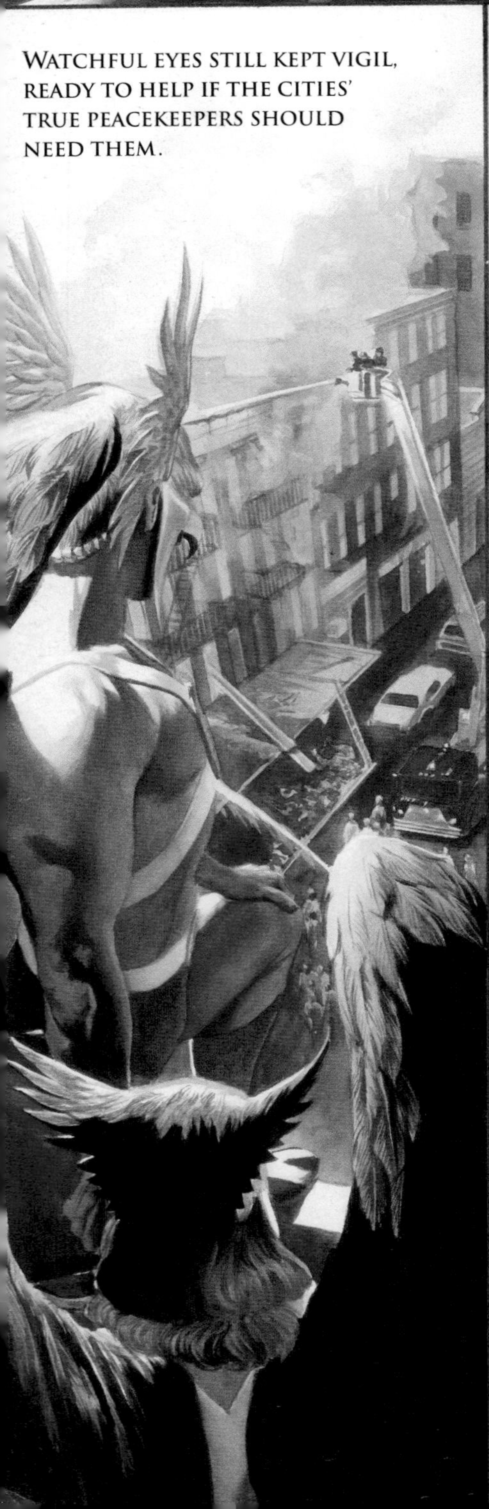
WATCHFUL EYES STILL KEPT VIGIL, READY TO HELP IF THE CITIES' TRUE PEACEKEEPERS SHOULD NEED THEM.
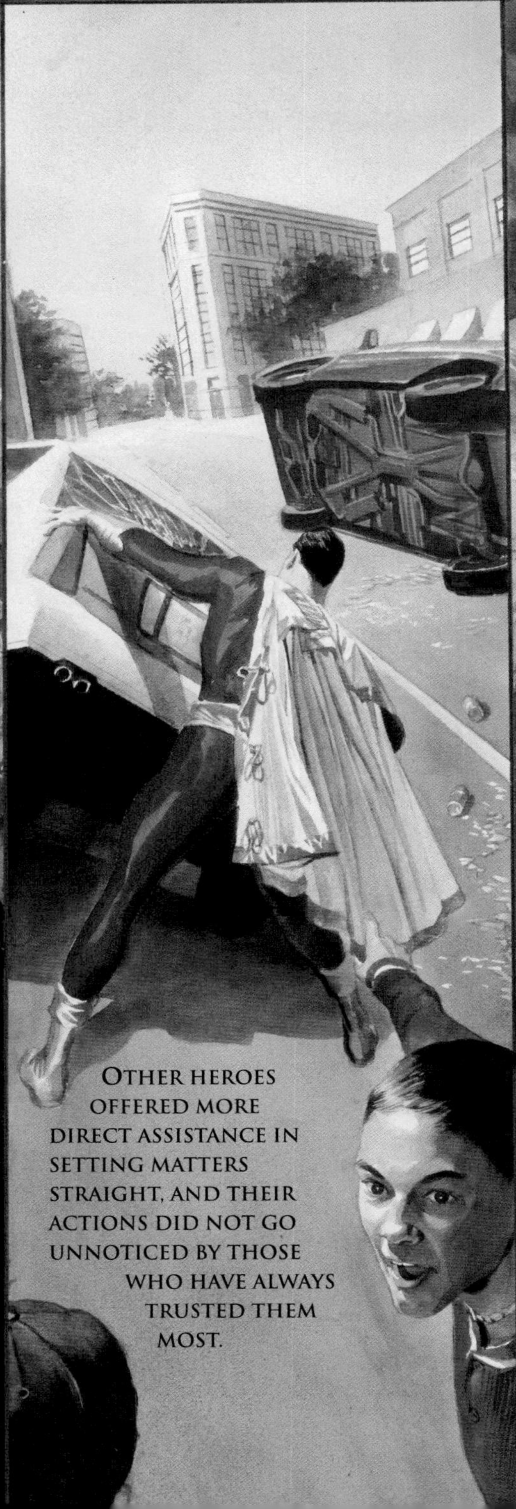
OTHER HEROES OFFERED MORE DIRECT ASSISTANCE IN SETTING MATTERS STRAIGHT, AND THEIR ACTIONS DID NOT GO UNNOTICED BY THOSE WHO HAVE ALWAYS TRUSTED THEM MOST.
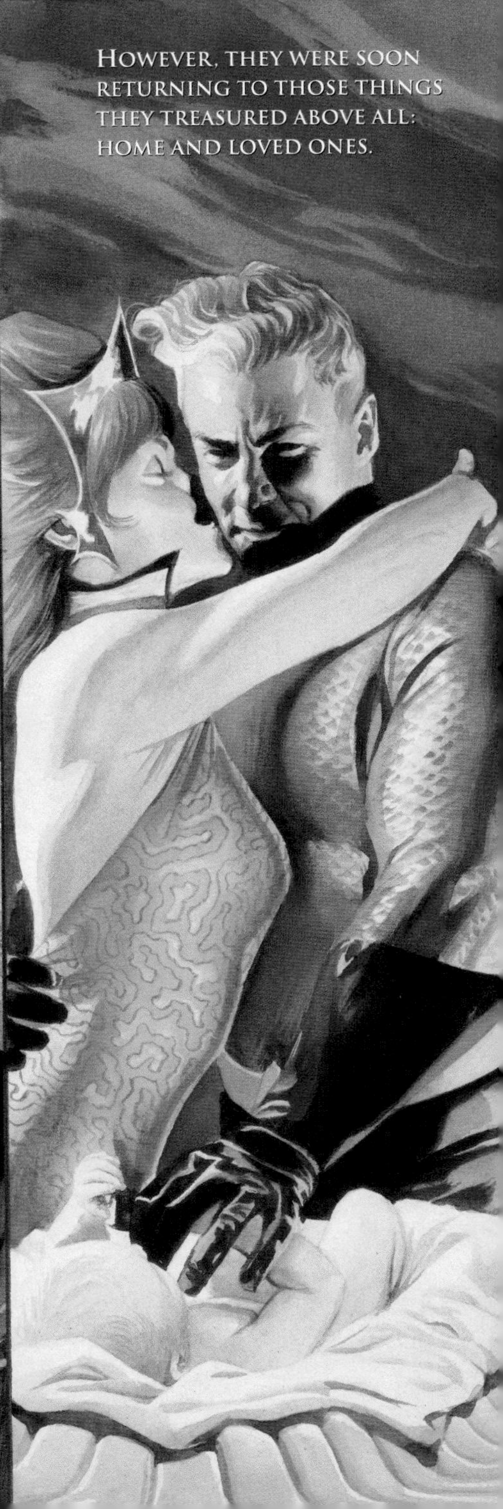
HOWEVER, THEY WERE SOON RETURNING TO THOSE THINGS THEY TREASURED ABOVE ALL: HOME AND LOVED ONES.

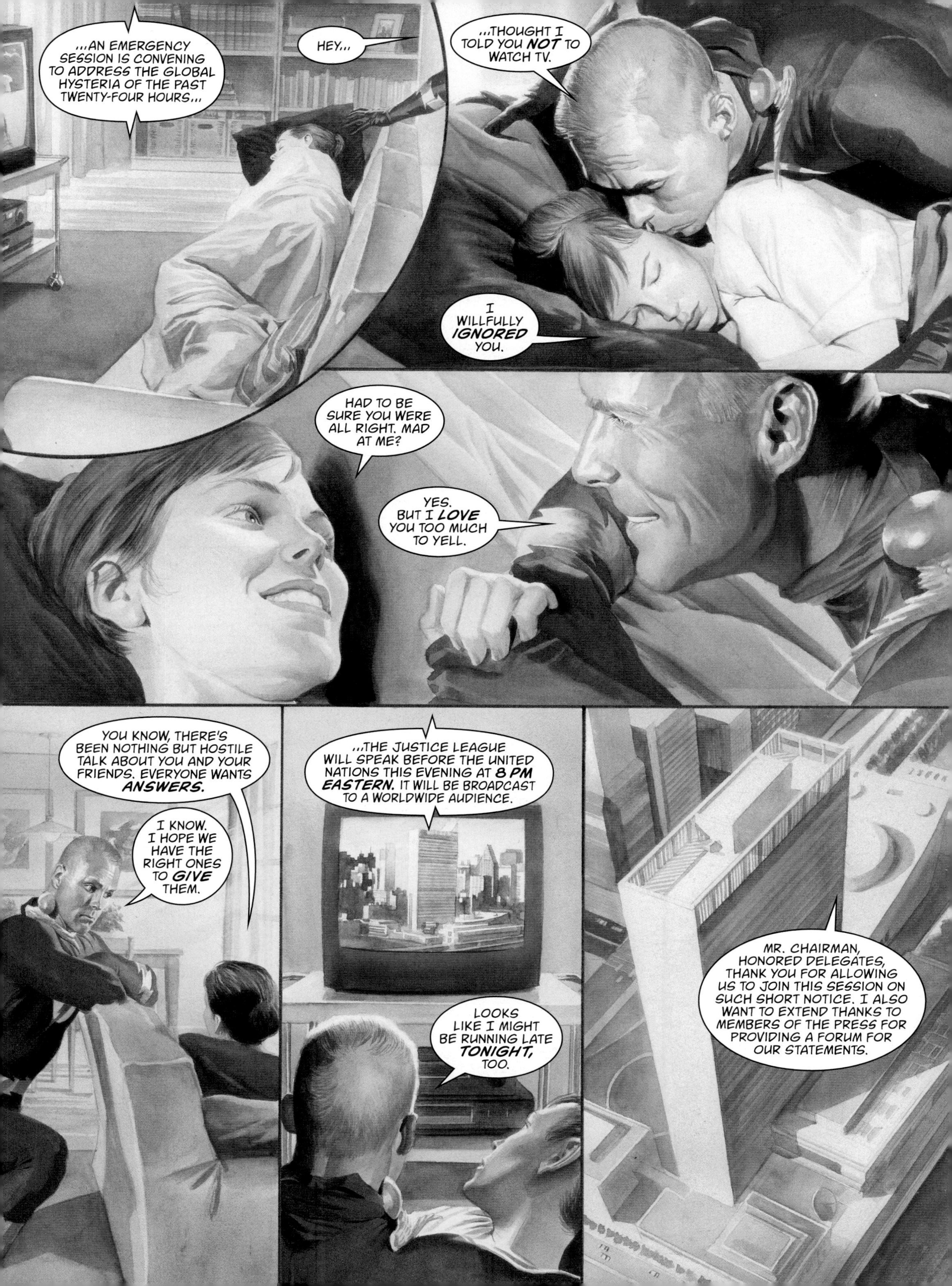
...AN EMERGENCY SESSION IS CONVENING TO ADDRESS THE GLOBAL HYSTERIA OF THE PAST TWENTY-FOUR HOURS...
HEY...
...THOUGHT I TOLD YOU **NOT** TO WATCH TV.
I WILLFULLY ***IGNORED*** YOU.
HAD TO BE SURE YOU WERE ALL RIGHT. MAD AT ME?
YES. BUT I ***LOVE*** YOU TOO MUCH TO YELL.
YOU KNOW, THERE'S BEEN NOTHING BUT HOSTILE TALK ABOUT YOU AND YOUR FRIENDS. EVERYONE WANTS ***ANSWERS.***
I KNOW. I HOPE WE HAVE THE RIGHT ONES TO ***GIVE*** THEM.
...THE JUSTICE LEAGUE WILL SPEAK BEFORE THE UNITED NATIONS THIS EVENING AT ***8 PM EASTERN.*** IT WILL BE BROADCAST TO A WORLDWIDE AUDIENCE.
LOOKS LIKE I MIGHT BE RUNNING LATE ***TONIGHT,*** TOO.
MR. CHAIRMAN, HONORED DELEGATES, THANK YOU FOR ALLOWING US TO JOIN THIS SESSION ON SUCH SHORT NOTICE. I ALSO WANT TO EXTEND THANKS TO MEMBERS OF THE PRESS FOR PROVIDING A FORUM FOR OUR STATEMENTS.

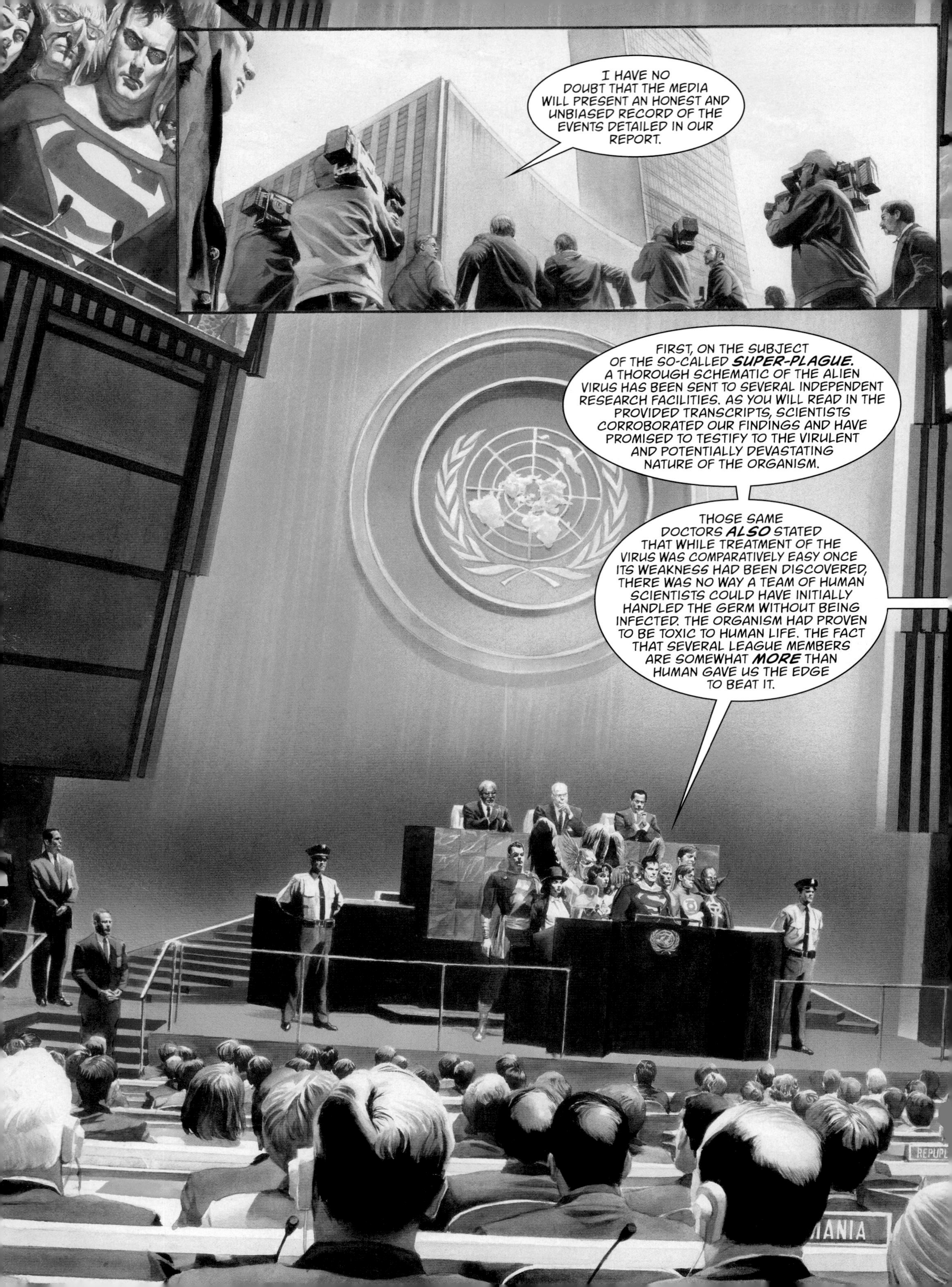
I HAVE NO DOUBT THAT THE MEDIA WILL PRESENT AN HONEST AND UNBIASED RECORD OF THE EVENTS DETAILED IN OUR REPORT.
FIRST, ON THE SUBJECT OF THE SO-CALLED SUPER-PLAGUE. A THOROUGH SCHEMATIC OF THE ALIEN VIRUS HAS BEEN SENT TO SEVERAL INDEPENDENT RESEARCH FACILITIES. AS YOU WILL READ IN THE PROVIDED TRANSCRIPTS, SCIENTISTS CORROBORATED OUR FINDINGS AND HAVE PROMISED TO TESTIFY TO THE VIRULENT AND POTENTIALLY DEVASTATING NATURE OF THE ORGANISM.
THOSE SAME DOCTORS ALSO STATED THAT WHILE TREATMENT OF THE VIRUS WAS COMPARATIVELY EASY ONCE ITS WEAKNESS HAD BEEN DISCOVERED, THERE WAS NO WAY A TEAM OF HUMAN SCIENTISTS COULD HAVE INITIALLY HANDLED THE GERM WITHOUT BEING INFECTED. THE ORGANISM HAD PROVEN TO BE TOXIC TO HUMAN LIFE. THE FACT THAT SEVERAL LEAGUE MEMBERS ARE SOMEWHAT MORE THAN HUMAN GAVE US THE EDGE TO BEAT IT.
REPUBL
MANIA

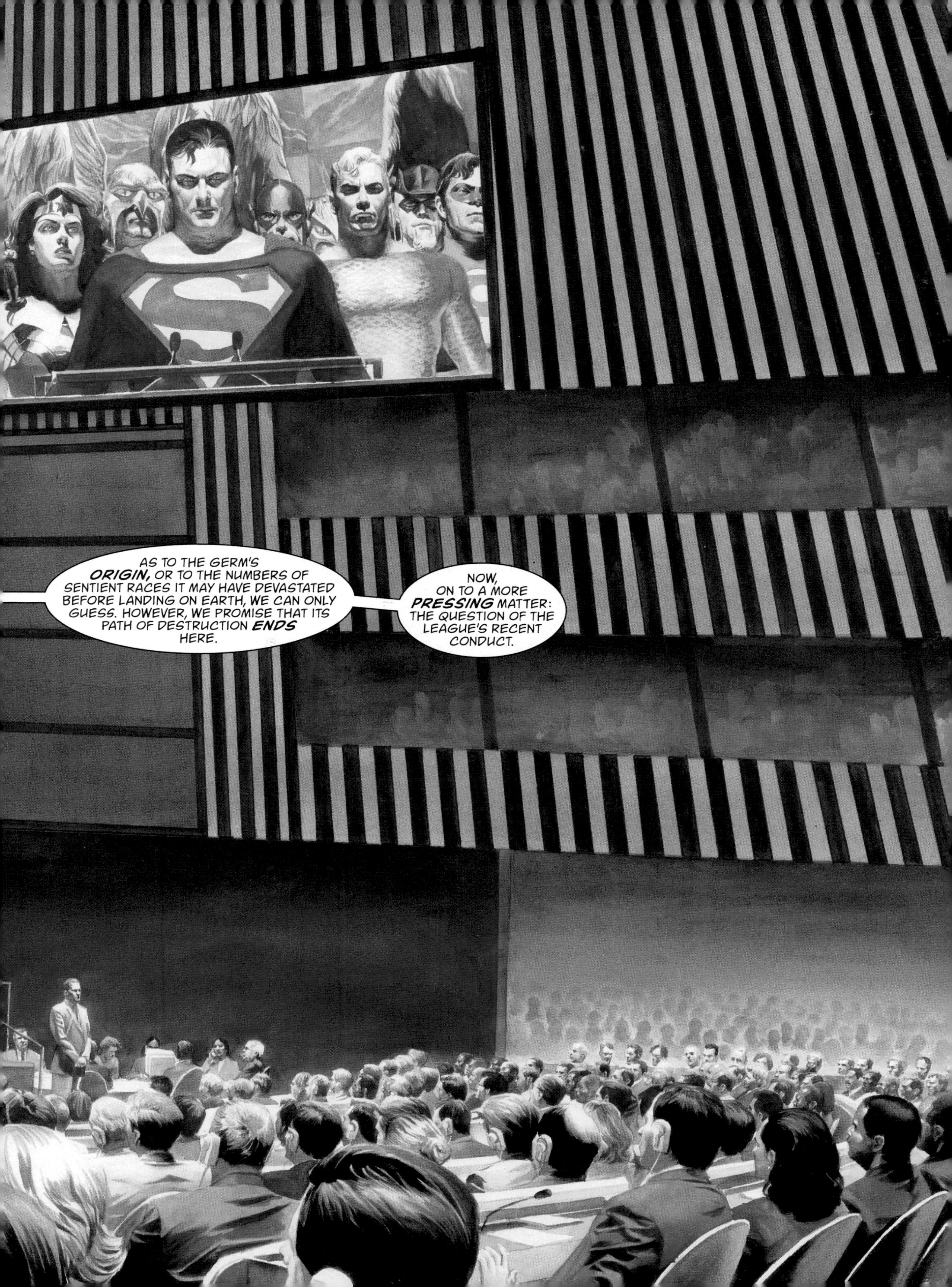
AS TO THE GERM'S ORIGIN, OR TO THE NUMBERS OF SENTIENT RACES IT MAY HAVE DEVASTATED BEFORE LANDING ON EARTH, WE CAN ONLY GUESS. HOWEVER, WE PROMISE THAT ITS PATH OF DESTRUCTION ENDS HERE.
NOW, ON TO A MORE PRESSING MATTER: THE QUESTION OF THE LEAGUE'S RECENT CONDUCT.

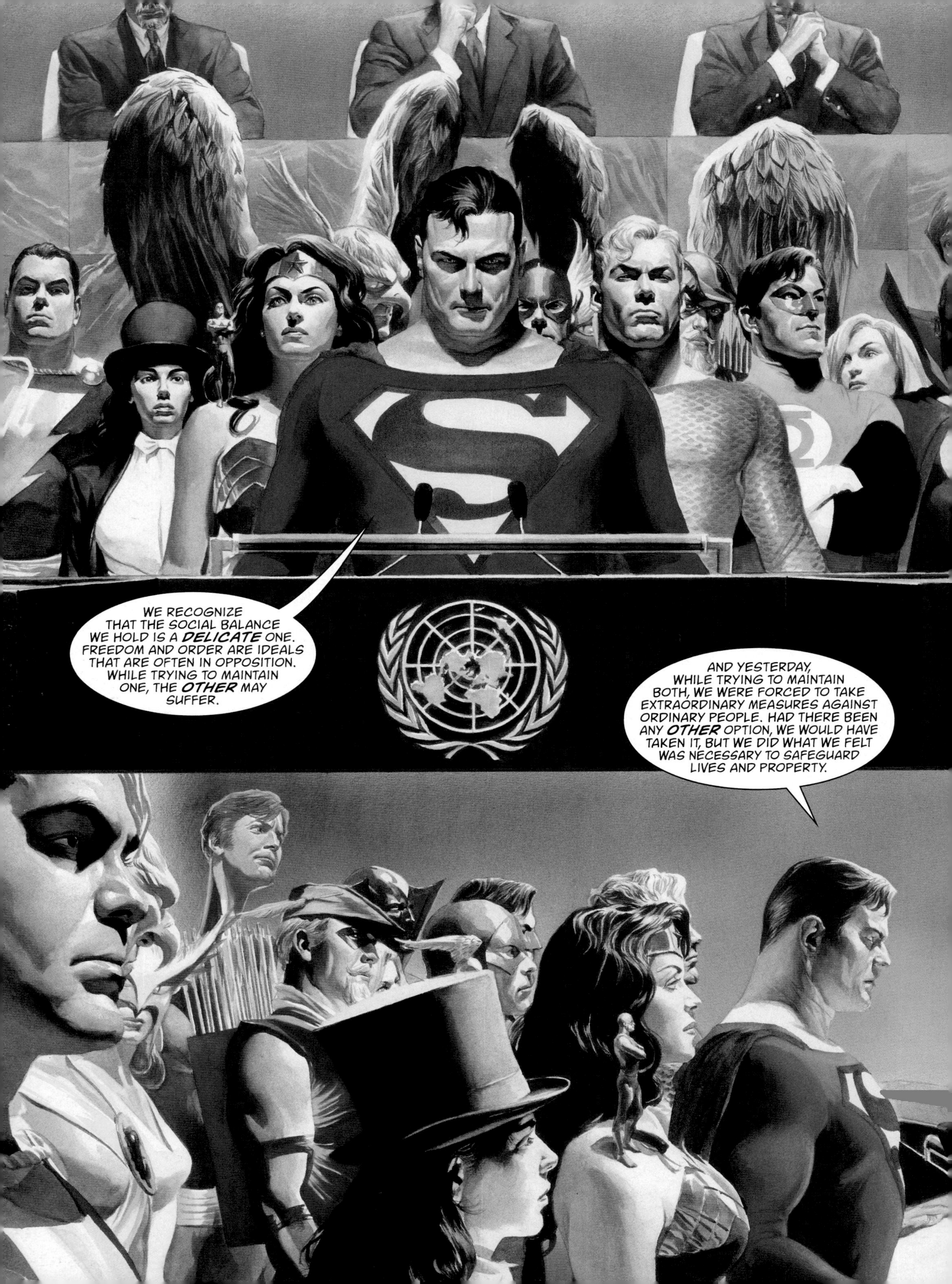
WE RECOGNIZE THAT THE SOCIAL BALANCE WE HOLD IS A *DELICATE* ONE. FREEDOM AND ORDER ARE IDEALS THAT ARE OFTEN IN OPPOSITION. WHILE TRYING TO MAINTAIN ONE, THE *OTHER* MAY SUFFER.
AND YESTERDAY, WHILE TRYING TO MAINTAIN BOTH, WE WERE FORCED TO TAKE EXTRAORDINARY MEASURES AGAINST ORDINARY PEOPLE. HAD THERE BEEN ANY *OTHER* OPTION, WE WOULD HAVE TAKEN IT, BUT WE DID WHAT WE FELT WAS NECESSARY TO SAFEGUARD LIVES AND PROPERTY.

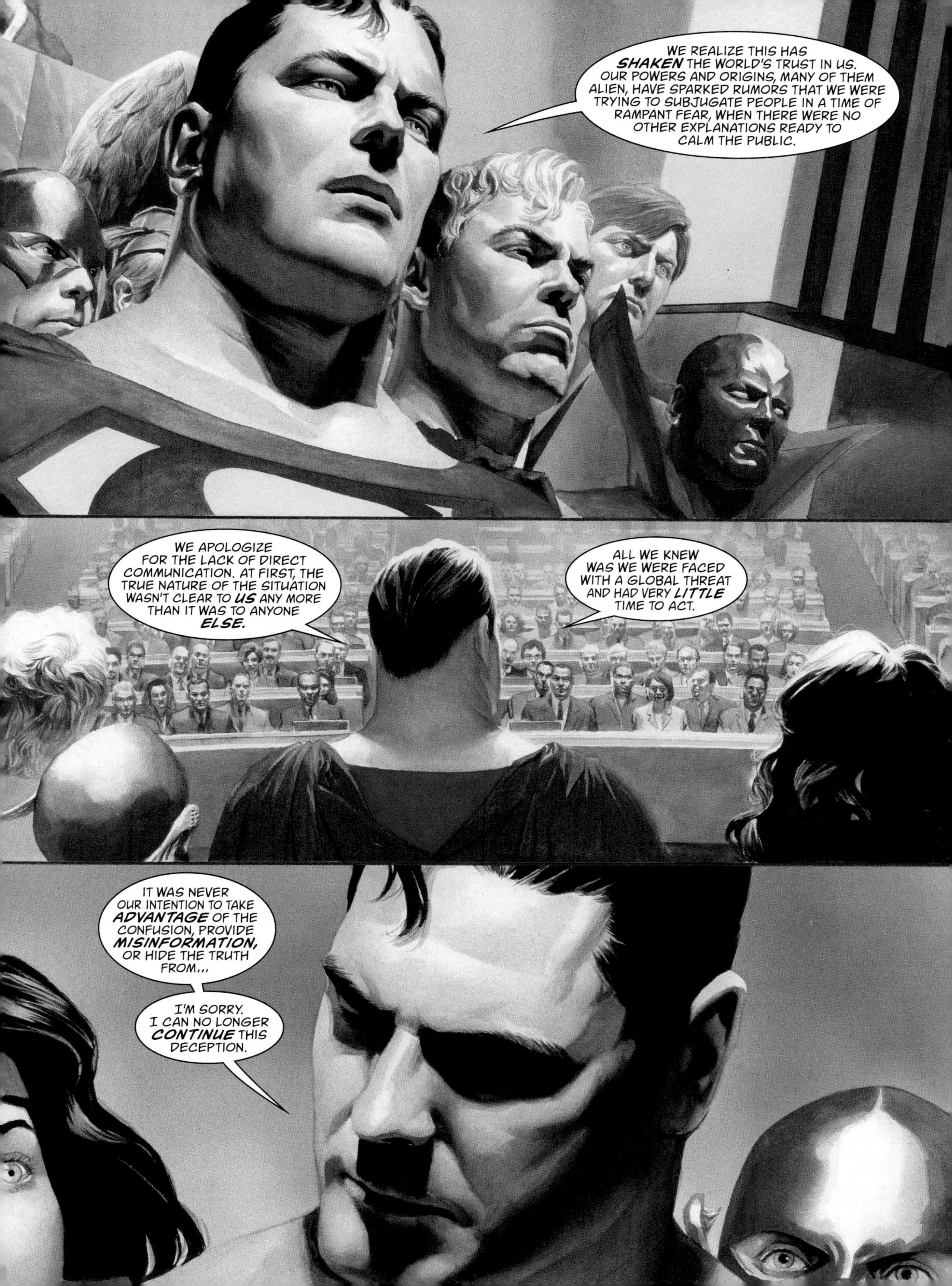
WE REALIZE THIS HAS SHAKEN THE WORLD'S TRUST IN US. OUR POWERS AND ORIGINS, MANY OF THEM ALIEN, HAVE SPARKED RUMORS THAT WE WERE TRYING TO SUBJUGATE PEOPLE IN A TIME OF RAMPANT FEAR, WHEN THERE WERE NO OTHER EXPLANATIONS READY TO CALM THE PUBLIC.
WE APOLOGIZE FOR THE LACK OF DIRECT COMMUNICATION. AT FIRST, THE TRUE NATURE OF THE SITUATION WASN'T CLEAR TO US ANY MORE THAN IT WAS TO ANYONE ELSE.
ALL WE KNEW WAS WE WERE FACED WITH A GLOBAL THREAT AND HAD VERY LITTLE TIME TO ACT.
IT WAS NEVER OUR INTENTION TO TAKE ADVANTAGE OF THE CONFUSION, PROVIDE MISINFORMATION, OR HIDE THE TRUTH FROM...
I'M SORRY. I CAN NO LONGER CONTINUE THIS DECEPTION.

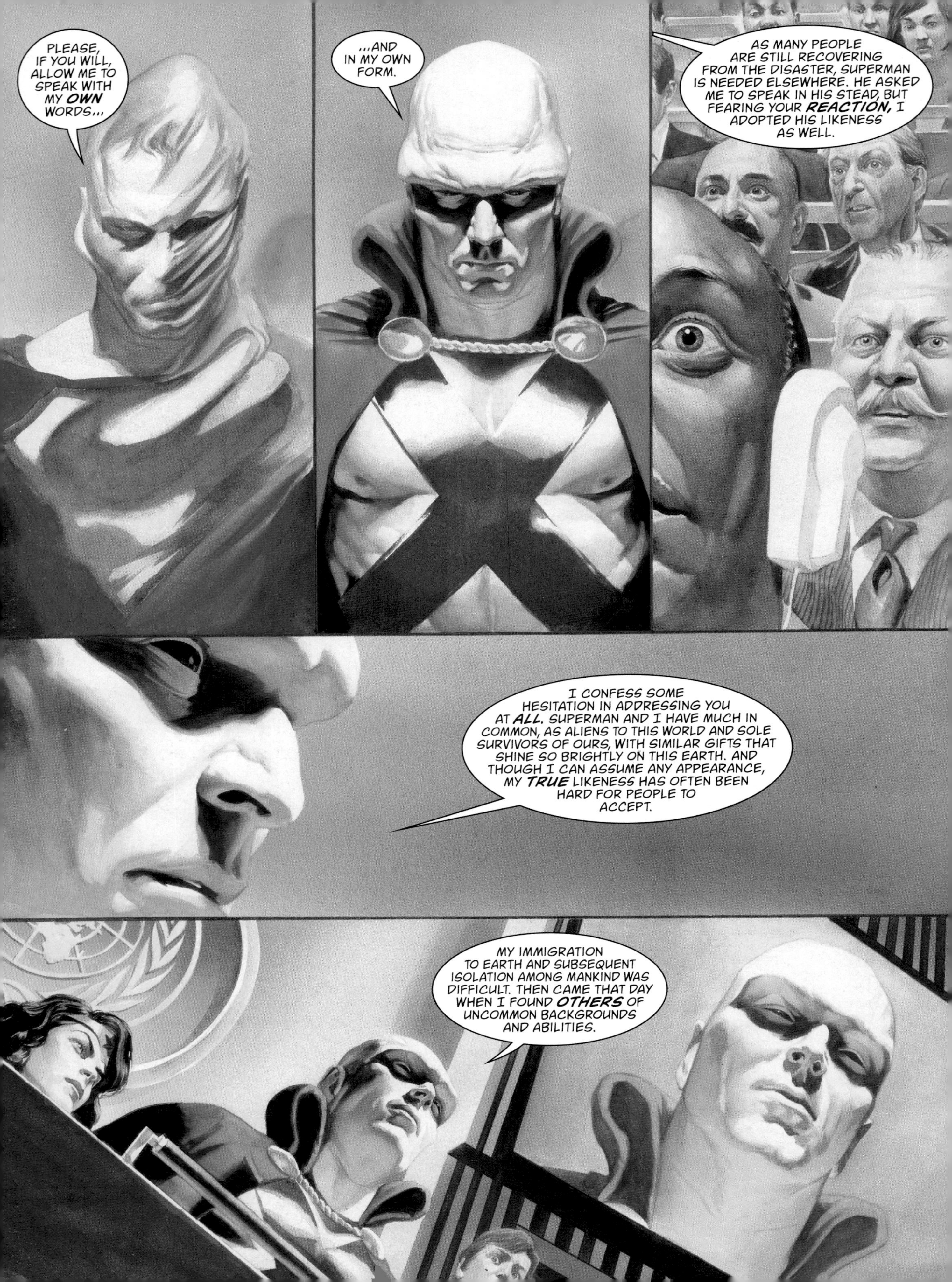
PLEASE, IF YOU WILL, ALLOW ME TO SPEAK WITH MY *OWN* WORDS...
...AND IN MY OWN FORM.
AS MANY PEOPLE ARE STILL RECOVERING FROM THE DISASTER, SUPERMAN IS NEEDED ELSEWHERE. HE ASKED ME TO SPEAK IN HIS STEAD, BUT FEARING YOUR *REACTION,* I ADOPTED HIS LIKENESS AS WELL.
I CONFESS SOME HESITATION IN ADDRESSING YOU AT *ALL.* SUPERMAN AND I HAVE MUCH IN COMMON, AS ALIENS TO THIS WORLD AND SOLE SURVIVORS OF OURS, WITH SIMILAR GIFTS THAT SHINE SO BRIGHTLY ON THIS EARTH. AND THOUGH I CAN ASSUME ANY APPEARANCE, MY *TRUE* LIKENESS HAS OFTEN BEEN HARD FOR PEOPLE TO ACCEPT.
MY IMMIGRATION TO EARTH AND SUBSEQUENT ISOLATION AMONG MANKIND WAS DIFFICULT. THEN CAME THAT DAY WHEN I FOUND *OTHERS* OF UNCOMMON BACKGROUNDS AND ABILITIES.

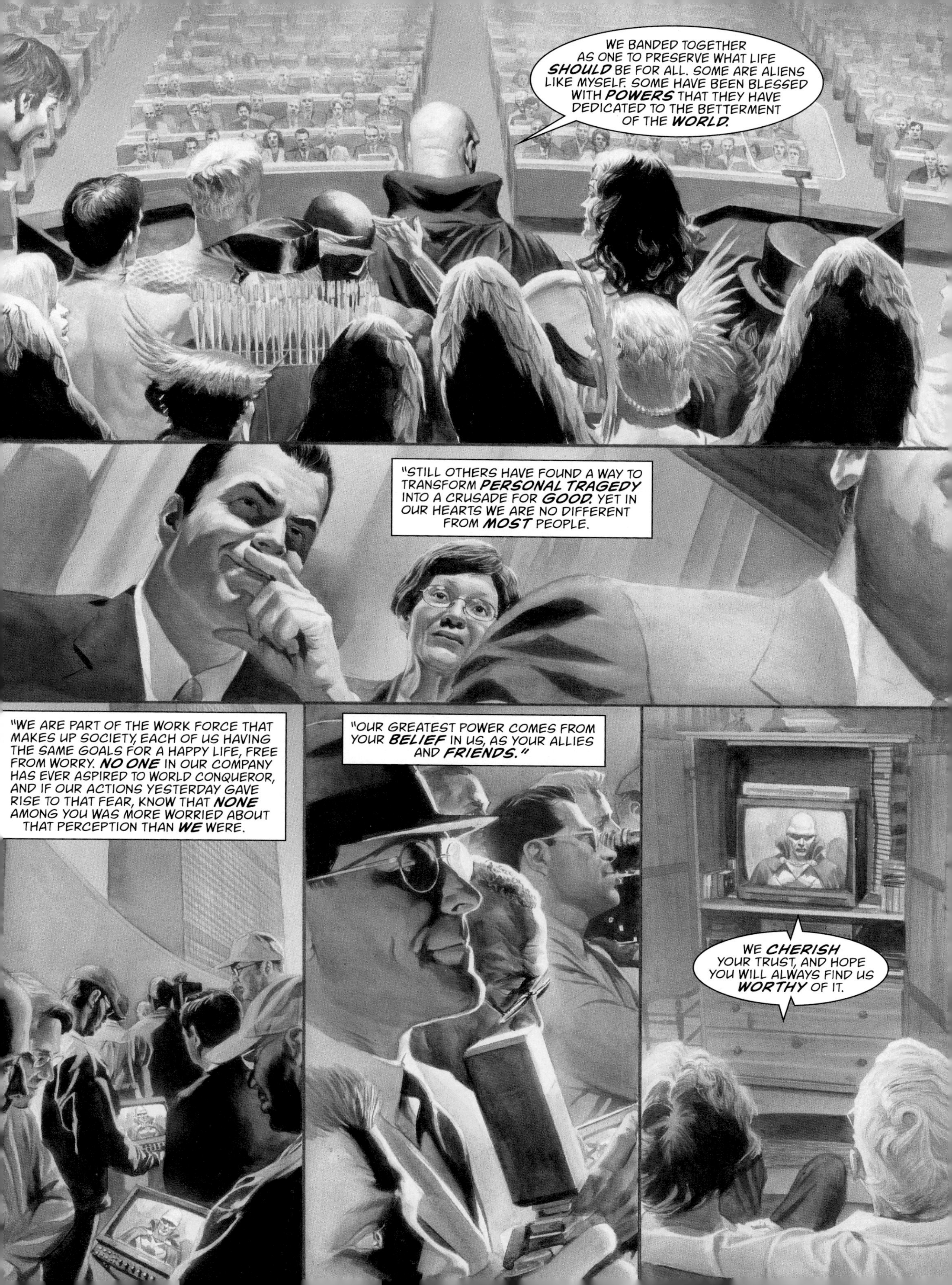
WE BANDED TOGETHER AS ONE TO PRESERVE WHAT LIFE **SHOULD** BE FOR ALL. SOME ARE ALIENS LIKE MYSELF. SOME HAVE BEEN BLESSED WITH **POWERS** THAT THEY HAVE DEDICATED TO THE BETTERMENT OF THE **WORLD.**
"STILL OTHERS HAVE FOUND A WAY TO TRANSFORM **PERSONAL TRAGEDY** INTO A CRUSADE FOR **GOOD.** YET IN OUR HEARTS WE ARE NO DIFFERENT FROM **MOST** PEOPLE.
"WE ARE PART OF THE WORK FORCE THAT MAKES UP SOCIETY, EACH OF US HAVING THE SAME GOALS FOR A HAPPY LIFE, FREE FROM WORRY. **NO ONE** IN OUR COMPANY HAS EVER ASPIRED TO WORLD CONQUEROR, AND IF OUR ACTIONS YESTERDAY GAVE RISE TO THAT FEAR, KNOW THAT **NONE** AMONG YOU WAS MORE WORRIED ABOUT THAT PERCEPTION THAN **WE** WERE.
"OUR GREATEST POWER COMES FROM YOUR **BELIEF** IN US, AS YOUR ALLIES AND **FRIENDS.**"
WE **CHERISH** YOUR TRUST, AND HOPE YOU WILL ALWAYS FIND US **WORTHY** OF IT.

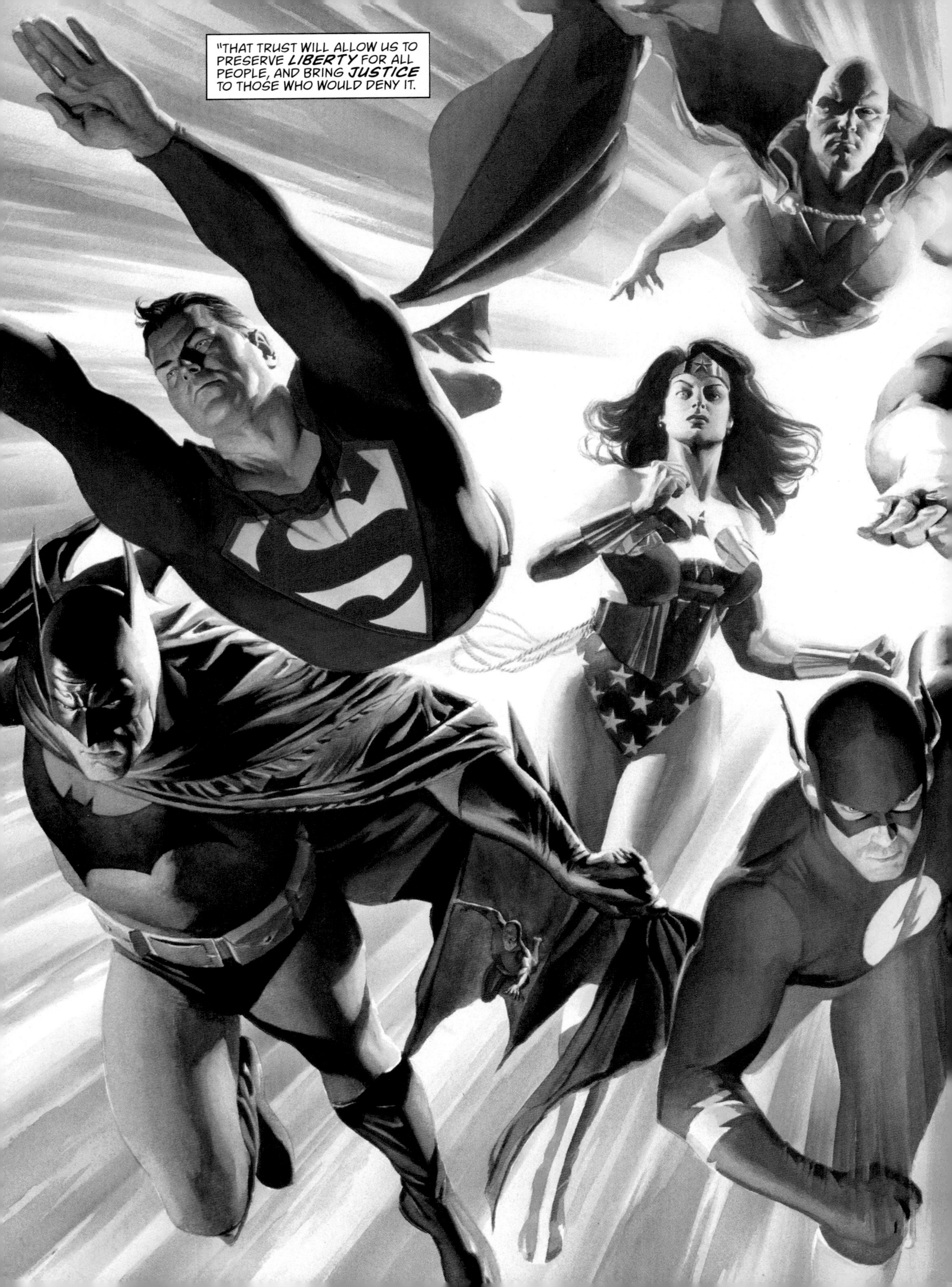
"THAT TRUST WILL ALLOW US TO PRESERVE LIBERTY FOR ALL PEOPLE, AND BRING JUSTICE TO THOSE WHO WOULD DENY IT.

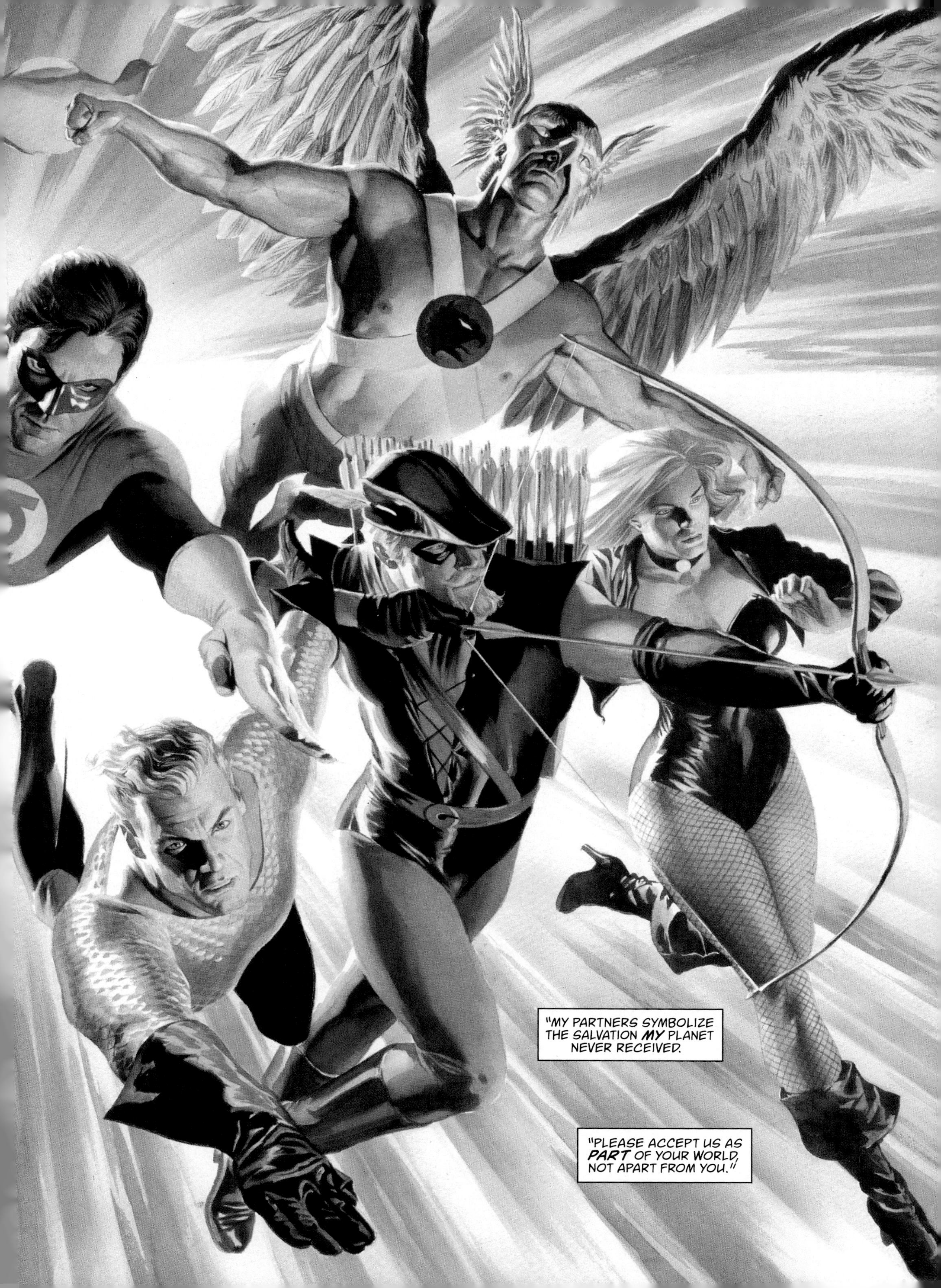
"MY PARTNERS SYMBOLIZE THE SALVATION MY PLANET NEVER RECEIVED.
"PLEASE ACCEPT US AS PART OF YOUR WORLD, NOT APART FROM YOU."

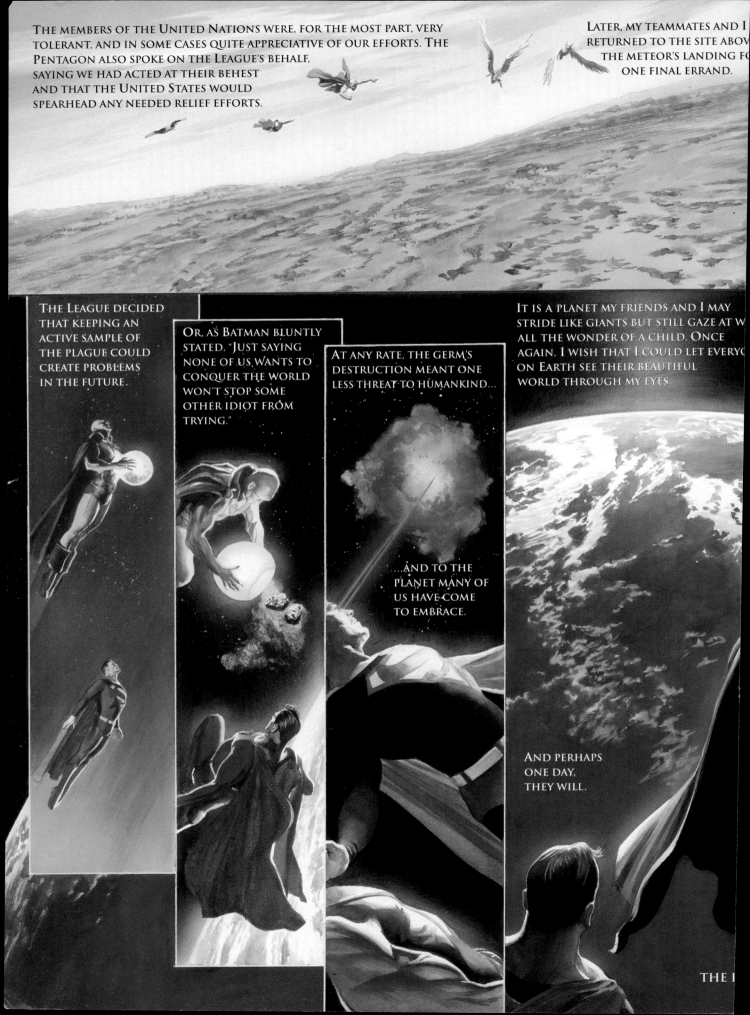

THE MEMBERS OF THE UNITED NATIONS WERE, FOR THE MOST PART, VERY TOLERANT, AND IN SOME CASES QUITE APPRECIATIVE OF OUR EFFORTS. THE PENTAGON ALSO SPOKE ON THE LEAGUE'S BEHALF, SAYING WE HAD ACTED AT THEIR BEHEST AND THAT THE UNITED STATES WOULD SPEARHEAD ANY NEEDED RELIEF EFFORTS.

LATER, MY TEAMMATES AND I RETURNED TO THE SITE ABOV THE METEOR'S LANDING F ONE FINAL ERRAND.

THE LEAGUE DECIDED THAT KEEPING AN ACTIVE SAMPLE OF THE PLAGUE COULD CREATE PROBLEMS IN THE FUTURE.

OR, AS BATMAN BLUNTLY STATED, "JUST SAYING NONE OF US WANTS TO CONQUER THE WORLD WON'T STOP SOME OTHER IDIOT FROM TRYING."

AT ANY RATE, THE GERM'S DESTRUCTION MEANT ONE LESS THREAT TO HUMANKIND...

...AND TO THE PLANET MANY OF US HAVE COME TO EMBRACE.

IT IS A PLANET MY FRIENDS AND I MAY STRIDE LIKE GIANTS BUT STILL GAZE AT W ALL THE WONDER OF A CHILD. ONCE AGAIN, I WISH THAT I COULD LET EVERYO ON EARTH SEE THEIR BEAUTIFUL WORLD THROUGH MY EYES.

AND PERHAPS ONE DAY, THEY WILL.

THE I

LOOKING AT THE WORLD
THROUGH X-RAY EYES

Storytelling in animation, while similar in many ways to comic book writing, follows its own set of rules. For example, while an heroic character on screen is often engaged in fast-paced action, there is little opportunity for the dialogue that is traditionally voiced by that same character when they are depicted in a comic book. I personally have always felt that Batman, and to a lesser degree Superman, in their animated forms, were heroes who did not need a lot of dialogue to explain what they were doing. Villain launches attack, hero leaps into action, defeats henchmen, dismantles bomb/freezing ray/giant robot, trounces main villain and finally vanishes as mysteriously as he arrived. That's all well and good in a cartoon, where the pivotal elements of the story are interpreted by the artists largely through expressive poses, character acting and sweeping visuals. But the comic book (along with its uptown cousin the graphic novel) have the luxury of telling a much more intricate story through the magic of the writer's text.

As a writer for animation, I am somewhat detached from the innermost thoughts of my characters. Certainly I put the words in their mouths and script the action that puts them through their heroic paces, but it's not quite the same as living in their skin. Therefore, it was a challenge for me to tell these stories of the world's greatest super-heroes from the perspectives of the heroes themselves.

There is a beautiful loneliness to the super-heroes' world. It is filled with beings of great power who have nobly taken upon their shoulders the welfare of the ordinary human. In most cases, they have given up their "normal" lives so that we could enjoy ours. They watch us from afar, save us from disaster and hold at bay the forces of evil, but rarely stick around for a thank-you. In disguises they walk among us, yet in their costumed identities they must remain forever apart.

Putting myself inside the heads of these iconic characters gave me a unique chance to see the world through their eyes. In their most intimate thoughts, the heroes sought to inspire rather than preach and to guide rather than rule, aspirations that form the very essence of humanity. Who better, then, to depict that humanity than Alex Ross? A generation of readers has now grown up with Ross's photo-realistic illustrations of super-heroes. He has rooted those fantastic characters in our reality and made them truly gods among mortals. Even so, Alex never discarded the emotions that made these super-humans human. He has given them strength tempered with compassion. Power held in check by wisdom. Disappointment mixed with optimism. If we could look at Ross's heroes with something akin to Superman's x-ray vision,

AFTERWORD

we would discover they are at heart very much like role models we have embraced since childhood: father, policeman, big brother, diplomat, and teacher. The heroes are like us because they *are* us, at least that part of us that looks to the good in each other.

PAUL DINI

PROJECT GENESIS

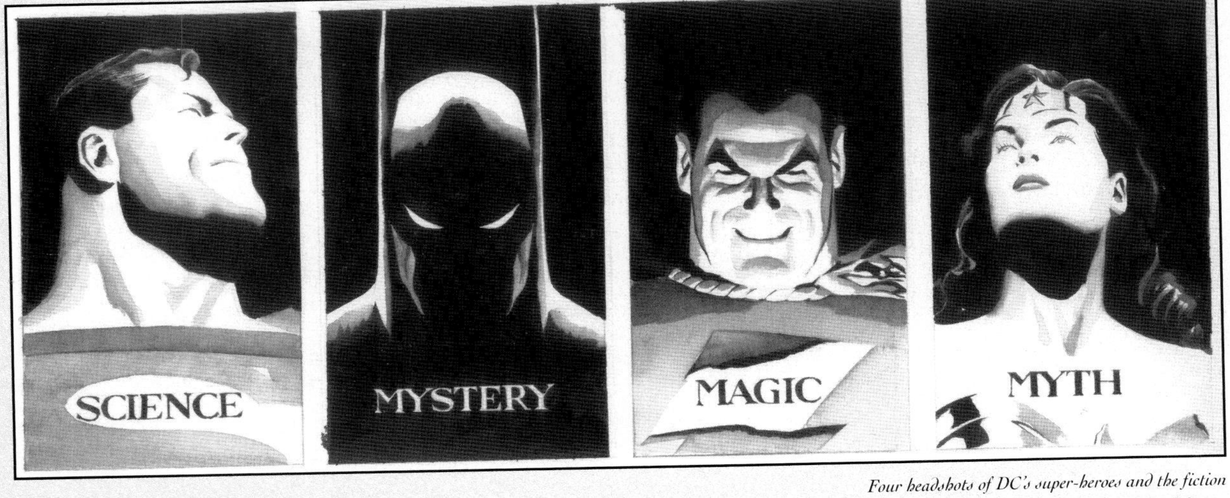
SCIENCE
MYSTERY
MAGIC
MYTH

Four headshots of DC's super-heroes and the fiction categories they symbolized as the proposed lineup for the "tabloid books" (1997).

As early as 1994, my friend and editor Charlie Kochman and I discussed plans to do a Superman book. Initially it was the idea of a children's storybook, with simple narrative text over large images, melded with the panel-to-panel storytelling found in comic books. Above all that I especially wanted to do a project spotlighting Superman alone, since I spent a great deal of time with the character in the ensemble cast of KINGDOM COME (1996). I had a desire to represent the first and greatest of all super-heroes in a manner truest to his earliest representation, devoid of all the trappings of sidekicks, villains, and accessory details that later stories would add. As this idea took hold between Charlie and me for a special approach to Superman, as well as a new format, the idea grew to include those other heroes we considered to be of seminal importance.

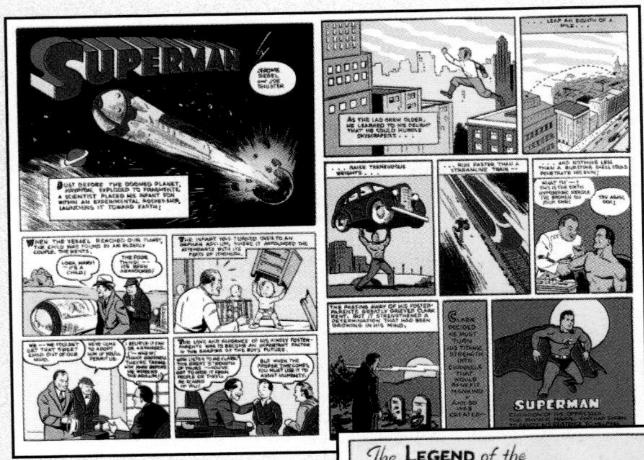
SUPERMAN
SUPERMAN

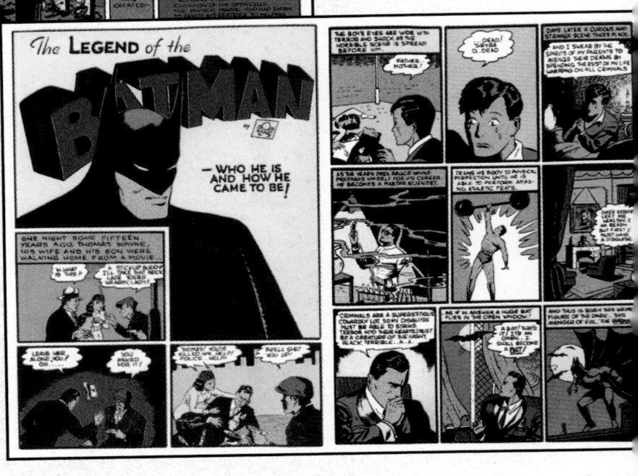
The LEGEND of the
BATMAN
—WHO HE IS AND HOW HE CAME TO BE!

The original two-page origins of ***Superman*** *by Jerry Siegel and Joe Shuster (1939) and* ***Batman*** *by Bob Kane (1940).*

Superman, Batman, Captain Marvel, and Wonder Woman were key super-hero archetypes. Nearly every character that came after them was shaped by their innovations in the genre. And as each of these great heroes was introduced in direct succession from 1938 to 1941, their sixtieth anniversaries were coming right up in time for our project. With a line plan in mind, I began to produce numerous sample pieces for presenting a group of books with an experimental style of storytelling and a special size format to separate the product. Harking back to the "Limited Collector's Editions" and "Famous First Editions" of the '70s, we recreated the tabloid-size format that was commonly used mostly for reprint material.

As many of these reprints introduced me to the first stories of these heroes, I wanted to create an homage to the two-page origins of Superman and Batman, as done by their original creators. Painted mock-ups of these were made as well as color cover roughs and tight ink layouts of double-page spreads to give examples of how the storytelling style might work.

Having all this in hand, in addition to an early SUPERMAN: PEACE ON EARTH outline I wrote, got us an audience with DC to consider developing the project. The clincher, though, was landing the writing talents of Paul Dini, who was then still writing and producing for the Superman and Batman animated series. Paul's coming on board, along with co-editor Joey Cavalieri, made a complete team to bring this ambition of Charlie's and mine to life, an ambition to hopefully make a memorable contribution to how these super-heroes are seen by a new generation.

ALEX ROSS

*early cover concept for **SUPERMAN: PEACE ON EARTH.***

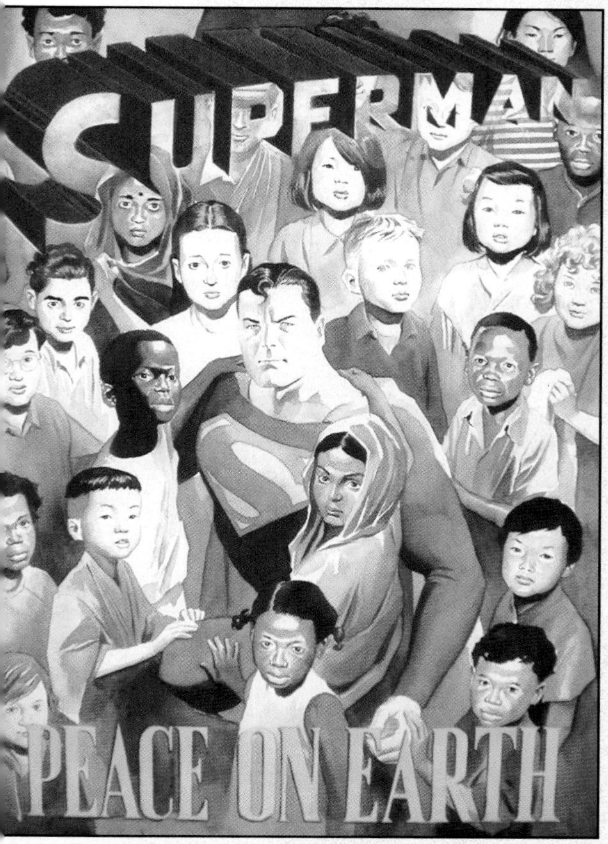
SUPERMAN
PEACE ON EARTH

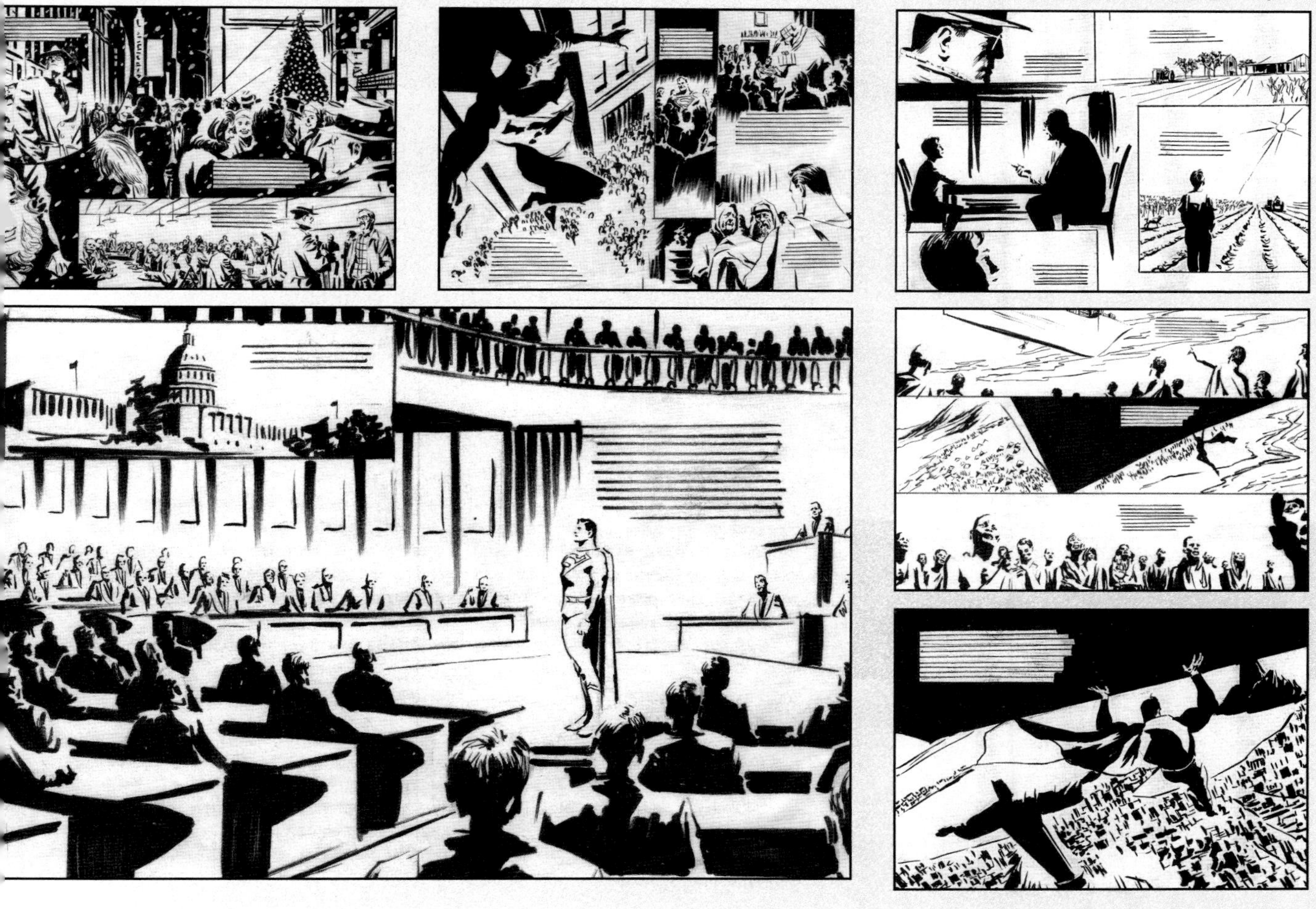

Pen and ink roughs for proposal to show layout style as similar to a children's storybook.

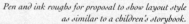

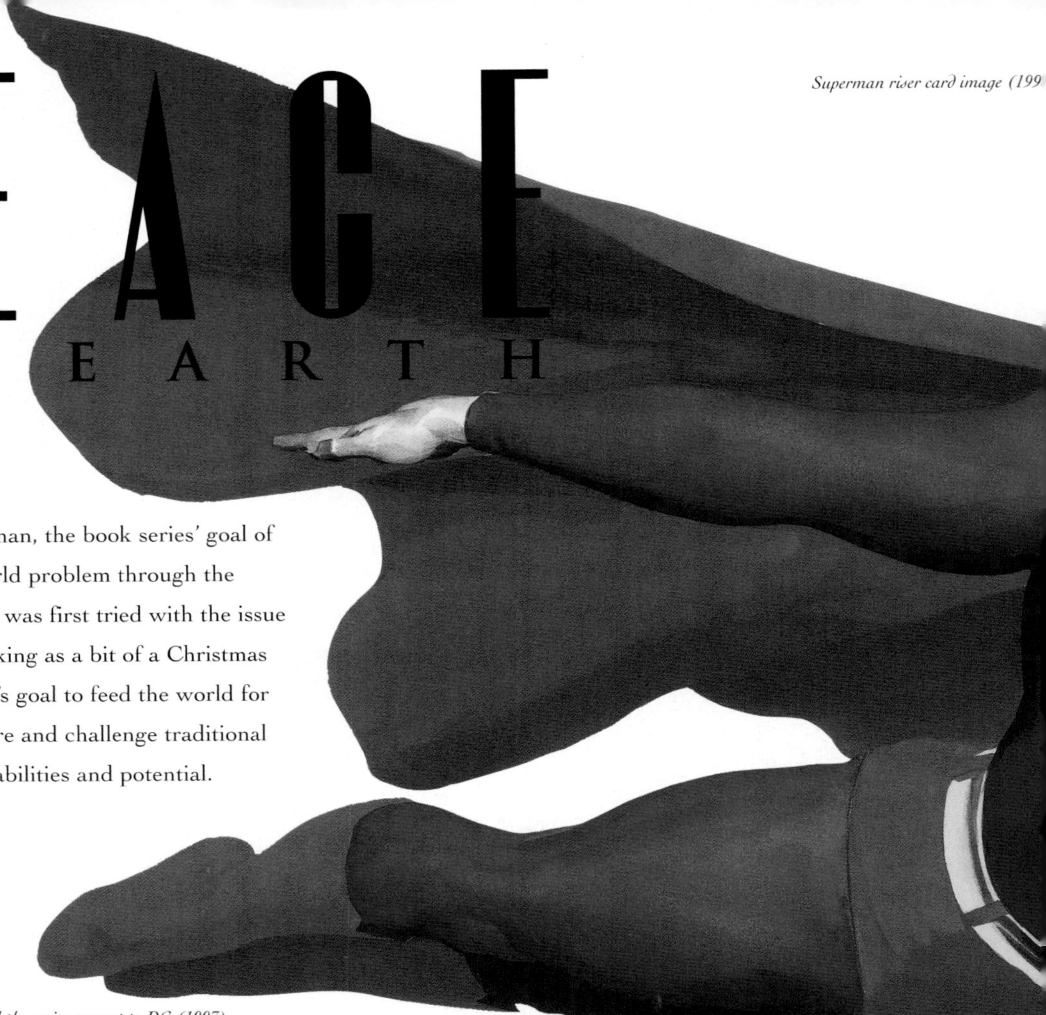

Superman riser card image (199

PEACE ON EARTH

Beginning with Superman, the book series' goal of addressing a "real" world problem through the actions of a super-hero was first tried with the issue of world hunger. Working as a bit of a Christmas tale as well, Superman's goal to feed the world for a day is meant to inspire and challenge traditional storyline focus for his abilities and potential.

Painted sample origin spread used to help sell the series concept to DC (1997).

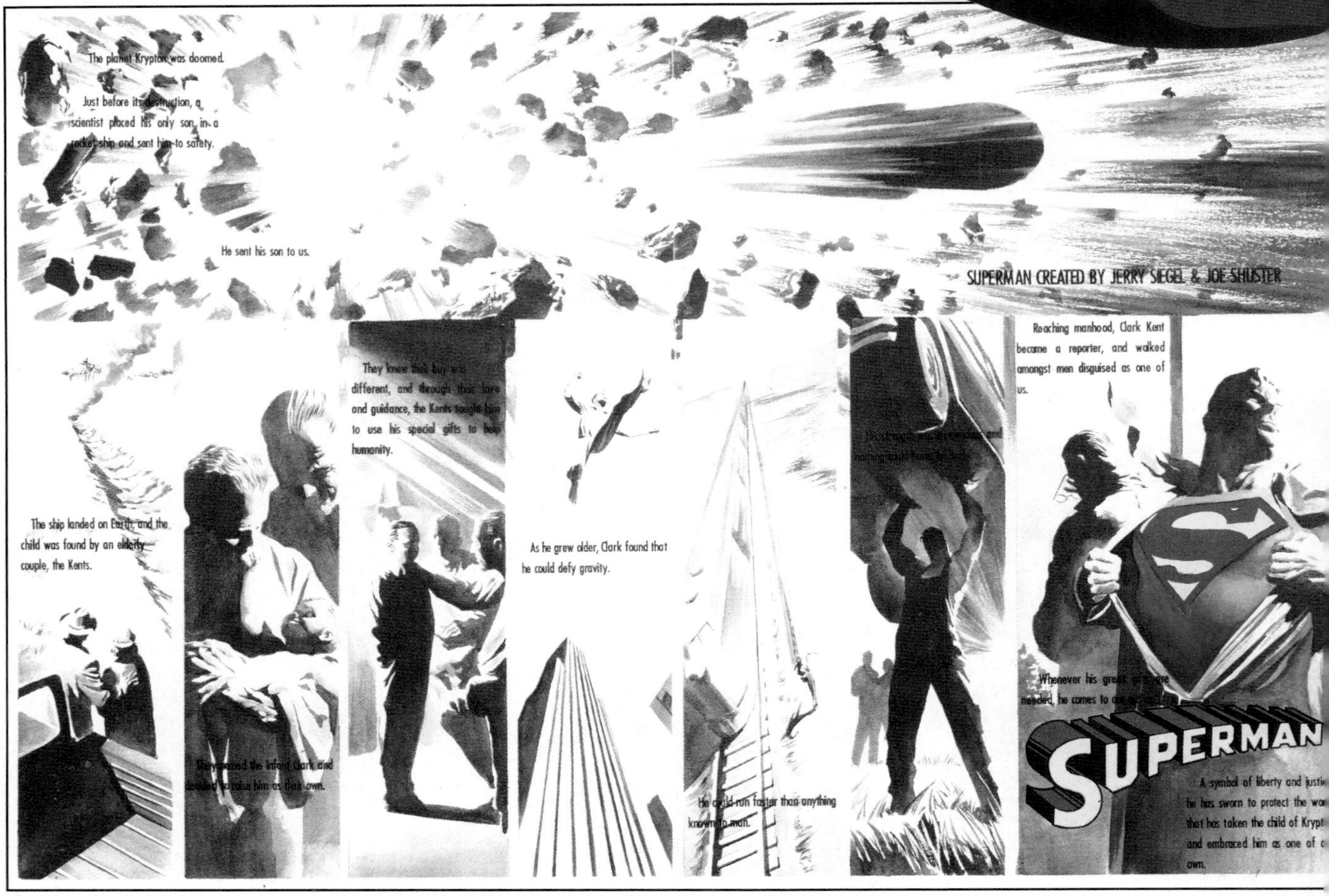
The planet Krypton was doomed.
Just before its destruction, a scientist placed his only son in a rocket ship and sent him to safety.
He sent his son to us.
SUPERMAN CREATED BY JERRY SIEGEL & JOE SHUSTER
The ship landed on Earth, and the child was found by an elderly couple, the Kents.
the infant Clark and
to raise him as their own.
They knew their boy was different, and through their love and guidance, the Kents taught him to use his special gifts to help humanity.
As he grew older, Clark found that he could defy gravity.
He could run faster than anything known to man.
Reaching manhood, Clark Kent became a reporter, and walked amongst men disguised as one of us.
Whenever his great
needed, he comes to
SUPERMAN
A symbol of liberty and justi
he has sworn to protect the wo
that has taken the child of Krypt
and embraced him as one of
own.

Painted sample cover layout used to help sell the series concept to DC (1997).

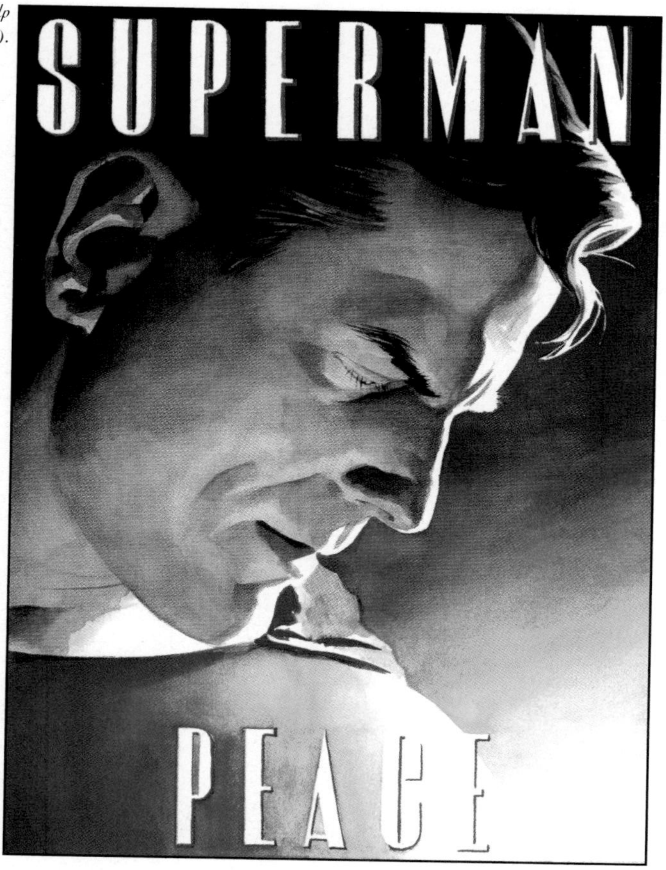
SUPERMAN
PEACE

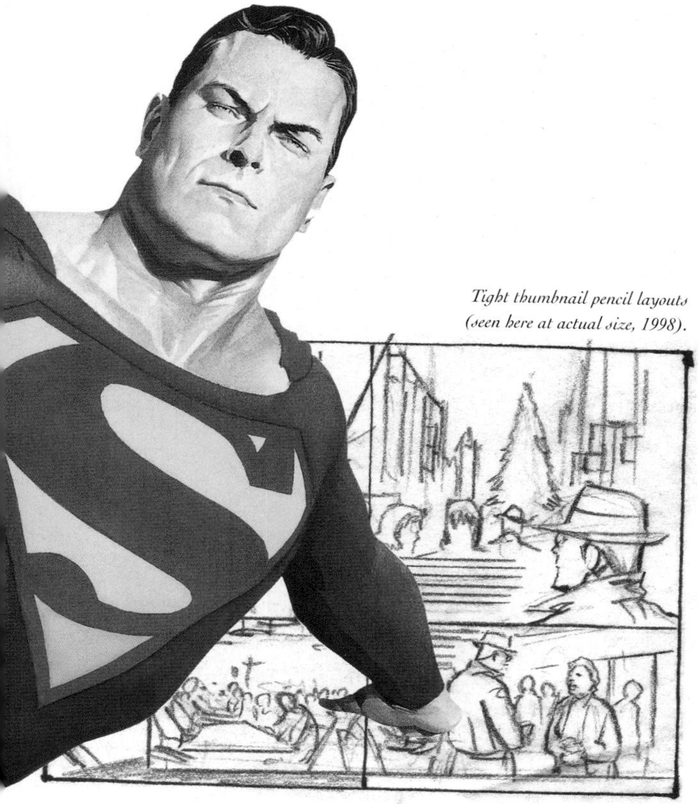

Tight thumbnail pencil layouts (seen here at actual size, 1998).

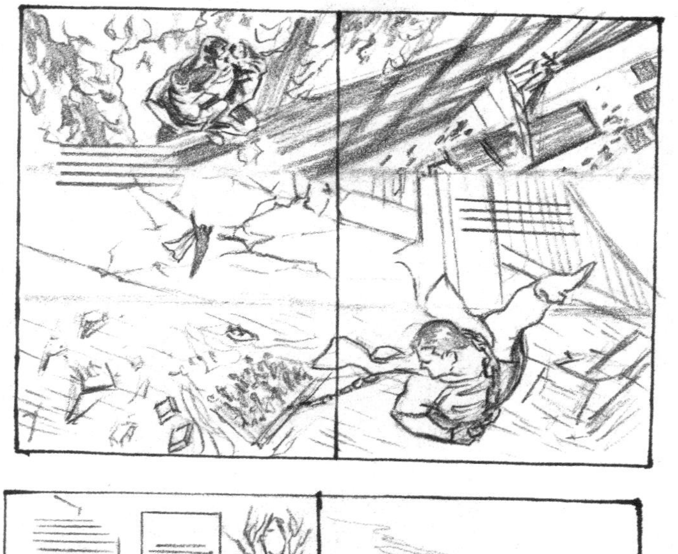

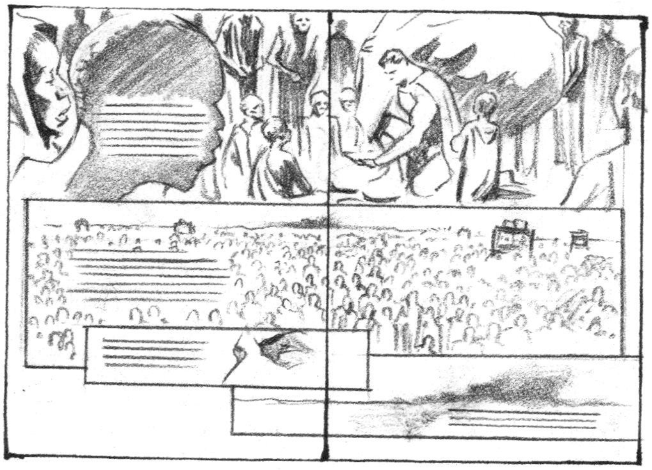

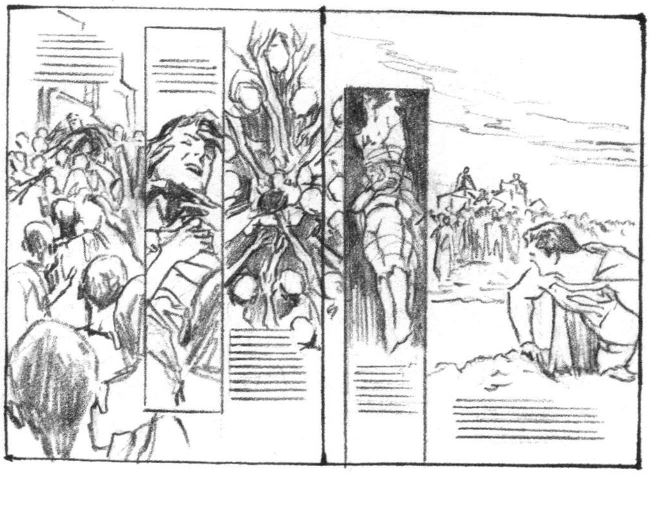

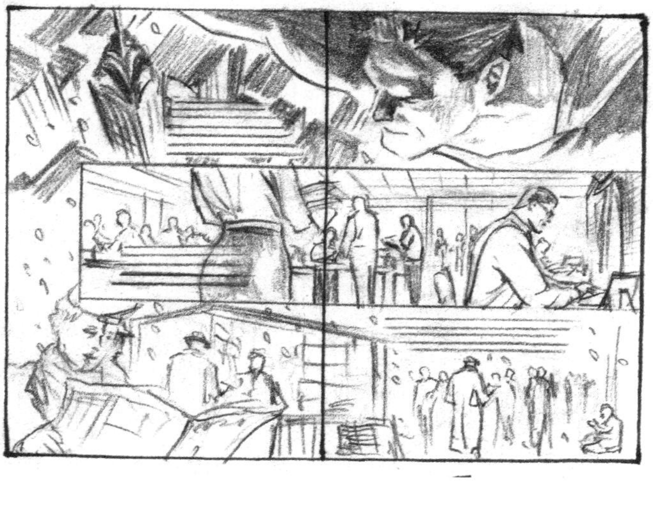

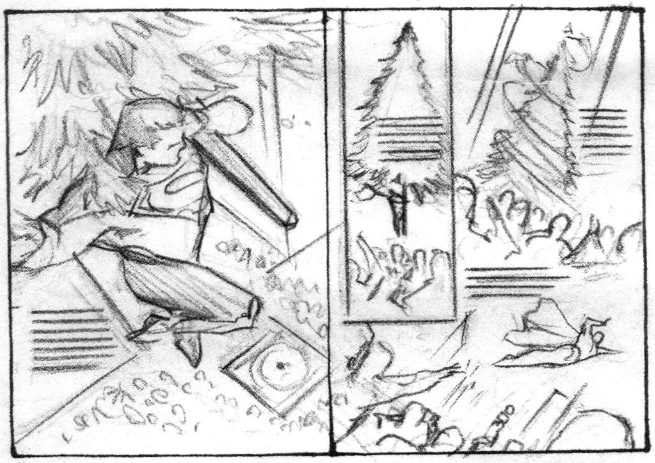

The art process follows in layers, beginning with tight thumbnail pencils for each double-page spread, which serve as a guide in photographing live models and researching other details.Here model Frank Kasy poses for Superman, matching the thumbnail's physical positioning as best as possible. Most often, two large photo lamps are used to light the model, following the shadows as described in Ross's early sketches.

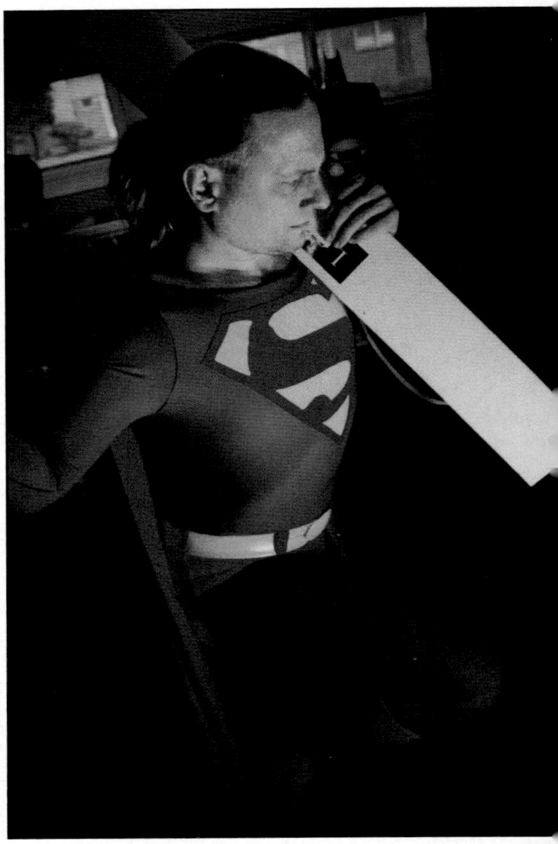

A new aim of Ross's at the time of the first oversized book was to create full costumes for his models to wear for each of the four main characters: Superman, Batman, Captain Marvel, and Wonder Woman. Ross commissioned costum maker Leman Yuen to sew a complete Superman outfit to fit Kasy. Ross picked out the colors of spandex with Yuen as well as drew the "S" shield at the size he desired.

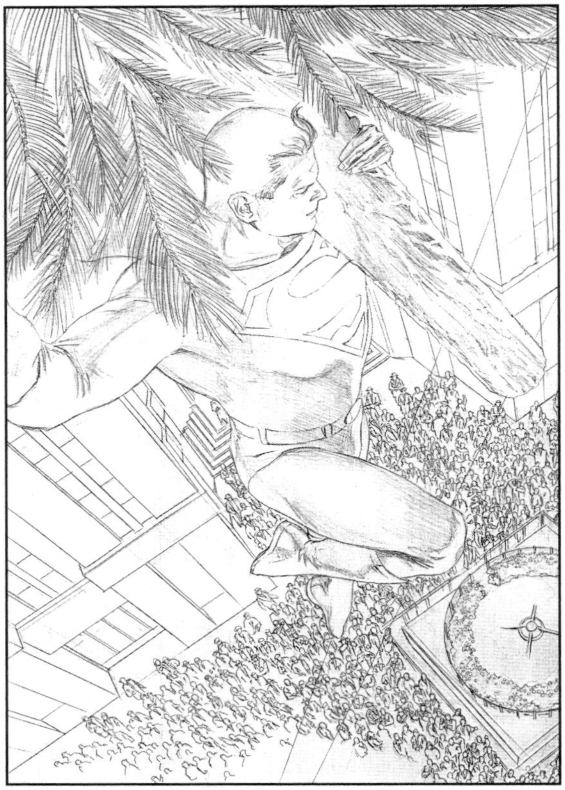

In the pencil drawing, the body's posture and proportion are transformed to match the needs of the character portrayed and the story's mood.

With gouache paint and a watercolor brush, all areas are painted by hand in black and white tonal value first. Near complete as a gray modeled image, the color stage is applied with the same paint, building up areas through transparent layers, alternately becoming opaque in certain areas based upon what looks best. Final color touches include airbrush colors sprayed in backgrounds as well as for various halo and monochromatic effects.

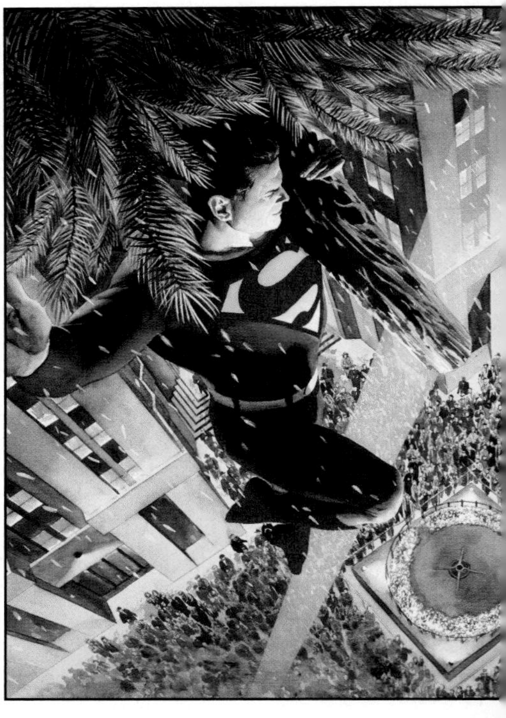

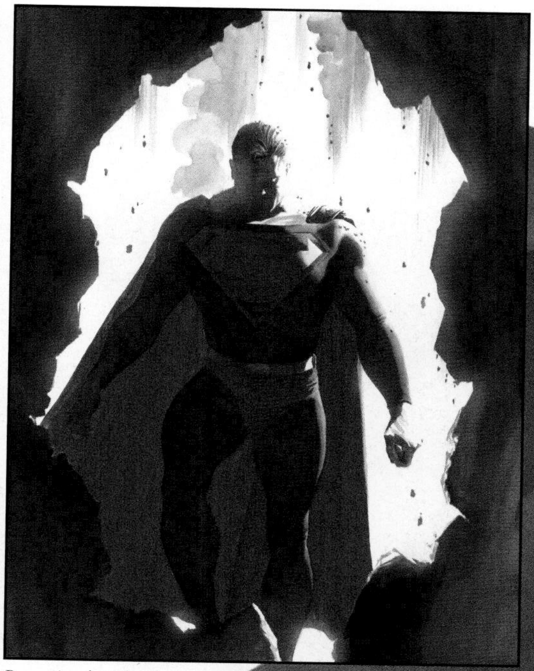

Promotional art for the cover of the San Diego Comic-Con convention program (1998).

A Superman doll provides the inspiration for this flying image.

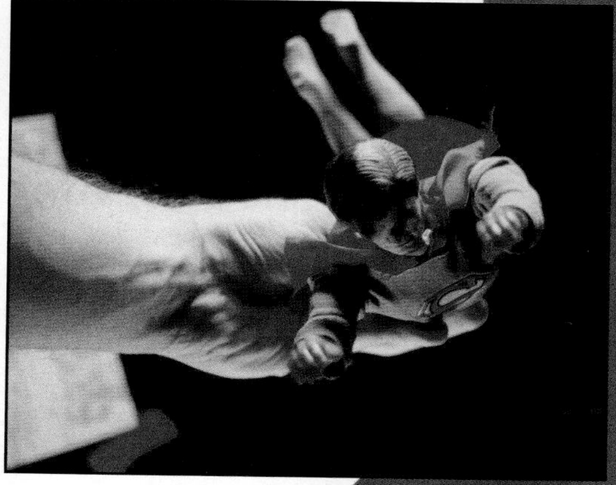

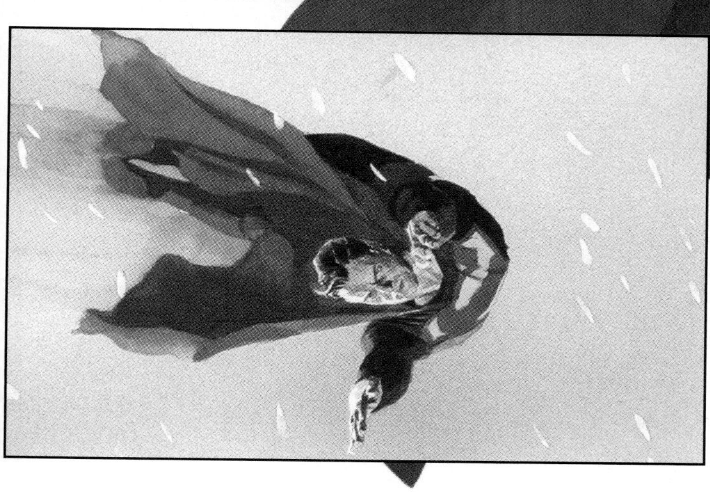

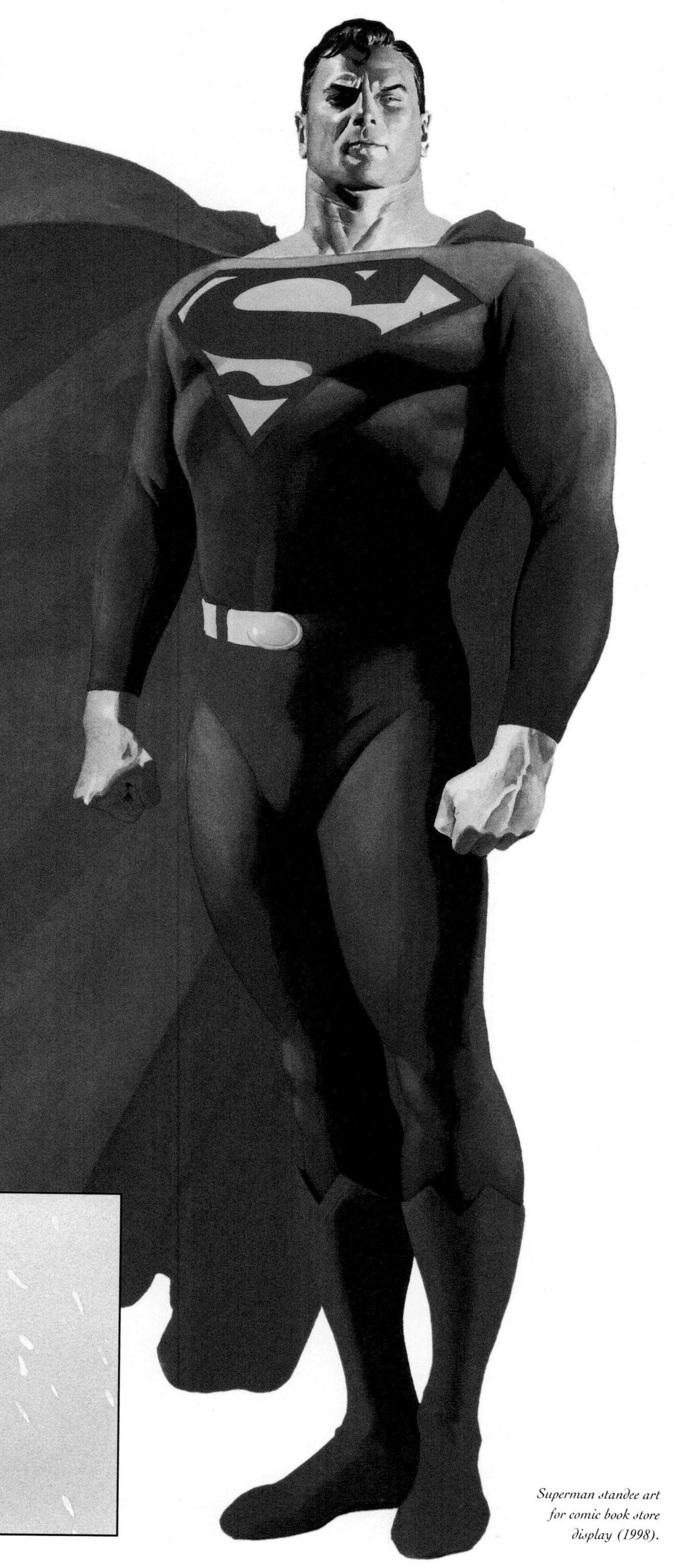

Superman standee art for comic book store display (1998).

WAR ON CRIME

Various sketches for the Batman riser card and the final Batman riser card image (1999).

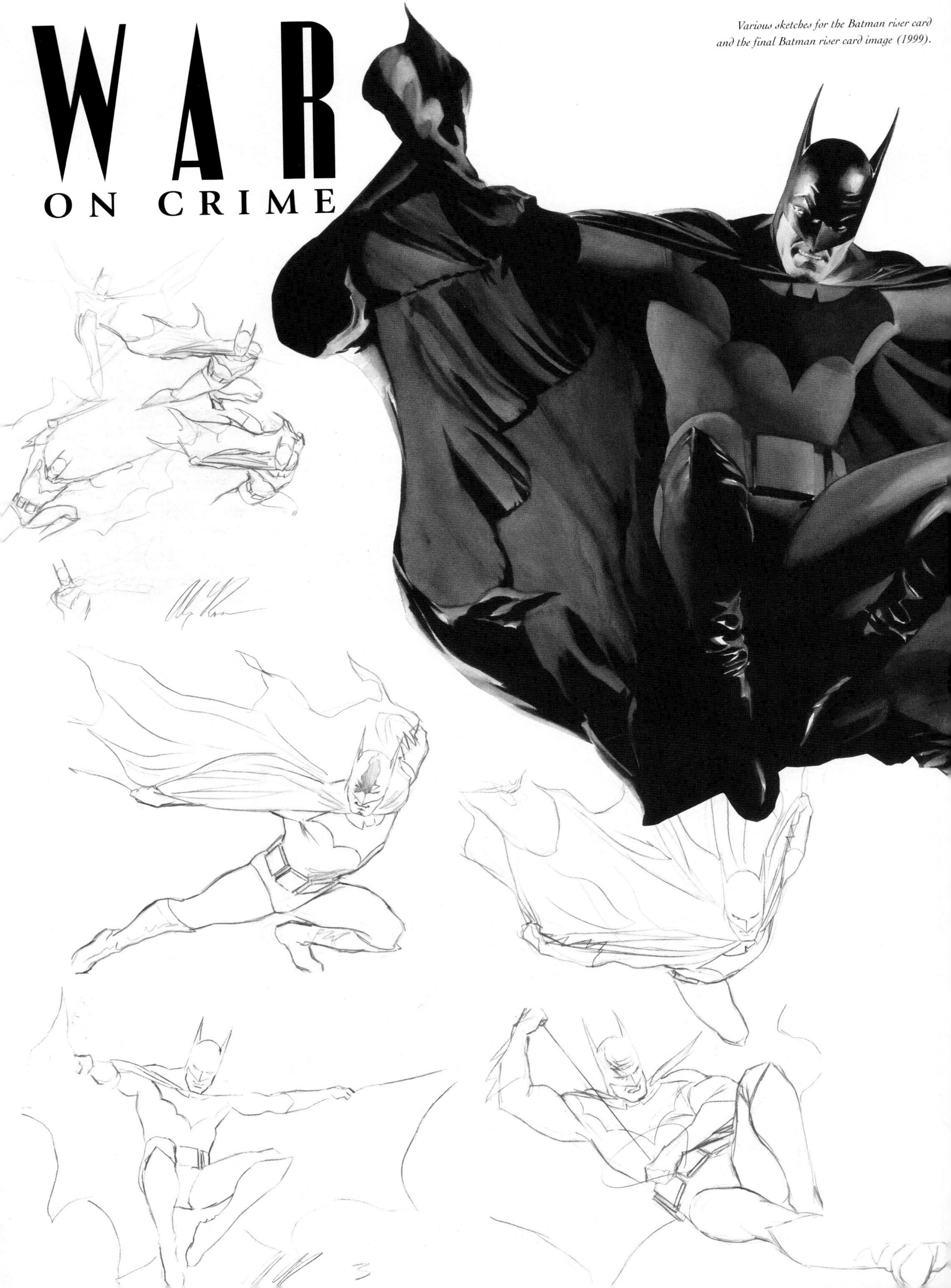

atman's focus has traditionally been the issue of crime that plagues our rger urban areas and the more colorful extremes of criminal behavior at comic books normally depict. The intent here was address the roots of crime as it pertains to environment and conomic disparity. Batman's goal in the story is one of nderstanding and to expose tragic circumstances that ne cannot easily make "war on."

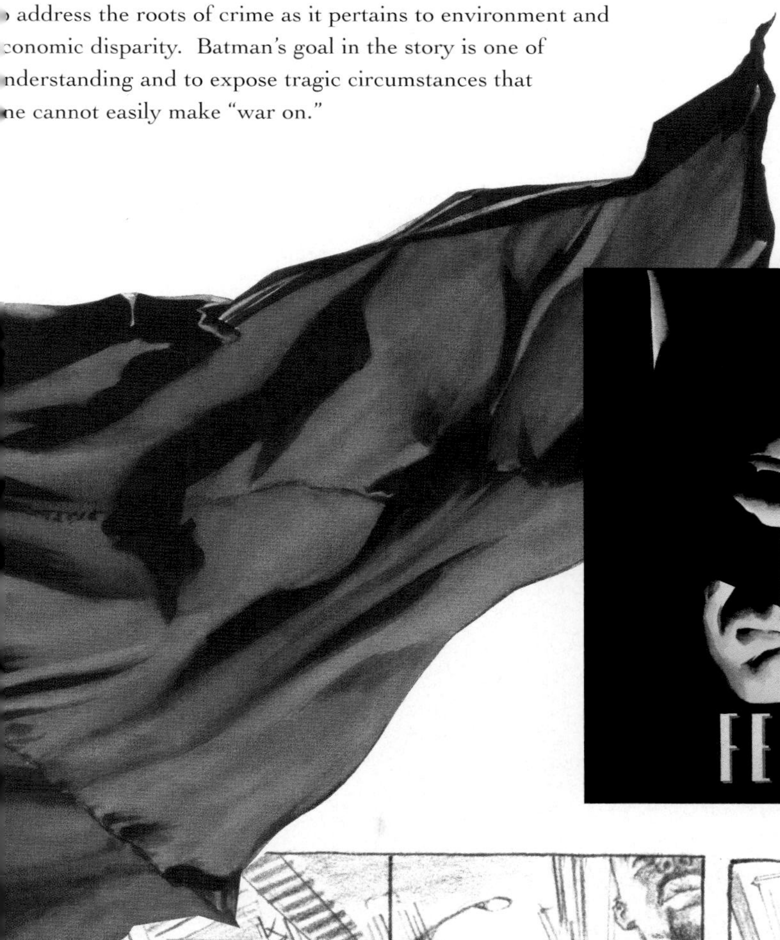

Cover layouts (1998).

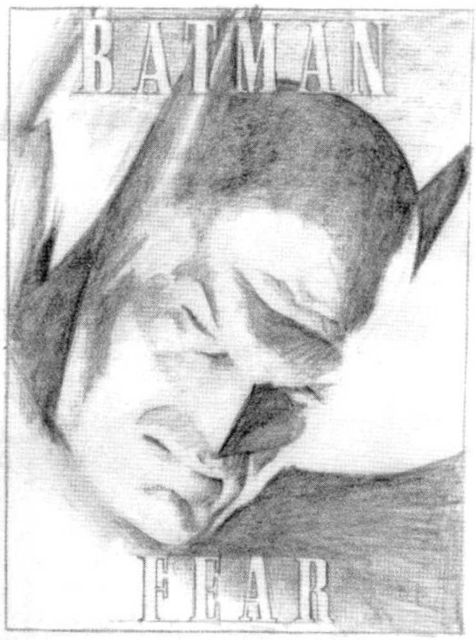
BATMAN
FEAR

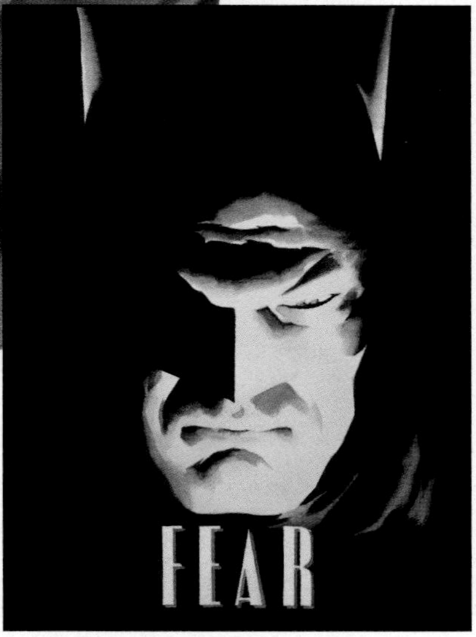
FEAR

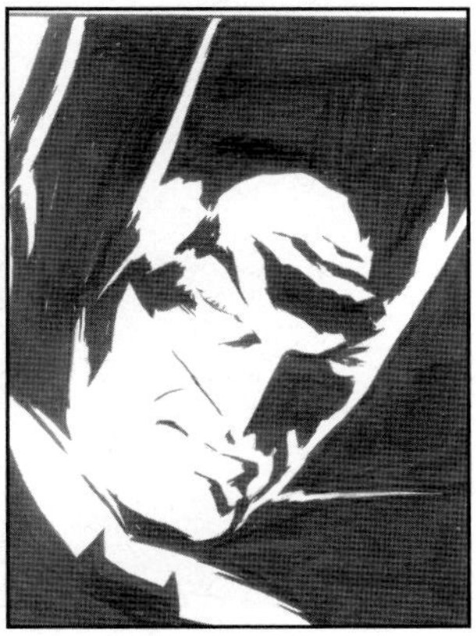

Tight thumbnail pencil layouts (seen here at actual size, 1999).

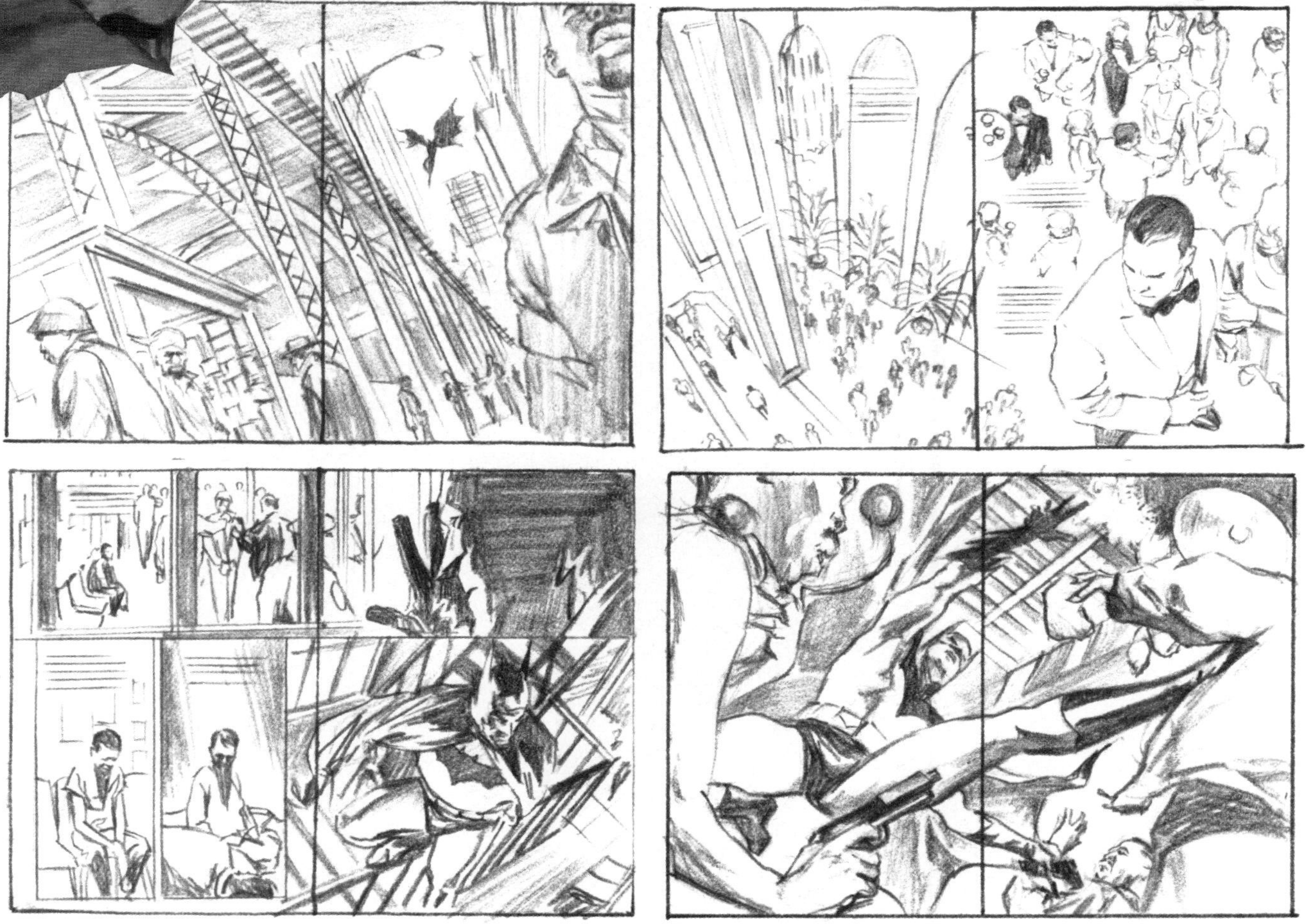

Promotional art for the cover of Wizard: The Comics Magazine #99 *(1999)*.

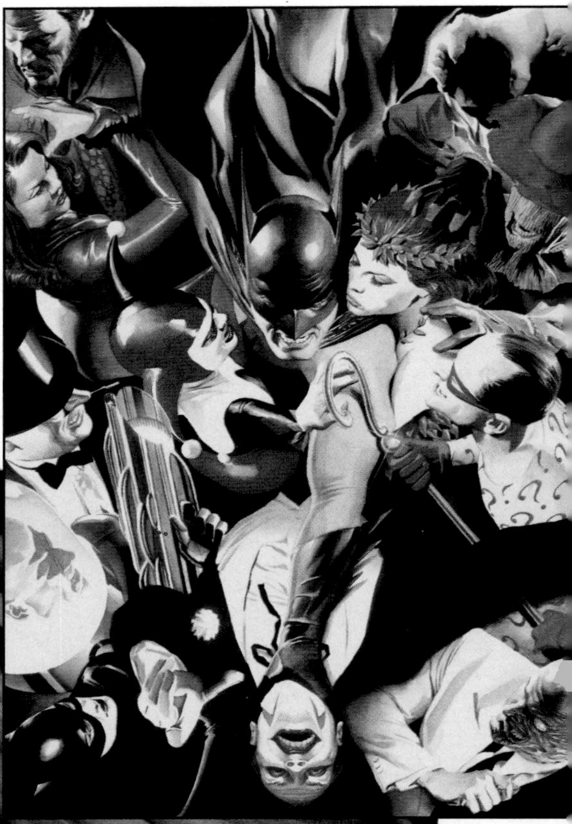

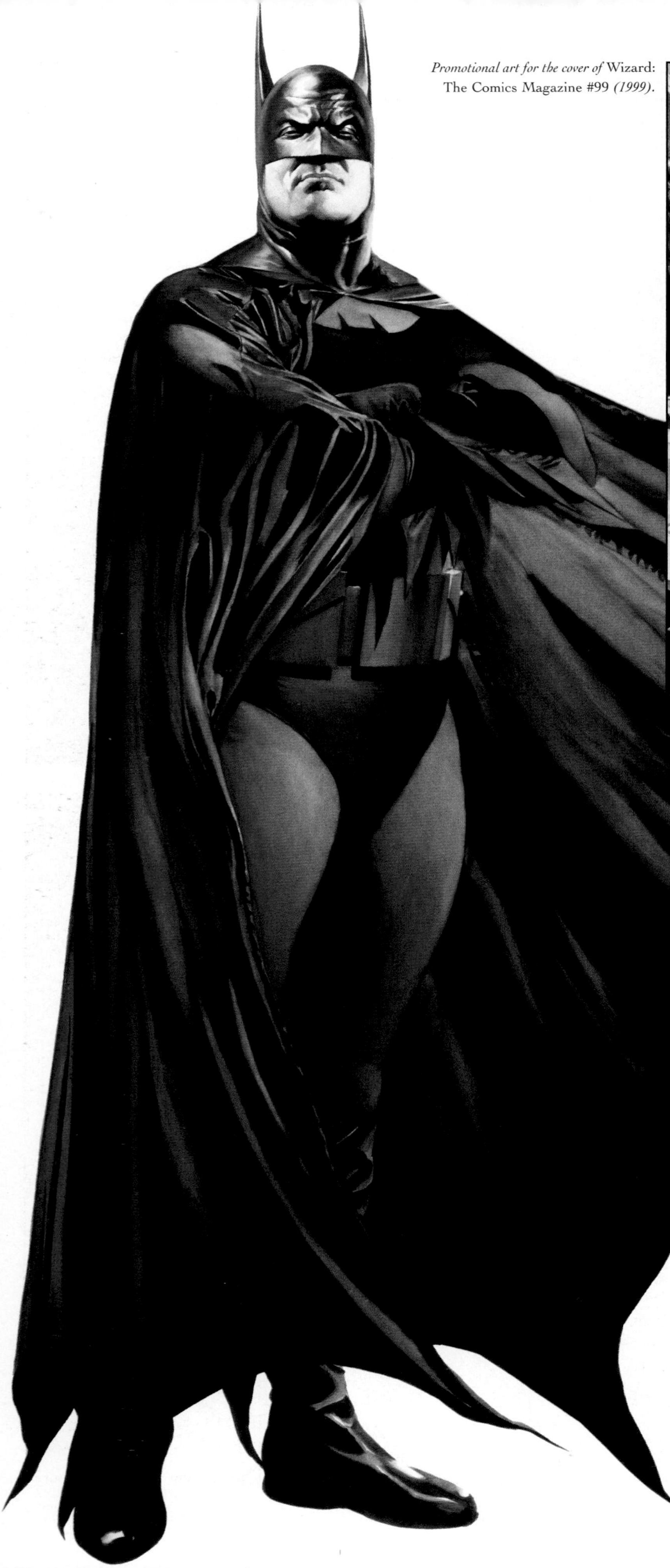

Batman retail poster (1999).

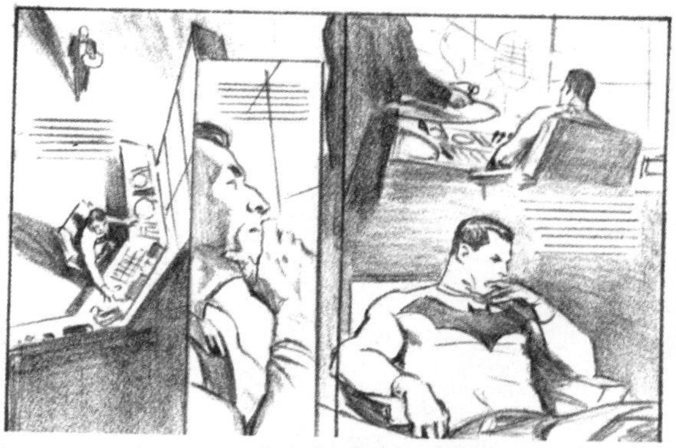

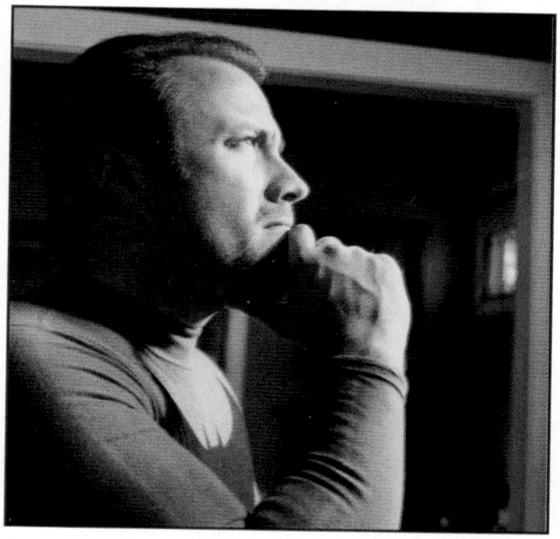

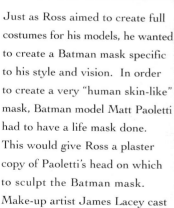

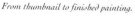

From thumbnail to finished painting.

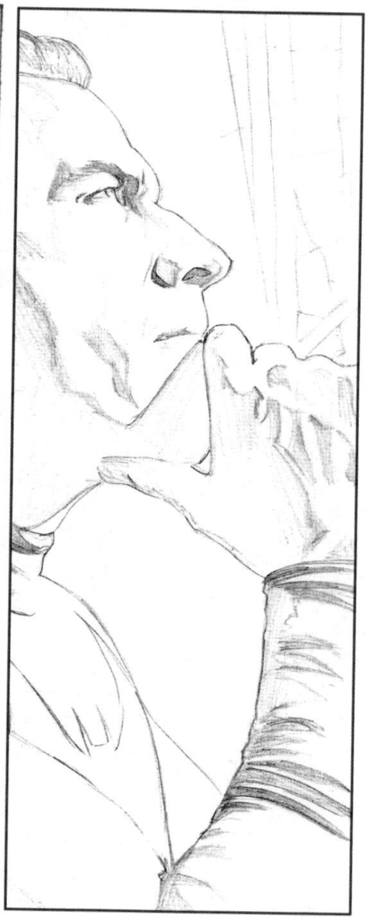

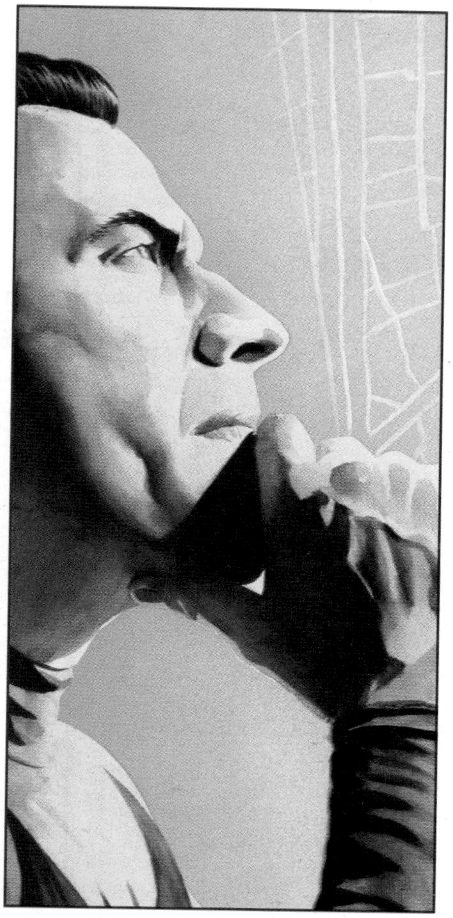

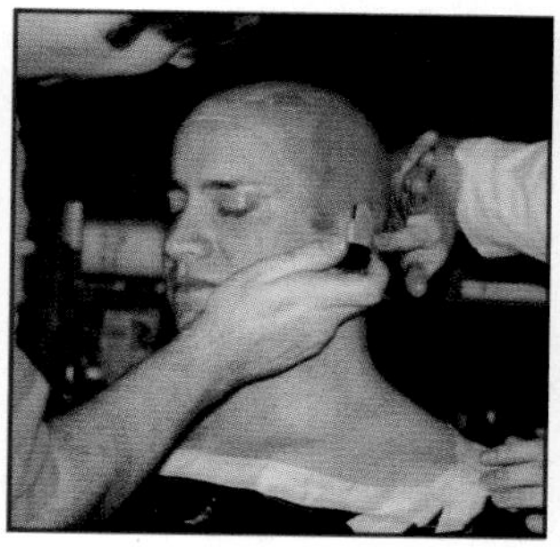

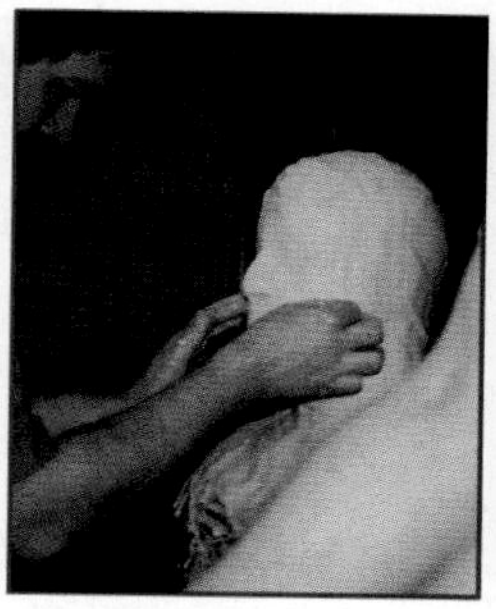

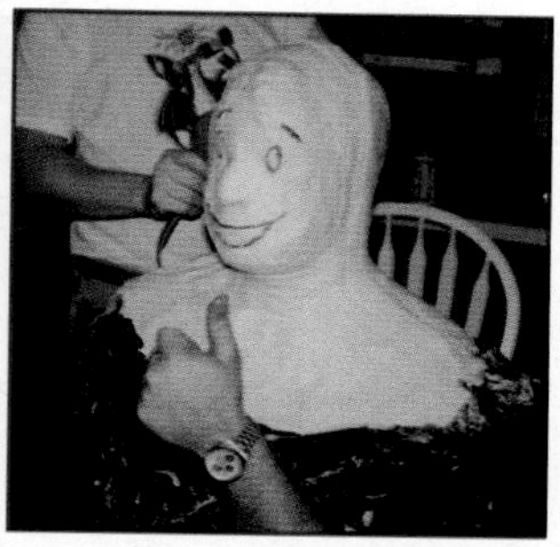

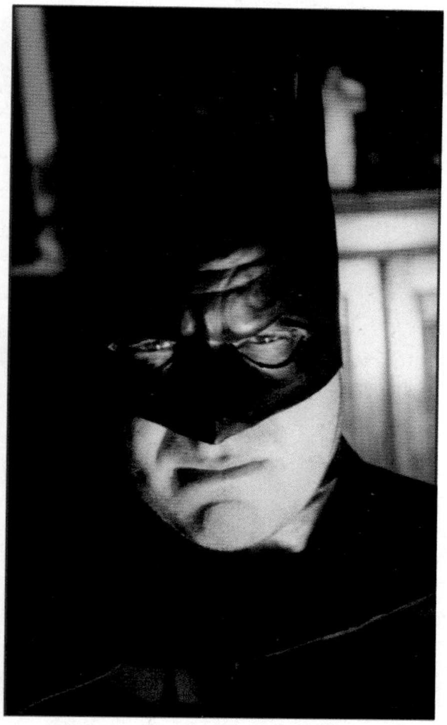

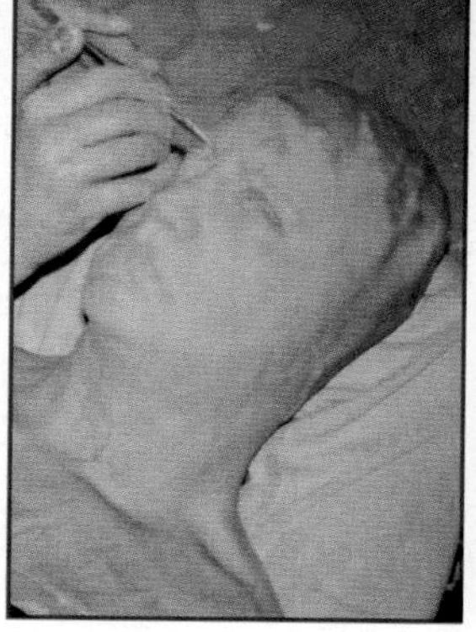

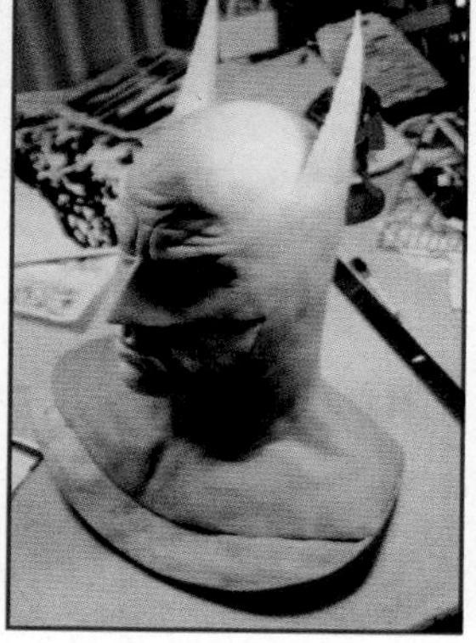

Just as Ross aimed to create full costumes for his models, he wanted to create a Batman mask specific to his style and vision. In order to create a very "human skin-like" mask, Batman model Matt Paoletti had to have a life mask done. This would give Ross a plaster copy of Paoletti's head on which to sculpt the Batman mask. Make-up artist James Lacey cast the life mask by creating an Imagel mold around Paoletti's head. Medical gauze was placed over the soft Imagel in order to hold the mold. After approximately four hours the mold was removed and later filled with plaster. After the plaster hardened, the mold was removed and the life mask was ready for sculpting. Ross sculpted clay on top of the cast to match his designs and to follow the model's face as closely as possible. Model-making company Acme Design, Inc. took the prototype sculpture to create yet another mold. They filled this new mold, of Paoletti's head and Ross's Batman cowl, with latex, resulting in the final latex rubber mask. Combined with other miscellaneous parts of Batman costumes donated by Kenn Kooi, Barry Crain, and Teresa Codie, the Batman outfit was the most complex undertaking Ross has made to realize a character.

POWER OF HOPE

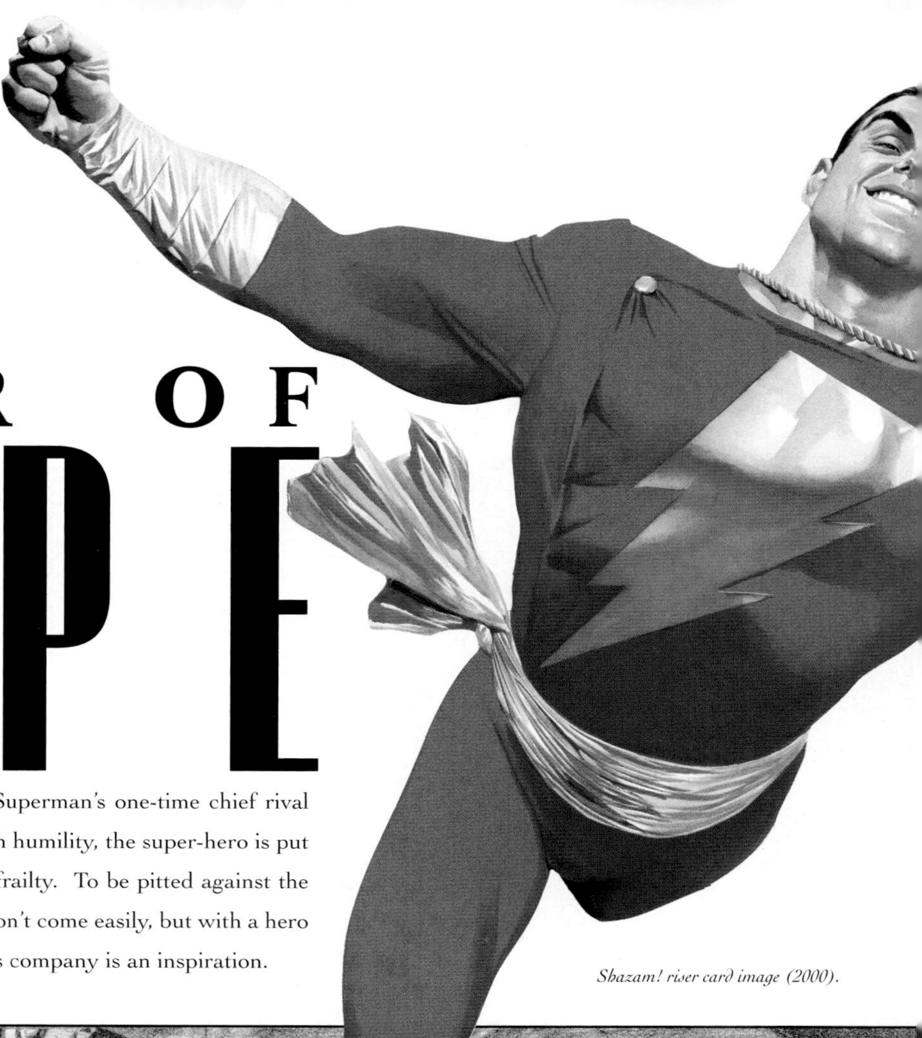

Given the joyful quality of Captain Marvel, Superman's one-time chief rival demanded a more lighthearted approach. With humility, the super-hero is put face-to-face with the human condition of our frailty. To be pitted against the plight of the sick and handicapped, solutions don't come easily, but with a hero of Captain Marvel's whimsy, the comfort of his company is an inspiration.

Shazam! riser card image (2000).

Tight thumbnail pencil origin spread (2000).

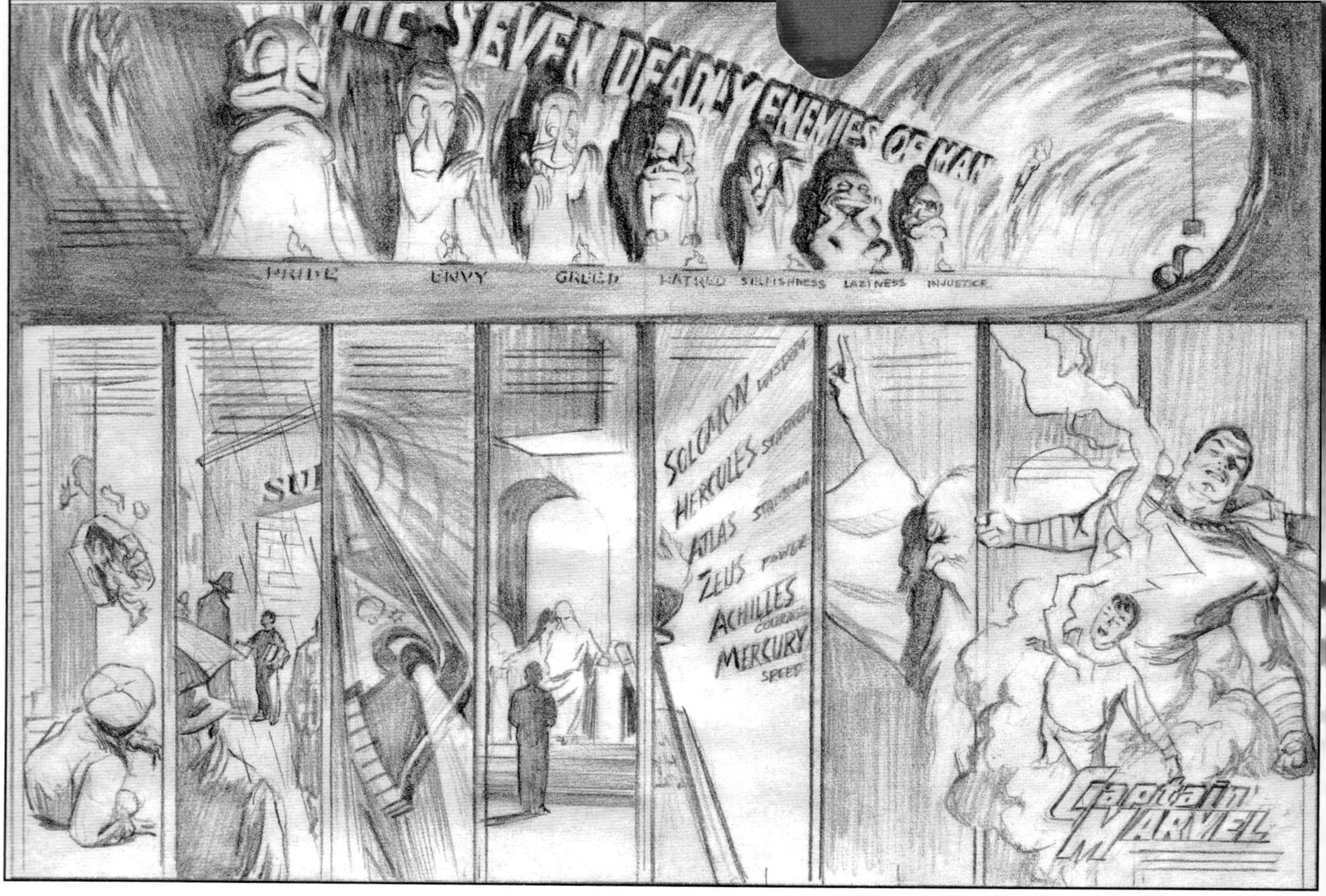
SEVEN DEADLY ENEMIES OF MAN
PRIDE
ENVY
GREED
HATRED
SELFISHNESS
LAZINESS
INJUSTICE
SOLOMON
HERCULES
ATLAS
ZEUS
ACHILLES
MERCURY
SPEED
Captain Marvel

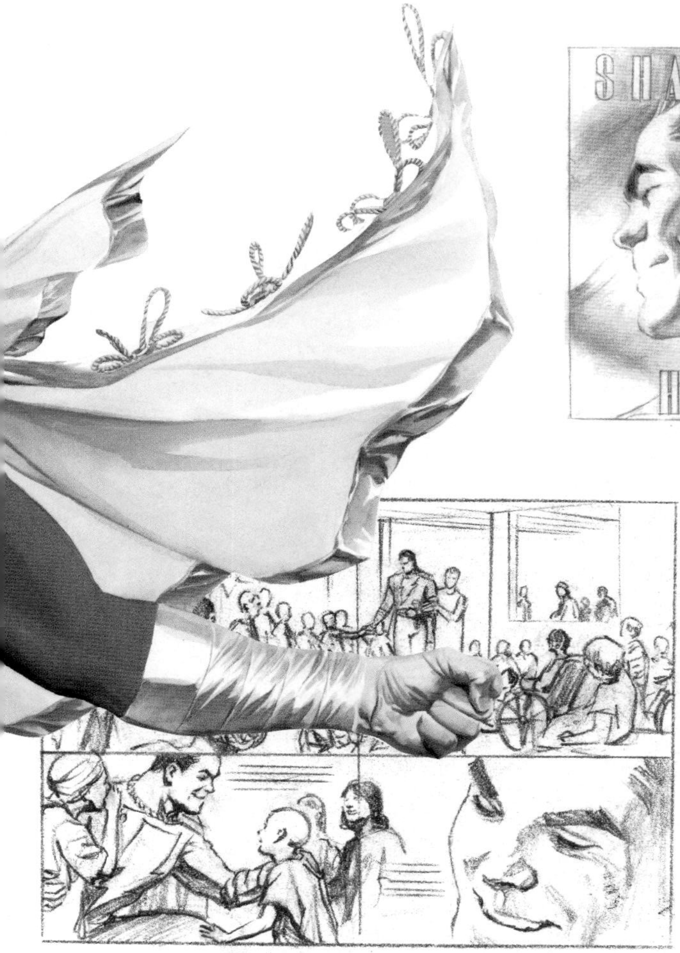

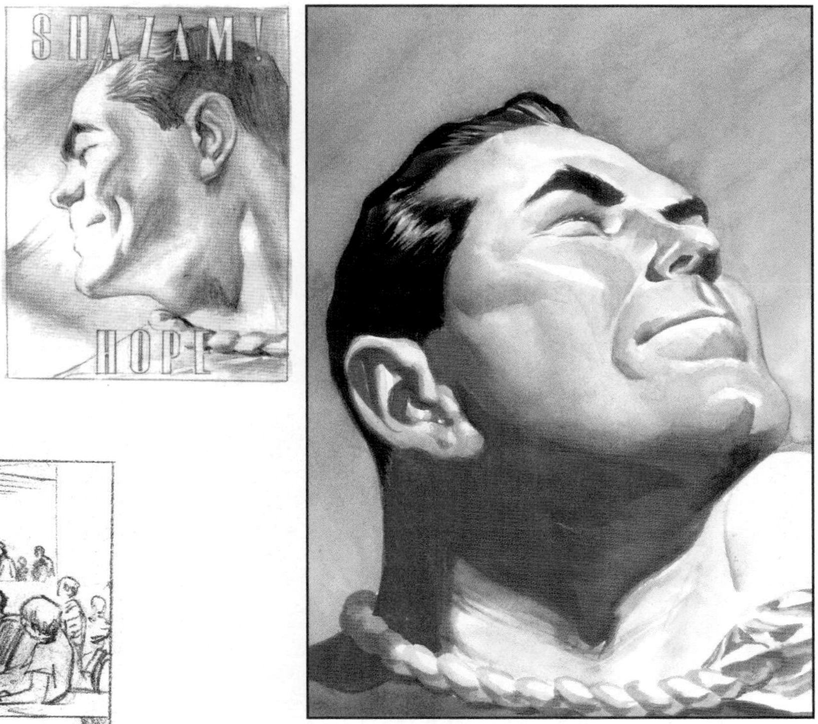
SHAZAM!
HOPE

Cover layouts (2000).

Tight thumbnail pencil layouts (seen here at actual size, 2000).

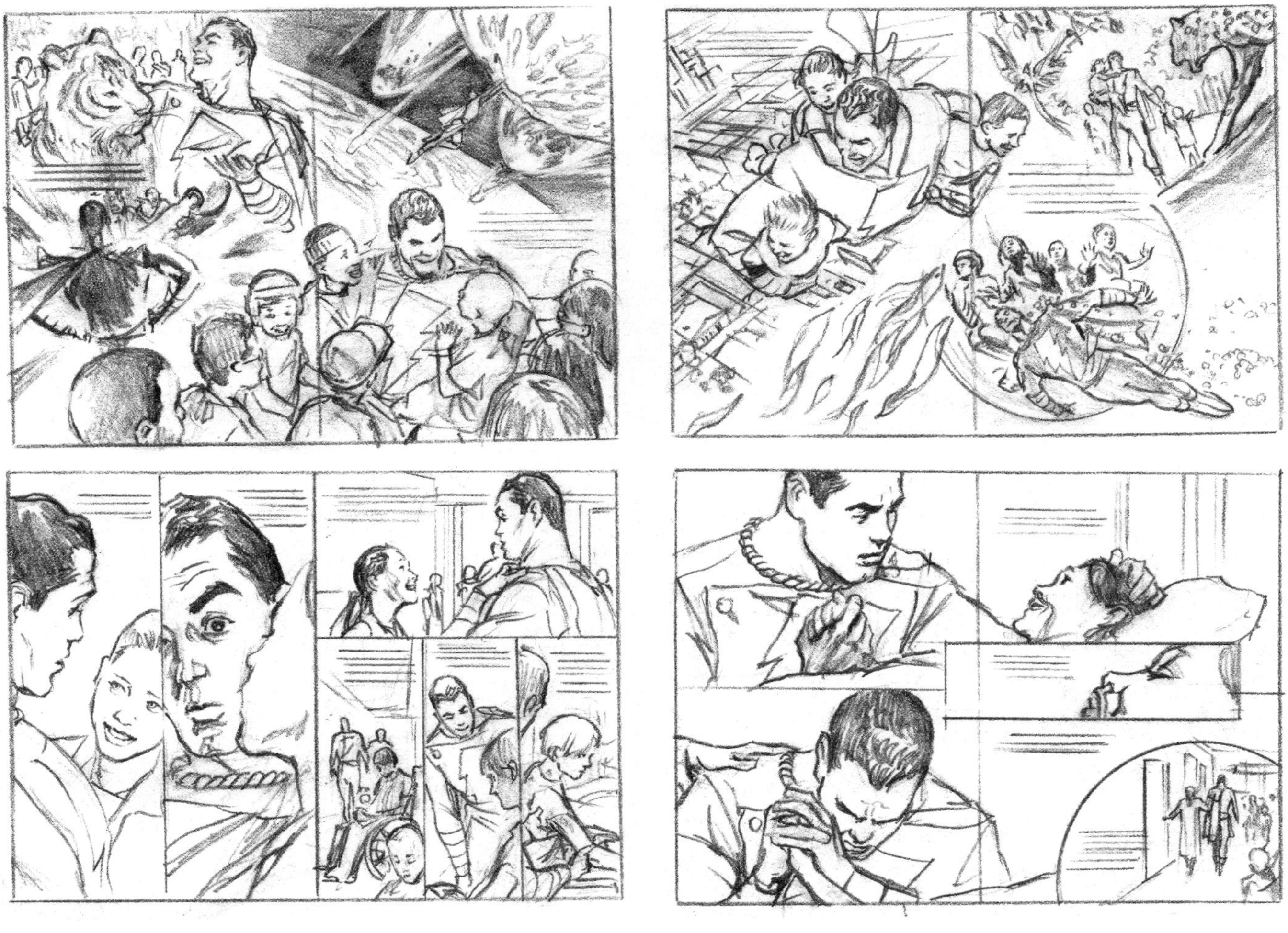

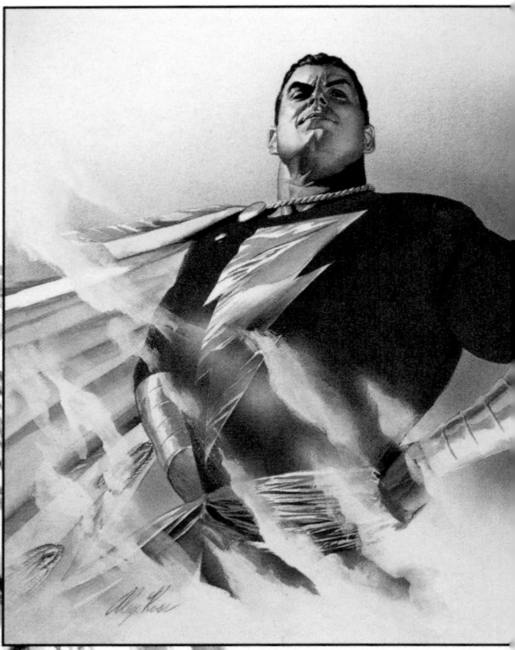

Promotional art for the cov
of Wizard: The Comi
Magazine #111 *(2000*

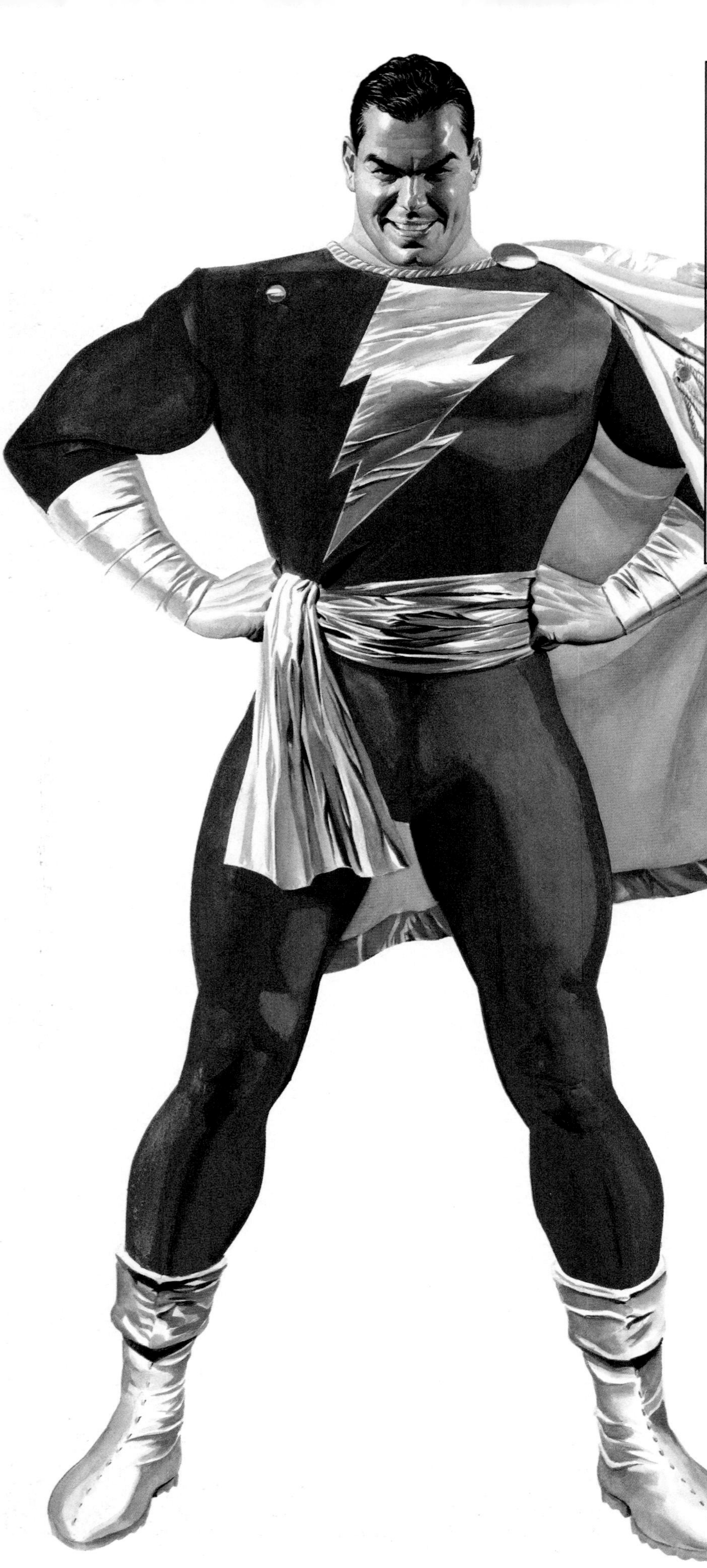

Shazam! retail poster (2000).

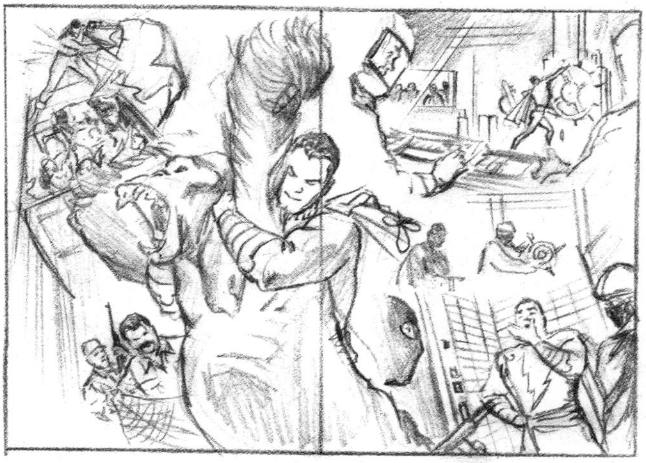

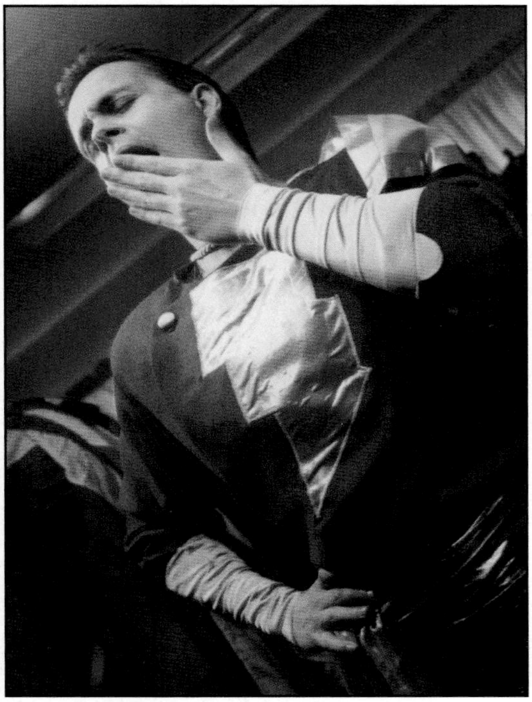

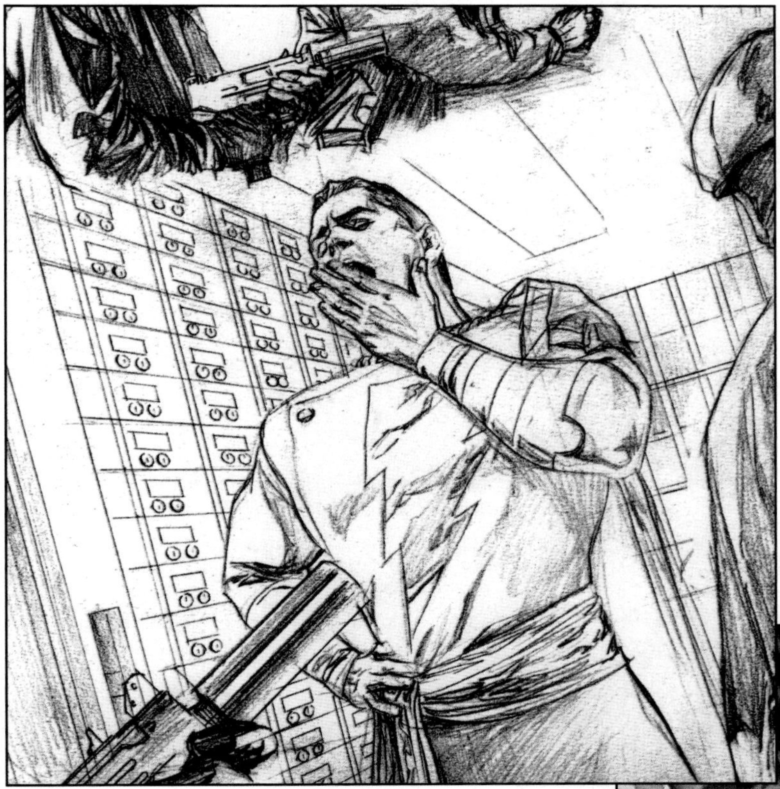

The use of live models for the series' heroes required Ross to make many alterations to his drawings. Most involved increasing the size and mass of the models' bodies to more idealized heroic proportions. Accentuating certain poses to more dramatic extremes was often required, and almost no single photograph would entirely match what was in the artist's mind's-eye. Always, though, the use of live models was vital in imagining legendary characters as real human beings. The models inspired as well as guided the art.

Ross commissioned costume-maker Teresa Codie to create a Captain Marvel costume for model Sal Abbinanti. This would be the first of many costumes Codie would go on to make for Ross. A series of life-sized posters was planned at the same time as the tabloid books, and Ross wanted to have full-body costumes upon which to base each poster illustration. These costumes were also intended for future use in other works involving the Justice League. Codie constructed outfits for Flash, Green Lantern, Green Arrow, Black Canary, Aquaman, Plastic Man, and many more.

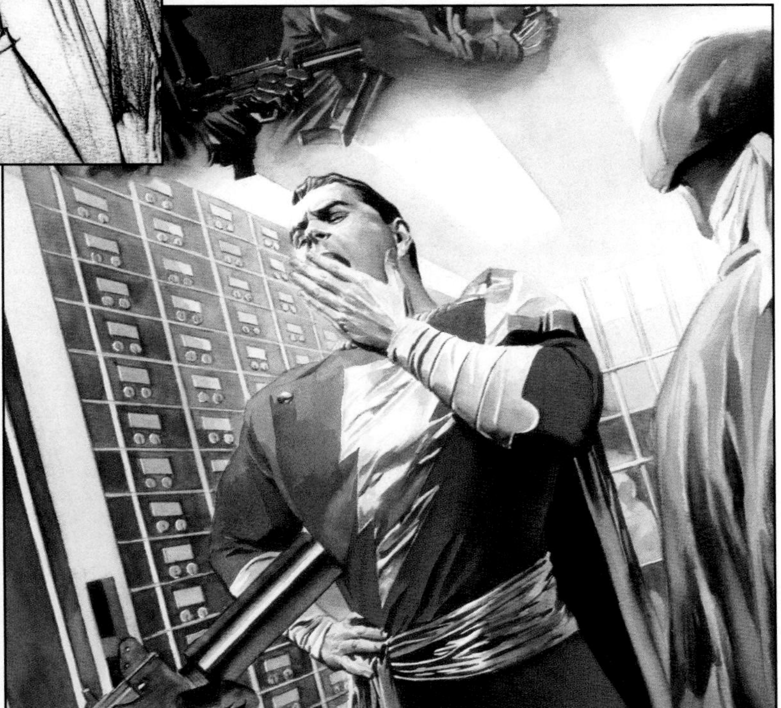

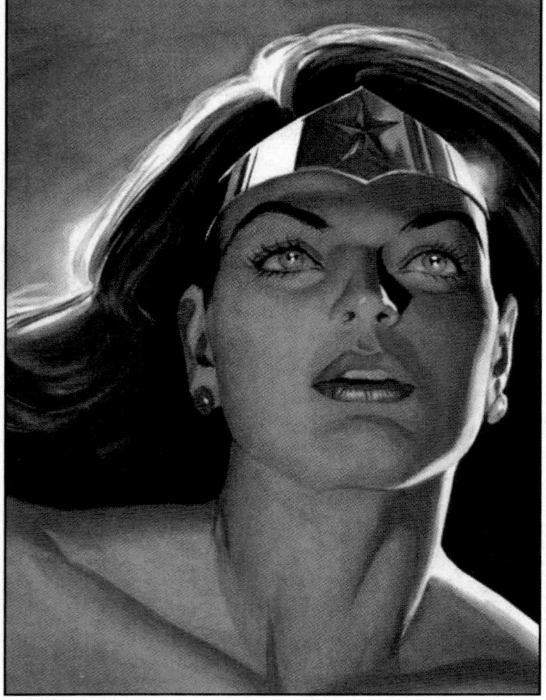

Painted cover layout (2001).

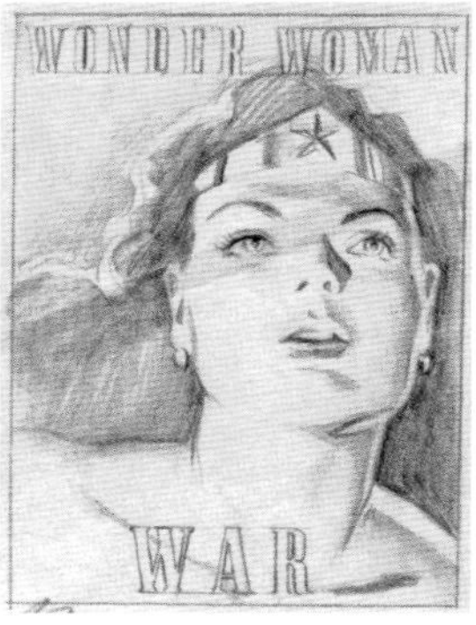
WONDER WOMAN
WAR

Wonder Woman
riser card image (2001).

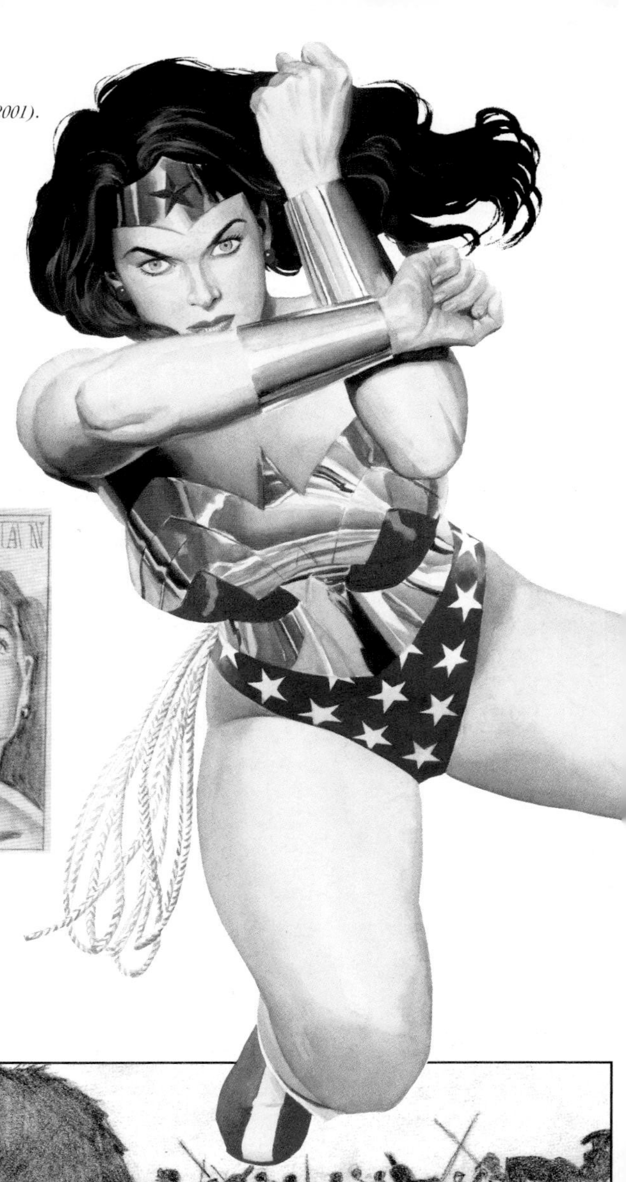

Tight thumbnail pencil origin spread (2001).

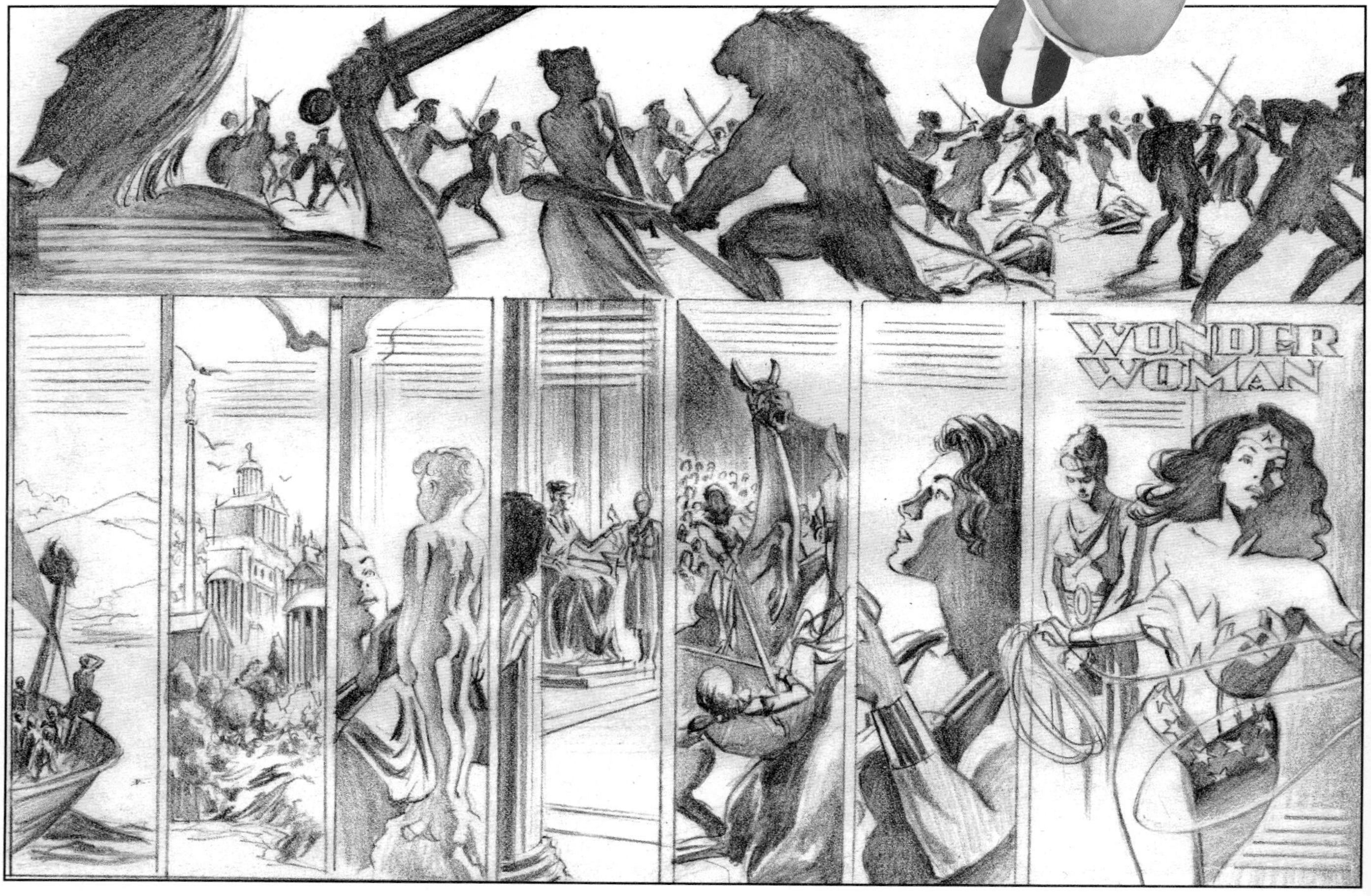
WONDER WOMAN

SPIRIT OF
TRUTH

The original issue planned for Wonder Woman's interest was man's predilection for war. This would evolve into a focus more on her role as an ambassador of sorts, dealing with cultural conflict, ideological separation, and prejudice. Her journey becomes one of personal revelation that not all symbols of liberation can be viewed as they are intended or that they can be appreciated the same way around the world.

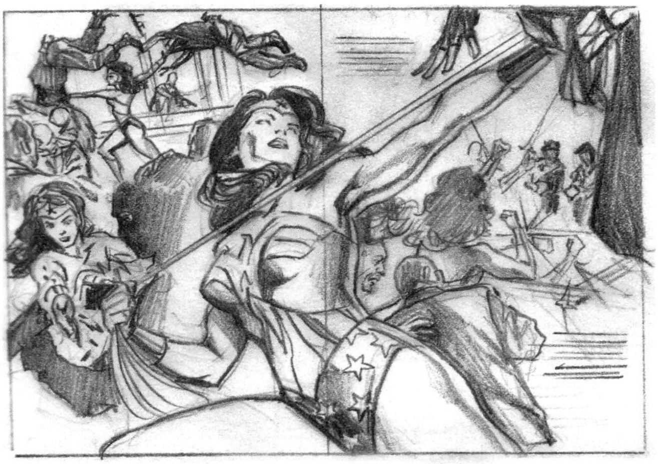

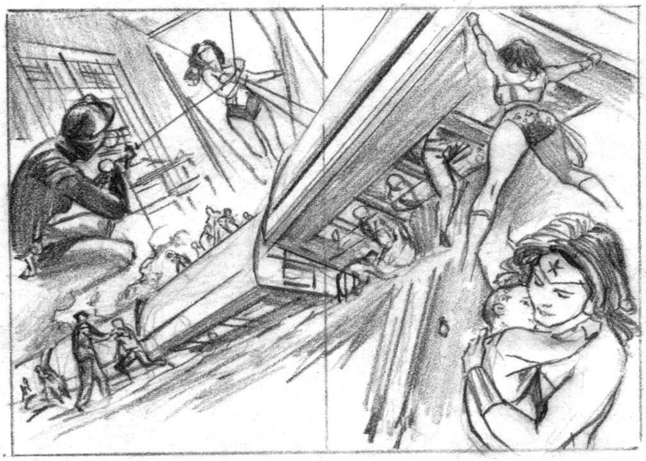

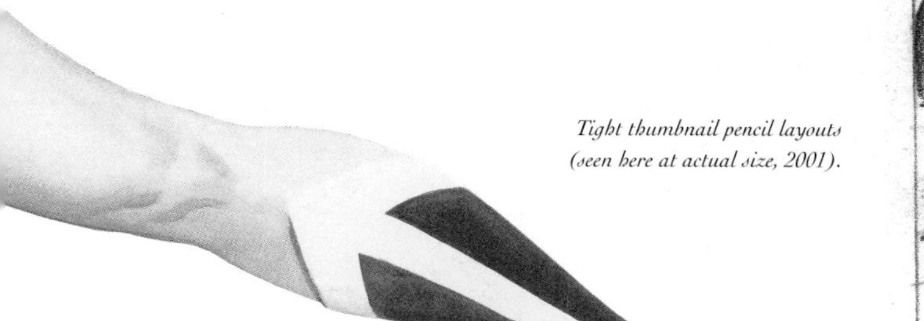

Tight thumbnail pencil layouts (seen here at actual size, 2001).

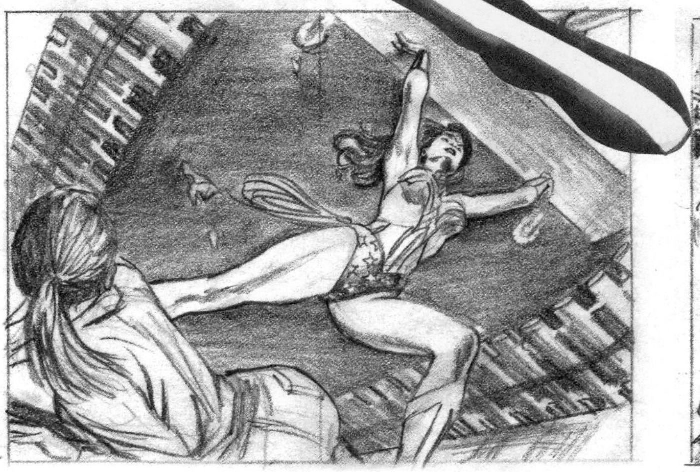

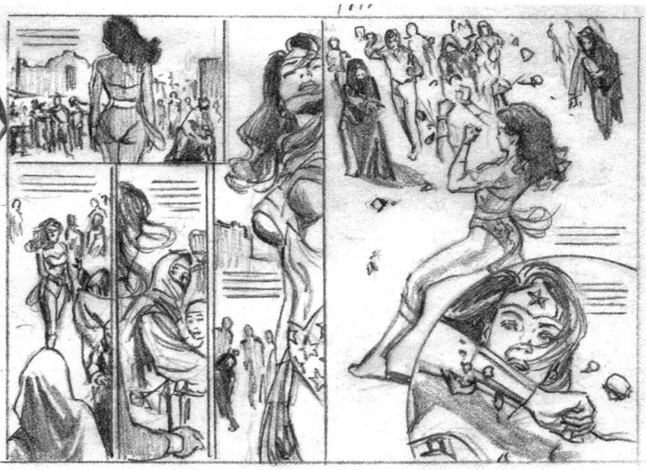

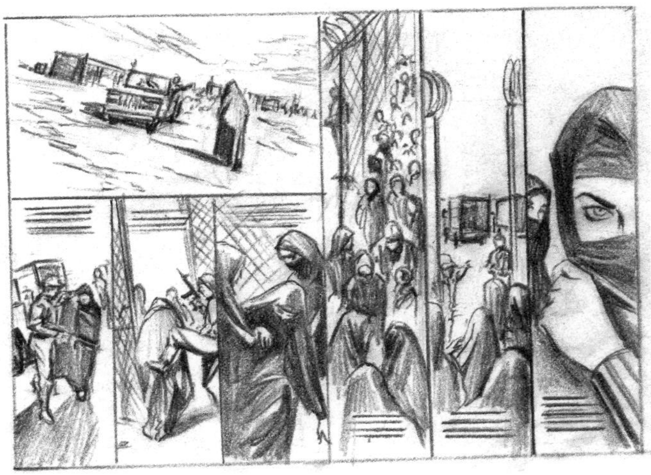

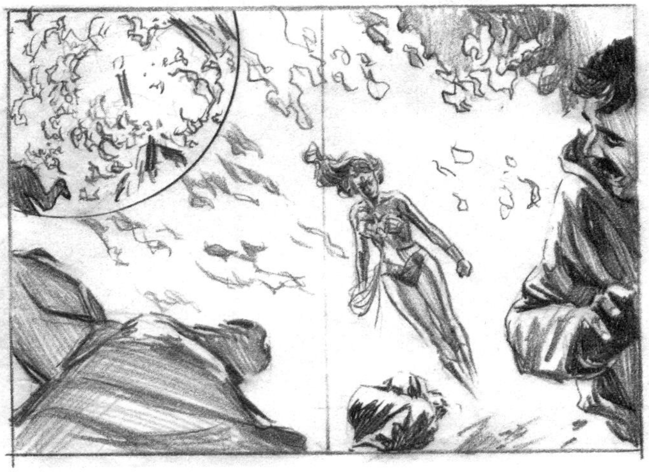

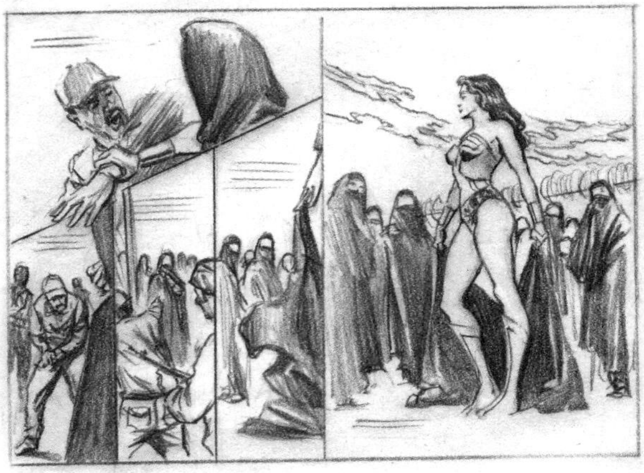

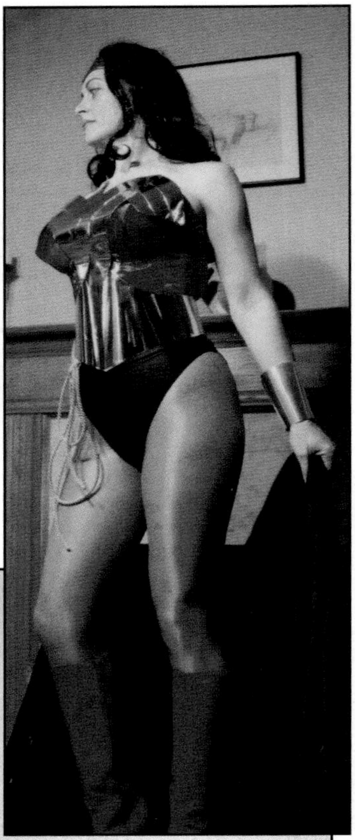

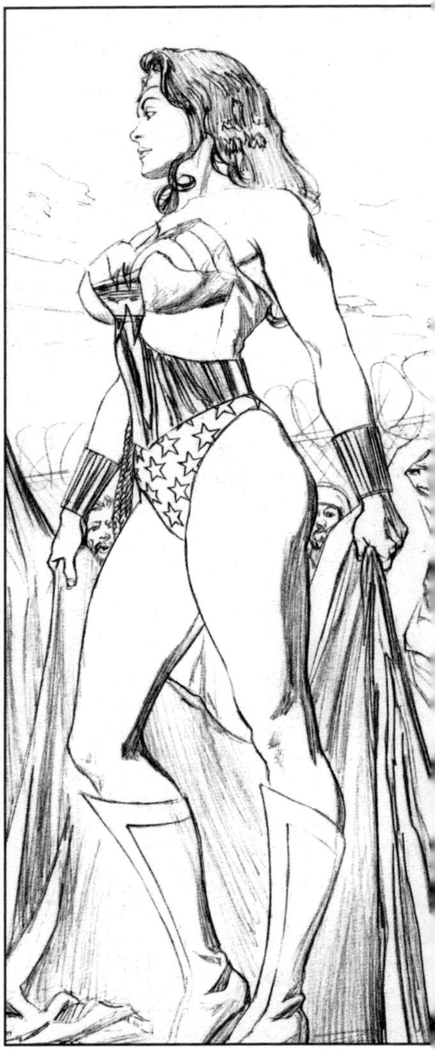

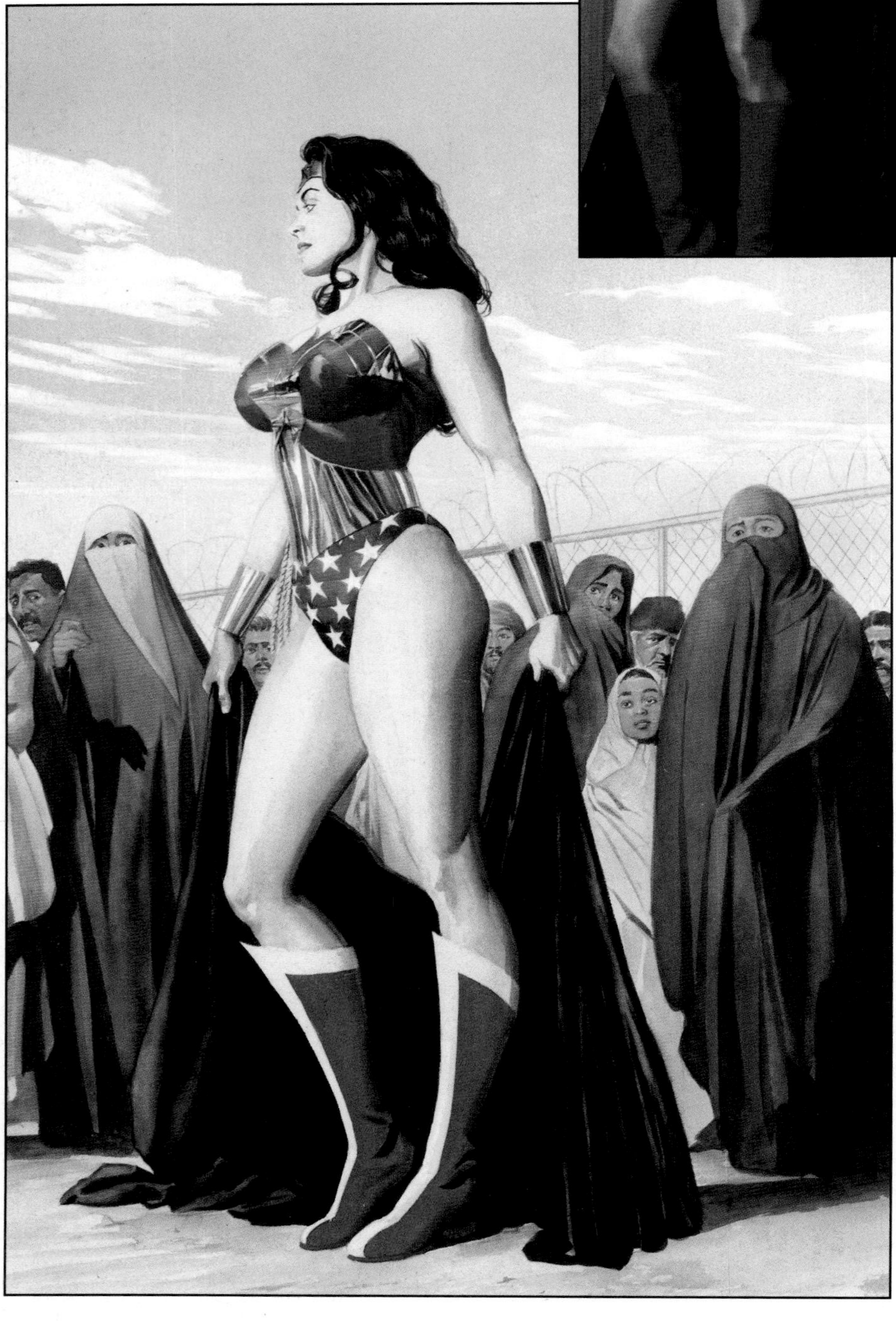

Although many new costumes for the series were created from scratch, Wonder Woman model Rhonda Hampton contributed her own costume, made previously for a Halloween party. Ross crafted an aluminum breastplate, belt, tiara, and bracelets to complete the outfit, covering the parts meant to be gold with a mirror-like contact paper. This would give the effect in photo reference of the kind of metallic reflections Ross wanted to depict. Ironically, like Superman model Frank Kasy, Hampton is a natural blonde who, in the case of Wonder Woman photo shoots, wore a dark brunette wig to capture the character's hair color and style.

At left: Three examples of the extensive model work and costuming for the individual League members juxtaposed with the final artwork. Models: Chris Fleming as Aquaman, Cory Smith as the Flash, and Tony Vitale as Green Lantern.

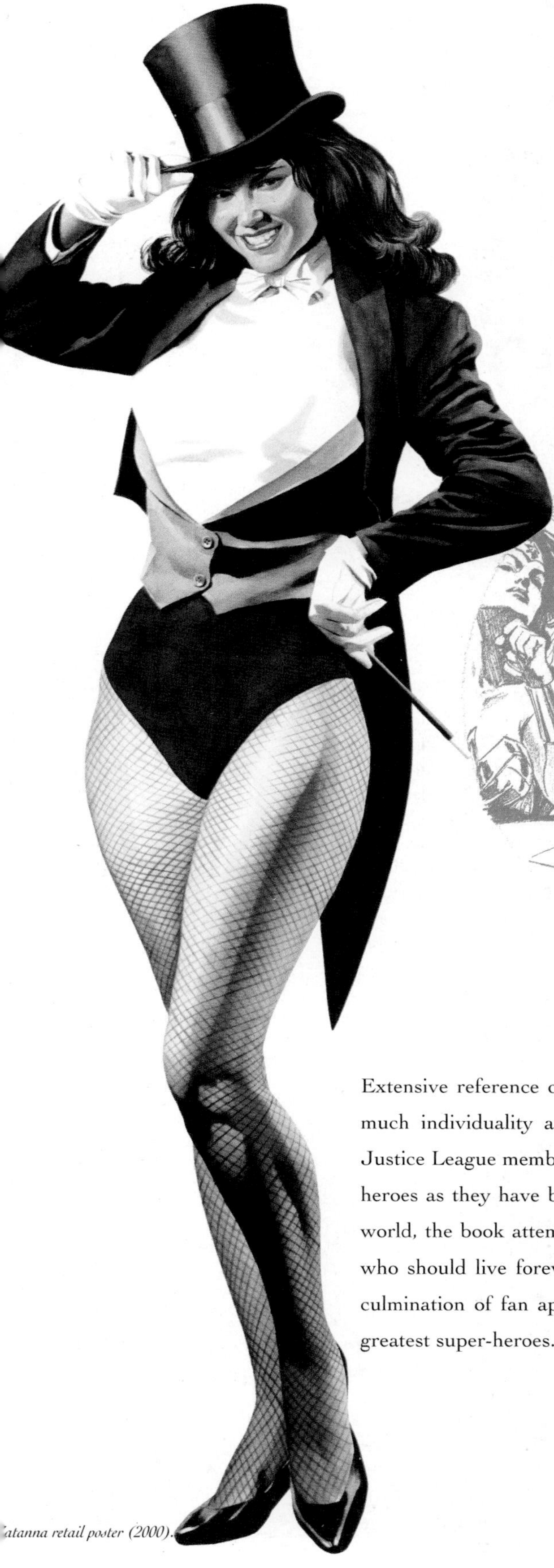

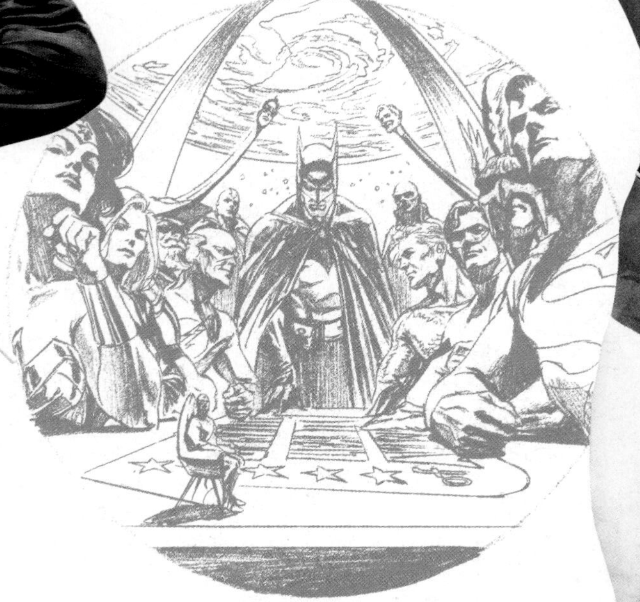

Tight pencil drawing of the JLA: LIBERTY AND JUSTICE plate (2002).

Extensive reference of numerous models was employed to add as much individuality as possible in the depiction of the various Justice League members. Done with an eye for the style of DC's heroes as they have been known for generations throughout the world, the book attempts to present a timeless version of legends who should live forever. LIBERTY AND JUSTICE stands as a culmination of fan appreciation felt by the authors for the world's greatest super-heroes.

atanna retail poster (2000).

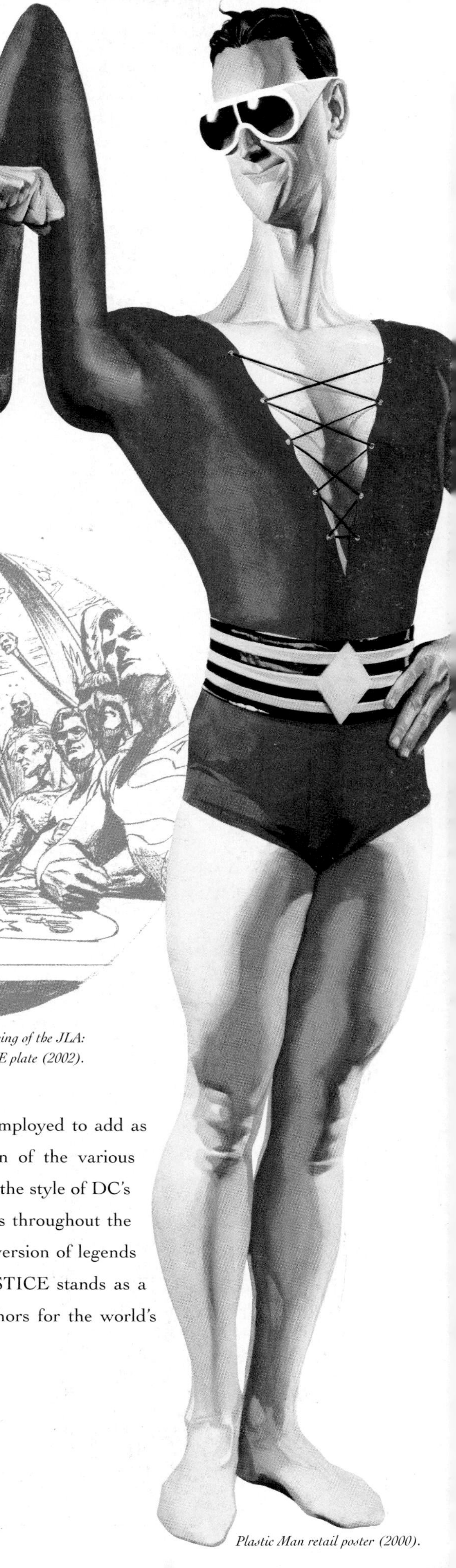

Plastic Man retail poster (2000).

For Alex, who gave me the call to adventure.
For Charlie, who kept me on the trail.
For Joey, who caught me when I eluded Charlie.
For Jenette, Paul, Rob, Dan, and the heroic DC support system.
For Chip and Alan, who each had a thousand good ideas and just as many kind words.
For Siegel, Shuster, Kane, Finger, Beck, Marston, Fox, Cole, Nodell, Infantino,
Schwartz and every talented soul who came before or since.
For my Dad, who taught me the wonder of Captain Marvel.
For T.J., who worked a million miracles.
For the fans, who enjoyed the stories.
And for Misty, who was there at the journey's end.

My deepest thanks and appreciation.

PAUL DINI
2005

ACKNOWLEDGMENTS

This product of six years' worth of work was built upon the strength of my friends who gave so much of themselves. Making my pantheon of super-heroes come to life with selfless dedication were: Frank Kasy as Superman, Matt Paoletti as Batman, Sal Abbinanti as Captain Marvel, Rhonda Hampton as Wonder Woman, Cory Smith as the Flash, Tony Vitale as Green Lantern, and Chris Fleming as Aquaman. Thank you all for your time.

For all the supporting roles and background faces, I had the pleasure of working with: Joey Abbinanti, Patrick Ahearn, Crystal Akins, Tony Akins, Keith Anderson, Lynn Armstrong, Arthur Banks, James Barnes, Tobey and Kris Bartel, Scott and Warren Beaderstadt, Kyle Bice, Ron Bogacki, Clint Borucki, Elizabeth, Laura, and Mark Braun, Lou Ann Burkhardt, Michael Burton, Gloria Chavez, Karen and John Cielo, Wil Clinger, Teresa Codie, Fraser Coffeen, Jerome Coloma, Malcolm Conyers, Coop, Michael Cortez, Steve Darnall, Eric DeCourcey, Dan DiDio, Tyler and Cydney Duff, Samantha Falbe, Chris Faulkner, Mark Ferreira, Rose Marie Garcia, Lorne L.Gary, Efstratios Gavas, Tom Gianni, Eddie Gorodetsky, Tony Goskie, Meg Guttman, Orlando Heard, Tom Hicke, Mike Hill, Jayson Huddleston, Brian Jacob, Jonathan Kasy, Rachel Kave, Charlie Kochman, Young, Sung, Doug, Kikumi, and Tabitha Koo, Rich Koz, Rich and Kathleen Kryczka, Jeff LaGreca, Edmond Lee, Tony Lenzo, Scott Vladimir Licina, Rick McCoy, Jr., Robert Miller, Jason Millet, T.J. Moore, Jose Munoz, Michael Naples, Zac Osgood, Joel Pace, Dave Pedroza, Kevin Reisberg, Dave Riske, Soul Rivera, James Robinson, Jason Rogers, Mary Jo Rogers, Jan C.Shimek III, Lisa Simone, Rob Simpson, Logan and Mason Smith, Ted Smuskiewicz, Valerie Studnick, Michelle Stutts, Marcia and Tony Thomas, Eric Thornton, Seth Tucker, Santonio Ussery, Karrie Varner, Ruth Waytz, Paul Zapata, and Debbie Zoumis. And my family, T.J., Indiana, Clark, and Lynette Ross, Michael and Geneva Ross Neberman, Tasha and Normandie Ross Rocans, and Nina and the late Steven Katz.

For costumes and props, I have to thank Teresa Codie, Leman Yuen, Barry Crain, and James Lacey, and Clint Borucki, Kenn Kooi, and Brian Busch of Acme Design, Inc. For additional reference material and insight, I am indebted to Tony Akins, Dave Riske, Holly Blessen, Ruth Waytz, Coop, Walt Grogan, David Olsen, and Richard Dillin, Jr.

Thanks to Rich Kryzcka and Lou Ann Burkhardt for access to my school, the American Academy of Art in Chicago, and to its students and teachers who helped with my many photo sessions.

Thanks to Steve Duff, Darlene Hanna, and Laura Miller of the Rehabilitation Institute of Chicago for providing exposure to a hospital environment and state-of-the-art treatments.

Thanks to Zac Osgood for opening a door at Children's Memorial Hospital, where I was given an exceptional tour by Beth Carona, Kathryn Carrico, Luis Duarte, and Mark Byrd.

For the childhood inspiration of the artistry of Dick Dillin, Neal Adams, Joe Shuster, and all of those who guided me throughout, I thank you.

And for T.J., who is the gift that Superman brought me.

ALEX ROSS
2005

To my parents and older brother,
and also my grandpa, whom I shall miss forever
Y. L.-Q.

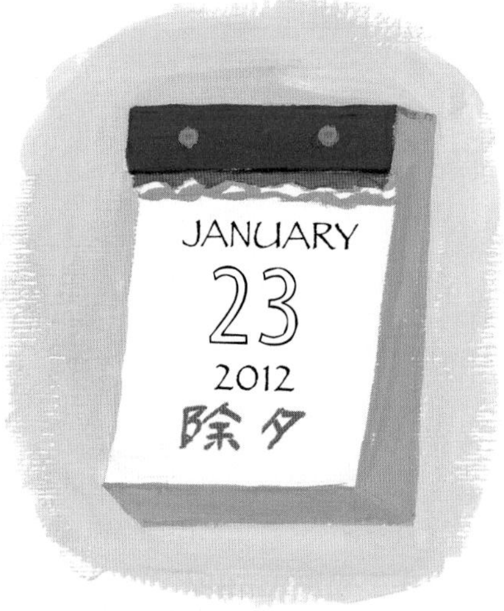
JANUARY
23
2012
除夕

First published in 2008 by Hsin Yi Publications, Taipei, Taiwan

First Candlewick Press paperback edition 2013

Library of Congress Catalog Card Number 2012947832
ISBN 978-0-7636-5881-6 (hardcover)
ISBN 978-0-7636-6748-1 (paperback)

17 18 19 20 21 22 APS 10 9 8 7 6 5 4 3

Printed in Humen, Dongguan, China

This book was typeset in Myriad Tilt.
The illustrations were done in gouache.

Candlewick Press
99 Dover Street
Somerville, Massachusetts 02144

visit us at www.candlewick.com

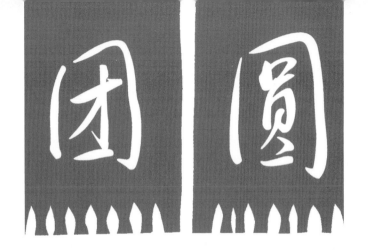

A NEW YEAR'S
REUNION

Yu Li-Qiong

illustrated by Zhu Cheng-Liang

CANDLEWICK PRESS

Papa builds big houses in faraway places.
He comes home only once each year,
during Chinese New Year.

Today, Mama and I wake up really early because . . .

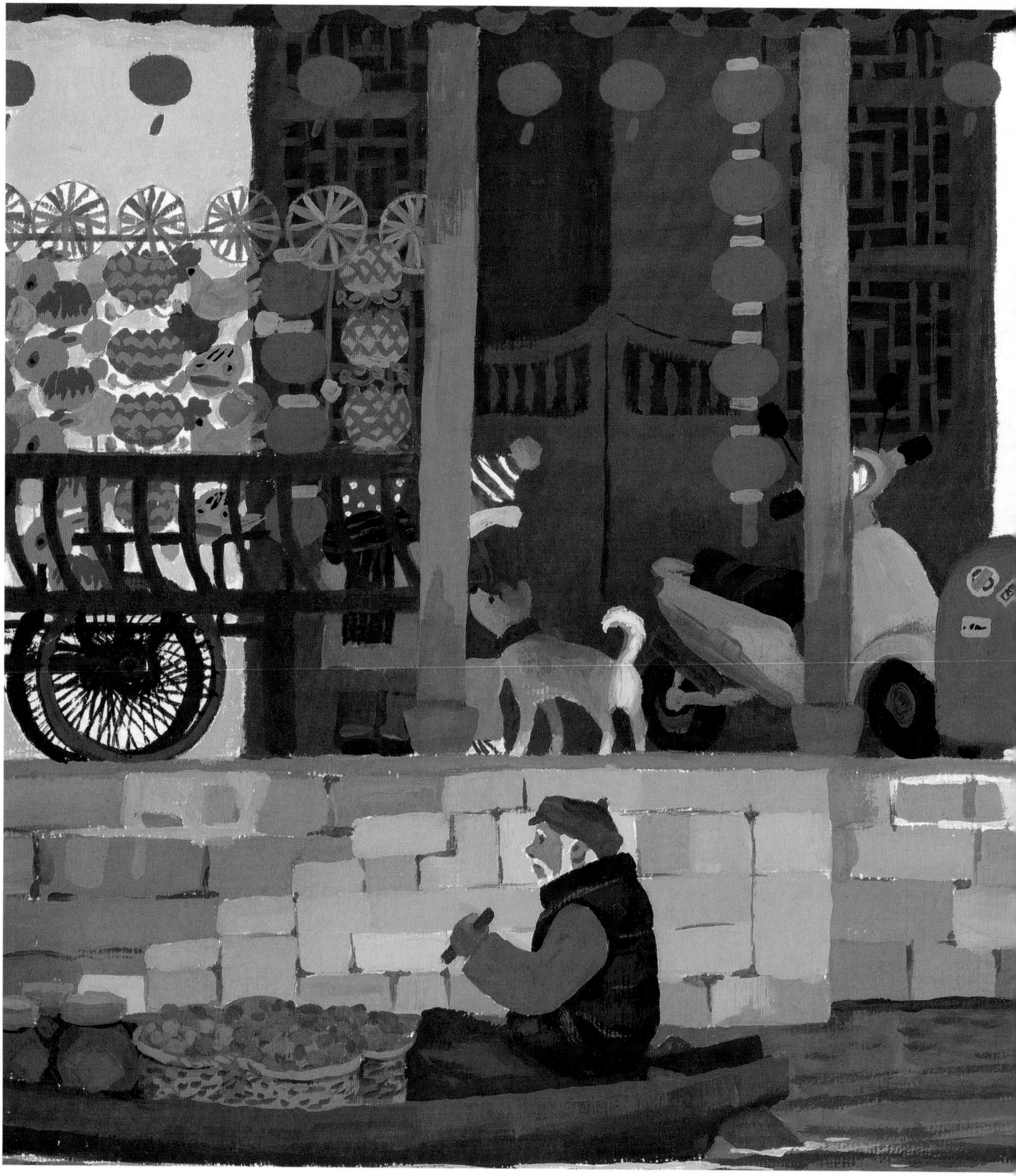

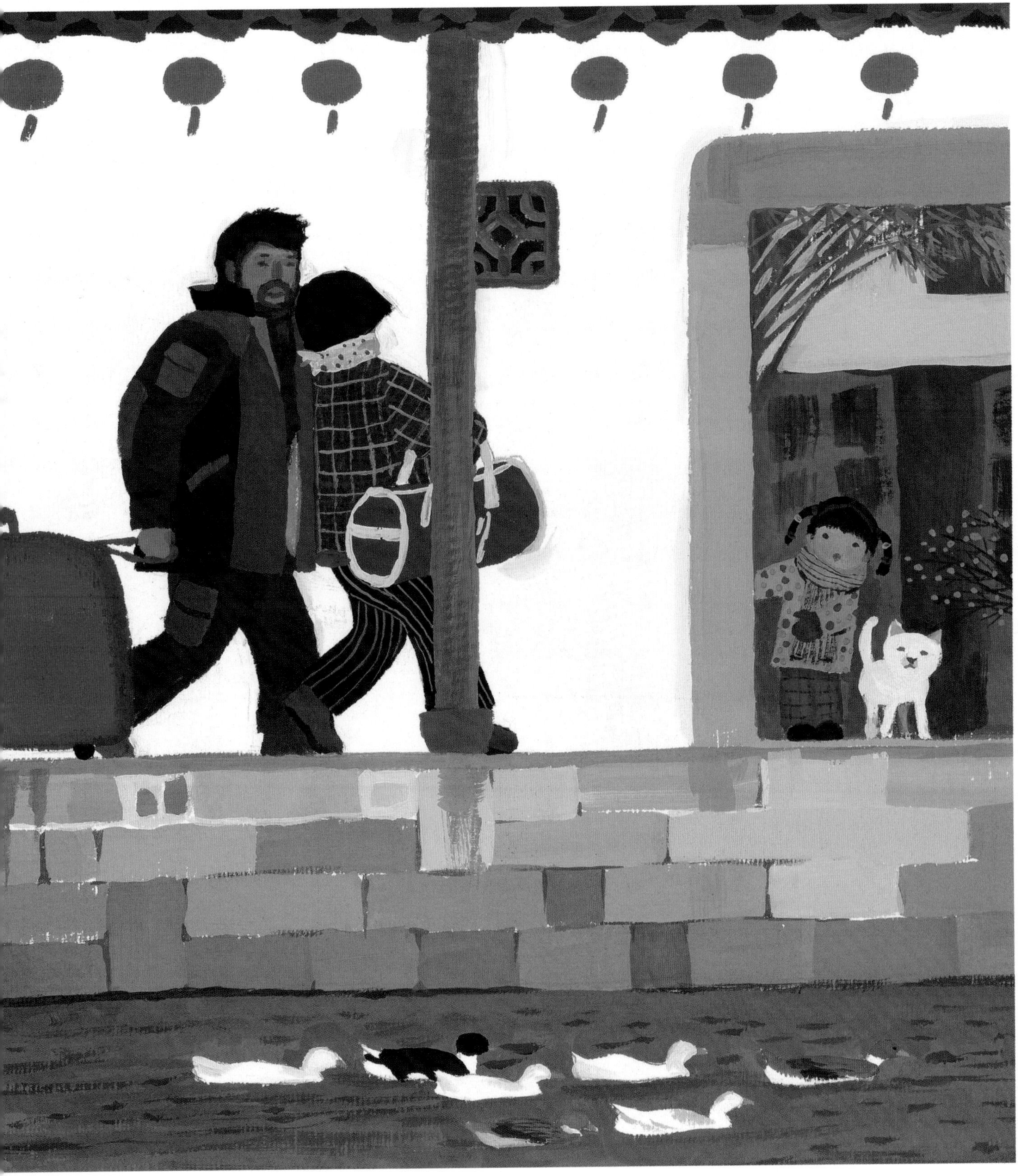

Papa is coming home.

I watch him from a distance, not daring to get close.
Papa comes over and sweeps me up in his arms,
prickling my face with his beard.
"Mama!" I cry in alarm.

"Look what I've got for you!" Papa rummages in
his big suitcase and takes out—ooh, what a pretty hat!
Mama has a new padded coat, too.

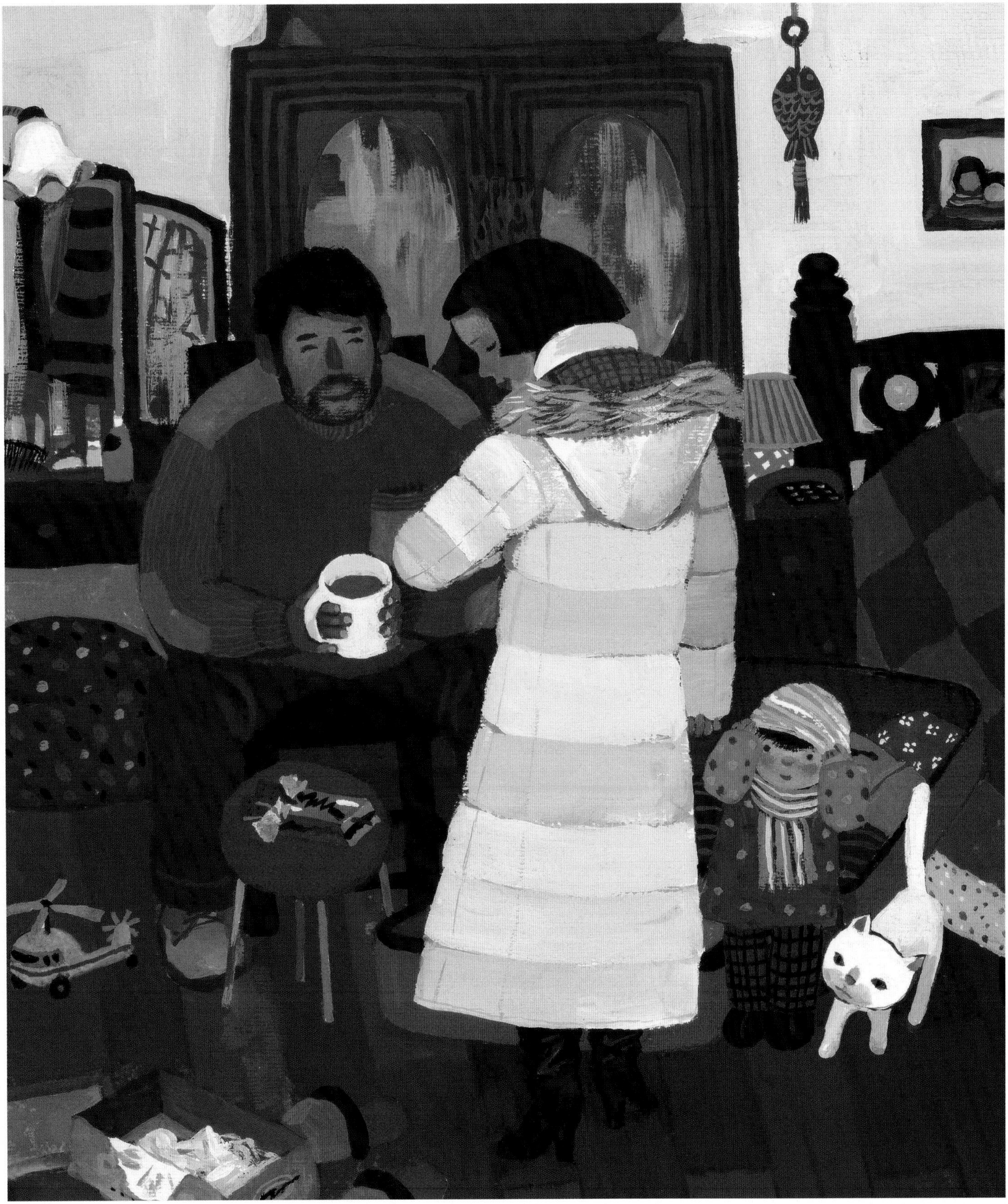

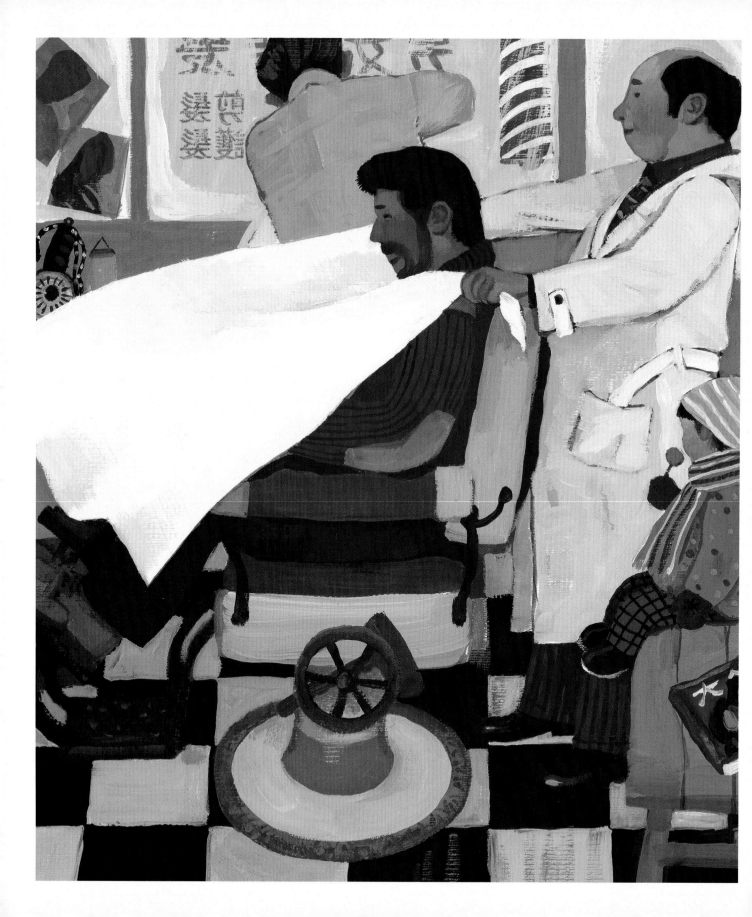

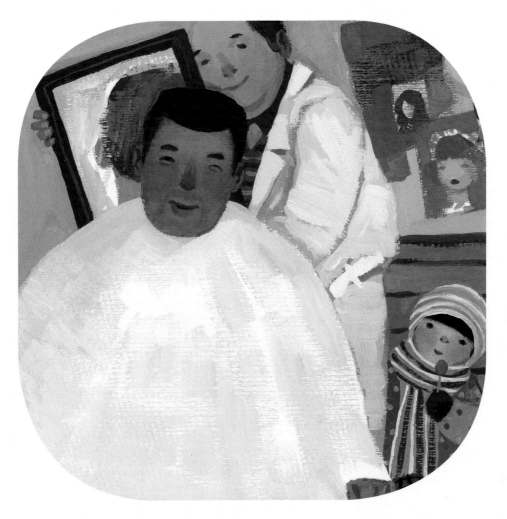

"Let's go and get me a haircut. Then everything will go
smoothly in the coming year," Papa says to me after lunch.
I sit on a chair, waiting.

The Papa in the mirror is getting more like
Papa the way he used to be.

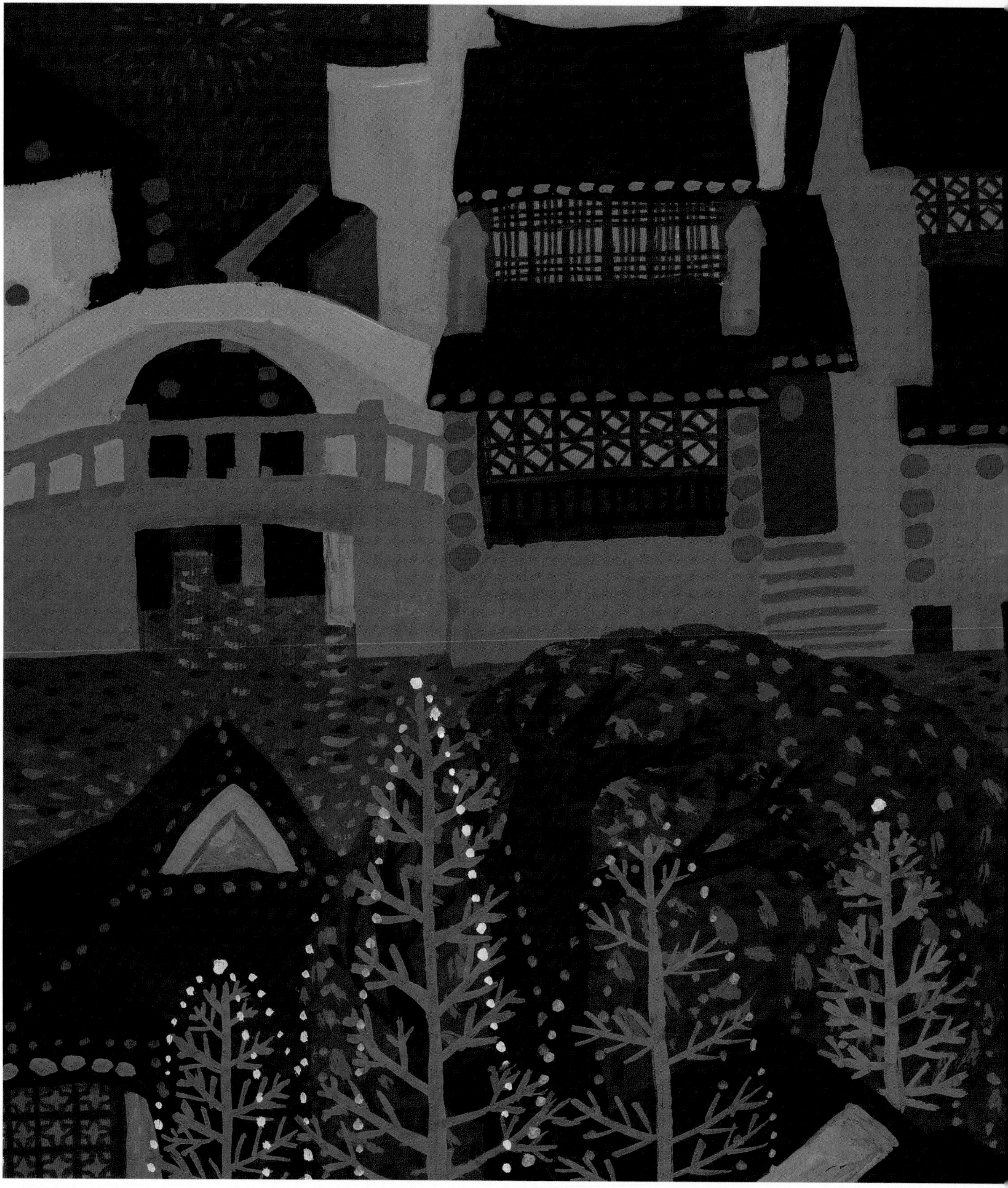

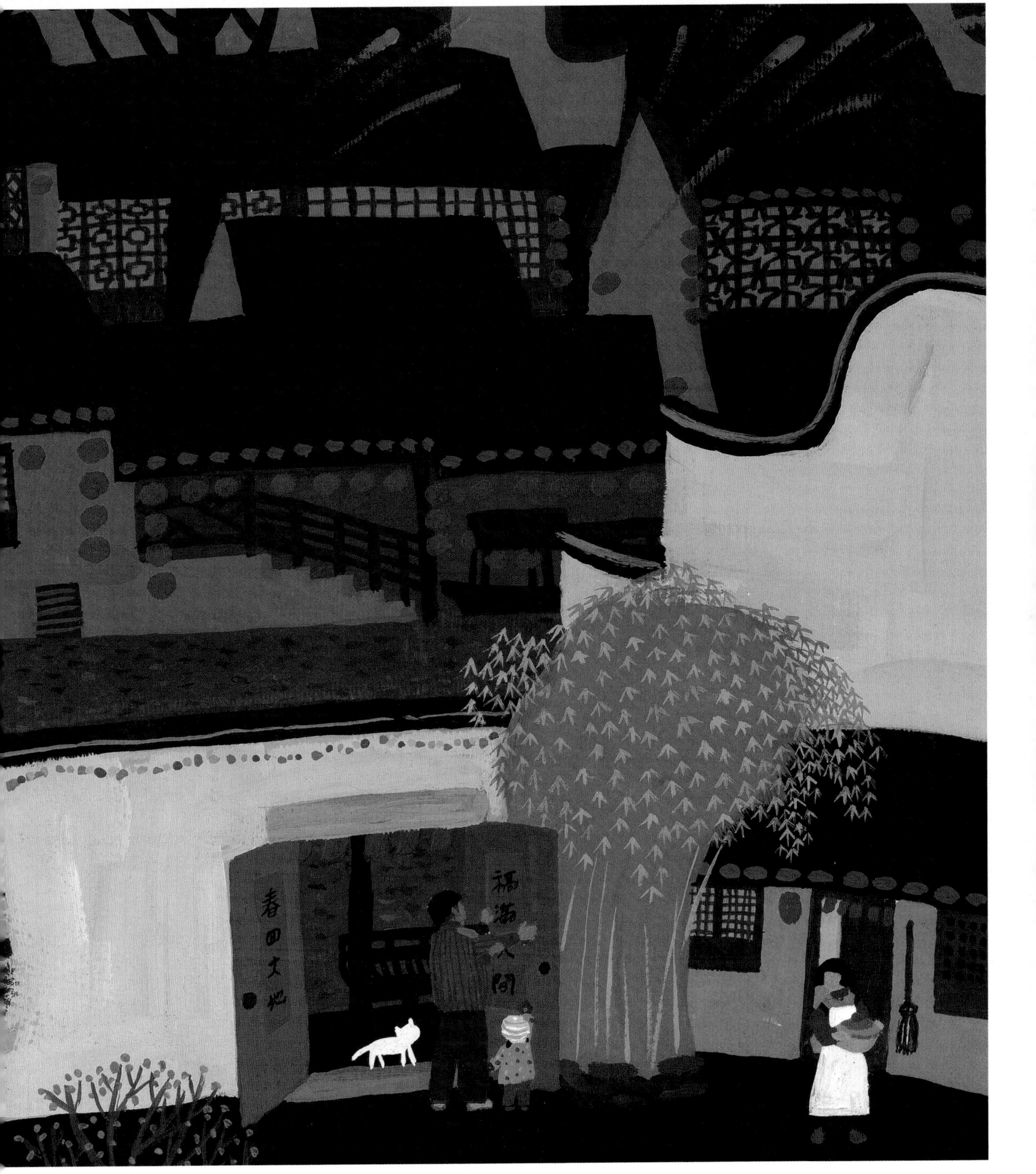
春回大地
福滿人間

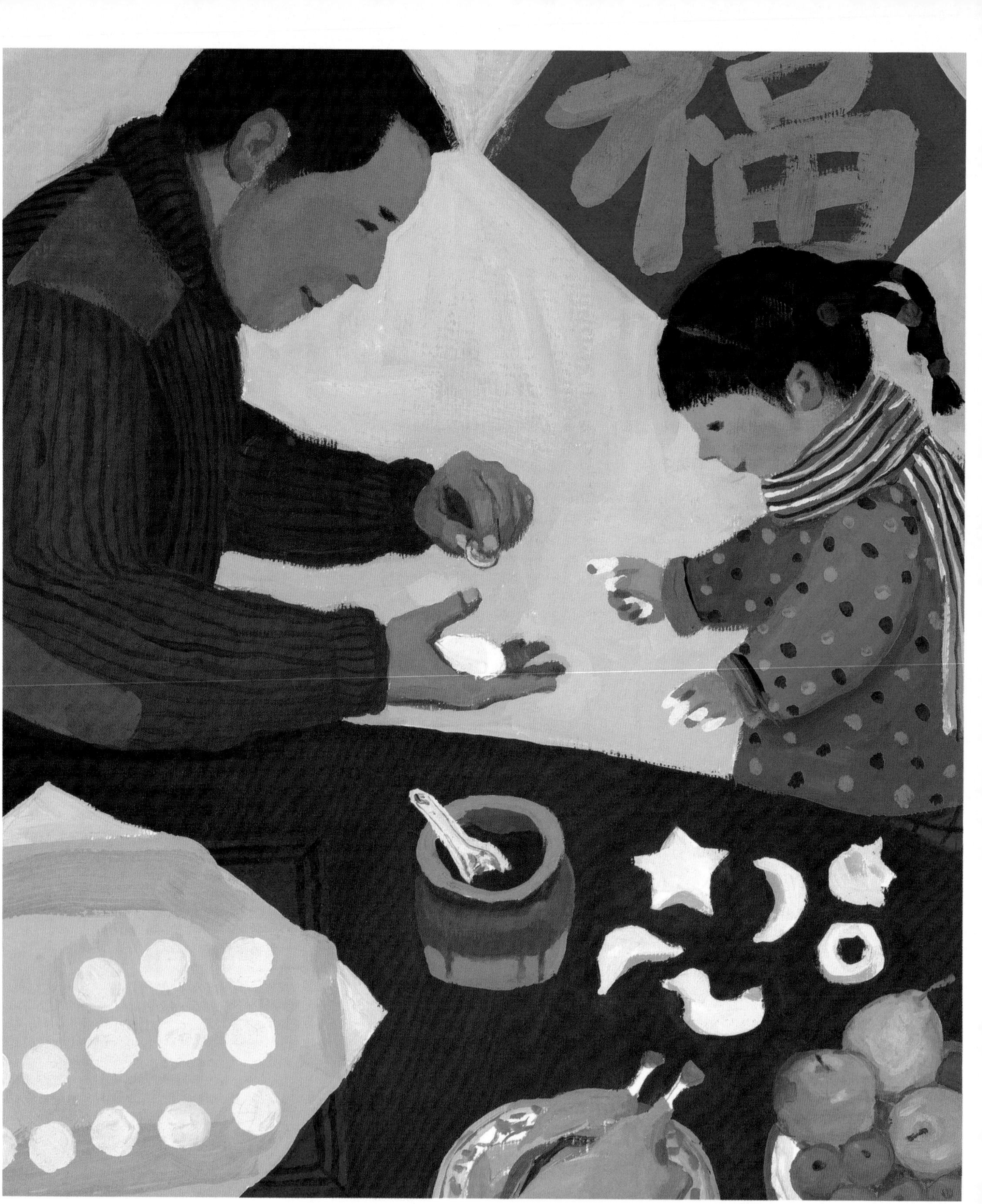

Later, it's time to make sticky rice balls. Papa buries
a coin in one of the balls and says, "Whoever finds
the ball with the coin will have good luck."

Pop, pop, pop, bang, bang, bang!

We hear firecrackers outside all night.
I lie between Papa and Mama and fall asleep,
drowsily hearing them whispering, whispering. . . .

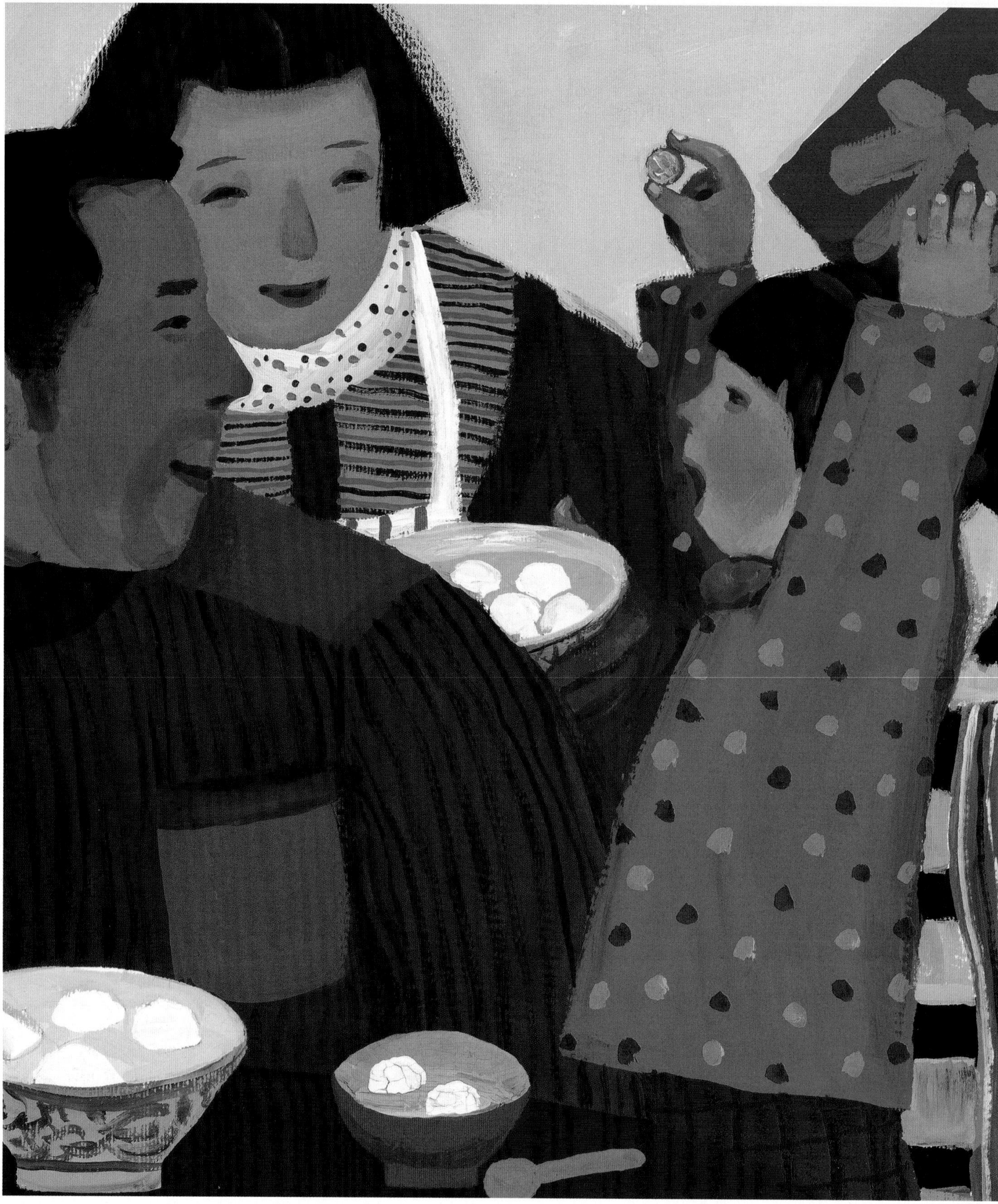

Early the next morning, Mama serves up piping-hot
sticky rice balls, and Papa feeds them to me with a spoon.
Suddenly, I bite on something hard. "The fortune coin!
It's the fortune coin!" I shout.
"Good for you, Maomao! Quick, put it away in your pocket so
the good luck won't escape!" Papa is more excited than I am.

Mama helps me into a brand-new jacket—
we're going New Year visiting!

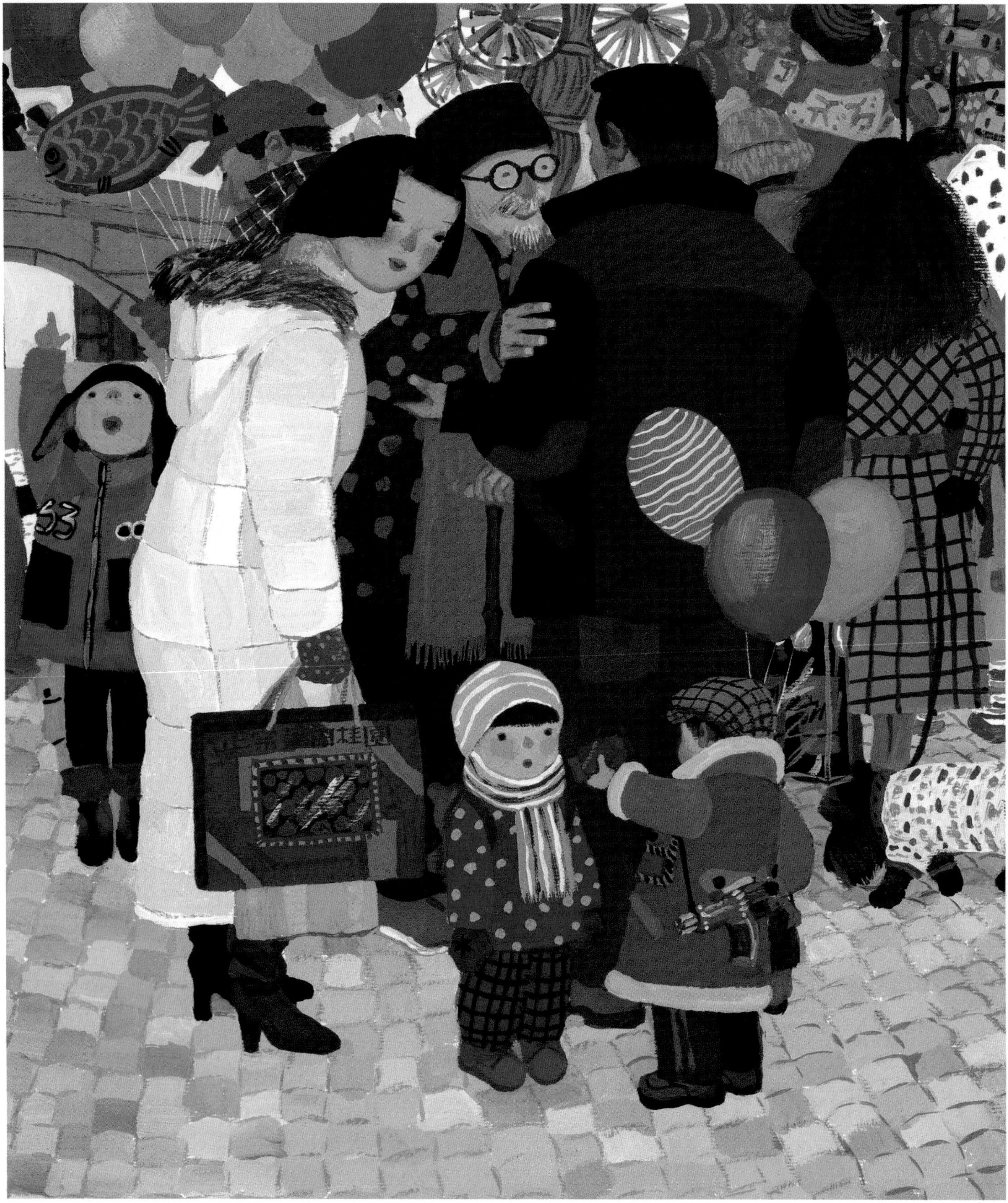
53

On the way, I meet my friend Dachun.

"Maomao, where are you going?"

"I'm out for New Year visits with my papa!"

"Me too. Look, I got a big red envelope!"

"Well, how about this?" I take the coin out of my pocket. "I have a fortune coin! My papa buried it in a sticky rice ball, and I found it!"

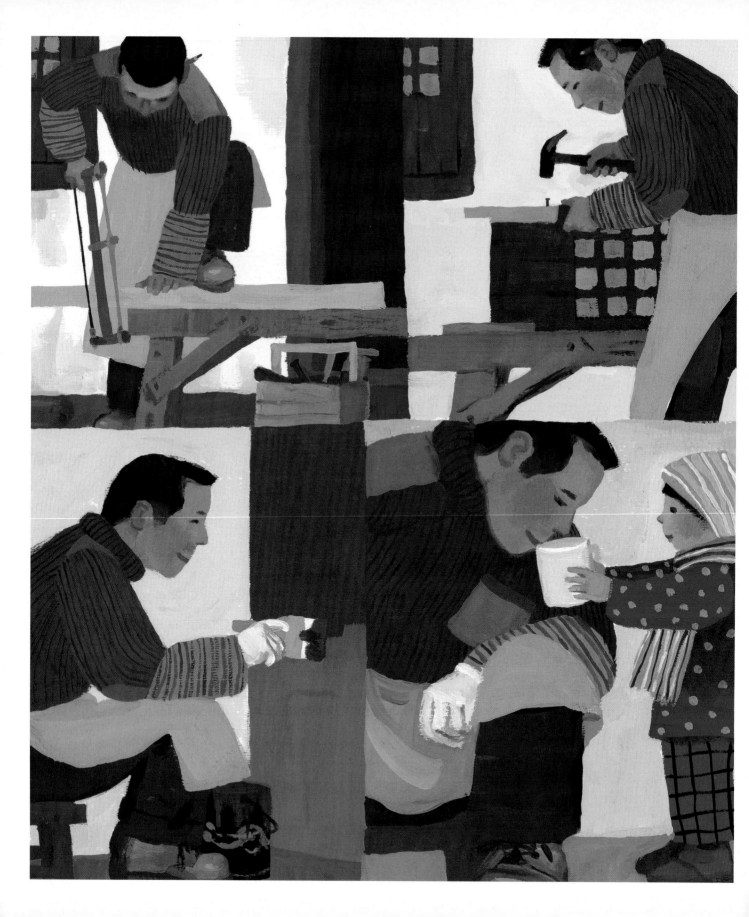

On the second day of New Year's, the sky is gloomy,
and it looks as if it's going to snow. Papa gets busy
fixing the windows, painting the door,
and changing the lightbulbs—
and the whole house brightens up.

"Come on, let's fix the roof!" Papa says with a wink.
Excellent! Mama never allows me up there alone!

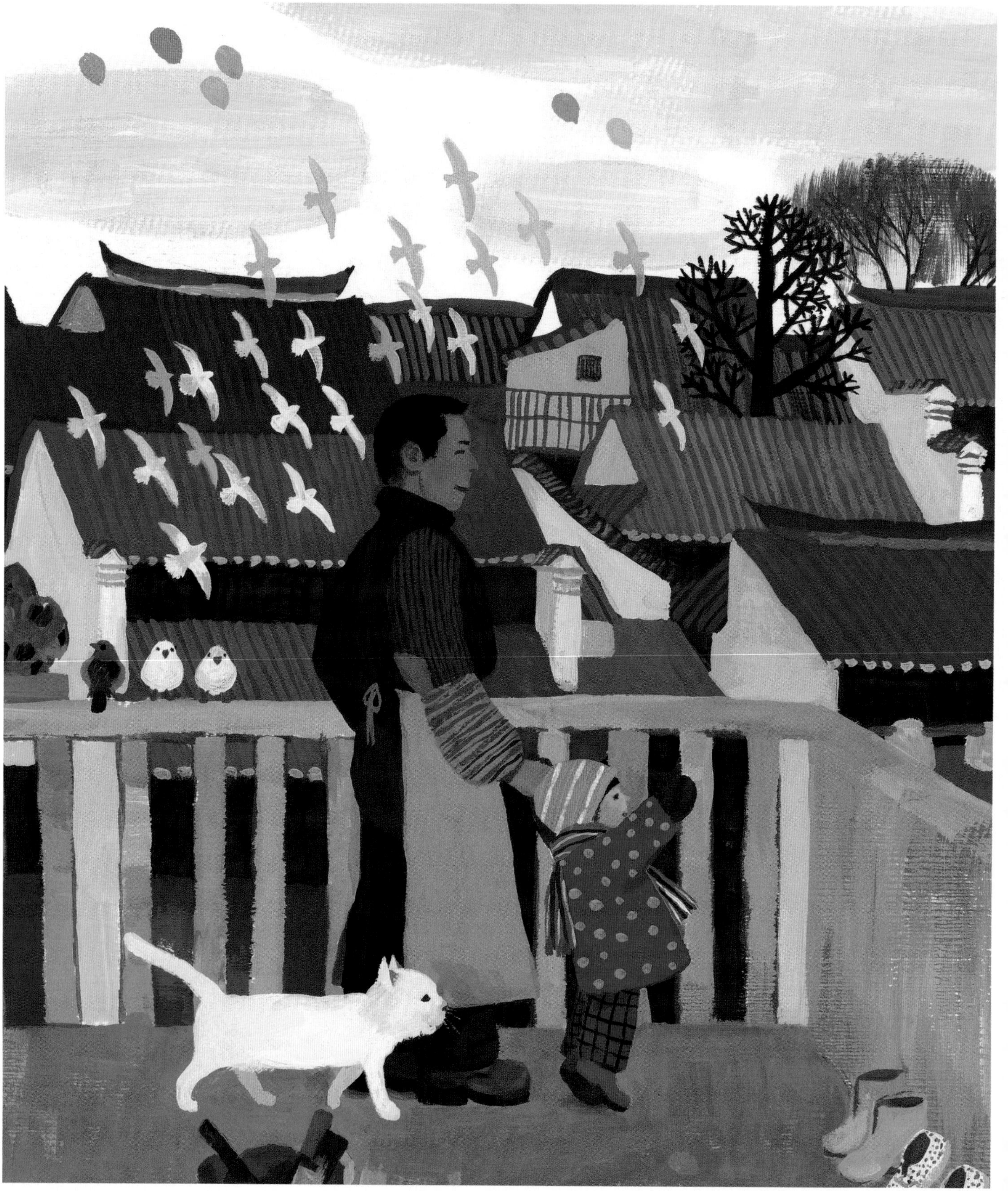

Hey, I can see Dachun's roof!

"Listen, what's that sound over there?" I say.

"Oh, it's the dragon dance on Main Street." Papa
straightens up and looks into the distance.

"Where is it? Where is it?" I stand on tiptoe,
stretching up as far as I can.

Papa puts me on his shoulders. "Now can you see it?" he asks.

"Yes, I can. They're coming!"

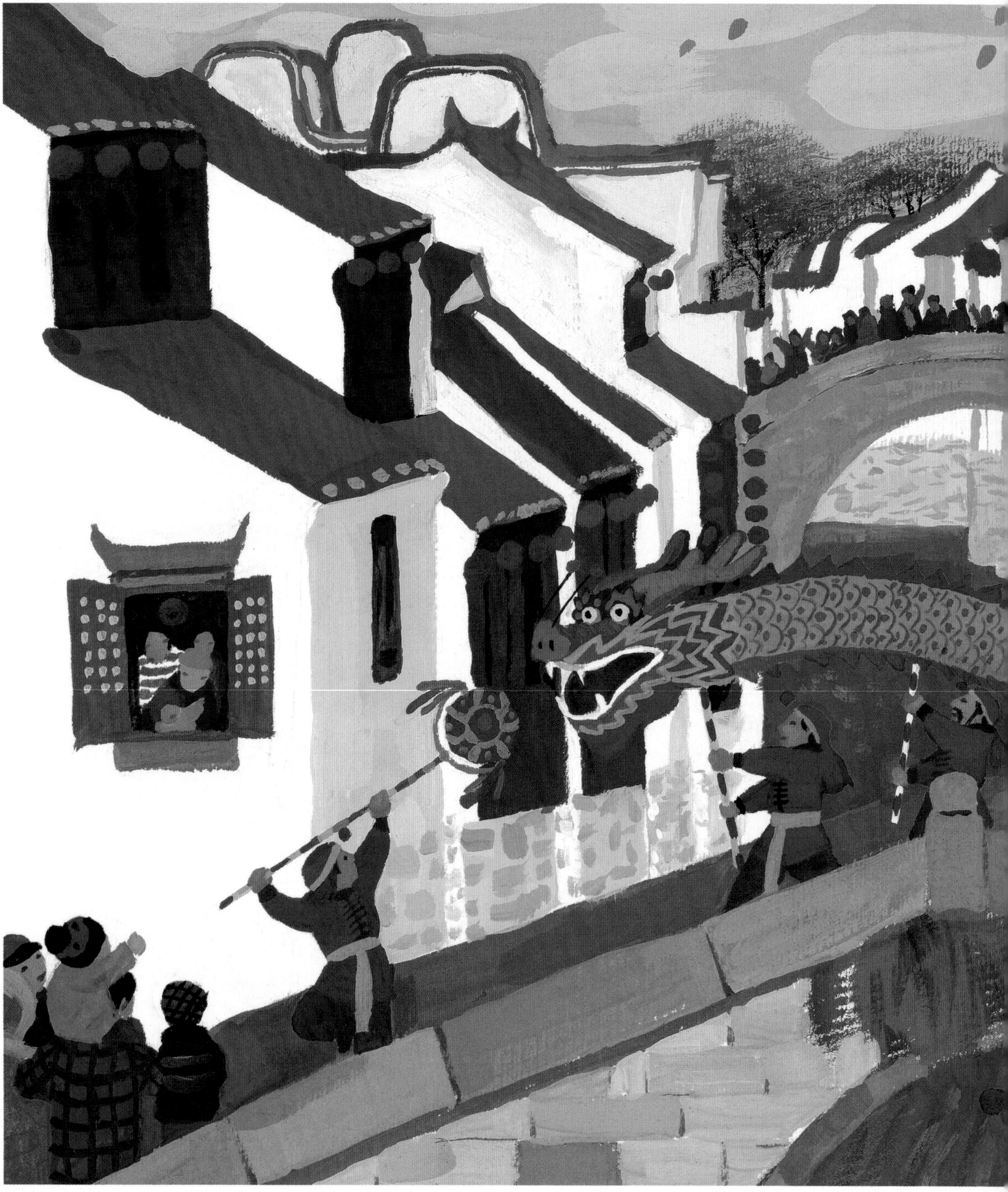

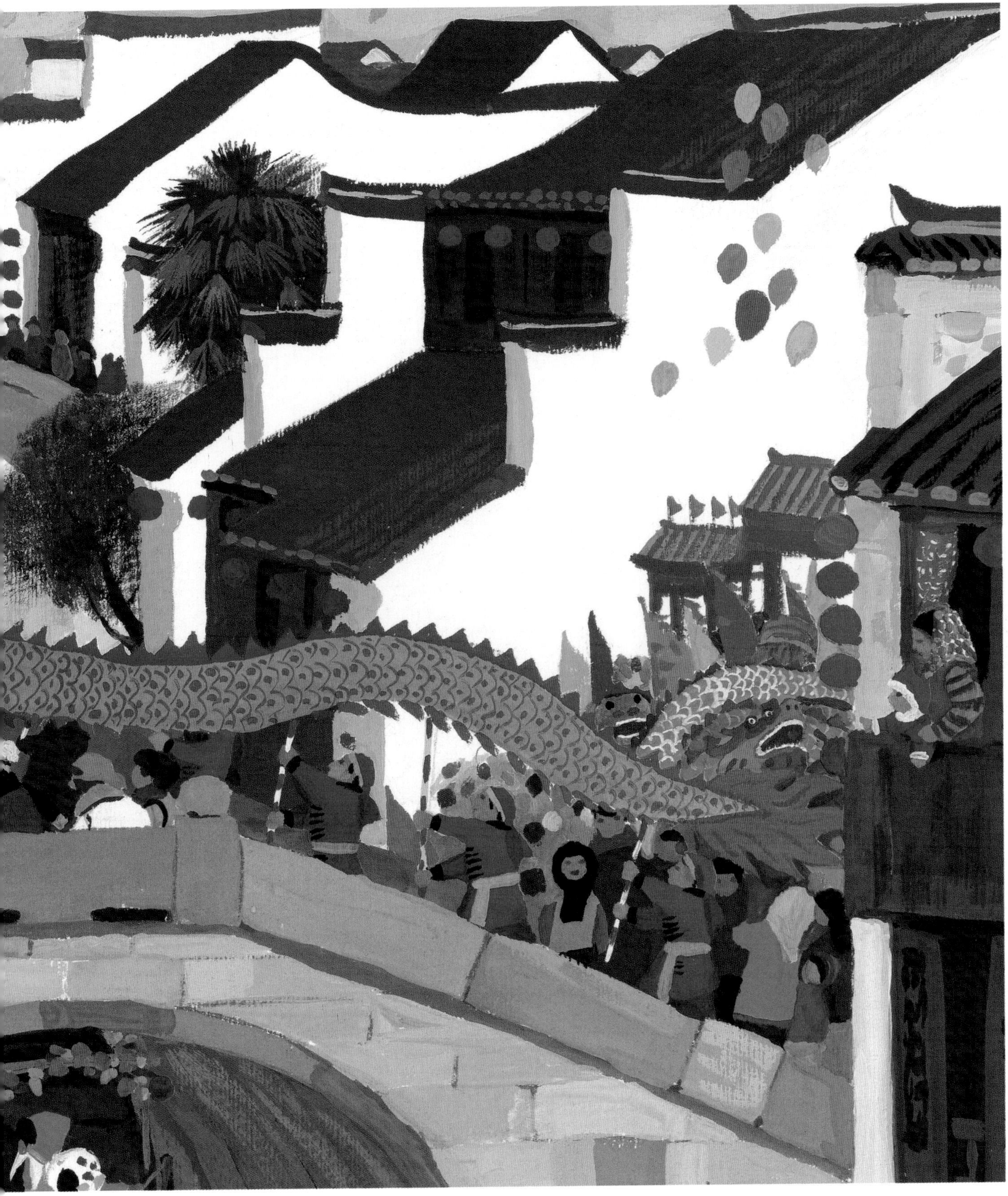

On the third day of New Year's, it snows—really hard!

When it finally stops, Dachun and the other children come and get me to play. We build a huge snowman in the courtyard and have a snowball fight.

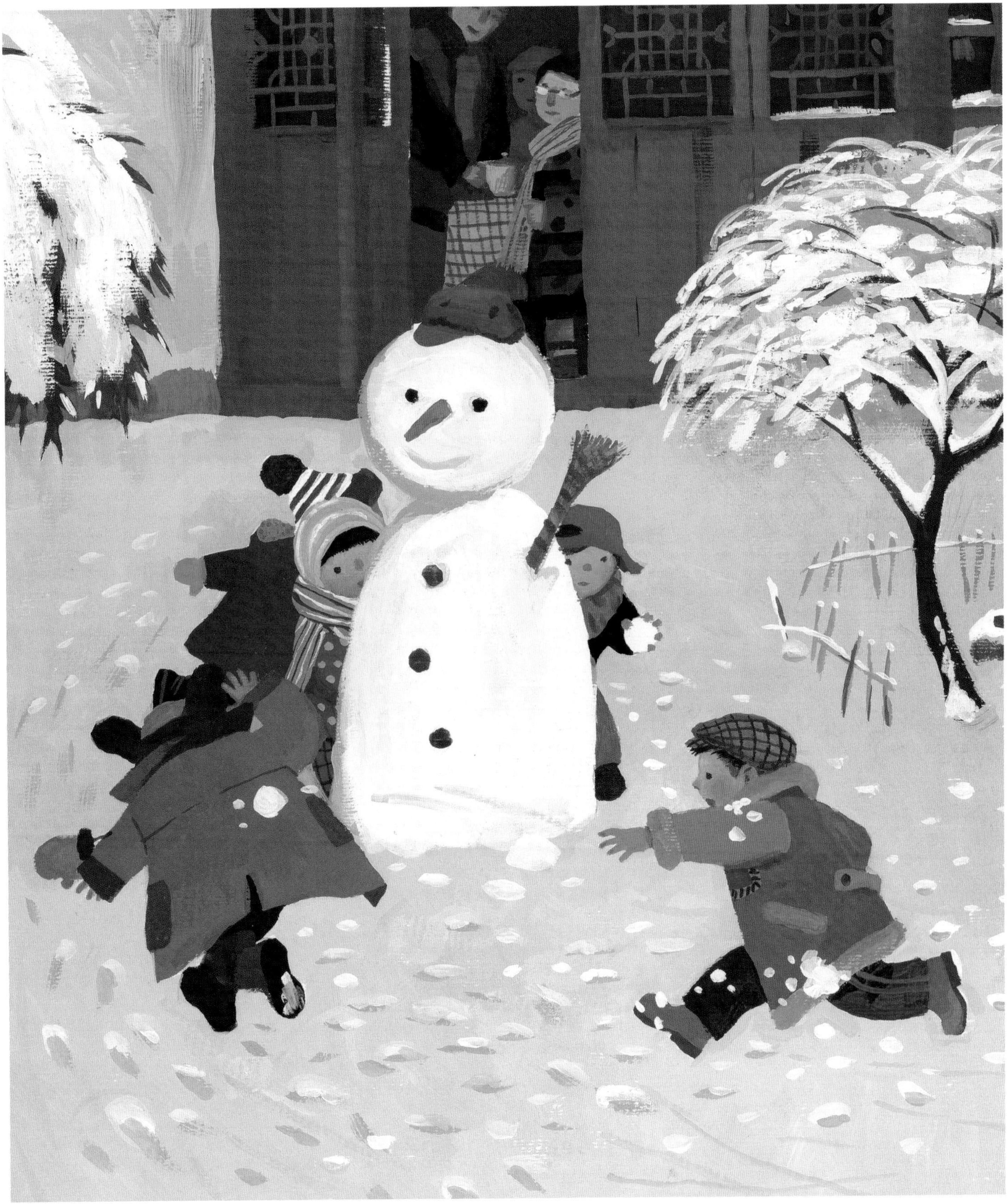

I don't go home till it's getting dark.
I feel inside my pocket and . . . I can't find the coin!
My fortune coin is gone!

I rush out to the courtyard, but it's all covered
in snow. Where is my fortune coin?

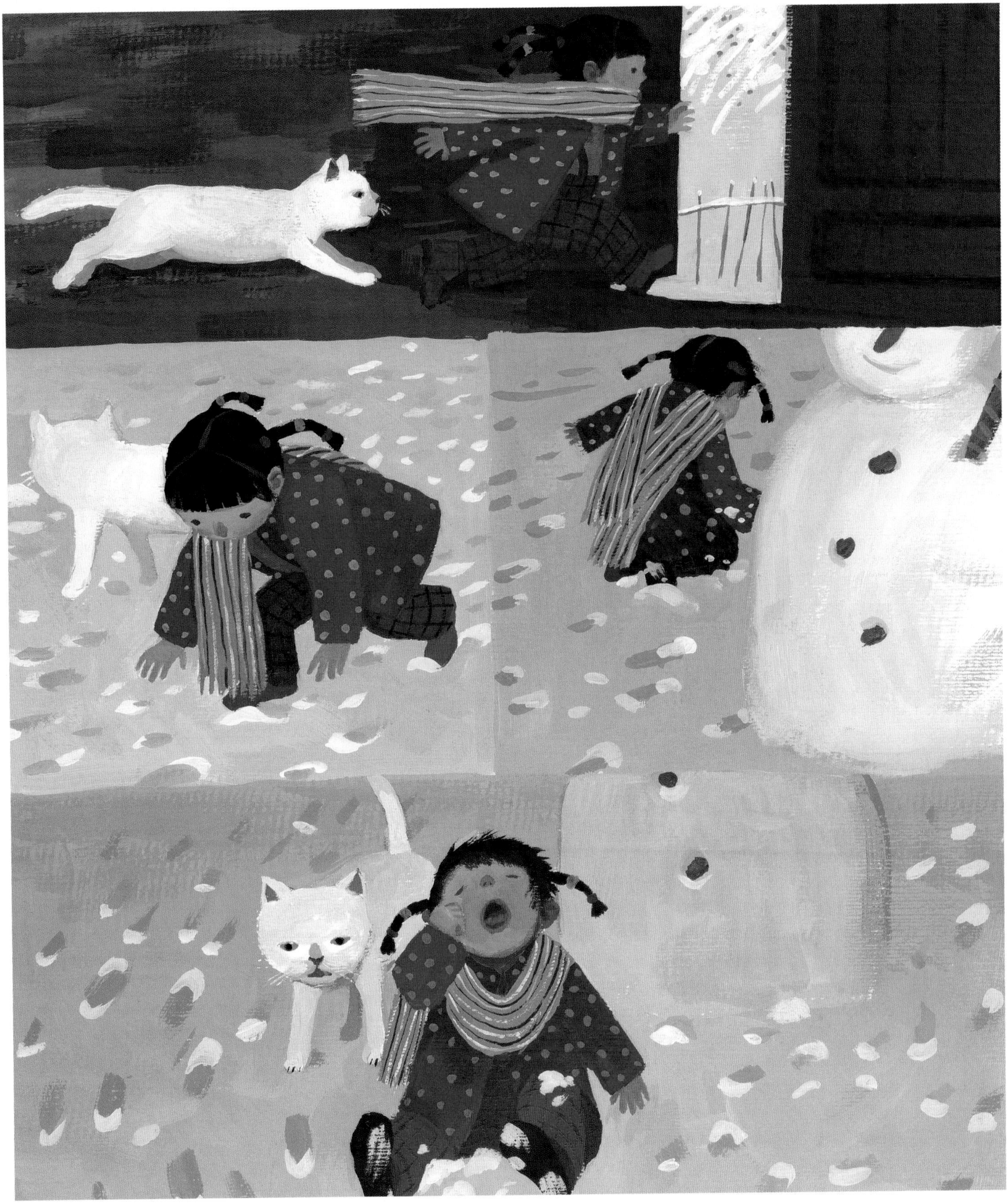

"Don't cry, sweetie. I'll give you another one.
Look, it's exactly the same!" Papa scoops another
coin out of his pocket.
"I don't want that one—I want the other one!" I bawl.

In the evening, I creep into bed, miserable, but as I take
off my jacket, *clink!* Something falls to the floor.
It's the coin! My fortune coin!
"Papa, come quick—come and see! I haven't lost
the fortune coin. It's been with me all the time."

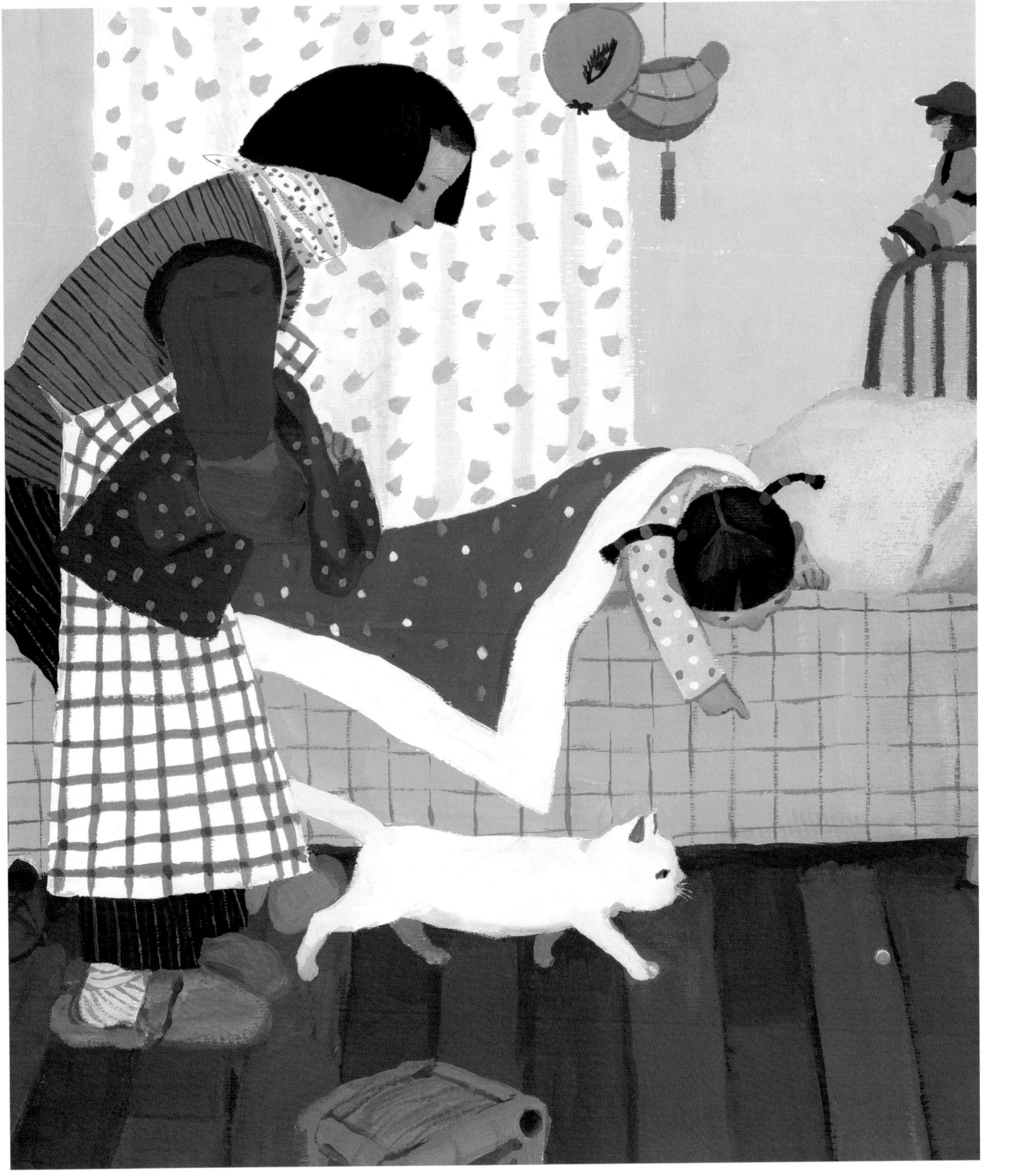

That night, I sleep very soundly.

When I get up the next morning,
I see Mama helping Papa pack.
He is leaving today.

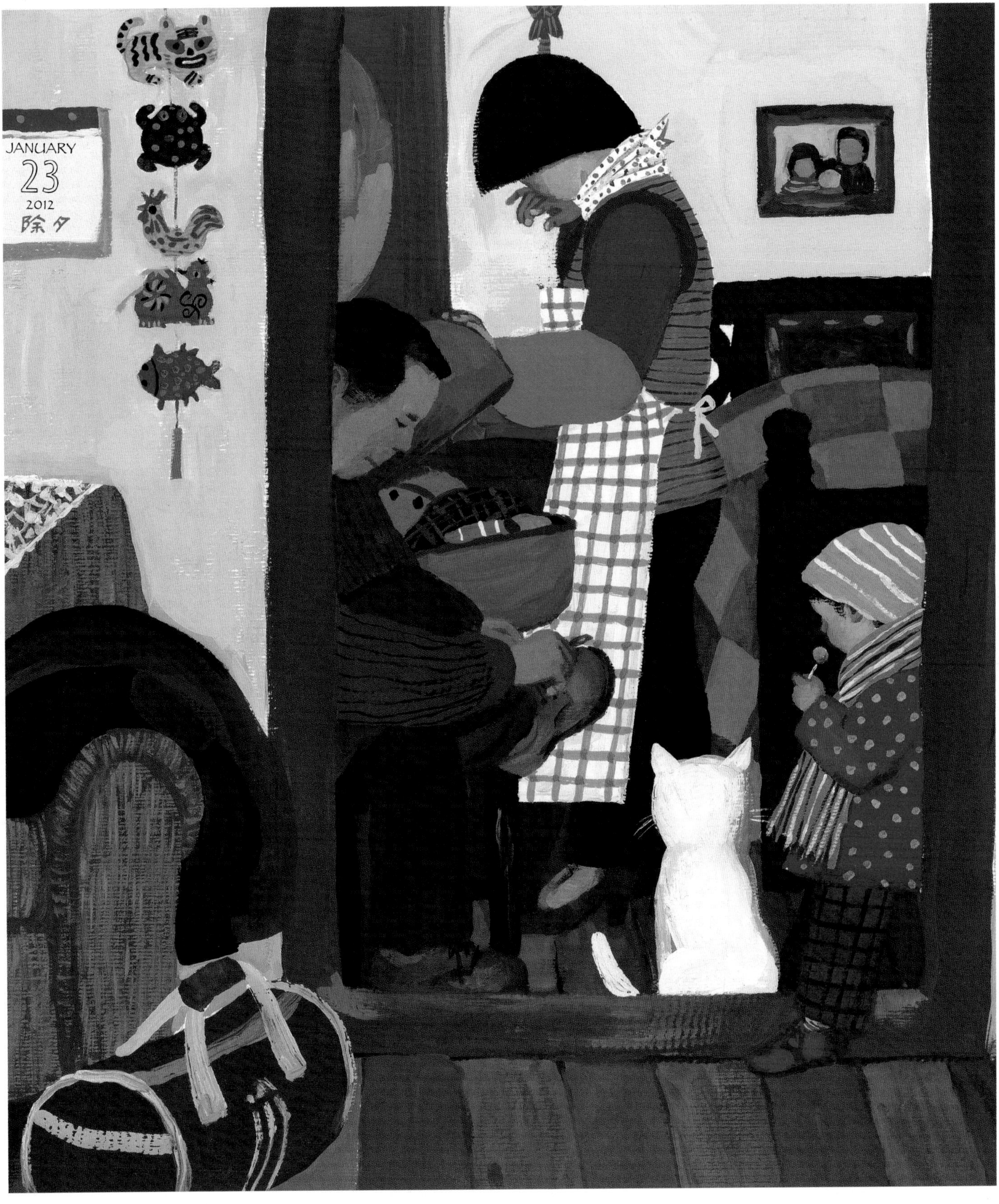
JANUARY
23
2012
除夕

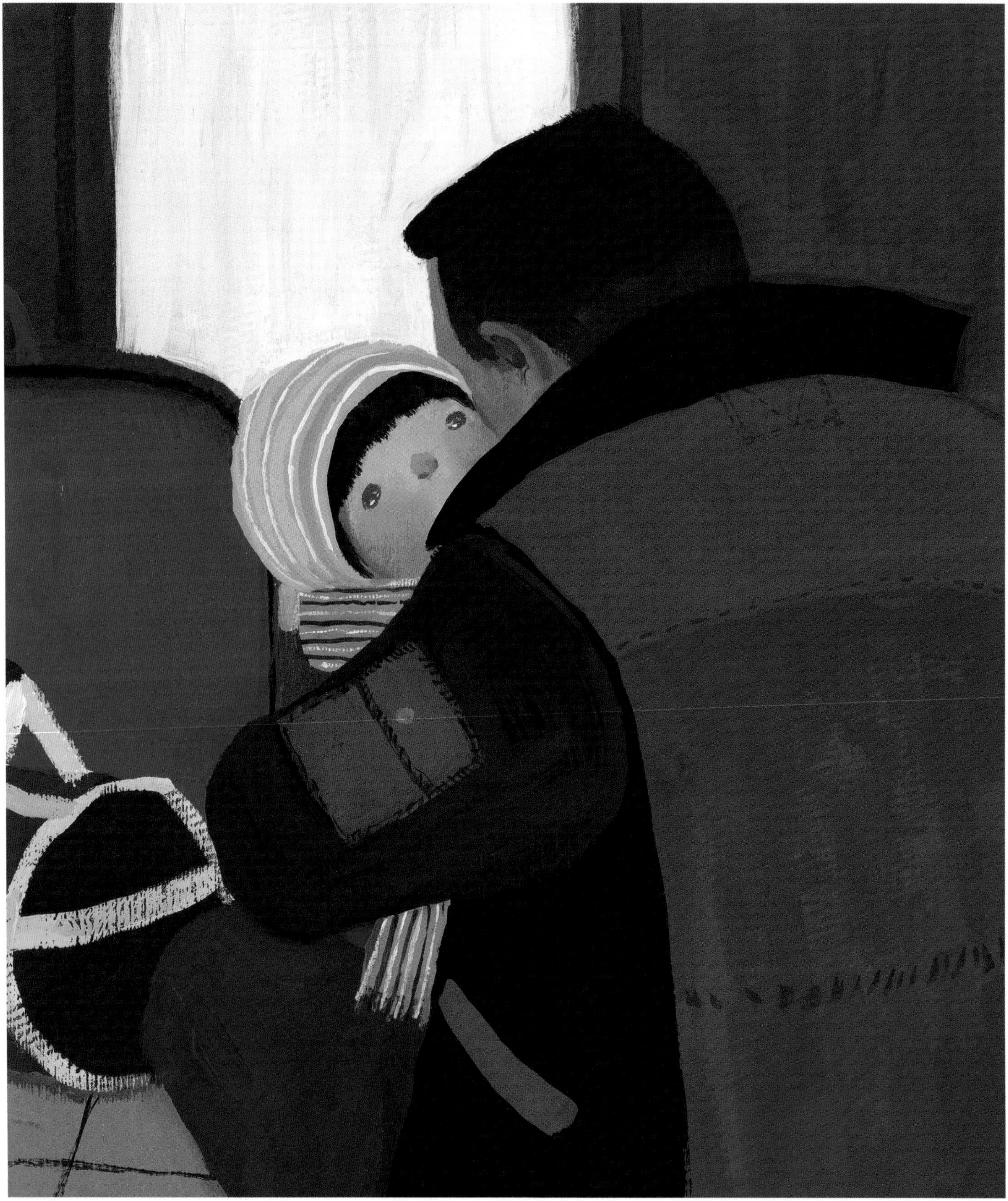

Soon, Papa's packing is done. He crouches down
and gives me a big hug, whispering in my ear,
"Next time I'm back, I'll bring you a doll, OK?"

"No, Papa." I shake my head hard.
"I want to give *you* something. . . ."

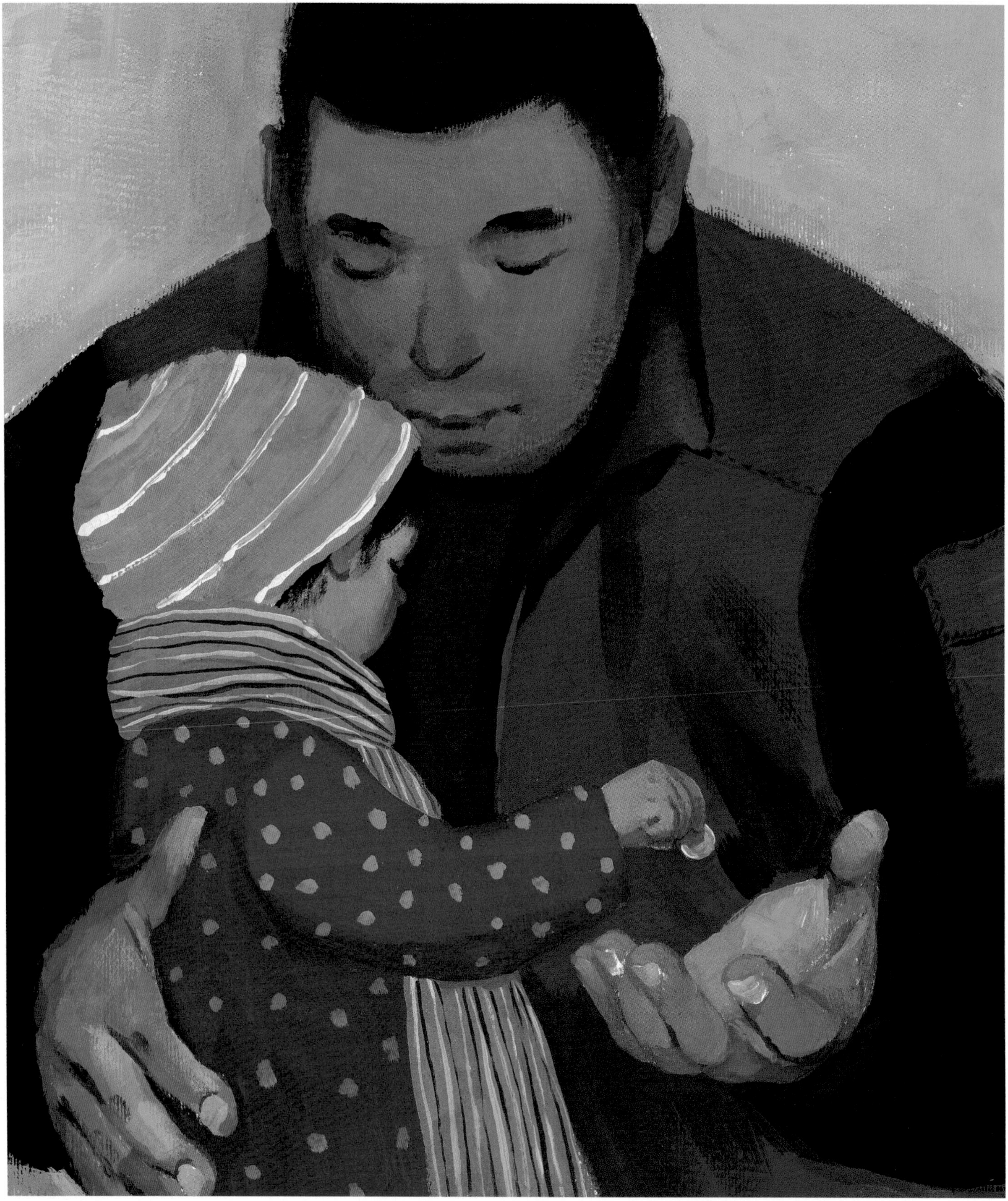

I put the coin, all warm from being held
in my hand for so long, in Papa's palm and say,
"Here, take this. Next time you're back, we can
bury it in the sticky rice ball again!"

Papa is very quiet.
He nods and hugs me tight.

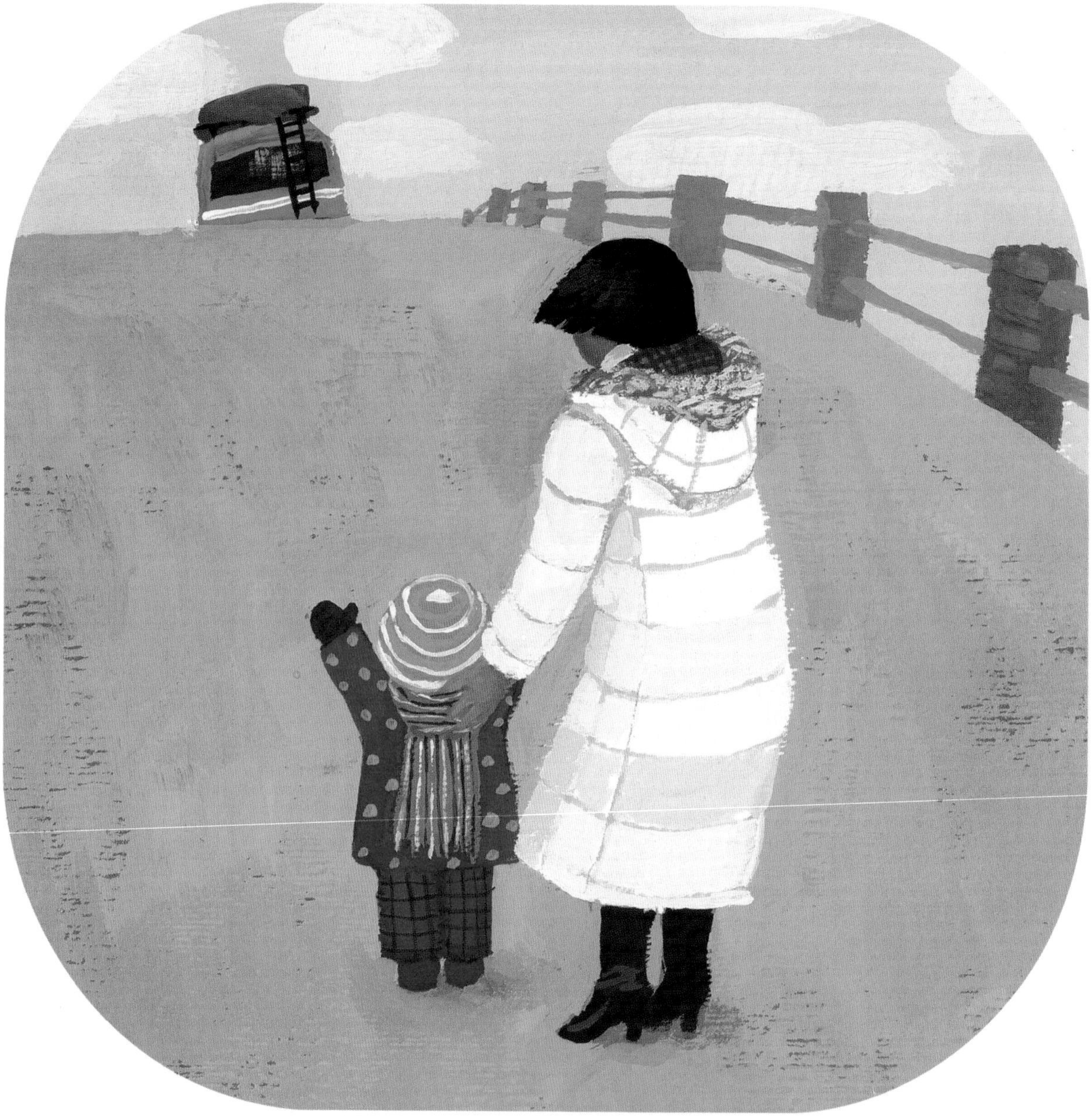